CORPVS CHRISTIANORVM

HAGIOGRAPHIES

VIII

CORPVS CHRISTIANORVM

HAGIOGRAPHIES

VIII

TURNHOUT
BREPOLS
2020

HAGIOGRAPHIES

*Histoire internationale de la littérature hagiographique latine et vernaculaire
en Occident des origines à 1550*

*International History of the Latin and Vernacular Hagiographical Literature
in the West from its Origins to 1550*

*Internationale Geschichte der lateinischen und einheimischen
hagiographischen Literatur im Abendland von den Anfängen bis 1550*

*Storia internazionale della letteratura agiografica latina e volgare
in Occidente dalle origine a 1550*

sous la direction de Michèle GAILLARD
Professeur émérite d'histoire du Moyen Âge
Université de Lille
(Institut de Recherche et d'Histoire du Septentrion – CNRS UMR 8529)

et

Monique GOULLET
Directeur de recherche
Université Paris 1 – Panthéon – Sorbonne
(Laboratoire de Médiévistique Occidentale de Paris)

VOLUME VIII

TURNHOUT
BREPOLS
2020

© 2020, Brepols Publishers n.v./s.a., Turnhout, Belgium

All rights reserved. No part of this publication may be reproduced,
stored in a retrieval system, or transmitted, in any form or by any means,
electronic, mechanical, photocopying, recording, or otherwise,
without the prior permission of the publisher.

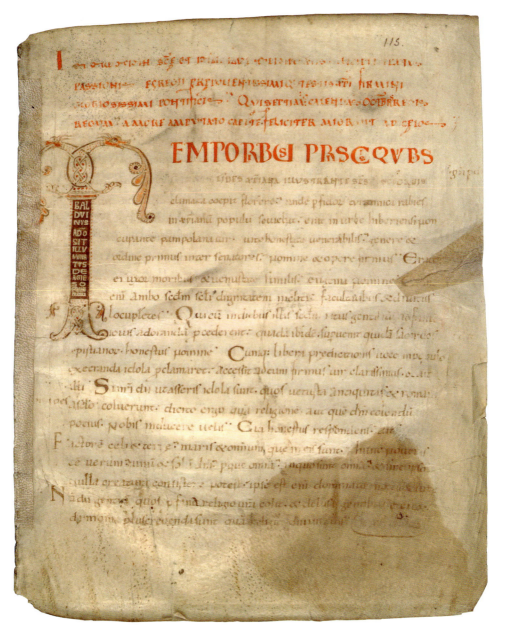

Montpellier, Bibliothèque interuniversitaire, BU historique de médecine, H 360, fol. 115r
Crédit photographique: BIU Montpellier / IRHT (CNRS)

Le manuscrit de Montpellier (BIU H 360), d'où est tirée l'image ici présentée (fol. 115r), forme un ensemble de cinq unités codicologiques distinctes réunies à une époque indéterminée et qui se clôt par une table confectionnée au xve siècle : celle-ci enregistre le contenu pour le moins hétéroclite du codex et rappelle combien l'hagiographie n'a pas été considérée au Moyen Âge comme une catégorie à part : les guerres des Romains, les conquêtes des Mérovingiens et de Charlemagne, les Vies d'évêques et les Passions de martyrs appartiennent toutes à l'Histoire.

Le fol. 115r débute la troisième unité codicologique (fol. 115-136), laquelle contient dans l'ordre un dossier relatif aux deux évêques d'Amiens prénommés Firmin (*BHL* 3003, 3008, 3012, voir *infra*, p. 410-421), un hymne noté en l'honneur de Germain d'Auxerre, la Passion de Pérégrin d'Autun (*BHL* 6623), un récit de l'Exaltation de la Croix (*BHL* 4178), une Passion de l'évangéliste Marc (*BHL* 5276) et une Passion d'Eusèbe de Rome (*BHL* 2740), à la suite de laquelle un labyrinthe a été figuré (exactement comme dans le ms. auxerrois BNF, lat. 1745, fol. 30v) et l'histoire du minotaure christianisée.

Le début de la Passion de Firmin d'Amiens (*BHL* 3003), s'ouvre par l'initiale T dans laquelle on lit l'inscription : *Balduinus a Deo sit illuminatus de agie sophie*, qui avait déjà attiré l'attention d'érudits du xviiie siècle, agacés par son usage incertain du grec (voir Jean Le Beuf *Recueil de divers écrits pour servir d'éclaircissemens à l'histoire de France...*, t. 2, Paris, 1738, p. 24). Qui est Baudouin ? S'agit de l'enlumineur, qui demanderait ainsi à être illuminé ? Le nom renvoie *a priori* au nord de la France : à Saint-Bertin, un moine Baudouin est connu pour avoir rassemblé vers l'an mil les *Dialogues* de Grégoire le Grand pour son abbé (Saint-Omer, BASO, ms. 168, fol. 161). Mais après tout, ce peut être ici un tout autre personnage, et peut-être le commanditaire : « Que Dieu éclaire Baudouin de sa sainte sagesse ! ».

Ce manuscrit a appartenu depuis une date indéterminée à l'abbaye cistercienne de Pontigny (où l'a vu Lebeuf, comme il le dit, *op. cit.*, p. 24), non loin d'Auxerre. D'après son sanctoral, il est bien originaire d'Auxerre, où l'on sait, grâce au calendrier d'Heiric († ca. 876) du ixe siècle (conservé à Melk, St, 412), que Firmin d'Amiens était fêté. La présence de Germain d'Auxerre et celle, dans la deuxième unité codicologique du manuscrit, d'une Passion d'Urbain Ier, évêque de Rome (fol. 47-67v) ainsi que d'un hymne (fol. 73-76) qui lui est consacré (*BHL* 8372/3, 8374), orientent plus précisément vers l'abbaye Saint-Germain, où les reliques d'Urbain arrivent en 862 (voir *BHL* 8391). Quant au nom « Baudouin », il est attesté en Bourgogne aux ixe et xe siècles, comme le montre une interrogation dans les bases du *Corpus Burgundiae Medii Aevi* [En ligne] http://www.cbma-project.eu. Deux ecclésiastiques de ce nom sont liés à Cluny au milieu du xe siècle : l'un est un moine qui transcrit des chartes et l'autre est co-abbé de Saint-Paul-hors-les-Murs à Rome. Celui-ci, mentionné dans la Vie d'Odon de Cluny (*BHL* 6292), demanda à ce dernier de réviser et commenter la Vie de Martin, et le remplaça un temps à Cluny comme prieur. A-t-il pu commander la copie d'autres récits hagiographiques, en partie rassemblés ensuite dans un codex factice ? L'hypothèse n'est pas à exclure.

Table générale des matières

INTRODUCTION: G. PHILIPPART
    Introduction [générale] .... I, 9-24
    L'hagiographie, histoire sainte des
    «amis de Dieu» .... IV, 13-40

I. ANTIQUITÉ
    Afrique latine (jusqu'en 540): V. SAXER .... I, 25-96
    Europe latine: F. SCORZA BARCELLONA .... III, 17-98
    Jérôme hagiographe († 420): A. BASTIAENSEN ..... I, 97-124

II. ITALIE
    300-550
        Passions: C. LANÉRY .... V, 15-369
        Vies: S. GIOANNI .... V, 371-445
    550-750
        Passions et vies anonymes: C. LANÉRY, G. VOCINO
        Grégoire le Grand hagiographe († 604):
            S. BOESCH GAJANO................................ VII, 11-94
    750-950/1000
        Nord: G. VOCINO
        Centre: G. VOCINO................................... VII, 95-268
        Ombrie (750-950): E. D'ANGELO .... VII, 269-344
        Midi: E. D'ANGELO .... IV, 41-134
    950-1130
        Nord: P. TOMEA.. III, 99-178
        Centre: P. LICCIARDELLO............................ V, 447-729
        Ombrie (950-1130): E. D'ANGELO.......... VI, 269-344
        Midi: O. LIMONE .... II, 11-60
    1130-1500/1550
        Nord (1130-1220): P. GOLINELLI............... I, 125-154
        Centre (1130-1220): A. DEGL'INNOCENTI. V, 731-798
        Centre et Nord (1220-1500): S. NOCENTINI
        Ombrie (1130-1500): E. D'ANGELO........ VI, 107-234
        Midi (1130-1220): O. LIMONE .... II, 11-60
        Midi (1266-1517): R. MANFREDONIA .... VI, 15-106
    1450-1550: S. SPANÓ-MARTINELLI .... II, 61-82

L'hagiographie grecque (VIIe-XIVe siècle):
S. Efthymiadis .... VII, 345-420

III. Espagne et Portugal

Péninsule ibérique
350-950: V. Valcárcel
Espagne, *Hagiographie latine*
950-1350
Asturie-Léon-Castille: J. C. Martin, P. Henriet
Catalogne-Valence: C. Pérez González
Aragon-Navarre: C. Pérez González ... VII, 421-503
1350-1500: B. Briesemeister
.... VI, 266-282, 326-375, 389-399
1450-1550: D. de Courcelles .... I, 155-188
Espagne, *Hagiographie vernaculaire*
1250-1350: A. García de la Borbolla ..... IV, 135-182
1350-1500: B. Briesemeister
.... VI, 266-269, 282-369, 375-399
1450-1550: D. de Courcelles .... I, 155-188
Portugal
950-1550: J. Mattoso .... II, 83-102
1350-1500: B. Briesemeister .... VI, 238-266

IV. Orient latin
J. Richard .... I, 189-198

V. Hongrie
G. Klaniczay, E. Madas .... II, 103-160

VI. Croatie et Slovénie
Croatie
400-1300: I. Petrović .... IV, 183-272
1300-1550: I. Petrović
Slovénie: M. Cerno .... VII, 505-564

VII. Bohême et Moravie
Hagiographie latine: M. Cerno, M. Betti ... VIII, 15-139
Hagiographie vernaculaire: M. Cerno

VIII. Pologne
T. Dunin-Wąsowicz .... III, 179-202

IX. Gaule et Germanie
300-750: M. Heinzelmann *et al.*

X. Aire germanique

Hagiographie latine
- 750-950: Th. Klüppel .... II, 161-210
- **750-1100: Supplément: K. Krönert.... VIII, 731-769**
- 950-1130: F. Lotter, S. Gäbe .... IV, 273-520
- 1130-1220: M. Rener .... VI, 401-520
- 1220-1450: M. Rener .... I, 199-266
- 1450-1550: D. Collins .... IV, 521-582

Hagiographie vernaculaire
- 850-1350: K. Kunze .... II, 211-238
- 1350-1550: W. Williams .... I, 267-288

XI. Aire française

Hagiographie latine

750-950

    Alcuin hagiographe († 804): J.-C. Poulin .... **VIII, 145-184**

    Province de Tours

        Hagiographie bretonne: J. C. Poulin .... **VIII, 189-242**

        Diocèses d'Angers et du Mans: L. Trân Duc, C. Mériaux .... **VIII, 243-257**

    Province de Rouen

        Diocèse de Rouen: L. Trân Duc .. VIII, 261-286

        Basse-Normandie: J. C. Poulin.... VIII, 287-309

    Province de Reims

        Diocèses de Reims, Soissons, Laon: M.-C. Isaïa .... **VIII, 315-365**

        Diocèse de Noyon: P. Chaffenet, M. Gaillard .... **VIII, 367-377**

        Diocèse de Châlons: K. Krönert, M. Gaillard .... **VIII, 379-387**

        Diocèses de Beauvais et Senlis: C. Mériaux .... **VIII, 389-407**

        Diocèse d'Amiens: F. Peloux .... VIII, 409-450

        Diocèses de Cambrai-Arras, Thérouanne, Tournai: C. Mériaux

    Province de Sens

        Diocèses de Sens, Troyes et Nevers: **M. Gaillard** .... **VIII, 453-471**

Diocèse d'Auxerre: A.-M. Verleysen
.... VIII, 473-492
Diocèse d'Orléans: H. Caillaud, M. Gaillard,
K. Krönert .... VIII, 493-514
Diocèse de Chartres: K. Krönert
Diocèse de Meaux: M. Gaillard
Diocèse de Paris
    Paris: K. Krönert .... VIII, 515-590
    Environs de Paris (Saint-Denis, Chelles):
    M. Gaillard, K. Krönert
Province de Lyon
    Diocèse de Lyon: M.-C. Isaïa .... VIII, 593-598
    Diocèses suffragants de Lyon: M. Gaillard,
    A. Rauwel .... VIII, 599-610
Province de Vienne
    Diocèse de Vienne: A.-M. Verleysen
.... VIII, 613-638
    Diocèses de Valence, Maurienne, Grenoble,
    Viviers: F. Peloux .... VIII, 639-680
    Diocèse de Genève: É. Chevalley
.... VIII, 681-694
Province de Tarentaise (750-1500): É. Chevalley
.... VIII, 695-720
    Diocèse de Besançon: A. Wagner
.... VIII, 721-727
Provinces d'Arles, Aix et Embrun: E. Magnani,
V. Olivier
Aquitaine: A.-M. Bultot-Verleysen
.... VI, 521-636, 688-704
Province de Cologne (région romane), diocèse de
    Liège: A. Dierkens
950-1130
Midi
    Provinces de Vienne, Tarentaise, Arles, Aix et
        Embrun: P.-A. Sigal .... I, 311-319
    Provinces de Bordeaux et Bourges (diocèses
        méridionaux): P. Bonnassie .... I, 291-311
    Provinces de Bordeaux, Bourges, Auch et
        Narbonne: A.-M. Bultot-Verleysen
.... VI, 637-694

Centre
- Province de Tours: I. van 't Spijker .... II, 248-258
  cf. aussi **J.-C. Poulin «L'Hagiographie bretonne»** .... **VIII, 189-242**
- Province de Sens
  - Orléanais: T. Head............................ I, 345-358
  - Autres diocèses

Nord et ouest
- Province de Cologne (région romane), diocèse de Liège: J. Webb .... VI, 809-904
- Province de Rouen: I. van 't Spijker ... II, 258-263
- Province de Reims: I. van 't Spijker ... II, 263-279

Est
- Provinces de Besançon et de Lyon: D. Iogna-Prat .... I, 319-338
- Province de Trèves (région romane), diocèse de Metz, Toul et Verdun: G. Philippart, A. Wagner .... IV, 583-742

1130-1350
- Sud-Ouest
  - Provinces de Bordeaux, Auch et Narbonne: C. Baillet, P. Henriet .... VI, 705-807
- Autres régions

1350-1550
Hagiographie imprimée: S. Bledniak .... I, 359-406
Hagiographie vernaculaire: G. Brunel-Lobrichon, M. Leurquin-Labie, M. Thiry-Stassin ...... II, 291-372

XII. Aire néerlandaise

Hagiographie latine
750-950
- Province de Cologne
  - Diocèse d'Utrecht: M. Carasso-Kok (à partir de 900) .... II, 373-411
  - Diocèse de Liège, cf. Aire française: A. Dierkens
- Province de Reims
  - Diocèses de Tournai, Thérouanne, Cambrai, cf. Aire française: C. Mériaux

950-1130
- Province de Cologne
  - Diocèse d'Utrecht: M. Carasso-Kok ... II, 373-411

Diocèse de Liège: J. Webb .... VI, 809-904
Province de Reims
   Diocèses de Tournai, Thérouanne, Cambrai:
      van 't Spijker (aire française, «La province
      ecclésiastique de Reims») .... II, p. 263-279
   1130-1350: J. Deploige
   1350-1550: V. Vermassen .... VII, 565-613
Hagiographie vernaculaire
   Les légendes rimées: W. Verbeke .... VII, 615-755
   La prose hagiographique: W. Verbeke

XIII-XV. Îles britanniques
   Angleterre, Pays de Galles
      Hagiographie latine: M. Lapidge, R. Love .... III, 203-326
      Hagiographie vernaculaire
         Old English: J. Cross .... II, 413-428
         Late Old English: G. E. Whatley .... II, 429-500
         Anglo-Normand: M. Thiry-Stassin .... I, 407-428
         Middle English: M. Görlach .... I, 429-486
   Écosse: A. D. Macquarrie .... I, 487-502
   Irlande: M. Herbert .... III, 327-360

XVI. Scandinavie
   Danemark et Suède: B. Carlé, A. Fröjmark ... II, 501-546
   Norvège et Islande
      Hagiographie latine
         Norvège: L. Jiroušková, A. Ommundsen,
            H. Antonsson .... VII, 757-874
         Islande: G. Jensson .... VII, 875-949
      Hagiographie vernaculaire: S. Filippusdóttir-Le Breton
         .... III, 361-452

Bilan
   Bilan et apport général du volume IV: G. Philippart
      .... IV, 743-780

Sigles et abréviations

AASS	*Acta Sanctorum*, de janvier à novembre, éd. par la Société des Bollandistes, Anvers, 1643-1794; 2ᵉ éd., 43 vol., Venise, 1734-1770; 3ᵉ éd., 60 vol., Paris – Rome, 1863-1868.
AASS OSB	*Acta Sanctorum Ordinis sancti Benedicti in sæculorum classes distributa*, éd. J. Mabillon, 6 vol., Paris, 1668-1701.
AB	*Analecta Bollandiana*.
BHL	*Bibliotheca hagiographica latina antiquae et mediae latinitatis*, 2 vol., Bruxelles, 1898-1899 (réimpr. 1949 en deux vol. et 1992 en un vol.) (Subsidia hagiographica, 6) et *Novum supplementum*, Bruxelles, 1986 (Subsidia hagiographica, 70).
BHLms	*Bibliotheca hagiographica latina manuscripta*.
BS	*Bibliotheca sanctorum*, Istituto Giovanni XXIII nella Pontificia università lateranense, 13 vol., 1961-1970.
Cat. Bruxelles	*Catalogus codicum hagiographicorum bibliothecae regiae Bruxellensis... ediderunt Hagiographi bollandiani*, 2 vol., Bruxelles, 1886-1889.
Cat. Paris	PONCELET, A., *Catalogus codicum hagiographicorum latinorum antiquiorum saeculo XVI qui asservantur in Bibliotheca nationali Parisiensi*, 4 vol., Bruxelles, 1889-1893 (Subsidia hagiographica, 2).
Cat. Vat.	PONCELET, A, *Catalogus codicum hagiographicorum latinorum Bibliothecae Vaticanae*, Bruxelles, 1910 (Subsidia hagiographica, 11).
CC CM	*Corpus Christianorum, Continuatio mediaevalis*.
CC SL	*Corpus Christianorum, Series latina*.
DHGE	*Dictionnaire d'histoire et de géographie ecclésiastiques*, Paris, à partir de 1912.
Hagiographies	*Hagiographies. Histoire internationale de la littérature hagiographique latine et vernaculaire en Occident des origines à 1550*, éd. G. PHILIPPART, t. I-V, Turnhout, 1994-2010, éd. M. GOULLET, t. VI-VII, Turnhout, 2014-2017 (Corpus Christianorum).
HBS	Henry Bradshaw Society.
LexMA	*Lexikon des Mittelalters*, Munich – Zurich, 1977-1999.
MGH	*Monumenta Germaniae Historica*.
	—, AA: *Auctores antiquissimi*.

—, *Conc.*: *Concilia Karolini aevi.*
—, *Epist.*: *Epistolae.*
—, *Poet. Lat.*: *Poetae Latini medii aevi.*
—, *SRG in usum scholarum*: *Scriptores rerum Germanicarum in usum scholarum.*
—, *SRG, NS*: *Scriptores rerum Germanicarum, nova series.*
—, *SRM*: *Scriptores rerum Merovingicarum.*
—, *SS*: *Scriptores* (in folio).

PL · *Patrologiae cursus completus... omnium SS. Patrum, doctorum scriptorumque ecclesiasticorum... Series Latina*, éd. J.-P. MIGNE, Paris, 1878-1891.

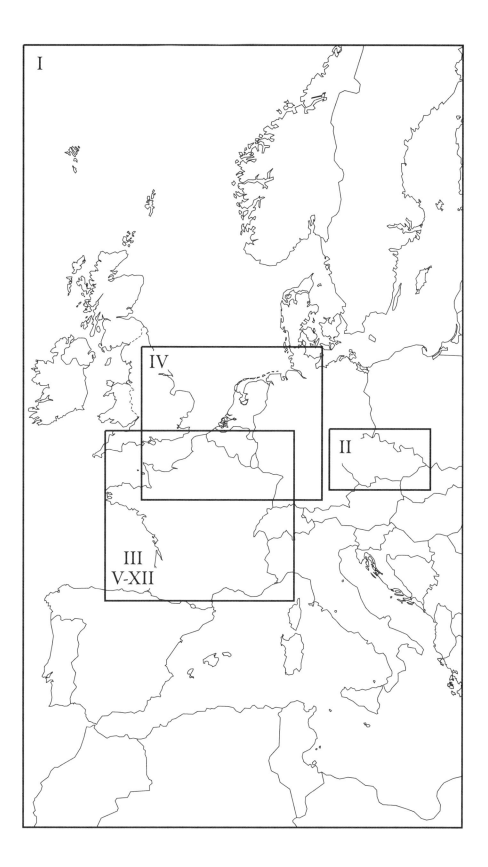

Latin Hagiography and the Cult of Saints in Czech Territories in the Middle Ages (tenth-fifteenth Centuries)

by

Marianna CERNO and Maddalena BETTI*

I. INTRODUCTION. – A. Geo-historical Framework and Terminology. – B. Political and Ecclesiastical History of Moravia and Bohemia in the Middle Ages. – 1. At First Great Moravia. – 2. Bohemia: Christianization and the Formation of the Přemyslid Duchy. – 3. The Foundation of the Bishopric of Prague. – 4. The Eleventh Century: Towards the Kingdom (and the Foundation of the Diocese of Olomouc). – 5. King Vladislav II and Jindřich Zdík, Bishop of Olomouc. The Hereditary Kingdom. – 6. The Last Přemyslids. – 7. Luxemburg's Dinasty. – 8. Jan Hus and the Hussite Wars.

II. LATIN HAGIOGRAPHY OF BOHEMIA AND MORAVIA. – A. Features and Protagonists of Bohemian and Moravian Latin Hagiography. – 1. Preliminary Note on Czech Modern Historiography. – 2. Latin Hagiography for the Czech Saints. – 3. Hussitica. – 4. Imported Sainthood (Vitus martyr. – Mauritius Agaunensis seu Thebaeus martyr. – Emmerammus episcopus martyr. – Godehardus Hildesheimensis episcopus. – Victorinus martyr. – *Legenda aurea*. – Clemens I papa. – Hieronymus Stridonius/Eusebius Hieronymus). – 5. Cyrillo-Methodiana. – 6. The Parodies of the Manuscript PRAHA, Národní Knihovna, III.E.27. – 7. The *Passio Iudeorum Pragensium*. – B. Alphabetical Inventory of the Czech Saints' Hagiographies. – 1. Adalbertus (Vojtechus) Pragensis episcopus. – 2. Agnes de Bohemia Ord. S. Cl. – 3. Arnestus seu Ernestus Pragensis episcopus. – 4. Benedictus, Iohannes et socii (Quinque fratres) in Polonia martyres. – 5. Guntherus eremita. – 6. Hieronymus de Praga magister. – 7. Hieronymus Stridonius (Eusebius Hieronymus). – 8. Hroznata Ord. Praem. martyr. – 9. Iohannes Hus. – 10. Iohannes de Ienzenstein Pragensis episcopus. – 11. Iohannes Milicius de Chremsir. – 12. Iohannes Nepomucenus Pragae presbyter. – 13. *Passio Iudeorum Pragensium*. –

---

* M. Cerno is accountable for the parts II and III of the present paper, and M. Betti for the part I. M. Cerno also translated in English the original Italian paper. The authors thank Guy Philippart for his useful advice on this article. The vernacular Czech hagiography is going to be presented in the next issue of *Hagiographies*, together with a list of the manuscripts of the Latin and vernacular hagiographies of the Czech saints.

14. Ivanus eremita. – 15. Ludmilla Bohemiae ducissa. – 16. Milada Pragensis abbatissa OSB. – 17. Procopius Pragensis abbas. – 18. Sigismundus rex Burgundionum m. – 19. Wenceslaus Bohemiae dux et martyr. – 20. Zdislava OP.

III. Selected Supplementary Bibliography. – A. Political and Ecclesiastical History of Moravia and Bohemia in the Middle Ages. – B. Latin Hagiography of Moravia and Bohemia. – 1. General Studies. – 2. Adalbertus (Vojtechus) Pragensis episcopus. – 3. Agnes de Bohemia Ord. S. Cl. – 4. Arnestus seu Ernestus Pragensis episcopus. – 5. Benedictus, Iohannes et socii (Quinque fratres) in Polonia martyres. – 6. Guntherus eremita. – 7. Hieronymus de Praga magister. – 8. Hieronymus Stridonius (Eusebius Hieronymus). – 9. Iohannes Hus. – 10. Iohannes Nepomucenus Pragae presbyter. – 11. *Passio Iudaeorum Pragensium*. – 12. Ivanus eremita. – 13. Karolus Magnus rex. – 14. Procopius Pragensis abbas. – 15. Sigismundus rex Burgundionum m. – 16. Wenceslaus Bohemiae dux et martyr. – C. Webography of the published sources.

Bibliography.

I. Introduction

A. Geo-historical Framework and Terminology

Bohemia (Čechy) and Moravia (Morava) are the two main historical regions of the Czech Republic, together with the Czech Silesia (České Slezsko). Bohemia occupies the Western part of the Czech Republic, including the main urban centre of the territory, the capital city of Prague. Moravia occupies instead the Eastern part, having as important centres the cities of Brno, Olomouc and Znojmo. The Czech Silesia is a part of the historical region of Silesia, which belongs to the actual North-Eastern territory of the Czech Republic (Silesia lays for the most part in the South-Western Poland).

Churches and monasteries of medieval Bohemia and Moravia

The present introduction offers a synthesis of the political events of Bohemia and Moravia, focusing on the ecclesiastical and monastic local history, aiming at providing an essential historical framework for the hagiographical culture and tradition, without claiming to be exhaustive.

The choice of considering together Bohemia and Moravia as a sort of twin reality is fully justified by their common historical and political background, at first within the Bohemia Duchy and then in the Kingdom, although both of them maintained their own peculiarities.

On the margins of the German Empire during its first centuries of life, in the fourteenth century the Slavic political formation, i.e. the Bohemian Kingdom, was at the centre of the imperial dynamics. Therefore, the constant and fluid relationship with the Empire played an essential role in starting the processes of construction of the Bohemian identity (*Identitätsbildungsprozessen*).

The hagiographical production was strategical in developing the identity issue, thanks to its flexibility in following the varying political circumstancies. The Přemyslid saints were the mainstay of the institutional authority during the reign of both Přemyslid and Luxembourg's dynasties, the latter being a successful heir of the other. The tradition of the Moravic dynasty of Mojmirid was also important, claiming a continuity between the past glory of the Great Moravia and the medieval history of the Bohemian Kingdom. In particular, the illustrious Moravian tradition of Cyril and Methodius played a crucial role in the local religious, cultural and ecclesiastical history, forming the basis for the claim of the autonomy of the local church, independent from the German clergy[1].

---

[1] The reference bibliography of the present chapter are the following general or introductory studies about medieval Bohemia and Moravia: BEREND – URBAŃCZYK – WISZEWSKI (2013) and CURTA (2019); on political history, PÁNEK – TŮMA (2018); on socio-economical transformations, KLÁPŠTĚ (2012); on the Bohemian identity, KALHOUS (2018); on the royal ideology, ANTONÍN (2017). On the history of the Czech territory and the Bohemian crown see also the first six volumes of *Velké dějiny zemí Koruny české*.

B. Political and Ecclesiastical History of Moravia and Bohemia in the Middle Ages

1. At first Great Moravia [2]

The denomination of Great Moravia occurs only in Constantine VII Porphyrogenitus's *De administrando imperio* to designate the political formation of the Mojmirids, leaders of the Slavic Moravians who appear in the Frankish Annals from the year 822. Nowadays, this denomination is less used, because of its connection to the nationalistic views of the nineteenth-century historiography.

Since the Seventies of the twentieth century, scholars have been debating the localisation of the Great Moravia: the archaeological data supported more convincingly the traditional opinion, according to which the heart of the political formation lied to the north of the river Danube, in the south-eastern part of the Czech Republic (present-day Moravia) and in western Slovakia [3].

Another issue is the political and socio-economic structure of the Great Moravia, which limited the expansion of the Franks in the middle Danube region. Great Moravia's political leaders Mojmir I (until 846), Rostislav (until 870) and Svatopluk (until 894) posed a serious threat to the Eastern Carolingian authorities. Great Moravia's decline is traditionally associated to the expansion of Magyars into the Danube basin at the beginning of the tenth century, but it was also tied to its fragile socio-economic foundations.

Great Moravia was the missionary territory of the Bavarian clergy. In 831 the bishop of Passau Regenharius celebrated a mass baptism for all the Moravians. However, Rostislav tried to prevent Moravia from falling into the jurisdiction of the Bavarian churches. Firstly, he turned to Rome to solicit the intervention of the Apostolic seat in vain, and then to the Byzantine emperor Michael III (842-867), who instead answered the plea, sending Constantine-Cyril and Methodius to Central Europe as missionaries. Rostislav warmly welcomed the brothers of Thes-

---

[2] On the political formation of Moravia, see BOWLUS (1995), EGGERS (1995) and TREŠTÍK (2001b). New approaches are offered by CURTA (2009) and MACHÁČEK (2009).

[3] The debate about the geographical position of Great Moravia started from BOBA (1971).

saloniki, and they trained the future Moravian clergy using the local language (863). They created the Glagolitic alphabet for the Slavic letters and translated the religious texts in Old Church Slavonic, a language based on a Macedonian dialect. Some years later, the brothers left Moravia and went to Rome to consecrate some of their Slavic disciples and introduce an ecclesiastical hierarchy independent of the Bavarian episcopate). Constantine-Cyril died in Rome, and there was buried in the church of St Clement, while Methodius obtained in 870 the title of archbishop of Pannonia by pope Hadrian II (867-872).

In the same year, Methodius was tried by the Bavarian bishops and subsequently imprisoned in the monastery of Reichenau for three years, for having exercised his episcopal functions in their missionary territories. Released in 873 thanks to the intervention of pope John VIII (872-882), Methodius suffered the hostility of the Latin clergy in Moravia at the time of Svatopluk, but in 880 obtained the title of archbishop of the Moravian church (*sancta ecclesia Marabensis*) by pope John VIII, which had also the suffragan diocese of Nitra (in today's Slovakia)[4].

Right after Methodius' death, the Slavic clergy was expelled from Moravia with the approval of the prince Svatopluk and the pope Stephen V, and took cover in the Balkans and Bulgaria. Between the end of the ninth century and the beginning of the tenth, the Magyars attacked Great Moravia, clouding the destiny of its church. Pope John IX (898-900) lastly attempted to revitalise the Moravian church by consecrating the archbishop John and the bishops Benedict and Daniel, but causing the negative reaction of the Bavarian clergy.

2. Bohemia: Christization and the Formation of the Přemyslid Duchy[5]

Bohemia is the name of the region ruled by the *Beihemi*, who carried out some raids in the Frankish territories and were firstly mentioned in 799-800, but more regularly since 850. The region ended up into the political sphere of influence of Svatopluk

---

[4] On the history of Cyril and Methodius, see DVORNÍK (1933), TACHIAOS (2001), VAVŘINEK (2014). On Methodius' archdiocese, see BETTI (2014).

[5] On the early history of the Přemyslid dynasty, see TŘEŠTÍK (1997); SOMMER (2009); CHARVÁT (2010); KALHOUS (2012).

in the Eighties of the ninth century. From this situation the tradition expressed in the *Legenda Christiani* blossomed (cf. *infra*, II.B.19), according to which the archbishop Methodius would have baptized in 894 in Moravia the duke of Bohemia Bořivoj of the Přemyslid dynasty (named by its legendary progenitor, Přemysl, alias Přemysl Oráč). After his return to Bohemia, Bořivoj founded the first local churches: in Levý Hradec near Prague a church dedicated to saint Clement (the pope Clement I, a cult related to the Cyril-Methodian tradition: cf. *infra*, II.A.4); in the castle of Prague a church dedicated to Virgin Mary. That was reported into the *Legenda Christiani*, a tradition accepted by Cosmas of Prague, who wrote the *Chronicon Boemorum* in the years 1119-1122. This chronicle, a chronological account of the deeds of the Czechs with a particular focus on their rulers, is an essential source for scholars who study the early Bohemian hagiography. The *Chronicon Boemorum* will be often mentioned in the present paper.

Instead, the *Annals of Fulda*[6] dated the first christianization of Bohemia back to the year 845, when fourteen dukes went to Regensburg, beseeching Louis the German (Louis II) to be baptized. The two versions of christianization thus reveal the political oscillation of the Bohemian leaders between Great Moravia and the kingdom of the Eastern Franks[7].

Moreover, the legend «Crescente fide» (cf. *infra*, II.B.19) reported that Spytihněv, Bořivoj's son, commissioned the building of a church in Budeč dedicated to the apostle Peter.

The duke Spytihněv allowed the first ecclesiastical organization in the territory by authorizing in 895 the foundation of the archpresbyterate of Prague, under the jurisdiction of the bishop of Regensburg.

The efforts to convert Bohemia to Christianity continued with Vratislav, Spytihněv's brother and successor (*c.* 915-921) and the founder of the church of St George in the castle of Prague. Married with the pagan princess Drahomíra, his sons were Wenceslas (Václav, born in 907) and Boleslav. According to the *Legenda Christiani*, Wenceslas was educated in Budeč by his paternal grandmother Ludmila, whom Drahomíra had got

---

[6] KURZE (1891), p. 35.
[7] On the christianization of the Bohemian people, see TŘEŠTÍK (1995); SOMMER – TREŠTÍK – ŽEMLICKA (2007).

murdered after Vratislav's death because of Ludmila's huge political influence over the future ruler. Once ascended to the throne, Wenceslas changed the political orientation of Bohemia, joining forces with the Saxons instead of the Bavarians. The symbol of this new ally was the dedication of the city cathedral to the martyr Vitus, the patron saint of Liudolfings of Saxony.

Wenceslas was murdered in 935 at Stará Boleslav by order of his brother Boleslav, who buried him in the same church of St Vitus and sanctified him, starting the long tradition of the saintly Přemyslid dynasty.

3. The Foundation of the Bishopric of Prague[8]

Boleslav I (935-972) strengthened his power by eliminating the families competing with the Přemyslids, excepting the Slavnikids (or Slavniks/Slavníks), who controlled the Eastern Bohemia. Forced to pledge allegiance to the emperor Otto I (950), Boleslav took part into the battle of Lechfeld against the Magyars. During Boleslav's reign, Prague became the centre of the long-distance trade and Bohemia acquired a sort of international dimension[9]. With the aim to ratify the new alliance with Poland, Boleslav gave his daughter Dobrava in marriage to Mieszko I Piast, who for this occasion converted to Christianism. Moreover, he put some effort into making the ecclesiastical organization of Bohemia more mature and independent: the diplomatic mission to Rome of Boleslav's daughter Mlada must be read in this context (about her cf. *infra*, II.B.16).

The bishopric of Prague was founded only in 973 and was put under the jurisdiction of the archbishop of Mainz, with the harsh opposition of the Bavarian bishops and a certain reticence of the emperors Otto I and Otto II. The first bishop of Prague, named Thietmar (maybe a monk of Corvey), was ordered only in 976, at the time of the duke Boleslav II (972-999), with the approval of the bishop of Regensburg Wolfgang, who in turn was worthily rewarded for having lost the jurisdiction over Bohemia. It is uncertain what remained of the prestigious archdiocese of Moravia in this period: maybe a bishopric with the

---

[8] On the foundation of the bishopric of Prague, see TŘEŠTÍK (2004) and KALHOUS (2012), p. 143-170.

[9] TŘEŠTÍK (2001a).

seat in Olomouc; the only extant source attested the existence of a Moravian bishopric in the year 976, without specifying its localisation[10]. In any case, the Moravian ecclesiastical organization needed a renewal.

Later, the territory of Moravia was under the jurisdiction of the second bishop of Prague – the first of Czech origins, of the Slavnikids family – Adalbert, born Vojtěch, who led a vaste diocese with a missionary vocation[11]. Boleslav II choose Adalbert-Vojtěch as a pastoral guide in 982, and he was consecrated in Verona by the archbishop of Mainz, at the presence of the emperor Otto II. Nonetheless, Adalbert's relations with the duke Boleslav II, the local clergy and the aristocracy of Bohemia were immediately difficult and nervous.

Adalbert stayed in Italy from 988 to 992, maybe as a legate of Boleslav II, in charge of promoting the elevation of Prague to archdiocese: he stopped over in Montecassino and in the monastery of St Nilus in Grottaferrata, before settling down in Rome, at the monastery of the SS. Boniface and Alexius. Back to Bohemia, in 993 Adalbert founded the first Benedictine male monastery in Břevnov, near Prague, dedicated to the saints Boniface and Alexius and composed at its beginnings by monks coming from the homonymous monastery of Rome[12]. But the crisis of the relationship between Boleslav II and Adalbert's family resulted in the slaughter of the Slavnikids, forcing Adalbert to leave Prague again. After a two-years stay in Rome, he chose to go to mission among the pagan Prussians, dying as a martyr near Gdansk. The polish Duke Bolesław I Chrobry (992-1025), who was hosting the surviving relatives of Adalbert, took his murdered body and translated it into the church of Gniezno. Gniezno became the see of a new archbishopric in 999 at the behest of the emperor Otto III and pope Sylvester II, having Adalbert's brother, Radim-Gaudentius, as its first arch-

---

[10] On the Moravian church, see JAN (2003) and WIHODA (2010), p. 94-104.

[11] On the historical figure of Vojtěch, see *Svatý Vojtěch* (1998).

[12] KUBÍN (2013) disagrees with this hypothesis, commented by KALHOUS (2015a). The monastery of Břevnov was abandoned right after Adalbert's death, and revived only at the beginning of the eleventh century, thanks to the efforts of the Bavarian monks of Niederaltaich.

bishop with the controversial title of *archiepiscopus sancti Adalberti*[13].

There was probably a widespread discontent in Bohemia at the foundation of an archbishopric in Poland due to Adalbert's prestige, since all the attempts of elevation of Prague's diocese were still failing at that time.

4. The eleventh Century: Towards the Kingdom (and the Foundation of the Diocese of Olomouc)[14]

After the death of Boleslav II, Boleslav III (999-1002, 1003-1004) ruled Bohemia and founded the second local Benedictine abbey in Ostrov around the year 1000. Being opposed by his brothers, the local bishop and the aristocracy, Boleslav asked for help to the Polish ruler Bołeslaw Chrobry, who occupied Prague and controlled Bohemia under the name of Boleslav IV, taking advantage of the political weakness of the duchy. Thanks to the alliance with the German king Henry II, Boleslav III's brothers regained the power: Jaromir (1004-1012) and Oldřich (1012-1033) respectively.

Oldřich's son Břetislav (1034-1055) ruled over Bohemia and Moravia in a stabler way: he occupied Silesia and attacked Poland. During the raid of the city of Gniezno in 1039, saint Adalbert's relics were stolen and transferred into St Vitus church, maybe to promote once again the elevation of the diocese of Prague to archbishopric. Even if Břetislav did not control Poland, and ruled over Bohemia and Moravia under the supervision of the German Empire, nonetheless the local reality became a stable, powerful and autonomous socio-political organization[15].

After Břetislav's death, there was once again a dynastic crisis: the seniority system of the Bohemian duchy caused continuous civil wars, while the freshly born Moravian duchies served to balancing and redistributing the hierarchical powers. Leaving five sons, who originated the five branches of the Přemyslid family, Břetislav tried to avoid the fight for the power by des-

---

[13] MICHALOWSKI (2016), p. 182-187.

[14] General studies on the eleventh-century Bohemia are WOLVERTON (2001) and WIHODA (2002b).

[15] On Břetislav's reign, see ŽEMLIČKA (1997), p. 55-75 and KRZEMIEŃSKA (1999).

ignating his son Spytihněv II (1055-1061) in succession to him, and giving to the others a partial ruling power over the Moravian zones of Brno, Olomouc and Znojmo, which after became all duchies.

After Spytihněv II, Vratislav II obtained the reign, ruling as a duke from 1061 to 1085, and as a king from 1085 to 1092[16]: he founded the new Moravian diocese, having its seat in Olomouc[17], and also the first Benedictine monastery of Moravia (1078) in Hradisko, near Olomouc[18].

Vratislav's brothers Konrad and Ota forced the ruler to appoint their younger brother Jaromír-Gebhard as the bishop of Prague (1068-1090)[19]. In turn, Jaromír tried to suppress the diocese of Olomouc; he fought against Vratislav's being in favour of the Chapter of the SS. Peter and Paul church in Vyšehrad, on the other side of the river Vltava, where Vratislav II had his headquarter. Jaromír also probably opposed to Vratislav's summoning again the monks of Sázava to Bohemia. Sázava was the only early-medieval monastery of Roman rite expressed in Old-Church Slavonic: Spytihněv II expelled the monks in 1056, and they would have been expelled again and definitively in 1095 (cf. chapter II, especially II.A.2 and II.B.17)[20]. Finally, Jaromír even refused to take part in Vratislav's incoronation in 1085, celebrated by the archbishop of Trier Egilbert: for the first time in Bohemian history, a duke obtained the (not dynastic) title of king by the German emperor Henry IV, as a reward for his help during the Investiture Controversy.

During the eleventh century, the dukes of Bohemia guaranteed a relevant international position by allying themselves to the Salian emperors, as well as by creating a crucial relationship with Rome. For this reason, Spytihněv II obtained the privilege of the miter, which then the popes Alexander II and Gregory II

---

[16] On Vratislav II, see REITINGER (2017).
[17] On the diocese of Olomouc, see ELBEL (2010).
[18] WIHODA (2002a).
[19] On Jaromír-Gebhard, see KALHOUS (2003).
[20] On the events, cf. SOMMER (2005) and the included paper by Peter Sommer at p. 157-172 dedicated to the history of the monastery in the eleventh century.

confirmed to Vratislav II, proving the special dignity of the Bohemian duchy to the eyes of the Roman curia[21].

5. King Vladislav II and Jindřich Zdík, Bishop of Olomouc. The hereditary kingdom

After Vratislav II's death, there was once again a problematic succession: the sons and the grandsons of the king, who were the rulers of the Moravian duchies, harshly fought against each other. Finally, Vladislav II defeated the other rivals (1140-1172), among whom the last one was the rebel duke of Moravia Konrád II Ota[22]. Vladislav II succeeded thanks to the support of the German king Conrad III Hohenstaufen, whom Vladislav II had helped during the second Crusade, and the bishop of Olomouc Jindřich Zdík (1126-1150), flanked by the papal legate Cardinal Guido of Pisa[23].

Jindřich Zdík was a reformer bishop, who promoted the entrance of the Premonstratensian monks in Bohemia. The Order had a great success, to the detriment of the Benedictine communities. The most important monasteries brought to existence in this period were Strahov, founded in Prague by Jindřich Zdík in 1142, Doksany and Milevsko. In 1193 the blessed Hroznata (about whom cf. *infra*, II.B.8) founded the Premonstratensian monastery of Teplá: the first members of this community were canons coming from Strahov. Soon after, in 1202-1210 Hroznata founded the female twin monastery of Chotěšov[24]. The duke Vladislav II and Jindřich Zdík then promoted the entrance of the Order of the Hospital of St John of Jerusalem, creating the first house in the district of Malá Strana in Prague, and of the Cistercians, founding Sedlec in 1142, Plasy in 1144, and Nepomuk in 1145[25].

Vladislav II was a faithful ally of emperor Frederick I Barbarossa. By assuring to Barbarossa military support, he was crowned in Regensburg in 1158. After Vladislav's death, Barbarossa intervened in the critical succession, aiming at main-

---

[21] ŽEMLIČKA (1992).
[22] Cf. MAŠEK – SOMMER – ŽEMLIČKA (2009).
[23] On the bishop Jindřich Zdík, see WIHODA (2010), p. 173-175, 186-199.
[24] On Premonstratensian monks in Bohemia, see HLAVÁČEK (2003).
[25] CHARVÁTOVÁ (1998).

taining his authority over Bohemia: he did not acknowledge Vladislav's son Frederick (Bedřich), for whom Vladislav abdicated in 1172. Instead, Barbarossa demanded as a ruler Vratislav II's grandson, Oldřich (Ulrich), who in turn immediately left the government over Bohemia to his elder brother Soběslav II. This latter faced the strong opposition of Konrad II Ota of Znojmo, who proclaimed himself margrave of Moravia, the administrator of a sort of independent state supported by the emperor Barbarossa (later, the Margraviate of Moravia was a subject territory of the Duchy of Bohemia). The emperor finally chose Přemysl I Otakar, another Vladislav II's son, as the duke of Bohemia (1192-1193, 1197-1230, king from 1198), and the brother of the latter, Vladislav Henry (Vladislav Jindřich), as the margrave of Moravia subject to the duke [26]. But in 1193 Barbarossa deposed even Přemysl I Otakar, and – in sharp contrast to the local use – appointed instead Henry Bretislaus (Henry Břetislav, 1193-1197), a member of the Přemyslid dynasty, who was at the time the bishop of Prague and as duke assumed the name of Břetislav III. After his death, Přemysl I Otakar was appointed again as the duke of Bohemia, being crowned by Otto IV Welf. Moreover, by supporting the election of Frederick II as king of Germany, in 1212 he obtained that the title of king of Bohemia became hereditary, even if still subject to the German emperor's authority, while to the other members of the dynasty were assigned the Moravian duchies, or remarkable roles at the court in Prague. Přemysl I Otakar also obtained the right of investiture and the control over the bishops of Bohemia and Moravia [27]. Nonetheless, Prague still remained a simple bishopric. The relationship with Rome became difficult when pope Innocent III contested Přemysl I Otakar's divorce and his new marriage with Constance (Konstancie), the daughter of the Hungarian king Béla III. The situation became even more complicated when Přemysl I Otakar refused to grant the privileges and the judicial autonomy obtained by the Bohemian church at the fourth Lateran council of the 1215. After having exiled the bishop of Prague Andrew (Ondřej), Přemysl I

---

[26] On the margrave of Moravia, see WIHODA (2016).

[27] The Golden Bull of Sicily (*Bulla aurea Siciliae*), a decree issued by Frederick II in September 1212, sanctioned such rights: cf. WIHODA (2012). On these events, cf. *Velké dějiny zemí Koruny Česke*, II (2000), p. 65-109.

Otakar finally accepted the conditions imposed by the papal legates (1221), aiming at preserving his son's succession to the throne.

6. The Last Přemyslids

After the death of Přemysl I Otakar in 1230, Wenceslas I, crowned by the archbishop of Mainz in 1228, ruled Bohemia until 1253, while his younger brother Přemysl was margrave of Moravia. Wenceslas I faced the attack of the Mongolians in Moravia, and expanded the Bohemian southern border by controlling the margraviate of Austria (entrusted to his heir Přemysl Otakar II) after the extinction of the Babenberg family[28]. Thanks to Wenceslas' political action, the Bohemian kingdom became the largest territorial entity of the Empire, and the only one with a hereditary royal title.

Přemysl Otakar II reigned over Bohemia from 1253 to 1278. In the first years of his government, he fought against Hungarians over the control of Styria, obtained in 1261 after having married Kunhuta, the daughter of the Hungarian king Béla IV. He also expanded the Bohemian kings' control over Carinthia and Carniola, undermining also Hungary after Béla IV's death, and being stopped only by the election of Rudolf I of Habsburg as king of Germany in 1273. Bohemia was definitively defeated by the German emperor Rudolf in the battle on the Marchfeld (Bitva na Moravském poli) of 1278, in which Přemysl Otakar II died[29].

His son Wenceslas II (1278-1305)[30], resigned to having lost the control over Austria (now ruled by the House of Habsburg), expanded the Bohemian territory over the Polish land, politically fragmented into different duchies or principalities. After having dominated the Upper Silesia and the duchy of Cracow, he was made king of Poland in 1300 thanks to the support of the noblemen of the Great Polonia and the Polish church[31].

The last members of the Přemyslid dynasty revitalised the religious local life by means of a close relationship with the Cis-

---

[28] On the expansion in Austria, see PRINZ (2003a).
[29] On the fight between Přemysl II Otakar and Rudolf I of Germany, see BLÁHOVÁ (1998).
[30] On Wenceslas II, see CHARVÁTOVÁ (2007) and JAN (2015).
[31] On the crowning, see ANTONÍN (2004).

tercian Order[32]: Cunigunde (Kunhuta) of Hohenstaufen, Wenceslas I's widow, founded in 1234 the monastery of Marienthal in Zittau; two years later, Constance of Hungary, widow of Přemysl I Otakar, founded the female monastery of Porta coeli in Tišnov; finally, Wenceslas II founded the monastery of Zbraslav. The last Přemyslid were often flanked by powerful Cistercian abbots, and they also promoted the entrance in Bohemia of the Mendicant Orders. Already in the Twenties of the thirteenth century, Dominicans settled in the church of St Clement «na Poříčí» in Prague, and shortly after also in Olomouc and in Brno[33]. The Minors (Franciscans) arrived during the Thirties, hosted by Wenceslas I in Prague, in the church of St James. Wenceslas' sister Agnes did even more, by founding a Poor Clare convent with an adjoining hospital (cf. *infra*, II.A.2 and II.B.2)[34].

At the end of the Přemyslid reign, there were twenty-one Franciscan male convents and five Poor Clare convents in Bohemia, as well as twenty-three male Dominican convents and two female ones.

7. Luxembourg's Dinasty[35]

The only male child of Wenceslas II became king of Bohemia and Poland after his father's death, but he was murdered after only a year (1305-1306). At first, the duke of Carinthia Henry, the husband of the eldest daughter of Wenceslas II Anna Přemyslovna, was the king of Bohemia, margrave of Moravia and king of Poland, even if he faced the opposition of Albert (Albrecht) I of Habsburg. Instead, the Czech noblemen promoted the succession of John of Luxembourg (John of Bohemia), the eldest son of the emperor Henry VII: John was king of Germany since 1308, and king of Bohemia since 1310, after having conveniently married the second daughter of Wen-

---

[32] CHARVÁTOVÁ (2002) and CHARVÁTOVÁ (2008).
[33] On the diffusion of the male and female Dominican foundations in the kingdom, see ANTONÍN (2019), p. 9-10.
[34] ANTONÍN (2019), p. 12 lists the Franciscan foundations in Bohemia until the thirteenth century.
[35] ŠMAHEL – BOBKOVÁ (2012).

ceslas II, Elizabeth (Eliška)[36]. As the new Bohemian king, John was flanked by the skilled archbishop of Mainz Peter von Aspelt and the archbishop of Trier Baldwin of Luxembourg, as well as supported by the bishop of Prague John IV of Dražice (1301-1343) and the abbots of the major Cistercian monasteries; but Bohemians harshly criticized his frequent absences and the exaggerated fiscal pressure.

After his father's death in 1314, John of Luxembourg supported the election of Louis IV of Bavaria against the rival Frederick the Fair, and expanded the Bohemian territory annexing the Upper Lusatia and Silesia. The relationship with Louis IV of Bavaria broke off because of the control of Tyrol, as well as because of their opposite positions on the Hundred Years' war: Louis endorsed England, while John supported France. In fact, John's family, the Luxembourg House, had a cultural perspective far distant from the Bohemian tradition, as they came from a territory very close to France and the related background.

During John I's reign, the bishop of Prague John IV of Dražice strengthen the properties of the diocese and stabilized the ecclesiastical administration, even if he stayed for a long time in Avignon. During his last years of life, he founded in Roudnice nad Labem the first Augustinian monastery of the Central Europe (1333), promoting the devotion for Ludmila and Adalbert pushed by a personal faith[37]. For his part, John of Luxembourg earned the favour of pope Clement VI: when John died fighting for the French king against England in the battle of Crécy in 1346[38], the pope excommunicated the German emperor and steered the election of John's son, Charles IV, who was administrating the Czech lands for many years. Moreover, Clement VI finally elevated Prague to archbishopric in 1344, having as suffragan seats the church of Olomouc and the newly created seat of Litomyšl: consequently, the churches of Bohemia were no longer under the jurisdiction of Mainz.

The crowning of Charles IV in Rome in 1355, and the promulgation of the Golden Bull (*Bulla aurea*) in 1356, which explicitly established the seven princes, who would have elected

---

[36] On these events, see BAUM (1998) and BOBKOVÁ (2013), who also describes the first difficult years of John's reign.

[37] On the bishop Jan IV. z Dražic, see HLEDÍKOVÁ (1991).

[38] On the reign of John I, see PAULY (1997) and BOBKOVÁ (2018).

the King (i.e. the four secular and three ecclesiastical *Kurfürsten*)[39], strengthen even more the Kingdom of Bohemia.

The first archbishop of Prague was (saint) Ernest (Arnošt) of Pardubice (1297-1364), capable administrator, faithful adviser of Charles IV, and emperor's legate at the papal curia of Avignon (cf. *infra*, II.A.2 and II.B.3)[40]. Ernest's successor Jan Očko of Vlašim (1364-1378) collaborated with the emperor Charles IV as well, substituting him during his absence in the year 1368. The bishop of Litomyšl John of Neumarkt, who was bishop of Olomouc since 1364, also had a very good relationship with the emperor (about his activity as a hagiographer, cf. *infra*, II.B.7 and II.B.19).

Charles IV aimed at making Prague the capital city of the Empire and its administrative centre; he founded the University in 1348[41]; he renewed the topography of the city, and created the district of Nové Město. He refurbished the royal castle and commissioned the building of the Karlštejn fortress and of new churches, promoting the entrance of new monastic Orders in Prague, such as the Carmelitans in the Church of Our Lady of the Snows; the Servite Order in the Church of Lady Day «Na trávníčku» (that is, «On the grass»); and the Augustinian Canons in Karlov[42].

With the intention of increasing the prestige of the city of Prague, Charles IV promoted his dynasty's legitimation by adopting successful strategies of political communication, and commissioning to the historians celebratory interpretations of the local past and tradition, from the Great Moravia to the latest kings of Luxembourg[43]. The imperial propaganda insisted on Charles' belonging to the Přemyslid dynasty, protagonist of the local hagiography (cf. *infra*, II.A.4-5 and II.B.15 and 19), since the emperor's mother was the daughter of the king of Bohemia Wenceslas II.

Wenceslas IV succeeded his father Charles IV in 1378: he was already king of Bohemia since 1363, and king of the Ro-

---

[39] Cf. HOHENSEE [*et al.*] (2009).

[40] On archbishop Ernest of Pardubice, see HLEDÍKOVÁ (2008).

[41] On the University of Prague, see ŠMAHEL (2007) and ŠMAHEL (2016).

[42] On the city of Prague at the time of the emperor Charles IV, see MORAW (1980).

[43] See BLÁHOVÁ (2006).

mans since 1376. Wenceslas' brother Sigismundus became the king of Hungary after his wedding with Mary, the daughter of the king of Hungary Louis I (Louis the Great), while Jobst (Jošt Lucemburský), Charles IV's nephew, became margrave of Moravia since 1375. Wenceslas IV was deposed as king of the Romans in 1400, and Ruprecht III, the Prince-elector of the Palatinate, came to the throne in place of him until 1419. He was a weak ruler in Bohemia, constantly being threatened by his brothers. From 1419 Sigismund ascended to the throne of Bohemia, being the last male member of the House of Luxembourg, who was also Holy Roman emperor from 1433 until his death in 1437.

8. Jan Hus and the Hussite Wars [44]

After the time of emperor Charles IV, the figure of Jan Hus dominated the history of Bohemia. He was a priest and a preacher, who promoted and leaded a huge and relevant reformist movement within the church, fighting against the ecclesiastical corruption and the immoral lay people, aiming at a fairer society. A sort of prelude of such revolution already showed up during the reign of Charles IV [45].

The background of the Hussite reform was composite: the struggles for the succession to the throne made the political situation unstable; the church was divided and in fight, because the Great Schism, which caused the so-called Avignon papacy, led to a contemporary reign of three popes from 1409 until the election of Martin V in 1417, at Constance. Moreover, the particular structure of the University of Prague composed by four nations (*nationes*) contributed to stir the cultural scene. The University's four nations were four groups corresponding to the main geographical provenances of the students. With specific regard to the subject of the present paper, the *nationes* discussed the controversial religious and theological issues of the Englishman John Wycliff. In this debate, the *natio Bohemica*, formed by Bohemian students of both Czech and German language, op-

---

[44] The reference study for this section is ŠMAHEL – PAVLÍČEK (2015).

[45] On the forerunners of Jan Hus, see HEROLD (2015). However, scholars recently argued against the continuity of a coherent reformist movement in Prague from 1360 to 1419, pointing out the simplistic approach of such view: cf. MARIN (2005).

posed to the other more conservative and pro-Rome three (Bavarian, Saxon, and Polish) for its own warm reception of Wycliff's reformist propositions.

Jan Hus was born between 1370 and 1372, studied at the Faculty of Arts in Prague as a member of the *natio Bohemica*, and became the dean of the same *natio* in 1401. After his ordination, he studied at the Faculty of Theology. In 1402 he became preacher at the Bethlehem Chapel of Prague, speaking in Czech vernacular not only to the aristocracy of the city, but to the entire population, and promoting his idea of a deep moral reform of the church[46]. In 1407 the *natio Bohemica* was denounced to the Roman pope for its appreciation of Wycliff's ideas: the shadow of heresy tarnished the English reformer's reputation, even if he died in perfect communion with the Roman church. Consequently, the apostolic seat forbade the diffusion of Wycliff's teaching and writings among the clergy and the population. For this reason, the archbishop of Prague Zbyněk Zajíc (1403-1411) had to contest the preaching in Czech language and forbid Hus' preaches against the clergy and Roman uses. At the same time, the king Wenceslas IV intervened shaking the balances of the University of Prague, fostering the activities of the *natio Bohemica* through the promulgation of the decrees of Kutná Hora in 1409, which caused the mass egress of the German students and masters[47]. Nonetheless, right before the council of Constance (Konstanz) of the years 1414-1418, Jan Hus lost Wenceslas' favour; being convoked to Rome, he sent some spokespeople on behalf of him, being consequently excommunicated[48]. Notwithstanding the favour of the new king, Sigismund, Jan Hus lost the support of his former followers, finding himself alone and isolated on the way to Constance in the fall 1414. There he was condemned, together with Wycliff's ideas, and executed at the stake the subsequent year. Shortly after, in 1416, Hus' major disciple Jerome of Prague died in the same way[49].

Jan Hus' death led to the Hussite war in Bohemia: an actual religion war[50] with several violent episodes, which took place

---

[46] SOUKUP (2015).
[47] NODL – ŠMAHEL (2009).
[48] On the trial of Jan Hus, see KEJŘ (2005) and FUDGE (2013b).
[49] On Jerome of Prague, see FUDGE (2016).
[50] On the Hussite wars, see KAMINSKY (1967) and ŠMAHEL (2002).

for about fifteen years starting with the so-called Prague defenestration, in the year of Wenceslas IV's death (1419). Not only the war broke out between the moderate faction of the Hussite movement (Utraquists) and the radical one (Taborits), but also external forces intervened, the so-called Crusades against Hussites, interfering in Bohemian politics.

The Catholic clergy endured the worst consequences: the archbishop of Prague Konrád z Vechty accepted in 1421 the so-called Four Articles of Prague, the Hussite manifesto, and for this reason he was deposed from the seat of Prague by the Roman Pope, who assigned the administration of the archdiocese to the bishop of Olomouc[51].

The Catholic church and the Utraquist faction reached a settlement of the conflict at the council of Basel in the years 1431-1436: the compromise called *Compactata* recognized the existence of the Hussite Christian church, the starting point of a semi-independent Bohemian church, which used Czech as the official language and celebrated the Holy Communion *sub utraque specie* (that means under both kinds of the bread and the wine), contrary to the Catholics (*sub una specie*, only under the kind of bread)[52].

Therefore, two different churches, the Catholic and the Utraquist, coexisted in Bohemia for two centuries. Out of the Kingdom, the Utraquist church had the fame of heretic and remained constantly isolated, in a condition that influenced also its literary production (cf. *infra*, II.A.3)

In the second half of the fifteenth century, George of Podebrady (Jiří z Poděbrad) dominated the scene: he ruled Bohemia from 1444 to 1453, and became king in 1458, reigning over Bohemia until 1470[53]. Although he was a capable politician, he had a hostile relationship with Rome because of his being explicitly Utraquist. He was a relevant ally of the German empire and the Hungarian crown (he was the son-in-law of Matthias Corvinus), and created a league against the Ottomans after the fall of Constantinople in 1453. At the same time, he impeded the Papal crusade, exacerbating the situation: in 1462 pope

---

[51] On the Catholic clergy and the administration of the diocese during the Hussite wars, see VODIČKA (2017).
[52] ŠMAHEL (2011).
[53] ŠMAHEL (1998).

Pius II condemned again the Utraquist church and rejected the *Compactata* pacts. Moreover, he declared George of Podebrady to be heretic and excommunicated him. In this context, the Catholic League of Zelena Hora arose in Bohemia, which helped the deposition of the Bohemian king, together with the Pope and the Hungarian army.

From 1471 the Jagiellon dynasty ascended to the throne of Bohemia: the new king Vladislav II (Wladislaw, Ulazlo), the son of Casimir IV Jagiellon, could not stop the fight started in 1468 between his father and Matthias Corvinus, until the peace of Olomouc of the year 1478. The war between Catholics and Utraquists ended in 1485 with the treaty of Kutná Hora («Treaty of Toleration»), after which Bohemia resumed the relationship with Rome[54].

The successor of Vladislav was Matthias Corvinus, and for few decades Bohemia tied up its history with the Hungarian kingdom, before Habsburg dynasty ruled the region from the second quarter of the sixteenth century until 1918. The advent of Habsburg dynasty closed the Bohemian Middle Ages and marked the slow but relentless decline of the autonomous Utraquist church, which did not find anymore the political support nor reached any agreement with the imperial authority.

II. LATIN HAGIOGRAPHY OF BOHEMIA AND MORAVIA

A. FEATURES AND PROTAGONISTS OF BOHEMIAN AND MORAVIAN LATIN HAGIOGRAPHY

1. Preliminary Note on Czech Modern Historiography

Sketching a picture of the hagiographies written in Moravia and Bohemia during the Middle Ages is not an easy task.

If on one hand there is a variety of cults and an abundance of texts in their chronological development, on the other hand scholars disagree on evaluating the hagiographies and their related context as valid sources. The highest attention is devoted

---

[54] On the relationship between the Roman church and the rulers of Central Europe, see KALOUS (2016).

to the major cults in particular, which are often connected to the historical and political situation in a very peculiar and complex way. Nonetheless, scholars recently gave more attention to hagiography, with also some examples of overall presentations. Beside this renewed interest in this literary genre, Czech scholars recently devoted some studies to the historiography's tendencies and ideologies of the last century and a half.

Any research in Czech hagiography must consider this historiographical matter and the complicated debate that is still underway about both the medieval historical context and the saints and their specific worship. As a consequence, texts and studies, which are mostly written in Czech language and sometimes difficult to be found from abroad, must be framed in the lively landscape of the scholarly discussions, which nowadays involve also the hagiographical subject.

Therefore, the present inventory aims at giving the most complete report of the actual *status quaestionis* of every single Latin hagiography of the Czech saints. This is the reason why for each saint of the catalogue only the essential textual data are offered, while Part III gives a supplementary selected bibliography as a starting point for any further research.

2. Latin Hagiography for the Czech Saints[55]

Czech hagiography arose at the beginning of the christianization of the territory: for this reason, as it happened in the entire Europe for the emperor Constantine and his moher Helena[56], the early local cults were directed to the ancestors of Přemyslid dynasty, that is to the princess Ludmila (or Ludmilla) and her grandson Wenceslas. They both lived between the end of the ninth century and the first third of the tenth, they were both martyrs, and they were both killed for political reasons and the struggle for the power. Ludmila died in 921, Wenceslas

---

[55] A summary of the medieval Czech cults is offered by KUBÍN (2017), which is the basis-study for the present paragraph, together with MARIN (2017).

[56] Cf. HOMZA (2017), p. 33-61. On Wenceslas as a model of medieval dynastic sainthood, a sort of evolution of the first examples of royal martyrdoms (like the Burgundian king Sigismundus, «the first saint-king of the Middle Ages», or like the English saint kings Oswaldus and Edmund) cf. KLANICZAY (2008), p. 254-255, 261-262 (p. 261 also about Ludmila).

in 935 (or 929 as written in the so-called *Legenda Christiani*, cf. *infra*, II.B.19).

To Ludmila and Wenceslas are dedicated the earliest Bohemian hagiographies, written around 970[57]. As only one of the Slavonic texts about Wenceslas is earlier than these two hagiographies, and as he is a royal martyr saint, Wenceslas soon personified the Czech national identity and state, and his cult symbolized the local institutions[58].

Ludmila's worship is instead less widespread, as it is limited to the Canoness – and after Benedictines – of the church of St George in the castle of Prague, a church founded by the blessed Mlada (or Milada). Ludmila's sainthood was officially recognized only in 1142, when the diocese of Prague used Ludmila's cult for political purposes. Only one hundred and fifty years later Ludmila became a national patron-saint, as her grandson Wenceslas already was.

Almost simultaneous to Wenceslas' death is the translation to Prague of the arm of saint Vitus, wanted by Wenceslas himself, who dedicated to Vitus the castle's *rotunda*. But the shortly subsequent violent martyrdom of Wenceslas hid Vitus' worship, compromising its destiny: in a few years Wenceslas' body was translated in the same place, and the promotion of his cult – due to his own killer, his younger brother Boleslav I – obscured Vitus' devotion for decades and centuries. Vitus' cult spread again in the fourteenth century, at the time of the emperor Charles IV, when Vitus also became a national co-patron saint.

Therefore, the first Wenceslas' co-patron saint was Adalbert (born Voytěch), the second bishop of Prague and a Benedictine monk, who founded the first male Bohemian monastery in Břevnov. Adalbert was in close contact with Rome and the Ottonian emperors, before dying as a martyr during a mission among the pagans in Prussia, near Gdansk, in 997. Because of his friendship with Otto III, two hagiographies had been written soon after his martyrdom, as well as his cult as a saint of the Empire had been promoted, similarly to Charlemagne. Nevertheless, Otto's premature death prevented the success of Adal-

---

[57] Some scholars assert that Ludmila's cult does not date back to the early Middle Ages: cf. HOMZA (2017), p. 91-92.

[58] Cf. MILADINOV (2013b), p. 24-25.

bert's devotion in the German Empire[59]. Adalbert's worship in medieval Europe soon succeeded in Poland and Hungary, while in Bohemia flourished soon after, when in 1039 duke Břetislav I stole Adalbert's relics from Gniezno and brought them to Prague, making Adalbert the co-patron national saint together with Wenceslas.

It means that Adalbert is a model of martyr and bishop saint venerated in a wide part of Central Europe during the Middle Ages[60]. His canonization in 999 by pope Sylvester II is traditionally accepted, even if it recently has been contested by some scholars as a mere fabrication (Petr Kubín).

The third Bohemian patron saint is abbot Procopius, who died in 1053. He founded the Benedictine monastery of Sázava, the only early medieval institution celebrating the liturgy in Old Church Slavonic[61]. Sázava also had a scriptorium where Slavonic texts were copied. All these are the only historical information about the saint, while any other detail derives from his hagiographies, written in a monastic milieu between the twelfth and the fourteenth century. From the second half of the thirteenth century, Procopius' cult spread throughout Bohemia, until he became a national co-patron saint.

A huge bibliography concerns Procopius, who is the only Bohemian saint whose hagiographies are completely studied and edited. In this regard, it should be noted the particular position of Petr Kubín, who affirms that the entire devotion for Procopius, as well as his hagiographical figure, is the result of a forgery of the mid-twelfth century, created with the aim of

---

[59] Cf. also MILADINOV (2013a), p. 187.

[60] KLANICZAY (2008), p. 255-256.

[61] Old Church Slavonic (or Slavic), also referred to as Paleo-Slavic (or Palaeo-Slavic), was the first Slavic literary language, born as a consequence of the translation of the Bible realised by Constantine-Cyril and Methodius. Old Church Slavonic was used also in Moravia for translating ecclesiastical works. The alphabet used to write the Paleo-Slavic language is the Glagolitic: it was created and used by Constantine-Cyril and Methodius during their mission of evangelisation among the Northern Slavs. Later and simplified is the Cyrillic alphabet, developed in the Balkan territories influenced by the Greek culture (Southern Slavs), and in the Bulgarian area in particular. Here and in other Slavic territories different linguistic varieties of the Paleo-Slavic developed, which had specific linguistic features and are known as «recensions» (for example in Dalmatia, the Croatian recension of the Paleo-Slavic). Cf. GARZANITI (2013); SMRŽÍK (1959).

preserving Sázava monastery from the new Orders' interferences.

In fact, in Kubín's view the proof of such historical and religious situation is the inclusion of the earliest attestation about Procopius in the *Exordium Zazavensis*, a typical example of *historia fundationis monasteriorum*. Procopius' description in the *Exordium Zazavensis* is the basis for any further hagiography devoted to the abbot: the *Vita minor* (beginning of the thirteenth century), the *Vita antiqua* (c. 1300), and the *Vita maior* (beginning of the fourteenth century). Any vernacular version derives from this latter[62]. As Kubín reports on Adalbert's canonization, a similar case occurs to Procopius, which should have been canonized by pope Innocent III in 1204: this should be a partial invention, even if some scholars accept it *in toto*[63]. Precisely, on one hand Procopius' canonization is historically attested in Bohemia for the year 1204; on the other hand, no Roman pope ever made its validity official. Procopius' cult flourished in Bohemia from the second half of the thirteenth century, and later he became a co-patron saint of the Kingdom.

Some other Czech cults are connected to the monastic milieu. Gunther/Vintíř was a hermit from Thuringia who died in 1045. He was buried near Prague, in Břevnov, after the monastery acquired his relics (Gunther spent his life between Bohemia and Bavaria). In Gunther's case, there are several contemporary prooves of his historicity, but his worship spread out from Břevnov much later, in the mid-thirteenth century, once again for political reasons and the ecclesiastical management of the area. This was the moment of the creation of his hagiography, which highlighted alleged connections to the Bohemian duke Břetislav I (that means, with the Přemyslid dynasty). Nonetheless, Gunther's canonization never took place and his cult remained circumscribed to the Bohemian territory, even if Břevnov monastery became a pilgrimage destination.

Another important saint monk is Hroznata, who founded the Premonstratensian monastery of Teplá, in Western Bohemia. His peculiar death in a cellar in 1217 caused his fame as a saint,

---

[62] The present chronology of Procopius' hagiographies differs from the traditionally accepted one, which considers the *Vita minor* as the earlier text about the saint. The new chronology is discussed by KUBÍN (2016b).

[63] For example NECHUTOVÁ (2007), p. 67-68; KLANICZAY (2008), p. 272.

and the abbot of Teplá commissioned his hagiography fourty years after, even if the text did not spread Hroznata's cult outside the monastery.

The Mendicant sainthood in Bohemia is represented by two female saints, of whom the major and more important is Agnes, a nun and a Přemyslid princess (she was the daughter of Ottokar I and the Hungarian Árpad princess Constance), cousin of Elisabeth of Thuringia (saint Elizabeth of Hungary) and niece of Hedwig of Silesia (saint Hedwig of Andechs). Agnes founded in Prague the first Clarisses' convent across the Alps, which had also an adjacent hospital dedicated to St Francis for poor people.

Agnes, who died in 1282, was very active in the European religious life of her time. The popes Gregory IX and Innocent IV wrote to her several letters about different aspects of the Rule of the Poor Clares and the management of both the convent and the hospital; pope Gregory IX officially acknowledged Agnes' foundation in 1244, giving her the title of abbess; Claire of Assisi personally wrote to Agnes four letters concerning the importance of the Rule of the Poor Clares and its reception in Bohemia between the fourteenth and fifteenth century.

Agnes' hagiographical dossier is characterised by a double and very distant tradition: the branch formed by the redaction *Candor lucis aeternae* (*BHL* 154b) and its middle-German translations, and the rest of the texts. These latter are connected to Claire of Assisi and her direct relationship with Agnes[64].

The second cult of the new Orders is dedicated to Zdislava, who died in 1252. Like Agnes, Zdislava helped poor and sick people as well. As she was considered as a Tertiary, she was venerated among the Dominican order, even if her worship remains marginal in the landscape of the Czech sainthood.

The age of Charles IV (1346-1378) is the period of the significant growing and development of the cult of saints, thanks to the emperor's active promotion and most of all to his acquiring of relics. As a consequence of Charles' travels, hundreds of saintly remains came to Bohemia, being a vehicle of the indulgences that were an instrument of the imperial authority[65].

---

[64] As discussed by FELSKAU (2017).

[65] MENGEL (2017), p. 58-59, 61; on Charles' activity in relics' acquirement and donation, cf. MACHILEK (1978); MENGEL (2004a), with further reference bibliography; the inventory of the copious relics kept in Prague in

Pushed by a personal faith, as he declared in a letter[66], Charles IV was particularly devoted to Wenceslas and Charlemagne, from which he took his forename and emperor's name respectively[67]. The emperor travelled over more than 400 places in order to honour the saints and acquire their relics, which were kept in Prague and in Karštejn fortress in particular, but also to give them as a present to several cities in Bohemia and elsewhere in the rest of Europe, as attested by some covering letters.

Scholars connect such Charles' fervent devotional activity to the purpose of increasing the fame and importance of both Luxemburg's dynasty and Prague, aiming at attracting more visitors and pilgrims to Bohemia, in a forward-looking picture of an economical, political and cultural development of the empire's capital city – where Charles IV founded the university in 1348, promoting the Czech translations and the diffusion of both classic and contemporary literature. In Charles' plan, Prague would have been a «new Rome»[68], in a «bicephalous» (he was both Czech king and Roman emperor) and officially bilingual reign (in Silesia, for example, German was the official language).

It has been said that the Roman martyr Vitus was chosen as co-patron saint by Charles IV because of the original dedication of Prague's cathedral wanted at the beginning of the tenth century by the duke (and saint) Wenceslas and rebuilt in a gothic shape on emperor's commission. Another non-Bohemian saint became co-patron in the same period: the martyr Sigismundus, the Burgundian king killed in the first quarter of the sixth century. Back from a travel to Agaune, the place of Sigismundus'

PODLAHA – ŠITTLER (1903). KLANICZAY (2008), p. 270, recalls the decoration of the Holy Cross Chapel, where almost all the 130 frames of the as many saints' pictures dominating the building contained the related relics.

[66] MENGEL (2004a), p. 148.

[67] MENGEL (2004a), p. 157, reminds us that the emperor spent his quite entire youth in France, at he court of his namesake king Charles IV. Nonetheless, it seems important to underline that the connection between Charles IV and Charlemagne was very popular, and that Charles IV intended to present himself as a reincarnation of the Carolingian ancestor: KLANICZAY (2008), p. 274; MENGEL (2007), p. 26-27. As for Wenceslas, Charles IV personally wrote a hagiography for the saint (cf. *infra*, II.B.19, penultimate text).

[68] Cf. for example KUBÍNOVÁ (2006).

burial, Charles IV brought to Prague some new relics, ten years after the first ones of the same martyr he acquired from the monastery of Einsiedeln. It was the year of Charles' hiring the title of «king of Burgundy» for the first time after Frederick Barbarossa's era, right there in Agaune, where Sigismundus' fame was being hidden for centuries by the most venerated martyrs of the Legio Thebaea, leaded by saint Maurice of Agaunum.

Sigismundus' cult was connected to Wenceslas' one, but differently from the case of Vitus, the association was intentionally made for political reasons (it is worth recalling here that both Sigismundus and Wenceslas were the names of Charles IV's sons). Planning the church's topography on the basis of the accounts of the saints' *post mortem* miracles, the emperor put the one's relics in front of the other's ones in the city cathedral, precisely on the eve of Wenceslas' feast[69]. Moreover, Charles IV promoted Sigismundus' worship in every way: he commissioned a splendid reliquiary; Sigismundus' celebration became mandatory; there were several artistic expressions, monumental buildings, and various architectural creations dedicated to the saint[70]. Very soon, the entire population grew fond of Sigismundus' cult, offering more and more attestations of miracles made by his relics: such success is attested by the *Libellus miraculorum*, of which only the fragmentary copy Paris, BnF, n.a.lat. 1510 still survives[71]. Another proof of Sigismundus' fame is the rich iconography of the saint, as reflected in the illuminated manuscript Wien, Österreichische Nationalbibliothek, ser. nov. 2633.

The emperor himself, who gave Sigismundus the title of co-patron saint of the Bohemian kingdom, attested such extraordinary power of miracles, which were most of all thaumaturgical. Among the hundreds of relics brought into Bohemia by Charles IV from around Europe, only Sigismundus had that much success, connected to a great amount of miracles and the related accounts (or, at least, survived accounts), and honoured by the national patronage[72]. Nonetheless, David C. Mengel observes that such promotion of Sigismundus' cult served also to

---

[69] Cf. also MENGEL (2007), p. 23-25.
[70] Cf. STUDNIČKOVÁ (2010).
[71] The text is published in *Cat. Paris*, III, p. 462-469.
[72] MENGEL (2007), p. 21 and 28-31 on the saint's miracles.

strengthen the worship of Wenceslas, first and native Bohemian patron-saint, whose devotion was quite weak among a part of the faithful[73]. However, the Hussite revolution inverted this trend, and while the national consciousness was arising, giving Wenceslas the preeminent place that Charles dreamt of, Sigismundus was increasingly put aside, if not even completely forgotten, in the same way as it already happened to him in Agaune.

Between the fourteenth and the fifteenth century the other important cults of Bohemia appeared, which are considered to be minor cults, if compared to the diffusion and the affection devoted to Wenceslas or Adalbert. They are, for example, the first archbishop of Prague, Arnošt/Ernest of Pardubice, on the seat from 1343 until 1364; John of Jenštejn, the third archbishop of Prague, a reformer that was forced to resign from his office; and Jan Milíc of Kromeriz, who died in Avignon in 1374 waiting for his trial. This latter was the one who scholars indicate as the forerunner of Jan Hus, since he was a very influential preacher of the emerging Bohemian Reformation (for each saint see also the related items of the hagiographical catalogue at chapter II.B). Some other saints of the last part of the Czech Middle Ages, whose cult is attested by liturgical but not hagiographical texts, are considered in section II.A.4.

From the beginning of the fifteenth century a deep change in the Czech spirituality occurred, which marked the subsequent two centuries and had its consequences until the contemporary era. The Hussite church developed its own vision of the sainthood, which was not unique and uniform, but differentiated among the parties of the movement itself, consequently influencing the contemporary sanctoral and hagiography. The texts about Jan Hus and Jerome of Prague, the two main protagonists of this long season of the Bohemian church, have peculiar characteristics. The Hussite period deserves a specific discourse, presented in section II.A.3.

The here proposed overview and the catalogue of the hagiographies of section II.B show the particular vitality and variety of both the Czech sanctoral and the related literary production, a situation that corresponds to the local cultural vivacity during the whole Middle Ages. As observed by Petr Kubín, the lack of

---

[73] MENGEL (2004a), p. 152-156; MENGEL (2007), p. 29.

Roman official canonizations of the saints do not affect this situation, and the immobilism of the worship that seems to remain anchored in the early Middle Ages with its ancient imported saints is only apparent[74].

3. *Hussitica*

Jan Hus and Hussitism characterised the last part of the Czech Middle Ages and the beginning of the Modern era. From the fifteenth century and for two hundred years, the Czech community remained on the fringes of the European Catholic life and church, due to the harsh conflicts, both theological and physical, against the Apostolic seat, which began with Hus' death at the stake in 1415, five years after his excommunication. At the Council of Basel in 1436, the Catholic and the Hussite churches reached an agreement, and the Utraquist church had its canonical recognition. As a matter of fact, the Utraquists claimed the lay right to receive the Holy Communion *sub utraque specie* (that means under both kinds of the bread and the wine, as the priests usually do): this is the reason why the chalice became the emblem of the Utraquists, which were also called Calixtines (from the Latin *calix*). In fact, the main and most substancial matters of the movement created by Jan Hus and continued by his supporters were the accusation against the clergy's corruption and the need of a deep moral reform of the daily life for both clerics and lay people.

At the beginning of the Hussite movement, the more radical supporters of Jan Hus, as for example Iacobellus of Stříbro (Jakoubek ze Stříbra) or Nicholas of Dresden, rejected the saints' cult and the veneration of the relics, reaching a form of actual iconoclasm. On the contrary, the moderate faction explicitly advocated the cult of saints. In fact, Jerome of Prague himself, the other thinker and main protagonist of the Hussite period together with Jan Hus, was charged with such form of refusal by the council of Constance (Konstanz), which condemned him and sentenced to the stake in 1416[75].

Jan Hus and Jerome of Prague immediately became Bohemian patrons, without any acknowledgement from the Pope:

---

[74] Kubín (2017), p. 38.
[75] Horníčková (2018), p. 62 and cited bibliography.

even if the moderate part of Hussite Bohemia reconciled with the Roman seat, the actual isolation of the Bohemian church caused a hagiographical season characterised by non-exportable saints[76]. Similarly, the hagiographical production had its peculiar features during the Hussite movement. While the memory of Jan Hus and Jerome of Prague as martyrs spread immediately after their death, the texts connected to their commemoration are richly differentiated, and embrace many literary genres. The contemporaneity of the protagonists and the impact of the Hussite movement in the cultural and religious life of that time leaded the whole Europe to a fervent discussion, both pro and against Hus and the proposed reform.

Moreover, the liturgy reveals such a peculiar situation as well, because only few texts are newly composed for the «new saints», while in most cases already existent songs and prayers were used, chosen among the ones for Vitus, for the feast of All Saints, or taken from the Common (*Commune sanctorum*) of the martyrs. Only the most polemic Humanist writings compare both Jan Hus and Jerome of Prague to the Apostles Peter and Paul, and they are consequently mentioned together. Contrary to the cult for Hus, the devotion for Jerome did not become popular, and his memory does not even appear in the calendaries.

Differently from hagiography and liturgy, Hussite iconography is later, starting at the beginning of the sixteenth century[77].

Another peculiarity of Hus' cult concerns his remains: Peter Mladenowicz's *Relatio* insists on their complete elimination, together with Hus' clothes. This is the reason why no cult of Hus' relics existed. Scholars still debate whether this situation also caused the total absence of Hus' miracles. In fact, the only mention of *post mortem* miracles accomplished by Jan Hus can be read in the anonymous *Relatio de delictis*, a generic report, which recounts some wonders without any detail, and once again with reference to Apostles Peter and Paul[78]. In the catalogue of the sections II.B.9 (Jan Hus) and II.B.6 (Jerome of Prague) are

---

[76] Cf. MARIN (2017), p. 28.
[77] HACK (2007), p. 138-139.
[78] The text is published by PALACKÝ (1869), p. 636-638 with the title *Anonymi relatio de delictis, quae in arce Kozí et vitate Ustie super Lužnic commit-*

listed the reference texts for the lectures during the commemorations and the celebrations of the two «new saints» of the Hussite period.

In the present paragraph are instead listed the most important other types of texts, which recount the story and the death of Jan Hus and Jerome of Prague, or concern non-official cults, but do not actually belong to the hagiographic genre. Indeed, the long Hussite period left a considerable legacy of heroic memories, in someway similar to the celebrations for the fallen of the wars or for the patriots, and sometimes at the limit of mythology.

Being actually descriptions of victims of a religious war, these protagonists often became hagiographical characters, at least in the narrative plots. For example, in the sermon by Iacobellus of Stříbro dedicated to Jan Hus and Jerome of Prague (cf. *infra*, II.B.9), other five martyrs are mentioned, but they remain anonymous. Another example is the one of the general Jan Žižka, who died in 1424, at the forefront of the defence of the reign from the crusades arriving in Bohemia in the aftermath of Jan Hus' death. Jan Žižka and the sort of cult of him among the Taborits (i.e. the radical Hussite faction) occupy some space in the *Historia Bohemica* by Enea Silvio Piccolomini, a five-book work written by the future pope Pius II when he was still a diplomat. While the end of the second book is devoted to Jan Hus, the third book is entirely dedicated to the Hussite wars[79].

More connoted and controversial is the episode of the three Hussite martyrs Jan, Martin and Stassko, killed even before Hus' death. Scholars debate whether such episode caused the tragic development of the events at the council of Constance. The three young men, after having listened to Jan Hus' discourse in the Bethlehem chapel, went to Prague demonstrating against the Roman absolution of the year 1411 and were arrested by the city council. Notwithstanding Jan Hus' intervention, the three boys were executed in 1412. Even if the episode is often remembered in scholarly studies, it has never been studied in depth, maybe because the cult of the three young men

---

tuntur a praedicatoribus et contra doctrinam christianam et contra ritus ab ecclesia approbatos.
[79] *Historia Bohemica* is edited by HEJNIC – ROTHE – UDOLPH (2005).

never established itself nor became official. Despite its relevance, then, the episode occurred to Jan, Martin and Stassko is one of the many violent events of the period. Some narratives in Czech language recount that a pious woman covered the three young dead bodies with linen fabric right after their execution, and then masters and students leaded by John of Jitschin brought them into the Bethlehem's chapel. There the three boys were buried right in front of the city council, while the procession sang the antiphon *Isti sunt sancti* and celebrated a liturgy for them. Notwithstanding their missed sanctification, many passages of the *Relatio* by Peter Mladenowicz, the most famous hagiography about Jan Hus (because Peter was an eyewitness of Hus' death; cf. *infra*, II.B.9), recounts that Jan Hus immediately recognised them as saints. In the later work *Tractatus de ecclesia*, Hus called them martyrs who fought against the Antichrist taking on the sword to oppose the devil's falsehood. Some other texts attested Jerome of Prague's attempt to promote their cult in the capital city[80]. Nonetheless, not even Jan Hus created an effective devotion toward the three boys, and in fact the same instable and high-tension moment caused soon after Jan Hus' death in Constance.

Even more limited and narrow seems to be the liturgical commemoration or the cult of the miners-martyrs of Kutná Hora, whose names were Šimon, Průša and Hana, which have an interesting and realistic iconography connected to the representations and the interpretations of Jan Hus' martyrdom[81].

Other works of this time, such as sermons, letters and chronicles, mention some other Hussite often anonymous martyrs[82], as well as liturgical fragments and hagiographical miniatures[83]. One of these mentions is about two young boys from Olomouc, a student of the Prague's University and a friend of him: they are remembered together in a sermon by Iacobellus of Stříbro devoted to Jan Hus, and also in another sermon by an anonymous preacher (cf. *infra*, II.B.9).

Several and varied works connected in different ways to the acts of the council of Constance are also devoted to Jerome of

---

[80] HACK (2007), p. 151.
[81] ŠÁROVCOVÁ (2015).
[82] Cf. *infra*, II.B.9, and HACK (2007), p. 146-147.
[83] HORNÍČKOVÁ (2018), p. 81-82.

Prague. For example, it is worth mentioning in this section the manuscript version of the *Fasciculi zizaniorum* (Oxford, Bodleian Library, e Musaeo 86), a collection of accounts of the trials of Jan Hus and Jerome of Prague, which lack in the printed version of the work. Another remarkable testimony is the Czech dossier about Jerome's trial, a composite collection maybe realized by the above-mentioned hagiographer and eye-witness Peter Mladenowicz. Staying in that period also in Constance, Peter should have gathered in the years 1416-1417 some trial papers and documents, for which any official record or transcript is missing. Peter's dossier includes the traslation of the last part of his own *Relatio*, as well as the translation of Poggio Bracciolini's letter of the year 1416, in which the Humanist reported to Leonardo Bruni the last phases of Jerome's trial and his death [84]. This is the *Epistula ad Leonardum Aretinum de magistri Hieronymi de Praga supplicio*, which does not belong to the hagiographical genre, not only for its epistolary form, but also for the type of description of the protagonist. Actually, in this letter Jerome is not a saint, nor a martyr: Poggio compared him rather to a classical hero of the Capitoline splendours at the times of the Roman Republic's integrity. The *Epistula* then belongs to the typical Humanistic works, both for its contents and the form [85].

In addition to the hagiographies dedicated to the founders, the Hussite church developed a peculiar concept of the saints and their own cult. Not only every faction had its own point of view (the most radical fringes completely refused the cult of saints, reaching forms of actual iconoclasm, as well as any kind of pilgrimage), but also the Hussite theology about the saints actually influenced the religious practice [86]. Except from the extremist positions, the most parts of the Hussite church, even the non-moderate ones, had a positive vision of the saints and their cult: certainly such development is in part due to the memory of Jan Hus and Jerome and their commemorations.

The more unanimous and shared devotion among the Hussites was the one for the Apostles, which represented the *ecclesia*

---

[84] FUDGE (2016), p. 169-171. Thomas A. Fudge's book includes a discussion of all the sources concerning Jerome, and indicates further bibliography.

[85] HACK (2007), p. 135-136; MONTECCHI (1995), p. 261-262, 264.

[86] The reference-study for the present section is HORNÍČKOVÁ (2018), which often refers in turn to HACK (2007).

primitiva, the Christianity of the origins, the ideal life and spirituality pursued by the entire movement. From this perspective, Jan Hus'death was a perfect imitation of Christ's Passion, exactly as Hus himself said while reaching the council, which convened him in Constance (cf. *infra*, II.B.9). Through such actualisation of Christ or saints's example in the present daily life, Hussites realised the real imitation of the perfect Christian behaviour: in this sense, for the Hussite church the cult of saints was not a commemoration of past events. Consequently, the immediate sanctification of Hus and Jerome of Prague was a natural fact, as well as the highest expression of the actual renovation of the *ecclesia primitiva* in the present. A more contentious matter among the different Hussite groups was the intercession of the saints and the Virgin, connected with the more general question of conferring divine prerogatives to them.

At the end of the Middle Ages, the synod of Hromnice of the year 1524 established the saints' cults admitted in the Utraquist church. They were: all the feasts devoted to Christ; part of the feasts dedicated to Mary; the commemoration of the Angels; All Saints day; the feasts for the saints included in the New Testament; John the Baptist, Mary Magdalene, and the martyr Lawrence; Jan Hus and all the Bohemian patron saints. The synod of Hromnice also established the admitted sacred images, which had a peculiar style and form, transmitting a precise significance: images of the saints of the early Christian period (Christian origins), the Bohemian patron saints and Jan Hus. They were all represented in the actual moment of their death (martyrdom), or as iconic characters with a didactical and commemorative purpose, never exceeding the supreme majesty, holiness and power of Jesus Christ, nor those of the Eucharist (if conserved in churches and houses of worship).

In addition to the sermons by Iacobellus listed in section II.B.9, it is worth mentioning here the letter of an anonymous canon of Olomouc of the year 1416 (the year of Jerome's death), which compared Jan Hus and Jerome – calling them «the new martyrs» – to Lawrence, the apostle Peter, and other saints of the Christian origins. Moreover, two other works listed in section II.B.9 compare somehow «the new martyrs» to the Passion of Christ and the martyrdom of Lawrence, who died burned on a gridiron: they are the *Relatio* by Peter Mladenowicz (which was actually read during the liturgical commemorations of Jan

Hus), and the *Passio* by John Barbatus respectively. In a sermon of the year 1419, Jan Želivský, former superior in the Premonstratensian monastery of Želiv and a member of the radical Hussite group, compared Hus and Jerome to the characters of the New Testament and martyr saints Peter and Paul, Jacob and John the Baptist, as well as to Job. This latter is an image, which recurred also in the fifteenth-century Czech iconography and liturgy. Among Jan Želivský's sources, together with the Fathers of the Church, there are the works and the sermons of the major representatives of the Hussite movement: Jan Hus himself, Nicholas of Dresden, Matthias of Janov, and Iacobellus of Stříbro[87].

With such characterization, the «new» Hussite saints are ready to join the pantheon of the major Czech patron saints, established in the fourteenth century: Wencleslas, Ludmila, Procopius, Adalbert, Sigismundus and Vitus. Wenceslas is the most important saint in the Utraquist sanctoral, but also Procopius had a significant cult, even if not connected to his relics nor to the pilgrimages to his monastery. Ludmila is the symbol of the claim of the chalice for the lay people; Vitus always accompanies Wenceslas because of the early dedication of the cathedral of Prague. Adalbert is the less venerated saint, maybe because of his strong connection to Rome and the Catholics, both during his life and after his death. Even minor was the cult for Sigismundus, maybe because of the bad fame and the negative memory of the emperor with the same name.

Together with the Bohemian patron saints, which were mentioned also in Hus' sermons, the limited horizon of the Hussite sanctoral shows the regional interest of these cults.

4. Imported Sainthood

In section II.A.1 it has been said that some of the major Czech saints were not born in Bohemia, nor in Moravia, and not even they died in this territory. Many saints of the Czech sanctoral share such feature: the present paragraph offers a brief presentation of the most important of them.

---

[87] CADILI (2012); HORNÍČKOVÁ (2018), p. 76 with additional bibliography.

Generally speaking, these minor imported saints are connected to historical, political, and religious events, but they do not have specific hagiographical texts. For example, some cults depend on the arrival and the presence in the Czech lands of the Mendicant Orders, which influenced and modified the religiosity and the hagiography of every territory they reached. The Hungarian saint kings Stephen, Emeric, and Ladislas give another example of a cult spread in the whole Central Europe, reaching also the western countries, as demonstrated by Edit Madas in a recent study[88]. Moreover, Hana Pátková studied the patron saints of the corporations and guilds, as well as of the confraternities, a devotion largely spread in Prague in the fourteenth century among both the Catholics and the Utraquists. Apart from the inevitable presence of Wenceslas, the patron saints of the corporations and guilds are in most cases imported saints, and their patronage quite never concerned a single or precise craft or profession. The exceptions are the Evangelist Luke, because of his «pictorial» connection with Virgin Mary (another extremely popular devotion), and Eligius, the saint of Noyon[89]. Pátková studied the cult of Eligius in particular, mentioning four manuscripts containing his hagiography and the Office (*Proprium*) offered by the emperor Charles IV in 1378 together with a reliquiary to the guild of goldsmiths. In fact, Charles IV imported the cult of Eligius into Prague, where the saint of Noyon soon became the patron saint of the guild of goldsmiths. With regard to this episode, Hana Pátková searched the sources proving the fact that in 1378 the king of France Charles V gave Charles IV the miter of saint Eligius as a gift, which the emperor would have in turn given to the guild of goldsmiths to be safeguarded. Such prooves are preserved in the *Sermo cum legenda abbreviata* copied in the manuscript Krivoklát, Krivoklásta Knihovna, I.A.26, and also in two other manuscripts containing the Office of the saint and the *Vita Eligii* by the bishop of Rouen Audoin, the main source of the *Sermo cum legenda abbreviata* itself. The common source for both hagiographical and liturgical testimonies seems therefore to be Paris, Bibliothèque historique de la Ville, Réserve 104[90]. Other

---

[88] MADAS (2017).
[89] PÁTKOVÁ (2017).
[90] PÁTKOVÁ (2006).

recurrent patron saints of the corporations were Wolfgang, who was bishop of Regensburg when the diocese of Prague was created as a suffragan of that seat in the tenth century[91], Barbara, and Catherine of Siena[92].

Vitus martyr

Scholars debated for a long time wether Vitus, the Christian martyr, should be identified with the pagan god Swantewit, which was venerated before the christianization. Since in Slavic language the two names are extremely similar, the Christian identity of the former patron would have spread throughout the Slavic world. About this matter, Herman Køllin reports the views of many scholars, which in general tend to assert the existence in Moravia of a deep cult for Swantewit, and try to set the date of the cult for the Christian Vitus to the Cyril-Methodian era. The presence of Vitus' name in some prayers in Old Church Slavonic seems to confirm this idea: at least it prooves a liturgical (vernacular) production regarding Vitus in the Cyril-Methodian era. Moreover, a church dedicated to Vitus in Staré Město (South Moravia), datable between the last quarter of the ninth century and the first quarter of the tenth, leaded scholars in concluding that Vitus' cult was a consequence of the first christianization of the territory, due to both Bavarian and Cyril-Methodian missions[93]. In fact, Vitus' relics arrived from Corvey to Prague at the latest in the first third of the tenth century, when the Saxon king Henry I the Fowler offered the saint's arm as a gift to his ally, the duke Wenceslas: as a consequence, Wenceslas dedicated to the martyr saint the *rotunda* of the Prague castle (a. 929)[94]. The connection between Prague and Corvey throughout Vitus' relics seems to be confirmed by the origins of the first bishops of the Bohemian capital city[95].

Even if no Latin Vitus' hagiography written in Czech territories survived, scholars considered its existence as certain, because of the surviving Old Church Slavonic version, which

---

[91] Cf. SCHWAIGER (1972).
[92] HERZIG (2013) studied the diffusion of the cult of Catherine of Siena in the Czech lands.
[93] KØLLN (2003), p. 47-49, with further bibliography.
[94] Cf. MENGEL (2017), p. 59-60.
[95] KRÜGER – DOLEŽALOVÁ (2009), p. 237.

ought to be a translation of the Latin one[96]. A testimony of the Vitus' cult in the Saxon Empire and in Corvey is included in the work *Rerum gestarum Saxonicarum libri tres* by the Corvey monk Widukind (tenth century), which also reports the contents of Vitus' hagiography. Widukind's passages are also recalled in a Corvey re-writing of Thiethmarus of Merseburg's *Chronicon* of the tenth-eleventh century[97].

Mauritius Agaunensis seu Thebaeus martyr

The cult for Maurice, the martyr leader of the Theban Legion in Agaunum (nowadays Saint-Maurice d'Agaune, Switzerland, Canton Valais), spread throughout Bohemia and Moravia during the eleventh century, thanks to the connections between the Benedictine monasteries of Břevnov and Ostrov and the one of Niederaltaich (in Bavaria). In the twelfth century, Vladislaus II of Bohemia took Maurice's relics from Milan to Prague: liturgical manuscripts and their iconography, as well as the local onomastics testify such devotion[98]. Later in 1354, during a visit to the monastery of Einsiedeln, the emperor Charles IV acquired some other relics of Maurice, namely a part of the arm, together with a part of the head of the Burgundian king Sigismundus (the first Sigismundus' relic obtained by the emperor). Both relics had come directly or indirectly to Einsiedeln from Agaune. Nonetheless, the acquisition became significant only a decade later, when the cult of Sigismundus increased its importance, as Charles IV assumed the title of king of Burgundy in 1365. Before this moment, none of the two saints had a specific cult. After his own crowning, Charles IV also visited the monastery of Saint-Maurice d'Agaune, which was both the centre of the cult of Maurice and his companions of the Theban Legion, and the monastery founded and dedicated to them by the martyr king Sigismundus at the beginning of the sixth century. From this place, the emperor Charles IV took into Prague some other relics of both Sigismundus and Maurice[99].

---

[96] NECHUTOVÁ (2007), p. 71.
[97] KRÜGER – DOLEŽALOVÁ (2009), p. 235-237.
[98] KUBÍN (2014b).
[99] MENGEL (2007), p. 21-24.

Emmerammus episcopus martyr in Baioaria (seventh-eighth centuries)

The creation, at the end of the ninth century, of the archpresbyterate of Prague led into the capital city several archpriests coming from the abbey of Sankt-Emmeram of Regensburg, in Bavaria, from where they imported the cult of their patron saint. By outlining the history of such devotion, Václav Bok highlighted the remarkable long life of the cult from the Early Middle Ages until the fifteenth century, even if with scarcer attestations in the later times[100]. From this perspective, it seems significant that the text of the *Vita Emmerammi* by the bishop Arbeo of Freising could have influenced the fundamental hagiography of Wenceslas, the so-called «Crescente fide» (cf. *infra*, II.B.19).

Godehardus Hildesheimensis episcopus (960/961-1038)

The cult for the bishop Gotthard (Gothard, Godehard) of Hildesheim is connected to the hagiographical figure of Gunther/Vintír, because the *Vita Godehardi posterior* (BHL 3582) by Wolfherius of Hildesheim recounts their meeting. This text is also a model for Gunther's hagiography, written in the thirteenth century (cf. *infra*, II.B.5). Contrary to the rest of Europe, where the cult for Gotthard was widespread and popular, as attested also by the rich manuscript tradition, in Bohemia this devotion did not last long; in fact, it seems limited to the specific political events of the first part of the twelfth century[101].

Victorinus martyr

The Czech devotions in the fourteenth century number a cult adopted in Prague in the second half of the century, only attested by liturgical traces: these seem to derive from a narrative merging of two notices taken from the Martyrology compiled by Ado of Vienne, referring to a confessor and a martyr respectively (inc. *Fuerunt autem duo fratres*; cf. BHL 7659-7664)[102]. The liturgical celebration of Victorinus' feast, on 5 September, was mandatory in Prague only since 1392, but the cult of the saint must have been earlier (and some liturgical manuscripts

---

[100] Bok (2006).
[101] Žemlička (2010); Kubín (1998).
[102] About this martyr and his dossier see Philippart (2010).

used in Prague attested so)[103], as it happened in the city of Litomyšl thanks to the relics gained by the bishop Albert of Sternberg in 1376. In fact, the martyr Victorinus had in Litomyšl a double celebration: on his *dies natalis* every 5 September, and on the day of the *translatio*, every 19 October (even if the actual translation took place the day before, in the feast of saint Luke the Evangelist). It is also known that from the year 1401 an annual market took place in Litomyšl in the week of the feast of saint Victorinus. As a consequence, the religious commemoration of the saint, connected to his relics' ostension, should have existed earlier also in Litomyšl, even if neither material nor liturgical traces survived in the city[104].

Legenda aurea (the Golden Legend)

The *Legenda aurea* by Jacobus de Varagine, the basis-text of the abbreviated rewriting of the hagiographical narratives according to the uses and tendencies of the fourteenth century, testifies to the new religiosity of the Mendicant Orders, proposing an active and locally rooted holiness, strongly linked to the expression of the identity[105]. The collection of *Legenda aurea* was very popular also in the Czech lands, where it was enriched with the local Latin hagiographies. In her 1984 study, Anezka Vidmanová listed 51 testimonies preserved in the Libraries of the Czech Republic, among which only four seem to have originated in other countries[106].

The Czech variant of the Latin *Legenda aurea* shows its rooting in Bohemian region through the geo-chronological coordinates of the Adalbert's hagiography. In the rest of the additional hagiographies (Procopius, Wenceslas, Ludmila and the Five Brethren, as well as Sigismundus and Cyril and Methodius), a Bavarian influence is evident, and especially from the spirituality of Regensburg.

The hagiographies of the Czech saints were added to the *Legenda aurea* at the end of the thirteenth century, and they are found in almost all the manuscripts of this collection used in the Czech territories. The erliest codex of the *Legenda aurea*

---

[103] VESELOVSKÁ – ADAMKO – BEDNÁRIKOVÁ (2017), p. 123.
[104] VEČEŘE (2014), p. 82-86.
[105] KLANICZAY (2008), p. 275-277.
[106] VIDMANOVÁ – BAHNÍK (1984); cf. also FLEITH (1991).

copied as a literary work and without practical purposes is Praha, Národní Knihovna, XII.D.19, dating back around the year 1300. It seems remarkable that the majority of the surviving manuscripts did not belong to any Hussite areas, with the exception of the codex Praha, Národní Muzeum, XIV.B.14[107].

The significant differences between the first Czech translation of the *Legenda aurea*, the *Pasionál*, and the Latin original work by Jacobus de Varagine, pretty freely used as a model by the Czech translator, led to a Latin re-translation of the *Pasionál* itself by a poorly learned anonymous author, who used an extremely literal method and a dialectical language. The *codex unicus* Brno, Moravská Zemská Knihovna (Universitní Knihovna), Mk 32 (II. 189) preserved this Latin translation of the *Pasionál*[108].

Clemens I papa

The imported hagiography, which had the most impressive impact in the religious and cultural tradition of Moravia and Bohemia, is related to the brothers from Thessaloniki Cyril and Methodius, a set of texts, which deserves a dedicated section (see *infra* II.A.5). Connected to the Cyril-Methodian hagiography is the figure of the pope Clement I (Clement of Rome, Clemens Romanus), whose relics Constantine-Cyril took from Cherson first to Great Moravia (861), where Clement became the patron saint, and then to Rome (867).

The so-called *Legenda Italica* (*BHL* 2073) recounts in detail the events of the translation, being focused almost exclusively on the *inventio* of Clement's relics in Cherson and the subsequent trip to Rome. The so-called *Legenda Moravica* (*BHL* 2074) is later and more concise, and describes carefully the means of the evangelization of the Slavs (cf. *infra*, II.A.5)[109]. The dossier also includes the account of the *inventio* written by Anastasius the Librarian in a letter to the bishop of Velletri Gaudericus (*BHL* 2072), having as sources the surviving Paleo-Slavic narratives[110]. The episodes of Clement's *inventio* and

---

[107] VIDMANOVÁ (1986a), p. 292-294.
[108] VIDMANOVÁ (1986a), p. 297.
[109] *AA.SS.*, Mart. II, Antwerpen 1667, p. *22-*23.
[110] Cf. BOYLE (1958), p. 363-364, PERI (1981), p. 21.

translatio to Rome also return in the Paleo-Slavic biographies of Cyril and Methodius[111].

At the time of the Great Moravia, the Slavic liturgy included the commemoration of both Clement's *dies natalis* on the 25 November, and his *inventio* on 30 January, and the dedications of several churches of that time testify this devotion in both Moravia and Bohemia. From the mid-thirteenth century circulated in Bohemia the rewriting of the hagiography of Clement, included at the end of the lectures of the Proprium celebrated by the Dominican Order and also in the *Legenda aurea* by Jacobus de Varagine. One of the manuscripts of the *Golden Legend* in which Clement's hagiography is included, dating back to the fourteenth century, served as a basis for the Modern rewritings of the legend. The mention of the liturgical commemorations of Clement's martyrdom (*dies natalis*) and his translation is included also in the *Legenda Moravica*[112].

Hieronymus Stridonius (Eusebius Hieronymus)

The figure of Jerome, the Father of the Church author of the most popular Latin translation of the Bible, the *Vulgata*, is connected to the liturgical use of the Slavic language and, therefore, somehow with the Cyril-Methodian heritage. The *inventio* of Jerome's relics and their *translatio* from the Holy Land to Rome at the end of the thirteenth century seem to have been the cause of the revitalization of his cult, contemporary to the official titling as Doctor of the Church formalized by pope Boniface VIII for Jerome, together with Augustine, Ambrose and Gregory the Great.

Jerome's Dalmatian-Illyrian origins produced a legend, according to which he was the first translator of the Bible in Paleo-Slavic: this is the reason why the Glagolitic alphabet used to be called *littera Hieronymiana*[113]. Such pious falsification is earlier than the *inventio* of the relics, as it dates back to the mid-thirteenth century[114]. In Bohemia, the emperor Charles IV warmly welcomed the legend. Firstly, he tried to involve pope Clement VI, settled in Avignon (a letter by the bishop of

---

[111] PERI (1981), p. 21 e 107.
[112] KØLLN (2003), p. 41-44.
[113] VERKHOLANTSEV (2014), p. 3-6.
[114] VERKHOLANTSEV (2012), p. 42-48.

Prague Arnošt/Ernest – afterwards a saint – testifies this attempt to raise awareness from the pope), and then in 1347 he founded the only Czech monastery for the Benedictine monks of the Eastern Rite approved by the pope[115], known as Emmaus monastery (but originally called monastery «Na Slovanech»). Notwithstanding its popular name, the Emmaus monastery was dedicated to Jerome, in which the monks were brought in from Dalmatia and Croatia. Using their Glagolitic alphabet and their Old Church Slavonic in the Croatian recension, in the Emmaus *scriptorium* the monks translated also into Czech language several theological Latin works. In the Emmaus' founding document, Charles IV proclaimed that Emmaus would have commemorated Jerome as the founder of the Slavic tradition, together with the memory of Cyril and Methodius, Adalbert and Procopius. Since Adalbert was the founder of the monastery of Břevnov and the most beloved Czech saint in the Central Europe, and Procopius was the promoter of the Slavonic Liturgy in Sázava, the only early-medieval monastery of Roman rite expressed in Old-Church Slavonic, it means that Charles IV strictly connected Jerome to the Bohemian culture and traditions. Moreover, he asserted the linguistic relationship between the Croatian recension of the Old Church Slavonic and the Slavic language spoken in the Czech lands[116]. In fact, in Charles' perspective, the affinity went beyond the linguistic sphere, involving the entire Czech identity, and this seems to have been the cornerstone of the emperor's personal devotion for Jerome. This Bohemian specific vision of Jerome's connection with the Cyril-Methodian tradition and the roots of the Czech culture is also expressed in the emperor's redaction of the Life of saint Wenceslas[117]. Several mentions about Jerome and his connection with the Slavic language also recurred in the works by Jan Hus and in many sermons written in the Czech lands[118].

---

[115] In the Emmaus monastery the monks used to celebrate the Roman liturgy in Old Church Slavonic: this is the so-called Roman-Slavonic Liturgy: SMRŽÍK (1959), p. 15. It is also known as Glacolitic liturgy, because of the use of the Glagolitic alphabet instead of the Latin one. As a consequence, the Slavonic liturgical books testify the Roman rite expressed in Old-Church Slavonic language.

[116] VERKHOLANTSEV (2014), p. 63-72.

[117] VERKHOLANTSEV (2014), p. 76-86.

[118] VERKHOLANTSEV (2013), p. 282-285.

5. Cyrillo-Methodiana
(Cyrillus et Methodius Slavorum apostoli)

The first christianization of Bohemia and Moravia took place between the ninth and eleventh centuries, similarly to Hungary and Poland, and followed the western models of sainthood, inspired by the Latin ecclesiastical organization. Nonetheless, the christianization of the Czech lands seems to follow a double guideline. On one hand, the Latin one, which firstly was Bavarian in particular, and then German (Ottonian), northern-Italian and Dalmatian; on the other hand, the one of the Cyril-Methodian mission, which was almost contemporary to the christianization fostered in the Great Moravia by the Bavarian church, but it was promoted by the Greek-Byzantines and strictly tied to the origin of the Old Church Slavonic and its liturgical use[119].

The sources testify the precedence of the Latin church in the evangelization of Moravia and Bohemia, referring to the peculiar diplomatic status of the mandate of Cyril and Methodius, which was endorsed by both Byzantium and Rome (so that some scholars questioned the definition of «mission» for the brothers' mandate of christianization)[120]. Consequently, part of the hagiographical production of the time of the origins in the Great Moravia (863-950) is bilingual, as it was soon rewritten (and not simply translated) from Latin into Old Church Slavonic. The hagiographies about Constantine-Cyril, Methodius and pope Clement I were all read and popular (with greater or lesser frequency depending on the historical moments), even if not each of them originated in Moravia or Bohemia, and they significantly influenced the hagiographies of the first local saints, namely Wenceslas and Ludmila (cf. chapter B: Alphabetical Inventory of the Czech Saints' Hagiographies).

Therefore, the memory of the Cyril-Methodian mission was alive and present in Czech territory, notwithstanding the subsequent ecclesiastical events, and in Moravia in particular, where the city of Olomouc mostly continued and preserved the

---

[119] WOOD (2013b); KLANICZAY (2008), p. 252-254; VERKHOLANTSEV (2014), p. 11-14.

[120] It is beyond the scope of this essay to return minutely to the Cyril-Methodian question, dealt with by an extremely wide bibliography. On the mentioned issues see TACHIAOS (2005).

legacies of the organization of the time of the Great Moravia, having Cyril and Metodius as the patron saints of the diocese. Not only the bishop of Olomouc, but also the Citercian monks of Velehrad promoted the cult of the brothers of Thessaloniki, as the Moravian city was the centre and the residence of the saints' mission in the Great Moravia. From the reign of Charles IV, i.e. from the second half of the fourteenth century, the cult for Cyril and Methodius renewed its popularity in the whole Bohemia, even if scholars disagree about its distribution among the population[121].

The Cyril-Methodian matter unfolds two important scenarios, which are briefly mentioned here. The first regards the polemic about the use of the Old Church Slavonic in the liturgy, a complex and structured theme over the centuries, where the question of the imprisonment of Methodius by the Bavarian clergy also plays a delicate role. Riccardo Picchio has shown how the struggle against the Slavic liturgy became harsher the more it moved away from the time of events, and how both Latin and Greek clergy felt the issue as much important[122].

The second scenario is the so-called «revisionist» debate introduced by Imre Boba at the beginning of the Seventies[123]. According to Boba's view, the geographical position of Moravia would be in a southern part of the Slavic territories, namely around Sremska Mitrovica in Serbia, the place of the supposed former seat of Sirmium, assumed as the episcopal seat of Methodius. In my opinion, such localisation of Moravia depends on a faulty reading of the sources, compromised by a historiographical prejudice. On a textual level, the whole issue is affected by the fact that later sources describe the ninth century Moravia,

---

[121] DOLEŽALOVÁ (2014); KALOUS (2014); MARIN (2017), p. 27. BARTOŇKOVÁ – VEČERKA (2010) offer an anthology of all the passages regarding Cyril and Methodius included in the medieval writings of Czech origins, both Latin and vernacular.

[122] PICCHIO (1991), p. 193-261. In the ninth century part of the Roman clergy denied the use of the Old Church Slavonic in the liturgy, while short after the Greek clergy did the same, mistrusting the validity of the Old Church Slavonic for the liturgy: PICCHIO (1991), p. 127. It is now accepted by scholars that the issue about the use of Old Church Slavonic for liturgical purposes falls within an overall Greek-Latin ecclesiastical framework, and should not be interpreted as a political-religious opposition between Rome and Byzantium.

[123] BOBA (1971).

each following the political, religious and ideological needs of the time when the texts were written[124].

Because of their connection to and influence with the earliest hagiographies of the Czech territory, it will be worth listing here briefly the major texts of the Cyril-Methodian tradition, even if they were not written in Bohemia or Moravia. Scholars still do not agree on dating such writings, whose mutual connections and dependencies are still not certain.

Legenda Italica: Vita cum translatione S. Clementis papa auctore Leone Hostiensi episcopo

BHL 2073

inc.: *Tempore igitur quo Michael imperator Novae Romae regebat imperium*

The *Legenda Italica*, written by the bishop of Ostia and Velletri Leo Marsicanus, dates back to the beginning of the twelfth century, as attested in a fourteenth century manuscript kept in Prague[125]. It is possible that Leo's source was the three books of the *Vita Clementis* written by the bishop of Velletri Gaudericus together with John Immonides, the late ninth century biographer of pope Gregory the Great. Leo certainly used some writings by Anastasius the Librarian as sources, as Johann Friedrich demonstrated at the end of the nineteenth century by highlighting several textual correspondencies. Consequently, the *Legenda Italica* descended from much earlier materials, which were contemporary to the Cyril-Methodian mission in the Great Moravia. The dating of these materials is closely linked to the Old Church Slavonic versions of the Lives of Constantine-Cyril and Methodius[126]. The *Legenda Italica* played an important role

---

[124] Cf. BETTI (2014), p. 27-34. On this regard, Jana Nechutová reminds us that the *Vita Procopii minor* and the chronicle of the anonymous monk of Sázava, who continued the *Chronicon* by Cosmas of Prague, show that the Cyril-Methodian tradition was not yet spread in the twelfth century Bohemia: NECHUTOVÁ (2007), p. 70.

[125] Praha, Archiv Pražského Hradu, Knihovna Metropolitní Kapituly, N. XXIII (1547), discovered by MEYVAERT – DEVOS (1955).

[126] On this matter see BETTI (2014), p. 96-104. A resume of the text in NECHUTOVÁ (2007), p. 55-56. There are several editions of the *Legenda Italica*: the latest is BARTOŇKOVÁ – VEČERKA (2010), p. 103-113; earlier editions are MEYVAERT – DEVOS (1955), p. 455-461, and EMLER 1 (1873), p. 93-99.

even after the Old Church Slavonic was assumed as a liturgical language.

Legenda Moravica

BHL 2074

inc.: *Tempore Michaelis imperatoris fuit quidam vir genere nobilis*

The basic sources for Cyril and Methodius' *Legenda Moravica*, written in Moravia in the thirteenth century, were the *Legenda Italica* and the *Vita Wenceslai* by Christian (*Legenda Christiani*), even if some scholars think that this text is earlier – from about eleventh century – and it is in turn a source for Christian. The *Legenda Moravica* also contains a mention of the *dies natalis* and the *translatio* of Clement I[127]. In his *Chronica Bohemorum* (*c.* 1125), Cosmas of Prague recounted the legend of Cyril and Methodius in a way that does not help the dating of the *Legenda Moravica*[128].

Passio «Diffundente sole»

BHL 5030

Cf. *infra*, II.B.14, *Ludmilla Bohemiae ducissa*.

Legenda «Beatus Cyrillus» (Epitome)

BHL 2075 = 5031

inc.: *Beatus Cyrillus natione graecus, tam latinis quam ipsis graecorum*

The hagiographical epitome «Beatus Cyrillus» has the same incipit of the Christian's extract from the *Vita Ludmilae*, and it is maybe the most controversial Latin hagiography of Czech origins. The affinity with Christian's text lead scholars to the hypothesis of the earlier dating of the epitome «Beatus Cyrillus», which would be in consequence a source for Christian himself, revealing itself as one of the most ancient hagiographical monuments of the Czech lands. Another *terminus* for the epitome is its connection with the *Privilegium Moraviensis ecclesiae* mentioned by Cosmas of Prague, which in consequence would lead to a

---

[127] Cf. NECHUTOVÁ (2007), p. 56. There are several editions of the text: the latest is BARTOŇKOVÁ – VEČERKA (2010), p. 232-241; an earlier edition in EMLER 1 (1873), p. 100-107.

[128] KØLLN (2003), p. 43.

dating back from the eleventh or twelfth century. Nonetheless, an early dating of the text contrasts with its contents about the Cyril-Methodian mission: according to the epitome «Beatus Cyrillus», the brothers of Thessaloniki went firstly to Rome, then to Bulgaria for the evangelization of the Khazars, and finally to Great Moravia. Moreover, the epitome's connection with *Legenda Moravica* is still controversial and unclear. It is also possible that the epitome «Beatus Cyrillus» dates back to the time of emperor Charles IV, being written in opposition to the emperor's support to the Slavic liturgy and to contrast the foundation of the Emmaus monastery for Slavic monks[129].

Legenda «Quemadmodum» (Epitome)
BHL 2076
inc.: *Quemadmodum ex historiis... colligitur, ss. Cyrillus et Methodius fratres germani de Alexandria...*

Formerly known from one only codex used by the first editor Beda Dudík, the *Legenda «Quemadmodum»* is copied in four medieval manuscripts, while seven other manuscripts contain a liturgical adaptation of the text[130]. It is not simple to clarify the connections between the *Legenda «Quemadmodum»*, which refers to Christian's legend, and the *Legenda Moravica*. The epitome *«Quemadmodum»* is really widespread, and several later writings, not necessarily hagiographical, recall the text.

6. The Parodies of the Manuscript Praha, Národní Knihovna, III.E.27

The manuscript Praha, Národní Knihovna, III.E.27, from the beginning of the fifteenth century, contains two very curious and still misterious hagiographical parodies. At fol. 61r-63r there is the *Passio raptorum de Slapanicz secundum Bartoss tortorem Brunensem*, a recount of the capture and execution by hanging of a few thieves in Šlapanice, in Southern Moravia, at Easter in

---

[129] NECHUTOVÁ (2007), p. 56-57 e 149. The most recent edition of the text is by BARTOŇKOVÁ – VEČERKA (2010), p. 272-275, with Czech translation; the earlier edition in *AB*, 81 (1963), p. 352-355.

[130] The manuscripts are listed by BARTOŇKOVÁ – VEČERKA (2010), p. 262-264, with a discussion on the existing editions and a new edition of the text at p. 264-268.

1401. For this text, the manuscript is a *codex unicus*[131]. The stylistic affinities with Christ's Passion and the scattered allusions to the Bible contribute to the typical solemn manner of the text.

Although some scholars think that it is a recount of a real event and try to identify the protagonists of the *Passio*, the author's ironic tone seems to reveal the facetious genre of the text, even if inspired by an actual episode. In fact, the author recalls apostle Thomas' incredulity and ask his public to believe in the story, even if he did not attend the described events. Lucie Doležalová underlined some similarities between the text and the *Passio Iudaeorum Pragensium* (cf. *infra*, II.B.12), even if this connection still needs an in-depth analysis[132].

In the manuscript Praha, Národní Knihovna, III.E.27, the same hand of the *Passio raptorum de Slapanicz* also copied the *Sermo de sancto Nemine*, one of the many redactions of the homiletic-hagiographical text devoted to the phantom saint named Nemo (that is: Nobody), halfway between a mythological character and a heretical figure[133]. Several sermons, tirades and accounts are devoted to Nemo in the last part of the Middle Ages and in the Modern Era, but he has no *dies natalis*, nor a liturgical commemoration, nor even a church or dedication in any sacred place. The *Sermo de sancto Nemine* includes sparse and fleeting Biblical references, without allowing any clue about its author or the background of the writing. Even if some variants of the Prague manuscript could testify a specific editorial phase or change, a coherent evaluation of the text must also take into consideration the *Sermo* both as a whole and in its context, which is often impossible to trace. In fact, the *Sermo de sancto Nemine* is often copied in heterogeneous, miscellaneous manuscripts, both in fictional and leisure books and in "serious" collections – a situation, which stresses the peculiarity of the text and its impossibility to fall under a specific literary genre.

---

[131] DOLEŽALOVÁ (2014), p. 253-256, with a list of the errors appeared in the edition by ŠUJAN (1885).

[132] DOLEŽALOVÁ (2014), p. 256-259.

[133] DOLEŽALOVÁ (2010), with bibliography for each redaction of the text and some observations about the relationship between the *Sermo de sancto Nemine* and the *Passio raptorum de Slapanicz*. The edition of the sermon in BAYLESS (1996), p. 292-300.

7. The *Passio Iudeorum Pragensium*

Another text deserves special attention in the present introductory chapter. Among the several accounts or hints included in historiographic sources about struggles, massacres and martyrdoms that took place in Bohemia in its violent late Middle Ages, with special reference to the Hussite wars, chronicles and annals often present short reports of mass murders of Jews occurring frequently in Bohemia, Moravia and Austria in the late fourteenth century. Such references are so poor, that we could only hypothesize how and why such persecutions happened. An exception to this lack of information is given by the *Passio Iudeorum Pragensium*, the account of the slaughter occurred against some Jewish inhabitants of Prague in Easter 1389 at the behest of Wenceslas IV. It refers to these violent deaths independently from the historiographic sources and it counts three different redactions and a poetic rework, but it is also very difficult to be evaluated, since it is partly ambiguous. Namely, the second redaction of the *Passio Iudeorum Pragensium* seems to be at the same time a historical account and a parody, if it is reliable to assert that the author tried to give a reason of the episode (often called «pogrom» by scholars). In fact, the same name of the putative author, John the Peasant, seems on one hand to parody the Passion of Jesus Christ recounted by John the Evangelist, and on the other hand to recall the actual ringleader of the mass murder, Ješko (Iešo, or Iohannes)[134].

Moreover, the *Passio Iudeorum Pragensium* stands out among other Christian and Hebrew sources about the Prague pogrom of 1398. Written right in the aftermath of the event and based on oral testimonies and a now almost lost documentation, the Latin hagiography was translated also into Czech, German and Hebrew (this latter version is very different from the corresponding Christian redactions)[135].

Lucie Doležalová highlighted some similarities between the *Passio Iudeorum Pragensium* and the hagiographical parody *Passio raptorum de Slapanicz* preserved in the manuscript Praha, Národní Knihovna, III.E.27 (presented in section II.A.6), but

---

[134] A detailed reading of the ambivalent text is offered by NEWMAN (2013).

[135] STEINOVÁ (2016) offers a study on the sources and the anti-Judaism of the year 1389, adding further bibliography.

the actual connection between the two texts deserves a deeper study[136].

B. Alphabetical Inventory of the Czech Saints' Hagiographies

1. Adalbertus (Vojtechus) Pragensis episcopus (n. ca. 956, m. 23-4-997)

In the aftermath of his martyrdom, for the second bishop of Prague two hagiographies were realised: the so-called *Vita prior*, surviving in three different redactions, and the hagiography by Bruno of Querfurt, in two redactions[137]. But the hagiographical dossier of this important Czech saint consists also of other texts.

Vita prior sive Vita antiquior sive Vita I auctore Iohanne Canapario (?)
BHL 37 – 37a – 37b
inc.: *Est locus in Germaniae partibus dives opibus*

John Canaparius wrote the *Vita Adalberti* around the years 998-1000, probably in Rome, in the monastery of SS. Boniface and Alexius located in the Aventine Hill, where Canaparius was abbot from 997 to 1004. Canaparius wrote the *Vita Adalberti* on the basis of the recount of Adalbert's younger brother, Gaudentius-Radim, who was also one of his companions in religious life. Canaparius' text (scholars almost agree on this attribution) did not survive in its original version: three different hagiographers reworked the *Vita Adalberti* immediately after its writing. All three redactions circulated already at the end of the eleventh century, as attested by the earliest manuscripts[138].

BHL 37: Redactio imperialis seu Ottoniana[139]

Written in Italy on commission of the emperor Otto III, it is probably the closest version to Canaparius' original text. It

---

[136] DOLEŽALOVÁ (2014), p. 256-263; DOLEŽALOVÁ (2010), p. 99-100.
[137] Cf. DUNIN-WĄSOWICZ (2001), p. 184-187, with additional bibliography.
[138] Reference study: KARWASIŃSKA (1996) (collection of studies); cf. also WOOD (2013a), p. 126-128.
[139] GAŞPAR (2013), with Latin text and English translation at p. 95-193.

quickly spread out of Italy in the German areas of the Empire, where Adalbert's cult promoted by the emperor became popular.

BHL 37a: Redactio Aventinensis (Romana) [140]

Written in the same monastery in the Aventine Hill where Canaparius wrote his original work, this version was written after the death of Otto III, occurred in 1002. Scholars think that this version was commissioned by pope Sylvester II (Gerbert of Aurillac), Otto's former tutor, but was not written by the pope, even if its origin dates back before his death in 1004. At least one of the surviving manuscripts of this version is earlier than the *Redactio imperialis*, dating back to *c.* 1060-1070: Cape Town, National Library, Grey Collection, 48 b 4 (it is the first of the two volumes of the «Legendary of St Cecily of Trastevere» [141]).

BHL 37b: Redactio Casinensis perperam adscripta Silvestro II papae [142]

This is a significant rewriting of the *Redactio Aventinensis* (*BHL* 37a), characterized by some negative passages concerning Adalbert's relationship with the monks of Montecassino. Moreover, the hagiographer added many further details about Adalbert's martyrdom and the beginnings of his cult, all elements that are missing in the other versions of the *Vita prior* (*BHL* 37 and 37a), but which appear instead in the anonymous *Passio Tegernseensis* (*BHL* 40, cf. *infra*). The *Redactio Casinensis* is explicitly ascribed to pope Sylvester II in the medieval tradition. The two earliest manuscripts are kept in Montecassino and date back to the year 1087.

According to another hypothesis, the *Redactio imperialis* (*BHL* 37) would be the earliest of the three rewritings, being the model for the other two. Specifically, the mention of Notker of Liège in the copy of *BHL* 37 Aachen, Bischöfliches Domarchiv und Domschatzkammer, G. 9 (XIX) would be the evidence of the origin of the text, written by Notker or by a member of his circle in the diocese of Liège [143]. A new edition

---

[140] Edition of the text by KARWASIŃSKA (1962), p. 51-67.
[141] STEYN (2002), 2, p. 196-202.
[142] Edition of the text by KARWASIŃSKA (1962), p. 71-84.
[143] FRIED (2002).

of the hagiography followed such hypothesis [144]. But in the studies by Jadwiga Karwasińska, who also paid a special attention to this testimony, the Aachen manuscript does not have any relevant position in the *stemma codicum*, nor seems to transmit a particular version of the text.

Vita sancti Adalberti episcopi Pragensis auctore Bruno Querfurtensi [145]

BHL 38-39

inc.: *Nascitur purpureus flos Bohemicis terris*

In 1004 Bruno of Querfurt, who lived in the last three decades of the tenth century, wrote another hagiography about Adalbert, using as a basis-source the *Redactio Aventinensis* (*BHL* 37a): it is the *BHL* 38 (*recensio longior*), which Bruno himself reviewed few years later, in 1008, during a stay in Poland (*BHL* 39, *recensio brevior*).

Passio anonyma (Passio Tegernseensis)

BHL 40 [146]

inc.: *S. Adalbertus primis Sclavorum natalibus Slawinihc patre*

Scholars think that the text was written between 1017 and 1038. The anonymous Passion includes some details of Adalbert's martyrdom and the beginnings of his cult, which return only in the *Redactio Cassinensis* (*BHL* 37b). As the *Passio Tegernseensis* mentions Adalbert's burial in Gniezno, scholars think that at least a copy of the *Vita prior* in the original version by Canaparius arrived into the Polish city, maybe around the year 1000, when the emperor Otto III visited the place, which had recently acquired Adalbert's relics [147]. In the most recent edition of the text, the editor Miłosz Sosnowski highlighted that the *Passio Tegernseensis* shortened the original *Vita prior*, that is the text which was the closest to Adalbert's brother Gaudentius-Radim, who later became the bishop of Gniezno. Two manuscripts kept in Munich preserve the text, one of which is

---

[144] HOFFMANN (2005), p. 125-159, with German translation at p. 160-179.
[145] Edition of the texts by KARWASIŃSKA (1969).
[146] SOSNOWSKI (2012).
[147] LABUDA (2004).

a copy of the other: München, Bayerische Staatsbibliothek, Clm 18897 and its copy Clm 23846.

Moreover, the *Passio Tegernseensis* is somehow connected to Bruno of Querfurt, one of Adalbert's biographers: in the earliest manuscript, the text is followed by the *Historia de predicatione episcopi Brunonis* (*BHL* 1471b), a brief account of Bruno's predication in Prussia and his sudden death written by Vibertus, his companion in the mission of evangelization and the only eyewitness who survived the martyrdom.

It is possible to recognize in the *Passio Tegernseensis* the *Liber de passione martyris* mentioned in the chapter 1, 6 of the *Chronicon et gesta ducum sive principum Polonorum* by the so-called Gallus Anonymus, who worked in Poland, and probably in Gniezno, at the beginning of the twelfth century[148].

Vita metrica perperam adscripta Cosmae Pragensi (Versus de passione sancti Adalberti)[149]

BHL 41

The text consists of 122 Leonine hexameters, with the addition of 22 supplementary verses entitled *Versus post missam, cum processit ad mensam Regis*.

inc.: *Quattuor immensi iacet inter climata mundi terra potens*

inc. suppl.: *Eia, dulcisonas persolvite carminis odas, alma dies mundum reddit*

The *Versus de passione sancti Adalberti* date back to the beginning or the first half of the twelfth century, and derive somehow from Canaparius' *Vita prior*, even if scholars are still unable to clarify the relationship between the two texts, nor agree on the identity of the author of the verses. They are actually attributed to Cosmas of Prague (c. 1045-1125) or Gaudentius-Radim, Adalbert's brother and archbishop of Gniezno (who lived between the tenth and the eleventh century); but there is also an alternative hypothesis about a later writing between thirteenth and fourteenth century.

---

[148] Cf. *Repertorium fontium*, III, p. 416-417. The *Chronicon* by the so-called Gallus Anonymus is one of the most important sources for the Polish medieval history: cf. WOŚ (1981).

[149] KARWASIŃSKA (1996), p. 159-189.

Vita de sancto Adalberto episcopo Pragensi
BHL 42
inc.: *Tempore illo, cum gentem Bohemicam caelestis gratiae splendor*

This hagiography is named «Perlbach Legend» after the surname of its second editor, who published it in the *MGH*[150]. The text seems to have been written in Poland in the years 1127-1248, and do not show any connections to the Czech versions of Adalbert's hagiographies, except for some general, inevitable similarities with the redactions by John Canaparius and Bruno of Querfurt[151].

Vita (De sancto Adalberto martyre)[152]
BHL 43
inc.: *In partibus Germaniae locus est opibus locuples*

In the year 1880 Augustin Kolberg published a hagiographical text about Adalbert entitled *De sancto Adalberto martire* [*sic*], including it in the *Legenda SS. patronum Bohemiae* printed in Cracow in 1507. This hagiography is based on the *Vita prior* and recounts the life of Adalbert until his consecration as a bishop of Prague, describing his pastoral care and his loving demeanor. After this orderly narration, the text turns suddenly into a series of disunited sentences extracted from the *Vita prior*, and namely from the chapters 11-16, 18, 20-23, then again 21, and finally 28-29. Some of the miracles *BHL* 44-45 follow this apparently unfinished part, precisely the ones numbered 1, 2 and 8 in the edition by Georg Heinrich Pertz[153]. For this text, the editor Kolberg formulated a possible comparison with the manuscript Bruxelles, KBR, 7773 (3444)[154].

---

[150] PERLBACH (1888); the first edition in *MPH*, 4 (1884), p. 206-221.
[151] NECHUTOVÁ (2007), p. 64.
[152] KOLBERG (1880), p. 26-32.
[153] PERTZ (1841), p. 613-615.
[154] A seventeenth-century manuscript coming from the former Bibliothèque des Bollandistes: VAN DEN GHEYN, *Catalogue des manuscrits de la Bibliothèque Royale de Belgique*, V: *Histoire – Hagiographie*, Bruxelles, 1905, p. 422-431.

Miracula

BHL 44-45

inc.: *Post mortem vero non defuerunt divina prodigia in miraculis etiam*

The account of some miracles carried out by Adalbert after his death was written in Poland during the second half of the thirteenth century[155].

Vita (Legenda «Sanctus Adalbertus ex regno Bohemiae missus»)

BHL 46

inc.: *Sanctus Adalbertus ex regno Bohemiae missus priusquam mundo*

Another text was included in the same collection printed in Cracow in 1507, from which Augustin Kolberg edited the above-mentioned hagiography *BHL* 43. It is an abbreviated legend, deriving its contents from the *Vita prior* and the *Vita* by Bruno of Querfurt, the two major hagiographies about Adalbert, which however did not spread largely in Poland[156]. As reported by the *BHL*, another copy of this shortened text is included in another liturgical book, printed in Cracow in 1511.

Vitae duae

BHL 47 and 48

inc. *BHL* 47: *Sanctus Adalbertus ex piis et religiosis parentibus oriundus fuit*

inc. *BHL* 48: *Sanctus Adalbertus nobilis progenie sed nobilior fide, natus in Bohemia*

These two texts, edited by Gelasius Dobner in 1768, are scarcely studied and considered by scholars. Dobner took the two hagiographies from a paper manuscript kept in Prague, in the Library of the Klementinum, when it still was a Jesuit college. The scholar dated back the manuscript between the end of the fourteenth century and the beginning of the fifteenth, and pointed out that the works included in it are ascribed to the «very illustrious man Jordan of Slavic origins» (*clarissimus vir Iordanus originum Sclavicarum*). Even if they derived once again

---

[155] NECHUTOVÁ (2007), p. 64; edition of the text in TRUHLÁŘ (1873h).
[156] DANIELSKI (1997), p. 238, which refers to KARWASIŃSKA (1997).

from the two major hagiographies about Adalbert (that is the writings by John Canaparius and Bruno of Querfurt), Dobner considered them worth publishing, because of the presence of previously unknown miracles. The contents revealed the Polish setting of the text, and consequently the geographical origin of its author, who worked in the Sixties of the thirteenth century, at the time of pope Urbanus IV[157].

Together with the collection printed in Cracow in 1507, these two hagiographies testify how the cult for Adalbert remained popular in Poland, even if it soon suffered the increasing development of the devotion for Stanislas, which was canonized in the mid-thirteenth century[158].

Vita

BHL 49

inc.: *Beatissimus Adalbertus martyr Christi in Bohemia provincia de nobilibus*

With reference to this text, Wojciech Danielski discussed about a breviary arrived in Poland from Hungary during the first half of the fifteenth century: the *Breviarium eremitarum s. Pauli* of the year 1428 now kept in Częstochowa, Biblioteka Klasztoru Jasnogórsiego (Klasztor OO. Paulinów, Jasna Góra), 617[159].

A liturgical rework of the hagiographies *BHL* 49 and 46 was written in Poland at the beginning of the sixteenth century, and it seems to be a sort of definitive rewriting, having the same incipit as *BHL* 46[160].

Vita

BHL 50

inc.: *Temporibus Boleslai ducis Boemorum et mortuo Dytmaro primo episcopo Pragensi*

---

[157] DOBNER (1764-1785), 2 (1768), p. 51; edition of the texts at p. 52-56 (*BHL* 47) and 57-59 (*BHL* 48).
[158] Cf. PLEZIA (1987), p. 14, 19.
[159] DANIELSKI (1997), p. 266.
[160] DANIELSKI (1997), p. 238. It seems to be one of the several texts adapted for the Polish liturgical use, for which Wojciech Danielski's study appears fundamental.

This brief text is the only Prussian hagiography of Adalbert of some resonance[161]. Probably the author was the Canon of Gniezno Sędziwoj of Czechła (Sandivogius de Czechel, Sandek sive Sandko magister), who collected several historical, hagiographical and liturgical texts and reworked and completed them all by using different sources. The result of this effort is the so-called «Codex Sedziwój», that is the manuscript Kraków, Biblioteka Muzeum Narodowego w Krakowie, Oddzial Zbiory Czartoryskich, 1310[162].

Another copy of the Vita «Temporibus Boleslai ducis» is included in the so-called «Rynsk Fragment», a 34-folios manuscript of the «last decades of the fifteenth century», from which Wojciech Kętrzyński, who had access to the private archive of the Iłowiecki family, published the text in 1870[163].

Translatio

BHL 51
inc.: *Hoc autem quod de beato Adalberti corpore postea*

From the same manuscript of the «Rynsk Fragment» kept in the private archive of the Iłowiecki family (cf. the previous item), Wojciech Kętrzyński published the anonymous account of Adalbert's *translatio* and a list of events happened after his death, an interesting information of a peculiar, almost folkloristic tradition about the saint. In the manuscript, the *Translatio* is copied at fol. 29r-v, right before the Vita «Temporibus Boleslai ducis» (fol. 29v-30v)[164].

Legenda

BHL 55
inc.: *Sanctus Adalbertus ortus fuit de Sclavonia*

---

[161] LABUDA (1997a), p. 222.
[162] DRELICHARZ (1995-96).
[163] KĘTRZYŃSKI (1870), p. 674, 676 and *passim* for the description of the manuscript and its contents; edition of the text at p. 690-692. The «Rynsk Fragment» also contains a copy of the *Vita Adalberti prior* by Canaparius (*BHL* 37 – 37a – 37b) slightly reworked: by comparing it to the text edited by PERTZ (1841), p. 581-595, Kętrzyński highlighted dozens of variants: KĘTRZYŃSKI (1870), p. 676-688.
[164] KĘTRZYŃSKI (1870), p. 688-690. The text is also edited in *MPH*, 5 (1888), p. 996-997 and in WAITZ (1888).

The scholarly studies about this text are really few. Brief mentions are given by Gerard Labuda[165], who inscribed the hagiogaphy among the fourteenth century production, and Georg Heinrich Pertz[166], who mentioned the manuscript München, Bayerische Staatsbibliothek, Clm 7642 as a testimony of this short hagiography[167].

Legenda

BHL 56
inc.: *Anno Ottonis III. quarto*

A brief annotation by Georg Heinrich Pertz informed of this hagiography, copied in five pages of a manuscript formerly kept in the monastery of Sint-Salvator in Utrecht[168].

Legenda aurea (Golden Legend)

A version of Adalbert's hagiography based on Polish materials appeared in the Czech adaptation of the *Legenda aurea* by Jacobus de Varagine: scholars recognize ten medieval copies of this text[169]. The setting of Adalbert's hagiography and its geo-historical connotation are the most peculiar among the Czech insertions in the original Latin collection[170].

2. Agnes de Bohemia Ord. S. Cl.
(n. ca. 1205, m. 6-3-1280/1283)

Despite the few surviving late medieval manuscripts, the spread of Agnes of Bohemia's dossier must have been significant, as attested by the rewritings, the Czech translations and the Modern reworks based on different versions of her hagiography. Agnes' dossier is divided into two branches, each one formed by several texts, corresponding to the two attempts of canonization. The first group of writings is formed by the so-called *Vita prima*, its embellishing rewriting known as *Vita se-*

---

[165] LABUDA (1997a), p. 222.
[166] PERTZ (1841), p. 581.
[167] The manuscript was written by Augustine of Indersdorf in the years 1479-1486: GLAUCHE – KNAUS (1979), p. 662.
[168] PERTZ (1841), p. 581, n. 72 no. 5. This manuscript is identified by HOFFMANN (2005), p. 29 with the codex Bruxelles, *KBR*, 7773 (3444).
[169] VIDMANOVÁ – BAHNÍK (1984).
[170] VIDMANOVÁ (1986a), p. 292.

cunda, and several brief redactions about the saint's life (cf. *infra*, *Compendium Pisanum*), as well as four letters addressed to Agnes by Clare of Assisi. The second branch of Agnes' hagiographical dossier includes instead only the hagiography *Candor lucis aeternae*, discovered at the beginning of the twentieth century.

The order of the miracles in the mentioned two branches of Agnes' hagiographical tradition allowed scholars to recognize the origin of the entire dossier, characterized by three editorial stages. In the first phase, the information about Agnes was collected in the double monastery founded by the saint herself, and did not receive any attention outside the monasteries' walls. In the second phase, the clergy of the court worked on some written hagiographical material, rewriting the documents in view of the first canonization process. The third and final stage consisted of the redaction *Candor lucis aeternae*, a hagiography strictly connected to the Franciscan environment, which was written in view of the second request of canonization[171].

Vita prima

BHL 154
inc. prol.: *Scripturus divae Agnetis Pragensis dominae et civis meae*
inc.: *Agnes inclita virgo Pragensis, filia Primislai Ottagari*

An ecclesiastical author, who however was not a monk, wrote Agnes' *Vita prima*, a hagiography, which pointed out the princess' illustrious Přemyslid dinasty and the kinship with Elisabeth of Hungary. According to the Bollandists, only a transcription from a now lost manuscript and a Czech translation are left, as well as a Modern Latin rewriting of the mid-seventeenth century[172]. But scholars have recently indicated that the dossier published in the *AASS* is a product of the Baroque era, even if based on medieval sources, of which the *Vita prima* would be an extract[173]. Scholars proposed – but did not prove – the text's attribution to Ulrich of Paběnic, vicar general of the bishop of Prague and master of the Knights of the Cross

---

[171] FELSKAU (2017), the reference study for this section, unless specified otherwise.

[172] Edition of the text in *AASS*, Mart. I, Antwerpen, 1668, p. 509-513.

[173] On the Baroque reworking, cf. KUBÍN (2015), p. 268-270, with additional bibliography.

(or Crusaders) with the Red Star, the Order of Hospitallers founded by Agnes herself.

Vita secunda
Not in *BHL*
inc.: *Annus millesimus ducentesimus quintus vertebatur cum primum lucem caelestem Agnes*

As already mentioned, the *Vita secunda* is an embellishment of the *Vita prima*, and this is maybe the reason why scholars hardly paid attention to this text. Moreover, the surviving version is actually a Latin re-translation from two lost manuscripts – one Latin and one Czech – and, similarly to *Vita prima*, seems to be a reworking of the Baroque era[174].

Compendium a Pisano scriptum (Compendium Pisanum)
BHL 154 no. 2
inc.: *Fuit alia in hoc Ordine insignissima genere et sanctitate, scilicet sancta Agnes de Bohemia*

The title *Compendium Pisanum* indicates the passage dedicated to Agnes of Bohemia and included in Bartholomew of Pisa's *De conformitate vitae beati Francisci ad vitam domini Iesu*. The text appeared in the *BHL* right after the *Vita prima*, but without a specific number.

Some other mentions of Agnes are included in different writings. In the *Chronicon Aulae Regiae*, Peter of Zittau recounted the first request of canonization of Agnes, promoted in 1328 by the last Přemyslid queen, Elisabeth, wife of John of Bohemia. The manuscript Šibenik, Samostan Sv. Franje, 36 contains the texts related to the second request for the canonization of Agnes[175]. In the *Chronicon Bohemorum*, John of Marignolli reported the third attempt to canonize Agnes, undertaken by the emperor Charles IV.

Legenda «Candor lucis aeternae»
BHL 154b
inc. prol.: *Crebris sacrarum virginum... precibus sum pulsatus*

---

[174] Edition of the text in *AASS*, Mart. I, Antwerpen, 1668, p. 513-532.
[175] The texts used for the request of canonization are edited by Kubín (2015), p. 287-289.

inc.: *Candor lucis aeternae et speculum sine macula*
BHL 154c
inc. prol.: *Omnipotens Deus, qui magno... pietatis munere*
inc.: *Regina Bohemiae, domina Guta*

A Bohemian Minor friar wrote the hagiography «Candor lucis aeternae» in view of the second attempt to canonize Agnes, as attested by the complete request's dossier included in the manuscript Šibenik, Samostan Sv. Franje, 36. It is still uncertain wether the request was actually presented, or if it was not enough to start the process. However, its internal incoherence is the result of the juxtaposition and/or reworking of different already existent accounts. From this perspective, the compiler's statement in the prologue assumes a further significance, when he says that his narration will not follow a chronological order, but a logical thread, in order to hold the readers' attention.

It is possible that a first monastic version of the hagiography would have been written right after Agnes' death by an author who scholars identified with the Franciscan chaplain Theodoricus. After this redaction, such prototype was reworked and integrated with some more passages. The compilation clearly reveals its composite nature in the earlier manuscript of the tradition, the codex Milano, Biblioteca e Archivio Capitolare della Basilica di S. Ambrogio, M 10, containing references of the years 1334b and 1339, the exact period of the canonization's request by the Order of Friars Minor[176]. Petr Kubín supposed that the dossier of Agnes' canonization was prepared by Nicholas Moravus, the Provincial Minister of the Franciscan Minors.

The anonymous compiler of the hagiography «Candor lucis aeternae» had both Bonaventuras's *Legenda sancti Francisci* and the anonymous *Legenda maior* of Hedwig of Silesia (saint Hedwig of Andechs, Agnes' aunt) as a model. Bonaventura's wrote both his *Legenda maior* and *Legenda minor* around the years 1260-1262, and Hedwig's *Legenda maior* was certainly written before the year 1300. The models used by the author of the hagiography «Candor lucis aeternae» emerged because of some textual correspondences between the recounts of Agnes' miracles and

---

[176] FELSKAU (2017); studies on the contents and the related historical and religious background are offered by FELSKAU (2000) and KUBÍN (2015). Reference edition: VYSKOČIL (1932).

some contents of the *Legenda sanctae Clarae* written by Thomas of Celano.

The number *BHL* 154c indicates the miracles published after the hagiography «Candor lucis aeternae» edited by Walter Warren Seton, who first discovered the text [177].

Laudatio

BHL 154d

inc.: *Fuit alia beata Agnes, virgo Deo placita et hominibus grata*

The number *BHL* 154d indicates a text transmitted by just one copy of the *Chronica XXIV generalium ordinis fratrum Minorum*, a writing ascribed to the Franciscan friar Arnaldus of Sarrant. This *Laudatio* is included in a letter by the cardinal Ugolino of Segni, later pope Gregory IX, to Clare of Assisi [178].

3. Arnestus seu Ernestus Pragensis episcopus

Scholars published several recent historical-biographical studies about Arnošt/Ernest, bishop of Prague from 1343 to 1364, while his hagiographic figure and the related texts received less attention [179].

Vita auctore Guilelmo de Lestkow

BHL 680 [180]

inc.: *Apparuit gratia Dei Salvatoris nostri*

Active in the first part of the fourteenth century, William of Lestkov (Vilem z Lestkova) well knew the life of Ernest/Arnošt,

---

[177] SETON (1915), recently reprinted (Cambridge 2010).

[178] *Analecta Franciscana*, 3 (1897), p. 183.

[179] It seems worth remembering here the miracle made by saint Apollonia concerning the teeth of Ernest (*BHL* 645): in 111 words the hagiography recounts the miracle of the punishment of Ernestus, who neglected to rebuild a chapel dedicated to saint Apollonia in Prague. The account is preserved at least in two fifteenth-century manuscripts from Utrecht (Bruxelles, *KBR*, 7917 [3189]) and Louvain (Paris, Bibliothèque Mazarine, 1736). Given her popularity as the patron saint of toothache sufferers and dental diseases in the high Middle Ages, it is likely that the protagonist of this tale was Apollonia of Alexandria, instead of Apollonia of Rome as listed in the *BHL*. I am grateful to Guy Philippart for this reference.

[180] Edited by TRUHLÁŘ (1873d), p. 387-398. The book *Vilém z Hasenburka* (1994) is a reprint of Truhlář's work.

thanks to his closeness to the church and his role as a diplomatic official of the emperor Charles IV. Consequently, this *Vita* could have been written in view of the canonization of the bishop. Nonetheless, or maybe exactly for this reason, William wrote the hagiography right after Ernest's death, in the years 1364-1368, mixing historical data with hagiographical cliches and typical images and rhetoric of this literary genre[181].

Visio

BHL 681

inc.: *Noverint universi... quod ego Arnestus ecclesiae Pragensis*

The *Vita Arnesti* by William of Lestkov is followed by a vision written in the first person, i.e. personally recounted by Ernest, who remembered a vision of Mary he had in Kłodzko (Kladsko, Glatz) when he was a young boy. Kłodzko is actually the place of Ernest' burial, although he died in Roudnice nad Labem. The *Visio* is copied right after William's *Vita*, without any pause or title, but introduced by the words *Sequitur miraculum domini Arnesti, archiepiscopi Pragensis*[182].

A different version of the same vision is included in Conrad of Megenburg's *Commentarius de laudibus B.V. Mariae*, in which the author referred to Ernest's episode by association of ideas, after having described the vivid memory of a personal vision of Virgin Mary during a Christmas night. This version of Ernest's vision is shorter than the one linked to William's hagiography, and it seems to be independent from this narrative, being instead the result of Conrad's personal researches, curiosity and interests, probably in connection to his tight relationship with Ernest's successor, the bishop John Ocko of Vlasim (Jan Očko z Vlašimi)[183].

Vita auctore Iohanne praeposito Glacensi

BHL 682

inc.: *Anno Domini 1364 obiit dominus Arnestus, primus Pragensis archiepiscopus, monasterii... Glacensis fundator. Fuit autem idem Arnestus natione Boemus, Arnesti militis de Pardubicz filius*

---

[181] NECHUTOVÁ (2007), p. 150-151.
[182] Edited by TRUHLÁŘ (1873d), p. 398-400.
[183] ZALUD (2013).

John, a provost of the Augustinian monastery of Kłodzko (Kladsko), wrote the second redaction of the Life of the bishop Ernest/Arnošt, probably inspired by the *Visio*, which follows the *Vita Arnesti* by William of Lestkov. Even if the relation between the two texts is still not clear, from John's *Vita* seems to derive the passage about Ernest included in the *Chronicon* by Benessius Krabice de Weitmühl (Beneš Krabice z Weitmile)[184].

A critical edition of this text is still missing, but it was published in the so-called «Mariale Arnesti», printed in 1651 in Prague by Bohuslav Balbín, a Czech Jesuit and a prominent intellectual, writer, and historian of his time, devoted to the Bohemian history and the Czech culture. The «Mariale Arnesti» is a Psalter dating back to the mid-fourteenth century, which included prayers written by different authors[185].

Narratio

BHL 683

inc.: *Reverendus in Christo pater dominus Arnestus... tantae erat contemplationis*

It is very difficult to find some information about this text, as well as the nineteenth-century edition mentioned in the *BHL*[186]. But a fine transcription is offered once again by Bohuslav Balbín, who studying the medieval reception of the *Bonum universale de apibus* (or *Apiarius*) by Thomas of Cantimpré († c. 1270) found a manuscript of the monastery of Třeboň containing some notes on the text written by the very same bishop Ernest[187]: Praha, Národní Knihovna, XII.F.3 (2189), a fourteenth-century copy of a codex of the Augustinian Canons' Monastery in Sadská. Our text *BHL 683*, which is very brief, preceeds these notes in the manuscript.

---

[184] SOBCZYK (2016), p. 54, on the basis of the studies by Wojciech Mrozowicz.

[185] BARTOŠ (1943); KOEHLER (1990).

[186] That is WATTENBACH (1851), p. 667-668.

[187] BALBÍN (1682), p. 89. Balbín's transcription is reprised by Nicolas Louis in his doctoral thesis: LOUIS 2013, p. 180. I am very grateful to Guy Philippart for this precious piece of information.

Vita

BHL 683b

inc.: *Fuit Arnestus natione Boemus...*

The *BHL Suppl.* indicated this redaction on the basis of a mention by Albert Poncelet[188]. Since it has the same *incipit* of the Life by John of Kłodzko (*BHL* 682), it could possibly be an adaptation. It is also followed by the *Visio* (*BHL* 681) and a recount of some miracles, which took place in the year 1468. Poncelet found this little dossier in the manuscript Roma, Biblioteca Alessandrina, 99, fol. 517r-522r.

A similar case could also be the one of the manuscript Augsburg, Universitätsbibliothek, II.1 2° 218, fol. 47vb, containing a text, which seems to recall once again John of Kłodzko's hagiography, with a little different *incipit*: *Anno domini 1364 obiit reverendus in Christo pater dominus Arnestus*[189].

Vita auctore Valentino Cratoaldi

Not in *BHL*

inc.: [tit.: *Ad lectorem*]. *Arnesti spectas tumulum, qui gloria, pastor, Pragensis cleri presul honorque fuit*

This hagiography, written in 1516 by the Polish Humanist Valentin Krautwald, was discovered, analyzed and edited in a single publication that still remains the scholars' reference study[190]. The *Vita*'s *codex unicus* is Città del Vaticano, Biblioteca Apostolica Vaticana, Chig. Q.II.51, fol. 143r-159v. To accomplish the canonization request for Arnošt, stopped because of the Hussite wars, Krautwald completed the bishop's dossier by using as a source the *Chronicon* of Michael Czacheritz, a regular canon of St Augustine of Kłodzko (Kladsko).

4. Benedictus, Iohannes et socii (Quinque fratres) in Polonia martyres

Vita auctore Brunone Querfurtensi

BHL 1147

inc. prol.: *Adiuva Deus ut magna parvus ingenio narrare valeam*

---

[188] PONCELET (1909), p. 189.
[189] Mentioned by HILG (1999), p. 369-373: 372.
[190] HLEDÍKOVÁ – ZACHOVÁ (1997).

inc.: *Quem res loquitur bene venisse, sanctus iste de Benevento venit*

During his first stay in Poland, around the years 1005-1006, or maybe already in 1004, that is in the aftermath of the saints' death, if not in 1009, right before his own martyrdom[191], Bruno of Querfurt wrote the hagiography of the Five brethren killed by some thieves in the monastery of Międzyrzecz, near Poznań, during a mission of evangelization[192]. Two of them were Polish and three of them Italian, and they all belonged to the ascetic circle of the Italian monk Romuald, the founder of Camaldoli[193]. Archaeological sites and researches attested that the five brethren were originally buried in Poland, but not all together, and then were translated to Bohemia in 1039, together with Adalbert's relics, and put once again in different places[194].

Bruno's hagiography is strictly connected with the literary tradition of Adalbert of Prague, but at the same time it has a peculiar biographical style drifting apart from the hagiographical genre. The Passion was discovered in the last part of the nineteenth century in the manuscript Berlin, Staatsbibliothek zu Berlin – Preußischer Kulturbesitz, theol. lat. 8° 162, which still remains the *codex unicus* of the tradition, dating back to the mid-twelfth century and including marginal minor variants[195].

Passio auctore Cosma Pragensi

BHL 1148

inc.: (*Anno dominicae inc. 1004 s. Benedictus cum sociis martyrizatus est*). *Temporibus Henrici imperatoris qui post Ottonem*

---

[191] MILADINOV (2013a), p. 186; DUNIN-WĄSOWICZ (2001), p. 185; NECHUTOVÁ (2007), p. 65.

[192] About the other historical sources, which recount the episode, WOOD (2013a), p. 128-129, and MILADINOV (2013a), p. 191.

[193] Quoting Sofia Boesch Gajano, KLANICZAY (2008), p. 257 reminds us that the five monks used to combine the Camaldolese spirituality with Eastern and Maronite hermit traditions, maybe with reference to abbot Zosimas.

[194] DUNIN-WĄSOWICZ (2001), p. 186; NECHUTOVÁ (2007), p. 65.

[195] The Latin text edited by Jadwiga KARWASIŃSKA (*MPHns*, 4.3, Warszawa, 1973, p. 27-84) was reprinted with parallel English translation by MILADINOV (2013a), p. 196-313; earlier editions: KADE (1888), p. 716-738; *MPH*, 6 (1893), p. 383-428; the text edited in *MPH* was reprinted and translated into Italian by IGNESTI (1951).

A second, brief redaction of the Passion of the Five brethren is the passage of the chapter I 38 of Cosmas' *Chronicon Bohemorum*[196]. From Cosmas' *Chronicon* this excerpt was also copied in the manuscript Würzburg, Universitätsbibliothek, M.p.th.q. 46, a twelfth-century collection of sermons and hagiographies[197].

5. Guntherus in Bohemia eremita (n. ca. 955, m. 9-10-1045)

Vita et miracula
BHL 3713-3719
inc.: *Fuit in partibus Thuringie quidam vir nobilis*[198]

The most recent edition on the hagiographical dossier of Gunther/Vintíř, realized by Petr Kubín[199], is the only study, which revealed the layered nature of the saint's *Vita*, reworked in three different phases. The stages of the redaction complicated Gunther dossier, so that the *BHL* listed seven versions of the hagiography, whose identification and sequence are not valid any more. According to Kubín's study, the only hagiography devoted to Gunther – formed by *Vita* and *miracula* – is the *BHL* 3713, written in the mid-thirteenth century by an anonymous monk of Břevnov in view of the canonization of the saint. All the other *BHL* variants are connected in different ways to this redaction.

Other original attestations about Gunther's life are included in different hagiographies: firstly, in the *Vita Godehardi posterior* (*BHL* 3582) by Wolfherius of Hildesheim, from which the *Vita Guntheri* itself quotes some sentences of the beginning; in the *De memoria beati Emmerami* by Arnald of Sankt Emmeram

---

[196] Cosmas of Prague's *Chronicon* is edited by BRETHOLTZ (1923), p. 1-241; KOEPKE (1851).

[197] THURN (1970-1994), 1 (1970), p. 77-79. I am grateful to Guy Philippart for the reference on this manuscript.

[198] The most recent editor, KUBÍN (2014a), p. 154, considered the incipit of *BHL* 3713 (*Regnante piissimo imperatore Henrico huius nominis secundo, cum beatus Godehardus Altahense coenobium regeret, fuit in Thuringiae partibus quidam vir*) as a later and shoddy variant.

[199] KUBÍN (2014a): bilingual (Czech-German) study at p. 11-71 and 73-145; edition of the text with Czech translation at p. 154-239.

(*BHL* 2541); finally, in the *Vita sancti Stephani regis Hungariae* by the bishop Hartwig (*BHL* 7921)[200].

Kubín's study also includes a discussion about the previous editions of the *Vita*, among which the best is the one included in the *Fontes rerum Bohemicarum*[201].

6. Hieronymus de Praga magister (n. 1370/1380, m. 30-5-1416)

De vita Magistri Hieronymi de Praga

inc.: *Magister Hieronymus sabbato post Ascensionem Domini hora quasi XI a media nocte computando*

The anonymous text appears to be as an account reported by an eye-witness of the last hearing of the trial and the execution of Jerome of Prague[202].

Narratio de Magistro Hieronymo Pragensi pro Christi nomine Constantiae executo

inc.: *Quia varietas affectuum humanorum plerumque interveniente odio*

The *Narratio de Magistro Hieronymo* is ascribed to Peter Mladenowicz, the author of the *Relatio de Magistro Iohanne Hus*, which seems to have the same style and structure as the *Narratio*. As Peter was not present at Jerome's trial in all its phases, and surely he did not attend at the saint's death, it seems that the author reworked an anonymous source[203].

Sermo habitus in Betlehem in memoriam novorum martyrum magistri Iohannis Hus et magistri Hieronymi auctore Iacobello de Mysa

Cf. *infra*, II.B.8, Iohannes Hus.

---

[200] KUBÍN (2014a), p. 77-81, 81-83 and 87-88 (Czech-German). A list of non-hagiographical sources about Gunther at p. 83-95.

[201] TRUHLÁŘ (1873g); KUBÍN (2014a), p. 115-136, discusses the different editions.

[202] FUDGE (2016), p. 171-172. The text is edited by EMLER 8 (1932), p. 335-338.

[203] SPUNAR 1 (1985), no. 723; FUDGE (2016), p. 172. The text is edited by EMLER 8 (1932), p. 339-350.

7. Hieronymus Stridonius (Eusebius Hieronymus)

Vita et Transitus Sancti Hieronymi (Hieronymus), sive Epistulae tres in laudem Hieronymi gloriosi auctore Iohanne de Novo Foro

BHL 3866d

inc. (epist. Ad Karolum IV): *Serenissime princeps... Eximiae virtutis beati Ieronimi merita gloriosa*

There are no attestations of saint Jerome's cult in Bohemia before the time of the emperor Charles IV. A Latin dossier about Jerome, formed by three pseudepigraphical letter ascribed to Augustine, Eusebius and Cyril, and usually entitled *Vita et Transitus Sancti Hieronymi* or simply *Hieronymus*, is dedicated to the emperor Charles IV and included in the writings by John of Neumarkt (Iohannes de Novo Foro/Noviforensis), the author of a remarkable part of the hagiographical dossier of Wenceslas (cf. *infra*, II.B.19)[204]. It is propably the rework of an already existing pseudepigraphical material, listed in the *BHL* under the numbers 3866-3868, which did not mention any Jerome's translation of the Bible into Old Church Slavonic.

This dossier had a widespread diffusion in late medieval Bohemia (fourteenth-fifteenth centuries).

Hieronymianus, sive Vita et miracula auctore Iohanne Andreae

BHL 3876

inc. (prol. I): *Secundam huius operis partem aggrediar, quae subdivisa*
inc. (prol. II): *Hieronymus a hiera, quod est sanctum*
inc.: *Hieronymus Eusebii viri nobilis filius*

Thanks to John of Neumarkt's work, around 1350 arrived in Bohemia the hagiography dedicated to saint Jerome written by Giovanni d'Andrea (Iohannes Andreae), an Italian canonist and intellectual who died in Bologna in 1348. The four chapters of the *Hieronymianus* completely describe the Father's figure, his biography and his miracles, and are followed by some praises about Jerome's several virtues and merits, and about the many different spheres and scopes of his holiness, as well as by a list of Jerome's translations from the Greek.

---

[204] The dossier is edited by KLAPPER (1932).

Even if the German translation of the *Hieronymianus* circulated much more widely across Bohemia than the Latin original[205], this hagiography influenced the poeticae and liturgical production about Jerome (offices, hymns, prayers), not only in the Czech lands but generally in Europe[206].

Vita et Gesta Sancti Hieronymi (lectiones sex)

These are six liturgical readings copied in the manuscript Praha, Národní Muzeum, XII.A.18 (1404) and connected to Jerome's *officium proprium*, which were widespread across Europe. The manuscript originated in the Czech city of Cheb on the occasion of the consecration of an altar to Jerome (*Chebské Officium sv. Jeronyma*). The primary sources for the readings are the *Legenda aurea* by Jacobus de Varagine, as shown by the beginning of the first lection, and the letters collected in the *Hieronymus* by John of Neumarkt, together with the *Chronicon* by Sigebert of Gembloux.

The Bohemian tradition of these lections is characterized by an insertion, which probably was added by John of Teplá, regarding Jerome's advanced knowledge of the Slavic, a language that he would have spoken more fluently than Greek or Hebrew[207].

8. Hroznata Ord. Praem. in Bohemia martyr (m. 1217)

BHL 3991[208]

inc. prol.: *Ut gemmae pretiosae nitorem* (al.: *Quemadmodum gemmae et pretiosi lapides*)

inc.: *Rege Premizl, qui et Ottacarus cognominatus fuit*

The blessed Hroznata (*c.* 1170-1217) is the founder of the important Premonstratensian monastery of Teplá and its twin female in Chotěšov. His hagiography was written in the thirteenth century, at the end of the Fifties, about thirty years after the saint's death, driven at an early grave by some thieves, who

---

[205] NECHUTOVÁ (2007), p. 180.
[206] See VERKHOLANTSEV (2014), p. 110-112.
[207] VERKHOLANTSEV (2014), p. 112-113; VERKHOLANTSEV (2013), p. 280-282. The text is edited by BLASCHKA (1937).
[208] NECHUTOVÁ (2007), p. 70-71. The text is edited by TRUHLÁŘ (1873e) and in *AASS*, Iul. III, Antwerpen, 1723, p. 804-810 (3ª ed., Paris – Roma, 1868, p. 770-776).

closed him in the cellar of his monastery and left him dying of starvation.

Written without any dialectical undertone, the Latin hagiography has a fluid enjoyable style, enriched by a certain rhetorical care and rhythmic refinement (*cursus*) in the *clausolae*. The peculiarity of this hagiography lies in the confirmation of the parallel historical documentation, attested by different sources: the deeds and documents of the foundation of the monastery; registers and papal documents relating to Hroznata's relations with the Roman Curia; Hroznata's last will and testament, dated 1197; the *Annals* of the two monasteries he founded; different passages in some historiographical works of that time, such as Gerlach's *Chronicon* (the chronicle by Gerlacus Milovicensis abbas, 1165-1228)[209].

9. Iohannes Hus (n. 1371 ca., m. 6-7-1415)

A discussion on the contents, the characteristics and the style of the fifteenth-century texts devoted to the figure of Jan Hus, which are listed in the present section, is offered by Thomas A. Fudge[210].

Relatio de Magistro Iohanne Hus auctore Petro de Mladonowicz

inc.: *Anno Domini M°CCCC°XIIII° serenissimus princeps et dominus dominus Sigismundus Romanorum et Hungariae rex*

Among the four works written in the aftermath of Jan Hus' death, two are in Latin and two in Czech language. They all belong to the hagiographical genre, since they imply that the protagonist has a heroic spirituality, the Christian ideal and the essence of the popular saint. Moreover, the core of each text is the protagonist's Passion, together with the opposition against the judges of the Council of Constance. Of the two Latin texts, the *Relatio de Magistro Iohanne Hus* by Peter Mladenowicz immediately became the reference writing for the event, consequently influencing the portrait of Hus and the perception of his story among the scholars. In fact, also the other texts contributed to build the protagonists' image and Hus' memory in the late medieval Bohemia. Sometimes these texts collected and

---

[209] For all references, see KUBÍN (2000).
[210] FUDGE (2013a), p. 190-209.

wrote down oral testimonies, originating an actual, peculiar and local new sub-historiographical genre about the story of Jan Hus[211]. The *Relatio de Magistro Iohanne Hus* by Peter Mladenowicz interpreted Hus' death as a martyrdom suffered in the name of Christian truth: such view is not only attested in the *Relatio*, when Peter Mladenowicz compares Hus' and Christ's Passions, but also in the epistles of Hus himself, especially among those written in his last year of life. Maybe Jan Hus did never compare his own experience to Christ's crown of thorns, as Peter wrote in his *Relatio*, but certainly Jerome of Prague expressed this same image the year after Hus' death, as reported in the acts of the Council of Constance[212].

With the title *Relatio de Magistro Iohanne Hus* scholars usually indicate the final part (*Finale de sancto viro et reverendo Magistro Iohanne Hus*) of a longer text somehow derived once again from the acts of the Council of Constance and reworked in three different stages, completed within the years 1415-1417[213].

Passio fidelis et christianissimi magistri Iohannis Hus auctore Iohanne Barbato[214]

inc.: *Judith 4°: Memores estote Moysi servi Domini. Ibidem 8°: Memores esse debent... Sic et carissimus magister vel frater noster zelo zelavit*

In the year 1418 Jan Bradáček, also referred to as Jan Bradatý or Jan of Český Krumlov (Jan z Krumlowa), and nicknamed Barbatus (in a letter of the year 1411, Jan Hus called him «steel beard»), wrote the *Passio fidelis et christianissimi magistri Iohannis Hus*. In this text, the author compared Hus to Jesus Christ, and the place of Hus' execution to Calvary. Barbatus also added some details lacking in Peter's *Relatio*, but on the other hand he seemed to emphasize the idealization and celebration of the protagonist, at the expense of the truthfulness of the events occurred – maybe because he wrote a text focused on Hus' death

---

[211] FUDGE (2013a), p. 185.

[212] HACK (2007), p. 133-134; the text of the *Relatio* is edited by NOVOTNÝ (1932b).

[213] SPUNAR 1 (1985), no. 722.

[214] The text is edited with a commentary by: FUDGE (2011). The text is edited with the title *Passio etc secundum Johannem Barbatum, rusticum quadratum* by EMLER 8 (1932), p. 14-24.

and did not take into account the facts that preceeded Hus' convocation to the Council of Constance.

Barbatus' *Passio* shows two redactional stages: it underwent in fact a second-hand rework, which some scholars identified with Iacobellus of Stříbro (Iacobellus de Misa, Jakoubek; cf. the here following item: *Sermo habitus in Betlehem*), and some others with Laurentius de Brzyezowa[215].

Sermo habitus in Betlehem in memoriam novorum martyrum magistri Iohannis Hus et magistri Hieronymi auctore Iacobello de Mysa

inc.: *Beati qui persecucionem patiuntur...* (Mt 5, 10). *Dominus noster Iesus Christus; Dominus noster Iesus Christus*

Among the hagiographies devoted to Jan Hus and Jerome of Prague, it is worth remembering also the sermon written by Iacobellus of Stříbro, the so-called «theologian of the first Hussitism»: talking about the protagonists of his own time, in this text Iacobellus contaminated the preaching with hagiographical elements. It is one of the very first examples of the hagiographies devoted to the new saints. By interpreting Mt 5, 10 («Blessed are those who are persecuted in the cause of uprightness»), Iacobellus sketched Jan Hus ascending into the sky greeted by the host of saints, as a new Elias and similarly to Jesus Christ. Inspired by the contents of the fifteenth-century Latin and vernacular Passions devoted to Jan Hus, this sermon also inherited their tones and hagiographic style[216].

In another sermon, written at the beginning of 1416 and still unpublished, Iacobellus commemorated Jan Hus together with the martyrs of Olomouc who died in 1415.

In addition to Jacobellus' sermons, there are at least another two anonymous homilies: one of those, written in the fifteenth century, is completely devoted to Jan Hus; the other one, of the

---

[215] FUDGE (2013a), p. 186-187; SPUNAR 1 (1985), nos. 736 e 624. DOLEŽALOVÁ (2014), p. 246-253 offered a comparison between the hagiography by Barbatus and the *Relatio* by Peter Mladenowicz.

[216] HACK (2007), p. 138 e 146; FUDGE (2013a), p. 190. The text of the *Sermo habitus in Betlehem* is edited by NOVOTNÝ (1932a).

end of the fifteenth century, also commemorated the two martyrs of Olomouc[217].

10. Iohannes de Ienzenstein Pragensis episcopus (m. 1400)

Vita domini Iohannis, Pragensis archiepiscopi tercii auctore Petro Clarificatore

BHL 4408

inc. prol.: *Iesus Christus heri et hodie*
inc.: *Deus igitur qui non vult mortem peccatoris*

The Life of the archbishop John of Jenštejn, a person who Jan Hus considered divine and deserving of the most holy memory, was written by his confessor Peter, nicknamed Clarificator, as demonstrated by František Michálek Bartoš in the first part of the twentieth century (the attribution is mostly accepted by scholars). Peter wrote John's hagiography in an epic style, on commission of both the archbishop Olbram (or Wolfram) of Škvorec, John's successor at the Prague's seat, and the prevost Matthew of Roudnice.

The *Vita Iohannis*, transmitted by the *codex unicus* Praha, Národní Muzeum, XVI.E.19, has above all a documentary inspiration: it begins with John's conversion, and it deals with his ascetic propensity, but also with the religious and political life of his time (for example recalling the contrasts with the king Wenceslas IV). Nonetheless, the 21st and last chapter describes the saint's miracles. The Hussite wars obscured both the hagiography and the cult of John of Jenštejn, also because his grave was not in the Czech territory, since he lived the last three years of his life in poverty in the St Praxedis monastery in Rome[218].

11. Iohannes Milicius de Chremsir (1320/1325-1374)

Narracio de Milicio auctore Matthia de Ianova

Not in *BHL*

inc.: *Nunc ad narrationem de probissimo Miliczyo remeabo*

---

[217] The texts are edited by EMLER 1 (1873), p. 368-372 (*Sermo de martyribus Bohemis*) and p. 373-376 (*Sermo de M. Iohanne Hus*).

[218] *BS*, VI, Roma, 1965, col. 816-818; NECHUTOVÁ (2007), p. 152-153. Most recent edition: KRMÍČKOVÁ (2006); previous edition: EMLER 1 (1873), p. 439-468.

Matthias of Janov, *magister Parisiensis* and canon of the Prague's cathedral, wrote the *Narracio de Milicio* as an introduction to the third book of his own work about the Antichrist, entitled *Regulae Veteris et Novi Testamenti*. In a study devoted to the *Narracio de Milicio*, a text written right after Jan Milíc's death, Olivier Marin underlined its hagiographical character[219].

Vita venerabilis Milicii
Not in *BHL*
inc. prol.: *Scripturus vitam servi tui ad honorem nominis tui*
inc.: *Cum ergo sol iustitiae erat sub nubilo et sui luminis claritatem absconderet*

Almost at the same time as Matthias of Janov, an anonymous disciple of Jan Milíc, wrote this *Vita Milicii*, which is a vivid report of an eye-witness of the preacher's activity. Inspired and connected to the second version of Wenceslas' hagiography «Oriente iam sole», this text has some peculiar characteristics, since its *pathos* refers to the genre of the *planctus*, and shows a special rhetorical care for the rhymes and the *cursus*.

Nonetheless, some scholars date back the (supposed) fourteenth-century text to the baroque era, since Bohuslav Balbín reworked it in the seventeenth century, without leaving any trace of the manuscript he used[220]; some others think that the *Vita Milicii* is a compilation of earlier material realised by Balbín himself[221].

12. Iohannes Nepomucenus Pragae in Bohemia presbyter (n. ca. 1340-1350)[222]

Even if the saint's cult was attested from the fifteenth century, only in the eighteenth century pope Benedict XIII officially canonized John Nepomucene (John of Nepomuk), acknowledging he was martyred in 1383 in obedience of the

---

[219] MARIN (2014). The text of the *Narracio* is edited among the *Regulae Veteris et Novi Testamenti* by KYBAL 3 (1911), p. 358-367; the text is also published by TRUHLÁŘ (1873b).
[220] NECHUTOVÁ (2007), p. 151-152. Edition by TRUHLÁŘ (1873f).
[221] MARIN (2014), p. 237, who recalled the discussion by MENGEL (2004b).
[222] LEROU (1991).

king Wenceslas IV's will. The reference text for John's canonization was a *Vita* compiled around sixty years earlier by Bohuslav Balbín and published in the *AASS*[223]. Balbín only cursorily referred to a homonymous canon of Prague of the same time as John Nepomucene, who was killed by drowning in 1393 after a fight between the king Wenceslas IV – who also killed Nepomucene – and the archbishop John of Jenštejn.

Shortly after Nepomucene's canonization, scholars found the acts of his trial and execution, drawn up by the archbishop John of Jenštejn in person right after the saint's death, in 1393, and included as third section of a dossier that Jenštejn addressed to the Roman Curia, describing the details of his fight against the king[224]. But in the dossier there was no mention of the confession, which was the basis for the recognition of his martyrdom: a multifaceted question arose, which affected the areas of devotion and history, not devoid of the ideological components that characterized the beginning of the twentieth century, and which also concerned the question of the second, homonymous martyr mentioned by Balbín.

Paule Lerou schematically listed the causes, which contributed to the genesis of the hagiographic legend of John Nepomucene: these are partly derived from the chronicler Václav Hájek of Libočany (first half of the sixteenth century), who clearly separated the two homonymous martyrs, and partly connected to the archbishop John of Jenštejn himself and to his successor (and commissioner of the hagiography) Wolfram, who both referred to John Nepomucene calling him *martyr*. Moreover, some other historiographical writings of the same time were very ambiguous about this matter[225]. In addition to that, a negative propaganda helped the developing of an unclear and ambivalent image of the king Wenceslas IV exactly in the years of his dispute with John of Jenštejn[226].

---

[223] *AASS*, Mai. III, 2ª ed., Venezia, 1738, p. 667-679.

[224] Edition by DE VOOGHT (1960), p. 422-441; study on the figure and «myth» of John Nepomucene at p. 400-421; about *Acta*'s structure cf. HÜBNER (2016), p 63-64.

[225] LEROU (1991), p. 282-284.

[226] Cf. HÜBNER (2016).

13. Passio Iudeorum Pragensium

Not in *BHL*

inc. (I): *Historia de cede Iudeorum Pragensi. Appropinquabat dies festus cristianorum insignior*

inc. (II): *Passio Iudeorum Pragensium secundum Iesskonem* (al. *Ieškonem*) *rusticum quadratum. Vespere autem sabbati, que lucescit in prima sabbati, ingressus sacerdos*

inc. (III): *Vespere autem sabbati, que lucescit in prima sabbati, in illo tempore ingressus sacerdos*

inc. (versus): *Sexto anno/iubileo romano* || *M semel tria CCC/bis LL XI removeto*

The editor of the *Passio Iudeorum Pragensium*, Evina Steinová, distinguished the three prosaic redactions by their incipit. The first version, entitled *De cede*, is very brief, maybe being the original writing, and quickly mentions the blasphemous act against the sacred host. The second version, entitled *Secundum Ieškonem*, is the longer and erudite redaction; it recounts a very different version of the event than the *De cede*, especially with regard to the responsibles for the massacre. The is a sort of hybrid composition, which mixes the traditional hagiographical genre and the *ludus paschalis*, creating a real *unicum* in the European medieval literary production. The third redaction, entitled *Secundum blasphemiam*, is an abbreviation of the *Secundum Ieškonem*, but it also has some peculiarities and it is the more similar to the poetic version of the text [227].

14. Ivanus in Bohemia eremita

BHL 4618 [228]

inc.: *Historia b. Ivani, qui communicatus est... Beatus Ivanus fuit natione Ungarus*

Several elements and aspects of the hermit Ivan are still unclear, because neither the hagiographical texts nor the history of the cult allowed scholars to clearly evaluate this figure [229].

---

[227] STEINOVÁ (2010) presented a study and the commented edition of all the Latin redactions of the text. An English translation is offered by NEWMAN (2013), p. 264-271.
[228] The text is edited by KOLÁŘ (1873-93).
[229] Cf. ZAPLETALOVÁ (2016).

The debated points are many: firstly, the degree of historicity of the known information, since his hagiography is the only reference source to recover any data about the saint. Secondly, the chronological origin of his cult; thirdly, the original language of the hagiography, being «Ivan» a name of clear Slavic origin, connected to the Cyrillic translation of the Greek name «John» (Ioannis). Finally, the details of the apparent overlap with the devotion – very spread in the early medieval Bohemia – to John the Baptist, adjoining Ivan also in the *dies natalis* (24 and 25 June respectively), and also another ancient martyr named John, the apostle's Paul Roman companion, commemorated on 26 June[230].

Three manuscripts preserved the Latin Life of Ivanus, whose provenances are from Břevnov, from the Library of the Klementinum in Prague, and from the chapter of St Vitus' church in Prague (the so-called «Chapter-redaction», dating back around the years 1465-1469)[231].

The setting of the legend refers to the second half of the ninth century, at the dawn of Bohemian Christianization, and still divides the scholars in the evaluation of its possible models and sources. Some scholars linked the text to the anti-utraquist controversy that raged in Bohemia in the middle of the fifteenth century, since the hagiography contains explicit references to a fight «against the heresy». Some others linked the text to the relics of the homonymous Bulgarian patron saint John of Rila (Ivan Rilski), who arrived to Bohemia in the year(s) of the «Chapter-redaction», a text sharing some passages with the hagiography of the Bulgarian hermit. Part of the scholars asserted instead that the original hagiographical nucleus of the *Vita Ivani* is much earlier, because of its still unclear connection with the eleventh-century *Vita Guntheri*[232], and/or because of the use of the hagiographies of Ludmila and Stephen as models and sources[233]. Nonetheless, some other elements of Ivan's hagiography clearly refer to the fourteenth century.

---

[230] KŘÍŽEK (2009), p. 103-105.
[231] ZAPLETALOVÁ (2016), p. 54.
[232] For this remark cf. NECHUTOVÁ (2007), p. 72.
[233] ZAPLETALOVÁ (2016), p. 54.

15. Ludmilla Bohemiae ducissa

Scholars still disagree on evaluating Ludmila's hagiographies, considering them as a tenth-century source – and consequently a hagiographical prototype for the female Czech sainthood –, or dating them back to the eleventh or twelfth centuries, notwithstanding the earlier appearance (in this perspective, the hagiographer's voluntary hints and alteration to an earlier era make the dossier a forgery in scholars' view).

The sharing of information and elements between the two most important Latin hagiographies of Ludmila (*BHL* 5026 and 5028) and the Old Church Slavonic version supports the earlier dating of the dossier and the idea of a common origin of the texts[234].

Nonetheless, scholars recently reconsidered the opposite opinion. Lastly debated by Petr Kubín with reference to the history of Ludmila's cult[235], the dating to the twelfth century seems to be connected to specific historical and ecclesiastical local events, acquiring more plausibility.

Passio «Fuit in provincia»

BHL 5026
inc.: *Fuit in provincia Boemorum quidam comes* [al.: *princeps*] *nomine Boriwoy*

The shortness of the text and the lack of miracles indicate an early origin of the hagiography, close to Ludmila's death. Some scholars think that it could derive from a now lost Old Church Slavonic Legend: the extant one, the so-called Ludmila's Prologue-Legend (Proložní legenda o sv. Ludmile), is later, dating back to the twelfth-thirteenth century. Part of the scholars remarked some similarities between the *Passio* «Fuit in provincia» and two hagiographies of Wenceslas, the *Passio* «Crescente fide» and the so-called «Lawrence's Legend» (the Montecassino Legend)[236].

Martín Homza recently confuted Dušan Třeštík's idea about the Bavarian authorship of the *Passio* «Fuit in provincia», which would be written by a monk from Regensburg inspired by the

---

[234] Cf. HOMZA (2017), p. 92.
[235] KUBÍN (2011), p. 81-124.
[236] NECHUTOVÁ (2007), p. 48.

hagiography of the local patron saint Emmeram in the last part of the tenth century[237].

BHL 5027 (Epitome)

inc.: *Fuit in provincia Bohemorum princeps quidam nomine Borziwoy; hic accepit uxorem*

The *BHL* listed the present hagiography as an abbreviation of the *Passio* «Fuit in provincia». Without knowing the version *BHL* 5026, in the *AASS* the Bollandist Constantin Suysken considered the text as an epitome of the following *BHL* 5028[238].

Passio auct. Ps.-Christiano de Scala

BHL 5028-5029

inc. prol. *BHL* 5028: *Domino... ecclesiae Dei Pragensis II pontifici Adalberto*

inc. *BHL* 5028: *Passionem beati Wenceslai simul cum avia sua*

inc. *BHL* 5029: *Mater beati Wenzlai quosdam proceres suos, filios iniquitatis*

inc. alter [*BHL* 5029]: *Subtrahente se*[239]

On *BHL* 5028 see *infra*, no. 19 (Wenceslaus Bohemiae dux et martyr m. 935), *BHL* 8825.

Josef Emler edited the redaction *BHL* 5029, also known as «Wattenbach Legend» from the name of its nineteenth-century editor, in the *Fontes rerum Bohemicarum* under the title *Utrpení sv. Lidmily*[240].

The redaction *BHL* 5029 derives from the *Legenda Christiani*[241]. Similarly, several other texts not included in the *BHL* originated in different places and times for liturgical needs.

Passio «Diffundente sole» et Sermo de Passione «Factum est»

BHL 5030 and *BHL* 5031d-f

inc. *BHL* 5030: *Diffundente sole iustitiae radios sanctae fidei*

---

[237] HOMZA (2017), p. 95-96, with reference to TŘEŠTÍK (1981).
[238] *AASS*, Sept. V, Antwerpen, 1755, p. 341, n. 10.
[239] NECHUTOVÁ (2007), p. 54.
[240] EMLER 1 (1873), p. 140-143.
[241] Some of these texts are mentioned by NECHUTOVÁ (2007), p. 54.

inc. *BHL* 5031d (rec. I): *Factum est (autem) ut* [al. *om.*] *post mortem venerabilis viri* [al.: *filii* vel om.] *sui assecla Christi*

inc. *BHL* 5031e (rec. II): *Factum est ut post mortem illustris principis*

inc. *BHL* 5031f (rec. III et IV): (a) *Factum est post mortem illustris principis*; (b): *B. Ludmilla, famula Christi, usque in finem vite sue*

For a long time, scholars considered the homily «Factum est» dedicated to Ludmila as a part of Cyril and Methodius' *Passio* «Diffundente sole», because so it was edited by Josef Truhlář[242], and the two texts are copied together in the manuscripts. The homily consists in a reworked passage of the *Legenda Christiani*, as suggested by the Bollandists and then demonstrated by Josef Pekař[243]. Václav Chaloupecký studied and edited the homily as an independent text, also discussing and newly editing the *Passio* «Diffundente sole»[244]. Given the affinities to the *Legenda Christiani* and the stratification of the text, scholars disagree on evaluating the origin of the *Passio* «Diffundente sole», dating it between the eleventh and the fourteenth century, similarly as the same *Legenda Christiani*[245].

Homilia auctore Carolo IV imperatore

Not in *BHL*

Scholars hardly considered this homily. As an early work of Charles IV, it must be evaluated with an eye to the vaste bibliography about the emperor, and in the context of his first writings, and the *Moralitates* in particular, a collection of various meditations inspired by Marian spirituality. The title refers to a

---

[242] TRUHLÁŘ (1873i).
[243] PEKAŘ (1905), p. 72.
[244] CHALOUPECKÝ (1939), p. 481-493 (*Passio* «Diffundente sole»); p. 538-556 (*sermo* «Factum est»); the edition of the sermonis also offered by BARTOŇKOVÁ – VEČERKA (2010), p. 251-256 with Czech translation.
[245] Cf. HOMZA (2017), p. 102-104; JAKOBSON (1985), p. 168, with further bibliography. In the mentioned study, Martín Homza discussed the contents of the text, its relationships with other hagiographies dedicated to Ludmila and Wenceslaus, and its importance in the history of the saint's cult.

specific section of the work, in which some Old Testament *exempla* are interpreted in moral sense[246].

16. Milada (Mlada, seu Maria) Pragensis abbatissa OSB (m. 994?)

Mlada, also called Milada or Mary (Maria), was the daughter of the duke of Bohemia Boleslav I, and the great-granddaughter of Ludmila. Grew up and educated in Regensburg, she became a Benedictine noun around 970, and founded with the papal permission a chapter of canonesses, later Benedictine nouns, at Hradčany, near Prague. It was the earliest Benedictine female monastery of Bohemia. As abbess, for the needs of the Order she commissioned the building of the church of St George at Prague's castle. The nouns of Hradčany strongly promoted Mlada's cult, until the monastery's suppression in 1782.

There are no hagiographies about Mlada. The medieval attestations of the saint are only liturgical and artistic, as bas-reliefs and paintings dating back from the first half of the thirteenth to the fourteenth century, and Mlada's mentions in the earliest calendar of Bohemia (fourteenth century), and in the Missals of the of the church of St George in Prague[247].

Listing the mentions of Mlada in the historiographical sources, the Bollandists noticed her absence in the Martyrology of the monastery of St George, and highlighted that she was always labelled as «blessed», even in the Martyrology itself, to underline her virtuous aura and the reputation for sanctity, which surrounded her when she was still alive[248]. Connected to this issue is the recent debate between Karel Pacovsky and Petr Kubín about Mlada's medieval cult. Against Kubín's study published in 2011, Pacovsky denied the medieval cult of Mlada, confuting Kubín's interpretation of the sources. Answering to Pacovsky's objections in the same issue of the journal «Studia Mediaevalia Bohemica», Kubín confirmed his position[249]. According to the latter, Mlada's cult flourished between the thir-

---

[246] KLANICZAY (2008), p. 274; NECHUTOVÁ (2007), p. 171-172. The edition of the *Moralitates* is offered by WÖDKE (1897).
[247] *BS*, IX, Roma, 1967, col. 477-479.
[248] *AASS*, Mart. III, 2ª ed., Venezia, 1736, p. 710 (3ª ed., Paris – Roma, 1865, p. 706).
[249] KUBÍN (2011); PACOVSKY (2016); KUBÍN (2016a).

teenth and the fourteenth century, and then declined until the baroque age (a similar destiny seems to have affected saint Zdislava, cf. *infra*, II.B.20). Kubín argued that scholars must read from a hagiographical perspective the extant historiographical sources, like Cosmas of Prague's *Chronicon Boemorum* or the work of the same title by Giovanni de' Marignolli. Moreover, Kubín suggested scholars to newly interpret the reliquiary of St George's church, commissioned by the abbess Kunhuta (1302-1321), in light of the act that its iconography presents many Přemyslid saints, and that the grave no. 102 located in the apse of Virgin Mary's chapel in St George's church would be exactly Mlada's grave.

17. Procopius Pragensis abbas (m. 1053)

Petr Kubín recently re-evaluated Procopius' hagiographical dossier. The state of the art of the present paragraph is based on his discussion, although the hagiographies will be listed following the order of the *BHL*. Kubín based his discussion on the 1953 edition of Procopius' Latin dossier sketched out by Václav Chaloupecký, and finished by Bohumil Ryba after the sudden Chaloupecký's death. One of Kubín's most insisted remarks referred to the distance between Chaloupecký's premises and Ryba's conclusions, due to the different methods and perspectives used by the two scholars[250]. Another remarkable innovation of Kubín's exam referred to the same figure of Procopius and his sanctity, also involving the relative chronology of his hagiographies, as it has been mentioned in the introduction (cf. *infra*, II.A.2). For this issue see the cited bibliography.

Countless are the epitomes and the reworkings of Procopius' hagiographies; the ones listed in the *BHL* refer (no longer reliably) to the *Vita maior*.

Vita sancti Procopii maior

BHL 6952 (interdum cum prol. 6952b)
inc. prol. I: *Domino ss. Severo... Dum mentis meae sagaciori speculatione*

---

[250] KUBÍN (2016b), with reference to CHALOUPECKÝ – RYBA (1953). Many extracts of Procopius' hagiographies are offered by BARTOŇKOVÁ – VEČERKA (2010), p. 211-213; KALOUS – STEJSKAL (2006) update the editorial status of the texts.

inc. prol. II: *Procopius dicitur quasi procus pius*
interdum datur prol. *BHL* 6952b, inc.: *Procopius dictus est quasi pius vel propicius*
inc. prol. III: *Benedicta sit pia sacrosancte Trinitatis*
inc.: *Beatus igitur Procopius nacione Bohemihena*

The *Vita maior* is the longest hagiography of Procopius, and the best-known one, since it was published in the *AASS*[251]. Among the 32 manuscripts, which preserve the text, even if sometimes incomplete, the earliest is the 1353 Premonstratensian breviary Praha, Národní Knihovna, VII.F.23. The earliest codex with the complete text is only 30 years later, and contains several hagiographies of Bohemian saints, like Gunther, Sigismundus, Ernest/Arnošt, Wenceslas and Adalbert (Praha, Národní Knihovna, XIII.D.20).

The *Vita maior* mixed and expanded the texts of the *Vita minor* and the *Exordium Zazavensis monasterii*, while its incipit recalled the *Vita Udalrici* in the version included in Jacobus de Varagine's *Legenda aurea*. With regard to this latter element, Petr Kubín remarked that the choice of Ulrich as a model could not be fortuitous, since the two saints share the same *dies natalis*.

The contents of the *Vita maior* reveal the later origin of the text compared to the rest of Procopius' dossier: a precise political and religious ideology altered the historical data, promoting the Old Church Slavonic and contrasting the Czech people of German origins. For this reason, Jana Nechutová asserted that the *Vita maior* originated in the Emmaus monastery «Na Slovanech» founded by Charles IV. Nechutová suggested that the addition of a prologue explaining the saint's name etymology would be another hint for a later dating of the hagiography, most likely contemporary to the earliest manuscript. Moreover, the first Czech translation of the *Vita maior* would further confirm the *terminus ante quem* to the mid-fourteenth century[252].

The last chapters of the *Vita maior* are devoted to Procopius' miracles, part of which explicitly happened after the saint's canonization. Only a few are an original addition by the hagiogra-

---

[251] *AASS*, Iul. II, Antwerpen, 1721, p. 139-148. KUBÍN (2016b), p. 56-58; CHALOUPECKÝ – RYBA (1953), p. 93-99 with edition at p. 239-267. The text is also published by EMLER 1 (1873), p. 360-366, completed by KRÁSL (1895).
[252] NECHUTOVÁ (2007), p. 148-149.

pher of the *Vita maior*, while some others date back to the thirteenth century, since they return also in the later version of the *Vita minor*.

Bohumil Ryba demonstrated that the text of the *Vita maior* enriched by a brand new miracle was the basis for the illustrated legend transmitted by the *Liber depictus* Wien, Österreichische Nationalbibliothek, 370, a manuscript dating back shortly before 1350, a period of a significant success of Procopius' cult[253].

Vita sancti Procopii minor

BHL 6952g

inc.: *Fuit itaque beatus abbas Procopius nacione Bohemus*

According to Václav Chaloupecký, the *Vita minor*, a text discovered by Josef Pekař, would be an embellishing reworking of the *Vita antiqua*. Although the manuscript tradition is quite large, only one codex preserves the entire text (Olomouc, Státní Archív, Kapitulní Knihovna, CO 54), while the other 23 manuscripts only transmit liturgical lections or selected chapters. The earliest manuscripts date back to the first half of the fourteenth century.

After the studies on the *Vita antiqua* (BHL 6953g, cf. *infra*), scholars by now agree on evaluating the *Vita minor* as the earliest existing hagiography about Procopius[254]. Since the accounts about the Sázava monastery end at the year 1061, scholars think that this Latin redaction was contemporary to the earliest Paleo-Slavic text about Procopius, even if not even its direct translation. Josef Pekař hypothesized the existence of this now lost Paleo-Slavic text on the basis of the prologues of the *Vita maior*, dating back the supposed text to the years 1061-1067[255].

Vita sancti Procopii antiqua (BHL: Vita dicta antiqua)

BHL 6953g

inc.: *Tempore Heinrici III imperatoris Romanorum... Fuit quidam Procopius nacione Boemus, Slavonicis apicibus*

---

[253] KUBÍN (2016b), p. 58-60.
[254] KUBÍN (2016b), p. 51-53; CHALOUPECKÝ – RYBA (1953), p. 61-69, with edition of the text at p. 121-161.
[255] SOMMER (2007), p. 140-142.

Václav Chaloupecký thought that the *Vita antiqua* was the earliest hagiography of Procopius' dossier, and that it was written shortly after 1096, the year of the entrance of a Latin community in the monastery of Sázava, in sostitution of the Slavic one. In Chaloupecký's opinion, the *Vita antiqua* would derive from a now lost Paleo-Slavic hagiography written between the years 1061 and 1067, the text hypothesized by Chaloupecký's master Josef Pekař on the basis of the contents of two prologues preserved in the manuscripts of the *Vita maior*[256].

According to Bohumil Ryba, the *Vita antiqua* would be instead a mid-thirteenth-century reworking of the *Vita minor*, as proved by the rhythmic clauses of the text. Jana Zachová's philological analysis confirmed such hypothesis[257], so scholars by now unanimously agree to consider the *Vita antiqua* as a hagiography derived from the *Vita minor*[258].

Exordium Zazavensis monasterii (BHL: Vita in Chronica Sazaviensi)

BHL 6953h
inc. prol.: *Hoc in loco congruum videtur non debere praetermitti*
inc.: *Tempore siquidem praefati Odalrici*

The *Exordium Zazavensis* is a writing about the history of monastery of Sázava, from the origin and beginnings until the year of the expulsion of the Slavic monks (i.e. 1096). Although it originated as an independent work, it is transmitted as a part of the continuation of Cosmas of Prague's *Chronicon Bohemorum*, written by an anonymous monk of Sázava (*Continuatio monachi Sazaviensis*). Since in the manuscripts the *Continuatio Sazaviensis* consists not only of a continuous writing about the years 1126-1162 added at the end of Cosmas' *Chronicon*, but also in scattered additions to the original work, the *Exordium Zazavensis* assumed the form of an added passage to Cosmas' *Chronicon* up to the year 1038.

Scholars dated the *Exordium* back to the twelfth century, but before 1173, because of its contents. In a second moment, then, the anonymous continuator of Cosmas' *Chronicon* incorporated

---

[256] KUBÍN (2016b), p. 50-51; CHALOUPECKÝ – RYBA (1953), p. 44-60, with edition of the text at p. 111-120.
[257] ZACHOVÁ (1971).
[258] Cf. also NECHUTOVÁ (2007), p. 70.

the *Exordium Zazavensis* to his own *Continuatio*, adding some more details. In fact, the Life of Procopius included in the *Exordium Zazavensis* is very similar, but not identical, to the *Vita minor*.

Six more Procopius' miracles, based on a *liber miraculorum* entitled *Cronica sancti Procopii*, are included in the *Chronicon* by the canon of Prague Beneš Krabice z Veitmile (Benessius Krabice), written in the last years of his life (he died in 1375)[259].

Narratio de canonizatione

BHL 6953m
inc.: *Igitur hiis et al.s b. patris quam plurimis miraculis*

Václav Chaloupecký thought that the *Narratio de canonizatione* was written shortly after Procopius' sanctification in 1204. But the studies by Bohumil Ryba demonstrated *Narratio*'s textual connections to the *Vita maior*, rather than to the earlier *Vita minor*. The manuscript tradition of the *Narratio* confirmed this fact: the text is actually copied in almost every testimony of the *Vita maior*, and never in the ones of the *Vita minor*. Since the same situation occurred for the prologues preserved in the manuscripts of the *Vita maior*, both these texts and the *Narratio* must belong to a later redactional phase[260].

18. Sigismundus rex Burgundionum m.

Legenda Temporibus Tiberii

BHL 7718b
inc.: *Temporibus Tiberii privigni magni Augusti... Pilatus Iudeae procurator ab eodem Tiberio dirigitur*

The *Passio* of the king Sigismundus counts several redactions, among which the earliest dates back to the eighth century. About this saint and his cult cf. *supra*, II.A.2 and II.A.4 (paragraph about saint Maurice of Agaunum). In the Czech Middle Ages the abbreviated redaction of the *Passio* circulated in Bo-

---

[259] KUBÍN (2016b), p. 58. The edition of the *Chronicon* is offered by EMLER 4 (1884), p. 457-548.
[260] KUBÍN (2016b), p. 60-62, with a discussion about *Narratio*'s contents at p. 74-78; CHALOUPECKÝ – RYBA (1953), p. 71-72, with edition of the text at p. 158-161.

hemia, commissioned by the emperor Charles IV and included in Jacobus de Varagine's *Legenda aurea* (extended version inclusive of the local saints)[261].

Miracula facta Pragae saec. XIV

BHL 7720

inc. prol.: *Splendoris lumine sempiterno*
inc.: *Nuper siquidem in die festi S. Wenczeslai*

The number BHL 7720 indicates Sigismundus' miracles included in the *Libellus miraculorum*, preserved in a fragmentary *codex unicus* (cf. *supra*, II.A.2). This work refers explicitly to the concurrent existence of the devotion for Wenceslas, and aims at promoting the two saints' cult to the same degree of popularity.

19. Wenceslaus Bohemiae dux et martyr (m. 935)

Passio auct. Gumpoldo ep. Mantuano[262]

BHL 8821

inc. prol.: *Studiorum igitur genera multiforma*
inc.: *Avulsa igitur ob insecabilis sacramentum Trinitatis*

Written in the last years of the Seventies of the tenth century on commission of the emperor Otto II, Gumpold's work is slightly later than the earliest hagiography of Wenceslas, the so-called «Crescente fide» (BHL 8823), which is the base-model for the entire dossier. Gumpold's insertions and amplifications highlighted the emperor's commission of the text, without altering the original hagiographical model, but completing the earlier narration and updating the social and religious function of the saint. Gumpold's Latin is rich and sometimes complex, studded with classical echoes. The author shows also a deep knowledge of the Slavic language and the Czech culture and environment.

---

[261] STUDNIČKOVÁ (2010), p. 300-301; KUBÍN (2014a), p. 106. According to the *BHL*, in some western manuscripts the incipit's first word of this *Passio* is *Tempore* instead of *Temporibus*.

[262] MILADINOV (2013b); with edition of the text and English translation at p. 28-75. Marina Miladinov offers Latin text derived from the most recent edition, ZACHOVÁ (2010b), compared to the most significant *loci critici* of the previous editions.

The most important manuscript of the tradition is Wolfenbüttel, Herzog August Bibliothek, 11.2 Aug. 4°, fol. 18v-37v, almost contemporary to the *Passio*'s writing. It was prepared before the year 1006 for Emma, the daughter of (saint) Adelaide of Burgundy and the king Lothair II of Italy, and the widow of the duke Boleslav II.

BHL 8821b

inc.: *Regnante felicis memoriae praeclarissmo rege Henrico primo*

In some manuscripts, Gumpold's hagiography does not have the prologue and begins with a different incipit.

BHL 8822: Appendix

inc.: *Hactenus sanctissimae ac imitabilis vitae et passionis*

The *Appendix* is a text added at the end of Gumpold's Passion in the manuscripts, and it was firstly edited by Tomáš Pešina z Čechorodu (Thomas Joannes Pessina de Czechorod). In 1819, Josef Dobrovský corrected some mistakes of this edition, but without re-editing the entire text. Dobrovský also remarked the literal correspondence between the text and the *Chronicon* by Cosmas of Prague, which would consequently be *Appendix*'s source [263].

Passio anonyma, translatio et miracula («*Crescente fide*»)

BHL 8823-8823a

inc.: *Crescente fide christiana in illis diebus Dei nutu*

Known as «Crescente fide» from its incipit, this text was written most likely in the Seventies of the tenth century [264], being one of the earliest Latin hagiography on Wenceslas and the basis for the rest of the saint's dossier. Its contents, which are partly inspired by the earlier Paleo-Slavic legend of Wenceslas, fix the *terminus post quem* to the years 872-873, the moment of

---

[263] DOBROVSKÝ (1819), p. 115-119.

[264] KØLLN (2003), p. 59, proposes the year 973 for the writing of the text, and KLANICZAY (2013), p. 389, the years 976-983. With regard to this issue, it is worth remembering that Gumpold's hagiography, a longer text based on the «Crescente fide», can be dated to the late Seventies of the tenth century, and certainly before 983, the year of Gumpold's death: MILADINOV (2013b), p. 21.

the murder of Boleslav I, and the *terminus ante quem* to the foundation of the diocese of Praga (973), an event that caused the writing of a new redaction of the saint's *Passio*[265].

Some scholars recognized two different redactions of this *Passio*, originated in Bavaria and in Bohemia respectively. The Czech redaction, which initially was only supposed[266], was discovered later, and acquired the number *BHL* 8823a, even if Bollandists considered this text as a «recensio quasi identica» to the Bavarian version *BHL* 8823[267].

The number *BHL* 8823b indicates instead a version that omitted the accounts of the translation and the miracles.

Passio auctore Laurentio monacho Casinensi

BHL 8824
inc. prol.: *Dominus ac redemptor noster humanis visibus*
inc.: *Quidam septemtrionalis axis indigenae*

This is one of the earliest texts about Wenceslas, together with the *Passio* «Crescente fide» (*BHL* 8823-8823a) and Gumpold's hagiography. The so-called *Legenda Casinensis* does not have any connection to the other two early hagiographies, instead the text is characterised by an autonomy in content and rhetoric. This rhythmic-prose Passion originated in Montecassino, and seems to belong to that group of eleventh-century

---

[265] KØLLN (2003), p. 59-60. NECHUTOVÁ (2007), p. 46, proposes to date the text back around 973, the year of the foundation of the diocese of Prague, reminding that the hagiographer used Arbeo of Freising's *Vita Emmerammi* (*BHL* 2538), written in the second half of the eighth century, as a source and a model.

[266] CHALOUPECKÝ (1939), p. 493-501.

[267] The Bavarian recension is edited by TRUHLÁŘ (1873a) with Czech translation. LUDVÍKOVSKÝ (1958) discovered the complete Czech redaction. With regard to the Bavarian recension, KØLLN (2003), p. 59, remarked that the author was an anonymous monk of Regensburg, which apparently aimed at presenting Wenceslas as the exemplar model of monastic perfection. According to Kølln, this version of Wenceslas' hagiography followed the unsuccessful writing of the Passion of Montecassino (*BHL* 8824), which the clergy of both Prague and Regensburg did not appreciate. These would be the reasons of the better knowledge of the Czech environment and the better mastery of the hagiographical style demonstrated by the compiler of the redaction «Crescente fide».

texts written for promoting the foundation of the diocese of Prague[268].

Oldřich Králík noticed some affinities between the *Legenda Casinensis* and the earliest Slavic legend of Wenceslas, the so-called *Pvrní staroslovenska legenda*, and consequently supposed that a common and now lost model had existed, which was known also by the compiler of the *Passio* «Crescente fide»[269]. However, the *Legenda Casinensis* was never popular, and maybe never used.

Notwithstanding the lack of success, the Passion was enriched with some added miracles, recounted to the monks of Montecassino by a Bohemian guest, which maybe was indeed the bishop of Prague (and then saint) Adalbert. But again, there are no attestations of any liturgical or devotional use of this augmented version, known as *Legenda Laurentii* from the monk, and then bishop of Amalfi, Lawrence of Montecassino[270]. At least, the *Legenda Laurentii* served as the basis-source for the *Vita Adalberti* written by John Canaparius.

The text of the Montecassino hagiography is divided into twelve liturgical lections and it is copied in the manuscript Montecassino (Frosinone), Archivio dell'Abbazia, 413[271]. The manuscripts Roma, Biblioteca Vallicelliana, H 13, fol. 53r-66v and Roma, Biblioteca Alessandrina, 95, fol. 778r-783v, used by the editor Francis Newton, are modern copies[272].

Passio ss. Wenceslai et Ludmillae auctore Christiano monacho (Legenda Christiani)[273]

BHL 8825 = BHL 5028
  inc. prol.: *Domino... ecclesiae Dei Pragensis II pontifici Adalberto... Passionem b. Wenceslai simul cum avia sua*
  inc.: *Moravia, regio Sclavorum antiquis temporibus*

---

[268] Cf. NECHUTOVÁ (2007), p. 48.
[269] KRÁLÍK (1959).
[270] KØLLN (2003), p. 59. NECHUTOVÁ (2007), p. 48, thinks instead that Lawrence may have known the Paleo-Slavic text or its lost model.
[271] From this manuscript the text was transcribed by DUDÍK (1855), p. 304-318. Another edition is offered by TRUHLÁŘ (1873c).
[272] NEWTON (1973), p. 23-42.
[273] KØLLN (1996); cfr. NECHUTOVÁ (2007), p. 43-46. The Latin text is edited by LUDVÍKOVSKÝ (1978); only chapters I-III are edited with Czech translation by BARTOŇKOVÁ – VEČERKA (2010), p. 165-175.

The *Legenda Christiani* is named after its author, who presents himself as a monk of Břevnov named Christian (Christianus), declaring to write the hagiography on the express wish of the bishop of Prague Adalbert.

The *Legenda Christiani* differs from the other hagiographies about Wenceslas because of its long digression about the origins of the Christianity in Moravia added at the beginning of the text. In particular, Christian talks about the first christianization of the Czech lands by Cyril and Methodius, who evangelized the area at the time of the stay in Moravia of the duke of Bohemia Bořivoj, hosted by the duke of Moravia Svatopluk. According to Christian, Methodius in person converted and baptized Bořivoj during this visit[274]. Neither the earliest Passions of Wenceslas («Crescente fide» and Gumpold's version), nor the hagiographies of Cyril and Methodius ever confirmed these data, instead delay the christianization of the Bohemian dukes to the time of Bořivoj's son and successor, the duke Spytihněv[275]. At least, Bořivoj appears as already converted in the *Passio* of Ludmila «Fuit in provincia» (*BHL* 5026), even if there is no mention of his baptism.

The problem in evaluating the *Legenda Christiani* is its sharing some contents of the earliest two hagiographies of Wenceslas, adding at the same time some new episodes, mostly related on the saint's miracles, which do not appear in any other version of the Passion. The weight of the consequences of any evaluation and solution of this textual dilemma still influences the scholars' debate, divided between a dating of the *Legenda Christiani* back to the end of the tenth century and the mid-

---

[274] Roman Jakobson reminds us that this preamble corresponds to the first two chapters of the *Legenda Christiani* according to the edition by PEKAŘ (1905), p. 88-125, and that this passages have a significant parallel in the first part of the so-called *Legenda Bodecensis* edited by CHALOUPECKÝ (1939), p. 521-536. The *Legenda Bodecensis* corresponds in turn, even if with some variants, to the first five chapters of the *Legenda Christiani*: JAKOBSON (1985), p. 168 with notes and additional bibliography.

[275] JAKOBSON (1985), p. 167, speaks of «distorsion» of the *Legenda Moravica* of Cyril and Methodius in the preamble of the *Legenda Christiani*, as well as in Ludmilas *Passio* «Diffundente sole» (this latter presented in section II.B.14, *Ludmilla Bohemiae ducissa*).

twelfth century. There is also a hypothesis of a later origin dating back to the fourteenth century[276].

Passio («*Oportet nos fratres*»)

BHL 8826[277]

inc prol.: *Oportet nos, fratres carissimi, vitam et passionem s. Wenceslai*

inc.: *Sub regno gloriosissimo Romanorum quandam regionem scimus esse, nomine Bohemiam*

This *Passio* is a reworking in rhythmic prose of the hagiography by Gumpold. Scholars disagree on evaluating the text and its dating: Josef Pekař affirmed that this «homily of hagiografical subject» originated in Italy at the end of the tenth century or at the latest in the first half of the eleventh century. Jaroslav Ludvíkovský instead proposed to date the text back to the beginning of the twelfth century based on the analyis of the style[278].

Passio «*Oriente iam sole*»

BHL 8827

inc.: *Oriente iam sole christianae religionis*

The Passion «Oriente iam sole» dates back to the thirteenth century: to the Seventies according to the *BHL*, to the first half of the century according to Jaroslav Ludvíkovský[279]. Jana Nechutová pointed out that there are two redactions of the hagiographies: the earliest would date back to the mid-thirteenth century, a time of a great success of Wenceslas' cult in Bohemia[280]. Nechutová based this dating on two elements: the account of the miraculous dream of the Danish king Eric, after which he commissioned the building of a church dedicated to Wenceslas (Eric died in 1250); and the use of Martin of Troppau's *Chronicon pontificum et imperatorum* as a source, written in

---

[276] KALHOUS (2015b) offers a systematic account of the historiographical debate on this hagiography.
[277] The text is edited by PEKAŘ (1905), p. 389-408.
[278] NECHUTOVÁ (2007), p. 51.
[279] LUDVÍKOVSKÝ (1942).
[280] DEVOS (1964), p. 104, dated back the first redaction of the *Passio* «Oriente iam sole» to the Fifties of the thirteenth century.

the decade 1268-1277[281]. The second recension is connected to a more extensive research made in view of the building of a monument devoted to Wenceslas. This recension originated around the mid-fourteenth century, and had an immediate success spreading very rapidly in the second half of the century. The use of the *Chronicae Pragensis libri III* by Francis of Prague (*c.* 1290-post 1355) as a model, the expressed new spirituality promoted in the first third of the fourteenth century by the Dominican friar Peregrinus of Oppeln, and the echoes of the first works by Jan Milíc of Kromeriz (1320/25-1374) confirmed the proposed dating[282].

The editor Josef Pekař published the entire dossier, consisting of the first redaction of the Passion (*BHL* 8827), the translation (*BHL* 8828), the miracles (*BHL* 8829), and the brief account *De socio sancti Wenceslai* (*BHL* 8830)[283], texts that are going to be briefly presented below.

Translatio et miracula

BHL 8828-8830

inc. (*BHL* 8828): *Post triennium vero passionis eius divina revelatione*

inc. (*BHL* 8829) (miracula XIII): *Licet ex antescriptis venerabilis viri sanctitas*

inc. (*BHL* 8830) (miracula de servo Podiven): *Quoniam in antecedentibus de fideli servo huius ducis*

The hagiograpical corpus consisting of three accounts about Wenceslas' translation and miracles (*BHL* 8828-8830) dates back to the second half of the thirteenth century, since it includes an explicit reference to Martin of Troppau's *Chronicon pontificum et imperatorum*, written around 1265 (cf. n. 281). The still fundamental study by Paul Devos on this corpus was based on one of the earliest manuscripts of the tradition, very close to the text's origin, the miscellaneous codex Bruxelles, Bibliothèque des Bollandistes, 433, fol. 75r-99v, of the second half of the thirteenth century[284].

---

[281] Cf. *Repertorium fontium*, VII: *L-M*, p. 489.
[282] NECHUTOVÁ (2007), p. 51-52.
[283] PEKAŘ (1905), p. 409-430.
[284] DEVOS (1964).

Quite surprisingly, these so to speak ancillary hagiographies of this short dossier derived from the first redaction of the *Passio* «Ut annuntietur» (*BHL* 8832, 8836, cf. below), a text similar to the *Passio* «Oriente iam sole». In the mentioned study, Paul Devos also discussed the still mysterious connection between these two Passions, asserting that the *Passio* «Ut annuntietur» would be written around thirty years before the other. The scholar edited all the hagiographical texts included in the manuscript kept in Bruxelles.

Various changes and the different repositioning in the sequence of the miracles were catalogued as *BHL* 8831 and its variants included in the *BHL Supplementum*[285].

Passio «*Ut annuntietur*» (BHL = *Passio, translatio, miracula, auctore Iohanne de Novo Foro ep. Olomucensi; Passio, translatio, miracula, auctore canonico ecclesiae Pragensis S. Viti?*)

BHL 8832 and 8836

inc.: *Ut annuntietur in partibus Bohemiae*

The *Passio* «Ut annuntietur» has two redactions, corresponding to the different titled used in the *BHL*, both dating back to the thirteenth century and connected to the above presented *Passio* «Oriente iam sole». The still mysterious link between the two hagiographies is directly connected to the discussion about their relative chronology.

The hagiography *BHL* 8832 is the second redaction of the *Passio* «Ut annuntietur». Its origin is somehow connected to a work by John of Neumarkt (*c.* 1315-1380), the above-mentioned author related to the hagiographical dossier of saint Jerome (cf. *supra*, II.B.7)[286]. Scholars know only one manuscript of the second redaction of the *Passio* «Ut annuntietur», the codex Praha, Národní Knihovna, VIII.A.3 (1406), together with its copy Bruxelles, Bibliothèque des Bollandistes, 152, f. 22r-47v[287].

Paul Devos confirmed the results of Josef Pekař's studies, which demonstrated that the version *BHL* 8836 of the *Passio* «Ut annuntietur» is the original one, or at least the earlier re-

---

[285] They are partly discussed by Devos (1964), p. 102, and *AASS*, Sept. VII, Antwerpen, 1760, p. 739, 840-842.

[286] Nechutová (2007), p. 52-53.

[287] Devos (1964), p. 88-90; the text is edited by Podlaha (1917).

daction, written by a canon of the cathedral of Prague in the Thirties-Forties of the thirteenth century[288]. Consequently, the redaction *BHL* 8832 is a much longer rework by John of Neumarkt, which nearly quadrupled the extension of his model[289].

Both redactions are followed by accounts of a translation (*BHL* 8833 e 8837 respectively) and miracles (*BHL* 8834 e 8838), forming two actual hagiographical booklets (*libelli*)[290].

Sometimes the *libelli* include also the *Sermo in traslatione BHL* 8835 (inc.: *Licet plurima*): the analysis of this sermon confirmed Paul Devos' conclusions about the precedence of *BHL* 8836 over the booklet *BHL* 8832-8834, as well as his accuracy in appreciating Jaroslav Ludvíkovský's work. Formerly ascribed to the bishop (and saint) Adalbert, the sermon dates back at least to the twelfth century[291].

Epitomae duae

BHL 8839, 8840

inc. *BHL* 8839: *Sanctus Wenceslaus athleta Christi egregius*

inc. *BHL* 8840: *Sanctus Wencezlaus dux Boemorum sic Deum dilexit ut... se applicaret. Qui postquam sacras litteras*

The Dominican General Chapter of the year 1296 introduced the cult of Wenceslas to the Order. According to the custom, at the General Chapter gathered two years later in Metz the Dominican of Bohemia presented the text of the saint's office, *BHL* 8839, to be officially included in the liturgy. But the proposed text did not satisfy the Order's requirements, and two years later a new suitable Office of Wenceslas was ready, *BHL* 8840[292].

The main difference between the two versions is the typology of Wenceslas's sainthood, which the Dominicans adapted to their own concept of holiness, expressed at the beginning of the text. Consequently, Wenceslas was no longer a royal saint, nor a fully virtuous man, as described in *BHL* 8839 accordingly to

---

[288] DEVOS (1964), p. 104.

[289] DEVOS (1964), p. 87-88.

[290] The edition of the redaction *BHL* 8836-8838 is offered by LUDVÍKOVSKÝ (1955); cf. *AASS*, Sept. VII, 3ᵃ ed., Paris – Roma, 1867, p. 721.

[291] Cf. NECHUTOVÁ (2007), p. 50.

[292] BARONE (1981); the text is edited by REICHERT (1898), p. 292-293 (*BHL* 8839) and p. 299-300 (*BHL* 8840).

the early medieval hagiographies of the saint. Wenceslas was rather a humble nobleman, who inherited his parents' wealth exclusively to benefit the others and be at the service of the poor people. The new text also recalled Wenceslas' work, but without the emphatic insistence of *BHL* 8839, which described Wenceslas working all night and preparing the holy host with his own hands. Moreover, in the newly adapted version *BHL* 8840 all the references to the political life and the imperial business of the time are missing, together with the allusion to Wenceslas' brother as a «new Cain».

The Dominican mentality emerged also in the reported miracles, which highlighted the divine manifestation through the intercession of the saint, rather than the power of Wenceslas' person or relics in making any miracle.

The Dominican epitomes contributed to the spread of the Wenceslas cult throughout Europe, as attested by the inclusion of the saint's mentions in the collection by Bernard Guy (*ante* 1330) and in the *Legendarium* by Peter Calo (*ante* 1340). This latter used exactly the version *BHL* 8840[293], which is also copied in some other Italian hagiographical collections, such as Napoli, Biblioteca Nazionale, VIII.B.9 and Torino, Biblioteca Nazionale Universitaria, I.II.28.

The redaction *BHL* 8841 is probably a mere interpolation of the *BHL* 8840[294], connected as it seems to the *Catalogus sanctorum* by Peter Nadal (Petrus de Natalibus), who realized his collection in the years 1369-1372.

Vita auctore Karolo IV imperatore (Historia nova de sancto Wenceslao martyre)

BHL 8842-8843

inc. rubr.: *Incipit historia nova de sancto Wenceslao martyre, duce Bohemorum, per dominum Karolum*

inc.: *Crescente religione christiana divina favente clementia baptizato Swatopluko*

The most recent surveys on the *Vita Wenceslai* written by the emperor Charles IV still refer to the fundamental 1934 study by

---

[293] Peter Calo's text corresponds to *BHL Suppl.*, p. 882, no. 9, mentioned as an abbreviation without any other detail about the text.
[294] Cf. VIDMANOVÁ (1986b), p. 44-45.

Anton Blaschka, who edited and critically examined the text[295]. Charles' hagiography includes a Life of Wenceslas and some miracles, but part of the manuscript tradition also transmits an account of *translatio*. Charles' Life and miracles, without the *translatio*, is also included in the *Liber viaticus* by John of Neumarkt, the compiler of Wenceslas' *Passio BHL* 8832. The *Liber viaticus* is the pocket-book, which John realized as a travel breviary for his personal use (Praha, Národní Muzeum, XIII.A.12).

The manuscript serves as a *terminus* for the dating of Charles' *Vita*, as it was realized between the years 1355-1361. Jana Nechutová indicated 1358 as the probable year of composition, because of the ideological contents of the hagiography[296]. Instead, Bernd-Ulrich Hergemöller proposed the year 1361 for the writing, because of the birth of Charles' son named Wenceslas: for this occasion, the emperor would have worked on the saint's Office[297].

Epitome e Vita auctore Carolo IV imperatore

BHL 8844

inc.: *Beatus Wenceslaus ex christianissimo patre Bohemorum duce*

Bollandists indicated with this *BHL* item an abbreviated reworking of Charles IV's hagiography on Wenceslas, transmitted by a manuscript of the Regular Canons of Corsendouk[298] and edited in several Central- and Western-European early printed books at the end of the fifteenth-beginning of the sixteenth century (listed in the *BHL*).

De sancto Wenceslao

Not in *BHL*

---

[295] BLASCHKA (1934); the most recent study by NAGY – SCHAER (2001) reprinted at p. 177-209 the edition by Anton Blaschka, without any alteration, but a division of the paragraphs different from the one in *AASS*, Sept. VII, 3ᵃ ed., Paris – Roma, 1867, p. 780-786, also recalling Blaschkas studies on the text. The only incipit is edited by BARTOŇKOVÁ – VEČERKA (2010), p. 270.
[296] NECHUTOVÁ (2007), p. 146-147.
[297] HERGEMÖLLER (1999), p. 392.
[298] Cf. DOBROVSKÝ (1819), p. 21.

inc.: *Inclitam et gloriosam festivitatem egregii et summi principis Bohemicae gentis*

This is a multi-redaction legend of Wenceslas, originated in the first half of the fourteenth century. The first version was a rewriting of the first redaction of the *Passio* «Ut annuntietur», while the following reworks added some materials taken from the *Legenda Christiani* and the *Passio* «Oriente iam sole». The text also appeared in a printed version of the *Legenda aurea* at the end of the fifteenth century[299], together with an account of translation beginning with the words *Anno Domini D CCCC XXXII quarto nonas Martii translatio gloriosi martyris*.

Some other hagiographies on Wenceslas, not included in *BHL*, were written during the high and late Middle Ages, often for liturgical use and needs, all across the Central and Western Europe. Such abbreviations often assumed the *Legenda Christiani* as primary source, but a complete inventory of these liturgical-hagiographic reductions is still missing[300].

20. Zdislava OP n. 1220 (m. 1252)

Zdislava was a Dominican Tertiary who lived in the thirteenth century, devoted to the care of poor and sick people, and famous as a benefactor of lepers. The chronicles of the thirteenth and the fourteenth centuries[301] reported Zdislava's miraculous power of healing and helping all people who accurred to her remains. After the obscuration of the devotion during the Hussite wars in the fifteenth-sixteenth century, the devotion for Zdislava flourished again at the end of the sixteenth century, and the will of canonize the saint arose. All the hagiographies

---

[299] Strasbourg, 1492 (GW M11283).

[300] Some of those texts, together with the ones dedicated to Ludmila, are listed by NECHUTOVÁ (2007), p. 54 and 146; some others in *BHL Suppl.*, p. 882, n. 9.

[301] For example, the *Chronica maior domus Sarensis* (i.e. *The major chronicle of the monastery of Žďár*) ascribed to the monk Henry and the so-called Dalimil-Chronicle: cf. NECHUTOVÁ (2007), p. 98. The *Chronica maior domus Sarensis* is edited by EMLER 1 (1873), p. 521-557 (cf. *Repertorium fontium*, IV: D-E-F-Gez, p. 705); the chronicle by Dalimil (a false name derived from a misunderstanding of the first editors) is an Old-Czech verse chronicle written right after the year 1310 and translated into Latin in the manuscript Praha, Národní knihovna České republiky, XII.E.17, fol. 1r-12v: cf. NECHUTOVÁ (2007), p. 160-161.

and biographies about Zdislava date back to the seventeenth century, together with her iconography, representing the saint in Dominican clothes holding in her hand a model of the monastery of Jablonné, founded by her husband. In the same century arose the legend of the saint's parental bond with the Berků family of Dubá, which at that time owned the Jablonné castle[302]. The official beatification and canonization of Zdislava date back to the twentieth century.

III. SELECTED SUPPLEMENTARY BIBLIOGRAPHY

A. POLITICAL AND ECCLESIASTICAL HISTORY OF MORAVIA AND BOHEMIA IN THE MIDDLE AGES

A preliminary, general bibliography about the history of medieval Bohemia and Moravia is offered among the notes of the chapter I. Here, few other useful studies are added:

FILIP, V. V., «Crociate, Ussiti e Osservanza nei territori della Corona di Boemia», in A. CACCIOTTI – M. MELLI, cur., *I Francescani e la crociata. Atti dell'XI Convegno storico di Greccio, 3-4 maggio 2013*, Milano, 2014, p. 323-342.

GRAUS, F., *Lebendige Vergangenheit. Überlieferung im Mittelalter und in den Vorstellungen vom Mittelalter*, Köln, 1975. (A chapter is devoted to the Hussite wars).

HUŇÁČEK, V., «Ostrov zwischen Brevnov und Sázava», in SOMMER (2001), p. 463-480.

MACHÁČEK, J. – WIHODA, M., ed., *The fall of Great Moravia. Who was buried in grave H153 at Pohansko near Břeclav?*, Leiden – Boston, MA, 2019.

ŠMAHEL, F., *Husitská revoluce*, 4 vol., Praha, 1995-1996.

—, Idea národa v husitských Čechách, Praha, 2000².

—, «The Divided Nation», in *Between Lipany and White Mountain. Essays in Late Medieval and Early Modern Bohemian History in Modern Czech Scholarship*, cur. J. R. PALMITESSA, Leiden – Boston, MA, 2014, p. 63-93. (English translation of the chapter 5 of the here above cited book of the same author, *Idea národa v husitských Čechách*, Praha, 2000²).

---

[302] *BS*, XII, Roma, 1969, col. 1460-1461; *Lexikon für Theologie und Kirche*, X, Freiburg – Basel – Rom – Wien, 2001, col. 1389.

SOMMER, P. – TREŠTÍK, D., – ŽEMLICKA, J. – DOLEŽALOVÁ, E., «The christianization of Bohemia and Moravia», *Annual of Medieval Studies at CEU Budapest*, 13 (2007), p. 153-163.
TREŠTÍK, D. – SOMMER, P. – ŽEMLIČKA, J., *Přemyslovci. Budování českého státu*, Praha, 2009.
VEPŘEK, M., red., *Velká Morava a velkomoravská staroslověnština*, Olomouc, 2014.
ŽEMLIČKA, J., *Přemysl Otakar II. Král na rozhraní věků*, Praha, 2011.

B. LATIN HAGIOGRAPHY OF MORAVIA AND BOHEMIA

1. General Studies

ADÁMKOVÁ, I., «Gli studi di storia, letteratura e agiografia cristiana antica nella Repubblica Ceca», *Sanctorum*, 7 (2010), p. 223-226.
BAUCH, M., *Divina favente clemencia. Auserwählung, Frömmigkeit und Heilsvermittlung in der Herrschaftspraxis Kaiser Karls IV.*, Köln – Weimar – Wien, 2015.
DERWICH, M. – DMITRIEV, M., dir., *Fonctions sociales et politiques de culte des saints dans les sociétés de rite grec et latin au Moyen Âge et à l'époque moderne. Approche comparative*, Wrocław, 1999.
HLAVÁČEK, I., «Schüler und Meister und Meister und Schüler in der frühen bömisch-tschechischen Reformation», in A. SPEER – T. JESCHKE, ed., *Schüler und Meister*, Berlin – Boston, MA, 2016, p. 829-849.
HLAVÁČEK, I. – BLÁHOVÁ, M., red., *Milénium brevnovského klástera (993-1993). Sborník statí o jeho významu a postavení v ceskych dějinách*, Praha, 1993.
KLANICZAY, G., «Le culte des saintes dynastiques en Europe centrale (Angevins et Luxembourg au XIVe siecle)», in *L'église et le peuple chrétien dans les pays de l'Europe du centre-est et du nord (XIVe-XVe siecles)*, Roma, 1990, p. 221-247.
—, «The Cult of the Saints in Recent Historiographies of Central Europe», in S. BOESCH GAJANO, cur., *Santità e sacralità. Fonti, metodi e prospettive della ricerca agiografica in Europa* Roma, 2014 [= *Sanctorum*, 10 (2013), p. 159-186].
—, «Saints' Cults in Medieval Central Europe: Rivalries and Alliances», in N. HOLGER PETERSEN – A. MÄND – S. SALVADÓ – T. R. SANDS, ed., *Symbolic Identity and the Cultural Memory of Saints*, Newcastle upon Tyne, 2018, p. 21-41.
KLOCZOWSKI, J., «L'érémitisme dans les territoires slaves occidentaux», in *L'eremitismo in Occidente nei secoli XI e XII. Atti della seconda Settimana internazionale di studio. Mendola 30 agosto – 6 settembre 1962*, Milano, 1965, p. 330-354.

Kubínová, K. – Kubín, P., «Bohemian Saints – Pilgrims to Rome», in *Wallfahrten in der europäischen Kultur. Pilgrimage in European Culture. Tagungsband Příbram 26.-29. Mai 2004 – Proceedings of the Symposium Příbram, May 26th-29th 2004*, H. Kühne – D. Dolezal et al., ed., Frankfurt a. M. – Berlin – Bern – Bruxelles – New York – Oxford – Wien, 2006, p. 97-107.

Ludvíkovský, J., «Latinské legendy českého středověku», *Sborník prací Filosofické fakulty brněnské univerzity. Studia minora facultatis philosophicae universitatis brunensis, Řada archeologicko-klasická*, 22-23 (1973-1974), č. 18-19, p. 267-308.

Machilek, F., «Böhmens Landespatrone im Mittelalter», in S. Samerski, hrsg., *Wenzel: Protagonist der böhmischen Erinnerungskultur*, Leiden – Boston, MA, 2018, p. 27-97.

Royt, J., «Kult a ikonografie svetcu uctívanych v benediktinskych klásterech v Cechách», in Lomičková – Jarošová (2013), p. 41-89.

Sommer, P., *Začátky křesťanství v Čechách. Kapitoly z dějin raně středověké duchovní kultury*, Praha, 2001.

Woock, E., «Antimendicancy in Central Europe and bishop Robert of Olomouc in historiography», *Mediaevalia Historica Bohemica*, 18, 2 (2015), p. 69-93.

Wood, I. N., *The Missionary Life. Saints and the Evangelisation of Europe, 400-1050*, Harlow – New York, 2001.

2. Adalbertus (Vojtechus) Pragensis episcopus (n. ca. 956, m. 23-4-997)

Bührer-Thierry, G., «Saint national ou saint européen? Les tribulations d'Adalbert de Prague et de ses reliques dans le temps et dans l'espace (x^e-xiie siècles)», in M.-M. de Cevins – O. Marin, éd., *Les saints et leur culte en Europe centrale au Moyen Âge (xie-début du xvie siècle)*, Turnhout, 2017, p. 247-260.

Dąbrowska, E., «Pierwotne miejsce pochowania i recepcja relikwii św. Vojciecha we wczesnym średniowieczu», in Z. Hilczer-Kurnatowska, red., *Tropami świętego Wojciecha*, Poznań, 1999, p. 147-158.

Dygo, M. – Fałkowski, W., red., *Bruno z Kwerfurtu: osoba, dzieło, epoka*, Pułtusk, 2010.

Engelbert, P., «Adalbert von Prag zwischen Bischofsideal, Politik und Mönchtum», *Römische Quartalschrift für christliche Altertumskunde und für Kirchengeschichte*, 92 (1997), p. 18-44.

Fros, H., «Les vies de St-Adalbert-Vojtech, attribuées à Sylvestre II», in *Gerberto. Scienza, storia e mito. Atti del «Gerberti Symposium» (Bobbio, 25-27 luglio 1983)*, Bobbio, 1985, p. 567-576.

GAŞPAR, C.-N., «(Re)claiming Adalbert: Patristic Quotations and Their Function in Canaparius' *Vita S. Adalberti*», in O. GECSER – J. LASZLOVSZKY – B. NAGY, ed., *Promoting the Saints: Cults and Their Contexts from Late Antiquity until the Early Modern Period. Essays in Honor of Gábor Klaniczay for his 60th Birthday*, Budapest – New York, 2010, p. 31-39.

GIEYSZTOR, A., *La porte de bronze a Gniezno. Document de l'histoire de Pologne au XIIe siècle*, Roma, 1959.

GOLINELLI, P., cur., *Il millenario di Sant'Adalberto a Verona. Atti del Convegno di Studi della Biblioteca Capitolare e delle Celebrazioni cittadine, Verona. 11-12 aprile 1997*, Bologna, 2000.

HENRIX, H H., hrsg., *Adalbert von Prag. Brückenbauer zwischen dem Osten und Westen Europas*, Baden-Baden, 1997.

KARWASIŃSKA, J., *Les trois redactions de Vita I de s. Adalbert*, Roma, 1960.

—, *Wybr pism. wity Wojciech*, Warszawa, 1996 (rist. di KARWASIŃSKA 1960).

LICCIARDELLO, P., «Agiografia latina dell'Italia centrale, 950-1130», in *Hagiographies*, V (2010), p. 587-593.

STRZELCZYK, J. – PEST, C. – POLAK, W., red., *Kanonizacja św. Wojciecha i dziedzictwo jego kultu*, Lublin, 2001.

TŘEŠTÍK, D., «'Gloria regni'. Vratislava II. Hymnus 'Versus post missam' a kronikář Kosmas», in M. NODL – P. SOMMER, red., adiuv. E. DOLEŽALOVÁ, *Verba in imaginibus. Františku Šmahelovi k 70. narozeninám*, Praha, 2004, p. 285-298.

3. Agnes de Bohemia Ord. S. Cl.
(n. ca. 1205, m. 6-3-1280/1283)

BOK, V., «Einige Beobachtungen zur lateinischen Legende über Agnes von Prag und zu ihren mittelalterlichen deutschen und tschechischen Übertragungen», in E. EICHLER, hrsg., *Selecta Bohemico-Germanica. Tschechisch-deutsche Beziehungen im Bereich der Sprache und Kultur*, Münster – Hamburg – London, 2003, p. 163-178.

FELSKAU, C.-F., *Agnes von Böhmen und die Klosteranlage der Klarissen und Franziskaner in Prag. Leben und Institution, Legende und Verehrung*, Nordhausen, 2008.

KALIVODA, J., «Rukopisná tradice anežské legendy 'Candor lucis aeternae'», *Listy filologické*, 127 (2004), p. 19-36.

SCHNEIDER, J., *«Candor Lucis Eterne – Glanz des ewigen Lichtes». Die Legende der heiligen Agnes von Böhmen*, Mönchengladbach, 2007.

SOUKUPOVÁ, H., *Svatá Anežska Česká. Život a Legenda*, Praha, 2015.

4. Arnestus seu Ernestus Pragensis episcopus

BOBKOVÁ, L., ed., *Arnošt z Pardubic (1297-1364). Osobnost, okruh, dědictví. Postać, środowisko, dziedzictwo*, Wrocław, 2005.

HLEDÍKOVÁ, Z., «Rukopis vatikánské Knihovny Chigi Q.II.51», *Studie o rukopisech*, 31 (1995-1996), p. 35-44.

MROZOWICZ, W., «Sredniowieczne żywoty Arnosta z Pardubic. Między historiografią a hagiografią», in R. GLADKIEWICZ, red., *Tradycja Arnošta z Pardubic w kulturze Ziemi Kłodzkiej*, Wrocław, 2008, p. 31-42.

ZACHOVÁ, J., «Ad Vitam Arnesti», *Acta Universitatis Carolinae, Philologica* 3, *Graecolatina Pragensia* X, 1983 (1986), p. 35-42.

5. Benedictus, Iohannes et socii (Quinque fratres) in Polonia martyres

TOMCZAK, R., red., *Męczennicy z Międzyrzecza, 1003-2003. Materialy z zympozjów*, 9-10 11 2001, 8-9 11 2002, Paradyż, 2003.

5. Guntherus in Bohemia eremita (n. ca. 955, m. 9-10-1045)

DENGLER, J., hrsg., *Tausend Jahre Rinchnach. Gunther-Symposium am 9./10.10.2010 an den 'Guntherorten' Rinchnach und Dobra Voda*, Rinchnach, 2011.

DRAGOUN, M., «Vintír a Radim – Lokální kulty českého vrcholného středověku», *Mediaevalia historica Bohemica*, 6 (1999), p. 65-75.

KUBÍN, P., «Der Heilige Gunther (m. 1054). Ein Thüringer in Böhmen», *Zeitschrift für Thüringische Geschichte*, 63 (2009), p. 11-38.

—, «Der Einsiedler Gunther und sein Weg zum Heiligenschein», *Deggendorfer Geschichtsblätter*, 32-33 (2010-2011), p. 37-72.

—, *Svaty Vintír: Poustevník, kolonizátor a diplomat. Der heilige Gunther: Einsiedler, Kolonisator und Diplomat*, Praha, 2017.

SOMMER, P., «Poustevník Vintír/Gunther a nejstarsí české benediktinské kláštery», in M. JAROŠOVÁ – R. LOMIČKOVÁ, red., *Ora et labora: vybrané kapitoly z dějin a kultury benediktinského řádu*, Praha, 2013, p. 9-26.

6. Hieronymus de Praga magister (n. 1370/1380, m. 30-5-1416)

KOŘÁN, I., «Knihovna Mistra Jeronyma Pražského», *Česky časopis historický*, 94 (1996), p. 590-600.

NEU WATKINS, R., «The Death of Jerome of Prague. Divergent Views», *Speculum*, 42 (1967), p. 104-129.

ŠMAHEL, F., «The Acta of the Constance Trial of Master Jerome of Prague», in H. BARR – A. M. HUTCHISON, ed., *Text and Controversy from Wyclif to Bale. Essays in Honour of Anne Hudson*, Turnhout, 2005, p. 323-234.

—, *Život a dílo Jeronyma Pražského. Zpráva o vyzkumu*, Praha, 2010.

ŠMAHEL, F., – SILAGI, G. (ed.), *Magistri Hieronymi de Praga Quaestiones, Polemica, Epistulae*, Turnhout, 2010. Bibliografia generale sull'autore e le opere alle p. cxliv-clx.

ŠRONĚK, M., «Sv. Jeroným Pražský v Chrudimi», in J. FROLÍK, red., *Jan Hus, husitství a východní Čechy. Příspěvky z konference, Chrudim 16.-18.9.2015*, Chrudim, 2015, p. 43-49.

STRNAD, A. A., «Die Zeugen im Wiener Prozeß gegen Hieronymus von Prag. Prosopographische Anmerkungen zu einem Inquisitionsverfahren im Vorfelde des Hussitismus», in J. PÁNEK – M. POLÍVKA – N. REJCHRTOVÁ, red., *Husitství, reformace, renesance*, 1: *Sborník k 60. narozeninám doc. Ph. Františka Šmahela Drsc.*, Praha, 1994, p. 331-368.

8. Hieronymus Stridonius (Eusebius Hieronymus)

IVIĆ, I., «The 'Making' of a National Saint: Reflections on the Formation of the Cult of Saint Jerome in the Eastern Adriatic», in *Supplementi: Visualizing Past in a Foreign Country: Schiavoni/Illyrian Confraternities and Colleges in Early Modern Italy in comparative perspective*, 7 (2018), p. 247-278.

KEJŘ, J., «Ioannis Andreae 'Hieronymianum opus' a jeho ohlas v českých zemích», *Studie o rukopisech*, 12 (1973), p. 71-88. Reprinted in S. PETR, red., *Vybor rozprav a studií z kodikologie a právních dějin. Auswahl von Mitteilungen und Studien aus Kodikologie und Rechtsgeschichte*, Praha, 2012, p. 153-168.

9. Iohannes Hus (n. 1371 ca., m. 6-7-1415)

DRDA, M. – HOLEČEK, F. J. – VYBÍRAL, Z., red., *Jan Hus na přelomu tisíciletí. Mezinárodní rozprava o českém reformátoru 15. století a jeho recepci na prahu třetího milénia*, Tábor, 2001.

HABERKERN, P. N., *Patron Saint and Prophet: Jan Hus in the Bohemian and German Reformations*, Oxford – New York, 2016.

HALAMA, O., S*vatý Jan Hus. Stručný prehled projevů domácí úcty k českému mucedníku v letech 1415-1620*, Praha, 2015.

ŠMAHEL, F., *Jan Hus: Život a dílo ve dvaceti kapitolách*, Praha, 2013.

ŠMAHEL, F. – PAVLÍČEK, O., eds., *A Companion to Jan Hus*, Leiden – Boston, MA, 2015.

SOUKUP, P., *Jan Hus: The Life and Death of a Preacher*, West Lafayette, IN, 2019.

10. Iohannes Nepomucenus Pragae in Bohemia presbyter (n. ca. 1340-1350)

DE VOOGHT, P., «Jean de Pomuk. Le mythe de Jean Nepomucène», in ID., *Hussiana*, Louvain, 1960, p. 400-421.

—, «Jean de Pomuk. Une ré-tractation», *Revue d'histoire ecclésiastique*, 67 (1972). p. 817-830.

11. Passio Iudeorum Pragensium

STEINOVÁ, E., «Jews and Christ interchanged: Discursive strategies in the *Passio Iudeorum Pragensium*», *Graeco-Latina Brunensia*, 17, 2 (2012), p. 73-86.

14. Ivanus in Bohemia eremita

KOŘÁN, I., «Legenda a kult sv. Ivana», *Umění*, 35 (1987), p. 219-235.

15. Karolus Magnus rex

CURTA, F. – STUCKEY, J., «Charlemagne in medieval East Central Europe (ca. 800 to ca. 1200)», *Canadian Slavonic Papers*, 53, 2-4 (2011), p. 181-208.

16. Procopius Pragensis abbas (m. 1053)

KADLEC, J. – CEREKEV, H., «Das Kloster des hl. Prokop an der Sasau», in J. HOFMANN, hrsg., *Tausend Jahre Benediktiner in den Klöstern Brevnov, Braunau und Rohr*, St. Ottilien, 1993, p. 297-307.

SOMMER, P., «Saint Procopius and Sázava Monastery», in P. KOUŘIL et al., *The Cyril and Methodius Mission and Europe. 1150 Years since the Arrival of the Thessaloniki Brothers in Great Moravia*, Brno, 2014.

17. Sigismundus rex Burgundionum m.

POLC, J., «Zapomenutý český patron», in F. DVORNÍK, red., *Se znamením kříže*, Řím, 1967, p. 127-131.

18. Wenceslaus Bohemiae dux et martyr (m. 935)

GRAUS, F., *Lebendige Vergangenheit. Überlieferung im Mittelalter und in den Vorstellungen vom Mittelalter*, Köln, 1975. (A chapter is devoted to saint Wenceslas).

—, «Der Herrschaftsantritt Sankt Wenzels in den Legenden (Zum Quellenwert mittelalterlicher Legenden für die Geschichte I)», in

Osteuropa in Geschichte und Gegenwart: Festschrift für Günther Stökl zum 60. Geburtstag, Köln – Weimar – Wien, 1977, p. 287-300.

LUDVÍKOVSKÝ, J., «Great Moravia Tradition in the 10th Cent. Bohemia and Legenda Christiani», in *Magna Moravia. Sborník k 1100. výročí příchodu byzantské mise na Moravu*, Praha, 1965, p. 525-563.

ŠMAHEL, F., «Die Verehrung des hl. Wenzel im hussitischen. Böhmen», in S. SAMERSKI, hrsg., *Wenzel: Protagonist der böhmischen Erinnerungskultur*, Leiden – Boston, MA, 2018, p. 99-120.

STEJSKAL, F., *Svatý Václav. Jeho život a úcta*, Praha, 1925.

C. Webography of the published sources

CMS – Centrum medievistických studií: https://sources.cms.flu.cas.cz/
Kujawsko-Pomorska Digital Library: http://kpbc.umk.pl/

Bibliography

Analecta Franciscana, sive Chronica aliaque varia documenta ad historiam Fratrum minorum spectantia, 3, Grottaferrata (Roma), 1897.

ANTONÍN, R., «Hnězdenská korunovace krále Václava II.», *Časopis Matice moravské*, 123, 2 (2004), p. 337-365.

—, *The Ideal Ruler in Medival Bohemia*, Leiden – Boston, MA, 2017.

—, «Mendikanti a české země za vlády posledních Přemyslovců», *Časopis Matice moravské*, 138, 1 (2019), p. 3-48.

BALBÍN, B., *Miscellanea historica regni Bohemiae*, decadis I, liber 4: *Hagiographicus*, Praha, 1682.

BÁRÁNY, A. – NOVÁK, Á. – GYÖRKÖS, A., eds., *The Jagiellonians in Europe: Dynastic Diplomacy and Foreign Relations*, Debrecen, 2016.

BARONE, G., «Les épitomés dominicains de la vie de saint Wenceslas (Bibliotheca Hagiographica Latina 8839 et 8840)», in *Faire croire* (1981), p. 167-187.

BARRALIS, C. – BOUDET, J.-P. – DELIVRÉ, F. – GENET, J.-P., éd., *Église et État, Église ou État? Les clercs et la genèse de l'État moderne. Actes de la conférence organisée à Bourges en 2011 par SAS et l'Université d'Orléans en l'honneur d'Hélène Millet*, Paris – Roma, 2014.

BARTOŇKOVÁ, D. – VEČERKA, R., red., *Magnae Moraviae Fontes Historici*, 2: *Textus biographici, hagiographici, liturgici*, Praha 2010^2.

BARTOŠ, F. M., «Mariale Servasancti et Mariale Arnesti de Pardubic», *Antonianum*, 18 (1943), p. 175-177.

BAUER, D. R. – HERBERS, K. – SIGNORI, G., hrsg., *Patriotische Heilige. Beiträge zur Konstruktion religiöser und politischer Identitäten in der Vormoderne*, Stuttgart, 2007.

BAUM, W., «Tirol und Böhmen im Zeitalter Johanns von Böhmen (1310-1346)», in BENEŠOVSKÁ (1998), p. 28-38.

BAYLESS, M., *Parody in the Middle Ages: The Latin Tradition*, Ann Arbor, MI, 1996.

BENEŠOVSKÁ, K., ed., *King John of Luxembourg (1296-1346) and the Art of his Era. Proceedings of the International Conference, Prague, September 16-20, 1996*, Praha, 1998.

BEREND, N., ed., *Christianization and the Rise of Christian Monarchy. Scandinavia, Central Europe and Rus' c.900-1200*, Cambridge, 2007.

BEREND, N. – URBAŃCZYK, P. – WISZEWSKI, P., *Central Europe in the high Middle Ages. Bohemia, Hungary and Poland c. 900-c. 1300*, Cambridge, 2013.

BETTI, M., *The Making of Christian Moravia (858-882). Papal Power and Political Reality*, Leiden – Boston, MA, 2014.

BIHRER, A. – SCHIERSNER, D., hrsg., *Reformverlierer 1000-1800. Zum Umgang mit Niederlagen in der europäischen Vormoderne*, Berlin, 2016.

BLÁHOVÁ, M., «Die Hofgeschichtsschreibung am Böhmischen Herrscherhof im Mittelalter», in SCHIEFFER – WENTA (2006), p. 51-73.

BLÁHOVÁ, M., hrsg., *Böhmisch-österreichische Beziehungen im 13. Jahrhundert. Österreich (einschließlich Steiermark, Kärnten und Krain) im Großreichprojekt Ottokars II. Přemysl, König von Böhmen. Vorträge des internationalen Symposions vom 26. bis 27. September 1996 in Znaim*, Prag, 1998.

BLASCHKA, A., *Die St. Wenzelslegende Kaiser Karls IV. Einleitung, Texte, Kommentar*, Reichenberg, 1934.

—, «Das St. Hieronymus-Offizium des 'Ackermann'-Dichters», in ERNSTBERGER – WOSTRY (1937), p. 107-155.

BOBA, I., *Moravia's History Reconsidered: A Reinterpretation of Medieval Sources*, The Hague, 1971.

BOBKOVÁ, L., «Das Königspaar Johann und Elisabeth. Die Träume von der Herrlichkeit in den Wirren der Realität», in PAULY (2013), p. 47-73.

—, *Jan Lucemburský. Otec slavného syna*, Praha, 2018.

BOESCH GAJANO, S., cur., *Omaggio all'Abruzzo*, Roma, 2010 (= *Sanctorum*, 7 (2010), p. 7-132).

BOK, V., «Zum Kult der regensburger Heiligen Emmeram und Erhard in den böhmischen Ländern», in FEISTNER (2006), p. 223-233.

BORGOLTE, M., hrsg., *Polen und Deutschland vor 1000 Jahren. Die Berliner Tagung über den «Akt von Gnesen»*, Berlin, 2002.

BOWLUS, C. R., *Franks, Moravians, and Magyars: The Struggle for the Middle Danube, 788-907*, Philadelphia, PA, 1995.

BOYLE, L., «Dominican Lectionaries and Leo of Ostia's 'Translatio s. Clementis'», *Archivum Fratrum Praedicatorum*, 28 (1958), p. 362-394.
BRETHOLTZ, B., «Cosmae Pragensis Chronica Bohemorum», *MGH, SRG, NS*, 2, Berlin, 1923.
CADILI, A., «'Ecclesia moderna' und 'ecclesia primitiva' in den Predigten des Jan Zelivský (Prag 1419)», *Archa Verbi*, 9 (2012), p. 86-135.
CEVINS (DE), M.-M. – MARIN, O., éd., *Les saints et leur culte en Europe centrale au Moyen Âge (XIe-début du XVIe siècle)*, Turnhout, 2017.
CHALOUPECKÝ, V., *Prameny X století: legendy Kristiánovy o svatém Václavu a svaté Ludmile*, Praha, 1939.
CHALOUPECKÝ, V. – LUDVÍKOVSKÝ, J., – RYBA, B., red., *Na úsvitu křesťanství: Z naší literární tvorby doby románské v století IX.-XIII.*, Praha, 1942.
CHALOUPECKÝ, V. – RYBA, B., red., *Středověké legendy prokopské: jejich historický rozbor a texty*, Praha, 1953.
CHARVÁT, P., *The Emergence of the Bohemian State*, Leiden – Boston, MA, 2010.
CHARVÁTOVÁ, K., *Dějiny cisterckého řádu v Čechách 1142-1420*, 1: *Fundace 12. století*, Praha, 1998.
—, *Dějiny cisterckého řádu v Čechách 1142-1420*, 2: *Kláštery založené ve 13. a 14 století*, Praha, 2002.
—, *Václav II. Král český a polský*, Praha 2007.
—, «Cisterciáci na dvoře posledních Přemyslovců», in DVOŘÁČKOVÁ-MALÁ – ZELENKA (2008), p. 327-346.
CONTÒ, A. – QUAQUARELLI, L., cur., *L'«antiquario» Felice Feliciano Veronese. Tra epigrafia antica, letteratura e arti del libro. Atti del Convegno di studi. Verona, 3-4 giugno 1993*, Padova, 1995.
CRUSIUS, I., hrsg., *Studien zum Prämonstratenserorden*, Göttingen, 2003.
CURTA, F., «The history and archaeology of Great Moravia: An introduction», in *Early Medieval Europe*, 17 (2009), p. 238-247.
—, *Eastern Europe in the Middle Ages (500-1300)*, Leiden – Boston, MA, 2019.
DANIELSKI, W., *Kult św. Wojciecha na ziemiach polskich w świetle przedtrydenckich ksiąg liturgicznych*, Lublin, 1997.
DAVID, Z. V., – HOLETON, D. R., ed., *The Bohemian Reformation and Religious Practice*, 5, Praha, 2004 (Series published as a special issue of the journal *Filosofický časopis*).
—, ed., *The Bohemian Reformation and Religious Practice*, 6, Praha, 2007.
—, ed., *The Bohemian Reformation and Religious Practice*, 10, Praha, 2015.
DE VOOGHT, P., *Hussiana*, Louvain, 1960.

DEVOS, P., «Le dossier de s. Wenceslas dans un manuscrit du XIe-XIIe siècle (Codex bollandianus 433)», *AB*, 82 (1964), p. 87-131.
DOBNER, G., *Monumenta historica Boemiae*, 6 vol., Praha, 1764-1785.
DOBROVSKÝ, J., *Kritische Versuche die ältere böhmische Geschichte von spätern Erdichtungen zu reinigen*, 3: *Wenzel und Boleslaw*, Praha, 1819.
DOLEŽALOVÁ, E., hrsg., *Die Heiligen und ihr Kult im Mittelalter*, Praha, 2010.
—, «The Cyrillo-Methodian tradition in Bohemia under the Luxemburgs», in KOUŘIL [*et al.*] (2014), p. 316-320.
DOLEŽALOVÁ, E. – NOVOTNÝ, R. – SOUKUP, P., red., *Evropa a Čechy na konci středověku: Sborník příspěvků věnovaných Františku Šmahelovi*, Praha, 2004.
DOLEŽALOVÁ, L., «Absolute Alterity in the Cult of Saints: Saint Nobody», in MARINKOVIĆ – VEDRIŠ (2010), p. 89-101.
—, «Passion and Passion: Intertextual Narratives in Late Medieval Bohemia between Typology, History, and Parody», in KRETSCHMER (2014), p. 245-265.
DRELICHARZ, W., «Sędziwój z Czechla (ok. 1410-1476)», in *Polski Słownik Biograficzny*, 36 (1995-1996), p. 394-399.
DUDÍK, B., *Iter Romanum. Im Auftrag des hohen mæhrischen Landesausschusses in den Jahren 1852 und 1853 unternommen und veröffentlicht*, Wien, 1855.
DUNIN-WĄSOWICZ, T., «Hagiographie polonaise entre XIe et XVIe siècle», in *Hagiographies*, III (2001), p. 179-202.
DUNN-LARDEAU, B., éd., *Legenda aurea: sept siècles de diffusion. Actes du colloque international sur la Legenda aurea: texte latin et branches vernaculaires à l'Université de Quebec à Montréal 11-12 mai 1983*, Montréal – Paris, 1986.
DVOŘÁČKOVÁ-MALÁ, D. – ZELENKA, J., red., *Dvory a rezidence ve středověku, 2: Skladba a kultura dvorské společnosti*, Praha 2008.
DVORNÍK, F., *Les légendes de Constantin et de Méthode vues de Byzance*, Prague, 1933.
EGGERS, M., *Das 'Großmährische Reich' – Realität oder Fiktion? Eine Neuinterpretation der Quellen zur Geschichte des mittleren Donauraumes im 9. Jahrhundert*, Stuttgart, 1995.
ELBEL, P., «Dějiny neúspěchu aneb úsilí Přemyslovců o zřízení arcibiskupství v českých zemích», in WIHODA – REITINGER (2010), p. 238-306.
EMLER, J. et al., red., *Fontes rerum Bohemicarum. Prameny dějin českých vydávané z nadání Palackého*, 8 vol., Praha, 1873-1932 (repr. Hildesheim 2004).
ERNSTBERGER, A. – WOSTRY, W., hrsg., *Heimat und Volk: Forschungsbeiträge zur sudetendeutschen Geschichte, Festschrift für Universitätsprofessor Dr. Wilhelm Wostry zum 60. Geburtstag*, Brno, 1937.

Faire croire. Modalités de la diffusion et de la réception des messages religieux du XIIe au XVe siècle. Actes de table ronde de Rome (22-23 juin 1979), Rome, 1991 (Publications de l'École Française de Rome, 51).

FEISTNER, E., hrsg., *Das mittelalterliche Regensburg im Zentrum Europas*, Regensburg, 2006.

FELSKAU, C.-F., «'Vita religiosa' und 'paupertas' der Premyslidin Agnes von Prag. Zu Bezügen und Besonderheiten in Leben und Legende einer späten Heiligen», *Collectanea Franciscana*, 70 (2000), p. 413-484.

—, «Shaping the Sainthood of a Central European Clarissan Princess. The Development and Fate of the Earliest Hagiographic Texts on Agnes of Bohemia and St Clare's Epistolary Tradition», in CEVINS (DE) – MARIN (2017), p. 125-171.

FLEITH, B., *Studien zur Überlieferungsgeschichte der lateinischen Legenda Aurea*, Bruxelles, 1991.

FRIED, J., «Gnesen – Aachen – Rom. Otto III. und der Kult des hl. Adalbert. Beobachtungen zum älteren Adalbertsleben», in BORGOLTE (2002), p. 235-279.

FUDGE, T. A., «Jan Hus at Calvary: The Text of an Early Fifteenth-Century 'Passio'», *Journal of Moravian History*, 11 (2011), p. 45-81.

—, *The Memory and Motivation of Jan Hus, Medieval Priest and Martyr*, Turnhout, 2013.

—, *The trial of Jan Hus. Medieval heresy and criminal procedure*, Oxford, 2013.

—, *Jerome of Prague and the Foundations of the Hussite Movement*, New York, 2016.

GARZANITI, M., *Gli Slavi. Storia, culture e lingue dalle origini ai nostri giorni*, a cura di F. ROMOLI [*et al.*], Roma, 2013.

GAŞPAR, C.-N., «The Life of Saint Adalbert Bishop of Prague and Martyr», in KLANICZAY (2013), p. 77-193.

GLAUCHE, G. – KNAUS, H., bearb., *Mittelalterliche Bibliothekskataloge Deutschlands und der Schweiz, 4.2: Bistum Freising. Bistum Würzburg. Mit Beiträgen von Bernhard Bischoff und Wilhelm Stoll*, München, 1979.

GROTHUSEN, K.-D. – LUDAT, H., hrsg., *Europa slavica – Europa orientalis. Festschrift für Herbert Ludat zum 70. Geburtstag*, Berlin, 1980.

HACK, A. T., «Heiligenkult im frühen Hussitismus. Eine Skizze», in BAUER – HERBERS – SIGNORI (2007), p. 123-156.

HAMBURGER, J. – SIGNORI, G., ed., *Catherine of Siena: The Creation of a Cult*, Turnhout, 2013.

HEJNIC, J. – ROTHE, H. – UDOLPH, E., *Aeneas Silvius Piccolomini, Historia Bohemica*, 3 vol., 1: *Historisch-kritische Ausgabe des lateinischen*

Textes; 2: *Die frühneuhochdeutsche Übersetzung (1463) des Breslauer Stadtschreibers Peter Eschenloër*; 3: *Die erste alttschechische Übersetzung (1487) des katholischen Priesters Jan Húska*, Köln – Weimar – Wien, 2005.

HERGEMÖLLER, B.-U., *Cogor adversum te. Drei Studien zum literarischtheologischen Profil Karls IV. und seiner Kanzlei*, Warendorf, 1999.

HEROLD, V., *The Spiritual Background of the Czech Reformation: Precursors of Jan Hus*, in ŠMAHEL – PAVLÍČEK (2015), p. 69-95.

HERZIG, T., «Italian Holy Women against Bohemian Heretics: Catherine of Siena and 'the Second Catherines' in the Kingdom of Bohemia», in HAMBURGER – SIGNORI (2013), p. 315-338.

HILG, H., *Lateinische mittelalterliche Handschriften in Folio der Universitätsbibliothek Augsburg: Cod. II. 1.2° 91-226*, Wiesbaden, 1999.

HLAVÁČEK, I., «Die Anfänge der Prämonstratenser im hochmittelalterlichen böhmischen Staat im Kontext der damaligen Ordensgeistlichkeit», in CRUSIUS (2003), p. 281-310.

HLEDÍKOVÁ, Z., *Biskup Jan IV. z Dražic*, Praha 1991.

—, *Arnost z Pardubic. Arcibiskup – zakladatel – rádce*, Praha, 2008.

HLEDÍKOVÁ, Z. – ZACHOVÁ, J., *Život Arnošta z Pardubic podle Valentina Krautwalda*, Pardubice, 1997.

HOFFMANN, J., *Vita Adalberti. Früheste Textüberlieferungen der Lebensgeschichte Adalberts von Prag*, Essen, 2005.

HOHENSEE, U. – LAWO, M. – LINDNER, M. – MENZEL, M. – RADER, O. B., hrsg., *Die Goldene Bulle. Politik-Wahrnehmung-Rezeption*, Berlin, 2009.

HOLGER PETERSEN, N. – MÄND, A. – SALVADÓ, S. – SANDS, T. R., eds., *Symbolic Identity and the Cultural Memory of Saints*, Newcastle upon Tyne, 2018.

HOMZA, M., *Mulieres suadentes – Persuasive Women. Female Royal Saints in Medieval East Central and Eastern Europe*, Leiden – Boston, MA, 2017.

HORNÍČKOVÁ, K., «Martyrs of 'Our' Faith: Identity and the Cult of Saints in Post-Hussite Bohemia», in HOLGER PETERSEN [*et al.*] (2018), p. 59-90.

HÜBNER, K., «Mord und Rufmord. Politische Propaganda und die Anfänge der Schwarzen Legende König Wenzels IV.», in BIHRER – SCHIERSNER (2016), p. 57-95.

IGNESTI, B., *Vita dei cinque fratelli e Lettera a re Enrico, S. Bruno di Querfurt*, Arezzo, 1951.

JAKOBSON, R., *Selected Writings, 6: Early Slavic Paths and Crossroads*, ed. by RUDY, S., Berlin – New York – Amsterdam, 1985.

JAN, L., «Počátky moravského křesťanství a církevní správa do doby husitské», in KORDIOVSKÝ – JAN (2003), p. 7-20.

—, *Václav II. Král na stříbrném trunů (1283-1305)*, Praha, 2015.

KADE, R., «Brunonis Vita quinque fratrum», *MGH, SS*, XV-2, Hannover, 1888, p. 709-738.
KALHOUS, D., «Jaromír-Gebhard, pražský biskup a říšský kancléř (1038-1090). Několik poznámek k jeho životu», *Mediaevalia historica Bohemica*, 9 (2003), p. 27-45.
—, *Anatomy of a duchy. The Political and Ecclesiastical Structures of Early Přemyslid Bohemia*, Leiden – Boston, MA, 2012.
—, «K otázce počátků břevnovského kláštera», *Časopis matice moravské*, 134, 1 (2015), p. 207-213.
—, *Legenda Christiani and Modern Historiography*, Leiden – Boston, MA, 2015.
—, *Bohemi. Prozesse der Identitätsbildung in frühpřemyslidischen Ländern (bis 1200)*, Wien, 2018.
KALOUS, A., «The Tradition of Saints Cyril and Methodius in the Late Mediaeval Bohemian Lands», in KOUŘIL [*et al.*] (2014), p. 322-328.
—, «Jagiellonian Kings of Bohemia and Hungary and papal legates», in BÁRÁNY – NOVÁK – GYÖRKÖS (2016), p. 159-169.
KALOUS, A. – STEJSKAL, J., «Několik poznámek k nové edici legend o svatém Prokopovi», in SOMMER (2006), p. 136-142.
KAMINSKY, H., *A History of the Hussite Revolution*, Berkeley, CA, 1967.
KARWASIŃSKA, J., *Św. Wojciecha biskupa i męczennika Żywot pierwszy. S. Adalberti Pragensis episcopi et martyris Vita prior*, Warszawa, 1962.
—, *Św. Wojciecha biskupa i męczennika Żywot drugi napisany przez Brunona z Kwerfurtu. Sancti Adalberti Pragensis, episcopi et martyris Vita altera auctore Brunone Querfurtensi*, Warszawa, 1969.
—, *Święty Wojciech. Wybór pism*, Warszawa, 1996.
—, «Drzwi gnieźnieńskie a rozwój legendy o sw. Wojciechu», in LABUDA (1997b), p. 271-289.
KEJŘ, J., *Die Causa Johannes Hus und das Prozessrecht der Kirche*, Regensburg, 2005.
KĘTRZYŃSKI, W., «Über eine neue Handschrift des Canaparius», *Altpreußische Monatsschrift*, 7 (1870), p. 673-702.
KLANICZAY, G., «Modelli di santità in Europa centrale negli ultimi secoli del Medioevo», in VOLPATO (2008), p. 251-288.
—, ed., *Vitae sanctorum aetatis conversionis Europae centralis (saec. X-XI). Saints of the Christianization Age of Central Europe (Tenth-Eleventh Centuries)*, transl. by GAŞPAR, C. – MILADINOV, M., intr. by WOOD, I. N., Budapest – New York, 2013.
KLAPPER, J., *Schriften Johanns von Neumarkt*, 2: *Hieronymus. Die unechten Briefe des Eusebius, Augustin, Cyrill. Zum Lobe des Heiligen*, Berlin, 1932.
KLÁPŠTĚ, J., *The Czech lands in medieval transformation*, Leiden – Boston, MA, 2012.

KOEHLER, T., «Onze manuscrits du 'Mariale' de Servasanctus de Faenza, ofm (d. ca. 1300)», *Archivum Franciscanum Historicum*, 83 (1990), p. 96-117.
KOEPKE, R., «Cosmae Chronica Bohemorum», *MGH, SS*, IX, Hannover, 1851, p. 31-132.
KOLÁŘ, J., «Život sv. Ivana», in EMLER 1 (1873), p. 112-120.
KOLBERG, A., «Analecta Warmiensia», *Zeitschrift für die Geschichte und Altertumskunde Ermlands*, 7 (1880), p. 1-78.
KØLLN, H., *Die Wenzelslegende des Mönchs Christian*, Copenhagen, 1996.
—, *Westkirchliches in altkirchenslavischer Literatur aus Grossmähren und Böhmen*, Copenhagen, 2003.
KORDIOVSKÝ, E. – JAN, L., *Vývoj církevní správy na Moravě. 27. mikulovské sympozium 9.-10. října 2002*, Brno, 2003.
KOUŘIL, P. *et al.*, eds., *The Cyril and Methodius Mission and Europe: 1150 Years since the Arrival of the Thessaloniki Brothers in Great Moravia*, Brno, 2014.
KRÁLÍK, O., «La leggenda di Laurentius di Montecassino su s. Venceslao ed il suo modello», *Ricerche slavistiche*, 7 (1959), p. 24-47.
KRÁSL, F., *Svatý Prokop, jeho klášter a památka u lidu*, Praha, 1895.
KRETSCHMER, M. T., éd., *La typologie biblique comme forme de pensée dans l'historiographie médiévale*, Turnhout, 2014.
KŘÍŽEK, P., «Iwan», in SAMERSKI (2009), p. 99-107.
KRMÍČKOVÁ, H., «Petri Clarificatoris Vita domini Iohannis, Pragensis archiepiscopi tercii», in KRMÍČKOVÁ – PUMPROVÁ – RŮŽIČKOVÁ – ŠVANDA (2006), p. 441-461.
KRMÍČKOVÁ – PUMPROVÁ – RŮŽIČKOVÁ – ŠVANDA, red., *Querite primum regnum Dei. Sborník příspěvků k poctě Jany Nechutové*, Brno, 2006.
KRÜGER, K. H. – DOLEŽALOVÁ, E., «Veit», in SAMERSKI (2009), p. 231-241.
KRZEMIEŃSKA, B.L., *Břetislav I. Čechy a střední Evropa v prvé polovině XI století*, Praha, 1999.
KUBÍN, P., «Die böhmischen Heiligen in den mittelalterlichen Handschriften Thüringens», *Zeitschrift des Vereins für Thüringische Geschichte*, 52 (1998), p. 271-281.
—, *Blahoslaveny Hroznata. Kriticky zivotopis*, Praha, 2000.
—, *Sedm přemyslovských kultů*, Praha, 2011.
—, «Založil břevnovský klášter opravdu sv. Vojtěch?», in LOMIČKOVÁ – JAROŠOVÁ (2013), p. 27-40.
—, *Legenda o sv. Vintířovi. «Vita s. Guntheri»*, Praha, 2014.
—, «Středověký kult sv. Mořice, v Čechách, a na Morave», *Studia mediaevalia Bohemica*, 6 (2014), p. 7-16.

—, «The Earliest Hagiography of St Agnes of Bohemia († 1282)» *Hagiographica*, 22 (2015), p. 265-290

—, «Byla Mlada středověkou světicí?», *Studia mediaevalia Bohemica*, 8 (2016), p. 133-135.

—, «Saint Procopius of Sázava between Reality and Fiction», *Revue Mabillon*, n.s. 27 (t. 88) (2016), p. 49-82.

—, «Saints fondateurs et saints modernes dans la Bohême médiévale», in CEVINS (DE) – MARIN (2017), p. 31-38.

KUBÍNOVÁ, K., *Imitatio Romae. Karel IV. a Řím*, Praha, 2006.

KURZE, F., «Annales Fuldenses sive Annales regni Francorum orientalis», *MGH, SRG in usum scholarum*, VII, Hannover, 1891.

KYBAL, V., *Matthiae de Janov dicti magister Parisiensis Regulae veteris et novi testamenti*, 4 vol., Praha – Innsbruck, 1908-1913.

LABUDA, G., «Św. Wojciech w literaturze i legendzie średniowiecznej», in LABUDA (1997), p. 212-226.

—, red., *Święty Wojciech w polskiej tradycji historiograficznej. Antologie tekstów*, Warszawa, 1997.

—, «W sprawie autorstwa i miejsca napisania 'Żywotu pierwszego' Świętego Wojciecha», *Studia Źródłoznawcze*, 42 (2004), p. 115-130.

LEROU, P., «Le culte de saint Jean Népomucène», *Mélanges de l'École française de Rome. Italie et Méditerranée*, 103, 1 (1991), p. 273-295.

LIBOR, J. – OBŠUSTA, P., red., *Ve stopách sv. Benedikta. Sborník příspěvků z konference Středověké kláštery v zemích Koruny české konané ve dnech 24.-25. května 2001 v Třebíči*, Brno, 2002.

LOMIČKOVÁ, R. – JAROŠOVÁ, M., red., *Ora et labora. Vybrané kapitoly z dějin kultury benediktinského řádu*, Praha, 2013.

LUDVÍKOVSKÝ, J., «Legenda o svatém Václavu počínající slovy 'Když vycházelo už slunce křesťanství' z prvé poloviny XIII století», in CHALOUPECKÝ – LUDVÍKOVSKÝ – RYBA (1942), p. 220-242.

—, «Václavská legenda 13. století 'Ut annuncietur', její poměr k legendě 'Oriente' a otázka autorství», *Listy filologické*, 3 [78] (1955), p. 196-209.

—, «Nově zištěný rukopis legendy *Crescente fide* a jeho význam pro datování Kristiána», *Listy filologické*, 6 [81] (1958), p. 58-68.

—, *Kristiánova legenda. Život a umučení svatého Václava a jeho báby svaté Ludmily*, Praha, 1978.

MACHÁČEK, J., «Disputes over Great Moravia: Chiefdom or State? The Morava or the Tisza River?», in *Early Medieval Europe*, 17 (2009), p. 268-285.

MACHILEK, F., «Privatfrömmigkeit und Staatsfrömmigkeit», in SEIBT (1978), p. 87-101.

MADAS, E., «À la recherche des sources liturgiques et hagiographiques du culte des 'saints rois' hongrois en Europe centrale», in CEVINS (DE) – MARIN (2017), p. 281-292.

MARIN, O., L'archevêque, le maître et le dévot. Genèses du mouvement réformateur pragois, Paris, 2005.

—, «Fin des temps et sainteté moderne: la "Narracio de Milicio" par Matthias de Janov († 1394)», in BARRALIS – BOUDET – DELIVRÉ – GENET (2014), p. 433-456.

—, «Introduction», in CEVINS (DE) – MARIN (2017), p. 5-28.

MARINKOVIĆ, A. – VEDRIŠ, T., eds., Identity and Alterity in Hagiography and the Cult of Saints: Proceedings of the 2nd Hagiography Conference organised by Croatian Hagiography Society 'Hagiotheca' and held in Split, 28-31 May 2008, Zagreb 2010.

MAŠEK, M. – SOMMER, P. – ŽEMLIČKA, J., red., Vladislav II. Druhý král Přemyslova rodu. K 850. výročí jeho korunovace, Praha, 2009.

MEYVAERT, P. – DEVOS, P., «Trois énigmes cyrillo-méthodiennes de la 'Légende italique' résolues grace à un document inédit», AB, 73 (1955), p. 375-461.

MENGEL, D. C., «A Holy and Faithful Fellowship: Royal Saints in Fourteenth-Century Prague», in DOLEŽALOVÁ – NOVOTNÝ – SOUKUP (2004), p. 145-158.

—, «A Monk, a Preacher and a Jesuit: Making the Life of Milíč», in DAVID – HOLETON (2004), p. 33-55.

—, «Remembering Bohemia's Forgotten Patron Saint», in DAVID – HOLETON (2007), p. 17-32.

—, «Bohemia's Treasury of Saints: Relics and Indulgences in Emperor Charles IV's Prague», in CEVINS (DE) – MARIN (2017), p. 57-76.

MICHAŁOWSKI, R., The Gniezno Summit. The Religious Premises of the Founding of the Archbishopric of Gniezno, Leiden – Boston, MA, 2016.

MILADINOV, M., «Life of the Five Brethren by Bruno of Querfurt», in KLANICZAY (2013), p. 183-313.

—, «Passion of Saint Wenceslas by Gumpold of Mantua», in KLANICZAY (2013), p. 17-76.

MONTECCHI, G., «Lo spazio del testo scritto nella pagina del Feliciano», in CONTÒ – QUAQUARELLI (1995), p. 251-288.

MPH = Monumenta Poloniae Historica, 6 vol., Lwów, 1864-1893 (availbale on-line).

MPHns = Monumenta Poloniae Historica, nova series, 16 vol. (till 2017), Kraków – Warszawa, 1946-.

MORAW, P., «Zur Mittelpunktsfunktion Prags im Zeitalter Karls IV.», in GROTHUSEN – LUDAT (1980), p. 445-489.

NAGY, B. – SCHAER, F., ed., *Karoli 4. imperatoris Romanorum vita ab eo ipso conscripta et Hystoria nova de Sancto Wenceslao martyre. Autobiography of Emperor Charles IV and His Legend of St. Wenceslas*, Budapest, 2001.
NECHUTOVÁ, J., *Die lateinische Literatur des Mittelalters in Böhmen*, trad. BOKOVÁ, H. – BOK, V., Köln – Weimar – Wien, 2007.
NEWMAN, B., *Medieval Crossover: Reading the Secular against the Sacred*, Notre Dame, IN, 2013.
NEWTON, F., *Laurentius monachus Casinensis archiepiscopus Amalfitanus. Opera*, Weimar, 1973.
LOUIS, N., *L'exemplum en pratiques: production, diffusion et usages des recueils d'exempla latins aux* XIIIe-XVe *siècles*, 1: *Enquête*, Thèse présentée à l'Université de Namur; Académie Universitaire Louvain, Faculté de Philosophie et Lettres, Département d'Histoire; École des Hautes Études en Sciences Sociales, Paris, Centre de Recherches Historiques, Namur, 2013. (available on-line: https://pure.fundp.ac.be/ws/files/12210171/PDF_01_Nicolas_LOUIS_th_se_enquete_annexe.pdf [last access 04/04/2020]).
NODL, M. – ŠMAHEL, F., «Kuttenberger Dekret nach 600 Jahren. Eine Bilanz der bisherigen Forschung», *Acta Universitatis Carolinae. Historia universitatis Carolinae Pragensis*, 49, 2 (2009), p. 19-54.
NOVOTNÝ, V., «Sermo habitus in Betlehem in memoriam novorum martyrum magistri Iohannis Hus et magistri Hieronymi», in EMLER 8 (1932), p. 231-242.
—, «Petri de Mladoniowicz Relatio de Magistro Iohanne Hus», in EMLER 8 (1932), p. 25-120.
PACOVSKY, K., «Kult první svatojiřské abatyše ve středověku», *Studia mediaevalia Bohemica*, 8 (2016), p. 125-132.
PALACKÝ, F., *Documenta Magistri Iohannis Hus vitam et doctrinam illustrantia*, Praha, 1869.
PÁNEK, J., red., *Vlast a rodný kraj v díle historika. Sborník prací žáků a přátel věnovaný profesoru Josefu Petráňovi*, Praha, 2004.
PÁNEK, J. – TŮMA, O., eds., *A history of the Czech land*, Praha, 2018[2].
PÁTKOVÁ, H., éd., *Z Noyonu do Prahy: kult svatého Eligia ve středověkých Čechách. De Noyon à Prague: Le culte de Saint Éloi en Bohême médiévale*, Praha, 2006.
—, «Les confréries, les métiers et le culte des saints dans la Bohême médiévale», in CEVINS (DE) – MARIN (2017), p. 311-325.
PATSCHOVSKY, A. – ZIMMERMANN, H., hrsg., *Toleranz im Mittelalter*, Sigmaringen, 1998.
PAULY, M., hrsg., *Johann der Blinde, Graf von Luxemburg, König von Böhmen, 1296-1346. Tagungsband der 9es Journées Lotharingiennes, 22.-26. ktober 1996, Centre Universitaire de Luxembourg*, Luxembourg, 1997.

—, hrsg., *Die Erbtochter, der fremde Fürst und das Land. Die Ehe Johanns des Blinden und Elisabeths von Böhmen in vergleichender europäischer Perspektive. L'héritière, le prince étranger et le pays. Le marriage de Jean l'Aveugle et d'Élisabeth de Bohême dans une perspective comparative européenne*, Luxembourg, 2013.

PEKAŘ, J., *Die Wenzels- und Ludmila-Legenden und die Echtheit Christians*, Prag, 1905.

PERI, V., *Cirillo e Metodio. Le biografie paleoslave*, Milano, 1981.

PERLBACH, M., «De sancto Adalberto episcopo Pragensi», *MGH, SS*, XV-2, Hannover, 1888, p. 1177-1184.

PERTZ, G. H., «Vita S. Adalberti episcopi», *MGH, SS*, IV, Hannover, 1841, p. 574-620.

PHILIPPART, G., «Un hypothétique recueil italien de "Vitae Patrum" du VIe siècle. À propos du dossier hagiographique de Victorin, ermite mystique de Septempeda, pseudo-évêque d'Amiternum», in BOESCH GAJANO (2010), p. 13-63.

PICCHIO, R., *Letteratura della Slavia ortodossa (IX-XVIII sec.)*, Bari, 1991. At p. 103-143 the paper «Lo slavo ecclesiastico», Italian translation of the original paper "Church Slavonic"», in A.-M. SCHENKER – E. STANKIEWICZ, eds., *Yale Concilium of International and Area Studies*, New Haven, CT, 1980, p. 1-33. At p. 145-261 the paper «Questione della lingua e Slavia cirillometodiana», reprint of the article originally published in R. PICCHIO, cur., *Studi sulla questione della lingua presso gli Slavi*, Roma, 1972, p. 7-120.

PLEZIA, M., *Średniowieczne żywoty i cuda patronów Polski*, ed. J. PLEZIOWA, Warszawa, 1987.

PODLAHA, A., *Vita sancti Wenceslai incipiens verbis «Ut annuncietur»*, Praha, 1917.

PODLAHA, A. – ŠITTLER, E., *Chrámový poklad u sv. Víta v Praze: jeho dějiny a popis*, Praha, 1903.

PRINZ, F., «Das Reich, Bayern, Böhmen und Österreich: Grundzüge einer historischen Nachbarschaft. Einige Vorüberlegungen», in PRINZ (2003), p. 50-68.

—, *Nation und Heimat. Beiträge zur böhmischen und sudetendeutschen Geschichte*, München, 2003.

PROVVIDENTE, S., «Hus's Trial in Constance: disputatio aut inquisitio», in ŠMAHEL – PAVLÍČEK (2015), p. 254-288.

REICHERT, B. M., *Acta Capitulorum Generalium ordinis Praedicatorum*, 1: *Ab anno 1220 usque ad annum 1303*, Roma – Stuttgart, 1898.

REITINGER, L., *Vratislav. První král Čechů*, Praha, 2017.

Repertorium fontium historiae medii aevi primum ab Augusto Potthast digestum, nunc cura collegii historicorum e pluribus nationibus emendatum et auctum, 11 vol., Roma, 1962-2007. The *Repertorium fontium* is now partly available on-line and enriched thanks to the project

Geschichtsquellen des deutschen Mittelalters (http://www.geschichtsquellen.de/start).
SAMERSKI, S., hrsg., *Die Landespatrone der böhmischen Länder. Geschichte – Verehrung – Gegenwart*, Paderborn – München – Wien – Zürich, 2009.
ŠÁROVCOVÁ, M., «The Execution of the Miners of Kutná Hora at Poděbrady and in Křivoklát in 1496: On the Veneration of the Miners of Poděbrady in the Sixteenth Century», in DAVID – HOLETON (2015), p. 259-278.
SCHIEFFER, R. – WENTA, J., hrsg., *Die Hofgeschichtsschreibung im Mittelalterlichen Europa*, Torún, 2006.
SCHWAIGER, G., «Der heilige Bischof Wolfgang von Regensburg 972-994», in SCHWAIGER – STABER (1972), p. 39-60.
SCHWAIGER, G. – STABER, J., hrsg., *Regensburg und Böhmen. Festschrift zur Tausendjahrfeier des Regierungsantrittes Bischof Wolfgangs von Regensburg und die Errichtung des Bistums Prag*, Regensburg, 1972.
SEIBT, F., hrsg., *Kaiser Karl IV. Staatsmann und Mäzen*, München, 1978.
SETON, W. W., *Some New Sources for the Life of Blessed Agnes of Bohemia: Including a Fourteenth Century Latin Version (Bamberg, Misc. Hist. 146, E. VII, 19) and a Fifteenth Century German Version (Berlin, Germ. Oct. 484)*, Aberdeen, 1915 (repr. Cambridge, 2010).
ŠMAHEL, F., «Pax externa et interna. Vom Heiligen Krieg zur Erzwungenen Toleranz im hussitischen Böhmen (1419-1485)», in PATSCHOVSKY – ZIMMERMANN (1998), p. 221-274.
—, *Hussitische Revolution*, I-III, Hannover, 2002.
—, *Die Prager Universität im Mittelalter*, Leiden – Boston, MA, 2007.
—, *Basilejská kompaktáta. Příběh deseti listin*, Praha, 2011.
—, *Alma mater Pragensis. Studie k počátkům Univerzity Karlovy*, Praha, 2016.
ŠMAHEL, F. – BOBKOVÁ, L., red., *Lucemburkové. Česká koruna uprostřed Evropy*, Praha, 2012.
ŠMAHEL, F. – PAVLÍČEK, O., eds., *A companion to Jan Hus*, Leiden – Boston, MA, 2015.
SMRŽÍK, S., *The Glagolitic or Roman-Slavonic Liturgy*, Cleveland, OH – Roma, 1959.
SOBCZYK, D., «Arnoszt z Pardubic w pamięci lokalnej Kłodzka», *Meluzyna*, 2 (5) 2016, p. 49-59.
SOMMER, P., hrsg., *Boleslav II. – der tschechische Staat um das Jahr 1000. internationales Symposium Praha 9.-10. Februar 1999*, Praha, 2001.
—, hrsg., *Der heilige Prokop, Böhmen and Mitteleuropa. Internationales Symposium, Benešov – Sázava 24.-26. September 2003*, Praha, 2005.
—, red., *Svatý Prokop. Čechy a střední Evropa*, Praha, 2006.
—, *Svatý Prokop. Z počátků českého státu a církve*, Praha, 2007.

—, «Der beginnende böhmische Staat und seine Heiligen», *Questiones Medii Aevii Novae*, 14 (2009), p. 41-54.

Sommer, P. – Treštík, D. – Žemlicka, J., «Bohemia and Moravia», in Berend (2007), p. 214-262.

Sosnowski, M., «Anonimowa *Passio s. Adalperti martiris* (BHL 40) oraz Wiperta *Historia de predicatione episcopi Brunonis* (BHL 1471b) – komentarz, edycja, przekład», *Rocznik Biblioteki Narodowej*, 43 (2012), p. 5-74.

Soukup, P., «Jan Hus as a Preacher», in Šmahel – Pavlíček (2015), p. 96-129.

Spunar, P., *Repertorium auctorum Bohemorum provectum idearum post Universitatem Pragensem conditam illustrans*, 2 vol., Wroclaw – Warszawa – Kraków – Gdansk – Lódz, 1985-1995.

Steinová, E., *Passio Iudeorum Pragensium: Kritická edícia Pašijí pražských židov*, Brno, 2010 (https://is.muni.cz/th/180028/ff_m/Steinova_diplomovapraca.pdf).

—, «*Passio Iudeorum Pragensium*: Tatsachen und Fiktionen über das Pogrom im Jahr 1389», in Teufel – Kocman – Řepa (2016), p. 159-186.

Steyn, C., ed., *The medieval and Renaissance manuscripts in the Grey collection of the National Library of South Africa, Cape Town*, 1: *Manuscripts 2.a.16 – 3.c.25*; 2: *Manuscripts 3.d.30 – 48.b.4-5*, Salzburg, 2002.

Stiegemann, C. – Kroker, M. – Walter, W., hrsg., *Credo. Christianisierung Europas im Mittelalter*, 1: *Essays*, Petersberg, 2013.

Studničková, M., «Kult des heiligen Sigismund (Sigmund) in Böhmen», in Doležalová (2010), p. 299-339.

Šujan, F., «Pašije šlapanických loupežníků», *Sborník historický*, 3 (1885), p. 245-252, 301-303.

Tachiaos, A.-E. N., *Cyril and Methodius of Thessalonica. The acculturation of the Slavs*, Crestwood, NY, 2001.

—, *Cirillo e Metodio: le radici cristiane della cultura slava*, Milano, 2005 (ed. it. a cura di M. Garzaniti).

Teufel, H. – Kocman, P. – Řepa, M., hrsg., «*Avigdor, Beneš, Gitl*» – *Juden in Böhmen, Mähren und Schlesien im Mittelalter. Samuel Steinherz (1857 Güssing – 1942 Theresienstadt) zum Gedenken*, Praha – Essen – Brno, 2016.

Thurn, H., hrsg., *Die Handschriften der Universitätsbilbliothek Würzburg*, 5 vol., Wiesbaden, 1970-1994.

Třeštík, D., *Počátky Přemyslovců: vstup Čechů do dějin, 530-935*, Praha, 1981.

—, «The Baptism of the Czech Princess in 845 and the Christianization of the Slavs», *Historica*, s.n. 2 (1995), p. 7-59.

—, «Eine große Stadt der Slawen namens Prag: Staaten und Sklaven in Mitteleuropa im 10. Jahrhundert», in SOMMER (2001), p. 93-138.
—, *Vznik Velké Moravy: Moravané. Cechové a stredni Evropa v letech 791-871*, Praha, 2001.
—, «K založení pražského biskupství v letech 968-976: pražská a řezenská tradice», in PÁNEK (2004), p. 179-196.
—, *Počátky Přemyslovců: vstup Čechů do dějin, 530-935*, Praha, 2007.
TREŠTÍK, D. – ŽEMLICKA, J., red., *Svatý Vojtech, Cechové a Evropa*, Praha, 1998.
TRUHLÁŘ, J., «Crescente fide: tzv. bavorská redakce», in EMLER 1 (1873), p. 183-190.
—, «Matěje z Janova Zpráva o Milíčovi z Kroměříže», in EMLER 1 (1873), p. 431-436.
—, «Vavřince, mnicha sv. Benedikta, Utrpení sv. Václava», in EMLER 1 (1873), p. 167-182.
—, «Život Arnošta z Pardubic», in EMLER 1 (1873), p. 387-400.
—, «Život blahoslaveného Hroznaty», in EMLER 1 (1873), p. 369-383.
—, «Život Milíče z Kroměříže», in EMLER 1 (1873), p. 403-430.
—, «Život Vintíře poustevníka», in EMLER 1 (1873), p. 337-346.
—, «Zázraky sv.Vojtěcha», in EMLER 1 (1873), p. 305-312.
—, «Život sv. Lidmily», in EMLER 1 (1873), p. 191-198.
URBAŃCZYK, P., ed., *The Neighbours of Poland in the 11th Century*, Warsawa, 2002.
VAJS, J., *Sborník staroslovanských literárních památek o sv. Václavu a sv. Ludmile*, Praha, 1929.
VAN DEN GHEYN, J., *Catalogue des manuscrits de la Bibliothèque Royale de Belgique*, 13 vol., Bruxelles, 1901-1948.
VAVŘÍNEK, V., *Cyril a Metoděj mezi Konstantinopolí a Římem*, Praha, 2013.
VEČEŘE, V., *Litomyšl Alberta ze Šternberka*, Doctoral thesis defended at the Praha University in 2014 (Thesis ID 123793). The complete thesis is available on-line: https://is.cuni.cz/webapps/zzp/detail/123793/?lang=en (last access 10/01/2020).
Velké dějiny zemí Koruny české, 1: *Do roku 1197*, Praha, 1999; 2: *1197-1250*, Praha, 2000; 3: *1250-1310*, Praha, 2002; 4a: *1310-1402*, Praha, 2003; 4b: *1310-1402*, Praha, 2003; 5: *1402-1437*, Praha, 2000; 6: *1437-1526*, Praha, 2007.
VERKHOLANTSEV, J., «St. Jerome, Apostle to the Slavs, and the Roman Slavonic Rite», *Speculum*, 87 (2012), p. 37-61.
—, *The Slavic Letters of St. Jerome. The History of the Legend and Its Legacy, or, How the Translator of the Vulgate Became an Apostle of the Slavs*, DeKalb, IL, 2014.

VESELOVSKÁ, E. – ADAMKO, R. – BEDNÁRIKOVÁ, J., *Stredoveké pramene cirkevnej hudby na Slovensku*, Bratislava, 2017.

VIDMANOVÁ, A., «La branche tchèque de la 'Legende dorée'», in DUNN-LARDEAU (1986), p. 291-298.

—, «Zlatá legenda Jakuba de Voragine a legendy o českých světcích», *Listy filologické*, 109, 1 (1986), p. 40-47.

VIDMANOVÁ, A. – BAHNÍK, V., *Jakub de Varagine, Legenda aurea*, Praha, 1984.

Vilém z Hasenburka. Vita venerabilis Arnesti primi archiepiscopi ecclesie Pragensis. Život ctihodného Arnošta, prvního arcibiskupa kostela Pražského, Praha, 1994.

VODIČKA, O., «Administrace dezintegrované pražské diecéze za hustiských válek», *Mediaevalia Historica Bohemica*, 20, 2 (2017), p. 153-187.

VOLPATO, A., cur., *Monaci, ebrei, santi. Studi per Sofia Boesch Gajano. Atti delle Giornate di studio «Sophia kai historia» Roma, 17-19 febbraio 2005*, Roma, 2008.

VYSKOČIL, J. K., *Legenda blahoslavené Anežky a čtyři listy sv. Kláry*, Praha, 1932.

WAITZ, G., «De translatione sancti Adalberti», *MGH, SS*, XV-2, Hannover, 1888, p. 708.

WATTENBACH, W., «Reise nach Österreich in den Jahren 1847, 1848, 1849», *Archiv der Gesellschaft für ältere deutsche Geschichtskunde*, 10 (1851), p. 426-693.

WIHODA, M., «Benediktinská kapitola v dějinách kláštera Hradisko u Olomouce», in LIBOR – OBŠUSTA (2002), p. 29-38.

—, «Between the Emperor and the Pope. A Traumatic Century of Czech History», in URBAŃCZYK (2002), p. 111-136.

—, *Morava v době knížecí 906-1197*, Praha, 2010.

—, *Die Sizilischen Goldenen Bullen von 1212. Kaiser Friedrichs II. Privilegien für die Přemysliden im Erinnerungsdiskurs*, Wien – Köln – Weimar, 2012.

—, *Vladislaus Henry. The formation of the Moravian identity*, Leiden – Boston, MA, 2016.

WIHODA, M. – REITINGER, L., red., *Proměna středovýchodní Evropy raného a vrcholného středověku*, Brno, 2010.

WÖDKE, K., «Moralitates Caroli quarti imperataoris», *Zeitschrift des Deutschen Vereines für die Geschichte Mährens und Schlesiens*, 1, 4 (1897), p. 41-76.

WOLVERTON, L., *Hastening Toward Prague. Power and Society in the Medieval Czech Lands*, Philadelphia, PA, 2001.

WOOD, I. N., «Hagiographie und Mission (700-1050)», in STIEGEMANN – KROKER – WALTER (2013), p. 121-129.

—, «The Hagiography of Conversion», in KLANICZAY (2013), p. 1-16.
Woś, J. W., «La 'Cronaca' di Gallo Anonimo», *Annali della Scuola Normale Superiore di Pisa. Classe di Lettere e Filosofia*, ser. III, 11, 1 (1981), p. 165-179.
ZACHOVÁ, J., «Zu zwei Legenden vom hl. Prokop», *Acta Universitatis Carolinae. Philologica et historica*, 1: *Graecolatina Pragensia*, 4 (1971), p. 19-26.
—, *Legendy Wolfenbüttelského rukopisu*, Praha, 2010.
—, «Passio sancti Venceslai martyris», in ZACHOVÁ (2010), p. 75-90.
ZALUD, Z., «Dalsí verze videní Arnošta z Pardubic u Konráda z Megenberka», *Mediaevalia historica Bohemica*, 16, 1 (2013), p. 7-13.
ZAPLETALOVÁ, D., «Mohl žít sv. Ivan český v raném středověku?», *Český kras*, 42 (2016), p. 54-61.
ŽEMLIČKA, J., «Mitra českych knížat», *Sborník společnosti přátel starožitností*, 3 (1992), p. 17-22.
—, *Čechy v době knížecí 1034-1198*, Praha, 1997.
—, «Die Verehrung des heiligen Gotthard (Godehard) im premyslidischen Böhmen», in DOLEŽALOVÁ (2010), p. 363-368.
ŽŮREK, V., «Les langues du roi. Le rôle de la langue dans la communication de propagande dynastique à l'époque de Charles IV», *Revue de l'IFHA*, 6 (2014), on-line: http://ifha.revues.org/8045.

L'hagiographie en France,
env. 750-950

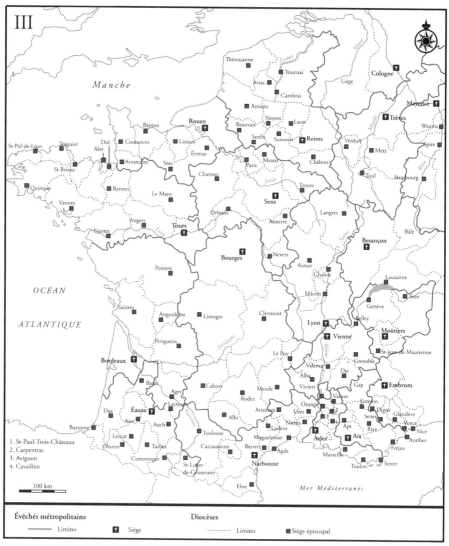

Provinces et diocèses de la Gallia à l'époque carolingienne

Avant-propos

Nous avions pensé ce volume VIII, en chantier depuis six ans, entièrement consacré à la *Gallia* du haut Moyen Âge, mais, hélas, ce ne fut pas possible. Il reste que les trois-quarts de ce volume s'y intéressent avec des contributions qui vont de la Bretagne à Besançon et des rivages de la Mer du Nord à la vallée du Rhône. De nombreux auteurs ont été sollicités pour couvrir cet immense espace, durant la période carolingienne (env. 750-950) et quelquefois un peu au-delà. En revanche, l'hagiographie latine en Gaule avant 750 prendra place dans le volume IX.

Outre un état de la question, chaque chapitre est donc le reflet des préoccupations de son auteur, de sa façon d'étudier l'hagiographie et de sa méthode de travail.

Espérons que cette grande diversité ne déroutera pas le lecteur mais qu'au contraire, elle sera stimulante et attrayante. Bien que tous les espaces prévus n'aient pas pu être traités dans ce volume, nous avons distribué la matière en provinces ecclésiastiques et en diocèses (selon la géographie de l'époque carolingienne, cf. la carte ci-contre), à une exception près, l'œuvre hagiographique d'Alcuin, qui, par sa qualité, son importance et sa diversité, méritait de figurer comme chapitre liminaire de l'ensemble du volume.

L'étude de certains diocèses de la *Gallia* à l'époque carolingienne n'a pu être terminée à temps, en particulier les diocèses provençaux, les diocèses de Liège, Cambrai, Thérouanne et Tournai ainsi que trois diocèses de la province de Sens, Meaux, Chartres et Paris; de ce dernier diocèse, seule la production hagiographique de la ville de Paris figure ici; l'importante production de Saint-Denis et celle de Chelles sont attendues pour le volume IX, de même que celle des diocèses de Meaux et de Chartres. On ne s'étonnera pas de ne pas voir traiter expressément ici les diocèses de Metz, Toul et Verdun, dont la production hagiographique ne commence véritablement que dans les années 930 et a donc été étudiée dans le volume IV par Guy Philippart et Anne Wagner, qui évoquent l'unique texte de la fin du IXe siècle, la *Vita prima* de sainte Glossinde de Metz, ainsi que le *Libellus de episcopis Mettensibus* de Paul Diacre, qui n'est pas à proprement parler une œuvre hagiographique.

En dehors de la *Gallia*, on trouvera ici un supplément sur la Germanie (étudiée dans les volumes II et IV de la collection), en particulier autour de Trèves et de Cologne, accompagné de l'étude du seul texte «carolingien» du diocèse de Strasbourg, la Vie de sainte Odile.

Nous souhaitons que la publication de ce volume incite les contributeurs sollicités pour les espaces encore non traités, en particulier dans la Gallia, à participer sans délai à la préparation du prochain volume qui sera dirigé par Fernand Peloux, près de trente ans après la publication du premier volume, sous la direction de Guy Philippart, en 1994.

Michèle GAILLARD et Monique GOULLET

Alcuin hagiographe

par

Joseph-Claude POULIN

INTRODUCTION.
I. HAGIOGRAPHIE EN PROSE. – A. Saint Willibrord († 739). – B. Saint Vaast († 540). – C. Saint Riquier († milieu VIIe s.). – E. Saint Martin († 397).
II. HAGIOGRAPHIE MÉTRIQUE
III. MESSES ET OFFICES PROPRES. – A. Saint Willibrord. – B. Saint Vaast. – C. Saint Riquier. – D. Saint Martin. – E. Autres saints.
CONCLUSION.
ANNEXE: Poèmes d'Alcuin pour des saints.
BIBLIOGRAPHIE.

INTRODUCTION

La *Vita Alcuini* (*BHL* 242; ALC 2), chap. 12 (24)[1], énumère les œuvres jugées les plus marquantes écrites par Alcuin; à côté de ses traités didactiques ou théologiques, ses commentaires de la Bible ou sa correspondance, l'hagiographie brille par son absence. Et pourtant, Alcuin a consacré beaucoup d'efforts à la louange des saints, comme on peut le constater facilement dans la récapitulation de sa production écrite dressée naguère par la *Clavis II*.

L'intérêt d'Alcuin pour la dévotion aux saints s'est manifesté assez tôt dans sa vie; il fut en effet témoin, sinon acteur, de l'implantation en Northumbrie d'une fête en l'honneur de tous les saints au 1er novembre. Une fois installé sur le continent, il se fit le promoteur d'une célébration de la Toussaint, comme en

---

[1] Composée dans les années 820, sous l'influence de son disciple et compatriote Sigulf, à l'abbaye de Ferrières, ou à Tours selon Christiane Veyrard Côme, auteure d'une nouvelle édition richement commentée; VEYRARD-COSME (2017).

Lieux mentionnés dans le chapitre « Alcuin hagiographe »

témoigne une de ses lettres à son ami l'archevêque Arn de Salzbourg, en 798[2].

Les écrits hagiographiques sortis de la plume d'Alcuin couvrent un large spectre de l'expression littéraire. Ses *Vitae* sont les plus connues – mais pas les plus étudiées[3]. Au-delà de ce volet strictement narratif, un Alcuin poète et un Alcuin liturgiste se sont également activés pour la plus grande gloire des saints. Ces trois dimensions de sa production seront traitées successivement.

I. L'Hagiographie en prose

Trois Vies en prose au moins sont attribuables à Alcuin: elles concernent saint Riquier (*Richarius*, BHL 7223-4, 7228), saint Vaast (*Vedastus*, BHL 8506-09) et saint Willibrord (*Willibrordus*, BHL 8935). La paternité d'une quatrième, consacrée à saint Martin de Tours (*BHL* 5625-6) est incertaine; son statut ne pourra être clarifié pour de bon que dans le cadre d'une enquête élargie aux *Martinelli*, une entreprise démesurée pour l'instant[4].

Elles sont toutes le résultat d'une opération de réécriture d'un hypotexte encore conservé, sauf celle de saint Willibrord:

–, **saint Riquier**: réécriture d'un *libellus* anonyme (*BHL* 7245) de la fin du VIIe siècle au plus tôt[5].

---

[2] *Ep.* 193 (= ALC 45.193). Wilmart (1934), p. 54 sq.; Deshusses (1979), p. 291-295; Lapidge (1984), p. 330 sq. Pour une réévaluation du rôle d'Alcuin dans la diffusion de la fête de Toussaint, voir Hammer (2004), p. 19-21. Il n'y a pas lieu de retenir ici un *Sermo in festivitate omnium sanctorum* parfois attribué à Alcuin (ALC 82).

[3] Les *Vitae* composées par Alcuin méritent certainement mieux que les jugements dépréciatifs recensés par Veyrard-Cosme éd. (2003), p. LIII sq. Parmi les chercheurs contemporains qui se sont attachés à l'étude de cette hagiographie, I Deug-Su et C. Veyrard-Cosme occupent une place éminente; voir les références dans notre étude de 2015, n. 2. Lapidge – Love (2001), p. 206 et 215 ont choisi d'omettre la production hagiographique continentale d'Alcuin.

[4] L'attribution à Alcuin de cette réduction de la Vie sulpicienne de saint Martin ne fait pas de doute pour Mullins (2011).

[5] Sur la possibilité qu'Alcuin ait d'abord effectué oralement cette transposition, peut-être en présence de Charlemagne, voir Berschin (2010), p. 171.

–, **saint Vaast**: réécriture d'une *Vita I^a* traditionnellement attribuée à Jonas de Bobbio, vers 642 (*BHL* 8501-03). Anne-Marie Helvétius a récemment mis en doute l'autorité de Jonas et proposé d'en ramener la composition vers 740-750[6].

–, **saint Willibrord**: l'idée de faire dépendre le travail d'Alcuin d'une version primitive (maintenant perdue) rédigée par un *Scottus* n'apparaît que vers 1100, sous la plume de Thiofrid d'Echternach[7]. Il est toutefois assuré qu'Alcuin a emprunté à Bède le Vénérable une partie de ses données biographiques pour la première partie de la vie du saint[8].

–, **saint Martin**: abrégé (ALC 89) des écrits de Sulpice Sévère sur saint Martin de Tours.

Toutes ces œuvres sont le résultat d'une commande, sauf celle de saint Martin, pour autant que nous puissions le savoir. Une lettre d'envoi coiffe chaque Vie, sauf celle de saint Martin; mais ce n'est pas en soi un motif suffisant pour refuser à Alcuin la paternité de cette dernière[9]. L'omission d'un élément péritextuel à pertinence locale est particulièrement prévisible dans le cas de copie d'un livret hagiographique destiné à l'exportation[10]; or cette *Vita Martini* est déjà présente dans un *Martinellus* copié à Lorsch aux environs de 800 (Merseburg, Domstiftsbibliothek 105, fol. 79v-83)[11], ce qui laisse peu de temps pour l'action d'un tiers, car Alcuin est décédé en 804.

Le lieu de composition des Vies est fonction de leur date. La Vie de saint Riquier est certainement postérieure à l'an 800, car elle fut offerte à Charlemagne empereur – seule biographie

---

[6] HELVÉTIUS (2011); sa conclusion ne s'impose pas encore.

[7] Thiofrid d'Echternach, *Vita s. Willibrordi* (en prose; *BHL* 8940), I-21. I DEUG-SU (1983), p. 21 et 31-3 considère cette possibilité encore envisageable. De même SCHROEDER, TRAUFFLER (1994), p. 37; et encore EID. (1996), p. 37. Dernièrement, acceptent encore cette hypothèse: BERSCHIN (1991), p. 116 et LOTTER (2006), p. 354 et 356; et surtout von PADBERG (1997), p. 19 sq. Plus dubitatifs sont DRÄGER (2008), p. 65 et PALMER (2009). p. 30 sq. et 69-71. Wilhelm Levison n'y croyait pas, suivi en cela par Maurice Coens: *AB*, 39 (1921), p. 186.

[8] BÈDE, *Historia ecclesiastica*, III, 13; V, 10 sq. et 19.

[9] *Contra*: GORMAN (2002), p. 101. Position plus nuancée sur ce point chez Fox (2008), p. 328 sq.

[10] Un exemple analogue est signalé par DECLERCQ (2005), p. 617.

[11] BISCHOFF (2004), n° 2753. Fac-similé numérique du manuscrit à l'adresse http://www.bibliotheca-laureshamensis-digital.de.

à lui être dédiée. La Vie de saint Willibrord, première dans l'ordre chronologique, fut composée entre 785 et 797[12]. On considère généralement que la Vie de saint Vaast fut rédigée entre les deux, encore que W. Berschin se demande s'il ne faut pas la rejeter en dernière position[13]. Aucun élément absolu ou relatif ne permet de dater la rédaction de la Vie de saint Martin. Au moins deux de ces *vitae*, sinon toutes, ont donc vu le jour à Tours, où Alcuin s'était retiré en 796. Mais pour autant, le point de départ de leur diffusion se situe essentiellement au lieu de culte principal du saint concerné: Centula pour saint Riquier, Arras pour saint Vaast, Echternach pour saint Willibrord et Tours pour saint Martin.

Chacune de ces quatre Vies en prose se termine par une homélie[14], qui n'a circulé que de concert avec la partie narrative – quand elle a survécu[15]. La candidature d'une Vie de saint Josse (*Judocus*) est définitivement écartée de la liste des œuvres d'Alcuin[16].

A. Saint Willibrord (†739)

La Vie de ce saint d'origine anglo-saxonne, compatriote et peut-être parent d'Alcuin, est la composition hagiographique la plus ambitieuse de notre auteur; elle se présente en effet sous la forme d'un *opus geminum* – Vie en prose suivie de sa transposition en hexamètres, conçues comme un tout. Ce dossier de saint Willibrord se compose des pièces suivantes:

–, **en prose**: une lettre d'envoi au commanditaire, l'archevêque de Sens et abbé d'Echternach Beornrad (d'origine anglo-

---

[12] Nous ne retenons pas la proposition de von Padberg (1997), p. 20, qui situe la rédaction de la Vie de saint Willibrord pendant le dernier séjour d'Alcuin en Angleterre, entre 789 et 793.

[13] Berschin (1991), p. 162 sq. et 174.

[14] Deux d'entre elles seulement sont répertoriées individuellement dans la *Clavis II*: *Homilia in die natali sancti Vedasti pontificis ad populum dicenda* (ALC 3; *BHL* 8509) et *Sermo de transitu sancti Martini* (ALC 81; *BHL* 5626). Les deux autres ne sont traitées séparément que dans la *BHL*: Riquier (*BHL* 7224) et Willibrord (*BHL* 8937).

[15] Un relevé de sa présence dans les manuscrits les plus anciens (avant 1200) se trouve dans Poulin (2013), p. 694-696.

[16] ALC 88; *BHL* 4504. Pour la démonstration, cf. Poulin (2009), p. 98-119.

saxonne lui aussi, †797) en guise de préface (*Ep.* 120; *BHL* 8935; ALC 45.120), une table des chapitres de 32 articles (incluant l'homélie finale), la Vie proprement dite en 31 chapitres (en comptant un *Appendix*); cet Appendice (*BHL* 8936) traite non pas du saint, mais de son père Wilgils (en contrepartie symétrique au premier chapitre de la Vie, lui aussi relatif à Wilgils); et une homélie finale (ou chap. 32 de la Vie; *BHL* 8937);

–, **en vers**: une table des chapitres de 33 articles (en comptant le *Carmen* final), une préface et une transposition métrique de la Vie en 33 chapitres (*BHL* 8938) incluant le *Carmen* final (*BHL* 8939) consacré au père du saint. En position terminale, une invocation personnelle d'Alcuin, en forme de distique.

ÉDITIONS: La meilleure édition complète est celle d'Albert Poncelet dans les *AASS* en 1910. Pour son édition de la Vie en prose dans les *MGH*, *SRM*, VII, Wilhelm Levison a utilisé en 1920 tous les témoins anciens survivants, sauf celui de Luxembourg, BnL 264 (tout comme Poncelet); il a connu le fragment *Parisinus* lat. 10837, mais n'a pas cherché à le rattacher à une famille de manuscrits (Poncelet lui attribue le numéro 1f). L'édition de la portion métrique de la Vie par Ernst Dümmler dans les *MGH*, *Poet. Lat.*, I, s'appuie sur trois des cinq manuscrits anciens conservés; il lui manque Trier, Seminarbibl. 75 et Würzburg, UB, M.p.th.f. 34, que Poncelet a connus (ses numéros 1c et 1a^2 respectivement). L'édition partielle de VEYRARD-COSME (2003), appuyée sur une sélection arbitraire de manuscrits, ne concerne que la Vie en prose; et encore, sans l'homélie finale (ou chap. 32). Une version numérique appauvrie de cette édition a paru dans un cédérom produit par la SISMEL en 2006. La lettre d'envoi est reprise séparément dans l'édition des *MGH*, *Epist.*, IV, Berlin, 1895, p. 175 et dans l'édition VEYRARD-COSME (2003), p. XLIXs.

B. SAINT VAAST († 540)

Les commanditaires et destinataires sont l'abbé Radon († en 797 au plus tard) et les moines de Saint-Vaast d'Arras. Dans sa lettre d'envoi (ALC 45.74), Alcuin utilise le verbe *emendare* pour caractériser son travail sur l'hypotexte; en fait, il va plus loin en modifiant sa source de manière intéressée. Alors que le biographe primitif plaçait la sépulture du saint dans la cité d'Arras, Alcuin la déplace *extra muros*, dans un oratoire au bord du Crinchon (recension A, *BHL* 8506), qui devait donner naissance à l'abbaye de Saint-Vaast[17]. Cette innovation dut plaire à la communauté monastique intéressée à la fin du VIIIe siècle; mais elle déclencha, dès le IXe siècle, deux réécritures de la finale afin de remanier les indications de sépulture (recension B, *BHL* 8907), puis allonger le texte jusqu'à 12 chapitres (recension C, *BHL* 8508). Ces deux derniers remaniements constituent cependant des témoins indirects de la composition d'Alcuin pour leurs huit premiers chapitres.

Le dossier alcuinien de saint Vaast se compose des pièces suivantes: une lettre d'envoi à l'abbé Radon, une table des chapitres en neuf articles, puis une préface[18], la Vie proprement dite en neuf chapitres (ALC 91), une homélie pour la fête du saint (ALC 3; *BHL* 8509)[19], un distique adressé à l'abbé Radon (ALC 85; ICL 10297); des compositions métriques et des inscriptions complètent le dossier. La Vie est couramment découpée en neuf chapitres (sans compter la lettre d'envoi), correspondant peut-être à des leçons pour l'office des Nocturnes; mais les chapitres paraissent trop longs pour un tel usage.

ÉDITIONS: l'édition de référence de la lettre d'envoi demeure celle de Dümmler dans *MGH, Epist.*, IV, n° 74 et celle de la Vie par B. Krusch dans *MGH, SRM*, III. Parmi les témoins antérieurs au XIIe siècle, Krusch ne tient cependant pas compte des manuscrits suivants: Arras, BM 734; Augsburg, UB, Cod. I.2.4° 6; Cambrai, BM 365, 546 et 854. Le manuscrit de Karlsruhe, BLB, Aug. XXXII n'apparaît que dans une addition de *MGH, SRM*, IV, 770; les témoins Cambridge, Corpus Christi College 9 et München, Bayerische Staatsbibliothek, Clm 4618 ne reçurent un signalement que dans le *Conspectus* de *MGH, SRM*, VII, p. 573 et 617 respectivement. Il faut chercher l'homélie finale dans la *Patrologie latine* (t. 101, col. 678-681), traduite par VEYRARD-COSME éd. (2003), p. XXXVIII-XL. L'édition partielle de la Vie par VEYRARD-COSME (2003) appelle les mêmes commentaires que pour saint Willibrord.

---

[17] Carte de l'agglomération d'Arras et du cours du Crinchon in PRÉVOT, GAILLARD et GAUTHIER (2014), p. 434.

[18] La tradition manuscrite est unanime à fusionner cette préface avec le premier chapitre de la Vie, sous un titre commun, au numéro un de la séquence des chapitres.

[19] GORMAN (2002), p. 126 doute de la paternité d'Alcuin; mais sa présence dans un témoin ancien, voisin de l'an 800 (Merseburg, Domstiftsbibl. 105), et la symétrie avec le cas de saint Riquier et de saint Willibrord nous ont convaincu de la retenir dans cet inventaire.

C. Saint Riquier († milieu viie s.)

À la demande de l'abbé Angilbert de Saint-Riquier († 814) – peut-être dans la foulée de la reconstruction de Centula après un incendie –, Alcuin s'est chargé de réécrire (*cultius adnotare*) une première Vie anonyme en 14 chapitres (*BHL* 7245) qu'on lui a communiquée sous forme de *libellus*. Une lettre d'envoi est adressée à Charlemagne empereur (*Ep.* 306; ALC 45.306; *BHL* 7223); elle n'accompagne jamais le reste du dossier dans les manuscrits antérieurs au xiie siècle. Une homélie finale (ALC 3) complète la Vie (ALC 90; *BHL* 7224) au 18e et dernier chapitre. Cet ensemble est encadré par deux distiques élégiaques (ICL 5595 et 3633 respectivement; *BHL* 7228). L'absence de titres de chapitres, tant sous forme de table liminaire que par insertion dans le corps du texte, ne résulte peut-être pas d'un accident de transmission[20].

Éditions: le dossier complet est publié par B. Krusch dans *MGH*, *SRM*, IV; parmi les manuscrits antérieurs au xiie siècle, il n'a pas pris en compte Cambridge, Corpus Christi College 9, ni Douai, BM 354. L'homélie finale n'est pas matériellement distinguée comme telle, ni dans les manuscrits, ni dans les éditions. L'édition partielle de Veyrard-Cosme (2003) appelle les mêmes commentaires que pour saint Willibrord.

D. Saint Martin († 397)

Cette version extrêmement condensée des écrits de Sulpice Sévère sur saint Martin de Tours se laisse découper en deux sections: une partie biographique (ALC 89; *BHL* 5625), suivie d'une homélie (ALC 81; *BHL* 5626). Elle entretient en outre un lien de dépendance formelle avec la *Vita s. Vedasti* d'Alcuin – ce qui ne suffit pas à prouver qu'il en est l'auteur. On peut imaginer qu'Alcuin ait voulu répondre aux attentes des Tourangeaux pendant son abbatiat sur place. Le témoin le plus ancien de la première partie se trouve dans un *Martinellus* des environs

---

[20] *Contra*: Berschin (1991), p. 150 sq.

de 800 (Merseburg, Domstiftsbibl. 105), peut-être copié du vivant d'Alcuin[21].

ÉDITION: la *Patrologie latine* (t. 101, col. 657-662) reproduit l'édition de Forster (1777), qui avait réuni les deux parties de l'œuvre, en 16 chapitres au total; d'après I Deug-Su[22], il semble qu'il faille plutôt les distinguer.

II. Hagiographie métrique

Le recours à des formes poétiques comme véhicules de la louange des saints se manifeste assez tôt dans la carrière d'Alcuin; les *Versus* d'York (ALC 87) en constituent un premier monument d'importance. Son dernier éditeur demeure toutefois hésitant sur la date et lieu de rédaction de ce long poème à la gloire des saints d'York: à partir d'un premier état rédigé à York peu après 782, il se peut que l'œuvre ait ensuite fait l'objet de révisions jusqu'à une date aussi tardive que 792-793[23]. Dès lors, les chercheurs se sont partagés entre deux scénarios: les partisans d'une composition à York d'une part[24] et les tenants d'une localisation sur le continent de l'autre[25]. L'enracinement nordique des *Versus* est en tout cas consolidé par le rapport de proximité qu'ils entretiennent avec le calendrier métrique d'York: les mêmes saints northumbriens sont en effet pour la plupart célébrés de part et d'autre. D'où l'hypothèse lancinante d'un rôle possible d'Alcuin (ou de son entourage) dans l'élaboration du dit calendrier[26].

---

[21] Bischoff (2014), n° 2754. E. A. Lowe croit y reconnaître des traces d'influences graphiques insulaires: *CLA* IX, n° 1232.

[22] I Deug-Su (1983), p. 191-193.

[23] Le titre complet est *Versus de patribus, regibus et sanctis Euboricensis ecclesiae*. Godman éd. (1982), p. XLII sq. et p. 2 note a.

[24] Lapidge (1990), p. 164; mais il ne fait pas place à cette œuvre dans Lapidge (2001)! James (1993), p. 36. Holtz (1997), p. 69. Coates (1996), p. 530, n. 2.

[25] F. Dolbeau, compte rendu de l'édition Godman (1982), in *Mittellateinisches Jahrbuch*, 20 (1985), p. 284. D. Ganz, compte rendu de l'édition Godman (1982), in *Speculum*, 60 (1985), p. 115 sq. Stapleton (2013), p. 205.

[26] Deshusses (1979), p. 293. Lapidge (1984), p. 331 sq. Lapidge – Love (2001), p. 215.

La proposition de Rosamond McKitterick, tentée de voir dans le manuscrit le plus ancien des *Versus* (Saint-Thierry de Reims, Xe siècle, maintenant perdu) un signe de l'arrivée relativement tardive du poème sur le continent[27] n'est guère recevable, au vu des nombreuses traces d'influence formelle des *Versus* sur des œuvres continentales du IXe siècle, et pas uniquement hagiographiques[28]. Le relevé de ces occurrences par l'éditeur de référence peut être complété par un cas certain de remploi dans une inscription funéraire angevine datable de 835[29].

Plus problématique est la reconnaissance d'un rôle d'Alcuin dans l'élaboration du florilège *De laude Dei* (ALC 30; encore inédit) vers 790, au moment de son dernier séjour à York. Cette compilation démarque un recueil insulaire postérieur à 709, date du décès d'Aldhelm de Sherborne. L'attribution de cette œuvre à Alcuin soulève cependant des doutes chez M. Gorman, qui la range dans la catégorie des *Dubia*[30]. Parmi les œuvres hagiographiques citées dans ce manuel de dévotion, Alcuin – ou un émule – a rassemblé un groupe d'extraits de Passions de martyrs de l'Antiquité, bon reflet de ses intérêts du moment en matière hagiographique[31]. En outre, une portion métrique placée à la fin du quatrième et dernier livre, consacrée à saint Ninian (14 *miracula* et une hymne alphabétique; *BHL* 6240b et 6240c respectivement), avait été qualifiée d'addition postérieure, parce qu'elle ne se trouve que dans le plus récent des deux manuscrits

---

[27] R. McKitterick, compte rendu de l'édition GODMAN (1982), in *Journal of Ecclesiastical History*, 85 (1984), p. 622.

[28] GODMAN éd. (1982), p. 147-154.

[29] DEBIAIS éd. (2010), p. 111 sq., n° 95; TREFFORT (2007), p. 212 sq.

[30] GORMAN (2002), p. 126. SHARPE (2001), p. 45 est également dubitatif. LAPIDGE – LOVE (2001), p. 215 attribuent le *De laude Dei* à Alcuin, mais ne discutent pas des *Versus*. Il n'est d'ailleurs pas complètement exclu que sa mise au point finale ait été faite sur le continent; voir les références rassemblées par HUSSEY (2008), p. 154 sq. n. 57.

[31] Un inventaire de cette documentation hagiographique a été dressé pour la première fois par CONSTANTINESCU (1974), p. 17 et 24-26. Voir dernièrement, LAPIDGE (2006), p. 233. Les martyrs concernés sont les suivants: Agatha (*BHL* 133), Agnes (*BHL* 156), Cosmas et Damianus (*BHL* 1970), Juliana (*BHL* 4522), Laurentius (dans les *Acta Polichronii*; *BHL* 4753-9) et Valentinus (*BHL* 8463-5). Tous ces saints, sauf Juliana et Valentinus, ont bénéficié d'au moins un poème par Alcuin, comme on pourra le constater dans l'Annexe.

conservés (Bamberg, Staatsbibl., Misc. Patr. 17 / B. II. 10, du XIe siècle)[32]. Elle pourrait cependant bien appartenir à l'œuvre, si l'on en croit l'annonce qui en est faite à la fin de la table des chapitres du seul autre manuscrit connu (El Escorial, Real biblioteca del monastero de San Lorenzo, B. IV. 17, du dernier tiers du IXe siècle)[33]. Ce petit dossier hagiographique correspond sans doute à la mention qui en est faite dans une lettre (ALC 45.273) «dans laquelle Alcuin remercie les moines de Witherne [*Candida Casa*] de lui avoir envoyé le poème sur saint Ninian»[34]. Il était certainement disponible à York à la fin du VIIIe siècle, car il entretient des rapports formels avec les *Versus* d'Alcuin[35] et sa Vie de saint Willibrord[36]; par la suite, il a aussi laissé quelques traces formelles sur les Vies de saint Martin et de saint Vaast par Alcuin[37].

Outre la partie versifiée de son *opus geminum* consacré à Willibrord, Alcuin a su créer ou saisir de nombreuses occasions de s'exprimer en vers dans le cadre de la dévotion aux saints. Sa propension bien connue à glisser des distiques ici ou là – y compris dans sa correspondance[38] – se retrouve déjà dans sa production hagiographique narrative:

–, **saint Riquier**: deux paires de vers élégiaques (*BHL* 7228) encadrent la *Vita s. Richarii*: le premier sert de lemme d'annonce en tête de la Vie (ICL 5595), le second conclut l'œuvre par un appel d'Alcuin à prier pour lui (ICL 3633);
–, **saint Vaast**: un distique adressé à l'abbé-commanditaire Radon, à la fin de la Vie (ALC 85);

---

[32] C'était la position de BULLOUGH (1983), p. 4, n. 11; p. 208, n. 11 de la réimpression.
[33] GANZ (2004), p. 388. D. Bullough n'a pas eu le temps de publier le *De laude Dei*, comme il l'avait annoncé; cette édition est maintenant en préparation par David Ganz et Susan Rankin.
[34] LEVISON (1940), p. 282 sq.; JULLIEN (1992), p. 173.
[35] LAPIDGE (1990), p. 166 sq.
[36] STRECKER (1922), p. 20.
[37] *Ibid.*, p. 23.
[38] Quelques exemples sont donnés par VEYRARD-COSME (1994), p. 142, 145 sq. et 153.

—, **saint Willibrord**: à la fin de la Vie métrique, un distique élégiaque d'invocation personnelle d'Alcuin, à l'instar de ce qui se trouve à la fin de sa Vie de saint Riquier[39].

Mais ces ornements métriques sont mal conservés dans la tradition manuscrite et dans les éditions imprimées, quand ils ne sont pas simplement copiés comme de la prose.

Pendant sa carrière continentale, l'intérêt d'Alcuin pour la dévotion aux saints a donc dépassé de beaucoup les trois ou quatre biographies qu'il a rédigées; à preuve ses très nombreuses compositions versifiées sous forme de *Carmina, Epitaphia, Hymni* ou *Inscriptiones* (voir l'Annexe). Dans certains cas, Alcuin a composé des groupes de poèmes, à l'intention d'un sanctuaire en particulier; ainsi pour Saint-Amand-en-Pévèle (peut-être à l'invite de l'abbé Arn; ALC 61.88), Saint-Vaast d'Arras (à la demande de l'abbé Radon; ALC 61.89-90.13)[40], Saint-Hilaire de Poitiers et Nouaillé (sur une requête de l'abbé Aton; ALC 61.99) ou Saint-Pierre de Salzbourg (encore pour satisfaire Arn, devenu évêque, puis archevêque; ALC 61.109).

De l'avis de MORDEK (1991), une liste de reliques transmise par un manuscrit du deuxième quart du IXe siècle[41] pourrait refléter à sa manière l'intérêt d'Alcuin pour le culte des saints; pour plus de la moitié de la quinzaine de saintes reliques nommées dans cette liste, Alcuin a en effet composé au moins un poème. Les saints qui se retrouvent de part et d'autre sont: Bonifatius, Brigida, Cheranus, Congallus, Columba, Maria Virgo, Patricius, Paulus apost. et Petrus apost.

III. MESSES ET OFFICES PROPRES

On a prêté à Alcuin la composition de bon nombre de messes et offices propres à des saints; la vérification de ces hypothèses

---

[39] Un appel analogue à se souvenir de lui est lancé par Alcuin dans le distique final d'un poème adressé à Beornrad, commanditaire de la Vie de saint Willibrord (ALC 11.8) et au début d'un poème à Angilbert de Saint-Riquier (ALC 11.16).

[40] C'est le seul cas où l'on voit Alcuin répondre à une commande pour des inscriptions versifiées, d'après TREFFORT (2004), p. 360. À propos de ces *inscriptiones*, voir l'Appendice de BROU (1957), p. 36-44.

[41] Sélestat, Bibliothèque humaniste 14 (104), fol. 45 (prov. Wissembourg).

est d'autant plus ardue que ces créations ont généralement circulé de façon anonyme. Il est pourtant assuré qu'il en a composé un certain nombre, car il en désigne certaines dans sa correspondance ; mais elles ne circulent jamais de concert avec les Vies des saints concernés, sauf sous la forme d'additions postérieures, à partir du XIe siècle.

Le sacramentaire progressivement élaboré par Alcuin à Tours à la fin du VIIIe siècle (ALC 68) contient plusieurs messes propres, entre autres celles qu'il a composées lui-même en l'honneur de plusieurs saints[42] ; comme le révèle la liste suivante, son intérêt pour la fête de la Toussaint y prend un relief particulier.

Cette liste recense les messes festives consacrées à des saints, ajoutées par Alcuin au sacramentaire grégorien à la fin du VIIIe siècle ; elle est dressée à partir des numéros d'ordre du répertoire établi par DESHUSSES (1988 et 1992 ; tomes II et III). Voir aussi DESHUSSES (1979), p. 288.

- Toussaint : n° 16, 385, 386, 387
- Benedictus : n° 343, 345
- Crux : n° 9
- Maria Virgo : n° 10, 336
- Rupertus : n° 347[43]
- Scholastica : n° 341

Certaines de ces messes propres, comme celle de la Vierge, furent tirées du sacramentaire de Tours et envoyées séparément à des correspondants de l'extérieur ; des indications expresses à cet effet sont fournies par des lettres adressées aux moines de Saint-Vaast d'Arras (ALC 45.296 ; a. 796-804) et de Fulda (ALC 45.250 ; a. 801-802). D'autres messes, absentes du sacramentaire de Tours, furent composées spécialement pour un patron local ; ainsi saint Vaast pour Arras, saint Boniface pour Fulda, saint Willibrord pour Echternach (ALC 67). Dans ces derniers cas, de telles messes propres étaient destinées à entrer dans le sacramentaire local, comme Alcuin le dit explicitement

---

[42] Le rôle d'Alcuin dans la mise au point de ce sacramentaire laisse toutefois sceptique GORMAN (2002), p. 187.

[43] Formulaire presque identique à celui d'une messe d'Alcuin pour la *depositio* de saint Vaast : DESHUSSES éd. (1992), t. I, p. 691, n°s 59*-63* et DESHUSSES (1988), p. 27, n°s 3478-3482.

aux moines de Saint-Vaast[44]. Alcuin a composé des messes propres pour chacun des saints dont il s'est fait le biographe – y compris saint Martin, selon N. Orchard[45]. Nous ne croyons pas qu'Alcuin ait composé une messe de saint Cuthbert[46], bien qu'il en ait utilisé une pour sa messe de saint Vaast, comme on le verra plus bas.

A. Saint Willibrord

Alcuin a probablement composé une (ou deux?) messe(s) en l'honneur de saint Willibrord, bien qu'il n'en parle pas dans sa correspondance: pour le *natale* au 7 novembre et pour l'*ordinatio* au 21 novembre. La paternité d'Alcuin paraît ici incertaine à M. Gorman; N. Orchard est plus affirmatif[47]. On trouve ces messes dans deux sacramentaires d'Echternach relativement anciens:

– Paris, BnF, lat. 9433 (vers 895-900), *natale* et *ordinatio*[48];
– Darmstadt, Hessische Landes- und Hochschulbibliothek 1946 (peu après 1028), *natale* seulement.

ÉDITIONS: aux éditions énumérées par la *Clavis II* (ALC 67), ajouter les deux suivantes: ROTH (1891), p. 282 sq. et HEN (1997), p. 311 sq. (*natale*) et p. 315 (*ordinatio*). Des éditions partielles de la messe de *natale* se trouvent aussi chez EIZENHÖFER – KNAUS éd. (1968), p. 38 = n°s 1504 et 1505 de l'édition HEN (1997). Et chez ORCHARD (2000), p. 261 sq.

B. Saint Vaast

Existe-t-il une messe propre pour saint Vaast composée par Alcuin? Dans sa lettre 296 envoyée aux moines de Saint-Vaast

---

[44] PALAZZO (1994), p. 148 sq.

[45] ORCHARD (1995), «Mass for St Willibrord», p. 7-9. GORMAN (2002), p. 126 sq. est plus dubitatif. De même LOCKETT (2000), p. 151.

[46] *Contra*: ORCHARD (1995), «Masses for St Cuthbert», p. 94.

[47] GORMAN (2002), p. 126; ORCHARD (1995), «Mass for St Willibrord», p. 8.

[48] D. A. Bullough n'est pas entièrement convaincu que cet exemplaire ait été destiné à Echternach, bien qu'il en émane très probablement; voir sa recension de l'édition de HEN (1997), *Journal of Ecclesiastical History*, 50 (1999), p. 776.

entre 796 et 804, Alcuin rappelle qu'il en a composé une: *dictavimus missam*[49]. W. Berschin la croit disparue[50]. Mais M. Lapidge pense la reconnaître dans un sacramentaire de Cambrai (BM 162 + 163) de la première moitié du IXe siècle[51]; on y trouve en effet une messe de vigile et une messe de *depositio* (6 février).

La messe de *depositio* se trouve aussi partiellement dans le sacramentaire d'Echternach (fin du IXe siècle), en association avec saint Remi de Reims, à la date du 1er octobre (anniversaire de saint Remi). Alcuin y remploie une oraison de postcommunion empruntée à une messe de saint Cuthbert, avec simple changement de nom; il a pu connaître cette dernière à York ou sur le continent, mais ne l'a sans doute pas composée lui-même[52]. Cette dernière messe était connue sur le continent depuis au moins la fin du IXe siècle, car elle est déjà présente dans un sacramentaire d'Essen à cette époque[53].

Les relations bien connues de Saint-Vaast et de Corbie avec l'Angleterre au Xe siècle auraient pu favoriser la diffusion de ce côté d'une messe de saint Vaast[54], par exemple du temps de l'épiscopat d'Æthelwold de Winchester (963-984). On la trouve en effet dans un missel de la fin du Xe siècle originaire de la région de Winchester (aujourd'hui partiellement conservé à Oslo, Riksarkivet, Lat. fragm. n° 208, f. [12]; connu sous le nom de Missel *Mi 1*)[55]. Le modèle de cette messe aurait aussi pu

---

[49] Exceptionnellement, cette lettre est recopiée dans le manuscrit Arras, BM 734, un livret de luxe du XIe siècle, contenant l'ensemble du dossier hagiographique de saint Vaast. Voir l'analyse de ce témoin dans POULIN (2015), p. 188-190.

[50] BERSCHIN (1991), p. 160. SHARPE (2001), p. 45 tient pour apocryphe son attribution à Alcuin.

[51] Éd LAPIDGE (1991), p. LXVs. et LXXXIV. GAMBER (1968), p. 356, n° 761. BISCHOFF (1998), p. 169, n° 773 date plutôt ce manuscrit du troisième tiers du IXe siècle.

[52] Cette messe de saint Cuthbert se trouve dans un sacramentaire de Fulda: Göttingen, Universitätsbibliothek, Theol. 231, fol. 29; RICHTER – SCHÖNFELDER éd. (1912), p. 31. ORCHARD (1995), «Masses for St Cuthbert», p. 87 et 94.

[53] Düsseldorf, Landes- und Stadtbibliothek, Cod. D.1. ELLARD (1930), p. 211.

[54] ORTENBERG (1992), p. 19; GANZ (1990), p. 104; PFAFF (2009), p. 82 sq.

[55] GJERLØW (1961), p. 46 et 66.

être importé dans cette région par Grimbald de Saint-Bertin (†903), par exemple[56]. Mais comment s'assurer de la paternité d'Alcuin? Henri Barré et Jean Deshusses pensent qu'elle n'appartient pas à la série des messes votives d'Alcuin[57]; mais elle aurait pu circuler séparément, de façon ponctuelle.

ÉDITIONS: DESHUSSES (1992), p. 690 sq. (vigile et *depositio*). La messe de *depositio* seulement dans les éditions suivantes: GJERLØW (1961), p. 66. HEN (1997), n°s 1460 et 1461. WILSON (1896), p. 161.

C. SAINT RIQUIER

Deux messes festives pour saint Riquier peuvent être attribuées à Alcuin: pour son anniversaire (26 avril) et pour une translation de l'ermitage de Forêt-Montier à Centula en 645 (9 octobre). Elles ont en commun de remployer partiellement la messe d'Alcuin pour le *natale* de saint Willibrord. Elles sont attestées par les manuscrits suivants, qui se rattachent de près ou de loin à la tradition de Saint-Riquier:

– London, BL Add. 34662: missel du milieu du XIVe siècle provenant de Saint-Valéry-sur-Somme, mais reflétant probablement l'usage de Saint-Riquier. N. Orchard estime que cette messe a pu être envoyée par Alcuin en même temps que la Vie du saint, peu après 800[58];
– Milano, Biblioteca Ambrosiana, DSP 10/27 bis: sacramentaire de Bobbio du début du XIe siècle, reproduisant un missel ou sacramentaire modèle venu de Saint-Riquier ou des environs, selon N. Orchard[59]. On y reprend l'oraison pour les vêpres et la préface de la messe de saint Willibrord.
– Paris, BnF, lat. 9432: sacramentaire d'Amiens du début du Xe siècle contenant la messe de *natale* de saint Riquier, calquée sur celle de saint Willibrord.
– Wien, ÖNB n. b. 1933, fol. 104 (*depositio* au 26 avril) et fol. 109v (*translatio* au 9 octobre): missel du XIVe siècle destiné à Saint-Riquier, reflétant un état du IXe siècle, selon Michel Huglo[60].

---

[56] GJERLØW (1961), p. 50. WILSON éd. (1896), p. XXXIV.
[57] BARRÉ – DESHUSSES (1968), p. 23.
[58] ORCHARD (2000), p. 262.
[59] ORCHARD (2000), p. 277.
[60] HUGLO (1959), p. 403-6.

Ces cas de remplois ne sont peut-être pas la seule marque d'influence du dossier alcuinien de saint Willibrord sur celui de saint Riquier: N. Orchard croit reconnaître un écho de la Vie en prose de saint Willibrord (chap. 6 et 12) sur celle de saint Riquier (chap. 4)[61].

ÉDITIONS: HUGLO (1959), p. 409 sq. (26 avril) et p. 410 sq. (9 octobre). Et 9 octobre seulement chez ORCHARD (2000), p. 264 sq. (d'après le manuscrit de Paris) et p. 277 (d'après le manuscrit de Milan); pour le 26 avril et le 9 octobre, p. 281 sq. (d'après le manuscrit de Vienne).

D. Saint Martin

Si Alcuin a composé des messes propres en l'honneur de saint Martin, elles pourraient faire partie des additions qu'il a apportées au sacramentaire grégorien pendant son abbatiat à Tours.

ÉDITIONS: OURY (1962), p. 86-89 (vigile, *natale* et octave). DESHUSSES (1972), n°s 26 (*natale*) et 27 (octave). ID. (1988), t. II, n°s 355 (vigile), 356 (*natale*) et 358 (octave), d'après des manuscrits tourangeaux, dont le plus ancien vient de l'abbaye Saint-Martin au troisième quart du IXe siècle (Tours, BM 184 + Paris, BnF, lat. 9430).

E. Autres saints

L'annonce faite aux moines de Fulda de l'envoi d'une messe en l'honneur de saint Boniface semble bien s'être concrétisée, car on trouve dans un sacramentaire de Fulda de la fin du Xe siècle deux messes (de vigile et d'anniversaire) qui sont les dérivés directs des deux messes correspondantes d'Alcuin pour saint Vaast, avec simple changement de nom[62]. Cette messe pour saint Boniface se trouve aussi dans un sacramentaire de Mayence; elle est contenue dans des additions ajoutées à la fin du Xe siècle, à l'aide de «cahiers provenant très vraisemblablement de Fulda»[63].

---

[61] ORCHARD (1995), «Mass for St Willibrord», p. 8.

[62] Göttingen, Universitätsbibliothek, Theol. 231, fol. 86v-88. RICHTER – SCHÖNFELDER éd. (1912), p. 119-121.

[63] Mainz, Bibliothek des bischöflichen Priesterseminars, ms. 1, fol. 191-204. PALAZZO (1994), p. 226 sq.; selon lui, ces additions fuldiennes seraient

Il existe une petite possibilité de voir en Alcuin l'auteur d'une messe en l'honneur de saint Rupert, patron de Salzbourg ; Alcuin aurait très bien pu l'envoyer à son ami Arn de Salzbourg, en démarquant la messe de *depositio* qu'il avait composée pour saint Vaast. Elle se trouve dans un manuscrit copié vers 830 pour Trente, mais sous l'influence manifeste de Salzbourg[64]. On peut en dire autant – mais pas plus – d'une messe pour saint Emmeran en bonne partie démarquée de celle de saint Vaast, compilée pour l'évêque Baturich de Ratisbonne ; ce dernier reçut en effet sa formation à Fulda, dans un milieu fortement marqué par l'influence alcuinienne[65].

Alcuin a-t-il en outre composé des pièces pour les offices consacrés à des saints ? Hariulf de Saint-Riquier lui en prête l'intention pour saint Riquier dans sa Chronique (II, 11) : *antiphonas quoque et responsoria vel hymnos de eodem sancto [Richario]* et en cite quatre vers (ALC 60.[3]). Le manuscrit d'Abbeville (XIIIe siècle ?) dans lequel J. Hénocque les a retrouvés est perdu. Dans les lettres qu'Alcuin a envoyées aux moines de Saint-Vaast (*Ep*. 296) et de Fulda (*Ep*. 250) pour leur annoncer l'envoi de messes, il ne fait pas allusion à de telles contributions. Que reste-t-il de reconnaissable dans tout cela, sachant que les traces éventuelles de cette nature ne sont jamais pratiquement accompagnées du nom de leur auteur ? La tâche de repérage de l'activité d'Alcuin dans ce domaine est encore compliquée par le fait qu'y règnent les remaniements, emprunts et remplois silencieux, à l'instar de l'hagiographie en général.

De tous les témoins antérieurs au XIIe siècle que nous avons analysés, seuls deux manuscrits de la Vie en prose de saint Willibrord possèdent des agencements explicites de première main destinés à alimenter les prières de l'office :

– Luxembourg, BnL 264 : la Vie, son *Appendix* et son homélie finale sont découpés en plusieurs séquences de leçons numérotées.

---

arrivées à Mayence non seulement textuellement, mais aussi matériellement (p. 155 sq.).

[64] Trento, Castello del Buon Consiglio, cod. 1590. DESHUSSES éd. (1988), t. II, p. 303 et ID., éd., t. III (1992), p. 85-87. GAMBER (1988), p. 79 sq., n° 709 (olim 724).

[65] UNTERKIRCHER – GAMBER (1962), p. 67 sq., n°s 114-117 (fol. 16-16v). Sur les liens possibles d'Alcuin avec ces dernières messes, voir aussi GJERLØW (1961), p. 16 sq.

– Paris, BnF, lat. 10837, fol. 1-1v: épave d'un montage d'extraits littéraux de la Vie, entrecoupés d'antiennes originales notées pour l'office de vêpres.

Ces deux témoins du XIe siècle, vraisemblablement élaborés à Echternach, ne constituent certainement pas un arrangement voulu par Alcuin lui-même[66].

Il en va de même pour le traitement de la Vie de saint Vaast par Alcuin: quand elle est découpée en leçons numérotées ou accompagnée de prières pour l'office, il s'agit à coup sûr de créations postérieures à Alcuin:

– Douai, BM 857, fol. 51v-55v: addition de prières pour l'office du saint, à l'occasion de la transformation au XIe siècle d'un livret hagiographique du Xe siècle.
– Cambrai, BM 864: dans ce légendier du troisième quart du XIe siècle, le début de la Vie a été découpé après coup en trois leçons.
– Arras, BM 734, fol. 81v-89: livret de luxe récapitulant l'ensemble de la documentation hagiographique relative au saint, rédigée par des auteurs variés, dont Alcuin. Les deux offices notés – de schéma monastique – sont des additions du XIe siècle, sans lien avec Alcuin[67], malgré Bacouël[68].

Il semble donc acquis qu'il n'entrait pas dans les vues d'Alcuin de formater ses *Vitae* de manière à fournir directement des prières pour l'office.

Le plus ancien office conservé de saint Vaast se trouve dans l'antiphonaire dit de Compiègne, daté des années 860/880 (Paris, BnF, lat. 17436, fol. 78v-79v). Il s'appuie manifestement sur la *vita* composée par Alcuin; ses neuf répons (schéma séculier) se succèdent en effet dans l'ordre des neuf chapitres de la Vie[69]. Mais cela ne suffit pas à prouver qu'Alcuin en soit l'auteur.

---

[66] Voir l'analyse détaillée de ces deux manuscrits dans POULIN (2016). LOCHNER (1988), t. I, p. 171.

[67] Voir l'analyse détaillée de ces trois manuscrits dans POULIN (2015), p. 188-190 et 193-195.

[68] BACOUËL (1872), p. 274.

[69] BROU (1961), p. 13-19.

Conclusion

L'œuvre écrite d'Alcuin, si abondante et diversifiée, comporte presque inévitablement un certain effet de redondance, en ce sens que l'auteur est fréquemment amené à se remployer lui-même; il assume d'ailleurs pleinement cette pratique de l'auto-remploi[70]. Le volet hagiographique de sa production procure de bons exemples de ce phénomène. Il n'est que de voir le nombre de rapprochements formels entre les *Versus* d'York et les Vies de saints composées par Alcuin: une quarantaine de points de contact formel avec la *Vita metrica s. Willibrordi*[71]. Seule la Vie de saint Vaast semble y avoir échappé. La proximité verbale des Vies de Riquier, Vaast et Martin est bien illustrée par les extraits rassemblés par I Deug-Su[72]. Alcuin a aussi pris sur lui de recycler certaines homélies ou messes propres au bénéfice d'autres saints que leur premier destinataire. Comme on l'a vu plus haut, Alcuin a remployé sa messe pour saint Willibrord au profit de saint Riquier; celle de saint Vaast fut probablement réutilisée pour saint Boniface, peut-être aussi pour saint Rupert et saint Emmeran. Pour le début et la fin de son homélie sur saint Vaast, Alcuin a emprunté à son homélie sur saint Willibrord.

L'union organique *vita* + homélie reflète bien la haute importance de la prédication aux yeux d'Alcuin; la même déclaration programmatique à cet effet apparaît dans ses Vies de saint Willibrord et saint Riquier[73]. Les copistes médiévaux ont ensuite généralement respecté cette association d'une hagiographie narrative avec une homilétique hagiographique[74]. Un distique

---

[70] WALLACH (1953), p. 152 sq.

[71] Cela étant, les deux œuvres auraient-elles été composées en même temps, se demande GODMAN éd. (1982), p. XLIV? Pour le détail des points communs, voir *ibid.*, p. 142 sq. Où l'on verra que le rayonnement formel des *Versus* d'York s'étend en outre largement sur les *Carmina* et les *Epistolae* d'Alcuin.

[72] I DEUG-SU (1983), p. 181-185.

[73] *Vita s. Willibrordi*, ch. 14 = *Vita s. Richarii*, ch. 9. BERSCHIN (1991), p. 124, 150, 153 et 174. WOOD (2001), p. 82. Cette position d'Alcuin n'est pas énoncée de façon aussi directe dans sa Vie de saint Vaast. DIESENBERGER (2010), p. 44.

[74] POULIN (2016), p. 24. C'est moins vrai pour la *Vita s. Martini* (BHL 5625) – si elle est d'Alcuin – dont le *Sermo de transitu* (BHL 5626) est

final prend place après l'homélie – ou après le *Carmen* qui lui correspond à la fin de la Vie métrique de saint Willibrord – et non pas après la biographie proprement dite; cette disposition manifestement voulue par Alcuin montre bien que Vie et homélie étaient fortement liées dans son esprit.

Car l'utilisation de distiques pour conclure ou encadrer ses œuvres fait également partie des habitudes d'écriture d'Alcuin, pas seulement en hagiographie[75]; c'est ainsi qu'il a conclu la Vie de saint Vaast et la Vie métrique de saint Willibrord – sa Vie de saint Riquier est gratifiée d'un encadrement par deux distiques. Il semble qu'Alcuin a innové sur ce point dans l'histoire de la biographie latine, prolongeant ainsi une habitude déjà manifeste dans sa correspondance[76]. Mais cette ornementation n'a pas toujours été respectée par les copistes médiévaux, puis les éditeurs modernes. Sur les quatre témoins complets de la *Vita s. Richarii* antérieurs au XIIe siècle, un seul a conservé les distiques d'encadrement (*Sangallensis* 563); et encore, en les copiant comme de la prose.

Enfin, il est remarquable de constater la place importante occupée par l'hagiographie dans l'abondante production épigraphique d'Alcuin, qu'elle ait été effectivement gravée ou non; le fait qu'il ait été plusieurs fois sollicité pour ce faire va de pair avec le fait que ses Vies de saints furent aussi des œuvres de commande. Il avouait d'ailleurs lui-même dans une lettre de 801 à Gisla et Rotruda (ALC 45.214) qu'il avait besoin d'un tel stimulus pour se mettre à son travail d'écriture[77]. Mais il n'est pas certain que les titres donnés à ses inscriptions versifiées dans les manuscrits soient sortis de sa plume[78]. Il faut plutôt retenir que messes propres et *tituli* destinés à des autels constituaient un ensemble à ses yeux[79].

La question a été soulevée à quelques reprises de savoir si les narrations hagiographiques d'Alcuin étaient délibérément structurées par une logique d'ordre numérique. Les 18 chapitres

---

souvent disjoint. Pour les manuscrits antérieurs au XIIe siècle des trois autres Vies, voir l'état de la présence concomitante des homélies dans POULIN (2013), p. 694-696.

[75] PABST (1994), t. I, p. 314 sq. et t. II, p. 610.
[76] BERSCHIN (2010), p. 177.
[77] BULLOUGH (1983), p. 16; p. 171 de la réimpression.
[78] Doute exprimé par BROU (1957), p. 40 sq.
[79] BARRÉ – DESHUSSES (1968), p. 40.

de la *Vita s. Richarii* (2 × 9) correspondent-ils à une intention de découpage du texte dans le but de fournir des lectures pour l'office du saint? Cette hypothèse paraît assez improbable, étant donné la longueur excessive de chaque chapitre. En tout cas, les copistes médiévaux n'y ont pas été sensibles, car aucun d'entre eux n'a cherché à mettre en évidence une telle fonction; un livret du IXe siècle ('s-Gravenhage, KB 071 H66) réaménage d'ailleurs sans vergogne la Vie de saint Riquier en 13 chapitres clairement découpés au lieu de 18. W. Berschin a pensé un moment que les 18 chapitres de la Vie de saint Riquier, tout comme les neuf chapitres de la Vie de saint Vaast, visaient à répondre aux besoins de l'office des Nocturnes; mais il semble y avoir assez vite renoncé[80].

Pour les Vies de saint Willibrord (en prose et en vers), il est possible qu'Alcuin ait cherché à atteindre le chiffre symbolique de 33[81]. Ernst Dümmler (en 1881) n'a pas été sensible à cette possibilité, qui a divisé en 34 chapitres son édition de la Vie métrique, là où Albert Poncelet (en 1910) s'en est tenu à 33 chapitres. Le démontage de la Vie en prose de saint Willibrord, de son *Appendix* et de son homélie finale en plusieurs séquences de leçons numérotées dans le manuscrit de Luxembourg, BnL 264 vise bien à procurer des lectures pour l'office, mais tardivement (dans la seconde moitié du XIe siècle) et sans égard au découpage en chapitres créé par Alcuin. Les copistes médiévaux ne numérotent pas forcément les chapitres de première main, ni dans la table des chapitres (quand elle est présente)[82], ni dans le corps du texte (quand il est découpé visuellement en chapitres). Il est donc difficile de s'assurer des intentions d'Alcuin sur ce point. H. J. Reichsmann a essayé de montrer que la Vie en prose de saint Willibrord fut composée par Alcuin selon un schéma prédéterminé[83].

Il paraît légitime d'inscrire Alcuin dans le cercle des hagiographes professionnels de son époque, dans la mesure où sa re-

---

[80] BERSCHIN (2010), p. 177; mais cet alinéa a disparu de la réimpression. L'hypotexte de la Vie alcuinienne de saint Vaast était déjà découpé en neuf chapitres.

[81] BERSCHIN (1991), p. 123. MEYER – SUNTRUP (1987), coll. 703-706.

[82] Pour un inventaire des tables de chapitres dans les Vies de saint Vaast et saint Willibrord dans les manuscrits antérieurs au XIIe siècle, voir POULIN (2013), p. 694 sq.

[83] REISCHSMANN (1989), p. 26-31 et 42.

nommée personnelle lui a attiré de nombreuses commandes; sauf peut-être pour saint Martin, il n'avait pas d'attaches personnelles particulières au lieu de culte principal des héros qu'il a célébrés. Sa contribution en la matière dépasse de beaucoup le volet narratif, pour inclure la liturgie, l'homilétique, l'hymnologie et l'épigraphie. La musicologie finit par être elle aussi concernée, car les cinq premiers vers de sa Vie métrique de saint Willibrord furent ajoutés à la fin du Xe siècle, puis ornés de neumes, au verso de la page couverture en tête d'un manuscrit originaire d'Echternach (Paris, BnF, lat. 9565, fol. 1v)[84]. Du XIe siècle, encore à Echternach, survit l'épave des prières d'un office de saint Willibrord (Paris, BnF, lat. 10837): des extraits de la Vie en prose d'Alcuin y alternent avec des antiennes notées.

Comme beaucoup de ses émules contemporains, Alcuin s'est adonné à la réécriture de biographies spirituelles plus anciennes. Son approche de l'hagiographie possède par certains côtés des traits assez conventionnels, comme son intérêt prioritaire pour les saints évêques et pour les saints du passé plutôt que ceux du présent. Mais il a en même temps su enrichir le discours hagiographique par des manières de faire qui firent école ou qu'il a contribué à populariser: addition de tables des chapitres en tête d'une Vie[85] et plus encore distribution des titres devant chaque chapitre du texte[86], encadrement d'une Vie par des distiques[87], application à l'hagiographie de la formule de l'*opus geminum*, adjonction d'une homélie à la biographie[88].

L'importance de la contribution d'Alcuin à l'hagiographie générale se laisse aussi apprécier par la vigueur relative des opérations de réécriture ou de remploi de ses écrits hagiographiques au cours des siècles qui ont suivi leur mise en circulation. Si les

---

[84] L'usage d'ajouter une notation musicale sur la première strophe d'une hymne devient courante au XIIe siècle: BOYNTON (2003), p. 132.

[85] La présence d'une table des chapitres en tête des compositions hagiographiques serait donc plus précoce que ce qu'a observé BULLOUGH (1998), p. 12. Et plus largement sur cette question: POULIN (2005).

[86] BERSCHIN (2004), p. 84. ID. (2010), p. 34.

[87] BERSCHIN (1991), p. 173 considère Alcuin comme un innovateur sur ce point; et encore ID. (2010), p. 177.

[88] Constatation déjà faite par Walter Berschin, en prologue de REISCHSMANN (1989), p. 7.

réécritures proprement dites sont déjà bien connues[89], l'enquête sur les remplois est loin d'être terminée. Au bilan que nous en avons dressé pour ses *vitae* jusqu'au XIIe siècle, il faut déjà ajouter les occurrences suivantes:

– dossier de **saint Martin**: la Vie de saint Martin fut remployée de manière à produire deux sermons dans un sermonnaire du XIe siècle[90]. Ælfric de Winchester († vers 1010) a remployé à deux reprises des passages de la Vie de saint Martin (*BHL* 5625) dans ses propres *Lives of Saints*, et en cinq occurrences dans ses *Catholic Homilies* (vers 991-992)[91];

– dossier de **saint Vaast**: une partie (anonymée) de la lettre d'envoi de la Vie à l'abbé Radon a été introduite (peu après 858) dans une version allongée de la *Regula canonicorum* de Chrodegang de Metz, puis traduite en vieil-anglais (dialecte saxon) dans les années 940/950[92];

– dossier de **saint Willibrord**: très tôt (avant 814), Raban Maur a effectué des emprunts à la Vie métrique pour son poème *In honorem sanctae Crucis* (ICL 9911), A-8, vers 9, 13, 18, 23, 26, 27 (= Alcuin, *V. metrica s. Willibrordi*, préf., vers 11, 14, 8, 13, 16, 19, 21, 23)[93]. La Vie métrique fut encore source d'ins-

---

[89] Voir le bilan dressé par POULIN (2013), p. 673-680.

[90] CROSS (1987), p. 39, n°s 65 et 66. Le manuscrit Pembroke 25 fut copié au XIe siècle (à Bury?), mais sa matière fut compilée vers la fin du deuxième quart du IXe siècle, peut-être sur le continent (CROSS [1987], p. 88-90). DOLBEAU (1988) a déployé une argumentation convaincante en faveur d'une localisation sur le continent (tourangelle?).

[91] Voir les références chez LAPIDGE (2006), p. 252. Mais Ælfric finit par préférer emprunter directement à Sulpice Sévère, comme l'a constaté BIGGS (1996), p. 302.

[92] Pour la date de la version latine allongée, nous suivons BARROW (2006), p. 204 sq. La traduction en vernaculaire du passage de la lettre 74 correspond aux p. 116, l. 8 – 117, l. 27 de l'édition de Dümmler; identification de la source par WALLACH (1953), p. 149-151; p. 266-269 de la réimpression. Édition référence de la Règle par LANGEFELD (2003), p. 326-329 et commentaire p. 11 sq. et 358. Pour la datation de la traduction, nous suivons DROUT (2006), p. 182 sq. et 193. Ce remploi d'Alcuin a été ignoré de l'édition BERTRAM (2005), p. 177, 181 et 280, n. 188. Ce n'est pas un cas unique de détournement de la correspondance d'Alcuin pour des fins étrangères (liturgie, prédication...) à la communication épistolaire; très tôt, en effet, elle a également été récupérée à d'autres fins, comme l'ont constaté BOUHOT (1974), p. 195 sq. (quatre sermons dérivés de la lettre 131) et DIESENBERGER – WOLFRAM (2004), p. 104-106.

[93] Éd. PERRIN (1997), p. 21 sq.; ID. (2004), p. 342.

piration pour Hrotsvitha de Gandersheim († vers 975) à six reprises au moins; l'éditeur se demande même si le distique final de la Vie métrique n'aurait pas influencé la péroraison du *De ascensione* (vers 147-150) et du *Basilius* (vers 260-264)[94]. Il est également possible qu'une charte d'Echternach (n° 164) porte une trace d'influence de la Vie en prose (chap. 3), peut-être par l'intermédiaire d'un répons de l'office des Nocturnes[95]. Enfin, on peut ajouter qu'Adam de Brême laisse paraître ouvertement à deux reprises sa connaissance de la Vie en prose: *Gesta Hammaburg. Eccl. Pont.* I-17 = *Vita W.* 9 et *Gesta* IV-3 = *Vita W.* 10[96].

Mais le rayonnement de l'hagiographie alcuinienne dépasse de beaucoup le domaine strictement biographique; le nombre imposant d'auteurs du IXe siècle qui ont emprunté à Alcuin des éléments puisés dans les *Versus* d'York en procure une bonne illustration[97]. La messe pour saint Willibrord remporte la palme du succès durable auprès des imitateurs d'Alcuin; au fil des siècles, on en trouve des calques au profit des saints Amandus d'Elnone, Ambrosius de Milan, Augustinus de Cantorbéry, Bertinus, Birinus de Winchester, Germanus de Paris, Marcus papa, Nicholas de Myre, Oswaldus de Worcester, Praecordius de Vailly-sur-Aisne, Provinus de Côme, Richarius de Centula[98]. La messe d'Alcuin pour le *natale* de saint Vaast a obtenu un peu moins de succès, partiellement démarquée au profit de saint Omer (Audomarus)[99], de saint Josse (Judocus)[100], de saint Ru-

---

[94] *Maria*, vers 618 = V. metr. W. I-1; *Agnes*, vers 71 = V. metr. W. I-2; *Pelagius*, vers 6 = V. metr. W. VI-6, et peut-être aussi I-13; *Primordia*, vers 176 = V. metr. W. XIII-10; *Basilius*, vers 258 = V. metr. W. XXIV-10; *Maria*, vers 213 = V. metr. W. XXII-17. HOMEYER éd. (1970), p. 16, n. 24 et p. 84. Les citations exactes sont dans EL KHOLI (1997), p. 23 et 84.

[95] LOCHNER (1988), t. I, p. 176.

[96] Ainsi chez KOHLMANN (1908), p. 65 et 111.

[97] Voir les relevés de GODMAN (1982), p. 147-154. Pour un bilan des emprunts puisés dans les Vies de saints d'Alcuin jusqu'en 1100, voir POULIN (2013), p. 680-690. HOMEYER (1970), p. 402 se demande si Roswitha a été influencée par les *Versus* d'York pour ses *Gesta Ottonis* et ses *Primordia*.

[98] ORCHARD (1995), «Mass for St Willibrord», p. 4-6 et 9; ID. (2000), p. 262.

[99] Éd. WILSON (1896), p. 210 sq.

[100] Une adaptation de la messe de saint Vaast pour saint Josse se trouve dans le missel de Winchester de la seconde moitié du XIe siècle: TURNER éd.

pert (Rupertus)[101], de saint Boniface et de saint Emmeran[102]. Une messe pour saint Martin, probablement attribuable à Alcuin, a fourni une oraison passée au Missel romain pour la messe des Docteurs de l'Église[103]. J. Deshusses se demande même si on ne pourrait pas attribuer au total 21 ou 22 messes votives à Alcuin; ou du moins les reconnaître comme influencées par celles qui sont à coup sûr sorties de sa plume[104].

Quant aux sermons d'Alcuin, ils ont connu un long retentissement sur l'homilétique médiévale, bien au-delà des saints pour lesquels notre hagiographe les avait conçus. Son sermon pour saint Willibrord (*BHL* 8937 = chap. 32 de la Vie en prose) a commencé à être remployé à partir du XIe siècle, au bénéfice de saint Canut de Danemark et de saint Taurin d'Évreux[105], pour continuer d'être ensuite recyclé au profit de plusieurs autres saints, comme l'avait déjà relevé François Dolbeau[106]. Le sermon d'Alcuin sur saint Vaast (*BHL* 8509) a connu plus de succès encore, dès le IXe siècle[107], au point d'être remployé (en latin ou en vernaculaire) pour plusieurs autres saints qui en étaient dépourvus[108]. Rien de tel n'a été observé pour le sermon de saint Riquier. Mais dans la plupart des cas, les emprunteurs ignoraient sans doute l'identité de l'auteur initial de leur source d'inspiration.

L'étude des Vies de saints d'Alcuin et de leur péritexte immédiat avait déjà conduit au constat d'une diffusion géographique relativement limitée de ce pan de son œuvre. La circulation de chaque Vie de saint se concentre pour l'essentiel autour de la région entourant le lieu de culte principal de chaque saint: Centula pour saint Riquier, Arras pour saint Vaast et Echternach pour saint Willibrord. La seule exception notable

---

(1962), p. 191 sq. Et encore dans un missel du Bec, entre 1265 et 1272: HUGHES éd. (1963), p. 223.

[101] GJERLØW (1980), p. 15 sq.
[102] DESHUSSES (1988), t. II, p. 27 sq.
[103] DESHUSSES (1972), p. 11 et 38. Éd. ID. (1988), t. II, n° 3517.
[104] DESHUSSES (1988), t. II, p. 25 sq.
[105] Références dans POULIN (2013), p. 685. Le remploi inédit pour saint Taurin d'Évreux se trouve dans Paris, BnF, lat. 989, fol. 30v-34v.
[106] DOLBEAU (1980), p. 386, n. 9: pour saint Babolenus, saint Donatianus et saint Vitonus (Vanne).
[107] Références dans POULIN (2013), p. 687 sq. Un premier repérage avait été effectué par DOLBEAU (1973), p. 276, n. 2. Et ID. (1980), p. 386, n. 8.
[108] HALL (2007), p. 261 sq.

à ce schéma concerne la Germanie méridionale, par effet des relations personnelles privilégiées d'Alcuin avec son ami Arn de Salzbourg[109]. Le regard élargi jeté ici sur la production hagiographique d'Alcuin ne remet pas en cause cette interprétation; on est loin de l'impact des écrits de «Jérôme hagiographe»[110].

Contrairement à ce qui s'est produit pour la correspondance d'Alcuin[111], ses *carmina* ou ses inscriptions, les médiévaux n'ont apparemment pas senti le besoin – ou vu l'intérêt – de regrouper sur un même support matériel l'ensemble de sa production hagiographique, pas même en la limitant à sa portion narrative. Ce n'est pas là que s'enracinaient les fondements de sa renommée personnelle de penseur et d'écrivain[112]; il n'est donc pas étonnant que la *Vita Alcuini*, composée une vingtaine d'années seulement après sa mort, n'en parle pas.

Annexe
Poèmes d'Alcuin pour des saints

Liste des saints pour lesquels Alcuin a produit une composition versifiée, d'après le répertoire de la *Clavis II*. Les poèmes appliqués à plus d'un saint à la fois sont énumérés sous le nom de chaque saint concerné, sauf quand il s'agit de couples généralement associés, comme Cosme et Damien. Le point d'interrogation marque une attribution incertaine à Alcuin. L'orthographe des noms suit autant que possible celle de la *BHL*.

---

[109] Poulin (2016), p. 28-32.
[110] C'est le titre donné à la contribution de Bastiaensen (1994), au premier volume de la présente collection.
[111] Sur la constitution précoce de collections de lettres d'Alcuin, voir maintenant Veyrard-Cosme (2013), p. 73-98. Une nouvelle édition de sa correspondance a commencé à paraître par les soins de Veyrard-Cosme (2018).
[112] Mais il faut dire que son nom est bien mal représenté dans la circulation médiévale de ses autres œuvres, comme l'a constaté Tischler (2004).

Anonymes: ALC 61.90.20;
    ALC 61.90.21
Adamnanus: ALC 61.110.15
Agatha: ALC 61.89.11[113];
    ALC 61.99.3; ALC 61.99.6;
    ALC 61.110.4[a]
Agnes: ALC 61.89.11
Aldegundis: ALC 61.89.21
Amandus: ALC 46.[11].88.15;
    ALC 61.88.3; ALC 61.88.5;
    ALC 61.88.14;
    ALC 61.89.24;
    ALC 61.90.8; ALC 61.99.6;
    ALC 61.109.15
Anastasius: ALC 61.109.19
Andreas apost.: ALC 61.88.10;
    ALC 61.89.20;
    ALC 61.99.16;
    ALC 61.109.5;
    ALC 61.110.1
Anianus: ALC 61.90.5;
    ALC 61.110.6
Ansfridus: ALC 61.110.8
Aper: ALC 46.[13].99.13
Apollinaris: ALC 61.110.14
Athanasius: ALC 61.110.6
Audoenus: ALC 61.89.6
Audomarus: ALC 61.89.[25d]
Autbertus: ALC 61.89[25d]

Bartholomeus: ALC 61.110.10
Bavo: ALC 61.106.3

Benedictus: ALC 11.51.6 (?);
    ALC 61.89.9[114];
    ALC 61.90.23;
    ALC 61.109.12;
    ALC 61.109.13[115];
    ALC 61.109.20
Bonifatius: ALC 61.86
Briccius: ALC 61.110.17
Brigida: ALC 61.110.16

Caecilia: ALC 61.89.11;
    ALC 61.99.1
Cheranus: ALC 61.110.15
Christophorus: ALC 61.110.17
Clemens: ALC 61.89.13
Columba: ALC 61.99.5;
    ALC 61.109.20
Columbanus: ALC 61.110.15
Congallus: ALC 61.110.15
Cornelius: ALC 61.110.11
Cosmas et Damianus:
    ALC 61.89.10[116];
    ALC 61.109.14[117]
Crispinus et Crispinianus:
    ALC 61.89.12
Crux (Sancta)[118]: ALC 11.6;
    ALC 61.89.12;
    ALC 61.109.10[a] (?);
    ALC 61.109.10[b] (?);
    ALC 61.109.11[119]
Cyprianus: ALC 61.110.11
Cyricus et Julitta:
    ALC 61.109.21

---

[113] Cette inscription correspond à ICL 1769, et non pas ICL 5759, comme dans la *Clavis II*. Voir aussi Agnes, Caecilia et Lucia.

[114] La même inscription a aussi été envoyée à Salzbourg: ALC 61.109.13.

[115] La même inscription a été envoyée à Saint-Vaast: ALC 61.89.9.

[116] L'incipit est identique à celui d'une inscription envoyée à Salzbourg: ALC 61.109.14.

[117] Inscription également envoyée à Poitiers. L'incipit est identique à celui d'une inscription envoyée à Saint-Vaast: ALC 61.89.10.

[118] Nous ne retenons pas le *Carmen* ALC 61.114.1.

[119] D. Schaller note que deux vers (14 et 15) sont empruntés à Bède (ICL 1151).

Dionysius: ALC 61.89.5;
    ALC 61.90.7;
    ALC 61.90.19;
    ALC 61.99.2; ALC 61.110.3

Elidius: ALC 46.[12].99.9
Eligius[120]: ALC 61.89.[25c]

Felix: ALC 61.110.13
Florianus: ALC 61.109.21

Gabriel[121]
Gaugericus: ALC 61.89.[25c]
Gelasius ep.: ALC 61.99.11
Genovefa: ALC 61.89.26
Georgius: ALC 61.89.15
Germanus: ALC 61.89.23;
    ALC 61.90.20;
    ALC 61.110.7
Gervasius et Protasius:
    ALC 61.99.14;
    ALC 61.110.10
Gislarius: ALC 61.110.4[b]
Gregorius martyr:
    ALC 61.110.14
Gregorius papa: ALC 61.89.8;
    ALC 61.90.25;
    ALC 61.110.3

Hieronymus: ALC 61.89.8;
    ALC 61.90.24;
    ALC 61.110.5
Hilarius: ALC 61.88.13;
    ALC 61.110.12
Hippolytus: ALC 61.110.1

Ita: ALC 61.110.16

Jacobus apost.: ALC 61.110.3;
    ALC 61.110.7
Jesus Christus Salvator:
    ALC 61.109.23
Johannes apost.: ALC 61.89.14;
    ALC 61.89.16;
    ALC 61.99.19[122];
    ALC 61.110.5
Johannes Baptista[123]:
    ALC 61.89.22;
    ALC 61.90.4[124];
    ALC 61.90.10;
    ALC 61.90.15 (?);
    ALC 61.99.9[125];
    ALC 61.99.19[126];
    ALC 61.106.1;
    ALC 61.109.8[127];
    ALC 61.109.19;
    ALC 61.109.22

---

[120] Nous ne retenons pas le *Carmen* ALC 11.[127.3.2].

[121] Nous ne retenons pas le *Carmen* ALC 61.90.14.

[122] La même inscription a été envoyée à Salzbourg (ALC 61.109.8) et à Saint-Vaast (ALC 61.90.4).

[123] Nous ne retenons pas le *Carmen* ALC 61.117[b].

[124] L'inscription *O Baptista potens* a été envoyée aussi à Salzbourg: ALC 61.109.8. Cette inscription correspond à ICL 10810, et non pas ICL 6918 comme dans la *Clavis II*.

[125] L'inscription *Hoc altare tenet* a été envoyée aussi à Saint-Vaast (ALC 61.99.19) et à Salzbourg (ALC 61.109.8).

[126] L'inscription *Hoc altare tenet* a été envoyée aussi à Poitiers (ALC 61.99.9) et à Salzbourg (ALC 61.109.8).

[127] L'inscription *O Baptista potens* a été envoyée aussi à Saint-Vaast: ALC 61.90.4. L'inscription *Hoc altare tenet* a été envoyée aussi à Poitiers (ALC 61.99.9) et à Saint-Vaast (ALC 61.99.19).

Johannes ep. Pictav.:
ALC 46.[13].99.13

Lambertus: ALC 61.89.7;
ALC 61.99.1; ALC 61.110.8
Laurentius[128]: ALC 61.88.8;
ALC 61.89.16;
ALC 61.90.16;
ALC 61.99.8; ALC 61.110.1
Leo papa: ALC 61.110.2
Leodegarius: ALC 61.110.4[b]
Leonius: ALC 46.[12].99.9
Lucia: ALC 61.89.11

Marcellus: ALC 61.110.9
Maria Virgo[129]: ALC 61.88.2;
ALC 61.89.13;
ALC 61.90.1; ALC 61.90.2;
ALC 61.99.12;
ALC 61.109.4;
ALC 61.109.16;
ALC 61.109.18;
ALC 61.110.4[a];
ALC 61.110.18
Martinus Turon.:
ALC 61.88.9[a];
ALC 61.88.9[b];
ALC 61.89.4; ALC 61.90.3;
ALC 61.90.11;
ALC 61.90.21 (?);
ALC 61.99.11;
ALC 61.109.22;
ALC 61.110.17

Matthaeus apost.:
ALC 61.89.14;
ALC 61.110.11
Mauritius: ALC 61.90.9;
ALC 61.90.18;
ALC 61.110.5
Maximilianus: ALC 61.109.19
Medardus: ALC 61.90.6;
ALC 61.110.9
Michael Archangelus[130]:
ALC 61.88.4;
ALC 61.88.12[131];
ALC 61.89.25[b];
ALC 61.91.4;
ALC 61.99.4 (?);
ALC 61.109.12[132];
ALC 61.110.18

Nabor: ALC 61.102[a]

Pancratius: ALC 61.110.14
Patricius: ALC 61.110.15
Paulus apost.[133]: ALC 61.89.16;
ALC 61.89.19[134];
ALC 61.109.6[135];
ALC 61.109.7; ALC.
61.109.9; ALC 61.109.17;
ALC 61.109.20;
ALC 61.110.2
Petronilla: ALC 61.110.4[a]
Petrus apost.[136]: ALC 61.88.11;
ALC 61.89.17;
ALC 61.89.18;
ALC 61.90.13;

---

[128] Nous ne retenons pas le *Carmen* ALC 61.114.6.

[129] Sur la dévotion d'Alcuin à la Vierge, cf. MEYER (1959), p. 343-350.

[130] Nous ne retenons pas une *Sequentia de sancto Michaele* (ALC 11.120), ni les *Carmina* ALC 61.90.14 et ALC 61.114.2.

[131] La même inscription a aussi été envoyée à Salzbourg: ALC 61.109.12.

[132] La même inscription a été envoyée à Saint-Amand: ALC 61.88.12.

[133] Nous ne retenons pas les *Carmina* ALC 61.114.4 et ALC 61.114.5.

[134] La même inscription a été envoyée à Salzbourg: ALC 61.109.6.

[135] La même inscription a été envoyée à Saint-Vaast: ALC 61.89.19.

[136] Nous ne retenons pas le *Carmen* ALC 61.114.3.

ALC 61.103.2;
ALC 61.107.2;
ALC 61.109.1;
ALC 61.109.2;
ALC 61.109.3
Philibertus: ALC 61.99.3
Philippus: ALC 61.110.9
Piatus: ALC 61.89.15

Quintinus: ALC 61.89.25[a][137];
ALC 61.90.7;
ALC 61.90.17; ALC 61.99.2

Raphaël[138]
Remedius/Remigius:
ALC 61.89.6;
ALC 61.90.22;
ALC 61.110.12
Richarius[139]: ALC 60.[3];
ALC 61.89.7
Rupertus: ALC 61.110.8

Salvius: ALC 61.90.8;
ALC 61.106.2

Samson: ALC 61.110.13
Scholastica: ALC 61.89.9[140];
ALC 61.109.13[141]
Silvester: ALC 61.110.2
Simon: ALC 61.110.12;
ALC 61.110.13
Stephanus[142]: ALC 61.88.6;
ALC 61.90.12;
ALC 61.99.18;
ALC 61.107.1;
ALC 61.109.9;
ALC 61.110.18
Sulpitius: ALC 61.99.5;
ALC 61.110.4[b]

Thaddaeus: ALC 61.110.13
Thomas: ALC 61.110.6

Vedastes: ALC 46.[14].89.2;
ALC 60.[1].89.26[c] (?);
ALC 61.89.1; ALC 61.89.3;
ALC 61.110.7
Victor: ALC 61.88.13
Virgilius: ALC 61.109.24

---

[137] Cette inscription correspond à ICL 9390, et non pas à ICL 6052, comme dans la *Clavis II*.

[138] Nous ne retenons pas le *Carmen* ALC 61.90.14.

[139] Nous ne retenons pas le *Carmen* ALC 11.[127.3.2]; ni cinq épitaphes de saint Riquier, plutôt attribuables à Angilbert de Saint-Riquier: ALC 11.[127.3.4-8].

[140] La même inscription a aussi été envoyée à Salzbourg: ALC 61.109.13.

[141] La même inscription a été envoyée à Saint-Vaast: ALC 61.89.9.

[142] Nous ne retenons pas le *Carmen* ALC 61.114.6.

Bibliographie

Instruments de travail

ALC = code de renvoi aux œuvres d'Alcuin dans la *Clavis II*.

BISCHOFF, B., *Katalog der festländischen Handschriften des neunten Jahrhunderts (mit Ausnahme der wisigotischen)*, 4 vol., Wiesbaden, 1998-2017.

Clavis II = JULLIEN, M.-H. – PERELMAN, F., *Clavis des auteurs latins du Moyen Âge. Territoire français, 735-987*, II: *Alcuin*, Turnhout, 1999 (*CC CM*).

EIZENHÖFER, L. – KNAUS, H., *Die liturgischen Handschriften der Hessischen Landes- und Hochschulbibliothek Darmstadt*, Wiesbaden, 1968 (Die Handschriften der Hessischen Landes- und Hochschulbibliothek, 2).

GAMBER, K., *Codices liturgici latini antiquiores. Pars II*, Fribourg, 2e éd. augm. 1968 (Spicilegii Friburgensis subsidia, 1).

—, *Codices liturgici latini antiquiores. Supplementum: Ergänzungs- und Registerband*, Fribourg, 1988 (Spicilegii Friburgensis subsidia, 1A).

ICL = SCHALLER, D. – KÖNSGEN, E., *Initia carminum latinorum saeculo undecimo antiquiorum. Bibliographisches Repertorium für die lateinische Dichtung der Antike und des früheren Mittelalters*, Göttingen, 1977; EID., *Supplementband*, Göttingen, 2005.

SHARPE, R., *A Handlist of the Latin Writers of Great Britain and Ireland before 1540*, Turnhout, 2e éd. corr. 2001 (Publications of the Journal of Medieval Latin, 1).

Sources

BERTRAM, J., éd., *The Chrodegang Rules: The Rules for the Common Life of the Secular Clergy from the eighth and ninth Centuries. Critical Texts with Translations and Commentary*, Aldershot, 2005 (Church, Faith, and Culture in the Medieval West).

DEBIAIS, V., éd., *Corpus des inscriptions de la France médiévale* (dir. C. TREFFORT), 24: *Maine-et-Loire, Mayenne, Sarthe (région Pays de la Loire)*, Paris, 2010.

DESHUSSES, J., «Les messes d'Alcuin», *Archiv für Liturgiewissenschaft*, 14 (1972), p. 7-41.

—, «Les anciens sacramentaires de Tours», *Revue bénédictine*, 89 (1979), p. 281-302.

— éd., *Le sacramentaire grégorien. Ses principales formes d'après les plus anciens manuscrits*, I: *Le sacramentaire, le Supplément d'Aniane*, Fribourg, 3ᵉ éd., 1992 (Spicilegium Friburgense, 16).
— éd., *Le sacramentaire grégorien. Ses principales formes d'après les plus anciens manuscrits*, II: *Textes complémentaires pour la messe*, Fribourg, 2ᵉ éd., 1988 (Spicilegium Friburgense, 24).
— éd., *Le sacramentaire grégorien. Ses principales formes d'après les plus anciens manuscrits*, III: *Textes complémentaires divers*, Fribourg, 2ᵉ éd., 1992 (Spicilegium Friburgense, 28).
DÜMMLER, E., éd., «Vita [metrica] sancti Willibrordi episcopi», *MGH*, *Poet. Lat.*, I, Berlin, 1881, p. 207-220.
GODMAN, P., éd., *Alcuin. The Bishops, Kings, and Saints of York*, Oxford, 1982 (Oxford Medieval Texts).
HEN, Y., éd., *The Sacramentary of Echternach: Paris, Bibliothèque nationale MS latin 9433*, Londres, 1997 (HBS, 110).
HOMEYER, H., éd., *Hrotsvithae Opera*, Munich – Paderborn – Vienne, 1970.
HUGHES, A., éd., *The Bec Missal* [Paris, BnF, lat. 1105], Londres, 1963 (HBS, 94).
KRUSCH, B., éd., «Vita Vedastis episcopi Atrebatensis duplex», *MGH*, *SRM*, III, Hanovre, 1896, p. 399-427.
— éd., «Vita Richarii confessoris Centulensis auctore Alcuino», *MGH*, *SRM*, IV, Hanovre – Leipzig, 1902, p. 381-401.
LANGEFELD, B., éd., *The Old English Version of the Enlarged Rule of Chrodegang. Edited together with the Latin text and English translation*, Francfort, 2003 (Münchener Universitätsschriften. Texte und Untersuchungen zur englischen Philologie, 26).
LAPIDGE, M., éd., *Wulfstan of Winchester. Life of Æthelwold*, Oxford, 1991 (Oxford Medieval Texts).
LEVISON, W., éd., «Vita Willibrordi archiepiscopi Traiectensis auctore Alcuino», *MGH*, *SRM*, VII, Hanovre – Leipzig, 1920, p. 81-141.
PERRIN, M. J.-L., éd., *Rabani Mauri In honorem sanctae crucis*, Turnhout, 1997 (*CC CM*, 100).
PONCELET, A., éd., «De sancto Willibrordo episcopo Traiectense et Fresonum apostolo», *AASS*, Nov. III, Bruxelles, 1910, p. 414-500.
RICHTER, G. – SCHÖNFELDER, A., éd., *Sacramentarium Fuldense saeculi X*, Fulda, 1912 (Quellen und Abhandlungen zur Geschichte der Abtei und der Diözese Fulda, 9). Réimpr. 1982 (HBS 101).
TURNER, D. H., éd., *The Missal of the New Minster, Winchester. (Le Havre, Bibliothèque municipale, MS. 330*, Londres, 1962 (HBS, 93).

UNTERKIRCHER, F. – GAMBER, K., éd., *Das Kollektar-Pontifikale des Bischofs Baturich von Regensburg (817-848) (Cod. Vindob. Ser. n. 2762)*, Fribourg, 1962 (Spicilegium Friburgense, 8).

VEYRARD-COSME, C., éd., *L'œuvre hagiographique en prose d'Alcuin. Vitae Willibrordi, Vedasti, Richarii. Édition, traduction, études narratologiques*, Florence, 2003 (Per verba, 21).

—, éd., *La «Vita beati Alcuini» (IXe s.). Les inflexions d'un discours de sainteté. Introduction, édition et traduction annotée du texte d'après Reims, BM 1395 (K 784)*, Paris, 2017 (Collection des Études augustiniennes, Série Moyen Âge et Temps Modernes, 54).

—, éd., *Alcuin. Lettres*, I: *Collection 1*, Paris, 2018 (Sources chrétiennes, 597).

WILSON, H. A., éd., *The Missal of Robert of Jumièges*, Londres, 1896 (réimpr. Woodbridge, 1994) (HBS, 11).

ÉTUDES

BACOUËL, «Manuscrits de la Bibliothèque d'Arras», in *Catalogue général des bibliothèques publiques des départements*, IV: *Arras – Avranches – Boulogne*, Paris, 1872, série in-4°, p. 9-426.

BANNIARD, M., «Les deux Vies de saint Riquier: du latin médiatique au latin hiératique», *Médiévales*, 25 (1993), p. 45-52.

BARRÉ, H. – DESHUSSES, J., «À la recherche du Missel d'Alcuin», *Ephemerides liturgicae*, 82 (1968), p. 5-44.

BARROW, J. S., «Review Article: Chrodegang, his Rule and its Successors», *Early Medieval Europe*, 14 (2006), p. 201-212.

BASTIAENSEN, A. A. R., «Jérôme hagiographe», in *Hagiographies*, I (1994), p. 97-123.

BERSCHIN, W., *Biographie und Epochenstil im lateinischen Mittelalter*, III: *Karolingische Biographie, 750-920 n. Chr.*, Stuttgart, 1991 (Quellen und Untersuchungen zur lateinischen Philologie des Mittelalters, 10).

—, *Biographie und Epochenstil im lateinischen Mittelalter*, V: *Kleine Topik und Hermeneutik der mittellateinischen Biographie. Register zum Gesamtwerk*, Stuttgart, 2004 (Quellen und Untersuchungen zur lateinischen Philologie des Mittelalters, 15).

—, «Alkuin († 804) und die Biographie», in E. TREMP – K. SCHMUKI, dir., *Alkuin von York und die geistige Grundlegung Europas (colloque de St-Gall, 2004)*, Saint-Gall, 2010, p. 169-182 (Monasterium Sancti Galli, 5); réimpr. in ID., *Mittellateinische Studien*, t. II, Heidelberg, 2010, p. 31-41.

BIGGS, F. M., «Ælfric as Historian: His Use of Alcuin's *Laudationes* and Sulpicius's *Dialogues* in his two Lives of Martin», in P. E. SZAR-

MACH, dir., *Holy Men and Holy Women. Old English Prose Saints' Lives and their Contexts*, Albany, NY, 1996, p. 289-315.
BOUHOT, J.-P., «Un sermonnaire carolingien», *Revue d'histoire des textes*, 4 (1974), p. 181-223.
BOYNTON, S., «Orality, Literacy, and the Early Notation of the Office Hymns», *Journal of the American Musicological Society*, 56 (2003), p. 99-168.
BROU, L., «Les sanctuaires védastins et les vers d'Alcuin», in ID., *The Monastic Ordinale of St. Vedast's Abbey, Arras. Arras, Bibliothèque municipale, ms. 230 (907) of the Beginning of the 14th Century*, Bedford, 1957, p. 36-44 (HBS, 86).
—, «L'ancien office de saint Vaast, évêque d'Arras», *Études grégoriennes*, 4 (1961), p. 7-42.
BULLOUGH, D. A., «Alcuin and the Kingdom of Heaven: Liturgy, Theology, and the Carolingian Age», in U.-R. BLUMENTHAL, dir., *Carolingian Essays: Andrew W. Mellon Lectures in Early Christian Studies*, Washington (DC), 1983, p. 1-69; réimpr. in ID., *Carolingian Renewal: Sources and Heritage*, Manchester, 1991, p. 161-240.
—, «Alcuin's Cultural Influence: The Evidence of the Manuscripts», in L. J. A. R. HOUWEN – A. A. MACDONALD, dir., *Alcuin of York, Scholar at the Carolingian Court* (colloque de Groningue, 1995), Groningue, 1998, p. 1-26 (Mediævalia Groningana, 22; Germania latina, 3).
COATES, S., «The Bishop as Benefactor and Civic Patron: Alcuin, York, and Episcopal Authority in Anglo-Saxon England», *Speculum*, 71 (1996), p. 529-558.
CONSTANTINESCU, R., «Alcuin et les *libelli precum* de l'époque carolingienne», *Revue d'histoire de la spiritualité*, 50 (1974), p. 17-56.
CROSS, J. E., *Cambridge Pembroke College MS 25: A Carolingian Sermonary used by Anglo-Saxon Preachers*, Londres, 1987 (King's College London Medieval Studies, 1).
DECLERCQ, G., «La *Vita prima Bavonis* et le culte de saint Bavon à l'époque carolingienne», in É. RENARD *et al.*, dir., *Scribere sanctorum gesta. Recueil d'études d'hagiographie médiévale offert à Guy Philippart*, Turnhout, 2005, p. 595-626 (Hagiologia, 3).
DIESENBERGER, M. – WOLFRAM, H., «Arn und Alkuin, 790 bis 804. Zwei Freunde und ihre Schriften», in M. NIEDERKORN-BRUCK – A. SCHARER, dir., *Erzbischof Arn von Salzburg*, Vienne – Munich, 2004 (Veröffentlichungen des IÖG, 40), p. 81-106.
—, «Der Prediger als Konstituent des sozialen Raumes», in D. R. BAUER *et al.*, dir., *Heilige – Liturgie – Raum*, Stuttgart, 2010, p. 27-48 (Beiträge zur Hagiographie, 8).
DOLBEAU, F., «Le légendier de l'abbaye cistercienne de Clairmarais», *AB*, 91 (1973), p. 273-286.

—, « À propos d'un sermon sur S. Possesseur, évêque de Verdun », *AB*, 98 (1980), p. 386.

—, « Du nouveau sur un sermonnaire de Cambridge », *Scriptorium*, 42 (1988), p. 255-257 (compte rendu de CROSS 1987).

DRÄGER, P., « St. Willibrord als ambulanter Wunderheiler in Trier: Alkuin und Thiofrid, *Vita sancti Willibrordi* », *Kurtrierisches Jahrbuch*, 48 (2008), p. 65-99.

DROUT, M. D. C., *How Tradition Works. A Meme-Based Cultural Poetics of the Anglo-Saxon Tenth Century*, Tempe, AZ, 2006 (Medieval and Renaissance Texts and Studies, 306).

EL KHOLI, S., *Lektüre in Frauenkonventen des ostfränkish-deutschen Reiches vom 8. Jahrhundert bis zur Mitte des 13. Jahrhunderts*, Würzburg, 1997 (Epistemata. Würzburger Wissenschaftliche Schriften, Reihe Literaturwissenschaft, 203).

ELLARD, G., « Remnants of a Tenth-Century Sacramentary from Fulda », *Ephemerides liturgicae*, 44 (1930), p. 208-220.

FOX, M., « Alcuin's Expositio in epistolam ad Hebræos », *Journal of Medieval Latin*, 18 (2008), p. 326-345.

GANZ, D., *Corbie in the Carolingian Renaissance*, Sigmaringen, 1990 (Beihefte der Francia, 20).

—, « Le *De laude Dei* d'Alcuin », *Annales de Bretagne*, 111/3 (2004), p. 387-391.

GJERLØW, L., *Adoratio Crucis. The* Regularis Concordia *and the* Decreta Lanfranci. *Manuscript Studies in the Early Medieval Church of Norway*, Oslo, 1961.

—, *Liturgica islandica*, I: *Text*, Copenhague, 1980.

GORMAN, M. M., « Alcuin before Migne », *Revue bénédictine*, 112 (2002), p. 101-130; réimpr. in ID., *The Study of the Bible in the Early Middle Ages*, Florence, 2007, p. 347-376 (Millennio medievale, 67; Strumenti e studi, n.s. 15).

HALL, T. N., « Latin Sermons for Saints in Early English Homiliaries and Legendaries », in A. J. KLEIST, dir., *The Old English Homily. Precedent, Practice, and Appropriation*, Turnhout, 2007, p. 227-263 (Studies in the Early Middle Ages, 17).

HAMMER, C. I., « "For All the Saints": Bishop Vivolo of Passau and the Eighth-Century Origins of the Feast », *Revue Mabillon*, n.s. 15 (t. 76), (2004), p. 5-26.

HELVÉTIUS, A.-M., « Clercs ou moines? Les origines de Saint-Vaast d'Arras et la *Vita Vedastis* attribuée à Jonas », *Revue du Nord*, 93 (2011), n°s 293-294, p. 671-689 (= *Mélanges Stéphane Lebecq*).

HOLTZ, L., « Alcuin et la réception de Virgile du temps de Charlemagne », in H. SCHEFERS, dir., *Einhard. Studien zu Leben und Werk. Dem Gedenken an Helmut Beumann gewidmet*, Darmstadt, 1997,

p. 67-80 (Arbeiten der Hessischen Historischen Kommission, N.F. 12).

Huglo, M., «Un missel de Saint-Riquier (Wien, Österr. N. B. 1933)», *Ephemerides liturgicae*, 73 (1959), p. 402-412 (réimpr. dans Id., *Les sources du plain-chant et de la musique médiévale*, Aldershot, 2006, n° VII).

Hussey, M. T., «*Transmarinis litteris*. Southumbria and the Transmission of Isidore's *Synonyma*», *Journal of English and Germanic Philology*, 107 (2008), p. 141-168.

I Deug-Su, *L'opera agiografica di Alcuino*, Spolète, 1983 (Biblioteca degli «Studi medievali», 13). [L'introduction et les chapitres relatifs à saint Willibrord, saint Vaast et saint Martin avaient déjà paru dans la revue *Studi medievali* en 1980 et 1981].

James, E., «Alcuin and York in the Eighth Century», in P. L. Butzer – D. Lohrmann, dir., *Science in Western and Eastern Civilization in Carolingian Times*, Bâle, 1993, p. 23-39.

Jullien, M.-H., «Les hymnes dans le milieu alcuinien», in L. Holtz – J.-C. Fredouille, dir., *De Tertullien aux Mozarabes*, II: *Antiquité tardive et christianisme ancien (VIe-IXe siècles). Mélanges offerts à Jacques Fontaine*, Paris, 1992, p. 171-182 (Collection des Études augustiniennes, Série Moyen Âge et Temps modernes, 26).

Kohlmann, P. W., *Adam von Bremen. Ein Beitrag zur mittelalterlichen Textkritik und Kosmographie*, Leipzig, 1908 (Leipziger historische Abhandlungen, 10).

Lapidge, M., «A Tenth-Century Metrical Calendar from Ramsey», *Revue bénédictine*, 94 (1984), p. 326-369 (réimpr. in Id., *Anglo-Latin Literature, 900-1066*, Londres – Rio Grande, 1996, p. 343-386).

—, «Ædilulf and the School of York», in A. Lehner – W. Berschin, dir., *Lateinische Kultur im VIII. Jahrhundert. Traube Gedenkschrift*, St. Ottilien, 1990, p. 161-178 (réimpr. in Id., *Anglo-Latin Literature, 600-899*, Londres – Rio Grande, 1996, p. 381-398).

—, *The Anglo-Saxon Library*, Oxford, 2006.

Lapidge, M. — Love, R., «The Latin Hagiography of England and Wales (600-1550)», in *Hagiographies*, III (2001), p. 203-325.

Levison, W., «An Eighth-Century Poem on St. Ninian», *Antiquity*, 14 (1940), p. 280-291.

Lochner, F. C., *La culture musicale de l'abbaye d'Echternach au Moyen Âge*, 2 vol., Bruxelles, 1988; thèse dactylographiée consultable au Département de musique de la BnF.

Lockett, L., «Alcuinus», in M. Lapidge et al., dir., *Compendium auctorum latinorum Medii Ævi: 500-1500*, t. I-2, Florence, 2000, p. 145-153.

LOTTER, F. – GÄBE, S., «Die hagiographische Literatur im deutschen Sprachraum unter den Ottonen und Saliern (ca. 960-1130)», in *Hagiographies*, IV (2006), p. 273-521.
MEYER, H. – SUNTRUP, R., art. «33», *Lexikon der mittelalterlichen Zahlenbedeutungen*, Munich, 1987, col. 703-706 (Münstersche Mittelalter-Schriften, 56).
MEYER, H. B., «Alkuin zwischen Antike und Mittelalter. Ein Kapitel frühmittelalterlicher Frömmigkeitsgeschichte», *Zeischrift für katholische Theologie*, 81 (1959), p. 306-350 et 405-454.
MORDEK, H., «Von Patrick zu Bonifatius... Alkuin, Ferrières und die irischen Heiligen in einem westfränkisches Reliquien-verzeichnis», in K. HERBERS *et al.*, dir., *Ex ipsis rerum documentis. Beiträge zur Mediävistik. Festschrift für Harald Zimmermann zum 65. Geburtstag*, Sigmaringen, 1991, p. 55-68.
MULLINS, J., «Tracing the Tracks of Alcuin's *Vita sancti Martini*», in J. ROBERTS – L. E. WEBSTER, dir., *Anglo-Saxon Traces*, Tempe, AZ, 2011, p. 165-179 (Medieval and Renaissance Texts and Studies, 405; Essays in Anglo-Saxon Studies, 4).
ORCHARD, N., «An Anglo-Saxon Mass for St Willibrord and its Later Liturgical Uses», *Anglo-Saxon England*, 24 (1995), p. 1-10.
—, «A Note on the Masses for St Cuthbert», *Revue bénédictine*, 105 (1995), p. 79-98.
—, «St Willibrord, St Richarius, and Anglo-Saxon Symptoms in three Mass-Books from Northern France», *Revue bénédictine*, 110 (2000), p. 261-283.
ORTENBERG, V., «Le culte de sainte Marie Madeleine dans l'Angleterre anglo-saxonne», *Mélanges de l'École française de Rome – Moyen Âge*, 104 (1992), p. 13-35.
OURY, G., «Les messes de saint Martin dans les sacramentaires gallicans, romano-francs et milanais», *Études grégoriennes*, 5 (1962), p. 73-97.
PABST, B., *Prosimetrum: Tradition und Wandel einer Literaturform zwischen Spätantike und Spätmittelalter*, 2 vol., Cologne, 1994 (Ordo, 4).
PADBERG, L. VON, *Heilige und Familie. Studien zur Bedeutung familiengebundener Aspekte in den Viten des Verwandten- und Schülerkreises um Willibrord, Bonifatius und Liudger*, 2e éd., Mayence, 1997 (Quellen und Abhandlungen zur mittelrheinischen Kirchengeschichte, 83).
PALAZZO, É., *Les sacramentaires de Fulda: étude sur l'iconographie et la liturgie à l'époque ottonienne*, Münster, 1994 (Liturgiewissenschaftliche Quellen und Forschungen, 77).
PALMER, J. T., *Anglo-Saxons in a Frankish World, 600-900*, Turnhout, 2009 (Studies in the Early Middle Ages, 19).
PERRIN, M. J.-L., «La poésie de cour carolingienne, les contacts entre Alcuin et Hraban Maur et les indices de l'influence d'Alcuin sur

l'*In honorem sanctae Crucis*», *Annales de Bretagne*, 111/3 (2004), p. 333-351.
PFAFF, R. W., *The Liturgy in Medieval England: A History*, Cambridge, 2009.
POULIN, J.-C., «Un élément négligé de critique hagiographique: les titres de chapitres», in É. RENARD *et al.*, dir., Scribere sanctorum gesta. *Recueil d'études d'hagiographie médiévale offert à Guy Philippart*, Turnhout, 2005, p. 309-342 (Hagiologia, 3).
—, *L'hagiographie bretonne du haut Moyen Âge. Répertoire raisonné*, Ostfildern, 2009 (Beihefte der Francia, 69).
— «Remanier Alcuin hagiographe (IXe-XIe siècles)», in J. ELFASSI *et al.*, dir., Amicorum societas. *Mélanges offerts à François Dolbeau pour son 65e anniversaire*, Florence, 2013, p. 665-697 (Millennio medievale, 96; Strumenti e studi, n.s. 34).
—, «La circulation des œuvres hagiographiques d'Alcuin (IXe-XIe siècles)», *Hagiographica*, 22 (2015), p. 167-216 et 23 (2016), p. 1-41.
PRÉVOT, F. – GAILLARD, M. – GAUTHIER, N., dir., *Topographie chrétienne des cités de la Gaule, des origines au milieu du VIIIe siècle*, XVI: *Quarante ans d'enquête (1972-2012)*, II: *Christianisation et espace urbain. Atlas, tableaux, index*, Paris, 2014.
REICHSMANN, H.-J., *Willibrord – Apostel der Friesen. Seine Vita nach Alkuin und Thiofrid*, Sigmaringendorf, 1989.
RICHARD, P., «"Sur la cendre et avec le cilice". Ornementation rhétorique et pudeur philosophique à l'âge carolingien», *Revue des sciences philosophiques et théologiques*, 100 (2016), p. 45-59; pour la *Vita s. Richarii* d'Alcuin.
ROTH, F. W. E., «Das Missale und Antiphonarium der Abtei Echternach o.s.b. saec. X in der Gr. Hofbibliothek zu Darmstadt», *Romanische Forschungen*, 6 (1891) (réimpr. New York, 1967), p. 271-284.
SCHROEDER, J. – TRAUFFLER, H., «Zu den Anfängen des Williborduskloster in Echternach», *Eiflia Sacra* (Mayence), 70 (1994), p. 29-53.
—, *Die Anfänge der Abtei Echternach. Von der «Villa Epternacus» zum frühmittelalterlichen Wallfahrtszentrum*, Luxembourg, 1996 (Publications de CLUDEM, 9).
STAPLETON, P. J., «Alcuin's York Poem and Liturgical Contexts: Oswald's Adoration of the Cross», *Medium Ævum*, 82 (2013), p. 189-212.
STRECKER, K., «Zu den Quellen für das Leben des hl. Ninian», *Neues Archiv*, 43 (1922), p. 1-26.

TISCHLER, M. M., «Alcuin, biographe de Charlemagne. Possibilités et limites de l'historiographie littéraire au Moyen Âge», *Annales de Bretagne*, 111/3 (2004), p. 443-459.

TREFFORT, C., «La place d'Alcuin dans la rédaction épigraphique carolingienne», *Annales de Bretagne*, 111/3 (2004), p. 353-369.

—, *Mémoires carolingiennes. L'épitaphe entre célébration mémorielle, genre littéraire et manifeste politique (milieu VIIIe – début XIe siècle)*, Rennes, 2007.

VEYRARD-COSME, C., «Littérature latine du haut Moyen Âge et idéologie politique. L'exemple d'Alcuin», *Revue des études latines*, 72 (1994), p. 192-207.

—, *«Tacitus Nuntius». Recherches sur l'écriture des «Lettres» d'Alcuin (730?-804)*, Paris, 2013 (Collection des Études augustiniennes, Série Moyen Âge et Temps Modernes, 50).

WALLACH, L., «The Origin of the Manuscript Collections of Alcuin's Letters», *Traditio*, 9 (1953), p. 149-154 (réimpr. In ID., *Alcuin and Charlemagne. Studies in Carolingian History and Literature*, Ithaca, NY, 1959, p. 266-274).

WILMART, A., «Un témoin anglo-saxon du calendrier métrique d'York», *Revue bénédictine*, 46 (1934), p. 41-69.

WOOD, I. N., *The Missionary Life: Saints and the Evangelisation of Europe, 400-1050*, Harlow, 2001.

L'écriture hagiographique dans la province de Tours (env. 750-950)

Une place tout particulière a été accordée à l'œuvre hagiographique d'Alcuin, abbé de Saint-Martin de Tours de 796 à sa mort en 804, car toute sa production hagiographique, qui touche à de nombreuses régions, n'a probablement pas été rédigée à Tours-même. Étant donné l'importance et la diversité géographique des objets de son œuvre, il nous a paru indispensable de lui consacrer un chapitre en tête de la section (du chap. XI: Aire française) consacrée à l'hagiographie latine 750-950[1].

Dans le diocèse de Tours proprement dit, aucune autre œuvre hagiographique que celle d'Alcuin n'est attribuable à cette période, excepté la Vita Alcuini (*BHL* 242), récemment éditée, traduite et étudiée par Christine Veyrard-Cosme qui établit qu'elle a été écrite vers 820 à Tours, à l'encontre d'une tradition qui voulait qu'elle fut rédigée à l'abbaye de Ferrières, dans le diocèse de Sens[2] et, peut-être, «La confession de saint Martin», une glose sur le Credo, qui n'est pas à proprement parler une œuvre hagiographique et apparaît dans la première série des *Martinelli* copiés à Tours sous l'abbatiat d'Alcuin[3].

Les diocèses bretons dépendant de la métropole tourangelle trouvent donc naturellement leur place dans cette section, ainsi que les diocèses du Mans et d'Angers.

En revanche, dans le diocèse de Nantes, presque aucune production hagiographique ne peut être attribuée à la période carolingienne. Selon A.-M. Bultot-Verleysen (*Hagiographies*, VI, p. 536-530), de l'œuvre d'Ermentaire relative à saint Philibert (*BHL* 6805-6809), seule la première partie des Miracles de saint Philibert a pu être rédigée vers 837-838, lors du séjour des

---

[1] Cf. POULIN, J.-C., «Alcuin hagiographe», *supra*, p. 145-184.
[2] *Ibid.*, n. 1, p. 145. Sur l'hypothèse sénonaise, *AASS*, Mai. IV, 1685, p. 333.
[3] Mise au point récente par W. PEZÉ, «Aux origines de la *Confession de saint Martin*», *Revue Mabillon*, n.s. 25 (t. 86) (2014), p. 5-44.

moines de Saint-Philibert à Déas (auj. Saint-Philbert); la Vie remaniée de saint Philibert a sans doute été élaborée à Noirmoutier et les autres Miracles dans le Poitou, lors du transfert du corps de Cunault à Messais[4]. La vie d'Aemilianus (*BHL* 105), supposé évêque de Nantes, inconnu des listes épiscopales[5] et tué par les Sarrasins à Bourbon-Lancy dans le diocèse d'Autun, au temps de Charles Martel, a sans doute été écrite au plus tôt au XIIe siècle[6]. Clarus (*BHL* 1824), censé avoir été le premier évêque de Nantes, est mentionné pour la première fois dans le catalogue épiscopal ajouté à la fin d'un manuscrit du XIIe siècle de la chronique de Saint-Aubin d'Angers[7]. Enfin, l'évêque Gunhardus (*BHL* 3712), tué par les Normands dans sa cathédrale en 843 n'a fait l'objet d'aucune *Vita*[8].

---

[4] A.-M. BULTOT-VERLEYSEN, «Hagiographie d'Aquitaine (750-1130)», in *Hagiographies*, VI (2014), p. 521-704, en part. p. 536-530.

[5] Cf. L. DUCHESNE, *Fastes épiscopaux de l'ancienne Gaule*, II: *L'Aquitaine et les Lyonnaises*, 2e éd., Paris, 1910, p. 369.

[6] Comme le suggère la mention de Charlemagne et de Roland (*AASS*, Iun. V, 1709, p. 81-82).

[7] Ce catalogue qui se termine avec la mention de l'évêque Robert († 1184?), a dû être rédigé à la fin du XIIe siècle; le premier témoin de sa légende se trouve dans un livre liturgique nantais de 1263 (DUCHESNE, II, p. 365).

[8] Toutefois, l'auteur de la «Chronique de Nantes» vraisemblablement rédigée peu après 1050, semble reprendre le récit d'un témoin oculaire (DUCHESNE, II, p. 369; R. MERLET éd., *La Chronique de Nantes*, 1896, p. 14-17).

Lieux mentionnés dans les chapitres sur la province de Tours

L'hagiographie bretonne
avant l'an mil

par

Joseph-Claude POULIN

I. PRÉSENTATION GÉNÉRALE. – A. Cadre géographique. – B. Cadre chronologique. – C. Typologie de la sainteté. – D. Sources et transmission. – E. Modalités de mise en écriture. – Conclusion. – Bibliographie.
II. RÉPERTOIRE DE L'HAGIOGRAPHIE BRETONNE ANTÉRIEURE À L'AN MIL. – A. Tableau de la production hagiographique. – B. Bibliographie générale complémentaire. – C. Dossiers individuels. – 1. Conwoion de Redon († 868). – 2. Ethbinus/Idunetus. – 3. Judocus de Saint-Josse-sur-Mer. – 4. Lenoverius/Leonorius. – 5. Machutes d'Alet. – 6. Maglorius de Dol. – 7. Melanius de Rennes († c. 530). – 8. Meroveus; – 9. Paulus Aurelianus de Saint-Pol de Léon – 10. Samson de Dol († c. 565?). – 11. Turiavus de Dol. – 12. Wenailus. – 13. Winnocus. – 14. Winwaloeus de Landévennec.

I. PRÉSENTATION GÉNÉRALE

A. CADRE GÉOGRAPHIQUE

Comment circonscrire l'espace visé par une enquête sur l'histoire de l'hagiographie bretonne la plus ancienne ? La structure diocésaine est peu efficace pour tracer des frontières claires. Trois diocèses d'origine tardo-antique sont en place de façon assurée au début de la période médiévale: Rennes, Nantes et Vannes relèvent de la province ecclésiastique de Tours. L'existence d'un diocèse gallo-romain à Alet (plus tard Saint-Malo) paraît en effet douteuse. Le reste de la péninsule armoricaine n'a connu que progressivement l'érection de sièges épiscopaux: Alet (à la fin du VIIIe siècle), Saint-Pol (au IXe siècle), Quimper, Saint-Brieuc et Tréguier (pas avant le Xe siècle). La mise en place d'un diocèse émietté en lien avec Dol-de-Bretagne résulta d'un processus mal élucidé, sans doute progressif jusqu'à son affirmation péremptoire au début de la seconde moitié du IXe siècle; mais on peut difficilement la faire remonter jusqu'à l'époque de son fondateur putatif, saint Samson († c. 565?).

La définition d'un espace propre à l'hagiographie bretonne est encore compliquée par deux facteurs adverses:

– D'une part, l'espace contrôlé par les Bretons a connu de fortes variations pendant la période considérée[1]. Pour autant, il n'y a pas lieu d'inclure dans ce panorama la production hagiographique des diocèses de Nantes ni d'Angers, et encore moins celle du Cotentin et de l'Avranchin (momentanément sous contrôle breton autour de 900)[2]: elle appartient à d'autres provinces d'écriture.

– Un second facteur encore plus puissant vient perturber l'établissement d'un répertoire raisonné de l'hagiographie bretonne: de nombreux cas se présentent en effet, de rédactions relatives à des saints bretons effectuées hors de la région de Petite Bretagne, par des hagiographes souvent non bretons. Cette production *in partibus* sera inventoriée, mais pas analysée ici comme telle; son énumération la plus complète possible permettra du moins de la tirer du quasi-oubli dans lequel son caractère marginal l'a souvent confinée. Quelques allusions partielles seulement la laissent entrevoir à l'état dispersé dans les chapitres déjà publiés de la présente *Histoire internationale*; mais cette production de la diaspora appartient plutôt à l'histoire des régions où elle est apparue.

Ce choix éditorial diffère donc de celui qui a été choisi pour l'hagiographie irlandaise dans la même collection; Máire Herbert a en effet décidé de laisser de côté les *Vitae* des saints irlandais *peregrini*, au bon motif qu'elles appartiennent plutôt à l'histoire de l'hagiographie continentale[3]. Le cas des saints bre-

---

[1] Ces fluctuations ont souvent fait l'objet de représentations cartographiques. Parmi les exemples récents, voir: TANGUY – LAGRÉE (2002), p. 63 et 67 (cartes n° 26 et 28); BÜHRER-THIERRY – MÉRIAUX (2010), p. 389, reprenant une carte de CASSARD (2002), p. 327. Ou encore CINTRÉ (2011), p. 31. Pour d'autres cartes plus anciennes, cf. les références de POULIN (2009), p. 33, n. 15.

[2] VAN TORHOUDT (2008), I, p. 84-141 et III (cartes). Ou, plus succinctement, LUNVEN (2014), p. 66 sq.

[3] HERBERT (2001), p. 329. La matière hagiographique bretonne a déjà été traitée pour la période 950-1130 par VAN 'T SPIJKER (1996).

tons se présente différemment, car aucune œuvre hagiographique ancienne n'a été composée à leur propos au Pays de Galles ni dans les Cornouailles quand leur carrière s'est déroulée en partie sur le continent.

La création hagiographique est une activité très décentralisée en Bretagne du haut Moyen Âge; aucun centre de production ne possède de prééminence significative, qu'il soit monastique ou épiscopal[4]. D'ailleurs, la distinction entre centre monastique ou épiscopal est peu significative, car des Vies de saints évêques furent aussi composées dans des monastères: Léhon pour saint Magloire, Landévennec pour saint Paul Aurélien. Cumulativement, les dossiers hagiographiques des saints Guénolé et Paul Aurélien constituent une masse documentaire inégalée; mais cela ne suffit pas à faire de Landévennec une école dominante dans l'espace breton, d'autant que ces textes ont assez peu circulé.

La frontière linguistique séparant les domaines breton et roman est aussi inadaptée au découpage d'une aire propre à la production hagiographique bretonne; suivre la «ligne Loth» en son tracé du IXe siècle[5] laisserait en effet de côté des centres de production qui font manifestement partie de l'espace hagiographique breton à l'époque carolingienne. La large réception de la *Vita s. Martini* de Sulpice Sévère un peu partout chez les hagiographes bretons amène à nuancer le clivage culturel qu'A. Lunven croit observer de part et d'autre de la frontière entre les zones bretonnante et gallo-franque[6].

B. Cadre chronologique

L'histoire générale de la péninsule armoricaine pendant le haut Moyen Âge est scandée par plusieurs phases remarquables susceptibles d'avoir influencé le rythme et le contenu de l'écriture relative aux saints bretons: l'héritage gallo-romain, les migrations bretonnes, les rapports avec les Mérovingiens, la

---

[4] Voir un essai de cartographie des centres de production hagiographique par MERDRIGNAC (1993), p. 13 ou encore MORICE (2007), t. II, p. 504.

[5] Représentation cartographique de cette ligne par GARAULT (2011), «L'abbaye de Saint-Sauveur de Redon», p. 53 ou LUNVEN (2014), p. 19.

[6] LUNVEN (2014), p. 355.

montée de l'influence carolingienne, le choc des agressions des vikings suivies de la dispersion des élites religieuses.

Ces moments successifs ont cependant agi avec une force inégale sur le travail des hagiographes. De l'époque gallo-romaine, seul le souvenir de saint Melaine de Rennes († vers 530) a suscité une création hagiographique narrative, mais guère avant le IXe siècle[7]. Par la suite, ce sont les saints d'origine bretonne (insulaire ou continentale), présumés actifs au VIe siècle, qui monopolisent l'attention des hagiographes bretons; mais cette mise en écriture ne s'effectue pas pendant la période dite mérovingienne, à l'exception probable d'une recension primitive (maintenant perdue) de la Vie de saint Samson de Dol (fin VIIe siècle?). Car c'est à la seconde moitié du IXe siècle que se situe l'âge d'or de l'ancienne hagiographie bretonne, soit bien plus tard que les débuts de l'hagiographie latine irlandaise (seconde moitié du VIIe siècle), mais bien avant les débuts de l'hagiographie galloise (fin du XIe siècle) ou cornouaillaise (plus tard encore). Les enjeux de l'intégration à l'espace carolingien ont agi comme un moteur puissant pour la mise en scène hagiographique des rapports parfois conflictuels (voir la querelle autour du statut métropolitain de Dol), mais le plus souvent sereins avec le monde franc. Les attaques vikings ont mis fin brutalement à cet essor vers la fin du IXe siècle, provoquant une dispersion (générale après 920) hors de la péninsule armoricaine des communautés ecclésiastiques, des textes, des manuscrits et des reliques[8]. Les hagiographes bretons ne reprendront pas la plume en Armorique avant la fin du Xe siècle au plus tôt, après le retour partiel des exilés, dans un contexte de restauration ecclésiastique complètement différent.

C. Typologie de la sainteté

L'histoire de la sainteté bretonne est d'abord une affaire d'hommes, qui seuls ont retenu l'attention des hagiographes

---

[7] Une exception mineure: un récit de miracle de saint Melaine à Rennes, raconté par Grégoire de Tours (*BHL* 5892).

[8] Nous ne croyons pas que cette césure puisse se réduire à un simple mirage historiographique, malgré SMITH (1992), p. 200 sq.; la Bretagne fut bien submergée par les vikings au début du Xe siècle, selon PRICE (2013), p. 733 et 739.

avant l'an mil; il n'y a pas de saintes femmes aux hautes époques – Leuférine[9], Ninnoca et Osmanna attendront[10]. Cette histoire ne commence qu'au VIe siècle; il ne s'y trouve donc pas de saints martyrs, pas même politiques. Les vieux saints bretons ne sont pas davantage des évangélisateurs, car ils débarquent ou circulent dans une contrée déjà chrétienne; quand ils se heurtent à une opposition, leurs épreuves viennent de mauvais chrétiens et non de païens récalcitrants. Une scène comme celle de la conversion de païens par saint Samson traversant les Cornouailles insulaires ne se répète pas sur le continent, ni pour lui ni pour les autres saints bretons. Saint Lunaire reçoit bien le mandat de traverser la Manche pour évangéliser les païens; mais il ne fait rien de tel une fois installé sur le continent. L'hagiographie bretonne n'est donc pas une hagiographie missionnaire. Elle concerne exclusivement des saints bretons (sauf le Gallo-Romain Melaine, et peut-être aussi saint Mervé, au nom plus franc que breton) actifs dans la péninsule armoricaine (saint Samson déborde en Neustrie), et non ceux de l'Église universelle[11].

La moitié des vieux saints bretons, sur lesquels on a écrit avant l'an mil, est d'origine insulaire; l'autre moitié est née sur le continent dans une famille d'immigrants. Mais il ne semble pas y avoir de différence de traitement entre les uns et les autres. Ils sont tous d'origine sociale élevée, sauf Mervé et Turiau, pour lesquels nous ne possédons aucune indication particulière. Dans deux cas seulement, il s'agit de saints prêtres, sans plus; mais l'appartenance de saint Mervé et saint Josse au corpus de l'hagiographie bretonne est plutôt marginale. L'ancienne hagiographie bretonne est avant tout une hagiographie épiscopale; majoritaires en nombre, les évêques se rapprochent cependant des saints fondateurs de monastères (Conwoion, Guénolé, Mervé, Josse) par leur goût prononcé pour la vie érémitique avant, pendant ou après leur épiscopat. La caractéristique principale du parcours de tous les saints bretons est leur inclination pour une vie érémitique; à telle enseigne que plusieurs évêques (Malo, Magloire, Paul Aurélien) ont fini par abdiquer leur charge pour se retirer hors du siècle, en ermites ou chefs de com-

---
[9] CHIRON (2018).
[10] CASSARD (2003).
[11] SMITH (1990), p. 357.

munauté monastique[12]. Pour le reste, les saints bretons sont des thaumaturges, sans spécialité particulière; ils ne manifestent pas de préférence marquée pour des prodiges en milieu urbain, rural ou maritime (sauf pour saint Magloire, plus souvent au bord de l'eau). Comme il est d'usage, les Vies bretonnes enregistrent les donations foncières accordées aux saints. En tant que personnalités publiques, les saints bretons entrent en relation avec des chefs politiques, bretons ou francs: Clovis pour saint Melaine, Conomor et Childebert Ier pour les autres saints de l'époque mérovingienne, Nominoé et Louis le Pieux pour saint Conwoion.

L'effort des hagiographes a porté essentiellement sur la vie des saints, assez peu sur leurs miracles *post mortem*; du moins sous la forme d'un recueil indépendant (comme pour saint Magloire et peut-être saint Melaine). Ces biographies possèdent souvent une valeur de «récit des origines», dans la mesure où la plupart des saints sont célébrés en tant que fondateurs de monastères (Samson, Guénolé, Conwoion) ou de diocèses (Malo, Paul Aurélien; Magloire et Turiau sont réputés être des successeurs de Samson sur le siège de Dol).

D. Sources et transmission

Une grande distance sépare généralement le parcours terrestre des saints bretons et la mise par écrit de leurs exploits. Cet écart chronologique n'a pas dissuadé les premiers biographes d'invoquer des sources écrites à l'appui de leur travail; mais de telles prétentions sont à ranger le plus souvent au rayon des lieux communs. Dans quelques cas seulement, l'existence d'un écrit antérieur à la première *Vita* conservée est digne de foi: c'est certain pour saint Melaine et saint Guénolé, probable pour saint Samson, possible pour saint Lunaire et saint Turiau. Partout ailleurs, il s'agit d'une reconstruction tardive, à laquelle l'invocation rituelle de sources orales n'ajoute pas beaucoup de crédibilité. La seule exception à ce *modus operandi* concerne saint Conwoion, dont les hauts faits furent consignés par un contemporain, témoin direct; et encore s'agit-il plus d'une histoire des

---

[12] N'entre pas dans ce compte le cas légendaire de saint Lunaire, devenu évêque au Pays de Galles à l'âge de 15 ans et qui, lors de sa mort, serait abbé d'un monastère continental non localisé.

débuts du monastère de Redon (fondé en 832) que d'une biographie de son saint fondateur à proprement parler.

Les premiers pas de l'hagiographie bretonne surviennent dans une pénombre documentaire qui complique grandement les efforts de datation et de mise en contexte; en tout cas, il ne faut les chercher ni en milieu insulaire, ni dans une autre langue que le latin (par opposition à l'ancienne hagiographie irlandaise). L'écriture hagiographique sur les saints bretons est une affaire continentale et non pas galloise, malgré l'origine des saints; elle appartient bien au domaine de la littérature latine, malgré quelques prétentions tardives et peu crédibles à l'existence de sources en langue vernaculaire (évidemment perdues). L'œuvre la plus ancienne est assurément la Vie de saint Samson; sa biographie dite «ancienne» est cependant déjà une réécriture, à notre avis[13]. Une version primitive, composée à Dol par un écrivain qui pourrait être d'origine insulaire (vers la fin du VIIe siècle?) n'est plus connue que par son remodelage et son allongement effectués encore à Dol, un siècle plus tard. Cette réécriture pourrait constituer une réponse à la pression carolingienne en vue d'une régularisation de l'organisation diocésaine en Bretagne.

Malgré sa précocité relative, la première hagiographie samsonienne n'a pas déclenché aussitôt un mouvement général de fixation de la mémoire des origines bretonnes par la voie hagiographique; il faut attendre la seconde moitié du IXe siècle pour voir éclore cette opération, au moment où une nouvelle réécriture de la Vie de saint Samson proclame ouvertement les ambitions métropolitaines de Dol, au détriment de Tours. Saint Magloire, et peut-être saint Turiau, en tant que successeurs supposés de Samson sur le siège de Dol, se voient alors attribuer à leur tour une dignité archiépiscopale. Mais contrairement à ce qu'on aurait pu attendre, le reste de l'hagiographie bretonne ancienne ne s'inscrit pas dans un climat polémique: ni Guénolé, ni Paul Aurélien, ni Melaine, ne prennent position dans ce débat d'actualité. Seul se distingue saint Malo, que son biographe Bili d'Alet envoie ostensiblement se faire consacrer évêque par le métropolitain de Tours; mais deux Vies anonymes de saint Malo prennent aussitôt le contrepied de ce contestataire. Le rédacteur

---

[13] C'est l'une des conclusions de notre communication au colloque de Sydney en 2013: POULIN (2017).

des *Gesta sanctorum Rotonensium* évite d'engager saint Conwoion trop clairement dans l'un ou l'autre parti: saint Samson et saint Martin de Tours y sont présentés sur un pied d'égalité en tant qu'«archevêques» (en III-3).

Pourtant, le dossier samsonien a largement circulé en Bretagne et fut fort apprécié des hagiographes bretons; à preuve, le caractère quasi général des emprunts formels qui lui furent faits. Ces emprunts prennent parfois un caractère massif, comme dans la Vie de saint Lunaire[14]. Une autre manifestation de la force d'attraction du dossier samsonien est révélée par la propension de plusieurs hagiographes bretons à imaginer des relations de cousinage de leurs héros respectifs avec le grand modèle ès sainteté: la diffusion progressive de cet apparentement flatteur se saisit d'abord dans la grande Vie de saint Magloire (et à sa suite dans la Vie anonyme brève de saint Malo), dans la grande Vie de saint Malo par Bili et la Vie de saint Paul Aurélien (cette fois au profit du duc Judual de Domnonée)[15].

Quelques saints bretons d'Armorique étaient connus hors de la péninsule avant la fin du IXe siècle[16], mais pas au point d'y susciter une production hagiographique narrative, à l'exception d'un miracle de saint Melaine par Grégoire de Tours[17]. C'est l'exode provoqué par les attaques vikings qui a entraîné l'ouverture de ce nouveau chapitre de l'histoire de l'hagiographie bretonne. Mais contrairement à ce qui s'observe ailleurs dans l'Occident carolingien, ces déplacements effectués dans l'urgence n'ont pas provoqué la mise par écrit de récits de translation; la plupart des quelques transferts racontés par l'hagiographie bretonne sont des vols (Malo, Magloire, Apothème d'Angers [dans les *Gesta* de Redon]) plutôt que des fuites devant les vikings. Le déplacement des reliques de saint Mai-

---

[14] Un tel air de famille reliant plusieurs Vies de saints issues d'un même milieu ne constitue pas un trait exclusif de l'hagiographie bretonne; un phénomène d'homogénéité relative se rencontre aussi dans l'hagiographie hispanique du VIIe siècle, par exemple. Cf. HENRIET (2012), p. 95.

[15] Essai de mise en tableau généalogique de ce réseau de parenté chez POULIN (2009), p. 174, n. 88. Ce cycle de cousinage imaginaire se prolonge au-delà de l'an mil: saint Méen est ajouté au XIe siècle.

[16] Cf. deux articles complémentaires sur ce sujet: MERDRIGNAC (1991) et POULIN (1993).

[17] Un sermon de Loup de Ferrières pour la fête de saint Josse ne parle pas du tout du saint lui-même.

xent de Plélan (une dépendance de Redon) à Poitiers relève d'une négociation complexe[18]. Il faut chercher dans le cartulaire de Redon un récit de la translation de saint Conwoion de Redon à Poitiers vers 920[19]. Il n'y a pas à tenir compte de la prétendue translation carolingienne des reliques de saint Brieuc à Angers, racontée dans un *additamentum* à sa Vie longue (*BHL* 1463) vers le milieu du XIe siècle[20]. Il est impossible de savoir si des reliques de saint Benoît de Macérac furent transportées à Redon dès le IXe siècle; sa mise par écrit est bien trop tardive (*BHL* 1145, XIIIe siècle). Vers 925, le prévôt Radbod de Dol a offert des reliques au roi anglais Æthelstan; mais ce transit n'est pas documenté sous la forme d'un récit de translation[21].

Les enjeux de défense territoriale ou de revendication foncière occupent une place modeste dans l'ancienne hagiographie bretonne, contrairement à ce qui s'observe parfois ailleurs[22]. C'est dans les Vies de saint Malo qu'on les voit affleurer le plus nettement[23]. L'auteur de la première Vie de saint Tugdual (*BHL* 8350) les avait peut-être aussi en tête, mais sa rédaction ne paraît pas antérieure à la seconde moitié du XIe siècle, et non pas du IXe comme on l'a longtemps pensé.

Les rédactions hagiographiques relatives à des saints bretons, mais effectuées hors de la péninsule armoricaine, se laissent ré-

---

[18] Dans ce dernier cas, d'après une notice du Cartulaire de Redon, acte n° 241, daté de 869: de POERCK (1962), p. 61 sq. et 94 sq. Article prolongé par MAZEL (2015).
[19] Cartulaire de Redon, acte n° 23, p. 228 sq. La BORDERIE (1898), t. II, p. 362 sq.
[20] *BHL* 1463. Inversion du rapport entre les versions longue et courte, proposée par MORIN (2010), p. 256. Si elle a existé, cette translation (partielle?) n'est pas forcément due aux attaques des vikings: JAROUSSEAU (2015), p. 219-221.
[21] Renseignement fourni par Guillaume de Malmesbury, *Gesta pontificum Anglorum*, II.85 et V.249; WINTERBOTTOM – THOMSON (2007), t. I, p. 292 et t. II, p. 597 sq. Le chapitre consacré aux translations dans la Bretagne carolingienne par DESELM (2009), p. 70-127 ne peut être invoqué ici, à cause de son défaut de critique documentaire et sa méconnaissance de l'historiographie récente du sujet. La compilation de DEUFFIC (2005) est partielle et manque parfois de critique. CASSARD (1996), p. 52-53 a dressé une carte des itinéraires hypothétiques de fuite des reliques de quelques saints bretons. Et encore, ID. (1998), p. 259 et (1999), p. 218.
[22] Par exemple chez DAVIES (1981).
[23] LUNVEN (2014), p. 52 et une carte de localisation à la p. 73 (fig. 12).

partir en deux catégories inégales. Dans une minorité des cas, l'écrivain pourrait être un Breton exilé du Xe siècle :

– la première Vie de saint Josse à Saint-Josse-sur-Mer (dép. Pas-de-Calais) ;
– la première Vie (mutilée) de saint Lunaire à Fleury-sur-Loire ;
– une longue interpolation de la Vie de saint Malo par Bili et un récit de sa translation à Paris ;
– une version abrégée et un *sermunculus* pour saint Guénolé à Montreuil-sur-Mer ;
– un récit (fragmentaire) de translation de saint Magloire à Paris.

Dans les autres cas, il est improbable, sinon exclu, de voir un Breton tenir la plume :

– une Vie de saint Ethbin (Idunet), à Montreuil-sur-Mer (?), au Xe siècle [24] ;
– une Vie métrique de saint Josse, à Winchester, à la fin du Xe siècle ;
– une traduction en vieil-anglais de la grande Vie de saint Malo par Bili, à Winchester, à la fin du Xe siècle [25] ;
– une translation de l'apôtre saint Matthieu en Bretagne, à Salerne à la fin du Xe siècle (et non pas à Saint-Pol-de-Léon par un évêque Mabbon) [26] ;
– une Vie de saint Mervé, sans doute hors de Bretagne, entre 860 et la fin du IXe siècle ;
– une réduction de la *Vita II^a s. Samsonis* dès la seconde moitié du IXe siècle (*BHL vacat*) ;
– une Vie longue de saint Guénaël (*Wenailus*) postérieure à la fin du XIe siècle, et non pas antérieure au Xe siècle ;
– la première Vie de saint Winnoc, par un moine de Saint-Bertin, avant 820 ;

---

[24] KERLOUÉGAN (1995).
[25] Pour des raisons d'ordre graphique, STOKES (2014), p. 87 et 136 est enclin à situer à Saint-Augustin de Cantorbéry la copie de ce manuscrit unique.
[26] POULIN (2009), p. 459-461. Pour une lecture différente de ce dossier, cf. BOURGÈS (2009) et (2019).

– un abrégé de la Vie de saint Guénolé (*BHL* 8956d), entre 913 et 1200, dans le nord de la France (Montreuil?) ou en Angleterre (Cantorbéry?).

Le cas de saint Émilion de Saujon est encore plus marginal: Armoricain (né à Vannes) – mais non Breton d'origine –, il a fait carrière en Aquitaine[27].

L'allusion à des sources orales fait partie de l'arsenal habituel destiné à inspirer confiance. D'une manière générale, l'écart important (plusieurs siècles!) qui sépare la vie terrestre des saints bretons et leurs premiers biographes ne peut que laisser sceptique. S'agissant des saints d'origine insulaire, quelle sorte de tradition orale aurait pu circuler sur le continent à leur propos, alors que leur pays natal s'est si peu souvenu d'eux aux hautes époques[28]? Le seul hagiographe breton qui soit très probablement allé outre-Manche n'a pu recueillir, au VIIIe siècle, que des échos sujets à caution sur saint Samson; il est possible que Bili ait incorporé dans son récit sur saint Malo des traditions insulaires parvenues jusqu'à lui par voie orale – ou écrite?[29].

La tradition manuscrite de l'hagiographie bretonne est quantitativement faible, sauf pour saint Samson, saint Magloire ou saint Malo; plus encore, aucun témoin ancien ne se trouve aujourd'hui en Bretagne avant le dossier de saint Guénolé dans le cartulaire de Landévennec (Quimper, BM 16; milieu du XIe siècle). Quand les saints bretons prennent place dans les compilations méthodiques des légendiers du XIe siècle, cette opération s'effectue hors de Bretagne, essentiellement dans la moitié nord de la France. Les cas les plus excentriques datent de

---

[27] Sa Vie la plus ancienne (version A; *BHL* 99) ne date que de la fin du XIe ou du début du XIIe siècle, selon DOLBEAU (2011), p. 133. Il n'y a pas lieu d'y chercher un noyau historique des VIIe-VIIIe siècles; *contra*, MERDRIGNAC (1992) ou YEURC'H (2016), p. 156 sq.

[28] La production hagiographique ne démarre pas avant le XIIe siècle au Pays de Galles et au XIIIe siècle dans les Cornouailles: LAPIDGE – LOWE (2001), p. 272 sq. et 278 sq. Plus optimiste sur la validité d'une tradition orale pour alimenter les hagiographes bretons: VAN 'T SPIJKER (1996), p. 250.

[29] Une version écrite de la *Navigatio Brendani* existait au moins depuis la fin du VIIIe siècle: ORLANDI – GUGLIELMETTI (2014), p. XCIV-XCVI, C-CI. Il n'est plus question de considérer cet épisode brendanien dans la Vie de saint Malo comme une interpolation du Xe siècle, comme l'a fait KENNEY (1920), p. 58 sq.

la fin du XIe siècle; ils concernent la Vie dite «d'Arezzo» de saint Guénolé, dans un célèbre légendier illustré de Toscane (Firenze, BNC, Fondo Nazionale II.I.412) et la première Vie de saint Josse à Worcester dans un exemplaire du Cotton Corpus Legendary (Cambridge, CCC 9). Aucun manuscrit breton, même tardif, n'a cherché à réunir l'ensemble des Vies des saints de la région; l'hagiographie ne semble donc pas avoir déclenché ou porté un réflexe identitaire qui s'exprime sous cette forme[30]. Il faut pourtant postuler une activité de *scriptoria* en Bretagne avant l'époque carolingienne[31].

Enfin l'étude de l'hagiographie bretonne est handicapée par un état de conservation des textes parfois incomplet; la plupart du temps, il s'agit de pertes accidentelles. Un recueil ancien de miracles de saint Melaine *in alia scedula* est disparu depuis longtemps, s'il a existé. Les *Gesta* de Redon (saint Conwoion) étaient déjà gravement mutilés à l'époque de Mabillon. La grande Vie de saint Guénolé interpelle à deux reprises une *beatitudo vestra* qui devait être identifiée dans un prologue ou une lettre d'envoi qui manquent aujourd'hui. La Translation de saint Magloire à Paris est maintenant réduite à l'état de cinq fragments. De la première Vie de saint Lunaire ne subsiste qu'un quaternion-épave (chap. 7-11). La Vie primitive de saint Samson a peut-être compté un prologue original, ensuite remplacé par la préface du premier remanieur avant la fin du VIIIe siècle; sa seconde Vie fit l'objet d'une réécriture condensée dont la fin est perdue par accident matériel.

E. Modalités de mise en écriture

Pour autant que nous puissions le savoir, les hagiographes au travail sont des moines; les diacres Hénoc (pour saint Samson) et Bili (pour saint Malo) sont les seules exceptions connues. Mais inversement, les commanditaires ou destinataires sont la plupart du temps des évêques:

– **saint Guénolé**: la version la plus longue semble destinée à une personnalité (*beatitudo vestra*) qui pourrait être un évêque de

---

[30] Pour un développement plus circonstancié sur l'état de la tradition manuscrite, cf. POULIN (2009), p. 47-49.
[31] DUMVILLE (2005), p. 52.

Quimper. Gurdisten adresse ensuite sa version abrégée dite « d'Arezzo » à l'évêque Jean d'Arezzo ;

— **saint Malo** : Bili a réalisé son travail à la demande de l'évêque Ratvili d'Alet ; une seconde lettre d'envoi salue aussi le clergé d'Alet ;

— **saint Paul Aurélien** : Gurmonoc offre sa biographie au *pater* Hinworet, qui pourrait être évêque de Léon ;

— **saint Samson** : à la demande de l'évêque Tigernomagle de Dol, la *vita primigenia* fut étoffée pour donner la Vie dite « ancienne » (ou *Vita I^a*). Autour de 900, la *Vita II^a* fut ornée de compléments métriques offerts à l'évêque Lovenan de Dol.

Les anciens hagiographes bretons ont utilisé principalement les ressources de la prose latine pour s'acquitter de leur tâche ; mais l'expression versifiée s'y ajoute assez souvent. Soit pour la rédaction de prosimètres (Guénolé, Paul Aurélien, Malo), soit par addition de pièces en vers distinctes (Guénolé ; Samson, en ornement de sa *Vita II^a*). Rares sont les Vies entièrement versifiées, comme celle de saint Josse ; mais c'est en Angleterre ! La plus réussie des compositions prose + vers est assurément l'*opus geminum* de Gurdisten de Landévennec consacré à saint Guénolé.

Comme d'habitude, la plupart des compositions hagiographiques consacrées à des saints bretons sont anonymes. Le diacre Hénoc, auquel on attribue la mise en écriture d'un premier état de la Vie de son cousin Samson n'est probablement qu'une figure emblématique, et non pas un vrai personnage historique. Gurdisten est sans doute déjà abbé de Landévennec au moment de la compilation de son grand œuvre sur saint Guénolé ; son disciple, le moine-prêtre Gurmonoc, est l'auteur de la première Vie de saint Paul Aurélien. Enfin le diacre Bili d'Alet a créé un long dossier sur saint Malo. Mais la première Vie de saint Tudual (*BHL* 8350), souvent datée du IXe siècle, n'est pas antérieure à la seconde moitié du XIe siècle, à notre avis[32] ; en attribuer la composition à un incertain Louénan, sur la foi du témoignage de la *Vita III^a s. Tutguali* du XIIe siècle (*BHL* 8353) est bien hasardeux. L'attribution des *Gesta sanctorum Rotonensium* à un Ratvili nous paraît incertaine. Aucun des auteurs non bretons, travaillant hors d'Armorique, ne peut être identifié nom-

---

[32] POULIN (2009), p. 374-377.

mément avant l'an mil, sauf pour un miracle de saint Melaine raconté par Grégoire de Tours et le sermon de Loup de Ferrières sur saint Josse.

La *Vita II^a* de saint Samson, organisée en deux livres (avant et après le passage sur le continent) a peut-être suggéré la structure bipartite des Vies de saint Guénolé et de saint Paul Aurélien. Mais un trait récurrent encore plus fréquent est la présence de compositions destinées à la prédication; soit à l'intérieur des biographies (Samson, Magloire, Guénolé), soit en pièces annexes distinctes (Malo par Bili, Guénolé, Josse). De ce point de vue, l'hagiographie bretonne s'inscrit bien dans une tendance observée ailleurs à la même époque[33].

Les pratiques d'intertextualité sont présentes dans l'ancienne hagiographie bretonne comme ailleurs dans l'hagiographie du haut Moyen Âge, mais avec des intensités et des contenus variables. Outre l'Écriture sainte, la source d'inspiration formelle la plus fréquemment mobilisée par les hagiographes bretons d'Armorique est assurément le dossier de saint Samson (*Vita I^a* ou *II^a*)[34]; mais ce rayonnement ne s'étend pas jusqu'aux hagiographes qui travaillent hors de la péninsule bretonne, ni au point de créer un véritable cycle littéraire. Le chef d'œuvre de Sulpice Sévère sur saint Martin de Tours a laissé des traces un peu partout dans l'hagiographie bretonne, mais nulle part de façon aussi soutenue que dans la Vie ancienne de saint Samson.

On a remarqué depuis longtemps la présence d'auteurs de l'Antiquité, profanes (surtout Virgile) et chrétiens, parmi les sources d'inspiration des hagiographes bretons; mais les contacts reconnus varient fortement en nombre et en nature[35]. La plus haute fréquence d'emprunts très diversifiés s'observe chez les hagiographes de Landévennec, pour raconter les Vies des saints Paul Aurélien et surtout Guénolé. D'autres auteurs,

---

[33] KRÖNERT (2010).

[34] Voir un tableau du réseau de ces dépendances formelles chez POULIN (2009), p. 70, corrigeant et complétant celui de POULIN (2003), p. 193.

[35] Des tableaux récapitulatifs des sources formelles repérées dans les Vies bretonnes se trouvent dans notre *Répertoire raisonné* de 2009 pour les saints suivants: saint Brieuc, p. 83 sq.; saint Lunaire, p. 137 sq.; saint Paul Aurélien, p. 300-307; saint Samson, p. 352-354; saint Guénaël, p. 395. Pour saint Guénolé, voir notre article de 2014, p. 203-218. D'autres tableaux récapitulatifs ont été compilés pour les saints Conwoion, Guénolé et Malo dans POULIN («Alet, Landévennec, Redon», à paraître).

pourtant moins éloignés des grands centres culturels du continent, s'abstiennent complètement de citer des auteurs profanes (Malo, Melaine, Mervé), pour s'inscrire dans un horizon strictement chrétien. Les *Gesta* de Redon se distinguent par leur caractère lourdement moralisateur (à coup de chaînes de citations bibliques) et leur recours à des données tirées des archives du monastère, à un point inégalé par les autres Vies de saints bretons.

Deux dossiers possèdent une structure plus ambitieuse qu'une biographie au sens courant du terme. Pour saint Malo, Bili d'Alet a monté un dossier où s'équilibrent et se complètent portions biographiques, séquences thaumaturgiques, poèmes, hymnes et sermons. Pour saint Guénolé, Gurdisten de Landévennec a construit un *opus geminum* (deux livres en prose et une *recapitulatio* en vers); à l'analyse, les deux premiers livres (prosimétriques) se révèlent encore plus complexes, par leur assemblage de sections tantôt biographiques, tantôt parénétiques, dont certaines parties ont dû exister séparément avant d'être assemblées sous la forme d'une Vie achevée[36]. Les compositions hagiographiques effectuées hors de Bretagne s'en tiennent à des récits plus simples et plus conventionnels.

L'origine familiale des saints bretons et le premier public de leurs Vies créent les conditions d'une mise en contact des traditions culturelles insulaires et continentales; mais l'ensemble de la documentation hagiographique conservée reflète un monde plus proche de la civilisation romano-franque que de l'univers celtique. Il n'est évidemment pas question de passer sous silence les origines bretonnes, ou même insulaires, des saints bretons; mais Samson est le seul à voir raconter plus longuement son parcours antérieur à la traversée de la Manche que sa destinée continentale.

C'est plutôt par les moyens mis en œuvre par les hagiographes qu'on perçoit le paysage culturel dans lequel s'inscrit leur travail. Gurdisten a utilisé couramment le *De excidio Britanniae* de Gildas et ponctuellement la Vie de sainte Brigitte par Cogitosus pour raconter saint Guénolé; il présente d'ailleurs Guénolé comme un dévot de saint Patrice. Son disciple Gurmonoc se vante lui aussi de connaître Gildas, dans sa Vie de saint Paul Aurélien. Bili a manifestement utilisé des récits re-

---

[36] Dernière mise au point sur ces questions chez POULIN (2014).

latifs à saint Brendan pour mettre en scène une navigation merveilleuse de saint Malo; deux remanieurs anonymes lui emboîtent aussitôt le pas sur ce point. Bili serait l'hagiographe breton le plus largement ouvert aux influences formelles insulaires s'il fallait reconnaître en plus des hispérismes dans une de ses hymnes à saint Malo[37]. Il convient d'ajouter à cette liste d'influences insulaires celtiques la légende galloise d'*Alba Trimamma*, évoquée par Gurdisten à propos de la mère de saint Guénolé[38]. Ces quelques points de contact ne permettent cependant pas de parler d'influence insulaire importante sur l'hagiographie bretonne, pas plus qu'Irène Snieders n'en a trouvé dans l'hagiographie des saints irlandais en Belgique[39].

En l'absence de manuscrits bretons anciens, il est impossible de savoir si les premiers manuscrits hagiographiques se rattachaient de façon visible à l'art du livre insulaire. La présence occasionnelle de mots bretons rendus en latin ne doit pas se lire comme un indice de l'existence de versions primitives en langue bretonne; au contraire, ce procédé révèle plutôt à quel point les hagiographes bretons avaient bien assimilé le latin comme langue de culture. Par exemple, Gurdisten a su créer un emploi nouveau pour le verbe latin *adscribere*; sa capacité à créer un néologisme témoigne de sa maîtrise de la langue classique (sa langue «paternelle»)[40]. Les Vies de saints bretons contiennent un bon échantillon d'onomastique celtique; mais leur apparence parfois ancienne ne peut pas servir directement à dater les œuvres ou leurs sources[41]. La prudence de mise dans l'utilisation des noms propres pour la datation des œuvres en hagiographie irlandaise doit s'exercer aussi pour l'hagiographie bretonne[42].

Mais l'essentiel est ailleurs: les traditions littéraires et spirituelles dans lesquelles s'inscrit l'hagiographie bretonne dérivent avant tout d'auteurs du monde méditerranéen ou romano-franc. C'est essentiellement dans cet encrier que les hagiographes bre-

---

[37] LEMOINE (1995), p. 10 sq.
[38] KOCH (2006), p. 880.
[39] SNIEDERS (1928).
[40] HARVEY (2013), p. 95-97; ou p. 8 sq. de la version numérique. Pour un relevé partiel des affleurements de la langue bretonne, cf. MERDRIGNAC (1998).
[41] Appel à la prudence de KOCH (2006), p. 879 sq.
[42] BREATNACH (2005), p. 99 et 101.

tons trempent leur plume quand vient le moment d'étoffer ou d'embellir leurs récits. Leurs interlocuteurs sont non seulement des auteurs de l'Antiquité tardive ou du début du Moyen Âge, comme Virgile ou Caelius Sedulius, mais aussi des écrivains de la première moitié du IXe siècle: Alcuin († 804) dans les Vies de Melaine, Malo et Guénolé[43]; Smaragde de Saint-Mihiel dans les Vies de Malo et Guénolé; ou la *Vita II[a] s.Carileffi* (*BHL* 1569-70; avant 843) dans les Vies de Malo et de Mervé[44]. Il est vrai que les hagiographes bretons ont connu certains auteurs insulaires, comme Cogitosus et Aldhelm chez Gurdisten (nous ne retenons pas Bède dans la Vie ancienne de saint Samson); mais la connaissance de ces auteurs a pu leur parvenir par l'intermédiaire d'un relais continental, plutôt que par une importation directe.

Ce bilan plutôt mince révèle à quel point le rapport de l'hagiographie bretonne à l'interface des mondes insulaire et continental est déséquilibré en faveur du second terme de l'équation, même si on se limite à observer les œuvres composées en Bretagne proprement dite. Déjà certains traits de forme mettent sur la piste de cette observation: des écrivains comme Bili et Gurdisten sont manifestement bien au fait des manières les plus actuelles sur le continent d'envisager la construction d'un dossier hagiographique. Pour saint Malo, Bili a combiné narration biographique et hymnes utilisables à l'office, à l'instar de ce que Hilduin a réalisé pour saint Denis dans les années 830, à la demande de Louis le Pieux (*BHL* 2172)[45]. Pour saint Guénolé, Gurdisten a eu recours à la formule de *l'opus geminum*, à l'instar de la *Vita s. Willibrordi* d'Alcuin; il a en outre utilisé un système de signalisation marginale de ses références couramment utilisé à l'époque carolingienne. La présence de tables de chapitres est encore un symptôme carolingien (Guénolé, Malo par Bili, Samson, peut-être Conwoion).

La quête de reliques à l'occasion d'un voyage à Rome – saint Conwoion ramène de Rome des reliques du pape saint Marcel-

---

[43] Pour le contexte plus large de l'influence de la *Vita s. Vedasti* d'Alcuin, cf. POULIN (2013), p. 686 et 688.

[44] Du point de vue de l'hagiographie, il serait donc paradoxal d'attribuer au patrimoine insulaire une influence prépondérante, comme le fait encore, après d'autres, JANKULAK (2006), p. 426.

[45] Sur ce dossier, voir maintenant LAPIDGE (2017).

lin – s'inscrit bien dans une pratique de l'époque carolingienne visant à renforcer les liens avec la papauté[46]. Cette démarche ne suffit cependant pas à faire des *Gesta* de Redon un monument de revendication autonomiste bretonne; les efforts déployés par saint Conwoion pour obtenir l'appui de Louis le Pieux montrent bien que son abbaye n'incarnait pas un irrédentisme breton[47]. Mais il est vrai qu'en l'absence de calendriers ou martyrologes bretons anciens, il est difficile de savoir jusqu'à quel point la Bretagne carolingienne épousait l'orientation de l'Église franque vers Rome[48].

Enfin la pratique de la réécriture, largement pratiquée à l'époque carolingienne, est bien représentée dans l'ancienne hagiographie bretonne, même en s'en tenant à la production armoricaine proprement dite:

– **saint Malo**: deux répliques rapides (anonymes) à la grande Vie de saint Malo par Bili laissent paraître une tension dans le clergé alétien, divisé entre partisans et adversaires de la suprématie de Dol;

– **saint Magloire**: abrégé d'un dossier trop long pour être commodément maniable;

– **saint Melaine**: plusieurs remaniements difficiles à dater entre le milieu du IXe et le milieu du XIe siècle, effectués d'un point de vue monastique;

– **saint Samson**: à la « Vie ancienne » qui est déjà une réécriture de la fin du VIIIe siècle, s'ajoutent celle de la *Vita II^a*, proclamation des ambitions métropolitaines de Dol, puis une réduction de celle-ci dès la fin du IXe siècle;

– **saint Turiau**: la *Vita brevior* pourrait dériver d'une *primigenia* perdue;

– **saint Guénolé**: la grande Vie s'inspire peut-être d'une première recension perdue. Gurdisten s'est ensuite chargé de se remanier lui-même à deux reprises: par une Homélie qui s'annonce comme un résumé de la version longue, à l'intention de lecteurs pressés ou moins exigeants; puis par un montage réduit de la grande Vie et de l'Homélie, expédié en guise de cadeau à son ami l'évêque Jean d'Arezzo.

---

[46] GAILLARD (2009), p. 30.
[47] *Contra*: HERBERS (1998), p. 152.
[48] Cette question en est une d'actualité pour toute l'Église carolingienne: HERBERS (2010), p. 25.

Le mouvement de réécriture des Vies armoricaines a peut-être commencé avant même la grande dispersion du début du Xe siècle; ainsi les Vies anonymes de saint Malo. La *Vita II^a s. Samsonis* fut condensée et en partie «débretonnisée» pour un public non breton dès la seconde moitié du IXe siècle, si l'on en croit un témoin fragmentaire, antérieur à 900 d'après André Wilmart[49].

Dans l'ensemble, l'ancienne hagiographie bretonne parle beaucoup plus d'intégration au monde carolingien que de revendication autonomiste. Il est vrai que les prétentions métropolitaines de Dol à partir du milieu du IXe siècle visaient à émanciper les Bretons de la tutelle ecclésiastique de Tours – bien qu'on ne voie pas exactement de quel poids pesait alors concrètement l'autorité du métropolitain de Tours. Mais la pointe samsonienne de cette ambition bretonne n'a pas renversé le cours général de l'hagiographie bretonne: la Vie de saint Magloire suit mollement les traces de Samson archevêque, la Vie brève de saint Turiau (peut-être tardive) suit de loin. Un parti opposé est tenu par Bili, qui lie saint Malo à Tours, suscitant aussitôt la contradiction de deux remanieurs anonymes.

Mais les autres hagiographes d'époque carolingienne n'entrent pas dans ces débats, pas même l'auteur des *Gesta* de Redon, pourtant contemporain du déclenchement de la crise du vivant de saint Conwoion. Ce dernier biographe se tient à distance prudente de la polémique; dans un récit de vision (III, 3), il fait apparaître le trio des saints Martin, Hilaire et Samson, tous trois qualifiés d'archevêques, ce qu'ils ne furent évidemment pas en leur temps[50]. Il est révélateur que la contestation de l'autorité tourangelle prenne, par la voie hagiographique, la forme de construction d'une métropole concurrente et non pas d'un recours à une quelconque forme celtique d'organisation ecclésiastique. Quand il s'agit de faire pièce à la pression institutionnelle du monde romano-franc, c'est au continent et non au

---

[49] Vatican, Reg. lat. 479. Présentation du manuscrit dans POULIN (2009), p. 337 sq.; BISCHOFF (2014), p. 430, n° 6685 est un peu plus précis: «Bretagne, IX. Jh., ca. 3. Viertel».
[50] KRAMER (2007), p. 34 sq.

monde insulaire que les écrivains bretons empruntent leurs meilleures armes hagiographiques[51].

L'hagiographie bretonne s'inscrit décidément dans un monde plus continental qu'insulaire. Les percées qu'elle a faites en retour outre-Manche au Xe siècle, dans le contexte des turbulences causées par les vikings, visent la partie anglo-saxonne de la Grande-Bretagne et non les régions occidentales d'où sont venus les saints bretons ou leurs familles:

– **saint Josse**: sa *Vita I^a* a traversé la Manche en même temps qu'un grand légendier du nord de la France; on en a tiré une version métrique à Winchester à la fin du Xe siècle;
– **saint Malo**: la Vie de Bili fut traduite en vieil-anglais à Winchester à la fin du Xe siècle;
– **saint Guénolé**: une version brève de la grande Vie de Gurdisten fut peut-être préparée à Cantorbéry, lieu de provenance de son manuscrit le plus ancien.

Nulle nostalgie d'un héritage celtique menacé, même chez Gurdisten, trop heureux d'introduire dans sa grande Vie de saint Guénolé un extrait d'une lettre de Louis le Pieux (monogramme inclus) datée de 818, enjoignant Landévennec de conduire le monachisme breton (teinté d'influences «scottiques») sur la voie de l'adoption du cadre bénédictin. Cet enchâssement paraîtrait un hors-d'œuvre s'il n'était ensuite fièrement répété (encore avec le monogramme impérial!) dans la version fortement condensée que Gurdisten a rapidement préparée vers 870 à l'intention de Jean d'Arezzo. Les liens d'amitié qui l'unissent à cet évêque italien illustrent bien le pouvoir d'attraction du continent sur les élites ecclésiastiques bretonnes au IXe siècle, jusqu'au bout du monde (dép. Finistère).

La présence de saints de Petite Bretagne dans les martyrologes historiques est modeste. Si Melaine prend déjà place dans le martyrologe hiéronymien (ordination au 6 janvier et déposition au 6 novembre) à la fin du VIe siècle[52], il faut attendre la fin du VIIIe siècle pour voir s'y ajouter saint Samson (au 28 juillet)[53] dans le manuscrit de Wissembourg (addition effectuée en 772) et dans le manuscrit de Berne (exécuté au dio-

---

[51] Ce constat est en accord avec le bilan dressé par GUIGON (2009).
[52] *AASS*, Nov. II posterior, 1931, p. 28 sq. et 588 sq.
[53] *AASS*, Nov. II posterior, 1931, p. 399 et 401.

cèse de Metz). Par la suite, ce sont ces deux saints qui sont les mieux représentés dans les martyrologes :

— on trouve **Melaine** (au 12 novembre, une date arbitraire) dans le martyrologe d'Adon de Vienne (sa première famille, en 855)[54], d'où l'a ensuite tiré Usuard de Saint-Germain-des-Prés (au 6 janvier) en 865[55]. Melaine est le seul saint de Bretagne à se maintenir dans le martyrologe de Notker le Bègue (au 6 janvier) vers 900[56] ;

— **Samson** : un martyrologe métrique — en fait plutôt un calendrier-obituaire — du Yorkshire composé au troisième quart du VIIIe siècle fut transporté sur le continent et interpolé entre 816 et 846 dans le diocèse de Reims ; c'est à cette occasion que fut ajouté le nom de Samson[57].

Les enquêtes personnelles d'Usuard lui ont permis d'ajouter à ses sources habituelles les noms de saint Turiau de Dol (au 13 juillet) et de saint Samson (au 28 juillet)[58]. Adon (deuxième famille, une compilation auxerroise du Xe siècle au plus tard[59]) lui a ensuite repris ces deux dernières notices.

Conclusion

Les relations de proximité que l'hagiographie bretonne entretient avec l'hagiographie continentale de l'époque carolingienne n'impliquent cependant pas qu'elle ait mis ses pas dans les traces exactes de tous les modèles dominants. Elle se distingue par son absence d'intérêt pour les saints martyrs de l'Antiquité ; elle n'a pas développé aussi vigoureusement la forme de la translation de reliques, qui vient justement à maturité à l'époque carolingienne[60] ; elle n'entre aucunement dans les débats à la mode sur l'apostolicité des Églises en Gaule[61], ni dans

---

[54] Dubois – Renaud (1984), p. 381.
[55] Dubois (1965), p. 155.
[56] *PL* 131, col. 1033.
[57] Quentin (1908), p. 124.
[58] Dubois (1965), p. 267 et 274 sq.
[59] Dubois (1984), p. xxvii.
[60] Heinzelmann (1979), p. 94.
[61] Bourgès (2013), p. 44. Sur le contexte historiographique de la question de l'apostolicité en Bretagne, cf. Guiomar (1987), p. 235 sq.

la tendance au dénigrement de l'époque mérovingienne. Dans sa pratique de l'intertextualité, elle ignore certains monuments mérovingiens beaucoup utilisés par les hagiographes carolingiens, comme les Vies de saint Colomban ou de saint Éloi.

Inversement, l'hagiographie bretonne possède un trait manifeste qui lui donne un air de famille original et bien reconnaissable: c'est l'influence samsonienne, qui colore la forme – et parfois aussi le fond[62] – d'une grande partie des sources hagiographiques composées en Bretagne avant l'an mil, mais sans créer de véritable cycle hagiographique pour autant. Ni inspirer les hagiographes non bretons du haut Moyen Âge; les seuls points de contact formel reconnus à ce jour sont une influence fugace de la *Vita s. Samsonis* sur la *Vita s. Geremari*[63] et peut-être sur celle de saint Marcouf[64], mais pas la *Revelatio ecclesiae Sancti Michaelis*[65]. Pour faire bonne mesure, on peut peut-être ajouter la préface historique d'une messe propre en l'honneur de saint Samson, dérivée de sa Vie ancienne, dans un sacramentaire (fin X^e/XIe siècle) d'une église du nord de la France[66]. Au Pays de Galles, il faut attendre le début du XIIe siècle avant de voir remployée la *Vita II^a s. Samsonis*[67] dans le *Liber Landavensis*[68]; mais c'est pour servir des intérêts locaux du moment, et non par curiosité pour la Bretagne continentale.

La question reste posée de savoir à quel titre l'ancienne hagiographie bretonne peut être considérée comme un récit des origines bretonnes en Armorique. L'historien régionaliste Arthur de La Borderie († 1901) – suivi de nombreux émules au XXe siècle – tenait beaucoup à y lire l'histoire des fondateurs de la Bretagne continentale; il est vrai qu'il avait tendance à attribuer aux Vies de saints bretons une date nettement plus haute que nous le faisons maintenant. À notre avis, la date de mise en écriture et les conditions d'élaboration du corpus hagiogra-

---

[62] Du coup, la dimension ascétique de la sainteté bretonne se trouve peut-être plus accentuée qu'il ne convient: STANCLIFFE (2005), p. 444 sq.

[63] Cf. les références dans POULIN (2009), p. 320.

[64] *Vita A* (*BHL* 5267), chap. 13-16; hypothèse proposée par FLOBERT (2004), p. 41, n. 7; p. 681, n. 7 de la réimpression.

[65] *BHL* 5951, leçons 4 et 7, d'après les relevés de BOUET (2003), p. 79.

[66] Paris, BnF, lat. 11589, fol. 96v. Cf. POULIN (2009), p. 336.

[67] Il s'agit bien de la *Vita II^a*, et non pas de la Vie dite ancienne, malgré SMITH (2004), p. 808.

[68] LAPIDGE – SHARPE (1985), n° 91 (ii).

phique breton constituent plutôt les conditions de construction carolingienne d'une telle mémoire. Mais quel fut le moteur de la brusque efflorescence hagiographique en Bretagne dans la seconde moitié du IXe siècle ? Expression du dynamisme d'un royaume breton en phase d'expansion ou manifestation de résistance à la pression carolingienne ? Anne Lunven opte pour la première réponse[69] ; mais les hagiographes bretons ne sont pas tous d'accord entre eux devant les débats de leur actualité. Le jugement serait plus facile à porter si l'expression hagiographique pouvait être confrontée à une documentation narrative profane ancienne – qui n'existe ni en latin ni en breton.

Les éditions disponibles des Vies de saints bretons sont loin d'être toutes satisfaisantes du point de vue de la critique documentaire actuelle[70] ; mais le seraient-elles, nous n'échapperions pas au fait que l'hagiographie bretonne reflète une écriture distanciée, une mise en scène idéalisée et un regard éminemment clérical sur le passé breton. Et ce discours typé parle d'intégration à la vie continentale bien plus que de revendication d'autonomie ou de résistance à l'influence romano-franque. Mais il serait excessif de demander à l'hagiographie de combler, à elle seule, le silence documentaire qui obscurcit l'histoire des origines bretonnes en Armorique.

Considéré comme un ensemble, le corpus de l'ancienne hagiographie bretonne reflète un monde qui n'est nullement fermé sur lui-même ; au contraire, les hagiographes bretons traitent leurs héros d'une manière qui les révèle bien à l'écoute de traditions spirituelles et littéraires plus continentales et méditerranéennes qu'insulaires. L'adoption de certaines manières de faire des hagiographes carolingiens se concilie chez eux avec une originalité régionale certaine[71]. Leur premier public est assurément breton ; mais le résultat de leur travail constitue de plein droit une page de l'histoire européenne de l'hagiographie. Contrairement à une certaine tradition historiographique, il faut donc conclure à une appartenance de l'ancienne hagiographie bretonne à l'hagiographie continentale bien plus forte

---

[69] LUNVEN (2014), p. 52.
[70] Pour un inventaire des éditions de sources hagiographiques bretonnes (partielles ou intégrales) depuis le milieu du XIXe siècle, cf. POULIN (2009), p. 470-482.
[71] BOSWORTH (2010), p. 1057.

qu'avec l'hagiographie insulaire[72]. À défaut d'avoir produit un chef-d'œuvre impérissable de la littérature universelle, les hagiographes bretons du haut Moyen Âge ont quand même réussi à composer des œuvres ambitieuses et remarquables, au premier rang desquelles nous placerions la grande Vie de saint Guénolé. L'hagiographie bretonne n'a pas fini de piquer la curiosité des chercheurs, ne serait-ce que par la difficulté persistante à dater précisément et remettre en contexte sa tête de série, le premier état de la Vie de saint Samson.

Bibliographie

Les liens vers les pages Web ont été vérifiés en août 2019.

AUBERT, R., «Leutiern», in *DHGE*, t. 31, Paris, 2013, col. 1175.

BISCHOFF, B., *Katalog der festländischen Handschriften des neunten Jahrhunderts (mit Ausnahme der wisigotischen)*, III: *Padua – Zwickau* (éd. B. EBERSPERGER), Wiesbaden, 2014.

BOSWORTH, A. K., «Learning from the Saints: Ninth-Century Hagiography and the Carolingian Renaissance», *History Compass*, VIII:9 (2010), p. 1055-1066.

BOUET, P., «La *Revelatio* et les origines du culte à saint Michel sur le Mont Tombe», in P. BOUET *et al.*, dir., *Culte et pèlerinages à saint Michel en Occident. Les trois monts dédiés à l'archange*, Rome, 2003, p. 65-90 (Collection de l'École française de Rome, 376).

BOURGÈS, A.-Y., «À propos d'hagiographie bretonne: l'ouvrage de L. Fleuriot sur Les origines de la Bretagne», *Hagio-historiographie médiévale*, (22 mai 2009), <http://www.hagiohistoriographiemedievale.blogspot.com> (22 mai 2009).

—, «À propos de la Translatio sancti Mathaei», *ibid*.

—, «Le dossier de la translation des reliques de saint Mathieu en Bretagne: une révision des hypothèses», *ibid*. (19 février 2019).

—, «Vicissitudes de la mémoire hagiographique bretonne au bas Moyen Âge: la fondation des évêchés en Bretagne», in H. BOUGET *et al.*, dir., *Histoires des Bretagnes*, 4: *Conservateurs de la mémoire*, Brest, 2013, p. 41-53: <https://ephe.academia.edu/ANDREYVESBOURGES>.

---

[72] Même pour la période antérieure à 800, ce diagnostic s'impose: en effet, il y a tout lieu de croire que la seule Vie bretonne assurément antérieure à cette date, la Vie ancienne de saint Samson, fut en effet composée à Dol. La Bretagne est encore rattachée aux îles britanniques dans l'essai de PHILIPPART – TRIGALET (2008), p. 116 sq.

BÜHRER-THIERRY, G. – MÉRIAUX, C., *La France avant la France: 481-888*, Paris, 2010 (réimp. 2014) (Histoire de France, 1).

CASSARD, J.-C., *Le siècle des Vikings en Bretagne*, Paris, 1996 (Les universels Gisserot, 14).

—, «En marge des incursions vikings», *Bulletin de la Société archéologique du Finistère*, 127 (1998), p. 258-262 et 128 (1999), p. 217-218.

—, *Les Bretons de Nominoé*, 2e éd. augm., Rennes, 2002.

—, «En Bretagne au Moyen Âge: l'impensable sainteté féminine?», in L. CAPDEVILA *et al.*, dir., *Le genre face aux mutations. Masculin et féminin du Moyen Âge à nos jours*, Rennes, 2003, p. 55-69.

BREATNACH, C., «The Significance of the Orthography of Irish Proper Names in the *Codex Salmanticensis*», *Ériu*, 55 (2005), p. 85-101.

CASTEL, Y.-P., «Les reliques de Paul Aurélien», in B. TANGUY – T. DANIEL, dir., *Sur les pas de Paul Aurélien,* Brest – Quimper, 1997, p. 103-118.

CHIRON, Y., «Leuférine ou Leuphérine», in *Dictionnaire de biographie française*, t. 22, Paris, 2018, col. 463 sq.

CINTRÉ, R., *Les marches de Bretagne. Une frontière du Moyen Âge à découvrir*, Rennes, 2011.

CONNER, P. W., *Anglo-Saxon Exeter. A Tenth-Century Cultural History*, Woodbridge, 1993 (Studies in Anglo-Saxon History, 4).

DAVIES, W., «Property Rights and Property Claims in Welsh *Vitae* of the Eleventh Century», in *Hagiographie, cultures et sociétés, IVe-XIIe siècles*, Paris, 1981, p. 515-533.

DESELM, D., *Unwilling Pilgrimage: Vikings, Relics, and the Politics of Exile during the Carolingian Era (c. 830-940)*. Thèse de doctorat de l'Université du Michigan, 2009: <http://deepblue.lib.umich.edu>.

DEUFFIC, J.-L., «L'exode des corps saints hors de Bretagne (VIIe-XIIe s.): des reliques au culte liturgique», in ID., dir., *Reliques et sainteté dans l'espace médiéval*, Saint-Denis, 2005, p. 355-423 (Pecia, 8-11).

DOLBEAU, F., «Le dossier hagiographique de saint Émilion», in F. BOUTOULLE *et al.*, dir., *Fabrique d'une ville médiévale. Saint-Émilion au Moyen Âge*, Bordeaux, 2011, p. 125-138 et 393-397 (Aquitania. Supplément, 26).

DUBOIS, J., éd., *Le martyrologe d'Usuard. Texte et commentaire*, Bruxelles, 1965 (Subsidia hagiographica, 40).

DUBOIS, J., – RENAUD, G., éd., *Le martyrologe d'Adon, ses deux familles, ses trois recensions. Texte et commentaire*, Paris, 1984 (Sources d'histoire médiévale).

DUMVILLE, D. N., «Writers, Scribes and Readers in Brittany, A. D. 800-1100», in H. FULTON, dir., *Medieval Celtic Literature and Society*, Dublin, 2005, p. 49-64.

FLOBERT, P., «Saint Marcouf, de Childebert Ier à Charles X», in L. LEMOINE – B. MERDRIGNAC, dir., *Corona monastica. Mélanges offerts au père Marc Simon*, Rennes, 2004, p. 41-46, *Britannia monastica*, 8, réimpr. dans ID., *Grammaire comparée et variétés du latin. Articles revus et mis à jour (1964-2012)*, Genève, 2014, p. 680-687 (n° 84) (ÉPHÉ, Hautes études médiévales et modernes, 105).

—, «Le remaniement carolingien de la Vie ancienne de saint Samson (*Vita II^a*, BHL 7481-7483)», in CIRDoMoc, éd., Rennes, 2005, p. 45-54, *Britannia monastica*, 9, réimpr. dans son recueil *Grammaire comparée et variétés du latin. Articles revus et mis à jour (1964-2012)*, Genève, 2014, p. 652-662 (n° 81) (ÉPHÉ, Hautes études médiévales et modernes, 105).

GAILLARD, M., «Pourquoi se rend-on à Rome pendant le haut Moyen Âge?», in S. CURVEILLER, dir., *Se déplacer, du Moyen Âge à nos jours*, Calais, 2009, p. 25-33.

GARAULT, C., *Écriture, histoire et identité. La production écrite monastique et épiscopale à Saint-Sauveur de Redon, Saint-Magloire de [Léhon], Dol et Alet/Saint-Malo (milieu du IXe-milieu du XIIe siècle)*. Thèse de doctorat, Université de Rennes II, 2011, 3 vol. dactyl. (dir. B. Merdrignac).

—, «L'abbaye de Saint-Sauveur de Redon: entre centre et confins. Débats historiographiques et enjeux identitaires», in H. BOUGET – M. COUMERT, dir., *Histoires des Bretagnes*, 2: *Itinéraires et confins*, Brest, 2011, p. 37-53.

GOUGAUD, L., «Notes sur le culte des saints bretons en Angleterre», *Annales de Bretagne*, 35 (1921), p. 601-609.

GUIGON, P., «The Archaeology of the So-Called "Celtic Church" in Brittany», in N. EDWARDS, dir., *The Archaeology of the Early Medieval Celtic Church*, Leeds, 2009, p. 173-190 (The Society for Medieval Archaeology Monographs, 29).

GUILLOTEL, H., «Genèse de l'*Indiculus de episcoporum depositione*», in C. LAURENT *et al.*, dir., *Mondes de l'Ouest et villes du monde. Regards sur les sociétés médiévales. Mélanges en l'honneur d'André Chédeville*, Rennes, 1998, p. 129-132.

GUIOMAR, J.-Y., *Le Bretonisme. Les historiens bretons au XIXe siècle*, Mayenne, 1987 (Archives historiques de Bretagne, 3).

HARVEY, A., «The Non-Classical Vocabulary of Celtic-Latin Literature: An Overview», in M. GARRISON *et al.*, dir., *Spoken and Written Language. Relations between Latin and the Vernacular Languages*, Turnhout, 2013, p. 87-100. Aussi accessible en mode numérique: <http://journals.eecs.qub.ac.uk/dmlcs/overview.pdf>.

HEAD, T., «The Diocese of Orléans, 950-1150», in *Hagiographies*, I (1994), p. 345-357.

Heinzelmann, M., *Translationsberichte und andere Quellen des Reliquienkultes*, Turnhout, 1979 (Typologie des sources du Moyen Âge occidental, 33).

Henriet, P., «Un horizon hagiographique d'opposition au pouvoir. Les milieux monastiques et ascétiques de l'Espagne septentrionale au VIIe siècle», in E. Bozóky, dir., *Hagiographie, idéologie et politique au Moyen Âge en Occident*, Turnhout, 2012, p. 93-109.

Herbers, K., «Rom im Frankenreich – Rombeziehungen durch Heilige in der Mitte des 9. Jahrhunderts», in D. R. Bauer *et al.*, dir., *Mönchtum – Kirche – Herrschaft 750-1000. Josef Semmler zum 65. Geburtstag*, Sigmaringen, 1998, p. 133-169.

—, «Hagiographie. Auswertungsmöglichkeiten seit Levison», in M. Becher – Y. Hen, dir., *Wilhelm Levison (1876-1947). Ein jüdisches Forscherleben zwischen wissenschaftlicher Anerkennung und politischem Exil*, Siegburg, 2010, p. 17-32 (Bonner historische Forschung, 63).

Herbert, M., «Latin and Vernacular Hagiography of Ireland from the Origins to the Sixteenth Century», in *Hagiographies*, III (2001), p. 327-360.

Huyghebaert, N., «Le *Sermo de adventu ss. Gudwali et Bertulfi*. Édition et étude critique», *Sacris erudiri*, 24 (1980), p. 87-113.

Jankulak, K., *The Medieval Cult of St Petroc*, Rochester, NY, 2000 (Studies in Celtic History, 19).

—, «Christianity in the Celtic countries. 5: Brittany», in J. T. Koch, dir., *Celtic Culture. A Historical Encyclopedia*, t. II, Santa Barbara, CA, 2006, p. 424-427.

Jarousseau, G., *Églises, évêques et princes à Angers du Ve au début du XIe siècle*, Limoges, 2015 (Cahiers de l'Institut d'anthropologie juridique, 42).

Kerlouégan, F., «Idunet (saint)», in *DHGE*, t. 15, Paris, 1995, col. 661-662.

Kenney, J. F., «The Legend of St. Brendan», *Proceedings and Transactions of the Royal Society of Canada*, section 2, 14 (1920), p. 51-67.

Koch, J. T., «Hagiography in the Celtic Countries. 4: Breton», in J. T. Koch, dir., *Celtic Culture. A Historical Encyclopedia*, t. III, Santa Barbara, CA, 2006, p. 879-881.

Krönert, K., «L'hagiographie entre historiographie et prédication. Étude sur une forme littéraire à partir de textes rédigés à Trèves (VIIIe-XIe siècle)», *Mélanges de science religieuse*, 67 (2010), p. 5-26.

La Borderie, A. Le Moyne de, *Histoire de Bretagne*, vol. 2, Rennes – Paris, 1898.

Lapidge, M., *Hilduin of Saint-Denis: The Passio S. Dionysii in Prose and Verse*, Leyde, 2017 (Mittellateinische Studien und Texte, 51).

Lapidge, M. – Lowe, R. C., «The Latin Hagiography of England and Wales (600-1550)», in *Hagiographies*, III (2001), p. 203-325.

Lapidge, M. – Sharpe, R., *A Bibliography of Celtic-Latin Literature, 400-1200*, Dublin, 1985 (Royal Irish Academy. Dictionary of Medieval Latin from Celtic Sources. Ancillary Publications, 1).

Le Huërou, A., *Baudri, archevêque de Dol et hagiographe (1107-1130)*, Thèse de doctorat, Université de Rennes 2, 2006, 2 vol. dactyl. (dir. B. Merdrignac).

Lemoine, L., «Maniérisme et hispérisme en Bretagne. Notes sur quelques colophons (VIIIe-Xe siècles)», *Annales de Bretagne*, 102/4 (1995), p. 7-16.

Lewis, B. J., «St Mechyll of Anglesey, St Maughold of Man and St Malo of Brittany», *Studia Celtica Fennica*, 11 (2014), p. 24-38 <http://ojs.tsv.fi/index.php/scf/article//view/45322>.

Loth, J., éd., «Les anciennes litanies des saints de Bretagne», *Revue celtique*, 11 (1890), p. 135-151.

Lunven, A., *Du diocèse à la paroisse: évêchés de Rennes, Dol et Alet/Saint-Malo, Ve-XIIIe siècle*, Rennes, 2014.

—, «Le pouvoir épiscopal en haute Bretagne avant le XIIe siècle (évêchés de Vannes, Alet/Saint-Malo, Rennes et Nantes», *Bulletin et mémoires de la Société archéologique et historique d'Ille-et-Vilaine*, 118 (2014), p. 113-138.

Mazel, F., «La translation des reliques de saint Maixent et le devenir de l'abbaye de Redon au Xe siècle», *Annales de Bretagne*, 122 (2015), p. 33-38 (excursus).

—, *L'évêque et le territoire. L'invention médiévale de l'espace (Ve-XIIIe siècle)*, Paris, 2016.

Merdrignac, B., «Bretons et Irlandais en France du Nord, VIe-VIIIe siècles», in J.-M. Picard, dir., *Ireland and Northern France A.D. 600-850*, Dublin, 1991, p. 119-142.

—, *Un enfant de Vannes: saint Émilion. Les relations entre la Bretagne et l'Aquitaine durant le haut Moyen Âge*, Vannes, 1992.

—, *Les Vies de saints bretons durant le haut Moyen Âge. La culture, les croyances en Bretagne (VIIe-XIIe siècle)*, Rennes, 1993.

—, «*Ut vulgo refertur...*: tradition orale et littérature hagiographique en Bretagne au Moyen Âge», in C. Laurent *et al.*, dir., *Mondes de l'Ouest et villes du monde. Regards sur les sociétés médiévales. Mélanges en l'honneur d'André Chédeville*, Rennes, 1998, p. 105-114.

Morice, Y., *L'abbaye de Landévennec des origines au XIe siècle à travers la production hagiographique de son «scriptorium». Culture monastique et idéologies dans la Bretagne du haut Moyen Âge*, Thèse de doctorat, Université de Rennes 2, 2007, 2 vol. dactyl. (dir. B. Merdrignac) <http://www.academia.edu/3538714>.

MORIN, S., «Réflexion sur la réécriture de la Vie de saint Brieuc au XIIe siècle: Briomaglus, Primael et Brioccius au temps de la réforme grégorienne», in J. QUAGHEBEUR – S. SOLEIL, dir., *Le pouvoir et la foi au Moyen Âge en Bretagne et dans l'Europe de l'Ouest. Mélanges en mémoire du professeur Hubert Guillotel*, Rennes, 2010, p. 243-259.

OHEIX, A., «Saint Benoît de Macérac», *Bulletin de la Société archéologique de Nantes et du département de la Loire-Inférieure*, 51 (1910), p. 61-80; réimpr. Nantes, 1910 (Études hagiographiques, 6).

ORLANDI, G. – GUGLIELMETTI, R. E., *Navigatio sancti Brendani. Alla scoperta dei segreti meravigliosi del mondo*, Florence, 2014 (Per verba, 30).

PADEL, O. J., «Gudwal», *Oxford Dictionary of National Biography*, 24 (2004), p. 165-166.

PICHOT, D., «Bretagne/Maine: de la marche à la frontière entre Vitré et Laval (VIe-XVe siècle)», in M. CATALA *et al.*, dir., *Frontières oubliées, frontières retrouvées. Marches et limites anciennes en France et en Europe*, Rennes, 2012, p. 87-100 (Enquêtes et documents, 41).

PHILIPPART, G. – TRIGALET, M., «Latin Hagiography before the Ninth Century: A Synoptic View», in J. R. DAVIS – M. MCCORMICK, dir., *The Long Morning of Medieval Europe: New Directions in Early Medieval Studies*, Aldershot, 2008, p. 111-129.

DE POERCK, G., «Les reliques des saints Maixent et Léger aux IXe et Xe siècles et les origines de l'abbaye d'Ebreuil en Bourbonnais», *Revue bénédictine*, 72 (1962), p. 61-95.

POULIN, J.-C., «Les relations entre la Bretagne carolingienne et le reste du continent d'après les sources hagiographiques», in G. CESBRON, dir., *Voix d'Ouest en Europe, souffles d'Europe en Ouest*, Angers, 1993, p. 65-81 et 773-774.

—, «Remanier Alcuin hagiographe (IXe-XIe siècles)», in J. ELFASSI *et al.*, dir., *Amicorum societas. Mélanges offerts à François Dolbeau pour son 65e anniversaire*, Florence, 2013, p. 665-697 (Millennio medievale, 96; Strumenti e studi, n.s. 34).

—, «L'intertextualité dans la Vie longue de saint Guénolé de Landévennec», *Études celtiques*, 40 (2014), p. 165-221.

—, «La circulation de l'information dans la "Vie ancienne" de saint Samson de Dol et la question de sa datation», in L. OLSON, dir., *St Samson of Dol and the Earliest History of Brittany, Cornwall and Wales*, Woodbridge, 2017, p. 37-82 (Studies in Celtic History, 10).

—, «Alet, Landévennec, Redon: trois ateliers d'écriture hagiographique vers 870», in C. EVANS, dir., *Monasteries, Convergences, Exchanges and Confrontations in the West of Europe in the Middle Ages, Colloque de Toronto* (à paraître).

PRICE, N., «Viking Brittany: Revisiting the Colony that Failed», in A. REYNOLDS – L. WEBSTER, dir., *Early Medieval Art and Archaeology in the Northern World. Studies in Honour of James Graham-Campbell*, Leyde – Boston, 2013, p. 731-742 (The Northern World, 58).

QUENTIN, H., éd., *Les martyrologes historiques du Moyen Âge. Étude sur la formation du martyrologe romain*, Paris, 1908 (réimpr. Aalen, 1969 et Spolète, 2002).

SMITH, J. M. H., «Oral and Written: Saints, Miracles and Relics in Brittany, c. 850-1250», *Speculum*, 65 (1990), p. 309-343.

—, *Province and Empire. Brittany and the Carolingians*, Cambridge, 1992 (réimpr. 2006) (Cambridge Studies in Medieval Life and Thought, IV, 18).

—, «Samson», *Oxford Dictionary of National Biography*, 48 (2004), p. 807-808.

SNIEDERS, I., «L'influence de l'hagiographie irlandaise sur les *Vitae* des saints irlandais de Belgique», *Revue d'histoire ecclésiastique*, 24 (1928), p. 596-627 et 828-867.

SCRAGG, D., «Old English Manuscripts, their Scribes and their Punctuation», in M. T. HUSSEY – J. D. NEES, dir., *The Genesis of Books. Studies in the Scribal Culture of Medieval England in Honour of A. N. Doan*, Turnhout, 2012, p. 245-260 (Studies in the Early Middle Ages, 9).

STANCLIFFE, C., «Christianity amongst the Britons, Dalriadan Irish and Picts», in P. FOURACRE, dir., *The New Cambridge Medieval History*, I: *C. 500 – c. 700*, Cambridge, 2005, p. 426-461.

STOKES, P. A., *English Vernacular Minuscule from Æthelred to Cnut, c. 990 – c. 1035*, Cambridge, 2014 (Publications of the Manchester Centre for Anglo-Saxon Studies, 14).

TANGUY, B., «Saints de l'ancien diocèse de Vannes dans l'hagiographie bretonne», in *Les saints bretons du pays vannetais*, Vannes, 2003, p. 119-136 (supplément au *Bulletin de la Société polymathique du Morbihan*, 129)

TANGUY, B., – M. LAGRÉE, dir., *Atlas d'histoire de Bretagne*, Rennes, 2002.

VAN TORHOUDT, É., *Centralité et marginalité en Neustrie et dans le duché de Normandie. Maîtrise du territoire et pouvoirs locaux dans l'Avranchin, le Bessin et le Cotentin (VIe-XIe siècles)*, Thèse de doctorat, Université Paris 7, 2008, 3 vol. dactyl.

VAN 'T SPIJKER, I., «Gallia du Nord et de l'Ouest. Les provinces ecclésiastiques de Tours, Rouen, Reims (950-1130)», in *Hagiographies*, II (1996), p. 239-290.

WHATLEY, E. G., «Late Old English Hagiography, ca. 950-1150», in *Hagiographies*, II (1996), p. 429-499.

WINTERBOTTOM, M. – THOMSON, R. M., éd. et trad., *William of Malmesbury. Gesta pontificum Anglorum. The History of the English Bishops*, I: *Text and Translation*, II: *Commentary*, Oxford, 2007 (Oxford Medieval Texts).

YEURC'H, B., «Le Vannetais [occidental] du IXe au XIe siècle», *Bulletin et mémoires de la Société polymathique du Morbihan*, 142 (2016), p. 155-191.

II. Répertoire de l'hagiographie bretonne antérieure à l'an mil

A. Tableau de la production hagiographique

Le tableau qui suit vise à mettre en lumière une des caractéristiques de la production hagiographique relative aux saints bretons du haut Moyen Âge: dès avant l'an mil, nombreux furent les auteurs non bretons, localisés hors de Bretagne armoricaine, à composer ou réécrire des pièces hagiographiques consacrées à des saints bretons. Une telle présentation en deux volets amène évidemment à énumérer des œuvres qui appartiennent à d'autres provinces culturelles que la Bretagne; elle avait déjà été adoptée pour un tableau à l'appui de notre essai sur la réécriture dans l'hagiographie bretonne ancienne[73]. Ce choix éditorial diffère donc de celui qui a été fait pour l'hagiographie irlandaise (HERBERT, *Hagiographies*, III, p. 329); mais il donne une visibilité minimale à plusieurs textes ou saints (habituellement de renommée modeste, il est vrai) qui sont passés presque complètement inaperçus dans les tableaux régionaux parus jusqu'à présent dans la collection *Hagiographies*. On pourra ainsi mesurer plus précisément l'attention portée aux saints d'origine bretonne dans l'hagiographie générale du haut Moyen Âge.

Ne figurent pas dans cette récapitulation les saints mineurs qui n'ont reçu qu'un traitement abrégé dans notre *Répertoire raisonné* (2009, p. 449-466), au motif que les écrits qui les concernent sont très probablement postérieurs à l'an mil. Pour

---

[73] POULIN (2003), p. 189 sq.

mémoire, la liste de ces saints marginaux peut d'ailleurs s'allonger comme suit:

– **Benedictus** de Macérac (Massérac): le cartulaire de Redon rapporte (Appendix, n° 52) qu'Alain le Grand aurait fait don de l'église de Macérac (*plebs Marczac*; dioc. de Nantes) à Redon en 894; faut-il y placer une translation de reliques de ce saint poitevin en faveur de la grande abbaye bretonne? Une *Vita*, peut-être rédigée à Redon (*BHL* 1145), mais probablement très tardive (XIIIe siècle), n'en parle pas[74].

– **Gudwalus** (Gurval): cet ermite du VIIe siècle (?) fut tardivement considéré comme successeur de saint Malo sur le siège d'Alet; il est parfois confondu avec saint Tudgual de Tréguier. Ses reliques font partie d'un lot de reliques bretonnes données par le roi Æthelstan au monastère de Notre-Dame et Saint-Pierre d'Exeter en 932[75]. Une *Vita* (*BHL* 3687), composée au milieu du XIIe siècle au plus tôt, par un moine de Saint-Pierre au Mont-Blandin (Gand), prétend s'appuyer sur une Vie primitive en livret – perdu, si même il a existé[76].

– **Leutiern**: cet évêque breton est mentionné dans une litanie bretonne du Xe siècle[77]. Ses reliques furent transportées de Bretagne à Paris, en même temps que celles de saint Magloire, pour fuir les attaques des vikings[78]; mais on ne lui connaît ni *Vita*, ni récit de translation.

– **Petroc**: ce saint cornouaillais aurait reçu un culte en Petite Bretagne aussi tôt que le Xe siècle; mais son dossier hagiographique aurait été composé dans les Cornouailles insulaires et non sur le continent[79].

Dans le tableau suivant, des références succinctes renvoient à la mention des textes concernés dans les instruments de travail que sont notre article sur les réécritures en 2003 et le *Répertoire raisonné* de 2009, ainsi que les dossiers déjà parus dans la présente collection: HEAD (1994) dans *Hagiographies*, I; VAN 'T

---

[74] OHEIX (1910); p. 6; p. 11 sq. de la réimpression.
[75] GOUGAUD (1921), p. 603. PADEL (2004), p. 165.
[76] Mention dans VAN 'T SPIJKER (1996), p. 249. PADEL (2004) croit en l'existence d'une documentation ancienne. HUYGHEBAERT (1980).
[77] LOTH (1890), p. 137 et 146.
[78] AUBERT (2013).
[79] *BHL* 6639. JANKULAK (2000), p. 74. LAPIDGE – LOWE (2001) p. 278.

Spijker (1996) et Whatley (1996) dans *Hagiographies*, II ; Lapidge – Lowe (2001) dans *Hagiographies*, III.

Rédaction en Bretagne armoricaine	*Rédaction hors de Bretagne armoricaine*
1. CONWOION	
Gesta ss. Rotonensium, Conwoionis et aliorum (*BHL* 1945) moine de Redon, vers 870 Poulin (2003), p. 177 Poulin (2009), p. 85-93 van 't Spijker (1996), p. 251	
2. ETHBINUS/IDUNETUS	
	Vita (*deperdita*) (*BHL* 2621) Montreuil-sur-Mer ? xe s. ? Poulin (2009), p. 439 et 452 sq. Rien dans van 't Spijker (1996)
3. JUDOCUS	
	Sermo in festivitate s. Judoci (*BHL* 4510d) Loup de Ferrières, milieu ixe s. Poulin (2009), p. 102-104
	Vita I^a (*BHL* 4504) moine breton (?), à Saint-Josse-sur-Mer, robablement autour de 925 Poulin (2003), p. 177 Poulin (2009), p. 104-113 et 118 sq. Rien dans van 't Spijker (1996)
	Vita metrica (*BHL* 4512) poète anonyme à Winchester, fin xe s. Poulin (2003), p. 178 et 194 Poulin (2009), p. 113 sq. Lapidge – Lowe (2001), p. 218
4. LENOVERIUS/LEONORIUS	
	Vita prima mutilata (*BHL vacat*) moine breton (?), à Fleury-sur-Loire, fin xe s. Poulin (2003), p. 179

Rédaction en Bretagne armoricaine	Rédaction hors de Bretagne armoricaine
	POULIN (2009), p. 120-133 et 137-141 Rien dans HEAD (1994)
5. MACHUTES[80]	
Vita (*BHL* 5116a et b) diacre Bili d'Alet (Saint-Malo), vers 870	Interpolation (?) de la Vie de Bili, de I-51 à I-76 (*BHL* 5116b) à Paris, au Xe s. (après 920) POULIN (2009), p. 166-168
Vita anonyma brevior (*BHL* 5117) moine d'Alet[81], vers 870	*Translatio de Sanctonica regione ad Britanniam* (*BHL* 5124) moine à Paris au Xe s. (après 920) POULIN (2003), p. 180 POULIN (2009), p. 184-188 et 197 sq.
Vita anonyma longior (*BHL* 5118a) moine d'Alet, fin IXe/début Xe s. (avant 920) POULIN (2003), p. 179-180 et 194 POULIN (2009), p. 142-184 et 189-197	Traduction de la Vie en vieil anglais, à partir du texte de Bili, à Winchester, fin Xe s. POULIN (2003), p. 180 POULIN (2009), p. 152 sq. WHATLEY (1996), p. 452 et 456
	Prière à saint Malo, par une moniale de Nunnaminster (St Mary's, Winchester), c.1000[82]
6. MAGLORIUS	
Vita longior, miracula et obitus (*BHL* 5139, 5140/5144) moine de Léhon, vers 860	*Translatio s. Maglorii Parisios* (*BHL* 5147) moines de Léhon, à Paris au Xe s. (après 920) POULIN (2009), p. 223-225 Rien dans VAN 'T SPIJKER (1996)
Vita brevior (*BHL* 5140/5144) lieu indéterminé, entre milieu IXe et XIIe s.	

---

[80] Pour une discussion récente sur les variations du nom latin de saint Malo, cf. LEWIS (2014), p. 29 sq. et 34.

[81] Claire Garault estime que les Vies anonymes s'adressent plutôt au clergé épiscopal d'Alet: GARAULT (2011), t. I, p. 125 et t. II, p. 360, 371 et 567.

[82] London, British Library, Royal 2.B.V, fol. 1; CONNER (1993), p. 57. SCRAGG (2012), p. 246-248.

Rédaction en Bretagne armoricaine	Rédaction hors de Bretagne armoricaine
Miracula in Sargia insula (*BHL* 5141) moine de Léhon, vers 860 *Translatio a Sargia insula ad Britanniam* (*BHL* 5142) moine de Léhon, vers 860 *Miracula post translationem* (*BHL* 5143) deux moines de Léhon, vers 900 *Aedificatio basilicae apud Lehonium* (*BHL* 5146) moine de Léhon, début Xe s. (avant 920) POULIN (2003), p. 181 POULIN (2009), p. 199-222 et 226-234	

7. MELANIUS

Vita I^a (*BHL* 5887-88) clerc de Rennes (?), fin IXe s. *Miracula* (*deperdita*) (*BHL vacat*) clerc de Rennes (?), fin IXe s.? *Vita II^a* (*BHL* 5891) moine de Bretagne, X^e ou XIe s. *Vita interpolata* (*BHL* 5889-90) moine de Saint-Melaine de Rennes, entre le Xe et le milieu XIe s. POULIN (2003), p. 181 sq. POULIN (2009), p. 235-259 Rien dans VAN 'T SPIJKER (1996)	*Miraculum* (*BHL* 5892) Grégoire de Tours, *Liber in gloria conf.* 54, entre 570 et 588 POULIN (2009), p. 237-240

8. MEROVEUS

	Vita (*BHL* 5941) peut-être hors de Bretagne, entre 860 et fin IXe s. POULIN (2009), p. 260-263

Rédaction en Bretagne armoricaine	*Rédaction hors de Bretagne armoricaine*
9. PAULUS AURELIANUS	

Vita I^a (*BHL* 6585)
    moine Gurmonoc de Landévennec; travail achevé en 884
    POULIN (2003), p. 182
    POULIN (2009), p. 264-290 et 298-307
	Vita II^a (*BHL* 6586)
	    Vital de Fleury (1005-1039)
	    VAN 'T SPIJKER (1996), p. 249 sq.
	    POULIN (2009), p. 294-298
	Translatio (*BHL* 6587)
	    Aimoin de Fleury (1004/1010)
	    HEAD (1994), p. 348
	    POULIN (2003), p. 182
	    POULIN (2009), p. 290-293

10. SAMSON	

Vita primigenia (*deperdita*) (*BHL vacat*)
    diacre gallois «Hénoc», travaillant sur le continent; fin VIIe s. (?)
Vita I^a (dite «ancienne») (*BHL* 7478-79)
    moine de Dol; fin VIIIe s.
Vita II^a (*BHL* 7481, 7483)
    moine de Dol, vers 860
Additamentum metricum[83]
(*BHL* 7480, 7482, 7484)
    clerc de Dol, entre fin IXe et c. 920
 	
POULIN (2003), p. 183-186 et 192
POULIN (2009), p. 308-354
LAPIDGE – LOVE (2001), p. 275
	Vita mutilata (*BHL vacat*), réécriture abrégée de la *Vita II^a*, hors de Bretagne, seconde moitié IXe s.[84]
	POULIN (2003), p. 184
	POULIN (2009), p. 337 sq.

11. TURIAVUS	

Vita primigenia (*deperdita*) (*BHL vacat*)
    peut-être à Dol, 2e moitié IXe s. au plus tôt, peut-être pas antérieure au XIe s.
	Vita longior et miracula (dite «de Paris») (*BHL* 8342-43)
	    moine de Saint-Germain-des-Prés, probablement première moitié du XIe s.

---

[83] KIRSCH (2001), p. 666 sq., estime qu'il a pu exister une version métrique complète.

[84] Inédite, connue par un témoin unique, mutilé à la fin par perte matérielle: Vatican, Reg. lat. 479, fol. 9-24v.

Rédaction en Bretagne armoricaine	Rédaction hors de Bretagne armoricaine
Vita brevior (*BHL* 8341) peut-être à Dol, nettement après le milieu du IXe s., peut-être pas antérieure au XIe s. POULIN (2003), p. 186 sq. POULIN (2009), p. 355-360 et 368-370	*Vita* (dite «de Clermont») (*BHL* 8342d) auteur certainement pas Breton; composition tardive, du XIIIe s. au plus tard POULIN (2003), p. 186 sq. POULIN (2009), p. 361-370 Rien dans VAN 'T SPIJKER (1996)

12. WENAILUS

	Vita longior et translationes (*BHL* 8818-19) peut-être à Corbeil, après la fin du XIe s. POULIN (2009), p. 382-395

13. WINNOCUS

	Vita *BHL* 8952 moine de Saint-Bertin, peu avant 820

14. WINWALOEUS

Hymnus ad vesperum (ICL 7989; *BHL vacat*) *Hymnus ad matutinum* (ICL 1437; *BHL vacat*) *Hymnus alphabeticus* (ICL 4219 + 614; *BHL vacat*) moine Clément de Landévennec (au moins pour la 3e hymne), dans les années 860 *Vita* (*deperdita*) (*BHL vacat*) brève composition hypothétique en prose, à Landévennec, milieu IXe s. (?) *Vita longior* (*BHL* 8957-58) abbé Gurdisten de Landévennec, entre 860 et 884 (plutôt au début de cette période) *Homelia* (*BHL* 8959) abbé Gurdisten, entre la *Vita longior* et la *Vita et homelia*	*Vita brevior* (*BHL* 8956d) dans le nord de la France (Montreuil?) ou en Angleterre (Cantorbéry?), entre 913 et 1200 *Sermunculus de vita* (*BHL* 8962) moine breton réfugié à Montreuil? entre 920 et XIIe s. au plus tard POULIN (2003), p. 188 POULIN (2009), p. 437-440 VAN 'T SPIJKER (1996), p. 249

Rédaction en Bretagne armoricaine	Rédaction hors de Bretagne armoricaine
Vita et homelia («Arezzo») (*BHL* 8960) abbé Gurdisten, vers 870	POULIN (2003), p. 187 sq. POULIN (2009), p. 396-436 et 440-445 VAN 'T SPIJKER (1996), p. 243 et 249

B. BIBLIOGRAPHIE GÉNÉRALE COMPLÉMENTAIRE

Les liens vers les pages Web ont été vérifiés en août 2019.

BOURGÈS, A.-Y., «Panorama de la littérature hagiographique bretonne médiévale», *Hagio-historiographie médiévale*: <http://www.hagiohistoriographiemedievale.blogspot.com> (3 décembre 2010).

—, «Hagiographie et langue bretonnes: quelques notes sur les apports des Mauristes au *Glossarium* de Du Cange», *ibid.* (25 mars 2018).

—, «Les Vikings dans l'hagiographie bretonne», in M. COUMERT – Y. TRANVOUEZ, dir., *Landévennec, les Vikings et la Bretagne. En hommage à Jean-Christophe Cassard*, Brest, 2015, p. 211-228.

—, «Retour sur les différents types d'approche du matériau hagiographique médiéval par les historiens de la Bretagne depuis le XIXe siècle», in M. COUMERT – H. BOUGET, dir., *Enjeux épistémologiques des recherches sur les Bretagnes médiévales en histoire, langue et littérature* (colloque de Brest, 2017), Brest, à paraître.

CASSARD, J.-C., «En marge des incursions vikings», *Annales de Bretagne*, 98/3 (1991), p. 261-272.

GARAULT, C., «Quelques perspectives de recherche. Autour de l'espace et du sacré dans sept Vies de saints bretonnes», in *Sacrée nature, paysages du sacré!* (colloque d'Orléans, 2009), à paraître.

GARAVAGLIA, C., «Les miracles des abeilles dans l'hagiographie bretonne», in A.-Y. BOURGÈS – V. RAYDON, dir., *Hagiographie bretonne et mythologie celtique*, Marseille, 2016, p. 293-315 (Au cœur des mythes, 4).

HOUDUS, É., *Actualisation du Mémento des sources hagiographiques de l'histoire de Bretagne de l'abbé Duine. Première partie: les fondateurs et les primitifs (V[e]-Xe siècles)*. Mémoire de maîtrise, Université de Rennes 2, 2001 (dir. B. Merdrignac).

Koch, J. T., « Hagiography, Breton », in J. T. Koch – A. Minard, dir., *The Celts. History, Life, and Culture*. I: *A-H*, Santa Barbara, CA, 2012, p. 406-407.

Le Hénaff-Rozé, C., « Les brittonismes au crible des concordances. La préposition *cum* dans les *vitae* composées à Landévennec au IXe siècle », in L. Lemoine *et al.*, dir., *Corona Monastica. Mélanges offerts au père Marc Simon*, Rennes, 2004, p. 227-238 (Britannia Monastica, 8).

Merdrignac, B., « Les saints et la "seconde migration bretonne" », in P.-R. Giot *et al.*, dir., *Les premiers Bretons d'Armorique*, Rennes, 2003, p. 93-120; aussi paru en anglais sous le titre « The Saints and the "Second British Migration" », in P.-R. Giot *et al.*, dir., *The British Settlement of Brittany. The First Bretons in Armorica*, Stroud, 2003, p. 119-154.

—, « La Neustrie/Normandie dans les Vies de saints bretons », in J. Quaghebeur – B. Merdrignac, dir., *Bretons et Normands au Moyen Âge. Rivalités, malentendus, convergences*, Rennes, 2008, p. 35-50.

—, « Hagiographes », in J.-C. Cassard *et al.*, dir., *Dictionnaire d'histoire de Bretagne*, Morlaix, 2008, p. 360-361.

—, « Châtiments et égarement dans quelques *Vitae* bretonnes », in J. Quaghebeur – S. Soleil, dir., *Le pouvoir et la foi au Moyen Âge en Bretagne et dans l'Europe de l'Ouest. Mélanges en mémoire du professeur Hubert Guillotel*, Rennes, 2010, p. 187-196.

—, « Présence et représentations de la Domnonée et de la Cornouaille de part et d'autre de la Manche d'après les Vies de saints et les listes généalogiques médiévales », *Annales de Bretagne*, 117/4 (2010), p. 83-119.

—, « Les origines antiques dans les *Vitae* de saints bretons du haut Moyen Âge », in M. Coumert *et al.*, dir., *Histoires des Bretagnes*, 1: *Les mythes fondateurs*, Brest, 2010, p. 43-58.

—, *D'une Bretagne à l'autre. Les migrations bretonnes entre histoire et légendes*, Rennes, 2012.

—, « D'une Bretagne à l'autre. Les migrations bretonnes entre histoire et légendes », in A. Goarzin – J.-Y. Le Disez, dir., *Bretagne/Cornouailles (britanniques): quelles relations? – Brittany/Cornwall: What Relations?*, Rennes, 2013, p. 15-32 (condensé de l'ouvrage précédent).

Poulin, J.-C., « Les réécritures dans l'hagiographie bretonne (VIIIe-XIIe siècles) », in M. Goullet – M. Heinzelmann, dir., *La réécriture hagiographique dans l'Occident médiéval. Transformations formelles et idéologiques*, Ostfildern, 2003, p. 145-194 (Beihefte der Francia, 58).

—, *L'hagiographie bretonne du haut Moyen Âge. Répertoire raisonné*, Ostfildern, 2009 (Beihefte der Francia, 69).

—, «Hagiographie bretonne ancienne (avant 1100)», in F. MORVAN, dir., *Histoire de Bretagne. Église, religion, croyances, du Moyen Âge à nos jours*, Pietraserena (Corse), 2018, p. 13-32 (Encyclopédie de la Bretagne).

—, «Présence d'une culture celtique insulaire chez les anciens hagiographes bretons», in C. BRETT, dir., Colloque de Cambridge, 2017, Turnhout, à paraître.

C. Dossiers individuels

Dans la revue suivante des dossiers individuels, les références bibliographiques et les renvois à des éditions ne font que compléter, corriger ou actualiser les bibliographies générale et particulières de notre *Répertoire raisonné* de 2009.

1. Conwoion de Redon († 868)

La Vie de Conwoion († 868) est incorporée (surtout au premier livre) dans une histoire plus vaste des origines de sa fondation monastique à Redon en 832 (*BHL* 1945). L'étude du texte est handicapée par la conservation incomplète de ses trois livres: il manque le début et la fin de l'œuvre, ainsi qu'un passage de longueur indéterminée à la fin du premier chapitre du premier livre. Le contenu des portions perdues peut être entrevu grâce à une réécriture abrégée du XIe siècle (*BHL* 1946) par un moine redonnais qui a connu une version complète des *Gesta*. Ce long document est la seule *Erlebnislegende* de l'ancienne hagiographie bretonne; Hubert Guillotel a cependant identifié une interpolation possible au chapitre 10 du deuxième livre, qui aurait pu être effectuée au premier quart du XIIe siècle[85]. Pour des raisons qui ne sont pas entièrement convaincantes, Eef Overgaauw pense que le troisième et dernier livre a pu être composé à Redon par un deuxième écrivain au début du Xe siècle[86]. De même, l'attribution des *Gesta* à Ratvili, évêque d'Alet, n'est pas du tout certaine[87].

---

[85] GUILLOTEL (1998), p. 134-136.

[86] E. A. OVERGAAUW, recension de l'édition BRETT 1989, dans: *Le Moyen Âge*, 101 (1995), p. 325 sq.

[87] Voir cependant GARAULT (2009), p. 149 et ses références.

Bibliographie complémentaire

GARAULT, C., «La mise en texte du passé: traditions locales et mémoire monastique. Le cas de l'abbaye de Saint-Sauveur de Redon», in *L'autorité de l'écrit au Moyen Âge (Orient-Occident)*, Paris, 2009, p. 148-152 (Histoire ancienne et médiévale, 102).

—, «L'abbaye de Saint-Sauveur de Redon, entre centre et confins. Débats historiographiques et enjeux identitaires», in H. BOUGET – M. COUMERT, dir., *Histoires des Bretagnes, 2: Itinéraires et confins*, Brest, 2011, p. 37-53.

KRAMER, R. D., «*In divinis scripturis legitur*»: Monastic Ideals and the Use of the Bible in the «Gesta sanctorum Rotonensium». Thèse de maîtrise, Université d'Utrecht, 2007: <http://dspace.library.uu.nl/handle/1874/25390>.

—, «*In divinis scripturis legitur*. Monastieke idealen en het gebruik van de Bijbel in de *Gesta sanctorum Rotonensium*», *Millennium. Tijdschrift voor middeleeuwse studies*, 22/1 (2008), p. 24-44. Résumé de la thèse de maîtrise de 2007.

—, «*...Quia cor regis in manu Dei est...*: The Pharaoh in Carolingian Monastic Narratives», in P. DEPREUX et al., dir., *Compétition et sacré au haut Moyen Âge: entre médiation et exclusion*, Turnhout, 2015, p. 139-163 (Coll. Haut Moyen Âge, 21).

MAZEL, F., «Entre mémoire carolingienne et réforme "grégorienne". Stratégies discursives, identité monastique et enjeux de pouvoir à Redon aux XIe-XIIe siècles», *Annales de Bretagne*, 122 (2015), p. 9-39. Avec un excursus intitulé «La translation des reliques de saint Maixent et le devenir de l'abbaye de Redon au Xe siècle» (p. 33-38).

ROBREAU, B., «Les Actes des saints de Redon. Christianisme et celticité», in A.-Y. BOURGÈS – V. RAYDON, dir., *Hagiographie bretonne et mythologie celtique*, Marseille, 2016, p. 229-271 (Au cœur des mythes, 4).

2. Ethbinus/Idunetus

Il est difficile de savoir si la Vie propre de saint Ethbin/Idunet (*BHL* 2621) a d'abord existé séparément, avant que son épisode principal soit interpolé au milieu du XIe siècle dans l'exemplaire de Quimper (BM 16) de la Vie de saint Guénolé (*BHL* 8957, au livre II, chap. 24), ou si au contraire elle constitue un développement postérieur à la rencontre de la mémoire de ces deux saints. Il est même difficile de savoir si la double dénomination correspond, ou non, à l'amalgame de deux personnages distincts, disciple(s) prétendu(s) de saint Guénolé.

Il semble en tout cas assuré qu'Ethbin est entré dans les traditions bretonnes à l'occasion du séjour de la communauté de Landévennec exilée à Montreuil, au Xe siècle, pour cause d'agressions vikings (Landévennec fut brûlé en 913)[88]. Au retour de cet exil, les moines de Landévennec ont fait une place anecdotique à Ethbin dans la Vie de leur saint patron, et plus complètement ensuite dans leur nouveau cartulaire. Pour autant, la dévotion à saint Ethbin n'a guère eu de succès en Bretagne; l'aire principale de son culte se situe plutôt dans le nord de la France.

Bibliographie complémentaire

BARBET-MASSIN, D., «Le miracle du lépreux dans l'hagiographie bretonne et irlandaise», in J.-C. CASSARD, dir., *Mélanges offerts au professeur Bernard Merdrignac*, Rennes, 2013, p. 27-52 (Britannia monastica, 10).

3. Judocus de Saint-Josse-sur-Mer

Frère de saint Judicaël, il n'a pas voulu lui succéder comme roi de Domnonée; son exil volontaire, puis son installation en Ponthieu (dép. Pas-de-Calais) l'ont fait sortir de l'orbite de l'hagiographie bretonne proprement dite. Dès le milieu du IXe siècle, Loup de Ferrières († 862) a composé un sermon (dépourvu de contenu biographique) en son honneur (*BHL* 4510d). Il faut attendre les environs de 900 pour qu'une première Vie (en prose: *BHL* 4504) soit rédigée à Saint-Josse-sur-Mer (Montreuil?); son dernier éditeur (LE BOURDELLÈS, 1993) pense pouvoir l'attribuer à un moine breton vers 920, pour des motifs peu convaincants. Le défaut d'apparentement de cette biographie avec le reste de l'ancienne hagiographie bretonne se révèle non seulement par l'absence de lien de dépendance envers la Vie de saint Samson, mais surtout par son inscription résolue dans le sillage formel du dossier de saint Fursy (*BHL* 3209 et 3213). Aucune trace d'un culte à saint Josse n'est décelable en Bretagne avant l'an mil. Des reliques de saint Josse ont traversé la Manche vers 900 (sans récit de translation connu), pour stimuler ensuite la composition d'une Vie métrique à Winchester

---

[88] Nous ne suivons pas ici TANGUY (2003), p. 123, qui place au IXe siècle la rédaction de la Vie de saint Ethbin.

(Hampshire) à la fin du Xe siècle (*BHL* 4512); ce long poème démarque la première Vie en prose.

Bibliographie complémentaire

GARRY, S. – HELVÉTIUS, A.-M., «De Saint-Josse à Montreuil: l'encadrement ecclésiastique du *vicus* de Quentovic», in S. LEBECQ *et al.*, dir., *Quentovic. Environnement, archéologie, histoire*, Lille, 2010, p. 459-473.

ORLANDI, G., «Lupus Ferrariensis abb.», in CHIESA, P. – L. CASTALDI, dir., *La trasmissione dei testi latini del Medioevo. Medieval Latin Texts and their Transmission. Te.Tra.3*, Florence, 2008, p. 432-454 (Millennio medievale, 75; Strumenti e studi, n.s. 18).

4. Lenoverius/Leonorius

Un premier état de sa Vie (sous le nom de Lenoverius) est connu par un quaternion-épave copié à Fleury-sur-Loire vers la fin du Xe siècle (*BHL vacat*); l'auteur est probablement un clerc breton, mais il est difficile de savoir s'il effectua sa rédaction en Bretagne ou à Fleury seulement, où il aurait trouvé refuge à cause des agressions vikings dans la seconde moitié du Xe siècle. À cette époque, la Vie de saint Samson était en tout cas disponible à Fleury; elle a fortement influencé l'écriture de la Vie de saint Lunaire. B. Merdrignac pense qu'une version primitive (maintenant perdue) aurait pu être composée à Saint-Jacut avant le Xe siècle[89]. Pour connaître un récit complet de la vie de saint Lunaire, il faut se reporter à la réécriture légèrement condensée effectuée au XIe siècle (*BHL* 4880; sous le nom de Leonorius), peut-être pour le prieuré de Beaumont-sur-Oise (dioc. Beauvais).

5. Machutes d'Alet

La prétention du diacre Bili d'Alet à réformer (*emendare*) une Vie primitive ne suffit pas à convaincre de l'existence d'une *Vita primigenia* perdue. Le dossier monté par Bili (*BHL* 5116a et 5116b) vers 870 a vite connu une circulation mouvementée; il est en effet très possible que le premier livre ait été largement interpolé en milieu parisien, au moment où le clergé d'Alet s'y

---

[89] B. MERDRIGNAC, «*Eppur si muove*: quelques notes sur le dos d'une enveloppe...», in B. MERDRIGNAC *et al.*, dir., *La paroisse, communauté et territoire. Constitution et recomposition du maillage paroissial*, Rennes, 2013, p. 423.

était réfugié vers 920. Il faut peut-être compter aussi comme contribution parisienne au même moment un récit de translation de Saintonge vers la Bretagne (*BHL* 5124), inspiré du dossier de saint Magloire. Il est également possible que certaines parties de la rédaction de Bili se soient perdues en cours de route[90]. À Alet, deux Vies anonymes (*BHL* 5117 et 5118a) ont bientôt donné la réplique à Bili vers 900, dans le cadre du débat sur les prétentions métropolitaines de Dol. Enfin, Malo fut un des saints bretons les mieux reçus en Angleterre: au xe siècle, à Winchester, la Vie de Bili fut traduite en vieil-anglais[91]. Il est possible que cette traduction recèle des portions du texte de Bili que les manuscrits latins ont laissé échapper. Vers l'an mil, une prière à saint Malo fut ajoutée à Winchester dans un psautier du milieu du xe siècle, par une moniale du Nunnaminster[92].

Bibliographie complémentaire

BOURGÈS, A.-Y., «Passage du diacre Bili à Lanmeur: une source possible de la *Vita* de saint Malo», *Bulletin de la Société archéologique du Finistère*, 123 (1994), p. 457-464.

—, «Trois siècles d'histoire littéraire: le dossier hagiographique médiéval de Malo», *Annales de la Société d'histoire et d'archéologie de l'arrondissement de Saint-Malo*, (2013) [2014], p. 287-291; résumé d'une communication parue sous le même titre in J.-L. BLAISE, dir., *Jean de Châtillon, second fondateur de Saint-Malo*, Saint-Malo, 2014, p. 157-185.

GARAULT, C., «Les rapports entre récits hagiographiques et matériel diplomatique à travers le dossier hagiographique de saint Malo (IXe-XIIe siècle)», in M.-C. ISAÏA – T. GRANIER, dir., *Normes et hagiographie dans l'Occident (VIe-XVIe siècle)*, Turnhout, 2014, p. 309-327 (Hagiologia, 9).

—, «La *Vita sancti Machutis* par Bili: reflets des enjeux territoriaux liés au pouvoir épiscopal dans les années 870 en Haute Bretagne», in G. BÜHRER-THIERRY – S. PATZOLD, dir., *Genèse des espaces politiques (IXe-XIIe siècle). Autour de la question spatiale dans les royaumes francs et postcarolingiens* (colloque de Marne-la-Vallée, 2013), Turnhout, 2018, p. 193-199 (Coll. Haut Moyen Âge, 28).

PETOUT, P., «La diffusion du culte de saint Malo», in P. d'ORNELLAS, dir., *Saint-Malo, la cathédrale des corsaires*, Strasbourg, 2017, p. 24-35 et 286 (La grâce d'une cathédrale).

---

[90] POULIN (2009), p. 154 et 165.
[91] WHATLEY (1996), p. 452 et 456.
[92] Cf. *supra*, p. 222 et n. 82.

PIETRI, L. – HEIJMANS, M. (avec la collaboration de B. MERDRIGNAC), «Maclovius», in *Prosopographie de la Gaule chrétienne (314-614)*, t. II, Paris, 2013, p. 1220 sq. (Prosopographie chrétienne du Bas-Empire, 4).

6. Maglorius de Dol

C'est au monastère de Léhon (dép. Côtes-d'Armor, ci-devant Côtes-du-Nord) que fut monté l'essentiel du dossier hagiographique ancien de saint Magloire, entre le début de la seconde moitié du IXe siècle et la fuite devant les vikings vers 920. (Vie, miracles, translation, construction d'une basilique: *BHL* 5139-44, 5146). Deux versions abrégées, obtenues par coupures importantes, assez difficiles à dater et à localiser, ont été tirées de la Vie longue; une seule de ces réductions a été publiée[93]. Ce réaménagement pourrait être aussi tardif que le XIIe siècle, date du manuscrit le plus ancien. Un récit de translation à Paris (*BHL* 5147) complète ce dossier, sans doute composé par des moines de Léhon réfugiés à Paris au Xe siècle.

Bibliographie complémentaire

GARAULT, C., «L'*Aedificatio basilicae apud Lehonium* (*BHL* 5146) ou la construction d'un nouveau sanctuaire par les moines de Saint-Magloire de Léhon», in J.-C. CASSARD *et al.*, dir., *Mélanges offerts au professeur Bernard Merdrignac*, Rennes, 2013, p. 227-246 (Britannia monastica, 17).

PIGEON, É.-A., «Saint Magloire. Et la translation de son corps de l'île de Serk au monastère de Lehon», *Mémoires de la Société académique du Cotentin. (Archéologie, Belles-Lettres, Sciences et Beaux-Arts)*, 12 (1896), p. 27-44 (réimpr. dans ID., *Texte français et latin des Vies des saints du diocèse de Coutances et Avranches, avec des notions préliminaires et l'histoire des reliques de chaque saint*, t. II, Avranches, 1898, p. 233-250).

LEVALET, D., «Des translations de reliques dans le diocèse d'Avranches aux IXe et Xe siècles. Nouvelles hypothèses», *Revue de l'Avranchin et du Pays de Granville*, 90 (2013), p. 169-189.

MORVAN, É., éd., *Le dossier hagiographique de saint Magloire. Texte, traduction et commentaire*. Mémoire de Master 2, Université de Bretagne occidentale (Brest), 2010 (dir. M. Coumert); comprend l'édition de passages inédits, absents des éditions précédentes.

---

[93] Par Joseph VAN HECKE dans les *AASS*, Oct. X, 1861 (*BHL* 5140/44).

—, *La fondation du monastère de Léhon d'après la Vie de saint Magloire.* Communication au colloque de Dinan, 29 mai 2010: <http://www.klewel.com/histoire-du-moyen-age-en-cotes-d-armor.php>.

SMITH, J. M. H., «Maglorius», *Oxford Dictionary of National Biography*, 36 (2004), p. 127-128.

7. Melanius de Rennes (†c. 530)

Outre un récit de miracle inséré par Grégoire de Tours dans son *In gloria confessorum* 54 (*BHL* 5892), c'est à Rennes que fut développé le dossier hagiographique de saint Melaine. Une première Vie (*BHL* 5887-5888), peut-être complétée par un recueil de miracles (maintenant perdu), pourrait être aussi ancienne que la fin du IXe siècle – en tout cas après 867 d'après A. Lunven[94]; il est impossible de la faire remonter jusqu'au VIIe siècle, car il faut au moins attendre que le *Vita s. Vedasti* d'Alcuin ait été connue à Rennes (au début du IXe siècle au plus tôt). Cette *Vita prima* a ensuite fait l'objet de deux réécritures indépendantes (*BHL* 5891 et 5889-90), probablement au monastère de Saint-Melaine de Rennes, au plus tôt au Xe siècle, mais peut-être aussi tard qu'au milieu du XIe siècle[95].

Bibliographie complémentaire

BONNAIRE, É., *La* Vita prima sancti Melanii. *Approche historique de la transmission du texte*, 1: *Introduction critique et édition*, 2: *Annexes*. Mémoire de Master 2, Université de Rennes 2, 2012, 2 vol. (dir. I. Rosé): <http://services.univ-rennes2.fr/memorable>; nouvelle édition de la première Vie au t. I, p. 153-180, à l'aide de l'ensemble des témoins.

[BONNAIRE-]LEFORT, É., «Le rayonnement de saint Melaine à travers l'étude de son dossier hagiographique: l'exemple de la *Vita prima*», in CIRDoMoc éd., Rennes, 2016, p. 93-107 (Britannia monastica, 18).

PIETRI, L. – HEIJMANS, M. (avec la collaboration de B. MERDRIGNAC), «Melanius 2», in *Prosopographie de la Gaule chrétienne (314-614)*, t. II, Paris, 2013, p. 1316-1317 (Prosopographie chrétienne du Bas-Empire, 4).

---

[94] LUNVEN (2014), «Pouvoir épiscopal», p. 128.

[95] Pour *BHL* 5891, voir LUNVEN (2014), *Du diocèse à la paroisse*, p. 65 sq. Et encore LUNVEN (2014), «Pouvoir épiscopal», p. 130.

8. Meroveus

La Vie de ce saint prêtre est assurément ancienne, car son témoin manuscrit unique est daté de 900 environ. Malgré l'origine rennaise du saint, son appartenance à l'hagiographie bretonne est marginale: son nom, l'aire de diffusion de sa renommée posthume, les emprunts de son biographe à la deuxième Vie de saint Calais (*BHL* 1569-70, composée vers 860) orientent plutôt vers le diocèse du Mans. Son témoignage a été surtout utilisé pour l'étude du tracé de la frontière entre les diocèses de Rennes et du Mans[96].

9. PAULUS AURELIANUS de Saint-Pol de Léon

La Vie de saint Paul Aurélien par le moine-prêtre Gurmonoc de Landévennec est la seule œuvre hagiographique bretonne ancienne datable avec précision: son auteur l'a achevée en 884 exactement. Il se place dans une dépendance formelle assumée du grand œuvre de son maître et abbé, Gurdisten de Landévennec, auteur d'un grand dossier sur saint Guénolé (cf. *infra*); Gurmonoc en imite jusqu'au régime intensif d'emprunts littéraux à de nombreux auteurs chrétiens et profanes. La translation des reliques du saint à Fleury-sur-Loire au milieu du Xe siècle par l'évêque Mabbon de Saint-Pol paraît sans lien avec les attaques des vikings; ce déplacement est évoqué vers l'an mil par Aimoin de Fleury dans ses Miracles de saint Benoît (*BHL* 6587, chap. 11 et 12). Une translation hypothétique de saint Paul Aurélien – ou du moins de son chef – à Nantes, puis à Saint-Florent-le-Vieil au Xe-XIe siècle n'a pas donné naissance à une documentation hagiographique[97].

Bibliographie complémentaire

«Wrmonocus Landevenecensis monachus», *Repertorium fontium historiae Medii Aevi*, XI-4: *Fontes W-Z*, Rome, 2007, p. 493-494.

BOURGÈS, A.-Y., «Du "métaréalisme" dans la *Vita sancti Pauli* de Wrmonoc? La description du chef-lieu épiscopal de Léon», in *Hagio-historiographie médiévale* (22 août 2017): <http://www.hagio-historiographiemedievale.blogspot.com>.

---

[96] PICHOT (2012). Et dernièrement sur ce point: LUNVEN (2014), *Du diocèse à la paroisse*, p. 65 sq. et 89. LUNVEN (2014), «Pouvoir épiscopal», p. 130, 138 et carte p. 129. MAZEL (2016), p. 260 sq. et 426, n. 76.
[97] CASTEL (1997), p. 103-106.

BRETT, C., « Paulus [Aurelianus] », *Oxford Dictionary of National Biography*, 43 (2004), p. 126-127.
HENRY, P., « Paul Aurélien, le costarmoricain ? », in J.-C. CASSARD *et al.* dir., *Mélanges offerts au professeur Bernard Merdrignac*, Rennes, 2013, p. 213-226 (Britannia monastica, 10).
PIETRI, L. – HEIJMANS, M. (avec la collaboration de B. MERDRIGNAC), « Paulus Aurelianus », in *Prosopographie de la Gaule chrétienne (314-614)*, t. II, Paris, 2013, p. 1457 sq. (Prosopographie chrétienne du Bas-Empire, 4).
POULIN, J.-C., « Gurmonocus Landevenecensis mon. », in M.-H. JULLIEN, dir., *Clavis des auteurs latins du Moyen Âge. Territoire français, 735-987*, III: *Faof – Hilduin*, Turnhout, 2010, p. 257-258 (*CC CM*).

10. SAMSON de Dol († *c.* 565 ?)

La *Vita* connue sous le nom de « Vie ancienne » (*BHL* 7478-79) est en fait le résultat de la réécriture d'une Vie primitive perdue. Cette *primigenia* est attribuable à un auteur gallois (connu sous le nom de « diacre Hénoc », cousin du saint) qui l'a composée sur le continent[98]. À ce texte de base, un moine de Dol a ajouté plusieurs compléments au premier livre et la plus grande partie du second livre (= *Vita I^a*) ; il travaillait vers la fin du VIIIe siècle, à la demande d'un évêque Tigernomagle. Peu après 860, un autre moine de Dol en a effectué une refonte complète (*BHL* 7481 et 7483 = *Vita II^a*) et ajouté la mention d'un archiépiscopat de Samson[99]; puis un clerc de Dol a joint à cette réécriture trois ornements métriques (*BHL* 7480, 7482, 7484) dédiés à l'évêque Lovenan de Dol entre la fin du IXe siècle et 920 environ. Comme le texte de la Vie est fort long, un auteur travaillant hors de Bretagne[100] a établi une réécriture abrégée de la *Vita II^a* dès la seconde moitié du IXe siècle, s'il faut en croire la date de son manuscrit unique (Vatican, Reg. lat. 479);

---

[98] Après avoir hésité à reconnaître l'existence de ce premier état (maintenant perdu), P. Flobert est finalement d'avis qu'il est un mythe: FLOBERT (2005), p. 53 (p. 661 de la réimpression).

[99] Le HUËROU (2006), t. I, p. 291 sq. estime que cette innovation (en II-24) a pu être ajoutée après coup.

[100] Voir par exemple la suppression, au chapitre 3 (fol. 10v), d'un éloge de Samson en tant que breton: *Huic vero de Britannorum genere similis non fuit, nec est, nec esse poterit*.

elle n'y est conservée que dans un état mutilé par perte matérielle, inédit à ce jour.

Bibliographie complémentaire

BIELER, L., «Silberstäbe als Weihgeschenk», *Anzeiger der Akademie der Wissenschaften in Wien. Philosophisch-historische Klasse*, 68 (1931), p. 1-12.

BOURGÈS, A.-Y., «En marge de la *vita* ancienne de Samson (*BHL* 7478-7479), le "royaume double" de Domnonée des deux côtés de la Manche: un faux débat mais de vraies interrogations», in *Hagio-historiographie médiévale* (23 avril 2019): <http://www.hagiohistoriographiemedievale.blogspot.com>.

—, «Quelques réflexions à propos du dossier hagio-historiographique de l'évêché et de la métropole de Dol», *ibid.* (22 juin 2019).

BRETT, C., «The Hare and the Tortoise? *Vita prima Sancti Samsonis, Vita Paterni* and Merovingian Hagiography», in OLSON (2017), *St Samson of Dol*, p. 83-101.

CHIRON, Y., «Leucher, ou Leucharus, Leucherus», *Dictionnaire de biographie française*, t. 22, Paris, 2018, col. 449 sq.

CORDO RUSSO, L., «La versión de la *Vita Samsonis* del *Liber Landavensis* (National Library of Wales Ms. 17110E)», *Temas Medievales* (Buenos Aires), 21 (2013), p. 49-96.

FLOBERT, P., *Grammaire comparée et variétés du latin. Articles revus et mis à jour (1964-2012)*, Genève, 2014 (ÉPHÉ, Hautes études médiévales et modernes, 105); comprend six articles relatifs à saint Samson et Dol (section VII, n°s 76 à 81), mais ignore les positions prises dans POULIN (2009).

HARVEY, D. C., «Constructed Landscapes and Social Memory: Tales of St Samson in Early Medieval Cornwall», *Environment and Planning*, D: *Society and Space*, 20/2 (2002), p. 231-248.

HARVEY, D. C. – JONES, R., «Custom and Habit(us): The Meaning of Traditions and Legends in Early Medieval Western Britain», *Geografiska Annaler*, B: *Human Geography*, 81/4 (1999), p. 223-233.

JANKULAK, K., «The Absent Saint: St Samson in Wales», in CASSARD, J.-C. et al., dir., *Mélanges offerts au professeur Bernard Merdrignac*, Rennes, 2013, p. 197-212 (Britannia monastica, 10).

—, «Present and yet Absent: The Cult of St Samson of Dol in Wales», in OLSON (2017), *St Samson of Dol*, p. 163-180.

KIRSCH, W., «Ausblick: *Vita metrica s. Samsonis*», in ID., *Laudes sanctorum. Geschichte der hagiographischen Versepik vom IV. bis X. Jahrhundert*, II: *Entfaltung (VIII.-X. Jahrhundert)*, I, Stuttgart, 2011, p. 661-669 (Quellen und Untersuchungen zur lateinischen Philologie des Mittelalters, 14).

LEWIS, B. J., «The Saints in Narratives of Conversion from the Brittonic-Speaking Regions», in R. FLECHNER – M. NÍ MHADNAIGH, dir., *The Introduction of Christianity into the Early Medieval Insular World. Converting the Isles I*, Turnhout, 2016, p. 431-456 (Cultural Encounters in Late Antiquity and the Middle Ages, 19).

MERDRIGNAC, B., «Saint Samson et saint Germain», in G. BURON et al., dir., *À travers les îles celtiques. Mélanges à la mémoire de Gwénaël Le Duc*, Rennes, 2008, p. 249-254 (Britannia monastica, 12).

MEWS, C. J., «Apostolic Authority and Celtic Liturgies: From the *Vita Samsonis* to the *Ratio de cursus*», in OLSON (2017), *St Samson of Dol*, p. 115-135.

OLSON, L., «The Early Hagiography of Saint Samson of Dol», in G. EVANS et al., dir., *Origins and Revivals: Proceedings of the First Australian Conference of Celtic Studies*, Sydney, 2000, p. 123-133 (Sydney Series in Celtic Studies, 3).

—, «The Date of the First Life of St Samson of Dol», in P. O'NEILL, dir., *The Land beneath the Sea. Essays in Honour of Anders Ahlqvist's Contribution to Celtic Studies in Australia*, Sydney, 2013, p. 171-182 (Sydney Series in Celtic Studies, 14).

—, dir., *St Samson of Dol and the Earliest History of Brittany, Cornwall and Wales*, Woodbrige, 2017 (Studies in Celtic History, 37).

—, «"Getting somewhere" with the First Life of St Samson», in OLSON (2017), *St Samson of Dol*, p. 1-18.

PIETRI, L. – HEIJMANS, M. (avec la collaboration de B. MERDRIGNAC), «Henocus» et «Samson», in iid. éd., *Prosopographie de la Gaule chrétienne (314-614)*, t. II, Paris, 2013, p. 971 et p. 1700-1701 (Prosopographie chrétienne du Bas-Empire, 4).

POULIN, J.-C., «La circulation de l'information dans la Vie ancienne de saint Samson et la question de sa datation», in OLSON (2017), *St Samson of Dol*, p. 37-82 et 181-208.

ROBREAU, B., «Saint Samson», *Bulletin de la Société de mythologie française*, 247 (2012), p. 29-38 (ignore POULIN 2009).

SMITH, J. M. H., «Samson», *Oxford Dictionary of National Biography*, 48 (2004), p. 807-808.

SOWERBY, R., «The Lives of Saint Samson. Rewriting the Ambitions of an Early Medieval Cult», *Francia*, 38 (2011), p. 1-31.

—, «A Family and its Saint in the *Vita prima Samsonis*», in OLSON (2017), *St Samson of Dol*, p. 19-36.

WOOD, I. N., «Columbanus, the Britons, and the Merovingian Church», in OLSON (2017), *St Samson of Dol*, p. 103-114.

WOODING, J., «The Representation of Early British Monasticism and *Peregrinatio* in *Vita Prima S. Samsonis*», in OLSON (2017), *St Samson of Dol*, p. 137-161.

11. Turiavus de Dol

Une Vie primitive (perdue) fut peut-être composée à Dol, au plus tôt dans la seconde moitié du IXe siècle (après 860); il en découle une *Vita brevior*, peut-être doloise elle aussi, mais nettement postérieure au milieu du IXe siècle, et peut-être pas antérieure au XIe siècle (*BHL* 8341). On s'est aussi intéressé à saint Turiau hors de Bretagne, car une Vie (allongée de miracles) fut composée par un moine de Saint-Germain-des-Prés, probablement dans la première moitié du XIe siècle (*BHL* 8342-43). Parallèlement à cette Vie dite «de Paris» existe aussi une Vie dite «de Clermont», composée par un auteur qui n'est certainement pas un Breton (*BHL* 8342d); sa date est postérieure, du XIIIe siècle au plus tard, date de son manuscrit unique.

12. Wenailus

Ce saint d'origine bretonne est demeuré méconnu en Armorique du haut Moyen Âge; sa première biographie (*BHL* 8818) fut probablement écrite après la fin du XIe siècle, peut-être à Corbeil (dép. Essonne). Il convient, à notre avis, de renoncer à voir dans cette Vie la plus ancienne composition hagiographique issue du scriptorium de Landévennec au début du IXe siècle, ou même à la fin de ce siècle[101]. C'est bien après une translation en région parisienne (*BHL* 8819) qu'il faut plutôt en placer la rédaction, même si l'auteur a probablement connu la grande Vie de saint Guénolé par Gurdisten.

Bibliographie complémentaire

MORVANNOU, F., «Saint Guenhaël», in *Les saints bretons du pays vannetais*, Vannes, 2003, p. 77-91 (constituant un supplément au *Bulletin de la Société polymathique du Morbihan*, 129 [2003]).

13. Winnocus

Ce saint d'origine bretonne n'appartient pas véritablement à l'hagiographie bretonne; sa première Vie est relativement ancienne (avant 820), mais composée par un moine de Saint-Bertin (*BHL* 8952); elle fait partie d'un ensemble qui n'a rien de breton, en continuation des Vies des saints Omer et Bertin.

---

[101] Ainsi chez MORICE (2007), t. I, p. 133 et 143 s.

Bibliographie complémentaire

Liot, R., «Un apôtre breton en Flandre: saint Winnoc», *Bulletin de la Société archéologique du Finistère*, 83 (1957), p. 102-105 et 84 (1958), p. 218-226.

Mériaux, C., *Gallia irradiata. Saints et sanctuaires dans le nord de la Gaule du haut Moyen Âge*, Stuttgart, 2006, p. 371-372 (Beiträge zur Hagiographie, 4).

14. Winwaloeus de Landévennec

L'abondant dossier de saint Guénolé s'ouvre par trois hymnes, dont la troisième au moins fut composée par le moine Clément de Landévennec, dans les années 860 (peut-être entre 863 et 867)[102]. Une Vie brève du milieu du IXe siècle, maintenant perdue, a peut-être existé. Mais le chantre principal de la renommée posthume de saint Guénolé est assurément l'abbé Gurdisten de Landévennec, autour de 870; nous lui devons en effet une Vie (très) longue (*BHL* 8957-58), une Homélie (*BHL* 8959) et enfin une réécriture condensée (*Vita et Homelia*, *BHL* 8960) offerte à l'évêque Jean d'Arezzo. Le souvenir de saint Guénolé fut aussi cultivé hors de Bretagne, notamment à Montreuil-sur-Mer, où s'étaient réfugiés les moines de Landévennec (en passant par Fleury?) après la destruction de leur monastère par les vikings en 913; c'est probablement par suite de cet exil que furent composés (au XIIe siècle au plus tard) une *Vita brevior* établie par coupures mécaniques de la Vie longue de Gurdisten (*BHL* 8956d) et un *Sermunculus de vita* (*BHL* 8962).

Bibliographie complémentaire

Édition des trois hymnes et de l'*Homelia* par Morice (2007), t. II, p. 525-539.

Édition de la lettre d'envoi de la Vie dite «d'Arezzo» par P. Licciardello, *Agiografia aretina altomedievale. Testi agiografici e contexti socio-culturali ad Arezzo tre VI e XI secolo*, Florence, 2005, p. 158-159 (Millennio medievale, 56; Strumenti e studi, n.s. 9).

Édition de la Vie dite «d'Arezzo» (*BHL* 8960) par C. Garavaglia, *Un monastero bretone nell'alto Medioevo: l'abbazia di san Guenole a Lan-*

---

[102] Morice (2007), t. I, p. 73 se demande si les deux hymnes anonymes pourraient avoir été composées par Gurdisten. Bardel – Pérennec (2015), p. 85 envisagent l'hypothèse d'une rédaction à l'occasion de la translation des reliques du saint dans une nouvelle église, dans la seconde moitié du IXe siècle.

devennec. Mémoire de maîtrise, Université de Milan, 2001, p. 121-131.
« Wrdistenus Landevenecensis abbas », in *Repertorium fontium historiae Medii Aevi*. XI-4: *Fontes W-Z*, Rome, 2007, p. 495-496.
BARDEL, A. – PÉRENNEC, R., « Le monastère de Landévennec au temps du cartulaire », in LEBECQ (2015), *Cartulaire*, p. 65-89.
BARRET, S., « Le manuscrit [Quimper, BM 16]: codicologie et paléographie », in LEBECQ (2015), *Cartulaire*, p. 17-24.
BOURGÈS, A.-Y., « Mythes fondateurs de la Cornouaille. La Quaternité cornouaillaise. Une construction idéologique à l'époque carolingienne en Bretagne », in A.-Y. BOURGÈS – V. RAYDON, dir., *Hagiographie bretonne et mythologie celtique*, Marseille, 2016, p. 273-291 (Au cœur des mythes, 4).
—, « De l'hagiographe au "cartulariste": le cartulaire de Landévennec », in *Hagio-historiographie médiévale* (25 avril 2016): <http://www.hagiohistoriographiemedievale.blogspot.com>.
DEUFFIC, J.-L., « L'étrange colophon du *libellus* de Château-du-Loir en l'honneur de saint Guénolé de Landévennec », in ID., dir., *Le manuscrit, entre écriture et texte. Deuxième partie*, Turnhout, 2016, p. 7-11 (Pecia, 18).
JOURDAN DE LA PASSARDIÈRE, F., « À propos du cartulaire de Landévennec », *Bulletin diocésain d'histoire et d'archéologie. Diocèse de Quimper et de Léon*, 21 (1922), p. 205-241, 268-278 et 327-335.
KIRSCH, W., « Bretagne: Wrdestinus von Landévennec: Vita s. Winwaloei », in ID., Laudes sanctorum. *Geschichte der hagiographischen Versepik vom IV. bis X. Jahrhundert*, II: *Entfaltung (VIII.-X. Jahrhundert)*, I, Stuttgart, 2011, p. 648-661 (Quellen und Untersuchungen zur lateinischen Philologie des Mittelalters, 14).
LEBECQ, S., « Landévennec, les vikings et Montreuil-sur-Mer », in *Avel Gornog. Histoire, nature et vie en presqu'île de Crozon*, 19 (juillet 2011), p. 50-53; réimpr. dans la *Chronique de Landévennec*, 49 (janvier 2012), p. 37-45.
—, « Les moines de Landévennec à Montreuil-sur-Mer. Retour aux sources », in M. COUMERT – Y. TRANVOUEZ, dir., *Landévennec, les Vikings et la Bretagne. En hommage à Jean-Christophe Cassard*, Brest, 2015, p. 157-169 (développement de l'article précédent).
—, dir., *Cartulaire de l'abbaye de Saint-Guénolé de Landévennec*, Rennes, 2015; avec un fac-similé du manuscrit de Quimper, BM 16 (Sources médiévales de l'histoire de Bretagne, 6).
—, « Autour de quelques chartes de Landévennec. Regards sur l'histoire de l'abbaye entre le IXe et le XIe siècle », in ID. (2015), *Cartulaire*, p. 53-64.

LOCKETT, L., «Clemens Landevenecensis monachus», in M. LAPIDGE et al., dir., *Compendium auctorum latinorum Medii Aevi (500-1500)*, II-5: *Cadurcus – Colmanus*, Florence, 2008, p. 644.

MORICE, Y., «Passés recomposés. L'hagiographie dans le cartulaire de Landévennec», in LEBECQ (2015), *Cartulaire*, p. 91-102.

PABST, B., «Wurdestin v. Landévennec», in *LexMA*, IX (1998), col. 372.

PIETRI, L. – HEIJMANS, M. (avec la collaboration de B. MERDRIGNAC), «Winwaloeus», in *Prosopographie de la Gaule chrétienne (314-614)*, t. II, Paris, 2013, p. 2032 (Prosopographie chrétienne du Bas-Empire, 4).

POULIN, J.-C., «Gurdistenus Landevenecensis abb.», in M.-H. JULLIEN, dir., *Clavis des auteurs latins du Moyen Âge. Territoire français, 735-987*, III: *Faof – Hilduin*, Turnhout, 2010, p. 253-257 (*CC CM*).

—, «L'intertextualité dans la Vie longue de saint Guénolé de Landévennec», *Études celtiques*, 40 (2014), p. 165-221.

—, «Les sources formelles de la grande Vie de saint Guénolé», in LEBECQ (2015), *Cartulaire*, p. 103-106 (condensé de l'article précédent).

SIMON, M., «Les trois fils de Catmael. Un extrait de la Vie de saint Guénolé», *Chronique de Landévennec*, 30 (avril 2007), p. 85-93.

—, «Benoît ou Guénolé?», *Chronique de Landévennec*, 31 (juillet 2007), p. 133-138.

—, «Gurdisten, un abbé pour Landévennec au IXe siècle», *Chronique de Landévennec*, 33 (janvier 2008), p. 41-48.

—, «*Vita sancti Winwaloei*. Une réplique aux *Dialogues* de saint Grégoire le Grand?», in G. BURON et al., dir., *À travers les îles celtiques. Mélanges à la mémoire de Gwénaël Le Duc*, Rennes, 2008, p. 241-247 (Britannia monastica, 12).

—, «Traduction de l'hymne alphabétique du moine Clément», in LEBECQ (2015), *Cartulaire*, p. 151-153.

SIMON, M. – COCHOU, L. – Le HUËROU, A., «Traduction de la Vie longue de saint Guénolé par l'abbé Gurdisten», in LEBECQ (2015), *Cartulaire*, p. 111-150.

VARIN, A., «The Relative Ages of Two Versions of the *Vita sancti Winwaloei*», *Proceedings of the Harvard Celtic Colloquium*, 3 (1983), p. 69-90.

WAQUET, A., «Clément, moine de Landévennec», in *DHGE*, t. 12, Paris, 1953, col. 1429.

L'écriture hagiographique dans les diocèses du Mans et d'Angers (env. 750-950)

par

Lucile TRÂN DUC

avec la collaboration de Charles MÉRIAUX

I. Le diocèse du Mans. – A. Les *Actus pontificum Cenomannis* et les *Gesta Aldrici*. – B. Les saints compagnons d'Avit. – C. Les saints fondateurs de monastères (par C. Mériaux).
II. Le diocèse d'Angers.
Bibliographie.

I. Le diocèse du Mans

A. Les *Actus pontificum Cenomannis* et les *Gesta Aldrici*

La production hagiographique du diocèse du Mans aux VIIIe-IXe siècles est dominée par la rédaction de ce que Florian Mazel nomme le « corpus carolingien »[1]. Celui-ci, qui se compose de quelques *Vitae*, récits de translations de reliques mais surtout des *Actus pontificum Cenomannis*[2] et des *Gesta Aldrici*, suscite de nombreux débats historiographiques. Les historiens associent d'abord sa réalisation à la rivalité qui oppose, de 838 à 863, la cathédrale à l'abbaye de Saint-Calais au sujet des droits de la première sur la seconde[3]. En effet, au début du IXe siècle,

---
[1] Mazel (2018), p. 31-40.
[2] Le Mans, BM 224; Weidemann (2002).
[3] Havet (1833-1894); Goffart (1966); Weidemann (2002).

l'évêque Francon (816-832) obtient du roi la jouissance de cette dernière pour une durée de neuf ans. Ce privilège est renouvelé par Louis le Pieux en 838 pour son successeur, Aldric (832-857), l'un de ses fidèles. Néanmoins, celui-ci le perd en 940, après la mort de l'empereur. La décision est contestée par la cathédrale et le prélat Robert (859-878) qui considèrent l'abbaye de Saint-Calais comme l'une de leurs dépendances. Le conflit perdure jusqu'en 863, date à laquelle l'affaire est réglée lors du plaid de la Verberie présidé par Charles le Chauve, ce dernier tranchant en faveur de Saint-Calais. Au cours de cette période, chaque camp affûte ses arguments et l'hagiographie participe pleinement de ce processus de légitimation. Toutefois, d'autres analyses, sans pour autant écarter cette dimension judiciaire, s'attachent davantage à souligner l'antériorité d'un projet destiné à mettre en valeur les origines du siège du Mans, le rayonnement de l'autorité épiscopale sur les fondations érémitiques et monastiques du diocèse mais aussi destiné à soutenir la récupération du patrimoine perdu depuis le début du VIIIe siècle. L'Église mancelle estime en effet avoir souffert de la politique menée par certains de ses évêques et des abus de grandes familles telles que celles des Hervéides, favorisés par le système de la précaire ainsi que par la multiplication des *Eigenklöstern*. Elle cherche alors à lutter contre les usurpations[4]. Les travaux récents de Florian Mazel sur le sujet mettent en évidence deux grandes phases dans cette production hagiographique[5]. La première, qui obéit à cette logique, est le fait d'Aldric, originaire d'Austrasie, issu de l'Église de Metz, l'un des foyers de la réforme carolingienne. La seconde, initiée par Robert, s'inscrit davantage dans le contexte du conflit qui oppose la cathédrale à l'abbaye de Saint-Calais.

Le propos d'Aldric est en effet de promouvoir une sainteté épiscopale. Afin d'atteindre cet objectif, il fait rechercher et exhumer les corps de saints locaux destinés à enrichir les autels de la cathédrale alors en reconstruction. Cette entreprise est soutenue par la composition du «corpus carolingien du Mans»[6]. Les *Actus*, inspirés du *Liber pontificalis* de l'Église romaine et rédigés au sein du chapitre cathédral, sont constitués d'une série

---

[4] Le Maître (1980), p. 56-57; Van der Straeten (1967), p. 496-497.
[5] Mazel (2018), p. 32.
[6] Mazel (2016), p. 57-58 et (2018), p. 34-35.

de notices biographiques retraçant l'histoire des évêques du Mans depuis l'épiscopat de Victeur (453-490), premier prélat attesté par sa présence aux conciles d'Angers (453) et de Tours (461). Chacune d'entre elles suit une trame similaire et insiste sur l'origine de son prélat et ses hauts faits parmi lesquels la construction d'édifices religieux dans la cité et ses faubourgs ou encore le nombre de cérémonies d'ordination auxquelles il participe. Elles sont parfois complétées par des chartes et des diplômes, souvent faux, faisant office de pièces justificatives. Les *Actus* sont ensuite repris, partiellement réécrits puis complétés sous l'épiscopat de Robert, vers 857-863, afin d'élaborer un dossier de preuves destinées à soutenir la cause de la cathédrale dans le procès qui l'oppose, comme on l'a vu, à l'abbaye de Saint-Calais. Robert fait ajouter les quatre premières biographies, celles de Julien, Turibe, Pavace et Liboire. La rédaction de l'ensemble, tant sous Aldric que sous Robert, est le fait d'une équipe de faussaires qui cherchent à faire passer ces textes pour contemporains des faits relatés. Ils ne savent en réalité que peu de choses de l'histoire du Mans et s'appuient essentiellement sur quelques traditions et mentions d'anniversaires d'évêques, sur des stèles et inscriptions funéraires, à l'instar de celles de Victeur et Turibe. Les *Actus* poursuivent ainsi plusieurs objectifs. Le premier est d'enraciner le siège épiscopal dans des temps lointains et glorieux. Ils soulignent ainsi les liens qui unissent les premiers évêques à des saints confesseurs prestigieux: Liboire et Vecteur à saint Martin, Principe à saint Rémi, Bertrand à saint Germain de Paris. L'ajout des quatre premières notices, à la demande de Robert, vise également à établir un lien avec les temps apostoliques: Julien et Turibe sont présentés comme des envoyés de Clément et comme des membres du groupe des soixante-douze disciples évoqués par les Évangiles. Le second objectif est d'ancrer les évêques dans un espace singulier. Les *Actus* mettent en avant l'œuvre bâtisseuse des prélats en évoquant la fondation et la consécration des lieux de culte qui constituent l'armature religieuse de la cité, à commencer par l'Église-mère. Il s'agit enfin de prouver et de sacraliser les droits de propriété de la cathédrale sur un ensemble d'églises, d'ermitages et de monastères ayant vu le jour entre le VIIe et le IXe siècle, d'où la production et l'insertion de nombreuses pièces d'archives, quatre-vingt-huit au total, qu'il s'agisse de sources authentiques, de faux ou de documents interpolés, actes de donation et de confirmation, en faveur de l'Église du Mans[7]. Il faut ensuite attendre les environs de 1060 pour que ce texte soit repris sous l'épiscopat de Vulgrin (1055-1065) et que soient ajoutées les notices des prélats succédant à Robert[8].

Les *Gesta Aldrici*, quant à eux, sont écrits du vivant même de leur protagoniste, l'évêque Aldric, et à son initiative. Ils sont destinés à prendre la suite des *Actus* et mettent l'accent sur les années 832-840, celles-ci correspondant à la reconstruction de la vieille *ecclesia* ainsi qu'à l'application de la réforme carolingienne dans le diocèse du Mans[9]. Il s'agit de consigner la mémoire des actes du prélat entrepris pour le bien de sa communauté de clercs, notamment de conserver le souvenir de la manière dont il applique la règle d'Aix avec la formation d'un chapitre cathédral et la construction d'un quartier canonial autour de l'église restaurée de Saint-Étienne, quartier comprenant cloître, maisons, celliers et autres bâtiments destinés à rassembler les chanoines à proximité de la cathédrale. Les *Gesta* s'arrêtent aussi sur la reconstruction de la cathédrale dont Aldric fait agrandir l'abside et remanier le massif occidental. Afin de doter son église de reliques, l'évêque fait rechercher et exhumer les corps des saints locaux. En juin 835, les restes des saints Julien, Turibe, Pavace et Liboire sont placés dans un premier autel, ceux de Victeur et Victeur II dans un second. Sont aussi évoquées la fondation et la rénovation d'établissements monastiques dans les faubourgs de la cité et à proximité, notamment le monastère de Saint-Sauveur au nord.

B. Les saints compagnons d'Avit

Plusieurs saints bénéficient aussi de la promotion de cette sainteté locale sous l'épiscopat d'Aldric, avec la rédaction de textes en leur honneur. C'est par exemple le cas d'un compagnon supposé de saint Avit[10], saint Almire († 560), dont la *Vita* (*BHL* 305), composée par un auteur désireux de se faire passer un contemporain des faits relatés mais qui appartient en réalité à l'équipe de rédaction des *Actus*, cherche à revenir sur les ori-

---

[7] Havet (1893-1894).
[8] Mazel (2018), p. 33
[9] Mazel (2016), p. 55-56.
[10] Sur la *Vita* d'Avit, cf. *infra*, «le diocèse d'Orléans», p. 502-505.

gines de Saint-Calais dans le but de soutenir les prétentions de la cathédrale face à cette abbaye[11]. Saint Julien et saint Liboire, respectivement premier et quatrième évêques supposés du Mans, profitent aussi de ce mouvement[12]. Ainsi, en 836, à la demande de Baduradus (815-862), évêque de Paderborn, et sous la pression de Louis le Pieux, Aldric accepte de céder un corps complet dont il se réserve le choix à l'Église de Paderborn[13]. C'est dans ce contexte qu'est écrite la *Translatio sancti Liborii* relatant l'évènement. Lors de la venue des envoyés de Paderborn, les corps sont exhumés et les sarcophages ouverts. Les restes de saint Liboire sont cédés avec quelques reliques des saints Pavace et Guinnisolus. Jusqu'au début du XXe siècle, seule une relation (*BHL* 4913) de cette translation est connue: celle d'un auteur saxon qui s'appuie sur le témoignage d'un prêtre de la même origine, Idon[14]. Il ressort néanmoins des recherches d'Alfred Cohausz qu'un premier récit existe: celui d'Erconrad, diacre de l'Église du Mans, composé du vivant d'Aldric et très certainement sous sa direction, au lendemain des faits relatés, c'est-à-dire avant 845 puisque l'évêque de Chartres, Bernoin († 845), est encore en fonction[15]. Ce texte vise à mettre en valeur le don de l'Église du Mans en insistant longuement sur les célébrations religieuses et les miracles accomplis par les reliques. Ce récit est suivi d'une autre relation, dite d'Avranches, rédigée elle aussi dans une optique mancelle, avant 860[16]. Néanmoins, les questions d'interdépendance entre ces trois œuvres sont loin d'être résolues et font toujours débat[17].

Dans le cadre du conflit qui l'oppose à l'Église-mère du diocèse, l'abbaye de Saint-Calais développe sa propre production hagiographique concernant son saint fondateur, originaire d'Auvergne et compagnon de saint Avit, dont les pérégrinations le conduisent dans le Maine. Ceci se traduit par la composition de deux *Vitae*[18]. La plus ancienne (*BHL* 1568) est un texte ano-

---

[11] PONCELET (1905), p. 36.
[12] MAZEL (dir.), à paraître.
[13] VAN DER STRAETEN (1967), p. 501-516.
[14] Sur les translations en Germanie, cf. *infra*, le Supplément «Germanie» par Klaus KRÖNERT, p. 753-761, avec la bibliographie y afférant.
[15] COHAUSZ (1967); Bielefeld, Ratsgymnasium, ms. II (5).
[16] BIARNE (2009), p. 109-119; VAN DER STRAETEN (1967), p. 515-516.
[17] VAN DER STRAETEN (1967), p. 515-516.
[18] PONCELET (1905), p. 36-44.

nyme datant de la première moitié du IXe siècle. Son auteur, sans doute un hôte de passage, s'appuie sur la *Vita* de saint Avit composée au début du siècle. Elle est aussi citée par Raban Maur dans son martyrologe. La seconde (*BHL* 1569), d'abord attribuée à un abbé du VIIe siècle, Siviard, voit sa date de rédaction réexaminée: elle est désormais considérée comme légèrement postérieure à *BHL* 1568, c'est-à-dire comme remontant au milieu du IXe siècle[19]. Les transformations sont essentiellement formelles et visent à répondre aux critères de la Renaissance carolingienne[20].

C. Les saints fondateurs de monastères
(par Ch. Mériaux)

En plus de la Vie d'Almire et des textes relevant de l'hagiographie épiscopale, on dispose d'un corpus assez abondant d'une dizaine de Vies de saints honorés comme fondateurs de petits monastères au cours du VIe siècle, en particulier les saints Alveus/Aleus (*BHL* 317), Boamirus (*BHL* 1382), Constantianus (*BHL* 1931), Erneus (*BHL* 2618), Lonochilius et Agnofleda (*BHL* 4966-4967), Meroveus (*BHL* 5941), Richmirus (*BHL* 7246) et Rigomerus (*BHL* 7256). Ces Vies entretiennent entre elles, ainsi qu'avec les *Actus pontificum Cenomannis* et les *Gesta Aldrici*, des relations qu'il reste encore très difficile d'éclaircir précisément en raison de leur tradition manuscrite souvent très incertaine. C'est la raison pour laquelle ces textes sommaires et de datation approximative attendent encore d'être étudiés pour eux-mêmes et pas seulement en marge d'autres dossiers textuels[21]. Ils ont cependant en commun de mettre en scène des saints fondateurs de monastères, placés dans une large

---

[19] *Ibid.* (1905), p. 37.

[20] Il existe encore quelques remaniements de la *Vita* de Calais (*BHL* 1570-1572). Le plus ancien manuscrit contenant *BHL* 1570 date du IXe siècle (Orléans, BM 191). *BHL* 1572 comprend une collection de *Miracula* dont le manuscrit le plus ancien remonte au Xe siècle (Paris, BnF, lat. 13763).

[21] On trouvera cependant quelques aperçus dans Le Maître (1976) qui exploite ces Vies pour décrire la situation religieuse du VIe siècle ce qui revient à leur accorder une valeur historique qu'elles n'ont pas; voir aussi Mériaux (2016). Pour l'étude de ces Vies en relation avec l'hagiographie de l'abbaye de Micy, voir Poncelet (1905); pour leurs rapports avec le corpus du Mans, voir Goffart (1966), p. 50-58 et 339-350.

palette de situations pastorales au point qu'il est difficile de penser que le public visé était exclusivement monastique. Il est partout question de l'obéissance à l'évêque, de la conversion des laïcs, de la lutte contre les superstitions, de la guérison des malades et des possédés, des rapports avec les *potentes* locaux, de l'administration de la pénitence, de la lutte contre les unions illégitimes et de la médisance dont les clercs étaient victimes concernant leurs relations avec les femmes. Ce sont autant de thèmes qui peuvent être rapprochés d'injonctions réformatrices figurant dans les textes pastoraux aussi bien carolingiens que grégoriens. On se contentera ici de présenter les trois Vies conservées dans des manuscrits antérieurs à l'an mille et dont la composition remonte donc indiscutablement aux IXe-Xe siècles.

La première Vie de saint Lonochilius (*BHL* 4966) est conservée dans un livret et un légendier de l'abbaye de Saint-Gall de la fin du IXe siècle (Saint-Gall Stiftsbibliothek 567 et 577). C'est la raison pour laquelle – en plus de considérations proprement stylistiques – on peut supposer une rédaction mérovingienne de ce texte relativement bref[22]. Une seconde version de la Vie (*BHL* 4967) a été produite au début du IXe siècle[23]. Les deux textes semblent avoir été écrit à Saint-Longis pour défendre l'autonomie de ce monastère qui fut ensuite rattaché à celui de Saint-Laumer, dans le Perche, sous le règne de Louis le Pieux. Il existe enfin une courte version «épiscopale» de la Vie insérée dans les *Actus*[24].

D'origine alémanique, né de parents aisés mais païens, Lonochilius gagna la Gaule au début du VIIe siècle (il est ensuite question du roi Clotaire et de son fils Dagobert) et fut baptisé à Clermont. Quelques temps plus tard, l'évêque du lieu l'ordonna prêtre. Il reprit ensuite son voyage et parvint dans le diocèse du Mans. Il s'installa dans un petit oratoire à *Buxiago* qui correspondrait à l'actuelle commune de Saint-Longis, près de Mamers dans la Sarthe. Les fidèles ne cessaient de lui rendre visite. Après un voyage à Rome, il aurait transformé cet oratoire en *monaste-*

---

[22] *Vita Lonoghylii* (*BHL* 4966), éd. W. LEVISON, *MGH*, *SRM*, VII, Hanovre – Leipzig, 1920, p. 432-437; cf. HEINZELMANN (2010), p. 76 et 82.

[23] *Vita Lonochilii* (*BHL* 4967), éd. J. BOLLAND, *AASS*, Ian. I, Anvers, 1643, p. 1120-1122; la datation est proposée par Wilhelm Levison (*op. cit.*) qui estime la seconde Vie antérieure aux *Actus*; voir aussi GOFFART (1966), p. 77.

[24] WEIDEMANN (2002), t. I, p. 66-67.

rium. Néanmoins la Vie ne donne jamais à Lonochilius le titre d'abbé et il n'est jamais fait mention de moines autour de lui. La fin de la Vie est d'ailleurs entièrement consacrée à un tout autre problème. Le prêtre répondit en effet au souhait d'une jeune fille, nommée Agnofleda, qui voulait échapper au mariage et recevoir le voile consacré. Son fiancé fit appel au roi Clotaire en calomniant le saint, accusé de lui avoir enlevé sa fiancée grâce à un sortilège. Le roi donna finalement raison à Lonoghylius et dota généreusement le monastère. Agnofleda mourut plus tard au *vicus publicus* voisin de *Vernum*. Il semble donc que la Vie donne surtout à imiter la sainte fréquentation d'un prêtre et d'une femme consacrée vivant non loin l'un de l'autre. Dans les *Actus* du Mans, la présentation de Lonochilius est tout à fait différente, principalement contrée sur les biens prétendument cédés au monastère par l'évêque Hadoindus dans le second quart du VIIe siècle.

Le culte de saint Rigomer apparaît à plusieurs reprises dans la documentation mancelle et la basilique suburbaine du Mans dans laquelle il fut enterré est déjà mentionnée dans le testament de l'évêque Bertrand (616)[25]. Sa Vie est aujourd'hui conservée dans un légendier de la première moitié du Xe siècle (Bruxelles, KBR 8550-8551)[26]. Rigomer aurait vécu au temps de Childebert Ier (511-568) et de son épouse Ultrogothe. Il est associé par l'auteur aux saints Calais et Laumer dont les Vies figurent aussi dans le manuscrit de Bruxelles, mais sans que l'on puisse repérer des emprunts formels à ces textes. Originaire du Sonnois – la région qui couvre les environs de Mamers –, il fut instruit par un prêtre nommé Launillus, puis élevé au sacerdoce (c. 1-4). Un bref paragraphe résume l'idéal sacerdotal carolingien: la prédication, l'administration de la pénitence, l'appel à l'hospitalité et à la charité, la guérison des malades par l'onction d'huile sainte (c. 5). La lutte contre les superstitions est illustrée par le récit de la destruction d'un *fanum* à la place duquel Rigomer fit édifier une église où les fidèles apportèrent leurs offrandes (c. 6). Toute la suite de la Vie est consacrée à une femme

---

[25] BIARNE (1987), p. 54-55; pour la mention d'un autel Saint-Rigomer dans la cathédrale au temps d'Aldric, voir les *Gesta Aldrici*, c. 3, éd. WEIDEMANN (2002), t. I, p. 125.

[26] *Vita Rigomeri* (*BHL* 7256), éd. J. PIEN, *AASS*, Aug. IV, Anvers, 1739, p. 786-788.

nommée Tenestina qui était alors fiancée mais refusait le mariage et voulait recevoir le voile consacré. Cette femme recevait les visites de Rigomer qui fut alors dénoncé au fiancé (c. 8). Il se justifia au palais du roi grâce à un miracle et Tenestina put finalement s'installer au Mans et y recevoir le voile de l'évêque. De toute évidence, l'auteur reprend ici le thème de la relation spirituelle entre un religieux et une religieuse qui se trouvait déjà développé dans la Vie de Lonochilius. Dans les deux cas, on peut y voir un petit *exemplum* sur le nécessaire respect du célibat.

Restée longtemps inédite, la Vie de saint Mervé (*Meroveus*) (BHL 5941) a retenu l'attention de Jean-Pierre Brunterc'h en 1983 en raison des renseignements topographiques précis qu'elle donne sur la frontière entre le Rennais et le Maine[27]. Sa datation carolingienne est incontestable puisqu'elle se trouve copiée dans un fragment de légendier de la fin du IXe siècle ou du tout début du Xe siècle originaire de Fleury. L'appartenance du texte au corpus des Vies de saints du Mans se justifie non seulement par des emprunts à la seconde Vie de saint Calais, mais aussi par quelques arguments supplémentaires exposés par Joseph-Claude Poulin[28]. Le *terminus post quem* de sa rédaction est fixé par les emprunts à la seconde Vie de saint Calais rédigée vers 860.

La Vie présente Mervé comme un ermite qui choisit de s'installer d'abord à *Coriacus* (dans le diocèse de Rennes, aujourd'hui Saint-M'Hervé), puis, en raison de l'affluence croissante des fidèles, à *Crucicula* (dans le diocèse du Mans, aujourd'hui La Croixille)[29]. Après sa mort, les Rennais et les Manceaux se disputèrent son corps qui fut emporté de nuit par les premiers et déposé au lieu de son premier ermitage. La Vie insiste aussi sur l'exercice du ministère sacerdotal. Elle donne même ce qui ressemble à une petite leçon d'économie paroissiale, en assurant que Mervé travaillait les peaux d'animaux et partageait ses revenus en trois parts: l'une pour le seigneur du lieu (*senior terrenus*) nommé Ghiso, l'autre pour les pauvres et la troisième pour

---

[27] BRUNTERC'H (1983), avec édition du texte p. 57-63 (d'après Vatican, Reg. lat. 318, fol. 222r-226v).

[28] POULIN (2009), p. 260-263, spéc. p. 262 et «L'hagiographie bretonne avant l'an mil», *supra*, p. 223 et 235.

[29] Saint-M'Hervé: dép. Ille-et-Vilaine, arr. Fougères-Vitré, cant. Vitré-Est; La Croixille: dép. Mayenne, arr. Laval, cant. Challiand.

sa propre subsistance. Le saint guérit un boiteux; il bénit les fidèles qui viennent à lui et apaise leurs querelles. Un épisode qui occupe une bonne partie de la Vie présente la colère du seigneur qui s'en prend à Mervée et se trouve miraculeusement immobilisé sur son cheval puis libéré par le saint. En somme, tous les acteurs de la vie «paroissiale» sont tour à tour mis en scène dans un texte qui rappelle à chacun ses droits et ses devoirs.

Si l'hagiographie carolingienne du diocèse du Mans est indéniablement dominée, voire écrasée, par la production issue du *scriptorium* cathédral qui a mis en valeur les grandes figures légendaires des évêques des premiers temps chrétiens, elle comprend aussi des textes qui sont autant de récits des origines monastiques du diocèse. Ceux-ci sont certes mis au service des prétentions épiscopales, mais, en reconstruisant le passé mérovingien, ils ne sont pas sans intérêt pour appréhender le processus d'encadrement à l'œuvre dans les campagnes carolingiennes.

II. Le diocèse d'Angers

L'époque carolingienne n'est pas une période riche en production hagiographique pour le diocèse d'Angers. Comme l'a rappelé Jean-Michel Matz, l'essentiel de la fabrique des saints a lieu entre le IVe et le VIIe siècle et met en valeur les premiers temps de l'Église d'Angers avec des figures telles que celles des confesseurs Maurille et Aubin. Il faut ensuite attendre les XIe-XIIe siècles pour observer une nouvelle phase avec le renouveau érémitique, celle-ci pouvant être qualifiée de «période de maturité»[30]. Entre les deux, la période carolingienne fait figure de parent pauvre ou de «traversée du désert» pour reprendre l'expression de Damien Heurtebise[31].

En effet, la production hagiographique épiscopale originale se limite à la composition de deux œuvres[32]. La première, la *Vita sancti Licinii* (BHL 4917), revient sur l'existence de saint Lézin, treizième évêque d'Angers. Elle reprend les codes des

---

[30] Matz (2006) p. 98.
[31] Heurtebise (2010), p. 112.
[32] Matz (2006), p. 100-101; Heurtebise (2010), p. 111-112.

Vitae du VIIIe siècle et promeut une sainteté aristocratique en présentant son héros comme un aristocrate, connétable et comte d'Anjou, faisant le choix d'entrer dans le clergé avant d'être élu évêque aux environs de 592. Ce texte est composé par un auteur anonyme s'inspirant des *Vitae* de saint Arnoul de Metz (*BHL* 689) pour la trame et de saint Lambert de Liège (*BHL* 4677) pour les vertus du personnage. Le *terminus post quem* peut être fixé à la première moitié du VIIIe siècle, époque à laquelle est composée la *Vita* de saint Lambert, tandis que le *terminus ante quem* pourrait ne pas dépasser la seconde moitié du IXe siècle si l'on se fie au titre «*dux atque comes Andecavensium*» attribué à Lézin, expression qui évoquerait en fait le grand commandement de Robert le Fort. La seconde, la *Vita* de *Magnobodus* (*BHL* 5151), peu documentée, est, elle, très certainement postérieure à 905. Elle revient sur l'existence de Mainbeuf, connu pour être le quinzième évêque d'Angers. Celui-ci reçoit la tonsure de Lézin et se voit confier l'abbatiat de Chalonnes avant d'accéder à l'épiscopat et de mourir vers 660-670.

Outre ces créations originales, on observe la réécriture de la *Vita* de Maurille († 453), originaire de Milan et disciple de saint Martin, élu évêque vers 423 et considéré comme le véritable évangélisateur du diocèse qu'il aurait dirigé durant une trentaine d'années[33]. Au texte composé vers 620 par Mainbeuf en son honneur (*BHL* 5730) succède un nouveau récit (*BHL* 5731) rédigé à la demande du prélat Rainon (881-906), par *Archanaldus*, écolâtre de Saint-Martin de Tours et personnalité littéraire de la province, vers 905-906. Celui-ci, afin de donner davantage de crédit à son propos, en attribue la paternité à Fortunat et le présente comme un remaniement contemporain de la *Vita prima* composée par Mainbeuf. Cette *Vita secunda* fournit à la légende de saint Maurille sa forme définitive en en faisant un personnage glorieux et surhumain, notamment grâce à l'épisode de la résurrection de son successeur légendaire, saint René, alors enfant mort sans baptême. Il s'agit, d'une part, de reformuler dans une langue conforme aux canons carolingiens les hauts faits de Maurille et, d'autre part, d'intégrer à la tradition hagiographique existante les éléments nouveaux de la croyance populaire, les cultes de Maurille et de René se développant considérablement au IXe siècle.

---

[33] MATZ (2006), p. 99-100; HEURTEBISE (2010), p. 108-110.

Ces textes, qui mettent à l'honneur la figure du saint évêque, permettent d'entretenir le mythe d'un certain âge d'or, de légitimer la fonction politique et sociale des prélats [34].

Il convient aussi de mentionner l'œuvre d'Odon, abbé de Glanfeuil, à qui l'on doit une *Vita* ainsi qu'un recueil de miracles en l'honneur de saint Maur, compagnon de saint Benoît et fondateur supposé de ce monastère [35]. Ces textes, composés à la fin des années 860, suivent de près la restauration de ce dernier dans les années 830. Tombé en désuétude sous les derniers Mérovingiens et les premiers Carolingiens, il est relevé par le comte du Mans, Rorigo, qui se le voit remettre par Louis le Pieux lorsqu'il exprime le désir de se convertir à la vie monastique. Le culte de saint Maur se développe ensuite sous l'abbatiat de *Gauzlinus*, appartenant lui-même à la famille des Rorigid. Celui-ci fait procéder à l'élévation des reliques de Glanfeuil. C'est à cette occasion que sont mis au jour les restes de saint Maur, de saint Pierre et de saint Étienne. Dès lors, Glanfeuil devient le centre de la dévotion envers saint Maur, moyen pour cette abbaye de s'imposer face à celle de Fleury où repose le corps de saint Benoît. Le culte de saint Maur culmine sous l'abbatiat d'Odon, à partir de 861, et prend de l'ampleur suite à la fuite de la communauté à Saint-Pierre-des-Fossés, à proximité de Paris, face aux incursions scandinaves. C'est dans ce contexte que sont rédigés les deux textes mentionnés [36].

D'après une lettre adressée par Odon de Glanfeuil à l'archidiacre du Mans et jointe au prologue de la *Vita sancti Mauri*, cette dernière serait la réécriture d'un récit antérieur dont il aurait fait l'acquisition lorsque, après avoir échappé à une attaque de Scandinaves, il croisa quelques pèlerins en provenance de Rome auxquels il acheta plusieurs volumes contenant des textes hagiographiques. Parmi ceux-ci figurerait une ancienne *Vita sancti Mauri* qu'il entreprend de rendre accessible aux hommes de son temps. Selon la version d'Odon, saint Maur voit le jour dans une famille romaine et entre comme oblat au monastère du Mont-Cassin où il devient rapidement le disciple de Benoît de Nursie en raison de ses dons et de son obéissance. Lorsqu'une délégation de l'évêque du Mans gagne le Mont-Cassin pour de-

---

[34] MATZ (2006), p. 102.
[35] WICKSTROM (2008).
[36] *Ibid.*, p. 11-55.

mander à un groupe de moines de venir fonder un monastère dans son diocèse, Maur est envoyé en Gaule. Après une traversée des Alpes ponctuée de miracles, il s'établit avec cinq compagnons sur la rive gauche de la Loire et y érige l'abbaye de Glanfeuil. Durant près de quarante ans, il préside ainsi une communauté de cent cinquante moines avant de mourir en 583. En dépit des affirmations d'Odon, aucun texte antérieur à ce récit n'a été retrouvé. En présentant ce dernier comme la réécriture d'une œuvre plus ancienne, due à l'un des compagnons de saint Maur, *Faustus*, témoin oculaire des faits relatés, l'abbé de Glanfeuil cherche à apparenter son patron au compagnon de saint Benoît évoqué par Grégoire le Grand dans ses *Dialogues II* et fait ainsi de Maur le propagateur de la règle bénédictine en Occident[37].

Après l'installation de la communauté à Saint-Pierre-des-Fossés, en 868, Odon composa également un petit recueil de miracles destiné à accompagner la *Vita sancti Mauri*. Celui-ci comporte deux parties retraçant l'histoire de Glanfeuil de 750 à 861. La première est une chronique rapportant les grands événements de cette abbaye depuis la donation faite par Pépin le Bref à *Gaidulf* de Ravenne au milieu du VIIIe siècle jusqu'à sa restauration, vers 830, par le comte Rorigo et l'abbatiat de *Gauzlinus*. La seconde relate les miracles survenus sous l'abbatiat d'Odon depuis 861, d'abord à Glanfeuil puis lors de la translation des reliques de saint Maur jusqu'à Saint-Pierre-des-Fossés en 868. Le texte se clôt sur l'arrivée des restes saints dans son refuge, à proximité de Paris, et sur la visite de Charles le Chauve qui s'ensuivit[38].

Ces deux récits rencontrent un écho considérable tout au long du Moyen Âge et contribuent à propager le culte de saint Maur hors de Glanfeuil. La *Vita sancti Mauri* en particulier connaît une très large diffusion dans nombre de monastères, les religieux y voyant une source précieuse leur permettant d'accéder à l'état originel de la règle bénédictine.

---

[37] *Ibid.*, p. 103-113.
[38] *Id.*, p. 112.

Bibliographie

Biarne J., « Le Mans », in *Topographie chrétienne des cités de la Gaule, des origines au milieu du VIIIe siècle*, V : *Province ecclésiastique de Tours (Lugdunensis tertia)*, Paris, 1987, p. 41-56.

—, « Les premiers évêques du Mans depuis les *Fastes épiscopaux* de Louis Duchesne », in S. Tison – H. Guillemain – N. Vivier, dir., *La foi dans le siècle. Mélanges offerts à Brigitte Waché*, Rennes, 2009, p. 109-119.

Brunterc'h, J.-P., « Géographie historique et hagiographie : la Vie de saint Mervé », *Mélanges de l'École française de Rome. Moyen Âge. Temps modernes*, 95-1 (1983), p. 7-63.

Cohausz, A., *La translation de Saint Liboire (836) du diacre Erconrad. Un document de l'époque carolingienne récemment découvert et les relations déjà connues du transfert des reliques*, Le Mans, 1967.

Goffart, W., *The Le Mans Forgeries. A Chapter from the History of Church Property in the ninth century*, Cambridge, 1966.

Havet, J., « Questions mérovingiennes. VII. Les actes des évêques du Mans », *Bibliothèque de l'École des Chartes*, 54 (1893), p. 597-692.

—, « Questions mérovingiennes. VII. Les actes des évêques du Mans », *Bibliothèque de l'École des Chartes*, 55 (1894), p. 5-60.

Heinzelmann, M., « L'hagiographie mérovingienne : panorama des documents potentiels », dans *L'hagiographie mérovingienne à travers ses réécritures*, éd. M. Goullet – M. Heinzelmann – C. Veyrard-Cosme, Ostfildern, 2010, p. 27-82.

Heurtebise, D., « L'intérêt historique de l'hagiographie angevine », dans D. Prigent – N.-Y. Tonnerre, dir., *Le haut Moyen Âge en Anjou*, Rennes, 2010, p. 105-113.

Le Maître, P., « Évêques et moines dans le Maine (IVe-VIIIe siècle) », *Revue d'histoire de l'Église de France*, 62 (1976), p. 91-101.

—, « L'œuvre d'Aldric du Mans et sa signification (832-857) », *Francia*, 8 (1980), p. 43-64.

Matz, J.-M., « La construction d'une identité : le culte des saints évêques d'Angers au Moyen Âge », *Hagiographica. Rivista di agiografia e biografia della Società internazionale per lo studio del Medioevo Latino*, 13 (2006), p. 95-120.

Mazel, F., *L'évêque et le territoire. L'invention médiévale de l'espace (Ve-XIIIe siècle)*, Paris, 2016.

—, « Les Actes des évêques du Mans », dans J.-M. Matz, dir., *Fasti Ecclesiae Gallicanae. Répertoire prosopographique des évêques, dignitaires et chanoines des diocèses de France de 1200 à 1500*, 18 : *Diocèse du Mans*, Turnhout, 2018, p. 31-40.

—, dir., *La fabrique d'une légende. Vie et culte de saint Julien du Mans au Moyen Âge*, Rennes, à paraître.

MÉRIAUX, C., «*Bonus agricola*. À propos de quelques figures de saints prêtres dans l'hagiographie carolingienne», dans *Gott handhaben. Religiöses Wissen im Konflikt um Mythisierung und Rationalisierung*, éd. St. PATZOLD, F. BOCK, Berlin – Boston, 2016, p. 115-130.

PONCELET, A., «La translation de saint Liboire», *AB*, 22 (1903), p. 156-172.

—, «Les saints de Micy», *AB*, 24 (1905), p. 5-97.

POULIN J.-Cl., *L'hagiographie bretonne du haut Moyen Âge. Répertoire raisonné*, Ostfildern, 2009.

VAN DER STRAETEN, J., «Hagiographie du Mans: note critique», *AB*, 85 (1967), p. 473-501.

WEIDEMANN, M., éd., *Geschichte des Bistums Le Mans von der Spätantike bis zur Karolingerzeit. Actus pontificum Cenomannis in urbe degentium und Gesta Aldrici*, Mayence, 2002.

WICKSTROM, J., éd., *Life and Miracles of Saint Maurus, disciple of Benedict and Apostle to France*, Collegeville, MN, 2008.

L'écriture hagiographique
dans la province de Rouen (env. 750-950)

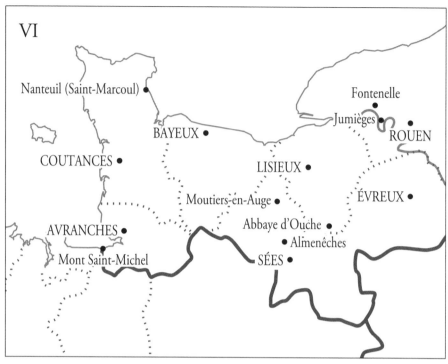

Lieux mentionnés dans les chapitres sur la province de Rouen

L'écriture hagiographique dans le diocèse de Rouen (env. 750-950)

par

Lucile TRÂN DUC

INTRODUCTION.
I. L'ÉCRITURE HAGIOGRAPHIQUE À L'ABBAYE DE FONTENELLE. – A. Les *Gesta abbatum Fontanellensium*. – B. Le dossier de saint Wandrille. – C. Le dossier des saints Ansbert et Lambert. – D. Le dossier de saint Vulfran. – E. Le dossier des saints Condède et Erembert.
II. L'ÉCRITURE HAGIOGRAPHIQUE À L'ABBAYE DE JUMIÈGES. – A. Le dossier des saints Aychard et Hugues. – B. Le dossier de sainte Austreberte.
III. DANS L'ORBITE DE LA CATHÉDRALE DE ROUEN: le dossier de saint Ouen.
CONCLUSION
BIBLIOGRAPHIE. – A. Sources. – B. Études.

INTRODUCTION

Lorsque débute la période carolingienne, la vie religieuse est largement développée dans le diocèse de Rouen et les monastères s'y sont multipliés: entre autres, Fontenelle fondé en 649 et Jumièges en 654. Dans leur sillage, les filiales féminines de Fécamp, Pavilly et Montivilliers ont vu le jour. Avec la mainmise des Pippinides sur la Neustrie au VIIIe siècle, ces établissements passent aux mains de ces derniers. À la faveur de la « Renaissance carolingienne », Fontenelle et dans une moindre mesure Jumièges s'imposent comme d'importants foyers culturels grâce à l'activité de leur *scriptorium*. Ceci profite largement à l'activité hagiographique destinée à soutenir les cultes rendus aux saints locaux et se traduit essentiellement par la réécriture d'œuvres antérieures. Il s'agit d'une part pour les nouveaux maîtres la basse vallée de la Seine de s'approprier des saints ayant déjà fait leur preuve, essentiellement des confesseurs. D'autre part, la captation de ces dévotions leur permet de légitimer et de sacraliser leur entreprise de conquête. Néanmoins, il convient également de noter la mise en valeur de figures proprement carolingiennes, en particulier à Fontenelle.

Qu'il s'agisse de réécritures ou d'œuvres originales, ces textes s'inscrivent dans un même mouvement destiné «à définir non seulement les normes qui doivent régir le monachisme régulier, mais aussi les vertus que doivent acquérir les serviteurs de l'État»[1]. En cela, les récits étudiés présentent des traits communs. Ils insistent en premier lieu sur l'appartenance à l'aristocratie des personnages auxquels ils s'intéressent, mettant à l'honneur la figure de l'*Adelsheilige*. Celle-ci va de pair avec un monopole du savoir et de la culture qui contribue à la formation du capital symbolique des élites. Bien souvent, les saints sont formés dans l'*aula regia* où ils se trouvent, de fait, attachés au pouvoir public: leur *cursus honorum* commence généralement par des charges temporelles auxquelles succèdent des fonctions ecclésiastiques. De tels parcours s'accompagnent parallèlement d'un refus du mariage, qu'il s'agisse d'unions manquées ou d'union rejetées, afin de mieux souligner un idéal de vie ascétique tourné vers le renoncement et la mortification. Malgré ceci, ce n'est qu'après avoir mené une existence prometteuse dans le siècle que les saints honorés optent pour une vie ecclésiastique, l'épiscopat et l'abbatiat constituant l'aboutissement d'une longue carrière. Ces charges sont alors exercées de manière exemplaire. L'obéissance à la *regula* en vigueur dans le monastère et le rétablissement en son état primitif de la règle bénédictine sont bien souvent soulignés. Ce *topos* doit être replacé dans le contexte de développement de l'idée de *correctio* permettant de tendre vers la perfection et la *renovatio* de la société. Les saints sont aussi présentés comme des héros soucieux du rayonnement de leur établissement. Les textes hagiographiques insistent ainsi sur leur intense activité bâtisseuse et sur la gestion du patrimoine de ces monastères. Ces confesseurs ne vivent néanmoins pas en vase clos mais se tournent vers l'extérieur et s'illustrent souvent par leur activité missionnaire. Celle-ci s'exerce la plupart du temps dans un périmètre proche mais aussi dans des régions plus lointaines, comme la Frise en ce qui

---

[1] HELVÉTIUS (2012), p. 40.

concerne saint Vulfran. Au fil de la période étudiée, le thème tend malgré tout à disparaître. Ceci s'explique par le succès de la *stabilitas loci* prônée par la règle bénédictine imposée par le capitulaire monastique de 816-817. Les moines se voient contraints à un mode de vie strictement cénobitique, séparés des laïcs et des clercs séculiers. Les cultes en vigueur dans le diocèse de Rouen reflètent en cela les réalités sociales et politiques de la période.

I. L'écriture hagiographique à l'abbaye de Fontenelle [2]

Après les victoires des Pippinides sur le camp neustrien à Tertry (687) et à Vinchy (717), le monastère de Fontenelle passe entre les mains de ces derniers. Ils imposent dès lors leurs hommes à la tête de l'abbaye, ce qui profite au *scriptorium* de l'abbaye [3]. Les abbés mettent en œuvre les réformes culturelles voulues par les Pippinides puis par leurs successeurs carolingiens [4]. Hugues (725-732) passe pour «être imbu de l'étude des lettres» [5]. Wandon (747-754) lègue à sa mort «une quantité de manuscrits considérable [6]». Gervold (789-807) fait de même et institue également une *scola* en application de l'*Admonitio Generalis* [7]. Anségise (823-833) fait exécuter des copies des Écritures et constitue une bibliothèque dont il complète les rayons scripturaires, patristiques et modernes [8]. C'est dans ce contexte que fleurit la production hagiographique de Fontenelle. Cette dernière met à l'honneur Wandrille, l'un de ses successeurs, Ansbert, ainsi que le moine Vulfran, dont les corps, d'abord inhumés dans l'église Saint-Paul, sont transférés dans l'église abbatiale Saint-Pierre en 704. Tous trois s'imposent dès lors comme les principaux saints du monastère. Autour d'eux gravitent un certain nombre de figures secondaires: Condède,

---

[2] Howe (2001), p. 127-192; Wood (1991), p. 1-14.
[3] Fontaine (1982), p. 31-54.
[4] Wood (1991), p. 3.
[5] Pradié (1999), chap. IV, §1, p. 60.
[6] *Ibid.*, chap. IX, §2, p. 106-109.
[7] *Ibid.*, chap. XII, §2, p. 140-141.
[8] *Ibid.*, chap. XIII, §4, p. 164-167.

Erembert, Lambert ou encore Hildemarque qui vivent à l'époque mérovingienne puis Wandon et Anségise, abbés carolingiens[9].

A. Les *Gesta abbatum Fontanellensium*[10]

Au sein de cette vaste production, il convient de distinguer les *Gesta abbatum Fontanellensium*, emblématiques de la production du *scriptorium* de Fontenelle. Il s'agit avant tout d'une œuvre destinée à construire la sainteté du lieu en mettant en exergue celle de ses abbés. Ce texte est composé en deux temps. La partie principale couvre une période allant de l'abbatiat de Wandrille à celui de Gervold (649-807). Elle est sans doute rédigée dans les années 823-833, sur ordre probable de l'abbé Anségise, dans la perspective de la réforme monastique qu'il introduit à Fontenelle à la demande de Louis le Pieux. L'auteur serait un moine fontenellien, tant sa connaissance de la topographie de l'abbaye est précise. D'après Pascal Pradié, il s'agit de l'archiviste de la communauté, celui-ci faisant un large usage de la documentation diplomatique. La seconde partie serait rédigée plus tardivement, entre 834 et 845, sous l'abbatiat de Foulques, nommé à la tête de Fontenelle et de Jumièges par Louis le Pieux. Elle ne couvre que le seul abbatiat d'Anségise. Néanmoins, en raison de la similitude des caractéristiques stylistiques avec la partie précédente, on aurait affaire à un même auteur. Si toutes les notices contenues dans les *Gesta abbatum Fontanellensium* n'ont pas nécessairement de rapport avec notre propos, c'est en revanche le cas des textes relatifs à Wandrille, Wandon et Anségise, considérés comme saints par la communauté.

La notice concernant Wandrille (*BHL vacat*) est la réécriture d'une *Vita prima* rédigée dans le dernier tiers du VIIe siècle et sur laquelle s'appuie largement l'auteur. Ce dernier en suit globalement la trame. Il s'attache à présenter le parcours de Wandrille qui renonce au siècle ainsi qu'au mariage pour suivre sa vocation religieuse, d'abord à Montfaucon et Saint-Ursanne, puis à Bobbio et Romainmôtier, et enfin dans le diocèse de

---

[9] Laporte (1939), p. 1-16.
[10] Pradié (1999).

Rouen où il fonde le monastère de Fontenelle qu'il dirige de manière exemplaire jusqu'à sa mort. Si l'auteur prend le soin d'amplifier certains épisodes tels que le séjour de Wandrille en qualité de *nutritus* à la cour de Dagobert, son passage à Bobbio pour insister sur la spiritualité colombanienne, et sa gestion de Fontenelle, et s'il prend soin de développer le thème des relations entretenues avec les autres figures marquantes du diocèse, les transformations apportées au texte sont essentiellement d'ordre sémantique et idéologique. En effet, ce récit vise avant tout à rattacher Wandrille aux Pippinides en faisant de lui un descendant direct de saint Arnoul par son père, un certain *Waltchisus*, oncle paternel de Pépin. Non seulement un tel lien contribue à sacraliser la parenté des Pippinides mais légitime également de fait leur mainmise sur un haut lieu de la résistance neustrienne.

Les *Gesta abbatum Fontanellensium* comportent également les seuls textes connus relatifs aux saints Wandon (*BHL* 8803) et Anségise (*BHL* 524). Wandon prend la direction de l'abbaye en 742 sur ordre de Pépin, après un exil à Maastricht. Le texte comporte de nombreuses informations sur les donations effectuées par l'abbé depuis son entrée en religion sous l'abbatiat d'Hildebert jusqu'à sa mort en 756. Anségise, dont la notice vient clore les *Gesta*, est présenté quant à lui comme le prototype de l'abbé bénédictin, serviteur de l'idéal impérial. C'est pourquoi, après avoir présenté les origines du personnage, le texte insiste longuement sur les liens entretenus avec le pouvoir carolingien: une fois tonsuré à Fontenelle, il est conduit au palais impérial pour y parfaire son éducation. Destiné à une carrière monastique, il se voit confier par Charlemagne plusieurs monastères à administrer, tout en étant nommé intendant des travaux du palais d'Aix-la-Chapelle. Louis le Pieux lui remet ensuite l'abbaye de Luxeuil, à titre de bénéfice, ainsi que celle de Fontenelle. S'ensuit alors une description de son activité à la tête de cet établissement. Sa volonté réformatrice passe par la mise en application de la règle de saint Benoît, tombée en désuétude sous les précédents abbés. Anségise s'illustre également par un grand nombre de donations et entreprend d'importants travaux. Lorsqu'il est frappé de paralysie, il entreprend de distribuer ses biens. À ces donations, l'auteur ajoute une transcription de la «Constitution d'Anségise», en d'autres termes du compte des recettes et des dépenses de Fontenelle. Selon Pascal

Pradié, cette notice est destinée à présenter l'abbé comme un serviteur fidèle du pouvoir impérial, mettant en œuvre la politique monastique initiée par Benoît d'Aniane. Son abbatiat est présenté comme l'aboutissement de ce mouvement réformateur[11].

B. LE DOSSIER DE SAINT WANDRILLE

Le dossier de Wandrille ne se limite pas à la notice des *Gesta abbatum Fontanellensium*. Il comporte également une *Vita altera* suivie de quelques *miracula* (BHL 8805 et 8807) ainsi que la *Translatio et miracula sancti Wandregesili* (BHL 8808-8809).

Comme la notice des *Gesta*, la *Vita altera sancti Wandregesili et miracula* respecte la trame de la *Vita prima* mais amplifie là encore certains épisodes : l'éducation reçue par Wandrille, le séjour à Bobbio, la fondation du monastère de Fontenelle, les rapports aux habitants des environs... Le nouveau texte apporte également des informations complémentaires sur la fondation de l'abbaye féminine de Fécamp. Il relate aussi la translation du corps de saint Wandrille, d'abord inhumé dans l'église Saint-Paul, puis dans l'église Saint-Pierre à l'initiative du cinquième abbé, Bain, en 704. S'ajoute à ce récit une série de miracles.

Il n'est guère possible de se fier au prologue de ce récit pour replacer celui-ci dans son contexte de rédaction. Il y est dit que cette *Vita altera* est rédigée à la demande du second abbé de Fontenelle, Lambert. Or ceci semble peu crédible dans la mesure où il est fait état de la translation des restes de Wandrille dans l'église Saint-Pierre à l'initiative de Bain. D'après John Howe, l'hagiographe travaille probablement à partir d'un texte intermédiaire perdu et surtout à partir de la notice des *Gesta abbatum Fontanellensium*. La rédaction de la *Vita altera* est donc postérieure. Elle est le fait d'un moine de Fontenelle puisqu'il désigne les membres de cette communauté comme «*fratres nostri*». Son initiative ne se comprend que dans le contexte de la mainmise des Pippinides puis des Carolingiens sur le monastère. En effet, le récit vise à intégrer à la documentation

---

[11] PRADIÉ (1999), p. XXVII.

cultuelle les informations relatives aux origines pippinides de Wandrille contenues dans les *Gesta abbatum Fontanellensium*[12].

Les manuscrits associent souvent à cette *Vita altera* la *Translatio* et les *Miracula sancti Wandregesili* (BHL 8808-8809)[13]. Ce texte relate la manière dont les religieux de Fontenelle exhument les corps de leurs saints les plus précieux, Wandrille et Ansbert, et prennent la fuite par crainte des vikings. Leurs pérégrinations les mènent d'abord momentanément à Quentovic avant un retour temporaire à Fontenelle, de nouveau à Quentovic, puis à Chartres et enfin à Boulogne. Chaque étape est marquée par de nombreux miracles.

Ce récit est composé en deux temps, sur la base de témoignages oraux, par des religieux ayant eux-mêmes participé au voyage et stationnant à Boulogne: entre 868 et le début du Xe siècle pour la partie qui relate le trajet de Fontenelle à Quentovic et entre 887 et le début du Xe siècle pour celle concernant le trajet de Fontenelle à Chartres puis à Boulogne, où la communauté trouve finalement refuge avant que le comte Arnoul de Flandre et Gérard de Brogne ne s'emparent de ses reliques pour les emporter au Mont-Blandin, à Gand[14]. L'œuvre doit être lue à l'aune de ce contexte particulier. Deux éléments en particulier retiennent l'attention. D'une part, force est de constater que le motif de la menace scandinave disparaît rapidement du récit. L'impression que donne ce dernier est plutôt celui d'un voyage parfaitement organisé et planifié[15]. D'autre part, les lieux mentionnés (Bloville, Quentovic, Outreau, etc.) renvoient aux domaines septentrionaux du monastère[16]. C'est avant tout à leurs dépendants que ces hagiographes s'adressent. Il s'agit probablement de leur démontrer la puissance des saints Wandrille et Ansbert. Tout porte donc à croire que ce texte sert les intérêts d'une communauté en exil luttant pour sa survie, se réfugiant derrière ses saints tutélaires, Wandrille et Ansbert, afin de préserver son identité et probablement son existence même.

---

[12] PRADIÉ (1999), chap. I, §2, p. 4.
[13] Se reporter à la liste présentée dans HOWE (2001), p. 183-190.
[14] HUYGHEBAERT (1978). Ce *sermo* est composé entre 945 et 950 dans le monastère Saint-Pierre au Mont-Blandin à Gand, par le *custos* du lieu. C'est pourquoi ce texte ne figure pas dans le dossier de saint Wandrille.
[15] MÉRIAUX (2006), p. 115.
[16] LOT (1913), p. XIII-XXIX.

C. LE DOSSIER DES SAINTS ANSBERT ET LAMBERT

On doit la *Vita sancti Ansberti* (BHL 519-520b) et la *Vita sancti Lamberti* (BHL 4675) à un auteur qui dit se nommer *Aigradus* et que l'on peut identifier comme un moine de Fontenelle si l'on se fie là encore à sa bonne connaissance de la topographie et de la documentation diplomatique du monastère.

La *Vita Ansberti* s'attache à faire de ce personnage un aristocrate originaire de Chaussy, sur l'Epte, ayant d'abord entamé une carrière dans l'administration palatine en qualité de chancelier. Selon un *topos* classique, Ansbert préfère y renoncer pour embrasser la vie monastique à Fontenelle où il s'adonne au travail manuel. Il est alors ordonné prêtre par l'évêque Ouen de Rouen puis il prend la succession de Lambert à la tête de Fontenelle lorsque celui-ci est nommé évêque de Lyon. En tant qu'abbé, Ansbert est l'incarnation même des paroles de Benoît. Il érige un *xenodochium* pour les pauvres et accroît les possessions du monastère. Après la mort de Ouen, il est nommé évêque de Rouen. En cette qualité, il organise un concile réformateur (688/689) et développe le culte de son prédécesseur en procédant à l'élévation de la tombe de ce dernier derrière le maître-autel de la basilique Saint-Pierre et en faisant de ce jour une fête pour l'ensemble du diocèse. Son implication dans les affaires du siècle lui vaut de s'opposer à Pépin. Il est exilé par celui-ci à Haumont-sur-Oise où il sent la mort le gagner. Néanmoins, il obtient de Pépin l'autorisation de voir sa dépouille inhumée à Fontenelle. La translation de son corps s'accompagne de miracles et il est finalement enterré dans la basilique Saint-Paul, aux côtés de Wandrille.

Aigrardus dédie ce texte à l'abbé *Hilbertus*, successeur d'Ansbert et quatrième abbé. Cette indication soulève plusieurs problèmes. En effet, la mort d'*Hilbertus* survient en 701, alors que certains événements mentionnés dans le texte ont lieu bien après. Il est par exemple écrit que le roi Thierry donne un domaine à Donzère, domaine sur lequel est fondé un monastère subordonné à Fontenelle jusqu'à ce que les relations se trouvent brisées du fait de la division du *regnum Francorum* et des incursions de la *gens Agarrenorum*, c'est-à-dire des Sarrasins. Or ceci a lieu aux environs des années 730. De même, la *Vita Ansberti* inclut des sources du VIIIe siècle, en l'occurrence le *Liber historiae Francorum* (726) et l'*Histoire ecclésiastique* de Bède (731). Tout porte donc à croire que la *Vita Ansberti* est probablement rédigée à la fin du VIIIe siècle et avant 811, date à laquelle l'ermite *Harduinus* lègue à Fontenelle un *Liber vitarum sancti Wandregisili, Ansberti ac Wlfranni confessorum volumen unum*[17]. Ainsi, le lien entre ce texte et Fontenelle est le seul aspect accepté de ce prologue, si l'on se fie à la bonne connaissance qu'a l'hagiographe de la documentation diplomatique du monastère et au fait qu'il se présente comme l'auteur de la *Vita Lamberti*, autre pièce de la production fontenellienne.

De cette *Vita sancti Ansberti* dépend directement une hymne alphabétique (*BHL* 523) de 23 versets de trois lignes, elles-mêmes composées de 15 syllabes. Son auteur insiste essentiellement sur l'exil de saint Ansbert et sur son apostolat dans la région de la Sambre avant de conclure sur sa mort et sur la translation de son corps vers Fontenelle, translation ponctuée de miracles. Ceci place le *terminus post quem* de cette hymne à la fin du VIIIe siècle ou au début du IXe siècle. Compte tenu de l'importance accordée au thème de l'exil, John Howe plaide pour une rédaction plus tardive, dans la seconde moitié du IXe siècle. Selon lui, il s'agit d'un moyen pour la communauté de Fontenelle de développer le culte d'Ansbert dans la région où elle trouve refuge[18]. Dans ce cas, ce texte obéirait à la même logique que la *Translatio et miracula sancti Wandrgesili*.

Il existe également un *Carmen de sancto Ansberto* (*BHL* 522) de 52 lignes divisé en deux chapitres portant sur la généalogie d'Ansbert et le mariage manqué de ce dernier. Là encore, ce *Carmen* s'appuie largement sur la *Vita sancti Ansberti* dont il est la versification. Sans doute est-il composé dans le courant du IXe siècle. Sa fin soudaine conduit John Howe à se demander s'il s'agit d'une *Vita* métrique inachevée ou si son auteur choisit délibérément de la laisser en l'état afin de ne pas dépasser cent lignes[19].

L'auteur de la *Vita sancti Ansberti*, on l'a précisé, se présente également comme étant celui de la *Vita sancti Lamberti* (*BHL* 4675). Celle-ci, telle qu'elle nous est parvenue, est incomplète. Elle relate l'existence de Lambert, noble originaire de la région de Thérouanne, qui fréquente la cour de Clotaire III

---

[17] PRADIÉ (1999), chap. XII, p. 142-143.
[18] HOWE (2001), p. 142.
[19] *Ibid.*, p. 143.

(657-673) avant de se convertir à la vie religieuse. Il gagne alors Fontenelle où il est tonsuré par Wandrille. À la mort de ce dernier, il est élu par les moines pour lui succéder. Sous son abbatiat, le monastère reçoit de nombreuses donations. Son auteur s'appuie sur les textes hagiographiques composés dans le monastère ainsi que sur sa documentation diplomatique, en l'occurrence sur les donations de Childéric III. Il utilise également la *Vita sancti Eligi* du pseudo *Audoenus*, la *Vita Columbani*, la *Vita Lupi* et la *Passio Leudegarii*. C'est pourquoi il est possible de proposer pour ce récit une fourchette de datation identique à celle de la *Vita sancti Ansberti*, à savoir fin VIIIe siècle-811.

D. Le dossier de saint Vulfran

Ce dossier se compose de deux pièces. Il comprend une *Vita sancti Vulframni* (*BHL* 8738) et une hymne alphabétique (*BHL* vacant).

La *Vita sancti Vulframni* s'arrête d'abord sur les origines aristocratiques de Vulfran et son entrée précoce dans la cléricature. Il est ensuite élu au siège métropolitain de Sens où il succède à Lambert avant de prendre la décision, à la suite d'une vision, d'aller évangéliser la Frise. Il se rend pour ceci auprès d'Ansbert, alors abbé de Fontenelle, à qui il offre son domaine patrimonial (688-687). Il recrute dans ce monastère quelques compagnons et gagne la Frise. Là, il prêche la parole de Dieu, baptise de nombreux païens et accomplit plusieurs miracles. Il sauve notamment quelques enfants d'exécutions rituelles parmi lesquels le jeune Ovon qu'il ramène à Fontenelle et qui s'illustre par la suite dans la copie de manuscrits. Il échoue toutefois à convertir le *princeps* Radbod. Après ce revers de fortune, il regagne Fontenelle où il prend l'habit monastique et termine sa vie le 13 des calendes d'avril 720. Il est alors inhumé dans l'église Saint-Paul, aux côtés de Wandrille et Ansbert, avant que leurs corps ne soient transférés dans l'église Saint-Pierre par l'abbé Bain (729).

La critique de ce texte s'avère délicate[20]. D'après son prologue, il est écrit par un dénommé Jonas qui dédie son œuvre à l'abbé Bain. Cette mention place en toute logique sa composition entre 701 et 710. Or il est question plus loin de l'abbé

---

[20] Lebecq (2000, 2004, 2011, 2018).

Wandon (747-754). De même, la *vita* stipule que Vulfran meurt en 720 et que son corps est transféré en 729 à l'initiative de Bain. Or l'abbatiat de Bain prend fin en 710 et on sait que cette translation a lieu en 704. C'est pourquoi Stéphane Lebecq date ce texte des années 788-811 : 788 marque le début de l'abbatiat de Gervold crédité de la fondation de la *scola* de Fontenelle ainsi que du développement des études dans le monastère ; 811 correspond au décès du moine *Harduinus*, auteur du *Liber vitarum sancti* [sic] *Wandregisili, Ansberti ac Wlfranni confessorum volumen unum* déjà cité. Quant à l'identité de l'hagiographe, elle vise à insinuer une confusion avec l'auteur de la *Vita Columbani*. D'après Stéphane Lebecq, il s'agit en réalité d'un moine de Fontenelle qui s'appuie largement sur la *Vita Columbani* de Jonas de Bobbio, la *Vita* et les *Miracula Amandi*, les *Decem Libri Historiarum* de Grégoire de Tours et l'*Historia ecclesiastica* de Bède.

Les analyses de Stéphane Lebecq démontrent que, en réalité, cette *Vita* résulte de l'intégration de plusieurs éléments. Ceci explique la dédicace à l'abbé Bain, le récit de deux miracles – sans doute recueilli auprès de l'abbé Wandon ou bien par celui-ci –, les traditions relatives à la mission frisonne probablement transmises par Ovon dont le témoignage est cité dès le prologue. Ce texte amalgame donc des éléments de tradition orale, transmis tant que vivent les témoins qui les recueillent et les véhiculent, en l'occurrence Ovon et Wandon. Leur mort fait sans doute ressentir la nécessité de cristalliser ces différents récits.

Cette *Vita* est accompagnée d'une hymne alphabétique (*BHL vacat*) reprenant les grandes lignes de l'existence de Vulfran, le menant d'un palais terrestre à la cour céleste. Il y est associé aux saints Wandrille, Ansbert et à l'abbé Bain[21]. Ce dernier est mentionné comme étant le commanditaire de ce texte.

Si pour François Dolbeau, il ne fait pas de doute que son auteur appartient à la communauté de Fontenelle, il n'en va pas de même de sa datation et de son lieu de rédaction, points qui soulèvent de nombreuses interrogations. Cette hymne figurant dans un manuscrit antérieur à 1012[22], établir un *terminus ante quem* n'est guère problématique. En revanche, dégager un *terminus post quem* s'avère plus délicat. Une datation basse conduirait à repla-

---

[21] DOLBEAU (2006), p. 279-283.
[22] Saint-Omer, BM 765.

cer la composition de cette hymne dans le contexte de l'exil des religieux de Fontenelle dans les régions septentrionales au cours de la seconde moitié du IXe siècle. Cette œuvre serait à rapprocher de l'hymne alphabétique en l'honneur d'Ansbert. Toutefois, si tel est le cas, la prière adressée à Bain, présenté comme vivant, conduit à faire de ce texte un faux manifeste, sans que l'on soit en mesure d'en présenter les enjeux. La mention du cinquième abbé de Fontenelle invite donc à envisager une datation haute. Néanmoins, cette option n'est pas non pleinement satisfaisante: remonter au début du VIIIe siècle suppose que ce texte, obscur par bien des côtés, survive à l'état de fossile sans faire l'objet d'une réécriture, jusqu'au début du Xe siècle. C'est pourquoi, si François Dolbeau se rallie, avec beaucoup d'hésitation, à l'idée d'une date haute, John Howe, quant à lui, défend l'idée d'une date basse[23].

E. Le dossier des saints Condède et Érembert

La *Vita sancti Condedi* (*BHL* 1907) et la *Vita sancti Eremberti* (*BHL* 2587) sont attribuées au même hagiographe.

Le premier texte relate l'existence de Condède, prêtre et ermite originaire de Bretagne, venu sur le continent à l'occasion d'un pèlerinage. Après avoir passé quelque temps dans un lieu nommé *Fontana Walarici*, il décide de visiter Fontenelle en raison de la réputation de ce monastère et se retire à proximité, sur l'île de Belcinnac qui lui est remise par le roi Thierry III. En 675, il cède à son tour l'île aux moines de Fontenelle. Après sa mort, ses reliques sont transférées dans l'abbaye pour être inhumées dans l'église Saint-Pierre.

Cette *Vita* est très certainement composée par un religieux qui a accès à la documentation diplomatique du monastère, en l'occurrence à la donation de Belcinnac à Condède par Thierry III, à celle de Belcinnac à Fontenelle par Condède, à la confirmation de ce don par Warraton, maire du palais, ou encore à l'épitaphe de Condède dans l'église Saint-Pierre. Il s'appuie également sur la *Vita sancti Lamberti* et utilise les Saintes Ecritures, la *Vita Willibrordi* d'Alcuin ou encore l'*Histoire ecclésiastique* de Bède. Ceci permet de fixer un *terminus post quem* aux

---
[23] Howe (2001), p. 160.

environs de 796-797, date de rédaction de la *Vita Willibrordi*, et un *terminus ante quem* en 840, date de rédaction de *Vita altera sancti Wandregesili* dont l'auteur exploite expressément la *Vita Condedi*.

Le second texte retrace la vie d'Erembert, originaire de *Villiolicortis*, à Poissy, et vivant sous le règne de Dagobert et de son fils Clovis. Il reçoit l'habit monastique à Fontenelle sous l'abbatiat de Wandrille avant de devenir évêque de Toulouse sur ordre de Clotaire III. Il revient néanmoins mourir à Fontenelle où il est inhumé dans l'église Saint-Paul tandis que son frère et ses neveux se font moines dans ce monastère. Puis son corps est transféré dans l'église Saint-Pierre et plus particulièrement dans l'oratoire Saint-Martin. Ce texte est probablement antérieur à la période 830-840 puisque la *Vita altera sancti Wandregesili* y fait expressément référence [24].

La répartition spatiale des différents manuscrits de ces *Vitae* s'explique par l'histoire de la communauté monastique et en particulier par ses pérégrinations face aux incursions scandinaves. En effet, ils se rencontrent bien souvent dans des manuscrits flamands [25]. Ceci correspond à la zone de diffusion des cultes fontenelliens suite à la translation des reliques du monastère à Gand en 944, à l'initiative du comte de Flandre et de l'abbé du Mont-Blandin. Wandrille intègre le groupe des saints protecteurs de la région. C'est sans doute par l'intermédiaire de la Flandre que ces textes regagnent ensuite Fontenelle à compter de la fin du Xe siècle, l'abbé Mainard qui restaure le monastère étant originaire de Gand. Il apporte avec lui les manuscrits et les chartes subsistants, restitués par l'abbaye du Mont Blandin [26]. C'est probablement sur cette documentation que s'appuie le moine Guillaume qui, dans la première moitié du XIe siècle, s'attache à collecter les pièces relatives au passé de Fontenelle [27]. Celles-ci sont retranscrites dans la première partie du *Maius Chronicon Fontanellense* [28]. En raison des liens entretenus par Fon-

---

[24] *Vita altera sancti Wandregesili*, chap. V, §26, p. 280.
[25] Pour la liste de ces manuscrits, se reporter à HOWE (2001), p. 127-192.
[26] GAZEAU (2007), p. 332.
[27] HOWE (2001), p. 133; VAN HOUTS (1996), p. 235-236.
[28] BM 332 (A 34). Ce manuscrit comprend la *Vita secunda sancti Wandregesili*, les *Miracula sancti Wandregesili*, la *Vita sancti Ansberti* et l'hymne en son honneur, la *Vita sancti Vulframni*, la *Vita sancti Condedi*, la *Vita sancti Eremberti* ainsi que la plus ancienne copie connue des *Gesta abbatum Fontanellensium*.

tenelle avec les autres monastères du diocèse, certains textes sont copiés dans des manuscrits composés à Jumièges, Fécamp, Saint-Ouen ou encore à la cathédrale de Rouen[29]. De même, certains d'entre eux se retrouvent dans des manuscrits composés en Francie ou en Angleterre[30]. Il est possible qu'une diffusion outre-Manche s'explique par l'implantation de Fontenelle au lendemain de la conquête du duc Guillaume (1066)[31]. À moins qu'elle ne soit le fait des liens entretenus par la Flandre avec l'Angleterre. En l'absence d'investigations plus poussées, il est difficile de trancher pour l'une ou l'autre de ces hypothèses.

Au sein de cet espace, tous les textes étudiés ne connaissent pas un égal rayonnement. Les récits relatifs à Wandrille, en particulier la *Vita altera* à laquelle est souvent associée la *Translatio et miracula*, sont les plus répandus, en raison du statut qu'acquiert le saint, suite au transfert de ses reliques en Flandre. De même, plusieurs manuscrits contenant la *Vita altera* comportent également la *Vita sancti Ansberti*, l'hymne alphabétique et le *Carmen* composés en l'honneur de ce dernier. Ceci est également vrai de la *Vita sancti Vulframni*. Seuls ces trois saints voient les textes les concernant copiés outre-Manche. La diffusion de la *Vita sancti Condedi* en Flandre est bien plus limitée. Ce récit est associé à la *Vita sancti Eremberti*, ceci s'expliquant certainement par le fait qu'ils sont composés par le même auteur. La *Vita sancti Lamberti*, elle, ne connaît qu'une diffusion locale.

Il est néanmoins nécessaire de ne pas oublier que ces différents récits sont connus par des manuscrits essentiellement composés entre le Xe et le XIIe siècle. C'est pourquoi le tableau brossé de la production hagiographique fontenellienne reste très certainement partiel, les pertes n'étant pas à négliger, qu'elles soient involontaires ou qu'elles résultent d'un tri délibéré. En effet, la *Vita altera sancti Wandregesili* mentionne un texte en l'honneur de sainte Hildemarque, première abbesse de Fécamp dont la fondation est soutenue par Fontenelle[32]. De même, elle fait état d'une *Vita* en l'honneur du mentor de Wandrille à Montfaucon, *Baltfridus*[33]. Or, aucune copie de ces deux œuvres

---

[29] Se reporter aux manuscrits recensés dans HOWE (2001), p. 127-192.
[30] Même remarque.
[31] PONCELET (1988), p. 149-171.
[32] *Vita altera sancti Wandregesili*, chap. III, §17, p. 277.
[33] *Ibid.*, chap. I, §5, p. 273.

n'est faite au Xe siècle. Peut-être sont-elles définitivement perdues lors de la fuite des moines. À moins qu'il ne s'agisse d'un oubli volontaire. Il semble qu'Hildemarque ne suscite que peu d'intérêt au lendemain de la restauration de Fontenelle. Ceci peut sans doute s'expliquer par le fait que la communauté qui s'installe à Fécamp à la fin du Xe siècle se construit largement sur le mythe de la table rase mobilisé par l'historiographie des débuts de la principauté normande[34]. Quant à *Baltfridus*, il ne fait l'objet d'aucun culte dans le monastère restauré de Fontenelle.

II. L'ÉCRITURE HAGIOGRAPHIQUE À L'ABBAYE DE JUMIÈGES[35]

La production hagiographique de Jumièges parvenue jusqu'à nous est plus modeste que celle de Fontenelle: elle se limite au dossier des saints Aychard et Hugues ainsi qu'à celui de sainte Austreberte. Pendant longtemps, les historiens ont vu dans cet état de fait le résultat des incursions scandinaves: le monastère est incendié en 841 et les religieux se réfugient dans l'un de leur prieuré, à Haspres, dans les années 850-860. Ces épisodes engendreraient d'importantes pertes. Néanmoins, cette hypothèse fait actuellement l'objet d'une remise en cause. Selon Rosamond McKitterick, il est fort possible que l'activité intellectuelle et la production de livres soient en réalité plus faibles qu'escomptées, auquel cas les vikings ne détruiraient ou n'interrompraient pas grand chose[36].

A. LE DOSSIER DES SAINTS AYCHARD ET HUGUES

Les historiens s'accordent pour attribuer la *Vita prima sancti Aychardi* (*BHL* 181) ainsi que la *Vita sancti Hugonis* (*BHL* 4032a) à un même auteur tant y sont observés de concordances (syntaxe, expression, vocabulaire, découpage des cha-

---

[34] ARNOUX (1991), p. 135-158; ID. (1999), p. 22-48; ID. (2000), p. 71-82; BAUDUIN (2001), p. 79-91.
[35] HOWE (2001), p. 92-125.
[36] MCKITTERICK (2014), p. 30-31.

pitres, formulation des titres et de l'index, contenu, références) et aussi un même goût prononcé pour la liturgie.

Selon la *Vita prima*, saint Aychard est un aristocrate originaire de la région de Poitiers, envoyé par ses parents dans le monastère de Saint-Hilaire pour y être éduqué par Ansfrid, un maître réputé. À 15 ans, il reçoit l'autorisation d'entrer dans le monastère d'Ansion, dans le Poitou et, à 20 ans, inspiré par une voix d'ange, il persuade sa famille d'offrir le domaine patrimonial afin de doter ce qui deviendra le monastère de Saint-Benoît de Quinçay. Lorsque saint Philibert se retire sur l'île d'*Herio* suite à son conflit avec le maire du palais Ebroïn, il appelle Aychard pour lui succéder à la tête de Jumièges. De nombreux miracles se produisent sous son abbatiat: il est notamment averti de la mort d'une partie de sa communauté et prépare cette dernière à cette calamité.

La *Vita sancti Hugonis* fait d'Hugues le fils de Charlemagne et d'*Anstrudis*, la fille de Tassilon de Bavière. Le récit s'attache d'abord à présenter l'éducation reçue par Hugues, à l'abbaye de Saint-Denis et à l'école palatine, puis relate comment, à l'occasion d'un pèlerinage à Rome, il est tonsuré, ordonné diacre et promet d'entrer à Jumièges. À la mort de l'évêque de Rouen, il lui succède en qualité de métropolitain et s'applique alors à réorganiser son diocèse, à relever ses églises et à prendre soin des pauvres. Lorsqu'il renonce au siège épiscopal, il entre à Jumièges comme simple moine et y passe neuf années avant de mourir et d'être inhumé à proximité de l'autel Sainte-Marie.

Les différents historiens, tout en attribuant ces *Vitae* au même auteur, s'accordent sur leur composition en milieu monastique en raison de l'omniprésence de la règle de saint Benoît et de la prééminence accordée à l'*ordo* monastique, jugé supérieur aux autres[37]. Ils s'opposent en revanche sur le lieu et la date de rédaction de ces textes. Il est possible d'établir un *terminus post quem* après 800: la *Vita Aichardi* évoque l'époque révolue de l'empereur Charlemagne; la *Vita Hugonis* s'appuie sur l'œuvre d'Eginhard et fait référence à la déposition de Louis le Pieux (833). Néanmoins, la confusion entre Hugues, abbé de Jumièges, et le fils illégitime de Charlemagne invite à penser que l'auteur écrit bien après la mort du second, survenue en 844.

---

[37] Van der Straeten (1969), p. 215-260; Id. (1970), p. 63-73; Howe (2001), p. 99-101; Le Maho (2006), p. 314-319.

Selon Joseph Van der Straeten, ces *Vitae* sont composées vers la fin du IXe siècle, à Haspres, dans le prieuré où les moines de Fontenelle trouvent refuge face aux raids scandinaves, car les auteurs semblent déconnectés de la tradition du monastère normand. Le rédacteur chercherait à célébrer les vertus de ces deux saints afin de promouvoir un culte local[38]. Pour John Howe, la rédaction de ces *Vitae* remonterait bien à la seconde moitié du IXe siècle mais serait antérieure à la fuite de la communauté de Jumièges, dans la mesure où les reliques de Hugues, Aychard, Constantin de Beauvais, Pérégrin et Flavius sont mentionnées comme étant inhumées à Jumièges[39]. Quant à Jacques Le Maho, il aboutit à des conclusions totalement différentes. S'il convient que les deux textes sont rédigés après le départ des moines de Jumièges, il propose au contraire une datation bien plus tardive: il lui semble difficile de croire que, au cours des années suivant la fuite des religieux de Jumièges, les traditions se perdent au point que les dépositaires du corps d'Hugues pensent détenir les reliques d'un simple moine et ignorent qu'il s'agit en réalité de leur ancien abbé[40]. Il estime également impossible de situer le lieu de rédaction à Haspres: aucun des textes ne fait mention de cette translation ou de *miracula post mortem*. Cette lacune cadre donc mal avec l'hypothèse d'une volonté de susciter le développement d'une dévotion autour de reliques. De plus, il est explicitement dit à la fin de la *Vita Aichardi* que les corps d'Aycadre et Hugues reposent au cimetière de l'abbaye de Jumièges. Aussi, si l'on en croit Jacques Le Maho, ces textes sont bel et bien destinés à l'abbaye de Jumièges même. Il plaide donc en faveur d'une rédaction au cours du milieu du Xe siècle, dans le cadre de la restauration du monastère. Il s'appuie pour cela sur la plus ancienne transcription connue de ces textes[41] et se fonde sur les analyses de François Avril selon qui, si l'écriture est bien de tradition carolingienne, le décor pourrait en revanche indiquer une date de composition plus récente, remontant probablement au milieu du Xe siècle[42]. C'est pourquoi, d'après Jacques Le Maho, ces *vitae* ne peuvent

---

[38] Van der Straeten (1970), p. 69-73.
[39] Howe (2001), p. 124.
[40] Le Maho (2006), p. 285-322.
[41] Rouen, BM 1377 (U. 108).
[42] Avril (1975), p. 7-8.

être rédigées que par l'un des religieux chargés de relever le monastère de Jumièges. Il se prononce en faveur d'Annon, alors à la tête du monastère de Micy: l'abbé chercherait à doter Jumièges des bases hagiographiques indispensables à la célébration de la mémoire de deux de ses principaux saints patrons. Le but ne serait pas de susciter le développement d'une dévotion autour des sépultures des saints Aycadre et Hugues mais de mettre à disposition de la communauté les textes à lire au réfectoire et aux offices festifs de ces saints[43]. Néanmoins, il est difficile d'oublier que, dans sa *Vita*, Aycadre est présenté comme reposant à Jumièges et qualifié dès le prologue de «patron». Or les moines qui relèvent le monastère ne nient pas la translation d'Aycadre à Haspres, ne cherchent pas à récupérer sa dépouille et ne semblent pas le considérer comme leur patron. De plus, lorsqu'il compose la *Vita Hugonis*, l'hagiographe semble avoir accès à la documentation diplomatique du monastère: il fait état de la générosité d'Hugues envers l'abbaye et nomme précisément plusieurs domaines. Ces différents arguments pouvant se voir opposer autant de contre-arguments, il est difficile en l'état de trancher en faveur de l'une ou l'autre des hypothèses avancées par les historiens. Tout au plus peut-on admettre une datation comprise entre le IXe et le Xe siècles.

Ces deux textes sont diffusés dans le diocèse de Rouen, sans surprise à Jumièges, dans le diocèse d'Avranches, au Mont Saint-Michel, et en Flandre[44]. Leur présence au Mont Saint-Michel s'explique probablement par les liens noués avec Jumièges puisque Thierry (1017-1027) cumule les deux abbatiats[45]. Quant à la présence de ces récits en Flandre, elle résulte sans doute de la translation des reliques d'Aychard et d'Hugues à Haspres. Cet événement constitue sans doute le point de départ du rayonnement de leur culte dans les régions septentrionales.

B. Le dossier de sainte Austreberte

C'est également à Jumièges que sont composés les textes en l'honneur de sainte Austreberte: la *Vita prima sanctae Austrebertae*

---

[43] Le Maho (2006), p. 303-306.

[44] Se reporter aux manuscrits recensés dans Howe (2001), p. 96-98 et 121-123.

[45] Gazeau (2007), p. 147-149 et 203-204.

(*BHL* 831), une *Vita* abrégée (*BHL* 833), ainsi qu'un recueil de *Miracula* (*BHL* 834/835).

La *Vita prima Austrebertae* s'attache en premier lieu à présenter les réalisations de saint Philibert, parmi lesquelles la fondation de Pavilly. Le texte s'arrête ensuite sur les origines d'Austreberte: fille de *Badefridus* et de Framehilde, elle se rattache au roi des Alamans par sa mère. En dépit de présages annonçant qu'elle est choisie par Dieu, ses parents arrangent son mariage. Refusant ce dernier, Austreberte fuit rejoindre Omer, évêque de Thérouanne, accompagnée de son jeune frère. Omer lui remet le voile consacré et la réconcilie avec ses parents. Austreberte gagne alors le couvent de *Portus* (Port-le-Grand, dép. Somme) dont elle devient abbesse en raison de ses mérites. Elle est ensuite invitée à Pavilly par Philibert mais se heurte rapidement à l'hostilité des religieuses et d'*Amelbertus*, le patron, qui fomentent un complot contre elle. Une fois celui-ci déjoué, l'abbaye de Pavilly prospère. Austreberte y mène une vie édifiante et connaît une mort exemplaire (704). Elle est inhumée dans l'église Saint-Pierre.

Dans son prologue, l'auteur dit écrire à la demande de l'abbesse Julia, qui succède à Austreberte à la tête de Pavilly. Si l'on se fie à l'emploi du masculin, il s'agit probablement d'un moine de Jumièges, Pavilly étant une fondation de ce monastère. L'hagiographe dit composer son texte plusieurs années après la mort d'Austreberte, principalement sur la base de témoignages relatés par des moniales ayant elles-mêmes assisté aux faits. Les témoins sont présentés comme encore vivants ou ayant vécu jusqu'à une époque récente. C'est pourquoi John Howe date ce texte des années 750[46].

Cette *Vita* est suivie d'un bref recueil de *Miracula* (*BHL* 834-835) associés au décès de l'abbesse. Ils se réfèrent explicitement au prologue de la *Vita prima*.

Existe également une *Vita abrégée* (*BHL* 833). Celle-ci suit fidèlement la trame de la *Vita* précédente tout en abrégeant certains passages par amputation ou par concision. Ce texte est difficile à dater et à localiser dans la mesure où il suit assez fidèlement la *Vita prima*. John Howe propose un *terminus post quem* dans la seconde moitié du VIIIe siècle, le récit original étant rédigé aux environs de 750, et un *terminus ante quem* dans

---

[46] HOWE (2001), p. 111.

le Xe siècle, époque à laquelle remontent les manuscrits les plus anciens contenant ce texte[47].

Ces récits connaissent un succès variable au cours du Moyen Âge. On constate une faible diffusion de la *Vita prima* puisqu'elle ne se rencontre que dans deux manuscrits composés au XIIe siècle, à Saint-Évroult et au Bec. La *Vita* abrégée est plus largement diffusée dans la mesure où il s'agit probablement d'une réécriture destinée à un public extérieur au diocèse de Rouen, moins intéressé par les détails de l'histoire locale. Comme les *Miracula sanctae Austrebertae*, elle se rencontre essentiellement dans des manuscrits provenant du diocèse de Rouen ou des manuscrits flamands, anglais et italiens[48]. La recherche et la copie de ces textes sont favorisées par le regain d'intérêt dont bénéficie le culte d'Austreberte au XIIe siècle, suite à l'*inventio* d'une partie de ses reliques à Pavilly et leur transfert à la Trinité-du-Mont de Rouen (1091) où elles font l'objet d'une campagne de valorisation. La diffusion de ces récits en Flandre s'explique probablement par les pérégrinations des restes de sainte Austreberte lors des invasions scandinaves, même si leur trajet reste obscur: les moniales semblent quitter Pavilly pour Marconne, lieu de naissance d'Austreberte, puis pour Sithiu et l'église Notre-Dame, proche de Saint-Bertin. Elles rejoignent de nouveau Marconne mais laissent une partie du corps d'Austreberte à Notre-Dame puis gagnent ensuite Montreuil où elles fondent un monastère quelques années plus tard. Ceci favorise sans doute la diffusion du culte dans la région. C'est par la Flandre que ces textes gagneraient ensuite l'Angleterre à compter du Xe siècle, par l'intermédiaire de Christ Church à Cantorbéry[49].

III. Dans l'orbite de la cathédrale de Rouen: le dossier de saint Ouen

À l'exception de celle de saint Ouen, la mémoire des évêques rouennais n'est pas cultivée par la cathédrale à l'époque pré-nor-

---

[47] *Ibid.*, p. 115.
[48] Se reporter aux manuscrits recensés *ibid.*, p. 109-116.
[49] Corrêa (1997), p. 107.

mande. Pour preuve, la *Vita sancti Gildardi* n'est rédigée qu'au Xe siècle, à Saint-Médard de Soissons. De même, c'est sous l'épiscopat d'Hugues (942-989) qu'un intérêt nouveau est porté à la figure de saint Romain. Il faut donc attendre le lendemain de la fondation de la principauté normande (911), plus précisément les Xe et XIe siècles, pour observer une vaste entreprise hagiographique en l'honneur des prélats rouennais[50].

À l'époque carolingienne, la *Vita prima sancti Audoeni* (*BHL* 750), composée au VIIe siècle par l'un des clercs desservant la basilique funéraire Saint-Pierre, future abbaye de Saint-Ouen de Rouen, fait l'objet d'entreprises de réécriture avec la rédaction d'une *Vita B* (*BHL* 751a) et d'une *Vita C* (*BHL* 753), successivement étudiées par Elphège Vacandard, Wilhelm Levison ou encore par Felice Lifshitz, Nancy Gautier et François Dolbeau. Ces différents travaux conduisent à des analyses contradictoires.

Globalement, à quelques exceptions près, la *Vita B* respecte la trame de la *Vita prima*. Elle s'attache à présenter les origines de saint Ouen, son parcours à la cour de Dagobert, ses qualités. Elle revient sur le séjour du saint dans la péninsule ibérique, son élection au siège épiscopal de Rouen et ses œuvres en qualité d'évêque. Elle s'arrête aussi sur son voyage à Rome et sa médiation entre l'Austrasie et la Neustrie. Néanmoins, de nombreux épisodes sont amplifiés, à l'instar des miracles accomplis en péninsule ibérique, de la mission diplomatique dont saint Ouen est chargé ou encore du voyage de la dépouille du prélat vers Rouen. Des épisodes sont aussi ajoutés: la bénédiction reçue de Colomban, le rôle joué par saint Ouen dans la fondation de l'abbaye féminine de Fécamp ou encore dans celle du monastère de Sainte-Croix, l'élévation de ses reliques à l'initiative d'Ansbert ainsi que le développement de son culte dans la basilique Saint-Pierre. Ce texte, datant de la première moitié du IXe siècle, est parfois attribué à tort à un dénommé *Fridegodus*. Il est composé à Rouen et non comme le soutient Felice Lifshitz, à Gasny, dans le Soissonnais, par des moines de Saint-Ouen qui s'y réfugient après 876[51]. Il s'agit, de loin, du texte hagiographique concernant saint Ouen le plus diffusé au cours du Moyen Âge, dans l'ouest de la Francie ainsi qu'en Angleterre où

---

[50] GAUTHIER (1992), p. 463-467; VIOLETTE (1997), p. 343-365.
[51] *Ibid.*, p. 450-451; LIFSHITZ (1995), p. 89.

l'évêque de Rouen est vénéré depuis que la reine Emma (1002-1052) a fait don de quelques reliques supposées lui appartenir à Christ Church de Cantorbéry.

La *Vita C*, quant à elle, paraphrase *B*, tout en faisant un usage sporadique de *A*. Elle est également enrichie de quatre miracles (chap. 47-53) dont le remanieur aurait pu prendre connaissance par tradition orale ou par l'intermédiaire d'un manuscrit interpolé de B. Contrairement à B, elle n'est pas rédigée à Rouen. Il s'agirait d'une commande effectuée auprès d'un lettré extérieur à l'abbaye de Saint-Ouen qui, jusque là, ignorait la geste de l'évêque de Rouen mais se voit charger de rénover une vie antérieure et d'en éclaircir les points obscurs dus à une brièveté excessive. Ce texte est antérieur à 850 puisqu'il est exploité dans la *Vita Leutfredi* (*BHL* 4899), datable de cette époque[52].

D'après Felice Lifshitz, B et C dériveraient de manière indépendante d'une *Vita* intermédiaire et perdue, œuvre d'Alcuin. Pour avancer cette hypothèse, l'historienne américaine se fonde sur les inscriptions rédigées par ce dernier pour plusieurs autels à Saint-Vaast d'Arras, dont celui de saint Ouen. Elle observe également une certaine proximité entre la trame narrative de *B* et *C* et d'autres œuvres du lettré anglo-saxon, de même que des similitudes dans les thématiques abordées, en particulier en ce qui concerne les relations entre Église et pouvoir, avec le couple Ouen-Dagobert, ou encore le concept d'*inimicus ecclesiae*[53]. Cette entreprise de réécriture s'expliquerait par une volonté de neutraliser le pouvoir de saint Ouen, saint neustrien par excellence, en minimisant le pouvoir de ses reliques et, à l'inverse, en valorisant son activité missionnaire dirigée contre les ennemis de l'Église. Néanmoins, cette analyse est loin de faire l'unanimité. Ainsi, François Dolbeau n'admet pas l'existence d'un prototype attribuable à Alcuin, faute d'arguments d'ordre philologique. De plus, la prise de contrôle de la vallée de la Seine par les Pippinides n'empêche pas saint Ouen de s'imposer comme principal patron de la région, et ce grâce au soutien même de métropolitains proches du pouvoir: Hugues est à l'origine de la fondation d'un premier collège de clercs à Saint-Pierre tandis que Remi (755-771), frère de Pépin le Bref, en fait une abbaye.

---

[52] DOLBEAU (2003), p. 235-236; sur Leutfredus, cf. POULIN, J.-C., *infra*, «L'hagiographie de Basse-Normandie», p. 291-292.
[53] LIFSHITZ (1995), p. 89.

Cette dernière est alors assez puissante pour émettre sa propre monnaie, sous forme de deniers frappés au nom de Saint-Ouen.

Conclusion

De manière générale, au IXe siècle les incursions scandinaves dans la vallée de la Seine poussent les clercs et les moines à fuir la région. Même si leur impact a pu être surestimé et même si le siège épiscopal se maintient dans le diocèse de Rouen, il est indéniable que ces raids portent un coup d'arrêt à l'activité de certains *scriptoria*, en particulier à celui de Fontenelle. Il faut attendre les Xe et XIe siècles et la fondation de la principauté normande (911) pour assister à un mouvement de restauration et de refondation monastique. Celui-ci s'accompagne d'une vaste entreprise hagiographique donnant lieu à la recherche et à la copie de textes d'époque mérovingienne et carolingienne, avec un inévitable phénomène de tri et d'oubli dont nous restons largement tributaires pour connaître l'état de la production hagiographique des VIIIe et IXe siècles.

Bibliographie

A. Sources éditées

Carmen de sancto Ansberto, éd. K. STRECKER, *MGH, Poet. Lat.*, IV-3, Berlin, 1923, p. 1004-1005.
Chronique des abbés de Fontenelle (Saint-Wandrille), éd. P. PRADIÉ, Paris, 1999.
Miracula sanctae Austrebertae, *AASS*, Feb. II, 1864, p. 427-429.
Miracula sancti Wandregesili, *AASS*, Iul. V, 1868, p. 291-302.
Vita sanctae Austrebertae, *AASS*, Feb. II, 1864, p. 419-424.
Vita sancti Ansberti, éd. W. LEVISON, *MGH, SRM*, V, Hanovre – Leipzig, 1910, p. 618-641.
Vita rythmica sancti Ansberti, éd. W. LEVISON, *Ibid.*, p. 641-643.
Vita sancti Aychardi, *AASS*, Sept. V, 1868, p. 85-100.
Vita B sancti Audoeni, *AASS*, Aug. IV, 1867, p. 810-819.
Vita sancti Condedi, éd. W. LEVISON, *MGH, SRM*, V, Hanovre – Leipzig, 1910, p. 644-651.
Vita sancti Eremberti, éd. W. LEVISON, *Ibid.*, p. 653-656.

Vita sancti Lamberti, éd. W. LEVISON, *Ibid.*, p. 608-612.
Vita sancti Vulframni, éd. W. LEVISON, *Ibid.*, p. 657-673.
Vita altera sancti Wandregesili, *AASS*, Iul. V, 1868, p. 272-281.
VAN DER STRAETEN, J., «Vie inédite de saint Hugues, évêque de Rouen», *AB*, 87 (1969), p. 215-260.

B. ÉTUDES

ARNOUX, M., «La fortune du *Libellus de revelatione, edificatione et auctoritate Fiscannensis monasterii*. Note sur la production historiographique d'une abbaye bénédictine normande», *Revue d'histoire des textes*, 21 (1991), p. 135-158.
—, «Before the *Gesta Normannorum* and Beyond Dudo: Some Evidence on Early Norman Historiography», *Anglo-Norman Studies*, 22 (1999), p. 22-48.
—, «Les premières chroniques de Fécamp: de l'hagiographie à l'histoire», in F. NEVEUX – P. BOUET (dir.), *Les saints dans la Normandie médiévale*, Caen, 2000, p. 71-82.
AVRIL, F., *Manuscrits normands XIe-XIIe siècle. Catalogue de l'exposition de la bibliothèque municipale, Rouen*, 1975.
BAUDUIN, P., «Autour d'une construction identitaire: la naissance d'une historiographie normande à la charnière des Xe-XIe siècles», *Cahiers du GHRIS*, 13 (2001), p. 79-91.
CORRÊA, A., «St. Austreberta of Pavilly in the Anglo-Saxon Liturgy», *AB*, 115 (1997), p. 77-112.
DOLBEAU, F., «Prose, rythme et mètre: réécriture hagiographique dans le dossier de saint Ouen», dans M. GOULLET – M. HEINZELMANN, dir., *La réécriture hagiographique dans l'Occident médiéval. Transformations formelles et idéologiques*, Sigmaringen, 2003, p. 231-250 (Beihefte der Francia, 58).
—, «Une hymne inédite en l'honneur de saint Vulfran», dans M. HEINZELMANN, dir., *Livrets, collections et textes. Études sur la tradition hagiographique latine*, Ostfildern, 2006, p. 279-283 (Beihefte der Francia, 63).
FONTAINE, J., «La culture carolingienne dans les abbayes normandes: l'exemple de Saint-Wandrille», dans L. MUSSET, dir., *Aspects du monachisme en Normandie (IVe-XVIIIe siècles), Actes du colloque scientifique de l'«année des abbayes normandes»*, Caen, 18-20 octobre 1979, Paris, 1982, p. 31-54.
GAUTHIER, N., «Quelques hypothèses sur la rédaction des vies de saints évêques de Normandie», in *Memoriam sanctorum venerantes. Mélanges Victor Saxer*, Rome, 1992, p. 449-468 (Studi di antichità cristiana, 48).

GAZEAU, V., *Normannia monastica*, II: *Prosopographie des abbés bénédictins (X^e-XIIe siècle)*, Caen, 2007.
HELVÉTIUS, A.-M., «Les modèles de sainteté dans les monastères de l'espace belge du VIIIe au Xe siècle», *Revue bénédictine*, 103 (1993), p. 51-67.
—, «Hagiographie et formation politique des aristocrates dans le monde franc (VIIe-VIIIe siècles), in E. BOZÒKY, dir., *Hagiographie, idéologie et pouvoir au Moyen Âge. L'écriture de la sainteté, instrument politique*, Actes du colloque international du CESCM de Poitiers (11-14 septembre), Turnhout, 2012, p. 59-79 (Hagiologia, 8).
HOWE, J., «The Hagiography of Jumièges (Province of Haute Normandie)», «The Hagiography of Saint-Wandrille (Fontenelle) (Province of Haute Normandie)», in M. HEINZELMANN, dir., *L'hagiographie du haut Moyen Âge en Gaule du Nord. Manuscrits, textes et centres de production*, Stuttgart, 2001, resp. p. 92-125 et 127-192 (Beihefte der Francia, 52).
HUYGHEBAERT, N., «L'énigme des reliques de saint Vulfran, archevêque de Sens», *Revue bénédictine*, 87 (1977), p. 180-194.
—, éd., *Une translation de reliques à Gand en 944. Le Sermo de Adventu Sanctorum Wandregesili, Ansberti et Vulframni in Blandinium*, Bruxelles, 1978 (Recueil de textes pour servir à l'étude de l'histoire de la Belgique).
LAPORTE, J., «Les recensions de Fontenelle du martyrologe hiéronymien et l'histoire du monastère de Fontenelle», *Revue Mabillon*, 29 (1939), p. 1-16.
LEBECQ, S., «Vulfran, Willibrord et la mission de Frise: pour une relecture de la Vita Vulframni», in M. POLFER, dir., *L'évangélisation des régions entre Meuse et Moselle et la fondation de l'abbaye d'Echternach (V^e-IXe siècle). Actes du colloque de Luxembourg, Centre luxembourgeois d'études médiévales*, 2000, p. 429-452.
—, «Mission de Frise et tradition orale: retour à la Vie de Vulfran», in M. GOULLET – L. MORELLE et al., éd., *Retour aux sources: textes, études et documents d'histoire médiévale offerts à Michel Parisse*, Paris, 2004, p. 669-676.
—, «Vulfran, Willibrord et la mission de Frise: pour une relecture de la *Vita Vulframni*» et «Traduction du prologue et des chapitres 6 à 10 de la Vie de Vulfran du pseudo-Jonas, moine de Fontenelle», in: ID., *Hommes, mers et terres du Nord au début du Moyen Âge*, 1, Vielleneuve d'Ascq, 2011, p. 75-104.
—, «Vulfran, clerc palatin, moine de Fontenelle, évêque métropolitain de Sens», in J.-M. DUVOSQUEL – J.-M SANSTERRE – N. SCHROEDER – M. DE WAHA – A. WILKIN, éd., *Religion, animaux et quotidien au Moyen Âge. Études offertes à Alain Dierkens* (*Revue belge de philologie et d'histoire*, 95 (2018)), p. 555-568.

LE MAHO, J., «Autour de la Renaissance monastique du Xe siècle en Normandie: les Vies des saints Aycadre et Hugues de Jumièges», in M. HEINZELMANN, dir., *Livrets, collections et textes. Études sur la tradition hagiographique latine*, Ostfildern, 2006, p. 314-319 (Beihefte der Francia, 63).

LIFSHITZ, F., *The Norman Conquest of Pious Neustria. Historiographic Discourse and Saintly Relics, 684-1090*, Toronto, 1995.

LOT F., *Études critiques sur l'abbaye de Saint-Wandrille*, Paris, 1913.

MCKITTERICK, R., «Postérité et transmission des œuvres historiographiques carolingiennes dans les manuscrits des mondes normands», in P. BAUDUIN – M.-A. LUCAS-AVENEL, dir., *L'historiographie médiévale normande et ses sources antiques (X[e]-XIIe siècle)*, Caen, 2014, p. 25-39.

MÉRIAUX, C., *Gallia Irradiata. Saints et sanctuaires dans le nord de la Gaule au haut Moyen Âge*, Stuttgart, 2006 (Beiträge zur Hagiographie, 4).

PONCELET, Y., «Les possessions anglaises de l'abbaye de Saint-Wandrille. Contributions à la connaissance de l'implantation monastique normande outre-Manche», *Annales de Normandie*, 37 (1987), p. 149-171.

VAN HOUTS, E., «Historiography and Hagiography at Saint-Wandrille: the *Inventio et Miracula sancti Vulfranni*», *Anglo-Norman Studies*, 12 (1989), p. 233-250.

VAN DER STRAETEN, J., «L'auteur des vies de s. Hugues et de s. Aycadre», *AB*, 88 (1970), p. 63-73.

VAN UYTFANGHE, M., «Le culte des saints et la prétendue *Aufklärung* carolingienne», in R. FAVREAU, dir., *Le culte des saints au IXe-XIIIe siècles*, Poitiers, 1995, p. 151-166 (Civilisation médiévale, 1).

VIOLETTE, L., «Une entreprise historiographique au temps de la réforme grégorienne: les *Actes des archevêques de Rouen*», *Revue d'histoire de l'Église de France*, 83 (1997), p. 343-365.

WOOD, I., «Saint-Wandrille and its Hagiography», in I. WOOD – G. A. LOUD – J. TAYLOR, dir., *Church and Chronicle in the Middle Ages. Essays Presented to John Taylor*, Londres, 1991, p. 1-14.

L'hagiographie de Basse-Normandie
(env. 750-950)

par

Joseph-Claude POULIN

INTRODUCTION.
I. EBRULFUS D'OUCHE. – Bibliographie spéciale.
II. LEUTFREDUS D'ÉVREUX. – Bibliographie spéciale.
III. MARCULFUS DE NANTEUIL. – Bibliographie spéciale.
IV. *MICHAEL ARCHANGELUS* – Bibliographie spéciale.
V. OPPORTUNA DE SÉES – Bibliographie spéciale.
VI. TAURINUS D'ÉVREUX – Bibliographie spéciale.
CONCLUSION.
BIBLIOGRAPHIE GÉNÉRALE SUR L'HAGIOGRAPHIE DE BASSE-NORMANDIE – 1. Catalogues, répertoires, instruments de travail – 2. Études d'ensemble pour l'hagiographie bas-normande, 750-950.

INTRODUCTION

La région visée par le présent bilan inclut – par commodité – les diocèses d'Avranches, Coutances, Bayeux, Sées, Évreux et Lisieux. Il importe cependant de ne pas attacher une importance démesurée à ce découpage de la partie la plus occidentale de la province ecclésiastique de Rouen, car il fut souvent perturbé ou oblitéré pendant la période ici considérée: pression bretonne du VIe au Xe siècle[1], agressions vikings aux IXe-Xe siècles, prise en main progressive par les autorités (civiles et religieuses) de Rouen à partir du Xe siècle.

La faiblesse de la production hagiographique dans cette portion nord-ouest de la Neustrie, puis Basse-Normandie, est liée au fait que cette région fut remarquablement ouverte aux flux et

---

[1] Cartographie de l'expansion bretonne (867-933) dans ce qui allait devenir la Normandie par Pierre BOUET, *Guillaume le Conquérant et les Normands au XIe siècle*, Caen, 2003, p. 15, fig. 4.

influences insulaires et continentales[2]. En effet, beaucoup de saints liés à la région par leur origine ou au moins par une étape significative de leur parcours terrestre l'ont quittée de leur vivant ou après leur mort; à telle enseigne que leur célébration hagiographique, quand elle existe, fut généralement mise par écrit après 950 et/ou hors de Basse-Normandie. Dans son panorama de la production hagiographique du nord-ouest de la Gaule, pour la période de 850 à 1150, van 't Spijker a expressément renoncé à en dresser un inventaire exhaustif[3].

Plusieurs traits bien connus de l'hagiographie générale à l'époque carolingienne sont remarquablement absents de la production locale bas-normande. Le nombre important de saints de la région morts martyrs est de peu d'utilité pour éclairer les origines chrétiennes de la région, car la mise par écrit de leur mort héroïque fut exécutée trop tardivement ou dans d'autres provinces d'écriture[4]. Le recours prétendu à des origines apostoliques fut bien entendu appliqué à quelques saints basnormands; que l'on entende l'apostolicité au sens strict (des saints disciples des apôtres) ou au sens atténué (mandat octroyé à la fin du Ier siècle par le pape Clément). Mais les hagiographes ne s'en sont occupés qu'après le Xe siècle, sauf pour saint Taurin[5]. Enfin, les translations de reliques n'ont pas manqué en Basse-Normandie – encore que ces remuements de reliques ne soient pas tous causés par les attaques vikings, comme l'a montré F. Lifshitz[6]. Mais la mise en écriture de ces transferts est trop tardive ou exécutée par des bénéficiaires extérieurs à la Basse-Normandie désireux d'authentifier leur possession de reliques.

L'expansion vers l'est de la zone d'influence des Bretons au IXe siècle a laissé de nombreuses traces dans l'hagiotoponymie régionale, comme l'a montré en détail la thèse de Van Torhoudt[7]; mais elle n'a pas produit de documentation hagiographique liée à la région, ni pour des saints bretons ou irlandais, ni pour des saints bas-normands. Les attaques des Vikings,

---

[2] FONTAINE (1982), p. 28.

[3] VAN 'T SPIJKER (1996), p. 247. Elle ne mentionne que les saints Ceronna (Sées), Marculfus (Coutances) et Vigor (Bayeux).

[4] Voir par exemple la liste dressée par MUSSET 1976, p. 142 sq.

[5] Cf. *infra*, p. 303-305.

[6] LIFSHITZ (1995), «Migration...», p. 177.

[7] VAN TORHOUDT (2008). Ce point avait déjà été signalé par JARRY (1999), p. 17.

quant à elles, ont provoqué des perturbations prolongées dans les diocèses de Basse-Normandie; l'interruption des listes épiscopales témoigne d'un contexte peu favorable au développement d'une hagiographie indigène.

D'un point de vue historiographique, l'étude méthodique de l'hagiographie régionale de Basse-Normandie à l'époque carolingienne accuse un retard certain par rapport à d'autres régions de la Gaule; peut-être à cause de sa modestie quantitative et qualitative, en l'absence de tout monument spécialement remarquable ou influent. La compilation de GAUTHIER (1992) ne concerne que l'hagiographie épiscopale; l'auteure se rallie à une opinion moyenne, sans fonder les propositions de datation des textes sur une recherche personnelle à nouveaux frais. Le répertoire préparé par VANGONE (2018) concerne en priorité la période 911-1204. Mis à part le cas d'Avranches (Mont-Saint-Michel), l'absence d'éditions critiques et d'études spéciales récentes handicape toute approche globale. Tout compte fait, il ne reste pour l'instant que six dossiers – dont un seul évêque – à traiter dans le cadre de ce chapitre; un démarrage bien timide après le silence quasi complet (hagiographiquement parlant) des siècles précédents[8].

I. EBRULFUS D'OUCHE

Le saint est né à Bayeux, mais sa fondation du monastère d'Ouche (*Uticensis*) fut rattachée au diocèse de Sées après la Révolution; elle fait présentement partie du diocèse de Bayeux. Évroult a vécu au VIe siècle (sous Childebert II) ou au VIIe (sous Childebert III); mais il est douteux que sa première Vie remonte au VIIIe siècle, malgré HOMMEY (1887), p. 263 sq. ou LIFSHITZ (1995), «Migrations», p. 191.

CHIBNALL (1980) a publié la version la plus ancienne et la plus brève de la *Vita s. Ebrulfi* (*BHL* 2376b), d'après deux ma-

---

[8] La célèbre Vie de saint Pair d'Avranches (*BHL* 6477) fut bien rédigée peu avant 600, mais à Poitiers par Venance Fortunat; il est possible qu'il ait disposé de traditions (orales?) locales, car sa composition fournit plus de précisions onomastiques qu'à l'accoutumée dans le reste de sa production hagiographique.

nuscrits anglais du XIIe siècle, ignorés des éditeurs précédents[9]: Oxford, Bodl. Lib., Fell 2, p. 432-439[10] et Hereford, Cathedral Library, P.VII.6, fol. 223-225v. Cette première recension n'est probablement pas antérieure au IXe siècle. C'est peut-être à elle qu'Adon fait allusion au 29 décembre dans la seconde famille de son Martyrologe (vers 900)[11]: *In pago Oximensi, s. Ebrulfi confessoris, cujus gesta habentur*; cette précision finale manque à la même date dans le Martyrologe d'Usuard.

Deux réécritures ont suivi, portées par des manuscrits de la fin du Moyen Âge: *BHL* 2374-75, puis son amplification[12] en style plus ampoulé (*BHL* 2377). L'appartenance du prologue *BHL* 2376 à l'un ou l'autre de ces remaniements est indécidable. L'absence de mention d'une translation au Xe siècle ne peut pas être invoquée pour vieillir ces recensions.

Bibliographie spéciale

CHIBNALL, M., « The Merovingian Monastery of St. Evroul in the Light of Conflicting Traditions », in G. J. CUMING – G. BAKER, dir., *Popular Belief and Practice*, Cambridge, 1972 (Studies in Church History, 8), p. 31-40; réimpr. in EAD., *Piety, Power and History in Medieval England and Normandy*, Aldershot, 2000, n° II.

—, « The *Vitae* of St. Évroul », in EAD., éd., *The Ecclesiastical History of Orderic Vitalis*, III: *Books V and VI*, Oxford, 1972 (réimpr. 2003), Appendix I, p. 363-364.

—, éd., « The Earliest Vita sancti Ebrulfi », in EAD., éd., *The Ecclesiastical History of Orderic Vitalis*, I: *General Introduction. Books I and II (Summary and Extracts). Index verborum*, Oxford, 1980 (réimpr. 2003), Appendix II, p. 204-211.

DELISLE, L., « Notice sur Orderic Vital », in A. LE PRÉVOST, éd., *Orderici Vitalis Angligenae, coenobii Uticensis monachi, Historiae ecclesiasticae libri tredecim*, t. V, Paris, 1855, p. I-CVI.

FOURNÉE, J., « Deux Saxons de Bayeux: saint Évroul et saint Marcoul », *Cahiers Léopold Delisle*, 17 (1968), p. 37-54.

---

[9] CHIBNALL (1972), p. 363, n. 5 avait d'abord annoncé la publication de cette édition dans le *Bulletin de la Société des Antiquaires de Normandie*.

[10] Une version numérisée de la page 439 de Fell 2 est consultable à l'adresse <https://digital.bodleian.ox.ac.uk>, diapo n° 8 (consulté le 27 avril 2020).

[11] DUBOIS – RENAUD éd. (1984), p. 37. Cette forme de référencement est usuelle dans la première famille du Martyrologe d'Adon, et plus encore dans la deuxième famille.

[12] Comme l'avait déjà constaté DELISLE (1855), p. LXXXII sq.

Hommey, L.-P., éd. et trad., «Une Vie de s. Évroult, écrite par un témoin oculaire de ses dernières années et de sa mort», *Bulletin de la Société historique et archéologique de l'Orne*, 6 (1887), p. 261-297. Édition d'après le ms. d'Alençon, BM 11, fol. 143-146 (XIIIᵉ s.).

Musset, L., «Evroul (saint)», in *DHGE*, t. 16, Paris, 1967, col. 219 sq.

II. Leutfredus d'Évreux

Ce saint du diocèse d'Évreux est réputé être mort vers 738, après 48 ans d'abbatiat. Il a en effet fondé un monastère sur le site d'une croix plantée par saint Ouen de Rouen, d'où le nom initial de la Croix-Saint-Ouen, plus tard nommé la Croix-Saint-Leufroy. Une Vie (*BHL* 4899) complétée de Miracles (*BHL* 4901) a été composée sur place vers le deuxième quart du IXᵉ siècle, par un auteur qui se présente comme contemporain de certains miracles. La Vie entretient des relations de dépendance formelle avec le dossier hagiographique de saint Ouen, et aussi avec les *Dialogues* de Grégoire le Grand; l'hypothèse d'un remploi (au chap. 18) tiré des Actes de Jean a également été soulevée[13]. Usuard a connu la Vie, car il démarque le titre de son chapitre 16 (dans l'édition des *MGH*) et le texte du chapitre 19 (dans l'édition des *AASS*) en date du 21 juin, dans une partie originale de son martyrologe.

Une brève notice résume en outre une élévation de reliques de Leufroy et de son frère Agofroy en 851 par l'évêque Gumbert d'Évreux (*BHL* 4900); il n'y est pas question d'une translation hors de Normandie. Cette cérémonie est distincte de celle (non datée, mais apparemment contemporaine de l'auteur) que relate le dernier chapitre de la Vie, placée sous le patronage de l'abbé-évêque Jean de Dol. Cette courte notice apparaît dans un manuscrit du XIᵉ siècle provenant de Saint-Germain-des-Prés; elle est intercalée entre la Vie et les Miracles (Paris, BnF, lat. 11750, fol. 123v)[14]. Elle pourrait n'avoir été rédigée qu'à Paris au Xᵉ siècle; en 918 en effet, Charles le Simple transféra à Saint-

---

[13] E. W. Brooks dans sa recension de l'édition de Levison: *English Historical Review*, 35 (1920), p. 439.

[14] Il existe un second témoin de cette «translation»: Vatican, Reg. lat. 1864, fol. 38-38v (XIᵉ-XIIᵉ s., provenant de Soissons).

Germain-des-Prés le résidu du patrimoine de la Croix-Saint-Leufroy, avec la charge de perpétuer le culte de ses saints.

Bibliographie spéciale

Éditions de référence: W. LEVISON, *MGH*, *SRM*, VII, Hanovre – Leipzig, 1920, p. 7-18; l'éditeur omet une quinzaine de chapitres, dépourvus d'intérêt historique à ses yeux. Il faut les chercher dans l'édition de G. HENSCHEN, *AASS*, Iun. IV, 1707, p. 105-112 (où les chapitres portent une numérotation différente).

CHIRON, Y., «Leufroy», in *DHGE*, t. 22, Paris, 2018, col. 464-465.

LAUER, P., «Les translations des reliques de saint Ouen et de saint Leufroy du IXe au Xe siècle et les deux abbayes de La Croix-Saint-Ouen», in *Bulletin philologique et historique (jusqu'à 1715)*, (1921) [1923], p. 119-136; et à part, Paris, 1924.

MESNEL, J.-B., *Saint Leufroy, abbé de La Croix, première moitié du VIIIe siècle*, Évreux, 1918 (Les saints du diocèse d'Évreux, 6).

III. MARCULFUS DE NANTEUIL

Il existe deux recensions relativement anciennes de la Vie de saint Marculf, communément appelées «version A» (*BHL* 5266) et «version B» (*BHL* 5267). Leur déroulement narratif est globalement le même; mais si elles dépendent l'une de l'autre, dans quel sens fonctionne la relation? Une dépendance commune d'une *Vita antiquissima* perdue du VIIe siècle est très improbable, malgré GROSSET (1979), p. 51. Leur tradition manuscrite respective ne peut servir à les dater plus précisément ni à les hiérarchiser, car elle ne remonte pas plus haut que les environs de l'an mil: version A: Vatican, Reg. lat. 490, fol. 57-64v [15] et version B: Cambrai, BM 865 (768), fol. 96v-102.

La référence au roi Childebert est habituelle dans l'hagiographie régionale[16], et aisément explicable par l'influence de la *Vita s. Paterni* de Fortunat (*BHL* 6477). La version A se distingue notamment par son style plus relevé et par un remploi littéral de Virgile[17]. LAPORTE (1951) p. 9, n. 1, croyait voir au chapitre 16 (*leguntur*) le signe de la présence d'une Vie ancienne

---

[15] PIGEON (1894), p. 11 renvoie par erreur au ms. Vatican, Reg. lat. 141.

[16] C'est par erreur que FONTAINE (1982), p. 27 renvoie ici à Childéric.

[17] Chap. 11 = *Énéide*, I, 87-89 + 86; et encore un écho au chap. 19 = *Énéide*, VI, 295.

comme racine de la version A; l'idée de BAEDORF (1913), p. 29 nous paraît plus satisfaisante, qui y reconnaît un écho de la *Vita s. Paterni* de Fortunat. Ici encore, l'auteur de la version A est porté par son élan emphatique coutumier[18].

La version B possède en propre (dans l'édition des *Acta Sanctorum*) un alinéa final (chap. 21) qui rapporte une tentative de translation de reliques de saint Marculf par saint Ouen de Rouen. Cette anecdote est manifestement inspirée de la *Vita III^a s. Audoeni*, chap. 47 (*BHL* 753); elle correspond à une volonté du siège métropolitain de reprendre le contrôle des diocèses de Basse-Normandie. Une telle initiative n'est guère pensable avant la fin du Xe siècle au plus tôt. Cet alinéa 21 semble donc une addition tardive, greffée sur une *vita* qui peut dater du IXe siècle, si tant est que le motif de la rencontre d'un saint avec une tentatrice (chap. 11-12) ne devienne fréquent dans l'hagiographie qu'à partir de ce siècle[19]. Par sa formulation recherchée, la version A pourrait correspondre à une réécriture plus ambitieuse.

Ces compositions ont pu être effectuées à l'abbaye de Nanteuil (lat. *Nantus*), la première fondation du saint et son lieu de sépulture, sur la côte orientale du Cotentin (dioc. de Coutances), bien que le saint soit né à Bayeux.

Bibliographie spéciale

FLOBERT, P., «Saint Marcouf, de Childebert Ier à Charles X», in L. LEMOINE – B. MERDRIGNAC, dir., *Corona monastica. Mélanges offerts au père Marc Simon*, Rennes, 2004, p. 41-46 (Britannia monastica, 8). Réimpr. in ID., *Grammaire comparée et variétés du latin. Articles revus et mis à jour (1964-2012)*, Genève, 2014, p. 680-687 (n° 84) (EPHE, Hautes études médiévales et modernes, 105).

FOURNÉE, J., «Deux Saxons de Bayeux: saint Evroul et saint Marcoul», *Cahiers Léopold Delisle*, 17 (1968), p. 37-54.

GROSSET, C., «Hypothèses sur l'évangélisation du Cotentin, IV: Saint Marcouf», *Revue du département de la Manche*, 21 (1979), p. 39-68; trad. en anglais sous le titre «A Theory on the Evangelisation of the Cotentin (Normandy Peninsula)»: <https://mem-

---

[18] *Vita B s. Marculfi*, 16: *Construxit etiam beatissimus sacerdos ibi monasterium* = *Vita A s. Marculfi*, 16: *multa monasteria in honorem DNJC ab ipso leguntur fundata* = *Vita s. Paterni*, 33: *multa monasteria per eum Domino sunt fundata*.

[19] C'est l'avis d'HELVÉTIUS (2001), §33 de la version numérique.

bers.societe-jersiaise.org/whitsco/gross0.htm> (consulté le 27 avril 2020).

Helvétius, A.-M., «Le saint et la sacralisation de l'espace en Gaule du Nord d'après les sources hagiographiques (VIIe-XIe siècle)», in M. Kaplan, dir., *Le sacré et son inscription dans l'espace à Byzance et en Occident. Études comparées*, Paris, 2001, p. 137-161.

Pietri, L. – Heijmans, M., «Marculfus 1», in *Prosopographie de la Gaule chrétienne (314-614)*, t. II, Paris, 2013, p. 1249 (Prosopographie chrétienne du Bas-Empire, 4).

Pigeon, É.-A., «Saint Marcouf. Notions préliminaires et critiques», *Mémoires de la Société académique du Cotentin (Archéologie, belles-lettres, sciences et beaux-arts)*, 10 (1894), p. 11-46. Réimpr. in Id., *Texte français et latin des Vies des saints du diocèse de Coutances et Avranches, avec des notions préliminaires et l'histoire des reliques de chaque saint*, t. 2, Avranches, 1898, p. 79-114.

Roche, P., «Saint Marcoul: légende et histoire», *Le Mantois. Bulletin de la Société «Les amis du Mantois»*, 27 (1976), p. 2-6.

IV. Michael Archangelus

Le plus ancien document hagiographique composé en Basse-Normandie à l'époque carolingienne raconte les circonstances de création, sur le Mont Tombe, d'un sanctuaire dédié à l'archange Michel par un évêque Aubert d'Avranches, à la suite d'une triple injonction angélique. La datation et la localisation de cet événement historique et de son récit (*Revelatio ecclesiae Sancti Michaelis archangeli in Monte qui dicitur Tumba*; *BHL* 5951) font encore débat.

La date de 708 habituellement attribuée à l'initiative de l'évêque Aubert (inconnu par ailleurs), est liée à la mention d'un roi Childebert, régnant alors sur l'ensemble de l'espace politique contrôlé par les Francs. L'évocation d'un Childebert pourrait n'être qu'un écho de sa présence (crédible) dans les œuvres de Venance Fortunat, et plus particulièrement dans sa Vie de saint Pair d'Avranches; un tel transfert s'est déjà produit au profit de la Vie ancienne de saint Samson de Dol (*BHL* 7478). Mais il ne saurait s'agir du même Childebert dans tous ces cas: au Childebert Ier (511-558) des saints Pair et Samson, l'hagiographe de saint Michel a substitué (sans le dire) un Childebert III (694-711), d'où la date de 708. Renvoyer la création d'un sanctuaire michaélien à l'époque d'un roi Childebert (sans précision de rang) permettait de rétro-projeter le lien entre Avranches et le Mont à une époque antérieure à la prise de contrôle de la région par les Bretons, telle qu'on la connaissait au milieu du IXe siècle. J.-M. Martin, puis J. C. Arnold, ont cru pouvoir inscrire cette date de 708 dans le contexte d'une rivalité avec le sanctuaire de Saint-Mihiel au diocèse de Verdun[20]. Mais dans la tradition montoise, la date de 708 n'apparaît explicitement qu'au milieu du XIIe siècle[21].

La rédaction de la *Revelatio* est communément fixée au début de la seconde moitié du IXe siècle; M. Simonnet, suivi par G. Gandy, croit pouvoir préciser «entre 851 et 867»[22], c'est-à-dire à un moment où la Sélune (et non le Couesnon) constituait une limite entre les domaines franc et breton. On pourrait allonger quelque peu cet intervalle, pour tenir compte du fait que l'auteur de la *Revelatio* a adopté comme modèle une légende de fondation du sanctuaire dédié à saint Michel sur le Mont Gargan dans les Pouilles (*Apparitio in Monte Gargano*; *BHL* 5948) – une rédaction de la seconde moitié du VIIIe siècle ou du début du IXe siècle[23].

D'après la *Revelatio* (leçons 5 et 6), l'évêque Aubert aurait envoyé au Mont Gargan une délégation chargée d'en rapporter des reliques de l'Archange. L'hypothèse d'un voyage d'Aubert lui-même au Mont Gargan est assez improbable, malgré BETTOCCHI (1994), p. 354. Mais l'*Itinerarium* du moine Bernard[24] raconte que ce pèlerin en Terre Sainte (vers la fin des années 860) est passé par le Mont Gargan, d'où il aurait pu ramener en Basse-Normandie une connaissance des lieux, sinon un exemplaire de *l'Apparitio*; car l'auteur de la *Revelatio* semble bien avoir eu accès à une version écrite (leçon 1: *sicut in scriptis habetur*)[25].

Une proposition récente de remonter la composition de la *Revelatio* jusqu'aux années 816-817, pour des motifs de qualité de

---

[20] MARTIN (2009), p. 407 sq. et 418; ARNOLD (2013), p. 112 sq.

[21] Dans les «Annales du Mont-Saint-Michel», in L. DELISLE, éd., *Chronique de Robert de Torigni*, Rouen, 1973, t. II, p. 215 et 280; BETTOCCHI (1994), p. 339.

[22] SIMONNET (1999), p. 19; GANDY (2016), p. 10.

[23] Ainsi chez OTRANTO (1988), p. 383, suivi par SIVO (1994), p. 105.

[24] *PL* 121, col. 569-574.

[25] GANDY (2020), p. 137, n. 24 est plus sceptique sur la disponibilité d'un exemplaire écrit en Normandie.

la langue et de contexte de réforme de l'institution canoniale[26], ne paraît pas susceptible de s'imposer. L'absence de mention d'attaques vikings n'est pas suffisante pour écarter la date traditionnelle[27]. Une suggestion de report de la rédaction de la *Revelatio* jusqu'au XIe siècle n'a pas trouvé d'écho[28]; le plus ancien témoin manuscrit est maintenant daté du XIe siècle, et non plus du Xe siècle[29]. Mais il faut prendre garde au fait que tous les manuscrits de la *Revelatio* n'ont pas la même valeur comme témoins de l'état le plus ancien du texte. C'est ainsi que l'exemplaire joint au Cartulaire du Mont a été interpolé: la leçon IV, 2 y est enrichie d'un renvoi à un crâne perforé réputé être celui de l'évêque Aubert[30].

Il est possible que la *Revelatio* ait été composée au Mont comme affirmation d'indépendance à l'égard du siège d'Avranches[31]. Le don de deux domaines offerts par Aubert (leçon VII, 2) témoignerait alors du désir des Montois de s'émanciper de l'autorité de l'évêque d'Avranches[32]. L'évêque Aubert y apparaît en effet comme simple exécutant de la volonté angélique, tout en faisant acte de générosité envers sa fondation. Qui plus est, ses successeurs sont présentés dans une lumière négative[33]. Mais A. Lunven inverse la proposition, à juste titre nous semble-t-il: la *Revelatio* constituerait une initiative de l'évêque d'Avranches pour asseoir son autorité sur le Mont, afin de contrer l'influence bretonne[34]. L'essai de localisation de la rédaction de la *Revelatio* à Saint-Denis de Paris, tenté par

---

[26] BOUET (2003), p. 71 sq.; BOUET (2004), p. 117-119.

[27] BOUET (2019), «Origines», p. 37.

[28] Une position adoptée séparément par AULISA (1994), p. 329 et 331, et POULLE (1999), p. 173 sq. LE MAHO (2015), p. 97 sq., propose d'en reporter la rédaction dans la seconde moitié du Xe siècle; et encore LE MAHO (2018), p. 409 sq.

[29] Paris, BnF, lat. 2873A, fol. 110v-114 (contient les cinq premières leçons seulement); MARTIN (2009), p. 405.

[30] Avranches, BM 210, fol. 7v (milieu XIIe siècle). BOUET (2019), p. 202.

[31] GANDY (2020), p. 145, n. 56.

[32] Ainsi chez LE MAHO (2015), p. 98. Pour la localisation des toponymes de la *Revelatio*, voir LEVALET (2010), p. 185 sq.

[33] GANDY (2015), p. 221; GANDY (2020), p. 145.

[34] LUNVEN (2014), *Du diocèse*, p. 52, n. 101; EAD. (2014), «Pouvoir épiscopal», p. 125 et carte p. 127. Dans le même sens, MAZEL (2015), p. 449, n. 17.

F. Lifshitz, a été réfuté efficacement par P. Bouet[35]; par conséquent, il devient moins probable que l'hagiographe se soit inspiré de la *Hiérarchie céleste* du Pseudo-Denis[36]. Il n'y a pas lieu, à notre avis, de voir dans la *Revelatio* un condensé de traditions mythologiques celtiques[37], ni la christianisation d'un lieu sacré antérieur[38].

La *Revelatio* est-elle une œuvre homogène? Selon P. Bouet, elle pourrait en effet avoir été mise au point en deux étapes: d'un côté un noyau primitif, narratif, reprenant une source perdue (leçons IV à VII), de l'autre un complément plus théorique (leçons I à III et VIII)[39]. À la jointure des leçons III et IV, se trouvent en effet des énoncés de raccordement. Il faudrait alors considérer la possibilité de distinguer deux auteurs et deux dates de rédaction. BOUET (2004) estime que la partie théorique constitue la phase initiale de création de l'œuvre; les deux strates textuelles sont en effet formulées sur un ton différent. Mais peut-on croire que la première partie a d'abord existé seule? Le tableau comparatif de la langue de la *Revelatio* avec celle de son modèle de l'*Apparitio* montre que les deux strates partagent bien des points de contact formel[40].

Divers chercheurs ont proposé de reconnaître dans la *Revelatio* une grande variété de sources. Outre les contacts prévisibles avec la Bible[41], le seul document écrit qui a inspiré à coup sûr l'auteur de la *Revelatio* est l'*Apparitio* italienne[42]; le Mont Gargan est d'ailleurs nommé à cinq reprises dans la *Revelatio*. Cependant, plusieurs des rapprochements suggérés ici ou là ne correspondent certainement pas tous à des remplois ou contacts assurés avec d'autres sources:

---

[35] LIFSHITZ (1995), p. 104-108; BOUET (2003), p. 77 sq.
[36] Comme l'a encore pensé ARNOLD (2007), §25-26.
[37] Ainsi chez DÉCENEUX (2002), «Mont», p. 62, et ID. (2002), *Bretagne*, p. 55-57.
[38] Comme le suggère FAURE (1988), p. 41 sq.; contra, BOUET (1998), p. 22 et 232, n. 5.
[39] BOUET (2004), p. 106-108.
[40] BOUET (2003), p. 73; BOUET (2004), p. 116. Et aussi OTRANTO (1994), p. 111-116.
[41] Voir le tableau récapitulatif de BOUET (2003), p. 75; ou BOUET (2004), p. 113.
[42] BETTOCCHI (1994), p. 344 et 354.

– L'auteur prétend avoir appris *a veracibus... narratoribus* (leçon III 2) l'existence d'un petit établissement monastique sur l'île avant même l'implantation d'un sanctuaire dédié à l'Archange.
– F. Duine a cru repérer dans la leçon III deux rapprochements avec le livre VI de l'*Énéide*[43].
– Bouet (2019), «Reliques», p. 195 estime que la *Revelatio* est déjà une réécriture, dans la mesure où l'hagiographe aurait intégré une source antérieure, écrite ou orale.
– Il est douteux que l'auteur de la *Revelatio* se soit inspiré de la Vie anonyme de saint Cuthbert (*BHL* 2019; vers 700) pour la description géographique du Mont[44]. Il serait plus vraisemblable d'y voir un écho de la Vie de saint Wandrille[45].
– Arnold (2007), §17-18 a repris les hypothèses trop hasardeuses de Hourlier (1967), p. 127 relatives à des liens de dépendance envers Flavius Josèphe (médiatisé par Eugippe) et les *Dialogues* de Grégoire le Grand.
– Les rapprochements avec la *Consolation* de Boèce, tels qu'entrevus par Arnold (2007), §21-24 sont beaucoup trop ténus pour être convaincants.
– Les ressemblances formelles de la *Revelatio* avec la Vie ancienne de saint Samson de Dol sont beaucoup trop topiques pour représenter des emprunts[46]. On peut en dire autant des liens supposés avec des écrits lériniens, malgré Gandy (2020), p. 144. C'est à juste titre que ce dernier chercheur a renoncé à voir des emprunts au *De laude eremi* d'Eucher de Lyon (*ibid.*).

Il est indémontrable que la leçon VIII provienne d'un recueil perdu de miracles, comme l'évoque Bouet (2003), p. 73 sq.; pourtant, il n'est pas impossible qu'elle constitue une addition postérieure, comme J. Hourlier en a fait l'hypothèse[47].

Bien que l'*Introductio monachorum* (*BHL* 5952) situe vers 965-966 la réforme de la communauté cléricale au Mont-Saint-Michel, sa mise en écriture au Mont ne date que du XIe siècle; c'est pourquoi elle n'est pas traitée ici.

---

[43] Duine (1921), p. 464, n° 94.
[44] À la leçon III, d'après Arnold 2007, §18.
[45] Simonnet (1999), p. 13.
[46] Malgré Bouet (2003), p. 79.
[47] Hourlier (1967), p. 126-128.

Bibliographie spéciale

Édition de référence: BOUET – [DESBORDES] (2003), p. 10-15; ou EID. (2009), p. 91-103 (pages impaires).

ARNOLD, J. C., trad., «The *Revelatio Ecclesiae de Sancti Michaelis* and the Mediterranean Origins of Mont St.-Michel», *The Heroic Age*, 10 (2007): <http://www.heroicage.org> (consulté le 27 avril 2020).

—, *The Footprints of Michael the Archangel. The Formation and Diffusion of a Saintly Cult, c. 300 – c. 800*, New York, 2013 (The New Middle Ages).

AULISA, I., «Le fonti e la datazione della *Revelatio seu Apparitio s. Michaelis Archangeli in Monte Tancia*», *Vetera christianorum*, 31 (1994), p. 315-331.

BETTOCCHI, S., «Note su due tradizioni micaeliche altomedievali: il Gargano e Mont Saint-Michel», *Vetera christianorum*, 31 (1994), p. 333-355.

BOUET, P., «Le premier millénaire», in *Le Mont-Saint-Michel. Histoire et imaginaire*, Paris, 1998, p. 21-29.

—, «La *Revelatio* et les origines du culte de saint Michel sur le Mont Tombe», in P. BOUET et al., dir., *Culte et pèlerinages à saint Michel en Occident. Les trois monts dédiés à l'archange*, Paris, 2003, p. 65-90.

—, «La *Revelatio ecclesiae sancti Michaelis* et son auteur», *Tabularia. Sources écrites de la Normandie médiévale. Études*, 4 (2004), p. 105-119: <http://www.unicaen.fr/mrsh/crahm/revue/tabularia/freculf.html> (consulté le 15 avril 2020).

—, «Les textes littéraires du Cartulaire du Mont Saint-Michel (manuscrit d'Avranches 210)», *Amis du Mont-Saint-Michel. Bulletin*, 111 (2006) p. 33-38 (dont la *Revelatio ecclesiae Sancti Michaelis*).

—, «Histoire des reliques de saint Aubert», *Revue des amis du Mont-Saint-Michel*, 124/4 (2019), p. 194-209.

—, «Des origines à l'arrivée des Bénédictins», in H. DECAËNS, dir., *Le Mont-Saint-Michel*, Paris, 2019, p. 36-47.

— et DESBORDES, O., éd., *Chroniques latines du Mont-Saint-Michel (IXe-XIIIe siècle). Les manuscrits du Mont-Saint-Michel: textes fondateurs*. Caen – Avranches, 2009 (Fontes et paginae): <http://www.unicaen.fr/services/puc/sources/chroniqueslatines/index.php>. (consulté le 15 avril 2020).

DÉCENEUX, M., «Le Mont-Saint-Michel», *Bulletin de la Société de mythologie française*, 208 (2002), p. 60-62.

—, *Bretagne celtique. Mythes et croyances*, Brest, 2002.

GANDY, G. N., «Dans quel but le Mont-Saint-Michel a-t-il été fondé?», *Revue de l'Avranchin*, 92 (2015), p. 219-234.

—, «Retour sur la fondation de l'abbaye du Mont-Saint-Michel et le rôle du duc Richard Ier de Normandie», *Annales de Bretagne*, 123/1 (2016), p. 7-33.

—, «*Revelatio* of the Origins of Mont Saint-Michel (Fifth-Ninth Century)», *Speculum*, 95 (2020), p. 132-166.

HOURLIER, J., «Les sources écrites de l'histoire montoise antérieure à 966», in R. FOREVILLE, dir., *Millénaire monastique du Mont-Saint-Michel*, II: *Vie monastique et rayonnement intellectuel*, Paris, 1967, p. 121-132.

LE MAHO, J., «Groupes ecclésiaux de Normandie, IVe-XIe siècle», in M.-L. PAIN, dir., *Groupes cathédraux et complexes monastiques: le phénomène de la pluralité des sanctuaires à l'époque carolingienne*, Rennes, 2015, p. 87-100 (Archéologie et culture).

—, «Sur les routes des pèlerins des Îles britanniques. Monastères des zones côtières de la Province de Rouen (VIe-VIIe siècles)», in S. BULLY et al. dir., *Colomban et son influence. Moines et monastères du haut Moyen Âge en Europe*, Rennes, 2018, p. 399-414.

LEVALET, D., *Avranches et la cité des Abrincates: Ier siècle avant J.-C. – VIIe siècle après J.-C. Recherches historiques et archéologiques*, Caen, 2010 (Mémoires de la Société des Antiquaires de Normandie, 45).

LUNVEN, A., *Du diocèse à la paroisse: évêchés de Rennes, Dol et Alet/Saint-Malo, Ve-XIIIe siècle*, Rennes, 2014.

—, «Le pouvoir épiscopal en Haute Bretagne avant le XIIe siècle et ses variations: évêchés de Vannes, Alet/Saint-Malo, Dol, Rennes et Nantes», *Bulletin et mémoires de la Société archéologique et historique d'Ille-et-Vilaine*, 118 (2014), p. 113-138.

MARTIN, J.-M., «L'axe Mont-Saint-Michel/Mont Gargan a-t-il existé au Moyen Âge?», in G. CASIRAGHI – G. SERGI, dir., *Pellegrinaggi e santuari di San Michele nell'Occidente medievale*, Bari, 2009, p. 402-420 (Bibliotheca Michaelica, 5); réimpr. in ID., *Byzance et l'Italie méridionale*, Paris, 2014, p. 547-562 (Bilan de recherche, 9).

MAZEL, F., «De Montfaucon-en-Argonne au Mont-Saint-Michel: fondations épiscopales, marquage des confins et appropriation de l'espace diocésain aux IXe-Xe siècles», in L. JÉGOU et al. dir., *Faire lien. Aristocratie, réseaux et échanges compétitifs. Mélanges en l'honneur de Régine Le Jan*, Paris, 2015, p. 443-452.

OTRANTO, G., «La montagna garganica e il culto micaelico: un modello esportato nell'Europa altomedievale», in *Monteluco e i monti sacri*, Spolète, 1994, p. 85-124.

POULLE, E., «Le crâne de saint Aubert entre mythe et légende», *Revue de l'Avranchin et du Pays de Granville*, 76 (1999), p. 167-188.

SIMONNET, N., «La fondation du Mont-St-Michel d'après la *Revelatio ecclesiae s. Michaelis*», *Annales de Bretagne*, 106/4 (1999), p. 7-23.

SIVO, V., «Ricerche sulla tradizione manoscritta e sul testo dell'*Apparitio* latina», in C. CARLETTI – G. OTRANTO, dir., *Culto e insediamenti micaelici nell'Italia meridionale fra Tarda Antichità e Medioevo*, Bari, 1994, p. 95-106 (Scavi e ricerche, 7).

—, «Un nuovo testo sul culto di san Michele (cod. Parisinus B. N. lat. 2873A)», *Vetera christianorum*, 32 (1995), p. 395-400.

V. Opportuna de Sées

Née en Hiémois dans la famille des Robertides, la sainte entre tôt au monastère de femmes appelé *Monasteriolum*; elle en devient bientôt abbesse et y meurt vers 770. Cet établissement a été couramment localisé à Almenèches, près d'Argentan (dép. Orne); mais si l'on en croit le chap. 11 de la Vie, *Monasteriolum* est distinct du monastère féminin d'Almenèches[48], où se trouvait Lanthilde, une parente d'Opportune.

Le dossier hagiographique carolingien d'Opportune a été achevé vers 886 par l'évêque Adelelme (Adelin) de Sées, un parent de la sainte; il écrivait, à la suite d'un vœu, à un moment où il se trouvait réfugié en région parisienne, pour cause d'agressions vikings. Il s'identifie nommément au début et à la fin de la Vie, et au début du recueil de miracles. Sa rédaction de la Vie (*BHL* 6339) à la première personne donne l'impression d'un sermon pour la fête anniversaire de la sainte; un découpage en leçons pour l'office n'apparaît que dans des manuscrits plus tardifs.

À défaut d'être bien informé sur la sainte, Adelelme lui prête force discours édifiants et surtout consacre beaucoup d'espace (chap. 8-15) à raconter le martyre de son frère, l'évêque Chrodegang (Godegrand) de Sées – un meurtre politique, en fait – au moyen d'une amplification de la narration établie quelques années plus tôt par l'archevêque Hérard de Tours (*BHL* 1782b). La présence de cette pièce rapportée est soulignée par une doxologie à la fin du chap. 15. La question a été posée de savoir à quel public s'adressait Adelelme[49]: des auditeurs lettrés (*dilectissimi filii*) ou l'assemblée chrétienne en général (*haec plebs*)? Ou les deux à la fois? La Vie pour les uns, les miracles pour les autres?

---

[48] Fleury (1974), p. 533 se rallie à cette correction, d'après une communication (inédite?) d'Henri Pellerin; *Monasteriolum* se trouverait plutôt à Moutiers-en-Auge (dép. Calvados).

[49] Heene (1991), p. 150 qs.; Van Uytfanghe (1991), p. 122.

Il est possible que les *Miracula* aient été composés avant la *Vita*, selon OURY (1970), p. 223. D'après l'analyse de FLEURY (1974), p. 582 et sq., ne sont sortis de la plume d'Adelelme que *BHL* 6340, chap. 1 à 11 + chap. 15 (*BHL* 6341); d'abord les miracles dont il a eu connaissance personnellement, ensuite les prodiges rapportés par des témoins fiables, à un moment où les reliques de la sainte reposaient à Moussy-le-Neuf (dép. Seine-et-Marne), apportées là par l'évêque Hildebrand de Sées, prédécesseur d'Adelelme (chap. 6). Seraient aussi tardifs que le XIIe siècle les chap. 12 à 14 de *BHL* 6340 + *BHL* 6343 (chap. 16) + *BHL* 6342 (chap. 17)[50].

Bibliographie spéciale

BLIN, J.-B.-N., «Sainte Opportune, vierge et abbesse d'Almenèches», in *Vies des saints du diocèse de Séez et histoire de leur culte*, t. II, Laigle, 1873, p. 120-133.

FLEURY, M., «Histoire de Paris, II: Les origines de l'ancienne église Sainte-Opportune», *Annuaire de l'École pratique des hautes études. 4e section: Sciences historiques et philologiques*, (1973-1974) [1974], p. 530-534.

GOLINELLI, M., «Sainte Opportune, une sainte normande en Goële», *Société d'histoire et d'archéologie de la Goële. Bulletin d'information*, 28 (1998), p. 12-17.

GOSSET, N., *La vie et les miracles de sainte Opportune, abbesse. La translation de ses reliques et fondation de son église à Paris. Tirée du cartulaire et archives de ladite église*, Paris, 1654 (réimpr. 1655 et 1659).

HEENE, K., «*Audire, legere, vulgo*: An Attempt to Define Public Use and Comprehensibility of Carolingian Hagiography», in R. WRIGHT, dir., *Latin and the Romance Languages in the Early Middle Ages*, Londres, 1991 p. 146-163 (Romance Linguistic Series).

LACHASSE, G., «Note sur Chrodegang ou Godegrand, évêque de Sées: un fragment d'un manuscrit de sa Vie à la Bibliothèque Mazarine», *Bulletin de la Société des Antiquaires de Normandie*, 57 (1963-64) [1965], p. 507-513.

OURY, G., «Le ms. Arsenal 632, premier témoin du culte de sainte Opportune?», *Études grégoriennes*, 10 (1969), p. 143-146.

—, «Sainte Opportune, sa vie et ses reliques», in Y. CHAUSSY, dir., *L'abbaye d'Almenèches-Argentan et sainte Opportune. Sa vie et son culte*, Paris, 1970, p. 221-236 (Bibliothèque d'histoire et d'archéologie chrétiennes).

---

[50] La numérotation des chapitres est celle de l'édition de Mabillon.

—, *Abbaye Notre-Dame d'Almenèches-Argentan*, Rouen, 1979 (Abbayes et prieurés de Normandie, 8).

POLIDORI, S., «Adalhelmus (Aldelelmus) Sagiensis ep.», in M. LAPIDGE *et al.*, dir., *Compendium auctorum latinorum Medii Aevi*, I-1, Florence, 2000, p. 19.

VAN UYTFANGHE, M., «The Consciousness of a Linguistic Dichotomy (Latin-Romance) in Carolingian Gaul: The Contradictions of the Sources and their Interpretation», in R. WRIGHT, dir., *Latin and the Romance Languages in the Early Middle Ages*, Londres, 1991, p. 114-129 (Romance Linguistic Series).

VI – TAURINUS D'ÉVREUX

Les pièces les plus anciennes du dossier hagiographique de saint Taurin sont une *Vita* (*BHL* 7990-91) et une *Inventio* (*BHL* 7992-94); une certaine parenté stylistique permet de penser que ces deux documents sont sortis d'une même plume[51]. Les éditions existantes donnent cependant à lire, sous une progression narrative identique, des versions légèrement décalées les unes par rapport aux autres. L'état de la Vie *BHL* 7991 présente en effet une latinité plus soignée que *BHL* 7990; leurs prologues respectifs sont toutefois complètement différents. Une distance un peu plus grande sépare les états de l'*Inventio*. Il reste donc à établir un classement relatif ou une hiérarchisation des liens éventuels de dépendance.

L'auteur s'identifie lui-même dans la Vie: un prêtre Déodat, disciple du saint – une prétention insoutenable, démasquée depuis plusieurs siècles. Il est possible que l'*Inventio* ait été composée avant la *Vita*, car Déodat y renvoie à un *libellus* qu'il aurait rédigé antérieurement. Il invoque en outre le témoignage d'une Vie de l'évêque Laudulphe d'Évreux, inconnue par ailleurs. Déodat prétend avoir vu personnellement certains miracles survenus à l'occasion de l'*Inventio*. Mais il ne faut chercher nulle cohérence chronologique ou factuelle dans ses récits; même la période de vie de Taurin demeure incertaine, quelque part entre le Ier et le VIe siècle. Taurin est tour à tour présenté comme simple évêque d'Évreux dans la *Vita*, mais comme premier évêque d'Évreux dans l'*Inventio* et contemporain du pape Clément Ier et de saint

---

[51] *Contra*: HERRICK (2007), p. 27.

Denis l'Aréopagite. Certains épisodes sont situés à l'époque des invasions hunniques, d'un roi Clotaire ou de Charles le Chauve.

Déodat annonce qu'il a achevé sa composition à Milan, auprès d'un saint Benoît; il est plus probable que l'œuvre fut composée à Évreux, là où Taurin est le *patronus noster*. Aux yeux de l'auteur de la *Translatio BHL* 7995 (XIIe siècle), *Vita* et *Inventio* constituaient un tout, ou du moins circulaient ensemble; en effet, il dit avoir lu dans la Vie que les reliques de s. Taurin furent transportées en Auvergne, ce qu'indique l'*Inventio*, mais pas la *Vita* proprement dite. Le témoin le plus ancien de ce dossier est un livret très soigné du XIe siècle (Paris, BnF, lat. 989).

La date de rédaction peut être fixée au deuxième tiers du IXe siècle: soit après le lancement de la légende carolingienne de saint Denis l'Aréopagite dans les années 830, et avant la mise au point de la deuxième famille du Martyrologe d'Adon au dernier quart du IXe siècle. En effet, Adon – ou son continuateur – ajouta alors (au 11 août) un lien entre Taurin et Denis, qu'il a dû trouver dans la Vie de Taurin[52], ce que ne disaient pas les martyrologes antérieurs.

Bibliographie spéciale

CHARLES, J., «Quelques réflexions sur le culte de saint Gaud, évêque d'Évreux», *Cahiers Léopold Delisle*, n° spécial 27 (1978), constituant le *Recueil d'études normandes en hommage au docteur Jean Fournée*, p. 75-82.

—, «Une relecture de la vie de saint Taurin, premier évangélisateur d'Évreux, illustrée par sa châsse», *Connaissance de l'Eure*, 68 (1988), p. 20-31.

CORDE, L.-T., *La châsse de Saint-Taurin, premier évêque d'Évreux, suivie de la légende du même saint, publiée et revue sur un manuscrit du XIe siècle de la Bibliothèque impériale de Paris*, Évreux, 1866 (réimpr. 1876). Édition d'après le manuscrit de Paris, BnF, lat. 989.

DELAPORTE, Y., «L'office fécampois de saint Taurin», in *L'abbaye bénédictine de Fécamp. Ouvrage scientifique du XXIIIe centenaire*, t. 2, Fécamp, 1960, p. 171-189 et 377.

---

[52] DUBOIS – RENAUD éd. (1984), p. 268 *et sq.*: «In civitate Ebroicas, natale sancti Taurini episcopi, quem beatus Dionisius ordinavit et eidem urbi destinavit episcopum. Ubi glorioso coronatus martyrio, multis miraculis fulget.» Les mots soulignés sont propres à la deuxième famille. Comme le saint a survécu à des tortures infligées par un persécuteur romain, il n'est pas vraiment traité comme martyr dans sa Vie. HERRICK (2005), p. 23 sq., date la Vie des années 1030.

Do, E.-S., *Saint Taurin, premier évêque d'Évreux au Ier siècle. Nouvelles recherches critiques et historiques*, Caen, 1887.

Jullien, M.-H. — Perelman, F., «Deodatus Sancti Taurini mon.», in *Clavis des auteurs latins du Moyen Âge. Territoire français, 735-987*, I: *Abbon de Saint-Germain – Ermold le Noir*, Turnhout, 1994, p. 293-294 (Deost 1).

Magne, C., «Saint Taurin au miroir de la tradition clunisienne. Histoire d'une captation liturgique», *Les Cahiers Bernon* (Lons-le-Saunier), 2 (2006), p. 77-102.

Mesnel, J.-B., *Saint Taurin, premier évêque d'Évreux*, Évreux, 1914 (Les saints du diocèse d'Évreux, 1).

Nocentini, S., «Deodatus Sancti Taurini monachus», in M. Lapidge et al., dir., *Compendium auctorum latinorum Medii Aevi*, III/1, Florence, 2009, col. 71.

Conclusion

La faiblesse de la production hagiographique locale en Basse-Normandie à l'époque carolingienne aide à comprendre pourquoi, avant le XIe siècle, les liturgistes ont eu recours au commun des confesseurs plutôt qu'aux Vies de saints pour bâtir des offices propres[53]. Il reste à évaluer dans quelle mesure l'hagiographie du XIe siècle peut recéler des éléments de tradition légitimement rattachables aux siècles antérieurs – une opération délicate à mener, sur laquelle nous avons fait l'impasse ici. Un exemple parmi d'autres illustrera les difficultés prévisibles: nous avons considéré que l'invocation du nom du roi Childebert (I, II ou III, peu importe) fait partie des lieux communs de l'hagiographie des saints bas-normands, tout comme dans l'ancienne hagiographie bretonne, à l'instar de la mise en scène – crédible et exemplaire – de Childebert Ier dans la Vie de saint Pair d'Avranches par Venance Fortunat. C'est pourquoi ces hagiographies nous paraissent apporter peu de matériaux solides pour la reconstitution d'un «moment Childebert» au VIe siècle[54]; nous y voyons plutôt une construction mémorielle postérieure, conduite par des hagiographes qui s'inspirent les

---

[53] Diard (2003), p. 211.

[54] Dumézil (2009). Les interventions de Childebert Ier dans l'hagiographie bas-normande sont prises au pied de la lettre par Roupsard (2017), p. 6 et 17 sq., après beaucoup d'autres.

uns des autres, tout en conservant un flou prudent sur l'identité de ce Childebert à trois têtes. N. Gauthier croit reconnaître ici ou là des Vies du IXe siècle sous des copies interpolées du XIe siècle[55]; à moins qu'il ne s'agisse de compositions du XIe siècle, tout simplement... Quoi qu'il en soit, la Basse-Normandie avant l'an mil ne constitue pas – au miroir de l'hagiographie – un paysage culturel aussi typé que la Bretagne armoricaine voisine; rien n'approche les ambitions ni la richesse des pratiques d'intertextualité des hagiographes bretons au même moment[56].

Bibliographie générale sur l'hagiographie de Basse-Normandie

1. Catalogues, répertoires, instruments de travail

Bouet, P., «Bibliographie. Sources relatives aux saints normands», in Bouet – Neveux (2000), p. 305-323.

Dubois, J. – Renaud, G. éd., *Le martyrologe d'Adon. Ses deux familles, ses trois recensions. Texte et commentaire*, Paris, 1984 (Sources d'histoire médiévale).

Duchesne, L., *Fastes épiscopaux de l'ancienne Gaule*, II: *L'Aquitaine et les Lyonnaises*, 2e éd., Paris, 1910.

Gazeau, V., *Normannia monastica (X^e-XIIe siècle)*, I: *Princes normands et abbés bénédictins*; II: *Prosopographie des abbés bénédictins*, Caen, 2007.

Pietri, L. – M Heijmans, dir., *Prosopographie de la Gaule chrétienne, 314-614*, 2 vol., Paris, 2013 (Prosopographie chrétienne du Bas-Empire, 4).

van 't Spijker, I., «Gallia du Nord et de l'Ouest. Les provinces ecclésiastiques de Tours, Rouen, Reims (950-1130)», in *Hagiographies*, II (1996), p. 239-290.

Van der Straeten, J., «Manuscrits hagiographiques du Mont Saint-Michel conservés à Avranches», *AB*, 86 (1968), p. 109-134.

Vangone, L., «Le ReTeHNor: un répertoire numérique de l'hagiographie latine de Normandie», *Tabularia. Les sources du monde normand à l'heure du numérique* (23 novembre 2018): <http://journals.openedition.org/tabularia/3167> (consulté le 22 avril 2020).

---

[55] Gauthier (1992), p. 468, suivie par Pezé (2014), p. 25.

[56] Voir notre chapitre consacré à cette page d'histoire littéraire dans le présent volume, p. 189-242.

2. Études d'ensemble
pour l'hagiographie bas-normande, 750-950

ARNOUX, M., «La conversion des Normands en Neustrie et la restauration de l'Église dans la province de Rouen», in F. BOUGARD, dir., *Le christianisme en Occident du début du VIIe siècle au milieu du XIe siècle. Textes et documents*, Paris, 1997, p. 269-281 (Regards sur l'histoire, 117).

BAUDRY, É., «Le pérégrin et le reclus. Ermites de Normandie, du VIe au IXe siècle», in *Voyageurs et ermites. Saints populaires et évangélisateurs de la Normandie*, Caen, 1996, p. 32-41.

BAEDORF, B., *Untersuchungen über Heiligenleben der westlichen Normandie (der Diözesen Avranches, Coutances, Bayeux und Seez)*, Bonn, 1913.

BEAUJARD, B., «Aux origines du culte des saints en Normandie», in N.-J. CHALINE, dir., *Histoire religieuse de la Normandie*, Chambray, 1981, p. 11-21.

BIRNS, N., «Medieval Historiography», *Clio*, 26 (1997), p. 230-242; recension de LIFSHITZ (1995) *Norman Conquest*.

BOUET, P. – NEVEUX, F., dir., *Les saints dans la Normandie médiévale (colloque de Cerisy-la-Salle, 1996)*, Caen, 2000.

DIARD, O., «Histoire et chant liturgique en Normandie au XIe siècle: les offices propres particuliers des diocèses d'Évreux et de Rouen», *Annales de Normandie*, 53 (2003), p. 195-223.

DUBOIS, J., «Hagiographie et culte des saints», in P. PÉRIN – L.-C. FEFFER, dir., *La Neustrie. Les pays au nord de la Loire, de Dagobert à Charles le Chauve (VIIe-IXe siècles)*, Rouen, 1985, p. 135-137.

DUMÉZIL, B., «La royauté franque et la christianisation des Gaules: le "moment" Childebert Ier (511-558)». in D. PARIS-POULAIN et al. dir., *Les premiers temps chrétiens dans le territoire de la France actuelle. Hagiographie, épigraphie et archéologie*, Rennes, 2009, p. 41-49.

FONTAINE, J., «Victrice de Rouen et les origines du monachisme dans l'ouest de la Gaule (IVe-VIe siècles)», in L. MUSSET, dir., *Aspects du monachisme en Normandie (IVe-XVIIIe siècles)*, Paris, 1982, p. 4-29.

FOURNÉE, J., «Propos sur les saints et la sainteté dans la province ecclésiastique de Rouen, avant les Vikings», in *Voyageurs et ermites. Saints populaires évangélisateurs de la Normandie*, Caen, 1996, p. 13-21 (et carte p. 12).

GAUTHIER, N., «Quelques hypothèses sur la rédaction des Vies des saints évêques de Normandie», in *Memoriam sanctorum venerantes. Miscellanea in onore di Monsignor Victor Saxer*, Vatican, 1992, p. 449-468 (Studi di antichità cristiana, 48).

HERRICK, S. K., *Imagining the Sacred Past in Hagiography of Early Normandy. The* Vita Taurini, Vita Vigoris *and* Passio Nicasii, PhD Harvard University, 2002.

—, «Heirs to the Apostles: Saintly Power and Ducal Authority in Hagiography of Early Normandy», in R. F. BERKHOFFER III *et al.*, dir., *The Experience of Power in Medieval Europe, 950-1350*, Aldershot, 2005, p. 11-24 (constituant les Mélanges Thomas N. Bisson).

—, *Imagining the Sacred Past: Hagiography and Power in Early Normandy*, Cambridge, MA, 2007 (Harvard Historical Studies, 156).

JARRY, T., « Les débuts du christianisme dans l'ouest de la Normandie», *Annales de Normandie*, 48 (1998), p. 115-149.

—, «Les débuts du christianisme en Cotentin», *Revue de la Manche*, 41:161 (1999), p. 7-31.

LAIR, J., «Étude sur les origines de l'évêché de Bayeux», *Bibliothèque de l'École des Chartes*, 23 (1862), p. 89-124, 24 (1863), p. 281-323, 29 (1868), p. 33-55 et 545-584.

LAPLATTE, C., «Un livre allemand sur les vieux saints de chez nous», *Semaine religieuse du diocèse de Coutances et d'Avranches*, 80 (20 juin 1946), p. 194 sq. et (27 juin 1946) p. 203 sq.; résumé de BAEDORF (1913).

LAPORTE, J., «Les origines du monachisme dans la Province de Rouen», *Revue Mabillon*, 31 (1941), p. 1-13, 25-41 et 49-68.

LE MAHO, J., «Un exode de reliques dans le pays de la Basse Seine à la fin du IXe siècle», *Bulletin de la Commission départementale des Antiquités de la Seine-Maritime*, 46 (1998), p. 137-188.

LIFSHITZ, F., *The Norman Conquest of Pious Neustria. Historiographic Discourse and Saintly Relics, 684-1090*, Toronto, 1995 (Studies and Texts, 122).

—, «The Migration of Neustrian Relics in the Viking Age: The Myth of Voluntary Exodus, the Reality of Coercion and Theft», *Early Medieval Europe*, 4/2 (1995), p. 175-192.

MUSSET, L., «L'exode des reliques du diocèse de Sées au temps des invasions normandes», *Société historique et archéologique de l'Orne. Bulletin principal* 88 (1970), p. 3-22.

—, «De saint Victrice à saint Ouen: la christianisation de la province de Rouen d'après l'hagiographie», *Revue d'histoire de l'Église de France*, 62 (1976) p. 141-152; réimpr. in P. RICHÉ, dir., *La christianisation des pays entre Loire et Rhin (IVe-VIIe siècles)*, Paris, 1993, p. 141-152.

—, «Autour des saints du haut Moyen Âge dans la future Normandie», in *Voyageurs et ermites. Saints populaires évangélisateurs de la Normandie*, Caen, 1996, p. 23-27.

—, «Les translations de reliques en Normandie (IXe-XIIe siècles)», in BOUET – NEVEUX (2000), p. 97-108.

Pigeon, É.-A., *Texte français et latin des Vies des saints du diocèse de Coutances et Avranches, avec des notions préliminaires et l'histoire des reliques de chaque saint*, Avranches, 1892-1898, 2 vol. Les 111 premières pages du t. I ont aussi paru à Avranches en 1891, sous le même titre (consultables sur Gallica). Tous les chapitres de ces deux volumes furent d'abord publiés sous forme d'articles dans les Mémoires de la Société académique du Cotentin (Archéologie, belles-lettres, sciences et beaux-arts) de 1891 à 1898.

Potts, C. W., *Monastic Revival and Regional Identity in Early Normandy*, Woodbridge, 1997 (Studies in the History of Medieval Religion, 11).

—, «When the Saints Go Marching: Religious Connections and the Political Culture of Early Normandy», in C. W. Hollister, dir., *Anglo-Norman Political Culture and the Twelfth-Century Renaissance*, Woodbridge, 1997, p. 17-32.

Roupsard, M., «Du paganisme au christianisme en Normandie occidentale (IVe-Ve siècles): premiers éléments de synthèse», *Annales de Normandie*, 67 (2017), p. 3-26.

Trân-Duc, L., «Les princes normands et les reliques (X^e-XIe siècles). Contribution du culte des saints à la formation territoriale et identitaire d'une principauté», in J.-L. Deuffic, dir., *Reliques et sainteté dans l'espace médiéval*, Saint-Denis, 2006, p. 525-561 (Pecia. Ressources en médiévistique, 8-11 [2005]).

Van Torhoudt, É., *Centralité et marginalité en Neustrie et dans le duché de Normandie. Maîtrise du territoire et pouvoirs locaux dans l'Avranchin, le Bessin et le Cotentin (VIe-XIe siècles)*, Thèse de doctorat, Université Paris 7, 2008, 3 vol. dactyl.

L'écriture hagiographique
dans la province de Reims (env. 750-950)

Lieux mentionnés dans les chapitres sur la province de Reims

NB: L'étude des diocèses de Cambrai-Arras, Thérouanne et Tournai paraîtra dans le vol. IX.

1 Abbeville
2 Avenay
3 Bazoches
4 Binson
5 Conchy-sur-Canche
6 Corbie
7 Coulombs
8 Fismes (Sainte-Macre)
9 Homblières
10 Lagny
11 Le Paraclet (comm. de Cottenchy)
12 Lillers
13 Loos
14 Montdidier
15 Mortemer
16 Orbais
17 Origny
18 Oroër
19 Paillart
20 Péronne
21 Pont-Sainte-Maxence
22 Ribemont
23 Sains-en-Amiénois
24 Saint-Basle de Verzy
25 Saint-Bertin
26 Saint-Germain-sur-Bresle
27 Saint-Germer-de-Fly
28 Saint-Josse-sur-Mer
29 Saint-Just-en-Chaussée
30 Saint-Riquier
31 Saint-Thierry au Mont d'Or
32 Saint-Valery-sur-Somme
33 Saint-Winnoc de Bergues
34 Vieux-Rouen-sur Bresle
35 Wailly

L'écriture hagiographique dans les diocèses de Reims, Soissons et Laon (env. 750-950)

par

Marie-Céline ISAÏA

INTRODUCTION.
I SOISSONS. – A. Les Vies de saint Voüé. – B. L'écriture hagiographique à Saint-Médard. – 1. Translation et Miracles de saint Grégoire le Grand et saint Sébastien. – 2. Vie de l'évêque saint Médard. – 3. Odilon de Saint-Médard hagiographe.
II. LES PASSIONS S'INSCRIVANT DANS LE CYCLE DE RICIOVARE. – A. La Passion de sainte Macre. – B. La Passion des saints Rufin et Valère. – C. La Passion des saints Crépin et Crépinien.
III. REIMS. – A. Les Vies des saints évêques de Reims. – 1. La Passion de saint Nicaise. – 2. La Vie de saint Remi de Reims. – 3. La Vie de saint Rigobert et le dossier des translations rémoises. – 4. La Vie de saint Maternien évêque de Reims. – B. Autour des monastères bénédictins du diocèse de Reims. – 1. Les Vies de saint Thierry et saint Thiou. – 2. L'œuvre d'Almann de Hautvillers. – 3. Les Vies des abbesses Bova et Doda. – C. Flodoard hagiographe.
BIBLIOGRAPHIE.

INTRODUCTION

L'histoire des diocèses de Reims, de Soissons et de Laon durant la période carolingienne est étroitement liée. La métropole rémoise tient sous surveillance les deux suffragants voisins. Les deux conflits d'autorité les plus acharnés de l'épiscopat d'Hincmar de Reims (845-882) l'opposent à Rothade de Soissons (833-868) et à Hincmar de Laon (858-871)[1] : il y a là deux sièges dont Reims ne tolérera pas qu'ils s'affranchissent de son

---

[1] DEVISSE (1975), en particulier p. 585-600 pour Rothade et p. 730-782 pour Hincmar de Laon; STRATMANN (1991); STONE, WEST (2015).

autorité. Les archevêques de Reims usent à leur profit dans ces débats de la manipulation des sources canoniques et de l'écriture de l'histoire. La spécialisation historiographique du siège rémois culmine ainsi au milieu du Xe siècle, avant Richer[2], avec l'œuvre de Flodoard, vaste réécriture du passé à des fins politiques bien contemporaines: dans une Histoire écrite depuis Reims vers 948-952[3] se trouve figée la légende d'une fondation de l'Église rémoise par saint Sixte, disciple de saint Pierre et maître de saint Sinice, premier évêque de Soissons[4]; la même Histoire affirme que le siège de Laon a pour sa part été fondé par saint Remi de Reims (m. 533/535) qui l'a confié à son premier évêque, l'indigne saint Génébaud[5]. On ne peut pas mieux dire que les sièges de Soissons et de Laon sont des annexes rémoises. Or la démarche de Flodoard attire l'attention sur la production hagiographique dans le diocèse: à côté de sources d'archive, le chanoine utilise majoritairement des textes hagiographiques, réécrits et agencés dans une trame chronologique et topographique explicative, pour connaître et raconter le passé de son Église. De fait, c'est l'*Historia Remensis Ecclesiae* [*HRE*] qui sert à dater la majorité des textes hagiographiques de la province, selon que Flodoard les a recueillis ou ignorés.

---

[2] LAKE (2013).

[3] FLODOARD DE REIMS, *Historia Remensis Ecclesiae* [*HRE passim*], éd. M. STRATMANN, *MGH*, *SS*, XXXVI, Hanovre, 1998; SOT (1993); ROBERT (2016) et aussi JACOBSEN (1978) pour la biographie de Flodoard.

[4] *HRE* I, 3, p. 66-67. La réinterprétation a commencé au moins sous Hincmar, voir STRATMANN (1990).

[5] *HRE* I, 14, p. 89-91. Là encore, la réinterprétation du passé date d'Hincmar, voir ISAÏA (2010), p. 151-156.

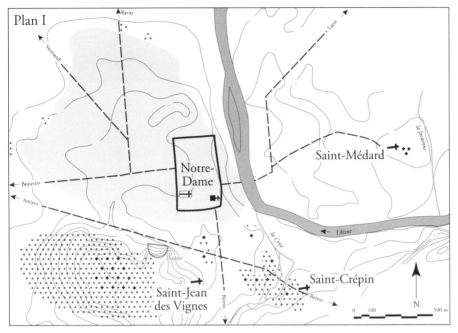

Les églises de Soissons

Plan d'après F. Prévot, M. Gaillard et N. Gauthier (éd.), *Topographie chrétienne des cités de la Gaule des origines au milieu du VIIIe siècle, Quarante ans d'enquête, 1972-2012*, XVI, 2: *Christianisation et espace urbain: atlas, tableaux, index*, Paris, De Boccard, 2014, p. 650.

Une telle perspective pose d'évidents problèmes de méthode: dans ce cas précis, selon qu'on voie en Flodoard un archiviste scrupuleux ou un fin politique, ses silences seront ignorance ou manipulation[6]. Plus largement, les historiens ont suivi le discours des sources, et concentré sur Reims toute leur attention[7]; c'est depuis Reims que les sources ont été étudiées par une forte tradition locale d'érudition[8], particulièrement efficace pour les

---

[6] Le débat est ouvert notamment par Roberts (2014).

[7] Il est assez symptomatique que les deux monographies classiques sur Soissons et Laon accordent l'essentiel de leur attention à l'époque mérovingienne: Kaiser (1973); Lusse (1992).

[8] Le Rémois Guillaume Marlot publie sa *Metropolis Remensis historia* (2 t., Reims) en 1666 et 1679. Sur l'activité rémoise de dom Anselme Le Michel, voir Dolbeau (1988).

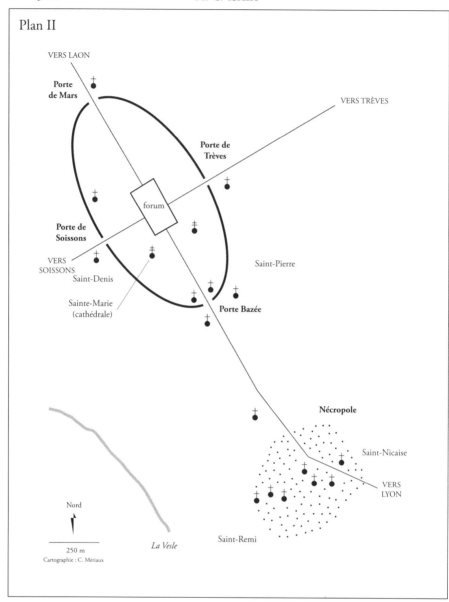

Les églises de Reims

Extrait de C. Mériaux dans: *Reims, une métropole dans l'histoire. La ville antique et médiévale*, dir. P. Demouy, Paris, Éditions Dominique Guéniot, 2014, p. 107.

textes hagiographiques du fait de la présence des Mauristes[9]. Avec un peu de recul cependant, les textes hagiographiques des trois diocèses pourraient donner une vision plus nuancée de la période: l'emprise de l'autorité épiscopale sur le diocèse de Reims conditionne peut-être la production hagiographique carolingienne, dans une optique historiographique et normative; il faut se demander cependant si cette impression révèle bien une politique concertée des archevêques du IXe siècle ou provient plutôt de l'interprétation donnée par Flodoard; dans les diocèses de Laon et surtout de Soissons perdurent d'autres traditions anciennes, dont l'hagiographie martyriale du cycle de Riciovare[10]. Le poids de cette tradition, joint à l'existence de liens personnels entre Laon, Soissons et Corbie contribuent à accroître les différences entre l'hagiographie plus monastique des diocèses occidentaux et l'hagiographie plus épiscopale de Reims. Ce chapitre s'attarde donc d'abord sur les textes hagiographiques moins étudiés produits dans les diocèses de Soissons et de Laon, avant de proposer une brève synthèse sur des textes rémois mieux connus.

---

[9] Dom Jean Mabillon est moine de Saint-Remi avant de rejoindre Saint-Germain des Prés, comme son collaborateur le Rémois dom Thierry Ruinart; même si l'érudition mauriste s'épanouit à Paris, Reims, avec Saint-Remi et Saint-Thierry, reste un point de collecte en vue de la rédaction des *Acta Sanctorum ordinis sancti Benedicti* comme des *Annales ordinis s. Benedicti*; en témoignent les documents conservés dans le manuscrit Paris, BnF, lat. 11777, dont les émouvantes lettres de Guillaume Robin fol. 4 ou fol. 5; ou la liste des textes hagiographiques disponibles à Saint-Remi, fol. 28-29v, etc. Sur l'activité rémoise des deux mauristes, voir l'édition par DOLBEAU (2007), p. 1766-1778. Les textes recherchés bien sûr ne concernent pas seulement les saints locaux: Luc d'Achery voulait par exemple trouver une Vie de l'abbesse [de Jouarre] Agilberte à Notre-Dame de Soissons (Paris, BnF, lat. 11777, fol. 67; la recherche semble avoir été vaine). Ruinart publie en outre les *Acta primorum martyrum sincera et selecta* en 1689; il ne dit pas dans sa préface avoir particulièrement puisé dans les bibliothèques rémoises mais il écrit comme ses collègues «à nos confrères et nos amis pour leur demander s'ils n'auraient pas dans leurs monastères ou les villes où ils vivent quelques vieux manuscrits qu'ils pourraient scruter attentivement, etc.», préface générale §10, p. 13 de la 2e édition (1713).

[10] J'adopte l'orthographe *Riciovare* en suivant GAILLARD (2014).

I. Soissons

L'hagiographie du diocèse de Soissons s'intéresse à partir de la fin du XIe siècle d'une part aux évêques contemporains Arnoul de Soissons (m. 1087)[11] et Geoffroy d'Amiens (m. 1115) enterré à Saint-Médard[12], d'autre part aux évêques antiques ou mérovingiens, dans l'ordre chronologique Onésime, Edibius, Principe, Bandry (enterré à Saint-Crépin), Anséric et Drausin (enterré à Notre-Dame)[13]. Les compositions culminent au cours des années 1070-1150, dans le double contexte d'une remise aux normes grégoriennes des comportements épiscopaux et d'un renforcement de l'autorité épiscopale sur la vie urbaine. La réécriture de l'histoire de l'Église soissonnaise inspire un retour aux sources de la cité épiscopale, jusqu'à l'évêque fondateur saint Sinice (*BHL* 7815)[14], tandis que Saint-Médard poursuit la mise en valeur de sa collection de reliques[15]. Les Vies et Miracles écrits aux XIe et XIIe siècle constituent donc une nouvelle étape d'hagiographie historiographique et épiscopale, qui contraste avec les temps carolingiens: il n'existe pas en effet de Vies ca-

---

[11] HARIULF D'OUDENBURG, *Vita s. Arnulfi* (*BHL* 703), éd. *AASS OSB*, VI-2 (1701), soit *Vita* p. 502-547 et *Miracula*, p. 547-555 par Lisiard évêque de Soissons, avec lettre d'envoi à Raoul le Vert archevêque de Reims, peu après le concile de 1119.

[12] NICOLAS DE SAINT-CRÉPIN, *Vita s. Godefridi Ambianensis* (*BHL* 3573-3574), éd. A. PONCELET, *AASS*, Nov. III, Bruxelles, 1910, col. 905-944.

[13] Après VAN 'T SPIJKER (1996), p. 276-277, voir surtout OTT (2006); pour Principe et Edibius, DOLBEAU (1991).

[14] ISAÏA (2008). Voir surtout dans la Vie de l'évêque Onésime (*BHL* 6333) le travail de l'hagiographe pour retracer toute la liste épiscopale après le martyre de Crépin et Crépinien, soit Sinice – disciple de Sixte de Reims –, Divitien, Rufin et Filanus (cap. 2). C'est l'essentiel de l'information recueillie sur Onésime.

[15] Dans une interpolation, qu'Ernst Müller situe au XIe siècle, du manuscrit des *Histoires* de Nithard (Paris, BnF, lat. 9768, fol. 11) alors à Saint-Médard, on trouve une liste complète des saints dont le monastère revendiquait les reliques: «les moines vinrent à la rencontre [de Charles le Chauve] le suppliant de transférer dans l'église qui était en majeure partie construite les corps des saints Médard, Sébastien, Grégoire [le Grand], Tiburce, Pierre et Marcellin, Marius, Marthe, Audifax et Abacuc, Onésime, Méresme [ou Méderasme, sœur de saint Médard]» [puis dans la marge] «Marian, Pélage et Maur, Florian et ses six frères, Gildard, Serein et le seigneur Remi, archevêque de Rouen.»; voir MÜLLER (1909) et surtout son commentaire par DE GAIFFIER (1953), p. 108-119.

rolingiennes des évêques de Soissons mais seulement une réécriture de la Vie mérovingienne de saint Médard évêque de Noyon, qui le rapproche de saint Bandry (*infra*)[16].

A. LES VIES DE SAINT VOÜÉ

Le premier foyer intellectuel soissonnais, avant que Saint-Médard ne produise quelques textes hagiographiques, est le monastère féminin Notre-Dame de Soissons fondé par Ébroïn, récupéré par les Pippinides, et qui reste ensuite dans la famille carolingienne sous les abbesses Gisèle (m. 811), sœur de Charlemagne, Théodrade sa cousine, Imma, fille de cette dernière, etc.[17]. C'est là qu'est composée une Vie longue de saint Voüé[18] (*BHL* 8727), publiée par Mabillon d'après un manuscrit qu'il date du Xe siècle – le manuscrit vient précisément de Notre-Dame. *Vodoalus* ou *Vodoaldus* aurait vécu dans la mouvance du monastère[19] sous l'abbesse Adalgarde, c'est-à-dire autour des années 680-720. Mabillon attribue ce texte à «un auteur soissonnais anonyme de la fin du IXe ou du début du Xe siècle»[20]. Il s'empresse de l'éditer parce qu'il dispose d'un texte plus complet que celui que le chanoine régulier de Saint-Jean des Vignes de Soissons, Nicolas de Beaufort (1554-1624), a transmis de son côté à Jean Bolland, à partir de sa collation d'un manuscrit de Soissons avec un manuscrit de Longpont[21]. Les deux Vies à la vérité sont presque identiques: *BHL* 8728 est l'abréviation de *BHL* 8727, notamment par la suppression de quelques longues méditations spirituelles sur les qualités de Voüé (catalogue des vices que Voüé a évités §4; vertus §5). La datation donnée par Mabillon s'accorde avec la présence de

---

[16] *Supplementum* (*BHL* 5865), éd. D. PAPEBROCH, *AASS*, Iun. II, Anvers, 1698, col. 82B-86E. *Bandaricus* accueille le convoi funèbre qui apporte le corps de Médard à Soissons, cap. 11, col. 84A.

[17] REINHOLD (1974).

[18] *Vita s. Vodoali*, *AASS OSB*, IV-2 (1680), p. 545-550.

[19] Voüé réside à l'extérieur de l'enceinte monastique, à la porte du côté est (§3, p. 546). Il reçoit sa subsistance du monastère (§7, p. 547) où il entre pour célébrer la messe (§12, p. 548).

[20] La datation n'est pas justifiée: elle reprend mot pour mot celle de GERMAIN (1675), p. 75.

[21] *Vita s. Vodali* [sic] (*BHL* 8728), éd. J. BOLLAND, *AASS*, Feb. I, Anvers, 1658, col. 691-693.

BHL 8727 dans un manuscrit aujourd'hui à Paris, BnF, lat. 17626, de la deuxième moitié du Xe siècle, fol. 25v-31v. Début de légendier *per circulum anni* (janvier-février) adapté aux besoins d'une communauté bénédictine du diocèse de Soissons, il contient un texte très proche du texte édité[22]; des variantes mineures montrent que ce n'est pas le manuscrit qu'a utilisé Mabillon[23].

Après des débuts relativement classiques, l'histoire de Voüé se révèle peu commune: prêtre d'origine *scot*, Voüé embrasse la *peregrinatio pro amore Christi* avec son compagnon Magnebert et vient s'établir à Soissons devant la porte du monastère, là où la tour Saint-Benoît garde sa mémoire[24]. Un jour qu'il n'est pas capable de rendre à l'abbesse le plat d'argent dans lequel elle lui a fait porter son repas – il l'a donné aux pauvres – il reçoit de vifs reproches, et reprend sa *peregrinatio* pendant neuf ans; il souhaite rentrer chez lui et se rembarque; il faut l'intervention d'un ange pour le guérir de la fièvre qu'il a contractée, le renvoyer à Soissons et lui donner le double privilège de guérir les fièvres et d'empêcher les incendies, par sa présence physique, son manteau ou son bâton. Voüé achève donc sa vie exemplaire à Soissons: il est enterré par les religieuses dans l'église monastique Sainte-Croix. Son premier miracle *post mortem* est d'empêcher son fidèle Magnebert, miraculeusement tué par une fièvre violente, de devenir un serf du monastère.

L'auteur de *BHL* 8727 explique dans son long prologue qu'un *libellus* racontant l'histoire du saint a été perdu par négligence à Laon. Il compense cette perte par une enquête locale, enregistre l'existence d'un culte vivace autour des reliques de

---

[22] Mabillon édite un texte meilleur que celui du légendier Paris, BnF, lat. 17626, mais où demeurent des bizarreries; l'hagiographe parle-t-il vraiment du serpent des origines «instigateur et restaurateur de tout mal», *instigator et reparator omnis malitiae*, §7, p. 547, en utilisant un mot qui qualifie d'ordinaire de Rédempteur? Un simple *parator* conviendrait, ou mieux un *repertor*; il est vrai que l'hagiographe aime la complication.

[23] Les formules de conclusion diffèrent. Surtout, là où Mabillon édite §9, p. 547: *ut quicumque hoc fuerint vexari incommodo nomenque tuum in suis memorauerint orationibus, statim inde medelam percipiant...* le copiste du manuscrit Paris, BnF, lat. 17626, fol. 28v, a fait un saut du même au même: *ut quicumque hoc fuerint orationibus statimque inde medelam percipiant*. Le copiste fait aussi de Voüé un *consul* (fol. 26) là où il aurait dû écrire *exsul*, §2, p. 545, etc.

[24] Voüé est surnommé *Benedictus*, par l'ange qui lui confirme sa vocation puis par tout son entourage.

«notre patron Voüé» (§2) sur la tombe duquel il voit des miracles se produire chaque jour (§9; §19), et utilise pour le reste ce qu'il lit à propos d'autres saints (§14):

> Nous prenons Dieu à témoin qu'avec les éloges de notre adoration, nous n'avons rien inséré ici de peur d'être mis en pièces par les morsures des critiques s'il nous arrivait d'encourir par témérité quelque reproche de mensonge, d'autant plus que, comme nous l'avons rappelé plus haut, le texte de l'histoire de ses actions n'est chez nous pas du tout conservé par écrit: mais ce que nous avons appris de l'histoire d'autres Pères – ce très saint homme appartient à leur collège – ou ce dont nous avons eu connaissance par le récit des fidèles, nous nous sommes appliqué à l'insérer, bien que dans un discours sans apprêt[25].

L'hagiographe est un bon élève, qui cite Virgile (explicitement au §3; *topos* de l'*Enéide* IV, 6-7 en §17) et utilise un lexique recherché (*dumeta* §3, *sulcus* §3 et 4, *juba* §6, *eructatio* §6 pour qualifier les eaux débordantes et vivifiantes, *pollinctor* §16), aux sonorités grecques (*cenodoxia* §4; *paedagogus* §5, *thorax* §6, *agape* §7). L'hagiographe partage ces traits avec les auteurs de la fin du IXe siècle ou du début du Xe, comme bien des images; il les enchaîne parfois un peu hardiment: «Il [Voüé] s'attacha inébranlablement aux quatre vertus cardinales comme aux quatre colonnes spirituelles qui soutiennent l'armature de l'édifice, la prudence, la justice, la force et la tempérance. Le saint homme se déplaçait donc avec constance sur ce quadrige des vertus et s'avançait sur la terre des vivants. Il irriguait les champs des cœurs à ces quatre fleuves, comme s'ils coulaient depuis le paradis, etc.[26]». La recherche dans le lexique et la syntaxe contrastent avec le caractère folklorique de certains épisodes, par exemple à l'occasion d'un incendie qui s'est déclaré dans la cellule de Voüé: «L'ange du Seigneur aussitôt l'attrapa par un toupet de cheveux au sommet de son crâne, et le transporta sur une île de l'Aisne»[27] – l'hagiographe raconte l'épisode sans doute en fonction de traditions locales, mais en se souvenant d'une vision

---

[25] *Vita s. Vodoali* (BHL 8727), §14, p. 549.
[26] *Ibid.*, §6, p. 547.
[27] *Ibid.*, §11, p. 548: *Statimque angelus Domini apprehendit eum cincinno verticis suis et transportavit in insulam Axonae fluminis.*

d'Ézéchiel 8, 3[28]. Il répète ce qu'on lui a appris, vraisemblablement dans un milieu monastique :

> Le savoir du monde rampe à terre comme un serpent, mais le savoir divin retentit depuis les cieux. Personne ne suffit à l'embrasser en totalité par les quatre chemins (*quadruuium*) de l'humaine raison, lui qu'aucun des hommes instruits ne parvient à atteindre sans la grâce du Saint Esprit, si bien qu'Il introduit ceux qui l'écoutent à la vérité toute entière [cf. Jn 8, 32] comme en suivant l'enseignement des arts libéraux (*disciplina liberalium artium*), auxquels, même si nous sommes finalement beaucoup aidés par leurs règles, nous ne devons cependant pas attribuer le don du Saint Esprit, par qui toute l'écriture sainte a été inspirée par Dieu et dévoilée aux saints hommes de Dieu dans les siècles[29].

La construction alambiquée, et l'emploi de *quadruuium* plutôt que de *quadriuium*,[30] s'expliquent quand on rapproche ce passage d'une œuvre tardive de Paschase Radbert (env. 785-865), *De benedictionibus patriarchum Iacob et Moysi*[31]. Paschase l'a destinée à Guntland moine de Saint-Riquier, abbaye où il a trouvé refuge vers 851/852 quand il a dû quitter son abbatiat à Corbie.

La tradition manuscrite du *De benedictionibus* est aujourd'hui limitée : on constate ici qu'un auteur soissonnais en a une connaissance directe, même si partielle. Comme l'abbé de Corbie a reçu toute sa formation à Notre-Dame de Soissons, sous l'abbesse Théodrade (m. 846) avec laquelle il a longtemps conservé des liens[32], il ne serait pas invraisemblable que Pas-

---

[28] Vision du prophète : *Et emissa similitudo manus apprehendit me in cincinno capitis mei, et elevavit me spiritus inter terram et cœlum : et adduxit me in Jerusalem, in visione Dei...*

[29] *Vita s. Vodoali* (*BHL* 8727), §15, p. 549.

[30] L'expression est utilisée sous la forme *humanae ratiocinationis quadriuium* par Jean Scot (*De praedestinatione liber*, §2, éd. E. S. MAINOLDI, Firenze, 2003, p. 8, l. 9) pour désigner les quatre branches de la philosophie.

[31] PASCHASIUS RADBERTUS, *De benedictionibus patriarcharum Iacob et Moysi*, Lib. 2, éd. B. PAULUS, Turnhout, 1993, l. 34-42 (*CC CM*, 96).

[32] Voir l'envoi du traité de Paschase, *De partu virginis*, « A Dame vénérable [abbesse] du Christ, comme aux vierges consacrées qui mènent une vie religieuse à Soissons, Paschase Radbert, rebut de tous les moines. Je me suis décidé à éclaircir entièrement pour vous la question que vous, qui m'êtes très chère, m'avez posée jadis sur l'enfantement de la bienheureuse Vierge Marie, puisque je n'ai pas de réticence à vous aimer beaucoup pour cette raison que vous savez combien je vous chéris, profondément naguère comme votre élève, amplement maintenant que je suis devenu adulte. », Paschasius Radbertus,

chase ait continué à envoyer à Soissons ceux de ses traités qui pouvaient intéresser clercs et religieuses. De plus, ses liens avec l'école cathédrale de Laon sont bien attestés[33]; or l'hagiographe anonyme, qui regrette de ne pas avoir pu trouver à Laon la Vie de saint Voüé qu'il était venu y chercher, en fréquente donc la bibliothèque sinon cette école épiscopale que John Contreni a caractérisée, entre autres, comme intéressée par le lexique grec et la présence de maîtres 'scots' (!).

Paschase Radbert	Vie de saint Voüé (§15)
Sed nemo tamquam utili honestoque humanae ratiocinationis quadruuio ad plenum conquadratus sufficere probatur disputando in talibus ut introducat auditores suos in omnem ueritatem ad quam nemo eruditorum sine Spiritus sancti gratia peruenire creditur quasi ex disciplina liberalium artium. Cuius etsi multum iuuamur quandoque regulis non tamen eis tribuere debemus Spiritus sancti donum a quo omnis Scriptura sancta diuinitus est inspirata et sanctis Dei hominibus a saeculo reserata.	Nemo namque humanae rationis quadruvio ad plenum conquadratus sufficere probatur, ad quem nullus eruditorum sine sancti Spiritus gratia pervenire dicitur, ut introducat auditores suos in omnem veritatem quasi ex disciplina liberalium artium, quarum etsi multum juvamur quandoque regulis, non tamen eis tribuere deberemus sancti Spiritus donum, a quo omnis Scriptura sancta divinitus est inspirata et sanctis Dei hominibus a saeculo reserata.

La langue et le lexique de l'hagiographe rappellent parfois l'écriture de Paschase, en plus pédant, ce qui n'est pas surprenant s'ils ont été formés au même endroit à quelques générations d'écart. La culture commune à ces hagiographes formés par des femmes se lit encore dans l'audacieux transfert que l'hagiographe ose, de sainte Paule vers saint Voüé; c'est en effet à la lettre de Jérôme à Eustochium, éloge funèbre de sa mère Paula, que l'auteur emprunte le nécessaire pour décrire convenablement la mort de Voüé[34]:

De partu virginis, éd. E. A. MATTER, Turnhout, 1985, p. 47-89, préface (*CC CM*, 56C).

[33] Laon, BM 67 est le manuscrit du *Commentaire sur Matthieu* de Paschase.
[34] JÉRÔME, Lettre 108, §27, *Epistulae*, éd. I. HILBERG, Vienne, 1996, p. 345 puis §28, p. 346-347 (*Corpus Scriptorum Ecclesiasticorum Latinorum*, 55). Les emprunts à cette lettre sont sans doute plus nombreux. Certains se devinent. Comparer à propos de Voüé, *quanto illum Dominus propensius exaltabat, tanto se amplius humilians dejiciebat*, §13, p. 548 avec Jérôme, *Et quanto se plus dejiciebat, tanto magis a Christo sublevabatur*. Jérôme, Lettre 108, §3,

Jérôme, Lettre 108	Vie de saint Voüé (§16)
Quid agimus, anima? Cur ad mortem eius uenire formidas? iam dudum prolixior liber cuditur, dum timemus ad ultima peruenire, quasi tacentibus nobis et in laudibus illius occupatis differri possit occubitus. [...] Sentiebat prudentissima feminarum adesse mortem et frigente alia parte corporis atque membrorum solum animae teporem in sancto et sacro pectore palpitare et nihilo minus, quasi ad suos pergeret alienos que desereret, illos uersiculos susurrabat: Domine, dilexi decorem domus tuae et locum habitationis gloriae tuae [...] Post haec obmutuit et clausis oculis, quasi iam humana despiceret, usque ad expirationem animae eosdem repetebat uersiculos, uix ut audirem, quod dicebat; digitum que ad os tenens crucis signum pingebat in labiis. Defecerat spiritus et anhelabat in mortem; anima que erumpere gestiens ipsum stridorem, quo mortalium uita finitur, in laudes Domini conuertebat.	Cur hinc diutius moras innectimus, et **quasi** ejus **differri possit occubitus** vertere stilum ad ejus obitum **formidamus**? [...] **Sentiens** autem **prudentissimus** sibi prope temporalem **adesse mortem clausis oculis, quasi iam humana despiceret, digitumque ad os tenens crucis signum pingebat in labiis. Defecerat spiritus et anhelabat in mortem, animaque erumpere gestiens ipsum stridorem, quo mortalium uita finitur, in laudem Domini conuertebat.**

Il s'agit assurément d'un texte qui avait sa place dans la bibliothèque de Soissons et dans les lectures de l'hagiographe, d'une part parce qu'il constitue un parfait modèle pour des religieuses de la plus haute l'aristocratie, d'autre part parce qu'il justifie par la figure de Jérôme la place que des hommes occupaient sans cesse à leurs côtés. Paschase, encore lui, avait créé une lettre fictive où il s'imaginait Jérôme écrivant à Paula et Eustochium Sur l'assomption de la Vierge Marie[35], ce qui dit assez l'importance de ce modèle à Notre-Dame de Soissons. L'hagiographe auteur de la Vie de saint Voüé est donc un admirateur de Paschase et son texte un important témoignage des liens intellectuels entre Soissons, Corbie et Laon.

Ibid., p. 309. L'emploi par l'hagiographe de certains mots un peu rares (*coluber*, *illido*) pourrait s'expliquer par l'inspiration hiéronymienne.

[35] PASCHASIUS RADBERTUS, *De Assomptione*, éd. A. RIPBERGER, Turnhout, 1985, p. 97-172 (*CC CM*, 56C). La lettre est aussi connue sous le nom *Cogitis me*. Voir maintenant *Lettera di Girolamo. Un saggio di spiritualità monacale*, introduzione, traduzione e note a cura di C. DEZZUTO, Milano, 2009.

B. L'ÉCRITURE HAGIOGRAPHIQUE À SAINT-MÉDARD

1. Translation et Miracles de saint Grégoire le Grand et saint Sébastien

Odilon moine de Saint-Médard de Soissons a rédigé au début du Xe siècle une Translation (*BHL* 7545) augmentée de Miracles (*BHL* 7546)[36], dans laquelle il raconte comment les reliques de saint Sébastien ont été portées de Rome à Soissons à l'époque d'Hilduin de Saint-Denis – l'archi-chapelain de Louis le Pieux était aussi abbé de Saint-Médard de Soissons et de Saint-Germain d'Auxerre. Selon les Annales royales, Hilduin avait obtenu les reliques de saint Sébastien du pape Eugène II[37]. Odilon connaît cette source; il dit utiliser surtout un compte-rendu du prévôt de Saint-Médard Rodoin, allé en personne à Rome chercher les reliques: « on trouve aujourd'hui encore dans nos archives le rapport que transmit Rodoin à l'abbé Hilduin, dans lequel il a inséré en personne, sous forme de notes brèves, la table qui énumère ses nombreux miracles. Leur somme additionnée monte à 1470 entrées[38]. » La Translation développe

---

[36] *Translatio s. Sebastiani* (*BHL* 7545), éd. J. BOLLAND, *AASS*, Ian. II, Anvers, 1643, col. 278-295 et *Miracula ss. Gregorii et Sebastiani* (*BHL* 7546), *AASS*, Mart. II, 1668, col. 749-752; ensemble avec lettre d'envoi donc attribution à Odilon dans *AASS OSB*, IV-1 (1677), p. 385-410; de larges extraits dans O. HOLDER-EGGER, *MGH*, *SS*, XV-1, Hanovre, 1887, p. 379-391; commentaire et citations traduites dans JUDIC (2001), p. 287-289. Proposition de datation précoce – « au plus trad en 900 » – par LIFSHITZ (1992), p. 335-336, au prix d'une attribution à Rodoin de la lettre dite d'Odilon (note suivante), pour dissocier son correspondant Ingrannus de l'homonyme prévôt de Saint-Médard reconnu par Mabillon, éd. cit. p. 383. Si on fait abstraction de cette lettre, qui donne pour *terminus ante quem* l'élévation d'Ingramnus au siège épiscopal de Laon (932), on doit toujours tenir compte d'une lettre dans laquelle Odilon remercie Hucbald de Saint-Amand pour son envoi de la Vie de saint Lébuin (*BHL* 4812, *PL* 132, col. 877-894, composée pour l'évêque d'Utrecht Baldéric, après 918) et mentionne ce qu'il a écrit sur Sébastien (Odilon à Hucbald, *PL* 132, col. 627D).

[37] Odilon de Saint-Médard, *Lettre d'envoi à Ingrannus*, éd. O. HOLDER-EGGER, p. 379, l. 41, citation des *Annales regni Francorum*, éd. F. KURZE, *MGH*, *SRG in usum scholarum*, VI, Hanovre, 1895, ann. 826, p. 171.

[38] *Enimuero superest hoditenus in cartofilacio nostro scedula Rodoino ad memorabilem Hilduinum abbatem transmissa, in qua numerosa plurimum capitulatione virtutum eius insignia breviata personaliter habentur inserta. Quorum summa in conum redacta, surgit in milibus quattuor centum septuaginta.* Éd. O. HOLDER-EGGER, cap. 46, p. 391.

les circonstances sociales et politiques des années 820 avec un luxe de détails qui rend vraisemblable l'existence d'un témoignage écrit de Rodoin. Odilon connaît encore la Vie de Louis le Pieux par l'Astronome. Il insère enfin au milieu des Miracles un récit où Louis le Pieux raconte à la première personne les circonstances de sa déposition de 833 (*Conquestio domni Hludowici imperatoris*): comment il a été conduit à Soissons après le Champ du Mensonge, tandis qu'on lui faisait croire que son épouse Judith était morte, et que leur fils Charles ‹le Chauve› avait reçu la tonsure; comment il est revenu à Soissons après son rétablissement qu'il attribuait à saint Sébastien, et y a trouvé une réponse à ses scrupules. Du fait de cette inclusion, l'œuvre d'Odilon a une tonalité politique marquée compatible avec l'hypothèse d'une datation haute: Herbert II de Vermandois est abbé laïc de Saint-Médard et l'un des appuis du Carolingien Charles le Simple jusqu'en 922; mais après la mort de Robert Ier, le même Herbert capture Charles le Simple (923) et permet l'accession au trône de Raoul, allié des Robertiens[39]. L'œuvre d'Odilon, qui est un discours à la gloire du «César Louis empereur Auguste de divine mémoire», dont «la dévotion envers saint Sébastien est considérable», et d'Hilduin et Rodoin ses serviteurs dévoués, vante sans ambiguïté le prestigieux passé carolingien de Saint-Médard. Louis le Pieux se distingue parmi les bienfaiteurs de Saint-Médard par des dons d'argent, de vaisselle liturgique venant de son père Charlemagne, un évangéliaire, un encensoir et un vase pour l'huile du luminaire. La Translation veut prouver non seulement la présence à Saint-Médard du corps entier de Sébastien (vision et châtiment d'Ostroald évêque de Laon, m. 826) mais aussi celles de Grégoire le Grand. Odilon raconte en effet comment Rodoin a ajouté subrepticement aux reliques de Sébastien qu'il a obtenu d'emporter – et sont les seules mentionnées par les *Annales royales* – les restes du pape Grégoire après les avoir fait sortir de nuit de leur tombeau à Saint-Pierre. Installées avec l'honneur qui leur est dû, les reliques accomplissent tous les miracles attendus. Elles attirent à Soissons des dons si nombreux que des prêtres expliquent aux fidèles qu'ils ne doivent pas être géné-

---

[39] Après SOT (1993), p. 246-248 pour les fluctuations de la politique d'Herbert II dans les années 920 pour l'activité historiographique à Saint-Médard de Soissons à la même époque, voir REIMITZ (2012).

reux ailleurs que dans leur paroisse. Dans la Translation, la dévotion envers Sébastien l'emporte sur celle qui concerne Grégoire; au XIIe siècle, des Miracles des saints Grégoire et Sébastien tendent à prouver que la dévotion envers saint Grégoire est considérée comme plus efficace ou mieux encouragée[40]. Dans la Translation enfin, Odilon associe Médard à Sébastien et Grégoire en tant que troisième patron de Soissons.

2. Vie de l'évêque saint Médard

De fait, un renouveau du culte de Médard est attesté à cette même époque par l'écriture d'une nouvelle Vie pour le saint évêque de Noyon (m. av. 561) après la Vie géminée écrite par Venance Fortunat[41]. Ses éditeurs en parlent comme une «addition», un *Supplementum* au dossier antérieur, parce que son auteur explique avoir cherché seulement à rassembler ce que Fortunat, un étranger écrivant depuis Poitiers, n'avait pas pu connaître[42]. C'est pourtant une Vie à part entière, destinée à donner une dimension topographique et patrimoniale au culte de Médard, et dont Radbod de Noyon conserve la trame pour sa propre réécriture de la deuxième moitié du XIe siècle[43]. L'hagiographe commence avec l'adolescence du saint pour ajouter au récit de Fortunat des miracles d'intérêt local. Il accorde la plus large part à l'inhumation du saint, en vue de célébrer Saint-Médard comme le monastère principal de Soissons: Médard mourant à Noyon consent à être enterré à Soissons parce que le roi Clotaire lui promet «qu'il construira une basilique [sur son tombeau] et bâtira une communauté» (cap. 9, col. 83E); au gré du convoi funéraire, le roi donne des terres fiscales (cap. 13, col. 84CD) et accroît encore ses générosités quand il choisit d'être lui-même enterré à Soissons (cap. 15, col. 85A). Le plus notable est la tonalité réformatrice tardo-carolingienne du texte (cap. 18-22). L'hagiographe fait longuement état d'un conflit entre Saint-Médard et l'évêque de Soissons, qu'il situe approxi-

---

[40] OTT (2006), p. 228-231.
[41] *BHL* 5863 et 5864, voir HEINZELMANN (2010), p. 62-63 et n. 157.
[42] *Supplementum* [*Vita III[a] s. Medardi*] (*BHL* 5865), éd. cit., cap. 2, col. 82C. Il ajoute aussi des miracles de guérison qu'il lit chez GRÉGOIRE DE TOURS, cap. 17, col. 85C.
[43] Radbod II évêque de Noyon (m. 1098), *Vita s. Medardi* (*BHL* 5866-5867), éd. G. HENSKENS, *AASS*, Iun. II, Anvers, 1698, col. 87C-94F.

mativement à la fin du VIIe siècle: Warinbert, un familier du roi, a succédé à Aubert comme abbé de Saint-Médard et à Drausin comme évêque de Soissons. Il détourne «les revenus et les redevances que la coutume accordait à ceux qui servaient Dieu dans ce monastère pour son propre usage, et celui des siens[44].» Mauvais évêque, indigne abbé, il se heurte à la résistance passive et à la prière des moines; l'hagiographe décrit sa mort lamentable devant le tombeau de saint Médard un jour qu'il a fait irruption dans le monastère pour récupérer un convoi de sel et de miel. Il conclut par une sévère admonestation aux mauvais évêques, qui risquent de finir comme Judas, Arius et Warinbert. La volonté de détailler et pérenniser le temporel monastique, tout en s'affranchissant de la tutelle épiscopale, renvoie à Soissons au contexte général du xe siècle: on procède alors à Saint-Médard à une réorganisation du temporel au prix de certaines forgeries, puis à une lente conquête de l'indépendance. Herbert II de Vermandois autorise l'élection d'un abbé régulier vers 980; Saint-Médard revendique l'exemption qui la mettrait à l'abri des usurpations de l'évêque Foulques (m. 1019)[45]. L'auteur a laissé d'autres indices pour dater son texte: il sait que le monastère a été reconstruit de fond en comble sous le prévôt Rodoin et l'abbé Hilduin déjà cités, à cause de l'afflux de pèlerins suscité par la présence des reliques de Sébastien (cap. 16, col. 85C); cette glorieuse époque révolue, il parle de son époque comme de «ces temps danois[46]», marqués par l'incendie récent de Saint-Médard[47]. L'événement est sans doute celui que ra-

---

[44] *...reditus atque fiscalia, quæ qui ibidem Domino militabant accipere soliti erant, suis suorumque usibus male sibi providus delegabat... Supplementum*, cap. 18, col. 86A.

[45] DELANCHY (1997) «Le siècle des *rectores*» (biographie d'Odilon p. 92-94) pour les forgeries; et «À la conquête de l'exemption» (aux p. 95 et 103 pour Herbert et Foulques). Warinbert ressemble à un double hagiographique de Foulques. Le domaine de *Matvallis* (Bonneveau) qui est l'enjeu du conflit entre Saint-Médard et l'évêque n'est pas mentionné dans les biens de la mense monastique délimités par le diplôme de Charles le Chauve (env. 866-869), Paris, Arch. Nat., K 14, n°9 (2).

[46] *...et usque haec Danorum tempora... Supplementum*, cap. 12, col. 84B.

[47] À propos de Saint-Médard qu'a construite le roi Sigebert d'Austrasie: «Que personne ne prétende que c'est là la basilique commencée jadis par l'empereur Louis, et qui fut il y a peu brûlée par les Marcomans.», *Nemo sane autumet hanc esse basilicam quae olim a Chludovico Caesare coepta, nuper est a Marcomannis exusta. Supplementum*, cap. 16, col. 85C.

content les *Annales* de Saint-Vaast pour 886: «[Après que l'empereur Charles le Gros est reparti sur ses terres], Siegfried [chef normand qui a assiégé Paris] ravagea par le feu l'église du bienheureux Médard, les habitations des moines, bourgs, résidences royales, après avoir tué ou fait prisonniers les habitants de cette terre[48].» À cause de la contemporanéité et de la concordance de vues entre la Translation de saint Sébastien et la Vie de saint Médard, l'attribution de la réécriture carolingienne à Odilon est possible.

3. Odilon de Saint-Médard hagiographe

La délimitation de l'œuvre hagiographique d'Odilon est un problème que l'érudition a quelques fois abordé. Mabillon est le premier responsable d'une définition trop large des œuvres d'Odilon. Dans les Actes des saints bénédictins, il a édité à la suite de l'authentique Translation des saints Sébastien et Grégoire[49], une Translation à Soissons des saint Tiburce, Marcellin et Pierre[50] qu'O. Holder-Egger renvoie au plus tôt au début du XIe siècle[51]. Démarqué de celui d'Odilon, ce texte sert à expliquer par une translation de la première moitié du IXe siècle la présence de toutes les reliques que Saint-Médard revendique. D'autres Mauristes ou héritiers des Mauristes pensent possible qu'Odilon soit l'auteur de trois sermons édités par Jean du Bois (m. 1626) du fait de similitudes entre le premier sermon et la Translation de saint Sébastien[52]. En vérité, c'est avec la Vie ca-

---

[48] *Annales Vedastini*, éd. G. PERTZ, *MGH, SS*, I, Hanovre, 1826, p. 524, l. 33-34. Les *Annales de Saint-Médard* (XIIIe s.), *MGH, SS*, XXVI, Hanovre, 1882, p. 518-522 connaissent des menaces danoises (898) et des invasions hongroises (917, 937, 954), p. 520, mais ne mentionnent aucun incendie de Saint-Médard en particulier.

[49] *Translatio s. Sebastiani*, *AASS OSB*, IV-1 (1677), p. 383-410.

[50] *AASS OSB*, IV-1 (1677), p. 411-414.

[51] *Translatio SS. Tiburtii, Marcellini et Petri ad S. Medardum*, éd. O. HOLDER-EGGER, *MGH, SS*, XV-1, Hanovre, 1887, p. 393-395. L'attribution de Mabillon s'explique par la présence en tête de cette Translation d'une lettre d'Odilon à Ingramnus qui est un décalque de la lettre qui figure avant la Translation authentique.

[52] Jean du Bois, *Floriacensis vetus bibliotheca benedictina*, Lugduni: apud H. Cardon, t. II, 1605, p. 136-153. L'éditeur parle des sermons comme d'œuvres de trois «anciens auteurs anonymes» distincts. Dans l'article «Odilon», RIVET DE LA GRANGE (1867), p. 173-176, considère que les sermons pourraient être d'Odilon, avec un glissement des constats faits sur le premier

rolingienne de saint Médard que les rencontres sont nombreuses, évidentes, continues et parfois littérales à partir du chapitre 9 de Vie. Seulement l'auteur du sermon parle en conclusion de l'auteur de la Vie qu'il suit méthodiquement avec éloges et à la troisième personne: «[l'hagiographe de la nouvelle Vie] n'a pas voulu en quoi que ce soit porter atteinte à cet homme illustre [Fortunat], qui avait publié auparavant une Vie métrique de ce père [Médard] d'un discours condensé à l'extrême: seulement ce que le premier avait effleuré comme en passant, le second considéra que cela valait la peine de laisser sa plume s'y attarder. Le rhéteur accompli n'a pas tout dit dans son récit: et ce sont ces choses que l'auteur récent s'est donné la peine de transmettre à la postérité, sans les avoir déformées par ses propres commentaires mais comme on les trouve mentionnées dans les antiques documents des anciens[53]». L'auteur de l'homélie ferait-il son auto-portrait en ces termes? Il est plus probable que le sermon ressemble à la *Vita* parce qu'il lui emprunte beaucoup; mais si la *Vita* est d'Odilon, il sera prudent de lui retirer le sermon, et inversement.

Une troisième attribution à Odilon dépend d'un manuscrit aujourd'hui conservé à Paris, composé de *libelli* réunis à Saint-Germain-des-Prés; le manuscrit contient un *corpus* hagiographique soissonnais d'une écriture du Xe siècle[54], soit une Vie de saint Grégoire inédite, la première Vie de Médard en prose

---

à l'ensemble des trois que Bois distingue. La *Patrologie latine* adopte la paternité d'Odilon pour les trois, présentés comme *Odilonis monachi sermones tres*, *PL* 132, col. 629B-642B; le deuxième, col. 634D-639D, est en l'honneur de Médard et Godard son frère, évêque de Rouen. Radicalement différent du premier, il s'agit d'une méditation spirituelle sans rapport historique avec le contenu des *Vitae* des saints concernés, sinon pour dire qu'il est providentiel qu'ils aient été consacrés le même jour. C'est par erreur que le troisième a été décrit comme un sermon: il s'agit des six premiers chapitres de la première *Vita* de Médard en prose (*BHL* 5864), qui adopte il est vrai le style homilétique habituel aux Vies épiscopales de Fortunat.

[53] *Nec in aliquo illi voluit viro derogare, qui ejusdem Patris vitam, metro jamdudum et arctissima edidit oratione, sed quae ille ac si in transitu tetigit, haec iste dilatare calamo, operae pretium duxit. Quae vero perfectus orator in relatione praeteriit, haec iste novus relator posteris tradere ad notitiam procuravit, haud suis commentis extorta, verumque veteribus antiquorum utcunque cartulis inserta.* Sermo 1, *PL* 132, col. 634A-B.

[54] Paris, BnF, lat. 13345 (X[e] et XIIe s.), cf. *Cat. Paris*, III, p. 191-193. L'homogénéité de la partie soissonnaise fol. 117-184v a été reconnue par LIFSHITZ (1992), p. 334.

(*BHL* 5864) puis la réécriture-*Supplementum* (*BHL* 5865) qu'on vient de décrire, une Vie de saint Godard de Rouen (*BHL* 3539) avec *Relatio* du transfert de ses reliques à Saint-Médard de Soissons (*BHL* 3540)[55], enfin la Translation de saint Sébastien due à Odilon. Selon Felice Lifshitz, le rapprochement de ces œuvres ainsi qu'une communauté d'inspiration impliquent que le dossier de saint Godard ait été écrit par Odilon[56]. Pour la *Vita* de Godard, le fait est très improbable: Godard et Médard sont réputés deux frères, mais la *Vita* de l'évêque de Rouen parle de Protagia sa mère comme d'une chrétienne romaine et de son père Nectardus comme d'un Franc païen converti au christianisme[57], détail qu'ignore la tradition sur Médard. La Vie de saint Godard, «notre vénérable patron archevêque du siège de la sainte Église de Rouen» (§1, p. 393) s'interrompt après avoir mentionné la sépulture du saint «dans la basilique Sainte-Marie, qu'on appelle à présent Saint-Godard» (§9, p. 401), sans jamais marquer intérêt, respect, ni révérence particulière pour Soissons ni Saint-Médard: en l'état, il semble qu'elle a été composée dans la province de Rouen. La *Relatio* pour sa part a été écrite par un hagiographe qui a la Translation de saint Sébastien sous les yeux: sa description d'Hilduin par exemple, en archichapelain que Louis le Pieux utilise pour toutes les missions de confiance – *ab imperatore Romam delegatus ignaviam quorundam compescuit*[58] – est empruntée à l'œuvre d'Odilon – *a piissimo Caesare ad quorumdam improbitatem compescendam... delegatus*[59]. La *Relatio* résume les démarches d'Hilduin et Rodoin pour obtenir des reliques romaines, en gardant quelques détails qui trahissent sa source[60]. À partir du moment où l'auteur a rappelé que Saint-Médard possède les reliques de Sébastien et Grégoire, il passe à l'éloge de Charles le Chauve: le roi, digne successeur de son père et dévot de saint Médard, a l'idée de réunir Godard et Médard

---

[55] Poncelet (1889), *Vita* p. 393-402, *Relatio*, p. 402-405.

[56] Lifshitz (1992) p. 337.

[57] *Vita s. Gildardi*, éd. A. Poncelet, «Vita sancti Gildardi episcopi Rothomagensis et ejusdem translatio Suessiones anno 838-840 facta», *AB*, 8 (1889), p. 389-405, §2, p. 395.

[58] *Relatio s. Gildardi*, ibid., p. 402, l. 18-20.

[59] Odilon, *Translatio s. Sebastiani* (*BHL* 7545), éd. J. Bolland, cap. 4, col. 279.

[60] Hilduin obtient des «lettres portant le seing de l'anneau royal», *Relatio* p. 402, l. 27-28 qui viennent de la *Translatio*, cap. 11, col. 279.

à Soissons. Il ordonne le transfert des reliques, Rouen n'obtenant de conserver que la tête de saint Godard, mais devant laisser aller celles de Remi et Romain de Rouen. On n'observe pas de trace évidente d'une communauté de style qui attribuerait la *Relatio* à Odilon. Il y a un intérêt certain à Saint-Médard au Xe siècle pour les reliques conservées par l'abbaye et leur histoire, mais Odilon n'est pas le seul hagiographe soissonnais.

II. Les Passions s'incrivant dans le « cycle de Riciovare »

A. La Passion de sainte Macre

La Passion de sainte Macre (*BHL* 5126)[61] appartient au cycle de Riciovare[62], qui apparaît dès la première ligne pour « faire disparaître la religion des chrétiens de Gaule » : dans la province de Soissons, il trouve Macre et leur dialogue, suivi des tortures puis de l'exécution de la chrétienne, constitue l'intégralité de la Passion conservée. Il n'y a ni prologue, ni précision topographique, ni aucun détail biographique sur la martyre, soit une structure brève qui rappelle directement la première Passion des saints Rufin et Valère[63] (*BHL* 7373). G. Henskens ne précise pas dans quels manuscrits il a lu cette dernière : peut-être dépend-il, comme Jean Bolland avec Macre, de manuscrits soissonnais transcrits par Nicolas de Beaufort (1554-1624). Par rapport à la première Passion des saints Rufin et Valère, la Passion de Macre est cependant un peu originale dans les discours prêtés à la sainte. Macre insiste sur la dimension purgatoire de sa passion : elle ne souffre pas pour rendre témoignage ou par une endurance exceptionnelle, mais pour obtenir la rémission de ses péchés (§ 2-3). Surtout, elle tient des propos extrêmes sur la médecine : alors qu'on lui a coupé les seins, Macre passe la nuit en prison ; un ange lui propose un onguent, qu'elle refuse : Dieu

---

[61] *Acta s. Macrae*, *AASS*, Ian. I, Anvers, 1643, col. 325-326.

[62] Gaillard (2014) ; Meijns, Mériaux (2009) pour l'histoire locale du culte.

[63] *Acta martyrii Ruffini* [sic] *et Valerii* (*BHL* 7373), éd. G. Henskens, *AASS*, Iun. II, Anvers, 1698, col. 796-797.

lui est témoin «qu'elle s'est toujours gardée de la médecine corporelle... Tu sais que je n'ai jamais usé pour mon corps ni d'un médicament, ni de quoi que ce soit de comparable que les hommes fabriquent et utilisent pour les malades... Si c'est Ta volonté que je sois guérie... que ce soit sur Ta seule parole que je guérisse» (§ 5). Ses seins repoussent donc et elle meurt brûlée vive. Selon la *Translatio* qui suit (*BHL* 5127)[64], le culte de sainte Macre naît au tournant des VIIIe et IXe siècle, quand une vision révèle à un certain Lendulphe le lieu d'inhumation de Macre à côté d'une église Saint-Martin, et que Dangulf fonde une église {à Fismes} où les reliques de la martyre sont transportées «sous le règne de l'excellent empereur très orthodoxe Charles». La répartition du texte en Passion et Translation vient de la présence d'une rapide doxologie après la mention de la date du décès de Macre «le 6 des nones de mars, sous le règne de notre Seigneur Jésus Christ, à lui l'honneur et la gloire pour les siècles des siècles. Amen». Néanmoins *BHL* 5126 et 5127 forment un tout cohérent et pourraient avoir eu le même auteur du IXe siècle. Flodoard utilise les deux, ce qui fixe leur terminus *ante quem* avant 950 environ[65]. L'entreprise de Flodoard constitue surtout une récupération rémoise du dossier: la Passion avait clairement indiqué que Riciovare avait retrouvé Macre «dans la province de la cité de Soissons» (§ 1), incipit que Flodoard rend par «La bienheureuse Macre mourut dans ce *pagus* de Reims sous le préfet Riciovare»[66]. Il y a une différence de but entre la topographie chrétienne de l'Église de Reims de Flodoard d'une part, qui le conduit à énumérer les sanctuaires de la vallée de la Vesle (Fismes, Bazoches), et l'hagiographe sans doute soissonnais d'autre part pour qui Macre est l'un des éléments d'un cycle qui rapproche Soissons de Saint-Quentin et Beauvais.

B. La Passion des saints Rufin et Valère

Le cycle mérovingien continue en effet de stimuler la production hagiographique carolingienne à Soissons. La première

---

[64] *Translatio s. Macrae*, AASS, Ian. I, Anvers, 1643, col. 326.
[65] *HRE* IV, 51, p. 453-454.
[66] *HRE* IV, 51, p. 453, l. 16.

Passion des saints Rufin et Valère (du VIIe siècle?[67]) est notamment réécrite par Paschase Radbert (m. *ca.* 860), alors abbé de Corbie, donc avant 851/852[68]. L'œuvre est précédée d'un prologue extraordinaire qui compare les reliques et les textes hagiographiques: «Est-ce qu'il n'est pas indigne que, tandis que les premières sont revêtues de châsses d'or et ornées de pierres précieuses, les autres restent dans un état déplorable et négligé?[69]» Paschase justifie ainsi la réécriture d'une Passion ancienne qu'il connaît dans un *libellus*, mais «dont l'histoire est sans queue ni tête du fait de son ancienneté ou de l'impéritie du copiste[70]». On n'a pas de mal à repérer ici la précédente Passion[71] pour la trame de laquelle Paschase manifeste en pratique le plus grand respect. Rufin et Valère sont contemporains de Quentin, Victoric et Fuscien, Crépin et Crépinien, tous Romains venus en Belgique seconde prêcher le Christ au IIIe siècle[72]; et comme dans toutes ces légendes du cycle de Riciovare, «le préfet des Gaules» est venu exterminer les fidèles de la région. Avant d'aller tuer Quentin à Vermand, Riciovare donc fait rechercher Rufin et Valère qui travaillent pour les greniers impériaux. Ils sont découverts dans la grotte où ils ont trouvé refuge, sont interrogés, torturés, exécutés et leurs corps, transportés en direction de Reims, s'arrêtent d'eux-mêmes à Bazoches où ils sont vénérés depuis. Paschase reprend à toutes ces étapes les mots mêmes de l'hagiographe antérieur[73]. Son

---

[67] GAILLARD (2014), p. 27: le VIIe siècle est présenté comme une hypothèse.

[68] *Passio ss. Rufini et Valerii* (BHL 7374), éd. J. SIRMOND, reproduite par J.-P. MIGNE, *Sancti Paschasii Radberti Abbatis Corbeiensis Opera Omnia*, PL 120, Paris, 1852, col. 1489-1506. Elle est d'ailleurs connue aujourd'hui dans un manuscrit originaire de Corbie, Paris, BnF, lat. 12602, fol. 142v-155r du XIIe s.

[69] PASCHASE RADBERT, *Passio ss. Rufini et Valerii*, col. 1490B/C.

[70] *Ibid.*, col. 1489B.

[71] *Acta martyrii Ruffini* [sic] *et Valerii* (BHL 7373), éd. G. HENSKENS, *AASS*, Iun. II, Anvers, 1698, col. 796-797.

[72] PASCHASE RADBERT, *Passio ss. Rufini et Valerii*, col. 1494B.

[73] Par ex. l'interrogatoire des martyrs par Riciovare, *Passio* BHL 7374, col. 1498 = *Passio* BHL 7373, §2, col. 797; les chaînes que les martyrs portent et qui leur semblent légères comme des plumes, *Passio* BHL 7374, col. 1503 = *Passio* BHL 7373, §3, col. 797; le détail des tortures avec chevalet? (*aculeus*) et fouet plombé (*plumbatae*), *Passio* BHL 7374, col. 1505 = *Passio* BHL 7373, §4, col. 797; même apparition angélique, mêmes couronnes offertes aux martyrs, même apparence «de roses et de lys», etc.

apport personnel consiste à ajouter une portée morale au texte antérieur, par une glose appuyée sur des citations bibliques: Rufin et Valère se sont cachés dans une grotte à l'approche des persécutions[74]? Ils ont bien fait de ne pas compter sur leurs propres forces, car «l'espérance naît des situations favorables, mais la prudence des situations contraires», etc. Une étape après l'autre, Paschase adapte ainsi le texte hagiographique initial, bref et plein de rebondissements concrets, à une compréhension spirituelle de la vie chrétienne, et surtout monastique: il ne faut pas placer son amour dans le monde, quelles qu'en soient les séductions passagères[75]; la patience et l'humilité de la Croix l'emportent sur tous les pouvoirs et toutes les violences[76]; les fidèles et les princes de l'Église ont mérité par leurs vices et leurs conflits mesquins la persécution de Dioclétien, symptôme de la colère de Dieu[77]. La mise en cause classique des dieux pervers du panthéon romain, adultères, parricides, incestueux, va cependant au-delà de la simple question morale: elle prouve que le paganisme est contraire même à la loi naturelle et à la raison[78]. À cause de l'opposition que Paschase construit entre l'âge d'or des débuts de l'Église apostolique et la décadence qui justifie la persécution, Gerda Heydemann voit dans la Passion des saints Rufin et Valère un texte de circonstance sur la crise de l'empire, comparable à la Vie d'Adlhard et à l'*Epitaphium Arsenii* du même Paschase[79]. S'il y a bien un contexte qui permet d'expliquer cette réécriture, c'est aussi la réflexion carolingienne sur les médiations légitimes du culte: parlant par la bouche des martyrs, Paschase polémique longuement contre les idoles (*simulacra*) et la foi dévoyée (*superstitio*) qui les prend pour des dieux[80]; il a pris soin en introduction de préciser qu'il n'était pas hostile au culte des reliques, tant qu'on ferait bien la différence entre une dévotion tangible tolérable et la contemplation de la sainteté qui seule est nécessaire. «Tout homme qui considère la chose avec sagesse comprend facilement combien elle est plus importante que les vêtements ou la poussière des corps, même

---

[74] PASCHASE RADBERT, *Passio ss. Rufini et Valerii*, col. 1497.
[75] *Ibid.*, col. 1505.
[76] *Ibid.*, col. 1499.
[77] *Ibid.*, col. 1492-1493.
[78] *Ibid.*, col. 1501 et 1502.
[79] HEYDEMANN (2011), p. 195-199.
[80] PASCHASE RADBERT, *Passio ss. Rufini et Valerii*, col. 1502-1503.

des saints: ils sont corruptibles, elle est inaltérable, etc[81]». Il combine de ce fait une instruction morale adaptée à des moines ou moniales, à un discours sur l'exercice de la raison en matière de religion: cet enseignement vise très peu le culte local des saints Rufin et Valère à Bazoches.

C. La Passion des saints Crépin et Crépinien

À côté de Notre-Dame et de Saint-Médard, Saint-Crépin de Soissons aurait pu être le lieu de rédaction de traditions hagiographiques: la Passion des saints Crépin et Crépinien (*BHL* 1990)[82] est cependant peu convaincante à ce propos. Paschase connaît son contenu: la Passion place aux origines de l'Église soissonnaise deux Romains laïcs, deux frères venus prêcher la foi chrétienne aux païens, et qui gagnent leur vie comme cordonniers. La Passion en tant que telle se comprend dans le cycle de Riciovare dont elle est un point d'aboutissement logique sinon chronologique: Crépin et Crépinien sont très vite confrontés au gouverneur fou qui obéit aux ordres de Maximin, puis à l'empereur lui-même, qui les fait soumettre à toute espèce de tortures. Comme Riciovare désespère de vaincre leur résistance, il se jette lui-même dans le brasier préparé pour les martyrs «et c'est ainsi par la pire des morts qu'il mit un terme à son indigne vie» (*Martyrium* §4, col. 536). Maximin cependant fait décapiter les deux frères. La Passion met alors en scène la préservation miraculeuse de leurs corps, transportés de nuit à contre-courant sur l'Aisne, puis réinstallés à l'endroit «où par la suite les chrétiens construisirent une grande église» (§7). En d'autres termes, le sanctuaire Saint-Crépin conserve à Soissons les reliques de deux martyrs insignes; il n'y a cependant dans la Passion aucun indice prouvant sa rédaction par un clerc du sanctuaire, ni aucun trait qui permette une datation précise sur critère internes[83].

---

[81] *Ibid.*, col. 1490.

[82] *Martyrium s. Crispinus et Crispinianus* (*BHL* 1990), éd. B. Bossue, *AASS*, Oct. XI, Bruxelles, 1864, col. 535-537; M. Gaillard, «*Passio Crispini et Crispiniani*», dans Goullet (2014), p. 311-323.

[83] *Contra* Gaillard (2014) qui avance l'hypothèse d'une datation haute (VIIe siècle?) fondée sur l'attestation du culte à la fin du VIe siècle et la pré-

D. LA PASSION DE SAINTE BENOÎTE D'ORIGNY

La Passion de sainte Benoîte en prose (*BHL* 1087)[84] a rencontré un certain succès au Moyen Âge; la base *BHL*ms en connaît 17 manuscrits; l'œuvre a été mise en vers (*BHL* 1088, avant le XIe siècle) et écrite en français (XIVe siècle)[85]; une version très brève a été rédigée pour s'intégrer à un légendier tardif (*BHL* 1089). Il faut dire qu'elle a une certaine allure bien qu'essentiellement remplie de lieux communs, avec son long prologue, ses catalogues de vertus, et le décalque, au profit d'un groupe de femmes, du schéma apostolique de diffusion de l'évangile depuis Rome. La Passion initiale est indissociable du monastère féminin d'Origny au diocèse de Laon, dont les origines sont obscures: on sait seulement qu'il a été l'objet des attentions des deux épouses successives de Charles le Chauve, les reines Ermentrude (m. 869) et Richilde (m. ap. 910/914). Sur l'avis de l'évêque de Laon Pardule (847-857), Hincmar de Reims a rédigé un acte de donation royal en faveur d'Origny à la demande d'Ermentrude[86]. En 876, sous l'abbesse Ricoara qu'a imposée Richilde[87], les reliques de sainte Benoîte sont placées dans l'église Saint-Pierre du monastère. C. Suyskens soupçonne que c'est dans ce contexte que la Passion de sainte Benoîte a été rédigée, ce que la datation des premiers manuscrits conservés rend vraisemblable[88]. Quand il a édité d'après le manuscrit Paris, BnF, lat. 8431, fol. 3-20, sa mise en vers sous la forme d'une Passion métrique de sainte Benoîte (*BHL* 1088), Paul von

---

sence de la *Passio* dans le «légendier de Turin», confectionné au début du IXe siècle et contenant nombre de Passions anciennes; cf. GOULLET (2014).

[84] *Acta fabulosa s. Benedictae*, éd. C. SUYSKENS, *AASS*, Oct. IV, Bruxelles, 1780, col. 219-222.

[85] HÉLOÏSE/HELUIS DE CONFLANS, Vie de sainte Benoîte d'Origny, à lire dans le Berlin, Museum Dahlem, 78.B.16 (XIVe s.), fol. 1r-57v; voir GARDILL (2005).

[86] Résumé de l'histoire d'Origny par une lettre d'Hincmar à Richilde, selon l'analyse de Flodoard, voir *HRE* III, 27, p. 350.

[87] Lettre d'Hincmar à Odon de Beauvais (860-881), sur le jugement qu'il a rendu avec Hédénulf de Laon (876-886) contre l'usurpatrice Ricoara, *HRE*, III, 23, p. 311, l. 1-4.

[88] Paris, BnF, lat. 584, fol. 118r-127, du Xe siècle; Vatican, Reg. lat. 488, env. 950-1050, fol. 117v-126: la Vie de sainte Benoîte est copiée après la Passion de saint Lucien d'Odon de Beauvais (*BHL* 5009), fol. 97-117.

Winterfeld pensait la lire dans une écriture du IXe siècle[89]; la datation de *BHL* 1087 s'en trouvait plus étroitement encadrée encore. Cependant, le manuscrit Paris, BnF, lat. 8431 date du XIe siècle seulement[90]. La séquence chronologique doit donc rester souple: rédaction vraisemblable de *BHL* 1087 dans la deuxième moitié du IXe siècle, versification au cours du Xe siècle après la rédaction du *Carmen de sancto Cassiano* (*BHL* 1633) de la fin du IXe siècle, à qui la Passion métrique de sainte Benoîte emprunte des vers[91]. Après un prologue passe-partout – et avant un épilogue rythmique guère plus original – l'hagiographe fabrique le passé qu'il faut à une vierge martyre: la romaine Benoîte a choisi la *peregrinatio* et la virginité consacrée avec onze compagnes; et comme elles ont entendu parler des saints Quentin et Lucien (§5), elles viennent chercher la palme du martyre en Gaule, où elles se séparent. Benoîte garde avec elle sa suivante Liobera/Limberia/Libaria et s'installe à Origny parce que les cultes païens y abondent. Elle est rapidement interrogée par gouverneur Matroculus et exécutée après des tortures qui n'ont pas pu la faire fléchir. Pour les décrire, l'hagiographe s'est inspiré directement de la Passion des saints Rufin et Valère (*BHL* 7373[92]: il remplace seulement Riciovare par Matroculus[93]. Son récit serait donc une redite sans intérêt ou une simple annexe au cycle de Riciovare s'il ne s'était pas lancé de son propre cru dans une polémique anti-juive plus originale. Dès leur première rencontre, Matroculus avoue à Benoîte être «de la race de Judas» (§10), un ennemi radical du Christ et de l'Église. Au cours de leur dialogue, la sainte l'exhorte donc à «préférer vivre et être sauvé en Christ, plutôt que partager la fange des juifs en ce monde puis être torturé pour l'éternité en

---

[89] *Carmen de sancta Benedicta*, *MGH*, *Poet. Lat.*, IV-1, Berlin, 1889, datation p. 178-181 et texte p. 209-231.

[90] Manuscrit rapidement évoqué dans DOLBEAU (2002), p. 133, n. 21. Pour les Vies métriques des Xe et XIe siècle, voir aussi TAYLOR (2005).

[91] *Carmen de sancto Cassiano* (*BHL* 1633), éd. P. VON WINTERFELD, *MGH*, *Poet. Lat.*, IV-1, Berlin, 1889, p. 181-196, d'après l'unique manuscrit Paris, BnF, lat. 12958, fol. 73-76v (fin d'un manuscrit qui ne contient pas d'autre texte hagiographique): manuscrit des IXe-Xe s., présent à Corbie au XIIe siècle; sur le *Carmen de sancta Benedicta* et le *Carmen de sancto Cassiano*, voir KIRSCH (2012), p. 898-905; voir aussi *infra*, p. 369, n. 6.

[92] *Acta martyrii Ruffini* [sic] *et Valerii* (*BHL* 7373), éd. G. HENSKENS, *AASS*, Iun. II, Anvers, 1698, col. 796-797.

[93] Comparer *BHL* 1087 §14-15 avec *BHL* 7373, §3-4.

enfer. Car c'est de nous, chrétiens, et de vous, juifs, qu'il a été écrit... 'Mieux vaut un chien vivant qu'un lion mort [Qo 9, 4]' Nous sommes le chien vivant, issu des Gentils; le peuple des juifs est le lion mort, séparé de l'alliance du Dieu tout-puissant, etc.» (§ 16-17). Le sujet n'appartient pas au cycle de Riciovare; dans le contexte de la province de Reims, il évoque en beaucoup moins subtil les préoccupations d'Almanne de Hautvillers et sa Vie de sainte Hélène[94]. À cause de la mention des saints Quentin et Lucien, et du recours aux stéréotypes du martyre sous les empereurs païens, la première Passion de sainte Benoîte appartient au contexte hagiographique des diocèses de Noyon, Beauvais voire Soissons.

III. Reims

A. Les Vies des saints évêques de Reims

L'hagiographie du diocèse de Reims est marquée entre le IXe et le début du Xe siècle par l'écriture de Vies d'évêques mérovingiens, par l'archevêque de Reims lui-même (Vie de saint Remi d'Hincmar) ou par des clercs anonymes qu'on place avec vraisemblance dans le chapitre cathédral (Vie de saint Rigobert). L'idée qu'on peut écrire une histoire de l'Église rémoise par l'hagiographie, à travers la promotion de certains évêques précède donc l'œuvre de Flodoard, qui la systématise.

1. La Passion de saint Nicaise

La Passion de saint Nicaise (*BHL* 6076)[95] n'entre qu'imparfaitement dans ce cadre d'analyse: bien que consacrée à un évêque de Reims fondateur de la cathédrale Sainte-Marie (fin IVe-Ve siècle) et intégrée dans l'*HRE* (*BHL* 6075)[96], cette Passion reste une interprétation morale de toute vocation chré-

---

[94] Almann de Hautvillers, *Vie de sainte Hélène* (*BHL* 377), éd. J. Pinius, *AASS*, Aug. III, p. 580-599.

[95] *Passio s. Nicasii*, éd. C. Narbey, *Supplément aux* Acta Sanctorum *des Bollandistes*, 2 (1900), p. 498-500.

[96] *HRE* I, 6, p. 72-77, qui rend mal compte de l'importance de la dépendance de Flodoard à l'égard de *BHL* 6076. Le chapitre de Flodoard est utilisé

tienne, sans ancrage historique réel ni portée institutionnelle, ce qui n'est pas le cas des autres textes composés sous les archevêques Hincmar (845-888) et Foulques (883-900). La Passion de Nicaise raconte comment il a été exécuté dans sa cathédrale par les Vandales; sa sœur Eutropie, vierge consacrée, a demandé à subir le même martyre. L'hagiographe écrit en prose rimée un texte destiné à la méditation, aux accents ascétiques, qui insiste sur l'importance de la chasteté et du combat spirituel contre le diable, et sur les dangers de la prospérité matérielle. Il manifeste une connaissance incertaine de la chronologie: plus qu'une histoire d'un Nicaise dont il ignore l'origine, les débuts, le contexte, il propose une réflexion sur le ministère épiscopal conçu comme sacrifice expiatoire[97]. Sans doute à cause de cette portée qui dépasse le cadre rémois, la Passion initiale, présente dans près de 20 manuscrits médiévaux, a connu un vrai succès et donné lieu à un bourgeonnement de textes apparentés moins répandus: une version abrégée sans prologue a été éditée par Surius qui la prenait pour la Vie originelle (*BHL* 6079) d'après un manuscrit non identifié[98]; une variante (*BHL* 6078) se lit avant le XIe siècle dans un manuscrit de Saint-Vaast d'Arras[99]. La Passion plus longue *BHL* 6077[100] réalise leur synthèse. Aucune de ces réécritures n'est une réinterprétation du destin de Nicaise: ce sont de simples adaptations aux contextes d'utilisation. À Reims même, le développement le plus intéressant se lit au début d'un manuscrit conçu à Saint-Nicaise au XIIe siècle[101]: on y lit une Passion du type *BHL* 6076 complétée de passages de Flodoard réagencés[102] et d'un récit de translation (inédit, *BHL vacat*); l'archevêque de Reims Gervais (1055-1067) a restauré Saint-Nicaise et fait revenir de Tournai à Reims les re-

---

comme *Passio* indépendante de saint Nicaise dans Paris, BnF, lat. 5333, fol. 239-247.

[97] Isaïa (2017).

[98] L. Surius, *De probatis sanctorum viris*, *December*, Cologne, 1618, p. 264-265.

[99] Arras, BP 199 (189), fin du Xe siècle, aux fol. 45-47. *Passio* éditée en annexe du *Catalogue des manuscrits hagiographiques de Namur*, AB, 1 (1882), p. 609-613.

[100] *Ibid.*, p. 341-342.

[101] Reims, BM 1411, fol. 1-10.

[102] Fol. 4: fin de *HRE* I, 6; fol. 4v: *HRE* I, 7 et retour aux vers du début de l'*HRE* I, 6 au fol. 5.

liques de saint Nicaise[103]. Les déplacements de ces reliques sont les seuls points d'ancrage chronologiques à peu près sûrs: comme elle ne mentionne pas la translation effectuée sous Foulques, la première *Passio* doit être antérieure à 900[104].

2. La Vie de saint Remi de Reims

Plus que le martyr Nicaise, l'archevêque Hincmar de Reims (845-882) promeut saint Remi (m. 533/535), quinzième évêque de Reims et contemporain du roi Clovis (m. 511), dont il élève les reliques à Saint-Remi en mai-octobre 852[105]. Il fait alors rédiger une Vie de saint Remi dont on devine le plan dans l'office de saint Remi des années 850 (av. 866): cette Vie liturgique réunit à la trame lacunaire classique de la *Vita brevis* (*BHL* 7150) du pseudo-Fortunat[106] l'histoire du baptême des Francs. Elle sert surtout de noyau à la très longue *Vita Remigii* (*BHL* 7153-7159) qu'Hincmar rédige lui-même entre 878 et 882 et accroît d'un prologue (*BHL* 7152) où il raconte l'histoire du texte: au récit des actions de saint Remi, connues par la tradition locale et la *Vita brevis*, par deux chapitres de l'*In gloria confessorum* (*BHL* 7151) et l'historiographie franque, Hincmar a ajouté des enseignements sous la forme d'extraits patristiques commentés, parfois originaux, parfois tirés de ses propres traités comme le *De praedestinatione Dei*[107]. La *Vita Remigii* se présente donc comme un texte à deux niveaux de lecture, le sens historique étant présenté en même temps que son interprétation morale ou

---

[103] OTT (2015), p. 175-177.

[104] Cf. *infra* sur les translations.

[105] ISAÏA (2010), p. 419-422.

[106] ISAÏA, «*Vita Remigii BHL* 7150», dans GOULLET (2014), p. 323-336.

[107] Même un hagiologue aguerri trouve le texte bizarre: «[la Vie] est si longue [dans le manuscrit principal qui guide l'édition de Suyskens pour les *AASS*] qu'elle occupe presque, testament de saint Remi compris, 66 grandes pages ou 132 colonnes, et ainsi composée cependant qu'à peine la moitié – et encore – relève de l'histoire, le reste étant des sermons pour l'instruction du peuple, intégrés à presque chaque chapitre, ou des éloges, adaptés à la célébration des vertus des saints, surajoutés.», ...*tam prolixa vero haec est, ut una cum S. Remigii testamento sexaginta et sex magnas paginas seu columnas 100 et 32 fere impleat; sic tamen ut vix aut ne vix quidem, media illius pars ad historiam pertineat, reliqua autem sermones ad instruendam plebem sint, singulis pene capitibus inserti, vel panegyrici, ad sancti virtutes pro suggestu celebrandas accommodati.* C. SUYSKENS, «Commentarius praevius», §24, *AASS*, Oct. I, 1765, p. 64.

théologique. Les deux niveaux exégétiques justifient la présence d'un guide de lecture (*BHL* 7154) qui promet d'indiquer par des signes marginaux quels passages de la *Vita* seront accessibles à tout lecteur, et quels passages doivent être réservés aux plus savants. La longueur du texte et son double niveau de lecture structurel expliquent aussi qu'il circule accompagné d'une table des matières détaillée (*BHL* 7153). Il est possible qu'Hincmar soit encore responsable de l'ajout en pièce jointe du testament authentique de saint Remi (*Vita Remigii*, cap. 32, *BHL* 7160) et des vers qu'il a lui-même fait inscrire sur le tombeau-reliquaire du saint (*Vita Remigii*, cap. 33, *BHL* 7161-7162). Ces ajouts font de la *Vita Remigii* un dossier hagiographique à elle seule. Son volume, sa complexité, son hétérogénéité ont très vite posé le problème de sa copie intégrale et des aménagements exigés par son utilisation liturgique. Bruno Krusch, qui a donné l'édition de référence de la *Vita Remigii* dans les *Monumenta*, le note avec malice: «...les copistes supportèrent mal le bavardage de l'auteur, ce qui explique que peu des nombreux manuscrits qui subsistent contiennent l'intégralité du texte avec tous ses éléments[108]». Krusch n'en connaît en vérité que deux, présents à Metz au xe ou xie siècle, soit un manuscrit de Saint-Arnoul qui a brûlé en 1944[109] et un recueil de Vies présent à Saint-Symphorien à la fin du Moyen Âge, mais sauvé par son exportation vers les collections de Berne[110]. On doit leur ajouter aujourd'hui le manuscrit conservé au Vatican, Reg. lat. 561, vraisemblablement un manuscrit de Saint-Remi des xie et

---

[108] *Loquacitatem autem auctoris... [non] librarii... satis patienter tulerunt. Itaque e multis qui supersunt codicibus pauci textum omnibus numeris perfectum continent* (éd. B. KRUSCH, *MGH, SRM*, III, Hanovre, 1896, p. 244, 10-12).

[109] Metz, BM 395, manuscrit à longues lignes, format carré, portant l'*ex-libris* de Saint-Arnoul, xie siècle pour KRUSCH, fin xe siècle pour J. QUICHERAT, dans le *Catalogue général des manuscrits des bibliothèques publiques de France*, V: *Metz, Verdun, Charleville*, Paris, 1879.

[110] Berne, Burgerbibliothek 168, x[e]-xie s., recueil de Vies de saints portant l'*ex-libris* de Saint-Symphorien dans une écriture du xive siècle, *Catalogus codicum Bernensium (Bibliotheca Bongarsiana)*, éd. H. HAGEN, Berne, 1878, p. 235-236, avec la *Vita Remigii* aux fol. 83v-142. Les collections de Berne doivent beaucoup de leurs manuscrits français à l'activité des humanistes Pierre Daniel et Jacques Bongars. Il faut rapprocher de ces deux témoins le légendier *per circulum anni*, auj. Paris, BnF, lat. 5308 du xiie siècle, qui vient de Metz et contient un texte presque intégral de la *Vita*, fol. 108v-140v.

XIIe siècles passé avec les Petau dans les collections de la reine de Suède[111]; il rendrait possible une nouvelle édition de la *Vita Remigii*. La faiblesse de cette tradition manuscrite intégrale contraste avec le pullulement de Vies abrégées, dont on est loin d'avoir fait l'inventaire. La plupart de ces copies partielles sélectionnent dans le texte les passages biographiques ou historiographiques (*Vita Remigii*, cap. 1-29), avec ou sans le prologue d'Hincmar, et jusqu'au récit de la translation de saint Remi en 852 (*BHL* 7152-7157): outre les pièces jointes, ces manuscrits excluent ainsi les chapitres spéculatifs (cap. 30-31, *BHL* 7158-7159) sur l'accomplissement par saint Remi de tous les types de sainteté illustrés par les neuf chœurs angéliques; elles conservent des fragments variables des commentaires. L'intérêt pratique de ces Vies amoindries pour être plus narratives est parfaitement illustré par un manuscrit copié à Fleury: la *Vita* sert d'*historia* à l'office de saint Remi qui la suit[112]. Les éditions modernes se sont donc heurtées à une tradition morcelée et leur qualité dépend du choix pragmatique de tel ou tel manuscrit: Surius n'édite ni la table des chapitres, ni le guide de lecture, qui ne doivent pas apparaître dans la copie dont il dispose[113]; Suyskens travaille à Bruxelles d'après un manuscrit incomplet, en l'abrégeant encore de tout ce qui «ennuierait le lecteur» — il renvoie à Surius pour plus d'information[114]. Saint Remi prit grâce à Hincmar une nouvelle stature: il est présenté dans la *Vita* comme le véritable refondateur de l'Église gauloise au moment de l'invasion franque, mais aussi le créateur du diocèse de Laon confié à l'évêque Génébaud, le président d'un concile général de lutte contre l'arianisme et le correspondant du pape Hormisdas, autant d'inventions qui font de Remi un archevêque métropolitain d'envergure plutôt qu'un petit pasteur rémois.

En fonction du renouveau du culte suscité par Hincmar, J.-C. Poulin a pu situer à Reims une réécriture de la Vie de

---

[111] STRATMANN (1994); DOLBEAU (1979), p. 353.

[112] Paris, BnF, lat. 5595, copié au Xe siècle à Fleury, en usage à Reims au XIe siècle, *Vita Remigii*, fol. 1-81 puis office de saint Remi fol. 81v-84v.

[113] SURIUS, *De probatis sanctorum historiis*, I, Cologne, 1576, p. 278-310.

[114] Bruxelles, KBR 7487-7491, passionnaire du XIIIe siècle, cote Q.ms.4 dans la collection des Bollandistes, pour l'éd. C. SUYSKENS, *AASS*, Oct. I, Anvers, 1765, p. 131-169; manuscrit et principes d'édition présentés p. 64.

sainte Geneviève (*BHL* 3338)[115] au cours des années 870: elle se distingue en effet par la datation de la vie terrestre de Geneviève à partir des épiscopats de saint Nicaise et de saint Remi. À la génération suivante, d'autres dossiers sont en effet mis à jour voire créés à partir de la *Vita Remigii*: son chapitre 16 devient une *Vita s. Genebaudi* (sans *BHL*) pour la célébration de l'évêque de Laon Génébaud; ses premiers chapitres servent à fabriquer une Vie liturgique pour la mère de Remi sainte Cilinie[116]; le culte de saint Montan dépend tout entier de ce qu'elle dit de cet ermite, qui prédit à Cilinie la naissance de Remi[117]. Enfin une Vie de saint Basle[118] longtemps attribuée à Séulf, archevêque de Reims[119], trouve son origine dans la *Vita Remigii*. Dans le chapitre (*lectio* 6) consacré à la description de la formation monastique de Basle, parvenu au terme de la pérégrination qui l'emmène d'Aquitaine à Reims mais pas encore retiré comme ermite, l'hagiographe a composé pour Basle un long patchwork du chapitre 4 du texte d'Hincmar[120]. Le texte s'en trouve daté d'après 882; il est en outre antérieur à sa réécriture par Adson de Montier en Der (m. 992).

3. La Vie de saint Rigobert et le dossier des translations rémoises

Un dossier hagiographique est composé à propos de l'évêque de Reims Rigobert sous l'épiscopat de Foulques (883-900), après l'élection d'Eudes (888)[121]. La Vie de saint Rigobert

---

[115] Vie E (*BHL* 3338), éd. et trad. ISAÏA-BRET (2020), p. 280-355. Datation par HEINZELMANN, POULIN (1986), p. 171, confirmée par HEINZELMANN (1992), p. 9-16, et Vie E p. 15-16; POULIN (1996).

[116] ISAÏA (2010), p. 587-591.

[117] VAN DER STRAETEN (1956) bien qu'il attache trop de crédit à l'ancienneté de l'office de saint Remi. La célébration liturgique de Montan n'est pas attestée avant Hincmar.

[118] Pour la première Vie de saint Basle, voir *infra* à propos de saint Sindulphe.

[119] *Vita s. Basoli* (*BHL* 1033a-b), éd. M. GOULLET, in EAD., *Adsonis Dervensis opera hagiographica*, Turnhout, 2003, p. 257-269 (*CC CM*, 198): Monique Goullet édite cette Vie parce qu'il s'agit d'une source qu'exploite Adson de Montier-en-Der pour sa propre Vie de saint Basle.

[120] À partir de *Nulla illi ex omnibus propensior cura...* jusqu'à *...ut ad uictoriam perueniret*, soit *Vita s. Remigii*, p. 265.

[121] Mention de la reine Théodrade, épouse du roi Eudes en *Vita BHL* 7253, cap. 28, éd. W. LEVISON, *MGH, SRM*, VII, Hanovre – Leipzig, 1920, p. 58-

(*BHL* 7253)[122] loue avant tout l'évêque d'avoir restauré la vie canoniale à Reims (cap. 2) et d'avoir su garantir la prospérité et l'indépendance financière du chapitre cathédral par la création d'un prototype de mense canoniale, un *communis aerarius* (cap. 3), ce qui permet de situer sans erreur son milieu de rédaction. Sans avoir l'ambition de la Vie de saint Remi, la Vie de saint Rigobert en suit le modèle : elle en a la table des matières détaillée, et le même équilibre entre *Vita* (cap. 1-19) et *Miracula* (cap. 20-28) intégrant récits d'élévation et translation par Hincmar (cap. 24-27), puis translation par Foulques (cap. 28) ; elle la cite à propos des dons accordés par les Mérovingiens à l'Église de Reims (cap. 4) ; elle mobilise de la même façon la correspondance pontificale comme pièce justificative (cap. 14)[123] ; elle copie comme elle le *Liber historiae Francorum* pour situer Rigobert sous le majorat de Pépin II (m. 714). Elle partage sa distance critique vis-à-vis du pouvoir laïc et contribue à la légende noire de Charles Martel (m. 741) (cap. 13), qui assiège Reims et expulse Rigobert, pourtant son parrain[124]. L'exil de Rigobert chez les Wascons puis son retour comme simple clerc sous Milo sont cependant moins importants pour l'hagiographe que l'état des lieux du patrimoine de l'Église rémoise dont la Vie est l'occasion : la Vie est en fait une leçon hagiographique sur l'inaliénabilité des biens ecclésiastiques (par ex. cap. 16) et leur saine gestion (cap. 18 pour l'*oeconomus*), dans l'exact prolongement des réflexions menées sous Hincmar[125].

Le dossier de Rigobert s'inscrit dans le contexte plus large des translations rémoises[126]. Les raisons conjoncturelles des raids normands de la fin du IXe siècle se combinent avec la politique d'exaltation du pouvoir archiépiscopal pour réunir des reliques immédiatement autour, voire à l'intérieur de la cité. Ri-

---

78, ici p. 77 ; translation des reliques, de Reims à Ennemain en Vermandois en 894 selon *Translatio s. Rigoberti* (*BHL* 7254), *ibid.* p. 78-79, rédigée avant le retour des mêmes reliques à Reims sous Hervé.

[122] *Vita Rigoberti episcopi Remensis* (*BHL* 7253), éd. W. LEVISON, *MGH, SRM*, VII, Hanovre – Leipzig, 1920, p. 58-78.

[123] La *Vie de Rigobert* renvoie à une lettre du pape Hadrien à l'évêque de Reims Tilpin ; pour le rôle d'Hincmar dans la réinterprétation de la correspondance entre Hadrien et Tilpin, voir SCHNEIDER (2010), p. 50-56.

[124] ISAÏA (2010), p. 542-545.

[125] Pour Hincmar sur les biens d'Église, voir PATZOLD (2007).

[126] SOT (1993), p. 209-211.

gobert, inhumé à Saint-Pierre de Gernicourt, est transféré le premier par Hincmar à Saint-Thierry, abbaye dont l'archevêque de Reims est l'abbé (14 juin 864) puis à Saint-Denis, dépendance du chapitre cathédral (14 juin 873)[127]; les mêmes reliques sont ensuite portées par Foulques à Sainte-Marie (883); la Vie de Rigobert est destinée à commémorer soigneusement ces déplacements et les évêques qui les accomplissent. Le même Foulques installe les reliques de saint Nicaise à Sainte-Marie, ce que la Passion de saint Nicaise ignore: elle situe toujours les reliques de l'évêque martyr à Saint-Agricole[128]. Ce qu'on appelle la Vie de saint Gibrien (*BHL* 3526)[129] est tout au plus un bref mémento sans diffusion manuscrite qui raconte comment un culte spontané s'est organisé et a gagné en importance sur la tombe d'un ermite *scot* mal connu, enterré à *Cosla* sur la Marne, au diocèse de Châlons. Le souvenir de miracles antérieurs s'est perdu, mais l'hagiographe est en mesure de citer les noms et le lieu d'origine des malades guéris à partir du règne de Charles le Chauve. Il écrit lui-même après qu'«au temps du roi des Francs Eudes», la petite église de *Cosla* a été incendiée par des Danois. Gibrien a sa place dans une présentation de l'hagiographie rémoise parce que les reliques de ce saint prêtre ont alors été réclamées par un comte Haideric à l'évêque Rodoard de Châlons (885-893); Haideric les a déposées au *vicus* de Bouzy (*Balbiacus*)[130], avant qu'elles ne soient placées trois ans plus tard à Saint-Remi. Haideric obtient alors de Foulques un droit de sépulture pour lui et sa femme Herisinde dans Saint-Remi[131]. Foulques enfin fait revenir dès juin 883, les reliques de saint Remi qu'Hincmar avait mises à l'abri à Orbais; cette fois, c'est un moine de Saint-Remi Rotgar qui célèbre l'action de son

---

[127] Saint-Denis semble être alors considérée comme l'église funéraire des chanoines. Sa destruction au moment où Foulques fait relever les murs de Reims explique le transfert des reliques de Rigobert, puis la refondation de l'église sous Hervé, voir DEMOUY (2005), p. 324-325.

[128] *HRE* IV, 8, p. 399.

[129] *Vita s. Gibriani*, éd. G. HENSKENS, *AASS*, Mai. II, Anvers, 1680, col. 301-302.

[130] Bougy (Marne, cant. Ay) plutôt que Balby (Ardennes, cant. Rethel) selon DEVROEY (2004), p. 826, n. 92.

[131] *HRE* IV, 9, p. 400-402.

évêque par une *Historia relationis* (*BHL* 7160) contemporaine des faits[132].

4. La Vie de saint Maternien évêque de Reims

Cette Vie (*BHL* 5677) a très peu retenu l'attention des Rémois. Flodoard écrit en tout et pour tout à propos de cet évêque qu'il situe au IVe siècle: « Après lui [Betausius], Aper, puis Maternianus, dont l'archevêque Hincmar rappelle qu'il a envoyé les restes mortels à Louis de Germanique, dans la lettre adressée à ce même roi à propos des reliques de ce même saint et d'autres[133]. » La Vie *BHL* 5677 que le chanoine ignore ou néglige est pourtant un texte long et dense de facture carolingienne[134]: tout le problème est de savoir s'il s'agit d'un texte rémois, ou d'une Vie rédigée ailleurs, par exemple dans l'entourage des évêques de Hambourg-Brême. Adam de Brême en effet date de l'épiscopat d'Anschaire (831-865) l'arrivée de reliques de saint Maternien de Reims à Heiligenstadt[135], ce que le contexte de l'épiscopat à Reims d'Ebbon comme la carrière d'Anschaire, ancien moine de Corbie, rendent très crédible. Plus tard, les mêmes reliques sont conservées à l'abbaye de Bücken (Basse-Saxe), fondée par Rimbert de Brême[136]. La tradition manuscrite connue des premiers Bollandistes oriente davantage vers la Germanie que vers Reims, puisque c'est « dans un manuscrit de Böddeken » au diocèse de Paderborn que Paperbroch a trouvé la *Vita*. Peut-être s'agit-il du grand légendier que les chanoines réguliers ont composé au XVe siècle et où puisent souvent les Bollandistes. Plus important est le manuscrit redécouvert à Hambourg qui ressemble à la reliure très tardive d'un *libellus* de saint Maternien du IXe siècle, pour former une col-

---

[132] Édition partielle de la Translation attribuée à Rotfrid par G. Suyskens, *AASS*, Oct. I, 1765, col. 170-172; histoire du texte et édition dans Isaïa (2009).

[133] *HRE* I, 5, p. 72; Sot (1993), p. 371.

[134] *Vita s. Materniani*, éd. D. Papebroch, *AASS*, Apr. III, Anvers, 1675, col. 759-763.

[135] Adam de Brême, *Gesta Hammaburgensis ecclesiae pontificum*, I, 18, éd. B. Schmeidler, *MGH*, *SRG in usum scholarum*, II, 3e éd., Hanovre, 1917, p. 25.

[136] *Ibid.*, p. 45.

lection de Vies de saints missionnaires de la Germanie[137]. La Vie de saint Maternien elle-même ne donne pas d'indication décisive sur son lieu de rédaction; elle ne sait rien en tout cas de la topographie rémoise. D'un point de vue thématique, elle construit le portrait d'un évêque à l'autorité irrésistible car surnaturelle: l'enfant âgé de huit jours rayonne de gloire au milieu de la nuit (§ 2), la même gloire qui le désigne plus tard comme évêque (§ 5 et § 7); il échappe au berceau à un incendie comme Daniel dans la fournaise (§ 3) et s'entretient familièrement avec des créatures célestes (§ 4, § 18). L'hagiographe remploie des motifs qui tiennent à la fois de la Transfiguration et de l'échelle de Jacob (§ 6) pour signifier, toujours par des manifestations lumineuses (§ 9), que Maternien jouit d'un contact direct avec le monde surnaturel; il est capable d'accomplir de nombreux miracles de son vivant. Ce n'est pas le portrait d'un saint ancré dans l'histoire, qui suivrait les étapes d'une formation scolaire ou cultiverait des vertus morales. La puissance de sa *virtus* épiscopale est démontrée par l'efficace de sa sentence d'excommunication (§ 11) et surtout par une confrontation avec un mage venu d'Afrique, Irénée, qui le met au défi de dompter cinq taureaux furieux (§ 12-16). Le duel public, où Maternien et Irénée démontre chacun sur le champ leur pouvoir par des signes, évoque directement les compétitions entre païens et chrétiens telles qu'on les raconte à la fin du IXe siècle dans les évêchés missionnaires[138]. La *Vita* se termine par la création invraisemblable d'une forte proximité entre Hilaire de Poitiers et Maternien. L'hagiographe n'en profite pas pour souligner l'engagement de l'évêque de Reims dans la promotion de la foi nicéenne contre l'arianisme, ce qui aurait eu du sens en Gaule, mais brode sur le sujet de la lutte contre le paganisme: «Les hérétiques, les magiciens, les devins, les sorciers, les augures et les haruspices, ils les vainquirent et les dominèrent; ils expulsèrent virilement les autres de leurs régions sous la condamnation et la sanction de l'anathème...» (§ 18). La tradition manuscrite comme le contenu

---

[137] Hambourg, Staats- und Universitätsbibliothek, Theol. 1579, 2e moitié du IXe siècle, avec la *Vita s. Materniani* fol. 1-8v; voir la description citée par J. VAN DER STRAETEN, *AB*, 118 (2000), p. 424: la *Vita* a été reliée avec la Vie de saint Boniface (*BHL* 1408) et celle de saint Swibert (*BHL* 7941).

[138] BÜHRER-THIERRY (2014); les manifestations surnaturelles (visions) rappellent aussi les débuts de saint Anschaire selon *BHL* 544.

de la *Vita* plaident donc en faveur d'une rédaction dans l'évêché de Hambourg-Brême dans la deuxième moitié du IXe siècle.

B. Autour des monastères bénédictins du diocèse de Reims

À Reims, il serait infondé d'opposer production hagiographique épiscopale et canoniale d'un côté, écriture monastique de l'autre. Les principaux établissements bénédictins du diocèse, de fondation mérovingienne, sont placés sous l'étroit contrôle des archevêques de Reims à l'époque carolingienne, pour des raisons présentées comme historiques dans les textes hagiographiques[139]: depuis sa réforme sous l'évêque Tilpin (748-794), Saint-Remi a ainsi l'évêque de Reims pour abbé – il s'agit de toute façon d'une ancienne basilique créé sur le lieu de sépulture du quinzième évêque de Reims; même situation à Saint-Thierry au Mont d'Or[140], que l'hagiographie présente comme un monastère fondé par saint Thierry sous la responsabilité de l'évêque saint Remi, tandis que Saint-Basle de Verzy aurait été fondé par un pèlerin attiré à Reims par la réputation du même saint évêque; Saint-Pierre d'Hautvillers passe pour une fondation de l'évêque saint Nivard (av. 657-673), dont la sœur sainte Berthe a créé l'abbaye féminine Saint-Pierre d'Avenay; Saint-Pierre d'Orbais est une création de l'évêque Rieul (ap. 689-av. 719). Pour ces grands établissements, le milieu du Xe siècle marque une nette césure, avec l'obtention progressive d'une forme d'autonomie institutionnelle (élection régulière de l'abbé à Saint-Remi en 945; réforme de Saint-Basle pilotée en 952 par l'archevêque Artaud[141]; restauration de la vie bénédictine à Saint-Thierry en 972). Jusqu'à ce tournant, des textes hagiographiques expliquent partout sauf à Orbais[142] les liens étroits entre monastères et évêques de Reims. Il importe de replacer ces textes dans leur contexte d'écriture.

---

[139] Sot (1991).
[140] Poirier-Coutansais (1974), p. 147-219.
[141] Demouy (2005), p. 297-298.
[142] Sot (1993), p. 438-447.

1. Les Vies de saint Thierry et saint Thiou

Le dossier hagiographique de l'abbé fondateur du Mont d'Or est composé de deux Vies de saint Thierry carolingiennes dont les relations sont très claires. La première (*BHL* 8060) est la Vie longue éditée par dom Mabillon[143]. Elle sert entre autres à situer dans quel contexte le roi Thierry (m. 534) fils de Clovis a donné «par un précepte revêtu de son autorité» le domaine de Vandières (*Vanderas*) à l'évêque de Reims Remi et le domaine de Jouy (*Gaugiacus*) à l'abbé Thierry en signe de gratitude pour la résurrection de sa fille; comme le roi Charles le Chauve (m. 877) voulait, dans son ignorance, donner le domaine de l'Église de Reims à son fidèle Angilram, l'évêque Hincmar l'en a dissuadé en produisant l'acte ou «charte-témoin» de Thierry. La Vie de saint Thierry *BHL* 8060 qui raconte tous ces détails est donc postérieure à la mort d'Hincmar (m. 882), mais antérieure à la composition d'un Office de saint Thierry par Hucbald de Saint-Amand[144]. Elle doit être datée de l'épiscopat de Foulques (883-900). De quelles traditions antérieures a-t-elle gardé mémoire? Saint Thierry a des traits qui ne sont pas ceux qu'on attend d'un abbé qui aurait été fabriqué pour l'occasion: il ne vient pas d'une famille noble, il a été marié ou presque, il fonde le Mont d'Or avec une femme, l'abbesse Susanne, comme s'il s'agissait d'une communauté double de type irlandais. L'existence d'un hypotexte mérovingien est probable[145]. Outre sa portée patrimoniale, la version carolingienne insiste sur la dépendance structurelle de saint Thierry à l'égard de saint Remi: Remi confirme le jeune homme dans son amour de la virginité consacrée, lui indique le lieu où il devra fonder son monastère, s'en sert comme d'un disciple doué auprès du roi Thierry, etc. C'est l'histoire des origines qui convient à une fondation placée sous l'autorité des archevêques de Reims. L'autre Vie de saint Thierry conservée (*BHL* 8059) est à l'examen un simple abrégé de la précédente, par un frère de la communauté du Mont d'Or[146]. L'abréviation est très imparfaite; elle conduit par

---

[143] *Vita s. Theoderici II*ᵃ (*BHL* 8060), *AASS OSB*, I (1668), p. 614-620.

[144] L'office est édité par CHARTIER (1995), p. 347-359.

[145] HOURLIER (1979).

[146] L'auteur s'adresse à ses frères, à propos de «notre Thierry»; il s'attarde à décrire la «dignité de ce lieu», *Vita s. Theoderici I*ᵃ (*BHL* 8059), Jean-Baptiste du Sollier reproduit en *AASS*, Iul. I, Anvers, 1719, col. 62-64, la Vie

exemple l'auteur à faire allusion à Marcard comme s'il s'agissait d'un personnage bien connu, oubliant qu'il a supprimé le passage où le père de Thierry était présenté. La Vie abrégée omet aussi l'épisode relatif à Vandières et Jouy ainsi que la résurrection de la fille du roi Thierry: elle y gagne une tonalité plus spirituelle, et beaucoup d'incohérences de détail. Sa présence dans un manuscrit de Saint-Remi de Reims (auj. Paris, BnF, lat. 13673, fol. 69v-80, qui pourrait être celui que dom Mabillon a consulté pour les *Annales*) date sa confection d'avant les xe-xie siècle. C'est cependant la comparaison avec l'*HRE* I, 24 qui est déterminante: Flodoard utilise les textes *BHL* 8060 et *BHL* 8059; l'abréviation a donc été réalisée avant le milieu du xe siècle.

Une Vie de saint Thiou abbé du Mont d'Or (*BHL* 8097)[147] figure dans un manuscrit au format hincmarien (Vatican, Reg. lat. 466, fol. 66-78v, xe siècle, avec additions au xie siècle), qui contient aussi deux pièces composées par Hucbald de Saint-Amand pour Saint-Thierry[148]; comme elle a été reprise pour l'essentiel par Flodoard[149], cette Vie rémoise est antérieure aux années 950. La *Vita* du deuxième successeur de saint Thierry n'est pas en harmonie avec le dossier hagiographique carolingien de ce dernier; destinée à la célébration annuelle de saint Thiou (§1), elle expose comment l'humble moine a été «établi abbé, avec l'accord de l'évêque, à la demande de la communauté des moines[150]», mais sans jamais faire mention de Reims, ni de Remi: Thiou, dit-elle seulement, «est entré dans le monastère du bienheureux Thierry» (§3). À première vue, elle fait le portrait concret d'un saint moine laborieux, capable d'aller rechercher un porc tombé dans un puits (§5); sans qu'il soit jamais question de son éducation, mais seulement du *topos* de sa naissance parmi les grands de ce monde, Thiou commence sa carrière monastique en travaillant la terre pendant 22 ans, avec un

---

éditée par Mabillon dans les *Annales OSB*, I, p. 681. L'hypothèse que j'avais formulée dans *Remi de Reims*, p. 575-581 d'une Vie résumant un hypotexte perdu partagé avec *BHL* 8060, est une complication inutile.

[147] *Vita s. Theodulfi*, AASS OSB, I (1668), p. 346-349.

[148] *Epistola de sancto Theoderico* et hymne pour le même: *Exultet Domino mente serena*, fol. 25; Y. CHARTIER, «Clavis operum Hucbaldi Elnonensis», *Journal of Medieval Latin*, 5 (1995), p. 202-224, n°10 et 18.

[149] *HRE* I, 25, p. 127-130.

[150] *Vita s. Theodulfi*, §4 p. 346.

attelage de deux bœufs infatigables et sa houe (§ 3); son araire fait encore des miracles (§ 7); c'est le saint thaumaturge d'un monde rural, pour lequel il a soin, sitôt élu, de faire construire une église Saint-Hilaire. Il se charge de la desservir, multipliant par deux le nombre des offices quotidiens[151]. Dans le détail, la *Vita* pourrait avoir gardé des informations remontant au VIe siècle qui serait celui du saint Thiou historique: elle mentionne ainsi le passage au monastère d'un «ambassadeur nommé Offo envoyé alors auprès du prince de ce royaume de la part des Austrasiens qui sont les Francs supérieurs» (§ 10) qui pourrait avoir existé à la cour de Childebert II[152]; l'hagiographe utilise cependant le vocabulaire typique du *Liber Historiae Francorum*[153], *a parte Austrasiorum qui sunt superiores Franci*, c'est-à-dire le vocabulaire politique du VIIIe siècle. Cela rend possible que la Vie *BHL* 8097 soit l'écriture carolingienne (IXe siècle) d'une tradition locale antérieure. Les deux autres versions presque jumelles de la Vie de saint Thiou (*BHL* 8098 et *BHL* 8099)[154] partagent avec *BHL* 8097 des citations littérales (dans le prologue notamment) tout en ne présentant pas les miracles dans le même ordre. Elles ajoutent deux éléments fondamentaux, l'origine aquitaine de Thiou (§ 3) et la fondation du Mont d'Or par Remi et son «bras droit et premier auxiliaire Thierry» (§ 5). Comme Flodoard est pour la lettre du texte très proche de *BHL* 8097, mais en présentant les épisodes dans l'ordre de *BHL* 8098-8099, l'hypothèse la plus économique est de penser que les deux dernières variantes sont des efforts postérieurs aux années 950 pour mettre la biographie de Thiou en cohérence avec la vulgate carolingienne sur saint Thierry[155]; Flodoard, il faut le souligner, ne connaît pas d'origine aquitaine à Thiou, ni ne présente le Mont d'Or comme une fondation épiscopale.

---

[151] Un résumé complet dans SOT (1993), p. 413-414.

[152] Peut-être Otto, référendaire de Childebert II que cite Grégoire de Tours (*Libri historiarum*, X, 19) à propos du procès d'Egidius de Reims en 590; SOT, *Flodoard*, p. 414, n. 156; *HRE* I, 25, p. 129, n. 6.

[153] *La geste des rois des Francs. Liber historiae Francorum*, trad. S. LEBECQ, Paris, 2015, p. 89, n. 186.

[154] *Vita s. Theodulphi abbati S. Theoderici in Or Remorum monte* (*BHL* 8099), éd. G. HENSKENS, *AASS*, Mai. I, Anvers, 1680, col. 96-99.

[155] Noter cependant que pour HOURLIER (1979), l'ensemble du dossier existait sous Hincmar. Sa datation de *BHL* 8098-8099 repose entre autres sur son utilisation supposée par Flodoard, qui ne me paraît pas évidente.

2. L'œuvre d'Almann de Hautvillers

À Hautvillers enfin, la présence d'un hagiographe exceptionnel en la personne d'Almann permet la composition de textes hagiographiques célébrant l'établissement: Hautvillers, dit Almann dans sa Vie de saint Nivard, est la fondation d'un évêque de Reims[156]. Hautvillers a le privilège d'abriter les reliques de sainte Hélène, mère de Constantin[157], mais aussi celles de saint Sindulfe[158]. Le nécrologe de Saint-Pierre fait de ces trois compositions les titres de gloire principaux du moine: «Il écrivit les Vies des saints Nivard, archevêque de Reims, Sindulfe, prêtre et solitaire, et de la bienheureuse Hélène impératrice, ainsi que la translation du corps de cette dernière depuis la ville de Rome jusqu'au monastère de Hautvillers, et d'autres œuvres[159]». Sans doute faut-il inclure dans cet «*et alia opera*» une Vie de saint Memmie évêque de Châlons (*BHL* 5909) que les moines de Hautvillers avaient moins de raison de citer mais qui n'en est pas moins l'œuvre d'Almann[160]. Selon les hypothèses d'E. Mainoldi, les différences de style qu'on observe entre ces textes s'expliquent par l'existence de phases assez distinctes dans l'œuvre du moine[161]. Almann écrit d'abord le dossier d'Hélène à la demande d'Hincmar de Reims[162], après avoir suivi l'enseigne-

---

[156] ALMANN, *Vita s. Nivardi ep. Remensis* (*BHL* 6243), éd. W. LEVISON, *MGH*, *SRM*, V, Hanovre – Leipzig, 1910, p. 160-171; *Clavis* I (1994): ALMA16, p. 112-113.

[157] ALMANN, *Vita s. Helenae imperatricis* (*BHL* 3772); le dossier comprend aussi une *Translatio* à Hautvillers (*BHL* 3773) et des *Miracula* (*BHL* 3774-3775), respectivement édités par J. PINIUS, *AASS*, Aug. III, Anvers, 1737, col. 580-599, col. 601-603, col. 612-617. *Clavis* I (1994): ALMA12, p. 109-110.

[158] ALMANN, *Vita s. Sindulfis* (*BHL* 7792) et du même, *Translatio* à Hautvillers (*BHL* 7793), éd. J. VAN HECKE, *AASS*, Oct. VIII, Bruxelles, 1853, col. 892-895, d'après *Vita s. Sindulfis*, *AASS OSB*, I (1668), p. 368-371. *Clavis* I (1994): ALMA17, p. 113.

[159] Cité par J. MABILLON, *Veterum analectorum tomus secundus*, Paris, 1676, p. 95.

[160] Sur Memmie, cf. K. KRÖNERT, *infra*, «Le diocèse de Châlons», p. 380-383.

[161] MAINOLDI (2009).

[162] «Sur la demande instante du seigneur apostolique Hincmar évêque de la cité de Reims», Almann conçoit d'emblée un triptyque hagiographique – *Vita, Translatio, Miracula*: il s'agit de «réunir... la naissance de sainte Hélène, le déroulement de sa vie et son terme, et comment elle fut portée de Rome

ment d'Heiric d'Auxerre: son texte est une démonstration de culture classique[163] à la préciosité grécisante et à visée théologique. Les Vies de saint Nivard et saint Sindulfe, plus simples et plus courtes, seraient aussi plus tardives, à placer entre la mort d'Hincmar (882) et celle d'Almann (904). Il ne faut cependant pas exagérer les différences entre ces textes: on retrouve dans la Vie de saint Sindulfe tout le raffinement d'Almann[164]; c'est moins net pour la Vie de saint Nivard, qui est avant tout, selon les observations de W. Levison, un décalque de la deuxième Vie de saint Wandrille (*BHL* 8805) et dont le style ni la méthode ne rappellent Almann.

La Vie de sainte Hélène mériterait une nouvelle édition, capable notamment de faire apparaître la dépendance de l'auteur à l'égard de deux sources historiques qu'il utilise différemment: d'un côté, il puise dans l'Histoire tripartite un récit de l'invention de la Vraie Croix sur lequel il brode assez librement; de l'autre, il emprunte scrupuleusement à Orose sa présentation de Constantin comme empereur des derniers temps, qui met un terme aux persécutions. Le recours à ces sources historiques s'impose à l'hagiographe puisqu'il est question de raconter la vie de la mère de Constantin; cependant, Almann ne s'embarrasse pas du contexte historique dans le détail; il réduit la guerre civile qui suit l'abdication de Dioclétien (305) à une opposition simpliste entre chrétiens et païens; il supprime des éléments gênants (Hélène est la concubine de Constance, non sa femme légitime). À la place, il développe une analyse typologique d'Hélène, femme, mère, épouse, qui est à la fois Marie et l'Église; de ce fait, parce qu'il construit des analogies constantes entre l'Ancien et le Nouveau testament, Almann tient à la fois

---

jusqu'à notre patrie, et par quels signes et miracles elle resplendit à notre époque», ALMANN, *Vita s. Helenae*, §2, col. 581.

[163] L'hagiographe justifie son entreprise dans le prologue en opposant les mérites et vertus d'Hélène [de Troie] que les Grecs ont chantée et de sainte Hélène, qui n'a pas encore eu de biographie à sa hauteur. Almann, *Vita s. Helenae*, §2, col. 581: il finit par expliquer que sainte Hélène est une descendante de la première (§10, col. 583). Almann évalue aussi la part de vérité que contient la philosophie platonicienne (§4, col. 581), etc.

[164] Par ex. utilisation d'*agonitheta* pour qualifier Sindulfe en §3, col. 893, avec le sens tardif d'*athleta*; voir aussi les variations théoriques sur le type de sainteté qu'illustre saint Sindulfe en §6, col. 893 et en conclusion de la *Vita* §10, col. 894.

le discours pénible des clercs contre l'aveuglement des juifs, mais tout en insistant sur la définition du judaïsme comme formation utile à la pleine intelligence du christianisme: sainte Hélène, selon Almann, est presque devenue juive, ce qui l'a préparée à découvrir la vérité de la Croix.

L'hagiographe n'avait apparemment à sa disposition pour écrire la vie d'un prêtre ermite du VIe siècle qu'une unique source, l'épitaphe de Sindulfe qu'il reproduit (ou invente?) en conclusion de la Vie (§10). Il compose donc un texte surtout spirituel sur les vertus de Sindulfe, et notamment son détachement de ce monde, sans aucun miracle. Almann utilise vraisemblablement pour le reste sans le dire le précédent de la Vie de saint Basle contemporaine. Une Vie de saint Basle[165] anonyme a en effet été rédigée après la translation des reliques du saint le 1er octobre 865 (mentionnée §13), mais aussi après le décès d'Hincmar (882) si c'est bien ainsi qu'il faut comprendre l'adjectif «vénérable» qui accompagne cette mention; et avant sa réécriture vers 991/992 par Adson de Montier-en-Der (m. 992). Mabillon, sans douter qu'elle soit l'œuvre d'un moine de Verzy, l'édite d'après un manuscrit d'Hautvillers non identifié. La Vie est sans prétention, et a peu circulé. Elle donne des coordonnées minimales pour Basle: noble né au *pagus* de Limoges, il est accueilli à Reims par l'évêque Egidius qui l'invite à rejoindre la communauté monastique de Verzy. Après une période de formation, Basle passe 40 ans dans un ermitage sylvestre, où il souhaite avant sa mort que son neveu Balsemius le remplace. L'allusion, non nécessaire, à la réputation de saint Remi pour expliquer le choix par Basle de Reims comme destination de sa pérégrination pourrait s'expliquer par une rédaction du texte à la fin du IXe siècle, dans le contexte de l'épiscopat de Foulques (883-900). Or on trouve dans la Vie de saint Basle et dans celle de saint Sindulfe des parallèles continuels: les deux hommes sont Aquitains; ils veulent suivre l'exemple d'Abraham et quitter le pays de leurs pères; ils viennent à Reims sous la conduite d'un ange; ils trouvent un endroit où vivre dans la plus grande solitude; ils y affrontent des tentations diaboliques; mais Dieu veut révéler leurs mérites au monde; ils meurent parvenus à un grand âge. La comparaison s'arrête là parce que l'auteur de la Vie de saint Basle n'a ni le talent ni la culture d'Almann, et

---

[165] *Vita s. Basoli* (BHL 1030), *AASS OSB*, II (1669), p. 65-67.

qu'il commémore aussi des miracles; elle témoigne, au minimum, d'une même inspiration, ce qui nourrit l'hypothèse d'une datation plutôt précoce (env. 882-900) de la Vie de saint Basle.

Avec la Vie de saint Nivard enfin, Almann donne un bon résumé des caractères de l'hagiographie dans le diocèse de Reims au IXe siècle: elle a pour sujet un évêque mérovingien réel (m. 673), qui a fondé un établissement bénédictin dans le diocèse (Hauvillers pour l'abbé saint Berchaire), et s'est illustré par sa noblesse et ses relations avec le pouvoir royal (la Vie commence par le situer sous Childéric II, m. 673; Nivard est choisi comme évêque de Reims par la faveur de Sigebert III, m. 656). La Vie sert aussi à esquisser une liste épiscopale, puisque Nivard est présenté comme le successeur de Lando (§4), le prédécesseur de son propre neveu par alliance Rieul (§1), le 25e évêque après Sixte et le 11e après Remi (§5). Elle raconte la composition du patrimoine de l'Église rémoise, y compris en invoquant des actes d'archive (§6), et la dotation d'Hautvillers décrit comme un monastère épiscopal et familial doté d'un privilège d'immunité (§9-10).

3. Les Vies des abbesses Bova et Doda

Les premiers Bollandistes ont édité une Vie de la sainte abbesse Bove et de sainte Dode de Reims (*BHL* 1435) d'après un manuscrit de la reine de Suède «n° 141», actuel Vatican, Reg. lat. 490[166]. La Vie n'a connu aucune autre diffusion à notre connaissance. Son auteur anonyme dit s'être informé auprès d'Ève et Gertrude, religieuses de Saint-Pierre de Reims, où les reliques des saintes sont conservées: elles lui ont raconté ce qu'elles tenaient elles-mêmes de sœurs décédées, puisque le très ancien volume qui contenait la première Vie des saintes Bove et Dode a brûlé (§2). On sait ce que vaut cette excuse en général: dans ce cas particulier, elle fournit l'occasion d'une description détaillée des trésors (disparus!) que contenait l'*armarium* calciné, avec une démonstration de compétence lexicale dans le meilleur goût du Xe siècle. Heureusement, l'auteur avertit son lectorat: il est inutile de chercher dans son texte «des expressions ornées de

---

[166] *Vita s. Bovae et Dodae*, éd. G. HENSKENS, *AASS*, Apr. III, Anvers, 1675, col. 283-290, dans le manuscrit Vatican, Reg. lat. 490, aux fol. 80v-95v (vers 950-1050).

fleurs de rhétorique [...], des mots enflés d'enthymèmes ou de sorites très obscurs » – ce qui ne l'empêche pas de placer encore plus loin « les eaux du Phlegethon » (§ 14) ou d'imaginer la formation de Bove « à l'école des lettres », *in gymnasio litterarum* (§ 4). La Vie, on l'a compris, dépasse de loin, en taille et en prétention, le niveau des Vies à usage liturgique. Bien qu'adressée par le prologue à tous les fidèles en général, elle interpelle régulièrement à partir du paragraphe 7 un « toi » qui pourrait bien être l'abbesse du monastère, ou l'une de ses religieuses. L'hagiographe lui destine un texte composite. Il déploie d'abord la glorieuse histoire d'un trio familial, ce dont le pseudo-titre de la Vie rend mal compte : Baudry (Baldericus) fonde pour sa sœur Bova, fille « du roi Sigebert qui était né de la souche des très nobles Césars » (§ 4), un monastère à Reims, dont elle devient abbesse. Bova y assure la parfaite éducation de sa nièce Doda que Baudry lui a confiée (§ 7). Baudry et Bova sont comparés à Benoît et Scholastique et pourraient même l'être à la Trinité tant ils sont unis dans une même dévotion avec Doda (§ 15). La mort édifiante de Baudry occupe plus du quart du texte, suivie de la mort de Bova, puis de Doda : ils sont enterrés dans une église Sainte-Marie *extra muros,* ruinée par le temps et les invasions (§ 20), d'où leurs reliques ont été rapportées à Saint-Pierre (§ 24). La méditation spirituelle, déjà importante quand l'hagiographe raconte les enseignements de Bova à ses sœurs sur le jeûne ou l'humilité, prend une place prépondérante dans les trois récits successifs des trépas admirables. Le début du texte en revanche rappelle les épisodes les plus romanesques de l'hagiographie mérovingienne. Bova élève Doda qui est promise en mariage à un grand noble (§ 7). Quand son fiancé vient la chercher, il découvre que Bova a imposé le voile en tout hâte à Doda pour lui permettre de suivre sa vocation de moniale : il reste brièvement paralysé pour avoir voulu la récupérer de force. Converti et guéri, il accorde au monastère les biens qu'il destinait à la dot de sa fiancée, avant de devenir lui-même moine (§ 9-10). C'est l'occasion inattendue d'une mise au point sur le patrimoine monastique : « [Le fiancé] accorda donc à ce monastère ces dons dont il a été question et bien d'autres, que la même église détient encore ; et pour qu'on ne juge pas sans aucune importance l'ensemble de ces biens qui t'ont été assignés, sont cités en particulier quelques-uns que, pour servir à rappeler tous les autres, nous avons énumérés sur ce feuillet seulement, de peur qu'accumulés en trop grand nombre, ils ne te causent de l'ennui lors de ta lecture, à savoir Nogent l'Abbesse... et Vaux-Montreuil.» (§11). Sous sa forme actuelle, la Vie *BHL* 1435 ressemble donc à l'écriture tardive d'une première tradition carolingienne typique de la manière rémoise (relecture d'un passé mérovingien; consolidation du patrimoine monastique par l'hagiographie). Fait remarquable, elle est en désaccord partiel avec l'Histoire de Flodoard: le chanoine connaît Baudry et sa sœur Bova, Doda leur nièce et leur famille royale, mais raconte comment le fiancé éconduit «est mort, dit-on, les vertèbres rompues, d'être tombé de cheval dans son emportement»; il pense que Doda a succédé à Bova comme abbesse, et qu'une révélation a été nécessaire pour faire connaître l'emplacement de leurs tombes[167]. C'est un argument en faveur d'une écriture de la Vie *BHL* 1435 après 952, mais pas une explication des choix qu'aurait alors effectués l'hagiographe.

C. Flodoard hagiographe

Déjà évoqué à propos de son Histoire de l'Église de Reims, le chanoine Flodoard est aussi l'auteur d'une immense épopée hagiographique *De triumphis Christi*, en 19 livres, 302 chapitres et 19939 vers[168]. Dans cet étonnant ouvrage dont on attend encore l'édition scientifique[169], Flodoard relate «les triomphes du Christ» à travers ses saints, en Palestine (3 livres, 2940 vers), à Antioche (2 livres 2490 vers) et en Italie (14 livres, 14509 vers). Selon P. C. Jacobsen[170], il a commencé à écrire vers 925, ce qui en fait l'œuvre de jeunesse d'un excellent élève. Flodoard systématise les expérimentations hagiographiques du IXe siècle, qui

---

[167] *HRE* IV, 38, p. 439; Sot (1993), p. 332-335.
[168] *PL* 135, col. 595-886.
[169] Denis Muzerelle a consacré une partie de sa thèse de l'École des Chartes à l'édition des livres I-IV et XII de la partie sur l'Italie, édition qui n'a pas été publiée et reste difficilement accessible, cf. Muzerelle (1969). Parmi les travaux récents, la thèse de Julie Leyronas sur les saints d'Antioche insiste sur les incohérences métriques du texte imprimé, qui rendent mal compte des compétences poétiques de Flodoard, et suggère de bonnes corrections.
[170] Jacobsen (1978); voir aussi le compte rendu par H. Platelle, *Cahiers de civilisation médiévale*, 24 (1981), p. 298-300, auquel nous empruntons en partie les termes de ce paragraphe, et l'analyse de Kirsch (2012), p. 861-866.

visaient à inclure dans une trame historique établie scientifiquement les exploits des saints tardo-antiques: le propos est théologique et vise à révéler l'organisation providentielle de l'histoire du monde. La proximité intellectuelle avec le travail d'Almann de Hautvillers sur Hélène est patente. Flodoard utilise donc les grands classiques historiographiques, la traduction par Rufin de l'Histoire ecclésiastique d'Eusèbe, la traduction par Cassiodore de l'Histoire tripartite, les Sept livres contre les païens d'Orose, le *Liber Pontificalis*; il a puisé également dans les œuvres de Grégoire de Tours et de Grégoire le Grand, dans le *De viris illustribus* de Jérôme, le martyrologe d'Usuard et les Fausses décrétales. En systématisant le schéma providentialiste de ses sources, et notamment d'Orose, il explique toute l'histoire de l'empire romain depuis la naissance du Christ par l'orthodoxie des empereurs. Outre sa forme poétique, l'originalité de l'œuvre tient à l'organisation géographique de sa matière, ce dont les titres des chapitres ne rendent pas bien compte: la démarche de Flodoard rappelle ici celle de Grégoire de Tours cartographiant les sanctuaires, notamment dans l'*In gloria confessorum*. Comme chez Grégoire, la chronologie s'en trouve malmenée au profit d'une structuration encyclopédique de l'œuvre hagiographique[171].

Bibliographie

Bührer-Thierry, G., «Qui est le dieu le plus fort? La compétition entre païens et chrétiens en Scandinavie au IXe siècle d'après la *Vita Anskarii*», in *Aux marges du monde germanique. L'évêque, le prince, les païens (VIIIe-XIe siècles)*, Turnhout, 2014, p. 223-236.

Chartier, Y., *L'œuvre musicale de Hucbald de Saint-Amand. Les compositions et le traité de musique*, Montréal – Paris, 1995

de Gaiffier, B., «Les sources latines d'un miracle de Gautier de Coincy: l'apparition de sainte Léocadie à saint Ildefonse», *AB*, 71 (1953), p. 100-132.

Delanchy, Abbé, «Le siècle des *rectores*», in D. Defente, dir., *Saint-Médard. Trésors d'une abbaye royale*, Paris, 1997, p. 83-98.

—, «À la conquête de l'exemption», *Ibid.*, p. 101-121.

Demouy, P., *Genèse d'une cathédrale*, Langres, 2005, p. 324-325.

---

[171] Kirsch (2012), p. 864.

DEVISSE, J., *Hincmar, archevêque de Reims*, Genève, 1975.

DEVROEY, J.-P., «La *villa Floriacus* et la présence de l'abbaye des Fossés en Rémois durant le haut Moyen Âge», *Revue belge de philologie et d'histoire*, 82 (2004), p. 809-838.

DOLBEAU, F., «Un exemple peu connu de conte hagiographique. La Passion des saints Pérégrin Mathorat et Viventien», *AB*, 76 (1979), p. 337-354.

—, «Un catalogue fragmentaire des manuscrits de Saint-Remi de Reims au XIIIe siècle», *Recherches augustiniennes et patristiques*, 23 (1988), p. 213-243.

—, «Hagiographie latine et prose rimée. Deux exemples de Vies épiscopales rédigées au XIIe siècle», *Sacris Erudiri*, 32 (1991), p. 223-268.

—, «Un domaine négligé de la littérature médiolatine: les textes hagiographiques en vers», *Cahiers de civilisation médiévale*, 45 (2002), p. 129-139.

—, «Notes prises à Saint-Remi de Reims par Mabillon et Ruinart», in «Quelques instruments de travail chez les Mauristes», *Comptes rendus des séances de l'Académie des Inscriptions et Belles-Lettres*, 151 (2007), p. 1729-1778.

GAILLARD, M., «Un 'cycle' hagiographique du haut Moyen Âge en Gaule septentrionale: les *Passions* des martyrs de Riciovare», *Hagiographica*, 21 (2014), p. 1-27.

GARDILL, I., *Sancta Benedicta. Missionarin, Märtyrerin, Patronin. Der Prachtcodex aus dem Frauenkloster Sainte-Benoîte in Origny*, Petersberg, 2005.

GERMAIN, M. *Histoire de l'abbaye royale de Notre Dame de Soissons, de l'ordre de saint Benoît... par un religieux bénédictin de la congrégation de Saint Maur*, Paris, 1675.

HEINZELMANN, M., «Manuscrits hagiographiques et travail des hagiographes: l'exemple de la tradition manuscrite des Vies anciennes de sainte Geneviève de Paris», in ID., dir., *Manuscrits hagiographiques et travail des hagiographes*, Sigmaringen, 1992 (Beihefte der Francia, 24).

—, «L'hagiographie mérovingienne. Panorama des documents potentiels», in M. GOULLET – M. HEINZELMANN – C. VEYRARD-COSME, dir., *L'hagiographie mérovingienne à travers ses réécritures*, Ostfildern, 2010, p. 27-82 (Beihefte der Francia, 71).

HEYDEMANN, G., «Relics and Text. Hagiography and autority in Ninth-Century Francia», *An Age of Saints? Power, Conflict and Dissent in Early Medieval Christianity*, éd. P. SARRIS – M. DAL SANTO, Leiden – Boston, 2011, p. 187-204.

Hourlier, J., «Le monastère de Saint-Thierry aux époques mérovingienne et carolingienne», in M. Bur, éd., *Saint-Thierry, une abbaye du VIe au XXe siècle*, Saint-Thierry, 1979, p. 15-38.

Isaïa, M.-C., «Nous sommes deux sœurs jumelles: Soissons, suffragante de Reims in l'hagiographie (XIe et XIIe s.)», *Publications de l'Académie Nationale de Reims*, 177 (2008), p. 337-352.

—, «Retour à Reims. L'*Historia relationis* de Rotgar de Saint-Remi. Édition critique et commentaire», in M. Goullet et al., *Prava pro magnis munera, Études de littéraire tardo-antique et médiévale offertes à François Dolbeau*, Turnhout, 2009, p. 453-494.

—, *Remi de Reims. Mémoire d'un saint, histoire d'une Église*, Paris, 2010.

—, «Saint Nicaise évêque de Reims et les barbares (IXe-Xe siècle)», in E. Bozoky, éd., *Des saints et des barbares*, Rennes, 2017, p. 53-67.

— et Bret, F., *Vie de sainte Geneviève*, Paris, 2020 (Sources chrétiennes, 610).

Judic, B., «Le culte de saint Grégoire le Grand et les origines de l'abbaye de Munster en Alsace», in *L'hagiographie du haut Moyen Âge en Gaule du Nord*, éd. M. Heinzelmann, Stuttgart, 2001, p. 263-295 (Beihefte der Francia, 52).

Kaiser, R., *Untersuchungen zur Geschichte der Civitas und Diözese Soissons in römischer und merowingischer Zeit*, Bonn, 1973.

Kirsch, W., *Laudes sanctorum. Geschichte der hagiographischen Versepik vom IV. bis X. Jahrhundert*, II: *Entfaltung (VIII.-X. Jahrhundert)*, 2 vol., Stuttgart, 2012 (Quellen und Untersuchungen zur lateinischen Philologie des Mittelalters, 14).

Lake, J., *Richer of Saint-Rémi. The Methods and Mentality of a Tenth-century historian*, Washington, D.C., 2013.

Lifshitz, F., «The 'exodus of holy bodies' reconsidered: the translation of the relics of St. Gildard of Rouen to Soissons», *AB*, 110 (1992) p. 329-340.

Lusse, J., *Laon et le Laonnois du Ve au Xe siècle. Naissance d'une cité*, Nancy, 1992.

Mainoldi, E. S., «Una proposta di nuova attribuzione ad Almanno di Hautvillers», *Archives d'histoire doctrinale et littéraire du Moyen Âge*, 76 (2009), p. 7-28.

Meijns, B. – Mériaux, C., «Le cycle de Rictiovar et la topographie chrétienne des campagnes septentrionales à l'époque mérovingienne», in D. Paris-Poulain – D. Istria – S. Nardi-Combescure, dir., *Les premiers temps chrétiens dans le territoire de la France actuelle. Hagiographie, épigraphie et archéologie*, Rennes, 2009, p. 19-33 (Archéologie et culture).

Müller, E., «Die Nithard-Interpolation und die Urkunden und Legendenfälschungen im St. Medarduskloster bei Soissons», *Neues Archiv*, 34 (1909), p. 683-722.

MUZERELLE, D., « Flodoard, *De triumphis christi apud Italiam*. Étude des sources. Édition des livres I-IV et XII », in *Positions des thèses de l'École des Chartes* (1969), p. 109-112.

OTT, J. S., « Educating the bishop: models of episcopal authority and conduct in the hagiography of early twelfth-century Soissons », in S. N. VAUGHN – J. RUBENSTEIN, éd., *Teaching and Learning in Northern Europe*, Turnhout, 2006, p. 216-253.

—, *Bishops, Authority and Community in Northwestern Europe, c. 1050-1150*, Cambridge, 2015 (Cambridge Studies in Medieval Life and Thought. Fourth Series, 102).

PATZOLD, S., « Den Raum der Diözese modellieren? Zum Eigenkirchen-Konzept und zu den Grenzen der *potestas episcopalis* in Karolingerreich », in P. DEPREUX – F. BOUGARD – R. LE JAN, dir., *Les élites et leurs espaces. Mobilité, rayonnement, domination (VIe-XIe siècle)*, Turnhout, 2007, p. 225-245.

POIRIER-COUTANSAIS, F., *Les abbayes bénédictines du diocèse de Reims*, Paris, 1974 (Gallia monastica, 1).

POULIN, J.-C., « Geneviève, Clovis et Remi: entre politique et religion », in M. ROUCHE, éd., *Clovis. Histoire et Mémoire*, t. 1, Paris, 1996, p. 331-348.

REIMITZ, H. « The social logic of historiographical *compendia* in the Carolingian period », in O. KANO, éd., *Herméneutique du texte d'histoire*, Nagoya, 2012, p. 17-28.

REINHOLD, K., « Aspects de l'histoire de la *civitas Suessionum* et du diocèse de Soissons aux époques romaine et mérovingienne », *Cahiers archéologiques de Picardie*, 1 (1974), p. 115-122.

RIVET DE LA GRANGE, A., *Histoire littéraire de la France*, VI, rééd. Paris, 1867.

ROBERTS, E., « Flodoard, the will of St Remigius and the see of Reims in the tenth Century », *Early Medieval Europe*, 22 (2014), p. 201-230.

—, « Hegemony, rebellion and history. Flodoard's *Historia Remensis ecclesiae* in Ottonian perspective », *Journal of Medieval History*, 42 (2016), p. 155-176.

SCHNEIDER, O., *Erzbischof Hinkmar und die Folgen: der vierhundertjährige Weg historischer Erinnerungsbilder von Reims nach Trier*, Berlin, 2010, p. 50-56

SOT, M., « La fonction du couple saint évêque / saint moine dans la mémoire de l'Église de Reims au Xe siècle », in *Les fonctions des saints dans le monde occidental (IIIe-XIIIe siècle)*, Rome, 1991, p. 225-240.

—, *Un historien et son Église. Flodoard de Reims*, Paris, 1993.

STONE, R. – WEST, C., dir., *Hincmar of Rheims. Life and work*, Manchester, 2015.

STRATMANN, M., «Wer weihte Hinkmar von Reims?», *Deutsches Archiv für Erforschung des Mittelalters*, 46 (1990), p. 164-172.

—, *Hinkmar von Reims als Verwalter von Bistum und Kirchenprovinz*, Sigmaringen, 1991.

—, «Die *Historia Remensis ecclesiae*. Flodoards Umgang mit seinen Quellen», *Filologia mediolatina*, 1 (1994), p. 111-129.

TAYLOR, A., «Just like a mother bee. Reading and writing *Vitae metricae* around the Year 1000», *Viator*, 36, 2005, p. 119-148.

VAN DER STRAETEN, J., «Saint Montan ermite honoré en Thiérache», *AB*, 74 (1956), p. 370-404.

VAN 'T SPIJKER, I., «Gallia du Nord et de l'Ouest. Les provinces ecclésiastiques de Tours, Rouen, Reims (950-1130)», *Hagiographies*, II (1996), p. 239-290.

L'écriture hagiographique dans le diocèse de Noyon (env. 750-950)

par

Paul CHAFFENET et Michèle GAILLARD

I. LES RÉÉCRITURES CAROLINGIENNES. – A. La Vie de saint Éloi.– B. Les Passions de saint Quentin (en vers et en prose)
II. DES TEXTES ORIGINAUX – A. Autour du culte de saint Quentin. – B. Les miracles de saint Fursy. – C. Le dossier hagiographique de sainte Hunégonde d'Homblières.
III. LA POURSUITE DE L'ACTIVITÉ HAGIOGRAPHIQUE AU MOYEN ÂGE CENTRAL.
BIBLIOGRAPHIE.

Dans le diocèse de Noyon, pour l'époque étudiée, l'écriture hagiographique reste une célébration des temps anciens (époque des persécutions et époque mérovingienne): aucun saint contemporain ne fait l'objet d'un culte et même les récits nouvellement écrits situent leurs héros à l'époque mérovingienne. Les récits hagiographiques antérieurs font l'objet de réécritures, en prose ou en vers, visant à les remettre au goût du jour. La rédaction de récits de translation et de miracles témoigne également de la vitalité de ces cultes anciens.

I. LES RÉÉCRITURES CAROLINGIENNNES
A. LA VIE DE SAINT ÉLOI

À l'époque carolingienne, un certain nombre de récits hagiographiques concernant des saints parmi les plus importants du diocèse font l'objet de réécritures. Tel est le cas de la Vie de saint Éloi dont deux réécritures sont connues: *BHL* 2477, conservée dans un manuscrit de Chartres du Xe/XIe siècle (détruit) et dans le manuscrit 48108 de la Bibliothèque royale de Bruxelles, du XIIe siècle[1] ainsi qu'une réécriture en vers, sans doute de l'époque carolingienne, dont le plus ancien manuscrit (Bibliothèque royale de Bruxelles, 5374-5375) est daté du IXe siècle[2]; il est probable que ce poème soit dû à la plume d'un moine de Saint-Éloi de Noyon[3].

B. Les Passions de saint Quentin (en vers et en prose).

Les textes les plus nombreux ont trait à saint Quentin dont le culte se développe considérablement au IXe siècle; ils ont été tout particulièrement étudiés par J.-L. Villette[4]. La deuxième version de la *Passio et Inventio Sancti Quintini* (*BHL* 7005-7006-7007) a probablement été rédigée au IXe siècle puisque le plus ancien manuscrit conservé est daté du Xe siècle (Paris, BnF, n.a.lat. 2164); il s'agit d'une amplification de la *Passio et Inventio* rédigée à l'époque mérovingienne (*BHL* 6999-7004)[5] mais la trame narrative reste inchangée. La troisième version (*BHL* 7008-7009), de taille intermédiaire entre la première et la seconde, se distingue par l'augmentation du nombre des compagnons de Quentin, qui passe de un à onze; la date de rédaction est difficile à préciser, puisque le manuscrit le plus ancien (Orléans, BM 197) est également daté du Xe siècle, mais elle est sans aucun doute postérieure à l'écriture de la *Passio Fusciani et Victorici* à laquelle elle emprunte la liste des disciples et dont le plus ancien manuscrit est du VIIIe siècle (Paris, BnF, lat. 12598). Au IXe siècle ont également été rédigées des pièces en vers (*BHL* 7010 et 7016): la plus récente (*BHL* 7016) a été dédiée

---

[1] http://www.manuscrits-de-chartres.fr/fr/manuscrits/chartres-bm-ms-27; description dans *Cat. Bruxelles*, II, p. 419, 54°. Parmi les Vies tardives, B. Krusch (*MGH, SRM*, IV, Hanovre, 1902, p. 657) évoque aussi celle (*BHL* 2477b), contenue dans Paris, BnF, lat. 11759 (fol. 267-277), du XIVe siècle, mais il est impossible d'en dater la rédaction.

[2] Édition dans *Cat. Bruxelles*, I, p. 470-483 et éd. K. Strecker, *MGH, Poet. Lat.*, IV-2, Berlin, 1923, p. 787-806.

[3] *Ibid.*, p. 784-785.

[4] Villette (1999), Villette-Gaillard (2011); ces articles sont issus de la thèse restée inédite de Villette (1982).

[5] Voir Gaillard (2014).

à Otger, chanoine de Saint-Quentin, probablement avant son élévation à l'épiscopat d'Amiens vers 890[6].

II. Des textes originaux

A. Autour du culte de saint Quentin

Outre ces réécritures, Quentin est l'objet de deux récits originaux aux IXe-Xe siècles, le *Liber miraculorum* (BHL 7017-7018) et le *Sermo in tumulatione ss. Quintini, Cassiani et Victorici* (BHL 7020).

Le *Liber miraculorum* (BHL 7017-7018) est la somme de deux textes hagiographiques de longueur fort inégale. On trouve tout d'abord un livre de miracles proprement dit. Plusieurs des événements qu'il rapporte ont eu lieu sous l'abbatiat de Fulrad († 826) à l'abbaye Saint-Quentin et sont contemporains de l'auteur dont tout porte à croire qu'il s'agit d'un moine de cette abbaye. Dans le *Liber*, les miracles de châtiment, certes moins nombreux que ceux de guérison, font l'objet d'une rédaction plus longue et plus détaillée. Ils concernent des laïcs (des paysans et aussi des aristocrates laïques) sacrilèges, irrespectueux envers saint Quentin ou encore usurpateurs de biens monastiques. Ils constituent dès lors un aspect fondamental du dis-

---

[6] Poncelet (1901); l'auteur met en évidence les quelques ressemblances entre des passages des *Carmina* édités dans les *MGH* (éd. P. von Winterfeld, *Poet. Lat.*, IV-1, Berlin, 1889, p. 178-221), *de sancto Cassiano* (BHL 1633), *de sancto Quintino* (BHL 7010) et *de sancta Benedicta* (BHL 1088) et la passion en vers (BHL 7016) dédiée au chanoine Otger dans les cinq derniers vers du poème, en forme d'acrostiche (p. 44). La dédicace à Otger (et non l'attribution comme auteur) a été établie par F. Dolbeau (2006) *contra* J.-L. Villette (2011): dans le plus ancien manuscrit recensé (Paris, BnF, lat. 17627, de la 2e moitié du XIe siècle et en provenance de Saint-Quentin de Beauvais), le *Carmen* dédié à Otger est encadré par ces deux autres poèmes (dont les passages relatifs à saint Quentin sont numérotés 7011 et 7012 dans la *BHL*). S'il est tout à fait vraisemblable que BHL 7010, dont le plus ancien manuscrit recensé (Paris, BnF, lat. 14143) est daté du IXe, et BHL 1633 (voir plus loin) sont antérieurs au poème dédié à Otger (BHL 7016), rien n'est établi pour BHL 1088.

cours moral du *Liber*, si ce n'est le premier[7]: au même titre qu'ils sont un avertissement lancé à ceux qui offenseraient le saint et ses représentants, ils servent les intérêts des moines de Saint-Quentin dans la défense de leur temporel. La première section du *Liber* est suivie d'un paragraphe beaucoup plus bref ne racontant pas d'épisodes miraculeux mais la translation des reliques de saint Quentin dans la crypte du monastère, sous l'abbé Hugues (833/834-844), en 834 ou en 835, dont l'auteur fut un témoin direct. Comme l'auteur du *Carmen* dédié à Otger (*BHL* 7016) semble s'en être également inspiré, on peut avancer que ce *Liber* a été écrit entre 835 et 890.

Le *Sermo in tumulatione* (*BHL* 7020) relate les transferts successifs des corps des saints Quentin, Cassien et Victoric jusqu'au tout début du Xe siècle. Reprenant les observations de Claude Héméré, de Louis-Paul Colliette puis du Père Benjamin Bossue qui s'étaient appuyés sur un catalogue de reliques pour affirmer que la *tumulatio* des trois saints faisait l'objet d'une célébration annuelle au 12 janvier[8], Jean-Luc Villette considère que la messe célébrée par l'évêque Raimbert de Noyon-Tournai (...902?-906...) devant les trois corps saints ne pouvait avoir eu lieu qu'un dimanche, ce quantième (dimanche 12 janvier) ne concordant qu'avec 906, le *Sermo* aurait donc été écrit au début du Xe siècle, entre le début de l'épiscopat de Raimbert, vers 902, et cette célébration de 906. L'organisation interne du récit correspond à un diptyque caractérisé par un balancement entre la vénération des saints et la déploration classique des méfaits normands interprétés comme une manifestation de la vengeance divine. Une grande partie des textes hagiographiques relatifs à saint Quentin mais aussi aux saints du cycle de Riciovare, ainsi que les Annales de Saint-Vaast ont été utilisés par l'auteur. Le début consiste en un long rappel (six chapitres sur dix-sept) du «cycle de Riciovare»[9]; le *Sermo* se concentre ensuite sur les translations des reliques de Cassien et de Quentin dans la

---

[7] *Contra* J.-L. VILLETTE (2011) pour qui les miracles de guérison sont primordiaux dans le *Liber* en raison de leur plus grand nombre.

[8] Claude HÉMÉRÉ, *Augusta Viromanduorum vindicata et illustrata*, 2 vol., Paris, 1643, p. 369: *Reliquiae sanctorum in ecclesia domini Quintini quiescentes, uno catalogo continentur sub finem libri [...] duodecim [januarii] tumulatio Quintini, Victorici, Cassiani facta per Rambertum praesulem Noviomensem post normannicam desolationem.*

[9] Cf. GAILLARD (2014).

première moitié du IXe siècle. Vient ensuite une évocation des dépradations normandes dans le nord du royaume de Francie occidentale, auxquelles le monastère Saint-Quentin n'a pas échappé puisqu'à deux reprises les dépouilles des deux saints doivent être mises à l'abri à Laon avant que le sanctuaire ne soit incendié en 883 et qu'une partie de la communauté religieuse ait été massacrée ou emmenée en captivité. Le monastère se relève ensuite grâce au retour en grande pompe des corps saints suite aux efforts de Thierry, comte et abbé laïque qui entame des travaux de fortifications en 886. Puis, en 893, Otger, ancien chanoine de Saint-Quentin et évêque d'Amiens, procède à la translation du corps de saint Victoric dans le sanctuaire du Vermandois; la réunion des corps des trois saints en un même lieu est l'objet d'une cérémonie de consécration orchestrée par l'évêque Raimbert: surgit alors du tombeau de saint Quentin un globe lumineux miraculeux qui vient en quelque sorte cautionner l'action épiscopale.

Au culte de saint Quentin, il faut sans doute associer l'écriture de la Vie en vers de Cassien[10] (*BHL* 1633) dont le plus ancien manuscrit recensé (Paris, BnF, lat. 12958, originaire de Corbie) est daté des IXe/X{e} siècles et qui, comme cela a été évoqué plus haut, a été utilisé dans le *Carmen* en l'honneur de saint Quentin.

B. Les miracles de saint Fursy

D'après sa *Vita* (*BHL* 3209-3210)[11], écrite peu de temps après sa mort, en 649-650, le corps de Fursy aurait été amené à Péronne par Erchinoald, maire du palais de Neustrie (638-657) et placé dans une église construite par ses soins. Le dossier hagiographique de saint Fursy a été amplifié au IXe siècle par des *Virtutes* (*BHL* 3213), probablement écrites à Péronne. La datation de ce texte a été établie par Bruno Krusch qui s'est avant tout fondé sur des arguments d'ordre lexical mais ses conclu-

---

[10] Dont les reliques ont été transférées à Saint-Quentin en 841. Sur les vies en prose (*BHL* 1630-1632), voir M. Gaillard, «Le diocèse d'Autun», *infra*, p. 604.
[11] Éd. B. Krusch, *MGH*, *SRM*, IV, Hanovre – Leipzig, 1902, p. 434-440 (§ 10, p. 439). Sur ce texte mérovingien, cf. Heinzelmann (2010), p. 76-77.

sions n'ont pas été remises en cause[12]. L'originalité des *Virtutes* tient au fait qu'elles narrent des miracles dus à l'intercession de saint Fursy à Péronne mais aussi, de son vivant, en Ponthieu et en Amiénois. Alors que la *Vita* accordait une certaine importance à la fondation du monastère de Lagny-sur-Marne, les *Virtutes* insistent au contraire davantage sur le séjour prolongé du saint irlandais à Péronne où il aurait été accueilli par le maire Erchinoald qui lui aurait demandé de baptiser son fils. Les connaissances de l'hagiographe sur le site de Péronne ainsi que les qualificatifs élogieux attribués à plusieurs reprises à Erchinoald plaident en faveur d'une rédaction locale. D'après ces *Virtutes* le maire du palais neustrien, venu rencontrer saint Fursy à Lagny, aurait déclaré vouloir lui céder une éminence appelée le « Mont des Cygnes » où leurs deux dépouilles seraient inhumées. À la différence de la *Vita*, les *Virtutes* placent le lieu du décès de Fursy à *Macerias*[13]; Erchinoald réclame son corps et celui-ci, chargé sur un chariot tiré par des taureaux, est emmené à Péronne et, après plusieurs péripéties, est placée aux côtés des restes de Patrice, Meoan et Meldan que le saint lui-même avait auparavant installés sur le mont où une église est bâtie dans les trente jours en l'honneur des douze Apôtres. La suite du récit reprend plus ou moins les données de la *Vita*: le 9 février, les restes du saint sont installés dans l'église à droite de l'autel des saints-apôtres (selon les *Virtutes, in porticu,* selon la *Vita*) et, quatre ans, plus tard, le saint corps fut transféré dans une *domuncola* (à l'est de l'autel selon la *Vita*), en présence des évêques Éloi de Noyon-Tournai, Aubert (de Cambrai ou de Senlis) et – ajoutent les *Virtutes* – de Médard de Noyon-Tournai[14]. L'auteur des *Virtutes* précise enfin que, eu égard à la multiplication des miracles du saint, Erchinoald et son épouse lui font construire une église et que le tombeau du saint est réalisé par Éloi.

---

[12] *Virtutes sancti Fursei abbatis Latiniacensis*, éd. B. KRUSCH, *MGH, SRM*, IV, Hanovre – Leipzig, 1902, p. 440-449 (pour la datation, p. 427); sur ce texte, cf. CHAFFENET (2017), p. 104-111.

[13] *Macerias* peut correspondre à Mézières-en-Santerre (Somme, arr. Montdidier, cant. Moreuil) ou encore à Mézières sur-Oise (Aisne, arr. Saint-Quentin, cant. Ribemont).

[14] Ce qui est impossible puisque Médard vécut un siècle avant les deux autres évêques!

C. Le dossier de sainte Hunégonde d'Homblières

Le second dossier hagiographique important pour cette période (quoique légèrement postérieur) concerne une sainte, Hunégonde d'Homblières († vers 690?), dont le culte semble avoir commencé très tard: la plus ancienne trace liturgique de la dévotion à sainte Hunégonde consiste en l'inscription de son *dies natalis* dans un calendrier de la fin du IXe siècle, originaire d'Arras puis adapté à l'usage de l'abbaye de Corbie. Ce dossier hagiographique se compose d'une *Vita* (BHL 4046) ainsi que de la *Translatio prima* (BHL 4047) et de *Miracula* (BHL 4048-4049) composés par Bernier, premier abbé bénédictin d'Homblières (949?-982)[15]. Selon la *Vita sanctae Hunegundis*, l'abbaye féminine d'Homblières aurait été fondée à la fin du VIIe siècle; native de Lambais, Hunégonde aurait été baptisée par saint Éloi, alors évêque de Noyon. Ses parents voulant la marier à un certain Eudalde, elle convainc ce dernier de l'accompagner à Rome où elle rencontre le pape Martin Ier (649-655) qui lui donne le voile consacré et la voue au célibat. La vierge s'attire les foudres de son fiancé qui entreprend de dilapider les biens de celle-ci. Grâce à un miracle, Hunégonde parvient à arrêter ces méfaits, ce qui conduit Eudalde à s'amender: il promet de ne plus pécher contre elle, donne des biens aux *sorores* du monastère d'Homblières où la jeune femme entend accomplir sa vocation religieuse et devient le gestionnaire (*procurator*) des affaires extérieures de la communauté. Enfin, il s'engage par testament à ce que tout son patrimoine soit cédé aux religieuses après sa mort et annonce son désir d'être inhumé à Homblières.

L'abbaye d'Homblières n'est connue avec certitude qu'à partir du court gouvernement de sa dernière abbesse, Berthe, promue en 946 afin de rétablir la pureté religieuse dans l'établissement féminin; la rédaction de la Vie d'Hunégonde, certainement écrite avant le récit de translation et les *Miracula*, daterait-elle de cette époque? L'échec de la réforme est sanc-

---

[15] Une *Translatio altera* (BHL 4050) a été écrite entre 1051 et 1060; son auteur anonyme (probablement un moine d'Homblières) est le premier hagiographe à attribuer à l'abbé Bernier la paternité des *Miracula* et de la *Translatio prima*. Il existait aussi une *Vita Rythmica* (BHL 4051) dont seuls des extraits ont été édités par J. STILTING dans le *Commentarius praevius* de la Vie de la sainte; le manuscrit qu'il a utilisé provenait de la Chartreuse de Cologne.

tionné en 949 par l'éviction des *sanctimoniales* au profit de moines bénédictins. Dans la *Translatio prima,* après avoir raconté les circonstances de l'invention des reliques de sainte Hunégonde en 946, Bernier relate des miracles faisant de la patronne la protectrice du monastère d'Homblières avant et après le remplacement des *sanctimoniales.* La *Translatio prima* rapporte trois miracles facilement datables: ils se sont produits dans l'intervalle de trente-deux jours séparant la découverte du saint corps (en octobre 946) de l'arrivée officielle de l'évêque de Noyon-Tournai (en novembre). Les *Miracula sanctae Hunegundis*, comme leur titre l'indique, sont exclusivement consacrés au souvenir d'intercessions surnaturelles de sainte Hunégonde. Un des miracles a lieu précisément en 964 et l'auteur, vraisemblablement l'abbé Bernier, prétend en avoir été un témoin oculaire. Jean Mabillon a considéré que la *Vita,* la *Translatio prima* et le recueil de miracles avaient été rédigés dans la foulée vers 965. Dans les *Miracula sanctae Hunegundis,* l'efficacité de la sainteté de la patronne est révélée dans toute son ampleur. Aux dires de l'hagiographe, son projet, annoncé d'emblée, est de porter à la connaissance du lecteur certains miracles récents, remarquables et dignes de mémoire. Par ailleurs, les *Miracula* de sainte Hunégonde insistent sur la nécessité de conserver le souvenir, au moyen de l'écrit, de miracles qui risquent d'être exposés à l'oubli. En mettant par écrit ces miracles survenus dans le passé puis au temps des moines bénédictins, l'abbé Bernier révèle la puissance de sainte Hunégonde sur une période d'au moins une vingtaine d'années jusqu'au miracle de 964. Dans ce recueil, il insiste sur les miracles de châtiment (cinq au total) qui fondent l'essentiel de son propos.

III. La poursuite de l'activité hagiographique au Moyen Âge central

La célébration de saint Quentin se poursuit au-delà de l'époque carolingienne avec deux autres textes:

– les *Miracula s. Quintini in coenobio Insulensi patrata* (*BHL* 7019) ont sans doute été rédigés dans le dernier quart du Xe siècle, à la demande de l'évêque de Noyon-Tournai Liudolphe (vers 978/979-vers 990/991), et relatent le développement de l'abbaye Saint-Quentin-en-L'Île ;

— le *Sermo de elevatione gloriosissimi martyris Quintini* (*BHL* 7021), rédigé à la fin du Xe siècle ou au début du XIe siècle, raconte une sortie des reliques lors d'un conflit qui s'est terminé par la donation de la terre de Sinceny par Herbert (III?), comte de Vermandois (987/988-1000?)[16].

Le *Sermo de adventu sancti Praejecti* (*BHL* 6918) relate la translation des reliques du saint auvergnat Prix, évêque de Clermont et martyr († 676), par l'abbé Fulrad de Saint-Quentin au temps de Charlemagne. Fulrad aurait décidé de confier les reliques à une communauté monastique qui ne peut être assurément identifiée à l'abbaye Saint-Prix-près-Saint-Quentin (cette dernière n'étant pas attestée avant la fin du Xe siècle). Le *Sermo* mentionne un miracle survenu à Béthune ; or les moines du prieuré clunisien Saint-Prix de Béthune (diocèse d'Arras) détenaient des reliques de Prix, ce qui est attesté par une charte délivrée en 1123 par Raoul le Vert, archevêque de Reims (1107-1124)[17]. Le *Sermo* aurait donc pu être rédigé au début du XIIe siècle par les moines de Saint-Prix-près Saint-Quentin, soucieux d'affirmer, face à leurs frères béthunois, leurs prétentions quant à la possession des reliques de leur saint patron.

Mentionnons, pour compléter ce tableau, des Vies dont la rédaction est attribuée à Radbod II, évêque de Noyon-Tournai (1068-1098) : la réécriture de la Vie de saint Médard (*BHL* 5866)[18] et la Vie de sainte Godeberte (*BHL* 3572)[19]. Quant à

---

[16] L'identification du comte donateur avec Herbert III de Vermandois n'est pas certaine : il pourrait aussi s'agir d'Herbert IV (1045-vers 1080), ce qui reviendrait à reculer d'environ un siècle la rédaction du *Sermo de elevatione*. Le plus ancien manuscrit connu (Paris, BnF, lat. 17627), en provenance de Saint-Quentin de Beauvais, est daté de la deuxième moitié du XIe siècle.

[17] Charte de Raoul le Vert, archevêque de Reims, réglant un litige entre les moines de Saint-Prix de Béthune et les Clunisiens du Saint-Esprit d'Abbeville (1123, avant le 3 août), éd. DEMOUY (1982), 3, n° 182 : *contigit a monachis Sancti Prejecti corpus ejusdem martyris in episcopatum Atrabatensem ad castellum deferri quod Betunia dicitur*.

[18] Aucun manuscrit antérieur au XVe siècle, n'en a été recensé. En revanche, la Vie *BHL* 5867 dont les plus anciens manuscrits sont du XIe siècle (Cambrai, BM 846 ; Vatican, Reg. lat. 496 ; Paris, BnF, lat. 18299), pourrait être antérieure, sans qu'on puisse la rattacher à un auteur quelconque, de Saint-Médard de Soissons, du diocèse de Noyon ou bien encore de Dijon où

la Vie de saint Montan (*BHL* 6010d), rattachée par la *BHL* au Vermandois, elle concerne un ermite vénéré à Laon dès avant le XIe siècle comme celui qui, selon la Vie de saint Remi par Hincmar[20], aurait prédit la naissance de Remi. Sa courte *Vita*, connue par une copie moderne, est indatable[21]. Il convient enfin de signaler le cas particulier qu'est la Vie de saint Geoffroy (*BHL* 3573), moine profès au Mont-Saint-Quentin (près de Péronne) dans les années 1070 puis évêque d'Amiens (1104-1115): cette *Vita* célèbree à un saint formé à la vie monastique en Vermandois, mais elle a été écrite en dehors du diocèse de Noyon, dans les années 1130 par Nicolas, moine de Saint-Crépin-le-Grand de Soissons[22].

Bibliographie

Chaffenet, P., *Aristocratie et communautés religieuses aux marges septentrionales du royaume de France (fin IXe-début XIIe siècles). Le cas du diocèse de Noyon*, thèse de doctorat sous la direction de Michèle Gaillard et d'Alain Dierkens, Université de Lille-Université Libre de Bruxelles, juin 2017.

Demouy, P., *Recueil des actes des archevêques de Reims d'Arnoul à Renaud II (997-1139)*, thèse dactylographiée, 3 vol., Nancy, 1982.

Dolbeau, F., «Beringus, hagiographe en Vermandois (fin IXe s.)», *AB*, 124 (2006), p. 259-260.

Gaillard, M., «Un 'cycle' hagiographique du haut Moyen Âge en Gaule septentrionale: les Passions des martyrs de Riciovar», *Hagiographica*, 21 (2014), p. 1-28.

---

des reliques de Médard ont été apportées (cf. Gaillard – Rauwel, «Le diocèse de Langres», *infra*, p. 600-603).

[19] Sont répertoriées dans le *CGM* et dans la *BHLms* seulement deux copies modernes; l'édition des *Acta Sanctorum* a été faite d'après un manuscrit de la cathédrale de Noyon, aujourd'hui disparu.

[20] Voir «Le diocèse de Reims», par M. C. Isaïa, *supra*, p. 341-361, et Isaïa (2010), p. 474-476.

[21] Van der Straeten (1956).

[22] Nicolas de Saint-Crépin-le-Grand de Soissons, *Vita sancti Godefridi*, éd. A. Poncelet, *AASS*, Nov. III, Bruxelles, 1910, p. 905-944. Sur cette œuvre, voit Ott (2005), et, sur la biographie de saint Geoffroy et sa production diplomatique en tant qu'évêque d'Amiens, voir Morelle (1991).

—, « La *Passio* de saint Quentin », in M. GOULLET, éd., *Le Légendier de Turin, Torino, Biblioteca Nazionale e Universitaria D.V.3*, Florence, 2014, p. 211-228.

HEINZELMANN, M., « L'hagiographie mérovingienne: panorama des documents potentiels », in M. GOULLET – M. HEINZELMANN – C. VEYRARD-COSME, *L'hagiographie mérovingienne à travers ses réécritures*, Ostfildern, 2010, p. 27-82 (Beihefte der Francia, 71).

ISAÏA, M.-C., *Remi de Reims: mémoire d'un saint, histoire d'une Église*, Paris, 2010 (Histoire religieuse de la France, 35).

MORELLE, L., « Un 'grégorien' au miroir de ses chartes: Geoffroy, évêque d'Amiens (1104-1115) », in M. PARISSE, dir., *À propos des actes d'évêques. Hommage à Lucie Fossier*, Nancy, 1991, p. 177-218.

OTT, J. S., « Writing Godfrey of Amiens: Guibert of Nogent and Nicholas of Saint-Crépin between sanctity, ideology, and society », *Mediaeval Studies*, 67 (2005), p. 317-365.

PONCELET, A., « Carmina de S. Quintino », *AB*, 20 (1901), p. 5-44 et p. 158.

VAN DER STRAETEN, J., « Saint Montan ermite honoré en Thiérache », *AB*, 74 (1956), p. 370-404.

VILLETTE, J.-L., *Hagiographie et culte d'un saint dans le haut Moyen-Age. Saint Quentin, apôtre du Vermandois (VIe s.-XIe s.)*, thèse de doctorat de IIIe cycle (dactylographiée) sous la direction de Pierre Riché, Université Paris X, 2 vol., 1982.

—, « *Passiones et Inventiones S. Quintini*, l'élaboration d'un *corpus* hagiographique du haut Moyen Âge », *Mélanges de science religieuse*, 56-2 (1999), p. 49-76.

—, « Saint-Quentin, un culte et un site au cœur de l'Europe », in *Aux origines de Saint-Quentin: de la tradition littéraire à la réalité archéologique, Saint-Quentin*, Musée Antoine Lécuyer, 2011, p. 59-62.

VILLETTE, J.-L. – GAILLARD, M., « L'histoire de Saint-Quentin entre textes et images », *ibid.*, p. 7-14.

L'écriture hagiographique dans le diocèse de Châlons (env. 750-950)

par

Klaus KRÖNERT
avec la collaboration de Michèle GAILLARD

I. MEMMIE, PREMIER ÉVÊQUE DE CHÂLONS: sa *Vita I^a* (*BHL* 5907).
II. LES LÉGENDES DE L'ÉVÊQUE ALPIN, DE PUSINNE ET DE SES SŒURS.
BIBLIOGRAPHIE.

L'agglomération, occupée depuis l'époque gallo-romaine, est nommée au IVe siècle, *Catelauni*; la *civitas Catelauni* n'est cependant attestée qu'à l'extrême fin du IVe siècle[1] mais, si l'on en croit la liste épiscopale de Châlons[2], le premier évêque Memmie aurait vécu au IVe siècle; sa *Vita* (*BHL* 5907) ne fut probablement rédigée qu'au IXe siècle. Une autre *Vita* concerne l'évêque Alpin († vers 510) (*BHL* 309-310), le huitième de la liste épiscopale; selon la Vie de Loup de Troyes, il s'est illustré par ses victoires sur des démons[3]. Au IXe/Xe siècle, sa *Vita* donna naissance à la légende de Pusinne et de ses six sœurs qui auraient été originaires de la région du Perthois[4] et auraient décidé, sous la

---

[1] BEAUJARD (2006), p. 62-63.
[2] Établie probablement au XIe siècle et connue par une copie de Mabillon (DUCHESNE, p. 92-93), cette liste donne huit noms avant Amandinus, qui signe les actes du concile de Tours de 461; le premier de cette liste, Memmius, est aussi mentionné par Grégoire de Tours, qui ne le situe pas dans le temps (cf. aussi BEAUJARD 2006, p. 64 *contra* RAUVAUX (1983), p. 64).
[3] *Vita s. Lupi ep. Trecensis* (*BHL* 5087-5088), c. 11, éd. B. KRUSCH, *MGH, SRM*, III, Hanovre, 1896, p. 124.
[4] Région située à plus de trente kilomètres au sud-est de Châlons, entre les villes actuelles de Vitry et Saint-Dizier.

conduite d'Alpin, de consacrer leur vie à Dieu[5]; ce cycle hagiographique déborda bientôt les limites du diocèse de Châlons[6].

I. MEMMIE, PREMIER ÉVÊQUE DE CHÂLONS: SA *VITA I^a* (*BHL* 5907)

La première Vie de Memmie[7], fondateur et premier évêque du siège de Châlons, est sans doute légendaire: originaire de Rome, Memmie a été envoyé en Gaule par saint Pierre, en même temps que Denis de Paris, Sixte de Reims, Euchaire de Trèves, Savinien de Sens et Sinice de Soissons. Lors du voyage, l'un de ses deux compagnons, Domitien, meurt, Memmie et l'autre compagnon, Donatien, rentrent à Rome, retournent en Gaule et ressuscitent le défunt à l'aide d'un vêtement que saint Pierre leur a donné; après une autre résurrection, les saints hommes arrivent à Châlons où Memmie exerce un épiscopat exemplaire durant vingt-quatre ans, ponctué d'autres miracles; après sa mort, Donatien et Domitien prennent sa succession.

Le culte de Memmie est ancien: il date au moins du VIe siècle[8] et il a pris de l'importance au VIIe siècle quand, le 5 juillet 677, ses reliques furent découvertes dans l'église Saint-Memmie à la suite d'un miracle de pluie. Cet événement est relaté dans un texte de l'époque, l'*Inventio Memmii* (*BHL* 5911), qui n'inclut cependant aucun élément biographique concernant le saint[9]. La *Vita I^a* du saint, fut-elle également écrite à cette occasion, comme complément au récit d'invention, ou est-elle une œuvre plus tardive? Les deux thèses ont eu leurs défenseurs: dans l'introduction à l'édition de l'*Inventio Memmii*, publiée en 1910, Wilhelm Levison a avancé que la Vie n'est pas anté-

---

[5] DE GAIFFIER (1958); RÖCKELEIN (2002), p. 392.

[6] KLÜPPEL (1996)

[7] Pour l'édition de la *Vita I^a Memmie*, cf. *AASS*, Aug. II, 1735, p. 11-12.

[8] Memmie figure dans la plus ancienne recension du martyrologe hiéronymien probablement complétée sous l'épiscopat d'Aunaire d'Auxerre (561-605), et Grégoire de Tours le présente comme «patron special» de Châlons (GRÉGOIRE DE TOURS, *Liber in gloria confessorum*, c. 65, éd. B. KRUSCH, *MGH*, *SRM*, I-2, Hanovre, 1885, p. 336-337.

[9] *Inventio Memmii*, éd. W. LEVISON, *MGH*, *SRM*, V, Hanovre – Leipzig, 1910, p. 363-367.

rieure au IXe siècle[10]. Plus tard, en 1930, il s'est demandé si elle n'avait pas été rédigée au VIIe siècle, avant l'*Inventio* de 677. Très courte, la Vie lui donnerait l'impression d'être ancienne[11]. Plus récemment Brigitte Beaujard a proposé une datation très tardive, la fin du IXe siècle[12], et Hans Hubert Anton a défendu l'idée selon laquelle le texte daterait du VIIe siècle environ[13].

Après avoir discuté l'ensemble de ces propositions, Damien Kempf et moi-même avons finalement argumenté pour considérer la *Vita I[a] Memmii* comme un texte de la fin du VIIIe ou du début du IXe siècle[14]. Un premier *terminus ante quem* est fixé par la *Vita II[a] Memmii* (*BHL* 5909), réécriture de la première Vie réalisée par Almann de Hautvilliers en 868[15]. Le manuscrit le plus ancien – Zurich, Zentralbibliothek, Ms. C10i, de la fin du IXe siècle, fol. 157r-157v – ne permet pas de préciser davantage le moment de la rédaction. Le premier argument en faveur d'une datation des les années 800 environ est tiré du texte: l'auteur mentionne la liste des évangélisateurs que saint Pierre aurait envoyés en Gaule en même temps que Memmie: Denis de Paris, Sixte de Reims, Euchaire de Trèves, Savinien de Sens et Sinice de Soissons. Étant donné que ces noms se trouvent, à une exception près, dans les trois manuscrits les plus anciens[16], il est vraisemblable qu'ils se trouvaient déjà dans la version originale de la Vie de Memmie et que l'auteur a repris des traditions déjà existantes. En effet, trois d'entre elles reprennent des légendes élaborées au IXe siècle ou seulement très peu de temps auparavant: celles de Sixte et Sinice, qui formaient une sorte de paire, et celle de Savinien[17]. Le deuxième argument concerne la *causa scribendi* du texte: à l'époque précarolingienne, les légendes des origines apostoliques aussi élaborées que celle de Memmie sont

---

[10] *Ibid.*, p. 363.
[11] LEVISON (1948), p. 21.
[12] BEAUJARD (2006), p. 60.
[13] Cf. ANTON (2014), p. 32.
[14] Kempf, Krönert (2017).
[15] *BHL* 5909; sur les œuvres d'Almann, cf. M.-C. ISAÏA, «Le diocèse de Reims», *supra*, p. 354-357.
[16] Paris, BnF, lat. 17002 (fol. 39v); Bruxelles, KBR 7984 (3191) (fol. 158v-159r); Zürich, Zentralbibliothek, Ms. C10i (fol. 157r).
[17] KEMPF, KRÖNERT (2017), p. 20-21; cf. également ISAÏA (2009) et BAUER (1997), p. 359-360 où l'on trouve les premières attestations. Pour Savinien, cf. M. GAILLARD, «Le diocèse de Sens», *infra*, p. 460-462.

attestées uniquement pour les villes aussi importantes que Paris ou Arles et les textes alors rédigés s'inscrivent généralement dans des contextes de revendication de droits. Rien de tel ne peut être attesté pour Châlons au VIIe siècle. Au début du IXe siècle, en revanche, la situation se présente différemment: Châlons profitait d'un certain essor économique, comme d'autres villes en Champagne. De plus, l'évêque Hildegrin (800/802-825/827) était un personnage d'importance: il fut chargé d'un district missionnaire en Saxe qui devint par la suite l'évêché de Halberstadt; il n'est pas exclu que ses préoccupations l'aient incité à commander une *Vita* qui insiste sur l'action évangélisatrice de Memmie[18]. La *Vita* de Memmie témoigne aussi de la volonté qu'eurent de nombreux sièges épiscopaux, à partir de la fin du VIIIe siècle, de revendiquer des origines apostoliques: Metz, Limoges, Périgueux, Angoulême, Reims, Beauvais, Trèves, Chartres, Le Mans, Orléans ou encore Paris, revendiquaient désormais une fondation par un apôtre ou par le disciple d'un apôtre[19]. Enfin, le dernier argument, qui est toutefois moins explicite, est linguistique: les deux manuscrits les plus anciens – celui de Zurich, de la fin du IXe siècle et de Bruxelles, Bibl. royale de Belgique, ms. 7984 (3191), fol. 168v-160v, du Xe siècle – sont écrits dans un latin fortement influencé par la réforme carolingienne. Seul le manuscrit Paris, BnF, lat. 17002, fol. 39v-40r, du début du XIe siècle, le légendier de Moissac, est truffé de graphies et de phonétismes typiques de la période mérovingienne et assez éloignés du latin classique[20]. C'est uniquement sous l'impulsion des réformateurs carolingiens, que le respect des règles de la grammaire antique fut rétabli, mais pas toujours avec des effets immédiats: jusque dans les années 820/830, on peut encore trouver des graphiques et phonétismes mérovingiens[21]. C'est probablement sur un tel modèle aujourd'hui perdu que le scribe du légendier de Moissac a copié son texte; on peut donc avancer le *terminus ante quem*

---

[18] Cf. KEMPF, KRÖNERT (2017), p. 21; cf. également RAUVAUX (1980), p. 58-61 et p. 68-69.
[19] Cf. BAUER (1997), p. 355-364.
[20] Sur ce légendier, cf. PELOUX (2018), en particulier GOULLET (2018).
[21] Voir par exemple, le «Légendier» de Turin, daté des environs de 825, dans GOULLET (2014), en particulier, p. 165-195.

de 825/830 pour la rédaction de la *Vita I^a Memmii*[22]. Ce texte semble donc faire partie du début de l'essor des récits apostoliques qu'on observe en Gaule sous les Carolingiens, dont la liste des évêques envoyés par Pierre en même temps que Memmie, au début de la *Vita*, est le reflet.

II. Les légendes de l'évêque Alpin, de Pusinne et de ses sœurs

C'est seulement au xve siècle que la légende de Pusinne et de ses six sœurs trouve sa forme définitive dans une Vie de la sainte (*BHL* 6993); l'auteur de ce texte s'est servi de plusieurs Vies datant des ixe-xe siècles qui avaient successivement enrichi la légende. La datation de ces écrits, faite le plus souvent en fonction de l'évolution de la légende, ainsi que la détermination des lieux de leur rédaction s'avèrent cependant aléatoires malgré les travaux successifs de B. de Gaiffier[23], H. Beumann[24] et H. Röckelein[25]; seules de nouvelles éditions de ces textes pourraient permettre d'aller plus loin.

Les textes les plus anciens sont les deux Vies d'Alpin: la très brève *Vita I^a* (*BHL* 309)[26] et la *Vita II^a* (*BHL* 310), sa réécriture, qui pourrait dater de la première moitié du ixe siècle[27]. Elles étaient complétées par une collection de miracles qui est toujours inédite (*BHL* 311)[28]. Les deux Vies rapportent que le jeune Alpin s'est fait remarquer lors de la mission que Germain d'Auxerre et Loup de Troyes ont menée pour lutter contre les Pélagiens en (Grande-) Bretagne, et elles relatent qu'une fois

---

[22] Pour une analyse stylistique très détaillée des trois manuscrits les plus anciens de la *Vita I^a Memmii*, cf. Kempf, Krönert (2017), p. 23-24.

[23] Cf. de Gaiffier (1958 et 1971).

[24] Beumann (1970).

[25] Röckelein (2002), p. 108-117, 203-305, 392-393.

[26] *Vita I^a Alpini ep. Catalaunensis* (*BHL* 309), *AASS*, Sept. III, 1750, p. 85-86.

[27] *Vita II^a Alpini ep. Catalaunensis* (*BHL* 310), *AASS*, Sept. III, 1750, p. 86-90; le plus ancien manuscrit de ce texte est Montpellier BIU H 002, de la deuxième moitié du xiie siècle (fol. 126r-130r). Pour la datation, cf. de Gaiffier (1958), p. 205 et Röckelein (2002), p. 116 et p. 392.

[28] Pour les *Miracula Alpini ep. Catalaunensis* (*BHL* 311), Cf. Commentarius praevius n° 4-6, *AASS*, Sept. III, 1750, p. 82-83.

accédé à l'épiscopat de Châlons, il aurait réussi à ce qu'Attila épargne son siège[29]. Dans la *Vita II^a*, il est dit qu'en visite dans le Perthois, Alpin consacra sept sœurs au service de Dieu[30]. Selon H. Röckelein, deux autres Vies du cycle semblent encore avoir été écrites à peu près à la même époque, également à partir de la Vie d'Alpin[31], la *Vita Hoyldis*[32] et la *Vita Manechildis*[33]. Manechildis (Magenhildis) et Hoyldis (Othildis) sont présentées dans leurs *Vitae* respectives comme des vierges qui se sont fait remarquer par Alpin de Châlons grâce à leur vie exemplaire et l'hagiographe d'Hoyldis a même ajouté que son héroïne avait six sœurs, dont deux sont mentionnées nommément: Ama/Ymma et Manechildis[34]. Ces deux Vies ainsi qu'une *Vita Liudrudis* aujourd'hui perdue[35] ont ensuite, selon beaucoup de probabilité, servi de modèle à Thierry, archevêque de Trèves (965-977) qui a composé à la fin du Xe siècle une *Vita rhythmica Liutrudis* (BHL 4952)[36].

Selon H. Röckelein, elles auraient aussi été utilisées pour l'écriture de la *Vita Pusinnae* (BHL 6992t), autour de l'an mil[37]. Dans son introduction à l'édition de cette dernière, B. de Gaiffier indique qu'un psautier de Notre-Dame de Soissons, de la fin de VIIIe siècle, contient une litanie pour des vierges parmi lesquelles figure le nom de Posinna; on pourrait trouver là un indice qui expliquerait le choix des reliques de Pusinne pour la

---

[29] KRÖNERT, MÉRIAUX (2017), p. 43.

[30] *Vita II^a Alpini ep. Catalaunensis* (BHL 310), *AASS*, Sept. III, 1750, c. 15, col. 89.

[31] RÖCKELEIN 2002, p. 392.

[32] La *Vita Hoyldis* (ou *Othildis*) (BHL 3990), éditée dans les *AASS*, Apr. III, 1675, p. 782-784, comme relevant du diocèse de Troyes, repose sur un manuscrit du XIVe siècle et évoque (c. 3, p. 783) une translation du bras de la sainte dans le monastère cistercein qui porte son nom, dans le diocèse de Toul.

[33] La *Vita Manechildis* (BHL 5207), éditée dans les *AASS*, Oct. VI, 1794, p. 531, repose sur un « vieux manuscrit de Sainte-Menehould » non spécifié et ressemble davantage à une compilation ou à une réécriture de l'éditeur bollandiste qu'à une édition au sens propre du terme.

[34] *Vita Hoyldis*, cap. 1, *AASS*, Apr. III, 1675, p. 783.

[35] Qui a pu être écrite à Herford ou à Reims selon BEUMANN (1970), p. 29.

[36] Ce texte est présenté dans le supplément pour la Germanie, *infra*, p. 743-744.

[37] Pour la datation de la Vie de Pusinne (BHL 6992t), cf. RÖCKELEIN (2002), p. 109 et 116 *contra* KLÜPPEL (1996), p. 196.

translation depuis Binson[38], non loin de Châlons, à Hereford (monastère fondé selon le modèle Notre-Dame de Soissons) en Saxe, en 860. Cet événement est bien documenté grâce à un récit de translation qui a été rédigé entre 862 et 877 (*BHL* 6995)[39]; mais l'auteur de cette œuvre semble tout ignorer de la vie et de la filiation de son héroïne. C'est aussi à cette époque qu'une collection de miracles attribués à Pusinne (*BHL* 6994d) a été rédigée, certainement en Saxe[40].

L'ignorance de l'auteur de la *Translatio* à propos de Pusinne a conduit H. Röckelein à dater la *Vita Pusinnae* (*BHL* 6992t) des environs de l'an mil. Cependant, l'édition de cette *Vita Pusinnae* (*BHL* 6992t) qui ne mentionne pas la translation à Hereford, par B. de Gaiffier, d'après un manuscrit de la Bibliothèque Sainte-Geneviève de Paris daté de la fin du xe ou du début du xie siècle, où seules sont nommées, parmi les sœurs de Pusinne, Emma et Othildis, autorise à poser l'hypothèse d'une rédaction de cette *Vita* avant la translation à Hereford[41]. En tout cas, il semble bien que le culte de Pusinne se soit développé parallèlement à Binson (où une inscription datée de 1069 atteste la permanence du culte[42]) et à Hereford.

D'autres Vies de ce cycle dédiées à Pusinne et à Liutrude ont encore vu le jour, mais elles datent toutes, autant que nous pouvons l'affirmer, du xive et du xve siècle. Elles dépassent donc le cadre chronologique de cette étude[43].

---

[38] À l'emplacement du prieuré de Binson (dont l'existence n'est attestée qu'à l'extrême fin du xie siècle), ont été découvertes, en 1838 puis en 1898, deux stèles ornées de chrismes inscrits dans un cercle et pourvues d'épitaphes de femmes (*Vrsicina* et *Melania*) datables du ve siècle; le culte de Pusinne et de ses sœurs pourrait donc reposer sur la découverte fortuite de telles épitaphes; cf. CHOSSENOT (2004), p. 327).

[39] Une nouvelle édition complète de ce texte fait toujours partie des *desiderata*; cf. pour des éditions partielles: *AASS*, Apr. III, 1675, p. 166-170 et *MGH*, *SS*, II, p. 681-683; Cf., pour la *Translatio Pusinnae* (*BHL* 6995), KLÜPPEL (1996), p. 195-196, et surtout RÖCKELEIN (2002), p. 108-117.

[40] Cf. KLÜPPEL (1996), p. 196, pour qui cette collection des *Miracula Pusinnae* a été écrite du vivant des évêques Liudbert de Münster († 871) et Badurad de Paderborn († 862).

[41] *Ibid.*, p. 196. Dans ce cas, on doit supposer, à la suite de B. de Gaiffier que c'est la *Vita Rythmica Liutrudis* qui se serait inspirée de la *Vita Pusinnae BHL* 6992t ; cf. DE GAIFFIER (1958), p. 200.

[42] DE GAIFFIER 1958, p. 194.

[43] C'est en particulier le cas de la *Vita Pusinnae* (*BHL* 6993) éditée dans les *AASS*; cf. RÖCKELEIN 2002, p. 392.

Bibliographie

Anton, H. A, *Regesten der Bischöfe und Erzbischöfe von Trier*, I-1: *Grundlegung der kirchlichen Organisation, die ersten Bischöfe – ihre Spiegelung in Zeugnissen von der Spätantike bis zum späteren Mittelalte*r, Düsseldorf, 2014 (Publikationen der Gesellschaft für Rheinische Geschichtskunde, 83).

Bauer, T., *Lotharingien als historischer Raum: Raumbildung und Raumbewusstsein im Mittelalter*, Cologne, 1977 (Rheinisches Archiv, 136).

Beaujard, B., «Châlons-en-Champagne», in N. Gauthier – B. Beaujard – F. Prévot, dir., *Topographie chrétienne des cités de la Gaule, des origines au milieu du VIIIe siècle*, XIV: *Province ecclésiastique de Reims (Belgica secunda)*, Paris, 2006, p. 59-66.

Beumann, H., «Pusinna, Liutrud und Mauritius. Quellenkritisches zur Geschichte ihrer hagiographischen Beziehungen», in H. Stoob, éd., *Ostwestphälisch-weserländische Forschungen zur Geschichte und Landeskunde*, Münster, 1970, p. 17-29 (Veröffentlichungen des Provinzialinstituts für westfälische Landes- und Volksforschung, I-15: Kunst und Kultur im Weserraum 800-1600, 3).

Chossenot, R. *et al.*, *Carte archéologique de la Gaule*, 51-1: *La Marne*, Paris, 2004.

de Gaiffier, B., «La plus ancienne Vie de sainte Pusinne de Bison, honorée en Westphalie», *AB*, 76 (1958), p. 188-223.

—, «À propos des Vies des saintes Pusinne et Liutrude», *AB*, 89 (1971), p. 311-318.

Goullet, M., dir., *Le légendier de Turin: ms. D.V.3 de la Bibliothèque nationale universitaire*, Florence, 2014 (Millennio medievale, 103).

—, «Sur la langue de quelques textes du Légendier de Moissac», in Peloux (2018), p. 152-175.

Isaïa, M.-C., «'Nous somme deux sœurs jumelles': Soissons, suffragante de Reims dans l'hagiographie (XIe-XIIIe siècle)», *Publications de l'Académie Nationale de Reims*, 177 (2008), p. 337-351.

Kempf, D. – Krönert, K., «La Vie de saint Memmie de Châlons et les légendes apostoliques des diocèses de Gaule au début du IXe siècle», *Revue d'histoire de l'Église de France*, 103 (2017), p. 5-25.

Klüppel, T., «Die Germania (750-950)», in *Hagiographies*, II (1996), p. 161-209.

Krönert, K. – Mériaux, C., «Saints et barbares en Gaule du Nord pendant le haut Moyen Âge», in E. Bozoky, éd., *Les saints face aux barbares au haut Moyen Âge. Réalités et légendes*, Rennes, 2017, p. 29-51.

Levison, W., «Die Anfänge Rheinischer Bistümer in der Legende», in Id., *Aus rheinischer und fränkischer Frühzeit: Ausgewählte Aufsätze*, Düsseldorf, 1948, p. 7-27.

PELOUX, F., éd., *Le légendier de Moissac et la culture hagiographique méridionale autour de l'an mil*, Turnhout, 2018 (Hagiologia, 15).

RAUVAUX, J.-P., «Histoire topographique de Châlons-sur-Marne (IVe-XVIe siècles)», *Mémoires de la Société d'agriculture, commerce, sciences et arts du département de la Marne*, 95 (1980), p. 57-87.

—, «Les évêques de Châlons-sur-Marne, des origines à 1789», *Mémoires de la Société d'agriculture, commerce, sciences et arts du département de la Marne*, 98 (1983), p. 29-121.

RÖCKELEIN, H., *Reliquientranslationen nach Sachsen. Über Kommunikation, Mobilität und Öffentlichkeit im Frühmittelalter*, Stuttgart, 2002 (Beihefte der Francia, 48).

L'écriture hagiographique dans les diocèses de Senlis et de Beauvais (env. 750-950)

par

Charles MÉRIAUX

I. Le diocèse de Senlis.
II. le diocèse de Beauvais. – A. Saint Lucien. – B. Saint Just. – C. Les saints d'Orër et de Fly: Germer, Angadrême et Évroult. – D. Le légendier de Saint-Quentin de Beauvais.
Bibliographie.

I. Le diocèse de Senlis

Dès l'époque mérovingienne, saint Rieul (*Regulus*) est associé par l'auteur de la plus ancienne Passion des saints Fuscien et Victoric d'Amiens (*BHL* 3226) au groupe des compagnons de saint Denis et mentionné explicitement comme premier évêque de Senlis[1]. Le culte de Rieul est ensuite bien attesté à l'époque carolingienne, même si son rayonnement est resté modeste: Eudes de Beauvais (860-881) le signale dans la Passion de saint Lucien (*BHL* 5009) qu'il réécrit au début de son épiscopat[2]. Rieul figure aussi dans les litanies, le calendrier et les listes épiscopales du sacramentaire (ou graduel) de Senlis exécuté peut-être à Saint-Denis entre 877 et 882[3]. Quelques années plus tôt, Usuard l'avait déjà inscrit dans son martyrologe au 30 mars avant de le déplacer au 23 avril. Mais la brièveté de l'éloge que

---
[1] Duchesne (1915), p. 147; Gaillard (2009).
[2] Moretus Plantin (1953), p. 95.
[3] Paris Bibliothèque Sainte-Geneviève 111; cf. Delisle (1886), p. 143-146; Duchesne (1915), p. 115-117; Krüger (2007), p. 143-151; Dubois (1965), p. 204.

compose le moine de Saint-Germain des Prés permet difficilement d'imaginer qu'il ait eu personnellement connaissance d'une Vie du saint[4].

Trois Vies ont été conservées dont surtout les deux premières nous retiendront ici. Elles ont été copiées dans une petite dizaine de manuscrits et n'ont pas fait l'objet d'étude approfondie depuis leur édition dans les *Acta Sanctorum* au XVIIe siècle[5]. Le texte le plus bref (*BHL* 7106) se lit dans des légendiers du XIIe siècle en usage dans des abbayes du nord de la France: Marchiennes (Douai, BM 840), Saint-Bertin (Saint-Omer, BSAO 715) et Clairmarais (Saint-Omer, BSAO 716). Il présente l'état le moins avancé de la légende du saint, considéré pour cette raison par les éditeurs bollandistes comme le plus ancien: *acta priora eaque breviora, imo antiqua ac sinceriora*[6]. Venu de Grèce avec saint Denis l'Aréopagite, Rieul aurait été envoyé en Gaule par le pape Clément, successeur de Pierre, puis, de là, au *castrum* de Senlis, tandis que Lucien parvenait à Beauvais où il fut martyrisé. Rieul entreprit avec succès de convertir la population de son diocèse en multipliant les miracles de guérison et en fondant des églises. À Rully, non loin de Senlis, comme l'église n'était pas assez grande pour accueillir la foule, l'évêque prêcha à l'extérieur et imposa miraculeusement le silence aux grenouilles du lac voisin. Rien n'est dit du lieu de sa sépulture. Il apparaît ainsi très difficile de préciser les circonstances dans lesquelles aurait été commanditée la rédaction de ce texte, même si on conçoit difficilement qu'une figure si locale, doublement éclipsée par la sainteté des martyrs Denis et Lucien, ait suscité de l'intérêt hors du diocèse de Senlis.

Il en va très différemment de la Vie *BHL* 7107, conservée, elle aussi, dans des manuscrits du nord de la France dont le plus ancien est un légendier de Saint-Pierre de Jumièges copié à la fin du XIe siècle, Rouen, BM 1383 (Y. 80). L'épisode des grenouilles de Rully n'y est pas repris. En revanche, on lit des développements très étendus sur l'épiscopat que Rieul aurait d'abord exercé à Arles, puis sur son séjour à Paris auprès de Ca-

---

[4] DUBOIS (1965), p. 203 (*Apud castrum Silvanectensium, depositio sancti Reguli episcopi et confessoris*) et 217 (*Castro Silvaenectis, sancti Reguli episcopi et confessoris*); voir aussi BORST (2001), I, p. 729-730 et II, p. 807.

[5] «De S. Regulo episcopo», p. 816-827.

[6] *Ibid.*, p. 816.

tulla, la pieuse femme qui, selon la plus ancienne Passion de saint Denis et de ses compagnons, avait procédé à leur inhumation. Celle-ci le recommanda à une parente nommée Callicia qui l'accueillit à Senlis. Par la suite, une apparition de saint Denis au préfet païen Quintilien facilita la mission de Rieul dans la cité. L'accent est mis aussi sur la fondation de l'église Saint-Pierre-Saint-Paul hors des murs dans laquelle Rieul fut inhumé. La Vie est complétée par plusieurs miracles dont le premier met en scène le roi Clovis venu subtiliser une dent du saint avant de la rendre et d'ordonner la reconstruction et l'embellissement de l'église. Le dernier miracle raconte la guérison de la fille du roi Charles le Chauve, Judith (donc dans le troisième quart du IXe siècle). L'absence d'un prologue permet difficilement de se montrer trop affirmatif, mais l'insistance sur le patronage de saint Denis, sur le lieu de sépulture du saint et sur les liens avec la royauté (mérovingienne puis carolingienne) suggère une commande locale au moment où la famille capétienne investit de manière plus prononcée Senlis et sa région. Helgaud de Fleury rappelle la fondation par le roi Robert le Pieux (996-1031) du *monasterium sancti Petri et sancti Reguli in civitate Silvanectensi* qui pourrait en fait correspondre à la restauration d'une communauté autour des reliques du saint évêque[7]. À l'évidence, la rédaction du texte entend inscrire dans un passé ancien et ininterrompu l'histoire de l'église fondée par Rieul pour accueillir son tombeau. Comme l'avait suggéré ses premiers éditeurs, la Vie pourrait bien être une composition contemporaine « de l'époque d'Hugues Capet et de Robert le Pieux »[8].

La dernière Vie de Rieul (*BHL* 7108) se présente comme l'œuvre d'un auteur irlandais du nom de Célestin écrivant à la demande de Clovis. Elle se trouve copiée dans le grand légendier de l'église d'Arles (Paris, BnF, lat. 5295). Sa rédaction s'inscrit dans un projet proprement arlésien qui explique qu'elle soit présentée avec les autres dossiers provençaux[9]. Il reste évidemment à préciser les rapports qu'entretient cette Vie avec la pré-

---

[7] BAUTIER – LABORY (1965), p. 130; sur la confusion possible entre les églises Saint-Rieul et Saint-Pierre, l'un comme l'autre bien attestées par la suite, voir VERCAUTEREN (1934), p. 255 et 258-259; PICARD et BIARNE (2006), p. 126.
[8] « De S. Regulo episcopo », p. 817.
[9] MAGNANI (2016).

cédente et à comprendre où et comment ont été ajoutées dans l'un comme dans l'autre texte les traditions ignorées de la Vie *BHL* 7106, faisant d'abord de Rieul un évêque d'Arles: ont-elles été d'abord développées à Arles pour gagner ensuite le nord du royaume ou l'inverse? Pour quelles raisons? Dans tous les cas, il est tentant de mettre cette circulation de traditions en rapport avec l'intensification des échanges consécutive au mariage de Robert le Pieux et de Constance d'Arles en 1003 dont on sait qu'il s'accompagna de l'arrivée de méridionaux à la cour, suffisamment importante pour bouleverser les modes vestimentaires et les comportements des gens du Nord et scandaliser certains contemporains si l'on en croit les *Histoires* de Raoul le Glabre (III 40)[10].

Selon Helgaud de Fleury, la reine Adelaïde, épouse d'Hugues Capet, fonda à Senlis un *monasterium sancti Franbaldi* desservi par douze clercs[11]. Pour autant, le culte de ce saint Frambaud, attesté à l'époque carolingienne dans le diocèse du Mans, n'a pas donné lieu à la rédaction d'une Vie[12]. Il faut enfin savoir que les érudits modernes ont considéré que l'évêque Liudhard qui, selon Bède le Vénérable, accompagna en Angleterre la princesse mérovingienne Berthe à l'occasion de son mariage avec le roi du Kent Aethelbert à la fin du VIe siècle, avait été évêque à Senlis[13]. Outre le fait que le principal texte hagiographique le concernant est un petit recueil de miracles rédigé à Canterbury (où se trouvait son tombeau) au tournant des XI-XIIe siècles par le moine Goscelin, aucune source ne le considère comme un évêque de Senlis avant la fin du XIVe siècle[14].

II. Le diocèse de Beauvais

Deux modèles de sainteté se laissent facilement distinguer dans le diocèse de Beauvais du haut Moyen Âge. Il s'agit d'une

---

[10] Arnoux (1996), p. 218.
[11] Bautier – Labory (1965), p. 82.
[12] À moins que l'on puisse considérer comme telle l'apographe conservé dans la bibliothèque des Bollandistes et tiré d'un manuscrit de Sainte-Marie de la Victoire de Senlis (*BHL* 3089).
[13] «De S. Letardo episcopo».
[14] de Vriendt (2013).

part des traditions martyriales attestées dès l'époque mérovingienne et bien enregistrées dans les grands martyrologes historiques du IXe siècle qui donnèrent lieu à une entreprise assez abondante d'écriture et de réécriture autour des saints Lucien et Just[15]. D'autre part, à une date plus difficile à fixer, entre le IXe et le XIe siècles, furent aussi mises par écrit des Vies de saints que l'on peut considérer comme les récits de fondations de deux petits établissements monastiques, Oroër et Fly avec les saints Germer, Angadrême et Évroult. Dès lors que la contribution d'Ineke van 't Spijker sur l'hagiographie de la Gallia du Nord et de l'Ouest entre 950 et 1130 n'avait pas pour ambition d'être exhaustive, le parti a été pris ici d'envisager les dossiers hagiographiques dans leur ensemble quand bien même leur composition avant 950 n'est pas absolument assurée[16].

A. Saint Lucien

Le nom de Lucius, puis de Lucianus, est associé aux martyrs dits de Riciovare dans les plus anciens textes (mérovingiens) qui relèvent de ce cycle hagiographique, même si, par la suite, les *Passiones Luciani* n'attribuent jamais à ce personnage imaginaire la mort du saint martyr de Beauvais. Le même nom de Lucius est mentionné comme compagnon de saint Quentin et des saints Crépin et Crépinien dans leurs plus anciennes Passions respectives; et celui de Lucianus dans la Passion ancienne des saints Victoric et Fuscien d'Amiens[17]. Le nom de Lucius est aussi cité parmi les martyrs dont les reliques furent inventées à Beauvais par saint Éloi, au même titre que celles des saints Quentin (au lieu-dit éponyme en Vermandois), Crépin et Crépinien (à Soissons) et Piat (à Seclin) et dont certaines reçurent à cette occasion une nouvelle châsse réalisée par l'ancien moné-

---

[15] *Le martyrologe d'Usuard. Texte et commentaire*, éd. J. DUBOIS, Bruxelles, 1965, p. 88, 156 et 324.

[16] VAN 'T SPIJKER (1996), spéc. p. 247. Les pages qui suivent développent certains points déjà présentés dans MÉRIAUX (2018).

[17] GAILLARD (2014), p. 2 et 10.

taire du palais de Clotaire II et Dagobert Ier devenu en 640 (jusqu'à sa mort en 660) évêque de Noyon et Tournai[18].

Le plus ancien récit de la Passion de Lucien (*BHL* 5008) se lit aujourd'hui dans les légendiers Paris, BnF, lat. 12598 (en provenance de Corbie et daté des environs de 800 pour les feuillets comportant la Passion), Orléans, BM 331 (originaire de Fleury, Xe siècle), Bruxelles, KBR 207-208 et British Museum, Harley, 2800 (tous deux du XIIIe siècle)[19]. Comme l'a noté Henri Moretus Plantin, son dernier éditeur, les copistes de ces trois témoins ont chacun cherché « à rendre moins incorrect le latin très barbare de l'auteur », à « rendre un texte mérovingien acceptable aux lecteurs plus cultivés de l'époque carolingienne »[20]. La Passion *BHL* 5008 représente donc à l'évidence un nouvel état d'un texte primitif que l'on datera par prudence du VIIIe siècle. Tel qu'il est conservé, il s'agit d'une Passion destinée à être lue le jour de la fête du saint (le 8 janvier), donc sans aucun doute à l'intention de la communauté et des fidèles rassemblés autour de son tombeau à Beauvais, même si rien n'indique que l'auteur soit à compter parmi eux. La Passion rapporte qu'à l'époque de l'empereur Néron, Lucien, qualifié de *presbiter* mais jamais d'évêque, fut envoyé de Rome par saint Pierre (c. 1-2) et convertit 12 000 païens à Beauvais. Alors un « empereur » (*caesar*, mais aussi *dux*) du nom de Julien envoya de Rome trois hommes nommés Latinus, Iarius et Antur qui firent d'abord périr les disciples de Lucien, Maximianus (ou Maxianus) et Julien, avant de lui trancher la tête. Sur son tombeau, une basilique fut construite à un mille de Beauvais. Henri Moretus Plantin a repéré des emprunts significatifs à la Passion des saints Julien et Basilisse (*BHL* 4529) fêtés le lendemain. Au milieu du IXe siècle, l'éloge que Raban Maur compose en l'honneur de Lucien dans son martyrologe montre qu'il a connaissance de cette première Passion[21].

---

[18] *Vita Eligii* (*BHL* 2474), éd. B. KRUSCH, *MGH*, *SRM*, IV, Hanovre – Leipzig, 1902, p. 663-741: I, 32, p. 688; II, 7, p. 700; MÉRIAUX – MEIJNS (2009); GAILLARD (2014), p. 8-9.

[19] *Passio Luciani* (*BHL* 5008), éd. MORETUS PLANTIN (1953), p. 66-70; commentaire: *ibid.*, p. 13-19; DE GAIFFIER (1954); AIGRAIN (1955).

[20] MORETUS PLANTIN (1953), p. 18.

[21] RABANUS MAURUS, *Martyrologium*, éd. J. McCULLOH, Turnhout, 1979 (*CC CM*, 44), p. 7 (4 janvier).

La deuxième Passion (*BHL* 5010) est un remaniement principalement formel mais qui vise aussi à établir une certaine cohérence chronologique en cherchant désormais à inscrire approximativement la mission de saint Lucien dans le contexte des IIIe-IVe siècles et en l'associant à celle de saint Quentin ainsi que, dans une moindre mesure, à celle de saint Denis qui aurait ordonné Lucien prêtre [22]. Le rapprochement entre Lucien et Denis est renforcé par l'introduction de l'épisode de la céphalophorie: décapité, Lucien aurait miraculeusement porté sa tête jusqu'au lieu de sa sépulture. Toutefois, aux yeux d'Henri Moretus Plantin, le rôle de saint Denis apparaît trop effacé pour considérer que la seconde Passion de ce martyr (*BHL* 2178) ait pu inspirer celle de Lucien. Il renonçait donc à préciser la datation de *BHL* 5010 autrement que par un emprunt aux *Dialogues* de Grégoire le Grand invitant à voir en l'auteur un moine bénédictin de Saint-Lucien, vraisemblablement contemporain de la réforme de l'établissement sous les règnes de Charlemagne (768-814) ou de Louis le Pieux (814-840). Dans sa récente édition de la seconde Passion anonyme de saint Denis qu'il date par ailleurs de l'abbatiat de Waldo (806-814), Michael Lapidge relève à son tour l'intérêt que porte son auteur à Lucien, mais, en se fondant sur des emprunts formels, il considère que la *Passio Dionysii* a servi de source à la *Passion Luciani* dont il situe sans autre précision la rédaction dans la première moitié du IXe siècle [23]. Il a été suivi sur ce point par Anne-Marie Helvétius qui serait toutefois encline à rajeunir la composition de la *Passio Dionysii* et à en dater la rédaction du milieu du VIIIe siècle [24], sans que ce point n'ait d'incidence sur la datation commune de la *Passio Luciani*. La fourchette reste donc très approximative dès lors qu'on ne sait rien de l'histoire de l'abbaye avant 833 et rien non plus de l'introduction de la règle bénédictine [25]. Comme on

---

[22] *Passio Luciani* (*BHL* 5010), éd. MORETUS PLANTIN (1953), p. 74-82; commentaire: *ibid.*, p. 20-28; DE GAIFFIER (1954); AIGRAIN (1955).

[23] LAPIDGE (2016), p. 52.

[24] HELVÉTIUS (2014), spéc. p. 35-36, n. 45.

[25] L'abbaye Saint-Lucien est mentionnée dans le testament d'Anségise: *Chronique des abbés de Fontenelle*, éd. P. PRADIÉ, Paris, 1999, XIII, 7, p. 180; l'abbaye est ensuite documentée par un diplôme de Charles le Chauve de 869: *Recueil des actes de Charles II le Chauve, roi de France*, éd. A. GIRY, M. PROU et G. TESSIER, Paris, 1943-1955, n° 325, p. 214-217; voir aussi VERCAUTEREN (1928), p. 107-108.

ne dispose d'aucun indice montrant que l'abbaye aurait disposé d'une école digne de ce nom, on ne peut écarter l'hypothèse d'un auteur appartenant à un autre établissement. On penserait alors volontiers à Saint-Denis.

La troisième et dernière Passion de saint Lucien (*BHL* 5009) se présente comme une œuvre anonyme, mais son attribution à l'évêque Eudes de Beauvais est solide et remonte au moins au XVIIe siècle[26]. Elle se fonde sur l'entrée du nécrologe de Saint-Lucien lui attribuant la rédaction ou du moins la commande d'une *Historia Christi militum in honorem Luciani, Maxiani et Iuliani*. Cette Passion longue a fait l'objet d'abréviations dans l'ensemble de sa tradition manuscrite, constituée d'une quinzaine de témoins. Après avoir eu une activité militaire (dont se ferait l'écho le vocabulaire parfois martial de la Passion), Eudes fut formé à l'abbaye de Corbie dont il devint abbé en 851 avant d'être élu évêque de Beauvais au plus tôt à la fin de l'année 859[27]. En 869, le diplôme de Charles le Chauve en faveur de Saint-Lucien rappelle que l'abbaye dépendait du siège épiscopal et procède à la restitution de la moitié de la *villa* de Luchy en Beauvaisis pour laquelle le souverain avait été sollicité par Eudes lui-même[28]. La mention de la translation des reliques des saints Lucien et Just à l'abbaye de Saint-Riquier le 12 juin 866 confirme le rayonnement du culte du martyr à ce moment-là[29]. De fait, le texte insiste sur les liens entre l'abbaye et l'évêché en attribuant à Lucien le titre d'évêque. Par ailleurs l'auteur inscrit beaucoup plus franchement le saint dans le contexte du Ier siècle en le présentant comme un envoyé du pape Clément, à l'évidence pour mettre en cohérence son texte avec la Passion de saint Denis (*BHL* 2175) composée vers 835 par l'abbé Hilduin qui identifiait le martyr de Paris avec le Denis converti par saint Paul à Athènes (Ac 17) auquel était attribué par la même occasion la paternité du corpus philosophique «dionysien» que l'empereur byzantin avait adressé à Louis le Pieux en 827. Pour

---

[26] Eudes de Beauvais, *Passio Luciani* (*BHL* 5009), éd. MORETUS PLANTIN (1953), p. 86-107; commentaire: *ibid.*, p. 29-34 et 83-85; DE GAIFFIER (1954); AIGRAIN (1955).

[27] Loup de Ferrières, *Correspondance*, éd. L. LEVILLAIN, II: 847-862, Paris, 1935, n° 106-107, p. 134-144; GRIERSON (1935).

[28] Voir *supra*.

[29] HARIULF, *Chronique de l'abbaye de Saint-Riquier (Ve siècle – 1104)*, éd. F. LOT, Paris, 1894, III, 12, p. 123-124.

en revenir à la troisième rédaction de la *Passio Luciani* qui a beaucoup emprunté à la *Passio Dionysii*, on notera l'affirmation de l'ancrage «parisien» du culte de saint Lucien de la part d'un évêque qui jouait alors un rôle politique de premier plan auprès d'Hincmar de Reims et de Charles le Chauve dans la construction du royaume de Francie occidentale.

B. Saint Just

Le culte d'un autre martyr, saint Just, est attesté depuis l'époque mérovingienne dans le diocèse de Beauvais, à Saint-Just-en-Chaussée, au croisement des routes Beauvais-Vermand et Senlis-Amiens[30]. Comme pour saint Lucien, le texte le plus ancien de la Passion de saint Just a longtemps été celui qui se trouve copié dans le légendier de Corbie de la fin du VIIIe siècle, dans deux anciens légendiers de Saint-Gall (Stiftsbibliothek, 548, fin du VIIIe siècle, et 566, début du Xe siècle) ainsi que dans une dizaine d'autres témoins (*BHL* 4590)[31].

En 1954 cependant, Bernhard Bischoff a découvert à la Bibliothèque de Düsseldorf un fragment de la Passion de saint Just dont l'étude et l'édition ont été confiées au Père Coens[32]. Un autre fragment provenant du même *codex* primitif, mais beaucoup plus mutilé, a été retrouvé très récemment au même endroit dans la reliure d'un incunable[33]. L'écriture de ces épaves est en caractères anglo-saxons du milieu du VIIIe siècle et semble pouvoir être attachée à un *scriptorium* de Northumbrie. Il est assuré que ces fragments ont autrefois appartenu à l'abbaye de Werden fondée en Saxe vers 800 par le frison Liudger. Or Liudger avait fait dans sa jeunesse un long séjour à York auprès d'Alcuin et, même s'il dut quitter précipitamment la ville en 773, il ne négligea pas d'emporter avec lui un grand nombre de manuscrits northumbriens sur le continent. De l'avis du Père

---

[30] Saint-Just-en Chaussée: dép. Oise, arr. Clermont, chef-lieu de cant.
[31] *Passio Iusti* (*BHL* 4590), éd. E. Carpentier, *AASS*, Oct. VIII, Bruxelles, 1853, p. 338-339; éd. C. Narbey, *Supplément aux Acta Sanctorum pour des Vies de saints de l'époque mérovingienne*, t. II, Paris, 1900, n° 15, p. 111-113 (d'après le légendier de Corbie), reproduite dans Röckelein (2006), p. 358-360; cf. Coens (1956), p. 86-90.
[32] Coens (1956), spéc. p. 94-96 pour l'édition du fragment.
[33] Zechiel-Eckes (2003).

Coens et, plus récemment, de Klaus Zechiel-Eckes, ces épaves semblent bien avoir fait partie du lot[34]. Ces fragments anglo-saxons de la *Passio Iusti* (BHL 4590c) témoignent ainsi de l'existence d'un texte plus ancien, composé sur le continent puisque son auteur écrivait auprès du tombeau du martyr et fait état de la fête et du pèlerinage qui avaient lieu le 18 octobre. Constatant un état très dégradé de la latinité du fragment de Düsseldorf, le Père Coens ne voyait pas d'inconvénient à faire remonter la rédaction primitive avant la fin du VIIe siècle[35].

La *Passio Justi* BHL 4590 correspond ainsi à la réécriture, avant la fin du VIIIe siècle, d'un texte qui circulait déjà. Il reste toutefois difficile de savoir qui fut l'auteur de cette nouvelle version et à quel usage elle était destinée puisqu'ont disparues toutes les précisions qui figurent dans les fragments de Düsseldorf. Subsiste toutefois la trame «d'une histoire d'allure presque grand-guignolesque» comme a pu l'écrire le Père Coens[36]. Né à Auxerre, Just accompagne son père Justin parti à la recherche de son frère Justinien qu'ils retrouvèrent à Amiens. Chrétiens, ils furent reconnus par des soldats du préfet Riciovare qui les retrouvèrent à la source Sirica. Just seul fut mis à mort alors que le père et l'oncle étaient réfugiés dans une grotte. Just put toutefois se saisir de sa tête tranchée et adresser une dernière prière. Il fit également savoir que son corps devait être enterré dans la grotte et sa tête rapportée à sa mère à Auxerre. Une fois arrivée dans la cité, celle-ci dégageait une telle lumière que l'évêque Amâtre eut connaissance du prodige et ordonna qu'elle fût déposée dans la basilique qu'il avait préparée pour sa propre sépulture. Une jeune fille venue y prier recouvra immédiatement la vue. Il est difficile de savoir si le lieu de la sépulture de Just est resté longtemps un lieu de vénération. Au milieu du IXe siècle, Usuard localise certes son culte *in territorio Belvacensi*, cela ne signifie pas nécessairement qu'une communauté était établie à cet endroit[37]. Comme on l'a vu, des reliques du saint

---

[34] COENS (1956), p. 91-92 et surtout ZECHIEL-ECKES (2002).
[35] COENS (1956), p. 96-97 et 105-106 («sans doute avant 700»); *ibid.* p. 104, à propos de la graphie *Rizoalis* employé par le fragment pour désigner Riciovare: «le copiste, un Anglo-Saxon, avait vraisemblablement sous les yeux un texte du VIIe siècle en semi-onciales où les *g* parfois se laissent prendre pour des *z*.»
[36] COENS (1956), p. 89.
[37] DUBOIS (1965), p. 324.

se trouvaient vraisemblablement à Beauvais en 866 puisqu'elles furent apportées à l'abbaye de Saint-Riquier avec celles de saint Lucien[38]. Il existe aussi un récit de translation de reliques à l'abbaye de Malmédy dans le premier tiers du Xe siècle, mais ce n'est assurément pas une production beauvaisienne; un miracle survenu à Cambrai montre toutefois que l'auteur connaissait le texte de la Passion de Just[39]. Enfin, comme l'a bien montré Hedwig Röckelein, le personnage et la vie de Just firent l'objet, vraisemblablement dès le IXe siècle, d'un étonnant dédoublement pour donner naissance à un nouveau culte, celui de saint Justin, qui ne se distingue que par le lieu de son martyre (à Louvres près de Paris) et la date de sa fête (le 1er août)[40]. La Passion (*BHL* 4579) fut calquée sur celle de Just et ses reliques furent ensuite largement diffusées en Saxe au Xe siècle[41].

Il reste à évoquer la dernière pièce du dossier de saint Just. Il s'agit d'une nouvelle réécriture de la Passion (*BHL* 4591) qui connut une diffusion restreinte et très locale[42]. Le plus ancien témoin est le légendier du chapitre Saint-Quentin de Beauvais (Paris, BnF, lat. 17627) sur lequel il faudra revenir. La Passion s'ouvre sur un court prologue rappelant que le martyre n'a pas été l'apanage des hommes mais que des femmes et des enfants se sont illustrés ainsi. Le texte est une réécriture fidèle sur le fond dont le découpage en douze leçons brèves suggère un usage liturgique. La Passion vient seulement préciser au c. 9 qu'une basilique avait été construite sur le lieu du martyre de Just, mais qu'en raison de l'affluence du peuple, ses reliques ont été apportées à Beauvais, dans le *sacrarium* de l'église Saint-Pierre qui

---

[38] Voir *supra*; COENS (1956), p. 108-109.

[39] *Translatio Iusti Malmundarium* (*BHL* 4594), éd. L. DE HEINEMANN, *MGH*, *SS*, XV-1, Hanovre, 1887, p. 566-567 (d'après l'édition prise par Dom Martène et Dom Durand sur un manuscrit de Malmédy aujourd'hui perdu); COENS (1956), p. 110; RÖCKELEIN (2006), p. 329. Il s'ensuivit la composition d'une nouvelle Passion dans le diocèse de Liège avant le XIIe siècle (*BHL* 4593).

[40] Louvres: dép. Val-d'Oise, arr. Sarcelles; Justin est mentionné dans le martyrologe Usuard (DUBOIS, 1965, p. 277) qui est le plus ancien témoin de son culte.

[41] RÖCKELEIN (2006), p. 333-347, avec édition *princeps* de la *Passio Iustini BHL* 4579 aux p. 352-356.

[42] *Passio Iusti* (*BHL* 4591), éd. E. CARPENTIER, *AASS*, Oct. VIII, Bruxelles, 1853, p. 340-342. La *BHL*ms signale trois manuscrits: Paris, BnF, lat. 5351, 16329 et 17627.

désigne sans aucun doute la cathédrale[43]. Pour quelle communauté fut-elle composée? Le chapitre cathédral? Le chapitre Saint-Quentin de Beauvais fondé dans les années 1060[44]? Le chapitre fondé ou restauré à Saint-Just-en-Chaussée dans la seconde moitié du XIe siècle, mais qui avait été établi sur des biens de la mense épiscopale et dont l'évêque conservait le titre abbatial[45]? La date de la composition est tout aussi incertaine, même si l'on serait enclin à mettre en avant les besoins liturgiques de ces nouvelles fondations dans le courant du XIe siècle.

C. Les saints d'Orër et de Fly: Germer, Angadrême et Évroult

En 863, une bulle du pape Nicolas Ier confirmait la donation par le roi Charles le Chauve à l'église de Beauvais de deux établissements qui étaient alors abandonnés: le monastère, autrefois féminin, d'*Oratorium* et le chapitre de Fly (*Flaviacum*)[46]. L'existence de l'un comme de l'autre était déjà bien attestée, surtout celle de Fly, dans l'orbite de l'abbaye de Fontenelle/Saint-Wandrille[47]. Passé 863, il n'est plus fait mention de ces deux établissements. Dans le cas de Fly, il faut attendre 1036 pour voir l'évêque Drogon y fonder un monastère[48]. Quant à *Oratorium* – identifié communément avec le village actuel d'Oroër[49] – on ne sait s'il a jamais été question d'y restaurer une communauté. La mémoire des origines de l'une et l'autre a cependant été conservée, sinon «inventée», dans l'hagiographie avec la rédaction des Vies des saints fondateurs: à Fly, Germer (*Geremarus*); à Oroër, Angadrême (*Angadrisma*) et Évroult

---

[43] Mériaux – Pietri (2006), p. 138.
[44] Voir *infra*.
[45] Lohrmann (1976), p. 45 et 63-64; Becquet (1989), p. 94-96.
[46] *PL* 119, p. 813; cf. Lohrmann (1976), p. 22 et *Recueil des actes de Charles II le Chauve, roi de France*, op. cit., t. II, n° 254, p. 78-79.
[47] *Chronique des abbés de Fontenelle*, op. cit., III, 1, p. 42 (au début du VIIIe siècle, Bénigne est abbé de Fly); XIII, 1, p. 148 (dans les années 820, Anségise est aussi abbé de Fly); XIII, 6, p. 170 (donation d'Anségise à Fly); XIII, 7, p. 180 (testament d'Anségise avec donations à Fly et *Oratorium*).
[48] Saint-Germer-de-Fly: dép. Oise, arr. Beauvais, cant. Grandvilliers; sur la communauté, voir Becquet (1989), p. 150-154.
[49] Voir *infra*.

(*Ebrulfus*), ce dernier à bien distinguer de son homonyme, fondateur du monastère d'Ouche au diocèse de Lisieux.

Les Vies de saint Germer (*BHL* 3437 et 3441) font vivre le fondateur de Fly au début du VIIe siècle[50]. Ami de saint Ouen, il aurait été admis à la cour de Dagobert avant de quitter cette existence séculière pour la vie monastique. Bien qu'il ait été originaire du *pagus* de Beauvais, l'essentiel de sa vie se déroule dans l'actuelle Normandie. Il aurait fondé le monastère d'*Insula* avant de rejoindre celui de Pentale. Saint Ouen lui-même l'aurait ordonné prêtre avant qu'il n'aille fonder le monastère de Fly où il mourut trois ans et demi plus tard et fut enterré. Si, en l'état, le texte ne permet guère de comparaisons stylistiques avec les Vies rédigées à Rouen et dans ses environs au haut Moyen Âge, sa caractéristique principale réside bien dans l'absence de tout lien avec les traditions hagiographiques beauvaisiennes antérieures et dans le fort tropisme rouennais exercé par la figure de saint Ouen. La situation est moins étonnante qu'il n'y paraît quand on connaît la position frontalière qu'occupait Fly entre les deux diocèses et l'influence très forte exercée par Fontenelle dès le haut Moyen Âge. Bruno Krusch datait la première Vie de la première moitié du IXe siècle (A = *BHL* 3441), révisée et complétée deux siècles plus tard pour les besoins de la restauration monastique de 1036 (B = *BHL* 3437).

La situation est un peu différente à propos des légendes de fondation du monastère d'*Oratorium* qui reposent sur un texte ancien, antérieur au IXe siècle, la Vie de saint Ansbert, abbé de Fontenelle puis évêque métropolitain de Rouen à la fin du VIIe siècle. On peut y lire qu'Ansbert avait été fiancé à une certaine Angadrême (*Angadrisma*). Refusant le mariage, elle fut momentanément frappée par la lèpre, ce qui mit un terme au projet. Elle aurait ensuite pris la tête du monastère d'*Oratorium* près de Beauvais[51]. Toujours inédite, la *Vita Angadrismae* contenue dans le légendier de Saint-Quentin de Beauvais (fol. 138v-

---

[50] *Vita Geremari* (*BHL* 3437), éd. J. Périer, *AASS*, Sept. VI, Anvers, 1757, p. 689-703; *Vita Geremari* (*BHL* 3441), éd. B. Krusch, *MGH, SRM*, IV, Hanovre – Leipzig, 1902, p. 628-633.

[51] Aigrade, *Vita Ansberti* (*BHL* 520), éd. W. Levison, *MGH, SRM*, V, Hanovre – Leipzig, 1910, p. 619-641, c. 3, p. 621: *Sequenti quoque tempore sancta gubernatrix efficitur coenobii Oratorii, quod est situm in pago Belloacensi prope muros urbis Belloacus*. La localisation du monastère d'Oratorium, «près des murs» de Beauvais, laisse planer un doute sur l'identification avec Oroër, situé non

143v) ne fait qu'ajouter des généralités à ces informations très brèves, mais le simple fait de les avoir rassemblées dans une Vie indépendante est révélateur de l'intention de son auteur ou de son commanditaire: insister sur le lien étroit entre Fontenelle et Oroër peut-être à un moment où il aurait été envisagé d'y restaurer une communauté[52].

L'auteur de la Vie de saint Évroult (*Ebrulfus*, à ne pas confondre, on l'a dit, avec son homonyme auquel est attribuée la fondation de l'abbaye d'Ouche au diocèse de Lisieux[53]) s'est chargé d'écrire une légende de fondation toute différente de l'abbaye d'Oroër, dans un sens exclusivement «beauvaisien», en omettant, sans doute délibérément, toute référence «normande»[54]. Originaire du Beauvaisis, ce saint prêtre est crédité de la fondation du monastère d'Oroër (c. 3) avant son ordination par l'évêque de Beauvais (c. 4). Il aurait aussi pris la tête de la communauté installée autour des reliques des martyrs Victoric, Fuscien et Gentien dans les environs d'Amiens (c. 5) et procédé à l'invention des reliques de saint Lucien à Beauvais (c. 6). Tout ceci le met explicitement en relation avec la tradition martyriale des victimes de Riciovare, tout en faisant de lui un contemporain de Germer et surtout d'Angadrême dont la figure se trouve éclipsée (c. 9). Le dernier chapitre précise que les reliques du saint sont désormais conservées dans la cathédrale Saint-Pierre de Beauvais (c. 10). La Vie d'Évroult, dont Wilhelm Levison a mis en évidence des emprunts à la Vie de saint Aubin par Venance Fortunat[55], est utilisée par l'auteur d'un faux diplôme du roi Chilpéric Ier pour Saint-Lucien que Fernand Vercauteren date du début du XIe siècle[56]. Le tropisme beauvaisien du texte invite à en chercher l'auteur au sein du chapitre cathédral.

---

pas dans le suburbium mais à une bonne quinzaine de kilomètres au nord de la cité (dép. Oise, arr. Mouy, cant. Beauvais).

[52] Pour les autres attestations du culte de la sainte, voir DE GAIFFIER (1980).

[53] Cf. POULIN, J.-C., «L'hagiographie de Basse-Normandie», *supra*, p. 289-291.

[54] *Vita Ebrulfi* (BHL 2372), éd. G. CUYPERS, G., *AASS*, Iul. VI, Anvers, 1729, p. 194-196.

[55] Aigrade, *Vita Ansberti, op. cit.*, p. 621, n. 2.

[56] VERCAUTEREN (1928), p. 102-103 et 109.

D. Le légendier de Saint-Quentin de Beauvais

Un bon nombre de textes que nous venons de présenter se trouvent copiés dans le légendier Paris, BnF, lat. 17627 de la fin du XIe siècle. Propriété de la cathédrale de Notre-Dame de Paris qui l'avait reçu du chanoine Claude Joly, il appartenait au XVe siècle à un certain Jean de l'hospice Saint-Just de Beauvais[57]. La collection comprend une bonne soixantaine de pièces. Elle s'ouvre sur l'ensemble du dossier textuel de saint Quentin (fol. 1r-55v)[58]. Elle comprend la seconde Passion de saint Just (fol. 124v-129r) ainsi que le début de la deuxième Passion de saint Lucien (fol. 260r-260v) dont le texte, mutilé, a été complété sur des folios ajoutés au XVIe siècle. On y trouve aussi des Passions de martyrs concernés de près ou de loin par la persécution légendaire du préfet Riciovare dans le Nord de la Gaule: Fuscien d'Amiens et ses compagnons (fol. 55v-61v), Firmin d'Amiens (fol. 193r-199r), Rufin et Valère de Soissons (fol. 201v-203v), Crépin et Crépinien de Soissons (fol. 207v-211r) et, enfin, la Passion de saint Denis par Hilduin (fol. 236r-260r). À ces textes, s'ajoutent la Vie d'Évroult (fol. 122r-124v), la seconde Vie de Germer (fol. 129r-138v) et celle d'Angadrême (fol. 138v-142v). On note également la présence de deux saintes du Vermandois: Benoîte d'Origny (fol. 71v-78r), au diocèse de Laon, et Hunégonde d'Homblières au diocèse de Noyon (83v-93v).

Tous ces éléments rattachent clairement la composition du légendier à la personne de Guy, chanoine et doyen de Saint-Quentin en Vermandois devenu évêque de Beauvais en 1063, et surtout à sa fondation: le chapitre Saint-Quentin de la cité connu aussi pour avoir reçu comme abbé Yves, avant son élection épiscopale à Chartres en 1090[59]. Outre la mise en avant du culte de saint Quentin, la présence d'un bon nombre de textes relevant du cycle dit de Riciovare ainsi que de légendes locales

---

[57] *Cat. Bruxelles*, III, p. 408-414; le manuscrit peut être consulté en ligne sur le portail Gallica.

[58] Pour le dossier de saint Quentin, voir CHAFFENET – GAILLARD «Le diocèse de Noyon», *supra*, p. 368-371.

[59] LABANDE (1892), p. 48-52; GUYOTJEANNIN, p. 70-71; VERCAUTEREN (1934), p. 284 et 286; BECQUET (1989), p. 61-64; *Recueil des actes de Philippe Ier, roi de France (1059-1108)*, éd. M. PROU, Paris, 1908, n° 94, p. 243-245 et n° 119, p. 303-304.

du Vermandois, le rassemblement des traditions hagiographiques beauvaisiennes (qui semble assez exhaustif) donne une bonne image de la culture hagiographique de la cité épiscopale dans la seconde moitié du XIe siècle.

Dès lors que le légendier ne fait pas mention des autres saints dont le culte serait attesté plus tard dans le diocèse de Beauvais, il y a tout lieu de penser qu'aucun texte ne leur avait été consacré avant le milieu du XIe siècle. Il s'agit de sainte Romaine, martyre, dont les reliques furent apportées en 1069 à l'initiative de l'évêque Guy depuis la cathédrale vers la collégiale Saint-Quentin (*BHL* 2795); et des saintes Maure et Brigide (*BHL* 5724). Plus étonnante est l'absence de traditions littéraires anciennes pour sainte Maxence (*BHL* 5797-5799) dont le culte est pourtant attesté dans la toponymie dès les VIIe-VIIIe siècles[60].

Replacée dans le cadre plus général de l'hagiographie carolingienne du nord de la Gaule, la production du diocèse de Beauvais apparaît assez effacée. On devine plus qu'on observe une activité au sein du chapitre cathédral et à Saint-Lucien. Il n'est pas exclu que plusieurs textes que nous avons passés en revue aient été composés par des personnalités extérieures. Paradoxalement, les auteurs les mieux identifiés sont les moines de Saint-Vaast d'Arras réfugiés à Beauvais entre 881 et 893 qui mirent par écrit quelques récits de miracles opérés sur place par leur saint patron[61]. On retiendra le rôle accordé aux deux martyrs, Lucien et Just, dans l'ensemble plus vaste des textes du cycle de Riciovare et, plus particulièrement du thème de la céphalophorie développé précocement par leurs Passions[62]. Quant à l'hagiographie monastique, d'inspiration « normande », elle reste peu développée, cantonnée dans des productions tar-

---

[60] Pont-Sainte-Maxence (dép. Oise, arr. Senlis) est mentionné dans le *Liber historiae Francorum* (que reprend la première continuation de la Chronique dite de Frédégaire) lorsqu'à la fin des années 670 le maire du palais Ébroïn quitta le monastère de Luxeuil pour renverser son rival Leudesius: *La Geste des rois francs*, texte latin édité par B. KRUSCH, introduction et commentaire de S. LEBECQ, Paris, 2019, p. 156; Frédégaire, *Chronique des temps mérovingiens*, traduction, introduction et notes par O. DEVILLERS et J. MEYERS, Turnhout, p. 204.

[61] MÉRIAUX (2018), p. 297-298.

[62] MORETUS PLANTIN (1953), p. 53-61; COENS (1956), p. 111-114; COENS (1962).

dives et mineures liées à la restauration du monastère de Fly, peut-être aussi de celle d'Oroër qui aboutit finalement à la récupération du culte d'Angadrême et d'Évroult à la cathédrale de Beauvais. On constate enfin l'absence d'une hagiographie épiscopale digne de ce nom qui reflète la très grande discrétion, dans le reste de la documentation, des évêques de Beauvais avant le IXe siècle[63].

Bibliographie

«De S. Letardo episcopo Silvanectensi in Gallia, Cantuariae in Anglia», in *AASS*, Feb. III, Anvers, 1658, p. 468-470.
«De S. Regulo episcopo Silvanectis in Gallia», in *AASS*, Mart. III, Anvers, 1668, p. 816-827.
Aigrain, R., «Une application de la méthode comparative en hagiographie», *Bibliothèque de l'École des Chartes*, 113 (1955), p. 201-208.
Bautier, R.-H. – Labory, G. (éd. et trad.), *Helgaud de Fleury. Vie de Robert le Pieux*, Paris, 1965.
Becquet, J., *Abbayes et prieurés de l'ancienne France. Recueil historique des archevêchés, évêchés, abbayes et prieurés de France*, 18: *Province ecclésiastique de Reims. Diocèse actuel de Beauvais*, Ligugé, 1989.
Borst, A., *Der karolingische Reichskalender und seine Überlieferung bis ins 12. Jahrhundert*, Hanovre, 2001, 3 vol.
Coens, M., «Aux origines de la céphalophorie. Un fragment retrouvé d'une ancienne Passion de s. Just, martyr de Beauvais», *AB*, 74 (1956), p. 86-114.
—, «Nouvelles recherches sur un thème hagiographique: la céphalophorie», in *Bulletin de la classe des Lettres de l'Académie royale de Belgique*, 5e série, 48 (1962), p. 231-253.
de Gaiffier, B., «Compte rendu de H. Moretus Plantin, *Les Passions de saint Lucien et leurs dérivés céphalophoriques*», *Le Moyen Âge*, 60 (1954), p. 237-243.
—, «Sainte Angadrisma (VIIe siècle). À propos de son culte», in E. Dassmann *et al.*, éd., *Pietas. Festschrift für Bernhard Kötting*, Münster, 1980, p. 280-283.
de Vriendt, F., «Léthard», in *DHGE*, t. 31, 2013, col. 1087-1091.
Delisle, L., *Mémoire sur d'anciens sacramentaires*, Paris, 1886.
Dubois, J., éd., *Le martyrologe d'Usuard. Texte et commentaire*, Bruxelles, 1965.

---

[63] Duchesne (1915), p. 119-120; Mériaux (2018), p. 296-297.

DUCHESNE, L., *Fastes épiscopaux de l'ancienne Gaule*, III: *Les provinces du Nord et de l'Est*, Paris, 1915.

GAILLARD, M., «Remarques sur les plus anciennes versions de la *Passio* et de l'*Inventio* des saints Fuscien, Victoric et Gentien (manuscrits Paris, BnF, lat. 12598 et Wien, ÖNB, 371)», in M. GOULLET, éd., *Parva pro magnis munera. Études de littérature tardo-antique et médiévale offertes à François Dolbeau par ses élèves*, Turnhout, 2009, p. 397-409.

—, «Un 'cycle' hagiographique du haut Moyen Âge en Gaule septentrionale: les Passions des martyrs de Riciovar», *Hagiographica*, 21 (2014), p. 1-28.

GRIERSON, P., «Eudes Ier évêque de Beauvais», *Le Moyen Âge*, 45 (1935), p. 161-198.

GUYOTJEANNIN, O., Episcopus et comes. *Affirmation et déclin de la seigneurie épiscopale au nord du royaume de France (Beauvais-Noyon, X^e – début XIIIe siècle)*, Genève – Paris, 1987.

HELVÉTIUS, A.-M., «La deuxième version latine de la Passion de saint Denis (*BHL* 2178)», *Bibliothèque de l'École des Chartes*, 172 (2014), p. 29-60.

KRÜGER, A., *Litanei-Handschriften der Karolingerzeit*, Hanovre, 2007.

LABANDE, L.-H., *Histoire de Beauvais et de ses institutions communales jusqu'au commencement du XVe siècle*, Paris, 1892.

LAPIDGE, M., «The 'anonymous *Passio S. Dionysii*' (*BHL* 2178)», *AB*, 134 (2016), p. 20-65.

LOHRMANN, D., *Papsturkunden in Frankreich*, Neue Folge, 7: *Nördliche Ile-de-France und Vermandois*, Göttingen, 1976.

MAGNANI, E., «Trophimus, Dionisus, Regulus, Felicissimus... Listes et vies des premiers évêques d'Arles (IXe-XIIe siècle)», *Provence historique*, 66 (2016), p. 103-118.

MEIJNS, B. – MÉRIAUX C., «Le cycle de Rictiovar et la topographie chrétienne des campagnes septentrionales à l'époque mérovingienne», in D. PARIS-POULAIN – S. NARDI COMBESCURE – D. ISTRIA, dir., *Les premiers temps chrétiens dans le territoire de la France actuelle. Hagiographie, épigraphie et archéologie: nouvelles approches et perspectives de recherche*, Rennes, 2009, p. 19-33.

MÉRIAUX, C., «Le culte des saints en Beauvaisis au XIe siècle», in P. BAUDUIN – G. COMBALBERT – A. DUBOIS – B. GARNIER – C. MANEUVRIER, éd., *Sur les pas de Lanfranc, du Bec à Caen. Recueil d'études en hommage à Véronique Gazeau*, Caen, 2018, p. 293-301.

MÉRIAUX, C. – PIETRI, L., «Beauvais», in L. PIETRI, éd., *Topographie chrétienne des cités de la Gaule, des origines au milieu du VIIIe siècle*, XIV: *Province ecclésiastique de Reims (Belgica secunda)*, Paris, 2006, p. 129-141.

Moretus Plantin, H., *Les Passions de saint Lucien et leurs dérivés céphalophoriques*, Namur, 1953.

Picard, J.-C. – Biarne, J., «Senlis»,», in L. Pietri, éd., *Topographie chrétienne des cités de la Gaule, des origines au milieu du VIIIe siècle*, XIV: *Province ecclésiastique de Reims (Belgica secunda)*, Paris, 2006, p. 117-127.

Röckelein, H., «Just de Beauvais alias Justin d'Auxerre: l'art de dédoubler un saint. Avec l'édition de la *Passio s. Iustini* (BHL 4579) par François Dolbeau et Hedwig Röckelein», in M. Heinzelmann, dir., *Livrets, collections et textes. Études sur la tradition hagiographique latine*, Ostfildern, 2006, p. 323-360.

van 't Spijker, I., «Gallia du Nord et de l'Ouest. Les provinces ecclésiastiques de Tours, Rouen, Reims (950-1130)», in *Hagiographies*, II (1996), p. 229-289.

Vercauteren, F., «Étude critique d'un diplôme attribué à Chilpéric Ier», *Revue belge de philologie et d'histoire*, 7 (1928), p. 83-112.

Vercauteren, F., *Étude sur les civitates de la Belgique seconde. Contribution à l'histoire urbaine du nord de la France de la fin du IIIe à la fin du XIe siècle*, Bruxelles, 1934.

Zechiel-Eckes, K., «Vom *armarium* in York in den Düsseldorfer Tresor. Zur Rekonstruktion einer Liudger-Handschrift aus dem mittleren 8. Jahrhundert», *Deutsches Archiv*, 58 (2002), p. 193-203.

—, «Unbekannte Bruchstücke der merowingischen *Passio sancti Iusti pueri* (BHL 4590c)», *Francia*, 30 (2003), p. 1-8.

L'écriture hagiographique dans le diocèse d'Amiens* (ca. VIIIe-XIIe s.)

par

Fernand PELOUX

I. L'HAGIOGRAPHIE ÉPISCOPALE AUX ÉPOQUES CAROLINGIENNE ET FÉODALE. – A. Les Passions de saint Firmin. – B. L'invention des reliques de Firmin. – C. La Vie de l'évêque et confesseur Firmin. – D. La Vie de l'évêque Sauve, découvreur des reliques de saint Firmin. – E. Les Miracles de saint Firmin. – F. Vie et miracles de l'évêque Honoré.
II. L'HAGIOGRAPHIE MONASTIQUE ET CANONIALE AU MOYEN ÂGE CENTRAL. – A. Corbie: les translations des reliques de Gentien et Précord. – B. Saint-Josse sur Mer et le dossier hagiographique de Josse. – C. Montdidier: le récit de la translation des reliques des saints Lugle et Luglien. – D. Saint-Germain sur Bresle: la Vie de Germain l'Écossais. – E. Saint-Valery-sur-Somme: Vie et translation de Walaricus. – F. Le monastère cistercien du Paraclet. Les Vies de la vierge Ulphe et de l'ermite Domice.
CONCLUSION.
BIBLIOGRAPHIE.

L'hagiographie antérieure à l'époque carolingienne se concentre dans ce diocèse sur la figure des saints Fuscien, Victoric et Gentien, missionnaires romains et martyrs du préfet Riciovare[1]. Les récits de la *Passio* (BHL 3226) et de l'*Inventio* (BHL 3229) de leurs reliques à l'époque de l'évêque d'Amiens Honoré (*Honoratus*), sous le règne du roi Childebert III, attendent toujours une édition critique. Ces textes, rédigés après 711 circulent dans les plus anciens légendiers conservés, dès le VIIIe siècle[2]. Dans un second temps seulement, après la constitution de ce dossier hagiographique consacré à des saints

---

* Il m'est agréable de remercier François de Vriendt qui m'a transmis plusieurs travaux qui ne m'étaient pas accessibles en raison du confinement ainsi qu'Aurélien André et Charles Mériaux pour leur relecture.

[1] MEIJNS, MÉRIAUX (2009) et GAILLARD (2014).
[2] Voir principalement GAILLARD (2009) et PARIS-POULAIN (2019).

dont les reliques sont chéries à l'extérieur de la ville (à Sains-en-Amiénois[3]), se développe une hagiographie qui exalte principalement les premiers évêques de la ville[4]. Cela dit, Fuscien, Victoric et Gentien ne furent pas délaissés: leur Passion fut encore réécrite «au XIe siècle probablement» (*BHL* 3224) pour des raisons qui restent à déterminer[5].

L'investissement hagiographique dans la figure des saints anciens du diocèse a perduré pendant tout le Moyen Âge: c'est pourquoi on abordera également dans les pages qui suivent des dossiers hagiographiques qui ont été constitués après l'époque carolingienne et qui n'ont pas été (ou à peine, dans le cas d'Honoré) abordés dans le volume II d'*Hagiographies*[6]. La production hagiographique dans les communautés monastiques du diocèse avait déjà été abordée, parfois succinctement: sans revenir sur chacun des dossiers alors listés, nous donnons dans une deuxième section un rapide aperçu de cette production en mentionnant plus longuement des textes qui n'avaient pas été mentionnés et en y ajoutant d'autres, produits dans d'autres sanctuaires.

I. L'HAGIOGRAPHIE ÉPISCOPALE AUX ÉPOQUES CAROLINGIENNE ET FÉODALE

A. LES PASSIONS DE SAINT FIRMIN

Firmin d'Amiens, fêté le 25 septembre est le principal saint de la cité d'Amiens. Son culte est attesté dès l'époque carolingienne à Amiens[7]. Simplement mentionné par Raban Maur

---

[3] Sur ce sanctuaire, voir NARDI COMBESCURE (2007).

[4] Sur ces figures et leur culte on pourra lire en dernier lieu MONTAUBIN (2012), p. 331-333 qui insiste sur l'époque carolingienne comme premier moment d'élaboration de leurs légendes. Pendant longtemps, la seule étude valable sur ce corpus hagiographique fut DUCHESNE (1915), p. 122-127.

[5] GAILLARD (2009). Les deux plus anciens manuscrits datent de ce siècle, il s'agit de Paris, BnF, lat. 17627 en provenance de Saint-Quentin de Beauvais et Cambridge, Corpus Christi College, 9, exemplaire du Cotton-Corpus Legendary, daté du milieu de ce siècle. Sur ce ms. voir en dernier lieu POULIN (2009), p. 105-107.

[6] VAN 'T SPIJKER (1996).

[7] DUBOIS (1968), p. 252-253.

entre 842 et 854, rattaché à Amiens par Wandelbert dans son martyrologe métrique en 848, il est considéré par Usuard comme un des martyrs de Riciovare, mais ce personnage n'a aucun écho dans les textes relatifs au saint[8]. Florus quant à lui a bien connaissance de la Passion ci-dessous[9].

D'après à la *BHL*, la Passion de saint Firmin est transmise dans deux versions principales (*BHL* 3002-3003) toutes deux reproduites par les Bollandistes en 1760[10]. Si l'on se fie aux manuscrits repérés dans les catalogues dressés par les Bollandistes, chacune de ces deux versions est attestée dès le Xe siècle[11]. La version *BHL* 3002 est transmise par douze manuscrits dont le plus ancien est un *libellus* français conservé dans un recueil composite à Gand (BU 244, fol. 25r-32v)[12] tandis que la seconde version *BHL* 3003, recensée dans 17 manuscrits, est attestée pour la première fois dans un manuscrit bourguignon provenant de l'abbaye cistercienne de Pontigny conservé à Montpellier (BIU, H 360, fol. 115r-121v). Il est possible que ce manuscrit vienne de la ville voisine d'Auxerre où le culte du saint est attesté dès la première moitié du IXe siècle[13].

Cependant, ces manuscrits ne sont pas les plus anciens à porter ces textes et on verra que leur examen invalide en partie la distinction faite entre *BHL* 3002 et *BHL* 3003: les liens entre ces deux versions sont nombreux et seul un examen approfondi

---

[8] *MGH, Poet. Lat.*, II, Berlin, 1884, p. 595; Dubois (1965), p. 309; Meijns, Mériaux (2009), p. 20, 24. Voir aussi sur ce dossier Gaillard (2014) qui mentionne le saint dans un tableau annexe (p. 24).

[9] Voir García-Villoslada (1982), p. 261.

[10] *AASS*, Sept. VII, 1760. Sur cette édition voir les remarques de Salmon (1861), p. CXIII-CXIV. On trouvera dans ce livre de très nombreux détails sur le culte du saint, tout comme dans Corblet (1872), p. 172-188.

[11] *Contra* van 't Spijker (1996), p. 275 qui pensait que ce texte avait été écrit «probablement au XIe siècle».

[12] La *BHL*ms indique à tort que cette version porte *BHL* 3003 alors qu'elle est porteuse de *BHL* 3002. Sur ce manuscrit voir *AB*, 3 (1884), p. 170-176 et en dernier lieu Derolez (2017), p. 109-110.

[13] Melk, St. 412, calendrier daté vers 820-840, cf. Borst (2001), p. 1324. L'hypothèse d'une origine auxerroise du manuscrit de Montpellier (cf. *supra* la page en frontispice de ce volume et son commentaire) a été émise par Cames (2004), p. 24. Je remercie Eliana Magnani qui m'en a confirmé l'origine. Sur ce manuscrit voir Moretus (1915), p. 266-267 et surtout la notice de Peyrafort-Huin, Stirnemann, Benoît (2001), p. 547-549. Voir aussi Dubois (1968), p. 155, Haggh (1998), p. 113-114 et Gilles-Raynal (2018), p. 338, n. 52.

de l'ensemble de la tradition manuscrite en vue d'une édition critique permettra de comprendre l'histoire de ce texte. La base *Légendiers latins* permet d'identifier d'autres manuscrits, dont le plus ancien recensé à ce jour: St. Gallen, Stiftsbibliothek, Cod. Sang. 563, daté des IXe-Xe siècles[14]. Son origine septentrionale est claire. Sur les 19 saints qu'il contient, on note 10 saints septentrionaux. Le manuscrit s'ouvre avec la Vie de saint Riquier par Alcuin (*BHL* 7228), suivie de la Passion de saint Denis (*BHL* 2171). On compte encore un dossier sur saint Quentin (*BHL* 7005-7007, 7014), la Passion des saints Crépin et Crépinien (*BHL* 1990), la Passion de Léger d'Autun (*BHL* 4851), la Vie d'Amand (*BHL* 332), la Passion de Sauve (*BHL* 7472) et la Vie de saint Vaast (*BHL* 8506). Le manuscrit se termine avec la Passion de Firmin, suivie du récit de son *inventio* (*BHL* 3009, sur ce texte voir *infra*) et de la Vie de saint Ouen (*BHL* 750). Signalons encore, dans la même chronologie, un fragment d'un légendier-homéliaire de Fleury conservé à Florence (Biblioteca medicea laurenziana, Ashburnham 38, fol. 3v-8v)[15]. Dans ce manuscrit non organisé de manière chronologique, la Passion de Firmin est suivie d'un dossier relatif aux saints amiénois Fuscien, Victoricus et Gentien (*BHL* 3226 et 3229) et de la Passion des saints Crépin et Crépinien (*BHL* 1990).

En fait, les principales variantes entre les deux familles résident dans l'*incipit* et le *desinit*: dans la première, *BHL* 3002 (Inc. *Temporibus maximiani et diocletiani imperatoribus*), la naissance du saint est placée sous la persécution des empereurs Maximien et Dioclétien, tandis que dans la seconde (*BHL* 3003 Inc. *Temporibus priscis, quibus fides christiana*) le nom des empereurs est tu, mais l'origine du saint clairement affirmée: Firmin est originaire d'une ville ibérique, Pampelune. Ensuite, toutes s'accordent pour en faire le fils du sénateur Firmus et de sa femme Eugenia, tous deux issus d'une famille très riche. Alors que tous étaient païens, un prêtre chrétien, Honest, vint prêcher la nouvelle foi. Le sénateur Firmus, et avec lui Faustin et Fortunat, veulent en savoir plus et demandent à Honest son origine: il a pour mère Honesta et pour père Emilius, et il est originaire de la ville de Nîmes. Il déclare être un disciple de l'évêque Saturnin (de Toulouse), lui-même disciple des apôtres et c'est ce der-

---

[14] Sur ce manuscrit voir dernièrement KREINER (2014), p. 260-261.
[15] GUGLIELMETTI (2007), p. 187-190.

nier qui lui a ordonné d'aller répandre la vérité de l'Évangile. Sept jours plus tard, Saturnin vient alors à Pampelune (dont le nom est là clairement cité) où il réside sous un pin (*terebintho*), dans un lieu où se trouvait autrefois un temple dédié à Diane. Après trois jours de prédication, il convertit plusieurs milliers de personnes (entre 20 et 40000 selon les versions) et ordonne la destruction du vieux temple de Diane. Une semaine plus tard, Fortunat, Firmus et Faustin, les trois sénateurs de la ville, décident de rompre avec les cultes anciens et de convertir Pampelune. Firmus, le père de Firmin transmet à son fils la foi chrétienne. Et, alors qu'il avait dix-sept ans, il l'éduque encore sept années dans la religion chrétienne. Le vieil Honest, venu amener la parole de Saturnin avant l'arrivée de Saturnin, l'envoie prêcher dans les cités et les bourgs environnants puis, l'expédie à Toulouse auprès de l'évêque d'alors, nommé Honorat. Ce dernier l'ordonne évêque. Firmin retourne auprès du prêtre Honest et, suivant les principes de l'Évangile, alors qu'il avait trente ans, quitte sa patrie, son frère et sa sœur (Faust et Eusébie selon certains manuscrits). Il arrive en Gaule, reste quelques jours à Agen avec un prêtre dénommé Eustache. Il convertit ensuite la majeure partie de la cité de Clermont, où il entre en conflit avec Arcadius et Romulus à propos du culte des idoles. Il traverse ensuite la Loire, aide l'évêque d'Angers dans sa mission d'évangélisation, en convertissant presque toute sa province en un an et trois mois. Ensuite, apprenant que le gouverneur des Gaules Valerius qui siégeait à Beauvais persécutait ses coreligionnaires, Firmin décide de s'y rendre. Il est jeté en prison, enchaîné et torturé mais ne cesse de prêcher. Comme le *praeses* Serge vint à mourir, Firmin est sorti de prison par les chrétiens et fonde une église en l'honneur de saint Etienne (et de saint Laurent selon la version *BHL* 3002). Le saint arrive enfin à Amiens, le 10 octobre, où il est reçu par le sénateur Faustinien qu'il baptise ainsi qu'Ausentius Hilarius. Le même jour, il baptise Attilia, la femme d'Agripinus, ses enfants et leurs serviteurs et, dans les trois jours qui suivent, près de trois mille autres habitants. Entendant les succès de cette évangélisation, les gouverneurs Longulus et Sébastien viennent depuis Trèves afin de présider un tribunal. Ils ordonnent que tous viennent *ad pretorium cimilianum*. Trois jours plus tard, soldats et prêtres viennent en nombre et le gouverneur Sébastien rappelle avec force le décret des empereurs en faveur du culte traditionnel. Le prêtre du temple de

Jupiter et Mercure dénonce alors l'action de Firmin, *hispanus genere*. Sébastien demande à ce qu'il soit présenté sous deux jours dans l'amphithéâtre (*ad spectaculum teatri*), à la porte *clippiana*. Après l'habituel «dialogue de sourd» entre le gouverneur et le saint, au cours duquel Firmin rappelle qu'il est un romain de rang sénatorial et un citoyen de Pampelune, le gouverneur hésite à prononcer la peine capitale car il craint que cela ne déclenche une émeute: le saint n'a-t-il pas prouvé ses pouvoirs de thaumaturge en guérissant, toujours à la *porta clippiana* des lépreux?

C'est à ce moment que les versions divergent dans les manuscrits. Si on se fie aux quatre plus anciens d'entre eux, chacun donne un texte différent. Pourtant, par leur *incipit*, et par la variante mentionnant l'église Saint-Etienne et Saint-Laurent à Beauvais, les manuscrits Saint-Gall, 563 et Gand, BU 344 se rattachent à *BHL* 3002 tandis que Montpellier, BIU, H 360 et Florence, Laur. Ashb. 38 portent *BHL* 3003. Le manuscrit de Montpellier se distingue en ce sens que la mort du saint est plus détaillée: Firmin est jeté en prison à nouveau et, la nuit suivante, alors qu'il priait, un des *milites* met à exécution la sentence et frappe le saint à la tête. Ensuite, Faustinien, que le saint avait baptisé plus tôt, récupère le corps de nuit et l'enterre dans le cimetière d'*Abladana* dans un monument nouveau, où personne ne fut inhumé jusqu'alors. Là, un autre saint Firmin, évêque et confesseur, construit une église en l'honneur de la Vierge où il vit plus tard le martyr Firmin alors qu'il célébrait la messe. De nombreux miracles ont lieu ensuite dans ce lieu. Dans les trois autres manuscrits, une phrase lapidaire, de type martyrologique, indique que Firmin souffrit le martyre le 25 septembre. Dans le manuscrit de Gand, elle est suivie d'une phrase indiquant que c'est Faustinien qui construisit une église en l'honneur de la Vierge, où l'on dit (*traditur*) que le corps du saint se trouve, mais il y a un doute sur l'endroit où Faustinien a déposé le corps en cachette en raison de la persécution. Toutefois, on ne doute pas que c'est bien dans cette église que l'autre Firmin, évêque et confesseur, a élu sépulture. Ce dernier a vécu 67 ans et il est mort le 1er septembre. Dans les manuscrits de Florence et Saint-Gall, Faustinianus vient chercher le corps mort du saint en prison, et l'enterre dans le cimetière d'*Abladana* (sans mention de monument), où des miracles ont lieu. Si le manuscrit de Florence s'arrête sur cette mention, le manuscrit de Saint-Gall poursuit en indiquant que le gouverneur Sebastianus est ensuite assassiné par des soldats de Beauvais, tandis que Faustinien, qui a enterré le corps, nomme son propre fils Firmin en l'honneur du martyr. Ce dernier Firmin, bien éduqué et digne de louanges est ensuite fait évêque par l'évêque de Lyon Jean et accomplit de nombreux miracles: il guérit ainsi le fils du patrice Calixte de ses fièvres. Ici, le manuscrit de Saint-Gall copie ensuite ce que l'on trouvait dans celui de Gand, mais attribue à Firmin le confesseur (non à Faustinien) le fait de construire l'église de la Vierge Marie où l'on dit que le corps du saint martyr repose. Comme dans le manuscrit de Gand, un doute est exprimé sur l'endroit où Faustinien a déposé le corps en cachette en raison de la persécution. Toutefois, là encore, on ne doute pas que c'est bien dans cette église que Firmin, évêque et confesseur, a élu sépulture et que ce dernier a vécu 67 ans; et il est mort le 1er septembre. La version du manuscrit de Saint-Gall apparaît à ce stade comme la plus cohérente. L'importance des variantes qui existent à propos du lieu de sépulture de Firmin et sa relation avec le confesseur Firmin montre combien les questions de localisation de reliques et de listes épiscopales furent importantes et justifièrent l'existence même de différentes versions de la Passion du saint.

En attendant une édition et une étude de la transmission et de la chronologie des différentes versions de ce texte qui a principalement circulé dans le nord de l'Europe – son insertion dans le *Legendarium Flandrense* en est une preuve [16] – quelques remarques s'imposent. L'auteur de ce texte cherche clairement à ancrer son récit dans un cadre antique: les fonctions (gouverneur, patrice), les lieux, la précision dans une des familles de manuscrits des empereurs, et surtout les noms des acteurs vont dans ce sens. L'anthroponymie est en effet exclusivement romaine et les noms sont relativement nombreux. Si on ne connaît aucun Eustache à Agen, un Arcadius est bien connu à Clermont dans la première moitié du VIe siècle: il s'agit du petit-fils de Sidoine Apollinaire qui invita Childebert Ier à prendre possession de l'Auvergne lorsque le roi Thierry était en Thuringe [17]. Romulus, nom évidemment hautement romain, est lui inconnu dans l'Auvergne de l'Antiquité Tardive. À Amiens, le sénateur

---

[16] DOLBEAU (1981), *passim*
[17] PIETRI, HEIJMANS (2013), p. 180-181.

Faustinien pourrait bien correspondre à celui qui est mentionné sur une épitaphe découverte dans la nécropole Saint-Acheul, occupée depuis le IVe siècle[18]. L'hagiographe a-t-il puisé les noms de son récit parmi les vestiges qu'il avait sous les yeux? Il est difficile de le dire car seul ce nom concorde avec les épitaphes aujourd'hui conservées. Quant à un évêque de Lyon prénommé Jean, aucun n'est connu parmi les listes épiscopales. Il est par ailleurs tout-à-fait curieux qu'un métropolitain lyonnais consacre un évêque d'Amiens dans la province ecclésiastique de Reims. S'agit-il de construire une histoire sainte autonome qui fasse fi des réalités ecclésiastiques? S'agit-il alors de se rattacher à la capitale antique des Gaules? Difficile de le dire.

En ce qui concerne les données topographiques de ce texte, les éléments relatifs à Amiens sont les plus précis: la mention de la porta *clippiana*, attestée uniquement par ce texte, renvoie à l'enceinte bien attestée archéologiquement et construite «à la fin du premier tiers du IVe siècle»[19]. L'amphithéâtre dans lequel le saint est conduit se situe bien à proximité de celle-ci: si celui-ci n'est déjà plus en activité au moment de la fortification de la ville, il doit être encore reconnaissable[20]. En ce qui concerne la topographie religieuse, la situation était peu claire dès l'époque carolingienne comme certains manuscrits l'expriment. Cela explique les variantes relatives au lieu et aux modalités d'inhumation du martyr. La nécropole *Abladana* n'est connue que par ce témoignage, et l'église construite en l'honneur de la Vierge pourrait se trouver dans le quartier Saint-Acheul, selon une série d'indices concordants, mais la chronologie et l'organisation du secteur est mal connue et repose sur des données archéologiques en partie anciennes et produites dans un contexte polémique[21]. Le fait que le groupe cathédral, mentionné en 850, soit composé de deux églises, dédiées justement à la Vierge et à saint Firmin vient encore obscurcir la situation[22]. En ce qui concerne enfin Beauvais, où le saint fonde une

---

[18] PICHON (2009), p. 50 et *CIL*, XII, n° 3520.

[19] D'après PICHON (2009), p. 48. Sur son tracé, voir encore MONTAUBIN (2012), p. 17-18.

[20] Voir en dernier lieu BAYARD, MASSY (1983) et PICHON (2009), p. 46-48.

[21] PIETRI (2006), p. 152. Sur les vestiges tardoantiques de cette nécropole, voir PICHON (2009), p. 242-249.

[22] PIETRI (2006), p. 151.

église tantôt dédiée à Saint-Étienne seul, tantôt dédiée au protomartyr et à Laurent, il est impossible de recouper cette information par d'autres sources: cette église n'est mentionnée que dans ce texte et ne semble pas avoir eu de postérité[23].

L'historiographie considère généralement que ce dossier a été forgé à l'époque carolingienne, d'où nous vient le plus ancien manuscrit connu. Cette datation, tout à fait possible, repose sur les invraisemblances du récit et sur les premières traces du culte de Firmin à cette époque. Une édition et une étude de la transmission écrite sont indispensables pour débrouiller ce dossier, mais, même fabriqué à l'époque carolingienne, il reste à expliquer l'itinéraire du saint depuis la Navarre, son parcours en Gaule, sa relation à Toulouse et à l'évêque Honorat dont c'est la première attestation[24]. La qualification de Saturnin comme disciple des apôtres (y compris dans les manuscrits qui placent clairement le martyre d'Amiens au IIIe siècle) a une origine tardo-antique (Césaire d'Arles, Grégoire de Tours) mais elle n'est semble-t-il pas utilisée dans le Midi de la France avant la fin de l'époque carolingienne lorsque des récits relatifs à Saturnin de Toulouse, reprenant justement les textes relatifs à Firmin d'Amiens, font de ce dernier une figure apostolique qui joua un rôle fondamental dans l'évangélisation du sud de la France et de l'Espagne. La relation entre tous ces textes n'a pas encore été débrouillée, faute là encore d'éditions solidement établies[25].

B. L'invention des reliques de Firmin

Outre la Passion du saint, on connaît aussi le récit de l'invention et de la translation de ses reliques au VIIe siècle. La version *BHL* 3008 a été éditée une première fois en 1670[26], reproduite ensuite par les Bollandistes et collationnée par Charles Salmon avec le manuscrit 46 de la BM d'Amiens qui contient des variantes importantes[27]. Près d'une quinzaine de

---

[23] MÉRIAUX, PIETRI (2006), p. 141.
[24] Sur la fortune légendaire de ce personnage, je me permets de renvoyer à PELOUX (2018), p. 294-297 dans lequel je m'appuyais uniquement sur les manuscrits inventoriés par les Bollandistes.
[25] Sur ces liens, voir principalement GILLES-RAYNAL (2006).
[26] LE COINTE (1670), IV, p. 181-182.
[27] SALMON (1861), p. 423 et sqq. Le texte se trouve au fol. 142.

manuscrits porte ce texte d'après la base *Légendiers latins*. Les plus anciens sont antérieurs à l'an mil: on y trouve Montpellier, BIU, H 360 et Gand, BU 244 (mais dans une unité codicologique plus tardive) que nous avons déjà rencontrés, ainsi que le manuscrit Paris, BnF, lat. 17625, du xe siècle, originaire de Compiègne. Une meilleure édition de ce texte est assurément souhaitable. Dans un court prologue, son auteur chante les louanges des corps saints et des miracles ayant eu lieu dans la ville d'Amiens, dont celui de la charité de saint Martin. Mais c'est bien de Firmin, le premier évangélisateur et martyr de la cité dont il veut parler. Depuis la prédication de Firmin, les miracles et la perfection dans la foi des habitants de la ville n'ont jamais cessé, jusqu'au temps du roi Thierry. Déjà l'évêque Honoré, contemporain du roi Childebert, découvrit miraculeusement les corps des saints Fuscien, Victoric et Gentien, à trois mille de la ville, conformément au lieu mentionné par leurs *gesta*. S'il trouva les corps de ces saints conformément à l'annonce du prêtre Lupicin, ne trouva pas le corps de Firmin, dont les miracles avaient éclairé la majeure partie de la Gaule comme un rayon de soleil. On comprend que l'auteur a bien sous les yeux le récit de l'invention des reliques de Fuscien, Victoricus et Gentien tel qu'il circule depuis le VIIIe siècle. Sous le règne de Thierry, un homme digne de toutes les louanges, Salvius, élu par le peuple d'Amiens à l'épiscopat savait que le corps du confesseur Firmin était enterré dans l'église dédiée à la Vierge mais il ignorait où se trouvait celui du martyr. Après de nombreuses prières en présence du peuple et de tous les clercs, un rayon de lumière vint indiquer le lieu où se trouvait le saint. Aussitôt, le prélat se met à creuser et découvre le corps dont l'odeur suave exhale dans l'ensemble du diocèse, mais aussi dans toutes les cités de la province: Thérouanne, Cambrai, Noyon et Beauvais, les cités limitrophes, furent touchées dans la même heure.

Il existe une autre version, plus courte, de cet événement (*BHL* 3009) signalée en note dans les *Acta Sanctorum*. Toujours inédite, elle est transmise par quatre manuscrits dont le plus ancien est le légendier du IXe siècle, conservé à Saint-Gall, qui comprend aussi la Passion (St. Gallen, Stiftsbibliothek, Cod. Sang. 563). Après un court prologue, l'auteur place aussi l'événement sous le règne de Thierry, grâce au bon évêque Salvius. Ce texte reprend les principaux éléments qu'on trouvait déjà dans le récit précédent: l'événement est situé après la découverte des corps des trois saints martyrs Fuscien, Victoricus et Gentien, sous le règne de Childebert. Dans cette version toutefois, ce sont les peuples et les prélats des cités voisines qui accourent et il y a une plus grande insistance sur la figure du roi Thierry: même sa femme, *Rodehildis* est mentionnée. La relation entre les deux versions mériterait clairement d'être établie.

C. La Vie de l'évêque et confesseur Firmin

Le confesseur Firmin, mentionné dès les plus anciens témoins de la Passion de son homonyme martyr est fêté le 1er septembre. Il fit aussi l'objet d'un récit hagiographique, très peu diffusé et connu dans deux versions (*BHL* 3012-3013), qui se distinguent seulement par la présence d'un court prologue (Inc. *Apostolica auctoritate sanctorumque traditione*), toujours inédit. La version *BHL* 3012 Inc. *Regnante Domino et saluatore nostro I. C. in saecula, anno ab Urbe condita* DCCCLXVII a été publiée par les Bollandistes en 1746 à partir de manuscrits non identifiés.

Le texte remonte à la fondation même d'Amiens sous Antonin le Pieux et fait de Faustinien un puissant préfet, contemporain du règne de Gratien. Conformément à ce que l'on trouvait à la fin de plusieurs versions de la Passion de Firmin, ce dernier appelle son fils Firmin en l'honneur du saint martyr d'Amiens. Et, comme l'indiquait déjà la Passion de Firmin telle qu'elle circule dans le manuscrit de Saint-Gall, ce dernier est fait évêque par le métropolitain lyonnais, mais ici le texte va plus loin: après la description des vertus de son héros, on apprend que ce dernier va à Rome auprès du pape Vigile qui lui transmet toute la *potestas* apostolique pour reconstruire et réorganiser ce qu'Attila et les Huns avaient détruit en Europe. Une telle description et la confirmation pontificale d'un évêque franc renvoient évidemment à une réalité plus tardive. Arrivé à Amiens après avoir ordonné différents clercs, réparé églises et monastères, le saint construit dans la nécropole de *Bladana* une église dédiée à la Vierge, conformément à ce que l'on trouve là encore dans la Passion du premier Firmin. Un jour qu'il célébrait la messe, il voir la palme du Seigneur et opère ensuite de nombreux miracles, guérissant la fille du patrice Calixte. Sa *uirtus* se fait aussi sentir dans les cités voisines et les bourgs qui en dépendent: ainsi il évangélise les habitants de Thérouanne, du Ponthieu, du Vimeu, de Saint-Bertin (*Talaonenses* pour *Taruanenses*?) et du pays de Caux. Cette précision montre probablement les prétentions des évêques d'Amiens au-delà de leur seul diocèse. Du reste, l'hagiographe précise que la *fama* du saint rayonne dans toutes les Gaules. Firmin, après avoir prévenu de sa mort prochaine et enjoint ses proches à poursuivre son œuvre, décède à 67 ans et enterré dans l'église qu'il avait construite en l'honneur de la Vierge. Il apparaît clairement que ce texte entretient des relations étroites avec la Passion de saint Firmin: est-ce cette Vie de saint Firmin le confesseur qui a été utilisée pour augmenter la Passion de saint Firmin martyr dans le manuscrit de Saint-Gall? La fin du texte dans ce manuscrit est en tout cas identique.

Il faut de toute façon fixer au Xe siècle le *terminus ante quem* de la rédaction puisque cette Vie est copiée dans le manuscrit de Montpellier, BIU, H 360[28], à la suite de la Passion et du récit de l'invention des reliques de Firmin martyr, mais le texte, découpé en neuf leçons, est acéphale à la suite de la perte d'au moins un feuillet (fol. 125): on ignore donc si ce manuscrit transmettait le prologue. Pour la version *BHL* 3012, la base *Légendiers latins* enregistre également un légendier de Saint-Laurent de Liège du XIIe siècle, où le texte circule sans le dossier consacré à Firmin (KBR 9636-9637 [Van den Gheyn 3228], fol. 142v-144) mais ce manuscrit porte bien le prologue et doit donc être rattaché à *BHL* 3013[29]. Sous ce dernier numéro *BHL*, la base *Légendiers latins* ne recense qu'un seul manuscrit, avec son prologue, le manuscrit latin 5270 (fol. 62-65), fragment d'un légendier de l'abbaye cistercienne de Beaupré du XIIIe siècle[30]. La distinction entre *BHL* 3012 et *BHL* 3013 apparaît donc en partie artificielle, même si la Vie de Firmin a bien circulé sans prologue: c'est le cas dans un lectionnaire amiénois du XIIIe siècle, Amiens, BM 149 (fol. 101-104v).

Pour Dom Dubois, c'est parce que les anciennes litanies hésitaient sur la place qu'il fallait donner à Firmin – parmi les martyrs, ou parmi les confesseurs – qu'un dédoublement eut

---

[28] *Contra* VAN 'T SPIJKER (1996), p. 275 qui pensait que ce texte avait été écrit «probablement au XIe siècle».

[29] Sur ce manuscrit: WEBB (2014), p. 835.

[30] Cf. DOLBEAU (1979), p. 196.

lieu et que des textes furent alors composés pour l'un et l'autre au milieu du IXe siècle[31]. Pour lui, la présence de ce texte à la suite de la Passion de Firmin et de son Invention dans le manuscrit de Montpellier, BIU, H 360 «est un indice sérieux en faveur de l'unité d'auteur» de ces récits qui s'accordent tout à fait entre eux (p. 255). Si cette hypothèse est possible, seule une édition résolument critique de l'ensemble de ces pièces permettrait de la corroborer.

D. La Vie de l'évêque Sauve, découvreur des reliques de saint Firmin

Salvius d'Amiens, que le récit de l'invention des reliques de saint Firmin mettait en scène, a fait aussi l'objet d'une Vie, éditée «à partir de trois vieux manuscrits» dans les *Acta Sanctorum* en 1643 (*BHL* 7470). Ce texte rapporte que Salvius a édifié un monastère en l'honneur de la Vierge et de Pierre. À la mort de son abbé, il est élu à la tête de ce dernier mais préfère vivre reclus. De sa cellule, il fait des miracles, et, alors qu'il est malade, ses frères le croient mort et préparent ses funérailles. Mais le saint se réveille, car Dieu a souhaité sa présence sur terre. Salvius prédit la mort de l'évêque Honoré, ce qui arriva sous le règne du roi Thierry. Ce dernier envoya alors ses émissaires à Amiens, dont l'évêque saint Antgaire de Noyon qui intima au peuple d'élire un autre évêque. Les habitants d'Amiens choisirent alors Salvius. Ce dernier construisit une église en l'honneur de Pierre et de Paul[32]. Comme la population ignorait où le corps du martyr Firmin avait été enterré, Salvius, levant les yeux au ciel, vit un rayon de soleil qui lui révéla l'emplacement du corps dont la découverte entraina l'exhalation d'un doux parfum. On trouve ici les mêmes mots que dans le récit de l'invention, mais le texte est encore plus précis: Salvius transfère le corps dans la crypte orientale qu'il a construit en l'honneur du martyr, dans l'église (Saint-Pierre et Saint-Paul) qu'il avait fait construire, dans un tombeau d'or et de pierres précieuses, à côté des saints Ache et Acheul. Alors, Thierry ordonna que les

---

[31] Dubois (1968), p. 254.
[32] Les chanoines de la collégiale Saint-Firmin-le-Confesseur revendiquent à la fin du Moyen Âge être les héritiers de cette église, cf. Abdi (2014), p. 41-42.

hommes que le patrice Mummole, après avoir pris la cité, avait rendus captifs et envoyé dans les Espagnes puissent rentrer chez-eux. Il se montra particulièrement généreux envers la cité. Il accomplit de nombreux miracles, guérissant la fille et la femme d'un noble nommé *Guado*: à la suite de cela, ce dernier céda perpétuellement une *villa*, à cinq mille de la cité d'Amiens. Il y construisit une église qu'il dédia au saint. Le saint vint ensuite dans le *pagus vimaccum*, le Vimeu, déjà mentionné dans la Vie du confesseur Firmin: il y séjourna et accomplit des miracles dans une *villa* donnée par le roi, nommée *Augusta*. À sa mort, *Salvius* est enterré dans une église dédiée à la Vierge, avant d'être transféré des années plus tard dans le *vicus* de *Monasteriolus*, Montreuil-sur-Mer, en raison de la dévotion des fidèles.

Ce texte est porté par sept manuscrits médiévaux: le plus ancien date du Xe siècle et se trouve être inclus dans un légendier factice (Paris, BnF, lat. 5275)[33], les autres appartiennent à la collection du Légendier de Flandres[34]. Luce Pietri a bien noté que ce texte «reproduit pour l'essentiel le chapitre consacré par Grégoire de Tours à Salvius d'Albi»[35]: même la mention des captifs du patrice Mummole en est issu. Pour Jacques Dubois, on rencontre dans cette «très mauvaise vie», les mêmes phrases que dans l'Invention de saint Firmin (*BHL* 3008), signe que la Vie de Sauve dépend de ce texte[36], à moins que ce ne soit l'inverse comme l'a proposé John Ott[37]. Quand il ne dépend pas de ces autres textes, l'auteur donne de curieuses informations: l'évêque Antgaire de Noyon n'est connu que dans cette Vie, tout comme le monastère que Sauve construisit en l'honneur de la Vierge et de Paul, ainsi que l'église dédiée à Pierre et à Paul dans laquelle le saint installa les reliques du martyr Firmin avec celles des saints Ache et Acheul[38].

---

[33] DOLBEAU (1979), p. 196 et POULIN (2006), p. 144. John Ott pense que ce manuscrit vient de Montreuil-sur-mer et signale deux copies modernes: OTT (2015), n. 89, p. 243.

[34] Cf. DOLBEAU (1981), tableau final. Aux manuscrits repérés dans la base *Légendiers latins*, on peut ajouter le lectionnaire du XIIIe siècle Amiens, BM 149, où le texte se trouve au fol. 243.

[35] PIETRI (2006), p. 150.

[36] DUBOIS (1968), p. 255.

[37] OTT (2015), p. 237, n. 70.

[38] Le texte ne précise nullement que cette église leur est dédiée, *contra* GILLON (2019), p. 59.

Ces précisions, absentes du récit de l'invention des reliques du martyr, complexifient encore l'image que l'on peut se faire de la topographie chrétienne d'Amiens dans le haut Moyen Âge : ces lieux, dont l'église Saint Pierre-Saint Paul, que l'on verra citée dans la Vie d'Honoré, ne sont pas identifiés par Luce Pietri qui indique que Salvius procède à « la translation de l'église cathédrale à l'intérieur de la ville », ce que ce texte ne mentionne pourtant pas[39]. En ce qui concerne enfin les miracles produits à l'extérieur d'Amiens, ils servent clairement à justifier des possessions épiscopales, ce qui est typique d'une hagiographie qui ne saurait être antérieure à l'époque carolingienne. L'existence de ce texte dans un manuscrit dès le Xe siècle ne permet pas pour l'instant d'être plus précis.

E. Les Miracles de saint Firmin

Le martyr Firmin fit plus tard l'objet de Miracles (*BHL* 3011), en partie reproduits dans les *Acta Sanctorum* à partir d'un bréviaire imprimé en 1554 par le bollandiste Jean Stilting dans son introduction au dossier du martyr Firmin en 1760[40]. Pour John Ott, il y a deux couches de rédaction : l'une après un incendie daté de 1106-1107 et l'autre sous l'épiscopat de l'évêque Garin (mort en 1144)[41]. La mention d'un synode (à laquelle on peut ajouter l'argument de la transmission de ce texte) l'invite à juste titre à penser que l'auteur est un clerc amiénois. Un examen approfondi des bréviaires du diocèse, tant manuscrits qu'imprimés devrait permettre, on l'espère, de retrouver l'exemplaire utilisé au XVIIIe siècle ou de repérer un autre témoin qui permettrait de mieux saisir cet ensemble de miracles très peu diffusés.

---

[39] Pietri (2006), p. 150. C'est une idée assez répandue dans l'historiographie : voir dernièrement Montaubin, p. 17. Sur la topographie chrétienne d'Amiens dans le haut Moyen Âge, voir encore Racinet (2002), p. 225-232.

[40] En 1910 (*AASS*, III, col. 897), le père Poncelet précise que la source de Stilting était une copie du XVIIe siècle conservée sous la cote 150 dans la bibliothèque bollandienne.

[41] Ott (2015), p. 243-244.

F. Vie et miracles de l'évêque Honoré

Parmi les figures des anciens saints évêques d'Amiens, Honoré, pourtant mentionné dès l'époque mérovingienne dans l'Invention des reliques des saints Fuscien, Victoric et Gentien, ne fit semble-t-il l'objet d'un récit que tardivement. Son culte s'ancre à l'époque carolingienne à Amiens: il se trouve cité dans plusieurs litanies de manuscrits du Nord de la France[42] et, dans le plus ancien calendrier amiénois, il côtoie les saints que nous avons abordés jusqu'alors (Paris, BnF, lat. 9432), vers 900[43].

Les Bollandistes ont publié en 1680 dans les *Acta Sanctorum* (Mai, III) un texte en précisant l'établir à partir d'un bréviaire d'Amiens et de divers manuscrits, notamment un manuscrit de l'église Saint-Honoré de Paris et un autre de la chartreuse Saint-Honoré de Thuisson-lès-Abbeville (*BHL* 3972)[44]. Ensuite, Victor de Beauvillé a également publié un texte (*BHL* 3973) à partir d'un manuscrit du XIVe siècle dont il ne donne pas la cote mais une brève description qui permet d'identifier un *libellus* consacré au saint[45]. Il y a entre les deux versions des variantes qu'il faudra relever et commenter, mais le texte de la Vita fourni par De Beauvillé, s'il contient tous les mots de celui des Bollandistes, est beaucoup plus prolixe et paraît plus tardif: il fait notamment du saint un boulanger[46]. Si la base *Légendiers latins* ne recense aucun manuscrit portant une Vie d'Honoré, il existe bien un témoin médiéval: le manuscrit Paris, Bibl. de l'Arsenal

---

[42] Une vingtaine de manuscrits ont été recensés avec ce nom par Krüger (2007), p. 486. Même si l'on peut dans certains cas avoir un doute sur l'identité de l'*Honoratus* mentionné à cause de son homonyme arlésien, la localisation de plusieurs manuscrits dans la France du Nord semble être un indice suffisant pour y voir le saint d'Amiens: voir notamment p. 347, 330 et 366 les manuscrits Montpellier, BIU, H 409, daté de 783-788 (Soissons) et surtout Amiens, BM 18, milieu du IXe siècle (litanies de Corbie) (p. 330) et Paris, BnF, lat. 12247, du IXe siècle (provenance Corbie ou Amiens).

[43] Sur ce manuscrit, voir Borst (2001), I, p. 138-139. Sur le culte du saint voir les éléments rassemblés par Corblet (1873), p. 38-77.

[44] Seul un extrait de ce texte se trouve copié à l'époque moderne dans le manuscrit Paris, BnF, lat. 3088, fol. 36v.

[45] De Beauvillé (1877), p. 181-191. Le texte a ensuite été traduit par Josse (1879).

[46] Charles Salmon considère également ce texte comme plus tardif, empreint de traditions orales dans son introduction à Josse (1879). Voir aussi dans le même sens Gaposchkin (2004), p. 223.

1032, du XIVe siècle, qui porte clairement la version publiée par les Bollandistes (*BHL* 3972)[47].

Dans ce manuscrit, comme dans le texte des Bollandistes, le saint, successeur de saint Firmin le confesseur est d'emblée placé à la fin du VIe siècle, au temps du prédécesseur du pape Grégoire le Grand, Pélage, alors que l'empereur Maurice, prédécesseur de Phocas, avait accueilli le roi Childebert. Honoré gouvernait alors de manière exemplaire l'Église d'Amiens. Un jour qu'il officiait, il vit la palme du Seigneur et, sous son épiscopat, on connut, par une révélation divine l'endroit où les corps des saints Fuscien, Victoric et Gentien avaient été ensevelis plus de trois cent ans auparavant. En effet, le prêtre amiénois Lupicin, guidé par un ange dans son sommeil, découvre les corps et chante une antienne qu'Honoré peut entendre à cinq milles de la ville. Alors que tous s'agglutinaient, le roi Childebert fit enterrer les martyrs avec honneur et amena de nombreux ornements à l'Église et lui donna le *vicus* de Mège. Le saint meurt dans le *pagus* de Ponthieu, dans la paroisse de Port-Le-Grand qu'il était en train de visiter. Son corps est ramené à Amiens.

S'ajoutent alors une série de miracles post-mortem, peu réécrits dans la version donnée par De Beauvillé, dont le premier est daté de 1060: le corps du saint est sorti le long des murailles pour faire cesser une sécheresse. Plusieurs miracles racontent ensuite différentes guérisons ou exorcismes. Le dernier rapporte que de retour de l'église des saints Pierre et Paul vers sa cathédrale, alors que son corps passe devant un crucifix, ce dernier s'incline[48]. Le texte se termine enfin par une exhortation à prier ce saint qui fait de l'église d'Amiens une sainte Église car elle possède ses reliques: cette mention doit indiquer selon John Ott que son auteur est un membre du chapitre cathédral[49]. Pour cet historien, il y a deux phases de rédactions dans les Miracles, l'une à la fin du XIe siècle et une autre plus tardive, qu'il date entre 1104-1115 en raison de la mention d'un enfant miraculé

---

[47] Ce manuscrit est signalé par HANSEN (2019), p. 157, n. 4. Ce recueil, composé principalement de textes patristiques n'a pas fait l'objet d'une description détaillée. J'ai pu consulter seulement une reproduction des feuillets finaux, qui portent la Vie et les miracles du saint (fol. 239v-241), signalés par des rubriques absentes du texte des Bollandistes.

[48] Sur la commémoration médiévale de ce saint et ce miracle voir GAPOSCHKIN (2004), p. 222 et sqq; GABORIT (2012) et ABDI (2014), p. 52.

[49] OTT (2015), p. 243.

devenu ensuite évêque de Thérouanne[50]. Une telle hypothèse, qui ferait de ce texte une production contemporaine de l'épiscopat de Geoffroy d'Amiens dont on connaît l'investissement dans les figures saintes du diocèse est basée sur l'identification de l'évêque de Thérouanne. Pour séduisante qu'elle soit, elle mériterait d'être mieux étayée, tout comme l'idée d'une rédaction des miracles en deux phases. Il est en tout cas certain que la Vie du saint entretient des relations étroites avec le récit de l'invention des reliques des saints Fuscien, Victoric et Gentien mais aussi avec la Vie de saint Firmin le confesseur: le récit de la découverte des reliques utilise en partie les mêmes mots que dans ces textes. La Vie d'Honoré a peut-être été composée, ou du moins remaniée à partir d'éléments plus anciens, au moment où des miracles post-mortem sont ajoutés. Cette rédaction tardive, de toute façon après 1066, expliquerait la mention précise de la paroisse dans laquelle le saint est mort: ce détail renvoie à une époque où cette entité est une réalité territoriale bien ancrée au sein du diocèse. De même, une datation tardive expliquerait également pourquoi l'auteur tient tant à fixer précisément dans le temps son héros, non seulement au sein de l'histoire des rois francs mais aussi dans la chronologie des différents papes.

Sous le numéro 3974, la *BHL* enregistre enfin un court texte édité par les Bollandistes dans les *Acta Sanctorum* mais sans attribution d'auteur. Ce texte se trouve aussi dans le manuscrit Paris, Bibl. de l'Arsenal 1032[51] et chez Victor de Beauvillé. Dans ces deux derniers cas, une rubrique donne une datation et une attribution claire: *Sermo Richardi, Ambianensis episcopi, de miraculis beati Honorati, episcopi et confessoris, tempore electionis eiusdem Richardi, fratris, XVII° kalendas iunii, anno Domini incarnati millesimo CC° V°*. Ce texte exhorte les frères qui gardent les reliques du saint à louer l'Église à travers ses miracles. Il donne ensuite le récit de la guérison d'un paralytique le jour de la fête du saint ainsi que celui de la guérison d'une femme dans l'hôpital qui jouxte l'église. Enfin, le texte se termine par l'évocation de la matrone Sybille (morte en 1204), fondatrice d'une église en l'honneur du saint à Paris. Les Bollandistes précisent que ce texte ne se trouve pas dans le bréviaire et le manuscrit d'Amiens qu'ils ont utilisés pour transmettre la Vie et les Mi-

---

[50] OTT (2000), p. 75-77.
[51] HANSEN (2019), p. 165, n. 29.

racles d'Honoré. Il se trouve toutefois bien chez De Beauvillé et dans le manuscrit de l'arsenal, dont l'existence justifierait bien une réédition de l'ensemble du dossier du saint.

II. L'HAGIOGRAPHIE MONASTIQUE ET CANONIALE AU MOYEN ÂGE CENTRAL

Dans le volume II d'*Hagiographies*, la production hagiographique monastique avait été évoquée, et notamment celle de l'abbaye de Saint-Riquier avec l'œuvre des hagiographes Angelramme, Hariulf (XIe siècle) et Anschaire (début du XIIe siècle)[52]. Je n'y reviendrai donc pas hormis pour signaler la rédaction, dans le sillage de la réécriture de la Vie de saint Riquier par Alcuin (*BHL* 7223), de deux livres de Miracles (*BHL* 7230) opérés par le saint patron de l'abbaye dans la première moitié du IXe siècle. Avec Saint-Riquier, Corbie est un des principaux lieux de production hagiographique monastique du diocèse: deux textes n'avaient pas été mentionnés en 1996. Il faut aussi mentionner des récits concernant d'autres sanctuaires et leurs reliques.

A. CORBIE: LES TRANSLATIONS DES RELIQUES DE GENTIEN ET PRÉCORD

L'abbé Adalhard, mort en 826, fait l'objet peu après sa mort d'une Vie par son successeur, Paschase Radbert (*BHL* 58)[53], mais ce n'est qu'«au XIe siècle qu'Adalhard de Corbie accède à la maturité hagiographique», selon Laurent Morelle[54], grâce à la réécriture de la première Vie sous l'impulsion du moine Géraud (*BHL* 60) entre 1058 et 1063, et à la composition simultanée d'un premier livre de miracles (*BHL* 61), complété ensuite à la

---

[52] VAN 'T SPIJKER (1996), p. 274-275. Sur les hagiographes de Saint-Riquier, voir depuis BOZOKY (2001); sur Hariulf en particulier voir depuis LEDRU (2017) et sa thèse de doctorat: LEDRU (2019), *passim*.
[53] Voir en dernier lieu VERRI (2009).
[54] MORELLE (2004), p. 171.

fin du XIe siècle par un second (*BHL* 62)[55]. On connaît aussi des récits de translation de reliques. Ainsi de celles de Gentien, cette fois détaché de ses compagnons Fuscien et Victoric. Elles furent transférées d'Amiens à Corbie dans les années 890, d'après un récit (*BHL* 3351) copié dans deux manuscrits de cette abbaye dans la seconde moitié du XIIe siècle[56]. Après un prologue qui indique clairement que ce texte a bien été rédigé à Corbie, l'auteur place son récit sous le règne du roi Eudes, sous l'abbatiat de Francon et sous l'épiscopat d'Otger. Comme ce dernier, dont un portrait laudatif est dressé, avait offert les reliques de Victoric à Saint-Quentin[57], l'abbé de Corbie souhaitait pareille générosité et demanda les reliques de Gentien. Les rapports d'amitié entre l'abbé et l'évêque sont longuement détaillés[58]. L'évêque, craignant les difficultés que causeraient la perte des reliques, trouva un stratagème: il demanda aux gardes du trésor d'aider l'abbé Francon et s'absenta d'Amiens. L'abbé et ses hommes arrivèrent de nuit, les reliques furent dérobées. Au petit matin les amiénois, prirent les armes pour poursuivre les voleurs, mais un épais brouillard les empêcha de voir leurs ennemis, si bien qu'ils rebroussèrent chemin, tandis que le corps du saint fut accueilli avec liesse à Corbie et installé dans l'église Saint-Pierre. Enfin, l'auteur compare cette translation avec le récit de l'Inventio (*BHL* 3229) de ces saints: Childebert souhaitait les transférer à Paris, mais la volonté divine en décida autrement. Ici, la volonté divine a voulu que les reliques de Gentien demeurent à Corbie. La datation de ce transfert de reliques méritera à l'avenir d'être précisée: l'analyse de l'image des relations qu'elle donne à voir entre Amiens et Corbie permettrait probablement de resserrer la chronologie. Il faudrait aussi expliquer

---

[55] Sur tout cela, voir l'étude fouillée de MORELLE (2013) dans laquelle on trouvera toute la bibliographie précédente.

[56] Paris, BnF, lat. 12607 et 13091. Le texte se trouve édité par Mabillon dans les *AASS OSB*, IV-2 (1682), p. 487-489 à partir d'un seul témoin. SALMON (1853), p. 138-145 se contente de reproduire le texte fourni par Mabillon.

[57] Sur ce transfert, voir *BHL* 7020 cf. CHAFFENET – GAILLARD, «Le diocèse de Noyon» qui le placent en 893 (*supra*, p. 371).

[58] Indéniablement, ce texte est à verser au dossier des relations complexes entre l'abbaye de Corbie et les évêques d'Amiens, cf. MORELLE (2011) qui ne mentionne pas ce texte. Voir aussi en ce sens les remarques de VAN METER (1996), p. 634, n. 6.

comment les reliques du saint sont entrées dans le trésor de la cathédrale d'Amiens depuis Sains-en-Amiénois avant ce vol.

L'autre récit de translation concerne le corps de saint Précord, ramené depuis une des possessions de l'abbaye, la *villa* de *Valliacus* (auj. Vailly-sur-Aisne) dans le *pagus* de Soissons vers 940[59], selon un récit incontestablement rédigé à Corbie, publié dans les *Acta Sanctorum Hiberniae* de John Colgan en 1645 et dans les *Acta Sanctorum* des Bollandistes en 1658 (Febr., I), d'après des manuscrits repérés par Nicolas Beaufort (*BHL* 6914). Ce récit résume en quelques mots la Vie du saint en faisant de lui un *scotus*, proche de Remi de Reims, qui vit en bon chrétien. Après sa mort, alors que le prêtre Thiard était chargé de veiller sur ses reliques, il préféra déléguer cette charge à un autre prêtre qui en profita pour voler les reliques pour les amener en Angleterre. Thiard se lance à sa poursuite, rapporte les reliques, et fait une halte à Fouilly où il laisse les reliques dans la maison de son ami *Seranus*. De nuit, ces dernières illuminent sa maison. *Seranus* court en informer l'abbé Béranger de Corbie qui finit par décider de transférer le corps du saint dans son établissement voisin. Alors, après trois mois de sécheresse dont eut à souffrir *tota terra Ambianensium*, une pluie abondante et réparatrice tomba. Le corps du saint fut installé dans l'Église Saint-Jean, une châsse fut ensuite fabriquée et le corps fut transféré dans l'Église Saint-Pierre. Thiard souhaita récupérer les reliques (l'abbé, après lui les avoir refusées, lui donna une somme d'argent en compensation), mais n'y parvint pas et mourut cette année. Les reliques du saint firent ensuite de nombreux miracles à Corbie, guérissant notamment un possédé de la ville d'Amiens. Ce dernier miracle a été judicieusement mis en relation avec la Paix d'Amiens-Corbie de 1034 et pourrait fournir un *terminus post quem* pour dater l'ensemble du récit[60].

Ce texte se trouve dans le manuscrit de Corbie du XIIe siècle (Paris, BnF, lat. 12607, fol. 190v-196) qui contient la Translation des reliques de Gentien. Sous le numéro *BHL* 6913, les Bollandistes recensent le texte contenu dans l'autre manuscrit hagiographique de Corbie qui contient la Translation des re-

---

[59] Cette date est donnée par la *BHL*. COENS (1963), p. 307, suivi par GILLON (2019), p. 53 indique 840, ce qui est une erreur car un autre abbé est connu à cette date: GANZ (1990), p. 30-31.

[60] VAN METER (1996), p. 637-638.

liques de Gentien, le manuscrit Paris, BnF, lat. 13091 (fol. 64v-66), du XIIe siècle également. Dans ce dernier manuscrit, toujours inédit, le récit de la translation de saint Précord est «un peu plus détaillé»[61]. Faut-il faire de la rédaction de ces deux récits de translation de reliques en faveur de Corbie des œuvres du XIe siècle? Alors, l'abbaye promeut son «capital sacré»[62], en manipulant des reliques (translation du corps de Paschase Radbert en 1058) et en investissant dans l'écriture hagiographique, comme en témoigne aussi la rédaction par le moine Gualdo d'une Vie métrique de saint Anschaire (*BHL* 546)[63]. Une étude plus poussée, qui prenne en compte également toutes les traces du culte des saints dans la célèbre abbaye de Picardie, permettrait de le savoir.

B. SAINT-JOSSE SUR MER
ET LE DOSSIER HAGIOGRAPHIQUE DE JOSSE

Localisée dans le Ponthieu, l'abbaye qui garde les reliques du breton Josse (*Iudocus*) a été le lieu d'une production hagiographique dédié à ce saint. Le dossier de saint Josse a fait l'objet de travaux récents et solides de Joseph-Claude Poulin auxquels on se contentera de renvoyer[64]. Une première Vie (*BHL* 4504), autrefois attribuée à Alcuin, y a peut-être été rédigée, «peut-être au IXe siècle (avant *c*. 870), mais plus probablement autour de 925»[65]. Ensuite, une seconde Vie (*BHL* 4505), le récit d'une *Inventio* sous l'abbé Sigebrand en 977 (*BHL* 4506 à 4509) et des Miracles (*BHL* 4510) ont été composés par Isembard de Fleury, pour les moines de Saint-Josse, peu après 1010[66]. Enfin, une

---

[61] MORELLE (1991), p. 288.
[62] MORELLE (2004), p. 172.
[63] Sur ce texte, voir en dernier lieu MORELLE (2011). Notons encore que c'est au XIe siècle qu'une messe pour la translation de Gentien est ajoutée au sacramentaire de Corbie (Paris, BnF, lat. 12051, fol. 1v-2r), cf. PARIS-POULAIN (2019), n. 70 qui indique par erreur qu'il s'agit d'un témoin du «récit de la translation».
[64] POULIN (2009), p. 98-119 dans lequel on trouvera toute la bibliographie antérieure et *supra*, p. 169-171, 193-208 et 230-231.
[65] POULIN (2009), p. 108 et *supra*, p. 149; pour une datation plus tardive dans le Xe siècle et une composition de la Vie à Saint-Benoît-sur-Loire, voir GARY – HELVÉTIUS (2010).
[66] Sur ce texte voir DE GAIFFIER (1979).

troisième Vie en prose (*BHL* 4511), inspirée des deux précédentes fut composée par Florent de Saint-Josse dans le courant du XIIIe siècle, et non au XIe siècle comme on le pensait avant que John Howe ne s'y intéresse[67]. Malgré l'existence de travaux récents, seule la première Vie a fait l'objet d'une édition. Il reste donc encore du travail pour comprendre les textes relatifs à ce saint qui connut un culte important au Moyen Âge[68].

C. Montdidier : le récit de la translation des reliques des saints Lugle et Luglien

La Vie de ces saints (*BHL* 5061) particulièrement fêtés à Lillers (Pas-de-Calais) est difficile à localiser et à dater, notamment car aucun manuscrit médiéval n'a été conservé. Elle est jugée «du XIIe siècle au plus tôt»[69]. Seule la translation des reliques des deux saints à Montdidier au Xe siècle concerne le diocèse d'Amiens. Le texte qui la rapporte (*BHL* 5063) est transmis d'abord par le Bollandiste Joseph Ghesquière d'après le récit qu'envoya Du Cange aux Bollandistes en 1666[70] : un prêtre breton nommé Paul qui se trouvait à Amiens fut frappé de cécité pour avoir osé perturber la fête de saint Matthieu (ou Maclou comme le corrige Ghesquière). Entendant les miracles que les saints faisaient, il se rend auprès de leur tombeau et il est guéri. Il décide d'emmener les reliques avec lui, et il est tenté de les vendre pour en tirer profit. Alors qu'il s'est arrêté chez un paysan dans le *vicus* de Paillart (*Pallardius*), des boules de feu s'échappent du coffre dans lequel se trouvent les reliques : le paysan se rend dans la localité voisine de Montdidier pour en informer les autorités religieuses. Les reliques, après une révélation divine, sont transférées à Montdidier sur l'ordre du comte

---

[67] Howe (1983).
[68] Signalons à cet égard le manuscrit Bruxelles, KBR 19052 (Van den Gheyn 3247) du XVIe siècle, non décrit dans le *Cat. Bruxelles*, II, 1889. Ce *libellus* peu connu, à l'usage de Saint-Winnoc de Bergues, contient une copie de miracles enregistrés à la toute fin du Moyen Âge.
[69] Voir les arguments de Mériaux (2006), p. 360-361. Sur ce texte voir encore l'étude de Bozóky (2011), qui ne reprend pas la question de la datation mais donne toute la bibliographie antérieure, ainsi que Gricourt, Hollard (2015).
[70] Ghesquiere (1794), p. 5 et sqq, reproduit ensuite dans les *AASS*.

Hilduin[71] et de son épouse Helwide, dans un prieuré clunisien dédié à la Vierge. Aux dires de Joseph Ghesquière, ce texte provient de ce prieuré. Il n'est pas impossible qu'il y ait été composé[72]. On doit donc situer sa datation après le rattachement effectif du prieuré à Cluny en 1130[73]. Ensuite, Louis Nicquet, prêtre célestin de Soissons, a transmis aux Bollandistes le récit d'un miracle placé à la même époque de la translation, durant lequel les reliques du saint furent sauvées d'un incendie, ce qui entraîna la construction par la comtesse Helwide d'une basilique en leur honneur et en celui de la Vierge. Ces deux récits sont difficiles à dater faute d'une tradition manuscrite ancienne. Par ailleurs, les traces du culte de ces saints à Montdidier semblent être rares avant la fin du XVe siècle[74].

D. SAINT-GERMAIN SUR BRESLE: LA VIE DE GERMAIN L'ÉCOSSAIS

C'est dans la collégiale Saint-Germain que fut écrite «probablement» la Vie de Germain l'Écossais (*BHL* 3452) par un des chanoines au Xe ou au XIe siècle[75]. Ce long texte a été édité

---

[71] Il s'agit du premier comte attesté à cet endroit, ce qui est confirmé par d'autres sources, cf. DE BEAUVILLÉ (1857), I, p. 50-52.

[72] Le récit se rapportant à cette même translation *BHL* 5062 est introuvable: les références de la *BHL* semblent erronées. BOZÓKY (2011), p. 761 écrit que «l'histoire de la translation des reliques des deux frères à Montdidier est racontée pour la première fois en 1656, dans la préface d'une pièce de théâtre consacrée aux saints par Bonaventure Fricourt», FRICOURT (1656). Elle indique par ailleurs (comme la *BHL*) que cette préface est reprise dans les *AASS Belgii*, ce qui est inexact. On trouve la même erreur chez GRICOURT – HOLLARD (2015), n. 257, p. 49. DE BEAUVILLÉ (1862), p. 14-16, dit que Ghesquière a reproduit la préface de Fricourt que lui a envoyé Du Cange «en paraissant ignorer la source où Du Cange avait puisé». De même, DANGEZ (1862), p. 307 explique que le récit de Fricourt est «rapporté par Du Cange» mais ce dernier, comme GRICOURT – HOLLARD (2015), p. 49, fournit (p. 160 et sqq) un récit qui diffère de celui transmis par Ghesquière et appelle le prêtre Paul «Paul Morand». On peut y reconnaître l'incipit de *BHL* 5062 tel que transmis dans la *BHL*: Inc. *Fuit quidam presbiter in Britannia nomine Paulus morans per spatium...* dans lequel le participe morans a été pris pour un nom de famille!

[73] DE BEAUVILLÉ (1857), III, ch. 1.

[74] DE BEAUVILLÉ (1862), p. 19-21.

[75] Selon LAPORTE (1959), p. 2 repris par FOUCHER (2019). Je n'ai pas eu accès à BASSEVILLE (1946)

par Jean Bolland dans les *Acta Sanctorum* en 1680 (Mai, I), à partir de copies de Rosweyde prises sur des manuscrits de l'abbaye de Doest près de Bruges (*monasterium thosanum*) et de Clairmarais[76], d'un exemplaire venant d'Amiens et d'un autre venant de Jean Cauchie qui avait transcrit le texte en 1646[77]. Philippe Labbe le publia également en 1657 à partir d'un manuscrit de Flamanville (mais sans le prologue et avec au moins une longue phrase en moins)[78]. La base *Légendiers latins* recense trois manuscrits médiévaux: un manuscrit de Fleury du XIIe siècle (Vatican, Reg. lat. 646)[79], et du XIIIe siècle, les manuscrits Bruges, SB 403 (fol. 172r-177) qui doit être le manuscrit de l'abbaye de Doest[80] et Paris, BnF, lat. 5075 (fol. 138v-144v), (amputé à la fin) ayant appartenu à l'abbaye bénédictine de Saint-Sauveur-le-Vicomte dans la Manche[81]. Tous mériteraient d'être inspectés.

Après un prologue, qui selon les *Acta Sanctorum* n'est pas présent dans tous les manuscrits, le récit indique que l'action du saint se déroule à l'époque de l'empereur Jovinien, successeur de Julien l'apostat dont l'action contre les chrétiens est longuement évoquée. La vie de saint Germain d'Auxerre est ensuite évoquée: ce dernier rencontra lors de sa pérégrination un *scotus* nommé Audin et sa femme *Aquila* ainsi que leur fils. Ils étaient païens, mais se convertirent au contact du saint, et nommèrent leur fils Germain. Celui-ci grandit en parfait chrétien, veillant, priant, prêchant. Il devient clerc et accomplit de nombreux miracles: guérisons, exorcismes. Il vient ensuite en Gaule, après une traversée miraculeuse sur la roue d'un char et il y prêche et convertit. En butte avec un gouverneur, ce dernier est frappé de mort; confronté à un dragon, il en vint à bout et entraine la conversion du gouverneur Maximien. Après plusieurs autres miracles, il se rend à Trèves et il est ordonné évêque par l'archevêque saint Séverin de Cologne. Ensuite, il part en pèlerinage à Rome, puis en mission en Espagne où il détruit des temples et construit églises et monastères et fut à l'origine de nombreuses

---

[76] Il s'agit du légendier reconstitué par DOLBEAU (1973), voir notamment, p. 280.
[77] Voir les références aux manuscrits de Cauchie données par FOUCHER (2019).
[78] LABBE (1657), I, p. 716-723.
[79] PELLEGRIN (1964), p. 21.
[80] Cf. *AB*, 3 (1884), p. 458.
[81] *Cat. Paris*, I, p. 388.

conversions. La ville de Toulouse en est témoin, qui commémore son passage[82]. Il retourne ensuite dans sa patrie accomplir d'autres miracles, puis revient en France.

Là, une pause a lieu dans la narration puisque l'auteur déclare insérer un récit de sa propre plume à propos de son action dans le port de Mogdunum (*in portum Mogduni*): il guérit une aveugle de ce lieu, et en convertit d'autres alors qu'il parcourt la Normandie. Il rencontre le comte de la cité de Bayeux qu'il punit pour lui avoir refusé du vin. Arrivé en ville, il détruit la muraille pour y pénétrer, comme en témoignent les ruines encore visibles. Là, il libère des captifs et convertit. Enfin, le saint vient dans le *pagus* d'Amiens, à Mortemer, où il apprend en songe son martyr. Il vient à Vieux-Rouen (Vieux-Rouen-sur Bresle, Seine-Maritime), dominé alors par le tyran Hubald qui lui refuse l'accès. Le saint évêque traverse alors la Bresle (*Auda*) qui sépare la Normandie de la France (*qui est limes medius Normanniae ac Franciae*), entre dans l'oratoire à proximité d'une église dédiée à la Vierge et y est décapité par Hubald. Le corps sans tête du saint est laissé à l'air libre, exposé aux bêtes sauvages et privé de sépulture sur l'ordre du tyran. La tête du saint se mit à parler à une jeune fille en lui demandant d'amener son corps auprès de son familier, le prince Sénard. Ce dernier organise alors des funérailles et enterre le saint, dans un sarcophage neuf sur lequel une église est construite.

Ce long texte regorge de lieux communs hagiographiques et a été pour cette raison souvent rejeté et trop peu étudié. La mention de la Normandie fait qu'il «a pu être composé au plus tôt au début du Xe siècle»[83]. Les épisodes de la vie du saint s'enchaînent rapidement, sans ancrage spatial particulier, jusqu'au passage relatif au port de *Mogdunum* et au martyre aux confins de la Normandie et de la Picardie. Bien que «les déplacements du corps mutilé sont insinués de façon singulièrement imprécise»[84], l'idée d'en faire un texte écrit près du sanctuaire Saint-Germain-sur-Bresle apparaît clairement justifiée. L'histoire de

---

[82] Cette curieuse mention avait déjà donné lieu à une note de Jean Bolland qui s'est fait confirmer par Pierre Poussines que le culte du saint n'existait pas dans la ville française, et qui se demandait s'il ne s'agissait pas d'un des toponymes *Tolosa* (comme Las Navas de Tolosa) ou d'une mélecture pour *Tortosa*.

[83] KERLOVEGAN (1984).

[84] LAPORTE (1959), p. 12.

ce sanctuaire reste à écrire, mais un dessin récemment découvert montre que le sarcophage du saint, dont le couvercle probablement du XIe siècle est peut-être inspiré d'un tombeau mérovingien, était percé de trous permettant aux fidèles de voir et toucher le saint corps[85]. C'est peut-être de ce siècle qu'il faut dater le récit[86]. D'après un texte composé au XVIIe siècle par Jean Cauchie pour l'office et qui est reproduit par les Bollandistes, une communauté de bénédictins qui s'était installée près du tombeau a transféré le corps à Ribemont dans le diocèse de Laon lors d'invasions normandes. En fait, il semble que le prieuré de Saint-Germain-sur-Bresle ne soit mentionné qu'au XIIe siècle, au moment donc où la Vie du saint apparaît pour la première fois dans un manuscrit[87]. Il y a là indéniablement un dossier à reprendre.

E. Saint-Valery-sur-Somme : Vie et translation de *Walaricus*

La Vie (*BHL* 8762) de Valery (Walaricus), fondateur au VIIe siècle de l'abbaye de Leuconay (aujourd'hui Saint-Valery-sur-Somme) et attesté chez Adon et Usuard, a été éditée par Bruno Krusch[88] qui considère, à la suite de Mabillon, qu'il s'agit d'un texte tardif, du XIe siècle, notamment parce que son prologue cite un archevêque Hugues, identifié comme étant l'archevêque de Besançon Hugues de Salins[89]. L'auteur déclare toutefois clairement abréger une Vie antérieure, de la main de l'abbé Raginbert, aujourd'hui perdue. Ce texte utilise notamment les Vies des saints Fursy et Colomban[90]. Il est très clairement influencé par le souvenir du saint irlandais, alors qu'aucune source ne permet de corroborer le fait que Valery fut un de ses compagnons[91]. La Vie présente un saint né en Auvergne qui rejoint

---

[85] Foucher (2019), p. 467.
[86] Kerlovegan (1984)
[87] Foucher (2019), p. 465.
[88] *MGH, SRM*, IV, Hanovre – Leipzig, 1902, p. 161-175.
[89] *Annales OSB*, I, 318 (cf. *AB*, 22 (1903), p. 105). Sur l'argumentation de Bruno Krusch sur ce texte voir Goullet (2010), p. 22. Bozoky (2001), p. 2 date ce texte du VIIIe ou du IXe siècle, sans s'en expliquer.
[90] *MGH, SRM*, IV, Hanovre – Leipzig, 1902, p. 158-159.
[91] Mériaux (2017), p. 5.

son oncle dans le monastère non localisé d'*Autumo* avant de partir pour Auxerre dans le monastère de l'évêque Aunachaire pour échapper à la proximité de ses parents. Ensuite, attiré par Colomban, il part pour Luxeuil, accompagné d'un certain Bobon. Après l'expulsion de Colomban par Thierry, il aida le saint abbé Eustase dans sa tâche. Il part ensuite prêcher avec un des frères, Waldolenus, en Neustrie. Ils arrivèrent dans l'Amiénois, à Wailly, où par son intermédiaire Dieu ressuscite un pendu condamné par le tribunal du comte Sigobard[92]. Ensuite, avec l'accord du roi et de l'évêque d'Amiens, ils s'installent à *Leucanaus*, où le saint évêque d'Amiens Berchundus avait l'habitude de se retirer. Suivent une série de miracles opérés par le saint, mentionnant quelques noms de personnes et de lieux de la région: la géographie du culte du saint – et avec elle, celle du rayonnement de l'abbaye – est ainsi en partie justifiée. S'ensuit encore des historiettes mettant en scène le catalogue de vertus du saint. Vient enfin le récit de sa mort: après une révélation, il désigne l'emplacement de sa tombe (auprès de l'arbre où le saint évêque d'Amiens Berchundus avait coutume de pendre des reliques de saints. Après les premiers miracles accomplis *post-mortem*, Berchundus décida de déplacer en grande pompe le corps du saint dans sa cité d'Amiens, ce qui fut miraculeusement refusé. L'abbé de Bobbio Athala fut aussi guéri par intermédiaire de Valery. Le texte s'achève enfin en mentionnant Blidmundus que le saint avait éduqué à la vie érémitique et qui demanda tant au roi qu'à l'évêque d'Amiens l'autorisation de construire un monastère: il en fut le second abbé.

La tradition manuscrite de ce riche texte permet de réviser la datation traditionnelle et invite à reprendre ce dossier: selon la base *Légendiers latins*, le texte est en effet transmis par trois manuscrits antérieurs à l'an mil: les manuscrits Turin, BN, F.III.16 (vers 900, originaire de Bobbio)[93]; Boulogne-sur-Mer, BM 106 où la Vie est «copiée à la fin du Xe siècle par deux mains flamandes» dans un «livret initial»[94]. Ces deux premiers manus-

---

[92] Cet épisode a été relevé par DE GAIFFIER (1943), p. 142-143.

[93] Voir en dernier lieu la description détaillée de ce manuscrit par VIRCILLO FRANKLIN (2004), p. 259-267. Le texte se trouve dans la partie du légendier qui ne respecte pas le *circulus anni* mais qui participe bien de la même campagne de copie.

[94] POULIN (2006), p. 157-158 (qui indique par erreur que ce manuscrit contient aussi une translation du saint).

crits ont bien été utilisés par Bruno Krusch pour son édition, mais il les datait du XIe siècle. Enfin, la base *Légendiers latins* enregistre Milan, BA, P. 113 sup, mais ce témoin date plutôt du milieu du XIe siècle[95]. Il n'a pas été utilisé par Bruno Krusch. Récemment, Charles Mériaux a émis à titre d'hypothèse l'idée que ce texte ait pu être composé « à l'issue de la restauration du monastère qui a dû suivre le retour des reliques en 981 », ce qui ne semble pas concorder avec la datation du manuscrit de Bobbio[96]. En réalité, une des clés de datation de ce texte réside dans la mention, dans le prologue, de l'archevêque Hugues, présenté comme le commanditaire de l'œuvre. Il serait plus logique de penser à un archevêque de Reims: dans ce cas, l'épiscopat d'Hugues de Vermandois (925-931 et 940-946), seul archevêque de Reims de ce nom, semble tout indiqué, même si son épiscopat semble postérieur à la datation proposée par C. Vircillo Franklin pour le manuscrit de Bobbio[97]. En fait, il n'est pas impossible que cette mention du prologue de la Vie de Valery constitue un *terminus* permettant de revoir la datation de ce manuscrit. Voilà de toute façon un texte dont la fabrique mériterait d'être explorée plus en avant.

En ce qui concerne la Translation du saint (*BHL* 8763), elle a été rédigée par un moine de Leuconay dans la seconde moitié du XIe siècle[98]. Le comte de Flandre Arnoul le Grand fit enlever les reliques de Valery à Leuconay (et avec elles, celles de saint Riquier à Saint-Riquier, selon les témoignages complémentaires des hagiographes de ce lieu, Angelramme et Hariulf, qui donnent une autre lecture de ces événements)[99]. Il les transféra

---

[95] Sur la datation de ce manuscrit: LAPIDGE (2017), p. 137. Le *Cat. hag. lat. Bib. Ambrosianae*, *AB*, 11 (1892), p. 360-362 le donne du Xe siècle. L'examen du manuscrit numérisé en ligne semble donner raison à M. Lapidge.

[96] MÉRIAUX (2017), p. 5.

[97] Sur l'épiscopat agité d'Hugues, on consultera: SOT (1993), p. 262-270, 279-293, 311-315.

[98] Le texte est édité dans les *AASS*, Apr. I, 1675, p. 23 sq., à partir d'un manuscrit fourni par Mabillon que ce dernier publia dix ans plus tard dans les *AASS OSB*, V (1685), p. 556 sq. O. HOLDER EGGER, dans les *MGH*, *SS*, XV-2, 1888, p. 693-696 se contente de reproduire des extraits à partir de ces deux éditions.

[99] BOZOKY (2001) a principalement analysé cela, mais en s'appuyant sur le texte incomplet des *MGH*. Voir aussi sur ce dossier MÉRIAUX (2006), p. 181-186.

dans l'abbaye Saint-Saulve de Montreuil vers 939, avant de les installer à Saint-Bertin (951-952), où elles sont attestées dans la *Geste des abbés de Saint-Bertin* par Folcuin en 955. Le récit produit à Saint-Valery-sur-Somme présente le comte Arnoul de manière négative: avec l'appui d'Erchembold, abbé de Leuconay poussé par le diable, il a volé le corps de Valery, après avoir commis des destructions. Ensuite, en 981, les reliques volées furent récupérées par Hugues Capet. Toujours selon le récit de la translation, le duc sut par une vision du saint qu'il fallait ramener les reliques de Valery à Leuconay. Il reprit le château de Montreuil et envoya des messagers réclamer les reliques au comte Arnoul qui refusa, en expliquant que les corps saints avaient été amenés sur ses terres par son grand-père et que depuis, ils faisaient l'objet d'un culte. Face à la menace militaire, Arnoul cède et fait fabriquer une châsse en argent dans laquelle il met les reliques de Valery pour les rendre au duc. Après le retour des reliques dans leur patrie d'origine, le récit se poursuit avec le récit de plusieurs miracles ayant eu lieu sous quatre des abbés de Leuconay.

Si on ignore quel fut le manuscrit utilisé par Mabillon et Henschens pour éditer ce texte, la base *Légendiers latins* recense deux *libelli* du XIIe siècle, désormais enchâssés dans des recueils plus larges: Rouen, BM 1407 (O. 55), fol. 57v-66, en provenance de Saint-Ouen de Rouen, et comprenant la Vie suivie de la translation, précédée de la rubrique *Corporis S. Walarici relatio et miraculorum quae tunc vel postmodum ab eo gesta sunt narratio*[100] et Paris, BnF, lat. 13092 (fol. 123-128v), en provenance de l'abbaye du Bec et également précédé de la *Vita* du saint. La version contenue dans ce manuscrit présente des variantes par rapport au texte édité dans les *Acta Sanctorum*. La datation de ce récit de translation dans la seconde moitié du XIe siècle repose depuis Henschens sur la mention dans les miracles de l'abbé Théodinus. À l'époque de son successeur l'abbé Bernard (à la tête de l'abbaye jusqu'en 1052), trois livres d'une Vie et des Miracles de Valery furent rédigés en vers par un moine du monastère, mais il n'en subsiste que des fragments reproduits par Henschens dans les *Acta Sanctorum*.

Enfin, sous le numéro *BHL* 8764, les Bollandistes enregistrent le récit d'un miracle uniquement transmis par

---

[100] Cf. *Cat. hag. lat. Rouen*, AB, 23 (1904), p. 151.

Henschens, à partir d'une source qu'on ignore. Centré sur le territoire de Faucourt, il permet d'éclairer les relations du sanctuaire de saint Valery avec l'aristocratie laïque (chevaliers, avoués), mais aussi l'utilisation qui est faite du corps saint au Moyen Âge central. Il est difficile de préciser la datation de ce texte dont aucun manuscrit n'a pour le moment été repéré: seule une analyse interne serrée permettrait d'aller plus loin. D'une manière générale pour les textes relatifs à Valery, et plus encore pour la Translation et les Miracles, l'établissement et la datation de ces récits remontant à des travaux forts anciens, une inspection systématique des manuscrits devrait être un préalable indispensable à une nécessaire reprise de l'analyse de ce riche corpus trop peu exploité.

F. Le monastère cistercien du Paraclet: Les Vies de la vierge Ulphe et de l'ermite Domice

Les dossiers de sainte Ulphe et de saint Domice ne font qu'un. Si l'historiographie place traditionnellement ces saints au VIIIe siècle, et en fait les contemporains d'un évêque nommé Chrétien, aucun document, pas même leurs récits hagiographiques, ne permet de corroborer ces éléments. Le culte le plus anciennement attesté est celui de Domice qui apparaît dans le plus ancien calendrier conservé du diocèse, copié vers 900 (Paris, BnF, lat. 9432)[101], tandis que celui de sainte Ulphe est attesté pour la première fois au milieu du XIe siècle par l'inscription de son nom dans les litanies d'un missel (Paris, BnF, lat. 17306, fol. 97). Les Bollandistes ont publié une Vie de la première en 1643 (Ian., II), à partir d'un légendier de la collégiale Saint-Wulfran d'Abbeville (*BHL* 8371). Le texte commence par énoncer les pratiques de cette vierge dans un catalogue de vertus relativement stéréotypé. Issue d'une riche famille, elle fuit le mariage promis par ses parents en se rendant la plus laide possible et quitte les siens pour entrer dans le *pagus* d'Amiens. Elle trouve une source à environ quatre mille de la ville, à côté de la rivière de La Nove (*Noyae*), dans un lieu éloigné de tous. L'ermite Domice habitait non loin de là et, mu par les mêmes principes chrétiens, il se joint à elle. Il l'aime comme

---

[101] Sur ce manuscrit, voir *supra* n. 43.

sa fille et elle le vénère comme son père. Ils prient ensemble la nuit et retournent dans leurs cellules respectives aux yeux des paysans qui s'inclinent devant eux. Vint enfin le récit de la mort de la sainte. Aurea, une autre vierge, vient dans sa cellule et trouve son corps. La cathédrale d'Amiens conserve un puits dans lequel se trouverait la source près de laquelle Ulphe a vécu et dans laquelle elle se baigna. Cette eau sert à la liturgie de l'église. Son corps fut ensuite transféré dans la cité d'Amiens avec celui de saint Domice. L'hagiographe précise que si une église fut construite en l'honneur de saint Domice au lieu où il trouva la mort, ce ne fut pas le cas pour sainte Ulphe: le lieu où elle est décédée resta vierge mais visité par des fidèles qui l'invoquaient pour guérir divers maux. Enfin, à l'emplacement de sa maison fut ensuite construit le monastère du Paraclet.

Cette dernière mention place la rédaction de ce texte après la construction de cet établissement cistercien en 1219. Pascal Montaubin estime que ce texte a été alors « rédigé au XIIIe siècle d'après une vie plus ancienne »[102]. Ce n'est pas impossible, si l'on considère l'ancienneté du culte. Si la base *Légendiers latins* ne recense pas de manuscrit, on peut noter la présence d'un texte abrégé dans un légendier de l'abbaye cistercienne de Loos du XIVe siècle composé pour supplémenter un exemplaire de la *Légende dorée* de Jacques de Voragine (Lille, BM 450 (216), 2e partie du manuscrit, fol. 53v)[103]. Ulphe fit en outre l'objet d'une Vie française au XVIe siècle (Amiens, BM 103): le traducteur déclare traduire en 1542 un texte qu'il a trouvé dans un manuscrit des Célestins d'Amiens. Ce même manuscrit contient une Vie latine de la sainte incomplète au début (fol. 231), écrite à cette même date au monastère du Paraclet d'Amiens, d'où ce manuscrit est issu[104]. À la fin du XVIe siècle, la Vie transmise par les Bollandistes se trouve aussi copiée dans un recueil d'hagiographie amiénoise ayant appartenu au XVIIe siècle à J. B. Hautin, conseiller du Châtelet (Aix-en-Provence, bibliothèque Méjanes, 353, fol. 26)[105].

---

[102] MONTAUBIN (2012), p. 496, n. 513.
[103] Sur ce manuscrit, voir DOLBEAU (2000), p. 376, 393.
[104] COYECQUE (1885), p. 45. Ce manuscrit est aussi connu de CORBLET (1873), p. 537 et sqq. La Vie française est éditée par JANVIER (1863), que je n'ai pu consulter.
[105] ALBANÈS (1894), p. 187.

Les Bollandistes ont aussi publié en 1861 une Vie de saint Domitius (*BHL* 2258), dont aucun manuscrit médiéval ne semble avoir été conservé[106]. Publiée à partir du légendier d'Abbeville où ils avaient déjà puisé la Vie d'Ulphe, ce texte rapporte que dans un temps de persécutions, un vieil homme, ancien chanoine de l'Église d'Amiens, vivait en ermite dans un lieu tenu secret à une quinzaine de milles de la cité d'Amiens. Ce dernier avait une petite prébende (*prebendula*), administrée par les chanoines de la cathédrale, qui lui permettait de survivre. Il avait par ailleurs pour habitude de se rendre de nuit à Amiens pour prier dans une église Sainte-Marie, à l'endroit où se trouve désormais le monastère Saint-Acheul. Le texte revient ensuite sur la figure de sainte Ulphe qui avait quitté sa famille et s'était installée sur le lieu du futur monastère de moniales cisterciennes du Paraclet, dans un lieu hérissé de ronces. Leur première rencontre et leurs premiers échanges sont détaillés, ainsi que leur souhait de vivre ensemble leur vie sainte. Un miracle rapporte ensuite qu'alors qu'ils allaient ensemble vers leur ermitage après avoir prié à Amiens, des grenouilles coassaient particulièrement fort. La sainte fit un signe de croix pour pouvoir dormir. Domitius, voulant réveiller la sainte pour qu'ils aillent prier ensemble n'y parvint pas, car ce n'est qu'une fois les coassements ayant cessé, qu'elle put s'endormir. Afin de ne pas manquer une nouvelle fois encore l'oraison du matin, elle pria pour que les grenouilles cessent définitivement leurs chants. Depuis, personne ne les a plus entendues. Enfin, le saint, sentant son trépas arriver, prépare ses funérailles et demande à la sainte de lui donner l'hostie. Ensuite, le prêtre de la paroisse dans laquelle ils se trouvent vient lui conférer l'extrême onction. Une fois mort, la sainte est affligée tandis que le saint est inhumé dans son oratoire, en présence d'une foule de fidèles. Puis, en raison des miracles qui ont lieu, le corps de Domitius est amené à Amiens.

L'articulation de ce récit avec la Vie de sainte Ulphe mériterait d'être creusée: malgré quelques mots communs, les épisodes sont différents. Il apparaît clairement que ce texte est tardif. L'insistance de l'auteur sur l'eucharistie, le viatique, le déroulement des rites à accomplir mais aussi les réalités institution-

---

[106] *AASS*, Oct. X, 1861, p. 145-148. Le bréviaire Amiens, BM 112 du XIIIe siècle, porte le saint dans son sanctoral, mais sans leçon propre.

nelles – des chanoines avec une prébende – excluent une datation haute. Reste qu'il s'agit d'un texte peu connu, qui mériterait l'attention des historiens de la sainteté: le miracle des grenouilles ainsi que l'étroite relation entre l'ermite et la vierge donnent à voir un modèle de vie sainte qui n'est pas banal. Ce dossier mériterait d'être repris, car outre le manuscrit du XVIe siècle de la BM d'Amiens et ses Vies française et latine, on trouve également, copiée dans un ensemble de copies prises pour Nicolas de Beaufort dans le manuscrit Paris, BnF, lat. 3088, fol. 89v-98, une longue Vie de la sainte, d'après un manuscrit des Célestins d'Amiens, dans lequel se trouve un prologue qui paraît inédit[107]: l'auteur, non sans incohérences chronologiques, explique avoir écrit son texte pour fortifier la dévotion envers les saintes vierges et évoque un incendie qui eut lieu en 1136 et détruisit en grande partie la ville d'Amiens. Le corps de la sainte se trouvait en 1208 dans la cathédrale avec un volume comprenant sa Vie qui disparut avec d'autres biens, ce qui pousse l'hagiographe à écrire cette Vie. Suit ensuite un texte qui a le même *incipit* que la Vie de la sainte publiée par les Bollandistes (*BHL* 8371), mais qui est beaucoup plus long et qui contient des éléments qu'on trouve dans la Vie de saint Domitius. Ensuite, on trouve copié (fol. 99) le miracle du chant des grenouilles ainsi qu'un récit de la fondation de l'abbaye cistercienne du Paraclet. Il reste à déterminer la place de cette copie dans la longue (et méconnue) tradition relative à cette sainte.

Conclusion

Dans le diocèse d'Amiens comme dans de nombreux autres diocèses à l'époque carolingienne et féodale, un des enjeux de l'écriture hagiographique fut de fournir une mémoire de la première évangélisation du diocèse; c'est dans cette période que cherchent à s'ancrer la plupart des dossiers que nous avons abordés[108]. Il reste encore beaucoup à faire pour les comprendre et

---

[107] Sur ce manuscrit et son contenu voir DOLBEAU (1976), p. 181.

[108] Un autre évangélisateur de l'Amiénois est saint Gatien qui fit l'objet d'un texte, intitulé *sermo de corylo* (*BHL* 3629) qui rapporte principalement le miracle de son bâton transformé en noisetier sur le lieu de son martyre. Il est écrit vers 1116 à Coulombs dans le diocèse de Chartres. Il est donc hors du

pour les replacer dans une chronologie la plus fine possible: des éditions critiques font défaut; les relations intertextuelles entre les différents récits sont encore à rechercher[109] et enfin la connaissance des manuscrits hagiographiques laisse encore à désirer. Par exemple, on ne dispose pas d'inventaire systématique des textes hagiographiques conservés dans les manuscrits de la bibliothèque municipale d'Amiens. L'examen des leçons du sanctoral des anciens bréviaires et lectionnaires de ce diocèse devrait permettre de restituer au mieux l'histoire des textes hagiographiques[110], si ce n'est d'en repérer d'autres, inconnus par ailleurs[111].

Dans l'état actuel des recherches, il apparaît bien – comme partout ailleurs – que l'étude des sanctuaires dans lesquels s'ancre l'écriture hagiographique permet de mieux comprendre le travail des hagiographes, ce qui nécessite de croiser les sources hagiographiques avec des données historiques et archéologiques[112]. Dans le cas de la cité d'Amiens, le lien entre topographie chrétienne et écriture hagiographique semble plus

---

cadre de cet article, cf. GILLON (2019), p. 52 et *AASS*, Oct. X, 1861. Dans le seul manuscrit recensé, le manuscrit Paris, BnF, lat. 13774 (dans la partie originaire de Saint-Honorine de Conflans, du XIIe siècle), ce texte, imparfaitement édité dans les *Acta Sanctorum*, est précédé de la Passion des saints italiens Gratilianus et Felicissima (*BHL* 3630) qui passe pour être la Passion de saint Gratien, cf. *Cat. Paris*, III, p. 207 et pour l'origine du manuscrit: DOLBEAU (1979), p. 229.

[109] Celle-ci a bien été relevée par OTT (2015), p. 237.

[110] Sur la liturgie médiévale de la cathédrale d'Amiens, on lira avec profit LEBIGUE (2012) et ANDRÉ (2012).

[111] CORBLET (1873), p. 162-175 a repéré dans le bréviaire du XIVe siècle Amiens, BM 113 une légende, toujours inédite, qu'il pense contemporaine de ce bréviaire, relative aux saints Just, Arthémie et Honesta (*BHL uacat*) martyrs à Monchel-sur-Canche (Pas de Calais, mais autrefois dans le diocèse d'Amiens). Enfants d'un roi de Toulouse resté païen, ils fuient la maison paternelle pour vivre en solitaires à Conchy. Alors que leur père vieillissait sans successeur, on envoya des émissaires chercher ses héritiers en Picardie. Les deux frères, refusant de suivre, sont décapités, Just portant sa tête jusqu'à sa tombe. Honesta, elle, pleura ses frères. Le culte est attesté dans la cathédrale d'Amiens dès le milieu du XIIIe siècle. Il existe également des copies modernes de cette légende, signalées par Jules Corblet (p. 175), notamment dans le manuscrit d'Aix-en-Provence (cf. *supra*, n. 105). Les Bollandistes reproduisent les leçons d'un bréviaire de 1554 et un texte transmis par le jésuite Jacques Malbranque (*AASS*, Oct. VIII, 1853, p. 369 et sqq).

[112] L'ouvrage dirigé par GILLON et SAPIN (2019) montre tout ce qu'on peut espérer de cette démarche.

resserré encore tant l'investissement dans l'hagiographie et les figures saintes dans l'espace urbain fut intensif dès l'époque carolingienne. Il semble avoir atteint un acmé au tournant des XIe et XIIe siècles: John Ott a compté cinq manipulations de reliques dans la ville entre 1096 et 1113[113]. Une telle utilisation du passé hagiographique local explique certainement pourquoi, au XIIIe siècle, il fut décidé de donner à la façade principale de la nouvelle cathédrale gothique le «premier portail entièrement dédié à un sujet hagiographique»[114], à la gloire de saint Firmin, puis quelques années après, de réitérer, avec la construction du portail Saint-Honoré[115].

Bibliographie

ABDI, S., «Les collégiales Saint-Firmin-le-Confesseur, Saint-Nicolas-au-Cloître et la cathédrale d'Amiens au Moyen Âge, une histoire partagée», *Bulletin de l'Association des Amis de la Cathédrale d'Amiens* (2014), p. 40-53.

ALBANÈS, J. H., *Catalogue général des manuscrits des bibliothèques publiques de France*, XVI: *Aix*, Paris, 1894.

ANDRÉ, A., «Processions et usages liturgiques amiénois du Moyen Âge au XVIIIe siècle», in ID. et X. BONIFACE, éd., *Amiens*, Strasbourg, 2012, p. 423-430 (La Grâce d'une cathédrale).

BASSEVILLE, M., «*Saint Germain Scot dit l'Escossoy... patron de la ville de Ribemont». Sa vie, ses reliques, son culte*, 3e éd., Nancy, 1946.

BAYARD, D. – MASSY J.-L., «Chapitre. IX. La ville fortifiée», in *Amiens Romain. Revue archéologique de Picardie*, 2-1 (1983), p. 221-246.

DE BEAUVILLÉ, V., *Histoire de la ville de Montdidier*, Paris, 1857.

—, *Examen de quelques passages d'une dissertation de M. l'abbé Dangez, sur la vérité du fait de la translation des reliques des saints Lugle et Luglien à Montdidier*, Amiens, 1862.

—, *Recueil de documents inédits concernant la Picardie*, 3 vol., Paris, 1860-1877.

---

[113] OTT (2015), p. 246.
[114] KASARSKA (2012), p. 194.
[115] Sur ces portails: GAPOSCHKIN (2004), KASARSKA (2012), p. 194-196; HANSEN (2019), PARIS-POULAIN (à paraître) ainsi que le projet de monographie de Barbara Abou-El-Haj, interrompu à sa mort en 2015, mais dont un état préparatoire a été mis en ligne: https://www.medievalart.org/lordship-and-commune [consulté le 30 mars 2020].

BORST, A., *Der karolingische Reichskalender und seine Überlieferung bis ins 12. Jahrhundert*, Hanovre, 2001.
BOZOKY, E., «Le recouvrement des reliques des saints Valéry et Riquier», in D. BUSCHINGER, éd., *Saint Riquier à Saint-Riquier. Actes du colloque du Centre d'études médiévales de l'université de Picardie-Jules Verne, Saint-Riquier, 9-10 décembre 2000*, Amiens, 2001, p. 1-13.
—, «La légende des saints Lugle et Luglien», *Revue du Nord*, 93 (2011), n°s 293-294, p. 761-777 (= *Mélanges Stéphane Lebecq*).
CAMES, G., «Un trésor manuscrit carolingien à la bibliothèque de la Faculté de Médecine de Montpellier», *Etudes héraultaises*, 35 (2004), p. 15-36.
COENS, M., «Anciennes litanies des saints», in *Recueil d'études bollandiennes*, Bruxelles, 1963, p. 129-322.
CORBLET, J., *Hagiographie du Diocèse d'Amiens*, 5 vol., Paris, Amiens, 1868-1875 (t. II en 1870; t. III en 1873).
COYECQUE, E., *Catalogue général des manuscrits des bibliothèques publiques de France*, XIX: *Amiens*, Paris, 1885.
DANGEZ, L., *La Vie des saints frères martyrs Lugle et Luglien: patrons de la ville de Montdidier en Picardie et de Lilliers-en-Artois*, Montdidier, 1862.
DE GAIFFIER, B., «Un thème hagiographique: le Pendu miraculeusement sauvé», *Revue belge d'archéologie et d'histoire de l'art*, 13 (1943), p. 123-148.
—, «Isembard de Fleury-sur-Loire auteur de la Vita *S. Iudoci* (*BHL* 4505-4510)», *Jahrbuch der Gesellschaft für niedersächsische Kirchengeschichte*, 77 (1979), p. 9-12.
DEROLEZ, A., *Medieval manuscripts: Ghent university library*, Gand, 2017.
DOLBEAU, F., «Le légendier de l'abbaye cistercienne de Clairmarais», *AB*, 91 (1973), p. 273-286.
—, «Notes sur la genèse et la diffusion du *liber de natalitiis*», *Revue d'histoire des textes*, 6 (1976), p. 143-195.
—, «Anciens possesseurs des manuscrits hagiographiques latins de la Bibliothèque Nationale de Paris», *Revue d'histoire des textes*, 9 (1979), p. 183-238.
—, «Nouvelles recherches sur le *Legendarium Flandrense*», *Recherches augustiniennes et patristiques*, 16 (1981), p. 399-455.
—, «Les prologues de légendiers latins», in J. HAMESSE, dir., *Les prologues médiévaux*, Paris, 2000, p. 345-393.
DUBOIS, J., *Le martyrologe d'Usuard*, Bruxelles, 1965.
—, «Firmin», in *DHGE*, t. 17, Paris, 1968, col. 251-257.
DUCHESNE, L., *Fastes épiscopaux de l'ancienne Gaule*, III: *Les provinces du Nord et de l'Est*, Paris, 1915.

FOUCHER, F., «Saint-Germain-sur-Bresle (Somme). Une crypte... médiévale?», in GILLON – SAPIN (2019), p. 465-468.

FRICOURT, B., *Sancti Luglius et Luglianus fratres martyres, tragoedia data apud Montemdesiderium in aula Mondiderina*, Paris, 1656.

GABORIT, J. R., «Quelques observations sur la statue dite du Saint-Sauve à la cathédrale d'Amiens», *Bulletin de la Société nationale des Antiquaires de France* (2012), p. 252-263.

GAILLARD, M., «Remarques sur les plus anciennes versions de la *Passio* et de l'*Inventio* des saints Fuscien, Victoric et Gentien: (manuscrits Paris, BnF, lat. 12598 et Wien, ÖNB, 371)», in M. GOULLET, éd., *Parva pro magnis munera. Études de littérature latine tardo-antique et médiévale offertes à François Dolbeau par ses élèves*, Turnhout, 2009, p. 397-409.

—, «Un 'cycle' hagiographique du haut Moyen Âge en Gaule septentrionale: les Passions des martyrs de Riciovar», *Hagiographica*, 21 (2014), p. 7-32.

GANZ, D., *Corbie in the Carolingian renaissance: Untersuchung zur monastischen Kultur der Karolingerzeit am Beispiel der Abtei Corbie*, Sigmaringen, 1990.

GAPOSCHKIN, C., «Portals, processions, pilgrimage, and piety: Saints Firmin and Honoré at Amiens», in S. BLICK – R. TEKIPPE, dir., *Art and architecture of late medieval pilgrimage in Northern Europe and the British Isles*, Leiden, 2004, p. 217-242.

GARCÍA-VILLOSLADA, R., «Leyendo la "Historia de los Obispos de Pamplona"», *Hispania sacra*, 34 (1982), p. 255-288.

GARY, S., HELVÉTIUS, A.-M., «De Saint-Josse à Montreuil: l'encadrement ecclésiastique du *vicus* de Quentovic», in S. LEBECQ – B. BÉTHOUART – L. VERSLYPE, éd., *Quentovic. Environnement, archéologie, histoire*, Villeneuve-d'Ascq, 2010, p. 459-473.

GHESQUIÈRE, J. H., *Acta sanctorum Belgii selecta*, 6 vol., Bruxelles, 1783-1794.

GILLES-RAYNAL, A.-V., «Le dossier de saint Saturnin de Toulouse dans le légendier de Moissac: aux origines du dossier légendaire?», in F. PELOUX, dir., *Le légendier de Moissac et la culture hagiographique méridionale autour de l'an mil*, Turnhout, 2018, p. 325-343.

GILLON, P., «Culte des saints et des reliques en Île-de-France et en Picardie», in GILLON – SAPIN (2019), p. 35-64.

GILLON, P. – SAPIN, C., dir., *Cryptes médiévales et culte des saints en Île-de-France et en Picardie*, Villeneuve-d'Ascq, 2019.

GOULLET, M., «Introduction», in EAD. – M. HEINZELMANN – C. VEYRARD-COSME, dir., *L'hagiographie mérovingienne à travers ses réécritures*, Sigmaringen, 2010, p. 11-26.

GRICOURT, D. – HOLLARD, D., *Les saints jumeaux héritiers des Dioscures celtes: Lugle et Luglien et autres frères apparentés*, Bruxelles, 2015.

Guglielmetti, R., *I testi agiografici latini nei codici della Biblioteca Medicea Laurenziana*, Florence, 2007.

Haggh, B., «The Office of St Germain, Bishop of Auxerre (d. 448, feast 31 July)», *Études grégoriennes*, 36 (1998), p. 111-134.

Hansen, H., «Constructing Episcopal Authority through Hagiography and Ritual in the Saint Honoré portal at Amiens Cathedral», in G. Boto Varela – I. Escandell – E. Lozano Lopez, dir., *The Memory of the Bishop in Medieval Cathedrals Ceremonies and Visualizations*, Bern – Berlin – Bruxelles etc., 2019, p. 149-182.

Howe, J., «The Date of the *Vita Judoci* by Abbot Florentius (*BHL* 4511)», *AB*, 101 (1983), p. 25-31.

Janvier, A., *La Légende de sainte Ulphe, fragment d'une histoire inédite de Boves*, Amiens, 1863.

Kasarska, I., «La sculpture des portails», in A. André – X. Boniface, éd., *Amiens*, Strasbourg, 2012 (La Grâce d'une cathédrale), p. 175-211.

Kerlovégan, X., «Germain l'Écossais», in *DHGE*, t. 20, Paris, 1984, col. 907-908.

Kreiner, J., *The social life of hagiography in the Merovingian kingdom*, Cambridge, 2014.

Krüger, A., *Litanei-Handschriften der Karolingerzeit*, Hanovre, 2007.

Josse, H., *La légende de saint Honoré, évêque d'Amiens, d'après un manuscrit de la bibliothèque de M. Victor de Beauvillé*, Amiens, 1879.

Labbé, P., *Nova bibliotheca manuscriptorum librorum, seu Collectio, historias, chronica, vitas sanctorum, ac similia antiquitatis monumenta, ex MSS. codd, eruta, copiose repraesentans*, Paris, 1657.

Lapidge, M., *Hilduin of Saint-Denis: The Passio S. Dionysii in Prose and Verse*, Leiden – Boston, 2017.

Laporte, J., *Saint Germain, apôtre du Cotentin, martyrisé dans le Val de la Bresle*, Saint-Riquier, 1959.

Le Cointe, C., *Annales ecclesiastici Francorum*, 8 vol., Paris, 1665-1683 (t. IV, 1670).

Ledru, T., «Hariulf de Saint-Riquier: un moine historien de la fin du XIe siècle», *Questes. Revue pluridisciplinaire d'études médiévales*, 36 (2017), p. 19-41.

—, *Saint-Riquier (VIIe-XIe siècles): histoire, mémoire, hagiographie*, Thèse de doctorat sous la direction de Michèle Gaillard, Lille, 2019.

Lebigue, J.-B., «La liturgie médiévale», in A. André – X. Boniface, éd., *Amiens*, Strasbourg, 2012, p. 387-391 (La Grâce d'une cathédrale).

Meijns, B. – Mériaux C., «Le cycle de Rictiovar et la topographie chrétienne des campagnes septentrionales à l'époque mérovingienne», in D. Paris-Poulain *et al.*, dir., *Les premiers temps chrétiens dans le territoire de la France actuelle. Hagiographie, épigraphie et ar-

chéologie: nouvelles approches et perspectives de recherche, Rennes, 2009, p. 19-34.

Mériaux, C., *Gallia irradiata: saints et sanctuaires dans le nord de la Gaule du haut Moyen Âge*, Stuttgart, 2006.

—, «Multorum coenobiorum fundator et innumerabilium pater monachorum. Le culte et le souvenir de saint Colomban et de ses disciples dans le Nord de la Gaule du haut Moyen Âge», in E. Destefanis, dir., *L'eredità di san Colombano. Memoria e culto attraverso il Medioevo*, Rennes, 2017, p. 85-98.

Mériaux, C. – Pietri, L., «Beauvais», in L. Pietri *et al.*, éd., *Topographie chrétienne des cités de la Gaule, des origines au milieu du VIIIe siècle*, XIV: *Province ecclésiastique de Reims (Belgica secunda)*, Paris, 2006, p. 129-141.

Montaubin, P., «Aux origines du quartier épiscopal», in A. André – X. Boniface, éd., *Amiens*, Strasbourg, 2012, p. 17-20 (La Grâce d'une cathédrale).

—, «Le clergé de la cathédrale jusqu'en 1500», *ibid.*, p. 331-348.

Morelle, L., «La liste des repas commémoratifs offerts aux moines de l'abbaye de Corbie (vers 986/989): une nouvelle pièce au dossier du "Patrimoine de saint Adalhard"?», *Revue belge de philologie et d'histoire*, 69 (1991), p. 279-299.

—, «Les deux Vies d'Adalhard, abbé de Corbie († 826)», in A. Wagner, dir., *Les saints et l'histoire: sources hagiographiques du haut Moyen Âge*, Rosny-sous-Bois, 2004, p. 163-175.

—, «Les évêques d'Amiens et l'abbaye de Corbie jusqu'au milieu du XIe siècle», *Bulletin de l'Association des amis de la cathédrale d'Amiens* (2011), p. 5-13.

—, «La réécriture de la *Vita Adalhardi* de Paschase Radbert au XIe siècle: auteur, date et contexte», in J. Elfassi *et al.*, éd., *Amicorum Societas. Mélanges offerts à François Dolbeau pour son 65e anniversaire*, Florence, 2013, p. 485-500.

Moretus, H., «Catalogus codicum hagiographicorum latinorum bibliothecae scholae medicinae in universitate Montepessulanensi», *AB*, 34 (1915), p. 228-267.

Nardi Combescure (S.), «Le culte de Victoric, Fuscien et Gentien et les recherches de l'abbé Messio à Sains-en-Amiénois (1863-1874). Chronique d'une fouille du 19e siècle», in G. Gros, *Champ fructueux. Images du legs esthétique et religieux de la Picardie de la latinité tardive au XIXe siècle*, Amiens, 2007, p. 17-36.

Ott, J., «Urban space, memory, and episcopal authority: The bishops of Amiens in peace and conflict, 1073-1164», *Viator*, 31 (2000), p. 43-77.

—, *Bishops, authority and community in Northwestern Europe, c. 1050-1150*, Cambridge, 2015.

Paris-Poulain, D., «Les origines du culte des saints martyrs Fuscien, Victoric et Gentien d'après les sources manuscrites», *Revue d'histoire de l'Église de France*, 105 (2019), p. 235-252.

Pellegrin, E., «Notes sur quelques recueils de vies de saints utilisés pour la liturgie à Fleury-sur-Loire, au XIe siècle», *Revue d'histoire des textes*, 12 (1964), p. 7-30.

Peloux, F., «La relique, le reliquaire et le récit hagiographique: des relations ambiguës (diocèses de Mende et de Toulouse)?», in *Corps saints et reliques dans le Midi*, Toulouse, 2018, p. 295-316 (Cahiers de Fanjeaux, 53).

Peyrafort-Huin, M. – Stirnemann, P. – Benoît, J.-L., *La bibliothèque médiévale de l'abbaye de Pontigny (XIIe-XIXe siècles): histoire, inventaires anciens, manuscrits*, Paris, 2001.

Pichon, B., *Amiens : 80/1*, Paris, 2009 (Carte archéologique de la Gaule).

Pietri, L., «Amiens», in Ead. et al., éd., *Topographie chrétienne des cités de la Gaule, des origines au milieu du VIIIe siècle, XIV: Province ecclésiastique de Reims (Belgica secunda)*, Paris, 2006, p. 143-153.

Pietri, L. – Heijmans, M., dir., *Prosopographie chrétienne du Bas-Empire*, 2 vol., Paris, 2013 (Prosopographie chrétienne du Bas-Empire, 4).

Poulin, J. C., «Les *libelli* dans l'édition hagiographique avant le XIIe siècle», in M. Heinzelmann, dir., *Livrets, collections et textes. Études sur la tradition hagiographique latine*, Ostfildern, 2006, p. 15-193.

—, *L'hagiographie bretonne du Haut Moyen Âge*, Ostfildern, 2009.

Racinet, S., *Peuplement et christianisation dans la partie occidentale de la province ecclésiastique de Reims*, Thèse de doctorat sous la direction de Charles Vuilliez, Reims, 2002.

Salmon, C., *Vies des saints Fuscien et Victoric, apôtres de la Morinie et de la Picardie, et Gentien, leur hôte, martyrs, et de saint Evrols, premier abbé du monastère de Saint-Fuscien-au-Bois*, Amiens, 1853.

—, *Histoire de saint Firmin, martyr, premier évêque d'Amiens, patron de la Navarre et des diocèses d'Amiens et de Pampelune*, Arras, 1861.

Sot, M., *Un historien et son Église au Xe siècle: Flodoard de Reims*, Paris, 1993.

Van Meter, D., «The Peace of Amiens-Corbie and Gerard of Cambrai's Oration on the Three Functional Orders: the Date, the Context, the Rhetoric», *Revue belge de philologie et d'histoire*, 74 (1996), p. 633-657.

van 't Spijker, I., «Gallia du Nord et de l'Ouest. Les provinces ecclésiastiques de Tours, Rouen, Reims (950-1130)», in *Hagiographies*, II (1996), p. 239-290.

VERRI, C., «L'arte del ritratto. La descrizione del santo nella Vita Adalhardi di Pascasio Radberto», in M. GOULLET, éd., *Parva pro magnis munera. Études de littérature latine tardo-antique et médiévale offertes à François Dolbeau par ses élèves*, Turnhout, 2009, p. 635-656.

VIRCILLO FRANKLIN, C., *The Latin dossier of Anastasius the Persian: hagiographic translations and transformations*, Toronto, 2004.

WEBB, J. R., «Hagiography in the diocese of Liège (950-1130)», in *Hagiographies*, VI (2014), p. 809-904.

L'écriture hagiographique
dans la province de Sens (env. 750-950)

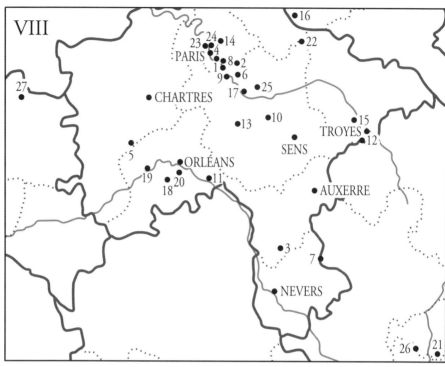

Lieux mentionnés dans les chapitres sur la province de Sens
(royaume franc uniquement, pour la Bretagne, cf. *supra*, p. 187)

NB: Seule est traitée ici la partie méridionale de la Province de Sens: les diocèses de Chartres, Paris et Meaux sont attendus pour le vol. IX.

1 Athis-Mons
2 Bonneuil-sur-Marne
3 Cessy-les-Bois (Nièvre)
4 Charenton-le-Pont
5 Châteaudun
6 Combs-la-Ville
7 Corbigny
8 Créteil
9 Draveil
10 Esmans
11 Fleury (abbaye de Saint-Benoît-sur-Loire)
12 L'Isle-Aumont
13 Larchant
14 Louvres-en-Parisis
15 Mantenay-Saint-Lyé
16 Marizy-sainte-Geneviève
17 Melun
18 Meung-sur-Loire
19 Mézières
20 Micy
21 Montméliant
22 Nogent-l'Artaud
23 Saint-Cloud
24 Saint-Denis
25 Saint-Martin de Champeaux
26 Tournus
27 Vandœuvre

L'écriture hagiographique dans les diocèses de Sens, Troyes et Nevers (env. 750-950)

par

Michèle GAILLARD

I. Diocèse de Sens. – A. Les Vies d'évêques. – B. Les Vies de saints du «cycle d'Aurélien». – C. La Vie de Sidronius – D. Les Passions des saints Savinien et Potentien.
II. Diocèse de Troyes. – A. Sabine et Sabinien. – B. Le lien avec Sens: Potentien et les deux Sabinien. – C. Écritures et réécritures attribuables sans certitude à l'époque carolingienne. – D. Le sermon de Prudence sur sainte Maure.
III. Diocèse de Nevers.
Bibliographie.

I. Diocèse de Sens [1]

Exceptés les poèmes hagiographiques d'Audradus Modicus, un poème en l'honneur de saint Pierre apôtre, un poème en l'honneur de saint Martin et la Pssion métrique de saint Julien et de ses compagnons (*BHL* 4534)[2], l'intérêt des hagiographes

---

[1] L'œuvre de Loup de Ferrières (*Vita sancti Wigberti et Vita sancti Maximini*), rédigée alors qu'il se trouvait encore en Germanie, n'est pas étudiée dans ce chapitre; pour la *Vita Wigberti*, cf. T. Klüppel, «Die Germania (750-950)», in *Hagiographies*, II (1996), p. 161-209 et pour la *Vita Maximini*, le supplément «Germanie», par K. Krönert, *infra,* p. 736-738. En outre, il semble qu'il faille définitivement situer la rédaction de la *Vita Alcuini* à Tours, vers 820, cf. *supra*, p. 185.
[2] Éd. L. Traube, *MGH, Poet. Lat.*, III, Berlin, 1896, p. 67-72 (introduction) et p. 84-121 (édition des poèmes hagiographiques). Audradus Modicus fut nommé chorévêque par un synode tenu à Sens en 847/848. Selon la chronique d'Aubry de Trois-Fontaines (éd. P. Scheffer-Boichorst, *MGH, SS*, XXIII, Hanovre, 1874, p. 735), il fit, à la suite d'une vision de saint Pierre,

se porte sur les écritures ou réécritures de Vies d'évêques; des liens serrés relient la production hagiographique sénonaise avec celle du diocèse de Troyes autour des saints Sidronius, Savinien/ Sabinien et Potentien.

A. Les Vies d'évêques

Trois évêques de Sens ont fait l'objet de *Vitae* à l'époque carolingienne.

La Vie de Loup (*BHL* 5082), évêque de Sens au début du VIIe siècle (présent au concile de Paris en 614) a été datée du VIIIe siècle par les Bollandistes et du IXe siècle par Krusch[3]; le plus ancien manuscrit connu (Wien ÖNB Cvp 420[4]) est daté du tout début du IXe siècle. Comme la Vie semble connue des auteurs des *Gesta* d'Auxerre du IXe siècle (vers 875)[5] et que Loup est mentionné dans les martyrologes d'Adon et d'Usuard[6], une rédaction carolingienne précoce est probable, peut-être dès la 2e moitié du VIIIe siècle, alors qu'un autre *Lupus* était archevêque de Sens (signataire de la confraternité d'Attigny en 765)[7].

---

un voyage à Rome au cours duquel il offrit son œuvre au Pape Léon IV et fut ensuite déposé par le concile de Paris de 848 qui voulait mettre fin à la fonction de chorévêque dans le royaume. Le petit nombre de manuscrits conservés (à Londres et à Munich) suggère que son œuvre fut guère diffusée et peut-être pas à Sens même. On peut déduire de la chronique de Clarius qu'il mourut après 853 et fut enseveli en l'église Saint-Didier, non loin de Nevers (BAUTIER, 1972, p. 54-57).

[3] *AASS*, Sept. I, 1746, p. 255-265; éd. B. KRUSCH, *MGH*, *SRM*, IV, Hanovre – Leipzig, 1902, p. 176-187. RÉAL (2001), p. 53 et HELVÉTIUS (2012, en part. p. 271, n. 82) la pensent plus ancienne à cause des détails circonstanciés qu'elle contient; la présomption d'ancienneté est confortée par sa copie dans le manuscrit Wien, ÖNB, Cvp 420, confectionné à Salzbourg vers 800, mais cela n'exclut pas totalement une écriture du milieu du VIIIe siècle; cf. DIESENBERGER (2010) et HEINZELMANN (2010), p. 72.

[4] Sur ce légendier, voir DIESENBERGER (2010).

[5] Les *Gesta* (*Les gestes des évêques d'Auxerre*), 1, M. SOT (dir.), G. LOBRICHON – M. GOULLET (éd.), Paris, 2006, §19, p. 64-67) tiennent de la *Vita Lupi* (§1 et 2, *AASS*, Sept. I, 1746, p. 256, éd. B. KRUSCH, *MGH*, *SRM*, IV, Hanovre – Leipzig, 1902, §3, p. 179) le fait que l'évêque Aunaire d'Auxerre et l'évêque Austrène d'Orléans étaient les frères de sa mère, Agia ou Aiga.

[6] DUBOIS (1965), 1er septembre, p. 295; DUBOIS – RENAUD (1984), 1er septembre, p. 295.

[7] DUCHESNE (1900), p. 414. En revanche, l'écriture des miracles (*BHL* 5085), connus par un manuscrit du XIVe siècle (Paris, BnF, lat. 5353)

La datation de l'écriture de la Vie d'Ebbon (*BHL* 5082-5083), archevêque de Sens (fin VIIe-début VIIIe), souffre d'une incertitude encore plus grande; récemment John Howes a tenté de démontrer que cette *Vita* a été rédigée avant l'*Historia Francorum Senonensis*, écrite en 1015; il admet la tradition selon laquelle elle fut écrite après «les invasions barbares des IXe et Xe siècles»[8] car il y est écrit que le récit des miracles a été détruit par les flammes à cause de la folie des païens. Cette hypothèse semble confortée par le passage de la *Vita* où sont décrites les invasions des «Vandales»: *Eo itaque tempore gens wandalorum suis confinibus egressa, Galliam profligatura prosiliit quæ per orbem dispersa hostili immanitate strages non modicas dedit. Urbes namque effregit, spolia diripuit, oppida diruit, monasteria subvertit, maximamque Galliæ partem in desolationem redigit.* Cette description fait en effet penser aux relations des invasions normandes ou hongroises chez certains auteurs monastiques, par les termes employés et l'ampleur de la dévastation décrite; il n'en reste pas moins que l'hagiographe, en utilisant le terme Vandales, suggère bien des peuples venus d'Afrique dont un des raids mit la cité de Sens en danger (en 731?). Certes, la réalité de cet épisode peut être aussi mise en doute, car seules les sources sénonaises (la chronique de Saint-Pierre-le-Vif, l'*Historia Francorum Senonensis* et la *Vita Ebbonis*[9]), qui se répètent les unes les autres en font état. Le plus troublant est que la description du siège de Sens par les Sarrasins dans la *Vita* d'Ebbon fait référence à des *machinata ignivomis speculis*, des machines aux flèches vomissant du feu, ce qui évoque le feu grégeois des Byzantins, que les Occidentaux découvrirent lors des croisades...[10], ce qui indiquerait une rédaction très tardive, au XIIe siècle... à moins qu'on suppose que l'auteur était déjà au fait des armes incendiaires utilisées par les Arabes et imitant le feu grégeois... En revanche J. Howe estime que la Vie aurait servi de source à la chronique

---

sont à coup sûr bien postérieurs puisqu'ils relatent des miracles survenus en 1102 (édition dans *Cat. Paris*, I, p. 311-312).

[8] HOWE (1986), p. 142: «written after the barbarian invasions of the ninth and tenth centuries».

[9] *Chronique de Saint-Pierre-le-Vif*, éd. et trad. BAUTIER – GILLES (1979); *Historia Francorum Senonensis brevis*, éd. G. WAITZ, *MGH*, *SS*, IX, Hanovre, 1851, p. 364-369; *Vita Ebbonis* (BHL 2360), *AASS*, Aug. VI, 1743, p. 94-100.

[10] MOUILLEBOUCHE (2010).

de Clarius (rédigée vers 1015) et non l'inverse parce que celle-ci mentionne des sœurs du prélat, inhumées à Saint-Pierre-le-Vif, dont la Vie d'Ebbon ne dit rien. En outre la chronique de Saint-Pierre-le-Vif de Sens mentionne une élévation du corps d'Ebbon effectuée entre 976 et 982:

> En ce temps-là, saint Ebbon reposait encore dans son premier tombeau en la chapelle Sainte-Marie, à droite de l'autel et resplendissait de ses innombrables miracles. C'est pourquoi, d'un commun accord, l'archevêque et l'abbé firent l'élévation de son corps, en grande pompe, devant un peuple innombrable qu'ils avaient convié[11].

La Vie ne faisant allusion ni à des miracles *post-mortem* ni à cette translation, on peut rejeter l'hypothèse de Hervé Mouillebouche selon lequel la chronique est la source de la *Vita*, on peut donc supposer une écriture antérieure de la *Vita*, liée au développement du culte d'un évêque dont la résistance au siège par les Sarrasins faisait un modèle pour ces temps troublés, probablement au temps des raids des Hongrois (autour de 935) dont les méthodes pouvaient évoquer celles des Sarrasins et dont l'origine géographique rappelait celle des vrais Vandales[12]. Il est donc possible, mais sans certitude absolue, de situer la rédaction de cette *Vita* vers le milieu du Xe siècle.

La Vie d'Aldric (*BHL* 263), archevêque de Sens jusqu'en 841 a été éditée par les Bollandistes, d'après un manuscrit retrouvé par Duchesne[13] qui n'a pu être identifié et l'édition de Mabillon faite à partir d'un manuscrit de l'abbaye de Ferrières[14]. Le seul manuscrit répertorié de la *Vita Adrici*, consiste en deux folios mutilés datés du XIe siècle qui donnent un texte (*BHL* 263b) partiel et mutilé, sensiblement différent de celui des *Acta Sanctorum* et probablement écrit antérieurement[15]. Les deux récits font état de la démission d'Aldric de sa fonction d'évêque et de

---

[11] BAUTIER – GILLES (1979), p. 99.

[12] Dans les récits contemporains les Hongrois sont souvent nommés Huns, par analogie avec ce peuple qui chassa sans doute les Vandales de Pannonie...; sur la réalité des attaques hongroises en Bourgogne voir MOUILLEBOUCHE (2006).

[13] *AASS*, Iun. I, 1695, p. 753-757.

[14] *PL* 105, col. 797-810.

[15] Vatican, Reg. lat. 598; le texte fragmentaire (*BHL* 263b) a été édité par A. Poncelet dans le catalogue des manuscrits hagiographiques de la bibliothèque vaticane (*Cat. Vat.*, p. 534-538).

son remplacement à l'épiscopat par Wenilon qui lui avait déjà succédé comme abbé à Ferrières (vers 840). Le plus ancien, dont les folios conservés interrompent brutalement le récit avant même la mort d'Aldric et donnent une version plus développée des chapitres 9 à 12 du texte *BHL* 263, a très certainement été écrit au temps de l'abbé Loup, probablement par un moine de Ferrières; en effet, au début du chapitre 12, est mentionnée la promotion de Loup, disciple d'Aldric à la tête du monastère[16], ce qui n'apparaît pas dans le texte *BHL* 263; les quelques mots suivants, semblables au texte *BHL* 263, laissent à penser que devait suivre, comme dans celui-ci, l'évocation de la translation à Saint-Pierre-le-Vif des reliques de Savinien et de ses disciples, qui eut lieu en 847[17]. Ces deux versions successives de la Vie d'Aldric peuvent donc être rapportées à l'époque carolingienne; la seconde a pu être écrite, en réutilisant la première, après la mort de l'abbé Loup (861), qu'elle ne mentionne pas, et en y ajoutant les récits de miracles, peut-être avant la fin de l'épiscopat de Wenilon († 865).

B. LES VIES DE SAINTS DU «CYCLE D'AURÉLIEN»

Parmi les Passions du «cycle d'Aurélien»[18], celle de Colombe est sans aucun doute la plus ancienne: deux versions très différentes (en particulier *BHL* 1894, version courte, et 1896, version longue) se trouvent dans des manuscrits du IXe siècle. Le fait que sainte Colombe soit mentionnée dans le martyrologe

---

[16] *Sed ne sancti pontificalisque laboris aliqua intercideret mora, predicte urbis cathedram sortitus est Vuenilo, quem ipse beatus abbatem sepe dicto prefecerat monasterio. Qui atiam eidem monasterio abbatem constituit Lupum, beati Aldrici discipulum adprime educatum et omnium artium liberalium studiis sagatissimum* (*ibid.*, p. 538).

[17] Cf. *infra* n. 38. Le texte *BHL* 263 mentionne aussi la translation des reliques de l'évêque Loup et de Colombe, qui, selon les annales de Sainte-Colombe de Sens, eut lieu en 853. *Annales Sancta Columbae Senonensis*, éd. G.-H. PERTZ, *MGH, SS*, I, Hanovre, 1826, p. 103-104: 853. *11. Kal. Augustas dedicatio basilicae sanctae Columbae, et 10. Kal. ipsius mensis translatio corporum sanctorum Columbae virginis et Lupi confessoris et episcopi* (...). La translation doit être consécutive à des travaux dans la basilique Sainte-Colombe qui est mentionnée pour la première fois dans le testament de l'évêque Desiderius d'Auxerre (attesté en 614).

[18] VAN DER STRAETEN (1962).

de Bède[19] et dans les plus anciens manuscrits du martyrologe hiéronymien[20] montre que le culte était ancien et que la Passion a pu être écrite aux temps mérovingiens (en particulier *BHL* 1894, contenue le manuscrit Paris, BnF, lat. 12598 fin VIIIe/début IXe siècle, en compagnie d'autres saints d'époque mérovingienne)[21]. Les Annales de Sainte-Colombe de Sens, mentionnant à l'année 853 la dédicace de la basilique Sainte-Colombe ainsi que la translation des corps de Colombe et de Lupus[22], attestent le renouveau du culte de sainte Colombe à cette époque, ce qui a pu susciter l'écriture d'une nouvelle version de la Vie, plus longue (*BHL* 1896), puis de *compendia* (*BHL* 1892, 1893 et 1895).

Au persécuteur Aurélien est aussi rattachée la Passion de Sanctianus, d'Augustin et de sa sœur Beata (*BHL* 7487) qui les associe à Colombe, à Savinien et à Potentien, dont l'auteur mentionne les *Gesta*[23]; quoique tardive, l'attestation d'une translation par l'archevêque de Sens Anségise, donc avant 883[24], suggère le développement du culte au IXe siècle et l'écriture de la Passion à cette période, peut-être avant cette translation qui n'y est pas mentionnée, d'autant que Beata figure au martyrologe d'Usuard, au 29 juin[25].

---

[19] Dubois – Renaud (1984), p. 4, au 31 décembre.

[20] Cf. Van der Straeten (1962), p. 117; Nouvelle édition du martyrologe hieronymien par H. Delehaye, P. Peeters, M. Coens, *AASS*, Nov. II, 1894, p. 16 (31 décembre).

[21] Ce dossier complexe nécessite le réexamen de tous les manuscrits. Sur deux des plus anciens manuscrits, Paris, BnF, lat. 12598 (fin VIIIe s.) et Montpellier, BIU, H 55 (IXe s.), voir respectivement Gaillard (2009) et Heinzelmann (2016).

[22] Cf. n. 16.

[23] L'édition (*AASS*, Sept. II, 1748, col. 669-672) a été faite d'après un légendier sénonais; la mention des *Gesta* de Savinien et de Potentin se situe à la col. 671.

[24] Éd. Bautier – Gilles (1972), p. 90-93: «L'an 883 mourut Anségise, le vénérable archevêque de Sens, et il fut enseveli au monastère Saint-Pierre. (...) C'est au temps de ce même archevêque que les corps des martyrs Sanctien et Augustin furent transférés de la ville appelée Sancceias au dit monastère (Saint-Pierre), translation faite par les frères de la dite abbaye et le prêtre desservant l'église de cette villa, nommé Éodald, le 24 juin».

[25] Van der Straeten (1962) a voulu discerner dans ce court texte trois strates d'écriture, celle du prologue, celle de la Passion proprement dite et celle du récit de la translation à Sancceias; rapportant, à la suite de Duru (1853), la rédaction de la Passion de Savinien et de Potentien au XIe siècle,

C. D'autres Vies mal datées

Le manuscrit le plus ancien de la Passio *Sidronii* (*BHL* 7702) est daté des X*e*/XI*e* siècles (Montpellier, BIU, H 360); cette Passion, inspirée de la Passion de saint Christophe et plagiée par la *Passio Sabiniani* (de Troyes), qui est conservée dans des manuscrits du X*e* siècle [26], peut être rapportée à l'époque carolingienne, d'autant qu'Usuard fait mention de Sidronius au 11 juillet [27].

La Vie de saint Mathurin de Larchant (*BHL* 5720) est un récit fabuleux qui fait vivre Mathurin à l'époque de l'empereur Maximien (fin III*e*-début IV*e* s.); sa renommée est telle que l'empereur le fait venir à Rome pour guérir sa fille possédée par le démon (en punition du martyre des saints d'Agaune); Mathurin meurt à Rome et son corps est ramené à Larchant. Cependant, le plus ancien manuscrit (Paris, BnF, lat. 5568) étant daté du X*e* siècle, ce récit peut avoir été écrit à l'époque carolingienne, d'autant que Mathurin, qui n'est pas mentionné par Florus et Adon, l'est par Usuard, au 1*er* novembre [28].

Un certain nombre de textes afférant à des saints mentionnés par les martyrologes carolingiens sont mal datés, voire indatables, dans la mesure où les manuscrits ayant servi aux éditions ne sont pas identifiés: la Vie (*BHL* 3820) d'Heraclius, évêque de Sens au début du VI*e* siècle et qu'Usuard mentionne au 8 juin [29],

---

il en conclut que le récit de la Passion et le prologue seraient postérieurs au paragraphe qui relate la translation à Sancceias (provoquée par les destructions des Vandales dans lesquels il faudrait voir les Sarrasins) et qui aurait donc été écrit entre 731 et 883. Si l'on pense, à la suite de Fliche (1912) (cf. *infra*), que le récit court de la *Passio Saviniani et Potentiani* a été rédigé dès le IX*e* siècle, il n'y a pas d'obstacle à dater l'ensemble de la Passion de Sanctianus de la fin du IX*e* siècle, ce qui est aussi l'opinion des Bollandistes (Jean Stilting, p. 669-670), qui soulignent cependant que Clarius affirme ne pas avoir d'actes de ces martyrs à sa disposition car ils ont été détruits par les païens (éd. Bautier – Gilles (1972), p. 64-65), et de Joseph Perrin (1929, p. 52-55). Dubois (1965), p. 257: *Interritorio Senonico, Beatae virginis.*

[26] Van der Straeten (1962), p. 121-123; sur saint Savinien de Troyes cf. *infra*, p. 463-464.

[27] Dubois (1965), p. 266.

[28] *Ibid.*, p. 333: *in pago Wastinensii Maturini confessoris.* J. Dubois remarque: «la Vie (*BHL* 5720) est très mauvaise; il n'est pas sûr qu'elle ait été écrite avant l'époque d'Usuard (p. 334)».

[29] Dubois (1965), p. 243: *Item senones, sancti Eraclii episcopis et confessoris.*

sans doute écrite après les invasions normandes qui ont, selon l'auteur, provoqué le transfert de ses reliques à la cathédrale Saint-Étienne; Vie de Paternus (*BHL* 6479), originaire de Coutances, qu'Usuard place le 12 novembre, à Melun (*Castello Miliduno*)[30]. Sans doute d'écriture postérieure à l'époque carolingienne est la Vie de Bond (Baldus, *BHL* 903), censé avoir prévenu l'évêque Artémius (attesté en 581 et 585[31] et mentionné par la *Vita Lupi*) de sa mort prochaine, inconnu des martyrologes médiévaux[32] et vénéré au prieuré Saint-Bond de Sens, fondé en 1096.

D. Les Passions des saints Savinien et Potentien

La datation des différentes versions de la Passion des saints Savinien (Sabinien) et Potentien dont le culte est attesté par Usuard au 31 décembre[33] n'est pas sans poser problème[34]. Ces récits sont tous contenus dans un manuscrit d'Auxerre du XIIe siècle (ou du début du XIIIe siècle), en provenance de la bibliothèque capitulaire de Sens, et édités par Duru[35]. Ce manuscrit écrit d'une seule main semble recopier à la suite différents *libelli* consacrés aux deux martyrs[36]. Se fondant sur le premier texte de ce manuscrit, mentionnant son auteur, le secrétaire de l'abbé Gerbert (1046-1079)[37], et l'ordre des textes qu'il pensait, comme plus tard Duchesne, refléter l'ordre d'écriture[38], Duru estimait que tous ces textes ne pouvaient être an-

---

[30] *Ibid.*, p. 340.

[31] Duchesne (1900), p. 412.

[32] Cf. Victor de Buck, *AASS*, Oct. XII, 1884, p. 872.

[33] Dubois (1965), p. 151: *Apud Senones, beatorum Sabiniani episcopi et Potentiani, qui a pontifice Romane ad praedicandum directi, eandem metropolim martyrii sui confessione illustrera fecerunt.*

[34] Balzamo (2012), chap. III: «Les débuts du mythe: Savinien, Potentien et leurs disciples».

[35] Ms. 198 de la bibliothèque municipale d'Auxerre, qui contient à la suite des textes relatifs à saint Savinien, un récit de l'invention de la sainte Croix (fol. 70-76) et l'*Historia ecclesiastica* d'Hugues de Fleury (fol. 77-203).

[36] Ou recopier un manuscrit plus ancien qui avait fait ce travail. Sur les *libelli* hagiographiques, cf. Poulin (2006). Voir l'analyse du manuscrit dans Fliche (1912), p. 1-9.

[37] Éd. Duru (1853), p. 290.

[38] Repris dans la numérotation de la *BHL*; Duchesne (1900), p. 400-410, en particulier p. 410.

térieurs au milieu du XIe siècle, aussi bien la «Grande Passion» (*BHL* 7415-7426[39]) aux fol. 5v-30v du manuscrit, qui datait de cet abbatiat, que les suivantes, le résumé de celle-ci (fol. 34v-43v) et la Passion (*BHL* 7432) suivie du récit de la translation de 847 (*BHL* 7433) situées aux fol. 43r-54v du manuscrit. En revanche Augustin Fliche[40], qui s'appuyait sur l'étude de plusieurs manuscrits des XIe et XIIe siècles de la BnF, pensait que la Passion *BHL* 7432-7433, contenue dans le ms. d'Auxerre, avait été rédigée après la translation (*BHL* 7419-7427) ayant eu lieu sous le roi Charles le Chauve en 847[41] et probablement après 876 (à cause de l'allusion à la primatie de Sens[42]) et que la Grande Passion qui, en revanche, datait bien du début du XIe siècle, lui était postérieure. Fliche a remarqué des différences importantes dans *BHL* 7432/7433 entre le manuscrit Paris, BnF, lat. 16735 (XIIe siècle, en provenance de Saint-Martin-des-Champs) et le manuscrit d'Auxerre édité par Duru: l'absence de table des matières, une phrase sur la fureur

---

[39] Cette «Grande Passion» inclut des textes spécifiques sur les disciples de Savinien, en particulier sur Potentin (*BHL* 7418), et le récit de la translation de Savinien, de Potentin et de leurs disciples au temps de l'archevêque Wenilon (vers 840-865) (*BHL* 7419); dans deux manuscrits du XIVe siècle, Paris, BnF, lat. 750 (folios ajoutés à un bréviaire, du XIIIe siècle, du monastère de Jouarre) et Paris, BnF, lat. 5360, on trouve le récit (*BHL* 7429) de la translation de reliques de Potentin à Jouarre et des miracles qui ont eu lieu à Jouarre, à Auxerre et à Orléans (éd. *Cat. Paris*, II, p. 340-49, c. 5-30, voir aussi III, p. 572); il n'est pas possible de dater ce récit, soit postérieur à tous les autres, soit propre à l'abbaye de Jouarre (dans le Ms. lat. 750, seule est présente la *Passio* de Potentin *BHL* 7418 et ce récit de translation à Jouarre) et peu diffusé (seul le Ms. lat. 5360 présente ce récit à la suite de la translation de Savinien et Potentien à Saint-Pierre-le-Vif de Sens *BHL* 7419); les légendiers cisterciens (Paris, BnF, lat. 16735 et 17007) qui contiennent un dossier consacré aux saints Savinien et Potentien ne contiennent pas *BHL* 7429 (*contra* BHLms); le dossier de Savinien et Potentien mérite sans doute un réexamen attentif des manuscrits.

[40] FLICHE (1912) n'utilise pas la numérotation de la *BHL*, ce qui rend difficile le repérage des textes qu'il étudie.

[41] DURU (1853), p. 316; la date est reprise par *Oderannus de Sens*, éd. et trad. BAUTIER – GILLES (1972), p. 87.

[42] *BHL* 7432, FLICHE (1912), p. 59; en 876, l'archevêque Anségise reçut du pape Jean VIII la dignité de vicaire apostolique, cf. DUCHESNE (1900), p. 418; mais cette allusion pourrait aussi refléter une revendication antérieure.

des Vandales[43], l'affirmation qu'il n'existe pas de récit ancien de la Passion de Savinien et une phrase qui précède la translation, attribuant l'*inventio* des reliques à l'archevêque Wenilon[44]. Pour lui, il ne fait aucun doute que cette Passion (*BHL* 7432/7433) est antérieure à la « Grande Passion » écrite sous l'abbé Gerbert. Malgré l'hypothèse de Duchesne, reprise récemment par Nicolas Balzamo[45], supposant, au temps de l'abbé Gerbert, une réaction critique qui aurait provoqué une nouvelle écriture de la Passion, beaucoup plus sobre, qui serait la *BHL* 7432-7433[46], il semble raisonnable, d'autant que Savinien et Potentien figurent dans le martyrologe de Wandalbert de Prüm rédigé dès 848, dans celui d'Adon[47] et dans celui d'Usuard rédigé vers 875[48], de suivre l'hypothèse de Fliche et de dater l'écriture de la Passion *BHL* 7432/7433 de l'époque carolingienne et plus précisément de la 2e moitié du IXe siècle, après la translation de 847 dont le récit (*BHL* 7419) pourrait lui être contemporain.

Curieusement, aucun de ceux qui ont étudié le dossier de saint Savinien n'a jugé nécessaire de s'interroger sur l'homonymie entre Savinien de Sens et Sabinien/*Savinianus*, honoré comme martyr à Troyes et frère de sainte Sabine[49].

---

[43] Éd. FLICHE (1912), p. 57; ce qui fait songer à la vie d'Ebbon et serait donc à rapporter aux invasions hongroises des alentours de 935.

[44] *Ibid.*, p. 71; Fliche fait de ce manuscrit la source du manuscrit d'Auxerre, ce qui ne peut être prouvé; il est plus probable que les deux manuscrits ont puisé directement ou indirectement à la même source.

[45] DUCHESNE (1900) p. 408-410, BALZAMO (2001), p. 55-56.

[46] Ce qui peut expliquer la réflexion d'Oderannus de Sens qui écrivait, vers 1030, ne rien savoir de la Vie et des missions des évangélisateurs, éd. BAUTIER – GILLES (1972), p. 113. BALZAMO (2001) utilise les éditions de FLICHE (1912) (celle de la « Grande Passion » qui est en réalité celle de Hénault, Paris – Chartres, 1884, et celle de *BHL* 7432/7433, faite d'après le ms. Paris, BnF, lat. 16735) mais il passe sous silence l'analyse critique de Fliche qui ne manque pourtant pas d'intérêt.

[47] Sur ce martyrologe, voir *infra*, p. 614-616.

[48] DUCHESNE (1900), p. 397; DUBOIS (1965), p. 151, DUBOIS – RENAUD (1984), 31 décembre, p. 40.

[49] Comme le manuscrit d'Auxerre édité par DURU (1853), les manuscrits que j'ai pu consulter (accessibles sur le site de la BnF) utilisent tous, pour le martyr de Sens comme pour celui de Troyes, la graphie *Savinianus*.

II. Diocèse de Troyes

A. Sabine et Sabinien

Comme l'a remarqué Isabelle Crété-Protin[50], le culte de sainte Sabine/*Savina* semble s'être développé à Troyes antérieurement à celui de son frère Sabinien, dès le VIIe siècle si l'on en croit la Vie de Frodobert rédigée par Adson[51]; toutefois le nom de Sabina n'est introduit que par Usuard au 29 août[52]; comme la *Vita Sabiniae* (BHL 7408) est contenue dans le manuscrit Montpellier, BIU, H 55 qui contient nombre de Vies anciennes[53], il est tout à fait probable que la Vie de Sabine soit antérieure à la période carolingienne, de la fin du VIIe siècle ou de la première moitié du VIIIe siècle. La *Passio Sabiniani* (BHL 7438), dont les manuscrits les plus anciens datent du Xe siècle (Orléans, BM 331 et Paris, BnF, lat. 1764), est un plagiat de la *Passio Sidronii* de Sens (BHL 7702), elle-même fortement inspirée de la passion de saint Christophe[54]. Comme Isabelle Crété-Protin, nous pensons que l'écriture de la *Passio Sabiniani* est postérieure à celle de sainte Sabine[55], d'autant que l'homonymie avec le Savinien de Sens ne peut manquer d'attirer notre attention[56].

---

[50] Crété-Protin (2002), p. 100-101.

[51] Cf. Goullet, M. (éd.), *Adsonis Dervensis opera hagiographica*, Turnhout, 2003, *Vita Frodoberti*, §1, p. 25 (*CC CM*, 198): Adson fait état de la construction de l'église Sainte-Sabine par Frodobert (*De quo fertur inter cętera quod basilicam beatę Savinę virginis in fundo sui iuris construxerit, ęcclesiam cui presidebat heredem instituens, in qua et honorifice sepultus iacet*).

[52] Dubois (1965), p. 293: *In pago Trecasino, sanctae Sabinae virginis, quae pro Christi amore laboriosissima peregrinatione suscepta, etiam virtutibus ac miraculis gloriosa quievit in pace*. À tort Usuard l'a inscrite au 29 août, *dies natalis* de Sabine de Rome, ce qui semble indiquer qu'il ne connaissait pas la *Passio* qui place son martyre au 29 janvier. Une Sabine est mentionnée dans le martyrologe de l'Anonyme lyonnais (antérieur à 806) à la date du 24 janvier, mais sans localisation, cf. Dubois-Renaud (1984), p. 22; le martyrologe de Bède ne connaît que sainte Sabine de Rome (*Ibid.*, p. 160).

[53] Sur ce manuscrit, cf. Heinzelmann (2016).

[54] Van der Straeten (1962), p. 1-124 et 128-129; l'unique témoin manuscrit en est le manuscrit de Montpellier, BIU, H 360 (manuscrit dont une page figure en frontispice de ce volume).

[55] Crété-Protin (2002), p. 101-102.

[56] Cf *infra*.

B. Le lien avec Sens : Potentien et les deux Savinien

Si on retient l'hypothèse d'une première rédaction de la *Passio Sabinani* (de Sens) au milieu du IXe siècle, le développement du culte de Savinien à Sens a pu provoquer, à Troyes, le développement du culte d'un autre Savinien (déjà mentionné par Usuard[57]), frère de la sainte déjà prestigieuse à Troyes, Sabine. La *Passio Sabiniani* de Troyes (*BHL* 7438-7441) a donc pu être rédigée dès la fin du IXe, créant ainsi un rival crédible au Savinien de Sens, pour mieux marquer l'autonomie du diocèse de Troyes par rapport à la métropole sénonaise. En retour, la rédaction de la «Grande Passion» de Savinien de Sens a pu être le moyen d'affirmer la prééminence du Savinien de Sens et surtout la dépendance de Troyes par rapport à Sens, en faisant de Potentien, successeur de Savinien à Sens[58], son évangélisateur[59].

C. Écritures et réécritures attribuables à l'époque carolingienne

Krusch attribue au début de la période carolingienne l'écriture de la *Vita* de saint Phal (Fidolus, *BHL* 2974-2975) dont les manuscrits les plus anciens, du XIIe siècle, sont conservés à Troyes (Ms. 1 et 7 de la bibliothèque municipale[60]) et à Paris (BnF, lat. 16737, *Liber de Natilitiis*). Cette vie relate comment Fidolus, otage des soldats du roi Thierry (Ier, puisque contemporain de l'évêque Loup), trouva refuge auprès d'Aventin, abbé d'un monastère de Troyes et auquel Fidolus succéda. L'hagiographe semble avoir voulu raconter, en brodant sur le récit de Grégoire (qui présente Aventin comme un disciple de l'évêque

---

[57] Dubois (1965), p. 170-171, 29 janvier; selon J. Dubois, Usuard utilise la *Passio Sabiniani BHL* 7438, ce qui ne peut être prouvé.

[58] Duchesne (1900), pour Sens, p. 391-396 et 411, pour Troyes, p. 449.

[59] Duru (1853), p. 303, en compagnie de Sérotin, de même qu'Altinus et Eodald à Orléans (*Ibid.*, p. 301). Ce qui n'est pas le cas dans la *Passio Sabiniani et Potentiani* (*BHL* 7432) considérée comme la plus ancienne par Fliche (1912) : Potentin, Altinus, Seroaldus et Edoaldus sont tués sur la route de Troyes, à un mille de Sens (éd. Fliche, p. 68 et 69; éd. Duru, p. 353-354).

[60] Le Ms. 7 de la BM de Troyes provient de Montieramey (abbaye fondée en 837 seulement, à 25 km de Troyes, au sud de la forêt du Der).

Loup mais ne dit mot d'une charge abbatiale ni de Fidolus[61]), la vie d'un saint vénéré à Troyes depuis longtemps en tant que prêtre et confesseur, puisque sa déposition figure dans le martyrologe hiéronymien au 16 mai[62]. Curieusement l'auteur ne donne pas le nom du monastère qu'étaient censés avoir gouverné successivement Aventin et Phal, ni le lieu de sépulture de son héros ; à quoi et à qui donc pouvait servir l'écriture de cette *Vita* ? Une autre version de la Vie (*BHL* 2976), qui rapporte la vie du saint à l'époque de Thierry II (595-613), a été éditée par Mabillon[63] : l'abbaye gouvernée successivement par les deux saints n'y est pas non plus indiquée mais il est précisé que saint Aventin, laissant l'abbatiat à Phal, s'est retiré tout près d'un lieu situé dans une île de la Seine, distante d'environ six milles (soit environ 10 km) de la ville de Troyes[64], ce qui correspond au site du prieuré de l'Isle-Aumont, fondé à la fin du XIe siècle au sud de Troyes, où les fouilles archéologiques ont attesté l'existence d'une église et d'une nécropole ainsi qu'une occupation intense à partir du VIe siècle[65] ; s'il y eut bien un monastère à cet endroit, comme le veut la tradition, c'est probablement lui qui fut à l'origine du développement du culte de saint Phal ; dans ce cas, l'écriture des deux versions de la *Vita Fidoli* a dû avoir lieu avant la disparition du monastère, dont on sait qu'il n'existait plus au milieu du IXe siècle[66].

---

[61] *In Gloria confessorum*, éd. B. KRUSCH, *MGH*, *SRM*, I-2, Hanovre, 1885, §67, p. 787-788 ; la version la plus ancienne de la Vie de Loup (*BHL* 5087) ne mentionne pas Aventin, seule la *Vita recentior* (*BHL* 5089) le fait.

[62] *In territorio Tricassinae civitatis loco Campellus depositio Fiduli presbiteri et confessoris* (*AASS*, Nov. II, Pars II, 1931, p. 257).

[63] *AA OSB*, I, Paris 1668, p. 196-202 ; les manuscrits utilisés n'ont pas été identifiés.

[64] *Ibid.*, §9, p. 198 : *deinceps ad locum quemdam iuxta vicum cui Insulae nomen dedit super ripam Sequanae situm, ab urbe sex fere distantem passuum millibue, usque ad viate suae terminum in eodem mansit solitarius.*

[65] CRÉTÉ-PROTIN (2002), p. 233-240, en émettant quelques réserves sur la méthode visant à démontrer l'historicité de la *Vita Fidoli* et à cause de son ignorance de *BHL* 2976. Sur l'Isle-Aumont, cf. SCAPULA (1975).

[66] Un diplôme de Charles le Chauve mentionne l'Isle parmi les possessions de Montier-la-Celle, sans qu'il n'y ait de référence à une quelconque communauté monastique (G. TESSIER, *Recueil des actes de Charles II le Chauve*, II: *861-877*, Paris, 1952, n° 356, p. 291-293, p. 293, l. 17).

La *Vita prima* de Lupus (*BHL* 5087-5087b-c) initialement attribuée par Krusch aux VIIIe-IXe siècles[67], doit sans doute être rapportée à l'époque mérovingienne, comme y incitent la datation dorénavant établie du plus ancien manuscrit complet, des années 780-820[68] et l'existence d'un fragment dans un manuscrit du VIIIe siècle en provenance de Corbie[69]. Ce n'est pas le cas des *Acta recentiora* de Lupus (*BHL* 5089), dont le plus ancien manuscrit recensé date du XIIIe siècle et qui développent considérablement les épisodes de la première Vie; on y voit aussi apparaître le nom d'Aventin[70], parmi ses disciples; enfin ce texte indique que Loup a été inhumé dans un monastère Sainte-Marie situé à l'est de Troyes. Comme Loup fut toujours considéré comme ayant été inhumé dans la basilique qui prit son nom, située à l'est de Troyes, l'auteur considérait que l'église du monastère était à l'origine dédiée à Sainte-Marie et il écrivait à un moment où la basilique était devenue un monastère[71]. Écrite en prose rimée, la Vie pourrait, peut-être, avoir été rédigée après le déplacement, consécutif aux invasions normandes, de l'abbaye Saint-Loup dans le centre de Troyes, à l'abri des remparts, et probablement avant la construction, au tout début du XIIe siècle, d'une église Saint-Martin à l'emplacement de l'ancienne abbaye[72].

La *Passio secunda* de Patroclus (*BHL* 6521), dont un seul manuscrit a été recensé[73], pourrait avoir été rédigée lors de la translation à Soest en 959, à l'initiative de l'archevêque Brunon

---

[67] *MGH*, *SRM*, III, Hanovre, 1896, p. 120-124 et VII, Hanovre – Leipzig, 1901, p. 284-302.

[68] EWIG (1978) en attribuait la rédaction au VIIe siècle, tandis que HEINZELMANN (2010, p. 53) la date du VIe siècle; voir aussi DIESENBERGER (2010).

[69] Saint-Petersbourg, BN, Fv, I-II.

[70] DUBOIS (1965), p. 174-175: *Trecas, sancti Aventini episcopi et confessoris;* introduit par Usuard d'après Grégoire de Tours (*In Gloria confessorum*, §67); le titre d'évêque n'est pas attesté par ailleurs.

[71] CRÉTÉ-PROTIN (2002) situe cette transformation à la fin du VIe ou au début du VIIe siècle, en s'appuyant sur la mention, dans la Vie de Loup de Sens (VIIIe-IXe, cf. *supra*), d'un abbé Winebaudus dirigeant cette basilique (p. 203); mais il pouvait évidemment s'agir d'un abbé de basilique; il n'est donc pas impossible que la création du monastère fut bien postérieure.

[72] CRÉTÉ-PROTIN (2002), p. 329-331.

[73] Münster UB 20, où sont aussi recopiées la *Passio prima* (*BHL* 6520) et l'*Historia Translationis* (*BHL* 6523).

de Cologne, et donc écrite en territoire germanique et non à Troyes[74].

Quant à la Vie de sainte Hoyldis (*BHL* 3990), rattachée par les Bollandistes au diocèse de Troyes et sœur de sainte Manechildis (*BHL* 5207, au diocèse de Châlons), elle a sans doute été rédigée après la translation de ses reliques au monastère qui porte son nom, fondé au plus tôt au XIIe siècle, dans le diocèse de Toul.

D. Le sermon de Prudence sur sainte Maure

La seule production datée sans conteste de l'époque carolingienne est un sermon de l'évêque Prudence relatant la Vie de sainte Maure (*BHL* 5725) dont aucun manuscrit ne semble avoir subsisté; chose exceptionnelle, il s'agit d'une nouvelle sainte que Prudence a connue et qui était la sœur du prévôt des frères auxquels s'adresse Prudence; il précise aussi que la sainte a été instruite et baptisée par l'abbé Léo qu'il qualifie de «vicinus noster» car il était abbé du monastère Saint-Gervais-et-Protais, situé à Mantenay-Saint-Lyé, à 6 km au nord de Troyes. Prudence rappelle aussi qu'il a prêché en présence de la sainte, dans l'église Saint-Aventin.

Ce texte est sans doute un éloge funèbre mis plus tard par écrit; d'où l'emploi de la première personne du singulier (Prudence, qui prononce le discours), de la deuxième du pluriel (adresse au public) et de la deuxième du singulier (adresse à chaque membre de la famille: le frère, Eutrope, la mère, le père, etc.). Ce texte est donc un beau témoignage de continuité des éloges funèbres au Moyen Âge[75]. L'originalité de cet éloge tient en sa forme littéraire, à la fois discours et récit[76], et en son objet: une jeune fille très pieuse qui fréquente le monastère de Mantenay et aussi l'église Saint-Aventin, est bien connue de l'évêque, mais ne s'est pas retirée dans un monastère. Prudence offre donc le modèle d'une sainteté féminine et laïque, en dehors du monastère, ce qui est un hapax pour cette période.

---

[74] Cf. Krönert, *infra*, p. 759-761.

[75] Réflexions communiquées par Monique Goullet; sur les liens entre la *laudatio* antique et l'hagiographie, cf. Goullet (2001).

[76] Pour une étude littéraire, voir Veyrard-Cosme (2013); on peut également consulter Castes (1990).

III. Diocèse de Nevers

À Nevers, la dédicace de la cathédrale aux saints Cyr et Julitte est attestée dans un acte de 817; trois deniers de Pépin le Bref portant la légende S(an)cti Cyrici ont été découverts dans la Nièvre en 1884[77]. Ces éléments attestant le culte à Nevers, ainsi que le récit de Grégoire de Tours qui relate que l'abbé Abraham, mort à Clermont en 477, avait ramené d'Orient des reliques de Cyricus[78], permettent de supposer que les traductions de la Passion de Cyr et Julitte (*BHL* 1802-1808), dont des versions orientales sont attestée à partir du Ve siècle, sont relativement anciennes[79]. Toutefois la translation de reliques au monastère d'Elnone (Saint-Amand-les Eaux), au IXe siècle, a suscité des réécritures, par Hucbald (*BHL* 1809)[80] puis par un certain Gunter, également moine d'Elnone, au XIIe siècle (*BHL* 1812-1813). Seul le prologue d'un récit perdu fait allusion à une translation de reliques, auparavant rapportées par l'évêque Amâtre à Auxerre, à la fin du IVe siècle, à Nevers (*BHL* 1811; attribué par les Bénédictins et par Duru à la fin du VIe siècle, il est en réalité indatable[81].

Falcon mentionne dans sa chronique (fin XIe siècle)[82] la translation, vers 880, des reliques de Leonardus à Corbigny depuis Tournus, en compagnie d'un certain Veterinus, inconnu par ailleurs; les différentes versions de sa Vie qui nous sont parvenues (*BHL* 4859-4861), grâce à l'édition des *Acta Sanctorum*[83] et des manuscrits des XIVe et XVe siècles, ne font état que de l'activité de Leonardus à Vandœuvre, au diocèse du Mans, au temps du roi Clothaire Ier, à tel point qu'on peut se demander s'il s'agit du même personnage, puisqu'on n'a aucune information

---

[77] Picard (1992).

[78] Grégoire de Tours, *Liber Vitae Patrum*, III, éd. B. Krusch, *MGH*, SRM, I-2, Hanovre, 1885, p. 222-223.

[79] Sur la *Passio Ciryci et Iulittae* voir l'étude de F. Dolbeau en introduction à l'édition du texte dans le manuscrit D.V.3, de la Bibliothèque Nationale Universitaire de Turin (du début du IXe siècle) dans Goullet (2014), p. 487-514.

[80] Cf. Le diocèse de Thérouanne, prévu pour le vol. IX de *Hagiographies*.

[81] Duru (1850), p. 132-134.

[82] Éd. Poupardin (1905), p. 89. Sur la translation de Léonard à Tournus, voir aussi Cartron (2009), p. 168-172.

[83] *AASS*, Oct. VII, 1845, p. 4759.

sur une éventuelle translation de reliques du Mans à Tournus, pas davantage sur une translation directe depuis Le Mans jusqu'à Corbigny, même si, au XIe siècle, les moines de Corbigny étaient persuadés de posséder les corps de saint Léonard de Vandœuvre, comme le montre la copie dans un manuscrit du XIe siècle (Paris, BnF, lat. 13765, fol. 95v-103r), peut-être à Corbigny, de la *Vita sanctissimi Leonardi confessoris Christi atque abbatis cui sacrum corpus in pago cynomannico olim conditur nunc Corbiniaco requiescit*[84].

La courte vie de Francovaeus (*BHL* 3142), moine à Saint-Martin de Nevers (monastère fondé au VIIIe siècle) puis ermite en compagnie de son frère, n'est connue que par l'édition des Bollandistes à partir d'un «ancien manuscrit» de l'Église de Nevers, non identifié. L'écriture en est sans aucun doute locale mais peut être très tardive, d'autant qu'aucun indice interne ne permet de situer chronologiquement l'existence de ce personnage.

Bibliographie

Balzamo, N., *Les deux cathédrales, mythe et histoire à Chartres*, Paris, 2012.

Bautier, R.-H. – Gilles, M. éd. et trad., *Oderannus de Sens, Opera omnia*, Paris, 1972.

—, *Chronique de Saint-Pierre-le-Vif de Sens, dite de Clarius*, Paris, 1979.

Cartron, I., *Les pérégrinations de Saint-Philibert: genèse d'un réseau monastique dans la société carolingienne*, Rennes, 2009.

Castes, A., «La dévotion privée et l'art à l'époque carolingienne: le cas de Sainte-Maure de Troyes», *Cahiers de civilisation médiévale*, 33 (1990), p. 3-18.

Crété-Protin, I., *Église et vie chrétienne dans le diocèse de Troyes: du IVe au IXe siècle*, Villeneuve d'Ascq, 2002 (Histoire et civilisations).

Diesenberger, M., «Der Cvp 420: die Gemeinschaft der Heiligen und ihre Gestaltung im frühmittelalterlichen Bayern», in M. Goullet – M. Heinzelmann – C. Veyrard-Cosme, éd., *L'hagiographie mérovingienne à travers ses réécritures*, Ostfildern, 2010, p. 219-248.

Dubois, J. éd., *Le Martyrologe d'Usuard: texte et commentaire*, Bruxelles, 1965 (Subsidia Hagiographica, 40).

---

[84] *BHL deest*, cf. Poncelet (1905), p. 85-87.

DUBOIS, J. – RENAUD, G. éd., *Le Martyrologe d'Adon. Ses deux familles, ses trois recensions. Texte et commentaire*, Paris, 1984 (Sources d'histoire médiévale, 14).

DUCHESNE, L., *Fastes épiscopaux de l'ancienne Gaule*, II: *L'Aquitaine et les Lyonnaises*, 2ᵉ éd., Paris, 1910.

DURU, L.-M., *Bibliothèque historique de l'Yonne*, 2 vol., Auxerre, 1850-1863.

EWIG, E., «Bemerkungen zur Vita des Bischofs Lupus von Troyes», in K. HAUCK – H. MORDEK, éd., *Geschichtsschreibung und geistiges Leben im Mittelalter. Festschrift für Heinz Löwe zum 65. Geburtstag*, Cologne, 1978, p. 14-26 (= ID., dans *Spätantikes und fränkisches Gallien*, 3, Ostfildern, 2009, p. 505-518).

FLICHE, A., *Les Vies de saint Savinien, premier évêque de Sens, étude critique suivie d'une édition de la plus ancienne Vita*, Paris, 1912.

GAILLARD, M., «Remarques sur les plus anciennes versions de la *Passio* et de l'*Inventio* des saints Fuscien, Victoric et Gentien (manuscrits Paris, Bnf, lat. 12598 et Wien, ÖNB, 371)», in M. GOULLET, éd., *Parva pro magnis munera: études de littérature tardo-antique et médiévale offertes à François Dolbeau par ses élèves*, Turnhout, 2009, p. 397-409.

GOULLET, M. dir., «La *laudatio sanctorum* dans le haut Moyen Âge, entre *Vita* et éloge», in M. SOT éd., *Le discours d'éloge entre Antiquité et Moyen Âge*, Paris, 2001, p. 141-152.

—, dir., *Le Légendier de Turin, Torino, Biblioteca Nazionale e Universitaria D.V.3*, Florence, 2014, p. 487-514.

HEINZELMANN, M., «L'hagiographie mérovingienne: panorama des documents potentiels», in M. GOULLET – M. HEINZELMANN – C. VEYRARD-COSME, éd., *L'hagiographie mérovingienne à travers ses réécritures*, Ostfildern, 2010, p. 27-82.

—, «Ein karolingisches Legendar vom Beginn des 9. Jahrhunderts: Montpellier, Bibl. Interuniversitaire Faculté Médecine H. 55», in C. ALRAUM – A. HOLNDONNER – H.-C. LEHNER et al., éd., *Zwischen Rom und Santiago: Festschrift für Klaus Herbers zu seinem 65. Geburtstag*, Bochum, 2016, p. 211-225.

HELVÉTIUS, A.-M., «L'image de l'abbé à l'époque mérovingienne», in S. PATZOLD – A. RATHMANN-LUTZ – V. SCIOR, dir., *Geschichtsvorstellungen. Bilder, Texte und Begriffe aus dem Mittelalter. Festschrift für Hans-Werner Goetz zum 65. Geburtstag*, Vienne – Cologne – Weimar, 2012, p. 253-276.

HOWE, J., «The date of the Life of Saint Ebbo of Sens», *AB*, 104 (1986), p. 131-143.

MOUILLEBOUCHE, H., «Un autre mythe historiographique: le cas d'Autun par les Sarrasins», *Annales de Bourgogne*, 82 (2010), p. 5-36.

PERRIN, J., *Le martyrium de saint Sanctien, de sainte Béate et de saint Augustin*. Sens, 1929.

PICARD, J.-C., «Nevers», in GAUTHIER, N. – PICARD, J.-C. – DUVAL, N. éd., *Topographie chrétienne des cités de la Gaule, des origines au milieu du VIIIe siècle*, VIII: *Province ecclésiastique de Sens (Lugdunensis Senonia)*, Paris, 1992, p. 147-148.

PONCELET, A., «Les saints de Micy», *AB*, 24 (1905), p. 85-87.

POULIN, J.-C., «Les *libelli* dans l'édition hagiographique avant le XIIe siècle», in M. HEINZELMANN, éd., *Livrets, collections et textes. Études sur la tradition hagiographique latine*, 2006, p. 151-193.

POUPARDIN, R., *Monuments de l'histoire des abbayes de Saint-Philibert (Noirmoutier, Grandlieu, Tournus), publiés d'après les notes d'Arthur Giry*, Paris, 1905.

RÉAL, I., *Vies de saints, vie de famille: représentation et système de la parenté dans le royaume mérovingien, 481-751 d'après les sources hagiographiques*, Turnhout, 2001 (Hagiologia, 2).

SCAPULA, J., *Un haut lieu archéologique de la haute vallée de la Seine. La butte de L'Isle-Aumont en Champagne*, Troyes, 1975.

VAN DER STRAETEN, J., «Actes des martyrs d'Aurélien en Gaule», *AB*, 80 (1962), p. 116-142.

VEYRARD-COSME, C., «Polyphonie énonciative et variations stylistiques dans le *Sermo de vita et morte gloriosae virginis Maurae* attribué à Prudence de Troyes», *Hagiographica*, 20 (2013), p. 79-92.

L'écriture hagiographique dans le diocèse d'Auxerre (env. 750-950)

par

Anne-Marie BULTOT-VERLEYSEN

I. La Vie et les Miracles de Germain, par Heiric.
II. Une œuvre composite : les Gestes des évêques d'Auxerre.
III. La translation de saint Baudille et la Vie de saint Marien.
Bibliographie.

À Auxerre, l'abbaye Saint-Germain produisit, entre autres œuvres réputées, les *Vita metrica* et *Miracula sancti Germani*, sous la plume de l'écolâtre Heiric. Comme en écho, les *Gesta* des évêques mobilisèrent l'autre pôle intellectuel et religieux de la ville, la cathédrale. Ce monument de la littérature historiographique n'est pas exempt d'une certaine coloration hagiographique qui sera mise en lumière.

I. La Vie et les Miracles de Germain, par Heiric

Heiric, né en 841 et entré tout jeune à Saint-Germain d'Auxerre, fut sans conteste l'hagiographe le plus fécond en Bourgogne au ixe siècle. Intellectuel confirmé et érudit, élève de Loup de Ferrières et d'Haymon d'Auxerre, disciple de Jean Scot dit l'Érigène, il enseigna vraisemblablement à Saint-Remi de Reims. Auteur d'une riche production littéraire et didactique, il mit ses talents d'écrivain au service du plus illustre évêque de la cité et patron de son abbaye[1]. Il existait pourtant une *Vita sancti*

---

[1] Sur la biographie d'Heiric, voir QUADRI (1990), p. 37-40 et CONTRENI (2006), p. 37-39. On trouvera un résumé de sa Vie, le répertoire commenté

Germani (*BHL* 3453) rédigée quelque trente ans après la mort du prélat (445-446) par le prêtre Constance de Lyon, correspondant de Sidoine Apollinaire; elle fut plusieurs fois remaniée et fit l'objet d'une substantielle amplification[2]. Le projet — apparemment non concrétisé — de la mettre en vers fut repris au IXe siècle et l'on s'adressa alors au *monachus et scholasticus* Heiric[3]. Les compositions en métriques étaient dans l'air du temps: Bède avait rédigé une Vie de Cuthbert en vers et en prose, Alcuin avait remanié en vers la Vie de Willibrord, mais c'est vraisemblablement Milon de Saint-Amand, auteur d'une Vie métrique en quatre livres du saint patron de son monastère qui fut le modèle du moine auxerrois[4].

Il s'agit, semble-t-il, d'une commande royale, sans doute par l'intermédiaire de l'abbé laïc de Saint-Germain, Lothaire, le fils infirme de Charles le Chauve, mort en 865, qui fut probablement l'élève d'Heiric[5]. Peut-être rédigé partiellement à Soissons[6], le travail fut achevé à Auxerre et dédicacé en 873 à Charles le Chauve[7]. L'hypotexte de la Vie métrique n'est pas l'œuvre de Constance mais bien la Vie amplifiée anonyme qui lui fut longtemps attribuée (*BHL* 3454). La *Vita metrica* de Heiric (*BHL* 3458)[8] est divisée en six livres rédigés en hexamètres.

---

de ses œuvres et une ample bibliographie dans VON BÜREN (2010), p. 375-405. Cette dernière conteste l'affirmation selon laquelle il fut très vraisemblablement le maître de Remi d'Auxerre; elle voit plutôt en Heiric un maître enseignant à Saint-Rémi de Reims. Son argumentation, basée entre autres sur l'interprétation des termes employés dans le manuscrit Paris, BnF, lat. 12949, fol. 25v (*Heiricus magister Remigii fecit has glossas*), est réfutée par DENOËL – CINATO (2015), en particulier p. 215-217. La date de décès d'Heiric est controversée; on ne possède plus aucun témoignage sur lui après 875.

[2] Voir la contribution de M. Heizelmann, attendue dans le vol. IX.

[3] C'est ainsi qu'il s'intitule lui-même dans l'*explicit* de la *Vita Germani* contenue dans le manuscrit Paris, BnF, lat. 13757. VON BÜREN (2010), p. 403-404.

[4] BERSCHIN (1991), p. 360.

[5] C. LEONARDI, «Conclusion», in IOGNA-PRAT – JEUDY – LOBRICHON (1991), p. 446; QUADRI (1990), p. 39.

[6] L'époque de la présence d'Heiric à Soissons n'est pas connue avec certitude: elle se situe aux environs de 865. Voir QUADRI (1992), p. 217-222.

[7] La date est déduite de l'épilogue de la *Vita* où l'auteur précise qu'il est âgé de 32 ans (Lib. VI, 638-639, éd. TRAUBE (1886), p. 516).

[8] *Ibid.*, p. 428-517. Voir l'analyse littéraire de BERSCHIN (1991), p. 358-361.

L'invocation à Dieu et les préfaces précédant chaque livre sont par contre composées en strophes lyriques, à la manière de Prudence[9]. Dans l'incipit du premier livre[10], l'auteur présente son œuvre comme *de prosa in metrum transfusa*, mais il ne se limite pas à cet exercice car il amplifie également le texte interpolé. Le talent poétique qu'il déploie dénote une réelle originalité pour son époque; il est proche de celui de Virgile, plus rigoureux même dans le respect des règles qui laissent peu de place aux variations dans la composition des hexamètres; les préfaces des livres 4 et 5 montrent également une inventivité dans la forme métrique, qui fit école[11].

Le premier livre aborde la carrière séculière de Germain jusqu'à sa désignation à l'épiscopat comme successeur d'Amator. Le deuxième relate la mort d'Amator (†418) et la succession de Germain: Heiric lui attribue comme thème les *operae morales* et tente de faire entrer l'évêque dans les catégories de martyrs, apôtres et vierges. Les quatre autres livres rapportent les miracles du saint durant son vivant, en particulier lors de ses voyages: en Bretagne (Lib. III et IV), en Gaule et en Armorique (Lib. V), en Italie où il meurt (Lib. VI). Le moine auxerrois complète son œuvre par deux livres de Miracles en prose (*BHL* 3462) et un Sermon pour la Saint-Germain (*BHL vacat*)[12]. C'est cet ensemble qui est offert à Charles le Chauve au plus tôt en 873[13]: la dédicace, «une des pièces les plus célèbres

---

[9] *Ibid.*, p. 361.

[10] Éd. TRAUBE (1886), p. 438.

[11] *Ibid.*, respectivement p. 474-476 et 488-489. Voir JACOBSEN (1991), p. 335, qui note son influence sur l'écriture de Dudon de Saint-Quentin, nous y reviendrons: «Die Strophenform der Praefatio zu Buch V gilt als Heirics Erfindung. Ihre erste, als Metrum Eolicum bezeichnete Zeile existierte zuvor offenbar nur als Möglichkeit in den Schriften spätantiker Grammatiker: ein akatalektischer daktylischer Pentameter mit spondeischer Basis. Diese Form Heirics wie schon die seiner 4. Praefatio imitierte – wie so vieles andere – Dudo von St-Quentin».

[12] Sur le *Sermo in solemnitate sancti Germani* (*BHL vacat*), partiellement repris dans le *Sermo de beato Maiolo* (*BHL vacat*), voir IOGNA-PRAT (1988), p. 55.

[13] Charles le Chauve est devenu empereur en 875, toutefois le fait qu'Heiric s'adresse à lui dans sa dédicace par l'apostrophe *Caesar invictissime* ne peut servir d'argument de datation: d'une part parce qu'au début de ce texte, Heiric le désigne comme *regumque omnium praecellentissimo Karolo* et d'autre part parce qu'il qualifie de Césars Charles et Louis (le Germanique) à une époque où ils étaient tous deux rois (859) (*Mir.*, Lib. II, c. 96), sans doute parce

parmi les panégyriques carolingiens», ainsi que la qualifie W. Berschin[14], évoque l'encouragement aux études prodigué par le roi, l'héritage de la Grèce, et met en valeur l'apport des philosophes irlandais passés sur le continent, allusion à peine voilée à Jean Scot; Heiric joint la lettre de l'évêque Aunaire demandant au prêtre Étienne l'Africain de mettre la Vie de Germain en vers et la réponse de celui-ci[15].

Concentré sur un objectif manifestement littéraire, l'auteur suit sa source sans guère en modifier le contenu[16]. L'influence du platonisme de Jean Scot est marquante en trois endroits de la *Vita Germani*: l'*Invocatio*, la préface du livre VI et les vers 536-566 du même livre. Elle est mise en valeur par les scholies qui accompagnent le texte dans plusieurs manuscrits; leur objectif est manifestement didactique: «Heiric y traduit les mots grecs, explique des mots par des synonymes, les noms propres de l'antiquité par des citations littéraires souvent empruntées à Fulgence le Mythographe, explicite le sens du texte par des renvois et des paraphrases et donne de longues explications philosophiques empruntées en grande partie au *De divisione naturae* de Jean Érigène»[17]. À côté de l'emploi de mots rares et recherchés ainsi que de termes grecs, alors qu'il ne maîtrisait vraisemblablement pas la langue et ses déclinaisons, Heiric fait preuve d'une réelle intelligence de la pensée de l'Érigène dans l'utilisation de citations dont les contraintes de versification et les lois de la quantité l'obligent à déplacer voire à substituer les mots[18].

---

qu'ils étaient fils de l'empereur Louis le Pieux (P. VAN DEN BOSSCHE, éditeur des Vies et Miracles de Germain d'Auxerre dans *AASS*, Iul. VII, Anvers, 1731 p. 278 note c.).

[14] BERSCHIN (1991), p. 359.

[15] Deux documents qui figurent également dans les *Gesta pontificum autissiodorensium* (c. 19).

[16] BOUCHARD (2009), p. 22 fait toutefois remarquer que seul Heiric présente Julius, gouverneur d'Autun au moment de la succession d'Amator, comme un chrétien dévot et un propagateur de la foi.

[17] VON BÜREN (2010), p. 402. Le principal témoin de l'œuvre (Paris, BnF, lat. 13757), très proche de l'original, présente ces scholies. POULIN (2006, p. 100) le qualifie d'«exemplaire très soigné et homogène sans être luxueux; copie de travail, sous la direction de l'auteur entre 873 et 875».

[18] Voir JEAUNEAU (2007), p. 361-367: l'auteur analyse les passages de l'*Invocatio* où Heiric combine avec habileté des extraits du Periphyseon et du poème *Si vis ογρανιας*. Voir aussi l'étude de IOGNA-PRAT (1988), p. 127-130, ainsi que celle de D'ONOFRIO (2006), p. 336-338, qui montre qu'Heiric

Il enrichit également son travail d'emprunts à la littérature latine et serait le premier auteur médiéval à citer Horace[19].

Dans les *Miracula*, la recherche de style s'efface devant l'intention de l'auteur qui entend bien accentuer le caractère monastique et la sainteté de Germain dont les pouvoirs sont exaltés et les miracles en faveur de son établissement rapportés en abondance[20]. Ils présentent également un intérêt historiographique certain par leur relation avec la première rédaction des *Gesta pontificum autissiodorensium*: se distinguant par une différence d'accentuation idéologique bien compréhensible – Heiric promeut la condition monastique, les *Gesta* affirment la prééminence des évêques –, les deux œuvres se sont nourries l'une l'autre[21]. Dans le prologue qui précède les *Miracula*, avant de

---

puise chez l'Érigène l'idée de la confluence de l'intelligence et de la foi dans la prière, tout en en renversant la fonctionnalité: «Heiric s'empare directement du texte de la prière de Jean Scot Érigène, le copie, l'abrège et le paraphrase en partie, puis l'enchâsse dans un ingénieux compendium de théologie néo-platonicienne, évidemment simplifié pour les lecteurs les moins préparés et les moins subtils» (p. 336-337).

[19] VON BÜREN (2010), p. 376 et 403. Quelques passages qui trahissent une connaissance directe de Catulle ont été signalés par ULLMAN (1960), p. 1030-1031. GÄRTNER (2002, p. 67-69) relève et commente un emprunt à Lucain (III, 426-445) au Livre I, 236-263; dans «Das Eintreten des heiligen Germanus für die Bretonen (Heiric von Auxerre, *Vita S. Germani* (*BHL* 3458) VI, 266-276)», *ibid.*, p. 70-71, le même auteur propose également une alternative à une correction d'une leçon fautive du manuscrit Paris, BnF, lat. 13757.

[20] CONTRENI (2006), qui analyse les miracles p. 39-48, fait cependant remarquer que s'ils sont souvent mentionnés dans les récits, les membres de la communauté de Saint-Germain sont singulièrement absents parmi les bénéficiaires (p. 44). Parmi les prodiges, notons en particulier deux résurrections: l'une est comparée à celle de Lazare (Lib. I, c. 8); la seconde valorise le pouvoir de Germain par comparaison à celui de l'évêque d'Orléans, Aniane (Lib. I, c. 11).

[21] La thèse traditionnelle d'une participation d'Heiric à la rédaction des *Gesta* est controversée. Selon JANIN (1976), les auteurs des Gestes ont utilisé les premiers *Miracula Germani*, tandis qu'Heiric s'est pour sa part servi des *Gesta* dans la seconde série des Miracles. M. Sot, dans l'Introduction de la dernière édition et traduction des *Gesta*, suit P. Janin en ce qui concerne le déroulement chronologique de la genèse des œuvres, mais n'y voit pas de contradiction quant au rôle potentiellement joué par Heiric dans l'élaboration des *Gesta*; il avance comme arguments la proximité géographique de la cathédrale et du monastère qui devait favoriser les contacts et la différence de genre littéraire qui peut expliquer la différence de respective rédactionnelle, cf. SOT – LOBRICHON – GOULLET (2006).

préciser son propos – rapporter des miracles de Germain opérés de son vivant, omis par son premier biographe, et y joindre ceux accomplis après sa mort[22]–, Heiric rappelle l'existence de l'œuvre de Constance et à cette occasion fait l'éloge de Lyon, ville où s'est réfugiée la science, elle qui est *hujus nostrae exitialiter perosa regionis*. On retrouve dans ce paragraphe les mots de Loup de Ferrières dans une lettre à Eginhard, qui résume la doctrine d'Alcuin: la science *propter seipsam tantum appetenda*. Cette idée, transmise de maître à élève, semble être, selon l'expression de L. Holtz, «comme la devise de l'école d'Auxerre»[23].

Les *Miracula* sont divisés en deux livres[24]. P. Janin a montré que la première version, qui accompagnait la *Vita*, comprenait le premier livre, le prologue du second livre et les vingt-quatre chapitres qui suivent dont le dernier relatait un miracle daté de 873[25]. Bien qu'Heiric soit muet sur les circonstances qui l'ont amené à poursuivre son ouvrage, selon toute vraisemblance c'est la translation de plusieurs évêques et martyrs autour du tombeau de Germain qui le décida car il consacra la plus grande partie de cette suite à relater l'acquisition des reliques et la translation proprement dite. P. Janin émet l'hypothèse que

---

[22] CONTRENI (2006, p. 43) note toutefois que la majorité des miracles ont lieu à l'époque d'Heiric; le souci principal de l'hagiographe était de montrer à ses lecteurs qu'il y avait des témoignages récents de la sainteté de Germain.

[23] HOLTZ (1991), p. 134-136 et comparaison des trois textes, p. 145-146.

[24] Voir VON BÜREN (2010), p. 398-400. Éd. *AASS*, Iul. VII, 1731, p. 255-283; ils sont suivis d'un *Sermo in solemnitate sancti Germani* (p. 284-285) (voir *supra* n. 12). La remarque de IOGNA-PRAT (1990, p. 101) selon laquelle les *Miracula* mériteraient une bonne édition critique est toujours valable. Il convient de prêter une attention spéciale à l'édition de P. LABBE (*Nova bibliotheca manuscriptorum librorum*, t. I, Paris, 1657, p. 531-568): bien qu'elle apporte des modifications mineures aux textes, elle respecte la division originale du plus ancien manuscrit (Paris, BnF, lat. 13757), contrairement à celle des Bollandistes, reprise par les autres éditeurs. Voir BOSWORTH (2013): l'auteure analyse en détail la structure des *Miracula*, compare la division en chapitres dans le plus ancien manuscrit et dans l'édition des *AASS* et étudie l'impact du non-respect de la répartition originale et de la relégation des titres dans la marge sur la compréhension de l'œuvre.

[25] *Éd. cit.*, Lib. II, c. 107; JANIN (1976), p. 95-96. La tradition manuscrite va dans le sens de la thèse de P. Janin car c'est à ce chapitre que se termine une partie des témoins, disparus de nos jours mais connus par P. Labbe. Voir aussi *supra* n. 21.

l'événement eut lieu le 25 septembre 875[26]. La conclusion des *Miracula*, soit les chapitres 123-128, a peut-être été ajoutée très peu de temps avant la mort de l'auteur, vers 876/877, ou après 883[27]. Ces chapitres ont particulièrement retenu l'attention: après un dernier éloge du sanctuaire, comparé au Saint des Saints, et une justification du culte des reliques inspirée de Jérôme (*Contra Vigilantium*), Heiric adresse un «Avertissement aux saints frères» (*Commonitorium sanctis fratribus*). Paraphrasant un sage païen, Fonteius de Carthage, dont la pensée a été relayée par Augustin, il leur enjoint de se purifier et de lutter contre l'Antique ennemi; il enchaîne avec l'importance de la conversion et du combat spirituel des moines qui assurent une mission propédeutique et un rôle d'exemple dans l'Église. Sa réflexion sur le service monastique culmine dans l'exposé du schéma des trois ordres fonctionnels au sein de la société, schéma qu'il a hérité de son maître Haymon, et qu'il modifie légèrement en «monachisant» l'ordre des *oratores*, et en le plaçant en troisième position, après celui des *belligerantes* et celui des *agricolantes*, pour mieux exalter le rôle des moines qui amènent toutes choses à la perfection[28]. «Riches d'une telle conclusion, commente D. Iogna-Prat, les *Miracula sancti Germani* représentent une sorte de monument d'illustration de la cause monastique», et l'historien de poser la question cruciale de l'utilisation de ce texte comme source pour la présentation du nouveau sanctuaire[29]. Car les *Miracula* sont une source importante pour l'histoire de la basilique d'Auxerre et en particulier des cryptes[30]. L'on n'y trouvera pas pour autant le souci du détail architectural. Tant l'emploi d'un vocabulaire volontairement archaïque et classique, et non technique – avec les risques de contresens qu'il

---

[26] Le 25 septembre est la date anniversaire de la translation d'un des évêques, Aunaire, qui allait occuper la place d'honneur près de Germain, et également le jour anniversaire de sa mort. Pour honorer les autres personnages – saints de Rome, d'Agaune et d'Auxerre –, il est vraisemblable qu'on choisit le dimanche comme jour de la translation commune; or il se fait que le 25 septembre 875 tombait un dimanche, cf. JANIN (1976), p. 100-101.

[27] QUADRI (1992), p. 218 et VON BÜREN (2010), p. 376. Rappelons que l'année de décès d'Heriric est inconnue.

[28] Éd. cit., Lib. II, c. 128. Voir IOGNA-PRAT (1990), p. 103-104 et (1986), p. 106-108 et 113-117, et ORTIGUES (1991), p. 207-208.

[29] IOGNA-PRAT (1990), p. 104.

[30] Voir PICARD (1990), qui traduit tous les passages concernés et PICARD – SAPIN (1990), p. 105-110.

implique[31] — que le refus de la description détaillée, inutile « puisque nous l'avons sous les yeux, et que presque tout le monde à l'entour la connaît bien »[32], montrent que l'intérêt de l'auteur se situe ailleurs, comme l'ont souligné J.-C. Picard et C. Sapin : « il désigne l'importance du geste monumental sans se soucier de son usage ou de son décor matériel »[33]. L'évocation des lieux et de leur aménagement a pour seul but la glorification du monastère tout entier, imprégné par la puissance miraculeuse de son saint patron[34]. S'il est par conséquent hasardeux de se fier au seul texte pour appréhender l'histoire du monument, celui-ci constitue par contre un complément, précieux et rare dans l'histoire, à l'analyse archéologique du site[35].

Si Heiric glorifie son héros en s'attardant aux lieux qui lui sont consacrés[36], en particulier son abbaye, il fait ressortir également les liens privilégiés de Saint-Germain avec les autorités séculières : la famille des Welfs, restaurateurs du sanctuaire[37], et

---

[31] Par exemple *secretarium* a chez Heiric le sens étymologique de lieu retiré, secret, alors qu'il désigne également la sacristie (*ibid.*, p. 105).

[32] *De cujus qualitate fabricae multa forent, quae ad laudem operis jure litteris mandarentur; verum quia et oculis subjecta est, et fere omnibus circumquaque notissima, parcendum in talibus paginae per magis necessaria posterius dilatandae* (Lib. II, c. 89). Trad. PICARD (1990), p. 98.

[33] PICARD – SAPIN (1990), p. 109.

[34] Voir également l'analyse lexicale de GOUT – IOGNA-PRAT (2004) : elle met en évidence la matérialisation et la spatialisation du sacré, en particulier dans les *Miracula*.

[35] PICARD – SAPIN (1990), p. 109. Heiric ne distingue pas suffisamment les informations sûres et ses interprétations personnelles. Il n'est pas certain qu'un petit oratoire ait réellement précédé la basilique construite par Clotilde, qui aurait pu avoir seulement embelli le monument ; il n'est par ailleurs pas sûr qu'il s'agisse bien de l'épouse de Clovis et non d'une autre Clotilde à qui il aurait attribué un titre royal comme il l'a fait pour une certaine Ingonde, bienfaitrice du monastère (*ibid.*, p. 106). Sur les témoignages des *Miracula* sur l'intérêt et la générosité des reines mérovingiennes en faveur de Saint-Germain, voir DEFLOU-LECA (2010), p. 131-135.

[36] Voir l'analyse des *Miracula* par CONTRENI (2006), p. 39-48. La mention d'une basilique construite en l'honneur de Germain par Remi de Reims *in loco, quo sepeliri decreverat* (Lib. I, c. 63) a retenu l'attention car elle constitue un argument en faveur de l'existence au IXe siècle d'une version intermédiaire — entre la courte originale et la longue interpolée — du testament de l'évêque. Voir LUSSE (1997), p. 459-460.

[37] Le premier miracle rapporté dans le Livre II (c. 87) est la guérison de Conrad l'Ancien qui fut à l'origine de la construction des cryptes. La relation entre Auxerre et les Welfs, installés en Bourgogne Transjurane, est égale-

Charles le Chauve, roi des Francs puis empereur en 875. Ce dernier apparaît en effet dans la dédicace générale de l'œuvre, mais on le retrouve plus précisément dans les *Miracula* où est relatée la translation de 859 (Lib. II, c. 98-102). Celle-ci a lieu lors de l'invasion du royaume par Louis le Germanique. La situation étant critique et l'issue de la confrontation très incertaine, Charles décide de s'en remettre à Dieu. Il se rend au monastère et ordonne la translation du corps saint dans la crypte rénovée. Ce geste de foi et de dévotion accompagné de largesses provoque le miracle qui donne la victoire au roi. Germain apparaît dès lors comme protecteur du trône et Charles comme protecteur et bienfaiteur du monastère[38]. A. K. Bosworth a montré pour sa part que l'insistance de Rémi à rapporter des miracles réalisés par Germain à l'extérieur des limites de la zone d'influence de l'abbaye, mais dans les limites du royaume de Charles le Chauve, avait pour objectif de renforcer l'allégeance d'Auxerre vis-à-vis du souverain carolingien[39]. Car loin de se cantonner à la mise en valeur du sanctuaire, par contraste avec ce qu'on lit dans les œuvres antérieures, l'action récente de Germain dans les *Miracula* se déploie bien au-delà; l'ensemble des prodiges est même structuré selon un ordre géographique[40]. Heiric se démarque des hagiographes carolingiens par ce qu'on pourrait appeler une délocalisation des pouvoirs du saint patron. La *virtus* bénéfique ou punitive de Germain ne s'exerce pas seulement au lieu de son repos, mais également dans les églises détentrices de reliques (Lib. I, c. 53 et 69), et, ce qui est plus rare, dans les oratoires qui lui sont simplement consacrés (Lib. I, c. 63, 64, 78) voire simplement dans les régions où il est honoré (Lib. I, c. 5, 80)[41]. Ce détachement du lieu central du culte va jusqu'à

---

ment mise en évidence par la présence à Saint-Germain des reliques de saint Maurice et de ses compagnons de la légion thébaine (Lib. II, c. 111). Sur les relations entre l'abbaye et les Welfs, voir IOGNA-PRAT (1986), p. 102-103, SASSIER (1991), p. 29-33, et VAN EGMOND (2006), p. 18-19.

[38] Voir l'analyse de cet épisode par SASSIER (1991), p. 33-34 et GROSS (2004).

[39] BOSWORTH (2015).

[40] CONTRENI (2006), p. 41.

[41] DEFLOU-LECA (2010) met en évidence l'utilisation du récit de miracle, en l'occurrence en faveur d'un pèlerin sourd, pour conforter le lien entre l'abbaye et sa dépendance de Moutiers-en-Puisaye (Lib. I, c. 5), p. 564.

créer des intrusions d'un saint éloigné sur le territoire d'un « concurrent »[42].

La forme littéraire de la *Vita Germani*, elle-même inspirée de celle de la Vie de saint Amand de Milon[43], fut imitée par différents auteurs dont Abbon de Saint-Germain (*Bella Parisiacae urbis*), Odon de Cluny (*Occupatio*), Flodoard de Reims (*Triumphi Christi*)[44]. Plus tardif, le cas de Dudon de Saint-Quentin (*De moribus et actis primorum Normanniae ducum*) a été bien étudié: adoptant essentiellement la structure poétique et le caractère virgilien du texte, il emprunte à l'œuvre hagiographique d'Heiric de nombreuses phrases et la totalité des termes grecs qu'il utilise[45]. Le style maniéré combinant grec et latin, cultivé au IVe siècle par Ausone, revint d'ailleurs à la mode dans le courant du IXe siècle[46]. Mais en dépit de ses qualités, la *Vita Germani* ne supplanta dans la liturgie ni l'œuvre de Constance de Lyon ni la Vie interpolée, vraisemblablement parce qu'elle n'apportait rien de neuf qui pût nourrir la dévotion au saint[47]. Elle apparaît plutôt comme un livre scolaire destiné aux niveaux supérieurs de grammaire et de poétique[48]. Elle inspira aussi Syrus, l'auteur de la Vie de l'abbé de Cluny, Maïeul (*BHL* 5179), qui la démarque en bonne partie[49]. Par ce biais, les clunisiens furent mis en

---

[42] Ainsi Germain ressuscite à Orléans un jeune garçon dont la mère s'était également adressée à Aignan (Lib. I, c. 11). S'il ne s'agissait d'un cas exceptionnel dans la littérature hagiographique de l'époque, ce décentrage des pouvoirs du saint conduirait même à appréhender différemment, de manière élargie, la notion de pèlerinage. Voir l'analyse d'ALBERT (1999), p. 162-163 et 225-228.

[43] BERSCHIN (1991), p. 360-361.

[44] JACOBSEN (1991), p. 333.

[45] Voir *supra* n. 94 et LECOUTEUX (2005), p. 26-33.

[46] Ermenrich d'Ellwangen en fut l'un des premiers témoins vers 850, cf. BERSCHIN (1991), p. 361.

[47] LOBRICHON (1991), p. 69.

[48] La Vie métrique se veut un livre scolaire pour les plus hauts niveaux de grammaire et de poétique comprenant des noms et des concepts théologiques et mythologiques et fournit de surcroît, tout à fait en phase avec son temps, un petit lexique grec qui se présente aussi sous forme de vers grecs et latins mélangés, cf. BERSCHIN (1991), p. 361.

[49] Voir IOGNA-PRAT – SAPIN (1990), p. 278 et surtout IOGNA-PRAT (1988), p. 124-126, où l'auteur compare les Vies de Maïeul (*BHL* 5177 et principalement 5179), la *Vita* et les *Miracula Germani*. Les emprunts sont littéraux ou révèlent une communauté de thèmes. La Vie de Maïeul donne l'impression d'avoir été «construite en référence directe à la *Vita sancti Ger-*

contact avec la pensée de Jean Scot. Les derniers chapitres des *Miracula* – le *Commonitorium fratribus* (c. 126-128) – de même que le Sermon pour la Saint-Germain connurent eux un retentissement certain: ils furent intégrés au Sermon pour le bienheureux Maïeul[50] et l'exposé d'Heiric sur l'ordonnancement de la société chrétienne s'y trouva radicalisé par l'accent porté sur le caractère virginal des moines et leur séparation d'avec le monde; le thème acquit ainsi une visée politique dans le contexte réformateur du XIe siècle[51].

II. Une œuvre composite: les Gestes des évêques d'Auxerre

Composés de notices biographiques, les gestes d'évêques constituent un genre particulier qui relève de la littérature historiographique, proche toutefois de l'hagiographie[52]: en effet les rédacteurs ne se contentent pas de livrer les données factuelles en leur possession, ils ont également le souci de faire l'éloge des prélats, insérant parfois avec habileté l'un ou l'autre miracle quand ils en ont connaissance; ils exploitent également toutes les sources disponibles, dont des œuvres hagiographiques qu'il leur arrive même de copier mot pour mot. La proximité entre *Gesta* et *Vitae* apparaît aussi dans les répertoires modernes,

---

mani... Ce parallèle a été voulu et on a voulu qu'il se remarque», ce qui est facilité par l'alternance prose/vers de la Vie de Maïeul.

[50] IOGNA-PRAT (1988), p. 55.

[51] IOGNA-PRAT – SAPIN (1990), p. 278 et IOGNA-PRAT (1986), p. 117-118, qui élargit la perspective: la réflexion sur les *ordines* menée par Adalbéron de Laon et Gérard de Cambrai pourrait avoir été une réponse épiscopale au schéma monastique d'Heiric (un des principaux manuscrits de la *Vita Germani*, Paris, BnF, lat. 13757, était peut-être déjà à Laon au IXe siècle). Voir également IOGNA-PRAT (1988), p. 353-354 et LECOUTEUX (2005), p. 32. Les *Miracula* d'Heiric furent enrichis de dix récits (*BHL* 3463, éd. cit., p. 285-287) par un moine d'Auxerre du début du XIe siècle. Un miracle rapporté par Grégoire de Tours (*BHL* 3460) fut aussi adjoint ainsi que des textes d'origine britannique: les extraits de l'*Historia brittonum* de Nennius (IXe s.) (*BHL* 3461) et le récit d'une translation du doigt de Germain à Selby datée de 1069 (*BHL* 3464).

[52] Voir SOT (1981) et VAN EGMOND (2006), p. 6-11. Plus spécifiquement à propos des *Gesta* des évêques d'Auxerre: M. GOULLET, «Étude littéraire et histoire du texte», in SOT – LOBRICHON – GOULLET (2006), p. XXVI-XXX.

comme la *BHL* ou, plus spécifiquement pour la région qui nous occupe, le *Corpus Burgundiae Medii Aevi*[53].

Les *Gesta pontificum autissiodorensium* ont fait l'objet de plusieurs campagnes de rédaction. La première et dans une moindre mesure la deuxième nous concernent car elles datent respectivement de 872-875, sous l'épiscopat de Wala (872-879), et de peu après 933[54]. La composition initiale, d'un seul tenant, est de la plume de deux chanoines, Alagus et Rainogala; elle couvre les six premiers siècles de l'évêché. La première continuation, d'un chanoine anonyme, est consacrée aux épiscopats de six évêques, de Wala jusqu'à Gualdric. L'on a évoqué plus haut la controverse relative à la participation ou non d'Heiric à la rédaction de la première partie; l'imbrication des deux œuvres est quant à elle certaine. Et le cas de Germain n'est pas isolé: d'autres sources hagiographiques ont été mises à contribution par les auteurs. Ainsi la notice d'Amator est signalée dans le Répertoire bollandien comme epitome de sa *Vita BHL* 356, tandis que celles de Pèlerin et d'Aunaire, qui utilisent des Vies préexistantes de ces prélats (respectivement *BHL* 6623 et *BHL* 805), sont considérées comme suffisamment originales pour être affectées d'un numéro propre (*BHL* 6625 et *BHL* 806).

III. La Translation de saint Baudile et la Vie de saint Marien

Mentionnons encore deux textes hagiographiques relatifs à des moines ayant vécu dans le diocèse d'Auxerre. La *Translatio*

---

[53] Dans le cas d'Auxerre, pour les évêques des origines à 950 reconnus comme saints, les notices d'une certaine ampleur sont affectées d'un numéro spécifique: outre Germain (*BHL* 3459), on relève Pèlerin (*BHL* 6625), Aunaire (*BHL* 806), Didier (*BHL* 2141), Angelelme (*BHL* 458), Héribald (*BHL* 3826), Hérifrid (*BHL* 3834), Géran (*BHL* 3420), Betton (*BHL* 1321), Guy (*BHL* 8875). Les autres, souvent brèves, sont mentionnées dans le répertoire mais ne sont pas affectées d'un numéro *BHL*. Voir par ailleurs le site http://www.cbma-project.eu consacré aux écrits médiévaux bourguignons, qui répertorie les notices des évêques sous l'onglet «Textes hagiographiques».

[54] Éd. in Sot – Lobrichon – Goullet (2006), p. 1-221.

Baudelii (*BHL* 1047) provient de Cessy[55], première dépendance monastique de Saint-Germain. Baudile est un martyr originaire de Nîmes, dont le culte est attesté dès le VIe siècle. Deux siècles plus tard, sous la pression des invasions sarrasines, un abbé nommé Romule, accompagné de quatre-vingt moines, aurait fui la ville: arrivé en Bourgogne, il aurait reçu le domaine de Cessy pour y bâtir un monastère en l'honneur du saint. En 878 l'abbé Trutgaud, à l'occasion d'une rénovation de l'édifice, envoya à Nîmes deux de ses moines, sous la protection de Bernard de Gothie, pour y chercher la plus importante partie des reliques, qui y avait été dissimulée[56]. Cette quête fait l'objet de la Translation. Le texte est exclusivement connu par la copie qu'en donna au XVIIIe siècle Jean Lebeuf, chanoine d'Auxerre, d'après un manuscrit qu'il data du XIIIe siècle et qui n'a jamais été retrouvé[57]. La première étape du voyage fut Narbonne où le comte Bernard exposa la requête des moines à l'archevêque Segebaud qui leur donna son assentiment et les gratifia même de reliques du premier évêque de la ville, Paul, et d'un autre prélat du nom d'Amans[58]. Les habitants de Nîmes par contre se montrèrent hostiles à l'exhumation du corps et durent être contraints par leur évêque et celui d'Uzès *cum aliis pluribus pontificibus et abbatis multis*, ainsi que le *civitatis princeps*, Ursus[59]. L'hagiographe rapporte ensuite les miracles qui se produisirent sur le chemin du retour, puis à Cessy même. L'œuvre se termine abruptement: soit le manuscrit était incomplet, soit, comme c'est fréquemment le cas pour les recueils de miracles, il était destiné à enregistrer d'autres récits.

---

[55] Auj. Cessy-les-Bois, dép. Nièvre. Sur le monastère et ses relations avec Saint-Germain, voir DEFLOU-LECA (2010), p. 87-106. Édition de la Translation par M. MÉNARD, dans son *Histoire civile, ecclésiastique et littéraire de la ville de Nismes*, t. 1, Paris, 1701, Preuves, p. 3-8.

[56] Sur Bernard, marquis de Gothie, dont la *Translatio*, éd. cit., p. 5, col. b, évoque discrètement la rébellion face à Louis le Bègue: *Bernardus... in comitatu suo, qui ut rex ibat...*, voir DHONDT (1948), p. 213 et 293-313.

[57] DEFLOU-LECA (2010), p. 98, n. 187. La formule finale laisse penser que le texte copié dans ce manuscrit est le témoin d'un usage liturgique (voir *infra* n. 144).

[58] Il pourrait s'agir du premier évêque de Rodez (situé une époque incertaine, peut-être dès la fin du IVe siècle ou le début du Ve), et ce d'autant plus que le diocèse de Rodez aurait été rattaché un temps à la Narbonnaise, dans la première moitié du VIe siècle. Voir DUFOUR (1989), p. 70, n. 26 et 73.

[59] Éd. cit., p. 3 col. B.

Quoiqu'il ne le dise pas explicitement, l'auteur semble bien appartenir à la communauté de Cessy ou en être fort proche[60] et écrire à l'époque des faits, en tout cas pour ce qui est de l'essentiel du texte[61]. La *Translatio* recèle quelques éléments de datation. Le *terminus a quo* est 878, année durant laquelle l'abbé Trutgaud entreprit de rénover le monastère. Toutefois l'un des derniers miracles fait mention de l'évêque d'Auxerre Wibald (879-887). Deux jeunes filles aveugles et affligées d'autres infirmités sont conduites au sanctuaire par leurs pères respectifs: guéries par Baudile, elles reçurent toutes deux le voile des vierges, l'une de l'évêque Wibald, l'autre du prêtre Aiglard. La seconde vécut encore sept ans, ce qui donne à penser que la mise par écrit remonterait à 886-887[62].

L'on sait que Cessy, quoique dépendance de Saint-Germain, avait des liens étroits avec les évêques d'Auxerre, en particulier Wala[63]. Peut-être faut-il voir un écho de cette proximité dans le rôle de premier plan que l'auteur confère à plusieurs évêques,

---

[60] Comme en témoigne la prière, éd. cit., p. 7, col. b: *Tua sunt hec, Christe, tua sunt hec, Domine, dona, propter que nobis sancta adducebas pignora, ut sanares videlicet per sanctum tuum Baudelium diversorum hominum corpora, eque et nostrarum animorum precordia.*

[61] L'avant-dernier paragraphe, éd. cit., p. 8, col. a, se termine par une phrase de conclusion: *Crescebant Dei signa, et crebrescebant laudum ejus preconia.* Pourtant, sans transition, un dernier prodige est rapporté: *De parte autem Curtevallis delata est puella in portitorio miserabilis...*; l'ajout peut bien sûr être du fait de l'auteur. Il se termine abruptement par *Tu autem Domine*: ces trois mots abrègent vraisemblablement la formule *Tu autem Domine miserere nobis*, par laquelle le lecteur achevait les leçons de l'office; cf. CALLEWAERT (1940), p. 185.

[62] Rien n'indique en effet que l'évêque Wibald est mort lorsque l'auteur rédige; d'autre part cette datation est compatible avec la mention de l'oncle de Bernard de Gothie, «*tunc inclito abbate, futuro autem episcopo*». Nommé *Gaudenus* dans le texte, il est identifié avec l'évêque de Paris, Gauzlin, qui accéda à la fonction en 884. Voir CROSNIER (1858), p. 162 et LE JAN (1995), p. 445, tableau n° 61.

[63] Attesté au temps d'Aunaire († 605) et Tétrice († 707), le monastère fut donné à Saint-Germain par une reine nommée Ingonde, non identifiée, à l'instigation de l'évêque Didier († 623) à qui l'usufruit fut réservé jusqu'à sa mort. Cessy n'apparaît effectivement dans l'orbite de Saint-Germain qu'au IXe siècle lorsqu'il est dirigé par l'écolâtre Haymon (865-878). À la même époque l'évêque Wala choisit le monastère comme dernière demeure. Plus tard c'est l'évêque Gualdric qui releva Cessy après sa destruction par les Normands en 911 et le fit bénéficier de ses largesses. Voir DEFLOU-LECA (2010), p. 91-105.

qu'ils soient contemporains (archevêque de Narbonne, évêques de Nîmes, Uzès, Auxerre) ou passés (Paul de Narbonne, Amans).

Un dernier texte nous retiendra brièvement. Il relate la vie du berrichon Marien[64]. Fuyant la menace des Goths, celui-ci gagna la Bourgogne, attiré par la réputation de Saint-Germain. Le monastère Saint-Côme-et-Saint-Damien, fondé par Germain lui-même sur la rive droite de l'Yonne, lui fut consacré avant la fin du VIe siècle et prit le nom de Saint-Marien[65]. L'œuvre, qui présente le héros comme un modèle d'observance de la Règle, est manifestement destinée à une communauté monastique. L'auteur, assez distant dans ses propos, rapporte que l'abbé Mamertin[66] voulut mettre à l'épreuve le moine, dont on louait l'humilité et l'obéissance, en l'envoyant garder des troupeaux. La suite du récit est consacrée aux miracles accomplis par le saint qui mourut à Fontenoy, où les frères lui avaient demandé de célébrer l'office pascal.

Dans son étude sur l'hagiographie auxerroise pré-carolingienne, W. van Egmond soulève le problème de la datation de la *Vita S. Mariani* (*BHL* 5523)[67], qui selon lui se heurte à une contradiction entre les *Gesta* – qui associent Marien au monastère qui lui sera dédicacé – et la *Vita* qui affirme que le moine fut inhumé *in ecclesia sancti Germani*. La parenté entre la mention de Marien dans la notice d'Alode et le début de la *Vita* est évidente[68], mais on s'interroge sur le sens de l'emprunt. Pour

---

[64] À ne pas confondre avec saint Marien, ermite en Berry. Voir BULTOT-VERLEYSEN (2014), p. 566 (n° 14).

[65] ATSMA (1983), p. 30-40.

[66] Mamertin est connu comme abbé de Saint-Cosme-et-Saint-Damien (voir *ibid.*, p. 37), mais ce monastère n'est jamais identifié par l'auteur de la *Vita*.

[67] VAN EGMOND (2006), p. 131-134.

[68] Édition de la *Vita Mariani* par G. HENSCHEN dans *AASS*, Apr. II, 3e éd., Paris et Rome, 1866, p. 758-759. Le texte commence ainsi: *Tempore beatissimi Allodii Pontificis, Germani reverendissimi successoris, idem monasterium antiquae beatitudinis retinens statum, odore suavissimo redolebat*. La notice d'Alode (in SOT – LOBRICHON – GOULLET (2006), p. 51) porte: *Huius presulatus tempore sanctus Marianus, a partibus Bituricensium adueniens, monasterio sancti Germani se sociari postulabat, quia idem monasterium antique beatudinis retinens statum, odore suauissimo redolebat*. On notera que le *idem* devant *monasterium* dans la *Vita* est curieux puisqu'on n'en a pas encore parlé, tandis qu'il est logique dans la notice d'Alode où il renvoie à Saint-Germain; ce pourrait être un indice que la notice est antérieure à la *Vita*. Alode est le premier évêque

W. Levison, les premiers rédacteurs des Gesta auraient utilisé la *Vita*, explicitement désignée dans la notice: elle serait donc antérieure à 872-875[69]. Selon l'historien néerlandais, c'est l'inverse: l'auteur de la Vie conservée aurait remanié l'œuvre mentionnée dans la notice; ne connaissant pas le monastère Saint-Marien détruit en 887, il aurait fait reposer le corps à Saint-Germain, témoignant peut-être ainsi d'une translation – inconnue par ailleurs – afin de protéger les reliques des incursions normandes dans la région à la fin du IXe siècle[70]. La *Vita* serait donc postérieure à cette date[71]. Cependant, Marien figure dans le martyrologe hiéronymien et dans celui d'Usuard[72]; la dédicace du monastère à Marien est attestée dès la fin du VIe siècle[73] tandis que les *Gesta* évoquent un livre écrit

---

à avoir été inhumé dans l'église Saint-Germain, c'est-à-dire l'ancienne église Saint-Maurice construite par Germain.

[69] LEVISON (1903), p. 165. Si la Vie était antérieure à la consécration de Saint-Marien, il aurait y pu avoir une première inhumation à Saint-Germain, suivie plus tard, lors de la dédicace, d'une translation à Saint-Marien, ce qui expliquerait que la notice d'Aunaire précise *monasterium quod domnus Germanus construxit, ubi sanctus Marianus requiescit*, cf. SOT – LOBRICHON – GOULLET (2006), p. 77.

[70] Remarquons aussi que l'auteur fait faire un curieux détour au cortège funèbre: le saint est décédé à *Fontanetum* (Fontenoy(-en-Puisaye), dép. Yonne), mais le corps part de *Meziclis* (Mézilles, dép. Yonne) et passe par *Leviaticum* (Levis, dép. Yonne) pour aller à Auxerre. Voir la carte dans ATSMA (1983), p. 81.

[71] VAN EGMOND (2006), p. 131, n. 234, et p. 133-134. Elle pourrait remonter à la première moitié du XIIe siècle, lorsque Saint-Marien fut reconstruit, cf. ATSMA (1983, p. 33). Au début du XIIIe siècle, la Chronique de Robert d'Auxerre, moine de Saint-Marien, fait allusion à un *libellus de vita* (introduction de l'édition de la *Vita Mariani*, p. 756). VAN EGMOND (2006, p. 134) fixe le XIVe siècle comme *terminus ante quem* sur base de la datation du manuscrit cité par G. Henschen dans l'introduction de son édition (*éd. cit.*, p. 757). Il s'agit du Vatican, lat. 1198, or il apparaît que ce manuscrit est un témoin du légendier de Jean de Mailly, compilateur du XIIIe siècle originaire de la région d'Auxerre, et qu'il présente un abrégé de la *Vita Mariani* (*BHL vacat*) et non le *BHL* 5523. Jean de Mailly s'est vraisemblablement servi du *libellus de vita* évoqué par Robert d'Auxerre. Voir MAGGIONI (2013), p. XII-XIII et 157-158 et CHAZAN (1998), p. 125 et n. 41.

[72] DUBOIS (1965), p. 286, 19 août; *Martyrologe Hiéronymien* (*codex Bernensis*), 19 août (XIV kal. Sept.) (*AASS*, Nov. II-1, 1894, p. 107 et *AASS*, Nov. II-2, 1931, p. 451).

[73] Dans le règlement liturgique de l'évêque Aunaire et dans le testament de l'évêque Didier (tous deux transmis par les *Gesta* du IXe siècle), cf. PICARD (1992), p. 57.

sur sa Vie[74]; il est donc probable qu'une Vie a été écrite assez tôt, entre le VIIe et le IXe siècle, mais il est peu probable que ce soit celle dont les Bollandistes ont fait l'édition et qui semble effectivement utiliser la notice des *Gesta*.

Bibliographie

Albert, B. S., *Le pèlerinage à l'époque carolingienne*, Bruxelles, 1999 (Bibliothèque de la Revue d'histoire ecclésiastique, 82).

Atsma, H., «Klöster und Mönchtum im Bistum Auxerre bis zum Ende des 6. Jahrhunderts», *Francia*, 11 (1983), p. 1-96.

Berschin, W., *Biographie und Epochenstil im lateinischen Mittelalter*, 3: *Karolingische Biographie, 750-920 n. Chr.*, Stuttgart, 1991 (Quellen und Untersuchungen zur lateinischen Philologie des Mittelalters, 10).

Bosworth, A. K., «Re-creating a Patron for the Ninth Century: Geography, Sainthood, and Heiric of Auxerre's *Miracula sancti Germani*», *Journal of Medieval Religious Cultures*, 41/2 (2015), p. 93-120.

—, «Representing the Saint: The Structure of Heiric of Auxerre's *Miracula sancti Germani*», in C. J. Chandler – S. A. Stofferahn, éd., *Discovery and Distinction in the Early Middle Ages. Studies in Honor of John J. Contreni*, Kalamazoo, MI, 2013, p. 251-272.

Bouchard, C. B., «Episcopal *Gesta* and the Creation of a Useful Past in Ninth-Century Auxerre», *Speculum*, 84 (2009), p. 1-35.

Bultot-Verleysen, A.-M., «Hagiographie d'Aquitaine (750-1130)», in *Hagiographies*, VI (2016), p. 521-636, 689-704.

Callewaert, C., «Tu autem Domine miserere nobis», in *Collationes Brugenses*, 28 (1928), p. 471-473; réimpr. Id., *Sacris Erudiri. Fragmenta liturgica*, Steenbrugge, 1940, p. 185-188.

Chazan, M., «Jean de Mailly et la Chronique de Robert d'Auxerre: hagiographie, histoire et "autorité"», *Archivum fratrum praedicatorum*, 68 (1998), p. 117-133 = Ead., *Études d'historiographie médiévale*, Metz, 2008, p. 361-377 (Publications du Centre Régional Universitaire Lorrain d'Histoire, Site de Metz, 35).

---

[74] Les éditeurs et traducteurs des *Gesta* se demandent (*Les Gestes*, p. 50, n. 71) si l'indication *vita ipsius* se rapporte à Marien ou à Allodius. Cependant la construction de la notice implique qu'il s'agit bien d'une Vie de Marien dont on vient de parler; en outre si les rédacteurs avaient disposé d'une Vie d'Allodius, ils n'auraient sans doute pas réduit leur récit aux quelques lignes sur l'arrivée de Marien qui semble le seul événement notable de l'épiscopat d'Allodius.

CONTRENI, J. J., «"And Even Today": Carolingian Monasticism and the *Miracula sancti Germani* d'Heiric of Auxerre», in D. BLANKS – M. FRASSETTO – A. LIVINGSTONE, éd., *Medieval Monks and their World: Ideas and Realities. Studies in Honor of Richard E. Sullivan*, Leyde – Boston, 2006, p. 35-48 (Brill's Series in Church History, 25).

CROSNIER, A., *Hagiologie nivernaise*, Nevers, 1858.

D'ONOFRIO, G., «Prière, philosophie et théologie durant l'Antiquité chrétienne et le haut Moyen Âge», in J.-F. COTTIER, éd., *La prière en latin de l'Antiquité au XVIe siècle: formes, évolutions, significations*, Turnhout, 2006, p. 317-350 (Centre d'études médiévales de Nice, 6).

DEFLOU-LECA, N., *Saint-Germain et ses dépendances (Ve-XIIIe siècle). Un monastère dans la société du haut Moyen Âge*, Saint-Étienne, 2010 (CERCOR, Collection «Congrégations, ordres religieux et sociétés»).

DENOËL, C. – CINATO, F., «Y a-t-il eu un scriptorium à Auxerre au temps d'Heiric (841-v. 876)?», in *Scriptorium. Wesen – Funktion – Eigenheiten. Comité international de paléographie latine, XVIII. Kolloquium, St. Gallen 11.-14. September 2013*, München, 2015, p. 199-230.

DHONDT, J., *Étude sur la naissance des principautés territoriales en France (IXe-Xe siècle)*, Bruges, 1948.

DUFOUR, J., *Les évêques d'Albi, de Cahors et de Rodez des origines à la fin du XIIe siècle*, Paris, 1989 (Mémoires et documents d'histoire médiévale et de philologie, 3).

GÄRTNER, T., «Zwei Beispiele unerkannter hagiographischer Lucanbenutzung, *AB*, 120 (2002), p. 67-69.

GOULLET, M., «Étude littéraire et histoire du texte», in SOT – LOBRICHON – GOULLET (2006), p. XXI-XXXIV.

GOUT, M.-L – IOGNA-PRAT, D., «Les lieux du sacré dans les Miracula sancti Germani d'Heiric d'Auxerre et les Gesta pontificum Autissiodorensium», *Bulletin du centre d'études médiévales d'Auxerre* (URL: http://journals.openedition.org/cem/982; DOI: 10.4000/cem.982).

GROSS, F., «La foi de Charles le Chauve», in J. HOAREAU-DODINAU – P. TEXIER, éd., *Actes des XXIIIe Journées d'histoire du droit*, Limoges, 2004, p. 175-188 (Cahiers de l'Institut d'anthropologie juridique, 11).

HOLTZ, L., «L'école d'Auxerre», in IOGNA-PRAT, – JEUDY – LOBRICHON (1991), p. 131-146.

IOGNA-PRAT, D., *Agni immaculati. Recherches sur les sources hagiographiques relatives à saint Maïeul de Cluny (954-994)*, Paris, 1988.

IOGNA-PRAT, D., «Le texte des *Miracula sancti Germani* et son intérêt pour l'histoire des idées politiques», in *Saint-Germain d'Auxerre:*

intellectuels et artistes dans l'Europe carolingienne, IXe-XIe siècles. Auxerre (Yonne), abbaye Saint-Germain, juillet-octobre 1990, Auxerre, 1990, p. 101-104.

IOGNA-PRAT, D. – JEUDY, C. – LOBRICHON, G., éd., *L'école carolingienne d'Auxerre de Murethach à Rémi, 830-908. Entretiens d'Auxerre 1989*, Paris, 1991.

IOGNA-PRAT, D – SAPIN, C., « L'héritage: d'Auxerre à Cluny », in *Saint-Germain d'Auxerre: intellectuels et artistes dans l'Europe carolingienne, IXe-XIe siècles. Auxerre (Yonne), abbaye Saint-Germain, juillet-octobre 1990*, Auxerre, 1990, p. 277-284.

JACOBSEN, P. C., « Die *Vita s. Germani* Heirics von Auxerre. Untersuchungen zu Prosodie und Metrik », in IOGNA-PRAT – JEUDY – LOBRICHON (1991), p. 329-351.

JANIN, P., « Heiric d'Auxerre et les *Gesta pontificum Autissiodorensium* », *Francia*, 4 (1976), p. 89-105.

JEAUNEAU, É., « Heiric disciple de Jean Scot », in IOGNA-PRAT – JEUDY – LOBRICHON (éd.) (1991), p. 353-370 = *« Tendenda vela ». Excursions littéraires et digressions philosophiques à travers le moyen âge*, Turnhout, 2007, p. 479-498).

LECOUTEUX, S., « À partir de la diffusion de trois poèmes hagiographiques, identification des centres carolingiens ayant influencé l'œuvre de Dudon de Saint-Quentin », *Tabularia* (En ligne), Écrire l'histoire au Moyen Âge, mis en ligne le 26 avril 2005.

LE JAN, R., *Famille et pouvoir dans le monde franc (VIIe-Xe s.). Essai d'anthropologie sociale*, Paris, 1995 (Publications de la Sorbonne – Histoire ancienne et médiévale, 33).

LEVISON, W., « Bischof Germanus von Auxerre und die Quellen zu seiner Geschichte », *Neues Archiv*, 29 (1903), p. 95-175.

LOBRICHON, G., « Les Vies de saint Germain d'Auxerre et les essais hagiographiques de l'école », in *Saint-Germain d'Auxerre: intellectuels et artistes dans l'Europe carolingienne, IXe-XIe siècles. Auxerre (Yonne), abbaye Saint-Germain, juillet-octobre 1990*, Auxerre, 1990, p. 69-70.

LUSSE, J., « À propos du testament de saint Remi », in M. ROUCHE, dir., *Clovis, histoire et mémoire. Le baptême de Clovis, l'événement*, Paris, 1997, p. 451-467.

MAGGIONI, G. P., *Jean de Mailly, Abbreviatio in gestis et miraculis sanctorum: supplementum hagiographicum. Editio princeps*, Florence, 2013 (Millennio medievale, 97; Testi, 21).

ORTIGUES, E., « Haymon d'Auxerre, théoricien des trois ordres », dans IOGNA-PRAT – JEUDY – LOBRICHON (1991), p. 181-227.

PICARD, J.-C., « Les *Miracula sancti Germani* d'Heiric d'Auxerre et l'architecture des cryptes de Saint-Germain: le témoignage des textes », in *Saint-Germain d'Auxerre: intellectuels et artistes dans* *l'Europe carolingienne, IXe-XIe siècles. Auxerre (Yonne), abbaye Saint-Germain, juillet-octobre 1990*, Auxerre, 1990, p. 97-101.

—, «Auxerre», in GAUTHIER, N. – PICARD, J.-C. – DUVAL, N., éd., *Topographie chrétienne des cités de la Gaule, des origines au milieu du VIIIe siècle*, VIII: *Province ecclésiastique de Sens (Lugdunensis Senonia)*, Paris, 1992, p. 47-65.

PICARD, J.-C. – SAPIN, C., «Une lecture archéologique du texte d'Heiric», in *Saint-Germain d'Auxerre: intellectuels et artistes dans l'Europe carolingienne, IXe-XIe siècles. Auxerre (Yonne), abbaye Saint-Germain, juillet-octobre 1990*, Auxerre, 1990, p. 105-110.

POULIN, J.-C., «Les *libelli* dans l'édition hagiographique avant le XIIe siècle», in M. HEINZELMANN, éd., *Livrets, collections et textes. Études sur la tradition hagiographique latine*, Ostfildern, 2006 (Beihefte der Francia, 63).

QUADRI, R., «Heiric», dans *Saint-Germain d'Auxerre: intellectuels et artistes dans l'Europe carolingienne, IXe-XIe siècles. Auxerre (Yonne), abbaye Saint-Germain, juillet-octobre 1990*, Auxerre, 1990, p. 37-40.

QUADRI, R., «Del nuovo su Eirico di Auxerre», *Studi medievali*, ser. 3, 33 (1992), p. 217-228.

SASSIER, Y., «Les Carolingiens et Auxerre», in IOGNA-PRAT – JEUDY – LOBRICHON, éd. (1991), p. 21-36.

SOT, M. *Gesta episcoporum, gesta abbatum*, Turnhout, 1981 (Typologie des sources du Moyen Âge occidental, 37).

SOT, M. (dir.), LOBRICHON, G. – GOULLET, M. (éd.), *Les gestes des évêques d'Auxerre*, 1, Paris, 2006.

ULLMAN, B. L., «The transmission of the text of Catullus», in *Studi in onore di Luigi Castiglioni*, t. II, Florence, 1960, p. 1025-1057.

VAN EGMOND, W. S., *Conversing with the Saints. Communication in Pre-Carolingian Hagiography from Auxerre*, Turnhout, 2006 (Utrecht Studies in Medieval Litracy, 15).

VON BÜREN, V., «Heiricus (Autissiodorensis) mon.», in M.-H. JULLIEN *et al.*, éd., *Clavis scriptorum latinorum Medii Aevi. Auctores Galliae, 735-987*, III: *Faof – Hilduin*, Turnhout, 2010, p. 375-405 (*CC CM*).

L'écriture hagiographique dans le diocèse d'Orléans (env. 750-950)

par

Hélène CAILLAUD
avec la collaboration
de Klaus KRÖNERT et Michèle GAILLARD

I. Des saints évêques: Aignan; Euverte et Eucher. – A. Les Vies d'Aignan et d'Euverte. – B. La Vie d'Eucher, une production orléanaise?
II. Des saints confesseurs. – A. Saint Avit. – B. Saint Mesmin. – C. Saint Liphard. – D. L'œuvre d'Adrévald de Fleury.
Conclusion.
Bibliographie.

Dès l'Antiquité tardive et durant tout le haut Moyen Âge, la cité et le diocèse d'Orléans jouissent d'une position politique et religieuse importante au sein des différents royaumes francs qui se sont succédé. Plusieurs fois capitale, la cité d'Orléans accueille également à plusieurs reprises des conciles et devient un lieu de réforme religieuse notamment sous les épiscopats de Théodulfe et de Jonas. Au temps de Charles le Chauve, il existe à Orléans quatre sites majeurs dotés chacun d'une communauté de moines ou de chanoines: la cathédrale Sainte-Croix, Saint-Aignan, Saint-Avit, Saint-Euverte auxquels il faut ajouter trois abbayes majeures: Fleury, Micy et Meung-sur-Loire.

Pendant toute la période carolingienne, de nombreux textes hagiographiques ont été écrits ou réécrits à un moment où chacune de ces communautés revendiquait des origines anciennes et prestigieuses, protégées par des saints puissants: Aignan, Euverte, Mesmin, Lifard, Avit et Benoît. Il est alors indéniable que ce développement hagiographique est à mettre en lien avec les (re)fondations et le développement de communautés dédiées à ces saints ce qui explique l'intérêt des hagiographes pour le passé, souvent rêvé, de leur communauté et de leur fondation.

I. Des saints évêques: Aignan, Euverte et Eucher

A. Les Vies d'Aignan et d'Euverte

Saint Aignan, évêque libérateur de la cité d'Orléans face aux troupes d'Attila, bénéficie très tôt après sa mort d'un culte et de la rédaction d'une *Vita* (*BHL* 473)[1]. Aujourd'hui, l'accord se fait sur une période d'écriture comprise entre la fin du Ve et le début du VIe siècle[2]. C'est le point de départ de la production hagiographique concernant Aignan mais aussi Euverte son prédécesseur, qui, sous la plume des auteurs successifs, est devenu celui qui a su reconnaître avant tous la *virtus* d'Aignan.

Le IXe siècle marque un moment important de production hagiographique dans le diocèse: deux Vies successives de saint Euverte sont rédigées (*BHL* 2799 et 2800). La mention du saint dans la première Vie de saint Aignan y est utilisée pour faire de saint Euverte le bâtisseur de la cathédrale Sainte-Croix et celui qui désigna Aignan comme son successeur. Se crée ainsi un lien indéfectible entre trois lieux importants de la cité d'Orléans, la cathédrale Sainte-Croix, la collégiale Saint-Aignan et la collégiale Saint-Euverte.

Euverte est ainsi donné comme le prédécesseur de saint Aignan ce qui contredit manifestement le récit de la première Vie de saint Aignan:

> Plusieurs années auparavant, le bienheureux Euverte, évêque de la cité d'Orléans avait fait construire de fond en comble, pour l'amour de Dieu, une grande église; et, après bien des années et la succes-

---

[1] *Vita s. Aniani I* (*BHL* 473) est attribuée à Sidoine Apollinaire par Cuissard (1886, p. 201-202) mais cette attribution est fortement discutée. Elle daterait probablement de la fin V^e-début VIe siècle et serait par là-même l'un des textes les plus anciens de la production hagiographique de l'Orléanais. Cette Vie n'existait pas vers 379 puisque Prosper cherchait alors à recueillir des témoignages sur l'invasion des Huns, mais c'est probablement à elle que Grégoire de Tours fait allusion quand il dit, un siècle plus tard, à propos de saint Aignan: *cuius virtutum gesta nobiscum fideliter retinentur*. Il est aussi possible que l'auteur de la Vie de sainte Geneviève, qui écrivait en 530, ait connu ce récit puisqu'il fait allusion au siège d'Orléans et aux prières de saint Aignan.

[2] Heinzelmann (2010), p. 61.

sion de nombreux évêques, le saint homme de Dieu Aignan, empli par le saint esprit et par le consentement du Seigneur, accéda à la charge pontificale[3].

Mais qu'importe, en à peine quelques décennies, cette tradition s'impose. Ainsi, on peut lire, dès les premières lignes de sa Vie, qu'Euverte est désigné miraculeusement, par une colombe, évêque d'Orléans tandis que la cité était bouleversée par des affrontements au sujet de l'élection du nouvel évêque. Même si aucune autre source ne le mentionne, L. Duchesne pensait qu'Euverte aurait pu être le quatrième évêque d'Orléans et aurait succédé à Desinianus. Il ajoute qu'un certain Eortius assista en 374 au concile de Valence[4]. Cependant, malgré l'ensemble des efforts des historiens et érudits pour rendre la chronologie cohérente, la véracité de cette succession ne peut être admise.

Le dossier hagiographique d'Euverte se compose de quatre récits hagiographiques: deux *Vitae*, un récit de translation et un récit d'*Inventio*. La première Vie du saint (*BHL* 2799) serait l'œuvre d'un certain Lucifer, sous-diacre de l'Église d'Orléans[5]. Cependant, cette mention n'apparaît que dans quelques manuscrits[6]. Pour J.-C. Picard, il s'agit-là de la plus ancienne Vie de saint Euverte; la seconde Vie (*BHL* 2800) ne serait pas le modèle mais un abrégé enrichi de quelques données supplémentaires[7]. La première Vie (*BHL* 2799), dont l'auteur avoue se servir d'une vie plus ancienne, était connue de Raban Maur et d'Usuard. Elle est contenue dans un manuscrit du tout début du IXe siècle qui contient nombre de récits hagiographiques an-

---

[3] *Vita I sancti Aniani* (*BHL* 473), *MGH*, *SRM*, III, Hanovre, 1896, p. 108-117, c. 2, p. 108.

[4] Duchesne (1907-1915), p. 456.

[5] *Vita s. Evurtii I* (*BHL* 2799), *AASS*, Sept. III, 1750, p. 52-58: L'auteur se présente au terme de son œuvre sous le nom de Lucifer, sous-diacre de l'église d'Orléans, c. 20: *Ego Lucifer subdiaconus haec gesta morum atque factorum sancti ac beatissimi Evurtii episcopi in veritate descripsi, nuhil neque superflue loquens.*

[6] En effet, l'édition des Bollandistes ne prend en considération seulement quatre manuscrits sur les trente-cinq existants et dont plus d'une vingtaine sont antérieurs au XIIIe siècle. Dans le cadre du PCR consacré à la cathédrale d'Orléans, il a été proposé de faire une nouvelle édition, traduction et commentaire des Vies de saint Euverte. Voir à ce propos, Caillaud (2018).

[7] Picard (1992), p. 84.

ciens[8], ce qui pourrait être l'indice d'une rédaction bien antérieure et permet d'avancer l'hypothèse d'une rédaction au VIIIe siècle, peut-être lors de l'épiscopat d'Eucher (démis de son siège en 732). Cet ordre de rédaction a été remis en question par G. Renaud qui pensait que la Vie II (*BHL* 2800)[9], dont le manuscrit le plus ancien sur les onze recensés par la *BHL*ms n'est pas antérieur au XIe siècle[10], est la plus ancienne. Elle s'appuyait sur la présence de certains détails architecturaux qui pourraient montrer qu'elle a été écrite au début du IXe siècle[11]: la description extrêmement précise d'un édifice cruciforme serait l'indice d'une rédaction carolingienne. Or, même si la période carolingienne est effectivement marquée par le développement de ce type d'édifice, cela n'implique pas que la rédaction ait été contemporaine de la contruction. Cette discussion au sujet de la datation de ces deux *Vitae* mériterait certainement d'être de nouveau ouverte. En effet, certaines lacunes de *BHL* 2800 s'expliquent volontiers si l'on considère qu'il s'agit d'un abrégé: l'auteur ne trouve pas utile de mentionner le nom (Tetradius) du bienfaiteur qui cède son champ pour la sépulture du saint et édifie un oratoire, ni l'emplacement du tombeau de saint Euverte, ce qui se comprend bien si cet abrégé était destiné à un public local[12]. De plus, en dépit de quelques différences, les deux auteurs suivent la même trame narrative: après avoir décrit longuement l'élection épiscopale de saint Euverte[13], qui n'est pas sans rappeler le miracle de la Colombe dans les

---

[8] Wien, ÖNB, Cvp 420, fol. 71-79; à propos de ce manuscrit, voir DIESENBERGER (2010).

[9] *Vita s. Evurtii II (BHL 2800)*, éd. dans *Cat. Paris*, II, p. 312-319.

[10] Montpellier, BIU 68, fol. 50-55v (XIe siècle), en ligne: http://www.calames.abes.fr/pub/#details?id=D01040655.

[11] RENAUD (1973), p. 747-748. Pourtant, chacun des deux auteurs détaillent de manière très précise la nouvelle cathédrale (*BHL* 2799, c. 10: Selon Lucifer, l'église a une forme de croix avec 170 coudées de longueur et 42 de largeur. Chaque bras de la croix comporte trois arcs. Il y a trois autels dont celui du milieu est dédié à la Sainte Croix. Selon *BHL* 2800, c. 10, l'église a une longueur de 177 coudées et 33 de largeur. Chaque bras du transept comporte trois arcs afin que, par leurs ouvertures, l'église apparaisse comme une seule, et sera d'une longueur de 34 coudées.).

[12] *Vita s. Evurtii II (BHL 2800)*, c. 16, p. 319: *Obiit ergo beatus Evurtius sub die septimo idus septembris, et sepultus in conspectu civitatis ad orientem.*

[13] *Vita s. Evurtii II (BHL 2800)*, c. 1-8; *Vita s. Evurtii I (BHL 2799)*, c. 1-7.

Évangiles[14], et qui met fin à une vive querelle qui déchirait les Orléanais, ils relatent comment Euverte éteignit un incendie par ses prières après avoir demandé aux habitants de construire une nouvelle cathédrale[15]. Viennent alors le miracle du trésor trouvé sur le chantier[16] et la construction de la nouvelle église[17]. Puis au terme d'une longue existence, Euverte, voulant éviter une nouvelle querelle, décide de désigner lui-même son successeur, Aignan[18]. Cependant, Lucifer est beaucoup moins avare en détails, précisant notamment la date de consécration de l'église (le 5 des Nones de Mai qui correspond à la célébration de l'invention du bois de la Croix[19]).

En réponse aux Vies de saint Euverte, un nouvel hagiographe, certainement un chanoine du chapitre de Saint-Aignan, rédige une nouvelle adaptation de la Vie d'Aignan (*BHL* 474)[20]. Il s'agit d'une réécriture de la première Vie (*BHL* 473) qui reprend la fin de la Vie de saint Euverte en précisant qu'Euverte désigna son successeur Aignan afin d'éviter une nouvelle querelle[21]. Ainsi, le thème de l'accession à l'épiscopat, qu'il s'agisse des Vies de saint Euverte ou de la seconde Vie de saint Aignan, apparaît comme un motif hagiographique important dans l'Orléanais carolingien[22]. L'épilogue de cette nouvelle Vie d'Aignan rapporte que le saint fut d'abord enterré à Saint-Laurent, puis transporté, de nombreuses années après, dans un temple prestigieux[23]. Nous avons conservé 30 manuscrits de ce texte, allant du Xe au XVe siècle[24] dont le Ms. Vatican, Reg. lat. 523 et le

---

[14] Mt. 3, 15-17; Mc. 1, 10; Lc. 3, 22; Jn. 1, 32.

[15] *Vita s. Evurtii II* (*BHL* 2800), c. 8; *Vita s. Evurtii I* (*BHL* 2799), c. 8.

[16] Cette anecdote est commentée par G. DUBY dans *Guerriers et paysans*, Paris, 1973, p. 183.

[17] *Vita s. Evurtii II* (*BHL* 2800), c. 9-11; *Vita s. Evurtii I* (*BHL* 2799), c. 9-13.

[18] *Vita s. Evurtii II* (*BHL* 2800), c. 11-15; *Vita s. Evurtii I* (*BHL* 2799), c. 14-20.

[19] Sur la date du 3 mai, voir notamment CORNET (1952).

[20] *Vita s. Aniani II* (*BHL* 474), R. HUBERT, *Antiquitez historiques pour l'histoire de l'Église de Saint-Aignan d'Orléans*, Hotot, 1661, p. 1-3.

[21] *Vita s. Evurtii I* (*BHL* 2799), c. 17, p. 57.

[22] Voir à ce propos, HEAD (1990), p. 105-107.

[23] Il ne s'agit sans doute pas de l'église construite par Robert le Pieux puisque deux témoins de ce texte se trouvent dans deux manuscrits datés de la fin du Xe ou du début du XIe siècle (cf. *infra*).

[24] RENAUD (1976), p. 252.

Ms. Paris, Bibl. Sainte-Geneviève, 3013, datant tous deux de la fin du Xe ou du début du XIe siècle. La deuxième Vie d'Aignan a pu être rédigée au IXe ou au Xe siècle. Enfin, une troisième Vie d'Aignan[25], le *Sermo de origine et prioribus gestis S. Aniani* (*BHL* 476) vient combler les lacunes des *Vitae* précédentes concernant la jeunesse du saint jusqu'à la mort de saint Euverte. G. Renaud signale douze témoins de ce texte datés entre le Xe et le XIVe siècle dont le plus ancien est Orléans, Bibl. mun. 197 (Xe s.). Ce manuscrit daterait du Xe siècle, selon l'étude de E. Pellegrin qui établit que ce manuscrit serait formé de parties diverses, toutes du Xe siècle, qui ont probablement été écrites à Saint-Benoît-sur-Loire[26]. Selon cette Vie, Aignan serait né à Vienne de parents nobles[27]. Dans son adolescence, il établit une cellule hors les murs de cette cité. Il entend alors parler de saint Euverte et décide de se mettre à son service. Euverte lui confère le sacerdoce et le fait abbé de Saint-Laurent. L'auteur continue par son élection épiscopale et arrête son récit ici.

Les hagiographes d'Euverte et d'Aignan ont ainsi créé des Vies de saints entrelacées qui établissent des relations privilégiées entre Aignan, Euverte et Dieu notamment à travers leurs élections épiscopales guidées par Lui (désigné par une colombe pour l'un, et par un enfant pour l'autre) et qui mettent en avant leur rôle au sein de leur communauté (citons par exemple l'incendie arrêté par Euverte et la construction d'une nouvelle cathédrale; la défense de la cité menée par Aignan face aux Barbares). Tout en rappelent le modèle antique du *defensor civitatis,* ces deux figures d'évêques correspondent au modèle de l'évêque tel qu'on le trouve à Orléans à l'époque carolingienne; qu'il s'agisse de Théodulfe, de Jonas ou encore d'Agius, chacun de ces évêques a rempli efficacement son rôle de relais de l'autorité impériale en matière religieuse comme en matière de défense. Ainsi, Théodulfe, avec le soutien de Louis le Pieux, entreprit la

---

[25] *Vita s. Aniani III* (*BHL* 476), R. Hubert, *Antiquitez historiques pour l'histoire de l'Église de Saint-Aignan d'Orléans,* Hotot, 1661, p. 4-5. Pour l'analyse complète de la Vie III de saint Aignan, voir RENAUD (1976), p. 252.

[26] RENAUD (1976), p. 252, n. 6.

[27] L'auteur mentionne également un frère, saint Léonien: *Sanctus Anianus Viennensis ciuitatis oppido fuit ex parentibus nobilibus oriundus; cuius germanus sanctus Leonianus ad Orientalem plagam foris iam dictae ciuitatis in Basilica Sancti Petri, ubi Sanctus Desiderius Martyr in corpore requiescit, est cum magno decore humatus* (Hubert (1661), p. 4). Sur ce saint, voir VAN DER STRAETEN (1972).

restauration de grands centres spirituels comme l'abbaye de Micy ainsi que des écoles. À sa suite, Jonas apparaît comme le seul garant de l'autorité impériale dans le comté. Enfin, Agius (843-867?) prend en charge la défense active et efficace de la ville aux côtés de Bouchard, l'évêque de Chartres[28].

Par la suite, le dossier hagiographique de saint Aignan est renforcé, au XIe siècle, par la rédaction d'un ensemble de *Miracula*[29] (BHL 476b). Ces *Miracula* ont été écrits au plus tard au XIIe siècle puisque le manuscrit le plus ancien que nous connaissons, le Vatican, Reg. lat. 585, remonte à cette époque, mais ils ne peuvent avoir été écrits avant la première moitié du XIe siècle, car il y est fait allusion très précisément à la Vie de saint Odilon de Cluny[30]. Le recueil de miracles, composé de seize miracles se situant à des époques différentes, ne semble pas avoir été connu en dehors d'Orléans: les deux seuls manuscrits aujourd'hui conservés au Vatican, en proviennent. Il s'agit de Vatican, Reg. lat. 585 (XIIe s.) et Reg. lat. 623.

Le dossier hagiographique d'Euverte est, quant à lui, complété par un récit de translation (BHL 2801)[31] qu'il est difficile de dater[32]. Pour T. Head, ce texte pourrait dater de la seconde moitié du XIIe siècle, moment où les chanoines de Saint-Euverte obtiennent la confirmation de leurs possessions par le pape Eugenius (1146)[33]. C'est également à cette époque que l'abbé Robert rédige un récit d'*Inventio* (BHL 2802)[34], une lettre adressée aux moines de Saint-Ouen annonçant la bonne nouvelle de la découverte des reliques du saint[35]. Mais il pourrait tout aussi bien dater de la seconde moitié du IXe ou du Xe siècle même si aucun élément tangible ne permet de l'affirmer. Le seul témoin

---

[28] Voir notamment MULLER (1987), p. 14-20.

[29] *Miracula s. Aniani* (BHL 476b et 476d), éd. G. RENAUD, «Les miracles de saint Aignan», *AB*, 94 (1976), p. 245-274.

[30] Miracles de saint Aignan, c. 9: *Inter quos fuit sanctae memoriae Odilo Cluniacensis monasterii abbas, qui quanti meriti sit quantumque apud Deum valeat, liber vitae eius et miraculorum declarat.* RENAUD (1976), p. 253.

[31] *Translatio s. Evurtii* (BHL 2801), AASS, Sept. III, 1750, p. 59-60.

[32] Ce texte mériterait une nouvelle étude. Il contient, en effet, outre l'accord de l'empereur pour procéder à la translation du saint, une charte de confirmation des biens et privilèges de la collégiale Saint-Euverte octroyée par *Carolus Dei gratia Francorum Rex et Romanorum patritius*.

[33] HEAD (1990), p. 52; *Gallia Christiana*, VIII, p. 508.

[34] *Inventio s. Evurtii* (BHL 2802), AASS, Sept. III, 1750, p. 61.

[35] HEAD (1990), p. 95-96.

médiéval date du XVe siècle[36]. Ce récit est vraisemblablement écrit par un chanoine de Saint-Euverte, communauté qui apparaît pour la première fois dans les sources en 840-843, dans un acte de Charles le Chauve[37]. Il y est fait référence à ses *Gesta*, certainement la *Vita* (*BHL* 2799), puisque le nom du bienfaiteur Tetradius est mentionné. Après avoir repris les éléments essentiels de la vie du saint, l'auteur rapporte le transfert des reliques du saint vers une église Saint-Étienne à l'intérieur de la cité face à la menace des Vandales (*vandalicae persecutionis*; *barbarorum inquietudine*)[38]. Puis avec l'accord de l'empereur Charles (*Carolus christianissimus imperator Francorum*), les reliques du saint regagnent Saint-Euverte. Afin de conserver la mémoire des biens octroyés à la collégiale, l'auteur insère une charte de confirmation des biens et privilèges cédés par un certain «Charles roi des Francs et Patrice des Romains». Cet acte est, sans aucun doute, une forgerie comportant plusieurs problèmes: la titulature tout d'abord qui comporte des éléments désignant Charlemagne et une erreur de chronologie avec la mention d'Agius, évêque d'Orléans de 843 à environ 867. S'inspirant sans doute du diplôme authentique de Charles le Chauve, l'auteur joue, volontairement ou non, de l'homonymie entre Charlemagne et Charles le Chauve pour attribuer la charte qu'il cite au grand empereur[39]. La construction d'un tel récit prend tout son sens dans le contexte orléanais de la seconde moitié du IXe siècle et le début du Xe siècle: après les nombreuses dépré-

---

[36] Vatican, Reg. lat. 623, fol. 93-99.

[37] HEAD (1990), p. 51; *Recueil des Actes de Charles le Chauve*, I, éd. G. TESSIER, Paris, 1943-1955, p. 64, n°25.

[38] La dénomination de «vandales» apparaît comme un terme générique désignant des païens, barbares, aux pratiques cruelles et féroces. Nombreux sont les établissements religieux qui profitèrent de ces attaques et déprédations commises pour revendiquer de nouvelles chartes de privilèges sur la base de documents perdus, comme Sainte-Croix d'Orléans. Elles sont également l'occasion de la rédaction de récits de translations et de miracles comme c'est le cas pour sainte Geneviève ou saint Germain de Paris. Voir à ce sujet, CAILLAUD (2016), «Les attaques menées contre les sanctuaires: le prétexte normand», p. 278-284.; voir également MALBOS (2012).

[39] Charles le Chauve pourrait convenir en termes de chronologie: il est le contemporain de l'évêque d'Agius. Il est couronné en 848 à Orléans et sa présence est plusieurs fois attestée en Orléanais entre 840 et 862. Voir MULLER (1987), p. 15.

dations causées par les vikings[40], les grands établissements monastiques, Fleury et Micy, ainsi que la collégiale Saint-Aignan revendiquent leur ancienneté et leurs origines prestigieuses. Bien qu'il soit certain que Saint-Euverte ne peut remonter aussi loin, ce texte veut affirmer la présence du corps saint au sein de la collégiale, renforcer son culte assuré par la communauté récemment fondée et conserver la mémoire de ses possessions et de sa tutelle épiscopale.

B. La Vie d'Eucher, une production orléanaise?

Eucher, évêque d'Orléans, exilé est mort en 732 à Saint-Trond. Né dans une noble famille d'Orléans, Eucher est baptisé par Ansbert, évêque d'Autun; après de brillantes études, il prend l'habit monastique; mais son oncle Savary, évêque d'Orléans, étant décédé, les habitants demandent à Charles Martel de le nommer à ce siège; Eucher accepte à contrecoeur mais fut un très bon évêque, humble et généreux, ce qui suscite la jalousie de certains conseillers de Charles; au retour de la bataille de Poitiers, ce dernier fait arrêter Eucher et l'envoie en exil dans le diocèse de Liège, où il est confié à la garde du duc Chrodebert; Eucher obtient l'autorisation de se retirer au monastère de Saint-Trond où il meurt en sa sixième année d'exil, donc en 738 et est enterré.

Malgré la tradition localisant la rédaction de la *Vita S. Eucherii* (BHL 2660)[41] à Saint-Trond, possession de l'évêque de Metz dans le diocèse de Liège, plusieurs historiens s'accordent aujourd'hui à localiser son écriture dans l'Orléanais. Selon Matthias Werner, suivi par Alain Dierkens, la Vie d'Eucher aurait été écrite à Orléans vers le milieu du VIIIe siècle[42]. Selon Jacques Le Maho, elle fut écrite au milieu du Xe siècle par le même auteur que les Vie des abbés de Jumièges Aycadre et Hu-

---

[40] Orléans est plusieurs fois touchées par les attaques normandes: en 841, 843 puis en 856 et 865. Voir à ce propos, MULLER (1987), p. 18. Notons que le terme de Vandales, utilisé dans la *Vita* pour désigner les barbares du très haut Moyen Âge, pouvait évoquer aussi les Normands.
[41] Éd. G. HENSKENS, *AASS*, Feb. III, Anvers, 1658, p. 208-219; éd. W. LEVISON, *MGH, SRM*, VII, Hanovre – Leipzig, 1920, p. 41-53.
[42] DIERKENS (1994), p. 281-282; WERNER (1980).

gues⁴³; il va plus loin en proposant comme auteur, Annon qui fut abbé de Jumièges à partir de 942/943 et décéda à Micy, où il devint abbé vers 950/960⁴⁴; il souligne la similitude des thématiques et remarque que cette *Vita* occulte la vision d'Eucher «au point que l'on peut se demander si la Vie n'a pas été écrite uniquement pour cela» et qu'un hommage particulier y est rendu à Charles Martel, *inclytus saeculi princeps*. Remarquons cependant que ces deux derniers arguments pourraient aussi aller dans le sens d'une écriture antérieure à celle de la *Visio Eucherii*, attribuée à Hincmar de Reims⁴⁵, comme le pensent M. Werner et A. Dierkens.

II. Des saints confesseurs

A. Saint Avit

Un autre saint mérovingien fait l'objet d'un culte important à Orléans⁴⁶ et bénéficie d'un dossier hagiographique conséquent. Il s'agit de saint Avit († vers 530) dont l'existence est solidement attestée; il est enterré près d'Orléans et les fidèles y ont élevé une église⁴⁷. C'était, selon Grégoire de Tours, un «abbé du pays chartrain qu'on appelle le Perche»⁴⁸. Grégoire relate également qu'il intervint auprès de Clodomir afin qu'il

---

⁴³ Sur ces *Vitae*, cf. *supra*, L. Trân Duc, «Le diocèse de Rouen», p. 275-278.

⁴⁴ Le Maho (2006), p. 311-321.

⁴⁵ La rédaction de la *Visio Eucherii* serait due à Hincmar de Reims. Éd. W. Hartmann, dans Id., *Die Konzilien der karolingischen Teilreiche, 843-859*, MGH, *Conc.*, III, Hanovre, 1984, p. 414-417. Cf., entre autres, C. Carrozzi, «Les Carolingiens dans l'au-delà», dans M. Sot (éd.), *Haut Moyen Âge, Culture, éducation et société, Mélanges Pierre Riché*, 1990, p. 367-376 (p. 368-369).

⁴⁶ Dès l'époque mérovingienne, Avit est célébré en grande pompe à Orléans: *Miraculum s. Aviti* (BHL 883), Grégoire de Tours, *Liber in gloria confessorum*, 97, éd. B. Krusch éd., MGH, *SRM*, I-2, Hanovre, 1885, p. 360-361.

⁴⁷ Poncelet (1905), p. 14; Grégoire de Tours, *Liber in gloria confessorum*, 97 (98): *Qui recedens a corpore, honorifice apud Aurelianensium urbem humatus est; super quem fideles christiani ecclesiam construxerunt*.

⁴⁸ *Miraculum s. Aviti* (BHL 883).

épargne la vie du roi des Burgondes (523)[49] et qu'il rencontra le roi Gontran lorsque celui-ci, en visite à Orléans, se rendit auprès du tombeau d'Aignan en sa basilique[50]. Avit figure également en tant que prêtre d'Orléans dans le *Martyrologe hiéronymien*[51].

Son dossier hagiographique, outre ce miracle rapporté par Grégoire de Tours, se compose de quatre *Vitae*: *BHL* 879 (Vie I), la plus ancienne des Vies d'où découlent *BHL* 881 (Vie II)[52], puis *BHL* 880 (Vie III)[53] pour finalement ne plus former qu'une seule, *BHL* 882 (Vie IV)[54], qui représente la synthèse de tous les éléments de la légende du saint. A. Poncelet reprend cet ordre des rédactions tout en montrant que ces trois recensions 879, 880, 881, bien que différentes sur la forme, ne diffèrent pas sur le fond[55]: seule *BHL* 882 s'écarte quelque peu des autres Vies.

Martin Heinzelmann date *BHL* 879 de la fin du VIe ou du début du VIIe siècle[56]. En 531, Childebert Ier lui aurait élevé une basilique à l'endroit où s'élevait une modeste structure de bois[57]. Rédigée donc au moment du développement du culte du saint à Orléans, cette Vie, qui fait d'Avit un abbé de Micy[58], est le point de départ de la tradition hagiographique autour du saint[59]; elle expose à ses lecteurs l'ampleur de sa renommée à

---

[49] Grégoire de Tours, *Libri historiarum X*, éd. B. Krusch et W. Levison, *MGH*, *SRM*, I-1, Hanovre, 1951, lib. III, c. 6, p. 102: *Cui a beato Avito abbate, magno tunc tempore sacerdote, dictum est.*

[50] *Ibid.*, lib. VIII, c. 2, p. 371: *Mane autem facto, dum rex loca sanctorum orationis gratia visitaret, ad metatum nostrum advenit. Erat enim ibi basilica sancti Aviti abbatis, cui in libro Miraculorum meminimus.*

[51] Martyrologe Hiéronymien, éd. H. Delehaye, *AASS*, Nov. II, 1894, p. 322-323: *In Aurelianis civitate Aviti presbyteri.*

[52] *Vita s. Aviti II* (*BHL* 880), inédite.

[53] *Vita s. Aviti III* (*BHL* 881), éd. B. Krusch, *MGH*, *SRM*, III, Hanovre, 1896, p. 380-385 (recension B).

[54] *Vita s. Aviti IV* (*BHL* 882), *AASS*, Iun. III, 1701, p. 351-359.

[55] Sur la datation de ces Vies, voir Auernheimer (2010).

[56] Heinzelmann (2010), p. 61.

[57] *Vita s. Aviti I* (*BHL* 879), c. 11: *Cui titulo superponitur villissima ligni memoria.*

[58] *Vita s. Aviti I* (*BHL* 879), *Cat. Bruxelles*, I, p. 57-63, c. 4: *sibi abbatem pontifice jubente constituunt.*

[59] D'autres textes hagiographiques, prenant pour base la Vie d'Avit (sans qu'on ait pu encore déterminer avec certitude s'il s'agissait de la première ou de la deuxième), ont été rédigées pour des saints qui ont fait partie du réseau de sainteté de l'abbaye de Micy. Pour la Vie de Calais (*BHL* 1568), qui aurait

travers ses différentes pérégrinations, ce qui lui permet de relier entre eux les sanctuaires qui lui sont dédiés: d'abord dans les environs d'Orléans[60], puis dans le Perche, près de Châteaudun où se trouve un monastère qu'il a fondé; à Châteaudun même, une basilique fondée en son honneur et enfin en Sologne, à Mézières.

Par la suite, *BHL* 881[61], texte encore inédit, puis *BHL* 880 reprennent globalement la trame narrative de *BHL* 879, même si l'auteur de *BHL* 880 insère vers la fin de son récit le miracle relaté par Grégoire de Tours, ce qui n'est pas le cas dans *BHL* 879 et 881.

Enfin, la quatrième Vie de saint Avit (*BHL* 882), qui a longtemps été vue comme la plus ancienne Vie du saint[62], a été réétudiée par A. Poncelet, qui a mis en évidence les emprunts de l'auteur à la Vie de saint Calais (*BHL* 1569)[63] pas antérieure au IXe siècle[64], ainsi qu'à *BHL* 880[65]. *BHL* 882 apparaît alors comme une copie presque mot pour mot de *BHL* 880 au sein de laquelle l'auteur inséra divers éléments connus sur le saint puisés dans d'autres récits comme la Vie anonyme de saint Mesmin (*BHL* 5814) et la Vie de saint Lubin (*BHL* 4847). Cette dernière Vie représente l'état le plus avancé de la légende de saint Avit. Reste la question de la datation.

Le dossier hagiographique du saint a récemment été repris par B. Auernheimer partant du principe que l'analyse des structures syntaxiques peut éclairer la datation des textes. Selon son

---

été écrite dans la première moitié du IXe siècle, et la Vie d'Almire dont l'auteur semble avoir œuvré pour les intérêts de l'évêché du Mans, cf. le chapitre sur le diocèse du Mans, par L. Trân Duc, *supra*. Parmi les compagnons d'Avit, on trouve aussi saint Viâtre (*BHL* 8551) qui aurait vécu au VIe siècle. Selon Poncelet (1905) la Vie semble écrite après la Vie d'Avit et celle de Calais, donc entre le IXe siècle et le premier quart du XIe siècle, car il a été utilisé par l'auteur de la Vie de Lié écrite à l'époque d'Odolric d'Orléans (1021-1035/36).

[60] Picard (1992), p. 92-93.

[61] Les Bollandistes ont identifié deux témoins: le manuscrit Paris, BnF, lat. 12606 et le manuscrit Vatican, Reg. lat. 585, du XIe siècle, qui contient également les Vies de saint Mesmin et de saint Aignan, ce qui suggère une origine orléanaise.

[62] *AASS*, Iun. III, 1701, p. 350, n. 2.

[63] Poncelet (1905), p. 53.

[64] Poncelet (1905), p. 17.

[65] *Vita s. Aviti IV* (*BHL* 882), c. 6.

étude, *BHL* 882 serait une réécriture carolingienne – et non une œuvre du XIe siècle comme il l'a été dit – dont l'auteur aurait corrigé et augmenté un texte plus ancien écrit dans une langue qui n'est plus acceptable du point de vue d'un auteur du IXe siècle.

B. Saint Mesmin[66]

Étroitement lié au dossier hagiographique de saint Avit, celui de saint Mesmin est entièrement constitué à l'époque carolingienne. En effet, les deux premières Vies du saint, l'une rédigée par un moine Bertold (*BHL* 5817)[67], l'autre par un auteur anonyme mais sans aucun doute moine de l'abbaye de Micy (*BHL* 5814-5816), ont toutes les deux été écrites successivement au cours du IXe siècle. La Vie de saint Mesmin *BHL* 5817, dédicacée à l'évêque Jonas († 843), a donc été rédigée dans les années 820-830, au temps de l'abbé Heiric (v. 828-842) sous la direction duquel les reliques des fondateurs furent déposées à Micy. Selon cette *Vita*, Jonas organise la translation des restes des trois abbés, Mesmin l'Ancien (le fondateur), Théodemir et Mesmin le Jeune. Le récit de cette translation termine l'œuvre de Bertold qui, par la suite, sert de modèle aux textes suivants. Bertold entend relater la Vie du saint fondateur de son monastère tout en exaltant les origines de sa fondation, les donations royales ainsi que les différents saints qui l'ont fréquenté voire même dirigé. À cette fin, il utilise clairement les Vies de saint Calais (*BHL* 1569)[68] et de saint Avit (très probablement *BHL* 880).

---

[66] Le dossier hagiographique de saint Mesmin a été récemment réouvert lors du séminaire d'Anne-Marie Turcan-Verkerk autour de Charles Vulliez et de Gisèle Besson qui préparent actuellement une nouvelle édition et traduction des Miracles de saint Mesmin par Létald.

[67] *Vita s. Maximini* (*BHL* 5817), *AASS OSB*, I (1668), p. 591-597. Tous les témoins de ce texte ne comportent pas le prologue en vers dans lequel Bertold se nomme en toutes lettres. En effet, Létald, qui écrit à la fin du Xe siècle à Micy semble utiliser une Vie sans ce prologue: *Bertoldum quoque virum eruditissimum, qui vitam veterem patris Maximini dicitur edidisse*; cf. Poncelet (1905), p. 46.

[68] Poncelet (1905), p. 47-50.

La Vie anonyme (*BHL* 5814-5816)[69] est dédicacée au roi dans un poème qui exalte l'action de Clovis. Cette entrée en matière confirme les enjeux de l'écriture avancés par Bertold: faire de Micy une fondation royale et encourager le roi à continuer l'œuvre de Clovis. Si les objectifs sont semblables et les textes quasi identiques, se pose alors la question des raisons qui ont pu présider à la rédaction de deux Vies.

Ces deux textes, sous prétexte de relater la Vie de leur saint patron, ont clairement pour objectif d'asseoir l'ancienneté de l'abbaye et ses origines prestigieuses ainsi que de retracer son histoire jusqu'au moment de sa (re)fondation par l'évêque Théodulfe d'Orléans et Benoît d'Aniane.

Pour autant, seul le texte de l'hagiographe anonyme (*BHL* 5814-5816) célèbre ouvertement ce moment; dans la Vie écrite par Bertold, il n'est question que de l'évêque Jonas. Notons que l'œuvre de Bertold étant dédicacée à l'évêque Jonas, il aurait été mal venu d'y mettre en avant l'œuvre de Théodulfe, son prédécesseur accusé de trahison et emprisonné jusqu'à sa mort en 820[70]. La vie anonyme, en revanche, met en avant l'action de Théodulfe. Selon Claire Tignolet, la vie anonyme, dédiée à un roi – vraisemblablement Charles le Chauve –, serait une réécriture de la Vie de saint Mesmin motivée par la volonté de mettre en avant l'action réformatrice de Théodulfe et, par là-même, de réhabiliter la mémoire de cet évêque, à une époque où il était possible de le faire – après la mort de Louis le Pieux et de Jonas.

La diffusion des deux *Vitae* est également très différente. En effet, si l'on ne conserve que deux témoins de la Vie écrite par Bertold, on en recense plus d'une douzaine pour la Vie anonyme dont la plupart provient de la région orléanaise: la Vie *BHL* 5817 est donc très rapidement supplantée par sa réécriture, *BHL* 5814-5816.

Par la suite, dans la seconde moitié du Xe siècle, le dossier hagiographique du saint est augmenté d'un recueil de Miracles

---

[69] *Vita s. Maximini II* (*BHL* 5814-5816), *AASS OSB*, I (1668), p. 580-591.

[70] TIGNOLET (2013). Théodulf d'Orléans est accusé de trahison, en 818, au moment de la révolte de Bernard d'Italie contre Louis le Pieux. Tombé en disgrâce, il est déposé et emprisonné. Il meurt probablement en 820, trop tôt pour bénéficier de la grâce générale décrétée en 821. C'est Jonas qui, dès 818, lui succède sur le siège épiscopal d'Orléans.

(*BHL* 5820) rédigé par un moine de Micy, Létald[71]. Les Vies de saint Mesmin – et plus tard, le recueil de Miracles écrit par Létald – participent à la mise en place d'un réseau de sainteté autour de l'abbaye de Micy et qui rayonne dans tout l'espace ligérien[72].

C. Saint Liphard

Selon sa *Vita* (*BHL* 4931)[73], après avoir occupé un poste dans la magistrature d'Orléans, Liphard embrasse une carrière ecclésiastique qui le porte à la vie érémitique. Il se retire à Meung avec son compagnon Urbicius où ils construisent une cellule. L'évêque d'Orléans l'autorise alors à fonder un monastère avec une église à l'endroit où s'élevait sa cellule[74]. Il meurt peu après et Urbicius devient le deuxième abbé de l'église de Meung-sur-Loire; la tradition locale veut que des vestiges conservés au bord de la Maure correspondent à cette première construction. Au IXe siècle, une communauté monastique est installée. L'écriture de la Vie de saint Liphard peut donc être mise en relation avec cette fondation dont l'église est dédiée à saint Liphard[75].

L'auteur de la Vie de saint Liphard, certainement un moine de Saint-Liphard, utilise plusieurs traditions issues d'autres récits hagiographiques pour forger son héros[76]. Il a recours à de nombreux *topoï* tel que l'attaque d'un serpent et d'un dragon, de nombreux miracles de guérison, et une relation quasi filiale avec son disciple, thème qui devint fréquent dans les récits hagiographiques relatifs à l'abbaye de Micy: Mesmin est le mentor de Théodemir, Avit, Viâtre...[77]

Les enjeux de l'écriture sont clairement exposés par l'auteur dans le prologue: «si je ne suis pas capable moi-même de l'imi-

---

[71] à propos de la datation du texte et de l'identification de Létald, cf. Vulliez (2012).

[72] Vulliez (2018).

[73] *Vita s. Liphardi* (*BHL* 4931) éd. J. Mabillon, *AASS OSB*, I (1668), p. 154-157.

[74] Mesqui (2014), p. 3-5.

[75] Mesqui (2014), p. 3.

[76] Head (1996), p. 38. C'est le même procédé dans l'œuvre de Bertold (*BHL* 5817) où il utilise les Vies de saint Avit et de saint Calais.

[77] Head (1996), p. 110.

ter, au moins je rends accessible par écrit ce qui doit l'être »[78]. Il s'agit là d'une *causa scribendi* classique dans la littérature hagiographique mais l'auteur va bien plus loin: il propose au lectorat et à la postérité un récit mettant en valeur la fondation ancienne de sa communauté et son lien spirituel avec la prestigieuse abbaye de Micy tout juste réformée – Liphard n'est pas un moine de Micy mais reçoit la vision de la mort de l'abbé Théodemir et participe à l'élection de Mesmin le Jeune. En effet, la référence à l'action épiscopale – c'est sur l'accord de l'évêque que Liphard fonda son monastère – et cette relation avec Micy pourraient trouver un sens plus politique si l'on considère, avec A. Poncelet, que cette Vie date du début du IXe siècle[79]. En effet, à ce moment, le comte Matfrid d'Orléans semble jouir de la possession du monastère Saint-Liphard de Meung[80]. Cependant, le monastère semble dépendre de l'évêché d'Orléans, puisque Théodulfe le compte parmi les monastères *quae nobis ad regendum concessa sunt* cédés par Charlemagne en personne[81]. Matfrid et Théodulfe, vivement opposés sur le plan politique, s'affrontent également lors de revendications de possessions et de droits. Le monastère de Meung-sur-Loire, place stratégique sur la Loire, a été âprement disputé entre le comte Matfrid et l'évêque Théodulfe durant le premier tiers du IXe siècle. Cette lutte a pu motiver les moines, favorables à l'évêque, soit pendant, soit juste après, à réaffirmer les origines anciennes de leur communauté et le rôle de l'évêque dans sa fondation.

Cette Vie a connu une diffusion relativement importante puisque les Bollandistes en recensent onze témoins dont les deux plus anciens sont datés du Xe siècle[82]. Le dossier hagiographique de Liphard est par la suite augmenté d'un recueil de

---

[78] *Vita s. Liphardi* (BHL 4931), c. 1: *si quem ipse imitari nequeo, reliquis imitandum patefacio scribendo.*
[79] PONCELET (1905), p. 90.
[80] Sur le comte Matfrid d'Orléans, voir en premier lieu DEPREUX (1994).
[81] DEPREUX (1994), p. 348-349. Par la suite, Charles le Chauve confirme à l'évêque d'Orléans la possession de biens restitués par Louis le Pieux après la révolte de 828.
[82] *BHL*ms: Chartres, BM 193 (507 5/B), fol. 173v-175v; Vatican, Reg. lat., 318, fol. 195v-199r.

Miracles (*BHL* 4932)[83] qui daterait du XIIe siècle et d'un récit de translation de 1104 (*BHL* 4933)[84].

D. L'œuvre d'Adrévald de Fleury

L'abbaye de Fleury, Saint-Benoît-sur-Loire, n'est pas en reste au sein de cette production hagiographique orléanaise. En effet, c'est à cette période qu'Adrévald de Fleury commença un recueil consacré aux Miracles de saint Benoît[85] qui est à la fois historiographique et hagiographique.

Ce recueil est composé de neuf livres écrits par cinq auteurs, tous moines de Fleury, entre le IXe et le XIIe siècle. Le livre I, dû à Adrévald (qui écrit vers 865), fait suite au récit de la translation des reliques de saint Benoît et est suivi d'un appendice de deux chapitres rédigés par son confrère Adelier. Après un intervalle d'un siècle, Aimoin reprend la rédaction des *Miracula* dans les premières années du XIe siècle et rédige les livres II et III. Après sa mort, vers 1010, l'œuvre est poursuivie par son confrère André, qui en rédige les livres IV à VII. Un livre VIII fut ensuite l'œuvre de Raoul Tortaire qui écrit dans la seconde moitié du XIe siècle et le début du XIIe (il est mort en 1122). Enfin le livre IX est l'œuvre d'Hugues de Sainte-Marie au cours du XIIe siècle. Ces neuf livres ne sont pas un simple recueil de Miracles qui se contenterait de relater les miracles accomplis par saint Benoît mais, comme pour l'œuvre de Létald, il s'agit d'une œuvre complexe mêlant politique et récit miraculeux. Cela témoigne d'une grande porosité entre nos différentes catégories de

---

[83] *Miracula s. Lifardi* (*BHL* 4932), *AASS OSB*, I (1668), p. 159-164. Les Bollandistes ne recensent pour ce texte qu'un seul manuscrit daté du XVIe siècle (Köln, HA, W. 261, fol. 19v-20r). Selon C. VULLIEZ (1994, p. 93), ce recueil de *Miracula* est difficile à dater sauf pour le dernier miracle qui serait l'œuvre de Bernard de Meung, un contemporain de l'évêque d'Orléans Manassès de Garlande (1146-1185); les précédents miracles pourraient avoir été mis par écrit au moment de la translation des reliques du saint et de la dédicace de l'église de Meung, le 14 octobre 1104.
[84] *Translatio s. Lifardi* (*BHL* 4933), *AASS OSB*, I (1668), p. 157-159. Un seul témoin de ce texte a été recensé: Köln, HA, W. 261, fol. 19v-20r.
[85] Une édition critique des *Miracula sancti Benedicti*, avec traduction française, vient de paraître sous la direction d'A. DAVRIL (2019).

classifications des sources, notamment dans la stricte distinction entre chronique, histoire et hagiographie[86].

Le recueil s'ouvre sur le récit de la translation des reliques de saint Benoît (*BHL* 1117)[87], récit qui tend à montrer que saint Benoît avait lui-même voulu le transfert de ses restes depuis le Mont-Cassin jusqu'aux rives de la Loire. Il suffit pour s'en convaincre de relire le discours qu'Adrévald prête à l'abbé Médon lorsque l'évêque de Rouen, Rémi, frère naturel de Pépin-le-Bref, se présenta au monastère avec la mission de prendre les reliques de saint Benoît pour les restituer au Mont-Cassin, conformément à la demande du pape Zacharie. «[...] Mais s'il lui plaisait, par suite de nos péchés, de quitter les Gaules et de regagner son pays natal, je le déclare clairement, c'est à lui de le manifester et je ne veux pas que nous y fassions obstacle d'aucune façon[88].» Et de fait, saint Benoît manifesta clairement sa volonté de demeurer à Fleury car, à peine l'évêque Rémi avait-il pénétré dans la basilique Notre-Dame où étaient conservées les reliques de saint Benoît, que lui et son entourage furent frappés de cécité[89].

Fermement attaché aux reliques du saint, Adrévald continue son récit dénonçant les exactions que subissent les moines de saint Benoît, d'autant que le IXe siècle est marqué par des tensions entre le comte d'Orléans et l'abbaye. Pour exemple, Adrévald livre le récit d'affrontements et de disputes opposant, au temps de Louis le Pieux, le comte et les moines dont saint Benoît fut le défenseur[90]. Le monastère de Fleury, comme l'ensemble de ses biens sont la propriété personnelle du saint, aussi lorsqu'une bande de soldats pillards s'apprête à s'emparer d'un troupeau de bovins «destiné à servir aux nécessités quotidiennes des frères», ils sont immédiatement châtiés. Adrévald conclut: «il retourne vers les siens et proclame partout ouvertement qu'il y a en ce lieu une vertu divine particulière et que personne ne restera sans punition s'il a molesté saint Benoît en quelque chose». Comme ces exemples le montrent, Benoît est défenseur

---

[86] DAVRIL (2001).
[87] *Historia translationis s. Benedicti* (*BHL* 1117), éd. E. DE CERTAIN, *Les miracles de Saint Benoît*, Paris, 1858, p. 1-14.
[88] *Miracula s. Benedicti* (*BHL* 1123), éd. E. DE CERTAIN, *Les miracles de Saint Benoît,* Paris, 1858, p. 15-83 (I, c. 16, p. 40).
[89] *Ibid.*, I, c. 17, p. 41-42.
[90] Parmi plusieurs exemples voir *Miracula s. Benedicti*, I, c. 20, p. 47-50.

efficace qui permet à Fleury de se développer notamment aux dépens de la puissance publique[91].

Nous pourrions multiplier les exemples tant l'enjeu principal de l'œuvre est là: affirmer le patrimoine et les privilèges de saint Benoît et de sa communauté. Le cas de ce recueil de Miracles comme une arme aux mains des moines n'est pas un cas isolé dans le royaume carolingien[92] C'est par ailleurs, les mêmes procédés que nous retrouvons sous la plume de Létald dans les Miracles de saint Mesmin visant là encore à défendre les possessions et les privilèges de l'abbaye[93].

Conclusion

La période carolingienne (750-950), surtout le IXe siècle, est une période florissante pour les communautés religieuses qui se développent autour du culte de saints importants tels qu'Aignan, Euverte, Avit, Liphard, Mesmin, Benoît. Il s'agit de saints mérovingiens, attestés historiquement ou pas, qu'on exhume ou dont on rénove la légende, ce qui témoigne d'un grand dynamisme hagiographique au sein du diocèse, sous l'impulsion des évêques et des communautés monastiques qui cherchent à s'affirmer et à développer leur sanctoral.

Ainsi, le IXe siècle est une période de grande production hagiographique qui témoigne du dynamisme culturel et religieux, porté notamment par deux figures épiscopales importantes,

---

[91] MULLER (1987), p. 13.

[92] Si l'on sort de l'Orléanais, le récit de Translation de saint Germain de Paris est particulièrement intéressant (cf. *infra*, p. 522-525). Irminon, abbé de Saint-Germain-des-Prés, fait rédiger dans la seconde moitié du IXe siècle le récit de la translation du saint que Pépin a organisée en 755. Ce récit, accompagné de miracles, participe d'une politique affirmée de l'abbé visant à définir précisément le patrimoine de l'abbaye et de réaffirmer, dans certains cas, sa domination. En effet, Irminon est également à l'origine de la composition d'un polyptyque recensant un très grand nombre de domaines ainsi que les hommes qui en dépendent. Dans ce cas, nous avons une complémentarité entre entreprise administrative et hagiographique. Exemple développé dans CAILLAUD (2016), p. 476-480. Pour d'autres exemples, voir BRUAND (2014).

[93] CAILLAUD (à paraître).

Théodulfe et Jonas[94]. Qu'il s'agisse de nouvelles fondations ou de refondations, ces communautés se dotent alors d'un sanctoral important qu'ils animent par l'écriture ou la réécriture de leur légende pour apporter la preuve des origines anciennes et prestigieuses de leur communauté et la puissance de leur saint patron. La période suivante n'est pas moins riche: Létald compose les Miracles de saint Mesmin, les moines de Fleury poursuivent les Miracles de saint Benoît, les moines de Micy continuent de se préoccuper des saints de tout l'Orléanais et au-delà[95].

Bibliographie

Auernheimer, B., «Étude de cas: proposition d'une méthode de datation de la Vie de saint Avit fondée sur l'analyse syntaxique», in M. Heinzelmann – C. Veyrard-Cosme – M. Goullet (éd.), *L'hagiographie mérovingienne à travers ses réécritures*, Ostfildern, 2010, p. 287-321.

Bruand, O., «Entre temps mérovingiens et post carolingiens: l'hagiographe avocat, défense des temporels et protection des réseaux de pouvoirs», in F. Laurent – L. Mathey-Maille – M. Szkilnik, éd., *Des saints et des rois. L'hagiographie au service de l'histoire*, Paris, 2014, p. 61-79.

Brunhölz, F., *Histoire de la littérature latine du Moyen Âge*, II: *L'époque carolingienne*, Turnhout, 1991.

Caillaud, H., *Violences hagiographiques. Discours et représentations de la violence dans les sources hagiographiques de la province ecclésiastique de Sens (V^e-XIIe siècle)*, thèse inédite sous la direction de P. Depreux, et St. Patzold, soutenue en 2016 à l'Université de Limoges.

—, «La production hagiographique dans le diocèse d'Orléans (IVe-XIIe s.)», in P. Martin (coord.), *PCR La cathédrale Sainte-Croix d'Orléans (Loiret). Site 45234025 AH. Rapport 2017*, SRA Centre-Val-de-Loire, Orléans – Grenoble, janvier 2018, p. 67-71.

—, «L'abbaye de Micy et le pouvoir épiscopal au prisme de l'hagiographie. Construction et déconstruction du discours hagiographique (IXe-XIe siècle)», in A. Massoni – N. Deflou-Leca, dir., *Évêques et communautés religieuses dans le royaume de France et ses marges*

---

[94] Jonas d'Orléans est aussi l'auteur d'une *Vita sancti Hucberti* (BHL 3994) et d'une Translatio (BHL 3995) écrite pour honorer une commande venant des moines d'Andage, au diocèse de Liège.

[95] Cette production a fait l'objet d'une synthèse par T. Head dans *Hagiographies*, I (1994); voir aussi Head (1990).

(*816-1563*). *Stratégies politiques, enjeux, confrontations*, Actes du colloque organisé à Grenoble les 10-12 mai 2017, à paraître.

CORNET, B., «La fête du 3 mai», *Revue belge de philologie et d'histoire*, 30 (1952), p. 837-848.

CUISSARD, C., «Les premiers évêques d'Orléans, examen des difficultés en présentant leurs actes», *Mémoires de la Société archéologique et historique d'Orléanais*, 21 (1886), p. 1-299.

DAVRIL, A., «Un monastère et son patron», *Cahier de recherches médiévales*, 8 (2001), p. 43-55.

—, éd., *Les Miracles de saint Benoît* (*Miracula sancti Benedicti*), textes édités, traduits et annotés par A. DAVRIL – A. DUFOUR – G. LABORY, Paris, 2019.

DIESENBERGER, M., «Der Cvp 420: die Gemeinschaft der Heiligen und ihre Gestaltung im frühmittelalterlichen Bayern», in M. HEINZELMANN – C. VEYRARD-COSME – M. GOULLET, éd., *L'hagiographie mérovingienne à travers ses réécritures*, Ostfildern, 2010, p. 219-248.

DIERKENS, A., «*Carolus monasteriorum multorum eversor et ecclesiasticarum pecuniarum in usus proprios commutator?* Notes sur la politique monastique du maire du palais Charles Martel», in J. JARNUT – U. NONN – M. RICHTER, éd., *Karl Martell in seiner Zeit*, Sigmaringen, 1994, p. 277-294 (Beihefte der Francia, 37).

DUCHESNE, L., *Fastes épiscopaux de l'ancienne Gaule*, II: *L'Aquitaine et les lyonnaises*, 2e éd., Paris, 1910.

HEAD, T., «Letaldus of Micy and the Hagiographic Traditions of Selles-Sur-Cher», *AB*, 107 (1989), p. 393-414.

—, *Hagiography and the cult of saints. The Diocese of Orléans, 800-1200*, Cambridge, 1990.

—, «The diocese of Orléans, 950-1150», *Hagiographies*, I (1994), p. 345-357.

HEINZELMANN, M., «L'hagiographie mérovingienne: panorama des documents potentiels», in M. HEINZELMANN – C. VEYRARD-COSME – M. GOULLET, éd., *L'hagiographie mérovingienne à travers ses réécritures*, Ostfildern, 2010, p. 27-82.

LE MAHO, J., «Autour de la renaissance monastique», in M. HEINZELMANN, dir., *Livrets, collections et textes, Études sur la tradition hagiographique latine*, Ostfildern, 2006, p. 285-322 (Beihefte der Francia, 63).

MALBOS, L., «Les raids Vikings à travers le discours des moines occidentaux. De la dénonciation à l'instrumentalisation de la violence (fin VIIIe-IXe siècle)», *Hypothèses* (2012), ⟨hal-01484789⟩.

MESQUI, J., «L'église de Saint-Liphard et la tour Manassès de Garlande à Meung-sur-Loire», dans *Bulletin monumental*, 172 (2014), p. 3-46.

Muller, F., «Les formes du pouvoir en Orléanais (814-923)», *Bulletin de la Société archéologique et historique de l'Orléanais*, 78 (1987) p. 7-26.

Picard, J.-C., «Orléans» dans Id., éd., *Topographie chrétienne des cités de la Gaule, des origines au milieu du VIIIe siècle*, VIII: *La province ecclésiastique de Sens (Lugdunensis Senonia)*, Paris, 1992, p. 81-95.

Poncelet, A., «Les saints de Micy», *AB*, 24 (1905), p. 5-104.

Renaud, G., «Les traditions de l'Église d'Orléans sur ses saints évêques Euverte et Aignan. Vie, miracles, culte», in *Annuaire 1972-1973 de l'EPHE*, 1973, p. 745-756.

—, «Les miracles de saint Aignan», *AB*, 94 (1976), p. 245-274.

—, «Vie et miracles de saint Aignan, évêque d'Orléans (V^e-XIe s.)», *Bulletin de la Société archéologique et historique de l'Orléanais*, 49 (1979), p. 83-110.

Tignolet, C., *«Exsul et exsul erat», Théodulfe (Vers 760-820/821): parcours biographique*, thèse sous la direction de Régine Le Jan, soutenue à l'Université Paris I en 2013.

Van der Straeten, P., «Vie arrageoise de saint Léonien, abbé à Vienne en Dauphiné», *AB*, 90 (1972), p. 110-116.

Vulliez, C., «Le miracle et son approche dans les recueils de «miracula» orléanais du IXe au XIIe siècle», dans *Miracles, prodiges et merveilles au Moyen Âge*, Orléans, 1994, p. 89-113 (Actes des congrès de la SHMESP).

—, «Des concurrents sérieux aux hagiographes fleurisiens. Culte des saints et productions hagiographiques à l'abbaye de Saint-Mesmin-de-Micy (fin X^e – début XIe siècle)», in A. Dufour – G. Labory, dir., *Abbon, un abbé de l'an mil*, Turnhout, 2008, p. 369-388.

—, «Les *Miracula sancti Maximini* de Létald de Micy: prolégomènes à une nouvelle édition», in M. Coumert – M.-C. Isaïa – K. Krönert – S. Shimahara, Rerum gestarum scriptor. *Histoire et historiographie au Moyen Âge. Hommage à Michel Sot*, Paris, 2012, p. 623-636.

—, «"Réseau de sainteté" et réseau cultuel d'une abbaye ligérienne, Saint-Mesmin de Micy, au Moyen Âge», in C. Senséby, dir., *L'écrit monastique dans l'espace ligérien (Xe-XIIIe siècle)*, Rennes, 2018, p. 255-270.

Werner, M., *Der Lütticher Raum in frühkarolingischer Zeit: Untersuchungen zur Geschichte einer karolingischen Stammlandschaft*, Göttingen, 1980, p. 184-196 (Veröffentlichungen des Max-Planck-Instituts für Geschichte, 62).

L'activité hagiographique à Paris à l'époque carolingienne (env. 750-950)

par

Klaus Krönert*

Introduction: Paris à l'époque carolingienne.
I. Saint-Germain-des-Prés. – A. Contexte historique. – B. Le martyrologe d'Usuard. – C. Des textes rédigés par des auteurs anonymes. – 1. *Translatio et Miracula sancti Germani episcopi Parisiaci anno 756* (BHL 3472-3473).– 2. Réécriture et continuation des récits de miracles de la *Translatio et Miracula sancti Germani sp. Parisiaci anno 756* (BHL 3474-3476). – 3. *Rhythmi* (BHL 3470, 3471, 3477) – 4. *Translatio sancti Germani espiscopi anno 845* (BHL 3479). – 5. *Vita et Miracula Turiani* (BHL 8342, 8343). – C. Les textes attribués à Aimoin. – 1. *Translationes an. 845, 857-863 et Miracula, auctore Aimoino* (BHL 3480). – 2. *Inventio et translatio beati Vincentii levitae et martyris* (BHL 8644-8645). – 3. *Carmen de translatione sancti Vincentii* (BHL 8646). – 4. *Translatio sanctorum Cordubensium martyrum Georgii atque Aurelii* (BHL 3409). – 5. *Translatio Savini martyris* (BHL 7450). – D. La *Vita Droctovei* rédigée par Gislemar (BHL 2336).
II. Sainte-Geneviève. – A. *Vita I^a Genovefae* (recension A), modèle des hagiographes carolingiens de sainte Geneviève (BHL 3335). – B. Les réécritures de la *Vita Genovefae*. – 1. *Vita Genovefae*, recension C (BHL 3336). – 2. *Vita Genovefae*, recension B (BHL 3334). – 3. *Vita Genovefae*, recension D (BHL vacat). – 4. *Vita Genovefae*, recension E (BHL 3338). – C. *Miracula Genovefae* (BHL 3341, 3342).
III. Textes parisiens dont le lieu exact de la rédaction n'a pas pu être identifié. – A. Textes carolingiens. – 1. *Marcellus: Vita II^a* (BHL 5249). – 2. *Justinus: Passio* (BHL 4579), *Passio rhythmica* (BHL 4580) et *Translatio Corbeiam anno 891* (BHL 4581). – 3. *Vita sancti Meredici et translatio a. 884* (BHL 5875-5876). – 4. *Chlodoaldus ou Chlodovaldus: Vitae I^a-II^a* (BHL 1732-1733). – B. Textes dont la datation est incertaine. – 1. *Translatio sancti Maglorii* (BHL 5147). – 2. *Aurea abb. Parisiis, Sermo de Vita* (BHL 814-

---

* Je remercie ici très chaleureusement Michèle Gaillard et Anne-Marie Helvétius pour leurs conseils, qui m'ont permis de mener cette recherche à bien, ainsi que Guy Philippart qui m'a communiqué des précieuses informations sur des manuscrits.

817). – 3. *Passio* en l'honneur d'*Agoardus, Aglibertus et soc. mm. Christolii in agro Parisiensi* (BHL 168).
BIBLIOGRAPHIE.

INTRODUCTION
PARIS À L'ÉPOQUE CAROLINGIENNE

Après la mort de Dagobert, la dynastie mérovingienne a connu un lent déclin qui l'a menée à la perte du pouvoir et à l'avènement des Carolingiens en 751 ; en conséquence, le Paris de l'époque carolingienne est souvent présenté comme une ville ayant perdu beaucoup de son importance, car la nouvelle dynastie et l'aristocratie dominantes étaient majoritairement originaires des régions de la Meuse et de la Moselle. Ainsi, le centre de gravité du royaume s'est-il déplacé de la Seine moyenne vers l'Austrasie, et ce furent d'abord Metz et, ensuite, Aix-la-Chapelle qui devinrent les nouveaux centres de pouvoir[1]. En réalité, Paris restait une ville de premier plan, comme le montrent les grands conciles qui y furent organisés en 825 et en 829. Ensuite, dans la seconde moitié du IXe siècle, la ville fut une cible privilégiée pour les Scandinaves, qui l'ont attaquée à plusieurs reprises. Pendant toute cette période, y compris lors des moments sombres, la cité s'est illustrée par une riche production hagiographique dans ses abbayes *intra* et *extra muros* à laquelle est consacré ce chapitre[2].

Outre les textes écrits à Saint-Germain-des-Prés et à Sainte-Geneviève, quelques écrits ne peuvent, pour l'instant, être attribués à un centre précis mais ont toutes les chances de provenir de l'un des établissements religieux de Paris de l'époque. Saint-Germain-des-Prés est en effet, et de loin, le centre de production hagiographique le plus actif de Paris à la fin du haut Moyen Âge. À côté des auteurs anonymes, plusieurs hagiographes de cette communauté sont connus par leur nom – Usuard, Aimoin et Gislemar – et les héros des textes ne sont pas uniquement les saints patrons – Germain et Vincent –, comme l'attestent le martyrologe d'Usuard, les écrits relatifs aux martyrs d'Espagne que le monastère a fait venir, la Vie du

---

[1] Cf. SOHN (2012), p. 27.
[2] La production hagiographique des monastères de Chelles et de Saint-Denis sera présentée dans le prochain volume d'*Hagiographies*.

premier abbé de la communauté, Droctovée, ainsi que, peut-être, une commande extérieure, la *Translatio Savini*. C'est aussi dans l'hagiographie germanopratine que les raids normands ont laissé le plus de traces. Dans les autres monastères – Sainte-Geneviève et peut-être aussi Saint-Marcel, Saint-Cloud et Saint-Éloi – l'écriture hagiographique s'est concentrée sur un saint particulièrement important pour la communauté, généralement le saint patron. Dans la cathédrale seule, un ou plusieurs auteurs ont encore écrit, semble-t-il, des textes relatifs à plusieurs saints, les anciens évêques de Paris Marcel et Justin et peut-être l'abbesse Aure et l'abbé Médéric. Cette vue d'ensemble de la production hagiographique parisienne contribuera donc à réévaluer l'importance de Paris à l'époque carolingienne.

I. Saint-Germain-des-Prés

A. Contexte historique

Les origines de l'abbaye Saint-Germain-des-Prés remontent au VIe siècle: Childebert Ier († 558) avait fait construire une basilique consacrée à saint Vincent afin d'y être enterré. Le patronage de l'église est certainement lié à l'expédition du roi en Espagne en 541, mais il est très peu probable que Childebert ait reçu, à ce moment-là, une relique de Vincent de Saragosse – sa robe –, comme le *Liber historiae Francorum*, du VIIIe siècle, veut le faire croire. L'évêque consécrateur de l'église fut Germain, qui a dirigé le diocèse de Paris entre 555 et 576 et qui y fut enterré, à l'extérieur de la basilique, sous un portique. Saint-Vincent accueillit plusieurs autres tombes royales de sorte qu'elle remplaça Saint-Geneviève comme principale nécropole mérovingienne, avant de céder sa place à Saint-Denis, après la mort de Dagobert († 639). Dans la deuxième moitié du VIIe siècle, Saint-Vincent devint un monastère, et il semble qu'à cette époque le patronage de Germain fût associé à celui de Vincent. C'est ce qui entraîna, en 756, la translation des reliques de l'évêque de Paris à l'intérieur de l'abbatiale[3]. Le monastère royal fut désormais désigné sous le nom de Saint-Germain. Richement doté – nous dispo-

---

[3] Cette translation est le sujet des textes *BHL* 3472 et *BHL* 3474.

sons d'un polyptyque rédigé sous l'abbatiat d'Irminon (811-829) –, il fut alors confié à des hommes aussi influents et proches du pouvoir qu'Hilduin, qui y exerça l'abbatiat entre 829 et 841. Puis, à partir de 845, les vikings assiégèrent Saint-Germain à plusieurs reprises. Détruite et incendiée en 845, en 857 et en 861, puis restaurée, l'abbaye fut encore pillée, saccagée et brulée par d'autres groupes vikings lors du siège de Paris de 885-886, célèbre grâce au récit d'un des moines de Saint-Germain, Abbon. Lors de cette période, la communauté fut contrainte de s'exiler au moins deux fois – de 845 à 846 et de 857 à 863 – et elle ne parvint à reconstruire l'abbaye qu'à la fin du Xe siècle. Malgré ces troubles, la production hagiographique germanopratine resta très riche durant toute la période carolingienne[4].

B. LE MARTYROLOGE D'USUARD

L'œuvre hagiographique la plus connue réalisée à Saint-Germain-des-Prés est un travail atypique qui, par sa globalité, nécessite d'être présenté ici en premier lieu, sans respecter l'ordre chronologique de la genèse de l'ensemble du corpus germanopratin. Il s'agit du martyrologe d'Usuard qui est aujourd'hui très bien connu grâce au travail monumental de dom Jacques Dubois, qui l'a édité de façon critique, à partir du manuscrit Paris, BnF, lat. 13745, sur lequel nous serons appelé à revenir[5].

Relativement peu connu, Usuard était moine, diacre et prêtre à Saint-Germain-des-Prés. Il a intégré cette communauté au plus tard au début des années 840, comme le prouve une liste de frères rédigée à ce moment-là, et il est mort un 13 janvier, sans doute en 877 ou très peu de temps après. En 858, il fit un voyage en Espagne en compagnie d'un autre moine de sa communauté, Odilard, pour récupérer, avec l'appui de Charles le Chauve, des reliques de saint Vincent à Valence. Ce périple ne lui a pas permis d'obtenir le corps convoité mais il n'est pas revenu les mains vides: lors du voyage, décrit par son élève Aimoin dans la *Translatio sanctorum Cordubensium martyrum Georgii*

---

[4] Pour les débuts de l'histoire de Saint-Germain-des-Prés, cf. DUVAL – PÉRIN – PICARD (1992), p. 119-122 et RIBADEAU-DUMAS (1958).

[5] DUBOIS (1965) et (1978), p. 45-56; BRUNHÖLZL, II (1992), p. 116 et 573; AIGRAIN (2000), p. 62-63; DUBOIS – LEMAITRE (1993), p. 116-117.

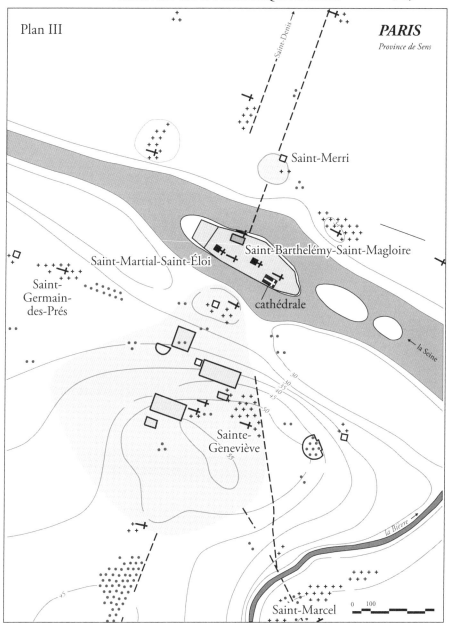

Les églises de Paris

Plan d'après F. PRÉVOT, M. GAILLARD et N. GAUTHIER (éd.), *Topographie chrétienne des cités de la Gaule des origines au milieu du VIIIe siècle, Quarante ans d'enquête, 1972-2012*, XVI, 2: *Christianisation et espace urbain: atlas, tableaux, index*, Paris, De Boccard, 2014, p. 650.

atque Aurelii (BHL 3409)[6], qui le conduisit aussi à Cordoue et à Tolède, il a obtenu des reliques de trois autres martyrs[7]. Il est fort probable qu'Usuard a également enseigné à l'école de son monastère: deux manuscrits du Xe siècle, de Ripoll, en Catalogne, contiennent une grammaire avec la dédicace suivante: *karissimo fratri Aimonio Usuardus conlevita et monachus*. Il est pratiquement sûr qu'il s'agit ici des deux moines de Saint-Germain-des-Prés qui se sont ensuite illustrés comme hagiographes. Le manuel, quant à lui, est destiné aux débutants: le nombre de citations est plutôt modeste, et l'ensemble de l'œuvre se veut pragmatique[8].

À la suite de ce voyage en Espagne, Charles le Chauve demanda à Usuard de rédiger un martyrologe pour «rétablir une certaine unité dans les solennités des saints», à un moment où la diversité des martyrologes existants – ceux qui sont attribués à Jérôme, à Bède, à Florus de Lyon et à Adon de Vienne notamment[9] – avait créé un certain désordre. À partir de ces modèles, Usuard a réalisé, jusqu'en 860, une vaste compilation. Si le roi a choisi Usuard pour ce travail c'est certainement parce qu'il savait qu'Usuard avait déjà commencé, vers 850, des recherches sur des martyrologes. Il était donc parfaitement préparé pour réaliser cette œuvre importante, qui nous est parvenue dans un grand nombre de manuscrits et dont l'attribution ne fait guère de doute: dans certains témoins, le martyrologe commence par une lettre-préface dans laquelle Usuard se mentionne lui-même[10].

La base de travail d'Usuard est le martyrologe de Florus de Lyon dans sa seconde recension, terminée vers 840. En effet, 572 éloges viennent directement de l'auteur lyonnais. Les lacunes des jours pour lesquels Florus n'avait pas de textes ou de fêtes à proposer furent comblées par l'hagiographe de Saint-Germain à l'aide des martyrologes de Jérôme, d'Adon de Vienne et de Wandalbert de Prüm, des emprunts à différentes Vies et Pas-

---

[6] Cf. *infra*, p. 546-550.
[7] DUBOIS (1965), p. 128-134.
[8] BRUNHÖLZL, II (1992), p. 116-117; la grammaire a été éditée par CASAS HOMS (1964), p. 77-129.
[9] Sur les martyrologes de Florus et d'Adon, cf. *infra*, «Le diocèse de Lyon», par M.-C. ISAÏA, p. 591-592 et «Le diocèse de Vienne», par A. M. BULTOT-VERLEYSEN, p. 608-610.
[10] DUBOIS (1978), p. 45.

sions et des informations qu'il avait obtenues oralement ou par d'autres voies. Pour résoudre le problème de la divergence entre ses sources quant aux dates des fêtes, Usuard a choisi de faire une confiance presque absolue au martyrologe d'Adon, qui était pour lui « le second livre de Florus »[11]. Après son voyage en Espagne, il a pris le temps d'insérer aux places adéquates différentes notices sur des saints espagnols, dont, notamment, quatorze notices de martyrs morts entre 825 et 857 et glorifiés par Euloge de Cordoue. D'autres notices reprennent des informations glanées dans les provinces qu'il a traversées lors de son voyage[12]. Ainsi l'auteur a-t-il rédigé, pour chaque fête, une notice biographique relativement succincte, mais tout de même assez fournie pour pouvoir servir lors des lectures à l'occasion des offices de matines. Dans cette perspective, beaucoup d'anciennes notices furent considérablement raccourcies et d'autres légèrement rallongées, de sorte que le martyrologe d'Usuard se caractérise par une homogénéité qui dépasse celle des autres œuvres de ce genre[13].

Le manuscrit le plus ancien du martyrologe d'Usuard est Paris, BnF, lat. 13745. Écrit à Saint-Germain-des-Prés à l'époque d'Usuard, il a parfois été considéré comme étant l'autographe de l'auteur mais la question n'est toujours pas tranchée. S'il est clairement l'archétype du martyrologe, il s'agit aussi de l'un des manuscrits les plus difficiles à étudier à cause de multiples corrections, retouches, mots grattés et parties entières poncées. On peut donc, avec vraisemblance, supposer que le fond primitif du texte est dû à un copiste anonyme et qu'Usuard a ensuite effectué des corrections de sa propre main. Hélas, comme nous ne connaissons pas, par ailleurs, l'écriture d'Usuard, cette hypothèse ne peut être irréfutable. C'est pour cette raison que dom Dubois a préféré parler du « manuscrit original d'Usuard » ; on ne peut pas non plus exclure que le texte du manuscrit ait été l'objet d'autres additions ou corrections après la mort d'Usuard[14].

La datation de l'élaboration du martyrologe d'Usuard dans la décennie 850-860 suscite des interrogations sur la méthode

---

[11] *Ibid.*, p. 47.
[12] *Ibid.*, p. 48.
[13] DUBOIS – LEMAITRE (1993), p. 116-117.
[14] DUBOIS (1978), p. 50-55.

de travail de l'hagiographe: face à la menace normande, la communauté de Saint-Germain-des-Prés a dû s'exiler à Combs-la-Ville puis à Esmans et enfin à Nogent-l'Artaud entre 857 et 863. Usuard, qui a retrouvé des frères après son voyage en Espagne en 858, a donc dû terminer son travail «hors scriptorium». Était-ce possible? Étant donné qu'une grande partie de l'œuvre était sans doute terminée et que ni le copiste, ni Usuard lui-même n'avaient encore besoin d'une grande bibliothèque, on peut facilement imaginer qu'ils ont finalisé le martyrologe lors de cet exil, dans un modeste refuge[15].

Le travail d'Usuard a connu un rapide et large succès, non seulement dans les monastères de l'ordre de saint Benoît, mais dans toutes les églises d'Occident, succès qui s'explique notamment par son homogénéité.

C. Des textes rédigés par des auteurs anonymes

1. *Translatio et Miracula sancti Germani episcopi Parisiaci anno 756 (BHL 3472-3473)*

Mort en 576 et vénéré le 28 mai, Germain nous est bien connu grâce à une Vie rédigée par son ami Venance Fortunat (*BHL* 3468). Comme nous l'avons vu, d'abord inhumé en dehors de l'église parisienne consacrée à saint Vincent, son corps fut transféré, en 756, à l'intérieur du sanctuaire. Le premier texte écrit sur lui dans le monastère de Saint-Germain porte sur cette translation et est connu sous le titre de *Translatio sancti Germani episcopi Parisiaci a*. 756 (*BHL* 3472); il est directement suivi d'une collection de trois miracles (*BHL* 3473). Ces écrits nous sont parvenus dans le manuscrit Rome, BN, Farfensis 29 (alias 341)[16], daté des années 875-925, et sont édités dans les *MGH*[17]. Selon N. Duval, P. Périn et J.-C. Picard, qui font partie des rares chercheurs à avoir travaillé sur ces récits, ils datent de la fin du VIIIe siècle[18].

---

[15] *Ibid.*, p. 50.
[16] Fol. 125v-128v.
[17] Éd. W. Levison, *MGH, SRM*, VII, Hanovre – Leipzig, 1920, p. 368-371 et 422-428.
[18] Cf. Duval – Périn – Picard (1992), p. 97-129, p. 102: *BHL* 3472-3473, écrits vers la fin du VIIIe siècle.

L'auteur anonyme de la *Translatio* (BHL 3472), sans aucun doute un moine de Saint-Germain, indique, au début de son texte, l'ancien emplacement de la tombe de l'évêque, sous un portique situé à l'extérieur de l'église et, selon la tradition, au sud de celle-ci[19]. Puis, il relate comment l'abbé du monastère, Lantfred, envisagea, vers 737, de transférer le corps de Germain, qu'il qualifiait *patronus*, à l'intérieur de l'abbatiale. Mais, choisi comme légat du roi, il fut envoyé en Aquitaine et, quand il revint douze ans plus tard, il dut d'abord rétablir la vie communautaire de ses moines, qui, entretemps, avaient négligé l'application de la règle. C'est donc en 755 – l'année suivant le sacre de Pépin III par Étienne II, comme l'auteur le précise – que Germain se serait manifesté dans une vision en faisant comprendre qu'il voulait désormais reposer derrière l'autel dédié à saint Étienne[20].

Curieusement, la translation elle-même, qui est datée par B. Krusch de 756[21], n'est pas relatée ici, et le récit passe directement aux miracles qui se sont produits auprès de la tombe de Germain: ils sont au nombre de trois et l'hagiographe les relate de façon très détaillée (BHL 3473). Le premier miracle s'est produit la même année que la translation: un jeune Italien souffrant de différents handicaps physiques, se rendit dans l'église de saint Germain, et après avoir passé une nuit auprès de la tombe, il bénéficia d'une guérison. Quand Pépin entendit cela, il fut si ému qu'il offrit un cadeau au miraculé. Mais, devenu très ingrat dans son comportement, celui-ci fut puni de cécité[22]. Le deuxième miraculé vint de l'Anjou; lui aussi handicapé par différents problèmes physiques, il se rendit à Tours où saint Martin le guérit de sa cécité, puis l'exhorta d'aller à Paris, sur la tombe de saint Germain, où l'Angevin retrouva entièrement la santé. L'hagiographe ajouta que Martin voulut ainsi mettre en valeur Germain[23]. Enfin, le dernier miracle de cette série porte encore sur un jeune homme paralysé, cette fois-ci originaire du Berry,

---

[19] *Translatio Germani* (BHL 3472), c. 1, éd. W. LEVISON, p. 422: *Etenim eum ducentis circiter vel eo amplius annis in porticu ecclesiae beati Vincentii martyris sanctum eius corpus iacuisset humatum*; à propos de l'emplacement de la tombe, cf. DUVAL – PÉRIN – PICARD (1992), p. 121.
[20] *Translatio Germani* (BHL 3472), c. 1, éd. W. LEVISON, p. 422-424.
[21] *Ibid.*, p. 370.
[22] *Miracula Germani* (BHL 3473), c. 2, éd. W. LEVISON, p. 424-426.
[23] *Ibid.*, c. 3, p. 426-427.

qui fut guéri après avoir passé une nuit auprès de la tombe du saint[24].

2. Réécriture et continuation des récits de miracles de la *Translatio et Miracula sancti Germani ep. Parisiaci anno 756* (BHL 3474-3476)

Ces deux récits – *BHL* 3472 et 3473 – ont connu, peu de temps après, une réécriture (*BHL* 3474 et 3475), qui fut complétée par l'ajout d'autres récits de miracles (*BHL* 3475 et 3476). Les textes *BHL* 3474-75 nous sont parvenus dans plusieurs manuscrits, dont le plus ancien est Vatican, Reg. lat. 581[25], datant du IXe siècle. Quant au *BHL* 3476, le manuscrit le plus ancien est Paris, BnF, lat. 5568[26], du Xe siècle. L'ensemble de ces écrits sont édités dans les *AASS*[27], et, de façon incomplète, en ce qui concerne les miracles, dans les *MGH*[28]. Selon N. Duval, P. Périn et J.-C. Picard, ils datent du IXe siècle[29], certainement d'avant 845. En effet, à partir de cette année-là, l'histoire du monastère de Saint-Germain a été fortement marquée par les raids normands, qui ne sont pas mentionnés dans ces textes, alors qu'ils sont très présents dans les écrits rédigés pendant cette période si mouvementée[30]. Ajoutons que, dans le manuscrit Paris, BnF, lat. 5568, les miracles (*BHL* 3476) précèdent immédiatement la *Translatio anno 845* (*BHL* 3479) qui a pour sujet la fuite des moines de Saint-Germain avec le corps de leur saint patron face à la menace viking ainsi que les miracles qui se sont produits à cette occasion[31].

Le début du récit de translation (*BHL* 3474) est quasi identique à son modèle et les rares modifications, toutes mineures,

---

[24] *Ibid.*, c. 4, p. 427-428.
[25] Fol. 87-106v.
[26] Sur les fol. 103-118v.
[27] *AASS*, Mai. VI, 1688, p. 788-796.
[28] Éd. G. WAITZ, *MGH*, *SS*, XV-1, Hanovre, 1887, p. 5-9.
[29] DUVAL – PÉRIN – PICARD (1992), p. 102.
[30] À une exception près, le poème rythmé sur saint Germain (*BHL* 3470, 3471, 3477).
[31] Paris, BnF, lat. 5568, fol. 103-118v: *BHL* 3476; fol. 119v-144v: *BHL* 3479; cf. aussi *infra*, p. 532-535; HEINZELMANN, *Translationsberichte* (1979), p. 115, n. 22, signale que pour l'année 845, la fête liturgique de la translation est déjà attestée.

sont exclusivement d'ordre stylistique[32]. À la fin de ce texte cependant, l'hagiographe anonyme – sans doute à nouveau un moine de Saint-Germain, peut-être l'abbé Irminon, nous y reviendrons – a ajouté un très long passage relatant, sans modèle direct et de façon détaillée, la translation de Germain elle-même[33]. Se référant à un témoignage oral de Charlemagne qui, alors âgé d'environ sept ans, aurait assisté à cet évènement avec son père, Pépin III, il rapporte comment les clercs, qui voulaient effectuer la translation, ont échoué à trois reprises[34] face à la difficulté de soulever le sarcophage: ce fut d'abord le roi, puis les évêques et enfin les moines qui n'arrivèrent pas à le déplacer. La solution est finalement venue de l'un des nobles – *optimates* – qui signala que les hommes du roi se comportaient mal sur le domaine royal de Palaiseau. Ayant appris cela, Pépin offrit ce bien au monastère[35] et il devint facile de déplacer le sarcophage dans la partie orientale de l'église[36], où il commença à dégager de fortes odeurs de sainteté de sorte que les présents pensèrent qu'il s'était fissuré, mais il n'en était rien: il s'agissait d'un miracle. Ce récit, entièrement mis dans la bouche du jeune Charlemagne, donne un indice sur les motivations de l'auteur pour réécrire cette *Translatio*. Le domaine de Palaiseau figurant dans le polyptyque de l'abbé Irminon, l'hagiographe voulait ainsi non seulement compléter l'ancien récit à qui manquait l'évènement central, la translation du corps, mais aussi confirmer la donation par Pépin de cet ancien domaine royal, au sud-ouest de Paris, qui faisait désormais partie des possessions de son monastère. C'est ce qui a conduit M. Heinzelmann à penser qu'Irminon lui-même, ou bien l'un de ses proches, a pu être l'auteur de cette nouvelle version[37].

La deuxième partie du texte, les *Miracula* (BHL 3475), reproduit assez fidèlement les trois guérisons miraculeuses telles qu'elles étaient relatées dans le texte BHL 3473, mais en en ral-

---

[32] *Translatio Germani* (BHL 3474), c. 1-2, éd. G. WAITZ, p. 5-6.
[33] *Ibid.*, c. 3-6, p. 6-8.
[34] *Ibid.*, c. 3, p. 4, où il est, pour la première fois, question d'une croix d'orfèvrerie, dont il sera encore question dans la Vie de Droctovée (cf. *infra*).
[35] *Ibid.*, c. 5, p. 5: «*Accipe*», inquit, «*o beatissime Germane, villam nostram Palatiolum cum omnibus appendicitis suis...*».
[36] *Ibid.*, c. 6, p. 7: *Ventum erat ad fossam in orientali parte huius ecclesiae, quae praeparata tantum onus expectabat suscipere.*
[37] HEINZELMANN (1979), p. 115, n. 22.

longeant à chaque fois la narration[38]. Sans autre forme de transition, l'hagiographe ajoute ensuite toute une série de nouveaux miracles dont les deux premiers notamment – en fait le quatrième et le cinquième de BHL 3475 – sont relatés avec beaucoup de détails[39]. Puis, les récits des quatre miracles suivants sont sensiblement plus brefs[40], et par la suite, l'hagiographe se contente même d'évoquer en seulement quelques mots trois autres guérisons[41]. Enfin, il termine cette série par un récit, où Martin conseille une fois de plus à un paysan de demander sa guérison à Germain[42]. Aucun de ces récits, détaillé ou pas, ne renferme des éléments susceptibles d'affiner la datation du texte, mais l'auteur – ou les auteurs car il est possible que ces récits aient été écrits au fur et à mesure que les miracles se produisaient – s'efforce de mentionner les noms propres et les régions d'origines des miraculés, ainsi que les problèmes physiques dont ils furent guéris, informations précises destinées à garantir l'authenticité du récit.

Cette collection de miracles a connu une nouvelle continuation, BHL 3476. Son début est indiqué par un très court prologue dans lequel l'auteur insiste sur le fait que de tels miracles doivent inciter le lecteur à craindre Dieu et à implorer le Seigneur et ses saints[43]. Cette collection peut être divisée en deux parties, peut-être rédigées par deux auteurs différents. D'abord, nous y trouvons sept récits de guérisons miraculeuses assez détaillés, indiquant toujours l'origine géographique des miraculés et leurs noms et attestant une ambition littéraire, certes modeste, de l'hagiographe, par exemple quand il compare le sauvetage d'un homme épargné par les flammes à l'épisode vétérotestamentaire des trois jeunes dans la fournaise[44]. Le début

---

[38] Du fait que G. Waitz ne les édite que partiellement, nous indiquons désormais les miracles selon l'édition des *AASS*. Les trois premiers miracles se trouvent dans c. II, 7-10, *AASS*, Mai. VI, 1688, p. 790-791.

[39] *Miracula Germani* (BHL 3475), c. 11-12 (4e miracle) et c. 13-15 (5e miracle), *ibid.*, p. 791-792.

[40] *Ibid.*, c. 16-18, p. 792-793.

[41] *Ibid.*, c. 18, p. 793.

[42] *Ibid.*, c. 19-20, p. 793.

[43] *Miracula Germani* (BHL 3476), c. III, 21, *AASS*, Mai. VI, 1688, p. 793: *ad Dominum Sanctosque ejus timendum rogandumque, Miracula Germani*.

[44] *Ibid.*, c. III, 21-27, p. 794-795; quant au miracle de sauvetage des flammes, cf. c. 22, *ibid.*, p. 794, et Daniel, III, 1-30.

de la deuxième partie de cette collection est marquée par un bref prologue, dans lequel l'auteur explique qu'il y aurait encore beaucoup d'autres miracles à raconter, mais qu'il préfère désormais de les énumérer très brièvement[45]. En effet, suivent quarante-neuf mentions de miracles, presque tous des guérisons physiques et, très rarement, des libérations des possédés, où l'auteur se contente de préciser, en une phrase seulement, les noms propres des bénéficiaires et les maux dont ils étaient libérés. Rien ne permet donc, dans cette partie du texte, de dater précisément ces miracles dont auraient bénéficié des personnes apparemment humbles, qui répondent aux noms répandus de Sirberga, Agembert, Ada ou Bernelinus[46]... Un très bref épilogue précisant que tout cela s'est produit après la translation du saint dans l'église, indique la fin de la collection et nous confirme en même temps que cette continuation a été bien conçue comme ajout au texte de *BHL* 3475[47]. Si ces récits de miracles suggèrent que la translation des reliques de Germain à l'intérieur de l'église a suscité un grand flux de pèlerins venus peu de temps après le transfert du corps, il est cependant plus probable que ces miracles se sont produits, en réalité, sur une période plus longue: la collection *BHL* 3476 a été écrite après les textes de *BHL* 3474 et 3475 qui, eux, datent au plutôt du début du IXe siècle, comme le suggère l'épisode de la donation de Palaiseau. *BHL* 3476 a donc sans doute été rédigé – peut-être à partir des notes prises par différents témoins – dans le deuxième quart du IXe siècle, mais avant 845, comme nous l'avons montré plus haut.

3. *Rhythmi* (*BHL* 3470, 3471, 3477)

Vers la fin du IXe siècle, un moine de Saint-Germain-des-Prés a réécrit plusieurs textes relatifs à saint Germain de Paris en mettant en vers la Vie de l'évêque écrite par Fortunat (*BHL* 3468) – la première partie d'un poème qui est répertoriée sous la cote *BHL* 3470 –, des récits de miracles, qui n'ont pas

---

[45] *Ibid.*, c. IV, 28, *AASS*, Mai. VI, 1688, p. 795.
[46] *Ibid.*, c. IV, 28-35, p. 795-796.
[47] *Ibid.*, c. IV, 35, p. 796: *Haec et alia non minus narratione digna Christus per eumdem Sanctissimum et Apostolicum virum Germanum, post videlicet sui corporis translationem, operari dignatus est qui cum Deo Patre et sancto Spiritu vivit et regnat ac nominatur Omnipotens, per innumera secula seculorum.*

de modèle – la deuxième partie de ce poème (*BHL* 3471) –, ainsi que le récit de la translation des reliques de Germain sous Pépin le Bref (*BHL* 3474) – la fin du même poème (*BHL* 3477). La *Vita sancti Germani*, des collections de *Miracula* et la *Translatio anno 756* étaient alors disponibles, en prose et en vers, dans la communauté parisienne, de sorte qu'il ne fait pas de doute que la communauté souhaita constituer, grâce à cette initiative poétique, un *opus geminum* sur son saint patron. Ces *Rhythmi* (*BHL* 3470, 3471, 3477), comme ils sont habituellement appelés, sont introduits par une préface dans laquelle l'auteur dit de façon explicite que les trois parties de l'œuvre constituent une unité, composée, par conséquent, par un seul auteur[48]. La troisième partie du poème, qui porte sur la *translatio anno 756* (*BHL* 3477), est introduite par une allocution et suivie par un bref *Carmen*, tous deux adressés au roi Eudes, ce qui permet d'être sûr que l'œuvre a été composée sous le règne de celui-ci, entre 888 et 897[49]. Il est donc possible que l'auteur du poème soit Aimoin, mort en 896 (dont il sera encore question par la suite), ou même le jeune Abbon, mort après 921, qui est connu pour avoir composé, vers 888-889, un poème sur «Le siège de Paris par les Normands»[50]. Mais étant donné qu'Aimoin et Abbon ont généralement pris soin de se mentionner comme auteur dans leurs œuvres et que ce n'est pas le cas ici[51], il est possible qu'un autre moine de la communauté pa-

---

[48] *Praefatio subnexa libris electionis Domni Odonis regis*, éd. P. VON WINTERFELD, *MGH, Poet. Lat.*, IV-1, Berlin, 1899, p. 124: 1. *Bene supra terminatis, lector constantissime, / Addam rithmum de ipsius vita pii praesulis.* (...) 3. *Hinc adiungam, sui sacri rex Pippinus corporis / Quomodo translationem digne celebraverit.*

[49] *Ibid.*, p. 132; *Incipit Praefationis alloquutio ad memoratum Domnum Odonem regem in translationem eiusdem sancti pontificis.* 1. *Credo, rex, vos delectari...*; *ibid.*, p. 136: *Carmen ad regem.* 1. *Deum semper, rex amate...*

[50] VON WINTERFELD ne pense cependant pas que l'auteur en soit Abbon; *ibid.*, p. 123: «Quis vero Fortunatum et translationem rhythmis explicuerit, ignoratur. Quod enim Gaudentius p. 8 de Abbone vel Aymoino monuit, recte ipse addidit etiam de aliis celeberrimi monasterii monachis cogitari posse; ego hoc addiderim de Abbone certe cogitari non posse. Neque tempus carminis angustioribus finibus circumscribitur quam Odonis regnum (a. 888-897), cum Kal. Ian. a. 898 Odo diem obierit».

[51] Cf. ABBON, *Le Siège de Paris par les Normands*, éd. et trad. H. WAQUET, Paris, 1942 (Les classiques de l'Histoire de France au Moyen Âge), et en particulier l'épître dédicatoire d'Abbon qui précède l'œuvre: *Abbon Scidula singularis cernui Abbonis dilecto fratri Gozlino. Cunctorum Dei plasmatum extimus et conlevita indignus Abbo*; cf. également la *Translatio Savini* (*BHL* 7450) ana-

risienne se soit ici illustré comme versificateur. Il est donc plus prudent de considérer les *Rhythmi sancti Germani* (*BHL* 3470, 3471 et 3477) comme une œuvre anonyme. Elle nous est parvenue dans un seul manuscrit, Bologne, BU, 1702, datant du XIe siècle[52], et l'édition de référence est celle des *MGH*[53]. Le mètre du poème est appelé «rythme»[54], très populaire au Moyen Âge et employé entre autres par Alcuin. À la différence des mètres antiques, il ne repose pas sur des syllabes longues et brèves, mais sur l'accent des mots. De plus, les élisions, telles qu'on les trouve chez l'hexamètre, sont abandonnées. Chaque vers se compose de deux parties. La première contient quatre pieds à deux syllabes chacun (= huit syllabes), dont l'une est accentuée et l'autre est inaccentuée. La deuxième partie est catalectique, c'est-à-dire incomplète: elle se compose également de quatre pieds à deux syllabes (toujours l'une accentuée et l'autre inaccentuée), à l'exception du dernier pied qui manque une syllabe (= sept syllabes).

Dans sa préface, composée de sept vers, l'auteur fait part de sa volonté d'ajouter aux autres textes relatifs à saint Germain une Vie et un récit de translation rythmés. La Vie rythmée (*BHL* 3470) est une assez fidèle reprise de la Vie écrite par Fortunat (*BHL* 3468)[55]: paragraphe par paragraphe, tous les événements de la Vie en prose sont ici repris et répartis en soixante-seize chapitres, comme Fortunat l'avait fait. Ainsi la Vie en vers commence également par le premier miracle du saint *ante natum* – il aurait empêché sa mère d'avorter –, et on relit, à une exception près, la totalité des miracles *in vitam* jusqu'à sa mort[56]. Le poète a même repris les miracles atypiques comme une gué-

---

lysée plus loin; dans la Translation des martyrs de Cordoue, il mentionne une autre œuvre qu'il a écrit et dans laquelle il s'est nommé.

[52] *BHL* 3470 et 3471 aux fol. 62-70; *BHL* 3477 au fol. 70v-74. Pour le manuscrit voir le catalogue dans *AB*, 4 (1924): ce manuscrit, qui séjourna à Limoges et à Rouen, n'est – chose curieuse – manifestement pas originaire de Paris.

[53] VON WINTERFELD, p. 123-136.

[54] Le poète l'indique lui-même dans son poème (*ibid.*, p. 132): 49. *Pedibus hoc carmen constat quattuor disyllabis. / Dymetrum acatalectum necnon catalecticum.*

[55] *Incipit rithmici de Vita et Miraculis beatissimi Germani Antistis, ibid.*, p. 124-130.

[56] Il manque la guérison du chapitre 55, sans doute un oubli; cf. *ibid.*, p. 128.

rison à distance à l'aide d'une lettre[57] et les quelques libérations de prisonniers[58]. Seul le dernier chapitre a connu une légère modification en rapportant une libération de prisonnier non relatée par Fortunat[59]. Le récit poétique est cependant plus condensé que la version en prose et il est suivi par ce qu'on peut appeler un complément, long de quarante-neuf vers (BHL 3471)[60]: notre poète explique d'abord que Fortunat avait omis plusieurs miracles que Germain avait réalisés avant sa mort, pour ensuite ajouter sept récits détaillés; il ne mentionne pas ses sources et, étant donné que nous n'avons aujourd'hui aucun modèle littéraire les rapportant, on peut supposer qu'il s'agissait des récits transmis oralement. Ce sont, pour l'essentiel, des miracles réalisés dans le monde rural: un sauvetage face à un serpent, des jugements lors de querelles de possession de bois et de vignes ou encore la punition d'un voleur. Seul le dernier miracle sort de ce contexte: Germain avait fait un signe de croix lors d'une consécration d'autel, signe qui aurait laissé une empreinte durant des siècles[61]. À la toute fin de cette partie, le poète indique dans un vers le mètre dans lequel il a composé son œuvre[62]. La troisième partie du Rythme, dédiée à la *Translatio anno 756* (BHL 3477)[63], est introduite, comme nous l'avons dit plus haut, par une brève allocution adressée au roi Eudes[64]. Notre hagiographe dit espérer lui faire plaisir – *delectari* – par la narration de si hauts faits, et ajoute quelques vers sur le sens qu'il faut donner aux récits de miracles. Le récit de la translation à proprement parler commence par onze vers sur l'histoire de Saint-Vincent/Saint-Germain-des-Prés, fondé par Germain suite à l'incursion du roi Childebert en Espagne, où il avait assiégé Saragosse. Ce bref rappel historique mentionne aussi la robe de saint Vincent que le roi aurait reçue à cette occasion[65] et qui est

---

[57] *Ibid.*, chap. 57.
[58] *Ibid.*, chap. 30, 61, 66, 67.
[59] *Ibid.*, chap. 76.
[60] *Incipit de certis praetermissis miraculis*, *ibid.*, p. 130-132.
[61] *Ibid.*, p. 131.
[62] *Ibid.*, p. 132; vers 49, cité plus haut.
[63] *Incipit Translatio Beatissimi Germani Praesulis*, *ibid.*, p. 133-135.
[64] *Incipit Praefationis alloquutio ad memoratum Domnum Odonem regem in translationem eiusdem sancti pontificis. 1. Credo, rex, vos delectari...*, *ibid.*, p. 132 .
[65] *Translatio beatissmi Germanis Praesulis*, 1-10, *ibid.*, p. 133.

également évoquée dans le *Liber Historiae Francorum*⁶⁶. À partir du onzième vers, notre poète reprend très fidèlement son modèle en prose, *BHL* 3474, avec, notamment, l'apparition au cours de laquelle Germain a manifesté sa volonté d'être transféré à l'intérieur de l'église et le long récit du jeune Charlemagne, ici aussi rapporté en discours direct, qui évoque, entre autres, la donation faite par Pépin du domaine de Palaiseau à Saint-Germain-des-Prés⁶⁷. Après avoir ainsi relaté la *Translatatio anno 756*, notre hagiographe se contente d'écrire que beaucoup de miracles se sont produits par la suite mais qu'il préfère se concentrer sur un seul récit transmis par Grégoire de Tours: une guérison effectuée à l'époque de Chilpéric (*BHL* 3478)⁶⁸. Un bref *Carmen* adressé à Eudes clôt cette œuvre: notre poète incite ici le roi à vénérer les saints, dont, en premier lieu, saint Germain⁶⁹. Curieusement, ce texte, écrit à la fin du IXᵉ siècle ne fait pas mention des raids normands qui ont marqué l'histoire de Saint-Germain-des-Prés dès les années 840 alors que presque tous les textes hagiographiques rédigés dans l'abbaye parisienne dans la seconde moitié du IXᵉ siècle leur accordent une place importante, comme le montrent les analyses qui suivent.

Quelle était la motivation de notre auteur pour composer ce long poème et le dédier au roi Eudes? Faute d'indication explicite de sa part, on ne peut que formuler cette hypothèse: en tant que comte, Eudes avait défendu Paris avec succès lors d'un siège normand qui avait duré pratiquement une année (885-886) et au cours duquel le monastère avait beaucoup souffert. Même si sa reconstruction n'a commencé qu'à la fin du Xᵉ siècle, sous l'abbé Morard (990-1014), l'abbaye a dû être remise en état dès la fin du IXᵉ siècle afin de permettre à la communauté de mener dignement la vie monastique. C'est certainement dans le cadre de ces premiers travaux de restauration que les *Rhythmi Sancti Germani* furent composés et dédiés à celui qui s'était avéré comme le défenseur le plus farouche de Paris et dont il valait mieux s'assurer la bienveillance.

---

⁶⁶ Cf. DUVAL – PÉRIN – PICARD (1992), p. 119.
⁶⁷ *Translatio beatissimi Germanis Praesulis*, 11-55, éd. VON WINTERFELD, p. 133-135.
⁶⁸ *Ibid.*, 56-64, p. 135.
⁶⁹ *Carmen ad regem*, 1-8, *ibid.*, p. 136.

4. *Translatio sancti Germani espiscopi anno 845* (BHL 3479)

Dès le début des années 840, les vikings ont intensifié leurs raids, et l'Empire carolingien fut constamment exposé à des attaques, de l'Elbe jusqu'à l'Aquitaine. L'année 845 est symptomatique de l'aggravation de la situation: au mois de mars, une flotte de 120 navires environ est entrée dans l'estuaire de la Seine, s'empara de Rouen et continua son raid jusqu'à Paris: Charles le Chauve ne put les empêcher d'occuper la ville ni de dévaster les monastères aux alentours. Le sort de l'abbaye Saint-Germain à cette époque nous est relaté par un texte contemporain, écrit par un auteur anonyme du monastère, la *Translatio anno 845* (BHL 3479). Face au grand nombre d'attaquants, les moines avaient préféré de quitter les lieux afin de se réfugier à Combs-la-Ville sur l'Yères (Seine-et-Marne) et n'en revenir qu'en 846[70]. C'est peu de temps après leur retour – selon Pierre Baudoin, après le printemps 849 – que l'hagiographe a décrit ces évènements, sur la demande de son abbé, Ébroin[71] dont la mort, en 854 au plus tard, nous donne le *terminus ante quem* de l'œuvre[72]. La *Translatio anno 845* nous est parvenue grâce à deux manuscrits: Paris, BnF, lat. 5568, du Xe siècle[73], et Namur, Fond de la Ville de Namur, 53, du XIIe siècle[74]. Elle est éditée, de façon lacunaire, dans les *MGH*, et de façon complète, dans les *Analecta Bollandiana*, où l'on trouve une transcription du manuscrit de Namur[75]. Souvent utilisée comme source pour les raids vikings, elle a fait récemment l'objet d'une analyse approfondie réalisée par Pierre Baudoin[76].

L'auteur de la *Translatio* a rédigé un texte qui entremêle différents sous-genres hagiographiques: récit de translation, récit de miracles, mais aussi sermon et texte historiographique. En effet, dans un bref prologue, il déclare vouloir faire connaître

---

[70] Cf. *Translatio anno 845*, c. 8, 21, éd. G. WAITZ, *MGH, SS*, XV-1, p. 12 et 15: *...ad ipsius sancti villam quae dicitur Cumbis delatum est. ...eos a propriis exulari sedibus, videlicet anno uno et duobus mensibus...*

[71] *Ibid.*, c. 1, p. 10: *...iubente Ebroino...conamur scribere...*

[72] BAUDOIN (2009), p. 158.

[73] Paris, BnF, lat. 5568, fol. 119v-144v.

[74] Namur, Fonds de la Ville de Namur. Dépôt à la Société archéologique de Namur, Cod. 53, du XIIe siècle, fol. 6-14.

[75] Éd. WAITZ, p. 10-16, et *AB*, 2 (1883), p. 69-98.

[76] Cf., par exemple, LUND (2005), p. 25-36, et surtout BAUDOIN (2009), p. 158-171.

sous forme de sermon les actes miraculeux de saint Germain et sa vertu protectrice pour les chrétiens, durant la période où le saint corps a été mis en sécurité face aux vikings[77]. Au début du récit, l'hagiographe expose le contexte de l'année 845: en cette année, la sixième du règne de Charles Chauve, l'empire, divisé en différentes parties (*varias in partes*) après la mort de Louis le Pieux, connut, à cause des péchés des hommes, une situation si grave que Dieu permit aux païens de rentrer dans les pays chrétiens. De la même façon qu'il avait fait punir les Israélites par les Babyloniens et les Égyptiens, désormais il «nous» faisait punir par les Danois[78]. Les péchés des hommes et le caractère punitif du raid normand sont par la suite constamment rappelés[79], ce qui justifie l'appellation de «sermon» bien que la suite du récit soit organisée – pour autant qu'on puisse le vérifier –, selon un plan chronologique et reprenne des événements qui sont essentiellement historiographiques et hagiographiques. En relatant de façon détaillée, avec un certain pathos, les opérations militaires qui ont permis aux Normands de prendre Rouen et d'avancer vers Paris et en expliquant pourquoi Charles le Chauve et Ébroin, l'abbé de Saint-Germain, ne pouvaient pas défendre la ville et ses abbayes – tous les deux étaient absents, le second en Aquitaine –, l'auteur explique pourquoi les moines ont décidé, sur le conseil de l'évêque, de quitter Saint-Germain en emmenant avec eux le corps de leur saint patron jusqu'à Combs-la-Ville[80]. Pendant ce temps, le saint a provoqué un certain nombre de miracles, tous relatés. À défaut du soutien des pouvoirs laïcs et ecclésiastiques, c'est le saint lui-même qui fut, d'après ce texte, l'unique défenseur de son lieu de culte parisien malgré l'absence de ses reliques[81]: trois Normands, qui avaient participé à la destruction de l'église le samedi précédant la fête de Pâques, sont morts devant l'autel de saint Étienne[82], un autre Normand, qui enfonça à treize reprises son épée dans une colonne de l'église, fut puni par un bras desséché et raide[83]. Et,

---

[77] *Translatio anno 845*, c. 1, éd. G. WAITZ, p. 10.
[78] *Ibid.*, c. 2, p. 10.
[79] *Ibid.*, c. 3, 4, 12 et 14, p. 10-13.
[80] *Ibid.*, c. 3-8, p. 10-12.
[81] Ibid., c. 15, p. 13: *Licet enim beatus Germanus absens iam corpore foret, tamen spiritu presens aderat ipsumque Dei templum protegebat.*
[82] *Ibid.*, c. 14, p. 13.
[83] *Ibid.*, c. 15-17, p. 13-14.

pour mentionner encore un troisième miracle, certains vikings furent la proie d'une crise de panique dans le monastère du fait qu'ils furent soudainement entourés d'un brouillard épais[84]. L'hagiographe insiste beaucoup dans ces passages sur les témoins grâce auxquels il a appris ces interventions divines et on comprend facilement pourquoi: comme il était avec ses autres frères à Combs-la-Ville, la crédibilité de son texte et le sérieux de son travail dépendent entièrement de ses sources[85]. Bien sûr, le retour des reliques de saint Germain et la déposition de son corps dans son ancienne tombe après une absence de quatorze mois sont également relatées avec minutie, en mêlant toujours des événements historiquement vérifiables et des faits miraculeux, qui concernent à la fois l'histoire de la communauté et l'histoire du royaume de la Francie occidentale[86]. Ainsi, apprenons-nous que les moines trouvèrent miraculeusement du vin dans leur abbaye au moment de leur retour pour être réconfortés[87]. Mais surtout, l'hagiographe détaille le sort des Normands auxquels le saint envoya l'épidémie de la dysenterie de sorte qu'ils moururent tous de façon plus ou moins épouvantable[88]. Ici, même lors de la libération du fléau viking, le salut ne semble guère être venu du pouvoir terrestre et les véritables actions politiques sont éclipsées. L'hagiographe préfère relater comment les punitions divines n'ont pas épargné les Normands les plus puissants, à commencer par le *dux* Ragnar: une fois tombé par terre et avant de mourir, il aurait crié qu'il avait été flagellé par saint Germain[89]. Quant à Horic Ier, *rex Normannorum*, il aurait ordonné de faire décapiter ceux des siens qui avaient survécu à la vengeance du saint et aurait envoyé leurs têtes aux chrétiens dans l'espoir de sauver ainsi la sienne[90]; puis

---

[84] *Ibid.*, c. 19, p. 14.

[85] Notamment le personnage de Cobbon qui fait l'objet d'une analyse détaillé de BAUDOIN (2009), p. 156-158.

[86] *Translatio anno 845*, c. 21-27-28, éd. G. WAITZ, p. 15.

[87] *Ibid.*, c. 21, p. 15.

[88] *Ibid.*, c. 19, p. 14: *Quorum corda ab illo die et deinceps ita sunt meritis et intercessione domini Germani valido pervasa timore, et ita dissenteria vel variis morborum afflicti generibus, ut quidam erorum cotidie morerentur, nullusque ex tanta populi multitudine infinitoque exercitu sese putaret evadere posse.*

[89] *Ibid.*, c. 30, p. 16.

[90] *Ibid.*, c. 31, p. 16: *Timens autem prefatus rex Normannorum, ne et ipse quemadmodum et alii morte pessima interiret, iussit omnes qui residui erant decollari eorumque capita christiano populo tradi.*

il aurait libéré tous les captifs chrétiens. Le véritable vainqueur était ainsi saint Germain[91].

Bien que la fin de l'œuvre soit indiquée par une formule finale et le terme «amen»[92], un ou plusieurs auteurs n'ont cependant pas tardé à ajouter d'autres récits de miracles attribués à saint Germain et réalisés dans l'abbaye parisienne. L'édition du manuscrit de Namur présente donc encore trois récits de guérisons, introduits par un bref prologue. Étant donné qu'ils sont repris par Aimoin dans sa réécriture de ce texte (*BHL* 3480) – daté d'entre 872 et 877 –, nous pouvons être sûr que les continuations ont été rédigées dans les années 850/860 ou, au plus tard, au début des années 870[93].

5. *Vita et Miracula Turiavi (seu Turiani*, BHL 8342, 8343)

Ce texte plus tardif concerne un saint breton, Turiau, qui est vénéré comme abbé-archevêque de Dol. Trois Vies – et sans doute une quatrième Vie perdue – ont été écrites à son sujet (*BHL* 8341-8342 et 8342d)[94]. Elles ne nous apprennent que peu de choses: le saint qu'il faudrait situer dans le VIIe-VIIIe siècle, serait né près d'un monastère fondé par saint Samson dans le *pagus* de Vallon. Très jeune, il alla à Dol où l'archevêque Tiarmaël l'adopta comme son successeur. Quelques faits miraculeux closent le récit. Ce dossier qui, dans son ensemble, fait partie de l'hagiographie bretonne, contient un double récit qui provient de Saint-Germain-des-Prés où furent transférées, probablement vers 920, les reliques de Turiau. Il s'agit de la *Vita* dite *longior* (*BHL* 8342) et des *Miracula* (*BHL* 8343) qui y sont rattachés[95]. Cette réécriture de la Vie réalisée par un moine germanopratin, reprend les mêmes éléments narratifs dans l'ordre de son modèle, *BHL* 8341. L'hagiographe connaît le lieu exact de la sépulture de Turiau à Saint-Germain et il ajoute, par rapport à son hypotexte, de nombreuses citations et réminiscences bibliques en faisant

---

[91] *Ibid.*, c. 31, p. 16.
[92] *Ibid.*, c. 31, p. 16: *...cui sit honor et potestas, decus et imperium per infinita secula seculorum. Amen.*
[93] *AB*, 2 (1883), p. 93-98.
[94] À propos de Turiau, cf. POULIN (2009), p. 355-370 et *supra*, «L'hagiographie bretonne avant l'an mil», p. 239.
[95] *Vita et Miracula Turiani seu Turiavi*, AASS, Iul. I, 1719, p. 619-625.

preuve de quelques ambitions stylistiques[96]. À la fin de la Vie, il ajoute directement, sans césure éditoriale, trois miracles de Turiau qui se sont produits à Paris et qui mettent en valeur l'efficacité du saint contre les incendies, miracles auxquels il n'a pas assisté personnellement, mais qui lui furent racontés. Le témoin unique de l'œuvre, Paris, BnF, lat. 11750, date du milieu du XIe siècle et provient de Saint-Germain-des-Prés. La Vie et les Miracles, quant à eux, ne sont certainement pas antérieurs au Xe siècle; Poulin situe leur écriture dans la première moitié du XIe siècle[97].

C. Les textes attribués à Aimoin

Moine depuis 845 environ, Aimoin († après 896) a été écolâtre et notaire à Saint-Germain-des-Prés. Considéré comme l'élève d'Usuard et le maître d'Abbon de Saint-Germain-des-Prés, il est aussi l'auteur de l'*Inventio et translatio beati Vincentii levitae et martyris ex Hispania in Castrense* (BHL 8644-8645), du *Carmen de translatione sancti Vincentii* (BHL 8646), de la *Translatio sanctorum Cordubensium Georgii, Aurelii et Nathaliae* (BHL 3409) et, peut-être, de la *Translatio Savini martyris* (BHL 7450)[98]. Toute l'œuvre d'Aimoin se caractérise par une haute valeur narrative et une prédilection pour de longues périodes dont la construction reste cependant très claire[99].

1. *Translationes an. 845, 857-863 et Miracula, auctore Aimoino* (BHL 3480)

Comme d'autres textes hagiographiques de Saint-Germain-des-Prés, la *Translatio anno 845* présentée plus haut (BHL 3479) a fait l'objet d'une réécriture, complétée pas les récits des évè-

---

[96] Poulin (2009), p. 362-363.

[97] *Ibid.* L'hagiographe est inconnu, mais François Dolbeau (2007), p. 43, a fait une observation qui suggère qu'il est peut-être identique à l'auteur de la Vie de sainte Aure: l'un comme l'autre utilise le mot rarissime *faust(issim)us/a* pour désigner le saint (cf. *Miracula Turiani*, c. 28, *AASS*, Iul. I, 1719, p. 624-625 et spécialement p. 624).

[98] Peut-être est-il aussi l'auteur du poème rythmé sur saint Germain (BHL 3470, 3471, 3477), dont il a été questionn ci-dessus.

[99] Pour Aimoin, cf. Brunhölzl, II (1992), p. 118, Saxer (2002), p. 274-282 et Silagi (1980), col. 242; *PL* 126, col. 1009-1010.

nements qui se sont produits par la suite. Intitulée *Translationes an. 845 et 857-863 et Miracula* (*BHL* 3480) et datable du milieu des années 870, après 872 et du vivant de Charles le Chauve (†877)[100], cette œuvre est issue de la plume d'Aimoin, comme il l'indique lui-même[101]. Elle nous est parvenue dans six manuscrits, dont trois datent du XIᵉ siècle: Mons, Université, Wins 4[102], Paris, BnF, lat. 12610[103] et Paris, BnF, lat. 12599[104]. Les éditions complètes les plus accessibles sont celles de Migne[105], réalisée d'après l'édition de J. Mabillon[106], et des *Acta Sanctorum*[107]. Plus récemment, ce sont surtout C. Gillmor, F. Brunhölzl et P. Baudoin, qui ont analysé cette œuvre[108].

Aimoin retrace lui-même la genèse de son travail dans une lettre introductive[109]; longtemps auparavant, selon Aimoin, Charles le Chauve avait demandé qu'on mette par écrit les hauts faits qui se sont produits lors du raid normand de 845 et l'abbé Ébroin avait alors confié cette tâche à deux moines de sa communauté dont chacun avait rédigé un texte: l'un est la *Translatio anno 845* (*BHL* 3479), l'autre est aujourd'hui perdu. Puis, plus tard, l'abbé Gauzlin (872-886) demanda à Aimoin d'en faire une seule œuvre, vraie et élégante, et celui-ci en avait profité pour rajouter le récit du deuxième exil des moines de son abbaye à Combs-la-Ville (857-863), lors d'un nouveau raid normand, et pour rapporter les miracles qui se sont alors produits[110].

---

[100] BAUDOIN (2009), p. 159-160 et HENRIET (2017), p. 111-126, en part. p. 118. Il se peut que le texte ait été rédigé à une date assez proche de la visite à l'abbaye de Charles le Chauve, de la reine Richilde et de l'évêque de Paris Ingelwin en 872, visite qui est mentionnée tout à la fin de l'œuvre (cf. *Translationes et Miracula*, Lib. II, c. 17, *AASS*, Mai. VI, 1688, p. 805).

[101] Cf. *infra*.

[102] Fol. 58r-70r.

[103] Fol. 72v-107r.

[104] Fol. 98-148v.

[105] *PL* 126, col. 1027-1050.

[106] *AASS OSB*, III-2 (1672), p. 104-118.

[107] *AASS*, Mai. VI, 1688, p. 796-805.

[108] BRUNHÖLZL, II (1992), p. 117 et 574; BAUDOIN (2009), p. 158-171; cf. également JULLIEN – PERELMAN (1994), 91 et GILLMOR (1988), p. 79-109, et GILLMOR (2001), p. 103-127.

[109] *PL* 126, col. 1027-1028.

[110] *Translationes et Miracula*, praefatio, *AASS*, Mai. VI, 1688, p. 796-797; ce second exil a été déjà évoqué *supra* dans la présentation du martyrologe d'Usuard, p. 516.

L'œuvre d'Aimoin est divisée en deux livres. Le premier reproduit le contenu de la *Translatio anno 845* (*BHL* 3479) et du texte perdu qui était consacré au même évènement; le second relate l'histoire des moines de Saint-Germain-des-Prés et les miracles auxquels ils ont assisté, jusqu'en 872. L'ensemble est écrit dans une langue très correcte, mais souvent un peu artificielle, ce qui s'explique certainement par le fait que l'hagiographe était habitué à rédiger des diplômes et des chartes[111].

Après un bref prologue insistant sur la valeur pédagogique des récits relatifs aux saints, Aimoin débute le premier livre en évoquant le contexte des années 845/846, marqué par un raid viking très dévastateur pour Rouen, Paris et leurs environs. Par rapport au texte de *BHL* 3479, on y trouve surtout quelques nouveaux miracles comme des miracles de lumière ou des visions annonçant, par exemple, le proche exil des moines lorsque les Scandinaves se rapprochèrent du monastère[112]. Il ne fait cependant pas de doute que ces passages reprennent assez fidèlement le modèle perdu: pourquoi Aimoin, qui reste, dans les paragraphes qui reposant sur le texte de *BHL* 3479, toujours très proche de sa source, aurait-il ici travaillé autrement? Il semble donc que la part originale de l'hagiographe dans ce livre soit minime et concerne seulement quelques accents, tout de même significatifs, sur lesquels nous reviendrons, ainsi que la disposition du matériel. Il modifie, par exemple, l'ordre dans lequel sont relatés le retour des moines à Paris et les punitions réservées aux Scandinaves à la fin et après leur raid[113]. Dans l'épilogue qui clôt le livre, l'hagiographe médite sur les punitions divines en rappelant, exactement comme l'auteur de *BHL* 3479, celles qu'a subies le peuple d'Israël[114].

Le second livre commence à nouveau par un bref prologue dans lequel Aimoin déclare raconter désormais les miracles qui se sont produits après le retour des moines à Saint-Germain-des-Prés, en 846[115]. En effet, on y trouve d'abord les récits de

---

[111] BRUNHÖLZL, II (1992), p. 118.
[112] *Translationes et Miracula*, Lib. I, c. 2-5, *AASS*, Mai. VI, 1688, p. 798.
[113] La mort des Normands dans les *Translationes et Miracula*, Lib. I, c. 10-13, *AASS*, Mai. VI, 1688, p. 799-800 (= *BHL* 3479, c. 20, 30 et 31); le retour des moines le 25 juillet 846 dans les *Translationes et Miracula*, Lib. I, c. 17, *AASS*, Mai. VI, p. 800 (= *BHL* 3479, c. 26, 27).
[114] *Translationes et Miracula*, Lib. I, c. 19, *AASS*, Mai. VI, 1688, p. 801.
[115] *Ibid.*, Lib. II, prologus, p. 801.

quatre interventions divines, toutes des guérisons de maux corporels[116]. Ils sont repris du récit de *BHL* 3479 où ils étaient ajoutés à la fin de l'œuvre, certainement par un ou plusieurs continuateurs, comme nous l'avons montré plus haut[117]. À partir du chapitre 5 seulement, Aimoin écrit en tant qu'auteur indépendant[118]. Il débute ce passage en expliquant que les Normands sont revenus quelques années plus tard – en fait depuis 856 – afin de «nous» affliger des punitions méritées. Le corps de Germain dut donc à nouveau être transféré dans son exil à Combs-la-Ville, évènement qui est daté de 857[119]. La suite du livre est essentiellement consacrée aux récits de miracles dont ont profité des malades, des handicapés et des possédés. Certaines interventions divines ont aussi comme toile de fond les Normands, par exemple un sauvetage de quelques frères qui ont osé célébrer Pâques à Paris dans l'abbaye Saint-Germain et qui ont miraculeusement échappé à une attaque viking[120]. Dans la deuxième moitié du livre nous apprenons enfin, de façon très factuelle, comment le corps du saint a été d'abord transféré à Esmans, puis à Nogent l'Artaud avant d'être ramené dans son abbaye parisienne[121]. Lors du retour, beaucoup d'autres miracles se sont produits et, pour montrer la joie que le retour du saint a provoquée, Aimoin a intégré à cet endroit un long hymne en son honneur[122]. Ce passage se termine par un paragraphe consacré à la mise au tombeau du saint, à l'endroit exact où il avait reposé avant son exil, à la datation précise de cet évènement, 863, et à la mention de la visite de Charles Chauve, de la reine Richilde et de l'évêque de Paris Ingelwin dans l'abbaye, visite qui est censée s'être produite en 872[123].

La mise en parallèle du texte d'Aimoin avec son modèle et l'analyse de la partie originale permettent de mieux saisir l'intention dans laquelle il a rédigé son œuvre: en plaçant désor-

---

[116] *Ibid.*, Lib. II, c. 1-4, p. 801-802.
[117] Seul le quatrième miracle de cette série ne se trouve pas dans le manuscrit de Namur 53, mais il ne fait pas de doute qu'Aimoin l'a également repris d'un modèle.
[118] BAUDOIN (2009), p. 167.
[119] *Translationes et Miracula*, Lib. II, c. 5, *AASS*, Mai. VI, 1688, p. 802.
[120] *Ibid.*, Lib. II, c. 10, p. 803.
[121] *Ibid.*, Lib. II, c. 11-13, p. 804.
[122] *Ibid.*, Lib. II, c. 14, p. 804.
[123] *Ibid.*, Lib. II, c. 17, p. 805.

mais la partie qui repose sur le texte de *BHL* 3479 sous le double patronage de l'abbé et du roi – l'auteur anonyme n'avait parlé que de l'abbé Ébroin comme commanditaire[124] – et en «oubliant» de préciser que, lors de l'attaque de 845, ni le roi, ni l'abbé n'étaient à Paris[125], il accorde à Charles le Chauve un rôle plus actif et plus positif que l'auteur du texte *BHL* 3479; ainsi l'action politique trouve-t-elle une place plus importante que dans le récit qui lui a servi de modèle. Ensuite, lorsque Aimoin fait œuvre originale, il tente aussi d'atténuer les aspects douloureux. La captivité de Gauzlin est donc passé sous silence et la fuite de la communauté, à Combs-la-Ville vers 857 puis vers Esmans et Nogent-l'Artaud, n'est que brièvement mentionnée en accordant davantage de place aux miracles qui se sont produits à ces occasions. Il ne fait pas de doute qu'Aimoin a cherché à donner une image «officielle» de la politique normande de Charles le Chauve, qui apparaît comme un roi martial, prêt à combattre. Bien sûr, saint Germain reste le héros principal, mais l'action du roi trouve ici une place qu'elle n'avait pas dans le récit de *BHL* 3479. Une telle vision prend tout son sens dans les années 872-873, quand Charles le Chauve dut faire face à une grave crise familiale et à la menace des Normands sur la Basse-Loire[126].

2. *Inventio et translatio beati Vincentii levitae et martyris* (*BHL* 8644-8645)

Aimoin est aussi l'auteur d'une œuvre intitulée *Inventio et translatio beati Vincentii levitae et martyris in monasterium Castrense an. 864, libri 2* (*BHL* 8644-8645). Il s'agit d'un récit consacré à Vincent, diacre à Saragosse et martyrisé sous Dioclétien à Valence. L'hagiographe décrit la translation du saint corps de Valence à Castres en deux livres, dont chacun a son propre numéro dans le répertoire de la *BHL* bien qu'ils représentent une unité. L'attribution du texte à Aimoin provient d'une lettre écrite par Aimoin et adressée à Bernon, abbé du monastère de Castres et commanditaire du texte, dans laquelle il évoque l'œuvre en question et se présente comme moine de Saint-Germain-des-

---

[124] BAUDOIN (2009), p. 160.
[125] *Ibid.*, p. 163.
[126] *Ibid.*, p. 168-170.

Prés[127]. La rédaction du texte date de l'an 869, comme l'a montré L. de Lacger[128]. L'œuvre a connu un grand succès comme le prouve la vingtaine de manuscrits qui nous sont parvenus[129] et dont les deux les plus anciens sont Paris, BnF, lat. 13760, du IXe siècle[130], et Vatican, Reg. lat. 490, du Xe siècle[131]. L'édition la plus répandue est celle de Migne[132], réalisée d'après le texte établi par Mabillon[133]. Parmi les analyses les plus importantes qui lui sont consacrées, il y celles de L. De Lacger[134], de P. J. Geary[135], de V. Saxer[136], de F. Brunhölzl[137] et d'A. Christys[138].

L'*Inventio et translatio Vincentii* est divisée en deux partie, dont la première (*BHL* 8644) est particulièrement captivante. Comme Aimoin le précise, l'acteur principal de la translation, Audald, lui a personnellement raconté les évènements, et de façon détaillée[139]. Ainsi, l'hagiographe rapporte qu'en 855 l'un des moines de l'abbaye de Conques, appelé Hildebert, a, lors d'une vision, entendu une voix lui demandant d'aller à Valence, sur la tombe de saint Vincent. Celle-ci avait été détruite par les païens, et il lui fallait transférer le corps dans un lieu paisible[140]. Hildebert demanda alors à un autre moine de sa com-

---

[127] *Epistola Aimoini ad Bernonem abbatis*, PL 126, col. 1011-1014: ...*domno abbati Bernonis, caeterisque sub eo fratribus, in pago Albiensi et monasterio beati Benedicti, quod Castrum cognominatur, sub eius regimine, regulari studio Deo commilitantibus, Aimoynus peccator, almi Germani Parisiorum praesulis monachorum novissimus...: quatenus adventum beati levitae et maryris Christi Vincentii ad vos ...litteris mandando posteris futurisque saeculis sciendum praeberem.*

[128] DE LACGER (1927), p. 307-358, en part., p. 307-308.

[129] La *BHL*ms a répertorié une bonne vingtaine de témoins sous le numéro de *BHL* 8644.

[130] Paris, BnF, lat. 13760, fol. 148r-187r.

[131] Vatican, Reg. lat. 490, fol. 65-71v; cf. plus loin, à propos des copies partielles de cette œuvre. Dans le *Cat. Vat.*, Poncelet ne précise pas s'il s'agit d'une copie partielle ou non.

[132] *PL* 126, col. 1011-1024.

[133] *AASS OSB*, IV-1 (1677), p. 644-651 (2e éd., p. 607-613).

[134] DE LACGER (1927), p. 307-358.

[135] GEARY (1993), p. 97-98 et 195-199.

[136] SAXER (2002), p. 257-357.

[137] BRUNHÖLZL, II (1992), p. 118 et 574.

[138] CHRISTYS (1998), p. 199-216.

[139] *Inventio et translatio Vincentii*, Lib. I, c. 2, *PL* 126, col. 1014: *Audaldus ...cuius ab ore quae dicuntur, et multo etiam ampliora nos in fide accepisse confidimus.*

[140] *Ibid.*, Lib. I, c. 1, col. 1013.

munauté, Audald, de l'accompagner et, avec l'autorisation de l'abbé Blandin et en compagnie de deux serviteurs, ils partirent; mais Hildebert, malade, dut rebrousser chemin. Arrivé à Valence, Audald a été hébergé par un Maure appelé Zacharie qui, en échange de cinq sous, lui dévoila l'emplacement de la tombe de Vincent. Une fois cette information vérifiée – Audald a finalement découvert une inscription mentionnant non seulement le nom du saint, mais aussi ceux de ses parents –, il préféra attendre la nuit suivante[141]. Dans l'obscurité et le silence nocturnes, le moine ouvrit sans difficulté la tombe, trouva un corps intacte et l'enleva – *de facto* un *furtum sacrum*[142]. Après avoir caché les reliques dans des feuilles de palmes, Audald, conforté par un miracle de lumière[143], arriva enfin à Saragosse; là, les choses se sont sérieusement compliquées: une femme, troublée de le voir prier devant un corps caché sous les feuilles, alerta le l'évêque Senior qui ordonna d'arrêter Audald et de lui ramener le mort. Il savait en effet qu'il y a longtemps un saint martyr, nommé Vincent, avait vécu à Saragosse[144]. Audald dut donc ruser: il prétendit d'abord ramener l'un de ses proches qui était mort pendant le voyage, puis, voyant que l'évêque ne lui croyait pas et sous la menace de la torture, il admit qu'il transférait un saint pour lequel il inventa le nom de Marin. Alors relâché par Senior, il rentra tristement, sans les reliques, à Conques, où personne ne le crût et où l'entrée lui fut refusée; c'est pourquoi il se rendit à Castres où la communauté l'accueillit[145]. Aimoin précise que rien ne se passa pendant huit ans et demi; il fallut l'initiative de Salomon, comte de Cerdagne[146], qui prétexta vouloir faire revenir l'un de ses proches, et un ordre du *regulus* de Saragosse, le gouverneur Abdilumar[147], un prince corruptible, pour ramener définitivement le corps de Vincent à Castres. Une délégation de la communauté de Castres, dont Audald fit partie, alla alors à nouveau à Saragosse pour rencontrer Senior,

---

[141] *Ibid.*, Lib. I, c. 2-3, col. 1014-1015.
[142] *Ibid.*, Lib. I, c. 4, col. 1015-1016.
[143] *Ibid.*, Lib. I, c. 5, col. 1016.
[144] *Ibid.*, Lib. I, c. 6, col. 1016.
[145] *Ibid.*, Lib. I, c. 7, col. 1017.
[146] *Ibid.*, Lib. I, c. 8, col. 1017.
[147] Aimoin était manifestement mal informé sur la situation politique en Espagne à cette époque, car le gouverneur était, à ce moment-là, Musa ibn Musa; cf. CHRISTYS (1998), p. 199-216.

l'évêque, et malgré de nouvelles menaces de torture, Audald ouvra la tombe dans laquelle se trouvait Vincent, enleva le corps et prépara la suite de la translation. Ici s'arrête le premier livre[148].

La second livre (*BHL* 8645) commence par un bref prologue où Aimoin annonce la suite du récit – la fin de la translation et les miracles – tout en insistant sur le fait qu'il voulait désormais être plus succinct[149]. En effet, cette partie de l'œuvre est bien plus classique: des récits de guérisons alternent avec des épisodes de voyage pour lesquels l'hagiographe prend la peine d'indiquer avec précision les lieux d'étape. Sous la conduite du comte Salomon et en passant par la ville de Balaguer et le fort de Berga, le cortège arriva ainsi en Cerdagne. Après une halte un peu plus longue, ils passèrent par Llivia et Carcassonne pour arriver enfin à Castres où il fut décidé de construire une nouvelle église accessible aux hommes et aussi aux femmes, qui avaient été exclues de l'ancien édifice[150]. C'est à ce moment-là qu'une femme mit en question l'authenticité des reliques, mais un miracle prouva qu'il s'agissait bien du corps de saint Vincent[151]. Les miracles qui se produisirent par la suite sont relativement divers: on y trouve, bien sûr, des guérisons de maux corporels, dont certaines à la suite du conseil de se rendre à Castres donné aux malades par l'évêque de Toulouse[152]. D'autres interventions divines concernent des restitutions de biens volés – par exemple une lance, déposée à l'entrée de l'église et dérobée à ce moment-là – ou des vols empêchés – comme celui de chevaux, laissés finalement sur place après la mort de l'un des malfaiteurs tombé de l'un des animaux[153]. Aimoin mentionne aussi un exil des reliques de Vincent qui furent mises en sécurité lorsque les Normands assiégèrent Toulouse[154]. Le rayonnement de saint Vincent est vite devenu supra-régional, comme l'atteste la guérison d'un homme paralysé qui a été transporté depuis Ro-

---

[148] *Inventio et translatio Vincentii*, Lib. I, c. 8, *PL* 126, col. 1017-1018: *...ad regulum saepe dictae civitatis, nomine Abdilam, chartam facere mandat.*

[149] *Ibid.*, prologue du Lib. II, col. 1018-1020.

[150] *Ibid.*, Lib. II, c. 1-4, col. 1019-1020; je remercie ici très chaleureusement Patrick Henriet qui a eu la gentillesse de m'aider pour l'identification des toponymes hispaniques.

[151] *Ibid.*, Lib. II, c. 5, col. 1020.

[152] *Ibid.*, Lib. II, c. 9, col. 1021-1022.

[153] *Ibid.*, Lib. II, c. 9, 12, col. 1021-1022, 1024.

[154] *Ibid.*, Lib. II, c. 11-12, col. 1022.

dez[155]. Ce second livre s'achève par un dernier miracle dont un sourd-muet a bénéficié et par un très bref éloge en l'honneur de Dieu, le Christ et les saints[156]. L'absence d'un épilogue était-elle destinée à encourager d'autres hagiographes à ajouter des miracles qui devaient se produire dans l'avenir? C'est peut-être pour cette raison qu'Aimoin a terminé son œuvre de façon aussi peu marquante.

S'il est clair que le récit contient certains faits vérifiables – notamment les mentions des évêques de Saragosse, Senior, et de Toulouse, Élisacher, et du comte de Cerdagne, Salomon[157] –, il ne fait pas de doute qu'il suscite un grand nombre de questions. Ainsi Castres aurait reçu les reliques si prestigieuses de saint Vincent par un simple hasard – Audald aurait très bien pu choisir un autre refuge. Or, nous savons que plusieurs monastères étaient intéressés par ses reliques. Outre Conques, Bénévent – même si celui-ci est, pour le IXe siècle, encore mal documenté –, et, bien sûr, Saint-Germain-des-Prés à Paris pouvaient également revendiquer ce corps du fait que Vincent fut pendant longtemps son premier saint patron[158]. La communauté parisienne a d'ailleurs fait un effort considérable pour obtenir ces reliques, comme l'atteste la *Translatio sanctorum Cordubensium martyrum Georgii autque Aurelii et Nathaliae* (BHL 3409). Par le manque de clarté et de transparence du récit de l'*Inventio et translatio Vincentii*, Aimoin aurait-il voulu cacher des tractations pour le saint corps entre différentes abbayes? Toujours est-il qu'il est impossible de bien comprendre ce qui s'est réellement passé dans les années 850 à 860 lors de ce transfert de reliques; nous ne pouvons que constater que l'œuvre d'Aimoin a beaucoup séduit ses lecteurs, surtout grâce à la si vivante première partie de son récit (*BHL* 8644). En effet – chose curieuse – nous avons plusieurs témoins médiévaux dans lesquels seule cette partie est copiée. Le rapport du voyage en Espagne, qui se lit par endroit comme un récit d'aventure, a manifestement plus séduit que le livre de miracles bien plus

---

[155] *Ibid.*, Lib. II, c. 16, col. 1023.
[156] *Ibid.*, Lib. II, c. 20, col. 1024.
[157] GEARY (1993), p. 195; Salomon a été nommé en 865 par Charles le Chauve gouverneur de la Marche d'Espagne qu'il venait de créer.
[158] Cf. l'excellent résumé sur les lieux de culte de saint Vincent au IXe siècle, par GEARY (1993), p. 196-197.

commun qui le suit[159]. De fait c'est le premier livre qui apporta la «preuve» que les reliques de Vincent avaient bien été transférées en Francie. Beaucoup copié et beaucoup lu donc, ce texte a servi de modèle à d'autres récits de translation du IXe/XI{e} siècles, comme les *Translationes S. Faustae, S. Maiani, S. Fidei et S. Bibani*, qui reprennent les grandes lignes de la *Translatio sancti Vincentii*[160].

3. *Carmen de translatione sancti Vincentii* (BHL 8646)

Peu de temps après, sur la demande d'un certain Theotgero, Aimoin a mis en vers l'*Inventio et translatio Vincentii* (BHL 8644-8645), comme il le dit lui-même dans une lettre[161] où il précise aussi qu'il s'agit d'une œuvre divisée en deux livres dont chacun est composé de trente hexamètres[162]. Le texte du poème, intitulé *Carmen de translatione sancti Vincentii* (BHL 8646), nous est parvenu dans le manuscrit Paris, BnF, lat. 13760, où il est copié directement après la version en prose du récit[163], et il est édité dans les *MGH*[164]. Peut-on parler d'un *opus geminum* qui a été créé par ce travail poétique? Probablement pas: les deux textes – celui en prose et celui en vers – sont inégaux, ne serait-ce que par leur longueur. Généralement négligé par la recherche, le poème est cependant pris en compte dans l'histoire de la littérature latine de Brunhölzl[165].

Chacun des deux livres est composé de trois chapitres qui portent tous des titres résumant le contenu des dix vers constitutifs du chapitre. Le premier chapitre du livre I reprend le

---

[159] Des exemples pour ces copies partielles (nous les avons repéré d'après les catalogues des Bollandistes sans avoir consulté les manuscrits nous-mêmes): Rouen, BM 1400 (U. 3), fol. 52v-53v; Rouen, BM 1379 (U. 42), fol. 180-184; Rouen, BM 1381 (U. 67), fol. 213-216, d'après le catalogue publié dans *AB*, 23 (1904), p. 129-275, qui signale pour ces manuscrits uniquement les textes BHL 8644.

[160] GEARY (1993), p. 178.

[161] *Epistola Aymoini*, éd. P. VON WINTERFELD, *MGH, Poet. Lat.*, IV-1, Berlin, 1889, p. 138. Il qualifie Theotgerus *comminister* et *laevitarum praecipuus domnus*.

[162] *Ibid.*, p. 138.

[163] Paris, BnF, lat. 13760, fol. 187-191. Les deux autres manuscrits connus datent de l'époque moderne.

[164] Éd. P. VON WINTERFELD, p. 138-140.

[165] BRUNHÖLZL, II (1992), p. 118 et 574.

voyage d'Audald en Espagne jusqu'à Valence, mais sans parler de Conques; le deuxième chapitre rappelle la découverte de la tombe grâce au Maure Zacharie; le dernier relate comment Audald a enlevé, de nuit, le corps de saint Vincent. Le premier chapitre du second livre passe plus ou moins sous silence les mésaventures d'Audald à Saragosse et à Conques pour se concentrer directement sur l'arrivé des reliques à Castres; le chapitre suivant reprend le «miracle d'authentification» – la punition par le saint d'une femme qui doutait de l'identité du saint et qui fut guérie après avoir reconnu son erreur; enfin, l'œuvre s'achève par dix vers consacrés à la déposition du saint corps derrière l'autel de saint Benoît. Étant donné que ce poème raccourcit considérablement le récit de la version en prose et qu'un grand nombre de détails est passé sous silence, le texte perd beaucoup de sa valeur narrative et est bien moins captivant que son modèle.

4. *Translatio sanctorum Cordubensium martyrum Georgii atque Aurelii* (BHL 3409)

Comme nous l'avons indiqué plus haut[166], au IXe siècle, les moines de Saint-Germain-des-Prés ont fait un effort considérable pour obtenir les reliques de saint Vincent, premier patron de la communauté. Tout à la fin de l'année 857 ou au début de l'année 858, Usuard fut envoyé en Espagne pour récupérer le corps du martyr, au moment-même où la communauté était en exil, probalement car le contexte politique semblait enfin favorable: Onfroi, un proche de Charles le Chauve, devint marquis de Gothie et gardien du *limes Hispanicus* et arriva à conclure un accord avec le gouverneur de Saragosse[167]. Pourquoi Usuard? Sans doute parce qu'il était déjà reconnu comme spécialiste des saints: durant les années 850 il était en train de mener ses recherches pour son martyrologue. Mais, comme trois ans plus tôt celle d'Audald, cette entreprise ne fut pas couronnée de succès[168]. Le voyage d'Usuard et de son compagnon ne fut pas un échec complet puisque les deux moines obtinrent d'autres reliques, celles de Georges, Aurèle et Nathalie. Cependant, le pro-

---

[166] Cf. *supra* nos analyses du martyrologe d'Usuard et des textes *BHL* 8644-8645.
[167] DUBOIS (1965), p. 129.
[168] Cf. *supra*, p. 540-545.

L'ACTIVITÉ HAGIOGRAPHIQUE À PARIS 547

logue ne parle que de Georgius et Aurelius, qui avaient subi le martyre à Cordoue en 852 et qui faisaient partie d'un groupe de quarante-huit chrétiens mozarabes exécutés par les autorités musulmanes sous la conduite d'Abd-al-Rahman II[169]. Le périple d'Usuard fut décrit par Aimoin dans un texte intitulé *Translatio sanctorum Cordubensium martyrum Georgii atque Aurelii* (*BHL* 3409) qui nous est parvenu dans le manuscrit Paris, BnF, lat. 13760, du IXe siècle[170] et est édité dans les *Acta Sanctorum* et dans la *Patrologie latine*[171]. Cette œuvre complète donc d'une certaine manière le récit de l'*Inventio et translatio Vincentii* (*BHL* 8644-8645). L'attribution se fait sans difficulté puisqu'en précisant dans le texte qu'il est l'auteur de l'*Inventio et translatio Vincentii*, l'hagiographe ne laisse aucun doute sur son identité[172]. Ce passage donne aussi un indice sur le moment de la rédaction de l'œuvre, après 869, année pendant laquelle Aimoin a écrit le texte relatif au transfert des reliques de Vincent. Dans la *Translatio sanctorum Cordubensium* (*BHL* 3409), c'est surtout le voyage en Espagne musulmane qui a attiré l'intérêt des chercheurs, comme l'attestent les travaux de dom Dubois[173], de B. de Gaiffier[174], d'A. Christys[175] et même une brève présentation faite par Brunhölzl dans son histoire de la littérature latine[176]. Ce voyage n'occupe cependant qu'une petite partie du texte, dont la majeure partie est consacrée à la translation des reliques à l'intérieur du royaume de Charles le Chauve – jusqu'à Esmans, où la communauté de Saint-Germain-des-Prés avait trouvé refuge durant les années 857 à 863 face à la menace normande –, ainsi qu'aux miracles qui se sont alors produits. La fin

---

[169] SÉNAC (2000), p. 27-28.
[170] Ce manuscrit contient la *Translatio sanctorum Cordubesnsium* (fol. 90v-147v) et l'*Inventio b. Vincentii* (fol. 148r-187r) (*AASS OSB*, IV-1 [1677], p. 644-651).
[171] *AASS*, Iul. VI, 1729, 459-469; cf. aussi *PL* 115, col. 939-960; les deux éditions sont établies d'après Mabillon, loc.cit. IV-2, Paris, 1680, p. 46-58.
[172] *Translatio sanctorum Cordubensium*, Lib. I, c. 3, *AASS*, Iul. VI, 1729, p. 460: *Sed qualiter id actum est, et quomodo a monachis monasterii beati Benedicti Albiensis post annos receptum, adque ad eundem locum translatum fuerit, in eiusdem sancti Levitae et Martyris translatione a nobis queque digestum sufficienti narration videri poterit.*
[173] DUBOIS (1965), p. 128-134.
[174] DE GAIFFIER (1937), p. 268-283.
[175] CHRISTYS (1998), p. 199-216.
[176] BRUNHÖLZL, II (1992), p. 574.

de l'œuvre consiste en un bref épilogue faisant mention d'un miracle attribué à la fois aux saints de Cordoue et à saint Germain de Paris, miracle qui a pour objectif d'attester le bon accueil fait aux nouveaux saints par le saint patron de la communauté[177]. On ne peut déterminer si ce miracle s'est produit à Esmans ou dans le monastère parisien, après le retour des moines à Paris en 863.

Cette *Translatio sanctorum Cordubensium*, texte remarquablement vivant comme la plupart des œuvres d'Aimoin, est divisée en trois livres; l'œuvre commence par une préface assez topique évoquant les nombreux miracles qui ne sont pas encore racontés, ce qui pousse l'auteur à relater ce qui s'est passé lors de la translation des martyrs de Cordoue[178]. Le premier livre a un caractère très historiographique: Aimoin commence par raconter comment, en 858 (ou peut-être peu de temps auparavant), les moines de sa communauté avaient décidé de faire venir le corps de saint Vincent de Valence du fait que les musulmans ne permettaient pas sa digne vénération et avaient désolé la ville. Avec le soutien royal, une délégation composée d'Usuard et d'Odilard se mit alors en route. Mais, lors du trajet, à Uzès, les deux moines apprirent que le corps avait déjà été transporté ailleurs – en fait à Saragosse, où il fut retenu de force par l'évêque Senior[179]. Après avoir renvoyé le lecteur à son propre récit sur la translation de Vincent à Castres, Aimoin raconte que les deux moines parisiens, qui avaient entre-temps continué leur voyage à Barcelone, décidèrent de chercher d'autres reliques; un certain Sunifrid leur apprit que des saints hommes nommés Georges et Aurèle avaient récemment subi le martyre[180]. Gardant leur nouvel objectif secret, ils poursuivirent vers Cordoue en passant par Saragosse, avec l'autorisation du gouverneur Abdilumar[181]. Une fois arrivés à destination, ils apprirent davantage de détails sur la mort de Georges et d'Aurèle grâce à une Passion écrite en

---

[177] *Translatio sanctorum Cordubensium*, Lib. III, c. 53, *AASS*, Iul. VI, 1729, p. 469: *Igitur praetermissis plurimis ponatur scribendis finis, admisso eo quo elucescat, beatum antistitem Germanum non solum de aeterno, verum et de praesenti laetari consortio... Collocatus autem ante eiusdem magni Praesulis altare, in quo superposita eorundem sanctorum Martyrum corpora servabantur, constitit...*
[178] *Ibid.*, Praefatio, c. 1, p. 459.
[179] *Ibid.*, Lib. I, c. 2-3, p. 460.
[180] *Ibid.*, Lib. I, c. 4-5, p. 460.
[181] *Ibid.*, Lib. I, c. 6-7, p. 460-461.

leur honneur par Euloge. Soutenus par un certain Léovigilde et Samson, futur abbé de Pinnamelaria, les deux moines de Saint-Germain acquirent finalement le corps complet de Georges et le corps d'Aurèle sans sa tête, ainsi que la tête de sainte Nathalie, elle aussi victime du même massacre de Cordoue en 852[182]. Le 11 mai 858, la vieille de l'Ascension, après un séjour de cinquante-six jours à Cordoue, accompagnés par des troupes de Maures[183], ils se rendirent enfin à Tolède pour rentrer ensuite en Francie en repassant par Alcala de Henarès, Saragosse, Barcelone, Gérone, Narbonne et Béziers[184].

Le début du deuxième livre consiste en quelques mots introductifs indiquant le sujet des chapitres suivants: les miracles survenus lors du transfert des reliques espagnoles de Béziers à Auxerre[185]. La *Translatio sanctorum Cordubensium* prend alors une tournure plus hagiographique, avec les récits de trois guérisons dont chacun des bénéficiaires est mentionné par nom propre[186]. Après presque deux mois – les translations sont généralement des voyages lents car ayant pour objectif d'attirer beaucoup de monde au passage – le convoi arriva à Viviers, puis poursuivit son périple jusqu'à Auxerre en passant par le Beaunois. Aimoin relate les miracles qui se sont produits en précisant toujours les noms des miraculés et les lieux des interventions des saints. Le miracle le plus original fut la restitution du pallium qu'un voleur avait enlevé des reliques hispaniques[187].

Un nouveau prologue assez bref marque le début du troisième livre, lui aussi consacré, pour l'essentiel, aux miracles réalisés par les nouveaux saints entre Auxerre et Esmans, dans le diocèse de Sens, où la communauté de Saint-Germain était alors établie. Usuard et Odilard l'ont ont enfin rejointe le 20 octobre 858[188]. Dans cette partie du texte, qui est bien plus

---

[182] *Ibid.*, Lib. I, c. 8-13, p. 461-462.
[183] Cf. aussi RÖCKELEIN (2002), p. 318, n. 430; DUBOIS (1965), p. 131-132.
[184] *Translatio sanctorum Cordubensium*, Lib. I, c. 14-16, *AASS*, Iul. VI, 1729, p. 462-463.
[185] *Ibid.*, Lib. II, c. 17, p. 463: *Hinc igitur digna gestorum ratione compellimur, quae in eadem civitate, quaeque per eos in frequenti itinere, superna agente clementia, patrata cognovimus...*
[186] *Ibid.*, Lib. II, c. 17-19, p. 463-464.
[187] *Ibid.*, Lib. II, c. 20-22, p. 464.
[188] *Ibid.*, Lib. III, c. 23, p. 464; DUBOIS (1965), p. 132-133.

longue que les deux précédentes, notre hagiographe relate une trentaine de miracles, avec, à chaque fois, le lieu exact de l'intervention et, le plus souvent possible, en donnant le nom et la *villa* d'origine du bénéficiaire. On y trouve, bien sûr, beaucoup de guérisons mais aussi des miracles de punition et deux visions. Un passage révèle même un fait surnaturel, qui se serait produit après le martyre des saints de Cordoue, et qui fut rapporté à Charles le Chauve, lequel, dans un premier temps, avait des doutes sur ces nouveaux saints: le «tyran Abdilumar» aurait laissé les corps des exécutés dans la rue afin que les animaux sauvages les dévorent mais ceux-ci ne les auraient pas touchés[189]. Aimoin précise aussi que, lors de la translation, les moines ont donné une partie des reliques au comte Eudes (le futur roi des Francs), et il évoque même une tentative de vol[190]. Le dernier miracle, que nous avons déjà évoqué, réalisé de concert par les saints de Cordoue et saint Germain, marque la fin de l'œuvre[191].

5. *Translatio Savini martyris* (BHL 7450)

Ce texte[192] est peut-être aussi issu de la plume d'Aimoin. Savin, mentionné dans le martyrologe d'Usuard[193], est considéré comme martyr au plus tard depuis la fin du IXe siècle. Selon sa Passion (*BHL* 7447) – un texte calqué sur les *topoi* des martyrs antiques et écrit au plus tard au XIe siècle, sans aucun doute après la *Translatio*, afin de stimuler le culte[194] –, il avait un frère, Cyprien, avec lequel il s'était enfui de leur ville, appelée «Amphipolis»[195], à cause des persécutions des chrétiens

---

[189] *Translatio sanctorum Cordubensium*, Lib. II, c. 51, *AASS*, Iul. VI, 1729, p. 468-469; DUBOIS (1965), p. 133.
[190] *Ibid.*, Lib. II, c. 52, p. 469.
[191] *Ibid.*, Lib. II, c. 53, p. 469.
[192] Je remercie chaleureusement Marie-Céline Isaïa, Eric Sparhubert et Cécile Treffort, dont les conseils furent fort utiles et stimulants pour la rédaction de ce paragraphe; sur les écrits relatifs à saint Savin, voir aussi la contribution d'A.-M. BULTOT-VERLEYSEN dans *Hagiographies*, VI (2014), «Hagiographie d'Aquitaine (750-1130)», p. 540-541.
[193] DUBOIS (1965), p. 266.
[194] DE GAIFFIER (1955), p. 323-341; POULIN (1975), p. 173.
[195] Selon la *Passio Savini et Cypriani*, cap I, 2, *AASS*, Iul. III, 1723, p. 193; cf. aussi le commentaire de cette Passion, *ibid.*, c. 5, p. 190: deux villes portant ce nom sont connues, en Macédoine et en Syrie.

sous l'empereur Maxime. Leur fuite fut vaine, car ils furent décapités en Gaule en un lieu nommé Cerisier – l'ancien nom de Saint-Savin – qui était alors un important *vicus* gallo-romain. Le lieu du prétendu martyre, localisé sur une hauteur au nord de Cerisier, porte aujourd'hui le nom de Mont-Saint-Savin[196]. Puis, selon la *Translatio,* à laquelle est consacrée cette notice (*BHL* 7450), les restes de Savin furent retrouvés vers la fin du VIIIe ou au début du IXe siècle et une nouvelle église, construite peu de temps après à Cerisier même – en fait, l'église qui est aujourd'hui celle de Saint-Savin-sur-Gartempe[197] – avait alors accueilli son corps. La *Translatio* est donc également le récit de fondation du monastère Saint-Savin.

L'attribution de la *Translatio* à Aimoin de Saint-Germain-des-Prés est cependant loin d'être assurée. Le principal argument pour le considérer comme auteur de l'œuvre repose sur la mention de son nom dans le titre de la préface du texte dans le manuscrit de Paris, BnF, lat. 13220, qui date du Xe siècle, copie qui est donc relativement proche de la rédaction du texte[198]. De plus, l'auteur demande, dans son avant-propos, de l'aide à «son seigneur saint Germain»[199]. Enfin, des liens entre Saint-Savin et Saint-Germain-des-Prés sont bien attestés pour l'époque carolingienne[200]. Quant aux arguments mettant en question l'attribution, il faut d'abord évoquer le fait que l'auteur de la *Translatio Savini* se désigne lui-même, toujours dans l'avant-propos, comme *presbyter* – qualité qui n'est pas attestée ailleurs pour Aimoin de Saint-Germain-des-Prés[201]. De plus, le style dans lequel ce texte est écrit, se distingue sensiblement de celui du

---

[196] *Passio Savini et Cypriani,* c. II, 29, *AASS,* Iul. III, 1723, p. 197: *...in loco, vel villa, cui prisca vetustas indiderat nomen Cirescus, ab Antiniaco villa videlicet vel vico, uno milliari*o; cf. FAVREAU, dir., *Saint-Savin* (1999), p. 11, et surtout BOURGEOIS – FAVREAU – RICHARD (2000) p. 85-105, en part. p. 92-93.

[197] Le lieu est appelé, selon la Translation, *Cerasus* et, selon la Passion, *Cirescus,* mais les deux toponymes latins désignent bien le même *vicus* de Cerisier.

[198] Paris, BnF, lat. 13220, fol. 20v: Praefatio Aimoini monachi in translationem almi Savini martyris.

[199] AIMOIN, *Translatio Savini martyris, praefatio,* c. 1, *PL* 126, col. 1051-1052.

[200] On trouve ainsi l'obit de la comtesse du Poitou Adda dans l'obituaire de Saint-Germain-des-Prés.

[201] AIMOIN, *Translatio Savini martyris, praefatio,* c. 1, *PL* 126, col. 1051-1052; cf. *supra* pour la biographie d'Aimoin.

moine parisien, comme l'a déjà remarqué Victor Saxer en notant que «leur style [celui des Actes de la translation de Savin] est plus simple que celui des ouvrages authentiques [d'Aimoin]»[202]. En effet, le lecteur de la *Translatio Vincentii* peut remarquer qu'Aimoin l'a écrite dans un latin très classique en utilisant de longues périodes oratoires et en ayant recours à une véritable mise en scène de dialogues rapportés en discours direct. En revanche, qualifier le style de l'hagiographe de la *Translatio Savini* comme 'simple' nous paraît un peu réducteur: on observe une syntaxe assez complexe, avec des ablatifs absolus recherchés, des *hyperbata* tels qu'on les trouve chez les auteurs classiques et un vocabulaire marqué par des mots rares et d'un recours aux expressions poétiques[203]. Si les styles dans lesquels les deux textes sont écrits se distinguent par le degré d'élaboration, il est clair que les deux écrits sont rédigés par un – ou des auteurs – de valeur. Sachant que les hagiographes médiévaux pouvaient, pour certains, considérablement modifier leur style[204], ce n'est pas un argument fort pour mettre en question l'attribution de la *Translatio Savini* à Aimoin de Saint-Germain-des-Prés, sans toutefois être en mesure de le prouver[205].

La préface du texte nous renseigne aussi sur le commanditaire du texte, Hubert de Saint-Savin[206]. La période de rédaction de l'œuvre peut être précisée par le fait qu'Usuard, dans son martyrologe, a qualifié Savin de confesseur tandis que l'auteur de notre *Translatio* le qualifie de «martyr, sur la foi d'une révéla-

---

[202] SAXER (2002), p. 257-357, et spécialement p. 274.

[203] À propos des mots et des expressions poétiques, cf. AIMOIN, *Translatio Savini martyris*, c. 2, 3 et 9, *PL* 126, col. 1051 et 1054: *eremi vastitate* (c. 2), *memoria volvebatur per ora* (c. 2), *longioris aevi defluxo iam spatio* (c. 2) et *remotiora silvarum* (c. 3), ainsi que, ibidem, les termes *karrale* et *mustus* (c. 9).

[204] Cf. Thiofried d'Echternach, auteur de la *Vita Irminae* écrite dans un style très simple et d'autres textes hagiographiques comme la Vie de Willibrord ou les *Flores Epitaphii*, rédigées dans un style extrêmement élaboré et complexe; cf. KRÖNERT (2003), p. 619-623.

[205] Une étude comparative des styles de toutes les œuvres attribuées à Aimoin, fondée sur des éditions scientifiques (qui manquent encore dans certains cas), pourrait éventuellement permettre de voir ici plus clair.

[206] AIMOIN, *Translatio Savini martyris, praefatio*, c. 1, *PL* 126, col. 1051-1052; Hubert de Saint-Savin n'est pas connu par d'autres textes, mais il a dû exercer son abbatiat après le célèbre abbé Dodon († 853), disciple et successeur de Benoît d'Aniane.

tion »²⁰⁷ et que la Passion le présente comme martyr. L'hagiographe de la Translation a donc rédigé son texte entre Usuard et l'auteur de la Passion, ce qui explique qu'aujourd'hui l'unanimité se fait autour d'une écriture de la *Translatio* entre le début du IXe et le Xe siècle²⁰⁸. Quant à la méthode de travail, l'hagiographe a eu recours à un témoin, comme nous le verrons dans l'analyse du texte. Le succès de la *Translatio Savini* fut manifestement très limité, car nous n'avons conservé que deux manuscrits, dont celui du Xe siècle mentionné plus haut²⁰⁹. Éditée dans la *Patrologie latine*²¹⁰, elle n'a pas beaucoup attiré l'attention des chercheurs²¹¹, sauf pour mieux comprendre les origines du monastère Saint-Savin²¹².

La *Translatio Savini maryris* commence par un rappel historique: l'hagiographe explique que lors de la période des Vandales, l'église qui abritait le corps de saint Savin est tombée en ruine et, pendant longtemps, le lieu resta complètement abandonné, jusqu'à ce que Dieu décidât que le sanctuaire devait être restauré²¹³. Un paysan s'aventura à l'endroit, désormais presque inaccessible à cause d'une végétation très dense: en cherchant l'un de ses animaux qui s'était égaré, il trouva, sans s'en rendre compte, la voûte de l'ancien sanctuaire, où l'animal était bloqué. Une fois la bête sauvée, il en parla partout²¹⁴. Bien que le lieu exact où le corps de saint Savin reposait ait été oublié depuis un certain temps, il devint alors manifeste qu'il devait se trouver là où le paysan avait retrouvé son animal²¹⁵. Un prêtre appelé Bonet décida donc de reconstruire l'église, entreprise qui fut approuvée par un miracle attribué à Savin, dont Bonet en personne fut le bénéficiaire; c'est Bonimius, le neveu du prêtre,

---

²⁰⁷ *Ibid.*, c. 10; POULIN (1975), p. 33.
²⁰⁸ DE GAIFFIER (1955), p. 329, et POULIN (1975), p. 173, préfèrent dater ce texte, de façon assez vague, d'entre le début du IXe et la fin du Xe siècle.
²⁰⁹ Paris, BnF, lat. 13220, fol. 20v-37v; le deuxième manuscrit est Arras, BM 344 (961), fol. 159-161, du XIVe siècle.
²¹⁰ *PL* 126, col. 1051-1056; corrections du texte par DE GAIFFIER (1955), p. 325-326.
²¹¹ Voir surtout DE GAIFFIER (1955), p. 323-341, et POULIN (1975), *passim*, qui se contente cependant de reprendre B. de Gaiffier.
²¹² Par exemple FAVREAU (1976), p. 9-37, FAVREAU, dir. (1999) et BOURGEOIS – FAVREAU – RICHARD (2000), p. 85-105.
²¹³ AIMOIN, *Translatio Savini martyris*, c. 2, *PL* 126, col. 1051.
²¹⁴ *Ibid.*, c. 3, col. 1051.
²¹⁵ *Ibid.*, c. 4, col. 1051-1052.

qui l'a raconté à l'hagiographe[216]. Peu de temps après[217], ayant entendu parler de Savin, un autre prêtre qualifié «clerc palatin», Badilon, également abbé de Marmoutier, décida de faire construire une nouvelle église en l'honneur de la Vierge sur un terrain qui lui appartenait, à Cerisier même. Puis il fit transférer le corps de Savin dans cette nouvelle église, la dota de riches donations et installa une communauté de clercs pour laquelle il fit construire d'autres bâtiments. Grâce à d'autres dons encore, effectués par les nobles des alentours, cette nouvelle abbaye – le monastère de Saint-Savin – devint de plus en plus grande et splendide[218]. La fin de l'œuvre d'Aimoin est consacrée à quelques miracles. Le premier de cette série prouvait que le saint n'avait pas abandonné le lieu de sa première sépulture puisque l'intervention divine se produisit sur le chemin sur lequel la translation avait eu lieu auparavant: bien qu'une charrette quittât accidentellement la route, aucune goutte de vin ne sortit des tonneaux. Une nouvelle fois Bonimius est mentionné comme garant pour ce récit: il l'aurait entendu de la bouche de son oncle Bonet[219]. Dans le dernier chapitre, l'hagiographe se contente de mentionner plus généralement quelques miracles – notamment des guérisons – qui se seraient produits au nouveau lieu de culte[220], puis, dans un très bref épilogue, il implore Savin de prier pour lui[221].

D. LA *VITA DROCTOVEI* RÉDIGÉE PAR GISLEMAR (*BHL* 2336)

Aimoin ne fut peut-être pas le dernier hagiographe à Saint-Germain-des-Prés à l'époque carolingienne. Nous possédons une Vie de saint, la *Vita Droctovei* (*BHL* 2336) qui pouvait être écrite à la fin de cette période. Droctovée est considéré comme premier abbé de la communauté germanopratine, institué dans

---

[216] *Ibid.*, c. 5, col. 1052. Bonitus s'est fait voler un cheval, qui lui fut restitué après avoir imploré Savin.
[217] L'hagiographe ne le précise pas, mais nous pouvons le supposer du fait que Bonimius et les acteurs de l'épisode suivant sont tous des contemporains d'Aimoin.
[218] AIMOIN, *Translatio Savini martyris*, c. 6-8, *PL* 126, col. 1052-1053.
[219] *Ibid.*, c. 9, col. 1053-1054.
[220] *Ibid.*, c. 10, col. 1054.
[221] *Ibid.*, c. 11, col. 1055-1056.

sa charge par saint Germain et mort vers 580. Fortunat, dans son *Carmen* IX, 11, fait mention de lui en le considérant comme disciple de Germain. La Vie qui lui est consacrée nous est parvenue dans deux copies, dont la plus ancienne se trouve dans le manuscrit Paris, BnF, lat. 11752, de Saint-Germain-des-Prés [222]. Le texte est édité dans les *Acta Sanctorum* [223] et, de façon partielle, dans les *MGH* [224]. L'auteur est un certain Gislemar qui dévoile son nom sous forme d'acrostiche dans un poème en l'honneur du saint, qui clôt le prologue. Hélas, ce Gislemar n'est pas identifié avec certitude: deux membres de la communauté portant ce nom sont attestés: d'abord, un moine sous l'abbatiat d'Ébroin, dans les années 840 [225], et ensuite un chancelier du monastère dans la deuxième moitié du XIe siècle [226]. Sans nous focaliser trop sur le nom de l'auteur – d'autres moines nommés Gislemar ont dû exister – nous pensons que la Vie de Droctovée date, au plus tôt, du Xe siècle: des textes rédigés systématiquement en prose rimée, comme c'est le cas ici, n'existent généralement pas avant 900 environ [227]. Le *terminus ante quem* est donné par le manuscrit de Paris du XIIe siècle, et N. Duval, P. Périn et J.-C. Picard proposaient ainsi le XIe siècle comme période la plus probable de l'écriture de cette œuvre [228]. Étant donné que le texte de la *Vita* est très tardif par rapport à la vie historique de son protagoniste, il a jusqu'à maintenant très peu intéressé les chercheurs. En effet, l'hagiographe ne sait presque rien de son héros malgré ses très sérieuses recherches de sources. Il reprend ainsi deux poèmes de Fortunat, dont celui cité plus haut [229], la Vie de Germain écrite par le même auteur, il connaît très bien le *Liber historiae Francorum* et sans doute aussi la Passion de saint Vincent, et il a eu recours à des diplômes trouvés

---

[222] Ce codex contient deux copies de la Vie de Droctovée: une première, sur les fol. 249r-251v, probablement du XIe/XIIe siècle, était presque effacée; c'est vraisemblablement la cause de la rédaction d'une nouvelle copie du texte au XIVe siècle, sur les fol. 252-256v.

[223] *AASS*, Mart. II, 1668, 37-40.

[224] Éd. B. KRUSCH, *MGH*, *SRM*, III, Hanovre, 1896, p. 537-543.

[225] KRUSCH, *ibid.*, p. 536, n. 3, renvoie à «Notices et documents publiés pour la société de l'histoire de France», Paris, 1884, p. 55.

[226] DUVAL – PÉRIN – PICARD (1992), p. 103 renvoient à DÉRENS (1972), p. 228-232.

[227] Par ex., LANGOSCH (1990), p. 26 et POHLHEIM (1925), p. 373-377.

[228] DUVAL – PÉRIN – PICARD (1992), p. 103.

[229] Le deuxième: FORTUNAT, *Carmen* II, 10, *De ecclesia parisiaca*.

dans la bibliothèque de son monastère[230]. Une analyse détaillée de la Vie confirme que l'auteur n'a pas trouvé de documentation spécifique sur la biographie de Droctovée: elle contient un grand nombre de passages généraux sur l'histoire du VIe siècle et beaucoup de *topoi* hagiographiques.

L'œuvre commence par un prologue dans lequel Gislemar présente Droctovée comme disciple de Germain qualifié de «notre patron» et explique que le «livre de vie» de son héros a brulé à l'époque des raids danois[231]. Un peu plus tard, il précise qu'il y eut même deux incendies[232]; étant donné que nous savons que le monastère a brulé, au moins partiellement, en 845, en 857, en 861 et en 885/886, nous ne pouvons pas déterminer de quelle catastrophe il parle ici. Évoquer une ancienne Vie perdue relève, de toute évidence, d'un *topos* hagiographique[233], à plus forte raison puisque les autres sources mentionnées sont bien réelles et encore aujourd'hui retrouvables[234]. Comme nous l'avons dit, un poème en vingt hexamètres clôt le prologue: chaque vers a sa césure après le penthémimère et chaque césure rime avec la fin de l'hexamètre. La Vie elle-même débute par un catalogue de vertus avant de révéler que Droctovée était originaire d'Autun où il fut consacré prêtre et nommé abbé du monastère Saint-Symphorien par Germain[235]. Après avoir dressé un catalogue de *topoi*, cette fois-ci sur la vie monastique parfaite menée par Droctovée, Gislemar raconte comment Childebert a fait de Germain le successeur d'Eusèbe sur le siège épiscopal de Paris[236], puis, en reprenant le *Liber historiae Francorum*, comment le roi a assiégé Saragosse. Lors de ce siège, la population aurait fait une procession avec la tunique de saint Vincent. C'est ce qui aurait attiré la bienveillance de Childebert, qui aurait par

---

[230] Cf. éd. B. Krusch, *MGH*, *SRM*, III, Hanovre, 1896, p. 536.

[231] *Vita Droctovei*, c. 3, *ibid.*, p. 538.

[232] *Ibid.*, c. 14, p. 541.

[233] Un tel texte aurait dû laisser des traces indirectes; d'autres hagiographes ont trouvé cette explication peu crédible: 1. le premier amplificateur de la *Vita Eucharii*, épilogue (BHL 2656, 2657); 2. l'auteur de la *Vita I*[a] *Paulini* (BHL 6562, 6563), prologue; 3. l'auteur de la *Vita Agritii* (BHL 178), prologue; 4 et 5. l'auteur *des Vitae II*[ae] *Paulini* et *Felicis* (BHL 6565, 6566, 2892), prologues.

[234] *Vita Droctovei*, c. 3, éd. B. Krusch, p. 538, comme Fortunat et le *Liber historiae Francorum*.

[235] *Ibid.*, c. 6, 7, p. 539.

[236] *Ibid.*, c. 10, p. 540.

la suite reçu cette relique pour l'église parisienne qu'il fit alors construire[237]. Puis, lors d'une autre expédition militaire, le roi aurait rapporté de Tolède une croix d'orfèvrerie, également destinée à son église Saint-Vincent[238]. Dans la *Translatio sancti Germani an.* 756 interpolée (*BHL* 3474), il est aussi question d'une croix en or conservée dans cette église, sans qu'on apprenne d'où elle vient[239]; la *Vita Droctovei* représente donc une nouvelle étape dans le développement de la légende, l'attribuant désormais à Childebert et en lui imputant une origine hispanique[240]. Après des descriptions de l'église Saint-Vincent, des reprises des poèmes de Fortunat et d'autres lieux communs, Gislemar rapporte comment Childebert a confié son église à Germain peu de temps avant de mourir[241]. D'autres longs passages sont ensuite consacrés aux funérailles royales[242], et c'est seulement après que l'hagiographe revient – on dirait presque, enfin – à son véritable sujet: Droctovée. Il explique comment Germain avait instauré une communauté de moines dans cette église et nommé Droctovée abbé de celle-ci, non sans préciser que cette intervention épiscopale ne pouvait servir de précédent puisque l'abbaye avait reçu des diplômes d'immunité[243]. Enfin, l'auteur précise que Droctovée est mort un 10 mars et que sa sépulture se trouve derrière l'autel de saint Germain[244].

---

[237] *Ibid.*, c. 11 et 12, p. 540, qui ont pour source le *Liber historiae Francorum*, c. 26, éd. B. KRUSCH, *MHG, SRM*, II, Hanovre, 1888, p. 284; cf. DUVAL – PÉRIN – PICARD (1992), p. 119.
[238] *Vita Droctovei*, c. 12, éd. B. KRUSCH, p. 541.
[239] *Translatio sancti Germani an* 756 (*BHL* 3474), c. 3, éd. G. WAITZ, *MGH, SS*, XV-1, p. 6.
[240] DUVAL – PÉRIN – PICARD (1992), p. 121.
[241] *Vita Droctovei*, c. 13-15, éd. KRUSCH, p. 541.
[242] *Ibid.*, c. 15-17, p. 541-542.
[243] *Ibid.*, c. 19, p. 548. L'édition de KRUSCH est ici lacunaire: l'édition des *AASS*, Mart. II, 1668, c. III, 14-15, p. 40, contient encore un éloge mettant en valeur les vertus du saint ainsi que ses facultés d'instruire les siens.
[244] *Vita Droctovei*, c. 20, éd. B. KRUSCH, p. 548 et *AASS*, Mart. II, 1668, c. III, 15, p. 40.

II. Sainte-Geneviève

D'abord sous le patronage des Apôtres, ou peut-être seulement de saint Pierre, l'abbaye Sainte-Geneviève a des origines qui remontent au début du vi^e siècle et sont liées à sainte Geneviève, native de Nanterre, qui est morte en 502. Celle-ci fut inhumée dans un oratoire en bois dans la nécropole antique installée sur la colline qui porta plus tard son nom. Ensuite, toujours sous le règne de Clovis, sa tombe a été englobée dans le périmètre d'une nouvelle basilique construite sur cette même hauteur et dédiée aux Apôtres, où son corps fut transféré depuis sa sépulture primitive. Cette basilique devint, très peu de temps après, la première église funéraire des Mérovingiens – Clovis lui-même s'y fit enterrer – avant d'être supplantée comme nécropole royale par Saint-Vincent/Saint-Germain-des-Prés et enfin par Saint-Denis ; elle accueillit aussi plusieurs conciles mérovingiens. À partir du milieu du viiie siècle environ, elle fut desservie par une communauté monastique et, au ixe siècle, les Apôtres commencèrent à partager le patronage de cette abbaye avec sainte Geneviève ; c'est seulement au xie siècle que celle-ci s'imposa comme unique sainte patronne de la communauté. Comme pour les autres abbayes parisiennes, les attaques scandinaves furent des moments particulièrement rudes pour les Génovéfains, qui sont partis à deux reprises en exil, en 845 et en 857. Ravagé lors de la grande attaque viking entre 857 et 862, le monastère ne fut reconstruit qu'au début du xiie siècle[245]. Il est aujourd'hui difficile à dire quels textes furent écrits ou commandés à Sainte-Geneviève – sa communauté est toujours très peu connue –, mais il est tout de même probable que plusieurs écrits relatifs à Geneviève en proviennent ou y furent au moins commandés.

---

[245] Cf. Duval – Périn – Picard (1992), p. 116-117 ; pour le patronage, voir Heinzelmann – Poulin (1986), p. 165.

A. Le modèle des hagiographes carolingiens
de sainte Geneviève:
la *Vita I^a Genovefae* (BHL 3335)

Sainte Geneviève († 502) est la première sainte à avoir été choisie par un roi franc, en l'occurrence Clovis, comme protectrice et accompagnatrice dans l'au-delà. Que le fondateur de la dynastie mérovingienne désirât être inhumé auprès d'elle, indique l'importance qu'elle avait acquise durant sa vie. Sainte Geneviève est aussi la première femme d'origine franque à avoir été honorée par une biographie composée seulement quelques années après sa mort, vers 520, sur la demande de la reine Clothilde, veuve de Clovis[246]. Bien que l'hagiographe, dont l'identité est inconnue, ait en recours à la Vie de saint Martin de Tours pour calquer quelques vertus épiscopales sur la sainte, le texte nous permet, notamment dans sa première partie, de saisir Geneviève en tant que personnage historique. Cette *Vita I^a* (BHL 3335), connue aussi comme recension A de la Vie, sera présentée dans un autre chapitre consacré à l'hagiographie mérovingienne, mais il convient de rappeler ici la trame narrative de l'œuvre, car elle a connu plusieurs réécritures à l'époque carolingienne[247].

Née à Nanterre, Geneviève rencontra Germain, évêque d'Auxerre, lorsque celui-ci effectua son premier voyage dans les Îles britannique (vers 430), et elle s'engagea alors à mener une vie chaste. Après la mort de ses parents, elle décida de vivre à Paris, où elle prédit que la ville ne subirait pas de dommage lors de l'attaque d'Attila (451). Alors accusée d'être une fausse prophétesse et menacée d'une condamnation à mort, elle est sauvée in extremis par Germain d'Auxerre. Ensuite, malgré la résistance d'une partie de la population, elle fait construire une basilique en l'honneur de saint Denis de Paris, pour lequel elle a une grande vénération[248]. Voilà la partie de la Vie qui présente le plus de traces historiques de la sainte. Dans la deuxième partie du texte, l'hagiographe cherche à souligner l'importance de son héroïne en relatant quelques miracles qui lui sont attri-

---

[246] Heinzelmann (2010), p. 27-82, en part. p. 62.
[247] La première Vie de Geneviève (BHL 3335) est éditée par B. Krusch, *MGH, SRM*, III, Hanovre, 1896, p. 215-238.
[248] Ce passage est relaté avec la légende clémentine (*ibid.*, c. 17).

bués – dont une résurrection à Orléans[249]. Parmi les épisodes remarquables de cette partie, il y a son voyage en Champagne, ayant pour objectif d'obtenir du blé et de sauver ainsi Paris d'une famine alors assiégé par des Francs, et un pèlerinage à la tombe de saint Martin de Tours[250]. Selon son biographe, Geneviève est morte âgée de plus que quatre-vingt ans, en 502, et elle fut d'abord inhumée dans un oratoire en bois. L'auteur termine son œuvre en précisant qu'il a écrit cette Vie dix-huit ans après la mort de la sainte et que Clovis († 511) avait commencé à construire une basilique en son honneur, travail que Clothilde, son épouse († 545), a terminé.

Ce récit existant en plusieurs versions fondées les unes sur les autres, il nous a paru nécessaire de présenter ici l'ensemble du dossier, bien qu'au moins un texte – *BHL* 3338 – ne provienne pas de Paris. Le mérite d'avoir classé ces différentes versions en cinq recensions revient à Bruno Krusch[251], dont seules les datations ont été revues depuis. Les travaux de référence à ce sujet sont ceux de Martin Heinzelmann et Joseph-Claude Poulin. Les deux chercheurs retracent aussi l'histoire érudite ayant permis d'établir les moments de rédaction de ces versions et leurs dépendances les unes des autres jusqu'aux conclusions qui représentent l'état actuel de la recherche[252]. Récemment, Marie-Céline Isaïa a fait deux nouvelles éditions des versions *BHL* 3336 et 3338 et les traductions de plusieurs textes du dossier en proposant une nouvelle datation pour la version *BHL* 3336[253].

---

[249] *Ibid.*, c. 42.
[250] *Ibid.*, c. 44.
[251] En utilisant encore l'ancienne nomenclature. Nous indiquerons par la suite la nomenclature actuelle, telle qu'elle est utilisée par HEINZELMANN – POULIN (1986), en part. p. 169.
[252] HEINZELMANN – POULIN (1988), p. 8-14; cf. HEINZELMANN (1992), p. 9-16 et également HARTMANN-PETERSEN (2007).
[253] ISAÏA – BRET (2020). Je remercie chaleureusement M.-C. Isaïa qui avait la gentillesse de me faire parvenir une version de travail de son ouvrage alors encore à paraître.

B. Les réécritures de la *Vita Genovefae*

1. *Vita Genovefae*, recension C (*BHL* 3336)

La rédaction C de la Vie de sainte Geneviève (*BHL* 3336/7) est aujourd'hui généralement considérée comme la plus ancienne réécriture de la *Vita I*$^{a\,254}$. La datation se fait à partir des manuscrits les plus anciens et du style. Les témoins les plus anciens que nous ayons conservés indiquent incontestablement une rédaction de l'œuvre durant le VIIIe siècle ou avant: Karlsruhe, Landesbibliothek, Augiensis perg. 32, du début du IXe siècle et originaire de la Reichenau[255]; et Vienne, ÖnB, Cvp 420[256], daté également du début du IXe siècle et provenant de Salzbourg. À cela s'ajoutent quelques fragments du légendaire de Wissembourg, de la fin du VIIIe ou des premières années du IXe siècle[257]. Le *terminus post quem* de la rédaction est plus difficile à déterminer: le principal argument réside dans le style. Poulin et Berschin ont ainsi remarqué que certains mots fétiches de la recension A, comme *quemadmodum*, ont disparu dans la réécriture. De même, l'hagiographe de la recension C ne prend pratiquement plus la parole à la première personne, comme l'avait fait l'auteur de son modèle. Puis, la plupart des discours directs sont désormais formulés en style indirect. Enfin, sur le plan de la syntaxe, l'auteur de la réécriture a remplacé par endroit des propositions subordonnées par des gérondifs. Berschin note aussi que l'auteur de la recension C connaissait bien les lois de l'*oratio obliqua*. C'est ce qui l'a conduit à conclure que le style est déjà influencé par la «réforme carolingienne»[258]. Heinzelmann propose ainsi une datation de la Vie dans la première moitié du VIIIe siècle[259], et, pour Berschin, ce texte prouve que le renouveau culturel sous les Carolingiens a commencé, dans certains centres, bien avant 800 et sans doute déjà

---

[254] Édition de la recension C: K. Künstle, *Vita sanctae Genovefae virginis Parisiorum*, Leipzig, 1910, p. 5-47 et Isaïa – Bret (2020).

[255] Fol. 76-80v.

[256] Fol. 131-140; sur ce manuscrit, voir Diesenberger (2010).

[257] Aujourd'hui conservés, principalement, à Hanovre, Kestnermuseum, 3959.

[258] Berschin, II (1988), p. 14; Heinzemann – Poulin (1986), p. 157.

[259] Heinzelmann – Poulin (1986), p. 155; cf. également Heinzelmann (2010), p. 27-82, p. 68, n. 180.

sous Pépin le Bref. La Vie de saint Riquier réécrite par Alcuin pour des raisons stylistiques et considérée comme premier exemple de ce genre et modèle pour d'autres, ne serait sans doute pas aussi précurseur qu'on le dit: elle aurait été précédée par d'autres œuvres composées par des auteurs anonymes et c'est ici que réside, pour le philologue allemand, l'importance de la recension C de la *Vita Genovefae*[260].

L'argument du style est cependant moins sûr qu'on pourrait le croire. En reprenant des idées déjà évoquées par la recherche ancienne, mais cette fois-ci avec une argumentation plus solide, M.-C. Isaïa invite à interpréter le style et les graphies de la recension C comme mérovingiens, avec, par endroits, des modifications introduites par des copistes carolingiens. À cela s'ajoute une autre observation: l'auteur de la Vie *BHL* 3336 emploie régulièrement et avec une maîtrise certaine le *cursus*, pratique qui a tendance à disparaître au tournant du VIe et VIIe siècles. C'est ce qui conduit M.-C. Isaïa à dater du VIe siècle cette Vie, qui serait donc écrite seulement quelques décennies après la *Vita I^a* (*BHL* 3335)[261]. La discussion pour la datation de la recension C est de ce fait rouverte.

Il reste alors la question de savoir où et pourquoi la *Vita I^a* a été réécrite. Dans l'hypothèse qui date *BHL* 3336 du VIIIe siècle, il se peut qu'un hagiographe parisien ait adapté la première Vie au style du moment. Les incertitudes sur l'installation d'une première communauté monastique dans la basilique de la future abbaye Sainte-Geneviève, dont nous savons seulement qu'elle a eu lieu au cours du VIIIe siècle, rendent cependant assez probable que le texte ait été écrit dans un autre établissement, peut-être sur la demande d'un clerc de la basilique parisienne qui abritait le corps de la sainte. Cet établissement pourrait être l'abbaye Saint-Denis, ce qui expliquerait la bonne diffusion de l'œuvre dès les années 800 dans le sud de la Germanie: Waldo († 814), abbé de Saint-Denis et de Saint-Gall,

---

[260] Ainsi, surtout: BERSCHIN, *Biographie und Epochenstil im lateinischen Mittelalter*, II (1988), p. 14. Cf. *supra*, «Alcuin hagiographe», par J.-C. POULIN, p. 152.

[261] Cf. l'introduction de *Vie de sainte Geneviève*, par M.-C. ISAÏA, dans ISAÏA-BRET.

assurait d'excellentes relations entre son monastère parisien et les abbayes du lac de Constance[262].

Il ne faut cependant pas exclure que la recension C de la *Vita Genovefae* ait été d'office écrite ou commandée pour le sud de la Germanie, ce qui expliquerait sa faible diffusion et réception en région parisienne au début du IXe siècle[263] et le fait que, durant la première moitié du IXe siècle, une nouvelle version de la Vie de la sainte parisienne a été écrite, plus vraisemblablement dans l'abbaye Sainte-Geneviève: la recension *B* (*BHL* 3334). Comme nous le verrons, cette version est relativement proche dans ses caractéristiques de la recension *C*. Aurait-il été nécessaire d'élaborer la version *B*, si la recension *C* avait été disponible à Paris?

Cependant, dans l'hypothèse d'une datation du VIe siècle de la recension *C*, on ne peut pas envisager une réécriture pour des raisons stylistiques. M.-C. Isaïa envisage donc une réécriture pour viser un nouveau public, plutôt laïc, pour lequel la *Vita I*[a] était inadaptée, peut-être pour la cour de Sigebert Ier (561-575) ou celle de Childebert II (575-595)[264]. En effet, les modifications du contenu, par rapport au modèle *BHL* 3335, quoique peu flagrantes, sont tout de même significatives: il s'agit, selon Poulin, d'omissions de passages et de condensations de la narration, qui cependant ne modifient pas l'ordre dans lequel les épisodes sont relatés. Plusieurs récits de miracles ont été ainsi complètement supprimés[265] et d'autres partiellement[266], tout comme des passages qui ne concernent qu'indirectement la biographie de la sainte[267]. L'ensemble de ces modifications

---

[262] ZETTLER (1997); HEINZELMANN – POULIN (1986), p. 155. Que le texte ait été écrit en Bavière nous paraît peu probable mais ne reste pas complètement à exclure, à cause de la provenance des manuscrits les plus anciens.

[263] *Ibid.*, p. 155.

[264] Cf. l'introduction de *Vie de sainte Geneviève*, dans ISAÏA – BRET (2020).

[265] HEINZELMANN – POULIN (1986), p. 158: les chapitres 29, 38, 47, 51, 54 et 55 de la *Vita I*[a] manquent dans la recension *C*.

[266] *Ibid.*, p. 158: les chapitres 31 et 32 de la *Vita I*[a] ont subi des coupures dans la recension *C*.

[267] *Ibid.*, p. 158: les chapitres 44 et 53 de la *Vita I*[a] manquent ou sont modifiés dans la recension *C* (44 ne concerne que saint Martin; dans 53 l'auteur de la *Vita I*[a] indique quand il a écrit son œuvre).

traduisent un désir de brièveté et de simplicité, qui est indirectement confirmé par la rareté des ajouts de l'hagiographe[268].

2. *Vita Genovefae*, recension B (BHL 3334)

La recension B de la *Vita Genovefae* (BHL 3334), écrite par un auteur anonyme dans la première moitié du IXe siècle, nous est parvenue dans vingt à trente manuscrits[269], dont les plus anciens sont Paris, BnF, lat. 17625, de Compiègne, daté de la fin du Xe siècle[270], et Rouen, BM 1381 (U. 67)[271], daté du XIe siècle et provenant de Paris comme beaucoup d'autres témoins de cette version[272].

Ces manuscrits ne nous permettent pas de dater la Vie avec précision, mais ils suggèrent que l'hagiographe était originaire de l'une des abbayes parisiennes, sans qu'on puisse déterminer laquelle avec certitude. La recension B a été éditée par Kohler en 1881[273]. La datation du texte se fait donc essentiellement à l'aide du style, désormais clairement influencé par la «réforme carolingienne» au point que Berschin parle d'un travail typique de grammairien. L'hagiographe a notamment remplacé les termes rares ou peu précis et les mots trop abstraits de son modèle, la recension A – il ignorait manifestement la version C –, par un vocabulaire plus courant et plus concret[274]. Le *terminus ante quem* se détermine par rapport à la version D, qu'elle précède, et à la recension E, qu'elle précède également et qui est datée, de façon assez sûre, de l'extrême fin des années 860.

La volonté de l'hagiographe de la version B d'adapter le latin de la *Vita I*[a] à l'idéal de son temps semble d'ailleurs avoir été l'une des motivations les plus importantes de l'auteur, car ses changements de contenu sont minimes: tout en restant très fidèle à son modèle, il s'est contenté de condenser et de supprimer quelques passages. Seule la suppression quasi totale du para-

---

[268] *Ibid.*, p. 161: chap. 27 dans la *Vita I*[a] et 22 dans la recension C, où l'hagiographe a, par exemple, précisé la destination de quelques négociateurs: *Germania*.

[269] HEINZELMANN (1992), p. 14.

[270] DOLBEAU (2000), p. 351-352.

[271] Fol. 37-42.

[272] HEINZELMANN (1992), p. 11.

[273] Éd. C. KOHLER, *Étude critique sur le texte de la Vie latine de sainte Geneviève de Paris*, Paris, 1881, p. 5-47.

[274] BERSCHIN, II (1988), p. 14; HEINZELMANN – POULIN (1986), p. 154.

graphe 17 de la version *A* pourrait révéler une intention politico-religieuse, comme l'a souligné Heinzelmann: dans ce passage, il est question de la légende clémentine selon laquelle saint Denis de Paris aurait été ordonné et envoyé en Gaule, où il subit le martyre, par le pape Clément. L'auteur de la version *B* se contente ici d'évoquer Denis et ajoute seulement les noms de ses compagnons, Rustique et Éleuthère, que l'auteur de la version *A* ne connaissait pas encore. Selon Heinzelmann, cette modification pourrait révéler une opposition des Génovéfains à Saint-Denis et à son puissant abbé Hilduin, qui, à cette époque, vers 835, avait écrit une *Passio Dionysii* (*BHL* 2175), dans laquelle il a insisté sur le fait que son héros avait été un évangélisateur apostolique consacré par saint Paul et envoyé en Gaule par le pape Clément[275]. Poulin est plus prudent dans ses conclusions sur ce passage. Selon lui, cette omission peut aussi s'expliquer par le simple fait que, dans les nouvelles versions de la *Passio Dionysii* écrites au VIIIe siècle et au début du IXe siècle (*BHL* 2178 et 2175), la légende de l'envoyé apostolique était trop éloignée de ce qui avait été écrit sur Denis dans la première Vie de Geneviève et, étant donné que ce paragraphe n'apportait rien à l'histoire et à la gloire de Geneviève, l'auteur de la recension *B*, dans sa volonté de se concentrer sur son héroïne, décida de le supprimer; c'est ce qui expliquerait aussi quelques autres suppressions de passages dans les paragraphes 40 et 44 qui n'apportent, eux aussi, rien à la légende de Geneviève[276].

Il semble donc que la recension *B* de la Vie de sainte Geneviève a été écrite au moment où le culte de la sainte a pris une telle importance à Paris qu'elle est devenue, aux côtés des Apôtres, la sainte patronne de l'abbaye parisienne. À condition que la recension *C* date bien du VIIIe siècle et qu'elle n'ait pas été disponible à Paris (car écrite en Germanie), la communauté de Sainte-Geneviève aurait pu penser indispensable d'avoir un texte écrit dans le style du temps.

---

[275] HEINZELMANN (1992), p. 12.
[276] Le fait que le c. 42 (résurrection à Orléans) a aussi disparu serait plutôt accidentel, cf. HEINZELMANN, POULIN (1986), p. 152.

566   K. KRÖNERT

3. *Vita Genovefae*, recension D (*BHL vacat*)

Peu de temps après la rédaction de la recension B, la Vie de sainte Geneviève a été réécrite une nouvelle fois. Cette nouvelle version, la recension D (*BHL vacat*), qui n'a pas encore connu d'édition complète, dépend en très grande partie de la *Vita I^a* comme le prouve une mise en parallèle de ces différentes versions: la recension D contient ainsi, comme la version A, la légende clémentine (cap. 17 dans A), un miracle de résurrection à Orléans (cap. 42 dans A) et un paragraphe relatif à saint Martin (cap. 44 dans A), qui manquent dans la version B. Comme la version B, l'auteur de la version D précise cependant les noms des compagnons de Denis, Rustique et Éleuthère (information qu'il a aussi pu obtenir des textes relatifs au premier évêque de Paris) et ajoute, vers la fin, quelques originalités: il mentionne la dédicace à saint Pierre de l'église funéraire de Geneviève, il précise les circonstances de la construction de l'église des Apôtres et il glose sur le rôle de Geneviève à cette occasion, faisant ainsi son éloge[277]. Cependant, il est exclu que la version D ait été écrite à partir de la recension E: les enrichissements de la légende génovéfaine dans la version E prouvent que celle-ci est plus tardive. La datation de la version D se fait donc essentiellement par rapport à l'état de la légende de Geneviève, intermédiaire entre l'écriture de B et celle de E[278]. C'est ce qui nous mène à une datation de cette Vie dans le deuxième tiers du IXe siècle.

Les trois manuscrits conservés[279] datent tous du XIIIe siècle et n'apportent donc rien à la discussion de la datation. Cette faible transmission indique cependant le peu de succès de cette version D, ce qui n'est pas une grande surprise. Les modifications du contenu sont minimes et seuls deux changements pourraient se révéler significatifs: la réintroduction de la légende clémentine pourrait avoir une signification politique et la description de la mort de la sainte, étonnamment brève dans la version A, occupe dans la version D bien davantage que ce à quoi on est habitué dans un texte hagiographique[280]. Ces change-

---

[277] HEINZELMANN – POULIN (1986), p. 165.
[278] *Ibid.*, p. 165-166.
[279] *Ibid.*, p. 165: Paris, BnF, lat. 5280; Paris, Bibliothèque de l'Arsenal, 996 (43 H.L.); Cambridge, University Library Ji III 30.
[280] HEINZELMANN (1992), p. 13.

ments n'ont cependant pas suffi pour juger ce texte meilleur que les autres versions précédemment écrites, ce qui fait que la version D est restée dans l'ombre de la version E qui constitue une refonte complète de la légende génovéfaine et qui, elle, a connu une large diffusion. La Vie illustre donc uniquement l'intérêt et l'importance du culte grandissant de la sainte au IXe siècle à Paris. On peut donc supposer que l'auteur en fut un ecclésiastique parisien, comme le suggère aussi l'ajout des noms des compagnons de saint Denis.

4. *Vita Genovefae*, recension E (BHL 3338)

La version E de la Vie de sainte Geneviève (BHL 3338)[281] a connu un succès aussi grand que les recensions A et C: nous en conservons aujourd'hui une trentaine de manuscrits dont le plus ancien est Paris, Bibliothèque Sainte-Geneviève, 3013 (HL [in-8°] 2), témoin qui date du XIe siècle et provient de Noyon[282]. Cette recension se distingue des autres non seulement par son style verbeux par endroits, mais surtout par le fait que l'hagiographe a réalisé un travail presque historiographique. Il a travaillé à partir d'autres versions de la Vie de sainte Geneviève et est le premier à avoir eu recours à des textes non génovéfains: la recension A lui a fourni la base, mais les versions C et D ont été aussi consultées, comme le montrent les citations et des reprises mises en évidence par Poulin[283]. La compilation de ces trois versions de la Vie de la sainte parisienne n'a cependant pas été systématique car l'auteur de la recension E conserva une certaine liberté dans l'usage de ses modèles, comme le montrent aussi les additions faites de mémoire ou des sources extérieures au dossier de Geneviève: ainsi a-t-il ajouté des précisions géographiques et historiques, comme les distances entre deux lieux ou les règnes

---

[281] Pour ce texte, voir la présentation de l'activité hagiographique dans M.-C. ISAÏA, «Les diocèses de Reims, Soissons et Laon, env. 750-950», *supra*, p. 345-346.

[282] Éditions: C. KOHLER, *Étude critique sur le texte de la Vie latine de sainte Geneviève de Paris*, Paris, 1881, p. 5-47; éd. et trad. ISAÏA – BRET (2020), p. 280-355.

[283] Poulin pense que l'hagiographe d'E a aussi repris la version B, mais, selon nous, les reprises éventuelles de B sont trop peu significatives pour prouver une dépendance, par exemple la mention des noms des compagnons de Denis, Rustique et Éleuthère; HEINZELMANN – POULIN (1986), p. 166, 169.

sous lesquels certains évènements se sont déroulés. L'origine du titre du consécrateur de Geneviève, Vilicus, évêque de Chartres, est cependant obscure et douteuse. En revanche, l'actualisation de la légende dionysio-clémentine repose sur les nouvelles Passions de saint Denis, sans qu'on puisse dire s'il s'agit de *BHL* 2178 ou de *BHL* 2175 rédigée par Hilduin, qui identifient toutes les deux l'évêque de Paris avec l'Aréopagite. Enfin, dans la version *E*, d'autres modifications encore sont significatives pour localiser et dater le texte. Ainsi, l'hagiographe évoque des nouveaux murs – *nove menia Parisii*[284] – à Paris; s'il n'est pas possible de savoir à quels travaux précis il fait ici allusion, il est probable qu'il s'agisse, soit des reconstructions de l'accès fortifié à Paris, soit de la reconstruction du monastère de Sainte-Geneviève détruit par les Normands après 857[285]. Certains passages établissent un lien très étroit entre Geneviève et Reims et plus particulièrement saint Remi. Des citations et des motifs hagiographiques rapprochent cette Vie de celle de saint Remi rédigée par Hincmar, sans qu'on puisse pour autant établir des dépendances directes et précises entre les deux écrits[286]; cependant l'hagiographe de Geneviève rappelle notamment que Remi a exercé son autorité sur Laon, comme Hincmar l'a affirmé entre 869 et 870, lors du conflit avec son neveu Hincmar de Laon[287]. Il y a donc de fortes chances que la version *E* de la Vie de sainte Geneviève ait été écrite à Reims à la toute fin des années 860 et qu'elle témoigne de l'activité hagiographique sous Hincmar. Que l'auteur en soit Félix, diacre à Saint-Vitus de Reims, comme le pense Krusch, reste cependant une pure hypothèse[288].

C. Miracula Genovefae (*BHL* 3341-3342)

Le dossier de sainte Geneviève contient aussi une collection de miracles (*BHL* 3341 et 3342) écrite par l'un des moines de

---

[284] Dans le c. 45 de la version *E*.
[285] Heinzelmann – Poulin (1986), p. 171 et 173.
[286] Isaïa (2010), p. 587-590; cf. Ead., l'introduction de *Vie de sainte Geneviève*, dans Isaïa – Bret (2020).
[287] Heinzelmann – Poulin (1986), p. 171-172.
[288] *Ibid.*, p. 171-172.

la communauté peu après 862[289]. En effet, entre 857 et 862, les moines de Sainte-Geneviève, fuyant les attaques normandes, avaient trouvé refuge dans le domaine de Marizy-Sainte-Geneviève (Aisne, cant. De Neuilly-Saint-Front) pendant cinq ans[290]. L'auteur de ces *Miracula Genovefae* décrit cet exil ainsi que le retour à Paris, lequel occupe le dernier paragraphe du texte[291]. L'œuvre pourrait donc s'intituler *Translatio et miracula* et même *Translationes et miracula*, car l'hagiographe relate aussi un premier exil des Génovéfains lors du raid viking de 845[292]. Malgré son grand intérêt, le texte n'a que peu attiré la curiosité des chercheurs[293]. Il manque notamment une édition moderne qui tienne compte des deux versions de l'œuvre ayant existé – *BHL* 3341 et 3342 – et de leurs éventuelles différences significatives. Seule la version de *BHL* 3342 est aujourd'hui accessible dans les *Acta Sanctorum*[294]. Les deux manuscrits les plus anciens connus sont Paris, BnF, lat. 14364[295] et Paris, BnF, lat. 5667[296], qui datent, tous les deux, du XIIIe siècle.

L'œuvre, telle qu'elle se présente dans les *Acta Sanctorum*, débute par deux miracles non datés qui se veulent anciens: l'hagiographe dit seulement qu'ils se sont produits après la mort de la sainte auprès de sa tombe; ils sont assez communs: il s'agit d'un miracle de lumière et d'une guérison[297]. C'est seulement à partir du troisième paragraphe que l'auteur devient plus précis, ajoutant davantage de détails à chaque récit, comme par exemple le nom de l'abbé de la communauté, Optatus, dont nous ignorons cependant quand il a exercé sa charge[298]. Aussi les interventions divines deviennent-elles par endroits, plus originales: à côté des guérisons, qui continuent à dominer la collection, on trouve deux récits, dont le premier concerne un

---

[289] L'auteur s'inclut régulièrement dans le nombre des moines: cf., par exemple, *Miracula Genovefae*, c. 36, *AASS*, Ian. I, 1643, p. 151: *Venismus ad villam...*; c. 37, *ibid.*: *Die eadem Redomarum venimus...* Selon LOT (1970), p. 719, 720, il s'appelait peut-être Martin.
[290] BAUDUIN (2009), p. 78.
[291] *Miracula Genovefae*, c. 37, *AASS*, Ian. I, 1643, p. 151.
[292] *Ibid.*, c. 10-12, p. 149.
[293] Cf. notamment LOT (1970), p. 713-780 et BAUDUIN (2009), p. 77-78.
[294] *AASS*, Ian. I, 1643, p. 147-151.
[295] Fol. 145-147.
[296] Fol. 15v-24v.
[297] *Miracula Genovefae*, c. 1, 2, *AASS*, Ian. I, 1643, p. 147.
[298] *Ibid.*, c. 3, p. 147-148.

ouvrier qui a été sauvé d'une chute du toit du monastère[299] et le deuxième traite d'une décrue de la Seine provoquée par le lit mortuaire de la sainte, quand Richaldus était évêque de Paris[300]. Hélas, les dates de l'épiscopat de ce dernier ne sont pas non plus établies. Puis, au dixième paragraphe, l'hagiographe précise que tous les miracles jusque là relatés datent de l'époque d'avant les raids vikings, annonçant en même temps que les suivants se sont produits lors de ceux-ci, c'est-à-dire à partir de 845. Pour éviter les pilleurs, les Génovéfains se sont alors retirés à *Ategiae* (lieu qui pourrait être aujourd'hui Athis-Mons), puis à Draveil. Lors de ce périple, la sainte a réalisé quelques interventions surnaturelles comme un miracle de lumière ou une punition de l'abbé des Génovéfains Herbertus, qui avait essayé de voler une dent de Geneviève[301]. Avec la retraite des Normands, les moines sont revenus à Paris et la sainte a continué à guérir des malades[302]. Les pilleurs sont finalement revenus – en 857 –, et les Genovéfains sont repartis une nouvelle fois en exil, cette fois-ci à Marizy, comme nous l'avons indiqué plus haut. C'est là que la sainte a accompli d'autres miracles, essentiellement des guérisons de possédés et de personnes souffrant des maux physiques[303]. Au bout de cinq ans seulement, les moines sont revenus à Paris, comme l'hagiographe le précise en relatant non seulement les miracles qui se sont produits sur le chemin, mais en indiquant aussi différents lieux d'étape dans les vallées de l'Ourcq et de la Marne. La réinstallation dans l'abbaye parisienne marque la fin de l'œuvre[304].

III. Textes parisiens dont le lieu exact de la rédaction n'a pas pu être identifié

Certes, le monastère de Saint-Germain fut de loin le centre d'écriture hagiographique le plus actif à Paris et plusieurs textes relatifs à sainte Geneviève sont issus de l'abbaye qui était sous

---

[299] *Ibid.*, c. 6, p. 148.
[300] *Ibid.*, c. 8, p. 148.
[301] *Ibid.*, c. 10-11, p. 149.
[302] *Ibid.*, c. 12-16, p. 149.
[303] *Ibid.*, c. 17-31, p. 149-150.
[304] *Ibid.*, c. 33-37, p. 150-151.

son patronage, mais il est aussi hautement probable que les clercs de la cathédrale et aussi les moines de Saint-Marcel et de Saint-Cloud ont rédigé ou fait rédiger des écrits en l'honneur de leurs saints patrons; peut-être encore à l'époque carolingienne ou, au plus tard, au début de l'ère capétienne, les communautés de Saint-Magloire et de Saint-Éloi se sont, elles aussi, procuré des Vies et des Passions. Non seulement la quantité de textes parisiens, mais aussi le nombre grandissant d'établissements qui, depuis la période carolingienne, ont célébré leurs saints avec des écrits laudatifs, ne laisse aucun doute sur le fait que Paris figurait alors parmi les hauts lieux religieux et littéraires de l'empire carolingien.

A. Textes carolingiens

1. Marcel: *Vita II^a* (BHL 5249)

Grâce à Venance Fortunat, nous possédons une Vie en l'honneur de Marcel, saint évêque de Paris au Ve siècle (*BHL* 5248), qui a été étudiée, pour son caractère légendaire, par J. Le Goff et J.-C. Picard[305]. Ce dernier a ainsi montré que l'ensemble du récit adopte la forme d'un «conte merveilleux», avec, comme apogée, le combat du saint avec un dragon.

Cette Vie a été réécrite, dans une forme relativement simple, par un auteur inconnu qui l'a considérablement raccourcie en ne gardant que la trame narrative des principaux évènements du modèle. Dans cette nouvelle version, la *Vita II^a Marcelli* (*BHL* 5249)[306], nous apprenons que Marcel était d'origine modeste[307] et qu'il s'est très tôt illustré par des miracles: il tint notamment dans sa main nue un fer incandescent afin de déterminer son poids, une sorte d'ordalie qui prouvait non seulement sa vie exemplaire, mais aussi son aptitude à sa future charge épiscopale[308]. Une fois nommé sous-diacre, il changea l'eau en vin, puis, une autre fois, en baume[309] – une nouvelle fois ces miracles qui sont en lien avec ses tâches sacerdotales à venir –,

---

[305] Le Goff (1967); Picard (1990).
[306] *Vita II^a Marcelli*, *AASS*, Nov. I, 1887, p. 266-267.
[307] *Ibid.*, c. 1, p. 266.
[308] *Ibid.*, c. 1, p. 266.
[309] *Ibid.*, c. 2-3, p. 266-267.

et il punit un évêque pécheur qui avait ordonné de fouetter un enfant[310]. Enfin, en tant qu'évêque de Paris, il délivra d'abord un autre pécheur repenti[311] et, finalement, – c'est le point culminant du récit –, toute la population qui était alors menacée par un immense serpent ou dragon qu'il chassa de ses terres[312].

Le manuscrit le plus ancien de ce texte, Chartres, BM 63 (115 1/G)[313], de la fin du IXe siècle, nous fournit le *terminus ante quem* de sa rédaction. Hélas, une datation plus fine et une localisation précise de l'œuvre se heurtent à l'absence totale d'autres indices, et nous devons nous contenter de constater qu'il est probable que l'hagiographe a composé cette deuxième Vie de Marcel dans l'une des églises parisiennes où l'intérêt pour ce pontife a dû être le plus grand, sans doute à l'époque carolingienne. Il se peut que ce soit la cathédrale – Marcel est le premier évêque de Paris qui ait été l'objet d'un culte et c'est là où ses reliques étaient temporairement mises à l'abri à la fin du IXe siècle lors de la menace normande –, ou bien le monastère Saint-Marcel, sur la rive gauche de Paris, au-delà du gué de la Bièvre, où est censé se trouver le saint corps. S'il est vrai qu'il faut attendre le IXe siècle pour avoir la preuve de l'existence d'une basilique de Saint-Marcel, il est cependant certain que celle-ci a très vite pris de l'importance, comme le montre la donation effectuée par Ingelvin, évêque de Paris entre 871 et 883/884, au «monastère de Saint-Marcel qui est desservi par une communauté de frères»[314].

2. Justinus: *Passio* (BHL 4579), *Passio rhythmica* (BHL 4580) et *Translatio Corbeiam anno 891* (BHL 4581)

Les légendes de saint Just de Beauvais et de saint Justin d'Auxerre sont si proches l'une de l'autre que H. Röckelein a parlé d'un «dédoublement» hagiographique. De ce fait, il est

---

[310] *Ibid.*, c. 4, p. 267.
[311] *Ibid.*, c. 5, p. 267.
[312] *Ibid.*, c. 6, p. 267.
[313] La *Vita II^a Marcelli* se trouve sur les fol. 15-21. Le manuscrit a brûlé en 1944.
[314] DUVAL – PÉRIN – PICARD (1992), p. 122, citent un diplôme de Charles le Simple de 918; cf. P. LAUER, éd., *Recueil des actes de Charles le Simple (893-923)*, Paris, 1940-1949, p. 223-225, n° 97.

L'ACTIVITÉ HAGIOGRAPHIQUE À PARIS 573

indispensable d'évoquer ici la Passion de Just, bien qu'elle n'ait aucun lien avec le diocèse de Paris[315]. Selon la *Passio Justi* (*BHL* 4590), un jeune garçon de neuf ans, Just, né à Auxerre et empli de vertus chrétiennes, partit avec son père à la recherche de son oncle qu'il trouva à Amiens. Capturé par des soldats de Riciovare, horrible mais fictif persécuteur, Just fut décapité dans une grotte à *Sinomovicus*, appelé plus tard Saint-Just-en-Chaussée. Il prit alors sa tête et se mit à marcher, ce qui est la plus ancienne occurrence d'un saint céphalophore. Puis Just demanda que son corps soit enterré «sur place» et que sa tête soit emportée à Auxerre, auprès de sa mère, ce qui fut fait; sa tête se trouve désormais dans l'église Saint-Symphorien[316]. D'après les recherches de M. Coens, cette *Passio I^a Justi* date de l'époque mérovingienne[317] et le culte du saint est bien attesté dès le VIIIe siècle, surtout à Saint-Just-en-Chaussée, à Senlis et à Beauvais[318] où le corps fut transféré, au plus tard vers 900, et qui devint le lieu principal du culte[319].

Au IXe siècle, un nouveau culte est né à partir de la légende de saint Just, celui de saint Justin d'Auxerre. Cette légende, relatée dans la *Passio Iustini* (*BHL* 4579) à laquelle cette notice est dédiée, préserve, avec peu de modifications, la trame de la légende de saint Just de Beauvais. Ici aussi, un jeune garçon de neuf ans, né à Auxerre mais qui s'appelle désormais Justin, part avec son père à la recherche d'un proche qu'il trouve à Amiens. Poursuivi par les persécuteurs de Riciovare, il est rattrapé et exécuté dans une grotte qui se trouve, cette-fois-ci, à *Lupera*, dans le *pagus Parisiensis*. Ce lieu est identifié avec Louvres-en-Parisis, dans le Val d'Oise, et faisait partie du domaine de Montméliant appartenant à Saint-Denis[320]. Et, comme dans la légende de Just, son corps fut enterré «sur place» et sa tête fut portée à Auxerre[321]. On voit donc clairement que la légende de Justin d'Auxerre est calquée sur celle de saint Just de Beauvais. Les corps des deux martyrs ont connu des destins posthumes

---

[315] Hedwig Röckelein a travaillé à deux reprises sur ces cultes: RÖCKELEIN (2002), p. 184-190.
[316] DOLBEAU – RÖCKELEIN (2006), p. 324-235, 328.
[317] COENS (1956), p. 86-114, en part. p. 105 et 106.
[318] DOLBEAU – RÖCKELEIN (2006), p. 327-328, p. 332.
[319] *Ibid.*, p. 328 et 332.
[320] STOCLET (1988), p. 94-105, en part. p. 102.
[321] DOLBEAU – RÖCKELEIN (2006), p. 333-334.

autonomes, mais les têtes des deux saints ne font qu'une à Auxerre[322].

Le plus ancien manuscrit de cette Passion (*BHL* 4579), Paris, BnF, lat. 15437[323], date du XIe siècle, mais le texte a certainement été écrit au IXe siècle, comme l'affirme H. Röckelein[324], qui en a réalisé, avec F. Dolbeau, l'*editio princeps*[325]. En effet, le martyrologe d'Usuard nous indique que la vénération de Justin remonte, en région parisienne, au IXe siècle et qu'elle est certainement liée à la translation du corps saint de Louvres à Paris où il fut déposé dans la cathédrale Notre-Dame. La date de ce transfert est inconnue, mais il est probable qu'il a eu lieu sous la pression normande, évidemment bien avant la translation du corps de Justin en Saxe vers 891 et sûrement bien avant que les raids normands aient atteint Paris, en 885, donc peut-être sous Gauzlin, abbé de Saint-Denis et évêque de Paris, dont la vie était fortement marquée par les attaques scandinaves[326]. Il est ainsi possible que la *Passio BHL* 4579 ait été écrite à Paris afin de lancer ou de soutenir le nouveau culte.

La *Passio BHL* 4579 a ensuite servi de base à une réécriture poétique: la *Passio rythmica Iustini* (*BHL* 4580)[327]. Négligée par la recherche jusqu'à maintenant, elle nous est parvenue en deux manuscrits médiévaux, dont le plus ancien est Trèves, Stadtbibliothek, 1159, du XIIe siècle[328]. Selon son éditeur, K. Strecker, toutes les caractéristiques linguistiques et poétiques plaident pour que son auteur fût un lettré de la «renaissance carolingienne» ou qu'il ait écrit sous son influence[329]. Sur le plan formel, il s'agit d'un poème rythmique d'une qualité moyenne, qui ne tient pas compte de la métrique antique. Chaque vers est composé de quinze syllabes, le premier hémistiche étant toujours de huit syllabes et le second hémistiche toujours de sept syllabes.

---

[322] Cf. *ibid.* p. 333.
[323] Paris, BnF, lat. 15437, fol. 89-92.
[324] DOLBEAU – RÖCKELEIN (2006), p. 333-351.
[325] *Ibid.*, p. 351-357.
[326] RÖCKELEIN (2002), p. 184-186.
[327] Éd. K. STRECKER, *MGH, Poet. Lat.*, IV-2, Berlin, 1923, p. 841-856.
[328] Trier, Stadtbibliothek 1382 (= 1159, ancien 1409), fol. 45-54v; le deuxième manuscrit est Bruxelles, Bollandinus 209, fol. 98-100v, du XVe siècle, en provenance de Bursfelde.
[329] Éd. STRECKER, p. 841.

Le texte a-t-il été composé à Paris? Ceci est tout-à-fait possible car les *opera gemina* sont relativement courants à l'époque carolingienne, et il n'est aucunement exclu que cette Passion rythmique ait complété la Passion BHL 4579. Hélas, ce n'est qu'une hypothèse et il ne faut pas exclure d'autres possibilités: le poème a pu être également écrit, un peu plus tard, à Corvey, après la translation du corps de Justin de Paris en Saxe, en 891, pour y stimuler le nouveau culte. Ce transfert, qui nous est relaté dans la *Translatio Iustini* (BHL 4581)[330], était, d'après H. Röckelein, un acte hautement politique car il faisait partie d'un pacte d'amitiés entre deux rois, Arnulf et Eudes[331]. Finalement nous ne pouvons même pas exclure que la *Passio rhythmica* date du milieu du xe siècle car c'est à ce moment-là, sous l'abbatiat de Gerbern (948-965), que le culte de Justin a atteint son apogée à Corvey, puisqu'en 949 Otton Ier avait offert à la grande abbaye saxonne la tête du saint, qu'il avait fait transférer d'Auxerre à Magdebourg peu de temps auparavant[332].

3. *Vita sancti Meredici et translatio a. 884* (BHL 5875-5876)

Patron de l'église Saint-Merri, Médéric n'a pas beaucoup attiré l'attention des chercheurs. Le personnage et son dossier hagiographique restent ainsi très peu connus. La première mention de son culte se trouve dans le martyrologe d'Usuard[333]. Sa Vie (BHL 5875) et le récit de translation qui la suit (BHL 5876) sont édités dans les *Acta Sanctorum*[334].

Entrecoupée de longs passages très généraux relatifs au culte des saints et aux miracles, la partie biographique de la Vie nous apprend que Médéric était – comme saint Germain – originaire d'Autun. Enfant, il a été offert à l'une des abbayes de la ville[335].

---

[330] Cf. aussi KLÜPPEL (1996), p. 195.

[331] RÖCKELEIN (2002), p. 187-188.

[332] *Ibid.*, p. 188: le transfert de la tête de Justin d'Auxerre à Magdebourg pourrait avoir eu lieu en 942, en 946 ou en 947.

[333] DUVAL – PÉRIN – PICARD (1992), p. 129, citent Usuard, au 29 août: *Parisius depositio sancti Mederici presbiteri et monachi*.

[334] *AASS*, Aug. VI, 1743, p. 520-525; les manuscrits les plus anciens sont: Paris, BnF, lat. 11749, fol. 15v-16v, du milieu du xie siècle, de Saint-Germain-des-Prés; et Paris, BnF, lat. 15437, fol. 144-145v, de la fin du xie siècle, de Saint-Marcel de Paris.

[335] *Vita Mederici*, c. 2, *AASS*, Aug. VI, 1743, p. 520: *monasterium iam dicti civitati*, donc: à Saint-Martin ou à Saint-Symphorien.

Grâce à sa discipline exemplaire et sa vie ascétique – il portait notamment un cilice sous sa bure –, il a été élu abbé par ses frères. Une foule de plus en plus nombreuse, attirée par ses multiples miracles, commençait cependant à le déranger dans sa communion avec Dieu. Il décida donc de se retirer dans un lieu désert avoisinant mais ses frères le retrouvèrent rapidement. Menacé d'excommunication par l'évêque d'Autun, il revint dans sa communauté et suscita encore beaucoup d'autres miracles. Finalement, il repartit avec l'un de ses proches, Frodulphe – aussi appelé Frou –, dans la région de parisienne afin d'y prier, mais lors du voyage, il tomba malade à Saint-Martin de Champeaux – *Campellae* – et ne put faire ensuite que de courts déplacements. C'est ainsi qu'il vint à Melun – *Milidunum* – où il libera – comme saint Germain – des captifs[336]. Finalement, il se fit transporter à Paris et, lors du voyage, en passant par Bonneuil-sur-Marne – *Bonoilum* – et Charenton-le-Pont – *Pons Karantonis* –, il accomplit encore beaucoup de guérisons, dont les bénéficiaires et leurs maladies sont désormais précisés[337]. Arrivé à Paris, il s'installa dans une église Saint-Pierre, où il mourut deux ans et neuf mois plus tard[338]. Dans la *Translatio*, l'auteur rapporte qu'en 884, le prêtre Teodelbertus, en charge de l'église funéraire de Médéric, demanda à Gauzlin, évêque de Paris (883/884-886), de transférer les reliques de Médéric en un lieu plus digne dans l'église Saint-Pierre. Une fois l'autorisation obtenue, cette translation se déroula la même année, le 29 août. La fin du récit se compose encore de quelques exhortations assez générales.

Vita et *Translatio* sont certainement issues d'une seule entreprise; l'hagiographe est inconnu, mais il est probable qu'il a écrit son œuvre peu de temps après la translation de 884 afin de promouvoir le culte, rendre la vénération du saint plus solennelle et garder une trace du transfert. Jean Stilting, l'éditeur dans les *Acta Sanctorum*, a ainsi daté les deux textes du tournant du IXe/Xe siècle[339], mais il n'est pas impossible que la date de

---

[336] *Ibid.*, c. 13, p. 522.

[337] *Ibid.*, c. 15, p. 523.

[338] *Ibid.*, c. 16, p. 523: *...venit ad suburban Parisii Urbis in cellula, quae sub nomine Petri principis Apostolorum fuerat consecrata.*

[339] Préface à la Vie de Médéric, par J. STILTING, *AASS*, Aug. VI, 1743, p. 519: *Nihil in illa (Vita) invenio, quod cogat nos credere, diu post translationem*

la rédaction doive être encore davantage rapprochée de celle de la translation: l'hagiographe n'évoque pas du tout le siège de Paris par les Normands en 885/886, à la différence de la plupart des auteurs ayant écrit après cette catastrophe. De plus, dans ce texte, rien n'indique que Gauzlin soit déjà mort. Le lieu de la rédaction n'est pas évoqué mais le fait que la légende de Médéric présente quelques parallèles avec celle de saint Germain et que l'un des manuscrits les plus anciens de l'œuvre – Paris, BnF, lat. 11749 – provienne du monastère de Saint-Germain-des-Prés, peut autoriser à y localiser l'auteur; cependant, celui-ci pourrait aussi être un membre de la cathédrale puisque la translation du saint s'est faite avec l'autorisation de l'évêque. Cette deuxième hypothèse est pourtant moins probable du fait que tous les transferts de reliques nécessitaient une telle permission et rien n'indique que Gauzlin était particulièrement attaché à Médéric.

Que pouvait savoir l'hagiographe de Médéric qui avait vécu deux siècles avant lui ? Le fait qu'il ait introduit dans son œuvre de longues réflexions générales sur le culte des saints, indique qu'il manquait manifestement de sources. Jean Stilting a tout de même supposé qu'il avait des anciens documents à sa disposition[340]. Cependant le lecteur peut remarquer que, dans la première partie de la Vie, l'hagiographe est assez imprécis: on y trouve beaucoup de *topoi* hagiographiques et aucun autre acteur majeur n'est mentionné avec son nom propre, ni même celui de l'abbé qui l'a accueilli dans le monastère d'Autun et dont il est devenu le successeur, ni celui de l'évêque de la même ville[341]. Dans la deuxième partie, en revanche, le compagnon de voyage de Médéric, Frodulphe, les toponymes des lieux traversés lors de ce périple, ainsi que les noms des miraculés et de leurs maladies sont précisés avec une grande exactitude, avec une si grande exactitude qu'on puisse ici, en effet, imaginer l'existence d'une documentation ancienne exploitée par l'auteur[342].

---

esse scriptam, ita ut verisimilius appareat, scriptam esse circa finem saeculi IX aut initium X.

[340] *Ibid.*, p. 519: *Fatendum tamen est, huic scriptori ab aetate non magnam esse auctoritatem; sed monumenta habere potuit antiquiora, ex quibus Sancti gesta hauserit.*

[341] *Vita Mederici*, c. 6, *AASS*, Aug. VI, 1743, p. 521.

[342] *Ibid.*, c. 10-16, p. 522-524.

4. Chlodoaldus ou Chlodovaldus: *Vitae I^a-II^a*
(*BHL* 1732-1733)

Saint Cloud (vers 522-560) – *Chlodoaldus* ou encore *Chodovaldus* – est un personnage bien connu: fils de Clodomer et petit-fils de Clovis, il a été frère de Thibaud et Gonthaire, assassinés tous les deux par leurs oncles Childebert et Clothaire, qui souhaitaient se partager le royaume de leur frère Clodomer après sa mort prématurée. Encore très jeune, Cloud a échappé au massacre du fait qu'il a été mis à l'abri à temps. Ensuite, il sauva sa vie en renonçant à ses droits royaux et en choisissant une vie de clerc. Grégoire de Tours, dans ses «Dix livres d'histoire», nous raconte cet épisode avec force détails qui ont contribué à discréditer les Mérovingiens[343].

Cloud a fait l'objet d'une première Vie (*BHL* 1732), qui est éditée dans les *Acta Sanctorum*[344] et dans les *MGH*[345]: dans une une sorte de traité d'hagiologie, l'hagiographe laisse entendre que son œuvre est destinée à une lecture lors de la fête du saint[346]. Les chapitres 5 à 7 reprennent le texte de Grégoire de Tours sur les dramatiques premières années du saint. Puis l'auteur raconte comment Cloud a vécu dans l'entourage d'un reclus, Séverin, installé sur la rive gauche de la Seine, dans l'actuel Quartier latin (chap. 9)[347], avant de partir en Provence (chap. 10). Une fois revenu à Paris, il a été accueilli par l'évêque Eusèbe (env. 551-555) et ordonné prêtre. Pour retrouver plus de calme, il s'est finalement retiré à Nogent – *Novigentum* –, lieu, qui a pris plus tard le nom de Saint-Cloud. Son *aura* ne cessait cependant de grandir et le nombre de ses disciples devint si important qu'il fonda un monastère où il mourut bientôt, un 7 septembre (chap. 12). Exceptés les épisodes qui reposent sur Grégoire de Tours et le passage sur sa mort à Nogent, le contenu de cette Vie ne se laisse pas vérifier et paraît ainsi peu fiable.

---

[343] Grégoire de Tours, *Libri historiarum X*, III, 1-18, éd. B. Krusch, *MGH*, *SRM*, I-1, 2e éd., Hanovre, 1951, p. 96-120.

[344] *AASS*, Sept. III, 1750, p. 98-101.

[345] *MGH*, *SRM*, II, Hanovre, 1888, p. 350-357.

[346] *Vita Chlodoaldi*, c. 1, *AASS*, Sept. III, 1750, p. 98: *Dies laetitiae et gaudii adest praecipuae vestrae urbi summa devotione celebranda, qua venerandus Christi confessor Clodoaldus vinculis corporeae fragilitatis exutus adire meruit gaudium aeternae beatitudinis...*

[347] À propos de cet ermitage, cf. Duval – Périn – Picard (1992), p. 124-125.

En effet, l'hagiographe est sans doute un homme de l'époque carolingienne: le *terminus ante quem* est donné par les deux manuscrits les plus anciens, Paris, BnF, lat. 15437, du XIᵉ siècle[348], et Paris, BnF, lat. 11749, également du XIᵉ siècle[349]. Quant au *terminus post quem*, il repose sur la dénomination du lieu dans lequel Cloud s'est retiré, Nogent, dont l'hagiographe précise que ce lieu s'appelle désormais Saint-Cloud, ce qui n'était pas le cas avant le milieu du VIIIᵉ siècle[350]. Krusch en a conclu que la Vie devait dater du IXᵉ ou du Xᵉ siècle[351], mais probablement pas de l'époque de Charles le Gros, quand les reliques de saint Cloud furent, semble-t-il, temporairement déposées à Paris, pour mieux les protéger contre les Scandinaves[352], puisque l'hagiographe laisse entendre que les reliques de Cloud étaient toujours là où le saint était mort[353]. L'auteur de la *Vita* était probablement un membre de la communauté de Saint-Cloud[354], mais ce n'était assurément pas un écrivain de grande qualité: Krusch lui attribue des connaissances grammaticales faibles[355].

---

[348] Fol. 161-164.

[349] Fol. 16v-19v.

[350] Dans le *Liber Historiae Francorum*, c. 24, nous pouvons encore lire: *Noviento villa Parisiaci suburbano depositus requiescit* (éd. B. KRUSCH, *MGH*, *SRM*, II, Hanovre, 1888, p. 282).

[351] *Ibid.*, p. 349.

[352] STILTING, dans son introduction à l'édition de la Vie de saint Cloud dans les *AASS*, Sept. II, 1748, p. 97-98, mentionne un cartulaire qui contient des chartes des évêques parisiens Inchadus et Erchanrad II et dont les compilateurs précisent qu'à leur époque, sous le règne de Charles le Gros, les reliques de Cloud étaient à Paris; cf. *AASS*, Sept. III, 1750, p. 98: *in praefatiuncula vero dictis chartis praefixa a compilatoribus, qui tempore Carolo Crassi seu memoratae obsidionis vivebant, affirmari, conservata eo temore fuisse in ecclesia cathedralis Parisiensi corpora Sanctorum Marcelli et Clodoaldi cum aliis huc non spectantibus. (...) Quod vero spectat ad S. Clodoaldum, translatio illa mihi probabilis admodum apparet. Certum tamen est, sacrum illius corpus non mansisse in cathedrali Parisiensi, sed ad propriam S. Clodoaldi ecclesiam fuisse cito relatum, si inde avectum fuerit.*

[353] *Vita Chlodoaldi*, c. 12, *AASS*, Sept. III, 1750, p. 101: *Cuius corpus in edam cella summo honore humatum est, ubi suffragantibus eius meritis completur votum ex fide petentis...*

[354] Éd. B. KRUSCH, *MGH*, *SRM*, II, Hanovre, 1888, p. 349: *Quam ob rem eorum opinioni accedo, qui Vitam saec. IX vel X compositam esse idque in monasterio S. Chlodovaldi contenderunt.*

[355] *Ibid.*: *Scriptor admodum rudis arte grammatica parum imbutus erat.*

Même si la Vie de Cloud n'est pas d'une grande valeur littéraire, elle reflète la solennité avec laquelle le saint était vénéré à Saint-Cloud à l'époque carolingienne. Le village et son monastère, peu connus pour cette période, avaient donc une certaine importance, comme le suggère aussi la décision de la communauté de mettre les reliques de leur saint patron à Paris, à l'abri des Normands. Cette importance ne doit cependant pas non plus être surévaluée: si Saint-Cloud avait attiré beaucoup de pèlerins, on y aurait sans doute rédigé un recueil de miracles. Il existe encore une deuxième Vie de Cloud (*BHL* 1733), attestée seulement dans le Sud-Est de la *Germania*, qui est restée inédite. Reprenant uniquement les passages qui reposent sur l'histoire de Grégoire de Tours, le texte a été jugé par Krusch «indigne» d'être publié[356]. Les deux manuscrits les plus anciens, tous les deux du XIe siècle[357], nous donnent un *terminus ante quem*, mais il n'est pour l'instant pas possible de préciser davantage à quel moment et où cette Vie a été composée. Dans la copie qui se trouve dans le *Magnum Legendarium Austriacum*, la fin diffère légèrement de celle des autres manuscrits[358].

B. Textes dont la datation est incertaine

1. *Translatio* de saint Magloire (*BHL* 5147)

Magloire fait partie des saints bretons qui seraient venus en Bretagne d'outre-Manche vers la fin du VIe siècle. Son dossier hagiographique qui est, à une exception près, issu de la production littéraire bretonne et qui a été étudié avec minutie par J.-C. Poulin[359], permet de retracer dans les grandes lignes sa vie ainsi que le parcours de ses reliques: cousin de saint Samson, il est devenu pontife de Dol, avant de démissionner aussitôt et se retirer dans la solitude avec soixante-deux moines. C'est ainsi

---

[356] *Ibid.*, p. 349: *Cum fere tota e Gregorio ad verbum exscripta sit, indignum eam iudicavi, quae publici iuris fieret.*

[357] Munich, Bayerische Staatsbibliothek, Clm 4547, fol. 249v-250 (Benediktbeuren, n° 47) et Clm 18583, fol. 170v-173 (Tegernsee, n° 583).

[358] *AB*, 17 (1898) p. 79.

[359] POULIN (2009), p. 199-234 et *supra*, «L'hagiographie bretonne avant l'an mil», p. 233-234.

qu'il est mort sur l'Île de Sercq, dans la Manche[360]. Puis, ses reliques furent transférées, sous le règne du roi breton Nominoé († 851), à Léhon, près de Dinan[361].

Seule la *Translatio s. Maglorii et aliorum Parisios* (BHL 5147) est un texte parisien qui rappelle comment les reliques de Magloire furent transférées, au Xe siècle, à Paris pour échapper aux Scandinaves. L'œuvre nous est parvenu dans un manuscrit du XIIIe siècle, Avranches, BM 210 (fol. 3v-4); les autres témoins sont sans exception postmédiévaux. L'édition de référence est celle de Guillotel, de 1982[362]. L'analyse de cette *Translatio* a révélé que le texte se présente en réalité de façon morcelée: on distingue ainsi cinq fragments dont les deux premiers reposent sans doute sur les informations consignées seulement peu de temps après l'arrivée des reliques à Paris vers 920-925. Ils rapportent comment Salvator, évêque d'Alet, s'est replié, sous la menace normande, sur Léhon avec le corps de saint Malo afin de continuer sa fuite avec Junan, abbé de Léhon. Les deux hommes emportèrent avec eux les reliques d'autres saints, dont celles de Magloire, et se joignirent à une caravane formée par les clergés de Dol et de Bayeux qui s'enfuirent aussi avec les restes des saints Samson, Seniers, Pair et Scubilion. Ils furent finalement accueillis à Paris par le duc Hugues le Grand, qui les installa dans l'église Saint-Barthélemy, sur l'île de la Cité[363]. Les trois fragments suivants, en revanche, ressemblent plutôt à une reconstruction plus tardive dans laquelle les intérêts du moment ont pris le dessus sur la véracité du récit: il y est question, entre autres, de la transformation de l'église Saint-Barthélemy en monastère, placé désormais sous le vocable de Magloire, par le duc Hugues et de la récupération d'autres reliques et de biens au profit de Saint-Magloire sous Hugues et Robert le Pieux[364]. Selon Guillotel, cette *Translatio* fut mis dans sa forme actuelle

---

[360] Cf. sa *Vita* ainsi que les Miracles et l'*obitus* qui lui sont joints (BHL 5139, 5140/5144) et qui datent des années 860.

[361] Cf. les *Miracula s. Maglorii in Sargia insula* (BHL 5141) qui sont de la même époque, suivis de de la *Translatio s. Maglorii a Sargia insula in Britanniam* (BHL 5142). D'autres écrits de 900 et du début du Xe siècle (BHL 5143, 5146) font part des faits miraculeux et d'une construction d'église à Léhon.

[362] GUILLOTEL (1982), 269-315, et ici p. 310-315.

[363] Cf. MERDRIGNAC (1993), p. 63-64.

[364] POULIN (2009), p. 225.

dans la seconde moitié du XIIe siècle à Saint-Magloire de Paris[365].

2. Aurea abb. Parisiis, Sermo de Vita (BHL 814-817)

Geneviève n'est pas la seule sainte parisienne qui ait fait l'objet d'une écriture hagiographique. Mais contrairement à celle qui est devenue la sainte patronne de la ville, Aure ou Aurée, à laquelle est consacrée cette notice, a fini par tomber dans l'oubli et son dossier hagiographique est resté quasi inédit jusqu'en 2007[366]. François Dolbeau est en effet le premier à avoir analysé et édité les trois écrits qui le constituent: la *Vita* et les *Miracula ante et post mortem* qui forment une unité (*BHL* 814α et β) et deux sermons panégyriques (*BHL* 815 et 816). Nous pouvons donc ici nous contenter de présenter ses principaux résultats[367].

Aure est bien attestée dans la Vie de Colomban (*BHL* 1898) écrite par Jonas de Bobbio et dans la Vie d'Éloi (*BHL* 2474) dont l'auteur est saint Ouen[368]. Selon ces écrits, elle a vécu à l'époque de saint Éloi († 660) qui l'avait choisie comme première abbesse d'un monastère parisien qu'il avait fait construire, sur des terres royales, entre 632 et 641. Situé sur l'Île de la Cité, à proximité du palais royal, avec une église cémétériale, Saint-Paul, qui se trouvait hors des murs dans le quartier actuel du Marais, ce monastère fut d'abord dédié à saint Martial avant de prendre le patronage de saint Éloi. Aure survécut à Éloi, et mourut lors d'une épidémie. Les données factuelles s'arrêtent à peu près là et il faut attendre le milieu du IXe siècle pour trouver la première attestation de son culte dans le martyrologe d'Usuard[369]. C'est aussi à cette époque que Charles le Chauve s'intéressa à l'abbaye Saint-Éloi qu'en 871 il donna à l'évêque de

---

[365] *Ibid.* et GUILLOTEL (1982), p. 293.
[366] Dans les *AASS*, Oct. II, 1768, p. 472-493, ne se trouve qu'un résumé.
[367] DOLBEAU (2007), p. 17-91; on y trouve, sur les pages 54-67, les éditions de la Vie et des Miracles (*BHL* 814β) et des chapitres de la version *BHL* 814α, qui diffèrent de la légende d'origine, ainsi que le Sermon *BHL* 815; le Sermon *BHL* 816 est resté inédit.
[368] Cf. éd. B. KRUSCH, *Ionae Vitae sanctorum Columbani, Vedastis, Iohannis*, *MGH, SRG in usum scholarum*, XXXVII, Hanovre – Leipzig, 1902, p. 746-749 et *Vita Elegii*, éd. B. KRUSCH, *MGH, SRM*, IV, Hanovre, 1902, p. 663-741; à propos de l'auteur de la Vie d'Éloi, WESTEEL (1999), p. 33-47.
[369] Pour l'histoire du culte de sainte Aure, DOLBEAU (2007), p. 22-28.

Paris. De ce fait, le culte de sainte Aure gagna considérablement en importance. Lors de son expulsion de l'abbaye de Saint-Éloi, en 1107, la communauté ne comptait qu'une douzaine de religieuses[370].

La Vie et les Miracles (*BHL* 814) ont été écrits durant la période faste de Saint-Éloi, dans les années 900 à 1050 au plus tard[371]. Le *terminus post quem* est déterminé par l'utilisation d'une lettre pseudo-hiéronymienne sur l'Assomption de Marie attribuée à Paschase Radbert qui date des années 825-836 et le *terminus ante quem* est à l'évidence l'expulsion des religieuses au début du XIIe siècle, car la Vie d'Aure, mettant en scène un idéal de sainteté féminine, a été destinée, sans aucun doute possible, à un public composé essentiellement de femmes[372]. L'identité de l'auteur est inconnue; on ne peut déterminer si c'était une femme ou un homme, s'il appartenait à Saint-Éloi ou à un autre établissement parisien, ou même à la cathédrale[373].

L'analyse des manuscrits montre qu'il existait deux versions de la Vie d'Aure. La légende primitive (*BHL* 814β)[374] débute par un chapitre panégyrique; puis l'auteur reprend, avec peu de modifications, les chapitres de la Vie d'Éloi qui lui permettent de présenter quelques données factuelles sur Aure (chap. II-IV). Les passages suivants sont consacrés à des vertus de la sainte ainsi qu'à trois miracles *ante mortem* qui mettent en valeur sa pénitence et son ascèse extrême. Le chapitre sur sa mort est à nouveau fondé sur la Vie d'Éloi et les trois miracles *post mortem* sont introduits par le récit de la translation du corps d'Aure depuis l'église Saint-Paul, lieu de son inhumation, au monastère de Saint-Éloi[375]. Les modifications de la deuxième version de la

---

[370] *Ibid.*, p. 44.

[371] Si l'auteur de ce texte est identique à celui de la Vie et des Miracles de Turiau (*BHL* 8342, 8343), le moment de l'écriture de la Vie d'Aure pourrait encore être précisé: elle daterait alors du début du XIe siècle ou, au plus tôt, de la fin du Xe siècle; cf. *supra*, notre présentation de la Vie et des Miracles de Turiau (*BHL* 8342, 8343), p. 535-536.

[372] Pour la datation, DOLBEAU (2007), p. 18 et 41-42.

[373] Pour l'auteur, *ibid.*, p. 18 et 42-43.

[374] Elle nous est parvenue dans le témoin Paris, BnF, lat. 11749, fol. 66-70v, du milieu du XIe siècle, de Saint-Germain-des-Prés; pour tous les manuscrits de cette première version, DOLBEAU (2007), p. 30-31.

[375] Pour l'analyse de la Vie, *ibid.*, p. 42-51.

Vie (*BHL* 814α)[376], réalisées sans doute à Saint-Éloi, concernent essentiellement les trois premiers chapitres; le remanieur a cherché à inscrire davantage la vie de la sainte dans une chronologie et a composé et introduit, à la place des passages panégyriques, un récit de sa jeunesse plus conventionnel en ajoutant, entre autres, des origines syriennes[377]. Le succès de cette Vie et des Miracles de sainte Aure était local et limité dans le temps: aucune copie complète, postérieure à 1200, n'est connue[378].

Quant aux Sermons (*BHL* 815, 816), ils sont d'un intérêt limité du point de vue hagiographique, car ils ne font aucun emprunt aux premiers chapitres de la *Vita*. La reprise de la lettre de Paschase Radbert qui avait permis de dater la Vie, dans le deuxième Sermon rend très probable que les deux panégyriques sont contemporains de la rédaction de la Vie (*BHL* 814β) et de ce fait témoignent de la solennité de la fête de sainte Aure à cette époque[379].

3. *Passio en l'honneur d'Agoardus, Aglibertus et soc. mm. Christolii in agro Parisiensi* (*BHL* 168)

Au milieu du IXe siècle, Usuard mentionne, au 24 juin dans son martyrologe, la vénération des martyrs de Créteil, Agoard et Aglibert[380]. L'absence de détails laisse supposer qu'il ne savait rien d'autre à leur sujet. Il existe aussi une *Passio Agoardi, Agliberti et soc. mm. Christolii in agro Parisiensi* (*BHL* 168), qui pose un problème de datation. Tenons-nous en donc pour l'instant uniquement aux données sûres.

La légende de ces deux martyrs est relatée, de façon succincte, mais avec un certain nombre de détails, dans la *Passio Saviniani et Potentiani* (*BHL* 7416), telle qu'elle a été élaborée par un moine de Saint-Pierre-le-Vif de Sens, sous l'abbatiat de Gerbert,

---

[376] Elle nous est parvenue dans les témoins Florence, Bibl. Nazionale, conv. soppr. J. VII. 48, fol. 85v-96 et 101v-102v, du XIIe siècle, provenant de Saint-Marc de Florence, et Paris, BnF, lat. 15436, fol. 12-14v, du XIe siècle, provenant de Saint-Marcel de Paris; pour tous les manuscrits de cette deuxième version, DOLBEAU (2007), p. 31-32.

[377] *Ibid.*, p. 37-38.

[378] Des copies plus tardives sont en réalité de Vies abrégées de plus en plus courtes; cf. DOLBEAU (2007), p. 30-36.

[379] *Ibid.*, p. 51-52.

[380] USUARD, *Martyrologe*, *AASS*, Iun. IV, 1707, p. 815-816.

entre 1046 et 1079[381]. Le principal intérêt de ce texte réside dans la présentation de Savinien et Potentien comme fondateurs de l'évêché de Sens[382], envoyés par saint Pierre et faisant partie des soixante-douze disciples du Christ. Selon ce récit, Savinien avait ensuite envoyé plusieurs de ses compagnons afin qu'ils prêchent l'Évangile à Orléans, Chartres et Troyes. Dans la région parisienne, ils passèrent à Créteil où ils ont baptisé une grande partie de la population, dont deux nobles, Agoard et Aglibert. La destruction des temples païens avait cependant suscité la colère du «préfet de la ville», Agrippin, qui, à défaut de pouvoir martyriser les missionnaires qui étaient déjà partis, a torturé et mis à mort Agoard et Aglibert[383]. Il va sans dire que cette légende est sans fondement historique et qu'elle est née dans le sillage du succès des légendes apostoliques qui ont pris de l'ampleur depuis le début du IXe siècle[384]. Pour revenir à la *Passio Agoardi et Agliberti*, elle relate les circonstances de la conversion des deux notables de Créteil, ainsi que leur mort violente, exactement comme elles étaient présentées par le moine de Saint-Pierre-le-Vif, en rallongeant cependant le récit de façon considérable grâce à des dialogues entre les saints et leur persécuteur.

Se pose alors la question de savoir si cette Passion a pu servir de modèle pour celle de Sens ou, au contraire, si elle a été écrite à partir de la Passion de Savinien et Potentien. La mention d'Agoard et Aglibert dans le martyrologue d'Usuard ne rend pas complètement impossible que la *Passio Agoardi et Agliberti* date du IXe siècle[385]. Mais il nous paraît bien plus vraisem-

---

[381] *Passio Saviniani et et Potentiani* (BHL 7416), éd. L.-M. DURU, *Bibliothèque historique de l'Yonne, ou collection de légendes, chroniques et documents divers pour servir l'histoire*, t. II, Auxerre, 1863, p. 294-312; cf. aussi BAUER (1997), p. 361-362 ; sur les différentes versions de cette Passion et le problème de leur datation, cf. M. GAILLARD, «Les diocèses de Sens, Troyes et Nevers», *supra*, p. 460-462.

[382] L'auteur les présente aussi comme fondateurs du monastère Saint-Pierre-le-Vif, avant même la fondation du siège épiscopal.

[383] Cf. *Passio Saviniani et Potentiani* (BHL 7416), éd. L.-M. DURU, dans *Bibliothèque historique de l'Yonne, ou collection de légendes, chroniques et documents divers pour servir l'histoire*, t. II, Auxerre, 1863, p. 302-303.

[384] KEMPF – KRÖNERT (2017).

[385] La *BHL*ms ne signale qu'une copie du XVIIe siècle (Bruxelles, KBR, 8990-8991, fol. 120-123v (VAN DEN GHEYN, *Catalogue des manuscrits de la Bibliothèque Royale de Belgique*: V: *Histoire – Hagiographie*, Bruxelles, 1905,

blable que cette Passion soit plus tardive et qu'elle soit contemporaine de la reconstruction (inachevée) de l'église et de la construction de la crypte à la fin du XIIe siècle; même si l'église attestée au Xe siècle est sans doute bien antérieure[386].

Bibliographie

ABELS, P. – BACHRACH, B. S., éd., *The Normands and their Adversaries at War. Essays in Memory of C. Warren Hollister*, Woodbridge, 2001.
AIGRAIN, R. – GODDING, R., *L'hagiographie. Ses sources – Ses méthodes – Son histoire*, Bruxelles, 2000 (Subsidia hagiographica, 80).
BAUDOIN, P., dir., *Les Fondations scandinaves en Occident et les débuts du duché de Normandie. Actes du colloque de Cerisy-la-Salle (25-29 septembre 2002)*, Caen, 2005 (Publications du CRAHM).
BAUDOIN, P., *Le monde franc et les Vikings, VIIIe-Xe siècle*, Paris, 2009.
BAUER, T., *Lotharingien als historischer Raum: Raumbildung und Raumbewusstsein im Mittelalter*, Cologne, 1997 (Rheinisches Archiv, 136).
BERSCHIN, W., *Biographie und Epochenstil, im lateinischen Mittelalter, II: Merowingische Biographie Italien, Spanien und die Inseln im frühen Mittelalter*, Stuttgart, 1988.
BOURGEOIS, L., dir., *Les petites villes du Haut-Poitou de l'Antiquité au Moyen Âge*, t. I, Chauvigny, 2000.
BOURGEOIS, L. – FAVREAU, R. – RICHARD, C., *Du Gué-de-Sciaux à Saint-Savin-sur-Gartempe*, in BOURGEOIS (2000), p. 85-105.
BRUNHÖLZL, F. *Geschichte der lateinischen Literatur des Mittelalters, II: Die Zwischenzeit vom Ausgang des karolingischen Zeitalters bis zur Mitte des elften Jahrhunderts*, Munich, 1992.
CASAS HOMS, J.M., «Una gramàtica inèdita d'Usuard», *Analecta Montserratensia*, 10 (1964), p. 77-129 (= Miscellània Anselm M. Albareda, II).
CHRISTYS, A., «St-Germain-des-Prés, St Vincent and the martyrs of Cordoba», *Early Medieval Europe*, 7 (1998), p. 199-216.
COENS, M., «Aux origines de la céphalophorie. Un fragment retrouvé d'une ancienne passion de s. Just, martyr de Beauvais», *AB*, 74 (1956), p. 86-114.

---

n° 3527, p. 637), tirée *De codicibus ms. ecclesiae parochialis Christoliensis*. Ce témoin contient aussi plusieurs textes sur Savinen et Potentien. Je remercie ici très chaleureusement Guy Philippart pour m'avoir communiqué ces informations.

[386] Sur l'actuelle crypte de l'église Saint-Christophe, voir GILLON – SAPIN (2019), p. 261-268 (par T. GALMICHE).

DE GAIFFIER B., «Les notices hispaniques dans le martyrologue d'Usuard», *AB*, 45 (1937), p. 268-283.

—, «Les sources de la Passion des saints Savin et Cyprien», *AB*, 73 (1955), p. 323-341.

DE LACGER, L., «Saint Vincent de Saragosse», *Revue d'histoire de l'Église de France*, 13 (1927), p. 307-358.

DÉRENS, J., «Gislemar, historien de Saint-Germain-des-Prés», *Journal des Savants* (1972), p. 228-232.

DIESENBERGER, M., «Der Cvp 420: die Gemeinschaft der Heiligen und ihre Gestaltung im frühmittelalterlichen Bayern», in M. GOULLET – M. HEINZELMANN – C. VEYRARD-COSME, éd., *L'hagiographie mérovingienne à travers ses réécritures*, Ostfildern, 2010, p. 219-248.

DOLBEAU, F., «Les Prologues de légendiers latins», in *Les Prologues médiévaux. Actes du Colloque international organisé par l'Academia Belgica et l'École française de Rome avec le concours de la F.I.D.E.M., Rome, 26-28 mars 1998*, Turnhout, 2000, p. 345-393 (Fédération Internationale des Instituts d'études médiévales. Textes et études du Moyen Âge, 15) [en annexe, édition de prologues inédits].

—, «Vie et miracles de sainte Aure, abbesse, jadis vénérée à Paris», *AB*, 125 (2007), p. 17-91.

DOLBEAU, F. – RÖCKELEIN, H., «Just de Beauvais alias Justin d'Auxerre: l'art de dédoubler un saint. Avec l'édition de la Passio s. Iustini (*BHL* 4579)», in M. HEINZELMANN, dir. (2006) p. 323-357.

DUBOIS, J., *Le martyrologe d'Usuard. Texte et commentaire*, Bruxelles, 1965 (Subsidia hagiographica, 40).

—, *Les martyrologes du Moyen Âge latin*, Turnhout, 1978 (Typologie des sources du Moyen Âge occidental, 26).

DUBOIS, J. – LEMAITRE, J.-L., *Sources et méthodes de l'hagiographie médiévale*, Paris, 1993.

DUVAL, N. – PÉRIN, P. – PICARD, J.-C., «Paris», in PICARD, J.-C. et al., *Topographie chrétienne des cités de la Gaule, des origines au milieu du VIIIe siècle*, VIII: *Province ecclésiastique de Sens (Lugdunensis Senonia)*, Paris, 1992, p. 97-129.

FAVREAU, R., «Les inscriptions de l'église de Saint-Savin-sur-Gartempe», *Cahiers de civilisation médiévale*, 19 (1976), p. 9-37.

—, dir., *Saint-Savin. L'abbaye et ses peintures murales*, Poitiers, 1999.

GEARY, P. J., *Le vol des reliques au Moyen Âge*, Paris, 1993.

GILLMOR, C. M., «War on the River: Viking Numbers and Mobility on the Seine and Loire, 841-886», *Viator*, 19 (1988), p. 79-109.

—, «Aimoin's *Miracula sancti Germani* and the Viking raids on St. Denis and St. Germain-des-Prés», in ABELS – BACHRACH, éd. (2001), p. 103-127.

GILLON, P. – SAPIN, C., dir., *Cryptes médiévales et culte des saints en Île-de-France et en Picardie*, Villeneuve-d'Ascq, 2019.

GOULLET, M. – HEINZELMANN, M. – VEYRARD-COSME, C., dir., *L'hagiographie mérovingienne à travers ses réécritures*, Ostfildern, 2010 (Beihefte der Francia, 71).

GUILLOTEL, H., «L'exode du clergé breton avant les invasions scandinaves», *Mémoires de la Société d'histoire et d'archéologie de Bretagne*, 59 (1982), p. 269-315.

HARTMANN-PETERSEN, G., *Genovefa von Paris – Person, Verehrung und Rezeption einer Heiligen des Frankenreiches. Eine paradigmatische Studie zur Heiligenverehrung im Frühmittelalter*, Hambourg, 2007.

HEINZELMANN, M., *Translationsberichte und andere Quellen des Reliquienkultes*, Turnhout, 1979 (Typologie des sources du Moyen Âge occidental, 33).

—, dir., *Manuscrits hagiographiques et travail des hagiographes*, Sigmaringen, 1992 (Beihefte der Francia, 24).

—, «Manuscrits hagiographiques et travail des hagiographes: l'exemple de la tradition manuscrite des Vies anciennes de sainte Geneviève de Paris», in ID., dir. (1992), p. 9-16.

—, dir., *Livrets, collections et textes. Études sur la tradition hagiographique latine*, Ostfildern, 2006 (Beihefte der Francia, 63).

—, «L'hagiographie mérovingienne. Panorama des documents potentiels», in GOULLET – HEINZELMANN – VEYRARD-COSME, dir. (2010), p. 27-82.

HEINZELMANN, M. – POULIN, J.-C., *Les Vies anciennes de sainte Geneviève de Paris*, Paris, Genève, 1986.

HENRIET, P. – HERBERS, K. – LEHNER H. C., *Hagiographie et prophétie (VIe-XIIIe siècles), études réunies*, Florence, 2017 (Micrologus Library, 80).

HENRIET, P. *Espace et temps dans les visions cosmiques des saints*, in HENRIET – HERBERS – LEHNER, p. 111-126.

ISAÏA, M. C., *Remi de Reims. Mémoire d'un saint, histoire d'une Église*, Paris, 2010 (Histoire religieuse de la France, 35).

ISAÏA, M. C. – BRET, F., *Vie de sainte Geneviève*, Paris, 2020 (Sources chrétiennes, 610).

JULLIEN, M.-H. – PERELMAN, Fr., *Clavis scriptorum latinorum Medii Aevi. Auctores Galliae, 735-987*, I: *Abbon de Saint-Germain – Ermold le Noir*), Turnhout, 1994 (*CC CM*).

KEMPF, D. – KRÖNERT, K., «La Vie de saint Memmie de Châlons et les légendes apostoliques des diocèses de Gaule au début du IXe siècle», *Revue d'histoire de l'Église de France*, 103 (2017), p. 5-25.

KLÜPPEL, T., «Die Germania (750-950)», in *Hagiographies*, II (1996), p. 161-209.

KRÖNERT, K., *La construction du passé de la cité de Trèves, VIIIe-XIe siècles. Étude d'un corpus hagiographique.* Thèse soutenue en 2003 à l'Université Paris X – Nanterre.

LANGOSCH, K., *Europas Latein des Mittelalters*, Darmstadt 1990.

LE GOFF, J., «Culture cléricale et traditions folkloriques dans la civilisation mérovingienne?», *Annales É.S.C.*, 22 (1967), p. 780-791.

LOT, F., «La grande invasion normande de 856-862», *Bibliothèque de l'École des Chartes*, 69 (1908) p. 5-62, réimp. in ID., *Recueil des travaux historiques de Ferdinand Lot*, II, Genève – Paris, 1970, p. 713-780.

LUND, N.«L'an 845 et les relations franco-danoises dans la première moitié du IXe siècle», in: BAUDUIN, dir. (2005), p. 25-36.

MERDRIGNAC, B., *Les Vies de saints bretons durant le haut Moyen Âge (VIIe-XIIe siècle)*, Rennes, 1993.

PICARD, J.-C., «Il était une fois un évêque de Paris appelé Marcel», in M. SOT, dir., *Haut Moyen Âge. Culture, éducation et société. Études offertes à Pierre Riché*, La-Garenne-Colombes et Paris, 1990, p. 79-91.

POHLHEIM, K., *Die lateinische Reimprosa*, Berlin, 1925.

POULIN, J.-C., *L'idéal de sainteté dans l'Antiquité carolingienne d'après les sources hagiographiques (750-950)*, Québec, 1975.

—, *L'hagiographie bretonne du haut Moyen Âge, Répertoire raisonne*, Ostfildern, 2009 (Beihefte der Francia, 69).

RIBADEAU-DUMAS, F., *Histoire de Saint-Germain-des-Prés*, Paris, 1958.

RÖCKELEIN, H., *Reliquientranslationen nach Sachsen. Über Kommunikation, Mobilität und Öffentlichkeit im Frühmittelalter*, Stuttgart, 2002 (Beihefte der Francia, 48).

SAXER, V., «Passion et translation de S. Vincent écrites à Saint-Germain des Prés au IXe siècle», in ID., *Saint Vincent diacre et martyr: culte et légende avant l'an Mil*, Bruxelles, 2002, p. 257-357 (Subsidia Hagiographica, 83).

SÉNAC, P., *L'Occident médiéval face à l'Islam. L'image de l'autre*, Paris, 2000.

SILAGI, G., «Aimoin von St Germain», in *LexMA*, I (1980), col. 242.

SOHN, A., *Von der Residenz zur Hauptstadt. Paris im hohen Mittelalter*, Ostfildern, 2012.

STOCLET, A., «Le temporel de Saint-Denis du VIIe au Xe siècle. La constitution du patrimoine foncier dans le Parisis», in *Un village au temps de Charlemagne. Moines et paysans de l'abbaye de Saint-Denis du VIIe siècle à l'an Mil*, Musée National des Arts et Traditions populaires, 29 nov. 1988 – 30 avr. 1989, Paris 1988, p. 94-105.

Westeel, I., «Quelques remarques sur la *Vita Eligii*, Vie de saint Éloi», *Mélanges de sciences religieuses*, 56-2 (1999), p. 33-47 (Vies de saints dans le nord de la France, VIe-XIe siècles, Lille, 1999).

Zettler, A., «Waldo von St. Gallen», in *LexMA*, VIII (1997), col. 1958.

L'écriture hagiographique
dans la province de Lyon (env. 750-950)*

---

* La bibliographie de l'ensemble de la province de Lyon figure à la fin de cette section.

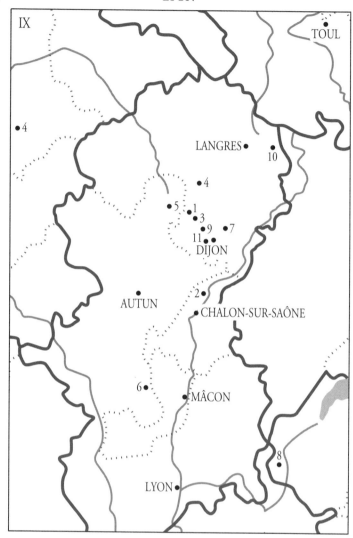

Lieux mentionnés dans les chapitres sur la province de Lyon

1 Alise
2 Beaune
3 Flavigny
4 Griselles
5 Moutiers-Saint-Jean
6 Paray-le-Monial
7 Saint-Apollinaire
8 Saint-Rambert en Bugey
9 Saint-Seine
10 Varennes
11 Vergy

L'écriture hagiographique dans le diocèse de Lyon (env. 750-950)

par

Marie-Céline Isaïa

Introduction.
I. De rares textes de datation incertaine concernant des saints d'époque mérovingienne.
II. Les martyrologes (Anonyme, Florus, Adon).

Introduction

Le diocèse de Lyon ne manifeste pas d'intérêt pour l'écriture hagiographique au moment de sa renaissance sous Leidrade (env. 798/804-814/816)[1] puis Agobard (816-840)[2], une situation d'autant plus remarquable que les clercs lyonnais élaborent durant cette même période des martyrologes historiques. Comme l'activité du diacre Florus (env. 825-855) permet de s'en apercevoir, l'Église lyonnaise s'est spécialisée au IXe siècle dans le travail intellectuel de récolte, critique et compilation

---

[1] Holtz (2013): la date de 798 est une déduction d'après une lettre d'Alcuin à Arn (éd. Dümmler, *Ep. Karolini Aevi*, II, Berlin 1895, n° 165, p. 267); Alcuin écrit à son ami en janvier 799 que Leidrade a été malade toute l'année et hésite entre le ministère de prédication et la vie plus tranquille [du moine]. Louis Holtz conclut que Leidrade était déjà évêque à cette époque; on peut aussi penser qu'il hésite à accepter la mission que veut lui confier Charlemagne et repousser à 799/800 sa consécration. La date de 804 dépend de l'interprétation des *Annales Lugdunenses*: si la personne qui a écrit en regard de l'année 804 «sans mérite de ma part, j'ai reçu la bénédiction» (Roma, Bibliotheca Vallicelliana E 26, fol. 31) est bien le co-évêque Agobard, alors Leidrade qui l'a choisi est entré en charge en 804 au plus tard.

[2] La meilleure synthèse sur Agobard est l'introduction de Michel Rubellin (2016).

des documents anciens davantage que dans la rédaction de textes nouveaux, surtout à portée historiographique[3]. Il est aussi possible que la réticence à l'égard des images et la prudence envers le culte des reliques qui caractérisent la réflexion d'Agobard aient limité l'inspiration hagiographique des clercs lyonnais[4]. Reste à considérer pour le diocèse de Lyon de rares textes de datation incertaine.

I. DE RARES TEXTES DE DATATION INCERTAINE CONCERNANT DES SAINTS D'ÉPOQUE MÉROVINGIENNE

L'écriture de ces textes est à situer plutôt avant le IXe siècle (deuxième moitié du VIIIe siècle?) ou nettement après la première moitié du IXe siècle[5].

La Passion de saint Rambert (*BHL* 7058) raconte la vie du grand aristocrate *Ragnebertus*, accusé de complot contre le maire du palais Ébroïn († 680)[6]. Grâce à l'intercession d'Ouen de Rouen, Rambert est seulement condamné à l'exil en Bugey (Ain); dans cette retraite forcée, il s'amende et fait pénitence, si bien qu'il est prêt à mourir en martyr quand Ébroïn envoie ses hommes de main l'assassiner. Le corps de Rambert est d'abord enterré à l'extérieur d'une église fondée par l'ermite saint Domitien en l'honneur de saint Genès d'Arles, puis placé à l'intérieur quand *Ragnebertus* commence à faire des miracles: la Passion décrit l'église devenue Saint-Rambert comme une basilique rurale de pélerinage[7]. Une publication collective a été

---

[3] En dernier lieu, CHAMBERT-PROTAT (2016).

[4] En préparation du concile de 825, Agobard a réuni un dossier d'autorités peu iconophiles et polémique contre une dévotion excessive envers les saints cf. *De picturis et imaginibus*, éd. L. VAN ACKER, *Agobardi Lugdunensis Opera omnia*, Turnhout, 1981 (*CC CM* 52), p. 151-181 et MITALAITÉ (2019).

[5] ISAÏA (2012).

[6] *Passio s. Ragneberti* (*BHL* 7058), éd. B. KRUSCH, *MGH*, *SRM*, V, Hanovre – Leipzig, 1910, p. 209-211.

[7] Auj. église Saint-Jean à Saint-Rambert-en-Bugey (Ain); cette région faisait partie du diocèse de Belley et donc, au Moyen Âge, de la province de Besançon; l'action de Leidrade dans ce monastère (cf. n. 11) fait supposer qu'il dépendait néanmoins du diocèse de Lyon tout proche.

consacrée en 1995 au culte de saint Rambert[8]. Elle donne une bonne idée de la difficulté qu'il y a à dater un texte, dont la langue serait mérovingienne[9] mais qui décrit l'organisation d'un palais assez carolingien[10]. La seule certitude est que la Passion de saint Rambert emprunte à la Passion de saint Léger écrite par Ursin peu avant 700 (*BHL* 4851). Situer l'écriture de la Passion entre le principat pippinide (années 740-750) et la réforme de Saint-Rambert (années 790-810) dans l'esprit de la réforme d'Aniane[11], est un compromis possible, même si Martin Heinzelmann n'exclut pas une datation mérovingienne[12]. Dans tous les cas, la *Vita* témoigne de l'existence d'un culte d'intérêt local: elle n'attache aucune importance à l'Église de Lyon ou à ses pasteurs, et les martyrologes lyonnais (*infra*) ignorent Rambert en retour.

Un résumé d'une Vie de saint Galmier/Germier – *Baldomerus* (*BHL* 899) a été édité par Henskens dans les *Acta Sanctorum*[13] d'après les notes que lui avait transmises Pierre-François Chifflet, à partir d'un manuscrit perdu de Saint-Just. Elle raconte comment Germier travaillait comme forgeron à *Auditiacus* quand l'abbé Viventius l'a rencontré et fait entrer dans la communauté de Saint-Just. Germier fut par la suite ordonné malgré lui sous-diacre par l'évêque de Lyon Gaudricus. Il accomplit encore des miracles. D'après les Bollandistes, la Vie existait dans un manuscrit hagiographique (IXe/Xe s.) qui portait l'*ex-libris*

---

[8] BAUD *et al.* (1995), en particulier TREFFORT (1995) pour le contexte d'élimination des élites régionales (Ennemond, Vulbas, Rambert) par le pouvoir neustrien, et BERTHELON – TREFFORT (1995, p. 41-46) pour le rôle joué par le monastère de l'Île-Barbe (Lyon) dans la diffusion du culte de Rambert.

[9] BERSCHIN (1988), p. 78-80.

[10] HEINZELMANN (1990), p. 115.

[11] Dans son rapport à Charlemagne, Leidrade commémore les travaux qu'il a menés à Saint-Rambert, à l'occasion de ce qui semble avoir été une reconversion d'une communauté de clercs ruraux en monastère de type bénédictin: «Un autre monastère, construit en l'honneur de saint Rambert, a été de la même façon repris de fond en comble, murs, toits, et même les églises; 56 moines l'habitent avec la Règle pour gardienne.», *Similiter aliud monasterium in honorem sancti Ragneberti aedificatum* [aj.: *ubi eiusdem sancti requiescit corpus*], *de novo totum reparatum est, sive in parietibus, sive in tectis vel eciam in ecclesiis, ubi nunc monachi numero* LVI *secundum regularem custodiam habitant.* LEIDRADE, *Lettre à Charlemagne*, éd. Coville (1928), p. 283-287, citation p. 287.

[12] HEINZELMANN (2010), p. 51.

[13] *Epitome vitae s. Baldomeri*, *AASS*, Feb. III, 1658, col. 683-684.

(Xe s.) de Saint-Père-en-Vallée (Chartres)[14]. Les vingt-sept *Vitae* que réunissait ce manuscrit témoignaient d'un intérêt certain mais non-exclusif pour le sanctoral bourguignon et rhodanien[15]; il a apparemment disparu dans l'incendie de la bibliothèque municipale. Impossible d'en dire plus sur une Vie dont le noyau peut être ancien, dans la mesure où elle parle de Saint-Just comme d'une communauté où certains vivent en ermites, un peu comme dans une laure; ce n'est donc pas le modèle canonial qui prévaut.

Les Actes de l'évêque martyr saint Ennemond posent des problèmes similaires de datation, qui ont été parfaitement explorés par Paul Fouracre et Richard A. Gerberding[16]: il n'existe pas de manuscrit faisant connaître la vie et l'assassinat politique de cet évêque attesté av. 653-av. 664, mais la seule édition de Jean Périer pour les *Acta Sanctorum* d'après une copie du XVIe siècle[17]. En l'état, les Actes de saint Ennemond sont vraisemblablement la réécriture tardive d'un texte de la deuxième moitié du VIIe siècle. Ils racontent comment Ennemond, dont le père puis le frère sont *praefectus* de Lyon, suscite la jalousie et la haine des élites locales qui le dénoncent comme traître au roi Clotaire III son filleul. Malgré l'appui de Waldebert abbé de Luxeuil, Ennemond est emmené sous bonne garde à Chalon-sur-Saône où il est assassiné. Les détails ne coïncident pas entièrement avec ce que la Vie de saint Wilfrid d'Eddius Stefanus[18], rédigée au dé-

---

[14] Chartres, BM 115 (63), fol. 110v-112, voir *Catalogue général des bibliothèques publiques des départements*, XI: *Chartres*, Paris, 1890, p. 63; description sous la cote Chartres 63, n°VII du *Cat. codic. hagiographic. latinorum Bibliothecae publicae Civitatis Carnotensis*, AB, 8 (1889), p. 92-98, texte 15 p. 94.

[15] Noter par ex. la présence des Vies de Philibert (*BHL* 6805, fol. 3-14v) et de Valérien (*BHL* 8488, fol. 175-178v) qui renvoient à Tournus, avec Aunaire d'Auxerre (*BHL* 805, fol. 89v-93v), puis d'Apollinaire de Valence (*BHL* 634, fol. 169-174v), des martyrs vénérés à Lyon Cyprien de Carthage (*BHL* 2040, fol. 130v-132v) et Pantaléon de Nicomédie (*BHL* 6429, fol. 94-101v), s'ajoutant à Galmier.

[16] *Acta Annemundi* (*BHL* 506), éd. J. PÉRIER, *AASS*, Sept. VII, 1760, col. 744-746; FOURACRE, GERBERDING (1996), p. 166-179 pour le commentaire, p. 179-192 pour la traduction anglaise.

[17] Périer reproduit au XVIIIe siècle l'édition du XVIIe siècle de P.-Fr. Chifflet, d'après les notes manuscrites d'un curé du XVIe siècle, à partir d'un manuscrit perdu: reconstitution de la chaîne, et identification des ajouts probables en fonction de chaque éditeur dans COVILLE (1928) p. 366-375.

[18] AEDDE DIT STEFANUS, *Vita sancti Wilfrithi* (*BHL* 8889), *The Life of Bishop Wilfrid by Eddius Stephanus*, éd. et trad. B. COLGRAVE, Cambridge, 1927.

LE DIOCÈSE DE LYON 597

but du VIIIe siècle, révèle du Lyon des années 660; quand elle dit que Wilfrid a séjourné trois ans à Lyon auprès d'un évêque puissant, assassiné sur l'ordre de la reine Bathilde, elle a néanmoins gardé l'essentiel du contexte d'élimination d'Ennemond. La mention de Viventiolus comme l'évêque de Lyon qui a choisi et consacré Ennemond (cap. 2, col. 744C) est l'un des anachronismes les plus manifestes qui ont fait douter de l'ancienneté des Actes[19]. Viventiolus en effet était évêque de Lyon au début du VIe siècle, correspondant d'Avit de Vienne, notamment présent au concile d'Épaone (517)[20]. La mise en scène de cet évêque suffit pour dire que la réécriture du noyau mérovingien a eu lieu assez tard, mais ne permet pas de choisir entre la deuxième moitié du IXe et le Xe siècle.

II. Les martyrologes (Anonyme, Florus, Adon)

Les clercs lyonnais du IXe siècle s'intéressent à l'hagiographie sous l'angle particulier des martyrologes dits historiques, c'est à dire présentés comme des calendriers (type martyrologe hiéronymien) mais augmentés de brèves notices topo-biographiques[21]. À Lyon, un anonyme complète d'abord avant 806 un récent martyrologe anglo-saxon du VIIIe siècle (tradition dite Bède II, apr. 755). Le diacre Florus révise ensuite le travail de l'Anonyme[22]. Adon enfin compose avant de devenir évêque de Vienne (860-875) son propre martyrologe à partir de celui de Florus[23]. Il n'y a pas lieu de rattacher aussi au *scriptorium* de Lyon le martyrologe contemporain de Saint-Quentin en Vermandois (martyrologe du pseudo-Florus). Malgré l'unité de lieu, il faut bien distinguer deux projets successifs: l'esprit de système qui caractérise le clergé lyonnais sous Leidrade puis

---

[19] Coville (1928) p. 387; Fouracre, Gerberding (1996), p. 171.
[20] Éd. C. de Clercq, Turnhout, 1963 (*CC SL*, 148C), mention de Viventiole p. 35; la lettre de convocation écrite par Viventiole en vue du concile (*Ibid.*, p. 23-24); l'évêque est encore en charge au moment du concile de Lyon de 518-523 (*Ibid.*, p. 40).
[21] Quentin (1908).
[22] Dubois, Renaud (1976).
[23] Dubois, Renaud (1984); sur le martyrologe d'Adon, cf. *infra* les p. 608-610 où A. M. Bultot-Verleysen avance une date et un lieu de rédaction différents.

Agobard conduit dans la première moitié du IXe siècle à tendre vers la rédaction d'un premier martyrologe historique complet (Anonyme puis les deux rédactions connues de Florus), en accord avec les impératifs carolingiens réformateurs; le martyrologe est un livre liturgique nécessaire au quotidien pour la célébration de l'office de nuit et la formation des moines[24]. Adon, quant à lui, parti de l'abbaye de Ferrières après l'élection de l'abbé Loup (840), réalise un projet personnel qui ne répond à aucune commande épiscopale; son martyrologe se rattache à l'Église de Lyon du fait de sa dépendance textuelle à l'égard du martyrologe de Florus, version II; il a vraisemblablement été rédigé alors qu'Adon réside dans la vallée du Rhône, mais révèle le goût d'Adon pour «les embellissements de la fiction» hagiographique[25] davantage qu'il ne rappelle la rigueur des entreprises lyonnaises précédentes.

---

[24] NIEDERKORN-BRUCK (2004).
[25] SCHILLING (2011), citation p. 78 dans le cadre d'une analyse globale des *Vitae* écrites par Adon.

L'écriture hagiographique dans les diocèses suffragants de Lyon (env. 750-950)

par

Michèle GAILLARD
avec la collaboration d'Alain RAUWEL*

INTRODUCTION.
I. LE DIOCÈSE DE LANGRES (avec A. RAUWEL). – A. La Vie de Valentin de Griselles. – B. La Passion de Gengoul. – C. L'activité hagiographique autour de Moutiers-Saint-Jean. – D. Une activité hagiographique autour de Saint-Bénigne de Dijon ?
II Le DIOCÈSE D'AUTUN. – A. *Translatio* et *Miracula* de sainte Reine. – B. Incertitudes d'attribution et de datation.
III. Le DIOCÈSE DE CHALON-SUR-SAÔNE. – A. L'activité hagiographique autour de l'évêque Girbaldus. – B. Gratus: une Vie tardive ? – C. La Passion de saint Valérien (Tournus).

INTRODUCTION

Les villes épiscopales, y compris la métropole et excepté peut-être Chalon à la fin de la période, ne paraissent pas particulièrement concernées par l'écriture hagiographique. Celle-ci se développe surtout en relation avec le culte de saints locaux, en milieu rural ou en milieu monastique. Cette production hagiographique n'a aucun lien avec celle des provinces voisines (Sens au nord, Vienne au sud). Dans le diocèse de Langres, les études critiques anciennes, en particulier celles du chanoine Jean Marilier[1], ont permis de repérer un petit nombre de textes hagiographiques attribuables à la période carolingienne sans

---

* Professeur agrégé à l'Université de Bourgogne et membre du Centre d'études en sciences sociales du religieux (CéSOR) de l'EHESS.
[1] Biographie et bibliographie dans CHAUVIN (1994).

qu'on puisse mettre en valeur une activité particulièrement riche autour de la cathédrale ou d'un monastère. Dans les diocèses d'Autun et de Chalon, qui sont issus, comme ceux de Nevers et de Mâcon, du démembrement du diocèse d'Autun de l'Antiquité tardive[2], la datation des récits hagiographiques est souvent complexe; seuls quelques textes peuvent être datés de l'époque carolingienne en fonction des manuscrits conservés ou de la teneur du récit, mais leur attribution à des hagiographes locaux, quoique probable, ne peut pas toujours être prouvée.

I. Le diocèse de Langres

A. La Vie de Valentin de Griselles

Une incertitude subsiste encore sur la datation de la Vie de Valentin (*BHL* 8457), objet d'un pèlerinage dans l'église rurale de Griselles[3], mais des indices pourraient conduire à la dater des alentours de 850/900 puisqu'elle est copiée dans plusieurs manuscrits datés des IXe/Xe siècles[4]; Valentin ne figure pas dans le martyrologe d'Usuard, ce qui fait supposer que l'écriture de la Vie n'est pas antérieure à l'époque carolingienne, même si les fouilles ont montré qu'un édifice engloba la tombe de l'ermite dès l'époque mérovingienne[5].

B. La Passion de Gengoul

La plus ancienne version de Passion de Gengoul (*BHL* 3328 a été récemment étudiée et datée par Monique Goullet), ainsi que les deux suivantes dont *BHL* 3329, poème écrit par Hros-

---

[2] Pour le diocèse de Nevers, ensuite ratttaché à la province de Sens, cf. *supra*, p. 464-465: aucun texte hagiographique ne semble avoir été rédigé dans le diocèse de Mâcon à cette période.

[3] Sapin – Deflou-Leca (2000-2001).

[4] Le manuscrit 63 de la BM de Chartres, en provenance de Saint-Père, détruit en juin 1944, fut autrefois daté des IXe-Xe siècles; le manuscrit Vatican, Reg. lat. 318, élément d'un passionnaire de Fleury, fut daté par dom Wilmart du début du Xe siècle; le manuscrit Autun BM 34 est daté dans le catalogue des IXe-Xe siècles.

[5] Sapin (2012), p. 334-335.

witha de Gandersheim[6]. Ce texte relate l'assassinat de Gengoul, aristocrate vivant au VIIIe siècle en Bourgogne, par sa femme et l'amant de celle-ci, un clerc; ce meutre passionnel, requalifié en martyre, donna lieu à l'écriture d'une légende qui eut un grand succès populaire jusqu'à l'époque moderne. Cette passion a très problement été rédigée à l'abbaye de Varennes, où était conservé le corps du saint, dans la seconde moitié du IXe siècle ou dans la première moitié du Xe siècle; elle ne peut en tout cas qu'être antérieure à la translation des reliques à Toul vers 970.

C. L'activité hagiographique autour de Moutiers-Saint-Jean

Parmi les textes concernant Jean de Réôme (mentionné dans les martyrologes d'Usuard, de Florus et d'Adon), certains pourraient avoir été rédigés à l'époque carolingienne. L'auteur de la *Vita prima* (*BHL* 4424) se présente comme étant Jonas de Bobbio († vers 660) dans les quelques lignes qui précèdent la préface dans le plus ancien manuscrit répertorié, datable des IXe-Xe siècles et utilisé par B. Krusch pour son édition[7]. Cette attribution pose évidemment question, de même que la datation des autres versions de cette Vie (*BHL* 4425 à 4428) et des récits de translation (*BHL* 4429-4430) dont le plus ancien manuscrit répertorié date du XIe siècle[8] et qui pourraient donc être carolingiens; quant à la Vie contenue dans le beau manuscrit de la bibliothèque municipale de Semur confectionné aux alentours de l'An mil, dont l'incipit est celui de *BHL* 4225, ce pourrait être une réécriture carolingienne de cette Vie[9].

---

[6] Goullet (2002), en part. p. 237-242; Guerreau-Jalabert (2002); Poly (1992).

[7] Paris, BnF, lat. 11748 (qui contient un certain nombre de Vies et de Passions réputées anciennes), fol. 151r-154r: éd. B. Krusch, *Vita Iohannis abbatis Reomanensis auctore Iona*, MGH, SRM, III, Hanovre, 1896, p. 505-517. La *BHLMs* identifie le texte, en partie illisible car effacé, du ms. Paris, BnF, lat. 11748 comme étant *BHL* 4727, ce qui est une erreur manifeste: l'incipit n'en est pas répertorié dans la *BHL*.

[8] Vatican, Reg. lat. 493 selon la *BHLMs*.

[9] Une édition de ce manuscrit est en cours par Eliana Magnani et Daniel Russo, et des études lexicologiques par Nicolas Perreaux, de l'université de Dijon. Pour Krusch (1893), il s'agit du même texte que celui du ms. Vatican, Reg. lat. 593 utilisé par Holder-Egger et que celui édité par Mabillon,

L'écriture de la Vie de saint Seine (*BHL* 7585), qui est mentionné dans le martyrologe d'Usuard et est censé avoir été un disciple de Jean de Réôme, est peut-être en rapport avec le séjour que fit Benoît d'Aniane au monastère de Saint-Seine, dans les années 780, ou bien encore avec la réforme qu'il propagea ensuite dans l'empire, mais les plus anciens manuscrits conservés datant du XIIe siècle[10], le débat reste ouvert, d'autant que c'est d'après un manuscrit de Moutiers-Saint-Jean que Pierre Rouvier en fit l'édition, en 1637[11].

D. Une activité hagiographique autour de Saint-Bénigne de Dijon?

Le récit de translation des reliques de saint Médard de Soissons à Dijon (*BHL* 5871) a été daté par Chaume[12] du début du Xe siècle: cette translation, selon l'auteur, aurait été causée par les incursions des «Marcomans», autrement dit des Hongrois[13]; en tout cas l'écriture de ce récit (*BHL* 5871) est antérieure au milieu du XIIe siècle[14]. Le manuscrit 640 de la BM de Dijon, en provenance de Cîteaux (XIIe-XIIIe s.), contient un récit de cette translation (*BHL* 5871) qui fait suite, d'une part, à une Vie de Médard (*BHL* 5867) dont le plus ancien manuscrit répertorié (dans la *BHLMS*) date du XIe siècle (Vatican, Reg. Vat. 596), et d'autre part, au *sermo* attribué à Odilon, moine de Soissons (*BHL* 5873)[15]; la datation proposée par Chaume est donc recevable, même si elle ne peut être prouvée.

---

mais découpé en leçons (*BHL* 4425); il s'agirait donc une version interpolée de la Vie attribuée à Jonas.

[10] Dijon, BM 641; Montpellier, BIU, H 30; Vatican, Reg. lat. 542; Paris, BnF, lat. 16733 et 17006.

[11] P. Rouvier, *Reomaus, seu Historia monasterii S. Joannis Reomaensis, in tractu Lingonensi, primariae inter gallica coenobia antiquitatis, ab anno Christi 425, collecta et illustrata*, Paris, 1637, p. 31-39.

[12] Chaume (1923), p. 30.

[13] Sur les Hongrois en Bourgogne, voir Mouillebouche (2006).

[14] Car citée dans la biographie du prévôt Garnier de Mailly, abbé de Saint-Étienne de Dijon (vers 1032-vers 1050), écrite dans le 3e quart du XIIe siècle; cf. Chassel (1993), p. 18, 84 et 156-157.

[15] Sur Odilon, qui a vécu au début du Xe siècle, voir *supra*, M.-C. Isaïa, «Les diocèses de Reims, Soissons et Laon», p. 330-333.

La Vie de l'évêque de Langres Urbanus (*BHL* 8407), dont les moines de Saint-Bénigne de Dijon possédaient les reliques, étant recopiée dans le manuscrit Paris, BnF, lat. 9376 dont les fol. 56-59 sont datables des environs de l'An Mil, il est probable que cette Vie fut écrite dans le courant du Xe siècle.

L'écriture, probablement par un moine de Saint-Bénigne, des Miracles de saint Apollinaire de Ravenne (*BHL* 627), vénéré au prieuré bourguignon du même nom, dépendant de Saint-Bénigne de Dijon, est sans aucun doute postérieure au début du Xe siècle: le récit décrit des Hongrois invoquant leur Dieu Wodan (chap. V) et raconte le transport des reliques pour ce qui ressemble fort à une assemblée de Paix (chap. IX); les plus anciens manuscrits répertoriés datant du XIIe siècle, une écriture dans le courant du XIe siècle est plausible, d'autant que c'est à la fin du Xe ou au début du XIe siècle que l'église Saint-Apollinaire fut rendue aux moines de saint-Bénigne[16].

II. Le diocèse d'Autun

A. *Translatio* et *Miracula* de sainte Reine

La *Passio Reginae* (mentionnée par Usuard au 7 septembre[17]) a été laissée de côté car indatable et plagiée de celle de Marina; en revanche la date de la translation depuis Alise jusqu'à Flavigny, en 866, sous l'abbé Egil, donne le *terminus post quem* pour la rédaction du récit de translation; selon le chanoine Marilier, ce texte a été rédigé par un témoin[18]. Il semble que les *Miracula* aient été écrits par le même auteur, sans doute un moine de Flavigny décidé à montrer que la sainte a approuvé son déplacement à Flavigny puisqu'elle y opère des miracles[19].

---

[16] *Chronique de Saint-Bénigne*, éd. BOUGAUD GARNIER (1875), p. 134.

[17] Usuard complète la notice du martyrologe hiéronymien, mais, à la différence de celui-ci, ne localise pas précisément la sainte: *In territorio Augustudunensi, sanctae Reginae virginis, quae sub proconsule Olibrio, equulei, cerceris ac lampadarum perpessa supplicia, tandem capitali sententia finiri est iussa*; cf. DUBOIS (1965), p. 298-299.

[18] MARILIER (1980), p. 147-156.

[19] COURTINE (1997), p. 35-40.

B. Incertitudes d'attribution et de datation

Grâce aux plus anciens manuscrits recensés[20], la Vie de Cassien [BHL 1630] est datable au plus tard de fin IXe/début Xe siècle. Il est probable que la Vie a été rédigée avant la translation à Saint-Quentin, en 841, puisqu'il n'en est pas question; quant aux deux autres versions fort proches l'une de l'autre [BHL 1631-1632], dont les plus anciens manuscrits recensés sont datés des Xe et XIe siècle, elles ne comportent pas non plus d'indices internes de datation et d'attribution. L'écriture peut avoir été l'œuvre d'un auteur «bourguignon» comme d'un moine de Saint-Quentin[21]. Quant à la Vie en vers (BHL 1633-1634), elle a très certainement été rédigée à Saint-Quentin (cf. *supra*, «Le diocèse de Noyon», p. 369).

La translation à Vergy, sous le comte Manassès de Chalon, à la fin du IXe siècle, des reliques de Vivant (Viventius) emmenées par des moines venus de Vendée donne le *terminus post quem* de la rédaction du récit de translation (BHL 8725-8726)[22]; la datation du plus ancien manuscrit[23] en donne le *terminus ante quem* (milieu XIe s.).

Les données concernant Floscellus, Leonardus, Racho et Reverianus sont encore plus fragiles.

Les reliques de Flocel (Floscellus), honoré à Beaune, auraient été transportées depuis le Cotentin jusqu'à Beaune au temps d'un comte Othon (Eudes), qui pourrait être Eudes, comte de Paris et comte d'Auxerre qui devint roi en 888 et mourut en 923[24]. La Vie de Flocel se trouve dans un manuscrit daté des

---

[20] Paris, BnF, lat. 5310 et 11748, IXe/Xe siècle (cf. n. 62). Pour la Vie en vers [BHL 1633], voir plus loin (diocèse de Noyon).

[21] Pour la Vie en vers [BHL 1633], voir plus loin (diocèse de Noyon).

[22] La première Vie de saint Viventius (BHL 8424), contenue dans le manuscrit 33 de la bibliothèque municipale d'Autun, du Xe siècle et dans le manuscrit Paris, BnF, lat. 13762 a probablement été rédigée en Vendée avant la translation; cf. RAUWEL (2010), p. 14.

[23] MS. Vatican, Ott. lat. 120 (fol. 84v-93r) selon la *BHLMs*.

[24] Le culte est attesté dans le Martyrologe de Beaune, au fol. 63, mais, dans ce même martyrologe, la seule translation mentionnée est celle de 1265, au fol. 179: *Quinto Idus Novembris. Eadem die Translatio corporis B. Floscelli martyris, in hac ecclesia Belnensi quiescentis, quod corpus per venerabiles patres, dominum Simonem, titulo S. Ceciliæ presbyterum Cardinalem, Apostolicæ Sedis legatum in Francia, et Girardum Dei Gratia Eduensem episcopum, de loco ad locum magis venerabilem die prædicta est translatum anno Domini millesimo ducentesimo sexagesimo*

IXe/Xe siècles²⁵; cette vie fut écrite au plus tard au IXe siècle mais rien ne dit qu'elle ait été rédigée en Bourgogne, puisqu'il n'y est fait aucune mention de la translation.

Quant à la Vie de l'évêque d'Autun Racho (ou Rocho), elle n'est connue que par un manuscrit du XVe siècle (Paris, BnF, lat. 916), dont la division en *lectiones* ne plaide pas pour l'ancienneté de l'écriture, du moins dans cette forme²⁶.

Le culte de Révérien (de Paul et de leurs dix compagnons) est mentionné dans les martyrologes d'Adon et d'Usuard²⁷ mais la Vie éditée par les Bollandistes, d'après un ancien manuscrit collationné par Chifflet, semble un avatar indatable du cycle d'Aurélien²⁸. Le seul manuscrit répertorié dans la *BHLMs* date du XIVe siècle.

III. Le diocèse de Chalon-sur-Saône

A. L'activité hagiographique autour de l'évêque Girbaldus

Les textes identifiés peuvent être plus ou moins précisément datés grâce aux actions de l'évêque Girbaldus, sous le règne de Louis le Bègue. Nous est parvenu, grâce à l'édition par les Bollandistes des Actes contenus dans «un ancien légendier de l'église de Chalon»²⁹, le récit de l'élévation des reliques des saints Agricola, Lupus, Sylvester³⁰ et Desideratus, par l'évêque Girbaldus; celui-ci commence par procéder à l'élévation des reliques de l'évêque Loup, dont on connaissait précisément l'emplacement de la tombe, à Saint-Pierre-hors-les-Murs, comme

---

quinto (*AASS*, Sept. V, 1755, *Commentarius praevius*, p. 478); Voillery (1886) tente de résoudre cette contradiction et place cette translation à la fin du IXe siècle.

²⁵ Montpellier, BIU H 156, fol.51-60v., ainsi que dans les manuscrits Paris, BnF, lat. 16733 et 17006, du XIIe siècle, et lat. 5353, du XIVe siècle. La Vie (*BHL* 3067) est éditée dans le *Cat. Par.*, II, p. 320-327.

²⁶ *Cat. Par.*, I, p. 50-52.

²⁷ Dubois (1965), p. 238 (1er juin).

²⁸ *AASS*, Iun. I, 1695, p. 40-41.

²⁹ *AASS*, Mart. II, 1668, p. 515-516.

³⁰ Seul Sylvestre est mentionné par Usuard, au 20 novembre: Dubois (1965), p. 344.

indiqué dans sa *Vita* (*BHL* 5081). Il est donc probable que cette écriture de la *Vita Lupi* est antérieure à cette élévation qu'on peut placer en 877; elle est conservée dans un lectionnaire du milieu du XIe siècle exécuté à la cathédrale Saint-Vincent de Chalon[31]; l'absence de repères chronologiques dans cette Vie consacrée à un évêque censé avoir vécu à la charnière des VIe et VIIe siècle incite à y voir une rédaction tardive, très probablement carolingienne[32]. Suite à cette première élévation, l'évêque Girbaldus rechercha les tombes des évêques Sylvestre et Agricola et celle du prêtre Desideratus. Comme l'indique l'auteur, ces trois personnages sont mentionnés par Grégoire de Tours[33]; Sylvestre siégea au concile d'Épaone en 517 et au concile de Lyon peu après; quant à Agricola, il procéda, selon Grégoire, à la translation du corps de Desideratus (que Grégoire avait rencontré au monastère de Gourdon[34]) dans le *xenodochium* qu'il avait fondé aux portes de Chalon. Selon ce récit, l'évêque Girbaldus procéda à l'élévation des reliques de Sylvestre et d'Agricola, retrouvées à Saint-Marcel de Chalon, peu avant le passage à Chalon du pape Jean VIII en route pour le concile de Troyes, en 879[35]; et c'est le pape lui-même qui replaça le corps d'Agricola dans son tombeau.

L'absence de manuscrit conservé rend la rédaction de ce récit difficile à dater; il est probable que l'écriture se fit peu après les événements, avant même la mort de l'évêque Girbaldus, qu'on doit situer après 885[36].

B. Gratus: une Vie tardive?

Quant à la Vie de Gratus qui assista en 650 au concile de Chalon, et dont le culte s'est développé à Saint-Laurent, qu'il aurait fondé, son écriture paraît très tardive: dans ses dernières lignes, elle évoque la reconnaissance par le pape Jean VIII (pro-

---

[31] Paris, BnF, lat. 3779.
[32] Duchesne (1910) p. 191; il fut destinataire d'une lettre de Grégoire le Grand en 601, *ibid.*, p. 193.
[33] Grégoire de Tours, *Liber in gloria confessorum*, éd. B. Krusch, *MGH, SRM*, I-2, Hanovre, 1885, §84 et 85, p. 352-353.
[34] Dép. Saône-et-Loire, arr. de Chalon.
[35] En fait, le concile eut lieu en août 878.
[36] Duchesne (1910), p. 194.

cédure qui paraît peu plausible à la fin du IXe siècle) de la sainteté de plusieurs personnages (dont Sylvester, Desiderius et Agricola); en outre dans le cours du texte, l'archevêque de Lyon est qualifié de primat, titre que la métropole lyonnaise ne revendiquait pas encore à la fin du IXe siècle et qui ne fut officiellement reconnu à l'archevêque de Lyon qu'en 1079, par Grégoire VII. Il est donc probable que cette Vie ne fut rédigée qu'au XIe siècle, dans le milieu des moines de Saint-Laurent, dont il est question dans la Vie et dont on ne sait à quelle date ils s'établirent dans cette église, ou bien encore à Paray-le-Monial où les reliques de Gratus ont été, selon l'auteur, transférées au temps du comte de Chalon Lambert († 978) et de l'évêque de Chalon Hugues (attesté en 1040); l'auteur semble confondre l'évêque de Chalon, Hugues et celui d'Auxerre du même nom (vers 1000-1039), fils du comte Lambert qui a fondé Paray-le-Monial. Cette confusion suggère une rédaction fort tardive, pas avant la fin du XIe siècle.

C. La Passion de saint Valérien (Tournus)

Valérien, compagnon de saint Marcel, et l'emplacement de son tombeau, à Tournus, sont mentionnés par Grégoire de Tours[37]; deux versions de sa Passion (*BHL* 8488 et 8489) nous sont parvenues: la première, contenue dans un manuscrit (détruit) de Chartres daté des IXe/Xe siècles[38] a sans doute été écrite avant l'*inventio* et la translation des reliques de Valérien par l'abbé Étienne vers 960/970[39]; la seconde Passion, suivie du

---

[37] Grégoire de Tours, *Liber in gloria martyrum*, éd. B. Krusch, *MGH*, *SRM*, I-2, Hanovre, 1885, §53, p. 75: *Huic martyri (Marcellus) adiungitur et sanguine et agone propinquus beatus athleta Valerianus, qui apud castrum Trinorciensim quadragesimo a Cavillonensi urbe miliario, consummato certamine, tumulatus est.*

[38] Chartres, BM 115, fol. 175r-178v; cette *Passio* figure aussi dans plusieurs manuscrits du Xe siècle: Vatican, Reg. lat. 318, Paris, BnF, lat. 17002 (légendier de Moissac) et lat. 11748, ce qui milite en faveur d'une écriture dès le IXe siècle et réduit à néant l'attribution traditionnelle à Baudry de Bourgueil. Sur la Passio de Valérien, voir, Mériaux (2018), en part. p. 433.

[39] Le moine Falcon indique, à la fin du XIe siècle, que la translation a eu lieu sous l'abbé Étienne (éd. R. Poupardin, *Monuments de l'histoire des abbayes de Saint-Philibert, Noirmoutier, Grandlieu, Tournus*, Paris, 1905, p. 97-99).

récit de translation, a été rédigée par un moine nommé Garnier, au début du XIIe siècle, à la demande de l'abbé Pierre II.

Les détails de la notice de Florus[40] montrent que celui-ci a, dès avant 840, connu un récit de la Passion; on peut en déduire que celle-ci fut rédigée avant 840. En revanche la notice rédigée avant 806 par l'Anonyme lyonnais[41] n'est qu'une adaptation du début de la notice de saint Marcel[42], ce qui suggère qu'il n'avait pas connaissance de la *Passio Valeriani*; on peut donc supposer que la Passion *BHL* 8488 a été rédigée dans les premières décennies du IXe siècle, même si l'on ne peut pas totalement exclure l'hypothèse d'une rédaction quelque peu antérieure dont l'Anonyme lyonnais n'aurait pas eu connaissance.

Aucun autre récit hagiographique concernant les saints vénérés à Tournus ne peut être rattaché à l'époque carolingienne: le récit des miracles de saint Philibert rédigé par le moine Ermentaire (*BHL* 6807-6809) s'arrête avant l'arrivée des moines à Tournus[43].

Bibliographie
(ensemble de la province de Lyon)

Baud, A. *et al.*, éd., *Saint Rambert. Un culte régional depuis l'époque mérovingienne*, Paris, 1995.

Berschin, W., *Biographie und Epochenstil im lateinischen Mittelalter*, 2: *Merowingischen Biographie*, Stuttgart, 1988.

Berthelon, B. – Treffort, C., «La diffusion du culte et la translation des reliques», in Baud (1995), p. 41-46.

Bougaud, E. – Garnier, J., éd., *Chronique de Saint-Bénigne*, Dijon, 1875.

Chambert-Protat, P., *Florus de Lyon, lecteur des Pères. Documentation et travaux patristiques dans l'Église de Lyon au IXe siècle*, Thèse de doctorat, dir. P. Mattei et A.-M. Turcan-Verkerk, EPHE, 2016.

Chassel, J.-L., *Vie de Garnier, prévôt de saint-Étienne de Dijon, étude, texte et traduction*, Asnières-sur-Seine (chez l'auteur), 1993.

---

[40] Copie du XIe-XIIe s. dans Paris, BnF, lat. 5254, en provenance de Saint-Pierre de Mâcon, fol. 52v-53r; cf. Dubois – Renaud (1976).
[41] Paris, BnF, lat. 3879, fol. 88v; cf. Dubois – Renaud (1976).
[42] *Ibid.*, fol. 88r.
[43] Cf. Bultot-Verleysen, in *Hagiographies*, VI (2014), p. 521-704.

CHAUME, M., «Les comtes de Dijon de la seconde race. Étude sur la translation des reliques de saint Médard de Soissons à Dijon en l'an 901», *Mémoires de l'Académie de Dijon*, 2 (1923), p. 27-65.
CHAUVIN, B., «*In memoriam* Jean Marilier (1920-1991)», *Cîteaux*, 45 (1994), p. 155-163.
COURTINE, N., «Sainte Reine et la tradition écrite. La *Passio s. Reginae*», in P. BOUTRY – D. JULIA, dir., *Reine au mont Auxois: le culte et le pèlerinage de sainte Reine des origines à nos jours*, Dijon – Paris, 1997, p. 29-60.
COVILLE, A., *Recherches sur l'histoire de Lyon du Ve au IXe siècle*, Paris, 1928.
DUBOIS, J., *Le Martyrologe d'Usuard: texte et commentaire*, Bruxelles, 1965 (Subsidia Hagiographica, 40).
DUBOIS, J. – RENAUD, G., *Édition pratique des martyrologes de Bède, de l'anonyme lyonnais et de Florus*, Paris, 1976.
—, *Le martyrologe d'Adon. Ses deux familles, ses trois recensions. Texte et commentaire*, Paris, 1984.
DUCHESNE, L., *Fastes épiscopaux de l'ancienne Gaule*, II: *L'Aquitaine et les Lyonnaises*, 2e éd., Paris, 1910.
FOURACRE, P. – GERBERDING, R. A., *Late Merovingian France. History and Hagiography 640-720*, Manchester, 1996.
GOULLET, M., «Les Vies de saint Gengoul, époux et martyr», in M. LAUWERS, éd., *Guerriers et moines. Conversion et sainteté aristocratiques*, Paris, 2002, p. 235-263.
GUERREAU-JALABERT, A., «Saint Gengoul dans le monde: l'opposition de la cupiditas et de la caritas», *ibid.*, p. 265-283.
HEINZELMANN, M., «*Studia sanctorum*. Éducation, milieux d'instruction et valeurs éducatives dans l'hagiographie en Gaule jusqu'à la fin de l'époque mérovingienne», in M. SOT, dir., *Haut Moyen-Âge. Culture, éducation et société. Études offertes à Pierre Riché*, La Garenne-Colombe, 1990, p. 105-138.
—, «L'hagiographie mérovingienne. Panorama des documents potentiels», in M. GOULLET – M. HEINZELMANN – C. VEYRARD-COSME, *L'hagiographie mérovingienne à travers ses réécritures*, Ostfildern, 2010, p. 27-82.
HOLTZ, L., «Leidrat, évêque de Lyon (798-814): ses livres, son écriture», in J. ELFASSI – C. LANÉRY – A.-M. TURCAN-VERKERK, éd., *Amicorum Societas. Mélanges François Dolbeau*, Firenze, 2013, p. 315-334.
ISAÏA, M.-C., «L'hagiographie contre la réforme dans l'Église de Lyon au IXe siècle», in *Réforme(s) et Hagiographie en Occident, VIe-XIIIe siècles*, *Médiévales*, 62 (2012), p. 83-104.
KRUSCH, B., in *Neues Archiv*, 18 (1893), p. 615-616.
MARILIER, J., *Alesia.Textes littéraires*, Paris, 2e éd., 1980, p. 147-156.

MÉRIAUX, C., «Les saints de Gaule du Nord et de Bourgogne dans le légendier de Moissac», in F. PELOUX, éd., *Le légendier de Moissac et la culture hagiographique méridionale autour de l'an mil*, Turnhout, 2018, p. 417-437.

MITALAITÉ, K., «Agobard et la question des images à l'époque de Louis le Pieux», in F. BOUGARD – A. CHARANSONNET – M.-C. ISAÏA, éd., *Lyon carolingien. Autour d'Agobard (816-840)*, Turnhout, 2019, p. 191-204.

MOUILLEBOUCHE, H., «Les Hongrois en Bourgogne: le succès d'un mythe historiographique», *Annales de Bourgogne*, 78 (2006), p. 127-168.

NIEDERKORN-BRUCK, M., «Wissensvermittlung im Kloster. Unterricht für den Gottesdienst – Unterricht im Gottesdienst. Wodurch und zu welchem Ende wurde den Mönchen historisches Wissen vermittelt», *Mitteilungen des Instituts für Österreichische Geschichtsforschung*, 112 (2004), p. 119-140.

POLY, J.-P, «Gengoul, l'époux martyr. Adultère féminin et norme populaire au Xe siècle», in *La femme au Moyen Âge*, Paris, 1992, p. 47-63 (Collection de la faculté de droit Jean Monnet).

QUENTIN, H., *Les martyrologes historiques du Moyen Âge: étude sur la formation du martyrologe romain*, Paris, 1908.

RAUWEL, A., «Reliques et légendes: les pérégrinations de saint Vivant», in ID., dir., *Saint-Vivant de Vergy: un prieuré clunisien au coeur de la Bourgogne*, Vosne-Romanée, Association Saint-Vivant, 2010, p. 10-19.

RUBELLIN, M., éd., *Agobard de Lyon, Œuvres*, Paris, 2016 (Sources chrétiennes, 583).

SAPIN, C., «La crypte entre mausolée et église aux Ve-VIe siècles. Réflexions à partir de sources historiques et archéologiques en particulier sur des cas bourguignons», *Hortus artium medievalium*, 18 (2012), p. 329-339.

SAPIN, C. – DEFLOU-LECA, N., «Saint-Valentin de Griselles: du culte érémitique à la fondation monastique», *Mémoires de la Commission des Antiquités du département de la Côte-d'Or*, 39 (2000-2001), p. 75-126.

SCHILLING, Beate, «Zu einem interpolierten Diplom Ludwigs des Frommen für die Kirche von Vienne (BM^2 570)», *Archiv für Diplomatik*, 57 (2011), p. 63-104.

TREFFORT, C., «Saint Domitien et saint Rambert: tradition et histoire», in BAUD (1995), p. 13-25.

VOILLERY, P., *Étude historique et critique sur les actes et le culte de saint Flocel, martyr*, Dijon, 1886, p. 32-58.

L'écriture hagiographique
dans les provinces de Vienne, Tarentaise
et Besançon
(env. 750-950)

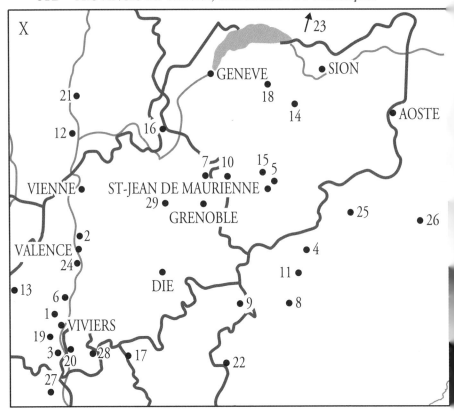

Lieux mentionnés dans les chapitres sur les provinces de Vienne et de Tarentaise

1 Alba-La-Romaine
2 Bourg-les-Valence
3 Bourg-Saint-Andéol
4 Briançon
5 Le Châtel
6 Cruas
7 Currière
8 Embrun
9 Gap
10 La Terrasse
11 La Roche-de-Rame
12 Lyon
13 Notre-Dame des Neiges
14 Octodure (Martigny)
15 Saint-Avre
16 Saint-Chef
17 Sainte-Jalle
18 Saint-Maurice d'Agaune
19 Saint-Montan
20 Saint-Paul-Trois-Châteaux
21 Savigny
22 Sisteron
23 Soleure
24 Soyons
25 Suse
26 Turin
27 Uzès
28 Vaison
29 Varacieux

L'écriture hagiographique dans le diocèse de Vienne (env. 750-950)

par

ANNE-MARIE BULTOT-VERLEYSEN

I. L'ŒUVRE D'ADON. – A. Adon compilateur: le Martyrologe. – B. Adon auteur: Les Vies de Theudère, Sévère (?) et Didier. – C. Adon éditeur: le manuscrit de Saint-Gall.
II. VIES ET MIRACLES D'ÉVÊQUES: AVIT ET BARNARD.
III. VIES D'ABBÉS: LÉONIEN, CLAIR ET MAXIME.
CONCLUSION.
BIBLIOGRAPHIE.

I. L'ŒUVRE D'ADON

La littérature hagiographique du diocèse de Vienne au IXe siècle est essentiellement marquée par la personnalité d'un de ses prélats les plus célèbres, Adon († 875)[1]. Les grandes étapes de sa vie sont connues par une lettre de son contemporain, Loup de Ferrières[2]. Vraisemblablement originaire du Gâtinais, Adon passa en effet quelques années à l'abbaye de Ferrières qu'il quitta pour Prüm. On le retrouve par la suite à Lyon, sans fonction précise, avant son élection, en 860, à la succession de l'archevêque de Vienne, Agilmar. Adon fut mêlé de près aux questions politiques et ecclésiastiques de son temps,

---
[1] Sur sa biographie, voir DUBOIS – RENAUD (1984), p. XII-XVIII; pour une vue d'ensemble de son œuvre, voir JULLIEN – PERELMAN (1994), p. 30-36.
[2] Cette lettre est adressée au comte Girart de Vienne au moment de la vacance du siège archiépiscopal de Vienne. Loup y affirme la régularité de la situation du candidat à la succession, Adon, moine de Ferrières, ayant quitté son abbaye depuis une vingtaine d'années. Voir DUBOIS – RENAUD (1984), p. XII-XIII.

dont le divorce du roi Lothaire II auquel il ne voulut jamais consentir.

L'activité littéraire d'Adon est hagiographique, mais aussi historique. Son *Breviarium de sex mundi aetatibus*, communément appelé *Chronicon*, auquel il mit la main jusqu'en 869, a été jugé avec sévérité. S'inspirant essentiellement de la chronique de Bède, l'ouvrage est complété par des données dont la chronologie est peu fiable, voire même truquée: ainsi la liste épiscopale des évêques de Vienne se trouve étalée sur cinq siècles, au lieu de trois, afin de faire d'un certain Crescent, disciple de saint Paul, le premier évêque et ainsi rehausser la renommée de l'Église de Vienne en lui attribuant une origine apostolique[3].

A. Adon compilateur: le Martyrologe

L'intérêt d'Adon pour les saints se concrétisa en premier lieu par l'élaboration d'un nouveau martyrologe[4]. Le jeune moine prit conscience que l'obligation, promulguée en 817, de lire à

---

[3] La Chronique est à lire dans *PL* 123, col. 23-138; on attend avec impatience l'édition critique dont la préparation a été annoncée par A. Dubreucq et N. Nimmegeers. Dans II Tim. 4, 10, il est dit que Paul envoya Crescent en Galatie, terme qui pourrait désigner la Galatie proprement dite ou la Gaule. Dans la première rédaction du Martyrologe, Adon fait d'abord passer le disciple par la Gaule avant de terminer ses jours en Galatie; son action à Vienne n'apparaît que dans les deuxième et troisième recensions et dans la Chronique, alors qu'Adon s'intéresse de plus près au prestige de la Viennoise. Et pour asseoir fermement la tradition, il fait de Martin et Verus, les supposés troisième et quatrième évêques de Vienne, également des disciples des apôtres (*PL* 123, col. 81 et 82). Voir Dubois – Renaud (1984), p. xix, p. 37-38 et 206-207; Nimmegeers (2014), p. 81-84. Toutefois cette version de la liste épiscopale de Vienne figure-t-elle bien dans le texte original d'Adon ou la mention des premiers évêques a-t-elle fait l'objet d'une interpolation, comme le suggère A. Grospellier sur la base d'un passage de la *Vita Theuderii* (voir n. 15)? Quoi qu'il en soit, ce type de falsification s'inscrit dans un large contexte: sa manifestation dans les textes hagiographiques aquitains dès le IXe siècle a été abordée dans notre contribution «Hagiographie d'Aquitaine (750-1130)», in *Hagiographies*, VI (2014); voir en particulier les dossiers de Front de Périgueux et de Martial de Limoges, n° 9, p. 555-560 et 17, p. 574-576. Notons que le premier évêque de Vienne attesté est Verus présent au concile d'Arles en 314 [Descombes – Février – Gauthier (1986), p. 24].

[4] Édition et commentaires Dubois – Renaud (1984). Voir également Quentin (1908), p. 465-681.

Prime le martyrologe et la Règle se heurtait à une difficulté: l'absence d'éloges pour chaque jour de l'année[5]. Son objectif fut de combler cette lacune. Il basa son travail sur celui de Florus dont il prit peut-être déjà connaissance à Prüm[6], mais c'est probablement à Lyon qu'il rédigea la première recension de son œuvre, vers 855[7]. Il ajouta 197 éloges à Florus et en modifia 188. Se vantant d'avoir rassemblé «ce que d'autres sont obligés de chercher avec beaucoup de peine à travers un grand nombre de livres», Adon s'est en fait contenté d'une dizaine de sources: la Bible, l'*Histoire ecclésiastique* d'Eusèbe dans la traduction de Rufin, le *De viris illustribus* de Jérôme, le *Liber Pontificalis*, les écrits de Grégoire de Tours et de Bède, et un seul passionnaire. Dom Quentin, relayé par J. Dubois, a mené une analyse détaillée de la méthode sciemment peu critique d'Adon qui n'hésite pas à manipuler ses sources pour remplir à tout prix le calendrier ou à étoffer des notices qu'il trouve trop sèches, au point de décourager les lecteurs par ses ajouts[8]. Confusions, voire créations pures et simples, de saints personnages à partir de vagues évocations sont légion et manifestent qu'Adon avait pour seul souci de répondre à la demande de clercs et de moines souhaitant disposer d'éloges quotidiens pour leurs offices. Il alla jusqu'à créer un faux martyrologe antique présenté comme sa source principale, le *Venerabile perantiquum martyrologium* dit *Parvum romanum*, pour conférer une autorité incontestable à une date d'anniversaire inusitée ou à un détail biographique inédit. Si la sévérité du jugement de H. Quentin, J. Dubois et G. Re-

---

[5] DUBOIS – RENAUD (1984), p. XX.

[6] Il est fort probable qu'un exemplaire du martyrologe de Florus se trouvait à Prüm car un moine de cette abbaye, Wandelbert, contemporain d'Adon, l'utilisa également (*ibid.*).

[7] Le martyrologe conservé existe en deux familles. La deuxième est l'œuvre d'un compilateur auxerrois presque contemporain d'Adon. La première dont on connaît trois recensions est authentique. Sur la première recension, élaborée à Lyon, voir la contribution de M.-C. ISAÏA, *supra*, p. 591-592. C'est dans la troisième recension que l'on trouve les additions viennoises, ce qui est un argument pour l'attribuer à l'archevêque de Vienne. Voir DUBOIS-RENAUD (1984), p. XX-XXVII. L'absence de Theudère et de Didier dans la première famille montre qu'Adon ne s'était pas encore intéressé à ces saints viennois dont il écrivit plus tard la Vie (voir *infra*).

[8] DUBOIS – RENAUD (1984), p. XXIII: «Adon s'était trompé s'il avait cru que clercs et moines entendraient avec plaisir des extraits de passions qui remplissent parfois des pages entières. Les compilateurs le résumèrent...».

naud se justifie pleinement selon nos critères contemporains, attirons toutefois l'attention sur la mentalité qu'elle révèle: Adon, dans la préface de la deuxième recension de son texte, explique qu'il a fait une œuvre utile non seulement parce qu'il a comblé les jours vides du calendrier mais aussi parce qu'il a rassemblé et résumé des lectures à l'intention de frères plus faibles et moins capables de lire, qui «auront de la sorte, en un volume de peu d'étendue, l'équivalent de ce que d'autres sont obligés de chercher avec beaucoup de peine à travers un grand nombre de livres»[9]. Il a dès lors donné libre cours à son intérêt pour la matière hagiographique, certes à moindres frais.

B. Adon auteur:
Les Vies de Theudère, Sévère (?) et Didier

À côté de ce travail de compilateur, Adon s'essaya à la composition hagiographique personnelle: il rédigea la Vie de Theudère, fondateur d'un monastère qui portera son nom et il remania les *Vitae* de son prédécesseur Didier de Vienne. Ces deux œuvres, dont l'ordre de succession n'est pas déterminé, sont les seules à lui être attribuées avec certitude.

Originaire d'Arcisse (commune de Saint-Chef, Isère), de famille noble, Theudère avait projeté de se faire moine à Lérins, mais l'évêque Césaire d'Arles le retint auprès de lui et l'ordonna prêtre. Quelque temps après, Theudère rentra dans son pays natal où il aurait construit plusieurs établissements dont la basilique mariale d'Arcisse au mont *Rupianus*, plus tard Saint-Theudère[10]. À la requête de l'évêque Philippe, il passa les dernières années de sa vie à Vienne même comme prêtre pénitencier reclus. Les seules informations que nous possédons sur le saint proviennent de la *Vita Theuderii* (*BHL* 8130)[11].

---

[9] *Ibid.*, p. XXV-XXVI, n. 2. La traduction est de Dom Quentin.

[10] Le vocable Saint-Chef est l'aboutissement de plusieurs déformations de *Theuderius* (B. de Vrégille, «Teuderio», in *BS*, XII, Rome, 1965, col. 443).

[11] Éd. *AASS*, Oct. XII, 1867, p. 840-842 qui reprend celle de Mabillon (*AASS OSB*, I, [1668], p. 678-681) plus répandue, mais moins fiable que celle publiée dans *La Vie de sainct Theudere*, Vienne, 1618 ou dans l'*Officium S. Theuderii*, Grenoble, 1667, p. 5-19 selon Grospellier (1900), p. 12. L'édition de B. Krusch qui suit le manuscrit de Saint-Gall, dont nous reparlerons, est de meilleure qualité mais omet le c. 8, quasi tout le c. 10 (à partir de *Pervenitur in suburbio*) et le c. 11 (jusque *plurima luminaria accreve-*

Sollicité vers 870 par les moines de Saint-Theudère, Adon entreprend la rédaction de l'ouvrage. S'appuyant sur les archives viennoises, des légendes locales et une Vie plus ancienne, il fait de son héros un contemporain du prêtre Sévère (VIe siècle)[12]. Il adresse son ouvrage aux frères de la communauté, qu'il exhorte ainsi: *Patris vestri Vitam, id est, Beati Theuderii, idcirco vestrae sanctitati scriptis meis comendare disposui, ut vos suis exemplis ad morem vitae aeternae amplius invitarem. Cupio enim ejus imitatores et aemulatores vos existere; cujus patrocinium Dei munere acquisivisse plurimum gaudeo.* À la fin de l'œuvre, il revient sur la nécessité pour les moines d'imiter la vie du saint s'ils désirent bénéficier de son patronage. Le texte a été analysé en détail par F. Descombes qui a souligné les nombreux parallélismes – enfance, accès à la prêtrise, rencontre avec un évêque illustre, activité de prêtre ou de moine bâtisseur –, avec la Vie de Sevère qui s'inspire elle-même de celles de Germain d'Auxerre (*BHL* 3453) et de Césaire d'Arles (*BHL* 1508-1509)[13]. Les *Vitae Theuderii* et *Severi* sont-elles pour autant toutes deux de la main d'Adon? Nous discuterons plus loin l'hypothèse de F. Descombes.

Dans le cours du récit, l'auteur met en avant deux aspects de la vie de Theudère: ses multiples fondations religieuses (c. 6)[14] et sa soumission à deux évêques, Césaire à Arles, Philippe à

---

rint), soit, selon ses propres mots dans l'introduction: *Laudes sancti miraculaque in translatione patrata praetermisi* (*MGH*, *SRM*, III, Hanovre, 1896, p. 526). Selon Descombes (1981), p. 364, «B. Krusch est le seul à avoir utilisé, dans son édition des *MGH*, le manuscrit de Saint-Gall, certainement le plus ancien et le meilleur; il a malheureusement éliminé sans justification les passages relatifs aux vertus du saint, à sa fonction de «prêtre pénitencier» et aux miracles opérés lors de la translation de son corps... on est tributaire, sur ce point, du texte des *Acta Sanctorum*».

[12] S'appuyant sur les archives viennoises, des légendes locales et une ancienne Vie, Adon situe Theudère au VIe siècle [communication inédite d'A. Dubreucq, citée par Nimmegeers (2014), p. 244 et n. 35].

[13] Descombes (1981), p. 365-368. La *Vita Caesarii* aurait influencé directement la *Vita Theuderii*: «tout le début de la *uita*, l'allusion à Lérins, l'activité de bâtisseur de monastères, tout cela baigne dans une atmosphère qui s'inspire visiblement de la *uita Caesarii*» (*ibid.*, p. 363).

[14] Excepté Saint-Theudère, d'abord dédié à Marie, ces édifices, s'ils ont existé, ont disparu. Lorsqu'ils sont attestés par d'autres sources, il n'est pas pour autant certain que Theudère soit leur véritable fondateur: voir Descombes – Février – Gauthier (1986), p. 31 et 33 au sujet de l'église Saint-Symphorien et de la chapelle Saint-Eusèbe de Verceil.

Vienne[15]. L'importance donnée à la relation entre Theudère et Césaire n'est sans doute pas innocente de la part d'Adon. Alors que Vienne était à l'origine capitale de la province romaine et du diocèse de la Viennoise, Arles avait dès le Ve siècle obtenu de devenir métropole d'une partie de ce territoire désormais dédoublé. Les limites des deux provinces avaient encore été débattues au concile de Francfort en 794. Avec les invasions, Arles vit son influence diminuer: elle perdit Viviers et Die. Dans la *Vita Theuderii*, si le saint se montre très obéissant envers Césaire, il le quitte néanmoins pour se consacrer à Vienne et se mettre finalement au service du peuple de la cité décrite avec précision et lyrisme par Adon. Qualifiée de *Galliarum nobilissima... metropolis illustrissima et inter Galliarum urbes insignissima* (c. 5) – Arles par contre n'est affectée d'aucun qualificatif –, Vienne, sous la plume de son archevêque, est doublement magnifiée aux dépens de son ancienne rivale[16]. L'intérêt de la *Vita Theuderii* pour la topographie de la ville au IXe siècle, en particulier ses fortifications antiques, est à souligner[17].

La Vie de Sévère (*BHL* 7692)[18] présente le saint comme un prêtre d'origine indienne, contemporain de Germain d'Auxerre, venu à Vienne pour convertir les païens qui y subsistaient et enseveli dans l'église Saint-Étienne qu'il aurait fondée. Signalée comme modèle de la Vie de Theudère, elle semble être un remaniement d'une *Vita* plus ancienne sur laquelle se base le

---

[15] Dans la *Vita Theuderii*, Philippe est explicitement mentionné comme 21e évêque de Vienne, alors qu'il figure en 23e position dans la liste épiscopale qu'on lit dans la Chronique. GROSPELLIER (1900), p. 14-23, suggère que cette liste a subi une interpolation visant à ajouter Crescent et Zacharias comme premiers évêques. L'argumentation n'a pas convaincu DUCHESNE (1907, p. 159, n. 1). La mention de Vienne en rapport avec Crescent apparaît dans la deuxième recension du martyrologe d'Adon: le supposé disciple des apôtres y aurait siégé et ordonné son successeur Zacharie. Enfin, dans le second éloge qui lui est consacré au 29 décembre, la troisième recension le qualifie de *Viennensis ecclesiae primi doctoris* [DUBOIS – RENAUD (1984), p. 37 et 206-207]. Cet ajout est vraisemblablement postérieur à la rédaction de la *Vita Theuderii* où la place de Crescent dans la liste épiscopale de Vienne n'est pas encore clairement définie.
[16] Voir DESCOMBES – FÉVRIER – GAUTHIER (1986), p. 23-24.
[17] Sur la rivalité entre les deux métropoles, voir CHEVALIER (1923), p. 5-11. Notons toutefois que dans la deuxième moitié du IXe siècle, la concurrence vient plus de Lyon que d'Arles [NIMMEGEERS (2014) p. 78].
[18] Éd. in *AB*, 5 (1886), p. 417-424.

martyrologe de Florus repris par Adon. F. Descombes repère méthodiquement les nombreux points communs entre les *Vitae Severii* et *Theuderii*, inspirées par celles de Césaire d'Arles et de Germain d'Auxerre[19]: le récit de l'enfance et de la jeunesse; l'accession à la prêtrise avec mention des différents degrés de l'*ordo*; la rencontre avec un évêque illustre, Germain d'Auxerre d'une part, Césaire d'Arles d'autre part, et même reconnaissance – quasi miraculeuse – entre les héros et les évêques qui se saluent par leurs noms alors qu'ils ne s'étaient jamais vus; l'activité de prêtre bâtisseur dans Vienne et dans les environs[20]; l'insistance sur la vie liturgique et sacramentelle; la mention de biens qui ont fait l'objet de restitutions. Ces deux œuvres, conclut F. Descombes qui leur associe plusieurs autres Vies viennoises[21], sont des témoins de la réorganisation de l'Église de Vienne à l'époque carolingienne, mise sous le patronage des principaux saints du diocèse qui se distinguent eux-mêmes par leur entière obéissance à leurs évêques. Cette promotion du pouvoir épiscopal apparaît dans chaque œuvre et reflète l'époque et le milieu dans lequel elles sont nées. Toutefois F. Descombes franchit un pas de plus en attribuant la révision de la *Vita Severi* à Adon lui-même[22]. Un des arguments avancés est la présence conjointe de ces Vies, aux côtés d'autres, dans un dossier hagiographique envoyé par Adon aux moines de Saint-Gall en 870, dossier sur lequel nous nous attarderons. Toutefois certains éléments incitent à la prudence. L'absence de revendication et de présentation de l'œuvre en premier lieu: la *Vita Theuderii*, comme la *Vita Desiderii*, ainsi qu'on le verra, est précédée d'une Préface où Adon se nomme et désigne les destinataires; il y met très fort en avant la valeur morale d'exemple des vies qu'il raconte et revient sur ce thème en bout d'œuvre; en outre, dans la *Vita Desiderii*, il signale l'existence de textes anciens qu'il va reprendre. À l'opposé, la *Vita Severii* commence assez abruptement et sans que l'auteur n'y manifeste aucune intention. On y trouve

---

[19] Descombes (1981), p. 365-368.
[20] Sévère fonde les églises Saint-Alban à *Vogoria*, Saint-Étienne et Saint-Laurent; la dernière est également mentionnée dans la *Vita Theuderii* (c. 7). Voir Descombes (1981), p. 367-368 et 371 et Descombes – Février – Gauthier (1986), p. 32. Sur les fondations de Theudère, voir *supra* n. 13.
[21] Celle de Didier, mais aussi celles de Clair et de Léonien sur lesquelles nous reviendrons.
[22] Descombes (1981), p. 374.

aussi rapporté un miracle – la délivrance de douze servants d'église incarcérés et enchaînés dans le but de susciter la colère de l'évêque Didier (c. 10) – qui n'apparaît pas dans la *Vita Desiderii*: or à cette occasion l'auteur dresse un bref portrait de la reine Brunehaut, très défavorable, essentiellement dans son attitude vis-à-vis des évêques qu'elle s'efforce de détourner de la religion chrétienne (il s'agit sans doute d'une allusion à l'origine arienne de la reine); son échec en ce qui concerne Didier fait croître sa haine à son égard. Dans la Vie de Didier, Adon ne fait aucune allusion à une influence néfaste de la reine dans des questions religieuses et axe son portrait sur ses écarts de conduite. Ces éléments quelque peu discordants laissent planer un doute sur l'attribution de la *Vita Severi* à l'archevêque de Vienne. Il est certain en revanche que les Vies de Theudère et de Sévère servent les mêmes objectifs: renforcer l'autorité de l'archevêque sur son clergé en promouvant le respect du droit canon et de la hiérarchie [23] et contribuer à légitimer les possessions et les revendications foncières de l'Église de Vienne [24].

Comme on vient de l'évoquer, Adon s'est également intéressé à son prédécesseur Didier († vers 610). D'origine bourguignonne, ce dernier reçut une solide formation littéraire. Jouissant de la confiance du pape Grégoire le Grand qui lui adressa plusieurs lettres, il fut également proche des souverains mérovingiens – la reine Brunehaut et son petit-fils Thierry –, mais ses discours moralisateurs déplurent. Il fut condamné à l'exil et mourut assassiné par des fonctionnaires trop zélés. Le premier auteur à mettre par écrit la Vie de l'évêque (*BHL* 2148) fut un roi wisigoth, Sisebut (612-620), lettré et correspondant d'Isidore de Séville: il y déploya des effets de style d'une qualité très

---

[23] «La rédaction de ces Vies s'inscrit dans un programme caractéristique de la Renaissance carolingienne qui vise à reprendre en main et à discipliner le clergé local. Elle permet aussi d'ébaucher un modèle de sainteté sacerdotale dans lequel l'attachement à la tradition et le respect de la hiérarchie constituent des éléments essentiels» [NIMMEGEERS (2014), p. 163].

[24] La mention de Sévère comme fondateur de Saint-Alban à *Vogoria* pourrait laisser entendre que la restitution à l'Église de Vienne décidée par Lothaire II en 863 n'aurait pas été immédiatement appliquée. De même l'attribution à Theudère de la fondation de Saint-Symphorien au-delà de la Gère, alors que Louis le Pieux avait restitué l'église dès 815, serait pour Adon une manière d'affirmer ses droits menacés par les convoitises laïques [NIMMEGEERS (2014), p. 164].

discutable et une prise de position politique résolument opposée à la reine des Francs[25]. Ce texte assez bien informé inspira peu de temps après un clerc de Vienne qui rédigea une œuvre anonyme (*BHL* 2149) dans laquelle il prit soin toutefois de se démarquer de son modèle et de le compléter par des précisions topographiques, le récit de la translation du corps du lieu du martyre, près de Lyon (Saint-Didier-sur-Chalaronne, Ain), à Vienne et des miracles posthumes[26].

La troisième Vie de Didier (*BHL* 2150) est signée par l'archevêque de Vienne[27]. Le début et la fin présentent le même schéma que la *Vita Theuderii*. Contrairement à ses prédécesseurs, Adon désigne les destinataires (Praef.): ce sont les frères et fils de l'Église de Vienne dont il souhaite augmenter la ferveur religieuse en mettant par écrit à leur intention la Vie de leur patron; ce souci d'exemplarité est encore rappelé à la fin du récit dans une sorte de postface intitulée *Dicta episcopi Adonis Viennensis*. Après une brève présentation stéréotypée du saint, l'auteur dresse un tableau concis des circonstances historiques et une généalogie précise des rois francs: l'un et l'autre ne détonnent pas sous la plume de l'auteur du *Chronicon* (col. 435-437).

L'œuvre suit les grandes lignes de la Vie anonyme. Bien qu'Adon se réfère explicitement à des *antiquis scriptis* (col. 435B) ou *membranis antiquioribus* (col. 442B), il paraît ignorer la première *Vita* dont on ne trouve pas d'écho direct dans son travail de réécriture[28]. Il partage toutefois et amplifie l'hostilité du roi

---

[25] Voir l'édition récente de Martín (2000) et l'arrière-plan politique dans Fontaine (1980).

[26] Éd. B. Krusch, *MGH*, *SRM*, III, Hanovre, 1896, p. 638-645. La position de Krusch selon lequel la *Vita secunda* ne serait pas antérieure au milieu du VIIIe siècle car l'auteur aurait commis de grossiers anachronismes, n'est plus défendue aujourd'hui par la critique. Voir Heinzelmann (2010), p. 49 et n. 99. Pour Martín Iglesias (1995), «Una posible datacion...», p. 448, elle aurait pu avoir été composée à l'occasion de la translation du saint à Vienne en 617; le même auteur (1995, «Un ejemplo...») analyse avec finesse le rapport entre cette *Vita* et celle composée par Sisebut.

[27] *PL* 123, col. 435-442.

[28] Il utilise par contre sa Chronique mot pour mot (comparer col. 439 et *PL* 123, col. 112) pour décrire la mort de Brunehaut; l'influence de Sisebut dans cet épisode, affirmée par B. Krusch (*MGH*, *SRM*, III, Hanovre, 1896, p. 628), est sujette à caution (limitée aux mots *equis* et *divaricata*) et peut-être indirecte. Pour décrire son travail (Praef. et col. 442B), Adon emploie les verbes *reuoluere* et *transponere*.

à l'égard de Brunehaut, dans la ligne du Pseudo-Frédégaire, dont pourtant il ne semble pas s'être servi[29]. C'est la caractéristique essentielle de ce remaniement: alors que Sisebut et l'Anonyme sont assez évasifs concernant les écarts de conduite de la reine et de son petit-fils, Adon présente sans ambages et abusivement Brunehaut comme incestueuse et fornicatrice[30]. Maigre compensation: il s'abstient de la qualifier de seconde Jézabel contrairement à l'Anonyme[31]. On remarquera que la réprobation morale violente d'Adon à l'égard du mariage de Brunehaut avec son neveu par alliance Mérovée est dans la ligne du rigorisme dont il a fait preuve dans l'affaire du divorce du roi Lothaire II[32]. Ni l'auteur anonyme de *BHL* 2149 ni Adon ne nomment le remplaçant de Didier sur le siège épiscopal pendant l'exil – à Livisio précise l'un (c. 3), *in quadam insula* indique vaguement l'autre (col. 437C) –: Domnole, qui fut également le successeur du saint martyr, est pourtant signalé dans le *Chronicon* (col. 112B)[33]. Ni l'Anonyme ni l'archevêque ne font non plus la moindre allusion à l'accusation portée contre Didier d'avoir violenté une dame de la noblesse, machination ourdie

---

[29] Frédégaire (éd. B. Krusch, in *MGH*, *SRM*, II, Hanovre, 1888, Lib. IV, c. 29) attribue un rôle actif à l'évêque de Lyon Arigius dans la condamnation de Didier lors de son procès et rend complice de cette machination le maire du palais Protadius, présenté comme amant de la reine (Lib. IV, 24). Adon ne transmet aucun de ces éléments.

[30] Selon Dumézil (2008, p. 186) le mariage de Brunehaut avec Mérovée, le neveu de son mari, avait pourtant été béni par l'évêque de Rouen Prétextat, parrain du prince, vraisemblablement pour des motifs politiques – s'assurer l'ascendant sur Mérovée si celui-ci renversait son père auquel il s'opposait – car l'évêque avait pourtant condamné le roi Charibert pour un comportement semblable.

[31] *Vita Desiderii secunda*, c. 2 et 8. Cette désignation infamante se trouve aussi sous la plume de Jonas de Bobbio dans la *Vita Columbani* (éd. B. Krusch, *MGH*, *SRM*, IV, Hanovre – Leipzig, 1902, c. 18).

[32] Dubois – Renaud (1984), p. XVI et M. Besson, «Brunehaut», in *DHGE*, t. 1, Paris, 1912, col. 585-586. Par contre, contrairement à ce qu'on lit dans la *Vita Severi*, Adon ne fait pas allusion à une influence néfaste de la reine dans les questions religieuses (voir *supra*).

[33] Selon Dubois – Gilet – Mérieux (1965), p. 45, n. 24, cette omission de la part de l'auteur de la deuxième Vie est due à la volonté de ne pas «rappeler de mauvais souvenirs concernant un évêque de son Église» que Sisebut traite de faux prêtre et de serviteur du diable. Toutefois Adon est élogieux pour cet évêque qu'il qualifie de *vir strenuus, et in captivis redimendis piissimus*.

par le palais qui entraîna la condamnation à l'exil, nous dit Sisebut (c. 4). L'Anonyme pour sa part n'explicite pas les raisons de la colère de la reine contre Didier, qui lui fit susciter contre lui un procès inique. Quant à Adon, il n'évoque même plus le procès et remplace l'épisode par une allusion encore plus voilée: les exhortations morales de Didier se seraient retournées à ses dépens (*Sed quia qui arguit impium generat maculam sibi*, col. 437C). Pourtant, dans sa Chronique, Adon, condensant l'affaire, rapporte que Didier a été tué sur l'ordre de Brunehaut *ex impietatibus suis arguens* (col. 111D): il connaissait donc probablement le motif de l'accusation. Dans la Vie par Sisebut (c. 15-18), après le retour en grâce de Didier, les discours moralisateurs de l'évêque reprennent de plus belle, entraînant la colère de la reine et de son petit-fils et la condamnation du saint. La version de l'Anonyme (c. 8-9) est différente: les miracles du saint opérés dans l'île où il avait été exilé auraient provoqué la jalousie des souverains qui l'auraient convoqué au palais pour lui tendre un piège; amené à affirmer la supériorité du mariage sur la débauche, il aurait à nouveau suscité l'ire royale et provoqué son arrestation. Adon reprend l'épisode mais ne met en cause que Brunehaut et ses amants (col. 438B-439B).

Adon étoffe son modèle en deux endroits: à propos de la translation, il raconte une pieuse altercation entre les Lyonnais qui ne voulaient pas se séparer du corps du saint et les Viennois qui le réclamaient (col. 440C), incident similaire à celui mettant en scène Poitevins et Tourangeaux à propos de saint Martin[34]. Il développe ensuite le récit d'un miracle sur le chemin de Vienne, la délivrance d'une possédée (col. 440D-441B): reléguant le prodige au second plan, l'auteur rappelle avec une lourde insistance l'origine de la localité où il se produit, la *villa Fasiana*, donnée à l'Église de Vienne par Didier dans son testament[35], frappant d'anathème quiconque ne respecterait pas cette disposition; cette terre effectivement contestée jusqu'en 815 suscitait probablement encore des convoitises à l'époque

---

[34] GREGORIUS TURONENSIS, *Historiae Francorum libri X*, Lib. I, c. 48.

[35] B. Krusch doute de la réalité de l'existence de cet acte (*MGH*, *SRM*, III, Hanovre, 1896, p. 628, p. 645, n. 1 et 647, n. 1). Voir aussi DESCOMBES (1981), p. 373.

d'Adon. Avant de terminer son ouvrage, l'archevêque précise l'époque et les dates de la passion et de la translation du saint[36]. Le fait de disposer des deux œuvres hagiographiques antérieures et d'autres informations, y compris d'Adon lui-même, relatives à la Vie et à la mort du héros permet de très bien cerner l'objectif de la réécriture entreprise par le prélat : il met en avant les questions morales, en accentuant le manichéisme des portraits. Il ne s'intéresse guère aux détails, excepté chronologiques, par contre, il profite de l'occasion pour insérer une argumentation destinée à défendre le droit de propriété de l'Église de Vienne, élimine ce qui pourrait susciter un doute quant à l'absolue pureté de son héros, évite d'évoquer un épisode qui pourrait jeter une ombre sur la qualité des occupants du siège épiscopal et insiste lourdement sur la valeur d'exemple de la Vie qu'il narre, comme il l'a déjà fait dans la *Vita Theuderii*. La comparaison, seulement esquissée ici, entre les Vies antérieures, les données de la Chronique et le remaniement d'Adon est révélatrice : ce qui est retenu, éliminé ou tu alors qu'on possédait l'information illustre bien la différence d'objectifs.

C. Adon éditeur : le manuscrit de Saint-Gall

Si Adon fut compilateur et auteur, il fut également éditeur de textes hagiographiques. Tout porte à croire en effet que le manuscrit Sankt-Gallen, Stifsbibliothek, Cod. Sang. 566 présente le reflet fidèle de l'ensemble, réuni et copié à l'instigation

---

[36] Deux autres Vies non datées portent les numéros *BHL* 2151 et 2152 ; une troisième inédite (*BHL vacat*) est contenue dans le manuscrit Berlin, Staatsbibliothek Preussischer Kulturbesitz, Ms. theol. lat. qu. 256 (voir G. Achten, *Die theologischen lateinischen Handschriften in Quarto der Staatsbibliothek Preussischer Kulturbesitz Berlin*, Teil 1: *Ms. theol. lat. qu. 141-266*, Wiesbaden, 1979, p. 186-288). Elles sont toutes les trois postérieures à la *Vita secunda* du clerc anonyme viennois dont elles dépendent. *BHL* 2152 (*AASS*, Mai. V, 1685, p. 252-253) insère également des extraits de la Chronique d'Adon et un épisode tiré de la *Vita Severi* ; *BHL* 2151 (éd. B. Mombritius, *Sanctuarium, seu vitae sanctorum*, nouv. éd. par D. H. Brunet et D. A. Quentin, t. I, Paris, 1910, p. 392-394) attribue l'exil de Didier à sa résistance face aux tentatives de séduction de la reine, puis reprend *BHL* 2152. Voir l'analyse dans Martín Iglesias (1995), p. 449-456 : «Apéndice: Las otras *Vitae y Passiones Desiderii*» et B. Krusch, *MGH, SRM*, III, Hanovre, 1896, p. 629.

de l'archevêque de Vienne, et destiné aux moines de l'abbaye de Saint-Gall qui lui avaient demandé des reliques de l'évêque martyr Didier[37]. C'est un recueil de Vies de saints intitulé au xve siècle, lors de la reliure, *Legende quam plurimorum sanctorum*. Les deuxième et troisième parties remontent aux IXe-Xe siècles. La première (p. 1) est une table des matières de la même époque que la reliure; à l'entame de la deuxième on trouve un calendrier (p. 2-21) qui a vocation à servir également de catalogue de bibliothèque: il indique en effet où on lira les textes qui concernent les saints du jour. La troisième partie du codex, la plus fournie (p. 97-326), est désignée dans le calendrier sous le titre *Collectariolum Passionis sancti Desiderii* ou *Collectariolum sancti Desiderii*[38]. Elle s'ouvre par la Passion de Didier de Vienne (p. 98-113) composée par Adon. Elle est immédiatement suivie par l'*Indiculum Isonis*, petit texte mis sous le nom de l'écolâtre Ison qui précise les circonstances de l'envoi à Saint-Gall par Adon d'un ensemble de reliques et de Vies de saints: *Hanc autem passionem praefatus Ado episcopus nobis fratribus in coenobio sancti Galli sub Grimaldo abbate Deo militantibus reliquiasque sancti Desiderii ab eo postulantibus cum ipsius aliorumque sanctorum reliquiis, actibus quoque et passionibus infra descriptis, anno supra memorato per nuntios satis fideles dirigere curavit*[39]. Bien que la liste de ces œuvres ne soit pas donnée, la critique s'accorde à y reconnaître les Vies de Didier, Theudère, Sévère, Julien de Brioude et Ferréol, qui forment un tout cohérent consacré aux saints viennois

---

[37] Le manuscrit numérisé peut être consulté sur «e-codices. Virtual Manuscript Library of Switzerland» (http://www.e-codices.unifr.ch/), de même que la notice de B. M. von Scarpatetti, *Die Handschriften der Stiftsbibliothek St. Gallen*, Bd. 1, Abt. IV: *Codices 547-669: Hagiographica, Historica, Geographica, 8.-18. Jahrhundert*, Wiesbaden, 2003, p. 61-65. Voir aussi Münding (1918), en particulier p. 19-42 (description du manuscrit).

[38] La quatrième, qui couvre les pages 327-342, est du XIe siècle.

[39] Voir l'analyse de Duft (1991), p. 112-114. Voir également la notice «Iso» par J. Pycke, in *DHGE*, t. 26, Paris, 1995-1997, col. 276-278. Les informations fournies par ce texte sont recoupées et complétées avec celles transmises par Notker le Bègue dans son martyrologe, au 10 des calendes de juin (manuscrit de Saint-Gall, 456, p. 154-155; éd. *PL* 131, col. 1087), cité, entre autres, par Dubreucq (2010) qui ajoute (p. 60, n. 22) que c'est un prêtre de Vienne, Berold qui a été chargé en 870 d'acheminer reliques et Vies.

et séparé des textes hagiographiques suivants par une page blanche (p. 156)[40].

L'*Indiculum Isonis* attribue l'initiative de l'entreprise à la communauté de Saint-Gall à l'époque de l'abbé Grimald. La demande portait avant tout sur les reliques de Didier. Comme on l'a vu, ce dernier avait critiqué la vie dissipée de Brunehaut et de son petit-fils Thierry, ce qui l'avait conduit au martyre. Saint Colomban et ses compagnons avaient également eu maille à partir avec les souverains mérovingiens, qui les avaient chassés du royaume de Bourgogne. Parmi eux, il y aurait eu Gall, dont les Vies rapportent qu'il avait emmené des reliques de Didier; l'évêque de Vienne jouissait donc d'une considération particulière à Saint-Gall[41]. A. Dubreucq met plus particulièrement cet intérêt pour les reliques et Vies de saints en relation avec la personnalité de l'abbé Grimald. Proche d'Adon par son parcours atypique et son rôle auprès du pouvoir politique, il partageait aussi le même idéal de réorganisation de l'Église. L'un et l'autre accordaient une grande importance aux fondations et constructions d'églises et de monastères et au rôle qu'y jouaient les reliques et leurs translations[42]. Adon ne se borna pas à répondre

---

[40] Ajoutons que les œuvres d'origine viennoise sont indiquées dans le calendrier comme se trouvant *in collectariolo Desiderii*, tandis que les autres – à l'exception toutefois des *Vita et actus Syri et Hiventii* (p. 219-251) – sont systématiquement signalées comme se trouvant *in collectariolo passionis Desiderii*; peut-être y avait-il là désir de distinguer la cohérence de l'ensemble viennois du support physique manuscrit, inauguré de fait par la Passion de Didier. La mention du calendrier concernant la Passion de Senesius (contenue dans un autre manuscrit) – *in collectariolo cuius principium est vita Silvestri* (p. 4) – vient à l'appui de cette hypothèse. Voir aussi les différents noms donnés à l'ensemble des œuvres qui suivent la Passion de Didier, dans MÜNDING (1918), p. 39 (description du manuscrit p. 19-42).

[41] Voir toutefois la notice de G. PHILIPPART dans le *DHGE* (t. 19, Paris, 1981, col. 800-801) qui expose les deux thèses en présence concernant l'identité du fondateur de l'abbaye de Saint-Gall: réel disciple de Colomban ou simple ermite local nommé Gallo (ou Gallonus) promu par un hagiographe compagnon du célèbre Irlandais, dont la Vie laisse entrevoir l'existence d'un certain Gallus?

[42] Formé à la cour de Charlemagne, Grimald fut chapelain de Louis le Pieux, avant de prendre la direction de la chancellerie royale sous Louis le Germanique. Prêtre séculier, il n'embrassa jamais l'idéal monastique et sa nomination à la tête de Saint-Gall fut controversée car elle allait à l'encontre du principe de libre élection. Adon pour sa part avait très tôt vécu hors de son monastère d'origine au point qu'il lui fallut une lettre de recommanda-

à cette requête: il joignit aux précieux restes la biographie du saint qu'il avait lui-même composée ainsi que la Vie de Theudère, également de sa composition, et trois autres œuvres: la *Vita Severi* que nous avons déjà présentée, la *Vita Ferreoli* et la *Vita Iuliani Briuatensis*[43].

Très tôt, les saints Ferréol et Julien ont été associés dans la littérature hagiographique. Ferréol est fonctionnaire impérial[44] à Vienne à une époque non précisée; il envoie le chrétien Julien fuir la persécution en Auvergne. L'un et l'autre sont toutefois décapités; le corps du premier est enseveli à Vienne, quoiqu'une version de sa Vie le fasse mourir près de Brioude, celui du second est ramené à Brioude, amputé de sa tête qui aurait été transportée à Vienne[45]. Les dossiers des deux saints ont donné lieu à plusieurs études critiques, synthétisées et enrichies par A. Dubreucq[46]; l'ensemble des textes a été récemment réexaminé par J.-P. Reboul dans un contexte de recherches archéologiques au nord-ouest de Vienne[47]. Nous nous concentrerons pour notre part sur la tradition carolingienne viennoise reflétée par le manuscrit de Saint-Gall. Ce dernier présente les Vies de Julien et Ferréol l'une à la suite de l'autre, ce qui n'est certainement pas dû au hasard.

---

tion de son abbé Loup de Ferrières pour justifier son mode de vie et rassurer le comte de Vienne qui hésitait à accepter sa candidature comme archevêque. Grimald et son représentant Hartmut eurent le souci de développer la bibliothèque abbatiale, de réorganiser le temporel de l'abbaye et de promouvoir le culte de saint Othmar, ancien abbé en l'honneur duquel fut construite une nouvelle basilique; il est possible que les reliques apportées de Vienne étaient destinées aux autels de l'édifice. Voir DUBREUCQ (2010), p. 61-62 et 66-67.

[43] Dans le manuscrit de Saint-Gall, elles occupent respectivement les pages: 98-113 (*Passio sancti Desiderii episcopi*); 113-126 (*Vita sancti Theuderii abbatis*); 127-144 (*Vita sancti Severi presbyteri*); 144-149 (*Passio sancti Iuliani Briuatensis* [sic]); 150-155 (*Passio sancti Ferreoli martyris*).

[44] Détenteur de la puissance tribunicienne dans les Vies de Julien de Brioude.

[45] Le premier témoignage de cette tradition se trouve chez Sidoine Apollinaire (430-486) dans une lettre à l'évêque de Vienne Mamert (*Ep.* VII, 1). Voir DIERKENS (2007), p. 36-37.

[46] DUBREUCQ (2007) et (2010).

[47] Sur le site de Saint-Romain-en-Gal où Ferréol aurait subi le martyre: voir PRISSET – BRISSAUD (2015); REBOUL (2015) compare les éditions existantes et offre une édition scientifique mais non critique des textes relatifs à Ferréol ainsi que leur traduction française.

Le texte relatif à Julien (*BHL* 4542d)[48], dont il y a tout lieu de penser qu'il correspond à celui utilisé dans la liturgie de l'Église de Vienne, dépend de la *Passio prior* (*BHL* 4540), du VIe siècle[49]; l'auteur semble aussi avoir connu le *Liber de passione et uirtutibus sancti Iuliani* (*BHL* 4541) de Grégoire de Tours, des années 580 (avec l'ajout du c. 50 vers 590-592)[50]. Mais il apporte des informations nouvelles, dont le lieu du martyre de Julien, aux environs de Brioude, *Vinicella*. Surtout, participant du mouvement contemporain de revalorisation de la fonction militaire, l'auteur transforme Julien en soldat, camarade ou subordonné du tribun Ferréol, alors que sa fonction n'était définie ni dans la *Passio prior* ni chez Grégoire[51]. Le texte, où l'on reconnaît des citations de l'Énéide de Virgile et des Métamorphoses d'Ovide, est rédigé dans un style recherché et rythmé qui incite à le dater du début de la renaissance carolingienne, avant 806 en tout cas car il a servi de base à la notice du martyrologe lyonnais[52]. La passion de Saint-Gall et le *Liber de passione et uirtutibus sancti Iuliani* ont été largement mis à profit par l'auteur de la *Passio posterior* (*BHL* 4542), qui n'est sans doute pas antérieure au Xe siècle, époque de son premier témoin manuscrit[53]. D'origine inconnue, il est possible que ce texte ait servi de lecture

---

[48] Éd. DUBREUCQ (2007), p. 210-212.

[49] Du début selon DUBREUCQ (2007), p. 196-199: elle est postérieure à la construction de la basilique de Victorius, vers 480; l'argument qui la faisait remonter au milieu du VIe siècle provient d'une interprétation discutable du mot *privilegium*. REBOUL (2015), p. 533-534, accepte la fourchette 532-582.

[50] C'est la position de DUBREUCQ (2007), p. 204-205, qui situe l'œuvre au tout début du IXe siècle. REBOUL (2015), p. 534, penche pour la fin du VIe siècle ou le début du VIIe siècle, époque d'efflorescence pour la poésie chrétienne de Gaule.

[51] Voir DEHOUX (2010), p. 279-281.

[52] Adon reprit intégralement la notice de l'Anonyme lyonnais dans son martyrologe au 28 août [DUBOIS – RENAUD (1984), p. 291]. Voir QUENTIN (1908), p. 176.

[53] Le plus ancien manuscrit est Chartes, BM 25(44), provenant de l'abbaye Saint-Père (éd. T. RUINART, *Gregorii Turonensis opera omnia*, Paris, 1699, col. 1265-1270, reprise dans *PL* 71, col. 1103-1106 et, sans le prologue presque entièrement emprunté à Grégoire, dans *AASS*, Aug. VI, 1743, p. 174-175). DUBREUCQ (2007), p. 205-206, a démontré la postériorité de la *Passio posterior* sur la Passion de Saint-Gall; à noter, entre autres, que les déformations des passages empruntés à Virgile et à Ovide leur font perdre tout rythme poétique.

liturgique, mais pas à Brioude qui est présentée comme un lieu extérieur[54].

La Passion de Ferréol contenue dans le manuscrit de Saint-Gall correspond à la première version, courte, de ce texte (*BHL* 2911), telle qu'elle est éditée par Surius, avec quelques variantes[55]. Cette version pourrait être contemporaine de la *Passio prior Iuliani* (*BHL* 4540, VIe siècle), qu'elle ignore toutefois[56]; Julien n'y est pas même nommé. Elle représente la tradition viennoise la plus ancienne concernant Ferréol, tandis que la Passion longue (*BHL* 2912), peut-être de la même époque, reprend la précédente dans les grandes lignes, mais évoque le martyre de Julien et fait mourir Ferréol à Brioude: il est probable qu'elle ait eu pour objectif de justifier le culte du saint dans la région brivadoise, où elle aurait été composée[57]. Adon n'a, selon toute vraisemblance, connu que la Passion courte à l'époque de l'envoi du dossier hagiographique viennois à Saint-Gall, tandis que dans la troisième recension du martyrologe il s'inspire de la Passion longue pour donner des précisions sur le fondateur d'une basilique en l'honneur de Ferréol à Vienne. On peut donc émettre l'hypothèse raisonnable qu'Adon n'a disposé de la Passion longue qu'après 870 et s'en est servi pour compléter la notice du martyrologe, dont la troisième recension pourrait dès lors être datée d'entre 870 et 875, année de la mort de l'archevêque[58].

---

[54] *Ibid.*, p. 203.
[55] L'édition des *AASS*, Sept. V, 1755, p. 764-765, reprend celle de T. Ruinart collationnée avec celle de Surius. Le texte de Saint-Gall (Cod. Gall. 566, p. 150-155) se lit dans Dubreucq (2010), p. 68-69.
[56] Seul est certain le *terminus ante quem*, l'envoi du *libellus* hagiographique à Saint-Gall, en 870, cf. Dubreucq (2007), p. 207-208. Reboul (2015), p. 534-540, argumente en faveur d'une datation haute (v. 450-473): elle aurait été rédigée sous l'épiscopat de Mamert (v. 449-v. 473) mais avant l'invention des reliques de Ferréol et de Julien par cet évêque. Des ressemblances entre les passions de Julien et de Ferréol, elles-mêmes fortement influencées par la Passion de Geniès d'Arles, ont été relevées par Franchi de' Cavalieri (1935), p. 210-213, réfutées par Fournier (1966), p. 25, n. 52, et acceptées par Fayard (1982) p. 18-25.
[57] Dubreucq (2007), p. 208.
[58] Dubreucq (2010), p. 66-67. Dans la seconde recension du martyrologe, Adon reprend le texte de l'Anonyme lyonnais. Ce dernier s'appuie sur la version longue qu'Adon ne connaît pas de première main à cette époque.

II. Vies et miracles d'évêques: Avit et Barnard

La forte empreinte d'Adon sur la littérature hagiographique a conduit à lui prêter des œuvres qui ne sont pas de sa main. Des doutes subsistent au sujet de la *Vita Severi,* on l'a vu. Par contre, en ce qui concerne les *Miracula* d'un de ses proches prédécesseurs, Barnard († 842), il est bien établi qu'il faut en rejeter l'attribution à Adon. Originaire du Lyonnais, ayant servi sous Charlemagne, Barnard fonda le monastère d'Ambronay (Ain) qu'il dirigea avant de succéder à l'archevêque Wulferius en 810. Plusieurs textes lui furent consacrés, dont quelques miracles (*BHL* 995)[59] sous la plume d'un auteur se présentant comme en charge de l'Église de Vienne (c. 7: *hanc Viennensem suscepi Ecclesiam*) et qualifiant Barnard d'*alitor meus* (c. 1). L'identification avec Adon fut proposée par le Père P. F. Chifflet qui avait transmis au Bollandiste G. Henschen les textes qu'il avait recueillis[60]. Toutefois l'on rencontre la mention d'un concile rassemblant un grand nombre d'évêques tenu à *Vetula Civitas* (c. 1), soit Saint-Paulien (Haute-Loire). Les reliques de Barnard y furent solennellement transportées. Selon toute vraisemblance, il s'agit du concile dit du Puy convoqué à Saint-Paulien par Guy d'Anjou en 993-994[61], qui fixe le *terminus a quo* de la relation écrite des Miracles. L'archevêque de Vienne était à l'époque Thibaud (957-1000): protecteur de l'abbaye de Romans, il fut absent au concile sans qu'on n'en connaisse la raison, mais il en ratifiera les dispositions après coup. Aucun indice ne permet d'identifier l'auteur des *Miracula* ni d'en préciser l'époque de composition[62].

Barnard est aussi connu par trois *Vitae* (*BHL* 991-993) et une *Translatio* (*BHL* 994)[63]. Vers la fin de sa vie, l'archevêque avait

---

[59] Éd. *AASS*, Ian. II, 1643, p. 547-548 et *AASS OSB*, IV-1 (1677), p. 588-589.

[60] *AASS*, Ian. II, 1643, p. 544-545.

[61] Voir Lauranson-Rosaz (1992), p. 318-321 et Giraud (1856) p. 24-26.

[62] Ils pourraient être tardifs: voir n. 65.

[63] La *BHL* mentionne encore sous le numéro 995d des *Lectiones* non datées et exclut une Vie tirée d'un office de l'ordre des Antonins édité en 1592, qui donne des informations originales (nom des parents, anecdote au sujet du

fondé à Romans un monastère dédié aux saints apôtres, où il se retira et fut inhumé. L'établissement fut détruit par les Normands en 860, relevé puis incendié lors de conflits entre les moines et l'archevêque Sobon vers 932. Dans les années qui suivirent, le monastère fit place à un chapitre de chanoines réguliers. En 944 les reliques de Barnard furent placées à gauche de l'autel des apôtres. Cet événement, suscité par le saint lors d'apparitions nocturnes, est rapporté dans une courte Translation vraisemblablement proche des faits. Le culte de saint Barnard prend son essor et le nom du fondateur est désormais ajouté à celui de la titulature ancienne de la collégiale[64]. Les *Vitae Barnardi* sont plus tardives. C'est certainement le cas du texte *BHL* 993 qui intègre une épitaphe datée d'à partir de 1100[65]. Toutefois, selon N. Nimmegeers, qui a étudié de manière approfondie le dossier hagiographique de Barnard, les deux autres Vies, qui viennent à l'appui des manœuvres des chanoines pour se soustraire au pouvoir archiépiscopal, ne sont pas non plus antérieures au XIIe siècle[66].

L'évêque Avit († 518), né dans une famille d'origine sénatoriale, et dont le père Isicius fut également évêque de Vienne, est surtout connu pour son œuvre littéraire et sa correspondance. Sa Vie (*BHL* 885)[67] est élaborée à partir de l'épitaphe du prélat

---

choix de Bernard comme prélat); elle est éditée par Mabillon (*AASS OSB*, IV-1, 1677, p. 545-546).

[64] Sur la fondation et les premiers siècles de Romans, voir THIRION (1974), p. 361-362. NIMMEGEERS (2014), p. 283-284, date la *Translatio* de la fin du Xe siècle, car après 995, toutes les chartes évoquent la fondation de Romans directement par Barnard ou en son honneur. Initialement l'abbaye était dédiée aux saints apôtres et aux martyrs viennois Exupère, Félicien et Séverin. Voir aussi BONNASSIE – IOGNA-PRAT – SIGAL (1994), p. 319.

[65] La Vie *BHL* 993 fait référence à la Translation et sans doute aussi aux Miracles: *Sunt tamen duo libelli compositi, in quibus et revelatio eius atque translatio, et pars miraculorum continentur* (éd. *AB*, 11 (1892), p. 415, l. 15-17); elle inclut dans le récit la deuxième épitaphe de Barnard composée vers 1100. Le manuscrit d'où est copié *BHL* 991 présente également cette épitaphe sans qu'on puisse être certain qu'elle était solidaire de la *Vita*.

[66] Deux d'entre elles, *BHL* 991 et 992, affirment sans ambages que l'abbaye de Romans fut dès sa fondation placée sous la protection pontificale; or c'est à la fin du XIe siècle ou au début du siècle suivant que « les chanoines de Romans modifient les actes qu'ils possèdent pour revendiquer leur sujétion directe à Rome » [NIMMEGEERS (2014), p. 261, n. 196].

[67] Éd. R. PEIPER, in *MGH*, *AA*, VI-2, Berlin, 1883, p. 177-181.

et de ses propres textes. Elle emprunte aussi à la Vie d'Apollinaire, évêque de Valence et frère d'Avit[68]. On y trouve enfin des similitudes avec la Chronique d'Adon mais le sens de l'emprunt n'est pas sûr: l'éditeur de la *Vita Aviti*, R. Peiper, l'estimait antérieure au IXe siècle, jugeant qu'Adon avait puisé dans la Vie de son prédécesseur les informations qu'il intégra dans son œuvre, tandis que M. Burckhardt, qui édita la correspondance de l'évêque, s'efforça de démontrer que la dépendance littéraire était inverse[69].

III. Vies d'abbés: Léonien, Clair et Maxime

Léonien et Clair auraient tous deux dirigé Saint-Marcel de Vienne, respectivement aux VIe et VIIe siècles[70]. De la *Vita Leoniani* (*BHL* 4879m) il n'existe qu'une recension conservée dans un lectionnaire d'Arras du XIIIe siècle, élaborée à partir d'un passage de la Chronique d'Adon. Non datée, elle ne semble pas antérieure au manuscrit qui la contient[71]. À Vienne même on ne trouve trace du culte du saint qu'à partir du Xe siècle: une inscription inspirée non par sa *Vita* mais par celle de saint Oyend[72]. La Vie arrageoise, seul témoin de l'abbatiat de Léo-

---

[68] Sur la Vie d'Apollinaire, peut-être elle-même carolingienne, voir la contribution de F. Peloux *infra*, p. 644-648.

[69] L'auteur s'inspire aussi de la liste épiscopale de Vienne, mais a-t-il connu la version remaniée du IXe siècle ou une version antérieure, dans laquelle Adon aurait pu également puiser ses informations? Voir Burckhardt (1938), p. 102-105, et Descombes (1985), p. 345-346. La datation basse est également adoptée par Heinzelmann (2010), p. 58, n. 136. Descombes (1981), p. 362, mentionne l'attribution par B. Krusch de cette Vie à Adon, mais sans référence. Signalons toutefois que l'absence de la Vie dans le manuscrit de Saint-Gall est un argument de poids contre cette hypothèse que nous n'avons pas trouvée chez un autre auteur. Par ailleurs, si Avit est présent dans le martyrologe d'Adon dès la première recension (au 5 février), la notice correspond à celle de Florus à trois mots près «qui résument curieusement les qualificatifs donnés par le martyrologe lyonnais: *admirandae fidei, doctrinae et eruditionis viri*», cf. Dubois – Renaud (1984), p. 80.

[70] L'histoire de cet établissement est mal connue; cf. Descombes (1981), p. 373 et Descombes – Février – Gauthier (1986), p. 32.

[71] Éd. Van der Straeten (1972), p. 133-135. Nimmegeers (2014), p. 18.

[72] Le saint était en outre mal connu à Vienne: la tradition locale ne permettait pas de lui attribuer avec certitude l'abbatiat de Saint-Marcel; il a

nien à Saint-Marcel, attribue au saint un frère du nom d'Aignan, passage pour lequel l'auteur s'inspire du *Sermo de origine et prioribus gestis S. Aniani* (*BHL* 476), de la fin IXe ou du début du Xe siècle[73].

La Vie de Clair (*BHL* 1825)[74] s'avère postérieure à 847, car elle mentionne l'église Saint-Sévère dédiée à Saint-Étienne avant cette date[75]; comme elle est inconnue d'Adon lorsqu'il envoie les Vies viennoises à Saint-Gall, elle est également postérieure à 870, l'auteur s'inspirant par ailleurs du *Chronicon*. En ce qui concerne son *terminus ante quem*, F. Descombes le fixe à 1036, si elle est bien mise à profit par Léger dans un acte de restitution de biens à Saint-Ferréol[76]. Dans cet acte, Léger (1030-1070) renvoie à la *Vita Clari* à propos de ce monastère. D'après N. Nimmegeers, l'œuvre, dépourvue de qualités littéraires[77], aurait au contraire pu être composée à l'instigation de l'évêque Léger afin d'appuyer sa reprise en main du monachisme

---

longtemps été considéré comme abbé de Saint-Pierre. Voir VAN DER STRAETEN (1972), p. 119-125, DESCOMBES (1981), p. 365 et NIMMEGEERS (2014), p. 241-242.

[73] RENAUD (1978).

[74] Éd. *AASS OSB*, II (1669), p. 483-485. Voir DESCOMBES (1981), p. 364-365. VAN DER STRAETEN (1972, p. 123) date la *Vita Clari* des VIIIe-IXe siècles sans justification.

[75] DESCOMBES – FÉVRIER – GAUTHIER (1986), p. 31.

[76] DESCOMBES (1981, p. 364) se réfère à un acte du 3 novembre 1036 (n° 1775 – et non 1875 – du *Régeste dauphinois*, éd. U. CHEVALIER, t. 1, fasc. 1, Valence, 1912, col. 299) où la phrase *ecclesia ipsius [domni Ferreoli] vel coenobium, quod vocant Griniensium quadragintorum simul in se habuit multitudinem monachorum* (éd. E. MARTÈNE – U. DURAND, *Veterum scriptorum... amplissima collectio*, t. 1, Paris, 1724, col. 402) ferait écho à celle de la *Vita Clari*: *Nam Grinianensium loca quadringentos monachos alebant* (c. 3). Les monastères griniens, en Dauphiné, sont appelés ainsi du nom du propriétaire gallo-romain de la terre où fut fondé le plus important d'entre eux, Saint-Ferréol (B. BLIGNY, «Griniens (Monastères)», in *DHGE*, t. 22, Paris, 1988, col. 286-287).

[77] «Sa composition est des plus décousues: au récit d'un miracle de jeunesse lié au monastère de la rive droite (Clair apaise les flots du Rhône au cours d'une traversée), sont juxtaposés, sans aucun lien, un tableau des édifices religieux de la ville de Vienne, sous l'autorité du saint pontife Cadeoldus, une suite de miracles opérés par le saint, la prédiction des raids sarrasins et de la ruine de l'église de Vienne, enfin le récit de la mort du saint et l'indication du lieu de sa sépulture, l'église de Sainte-Blandine», cf. DESCOMBES (1981) p. 365.

viennois[78]. Elle présente en effet une liste d'établissements destinée à montrer l'efflorescence de l'Église de Vienne sous l'évêque Chaoalde au milieu du VIIe siècle par opposition aux malheurs de l'époque qui suit; elle insiste sur la décadence du monachisme pour justifier sa réforme, or cette prétendue décadence n'est en rien attestée par l'archéologie.

Mentionnons encore la Vie consacrée à Maxime, abbé de Saint-Jean *Limonici* (*BHL* 5850)[79]. Le héros, né à la fin du VIe siècle, aurait étudié à l'école épiscopale de Cahors. Après une expérience érémitique, il se serait rendu à Vienne à la suite d'une apparition angélique. Il fut admis au monastère Saint-Jean de Limony, dont il devint abbé. Entré en conflit avec un fonctionnaire royal, il fut assassiné puis honoré comme martyr. L'établissement religieux n'est pas clairement identifié: on le situe à Limony (Ardèche)[80] ou à Simandres (Rhône), où une chapelle Notre-Dame de Limon aurait succédé à Saint-Jean[81]. Toutefois cette dernière hypothèse ne tient pas compte de la mention dans la *Vita* des *Limona fluentia* qui pourraient désigner la Limony qui traverse la localité ardéchoise homonyme. La Vie, non datée, est vraisemblablement fort éloignée des événements. Comme l'a fait remarquer avec pertinence N. Nimmegeers, elle ne peut pas remonter au-delà du VIIIe siècle «puisqu'elle mentionne un archevêque, titre porté une première fois par Wilchaire (vers 726) puis régulièrement seulement à partir de Barnard (810-840). La longueur du récit, ses incohérences, son sens du détail plaident pour une datation large comprise entre le Xe et le XIIIe siècle»[82]. La présence d'une généalogie bien dis-

---

[78] Nimmegeers (2014), p. 255-256, qui, dans un article postérieur [Baud – Nimmegeers – Flammin (2016)], élargit la datation à la fin du Xe siècle sans explication.

[79] Éd. *AASS*, Ian. I, 1643, p. 91-94.

[80] Ponton d'Amécourt (1875), p. 52; dans l'*Histoire littéraire de la France*, t. VI, Paris, 1867, p. 226, le lieu est traduit par «Limours» (toponyme non identifié) et situé sur le Rhône.

[81] Allmer – de Terrebasse (1875), p. 218. Cette identification est acceptée par Nimmegeers (2014), p. 244, qui ajoute «À condition de considérer qu'il mérite un certain crédit, ce récit suggère l'existence d'une communauté régulière implantée vers la fin du VIe siècle dans voisinage de celles de Grigny dont elle pourrait suivre la règle».

[82] *Ibid.*, p. 18.

tincte (c. 1) précédant la Vie proprement dite donne à penser que l'œuvre n'est pas antérieure au XIe siècle[83].

Conclusion

Telle que nous pouvons la connaître, l'activité hagiographique dans le diocèse de Vienne du VIIIe au Xe siècle est dominée par la personnalité de l'archevêque Adon. Celui-ci fait de son travail original, de réécriture ou d'édition un outil de propagande de la réforme carolingienne fortement arrimée au rôle de l'évêque dans la cité. À côté de ses préoccupations morales, le prélat doit également faire face à des soucis d'ordre matériel: les compositions hagiographiques sont alors prétextes à réaffirmer les droits de propriété de l'Église de Vienne. Comme on l'a entrevu, ces pratiques seront poursuivies par ses successeurs, soucieux également de défendre leurs prérogatives.

Bibliographie

Allmer, A. – de Terrebasse, A., *Inscriptions antiques et du moyen âge de Vienne en Dauphiné*, 2e partie: *Inscriptions du moyen âge antérieures au XVIIe siècle*, I, Vienne, 1875.

Baud, A. – Nimmegeers, N. – Flammin, A., «L'abbaye de Saint-André-le-Haut à Vienne. Origine et développement d'un monastère de moniales», *Bulletin du Centre d'Études médiévales d'Auxerre / BUCEMA* [En ligne] Hors-série 10 (2016).

Bonnassie, P. – Sigal, P.-A. – Iogna-Prat, D., «La Gallia du Sud, 930-1130», in *Hagiographies*, I (1994), p. 289-344.

Burckhardt, M., *Die Briefsammlung des Bischof Avitus von Vienne († 518) (Anhang Zur Vita Aviti)*, Berlin, 1938 (Abhandlungen zur mittleren und neueren Geschichte, 81).

Chevalier, U., *Étude historique sur la constitution de l'église métropolitaine et primatiale de Vienne*, t. II, Vienne, 1923.

de Gaiffier, B., «L'hagiographie dans le marquisat de Flandre et le duché de Basse-Lotharingie au XIe siècle», in *Études critiques d'hagiographie et d'iconologie*, Bruxelles, 1967, p. 463-474 (Subsidia hagiographica, 43).

---

[83] Voir les observations de B. de Gaiffier (1967), sur les généalogies de saints.

DEHOUX, E., «À l'épreuve de l'an mil. Grandeur et déclin du culte de saint Julien de Brioude (IXe-XIe siècle)», in A. DUBREUCQ – C. LAURANSON-ROSAZ – B. SANIAL, éd., *Brioude aux temps carolingiens – Actes du colloque international organisé par la ville de Brioude, 13-15 septembre 2007*, Brioude, 2010, p. 279-281.

DESCOMBES, F., «Hagiographie et topographie religieuse: l'exemple de Vienne en Dauphiné», in *Hagiographie, cultures et sociétés, IVe-XIIe siècles. Actes du Colloque organisé à Nanterre et à Paris (2-5 mai 1979)*, Paris, 1981, p. 361-379.

—, *Recueil des inscriptions chrétiennes de Gaule antérieures à la Renaissance carolingienne*, XV: *Viennoise du Nord*, Paris, 1985.

DESCOMBES, F. – FÉVRIER, P.-A. – GAUTHIER, N., «Vienne», in *Topographie chrétienne des cités de la Gaule, des origines au milieu du VIIIe siècle*, III: *Provinces ecclésiastiques de Vienne et d'Arles (Viennensis et Alpes Graiae et Poeninae)*, Paris, 1986, p. 17-35.

DIERKENS, A., «Christianisation et culte des saints en Gaule: quelques réflexions sur saint Julien, Brioude et l'Auvergne du IVe au VIIe siècle», in A. DUBREUCQ – C. LAURANSON-ROSAZ – B. SANIAL, éd., *Saint Julien et les origines de Brioude: actes du [1er] Colloque de Brioude, 22-25 septembre 2004*, Brioude, 2007, p. 36-37.

DUBOIS, J. – GILET, R. – MÉRIEUX, F., «Le dossier historique d'un saint du haut Moyen Âge. Saint Didier, évêque de Vienne et martyr», *Bulletin d'histoire et d'archéologie du diocèse de Belley*, 40 (1965), p. 33-57.

DUBOIS, J. – RENAUD, G., *Le martyrologe d'Adon: ses deux familles, ses trois recensions*, Paris, 1984 (Sources d'histoire médiévale, 14).

DUBREUCQ, A., «Les textes de la passion de saint Julien de Brioude: un état des lieux», in A. DUBREUCQ – C. LAURANSON-ROSAZ – B. SANIAL, éd., *Saint Julien et les origines de Brioude: actes du [1er] Colloque de Brioude, 22-25 septembre 2004*, Brioude, 2007, p. 195-212.

—, «La transmission des passions de saint Julien et de saint Ferréol à l'époque carolingienne», *ibid.*, p. 57-69.

DUCHESNE, L., *Fastes épiscopaux de l'ancienne Gaule*, I: *Provinces du Sud-Est*, 2e éd., Paris, 1907.

DUFT, J., «Isos Schriftum», in ID., éd., *Die Abtei St. Gallen. Ausgewählte Aufsätze in überarbeiteter Fassung*, II: *Beiträge zur Kenntnis ihrer Persönlichkeiten*, Sigmaringen, 1991, p. 109-117 (article d'abord paru sous le titre «Iso monachus – doctor nominatissimus», in *Churrätisches und st. gallisches Mittelalter* [= *Festschrift für Otto P. Clavadetscher*], Sigmaringen, 1984, p. 129-171).

DUMÉZIL, B., *La reine Brunehaut*, Paris, 2008.

FAYARD, A., «L'énigme de saint Julien ou les deux martyrs de Brioude», in *Almanach de Brioude*, 62 (1982), p. 18-28.

FONTAINE, J., «King Sisebut's *Vita Desiderii* and the Political Function of Visigothic Hagiography», in E. JAMES, éd., *Visigothic Spain: New Approaches*, Oxford, 1980, p. 93-129.

FOURNIER, G. – FOURNIER, P.-F., «Saint-Julien de Brioude, saint Ferréol de Vienne, saints Ilpide et Arcons», *Almanach de Brioude*, 46 (1966), p. 9-49.

FRANCHI DE' CAVALIERI, P., «S. Genesio di Arelate, S. Ferreolo di Vienna, S. Giuliano di Brivas», in *Note agiografiche*, VIII, Cité du Vatican, 1935, p. 210-213 (Studi et testi, 65).

GIRAUD, M., *Essai historique sur l'abbaye de Saint-Barnard et la ville de Romans*, Première partie: Lyon, 1856, p. 24-26.

GROSPELLIER, A., «Mélanges d'hagiographie dauphinoise, I», *Bulletin d'histoire ecclésiastique et d'archéologie religieuse des diocèses de Valence, Gap, Grenoble et Viviers*, 20 (1900), p. 5-36.

HEINZELMANN, M., «L'hagiographie mérovingienne. Panorama des documents potentiels», in M. GOULLET – M. HEINZELMANN – C. VEYRARD-COSME, dir., *L'hagiographie mérovingienne à travers ses réécritures*, Ostfildern, 2010, p. 27-82 (Beihefte der Francia, 71).

JULLIEN, M.-H. – PERELMAN, F., éd., *Clavis des auteurs latins du Moyen Âge: territoire français, 785-987*, I: *Abbon de Saint-Germain – Ermold le Noir*, Turnhout, 1994 (*CC CM*).

LAURANSON-ROSAZ, C., «La paix populaire dans les montagnes d'Auvergne au Xe siècle», in *Maisons de Dieu et hommes d'Église. Florilège en l'honneur de Pierre-Roger Gaussin*, Saint-Étienne, 1992, p. 289-333.

MARTÍN IGLESIAS, J. C., «Un ejemplo de influencia de la *Vita Desiderii* de Sisebuto en la hagiografía merovingia», *Minerva*, 9 (1995), p. 165-185.

—, «Una posible datacion de la *Passio sancti Desiderii BHL 2149*», *Euphrosyne*, NS 23 (1995) p. 439-456.

—, «Une nouvelle édition critique de la *Vita Desiderii* de Sisebut, accompagnée de quelques réflexions concernant la date des *Sententiae* et du *De uiris illustribus* d'Isidore de Séville», *Hagiographica*, 7 (2000), p. 127-180.

MÜNDING, E., *Das Verzeichnis der St. Galler Heiligenleben und ihrer Handschriften in Codex Sangall. 566: ein Beitrag zur Frühgeschichte der St. Galler Handschriftensammlung*, Hohenzollern, 1918 (Texte und Arbeiten, 1; Beiträge zur Ergründung des älteren lateinischen christlichen Schrifttums und Gottesdienstes, 3-4).

NIMMEGEERS, N., *Évêques entre Bourgogne et Provence (V^e-XIe siècle). La province ecclésiastique de Vienne au haut Moyen Âge*, Rennes, 2014 (Collection «Histoire»).

PONTON D'AMÉCOURT, G de, *Vies de saints traitées au point de vue de la géographie historique*, Paris, 1875 (extrait des Mémoires de la Société française de numismatique et d'archéologie).

PRISSET, J.-L. – BRISSAUD, L., avec la coll. de REBOUL, J.-F., «Première partie: étude archéologique», in J.-L. PRISSET, dir., *Saint-Romain-en-Gal aux temps de Ferréol, Mamert et Adon. L'aire funéraire des thermes des lutteurs (IVe-Xe siècles)*, Turnhout, 2015, p. 310-321 (Bibliothèque de l'Antiquité tardive, 28).

QUENTIN, H., *Les martyrologes historiques du moyen âge. Étude sur la formation du martyrologe romain*, 2e éd., Paris, 1908.

REBOUL, J.-P., «Le martyr Ferréol dans les sources écrites», in J.-L. PRISSET, dir., *Saint-Romain-en-Gal aux temps de Ferréol, Mamert et Adon. L'aire funéraire des thermes des lutteurs (IVe-Xe siècles)*, Turnhout, 2015, p. 479-554 (Bibliothèque de l'Antiquité tardive, 28).

RENAUD, G., «Saint Aignan et sa légende, les "Vies" et les "Miracles"», *Bulletin de la Société archéologique et historique de l'Orléanais*, 49 (1978), p. 83-109.

THIRION, J., «L'ancienne collégiale Saint-Barnard de Romans», *Congrès archéologique de France*, 130 (1972), p. 361-410.

VAN DER STRAETEN, J., «Vie arrageoise de S. Léonien, abbé à Vienne en Dauphiné», *AB*, 90 (1972), p. 119-136.

L'écriture hagiographique dans les diocèses suffragants de la métropole viennoise* (c. VIIIe-XIe s.)

par

Fernand Peloux

I. Die: Marcel.
II. Grenoble. − A. Aper. − B. Ferréol.
III. Maurienne. − A. Marin. − B. Tigre.
IV. Valence. − A. Apollinaire. − B. Galla.
V. Viviers. − A. La transmission destextes. − B. Andéol. − C. Aule. − D. Hostian. − E. Montan. − F. Venance.
Conclusion.
Bibliographie.

Le 28 juin 1119, le pape Calixte II fixe le ressort de la province ecclésiastique de Vienne aux diocèses de Die, Genève, Grenoble, Maurienne, Valence et Viviers. Avant cette date, la situation est complexe en raison des fluctuations de la géographie ecclésiastique, du fait notamment des rivalités entre les métropoles d'Arles et de Vienne depuis l'Antiquité Tardive[1]. Une partie des dossiers recensés ici a déjà été appréhendée par Pierre-André Sigal dans le premier volume de cette entreprise. La production hagiographique est peu abondante et peu de manuscrits hagiographiques médiévaux sont parvenus pour cet espace, si bien qu'un recours aux bréviaires ou aux travaux d'érudits de l'époque moderne s'avère souvent essentiel[2].

---

* À l'exception de Genève, traitée par Éric Chevalley, *infra*, p. 675-688.

[1] Bonnassie − Iogna-Prat − Sigal (1994). On trouvera des éléments dans Nimmegeers (2014) et Poupardin (1907), p. 320 qui signalait déjà la difficulté qu'il y a à établir clairement la liste des suffragants de Vienne au Xe siècle (p. 320). Je remercie Noëlle Deflou-Leca pour son aide et sa confiance dans la rédaction de cette notice ainsi que Michèle Bois et Laurent Ripart qui ont bien voulu discuter certains dossiers.

[2] Je me permets de renvoyer à Peloux (2018).

I. Die: Marcel

L'évêque de Die Marcel, mort en 510 et absent des martyrologes historiques, a fait l'objet d'au moins deux Vies: une en prose (*BHL* 5247b) et une en vers (*BHL* 5247c). Toutes deux dépendent d'une *Vita derperdita*. Giuseppe Kirner identifia ces Vies de saint Marcel dans un recueil factice et lacunaire de Bologne (Bibl. univ. 1232), copié aux XVIIe siècle, et montra que les deux textes remontaient à l'époque carolingienne[3]. Il ne reste que 199 distiques élégiaques de la vie métrique, soit moins des deux tiers[4]. Son auteur est l'évêque de Die Posthumus Vulfinus: ses liens avec Theodulfe d'Orléans, mort en 821, permettent de dater avec certitude ce texte du début du IXe siècle. Quant à la Vie en prose, elle est en outre connue par un manuscrit du milieu du XIIe siècle en provenance de la chartreuse de Currière dans le diocèse de Grenoble (Grenoble, BM 49) et par quelques leçons de bréviaires de Die. François Dolbeau a proposé l'édition et l'étude de ce texte rare du fait de sa diffusion très locale[5]. Ce récit, dont la «structure est plus savante qu'il ne semble au premier abord»[6] rapporte que Marcel, originaire d'Avignon, est éduqué par son frère Pétrone, lui-même évêque de Die. Ce dernier le désigne comme son successeur, mais à sa mort, une partie importante des habitants préfère un autre successeur, tandis que Dieu choisit Marcel. Le roi des Wisigoths, Euric, déporte les habitants de Die et envoie Marcel à Arles, puis en Couserans. Deux ans après, le roi l'appelle à Toulouse pour guérir son fils et, en échange de sa guérison, permet son retour à Die. Il opère ensuite plusieurs miracles, rencontre à Lyon Caratène, la reine des Burgondes et obtient une exemption fiscale en échange d'un miracle[7]. Enfin, lors de la construction d'un baptistère à Die, il maintient miraculeusement en suspension dans l'air une colonne qui avait

---

[3] Kirner (1900).
[4] Éd. K. Strecker, *MGH, Poet. Lat.*, IV-3, Berlin, 1923, p. 965-975. Voir sur ce texte Desaye (1990), «Une relecture...», et Gärtner (2001).
[5] Dolbeau (1983). Lire aussi les compléments apportés dans la réédition de cet article dans Id. (2005), p. 205-206.
[6] Dolbeau (1983), p. 107.
[7] Voir le commentaire de cet épisode par Favrod (1997), p. 368-371 et Escher (2006), p 120.

commencé sa chute[8]. L'auteur conclut en précisant que l'épiscopat de Marcel a duré quarante-six années et que de nombreux miracles ont eu lieu auprès de son tombeau. François Dolbeau a montré que la Vie perdue réécrite ici, explicitement mentionnée par l'auteur, empruntait abondamment à la Vie de Vivien de Saintes (*BHL* 1324) et qu'elle pouvait tout à fait avoir eu pour auteur le même Posthumus Vulfinus qui rédigea la Vie métrique: tous deux utilisent en effet Venance Fortunat et Jérôme.

II. Grenoble

Les textes hagiographiques ne sont guère plus nombreux pour le diocèse de Grenoble: La Vie de Cérat (*BHL* 1727), évêque de Grenoble du milieu du Ve siècle, connu de Paulin de Nole et inscrit le 6 juin dans le martyrologe hiéronymien, a en fait été produite en Gascogne avant le dernier tiers du XIIe siècle: elle ne rentre donc pas dans le cadre de cette étude[9].

A. Aper

Mentionnons la Vie rarissime de l'ermite du VIIe siècle, Aper (*BHL* 615)[10], dont Pierre-André Sigal écrit qu'elle «ne repose sur aucun fait précis» et qu'elle a été composé au XIIe siècle[11]. Il faut probablement réviser cette datation trop tardive, notamment parce que le légendier d'Uzès, unique manuscrit à porter ce texte (Paris, BnF, lat. 5315), date de la première moitié du XIIe siècle[12]. Le texte a très clairement été rédigé pour être lu lors de la fête du saint dans l'église qui conserve son corps (*Ideo,*

---

[8] L'intérêt topographique de ce texte a bien été vu par Paul-Albert Février dans Biarne – Colardelle – Février (1989), p. 66-67 et Desaye (1990), «Die».

[9] Voir l'étude de Christophe Baillet dans Baillet – Henriet (2014), p. 754, n. 26. Sans preuve, Nimmegeers (2014), p. 18, la date du VIIe siècle. Sur les premiers évêques de la ville, voir en dernier lieu Colardelle (2008), p. 21-26.

[10] Éd. in *Cat. Paris*, II, p. 89-93 et Chevalier (1895), p. 33-37.

[11] Bonnassie – Iogna-Prat – Sigal (1994), p. 315.

[12] Sur ce manuscrit voir Peloux (2018). Le saint est absent du sanctoral du bréviaire grenoblois, Grenoble, BM 784.

dilectissimi, qui ad festum preclari viri convenitis [...] *cuius sanctum corpus in presenti ecclesia requiescit*). Le saint est présenté comme originaire d'une cité appelée *Sennico*. S'agit-il de Senez en Provence comme le pensent les Bollandistes, ou bien de Sens (*Senonica*) comme le transmettent plusieurs bréviaires tardifs?[13] Toujours est-il qu'il quitte sa cité d'origine pour rejoindre celle de Maurienne où siégeait l'évêque Leporius, connu en 650 et qualifié ici de *beatissimus*, comme dans une version de la Vie de sainte Tigre (*BHL* 8290)[14]. Aper le rencontre dans sa *villa* de *Miliciano*[15] et s'installe dans une cellule sur un territoire qui appartenait à l'évêque. Leporius dédicace dans ce lieu une église dédiée à saint Nazaire. Celle-ci n'a pas encore été identifiée. Là, Aper vit en ermite, attirant auprès de lui pauvres et pèlerins.

Une *fama* négative atteint toutefois l'évêque Isicius de Grenoble, à qui on apprend que le saint ne respecterait pas la liturgie des heures pour pouvoir manger plus tôt[16]. Ce dernier envoie donc des témoins à sa rencontre, qui refusent de recevoir la bénédiction en compagnie du saint, prétextant devoir retourner à Grenoble. Sur leur chemin, ils sont frappés d'une soif ardente, dans un lieu nommé *Alanter* ou *Ambous*. Ils ne sont guéris que par l'intercession du saint et, topos hagiographique, une biche, venant du mont *Alander* (*montis alandri*) dans un lieu appelé *Ambias* les nourrit. Apprenant ce miracle, l'évêque Isicius se rend en bateau (le long de l'Isère donc) auprès du saint, rencontre l'évêque de Maurienne Leporius et, suivant son bon gouvernement, termine sa vie en bon évêque. Ensuite, un serviteur d'Aper (*famulus*) qu'il avait adopté, nommé Apruncule (c'est-à-dire le petit Aper) est sauvé alors qu'il faillit être noyé en puisant de l'eau dans l'Isère. À l'endroit du miracle, Aper ordonne

---

[13] Un bréviaire de 1552 donné en note par Ulysse Chevalier ainsi que deux bréviaires de Genève datés de 1487 et 1525 signalés par GROS (1932), p. 486.

[14] Sur ce dossier voir *infra*. DUCHESNE (1907), p. 241.

[15] GROS (1932), p. 489 se demande s'il ne faut pas voir dans ce lieu la *villa Malencianum* cédée à l'évêque de Maurienne par le testament du patrice Abbon en 739, cf. GEARY (1985), p. 70.

[16] Deux évêques de ce nom sont attestés sur le siège épiscopal de Grenoble: le premier entre 573 et 589 et le second est connu par sa mention dans une liste épiscopale copiée dans le cartulaire de l'évêché, parmi les évêques du VIIe siècle: DUCHESNE (1907), p. 231-232. Il doit donc s'agir du second, contemporain de Leporius de Maurienne.

que le cours du fleuve change, et un cercle, toujours visible, apparaît à côté de la cruche du serviteur miraculeusement retrouvée.

Ce texte relatif à un saint inconnu des martyrologes s'apparente davantage à une liste de miracles, et peut être rattaché à la catégorie hagiographique qu'est l'*Episodenerzählung*, où il y a peu d'éléments biographiques importants mais plutôt une succession d'épisodes miraculeux[17]. On notera l'importance de la relation entre les évêques de Grenoble et de Saint-Jean de Maurienne, mais aussi les mentions d'anthroponymes, et plus encore de toponymes, difficiles à localiser aujourd'hui. En raison de ce fonds ancien qui peut en effet remonter à l'époque mérovingienne, il n'est pas à exclure que ce texte puisse être une rédaction de l'époque carolingienne et avoir été mis par écrit dans un moment de conflit territorial entre les diocèses voisins de Maurienne et de Grenoble[18], à moins qu'il ne soit plus tardif et accompagne la territorialisation du diocèse de Maurienne: c'est dans ce contexte que fut rédigée la Vie de sainte Tigre (*BHL* 8290) dans laquelle Leporius apparaît aussi comme saint (voir *infra*). Des paroisses portant le nom d'Aper sont attestées dans chacun des deux diocèses: en Maurienne celle de Saint-Avre, qui a donné le nom à une commune toujours existante, au nord de Saint-Jean de Maurienne depuis le XIe siècle, tandis que dans le diocèse de Grenoble, dans le Grésivaudan, l'ancienne paroisse de La Terrasse portait aussi ce nom au XIIe siècle[19].

Par ailleurs, rien ne prouve l'origine grenobloise de ce texte, en raison de la place positive qu'y occupe le saint évêque Leporius de Maurienne, présenté en exemple pour l'évêque de Grenoble qui doutait de la *virtus* du saint. Cette situation explique peut-être le curieux incipit du texte dont le sujet est manquant et qui fait à la fois d'Aper un prêtre du diocèse de Grenoble et du territoire de la Maurienne: *Beati et religiosi sacerdotis, Apri no-*

---

[17] HEINZELMANN – POULIN (1986), p. 72-73.

[18] On sait ainsi qu'en 882, l'évêque Adalbert de Maurienne fut convoqué par Jean VIII à Rome pour avoir agressé l'évêque de Grenoble: DUCHESNE (1907), p. 241.

[19] GROS (1932), p. 487 et 489. Des vestiges datant de l'époque burgonde y ont été repérés: BERTRANDY *et al.* (2017), p. 336-337.

mine, suam clementiam sibi praescivit et preordinavit sacerdotem et confessorem parrochiae Gratianopolim et territorio Maurigenensi[20].

B. Ferréol

Cet évêque du VIIe siècle, attesté dans les listes épiscopales de Grenoble dès le Moyen Âge, a fait l'objet d'une Vie que Pierre David a édité à partir d'un bréviaire manuscrit de Grenoble (Grenoble, BM 136 (784), *BHL vacat*) en la complétant grâce au *De Allobrogibus* rédigé par Aymar du Rivail en 1553 qui donna un résumé de ce texte[21]. L'auteur ne connaît pas la date de l'épiscopat de son héros, il indique que ce dernier avait fait construire une estrade pour prêcher dans une plaine du Mont-Esson. Un jour, alors qu'il prêchait, l'un de ceux qui étaient près de lui le fit chuter avec une perche de saule, avant d'être précipité dans un four où l'on cuisait du pain. Des fidèles recueillirent ses restes, les déposèrent le long de l'Isère dans un tombeau de pierre. De nombreux miracles eurent lieu et on construisit une église en son honneur, église désormais ruinée et dépourvue des précieuses reliques. Aymar du Rivail ajoute que ses reliques furent transférées à Varacieu, dans le diocèse de Vienne mais «il est difficile de dire si ce nom est emprunté au panégyrique»[22]. Surtout, il rapporte que la ville fut ensuite ravagée et détruite, ce dont fait écho le cartulaire B de l'église de Grenoble rédigé au début du XIIe siècle. Comme le saint est appelé *Fergeolus* dans ce texte et que cette forme n'est pas attestée dans la documentation avant le XIIIe siècle, Pierre David date la version du bréviaire de ce siècle-là mais suppose l'existence d'un texte antérieur. Prenant comme preuve le fait que l'évêque Arconce de Viviers a été assassiné également par Ébroïn à cette période au mois de janvier, Pierre David veut faire de

---

[20] On peut raisonnablement rétablir le sujet grâce à la première leçon d'un bréviaire manuscrit de Grenoble du XVe siècle dans le sanctoral duquel le saint se trouve: ms. 136 (784), fol. 348v: «Sancta et indiuidua Trinitas beatum et religiosum sacerdotem Aprum nomine sua sibi prescivit». Le manuscrit est décrit par Leroquais (1934), II, p. 123-125.

[21] David (1930).

[22] David (1930), p. 10.

Ferréol une victime de ce maire du palais[23]. Or il semble que ni le peu qu'on sache d'Arconce de Viviers (*infra*), ni cette proximité de date ne soient des arguments suffisants pour permettre une construction aussi audacieuse[24].

III. Maurienne

Cet évêché est une fondation nouvelle du VIe siècle[25].

A. Marin

Fêté le 28 novembre, cet ermite et martyr céphalophore a été évoqué dans le vol. VI d'*Hagiographies*, car sa Vie (*BHL* 5536) et le récit de la *Translatio* de ses reliques (*BHL* 5537) ont été édités par Mabillon à partir d'un bréviaire de Saint-Savin au diocèse de Poitiers, où ses reliques sont attestées avant le XIe siècle[26]. Le second texte est bien un texte poitevin, et Baudouin de Gaiffier pensait que la Vie l'était aussi en notant qu'elle dépendait en grande partie de celle de l'évêque de Clermont Priest (*BHL* 6915-6916)[27]. L'inventaire des manuscrits hagiographiques d'Angers a permis à Joseph Van der Straeten de découvrir dans un manuscrit du XIIe siècle une version longue de cette Vie, uniquement tournée vers la Maurienne (Angers, BM 308, *BHL* 5536a)[28]. Dans ce manuscrit, dont la provenance n'est guère établie, après et avant la copie de différentes œuvres d'Augustin, on trouve douze textes hagiographiques, sans ordre

---

[23] Hypothèse déjà présente dans le martyrologe de Du Saussay puis dans les *AASS* (Ian. 1, 1643), cf. David (1930), p. 14.

[24] Elle est suivie sans critique par Nimmegeers (2014), p. 134, 177 et 187. Voir Coens (1935), p. 432 qui considère bien qu'il ne s'agit que d'une hypothèse.

[25] Parron-Kontis (2002).

[26] Éd. *AASS OSB*, III-2 (1672), p. 535-537 (*BHL* 5536) et p. 537-538 (*BHL* 5537), cf. Bultot-Verleysen (2014), p. 639-640. Il n'existe pas de témoin médiéval de *BHL* 5536, contrairement à ce qu'indique la base *Légendiers latins* qui note le ms. Trier, SB, 550, fol. 8-47v qui contient en réalité *BHL* 5336, relatif à la vierge.

[27] de Gaiffier (1955), p. 326-327, n. 4, 334. L'auteur ne donne pas ses arguments quant à l'origine poitevine de la Vie.

[28] Van der Straeten (1982), p. 283-288.

liturgique, tous très diffusés et connus par ailleurs, à l'exception notable de celui relatif à saint Marin. Son éditeur indique que «les emprunts à des textes analogues sont patents», ajoutant hélas «il n'y a pas lieu de les relever ici». En outre, le bollandiste n'a publié que la seconde partie du texte: il faut pour la première se reporter à l'édition de Mabillon à partir d'un bréviaire de Saint-Savin. Pour plus de clarté, une réédition et un repérage systématique des sources serait souhaitable.

L'action se situe sous le pontificat du pape Alexandre. Âgé de onze ans, Marin est laissé à Rome par ses parents, confié à saint Ellidius qui l'éduque et l'ordonne prêtre à vingt ans. À la mort d'Ellidius, Marin refuse de lui succéder et part en Bourgogne (*in partes Burgundiae*) dans le monastère bénédictin dédié à la Vierge de *Juga montium*, vulgairement appelé *Candorensis* où saint Eusippe avait passé sa vie. Là, l'abbé Erillius le prie de rester auprès des moines pour qu'ils profitent de son enseignement. Victime de son succès, Marin attire des pèlerins et décide donc de se retirer et vivre en solitaire, dans un lieu appelé *Magnus*. Le saint atteint alors la ville de Maurienne, près de la rivière *Suriae*. Deux ours viennent le nourrir chaque jour, jusqu'à ce que le roi des Vandales, à l'assaut des Lombards et des Burgondes, ne vienne dévaster la région, entraînant la fuite des moines de leur monastère. Il part ensuite avec ses troupes en direction de la ville de Maurienne pour l'incendier. Marin va à leur rencontre pour les en dissuader et prêcher l'Évangile. Il est conduit auprès du gouverneur Acquirinus qui lui demande de sacrifier à ses dieux, en échange de quoi son roi, Engald, le rendra riche et puissant. Devant son refus, il commence à être torturé.

Là, le manuscrit d'Angers poursuit en indiquant qu'il est jeté dans un four mais les flammes ne le consument pas, entraînant la conversion d'un certain nombre de ses bourreaux qui demandent le baptême: trois-cent cinquante d'entre eux sont alors baptisés. Le préfet demande à ce que Marin soit enfermé. Ce dernier lui dit que, s'il se convertit au christianisme, alors il pourra ressusciter tous ceux qui ont péri par les flammes. Le préfet accepte, Marin s'exécute et les morts ressuscitent. Ne tenant pas sa parole, le préfet le fait amener dans la vallée de la Maurienne pour lui trancher la tête, au-dessus du fleuve *Suria*. Il porte sa tête lui-même jusqu'au mont *Rigidus* et la pose sur une pierre de meulière tandis que son bourreau se suicide en se jetant du haut de la montagne. Trois mille hommes se convertissent à la suite de cela et sont baptisés par l'évêque Eusippe. Ensuite, l'évêque Urbain de Turin et le même Eusippe de Maurienne recueillent le corps du saint et l'installent dans l'église Sainte-Marie où de nombreux miracles, bien trop long à rapporter, ont lieu.

Ce texte curieux mériterait une étude approfondie: écrit dans un style très simple, il s'apparente bien à une Passion épique pour reprendre la typologie d'Hippolyte Delehaye. Bien que l'action se déroule principalement en Maurienne, l'auteur n'en n'est pas nécessairement originaire: aucun des toponymes, à commencer par celui du monastère *Candorensis*, n'a été formellement identifié. L'historiographie locale situe le martyre sur la commune du Châtel, près de Saint-Jean de Maurienne, mais le culte du saint n'y est attesté que depuis le XVIe siècle[29]. L'abondance des noms n'aide guère: qui est le pape Alexandre? Celui du début du IIe siècle? Ou bien s'agit-il de renvoyer à Alexandre II qui siégea entre 1061 et 1073? Cela pourrait-il être un indice de datation? Difficile de le dire. Rien ne permet en tout cas de faire de Marin une victime des Sarrasins[30]. Quant aux deux évêques présents pour recueillir son corps, ils sont inconnus par ailleurs, absents des listes épiscopales médiévales. Face à de telles difficultés, faut-il alors revenir à l'intuition première de Baudouin de Gaiffier, qui pensait que ce texte (dont il ne connaissait que le début) était une production poitevine? Une étude plus approfondie permettrait de le savoir.

B. Tigre

Grégoire de Tours raconte qu'une femme de la ville de Maurienne a rapporté un pouce de saint Jean-Baptiste dans sa ville qui dépendait autrefois de l'évêché de Turin (*In gloria martyrum*, XIII). Un manuscrit de droit canon, comprenant une version pro-viennoise de la *Notitia Galliarum* et copié à Vienne au Xe siècle, porte un texte donnant à cette femme le nom de Tigre (*BHL* 8289). La rubrique du récit indique clairement les raisons

---

[29] Gros (1948), p. 92-98. Aucun vestige n'est recensé par Rémy – Ballet – Ferber (1997), p. 148.

[30] *Contra* Gros (1948), p. 92-94.

de sa copie: *Auctoritas quod ex antiquo Mauriennensis ecclesia Viennensi ecclesiae metropoli subdita fuit*. La copie intervient en effet alors qu'en 908, Serge III, à la demande de l'archevêque de Vienne, affirme que le diocèse de Maurienne dépend bien de la métropole viennoise[31]. On trouve plus tard, vers 1100, une copie de ce texte avec des variantes assez peu significatives dans un document intitulé *Carta de Maurienna et de Seusia*[32].

Ce récit fait de Tigre une contemporaine de Gontran, originaire d'un *oppidum* de Maurienne non identifié (*Volacis*), sœur d'une certaine Pigménie. Elles rencontrèrent des moines qui allaient de Jérusalem à l'Irlande et parlèrent des reliques de Jean-Baptiste que la sainte femme réussit à aller chercher, ce qui lui permit d'édifier une église pour les vénérer (i. e. la future cathédrale Saint-Jean), avec l'appui soutenu du roi Gontran. Et comme le diocèse dépendait alors de la métropole de Vienne, ce fut le métropolitain de ce lieu, Isicius, qui la consacra avant que Gontran ne réunisse les évêques de son royaume à Chalon. Alors, saint Felmasius fut consacré premier évêque par le métropolitain de Vienne. De même, la ville de Suse fut assujettie à ce nouveau diocèse, le tout avec l'accord du pape.

Voilà donc un texte dont la seule rédaction a pour but de montrer l'ancienneté et la légitimité de la géographie ecclésiastique, qui n'est autre qu'une hagiogéographie[33]. Tigre intéresse finalement peu son auteur: a-t-il puisé à une *Vita* qui aurait disparu? On peut le croire car le début du texte y ressemble clairement: les origines géographiques et sociales de la sainte sont rappelées, son comportement de bonne chrétienne avec sa sœur. Rapidement toutefois, l'auteur abandonne sa source. Pierre le Mangeur, à la fin du XIIe siècle, se fait l'écho de la légende de la sainte rapportant les reliques du Précurseur mais, peut-être sous l'influence du dossier hagiographique de la sainte d'Iconium, transforme Tigre en Thècle[34]. À partir de cette date, l'association entre Thècle, la Maurienne et les reliques de Jean-Baptiste

---

[31] JAFFÉ (1885), t. I, n°3544, p. 447 Sur ce dossier, on consultera GROS (1948) ainsi que le riche mémoire de DERRIER (2019) que l'auteur a eu l'amabilité de me transmettre avant sa soutenance.
[32] BILLIET – ALBRIEUX (1861), p. 7-8.
[33] Voir les intéressantes remarques de ROMAN (1898), p. 13-15.
[34] Cf. *PL* 198, Paris, 1855, Cap. LXXIII.

circule chez plusieurs auteurs dont Jean Beleth[35], Sicard de Crémone[36] et enfin Jacques de Voragine[37].

Daniel Papenbroeck édita pour sa part une Vie, à partir d'un manuscrit venant de Saint-Jean de Maurienne «en écriture gothique» et que lui avait envoyé par Charles du Cange (*BHL* 8290)[38]. Ce texte se trouve aussi dans une copie manuscrite de Jacques Damé de 1681[39]. Cette *Vita* est abrégée dans un bréviaire à l'usage de Maurienne de 1512[40]. Ce texte reprend les origines sociales et géographiques de la sainte. La trame narrative et le vocabulaire du début du texte sont très proches de *BHL* 8289. S'agit-il alors de la source du manuscrit viennois, d'une réécriture par amplification de cette dernière, ou bien d'une réécriture d'un texte source disparu? Seule une édition critique et une analyse détaillée permettrait de le dire.

Cette version détaille les épisodes du voyage de la sainte et les circonstances qui lui permirent de ramener les reliques du Précurseur, rapporte le miracle des trois évêques qu'on trouvait déjà chez Grégoire de Tours, puis revient sur la construction de l'église avec l'aide de Gontran telle que rapportée dans le document viennois. Ensuite, il est précisé que Gontran délimita très clairement le diocèse, en particulier depuis un lieu nommé *Vologia* jusqu'à un mille de *Rama* (La Roche-de-Rame). Mais comme cette limite fit l'objet d'un conflit entre l'évêque de Maurienne Leporius et l'évêque d'Embrun, Gontran fit planter une borne à *Avigliana*. Le texte précise ensuite qu'il y a une autre limite depuis l'endroit où la rivière *Baisdra* se jette dans l'Isère jusqu'au *castrum* de Briançon. Et l'auteur d'ajouter que

---

[35] Iohannis Beleth, *Summa de ecclesiasticis officiis*, éd. H. DOUTEIL, Turnhout, 1976 (*CC CM*, 41), chap. CXLVII.

[36] *Sicardi Cremonensis episcopi Mitralis de officiis*, éd. G. SARBAK, L. WEINRICH, Turnhout, 2008 (*CC CM*, 228), p. 660.

[37] *La Légende dorée*, texte traduit, présenté et annoté par A. BOUREAU *et al.*, Paris, chap. 121, p. 708-717 et notes p. 1363-1365.

[38] *AASS*, Iun. 5, 1709, col. 73 et sqq. Par erreur, la *BHL*ms recense le manuscrit Paris, BnF, lat. 1452 sous ce numéro alors qu'il s'agit de l'unique exemplaire de *BHL* 8289.

[39] Archives départementales de Savoie, 3G 184, transcrit dans DERRIER (2019). BILLIET (1861), p. 307-308 donne aussi une version qu'il indique tirer d'un manuscrit de Combet qui le tirerait du manuscrit de la BnF n° 3887 (qui n'est autre que le ms. lat. 1452 comprenant *BHL* 8289). Voir aussi ROMAN (1898), p. 18.

[40] On en trouvera la transcription dans DERRIER (2019).

quiconque enfreindrait cet écrit s'attirerait les foudres de sainte Tigre et de saint Jean-Baptiste.

L'hagiographe termine en rapportant enfin brièvement la mort de la sainte. Très clairement, comme dans tout le dossier de sainte Tigre, l'hagiographe écrit pour des raisons territoriales liées à la définition du diocèse de Maurienne. L'existence de plusieurs versions, donnant parfois des noms de lieux discordants, empêche pour le moment de préciser la datation de ce texte, même si on peut penser, avec Georges de Manteyer, qu'il est bien postérieur au texte viennois: il ne s'agit plus seulement de montrer que Vienne est la métropole de la Maurienne mais que les limites de ce dernier diocèse sont bien délimitées, ce qui semble correspondre à un texte qui n'est pas antérieur à la seconde moitié du XIe siècle[41].

IV. VALENCE

A. APOLLINAIRE

Après la Passion des saints Félix, Fortunat et Achillée de Valence (*BHL* 2896-2897) qui est antérieure à l'époque carolingienne[42], il faut mentionner le dossier de l'évêque de la première moitié du VIe siècle, Apollinaire, inscrit au martyrologe hiéronymien[43]. Il est composé d'une Vie et de Miracles. La datation de sa Vie (*BHL* 634) ne fait pas l'objet d'un consen-

---

[41] DE MANTEYER (1908), p. 175-187. Ce dernier situe le texte dans les années 1060. Voir aussi MAZEL (2016), p. 198-201. Ces auteurs signalent l'existence d'une notice relative à l'affaire de cette délimitation reproduite par BESSON (1759), preuve n° 09. Ce dernier texte comprend des variantes importantes par rapport à ce que l'on trouve dans la Vie transmise par les Bollandistes. Voir enfin NIMMEGEERS (2014), p. 80-81 qui reprend exactement l'argumentation de DE MANTEYER (1908), sans le citer. Il faut encore ajouter à ce dossier un court miracle de la relique de Jean-Baptiste transmis par les Bollandistes à partir de documents venant de Saint-Jean de Maurienne (*BHL* 4313), mais la mention d'un miraculé captif chez les Turcs renvoie plutôt à l'époque moderne.

[42] HEINZELMANN (2010), p. 42.

[43] Différentes sources permettent de le documenter, cf. PIETRI – HEIJMANS (2013), p. 167-170.

sus[44]. Ce texte a ensuite servi à la composition de la Vie du frère du saint, le célèbre Avit de Vienne (*BHL* 885), qui n'est «guère plus ancienne que le IXe siècle» d'après Martin Heinzelmann, mais qui pourrait être encore postérieure[45]. L'auteur de la Vie d'Apollinaire se présente comme un contemporain de son héros, un témoin de ses miracles, ce que Bruno Krusch contesta fermement sur la base d'arguments remis en cause par Martin Heinzelmann qui indique que «les critères de Krusch sont des prétendues fautes historiques de l'hagiographe et une latinité jugée carolingienne»[46]. Quoi qu'il en soit, il semble qu'Agobard ait bien eu connaissance des *gesta scripta* du saint[47]. On notera au préalable que le plus ancien manuscrit est daté du Xe siècle (Vatican, Reg. lat., 711, II, fol. 41r-43v).

Le saint est présenté comme originaire d'une noble famille de Vienne. Un officier du roi Sigismond, chargé du fisc et nommé Étienne, épousa la sœur de sa défunte femme, si bien qu'Avitus et Apollinaire décidèrent de l'excommunier lors d'un synode. Cela entraîna la fureur du roi Sigismond, qui les envoya dans un *oppidum* de la cité de Lyon appelé *Sardinia*. Voyant que ces derniers refusent toujours de céder, Sigismond les renvoie chacun dans leur siège. L'eau du Rhône devient alors imbuvable. Saint Apollinaire découvre une source miraculeuse qui, à la demande de la reine, permet de guérir Sigismond tombé malade. Le roi se repent[48]. Ensuite, Apollinaire souhaite aller à Arles sur le tombeau de Genès, un miracle lui permet un voyage fluvial paisible. Un autre miracle a lieu près d'Avignon en présence de son diacre Claudius et d'un de ses serviteurs, Alifius, qui est exorcisé. Arrivé à Arles, le saint est accueilli par Césaire et le patrice Libère. Des membres de sa famille, Partemius et Ferréol sont

---

[44] Le texte est édité une première fois dans les *AASS* en 1770 (au 3 oct.), puis par B. Krusch dans les *MGH*, *SRM*, III, Hanovre, 1896, p. 197-203.

[45] Voir HEINZELMANN (2010), p. 58, n. 136; éd. R. PEIPER, *MGH*, *AA*, VI-2, Berlin, 1883, p. 177-181. Les Bollandistes utilisent le légendier de Bödekken et un manuscrit de Vienne transmis à eux par Chifflet pour éditer ce texte. Pour NIMMEEGERS (2014), p. 17, ce texte s'inspire aussi du catalogue épiscopal transcrit au XIe siècle dans la Bible de Berne.

[46] *Ibid.* Voir B. KRUSCH (1895), p. 52.

[47] *MGH*, *Epist.*, V, Berlin, 1899, p. 187.

[48] Les paragraphes 2 à 4 de la *Vita* d'Avit sont identiques aux chapitres 2 à 6 de la *Vita* d'Apollinaire (numérotation des *AASS*), ils portent l'épisode du chargé du fisc Étienne, suivis du miracle qui pousse Sigismond à se repentir.

aussi présents. Une sénatrice proche de lui (*propinqua sua*) Arcutamia, l'invite à Marseille, en présence d'un certain Léon. Apollinaire guérit alors un sourd-muet. Affaibli, il ne peut participer aux offices mais exorcise un certain Paragorius, venu le frapper au visage. Enfin, le diacre Leubaredus est témoin de sa mort et de la grande lumière qui sortit alors de sa cellule. Et l'auteur conclut son texte en expliquant combien Valence doit se réjouir d'avoir un tel patron.

Angela Kinney a réévalué ce texte de manière convaincante en montrant que la langue employée était tout à fait conforme au latin de l'Antiquité tardive, et que l'affaire d'Étienne est corroborée par ce qui est contenu dans les canons d'un concile tenu justement à Lyon entre 518 et 523[49]. Elle se demande si le lieu de *Sardinia* ne pourrait pas être en fait *Sarbiniacum*, Savigny, où l'on sait que Gondebaud possédait une *villa*, à moins qu'il ne s'agisse en fait du monastère de l'Ile-Barbe (*insula barbari*), transformé en une île littéraire d'exil, la Sardaigne. Enfin, elle note aussi l'intérêt prosopographique de ce texte. Reste que ce court récit concerne assez peu la cité de Valence dans laquelle l'action du saint n'est pas même évoquée. Tout porte à croire que son auteur, centré sur l'épisode mettant en scène les relations de Sigismond avec les évêques et les miracles du saint à Arles et à Marseille, est extérieur à cette cité. S'agit-il de rappeler la primauté arlésienne, en rapportant l'accueil favorable de Césaire? Il y a clairement eu un tri opéré, soit par un contemporain du saint qui n'a mis par écrit que ces quelques épisodes, soit par un auteur plus tardif qui n'a tiré d'une *Vita* plus ancienne que ce qui ne concernait pas l'action de l'évêque dans sa cité...tout en l'encourageant en conclusion à se réjouir d'avoir un tel patron[50]. L'idée que ce texte date de l'époque carolingienne,

---

[49] KINNEY (2014), p. 161-162. Sans exclure une rédaction carolingienne, FAVROD (1997), p. 15, 22, 425-427 considère également ce texte comme digne d'intérêt pour documenter le VIe siècle, en particulier en raison de l'affaire d'Étienne.

[50] COLUMBI (1638), p. 9 indique qu'Apollinaire résidait dans l'agglomération de hauteur de Soyons où il avait édifié un sanctuaire en l'honneur des saints Gervais et Protais, mais il ne s'appuie sur aucun document: c'est à tort que son texte a été pris pour une Vie par GILLES *et al.* (2013), p. 193). Le sanctoral du bréviaire de l'abbaye de Soyons (XVe siècle) porte bien une abréviation de la Vie *BHL* 634 (Paris, BnF, n.a.lat. 718, fol. 395v-397). C'est aussi sur ce texte que sont construites les leçons du sanctoral du lectionnaire

mais a été construit à partir de documents bien réels, est aussi défendue par Frederic Paxton pour qui l'auteur utilise la Vie de Séverin d'Agaune dans laquelle Clovis est guéri miraculeusement de fièvres[51]. Pourtant, nous n'avons repéré aucun parallèle textuel net entre ces textes.

On sait d'après la *Chronique des évêques de Valence*, composée au XVIe siècle, que l'évêque Bonitus procéda à la translation des reliques d'Apollinaire depuis l'église Saint-Pierre du Bourg jusqu'à l'église Saint-Étienne[52]. D'après Louis Duchesne, ce Bonitus «figure au bas du faux concile de Narbonne (788)»[53]. Si cette translation de reliques a bien eu lieu, cet événement n'aurait-il pas pu conduire alors à fixer par écrit la mémoire d'Apollinaire?[54] L'hypothèse demeure fragile.

Plus tard, des *Miracula* d'Apollinaire (*BHL* 636) sont rédigés, transmis uniquement dans le légendier d'Uzès à la suite de la Vie du saint (Paris, BnF, lat. 5315)[55]. Ils sont clairement datés de l'année 911, lorsque l'évêque Remegarius découvre une jeune fille miraculeusement guérie sur le tombeau du saint situé dans sa basilique pleine de vin et de blé en raison de la peur des raids musulmans. À la même époque, une autre jeune fille possédée, Ermengarde, fille de Ragambert, se réfugie dans la basilique où le démon n'entre pas: ses parents promettent des biens en échange de sa guérison. Une fois guérie, son frère Richard ne respecta pas la promesse et sa sœur fut de nouveau possédée par le démon, ce qui entraîna une seconde intervention du saint

---

de l'office de l'abbaye de Cruas (Paris, BnF, lat. 1019, fol. 281-281v) et des bréviaires de Valence du XVe siècle, Valence, BM 80, fol. 275-276v et Arras, BM 1143 (552), fol. 344v; sur les manuscrits liturgiques de Valence voir en dernier lieu MERCIER (2006).

[51] PAXTON (2008). Sur la datation de la *Vita Severini*, cf. HEINZELMANN (1996), p. 106 et en dernier lieu CHEVALLEY et RODUIT (2015), p. 50-52. Jean-François Reynaud penche aussi pour une datation carolingienne (dans PARRON, SOLEIL et TARDIEU (2006), p. 73).

[52] Sur ce texte voir surtout l'étude et l'édition de FONT-RÉAULX (1925 et 1926). Voir aussi les remarques de PLANET (2006). Sur l'église tardo-antique du Bourg cf. les éléments rassemblés par SCHILLING (2018), p. 316.

[53] DUCHESNE (1907), p. 220, 224.

[54] L'événement est retenu (sans indication de sources) par FRACHETTE (1998), p. 495.

[55] Le texte a été édité par les Bollandistes, *Cat. Paris*, II, p. 93-94 puis par CHEVALIER (1895), p. 38-40 et enfin dans les *MGH*, *SS*, XXX-2, Leipzig, 1934, p. 1343-1346.

dont fut témoin l'évêque Remegarius. La même année, le marquis Hugues, sur la route de l'Italie, s'arrêta à Valence et conduisit un muet nommé Pasturellus auprès du saint dont le corps reposait dans l'église Saint-Etienne[56]: après avoir reçu de l'évêque la bénédiction, il fut guéri.

Voilà donc un texte très court qui met en valeur le saint, mais aussi son successeur sur le siège épiscopal et le marquis de Provence. On pourrait se demander, face à une telle brièveté, si on n'a pas à faire à un extrait de *Liber miraculorum* plus large, mais on n'en trouve nulle trace ailleurs[57]. S'il y a quelques erreurs de datation, les personnages mentionnés renvoient bien au tout début du Xe siècle[58]. Il y a fort à parier que ce texte a été rédigé dans l'entourage même de l'évêque Remegarius. On notera que la première mention d'une dédicace de la cathédrale à Apollinaire remonte justement à un diplôme de 912[59]. Dans la *Chronique des évêques*, il est indiqué que ce dernier procéda à la translation des reliques des martyrs Félix, Fortunat et Achillée, sans nulle mention d'Apollinaire mais ce document pose bien des problèmes. On a en tout cas bien un épiscopat important pour le culte des saints à Valence.

B. Galla

Le culte de sainte Jalle est resté localisé dans la commune drômoise de Sainte-Jalle, dans une enclave du diocèse de Sisteron située aux confins des diocèses de Gap, Die et Vaison[60]. La géographie ecclésiastique de cette région est particulièrement mouvante et l'inclusion de cette sainte dans la présente synthèse s'explique uniquement par les coordonnées hagiographiques qui lui furent conférées dans la *BHL*: *Galla v. in dioecesi Valentina*. Seule une *Vita* a été repérée (*BHL* 3235), aujourd'hui

---

[56] Sur cette église du groupe épiscopal voir PARRON, SOLEIL et TARDIEU (2006) et les éléments rassemblés par SCHILLING (2018), p. 299-300.

[57] Les bréviaires de Valence (Valence, BM 80, XVe siècle, fol. 234v et Arras, BM 1142 (542), fol. 291) portent au 17 juin, fête de la translation du saint, une version abrégée de ces trois miracles, datés par erreur de 1011: le nom de la première miraculée est donné: Richilde.

[58] De MANTEYER (1908), p. 118-119 et GANIVET (2000), p. 155-156.

[59] POUPARDIN et PROU (1920), p. 96 et sqq.

[60] Voir BOIS (1997), p. 94-101 et VARANO (2011), p. 172-176.

transmise par un unique manuscrit (Vatican, Ott. lat. 120, du XIe siècle), un important légendier dont ne subsistent que 48 textes pour le mois de janvier et le début du mois de février. La sainte y apparaît au premier février, alors qu'elle est fêtée le 16 novembre dans les manuscrits liturgiques du diocèse[61]. Ce manuscrit de provenance inconnue servit de base à l'édition du texte dans les *Acta Sanctorum*[62]. Sans donner plus de détails, Martin Heinzelmann considère ce texte comme rédigé «pas avant le VIIe, voire le VIIIe siècle»[63]. Dans un court prologue, l'auteur explique que lire ou entendre des Vies de saints permet d'augmenter la foi. Aussi tentera-t-il dans un style rustique de rapporter la Vie de Jalle. Issue d'une famille illustre, elle refuse le mariage pour servir le Christ et atteint la cité de Valence où sept évêques la voilent. De retour, elle demeure dans l'église (non précisément localisée), où elle accomplit des miracles, guérit, exorcise ou punit. Ainsi, un miracle a lieu pour punir un prêtre qui lui dérobe sa condamine avec sa récolte[64]: la foudre détruit le champ de telle sorte que son nom même est effacé, et on l'appelle depuis *Aruinolus*.

Une guérison a lieu alors que la patrie (*patria*) de la sainte est encerclée par la multitude des barbares (*multitudo barbarorum*) entraînant la fuite de tous dans un *castrum*. Dans celui-ci, on trouve une basilique Saint-Pierre dans laquelle la sainte prie pendant que la *gens barbarorum* dévaste sa patrie. Tandis que les Barbares tentent de forcer les murs du *castrum*, elle les met en déroute par ses prières. Comme les habitants se réjouissent, la sainte, alors âgée de 90 ans et sentant sa mort approcher, demande à être enterrée. Morte, elle est conduite dans le *vicus* de *Bageno*, dans la basilique Saint-Étienne, et de nombreux miracles ont lieu sur le trajet.

Ce *vicus*, attesté dès l'Antiquité correspond au village de Sainte-Jalle dans l'église duquel on a découvert les traces d'un

---

[61] Voir les bréviaires de Valence, BM 80, fol. 299v et Arras, BM 1172 (552), fol. 363 (sanctoral, mais sans leçon propre).

[62] *AASS*, Feb. I, 1658, col. 940.

[63] HEINZELMANN (2010), p. 58.

[64] Leçon non comprise par les *Acta Sanctorum* qui ont rendu *son da nimam suam* et expliquent en note lire *con da nimam*, ce qui est juste, mais qu'il faut rendre par *condaminam*. Le mot est très rare au haut Moyen Âge, seulement attesté chez Césaire d'Arles, puis à l'époque carolingienne. Voir BILLY (1997), p. 142 sq. (qui date le texte du VIIe siècle, sans raison).

sanctuaire ayant précédé ce lieu de culte[65], mais le corps de la sainte a probablement été accueilli dans la chapelle voisine Saint-Anastase, qui portait autrefois le nom de Saint-Étienne et où un coffre reliquaire a été fouillé en 1987[66]. En fait, la mémoire hagiographique de Jalle s'inscrit bien dans une atmosphère tardo-antique: le nom de la sainte rappelle celui de la mère de Consorcia qui, d'après le *Vita* de celle-ci, antérieure au début du IXe siècle, se convertit à la vie religieuse avec toute sa famille vers 600 (*BHL* 1925-1925b)[67]. Or d'après ce texte, cette famille est aussi implantée dans le diocèse de Sisteron, comme Jalle. En fait, on peut se demander si *Galla* ne pourrait pas appartenir au même groupe familial que Consorcia[68]. Reste que contrairement aux textes relatifs à Consorcia, les éléments chronologiques sont presque inexistants dans la Vie de sainte Jalle, son auteur ne sachant pas la placer dans le temps. Cet élément ne va pas en faveur d'une rédaction très ancienne. Les barbares sont-ils un souvenir de l'invasion lombarde des années 570 documentée par Paul Diacre (*Histoire des Lombards*, III, 8)? Difficile de l'affirmer. L'auteur ne semble pas écrire pour exalter un sanctuaire et ne précise pas la localisation du *castrum* où se trouvait l'église Saint-Pierre[69].

Le seul lieu précis est bien la cité de Valence où la sainte a pris le voile, en présence de sept évêques. S'agit-il des évêques des sept diocèses qui forment la province de Vienne (Genève, Grenoble, Die, Maurienne, Valence, Vienne, Viviers)? Peut-être, mais il est difficile de rattacher cette situation à une époque donnée, tant la géographie ecclésiastique fut fluctuante. S'agit-il de montrer que c'est bien l'évêque de Valence qui domine la *patria* de la sainte et non l'évêque de Sisteron? On ne connaît pas de revendications des évêques de Valence dans cet espace qui concerne plutôt les diocèses de Die, Gap, Vaison et Sisteron. Il n'est toutefois pas impossible que notre auteur puisse être un membre du clergé valentinois, ce qui expliquerait ses faibles connaissances de cette région méridionale, même s'il a bien

---

[65] Desaye – Lurol – Mège (2000).

[66] Sur cette église voir Barruol (1981), p. 329-335 et Tardieu (2006) qui indique à tort que la Vie de la sainte se déroule à Valence.

[67] Sur ce dossier voir Magnani (2018), p. 11-12.

[68] Sur cette Galla, voir Pietri et Heijmans (2013), p. 842.

[69] Voir les propositions de localisations proposées par Barrillon (1998), p. 225 (qui traduit le texte p. 226-231).

connaissance des miracles de la sainte, et que celui de la condamine est relativement précis. En même temps, il écrit dans un latin très simple, dans un style qu'il qualifie lui-même de rustique, pour faire connaître l'expérience de cette sainte femme dont le culte fut très localisé et qui risquait, au dire même de l'auteur, de tomber dans l'oubli. La très faible diffusion de sa *Vita*, lui a, semble-t-il, donné raison[70].

V. Viviers

Ce diocèse a en partie été traité par Pierre-André Sigal dans le premier volume d'*Hagiographies* paru en 1994. Des diocèses considérés ici, celui de Viviers est le plus riche d'un point de vue hagiographique, même si la transmission des textes pose un certain nombre de problèmes, sur lesquels il est utile de s'arrêter au préalable avant de passer à l'examen de chaque dossier.

A. La transmission des textes

Signalons tout d'abord l'importance du manuscrit Bruxelles, KBR 1791-1794, du dernier quart du IXe siècle, et de son presque jumeau et contemporain Séville, Bibliothèque colombine, ms. 5-3-4. Tous deux renferment une partie essentielle des dossiers hagiographiques du diocèse, toujours dans leur plus ancienne version manuscrite et permettent bien souvent de proposer un terminus pour les dater. L'hypothèse d'une origine bourguignonne de ces manuscrits a été émise à plusieurs reprises, car les textes hagiographiques contenus sont liés à la figure de Girard de Vienne, fidèle de Louis le Pieux devenu ensuite un personnage légendaire[71]. En effet, parmi les quelques

---

[70] La sainte ne se trouve pas non plus dans le sanctoral du bréviaire de Sisteron imprimé en 1513 (Paris, BnF, B 6328).
[71] Voir notamment Louis (1951), p. 91, n. 1 repris par de Gaiffier (1951), p. 132-134 et Id. (1970), p. 285-288. Guerreiro (1990), p. 72 rapporte l'opinion de Bischoff selon qui le manuscrit de Bruxelles-KBR aurait été produit entre Auxerre et Lyon; ce manuscrit a été envoyé à Henschens par Scriverius. Voir enfin la description du second manuscrit par Marín (1959), qui plaide pour une écriture à la fois influencée par la région tourangelle et par l'Italie du nord mais qui ignore le manuscrit de la KBR.

saints dont on trouve un récit copié, on note un petit dossier relatif à Eusèbe et Pontien de Rome, qui comprend notamment dans le manuscrit de Bruxelles le récit de la translation de leurs reliques en Gaule par Girard (*BHL* 2747)[72]. Ce texte, dédié à Girard, raconte comment le comte profita de l'invention des reliques du saint patron de Viviers, Andéol, pour s'emparer de ses reliques, ainsi que de celles d'Hostian, autre saint du diocèse de Viviers. Les reliques de ce dernier se trouvent ensuite à Pothières, tandis que celles de Pontien et Andéol sont attestées à Vézelay, soit deux fondations dues à Girard[73]. Outre ce récit, les manuscrits de Bruxelles et de Séville comprennent justement la Passion d'Andéol et la rarissime Vie d'Hostian, mais aussi la Passion des saints bourguignons Florentin et Hilaire (*BHL* 3033), martyrs du légendaire Chrocus, dont un cartulaire épiscopal composé au Xe siècle à Viviers évoque l'action destructrice dans le diocèse[74]. Enfin, tandis que le manuscrit de Séville se termine avec la Passion de saint Romain d'Antioche (*BHL* 7298), celui de Bruxelles s'ouvre par la copie du martyrologe d'Adon puis par la Passion d'Ignace d'Antioche (*BHL* 4256)[75]. Une étude comparative plus fine de ces manuscrits hagiographiques est souhaitable pour mieux étudier leur parenté, mais dans l'état actuel des recherches, ils semblent bien porter une petite collection thématique, particulièrement précieuse pour documenter l'hagiographie du diocèse de Viviers.

On sait grâce à BEAUJOUAN (1960), p. 146-148, que la provenance lyonnaise du manuscrit sévillan est bien assurée. Voir aussi la notice dans GUILLÉN (2002), p. 145-146.

[72] Éd., *AB*, 2 (1883), p. 368-377.

[73] Sur cette affaire, outre les travaux de Baudouin DE GAIFFIER, cités à la n. 71 voir les remarques de BOZÓKY (2007), p. 177-178 et VOCINO (2011), p. 211-213.

[74] Sur Chrocus, voir RÉGNÉ (1914), t. I, BARDY (1935) et DEMOUGEOT (1962); sur Florentin et Hilaire, voir les remarques de BERGER (à paraître).

[75] Il ne s'agit pas là des seules différences entre ces manuscrits. Celui de Séville ne contient pas de martyrologe, ni d'homélie de Cyprien mais s'ouvre avec le *De promissionibus Dei* attribué à Prosper d'Aquitaine (*PL* 51, col. 733). Quant au manuscrit de Bruxelles, il se termine ensuite avec la copie de l'histoire de la persécution vandale de Victor de Vita, ainsi qu'avec la Vie d'Eugène de Carthage dans le *De Viris illustribus* de Gennade, un extrait de la chronique de Bède, la *Narratio de imperatoribus domus Valentinianae et Theodosianae*, une lettre de Jérôme, et un extrait de la chronique de Prosper d'Aquitaine. Voir la description de ce manuscrit par VAN DEN GHEYN (1901), p. 304-305.

Il faut ensuite mentionner un manuscrit perdu appelé tantôt *charta vielha*, *carta vetus* ou *charte vielhe* qui transmettait un certain nombre de textes hagiographiques du diocèse. Sa compilation s'est faite en deux temps sous l'évêque Thomas II, évêque de Viviers en 950-951 et sous son successeur Gaucerand (1133-1146). Ce document se trouve reproduit en 1407 dans le cadre d'une enquête elle-même connue par des copies faites par le chanoine Jacques de Banne au XVIIe siècle, transmises par deux manuscrits conservés à l'évêché de Viviers et par d'autres allusions faites par différents érudits[76]. Ce document composite s'ouvrait par une liste des évêques d'Alba puis de Viviers, qui précède une série de vingt-sept donations échelonnées entre le Ve et le début du VIIIe siècle. À la fin de cette pièce, intitulée *Dotatio sanctae et insignis Ecclesiae Vivariensis*, l'évêque Thomas se nomme et déclare avoir trouvé ce «pouillé» (*poleticum*) dans les archives de son église, sous le règne de Conrad. On y trouvait ensuite une liste des prébendes des chanoines de Viviers du Xe siècle (*Breve de obedientiis canonicorum vivariensium*). Enfin, après un recueil de diplômes carolingiens et une quinzaine de chartes (du IXe au début du XIIe siècle), ce document composite se clôturait par des Vies de saints locaux[77].

La liste épiscopale commence par rappeler que la cité d'Alba fut détruite par Chrocus, dont on sait l'importance de la figure dans les dossiers hagiographiques bourguignons. Suit une première série d'évêques qui ne sont pas qualifiés de saints mais c'est tout comme, puisque l'auteur précise que le Christ accomplit des miracles à travers eux. Ensuite, une fois le siège épiscopal transféré par l'évêque Promotus, la liste des évêques de Viviers débute. La grande majorité des évêques porte le qualificatif de *sanctus*: Lucien, Valère, Venance, Rustique (non qualifié de saint), Melanius, Firmin, Eucher, Aule, Eumachius et enfin Longin et Jean. Dans la *Dotatio*, plusieurs de ces évêques sont de nouveau cités (Melanius, Lucien, Valère, Venance, Lon-

---

[76] Voir la présentation de ce document dans LAUXEROIS (1983), p. 223, n. 1 et son édition partielle dans LAFFONT (2009), p. 34, 40-41, p. 49, n. 5, p. 60-61 qui s'appuie sur les travaux d'Olivier Darnaud, qui prépare une édition critique qu'il a bien voulu me transmettre. Voir sa présentation: DARNAUD (2012). Je remercie l'auteur pour ses remarques.

[77] DARNAUD (2012), p. 12.

gin), mais seul Firmin est qualifié de saint. Or il n'a laissé aucun récit hagiographique.

Restent enfin les manuscrits liturgiques du diocèse. On connaît un bréviaire de Viviers du XIVᵉ siècle (Grenoble, BM, R. 8691) et trois autres du XVᵉ siècle (Avignon, BM 128; Grenoble, BM, R. 8692; Paris, BnF, n.a.lat. 659)[78]. Il faut ajouter à cette liste deux bréviaires que nous n'avons pas pu consulter[79]. L'un, très peu connu, était localisé en 1964 à l'abbaye Notre-Dame des Neiges, et daté de 1420. Le second, du XIVᵉ siècle, se trouvait à la même époque à la bibliothèque du Grand Séminaire, mais n'a pu être retrouvé par Pascal Collomb[80]. Enfin, bien que dans le diocèse voisin de Valence, le bréviaire de l'abbaye bénédictine de Soyons du XIVᵉ siècle, à la limite du diocèse de Viviers, est tout à fait précieux (Paris, BnF, n.a.lat. 718)[81].

Il faut enfin signaler un martyrologe du XVIᵉ siècle, redécouvert tout récemment. Ce manuscrit est daté entre 1538 et 1542 et a pour modèle le martyrologe d'Usuard. Parmi les saints ajoutés, on trouve des fêtes propres au diocèse de Viviers, notamment pour les saints Arconce (8 janvier), Aule (fête le 29 avril et translation le 20 février), Andéol (1ᵉʳ mai) Montan (9 novembre) mais aussi pour la dédicace de la cathédrale (27 février). Pour Pascal Collomb, ce martyrologe fut effectué dans le contexte du concile de Trente qui uniformisa les pratiques liturgiques des églises d'Occident. L'auteur du martyrologe cherche clairement à accorder les traditions locales avec la topographie de son temps, à combler les lacunes des traditions hagiographiques préexistantes, et à vieillir le culte des saints locaux qu'on y trouve, en invoquant notamment l'ancienneté des documents qui l'atteste. Ainsi pour Venance, qui avait selon sa *Vita* commencé sa vie comme moine dans un monastère indéterminé, celui-ci se trouve clairement localisé à Viviers. Pour la première fois, un évêque qualifié de saint dans la *charta vetus* et

---

[78] Voir leur description dans LEROQUAIS (1934), I, 94-97; II, 130-133; III, 399-400.

[79] Ils sont signalés par ANDRÉ (1964). Voir ensuite les remarques de COLLOMB (2012), p. 145-146 et 158. Le bréviaire imprimé en 1503, signalé par DELISLE (1892), dont un exemplaire est conservé à la BnF (Vélins 2876), ne contient pas de sanctoral.

[80] Maurice André y consacre la majeure partie de son petit ouvrage mais ne dit hélas rien du sanctoral: ANDRÉ (1964), COLLOMB (2002).

[81] LEROQUAIS (1934), III, p. 400-403.

dans la Vie du même Venance, apparaît avec un culte: il s'agit de Valerius, mais l'auteur se contente de renvoyer à la fameuse *charta vetus*. Quant à l'évêque Arconce, une courte notice lui est consacrée dans le martyrologe qui indique qu'il fut décapité par des habitants de Viviers[82]. S'il apparaît dans le sanctoral des bréviaires que nous avons consulté, on renvoie à chaque fois au commun des martyrs, si bien que l'existence d'un récit ancien est tout à fait hypothétique et rien ne permet d'en faire une victime d'Ébroïn comme le pensait Pierre David[83].

B. Andéol

Fêté le 1er mai, le sous-diacre Andéol a fait l'objet d'une Passion qui le rattache à la mission lyonnaise de saint Polycarpe qui, après une apparition de saint Irénée, envoie Andéol avec Bénigne, Andoche et Thyrse en Gaule: il arrive à Lyon en passant par la Corse, à une époque où peu d'évêques s'y trouvaient (*BHL* 423)[84]. En chemin vers Carpentras où il se rendait dans un bateau de marchands sur le Rhône, le saint s'arrête prêcher dans le *vicus* de Bergoiata lorsque l'empereur Sévère intervient, le frappe d'une pierre et est aussitôt puni pour son acte. L'interrogatoire du saint s'ensuit qui aboutit à la distension de ses membres, à la flagellation et à l'enfermement dans l'obscurité. Là, un soldat nommé *Cerecius* indique que de l'autre côté du Rhône, sous le temple de Mars, se trouve une crypte dédiée aux démons, dans laquelle il sera en sécurité[85]. Après l'exécution du saint son corps est jeté dans le fleuve, lesté par une pierre, mais échoue miraculeusement sur l'autre rive, où il est enseveli par une *matrona*, sainte *Tullia*, dans un lieu appelé *Gentibus*. L'hagiographe décrit ici un double pôle, de part et d'autre du Rhône, ce qui est bien attesté dans la région pendant l'Anti-

---

[82] Martyrologe conservé à la bibliothèque du Grand Séminaire de Viviers, fol. 1. Je remercie Nicolas Clément de m'avoir transmis une reproduction de ce document et d'avoir discuté avec moi les dossiers de ce diocèse.
[83] David (1930), voir *supra*. Les commentaires de Régné (1914), t. I, p. 367-369 sont sans valeur.
[84] Sur ce qui suit voir Chalon (1972).
[85] Depuis Franz Cumont, on a supposé que ce devait être en réalité le *Mithraeum* conservé actuellement à Bourg Saint-Andéol, cf. *Ibid.*, p. 75-76.

quité et le haut Moyen Âge[86]. Le *vicus* de Bergoiata est identifié à l'actuel Bourg-Saint-Andéol où une occupation du haut Moyen Âge est bien attestée archéologiquement[87].

Ce texte est édité dans les *Acta Sanctorum* en 1680 à partir d'une copie envoyée par François Bousquet et collationnée avec quelques manuscrits indéterminés[88]. Cette *Passio* est attestée avant 837-842 dans la recension M du martyrologe de Florus, avant qu'Adon ne l'utilise également dans son martyrologe[89]. Le terminus *a quo* est donné par le plagiat de la Passion des saints Bénigne, Andoche et Thyrse du premier quart du VIe siècle, envoyés eux aussi dans les mêmes conditions en Gaule (*BHL* 424)[90]. Bref voilà un texte apparenté au cycle des martyrs de Bourgogne qui évoque des *realia* tardo-antiques et qui pourrait peut-être remonter à l'époque mérovingienne, à moins que sa rédaction finale ne se situe à l'époque carolingienne, au moment de la redécouverte de ses reliques[91]. Quoi qu'il en soit, l'existence d'une quinzaine de manuscrits portant cette Passion (dont trois antérieurs à l'an mil) devrait inviter à une réédition de ce texte essentiel pour l'histoire du christianisme ardéchois[92].

La découverte des reliques d'Andéol en 858 est au cœur d'un récit d'*Inventio* (*BHL* 423c), qu'on peut recouper avec l'épitaphe de l'évêque Bernoin de Viviers, conservée à Bourg-Saint-Andéol qui mentionne cette découverte sous son épiscopat[93], mais également avec le fameux récit fait par Aymoin du voyage des moines Usuard et Odilard de Saint-Germain-des-Prés depuis l'Espagne (*BHL* 3409): de passage en Vivarais, ils ont vent de la

---

[86] BÉAL et ODIOT (1999).
[87] Cf. RÉGNÉ (1914), t. I, p. 290-295 et CLÉMENT (2011), t. III-1, p. 9-10, 117-122. Sur l'église voir encore ESQUIEU (1995).
[88] *AASS*, Mai. I, 1680, col. 35-39.
[89] QUENTIN (1908), p. 253-254 et CHALON (1970), p. 70.
[90] Sur ce texte, bibliographie relais dans HEINZELMANN (2010), p. 41-42.
[91] Voir l'analyse de LAUXEROIS (1983), p. 205-215 qui renvoie à toute la bibliographie antérieure.
[92] Il s'agit du manuscrit Bruxelles, KBR 1791-1794 et de son jumeau sévillan cités plus haut, et du Vatican, Reg. lat. 274, fol. 97-101v dernière unité codicologique d'un recueil composite composé à Fleury, dans lequel la Passion d'Andéol suit la Vie de Maxime de Riez par le patrice Dynamius. Il faut encore ajouter le légendier de Saint-Gall du Xe siècle, ms. Sangallensis, 577, fol. 374-390.
[93] FAVREAU – MICHAUD – MORA (1992), p. 51.

«révélation du corps du saint martyr Andéol, disciple du grand Polycarpe», et s'empressent d'aller prier sur ses reliques dont ils emmènent une partie[94]. Enfin, cette découverte est surtout corroborée dans le long récit présent dans la *Translatio Eusebii et Pontiani* (*BHL* 2747) attestée dès la fin du IXe siècle, qui indique que le corps du saint était resté six cent ans enseveli en profondeur jusqu'à sa découverte.

Le récit de la Translation d'Andéol, recensé sous le n° *BHL* 423c est loin de s'appuyer sur une tradition manuscrite aussi ferme, puisqu'aucun manuscrit ne subsiste[95]. Ce petit texte ne dépend toutefois pas de la *Translatio Eusebii*, puisqu'il ignore la translation en Bourgogne mais date bien l'événement du règne du roi de Bourgogne Charles. Reprenant brièvement des éléments de la Passion du saint, le texte insiste clairement sur le rôle de l'évêque Bernoin à qui Polycarpe est apparu pour lui faire connaître le corps du saint enterré par Tullia dans une crypte profonde. L'évêque fait élever le corps et l'installe dans l'église Saint-Étienne et Saint-Jean érigée au bord du Rhône, toujours au lieu-dit *Gentibus*[96]. On a donc là un texte qui dépend principalement de la Passion du saint et qui est composé localement pour justifier un déplacement de reliques, très probablement dans le milieu épiscopal.

C. Aule

La Vie de cet évêque mentionné dans la *charta vetus* et fêté le 29 avril dans les manuscrits liturgiques (qui ne donnent aucune leçon propre) se trouve copiée en plusieurs endroits dans des manuscrits modernes du chanoine de Banne (lui-même s'appuyant sur un graduel de l'Église de Viviers) et chez Jean Columbi[97]. Auguste Le Sourd, considère que la version transmise par Columbi est meilleure et il en donne une traduction, tout en

---

[94] DE GAIFFIER (1951), p. 132-134 et LAUXEROIS (1983), p. 217-219.

[95] Le texte est édité *ex veteri manuscripto* dans RÉGNÉ (1914), t. I, p. 645-647.

[96] Sur ces lieux voir *Ibid.*, p. 302-303 et LAUXEROIS (1983), p. 219-220. Un sarcophage du saint est sculpté au début du XIIe siècle, cf. SAINT-JEAN (1971).

[97] COLUMBI (1668), p. 195-196 et la transcription de CLÉMENT (2011), t. II, p. 18.

reproduisant le texte transmis par De Banne[98]. Olivier Darnaud prépare une édition critique de ce texte qu'il a bien voulu nous transmettre. Après un prologue, l'auteur indique que saint Firmin succéda à saint Eucher sur le siège épiscopal. Firmin est le père d'Aule. Le saint mène une vie de bon pasteur et d'ascète, libère les captifs, et œuvre à la construction de sa cité. L'évêque Eumachius lui succède. Un portrait tout à fait positif de ce dernier est alors dressé, puis l'auteur revient à saint Aule pour raconter sa mort et la douleur qu'elle causa. Alors que son corps est emmené pour être enseveli, de nombreux miracles ont lieu. Ce petit récit regorge de lieux communs, et, par l'attention qu'il donne à la succession des évêques, on comprend que son auteur a peut-être eu sous les yeux le texte de la *charta vetus*, même s'il ne respecte pas scrupuleusement l'ordre épiscopal[99]. Le fait que le texte n'apparaît pas dans les leçons des bréviaires et qu'une inscription (aujourd'hui perdue) a dû être apposée tardivement sur un tombeau au moment de son transfert depuis l'église suburbaine Saint-Aule (attestée dès le haut Moyen Âge par la *Dotatio*) jusque dans la cathédrale de Viviers semblent être un indice supplémentaire du caractère tardif de ce texte[100].

D. Hostian

La Vie de l'ermite du début du VIe siècle Hostian est un texte court, uniquement transmis dans les deux manuscrits bourguignons de la fin du IXe siècle présentés plus haut (*BHL* 3989)[101]. Après un court prologue dans lequel il est rappelé qu'Hostian est un proche de saint Venance, évêque de Viviers[102], les liens familiaux entre les deux saints et le roi burgonde et martyr Si-

---

[98] Le Sourd (1917), p. 82-84.
[99] Darnaud (2019) considère que l'inverse est possible car les données généalogiques sont plus justes dans la *Vita* : ce serait l'auteur de la *Charta vetus* qui utiliserait la Vie du saint.
[100] Clément (2011), t. II, p. 112 et t. III-2, p. 193 indique, sans donner de preuve, que le transfert a lieu au moment de la Guerre de Cent Ans. Est-ce à cela que renvoie la fête de la translation qu'on trouve au 20 février dans les manuscrits liturgiques (sans leçon propre, à l'exception du martyrologe qui reprend les éléments de la *charta vetus* et qui renvoie à cette Vie) ?
[101] Éd., *AB*, 2 (1883), p. 355-358 à partir du manuscrit Bruxelles, KBR 1791-1794.
[102] Sur ce dossier, voir *infra*.

gismond sont évoqués. Élevé dans la foi chrétienne, Hostian vend tous ses biens pour les pauvres et pour l'Église et se retire vivre en ermite. Venance, évêque d'alors et fils du roi Sigismond, décide de lui faire faire sa cellule. Le saint s'installe au pied du mont Bayne dans un lieu nommé *Ticinus*, où il vécut quinze années durant en ascète et fit plusieurs miracles. Ainsi, un jour de Pâques, un prêtre du nom de Maxime vit par la fenêtre de sa cellule le saint bénir l'hostie en présence d'un ange. À la mort d'Hostian, alors que son corps rejoignait son tombeau, plusieurs miracles eurent lieu.

Martin Heinzelmann considère que cette Vie n'est pas antérieure au VIIe siècle, voire au VIIIe siècle, sans donner d'arguments [103]. En tout cas, Usuard, qui a probablement séjourné à Viviers lors de son retour d'Espagne, a introduit Hostian dans son martyrologe [104]. L'église où repose son corps se situe dans la vallée de Couspier, au bord du ruisseau de l'Enfer, dans une vallée perpendiculaire à l'Escoutay: dédiée à Saint-Martin et à Saint-Hostian, elle est mentionnée dès le *Breue de obedientiis* et des sarcophages tardo-antiques y ont été découverts [105]. Même s'il est difficile à dater, on note avec Charles Mériaux que ce texte correspond aux «préoccupations exprimées régulièrement par les autorités carolingiennes» [106].

E. Montan

«Ce saint obscur s'ajoute à la cohorte des nombreux autres dont le cas laissera sans doute l'historien toujours perplexe» conclut Joseph Van der Straeten après une savante étude [107]. Son culte n'est pas attesté avant le XIIe siècle, date à laquelle apparaît un village qui porte son nom. Dans les bréviaires de la fin du Moyen Âge, il n'y a aucune leçon hagiographique. Comme Joseph Van der Straeten l'avait déjà remarqué, il faut attendre le martyrologe du XVIe siècle au 9 novembre pour voir les éléments d'une *Vita* que l'auteur dit puiser dans un homéliaire.

---

[103] Heinzelmann (2010), p. 58. Beck (1950), p. XLIII, date le texte de la fin du VIe siècle.
[104] *Le martyrologe d'Usuard*, éd. J. Dubois, Bruxelles, 1965, p. 258.
[105] Clément (2011), t. I, p. 167-168 et t. III-2, p. 195.
[106] Mériaux (2016), p. 119.
[107] Van der Straeten (1975b).

Le chanoine De Banne copie des leçons d'un bréviaire de Saint-Paul-Trois-Châteaux, mais «les neuf dixièmes du contenu sont des lieux communs truffés de citations scripturaires»[108]. Cela dit, Montan serait un germain (*theothonicus*) originaire de la vallée dite *Laudonensi*, ce qui doit renvoyer à Laon et rapproche donc Montan d'un homonyme connu par ailleurs[109]. Il se retire du monde et aboutit en Vivarais, dans une grotte du Val-Chaud. La fin de cet unique texte est tirée de la Vie de Remi par Hincmar de Reims, dans laquelle on trouve également l'histoire du moine Montan du Nord-Est de la France. Il est difficile dans ces conditions de dater une tradition vivaroise mal établie qui a réutilisé de nombreux éléments et qui n'émerge que trop tardivement dans la documentation.

F. Venance

Évêque de Viviers dans le courant du VIe siècle, Venance est bien attesté par sa signature aux conciles d'Épaone en 517 et de Clermont en 535. Toutefois, contrairement à son compagnon Hostian, ce dernier n'est connu d'aucun martyrologe[110]. On connaît aussi Venance grâce à l'épitaphe du prêtre Paschase, qualifié de «patron» où ce dernier est présenté comme un disciple de saint Venance. Très clairement, avec cette épitaphe, on se situe déjà dans le discours hagiographique et ce texte pourrait faire office de *Vita* pour ce Paschase, inconnu par ailleurs[111]. Pour les archéologues qui en ont repris l'étude, cette inscription date du VIe siècle et la fouille d'une basilique funéraire à Viviers a permis de retrouver l'encoche ou venait s'encastrer cette épitaphe[112]. Venance est aussi mentionné dans le catalogue épiscopal rédigé vers 950 qui ouvre le cartulaire de l'église de Viviers dit *charta vielha*[113].

---

[108] *Ibid.*, p. 65.
[109] Van der Straeten (1975a) et Isaïa (2010), *passim*.
[110] *Le martyrologe d'Usuard*, éd. J. Dubois, Bruxelles, 1965, p. 258.
[111] Le texte est reproduit par Régné (1914), t. I, p. 379-380 et Dupraz et Fraisse (2001), p. 436-437. On en trouve une traduction dans Godding (2001), p. 426-427.
[112] Voir Dupraz (1988), Clément (2011), t. I, p. 288; t. II, p. 118; t. III-2, p. 179-206 et Dupraz (2012).
[113] Laffont (2009), p. 34.

La Vie de Venance a été éditée dans les *Acta Sanctorum* (*BHL* 8528) à partir d'une copie de Godefroid Henschen (1600-1681) qui a lui-même précisé qu'il tirait son texte d'un vieux manuscrit copié par son contemporain Pierre-François Chifflet[114]. Le chanoine de Banne a également copié une *Vie* de saint Venance, à partir d'un bréviaire du XIVe siècle, qui abrège le texte des Bollandistes[115]. Cette *Vita* assez longue commence par faire de Venance le fils du roi de Vienne Sigismond, ce qui a jeté la suspicion sur ce texte[116]. À la mort de l'évêque saint Valère, Venance est sorti de son monastère et élu évêque à la demande du peuple, qui a vent de sa *fama* et se rend auprès de son père. Venance arrive à Viviers où il travaille à la prospérité de l'Église, avec l'aide de son père. Il fait œuvre d'évergète: il agrandit la cathédrale Saint-Vincent, orne l'église Saint-Julien de colonnes de marbre, d'un pavement, la dote d'un baptistère, et prépare tout un système hydraulique pour que l'eau desserve ce lieu par des tuyaux en plomb. Au milieu, il fait installer un cerf en bronze qui crache l'eau. Il construit aussi l'église Saint-Saturnin et Sainte-Marie, refait faire les murailles de la ville, fait construire des maisons et organise le clergé. Après vingt-sept ans d'épiscopat, il meurt.

Ensuite, dans une deuxième partie, le même auteur entend rapporter ce qu'il advint par la suite. Après sa mort, un évêque romain du nom de Rusticus détruit ou s'approprie toute l'œuvre de son prédécesseur. Neuf mois après le début de son épiscopat, il est alors frappé du jugement divin et meurt: on comprend donc tout à fait pourquoi il n'est pas qualifié de saint par l'auteur du catalogue épiscopal de la *charta vetus*. L'auteur rapporte qu'à la mort de Venance, son corps avait été transféré dans un

---

[114] La copie est actuellement conservée chez les Bollandistes sous la cote 127. Le texte de la main de Chifflet se trouve copié à la BnF, dans la Collection Baluze, 144, fol. 296-299.

[115] Signalé par RÉGNÉ (1914), t. I, p. 338, retranscrit dans CLÉMENT (2011), t. II, p. 14-16. Est-ce le bréviaire qui se trouvait à la bibliothèque du Grand Séminaire? Cette abréviation commence avec l'accession à la cathèdre du saint (on ignore donc si Sigismond est qualifié de *rex viennensis*). Il en est de même dans les bréviaires Avignon, BM 128, fol. 326, Grenoble, BM 8691, fol. 68v et BM 8692, fol. 606 et Paris, BnF, n.a.lat. 659, fol. 256v-257. Le sanctoral du bréviaire de Valence, BM 80, fol. 258v ne contient pas de leçon propre.

[116] Voir FAVROD (1997), p. 15.

sarcophage dans l'église Sainte-Marie Saint-Saturnin qu'il avait fait construire. Le corps a été oublié et négligé, si bien que Dieu a décidé de son transfert dans une autre patrie. Une noble, épouse du comte des Bourguignons Guillaume, est guérie par lui: elle procède donc à la translation des reliques dans le monastère féminin de Soyons. Et l'auteur ajoute qu' « il y avait à [son] époque dans les confins du royaume de Lothaire un homme très noble et puissant du nom de Guillaume », très malade, qui a fait en vain le pèlerinage à Rome sur la tombe de saint Pierre. Le saint lui apparaît et lui ordonne de se rendre en direction de Lyon dans sa basilique près du Rhône: il fut guéri après un miracle.

Ce récit appelle plusieurs remarques. Notons tout d'abord l'importance de la figure de Sigismond. Aucun autre texte ne permet d'assurer que Venance est le fils de Sigismond, mais la présence d'une telle idée dès la fin du IXe siècle au plus tard dans la Vie de saint Hostian est tout à fait curieuse. L'utilisation de la figure du saint roi peut être une clé pour dater ce texte: si la domination burgonde est tout à fait attestée en Vivarais, il n'est pas non plus improbable que, plus tardivement, à l'époque du royaume de Bourgogne, se rattacher à une figure royale et sainte ait pu servir le clergé. En fait, « la capitale d'un nouveau *regnum Burgundiae* » dans la seconde moitié du IXe siècle est bien Vienne où le culte de Maurice se développe et sert à légitimer les prétentions de Boson et ses successeurs. Or leur concurrent est Rodolphe, qui manipule justement la figure de Sigismond auprès duquel il se fait inhumer. N'est-il pas lui aussi roi depuis 888 et donc successeur du saint roi martyr[117]? La figure de Sigismond aurait pu être utilisée alors en Bourgogne méridionale, dans la province de Vienne, pour récupérer aussi ce prestigieux héritage? Une telle captation aurait pu se faire également au moment de fondre l'héritage bosonide dans la Bourgogne rodolphienne à partir de 942[118]. Des reliques de saint Sigismond sont en tout cas attestées au Xe siècle à Arles[119]. Mais il faut bien prendre en compte les plus anciens manuscrits à porter cette idée, et ceux qui portent la Vie d'Hostian sont bien de la fin du IXe siècle, d'où l'intérêt d'étudier à

---

[117] RIPART (2002), CASTELNUOVO (2003), p. 195.
[118] Sur les transformations politiques dans cet espace voir RIPART (2013).
[119] CORBET (1991), p. 108.

LES DIOCÈSES SUFFRAGANTS DE VIENNE 669

l'avenir de plus près ces témoins, et notamment celui de la KBR qui porte justement une œuvre viennoise, le martyrologe d'Adon. Dans la Vie de Venance, Sigismond est bien qualifié de *rex Viennensis*, ce qui pour Laurent Ripart permet justement une assimilation entre le roi burgonde et les Rodolphiens (ou alors les Bosonides?)[120]. Comme Justin Favrod l'a noté, ce titre n'apparaît pas avant le IXe siècle et il «fut parfois appliqué aux rois de Bourgogne quand ils héritèrent du royaume de Provence vers 933»[121].

Si le lien de filiation entre Venance et Sigismond est bien attesté dès la fin du IXe siècle, la Vie de Venance telle qu'on la connaît par les Bollandistes pourrait être plus tardive, ce qui correspondrait à la mention du comte dans le récit de la translation des reliques. On a un texte dont on entrevoit au moins deux phases de rédaction, à la fin du IXe siècle, puis au XIe siècle. Pour Pierre-André Sigal, le chapelain de Soyons, moine du monastère Saint-Jean de Valence est l'auteur de ce texte, ce que rien ne prouve, même s'il est clair que l'ensemble fut mis en forme après la translation des reliques à Soyons[122]. On a au moins deux strates narratives, avec d'abord une première *Vita*, peut-être elle-même réécrite au moment de la mise par écrit du récit de la translation des reliques à Soyons.

Cette *Vita* a pu être ancienne. On peut en effet recouper les éléments rapportés dans ce texte par des données archéologiques précises[123]. Si la localisation de l'église Saint-Julien est peu assurée[124], l'église Sainte-Marie Saint-Saturnin que le saint aurait fait construire et où son corps a été accueilli a été fouillée: c'est de là que provient l'épitaphe de Paschasius, parmi des tombes privilégiées situées dans le chœur d'une basilique construite au

---

[120] RIPART (2018), p. 362.
[121] FAVROD (1997), p. 14 et 480 d'après POUPARDIN (1907), p. 183 et CHAUME (1937), p. 33.
[122] BONNASSIE – IOGNA – PRAT – SIGAL (1994), p. 313.
[123] Le texte est ainsi abondamment exploité par CLÉMENT (2011). Pour PIETRI et HEIJMANS (2013), p. 1920, sa «documentation, dans l'ensemble cohérente, concorde avec celle donnée par d'autres documents».
[124] CLÉMENT (2011), t. I, p. 141-142, t. III-2, p. 181-182; DARNAUD (2012), p. 22-23 et (2019) pense que cette église désigne la cathédrale avant qu'elle ne soit dédiée à Vincent, mais pour l'hagiographe, il s'agit de deux églises distinctes. Voir les données rassemblées par PIETRI et HEIJMANS (2013), p. 326 et déjà dans BIARNE, COLARDELLE et FÉVRIER (1986), p. 60.

VIe siècle. Fouillée en partie à la fin des années 1980 par Joëlle Dupraz, cette basilique a été également utilisée comme nécropole jusque vers le VIIIe siècle[125]. C'est donc à une réalité tout à fait tangible que renvoie la *Vita* de Venance[126].

Dans un second temps, le texte a été poursuivi, et peut-être réécrit ou remanié dans sa rédaction finale qui semble typique de la fin du XIe siècle ou du début du XIIe siècle, comme le montre l'épisode de l'évêque romain Rusticus, figure du mauvais réformateur imposé. La mention d'un royaume de Lotharingie pourrait se comprendre dans ce contexte, tout comme la mention d'un comte des Bourguignons Guillaume qui pouvrait alors être Guillaume Ier (1057-1087) sous l'impulsion duquel aurait lieu cette translation. Dans ce cas, son épouse, qui n'est pas nommée dans ce récit, serait Étiennette, qualifiée sur son épitaphe d'*Allobrogum comitissa*[127].

Cependant, le témoignage des bréviaires, qui offrent des textes abrégés mais dont la tradition manuscrite est plus ancienne que la copie reçue par les Bollandistes permet de proposer une hypothèse mieux établie encore. Dans les bréviaires du diocèse de la fin du Moyen Âge, c'est bien le texte des Bollandistes qui est abrégé avec la mention de la filiation à Sigismond[128], mais on dispose d'un bréviaire du XIVe siècle de l'abbaye de Soyons qui accueillit ses reliques. Dans celui-ci, la fête de la translation est célébrée et c'est bien le récit de la translation par la femme du comte qu'on trouve copié; mais ici, la qualité bourguignonne dudit comte est tue (Paris, BnF, n.a. lat. 718, fol. 345v-346), et celui-ci ne s'appelle pas *Guillelmus* mais *Gillinus*[129]. La mention est importante car Gillinus est le

---

[125] Dupraz (1988), Clément (2011), t. III-1, p. 285-290, Dupraz (2012) et en dernier lieu la notice de Marc Heijmans dans Prévot, Gaillard et Gauthier (2014), p. 326-327 et les réflexions de Darnaud (2019).

[126] Aussi le jugement de Favrod (1997), p. 15, est-il excessif: «La fausseté et la mauvaise qualité des informations y sont patentes: les auteurs multiplient à l'envi anachronismes et invraisemblances». On notera aussi la découverte d'une inscription fragmentaire en 1735, reproduite par Le Blant (1865), n° 483, p. 210, citée par Clément (2011), t. II, p. 139 et t. III-2, p. 184-185 et Darnaud (2019) qui comprenait textuellement les mots de la *Vita* consacrés à l'action évergétique du saint dans sa cité.

[127] De Vajay (1960).

[128] Voir *supra* n. 115.

[129] Dans ce bréviaire, pour la fête du saint, si le texte est bien tiré de la Vie éditée par les Bollandistes, il est largement réécrit et abrégé: il passe rapi-

nom de plusieurs comtes de Valence, attestés au Xe siècle par divers documents[130] et encore dans la première moitié du XIe siècle[131]. Vu que l'abbaye de Soyons est localisée dans le diocèse de Valence, la présence d'un comte Gilinus apparaît plus logique. Dans ce cas, le texte du bréviaire serait meilleur que celui des Bollandistes où le génitif *Gilini* aurait été pris par un lecteur pour l'abréviation de *Guillelmi*, puis transformé dans un second temps en comte de Bourgogne.

En ce qui concerne cette translation, il y a une idée récurrente dans l'historiographie locale qui indique qu'il y avait une communauté féminine auprès des reliques du saint à Viviers avant son transfert à Soyons. Ce texte ne permet pas de corroborer cette assertion[132]. Enfin, Le *novum supplementum* de la *BHL* recense au numéro 8528b un récit de translation perdu, issu du

---

dement sur l'action d'évergète et n'évoque qu'à la fin le lien de filiation entre Sigismond et Venance. Il y a en outre des répétitions entre la première et la dernière leçon qui permettent peut-être d'insister sur la qualité de moine de Venance, avant qu'il ne fût évêque. Le texte se termine par l'évocation d'un miracle qu'on ne trouve pas ailleurs, celui de la guérison d'un paralytique venu de Lyon au bord du Rhône auprès des reliques du saint (fol. 366v-367v et sqq).

[130] Notamment par l'inscription de ce nom dans un obituaire de l'église de Vienne: CHEVALIER (1913-1926), n° 1281. Pour les autres attestations de ce comte voir VAISSÈTE et DE VIC (1874), II, p. 73, 91, 568. Voir aussi GANIVET (2000), p. 295-297. LAFFONT (2008), p. 165 pense même qu'il est le fondateur de l'abbaye de Soyons. Voir aussi ID. (2009), p. 58-60, et surtout p. 93 à partir du texte du bréviaire. Il semble plutôt qu'il s'agisse d'une fondation remontant au moins à l'époque carolingienne: BUIS (1984).

[131] CHEVALIER (1897), p. 162-163 et VAISSÈTE – DE VIC (1874), II, p. 232, 271.

[132] DUPRAZ (2012), p. 75. Cette idée semble reposer sur un «livre de chœur» du XIVe siècle disparu, copié par le Chanoine de Banne et dans lequel «est inséré qu'autrefois il y a eu un couvent de religieuses de St. Benoit à Nôtre Dame du Rhône, sous le château de Viviers au Bourg inférieur, et que ces religieuses emportèrent en s'en allant le corps de S. Venant, évêque de cette ville, en cachette, qui étoit enseveli en la dite église de Nôtre Dame [...] La tradition et les vieux écrits des Dames de Soyons disent que S. Venant étoit fils du roi de Bourgogne et qu'il étoit évêque de Viviers, et que venant à mourir, il ordonna que son corps fut porté à Lyon, siège des rois de bourgogne et qu'il fut baillé aux religieuses pour le porter en ladite ville, ce qui fut fait», transcrit par CLÉMENT (2011), t. II, p. 39-40. Ce document pourrait correspondre à celui indiqué par ROUCHIER (2009) et COLLOMB (2012), p. 153-157 qui ignorent toutefois les copies de De Banne reproduites par Nicolas Clément. Sur ces légendes divergentes relatives au corps de Venance, voir encore RÉGNÉ (1914), t. I, p. 364.

grand légendier de Boedekken, mais il concerne plus certainement des reliques du saint homonyme Venance de Rimini à l'abbaye de Fulda[133]. Ce texte, édité par les bollandistes dans la notice relative au saint italien est selon eux *desumpta ex BHL 7044*, c'est à dire tiré du récit rédigé par Raoul de Fulda sur les miracles survenus durant les travaux et translations de reliques orchestrées à Fulda[134].

Il faut encore ajouter à ce dossier un autre texte, une Vie de Venance non repérée jusqu'alors, mais dont l'intérêt ne saurait être négligé car elle est portée par un manuscrit du XIIIe siècle: c'est donc à ce jour le plus ancien témoin relatif à la vie de ce saint. Elle est contenue dans un lectionnaire de l'office de l'abbaye bénédictine de Cruas, dans le diocèse de Viviers, mais sous la domination des évêques d'Arles: Venance est le seul saint du diocèse de Viviers à y faire l'objet d'un texte[135]. Ce récit abrégé, s'il entretient des liens avec la version jusqu'alors connue par les Bollandistes, comporte aussi des différences. Il gomme le lien de paternité entre Sigismond et Venance, même si Sigismond est toujours présenté comme celui qui permet à Venance son action d'évergète. Il comprend aussi des passages qu'on ne trouve pas dans la version publiée par les Bollandistes: ainsi, il est rappelé l'action de Sigismond à Agaune auprès des reliques de saint Maurice et ses compagnons, mais aussi son martyre et les miracles qui ont lieu auprès de son corps. Ensuite, on trouve un passage rappelant que le saint a été proche d'Hostian: il s'agit là probablement de la réutilisation de la Vie d'Hostian dont on a vu qu'elle mentionnait Venance en en faisant bien un fils de Sigismond. Enfin, il est indiqué que Venance décide finalement de se retirer dans une cellule construite en pisé, dans une petite vallée donnant sur le fleuve Escoutay, confluent avec le Rhône à Viviers, où il meurt. On ne trouvait pas cet élément dans le récit précédent: il y a probablement eu une fusion de la légende de Venance avec celle d'Hostian qui comprenait ces éléments. La suite change elle aussi radicalement de la version des Bollandistes: le successeur de Venance, Melanius (lui aussi attesté dans la *Carta vetus*) y construit une église en l'honneur de saint

---

[133] Münster, UB 21 (fol. 1-2).
[134] *AASS*, Apr. I, 1675, col. 7 et *MGH, SS*, XV-1, Hanovre, 1887, p. 333-334.
[135] Étaix (1994).

Martin qui s'appelait autrefois Saint-Hostian[136]. Ensuite, c'est l'évêque Bernoin qui, au IXᵉ siècle, fit élever son corps, comme il l'avait fait pour le corps de saint Andéol. On a vu que l'intervention de Bernoin, si elle est effectivement bien attestée pour Andéol, l'est aussi pour le corps d'Hostian, d'après le récit de la translation des reliques d'Eusèbe et Pontien par le comte Girart (*BHL* 2747). Mais ici, l'événement est rapporté à propos de Venance. On a donc un petit récit qui apparaît cohérent, qui est bien attesté dans un manuscrit médiéval, mais qui semble déplacer les lieux de sépulture et les acteurs du culte du saint en fusionnant deux dossiers hagiographiques en un.

Conclusion

Malgré l'existence de dossiers hagiographiques fournis pour le diocèse de Viviers, les diocèses de la province de Vienne ne se caractérisent pas par la richesse de leur production hagiographique. Les manuscrits hagiographiques locaux sont rares et il faut bien souvent se contenter des leçons des bréviaires. Les uns comme les autres restent toutefois peu étudiés et un examen approfondi permettrait des avancées significatives. On peut toutefois souligner l'importance des enjeux territoriaux, en partie liés à la question de l'héritage du royaume burgonde et aux prétentions de la métropole de Vienne. Ils semblent avoir conditionné une part essentielle de la rédaction des récits hagiographiques locaux dans lesquels les informations relatives à la topographie chrétienne sont particulièrement précieuses. En l'état actuel des recherches, à défaut de pouvoir dater avec précision la majeure partie de ces textes, force est donc de constater qu'ils ont souvent pour but de fournir une histoire sainte à une topographie bien visible, d'où la nécessité de les confronter aux données archéologiques, lorsqu'elles existent.

---

[136] Une église Saint-Hostian et Saint-Martin est bien attestée parmi les biens des chanoines de l'église de Viviers au milieu du Xᵉ siècle, cf. LAFFONT (2009), p. 60. Il s'agit bien de celle qui accueillit le corps d'Hostian.

Bibliographie

André, M., *Textes liturgiques anciens du diocèse de Viviers au XIVe siècle*, Privas, 1964.

Baillet, C. – Henriet, P., «Gallia, 1130-fin XIIIe siècle. Provinces de Bordeaux, Auch et Narbonne», in *Hagiographies*, VI (2014), p. 521-704.

Bardy, G., «Recherches sur un cycle hagiographique. Les martyrs de Chrocus», *Revue d'histoire de l'Église de France*, 21 (1935), p. 5-29.

Barrillon, F., *Sainte-Jalle: une autre histoire de la Provence*, Pont-Saint-Esprit, 1998.

Barruol, G., *Provence romane. La haute-Provence*, La-Pierre-qui-Vire, 1981.

Béal, J.-C. – Odiot, T., «Les "sites doubles" drômois et ardéchois de la vallée du Rhône dans l'Antiquité: Le Rhône romain. Dynamiques fluviales, dynamiques territoriales», *Gallia*, 56 (1999), p. 91-98.

Beaujouan, G., «Fernand Colomb et l'Europe intellectuelle de son temps», *Journal des Savants*, 1960, p. 145-159.

Beck, H., *The pastoral care of souls in south-east France during the sixth century*, Rome, 1950.

Berger, J., «L'*ecclesia matrix* de Mornant: apparition d'une succursale savinienne entre Lyonnais et Jarez (Xe-XIIIe siècle)», in O. Puel – P. Ganivet, *Saint-Martin de Savigny. Un monastère lyonnais et ses territoires*, à paraître (*Revue archéologique de l'Est*).

Bertrandy, F. *et al.*, *L'Isère*, Paris, 2017 (Carte archéologique de la Gaule).

Besson, J. A., *Mémoires pour l'histoire ecclésiastique des diocèses de Genève, Tarantaise, Aoste et Maurienne, et du décanat de Savoye*, Nancy, 1759.

Biarne, J. – Colardelle, R. – Février, P. A., *Topographie chrétienne des cités de la Gaule, des origines au milieu du VIIIe siècle*, III: *Provinces ecclésiastiques de Vienne et d'Arles (Viennensis et Alpes Graiae et Poeninae)*, Paris, 1986.

Billiet, A., *Mémoire sur les premiers évêques du diocèse de Maurienne tiré des mémoires de l'Académie de Savoie*, Chambéry, 1861.

Billiet, A. – Albrieux, A., *Chartes du diocèse de Maurienne*, Chambéry, 1861.

Billy, P.-H., *La «condamine», institution agro-seigneuriale: étude onomastique*, Tübingen, 1997.

Bois, M., «L'organisation des terroirs du haut Moyen Âge entre Rhône et Durance», in M.-P. Estienne, éd., *Les Baronnies au Moyen Âge: femmes, hommes, territoires, villages, châteaux et églises*, Mane, 1997, p. 94-101.

BONNASSIE, P. – IOGNA-PRAT, D. – SIGAL, A., «La Gallia du Sud (930-1130)», in *Hagiographies*, I (1994), p. 289-344.
BOZÓKY, E., La *politique des reliques de Constantin à Saint Louis: protection collective et légitimation du pouvoir*, Paris, 2007.
BUIS, M., «Les sculptures carolingiennes de l'église de Soyons (Ardèche)», *Revue du Vivarais*, 88 (1984), p. 65-72.
BULTOT-VERLEYSEN, A.-M., «Hagiographie d'Aquitaine (750-1130)», in *Hagiographies*, VI (2014), p. 521-704.
CASTELNUOVO, G., «La Burgondie carolingienne et rodolphienne. Prémices et développements d'un royaume», in P. PARAVY, éd., *Des Burgondes au Royaume de Bourgogne (V^e-Xe siècle). Espace politique et civilisation*, Grenoble, 2003, p. 183-210.
CHALON, M., «Le martyre de saint Andéol et les origines chrétiennes chez les Helviens», in *Vivarais et Languedoc*, Montpellier, 1972, p. 69-79.
CHAUME, M., *Les origines du duché de Bourgogne*, II: *Géographie historique*, Dijon, 1937.
CHEVALIER, J., *Mémoires pour servir à l'histoire des comtés de Valentinois et de Diois*, t. I: *Les anciens comtes de Die et de Valence, les comtes de Valentinois de la maison de Poitiers*, Paris, 1897.
CHEVALIER, U., «Vies des saints dauphinois», *Bulletin d'histoire ecclésiastique et d'archéologie religieuse des diocèses de Valence, Gap, Grenoble et Viviers*, 15 (1895), p. 33-37.
—, *Regeste dauphinois, ou répertoire chronologique et analytique des documents imprimés et manuscrits relatifs à l'histoire du Dauphiné, des origines chrétiennes à l'année 1349*, Valence, 1913-1926.
CHEVALLEY, É. – RODUIT, C., «La naissance du culte des saints d'Agaune et les premiers textes hagiographiques», in B. ANDENMATTEN – L. RIPART, éd., *L'abbaye de Saint-Maurice d'Agaune, 515-2015*, I, *Histoire et archéologie*, Gollion, 2015.
CLÉMENT, N., *L'occupation du sol dans le pagus d'Alba-Viviers (Ardèche) entre le Ve et le Xe siècle*, Thèse de doctorat, Université Lyon II, 2011.
COENS, M., «Bulletin des publications hagiographiques», *AB*, 53 (1935), p. 140-224.
COLARDELLE, R., La *ville et la mort: Saint-Laurent de Grenoble, 2000 ans de tradition funéraire*, Turnhout, 2008.
COLLOMB, P., «Deux manuscrits liturgiques médiévaux à l'usage du diocèse de Viviers», in *L'Église cathédrale de Viviers du haut Moyen Âge à l'époque moderne. Une Église du Midi*, *Revue du Vivarais*, 116-1 (2012), p. 145-158.
COLUMBI, J., *De Rebus gestis Valentinorum et Diensium episcoporum libri quatuor*, Lyon, 1638.
—, *Opuscula varia*, Lyon, 1668.

Corbet, P., «L'autel portatif de la comtesse Gertrude de Brunswick (vers 1040). Tradition royale de Bourgogne et conscience aristocratique dans l'Empire des Saliens», *Cahiers de civilisation médiévale*, 34 (1991), p. 97-120.

Darnaud, O., «La charta vielha de l'église de Viviers. Essai de reconstitution d'un cartulaire disparu», in *L'Église cathédrale de Viviers du haut Moyen Âge à l'époque moderne. Une Église du Midi, Revue du Vivarais*, 116-1 (2012), p. 9-36.

—, «Les premiers évêques de Viviers (fin V^e-VIe s.)», *Mémoire d'Ardèche et Temps Présent*, 143 (2019), p. 7-16.

David, P., *Saint Ferjus, évêque de Grenoble au VIIe siècle*, Grenoble, 1930.

de Gaiffier, B., «Hagiographie bourguignonne», *AB*, 69 (1951), p. 131-147.

—, «Les sources de la Passion des SS. Savin et Cyprien», *AB*, 73 (1955), p. 323-341.

—, «Un dossier hagiographique réuni pour Girart de Vienne?», *AB*, 88 (1970), p. 285-288.

Delisle, L., «Note sur un bréviaire de Viviers imprimé à Privas en 1503», *Bibliothèque de l'École des Chartes*, 53 (1892), p. 88-94.

De Manteyer, G., *La Provence du Ier au XIIe siècle: études d'histoire et de géographie politique*, Paris, 1908, p. 175-187

Demougeot, É., «Les martyrs imputés à Chrocus et les invasions alamanniques en Gaule méridionale», *Annales du Midi*, 74 (1962), p. 5-28.

Derrier, J.-P., *Thècle de Maurienne, aux fondements d'une tradition hagiographique*, mémoire de master soutenu à l'université de Savoie, Chambéry, 2019.

Desaye, H., «Die à l'époque burgonde d'après une nouvelle version de la vie de saint Marcel évêque de Die (463-510)», *Revue Drômoise*, 87 (1990), p. 2-19.

—, «Une relecture de la vie en vers de saint Marcel, évêque de Die (463-510)», *ibid.*, p. 375-380.

Desaye, H. – Lurol, J.-M. – Mège, J.-C., «Découverte d'autels aux déesses Baginatiae à Sainte-Jalle (Drôme)», *Revue archéologique de Narbonnaise*, 33-1 (2000), p. 178-193.

De Vajay, S., «Étiennette dite de Vienne, comtesse de Bourgogne, Lorraine et Espagne au XIe siècle», *Annales de Bourgogne*, 32 (1960), p. 233-266.

Dolbeau, F., «La Vie en prose de saint Marcel de Die», *Francia*, 11 (1983), p. 97-130.

—, *Sanctorum societas: récits latins de sainteté (IIIe-XIIe siècles)*, Bruxelles, 2005.

Duchesne, L., *Fastes épiscopaux de l'ancienne Gaule*, I: *Provinces du Sud-Est*, 2e éd., Paris, 1907.

Dupraz, J., «Chapitre II. Une basilique funéraire suburbaine», in Y. Esquieu, dir., *Viviers, cité épiscopale: Études archéologiques*, Lyon, 1988, p. 23-30.

—, «Archéologie préventive à Viviers (1987-2009): contribution à la connaissance de la topographie urbaine de Viviers, de l'Antiquité tardive au XIXe siècle», *L'Église cathédrale de Viviers du haut Moyen Âge à l'époque moderne. Une Église du Midi, Revue du Vivarais*, 116-1 (2012), p. 55-67.

Dupraz, J. – Fraisse, C., *L'Ardèche*, Paris, 2001 (Carte archéologique de la Gaule).

Escher, K., Les *Burgondes, Ier-VIe siècles apr. J.-C.*, Paris, 2006.

Esquieu, Y., «Bourg-Saint-Andéol. L'église de Saint-Andéol», in *Congrès archéologique de France. 150e session, 1992, Moyenne vallée du Rhône*, Paris, 1995, p. 33-47.

Étaix, R., «Le lectionnaire de l'office de Cruas», *Revue du Vivarais*, 98 (1994), p. 15-22.

Favreau, R. – Michaud, J. – Mora, B., *Alpes-de-Haute-Provence, Hautes-Alpes, Ardèche, Drôme*, Paris, 1992 (Corpus des inscriptions de la France médiévale, 16).

Favrod, J., *Histoire politique du Royaume burgonde (443-534)*, Lausanne, 1997.

Font-Réaulx, J. de, «Les chroniques des évêques de Valence», *Bulletin de la Société d'archéologie et de statistique de la Drôme*, 59 (1925), p. 289-296 et 60 (1926), p. 62-71, 107-120, 177-201, 266-283.

Frachette, C., «Évêques et comtes en Valentinois au Xe siècle (879-1029): concours et concurrence pour le pouvoir», in N. Coulet – O. Guyotjeannin, dir., *La ville au Moyen Âge*, Paris, 1998, p. 487-500.

Ganivet, P., *Recherches sur l'évolution des pouvoirs dans les pays lyonnais, de l'époque carolingienne aux lendemains de l'an mil*, thèse de doctorat, Lyon, 2000.

Gärtner, T., «Kritisch-Exegetisches zur Marcellus-*Vita* des Vulfinus von Die», *Eranos*, 99 (2001), p. 18-27.

Geary, P., *Aristocracy in Provence: the Rhône Basin at the dawn of the Carolingian Age*, Stuttgart, 1985.

Gilles, A. *et al.*, «L'établissement de hauteur du Malpas à Soyons (Ardèche) durant l'Antiquité Tardive (IVe-VIe siècle)», *Revue archéologique de Narbonnaise*, 46 (2013), p. 179-199.

Godding, R., *Prêtres en Gaule mérovingienne*, Bruxelles, 2001.

Gros, A., «Saint Avre, confesseur non pontife», *Revue d'histoire de l'Église de France*, 18 (1932), p. 486-491.

—, *Histoire du diocèse de Maurienne*, I: *Des origines au XIVe siècle*, Chambéry, 1948.

GUERREIRO, R., « Passion de saint Fructueux de Tarragone », in *Saint-Germain d'Auxerre. Intellectuels et artistes dans l'Europe carolingienne (IXe-XIe siècles)*, Auxerre, 1990, p. 133-136.
GUILLÉN, J. F. S., *Catálogo de manuscritos de la Biblioteca Colombina de Sevilla*, Séville, 2002.
HEINZELMANN, M., « Clovis dans le discours hagiographique du VIe au IXe siècle », *Bibliothèque de l'École des Chartes*, 154 (1996), p. 87-112.
—, « L'hagiographie mérovingienne: panorama des documents potentiels », in M. HEINZELMANN – M. GOULLET – C. VEYRARD-COSME, dir., *L'hagiographie mérovingienne à travers ses réécritures*, Ostfildern, 2010, p. 27-82.
HEINZELMANN, M. – POULIN, J.-C., *Les Vies anciennes de sainte Geneviève de Paris: études critiques*, Paris, 1986.
ISAÏA, M.-C., *Remi de Reims mémoire d'un saint, histoire d'une Église*, 2010.
JAFFÉ, P., *Regesta Pontificum Romanorum*, Leipzig, 1885.
KINNEY, A., « An Appeal Against Editorial Condemnation: a Reevaluation of the *Vita Apollinaris Valentinensis* », in V. ZIMMERL-PANAGL – L. J. DORFBAUER – C. WEIDMANN, éd., *Edition und Erforschung lateinischer patristischer Texte. Festschrift für Kurt Smolak zum 70. Geburtstag*, Berlin, 2014, p. 157-178.
KIRNER, G., « Due Vite inedite di S. Marcello vescoco die Die », *Studi Storici*, 9 (1900), p. 289-327.
KRUSCH, B., « La falsification des vies de saints burgondes », in *Mélanges Julien Havet*, Paris, 1885, p. 35-56.
LAFFONT, P.-Y., « Sur les marges occidentales du royaume de Bourgogne: le Vivarais (IXe-XIe siècle) », in C. GUILLERÉ – J.-M. POISSON – L. RIPART, dir., *Le royaume de Bourgogne autour de l'an mil*, Lyon, 2008, p. 153-174.
—, *Châteaux du Vivarais: pouvoirs et peuplement en France méridionale, du haut Moyen Âge au XIIIe siècle*, Rennes, 2009.
LAUXEROIS, R., *Le Bas Vivarais à l'époque romaine: recherches sur la Cité d'Alba*, Paris, 1983.
LE BLANT, E., *Inscriptions chrétiennes de la Gaule antérieures au VIIIe siècle*, II, Paris, 1865.
LEROQUAIS, V., *Les bréviaires manuscrits des bibliothèques publiques de France*, 3 vol. Paris, 1934.
LE SOURD, A., *Mémoires de Jacques de Banne, chanoine de Viviers*, Aubenas, 1917.
LOUIS, R., *Girart, comte de Vienne (...819-877) et ses fondations monastiques: de l'histoire à la légende*, Auxerre, 1946.

MAGNANI, E., «La vie consacrée des femmes et l'ascétisme domestique. Normes, liturgies, pratiques (fin IVe-début XIIe s.)», *Revue Mabillon*, n.s. 29 t. 90 (2018), p. 5-25.
MARÍN, T., «Un nuevo códice carolino (Bibl. Colombina, ms. 101)», *Hispania Sacra*, 12 (1959), p. 165-189.
MAZEL, F., *L'évêque et le territoire: l'invention médiévale de l'espace*, Paris, 2016.
MERCIER, A., «Les manuscrits liturgiques de la cathédrale Saint-Apollinaire et de l'abbaye Saint-Ruf», in PARRON – SOLEIL – TARDIEU (2006), p. 248-263.
MÉRIAUX, C., « *Bonus agricola*: À propos de quelques figures de saints prêtres dans l'hagiographie carolingienne», in S. PATZOLD – F. BOCK, dir., *Gott handhaben: religiöses Wissen im Konflikt um Mythisierung und Rationalisierung*, Berlin, 2016, p. 115-130.
NIMMEGEERS, N., *Évêques entre Bourgogne et Provence: V^e-XIe siècle*, Rennes, 2014.
PARRON, I. – SOLEIL, P. – TARDIEU, J., dir., *De mémoires de Palais: archéologie et histoire du groupe cathédral de Valence*, Valence, 2006.
PARRON-KONTIS, I., «Chapitre 1. Les structures du pouvoir», in *La cathédrale Saint-Pierre en Tarentaise et le groupe épiscopal de Maurienne*, Lyon, 2002, p. 12-33.
PAXTON, F., «Power and the power to heal. The cult of St Sigismund of Burgundy», *Early Medieval Europe*, 2 (1993), p. 95-110.
PELOUX, F., «Deux légendiers de l'ancien royaume bosonide? Réflexion sur la transmission manuscrite de l'hagiographie du sud de la province ecclésiastique de Vienne (IXe-XIIe siècle)», *Bulletin du centre d'études médiévales d'Auxerre, BUCEMA* [En ligne], 22.2 (2018): http://journals.openedition.org/cem/15670.
PIETRI, L. – HEIJMANS, M., *Prosopographie de la Gaule chrétienne, 314-614*, 2 vol., Paris, 2013 (Prosopographie chrétienne du Bas-Empire, 4).
PLANET, A., «Les origines chrétiennes de Valence dans les textes du haut Moyen Âge», in PARRON – Soleil – TARDIEU (2006), p. 68-72.
POUPARDIN, R., *Le Royaume de Bourgogne (888-1038), étude sur les origines du royaume d'Arles*, Paris, 1907.
POUPARDIN, R. – PROU, M., *Recueil des actes des rois de Provence: 855-928*, Paris, 1920.
PRÉVOT, F. – GAILLARD, M. – GAUTHIER, N., éd., *Topographie chrétienne des cités de la Gaule, des origines au milieu du VIIIe siècle*, XVI-1: *Images nouvelles des villes*, Paris, 2014.
QUENTIN, H., *Les martyrologes historiques du moyen âge: étude sur la formation du martyrologe romain*, Paris, 1908.

RÉGNÉ, J., «L'invasion de Crocus roi des Alamans et les origines de l'Église de Viviers», *Revue du Vivarais*, 22 (1914), p. 241-246.

—, *Histoire du Vivarais*, 2 vol., Largentière, 1914-1921.

RÉMY, B. – BALLET, F. – FERBER, E., *La Savoie*, Paris, 1997 (Carte archéologique de la Gaule).

RIPART, L., «Saint Maurice et la tradition régalienne bourguignonne (443-1032)», in P. PARAVY, éd., *Des burgondes au royaume de Bourgogne (V^e-Xe siècle)*, Grenoble, 2002, p. 211-250.

—, «Le premier âge féodal dans les terres de tradition royale l'exemple des pays de la Bourgogne rhodanienne et lémanique», in D. IOGNA-PRAT et al., éd., *Cluny. Les moines et la société au premier âge féodal*, Rennes, 2013, p. 229-248.

—, «Le royaume rodolphien fut-il un royaume burgonde?», in A. WAGNER – N. BROCARD, éd., *Les royaumes de Bourgogne jusqu'en 1032 à travers la culture et la religion*, Turnhout, 2018, p. 345-372.

ROMAN, J., *Le Briançonnais, sa formation et son rattachement à l'archevêché*, Embrun, 1898.

ROUCHIER, J., «Le livre du Maître de chœur ou rituère de l'église de Viviers», *Revue du Vivarais*, 113-2 (2009), p. 117-120.

SAINT-JEAN, R., «Un témoin de la première sculpture romane rhodanienne: le sarcophage de Saint-Andéol», *Revue d'études ligures*, 37 (1971), p. 189-199.

SCHILLING, B., *Gallia pontificia: répertoire des documents concernant les relations entre la papauté et les églises et monastères en France avant 1198*, III: *Province ecclésiastique de Vienne*, 2: *Diocèses de Grenoble et de Valence*, Göttingen, 2018.

TARDIEU, J., «Sainte Galle et Sainte Jalle», in PARRON – SOLEIL, – TARDIEU (2006), p. 79-81.

VAISSÈTE, J. – DE VIC, C., *Histoire générale du Languedoc, avec des notes et des pièces justificatives*, Toulouse, 1874.

VAN DEN GHEYN, J., *Catalogue des manuscrits de la Bibliothèque Royale de Belgique*, I: *Écriture sainte et liturgie*, Bruxelles, 1901.

VAN DER STRAETEN, J., «Saint Montan ermite honoré en Thiérache», *AB*, 74 (1956), p. 370-404.

—, «Saint Montan, ermite du Vivarais», *AB*, 75 (1957), p. 47-65.

—, *Les manuscrits hagiographiques d'Orléans, Tours et Angers: avec plusieurs textes inédits*, Bruxelles, 1982.

VARANO, M., *Espace religieux et espace politique en pays provençal au Moyen Âge (IXe-XIIIe siècles): l'exemple de Forcalquier et de sa région*, Thèse de doctorat, Aix-en-Provence, 2011.

VOCINO, G., «Le traslazioni di reliquie in età carolingia (fine VIII-IX secolo). Uno studio comparativo», in D. SCOTTO, éd., *Del visibile credere. Pellegrinaggi, santuari, miracoli, reliquie*, Florence, 2011, p. 217-264.

La Passion des saints Victor et Ours (Genève)

par

Éric CHEVALLEY

I. ÉCRITURE, TRADITION MANUSCRITE ET ÉDITION DE LA PASSION.
II. STRUCTURE ET CONTENU DE LA PASSION.
III. VALEUR HISTORIQUE.
BIBLIOGRAPHIE.

De l'ancien évêché de Genève nous est parvenue une abondante documentation permettant de faire remonter sa création à la fin du IVe siècle et de suivre une bonne partie de son histoire au fil du temps. Le rôle de capitale que cette cité joua au sein du royaume burgonde explique en partie cette richesse, illustrée notamment par les lettres et les homélies d'Avit de Vienne[1]. En outre, l'Église de Genève a conservé une trace de ses anciens pasteurs sous la forme d'un catalogue, appelé Catalogue de Saint-Pierre[2]. Les fouilles archéologiques entreprises sur le site de la cathédrale Saint-Pierre à partir de 1976 ont mis au jour un remarquable complexe épiscopal doté d'une cathédrale double, d'un baptistère et d'une résidence épiscopale. Ainsi la Genève chrétienne fait partie des cités de la Gaule les mieux documentées pour la période de l'Antiquité tardive et du haut Moyen Age[3]. Par ailleurs, bon nombre de ses évêques furent impliqués à divers titres dans le culte de saint Maurice et de ses compagnons martyrs, tel Maxime qui, selon la Vie des Abbés d'Agaune, incita Sigismond à fonder un monastère à l'endroit qui avait été consacré par le sang des Thébains[4]. De cette façon, les sources relatives au culte des martyrs d'Agaune viennent en-

---

[1] *Alcimi Ecdicii Aviti Viennensis episcopi opera quae supersunt*, éd. R. PEIPER, MGH, AA, VI-2, Berlin, 1883.
[2] BINZ – ÉMERY – SANTSCHI (1980), p. 51-60.
[3] BONNET – SANTSCHI (1986), p. 37-48; BONNET – PEILLEIX (2012).
[4] CHEVALLEY – RODUIT (2014), p. 156.

richir les informations dont nous disposons sur les évêques de Genève⁵. Parmi ceux-ci, certains se sont distingués par leur origine sociale, leurs vertus et leurs capacités intellectuelles: Salonius, fils d'Eucher de Lyon, avait composé des commentaires de plusieurs textes bibliques⁶. Maxime était, selon le témoignage de la Vie des Abbés d'Agaune, un prédicateur hors pair. Malgré cela, nous n'avons que peu de traces d'une production hagiographique issue du diocèse de Genève: aucun de ses évêques ne fut honoré par la composition d'une Vie. Du moins nous n'en avons pas conservé le souvenir et seuls les martyrs Victor et Ours ont fait l'objet d'une composition certainement réalisée à Genève ou pour Genève.

De plus, les traces manuscrites de cette maigre production hagiographique ne sont pas à rechercher dans le diocèse lui-même. Le passage à la Réforme et la sécularisation des monastères ont amené la dispersion des bibliothèques et la perte des témoins manuscrits d'origine locale. Aujourd'hui, c'est en dehors du diocèse de Genève que se trouvent les derniers témoins d'une écriture hagiographique genevoise de haute époque.

I. Écriture, tradition manuscrite et édition de la Passion

Ours et Victor sont mentionnés pour la première fois vers la fin de la première moitié du Vᵉ siècle par Eucher de Lyon dans sa Passion des martyrs d'Agaune: l'auteur précise que, selon une tradition établie, les deux martyrs de Soleure, Ours et Victor, appartenaient également à la Légion thébaine⁷. Par la suite, plusieurs Passions furent composées en l'honneur des deux

---

⁵ Isaac, premier évêque connu de Genève, est mentionné par Eucher de Lyon comme l'un des garants des informations qu'il donne sur le martyre des Thébains: *Porro ab idoneis auctoribus rei ipsius ueritatem quaesiui, ab his utique qui adfirmabant, se ab episcopo Genauensi sancto Isaac hunc quem praetuli ordinem cognouisse; qui, credo, rursum haec retro a beatissimo episcopo Theodoro uiro temporis anterioris acceperit. Passio Acaunensium martyrum auctore Eucherio episcopo Lugdunenss* (éd. B. KRUSCH, *MGH, SRM*, III, Hanovre, 1896, p. 40).

⁶ BINZ – ÉMERY – SANTSCHI (1980), p. 63-64.

⁷ *Ex hac eadem legione fuisse dicuntur etiam illi martyres Ursus et Victor, quos Salodorum passos fama confirmat. Salodorum uero castrum est super Arulam flumen neque longe a Rheno positum* (Éd. KRUSCH, p. 38).

saints, compositions recensées par la *BHL* sous les numéros 8584-8588. Les Bollandistes ont édité au tome VIII du mois de septembre deux textes différents : une Passion que l'on qualifie de Soleuroise, car elle accorde une forme de préséance à Ours qui est toujours cité en premier (ou seul) et porte une attention soutenue à la topographie sacrée de Soleure. Elle mentionne en particulier le pont du haut duquel les martyrs furent précipités après avoir été décapités et l'endroit où ils sortirent de la rivière portant leur tête dans leurs mains (*BHL* 8588)[8]. À la suite de ce texte figure une autre version (*BHL* 8584) qui, au contraire, privilégie Victor et rapporte la translation de ses reliques de Soleure à Genève où une basilique lui fut consacrée aux abords de la cité[9].

Depuis l'étude déjà ancienne d'Alois Lütolf et celle, plus récente, de Berthe Widmer, il est démontré que la version genevoise, centrée sur Victor, représente la plus ancienne et la plus autorisée des deux traditions[10]. Elle daterait du VIIe siècle, alors que la Passion d'Ours et Victor (soleuroise) résulterait d'une forme de réécriture plus tardive, largement inspirée de la Passion de Felix et Regula[11]. Le crédit de la Passion genevoise est en effet conforté par le témoignage de la Chronique de Frédégaire qui rapporte dans des termes très proches un événement décrit par la Passion : la redécouverte des restes de saint Victor sous le règne de Thierry II, en présence des évêques Aeconius, Rusticius et Patricius soit en 602[12]. La précision des indications

---

[8] *AASS*, Sept. VIII, 1762, p. 291 ; il s'agit d'une reprise de l'édition de Surius, VII (1581), p. 736-37.

[9] *Ibidem*, p. 292-293 ; l'édition est fondée sur un manuscrit de Notre-Dame de Signy dont la datation n'est pas précisée.

[10] LÜTOLF (1871), WIDMER (1990), p. 33-81.

[11] WIDMER (1990), p. 78-80, appuie sa démonstration en présentant vis-à-vis les passages correspondants des deux textes.

[12] *Chronicarum quae dicuntur Fredegarii Scholastici liber IV* (éd. B. KRUSCH, *MGH, SRM*, II, Hanovre, 1888, p. 129): *Eo anno corpus sancti Victoris, qui Salodero cum sancto Ursio passus fuerat, a beato Aeconio pontifice Mauriennense inuenitur. Quadam nocte in suam ciuitatem ei reuelatur in sompnium, ut surgens protinus iret ad eclesiam, quam Sideleuba regina suburbanum Genauinse construxerat; in medium eclesia designatum locum illum sanctum corpus adesset. Cumque Genaua festinus perrexisset cum beatis Rustico et Patricio episcopis, triduanum faciens ieiunium, lumen per noctem, ubi illum gloriosum et splendidum corpus erat, apparuit. Quem cum selencio hii tres pontifecis, cum lacrimis et orationibus, eleuato lapide, in arcam argentiam inuenerunt sepultum, cuius faciem robentem quasi uiuum repperunt. Ibique*

fournies par ce chapitre de la Passion laisse penser qu'il a été rédigé peu après les événements rapportés, à Genève certainement, qui était devenu le centre du culte de saint Victor martyr de la Légion Thébaine [13]. Ainsi, il paraît légitime de considérer que la Passion a été composée au VIIe siècle.

Bien que la Passion genevoise soit éditée dans les *Acta Sanctorum*, son texte semble cependant problématique. Pour cette raison, Lütolf et Widmer ont choisi de fonder leur étude sur la transcription d'un manuscrit de Saint-Gall (Sankt-Gallen, Stiftsbibliothek, 569, IXe/Xe siècle) qui présente un texte assez éloigné de celui que propose l'édition des Bollandistes: la *BHL* recense cette variante sous le numéro 8586. En l'absence d'édition critique, il peut sembler difficile de préciser les rapports qu'entretiennent ces deux traditions. Cependant, la préférence accordée par Lütolf et Widmer au témoin de Saint-Gall paraît justifiée car, en plus de l'absence de donnée sur la datation du manuscrit utilisé par les Bollandistes, son texte semble contenir une forme d'abrégé et de réécriture, en particulier du chapitre d'introduction centré sur les exploits de la Légion Thébaine. Nous y apprenons qu'au moment où Maximien conduisait son armée à Genève (!), Victor et Ours se seraient séparés du reste de la Légion pour chercher refuge à Soleure où ils auraient été retrouvés par les bourreaux. De façon générale, hormis le dernier chapitre dont la rédaction est identique, le texte édité dans les

---

princeps Theudericus presens aderat, multisque rebus huius eclesiae tribuens, maxemam partem facultates Warnacharii ibidem confirmauit. Ad sepulchrum illum sanctum mirae uirtutes ex ipsa diae, quo repertum est, prestante Domino, integra adsiduaetate ostenduntur.

[13] WIDMER (1990), p. 43. Cependant LÜTOLF (1871), p. 151, a envisagé l'idée que la fondation d'une église en l'honneur d'un martyr nommé Victor par une princesse qui aurait pris le voile sous le nom de Chrona peut trouver une forme d'explication dans l'association que l'on rencontre habituellement entre les martyrs Corona et Victor (d'Alexandrie). VAN BERCHEM (1956), voulant donner plus de crédit à son hypothèse de l'origine orientale du culte des martyrs d'Agaune, considère que le martyr pour lequel la princesse Sédéleubeude (devenue Chrona) a fait construire une église était Victor de Syrie dont le culte est associé à celui de Corona (p. 44). La notice de SANTSCHI (1991), p. 239, reprend cette idée et considère que le dédicataire de la fondation était initialement Victor de Syrie. Pour une réfutation de cette hypothèse voir FAVROD (1997), p. 298, n. 66.

Acta Sanctorum ressemble à une forme de réinterprétation plus concise du texte transmis par le témoin de Saint-Gall[14]. Par ailleurs, un manuscrit provenant de Saint-Bénigne de Dijon, conservé aujourd'hui à Montpellier (Montpellier, BIU, H 238, IXe/Xe siècle) présente un texte extrêmement proche du témoin de Saint-Gall, sans en être une copie exacte[15]. Cela suffit déjà à démontrer que la version transmise par Saint-Gall 569 n'est pas dépendante de ce seul témoin, mais reflète une tradition plus répandue qui doit correspondre à la version originale de la Passion des saints Victor et Ours. Selon Lütolf, le témoin de Saint-Gall daterait du IXe, alors que selon Krusch il serait du Xe siècle[16]. Scarpatetti pense que la partie de ce manuscrit contenant le corpus consacré aux saints Victor et Ours a été copiée à la fin du IXe ou au début du Xe par deux mains différentes qui ne sont pas attribuables au scriptorium de Saint-Gall[17].

II. Structure et contenu de la Passion

La Passion est constituée de plusieurs épisodes situés à des moments différents. Elle présente d'abord les exploits de la Légion thébaine engagée par Maximien dans la persécution des chrétiens. Plutôt que de commettre un tel crime, les soldats chrétiens préférèrent confesser leur foi et mourir par l'épée.

---

[14] Il faut noter que Krusch (1896), p. 31, pense au contraire que la version transmise par les témoins de Saint-Gall et Montpellier est une amplification de celle qui figure chez les Bollandistes. Selon lui, l'auteur aurait complété ses informations à partir d'éléments supplémentaires fournis par Adon dans son martyrologe.

[15] On le constate par exemple dans un passage où le témoin de Saint-Gall présente un texte lacunaire: *Hyrtacus magistoribus* (lacune) *hoc totum deputans sancis martyribus Victori et Ursi ignem amoueri iubet*; Montellier: *Hyrtacus furoribus magnis incitatus sanctis martyribus Victori et Urso ignem inferri iubet*. Selon Krusch, le manuscrit de Montpellier a été copié au XIe siècle; Heinzelmann – Poulin (2006) le datent de la fin du Xe ou du début XIe siècle (p. 162).

[16] Lütolf (1871), p. 172; Krusch (1896), p. 32.

[17] Scarpatetti (2003), p. 70-74. Selon Heinzelmann – Poulin (2006), le manuscrit 569 de Saint-Gall contient aux pages 224-239 la Passion «genevoise» de saint Victor copiée par une main française vers 900, la deuxième Passion a été ajoutée sur les pages laissées libres plus tardivement (X^e) probablement à Soleure (p. 156).

Parmi les saints qui subirent le martyre à Agaune sont nommés, en plus de Maurice, Exupère et Candide, les saints Innocent et Vital[18]. Pour éviter de subir la fureur du tyran, Victor et Ours se retirèrent à Soleure. C'est également le choix que firent d'autres soldats de la Légion thébaine, Géréon et ses compagnons qui rejoignirent Cologne[19]. Victor et Ours furent néanmoins rejoints par un lieutenant de Maximien nommé Hyrtacus. Malgré les menaces de celui-ci, ils refusèrent de participer à la persécution de leurs coreligionnaires. Soumis à la torture, Victor et Ours surent rester fermes et entrèrent sans hésitation dans le bûcher auquel on les avait condamnés, mais une pluie miraculeuse mit fin au supplice. Loin de se laisser fléchir par ce miracle, Hyrtacus ordonna que les deux soldats fussent frappés par le fer. Tous deux accueillirent la sentence avec joie. Leurs dépouilles, emportées avec respect par des chrétiens, furent dignement ensevelies non loin du bourg de Soleure. Cette première partie est nettement inspirée de la Passion des martyrs d'Agaune d'Eucher de Lyon, mais dans une version déjà évoluée qui avait associé aux martyrs mentionnés par Eucher dans sa rédaction primitive les saints Innocent et Vital[20].

---

[18] *Ex hac ipsa primi, ut maximi ceteram uniuersam dignitatem praeirent et in castris signa, ut incessus armorum ordinando disponerent, Mauricius, Exuperius, Candidus, Victor, Innocentius, Vitalis* (Sankt-Gallen, 569, p. 224).

[19] *Tunc beatissimi Victor et Ursus ut furorem tyrannicam declinarent, ad castrum Salodorum qui est super Arulam fluuium secesserunt. Sicut hac eadem causa ipsa Gereon cum sociis ad Colonicam urbem transitum fecerunt in qua postmodum martyrum Christi gratia implere meruerunt* (Ibid., p. 225).

[20] La mention d'Innocent montre que l'auteur de la Passion de Victor et Ours connaissait la tradition relative aux martyrs d'Agaune à travers un texte où figurait le passage relatant la découverte de ce nouveau martyr. KRUSCH (1896), p. 40-41. On date généralement cette interpolation au texte d'Eucher de la fin du Ve siècle, voir BESSON (1913), p. 49. Quant à Vital, dont le nom figure dans bon nombre de manuscrits de la Passion anonyme de saint Maurice, en particulier Turin, Biblioteca Nazionale, D.V.3 (CHEVALLEY – RODUIT (2014), p. 31), sa présence dans la liste montre peut-être que le texte à disposition contenait également la Passion anonyme ce que laissent penser d'autres indices, telle l'obligation d'accomplir un sacrifice aux dieux de Rome. *Iussu itaque impiissimi Maximiani ab Hirtaco executore supradicti Victor et Ursus tenti conuentis ab aparatoribus, ut sacrificando demonibus parerent impiissimis iussis Maximiani* (Sankt-Gallen, 569, p. 225). Par ailleurs, le parallèle établi avec Géréon et ses compagnons atteste que la tradition relative aux martyrs thébains de Cologne est bien connue de l'auteur de la Passion. Les premières traces de cette tradition se trouvent chez Grégoire de Tours (*In gloria Mar-*

La deuxième partie du texte est consacrée au récit de la translation des reliques de Victor de Soleure à Genève. Elle eut lieu sous le règne de Godégisèle et à l'instigation de la reine Théodelinde qui bénéficiait de l'appui de l'évêque Domitien. Ainsi la dépouille du saint fut solennellement transférée à Genève, dans la basilique que la reine avait fait construire aux abords de la ville. Les reliques furent déposées dans l'autel où elles restèrent assez longtemps enfermées et cachées.

Sous le règne du roi Thierry, alors que le souverain résidait à Genève, les évêques Hiconius de Maurienne, Rusticius d'Octodure et Patricius de Tarentaise, qui s'étaient rendus à la cour, obtinrent de retrouver les restes du saint qu'ils découvrirent à l'intérieur d'un coffre de bois recouvert d'argent. Cette redécouverte se produisit alors que Papolus, déjà très âgé et grabataire, était évêque de Genève.

À la faveur de ces événements, des miracles apparurent à nouveau sur le tombeau du saint. Ainsi, une femme qui avait dérobé un cierge ne put le faire tomber de sa main qu'après avoir fait pénitence sur la tombe du martyr. Un marchand qui tentait de tromper un autre en prêtant un faux serment fut précipité à terre, révélant ainsi sa malignité. Par le pouvoir du saint toujours, une jeune servante fut délivrée du démon qui sortit de son corps en prenant la forme d'un lézard, s'échappant par l'oreille de sa victime. Nombreux sont les miracles que Dieu réalisa pour la gloire de son martyr.

Le texte précise enfin que Victor et Ours subirent le martyre sous le règne de Maximien la veille des calendes d'octobre (30 septembre).

Cette structure témoigne peut-être de plusieurs étapes de rédaction: il n'est pas exclu qu'une Passion primitive (mais déjà centrée sur Victor, donc rédigée à une époque proche de la translation) accompagnée du récit de la translation ait été complétée par le récit de la redécouverte des reliques sous Thierry II et des miracles consécutifs. Il se pourrait aussi que l'ensemble ait été élaboré après la redécouverte à partir de témoignages plus an-

---

tyrum, 61, éd. B. KRUSCH, *MGH*, *SRM*, I-2, Hanovre, 1885, p. 80) et dans certains témoins de la Passion anonyme de saint Maurice, cf. CHEVALLEY – RODUIT (2014), p. 100-101.

ciens. L'attribution du martyre à la veille des calendes d'octobre me semble en revanche relever d'un ajout plus tardif[21].

III. Valeur historique

Dans son étude du dossier des martyrs d'Agaune, B. Krusch avait porté un jugement sur la valeur de la Passion des saints Victor et Ours qui a influencé pour longtemps la critique historique. Selon lui, la Passion genevoise (dont l'original lui semble être le texte édité par les Bollandistes) ne fait que compléter les indications fournies par Frédégaire, en expliquant notamment comment le corps de Victor, martyr de Soleure, s'est retrouvé à Genève. Aussi les indications fournies par la Passion seraient-elles soit empruntées à Frédégaire, soit pour le moins douteuses. Ainsi, lorsqu'une variante se présente, Krusch accorde sa préférence au texte historique, par définition plus autorisé. Pour cette raison, il n'a pas trouvé judicieux d'éditer le texte de la Passion. Quant à la version transmise par le manuscrit de Saint-Gall, Krusch considère qu'elle reflète un état postérieur: la partie consacrée au martyre des deux héros aurait été complétée à partir du martyrologe d'Adon, alors que de nombreux détails erronés auraient été introduits, telle la mention d'un évêque de Genève du nom de Papolus, dont nous ne trouvons aucune trace chez Frédégaire. Celui-ci mentionne pourtant deux évêques, en plus d'Aeconius de Maurienne, dont l'un devait bien être celui de Genève[22].

Bien que les historiens aient globalement repris les conclusions de Lütolf sur l'importance du manuscrit de Saint-Gall dans l'établissement du texte de la Passion de Victor et Ours, ils

---

[21] La date du martyre est indiquée à la fin de la Passion, après le récit des miracles: *Passi sunt autem sancti martyres Victor et Ursus sub Maximiano imperatore pridie kalendas octobris*. WIDMER (1990), p. 40, fait remarquer que le martyrologe hiéronymien indique au 30 septembre une translation de la dépouille de Victor de Milan. Il se pourrait donc que le choix du 30 septembre pour la commémoration des martyrs de Soleure ait été en quelque sorte suggéré par l'évocation du martyr homonyme de Milan. Quoi qu'il en soit, il fallait que la date retenue s'intègre dans la chronologie d'ensemble du martyre de la Légion thébaine, le massacre d'Agaune étant situé au 22 septembre, celui des Thébains de Cologne au 10 octobre.

[22] KRUSCH (1896), p. 31.

ont majoritairement suivi le point de vue négatif de Krusch quant à la valeur des informations transmises par le texte hagiographique, auquel on préfère systématiquement le témoignage du chroniqueur. Ainsi les notices de la *Topographie chrétienne de la Gaule*, du volume d'*Helvetia Sacra* consacré aux prieurés clunisiens et, plus récemment, du *Dictionnaire historique de la Suisse* attribuent la fondation de l'église à la princesse Sédeleubeude (*Sideleuba regina* dit le chroniqueur) que l'on considère comme la sœur aînée de Clotilde [23]. Ainsi, lorsque les deux traditions sont opposées, le choix des variantes est toujours en faveur du texte historique [24].

Toutefois, le témoignage de la Passion ne semble pas pouvoir être réfuté aussi facilement. Pourquoi dans le récit de la fondation écarter en faveur d'une princesse (dont l'identité n'est pas si bien établie [25]) l'intervention de la reine Théodelinde, qui en tant qu'épouse de Godégisel devait exercer à Genève une influence déterminante pour mener à bien une telle entreprise? Justement, la reine est connue par un document relatif au monastère Saint-Pierre de Lyon, qui attribue la fondation de cet établissement au roi Godégisel et à sa très pieuse épouse, la reine Théodelinde [26].

---

[23] BONNET – SANTSCHI (1986), p. 37-48, SANTSCHI (1991), p. 239-244. L'article de HUBLER (2010) consacré au prieuré Saint-Victor dit avec prudence que l'église a été fondée à la fin du Ve siècle par une princesse burgonde.

[24] En revanche, FAVROD (1997), p. 294-296, rapporte la fondation de l'église Saint-Victor de Genève en se basant sur les indications fournies par la Passion. Il cite également une hypothèse de CHAUME (1947), p. 156-157, permettant d'expliquer les variantes transmises par Frédégaire.

[25] La question est assez complexe du fait que Frédégaire indique comme fondatrice *Sideleuba regina*, qu'il avait au préalable (III, 17, éd. B. KRUSCH, p. 99) présentée comme fille ainée d'Hilperic, condamnée à l'exil par Gondebaud en même temps que sa sœur Clotilde. Frédégaire indique aussi (IV, 22, *Ibid.*, p. 129) qu'elle prit l'habit pour se vouer à Dieu. Or, Grégoire de Tours, source principale de Fédégaire, donne à la princesse qui prit l'habit le nom de Chrona (*Gregorii episcopi Turonensis libri historiarum X*, II, 28, éd. B. KRUSCH, *MGH*, *SRM*, I-1, 2e éd., Hanovre, 1951, p. 73-74). On a souvent tenté de résoudre cette difficulté en disant que le nom de Chrona est une forme germanisée du nom Corona que Sédéleubeude aurait pris en entrant en religion. Pour une réfutation de cette approche voir FAVROD (1997), p. 297-299.

[26] FAVROD (1997), p. 345-348. Il n'est pas impensable que la fondation d'un édifice dédié au culte catholique sous le patronage de la reine ait re-

Quant à l'évêque Domitien de Genève, avant d'évoquer son rôle dans la translation des reliques du saint martyr, la Passion précise l'étendue du territoire dont il était titulaire « son diocèse englobait non seulement les villages et les bourgs situés sur les deux côtés du lac, mais aussi le bourg de Soleure situé sur l'Aar »[27]. Krusch considérait que l'existence de ce prélat avait été suggérée à l'auteur de notre texte par un ajout à la Passion des martyrs d'Agaune. Un passage interpolé évoque effectivement la découverte du corps de saint Innocent, Thébain jusqu'alors inconnu, révélé par une crue du Rhône, et sa translation en présence des évêques Domitien de Genève, Gratus d'Aoste et Protais d'Octodure[28]. Ainsi le rôle que la Passion attribue à l'évêque Domitien relèverait davantage d'un emprunt littéraire que d'une tradition historique véritable. Cependant, en plus de la synchronie entre son existence et celle de la reine Théodelinde, les précisions données sur l'étendue du diocèse de Genève au temps de Domitien ne se bornent pas à rendre plus vraisemblable la translation, mais témoignent véritablement de la situation complexe des anciens évêchés de l'actuelle suisse romande[29]. D'ailleurs le rôle de ce prélat dans l'établissement du culte de saint Victor à Genève semble confirmé par l'existence d'un document aujourd'hui perdu, mais édité par Josias Simler en 1576. Selon le témoignage de l'historien zurichois, une inscription qui se trouvait dans l'église Saint-Victor attestait que la translation avait eu lieu sous l'épiscopat de Domitien dont le diocèse englobait alors le bourg de Soleure[30]. La fondation de

---

présenté une forme d'ouverture de la part du souverain burgonde à l'intention de ses sujets catholiques.

[27] *Eodem tempore sanctus Domicianus episcopus in eadem ipsa urbe erat; ad cuius diocesym non solum uici et castra supra lacum ex utraque parte posita, sed et castrum Solodorum super Arulam situm pertinebant* (Sankt-Gallen, 569, p. 227). Le témoignage du manuscrit de Montpellier confirme l'authenticité de ce passage (fol. 123v).

[28] *Passio Acaunensium martyrum*, 1896, p. 41: *Cuius translationem a sanctae recordationis Domiciano Genavensi et Grato Agustane urbis uel Protasio tunc temporis huius loci episcopis caelebratam recolentes, cotidiana deuotione et laudibus frequentamus.*

[29] Chevalley – Favrod (1992), p. 47-68.

[30] SIMLER (1576), p. 69: *tradunt enim in fano D. Victoris prope Genevam scriptum esse: Acta sunt haec regnante Domitiano episco Genavensi quo tempore etiam castrum Salodorense episcopatui Genevensi subditum erat* etc. Le texte cité par l'historien zurichois reprend l'indication fournie par la Passion à propos de

cet établissement constitue donc un jalon important dans l'établissement du culte des martyrs thébains en dehors du Valais et dans le rapport de collaboration et d'échange qui s'instaura entre Agaune et l'évêché de Genève[31]. À l'époque carolingienne, l'église Saint-Victor servit de basilique funéraire. Vers la fin du second royaume de Bourgogne, elle entra dans l'orbite de Cluny pour devenir un prieuré destiné à jouer un rôle significatif dans l'histoire de Genève[32]. Aujourd'hui, les seules indications dont nous disposons sur l'architecture et la décoration de l'ancienne église proviennent des sources historiques, Chronique de Frédégaire et Passion de Victor et Ours : elles ont été exploitées par L. Blondel dans un article paru en 1958[33].

Quant à la redécouverte des reliques du saint sous le règne de Thierry II, Widmer a montré que les précisions de l'Anonyme lui confèrent une valeur supplémentaire. Ainsi le coffre dans lequel se trouvaient les reliques du saint est décrit par la Passion avec plus de précisions : *inuenerunt summo honore compositum infra thecam ligneam argento decentissime preparatam sancti martyris corpus*[34]. De même, les indications concernant les évêques présents lors de cette cérémonie ne sont pas si contournées, telle la mention de l'évêque de Genève Papolus, qui n'aurait pu assister à la cérémonie car il était très âgé et infirme[35]. Selon la Passion, l'évêque Hiconius de Maurienne aurait été secondé par les

---

l'étendue du diocèse de Genève à l'époque de Domitien. Malheureusement, il est aujourd'hui impossible de proposer une datation pour cette inscription.

[31] Les évêque de Genève furent impliqués dès l'origine vraisemblablement dans le culte des martyrs d'Agaune, cf. CHEVALLEY (2018).

[32] SANTSCHI (1991), p. 240-243.

[33] BLONDEL (1958), p. 211-258. À la Réforme, l'église fut progressivement détruite pour des raisons de défense, en raison de sa proximité avec les remparts. Aujourd'hui, ses vestiges se trouvent enfouis sous l'actuelle église orthodoxe russe.

[34] Sankt-Gallen, 569, p. 229.

[35] *Ibid.*: *Tunc temporis sanctus Papolus mirae sanctitatis uir senior iam grauatus Geneuensium habebatur episcopus.* Helvetia Sacra mentionne deux évêques du nom de Pappolus, l'un attesté entre 541 et 549, l'autre vers 650. En revanche, pour la période concernée par la découverte des reliques, l'existence d'un évêque du nom de Rusticius ou Patricius est envisagée à partir de Frédégaire, qui toutefois ne précise pas les sièges des deux évêques présents au côté d'Hiconius de Maurienne. Comme leur nom figure au *Catalogue de Saint-Pierre*, on a pris l'habitude de penser que l'un des deux devait alors être titulaire de l'évêché de Genève, cf. BINZ – ÉMERY – SANTSCHI (1980), p. 66-67.

évêques Rusticius et Patricius, le premier étant titulaire de l'évêché d'Octodure et le second de Tarentaise[36]. Même si la dénomination du siège du Valais peut sembler problématique à une époque où le siège épiscopal devait se trouver à Sion et plus à Martigny, l'ensemble des détails a le mérite d'offrir une certaine cohérence[37].

À la suite de la Passion, le manuscrit de Saint-Gall (p. 231-233) contient, de la même main, une homélie signalée par l'incipit: *Omelia breuiter dicenda et legenda in festiuitate sanctorum martyrum Victoris et Ursi*. On le voit, Victor occupe d'emblée le premier rang. Un passage figurant à la dernière page lui accorde également la préséance, tout en précisant que son corps fait l'objet d'un culte à l'endroit-même: *Ecce sanctus iste Victor cuius sacratissimum corpus hic honoramus*. Plus loin, l'auteur semble s'adresser à une communauté de frères. Il est donc fort probable que cette homélie ait été composée à Genève afin être prononcée dans la basilique qui conservait les reliques du saint martyr[38]. Le prédicateur propose à l'assemblée d'imiter la constance et l'innocence des bienheureux martyrs, il célèbre la victoire de celui que son nom destinait à mépriser la pourpre des empereurs et toutes les formes de tourments. L'orateur termine la pièce en invitant les frères à placer leur confiance en l'intercession du bienheureux Victor.

---

[36] Sankt-Gallen, 569, p. 228-229: *Hiconium Mauriennensem, discipulum olim beati Cadooldi Vienensis episcopi, et ab eodem episcopo Maurienensi ordinatum, Rusticium atque Patricium cum aliis simul sacerdotibus et nobilibus undecumque uiris. Ex duobus supradictis episcopis alter Hocthodorensium, alter ex oppido Darentensium fuit*.

[37] *Helvetia Sacra*, I, 5: *Le diocèse de Sion*, éd. P. BRAUN, B. DEGLER-SPENGLER, E. GILOMEN-SCHENKEL, Bâle, 2001, p. 135-136, indique, à partir du témoignage de la Passion de Victor et Ours, un évêque du Valais du nom de Rusticius. Toutefois, la mention du siège d'Octodure est problématique, puisqu'à partir de 585 au moins les évêques du Valais ont établi leur résidence à Sion. De même, l'impossibilité d'étendre la durée de vie des deux évêques de Genève nommés Pappolus à l'époque concernée inciterait à considérer Rusticius comme un évêque de Genève et non du Valais.

[38] En l'absence de référence permettant de situer dans le temps la composition de l'homélie, on ne peut que la considérer comme antérieure à la fin du IXe siècle, date du témoin de Saint-Gall.

Bibliographie

Binz, L. – Émery, J. – Santschi, C., *Le diocèse de Genève*, in *Helvetia Sacra*, I, 3: *Archidiocèses et diocèses III*, Berne, 1980.
Besson, M., *Monasterium Acaunense*, Fribourg, 1913.
Blondel, L., «Le prieuré de Saint-Victor. Les débuts du christianisme et la royauté burgonde à Genève», *Bulletin de la société d'archéologie de Genève*, 11 (1958), p. 211-258.
Bonnet, C., – Peilleix, A., éd., *Les fouilles de la cathédrale Saint-Pierre de Genève. Les édifices chrétiens et le groupe épiscopal*, Genève, 2012.
Bonnet, C. – Santschi, C., «Genève», in *Topographie chrétienne des cités de la Gaule, des origines au milieu du VIIIe siècle*, III: *Provinces ecclésiastiques de Vienne et d'Arles (Viennensis et Alpes Graiae et Poeninae)*, Paris, 1986, p. 37-48.
Braun, P. – Degler-Spengler, B. – Gilomen-Schenkel, E., éd., *Helvetia Sacra*, I, 5: *Le diocèse de Sion*. Bâle, 2001.
Chaume, M., «Francs et burgondes au cours du VIe siècle», in *Recherches d'histoire chrétienne et médiévale*, Dijon, 1947, p. 156-157.
Chevalley, É., «Le culte des martyrs thébains en prélude à la fondation de 515», in A. Wagner – N. Brocard, éd., *Les royaumes de Bourgogne jusqu'en 1032. À travers la culture et la religion*, Turnhout, 2018, p. 140-147.
Chevalley, É. – Favrod, J., «Soleure dans le diocèse de Genève ? Hypothèse sur les origines du diocèse d'Avenches/Vindonissa», *Revue d'histoire ecclésiastique suisse*, 86 (1992), p. 47-68.
Chevalley, É. – C. Roduit, C., *La mémoire hagiographique de l'abbaye de Saint-Maurice d'Agaune, Passion anonyme de saint Maurice, Vie des abbés d'Agaune, Passion de saint Sigismond*, Lausanne, 2014 (Cahiers lausannois d'histoire médiévale, 53).
Favrod, J., *Histoire politique du royaume burgonde (443-534)*, Lausanne, 1997.
Heinzelmann, M., – Poulin, J.-C., *Les libelli dans l'édition hagiographique avant le XIIe siècle. Études sur la tradition hagiographique latine*, Ostfildern, 2006.
Hubler, L., «Saint-Victor», *Dictionnaire historique de la Suisse*, t. 10, Hauterive, 2010, p. 862.
Lütolf, A., *Die Glaubensboten der Schweiz vor St. Gallus*, Lucerne, 1871.
Santschi, C., «Saint Victor de Genève», in *Helvetia Sacra*, III, 2: *Die Orden mit Benediktinerregel*, H.-J. Gilomen – E. Gilomen-Schenkel, red., Basel – Frankfurt am Main, 1991.
Scarpatetti, B. M. von, *Die Handschriften der Stiftsbibliothek St-Gallen*, Bd. 1, Abt. IV, Wiesbaden, 2003.

SIMLER, J., *De Republica Helvetiorum*, Libri duo, Tiguri, 1576.
VAN BERCHEM, D., *Le martyre de la légion thébaine. Essai sur la formation d'une légende*, Bâle, 1956.
WIDMER, B., «Der Ursus- und Victorkult in Solothurn», in *Solothurn. Beiträge zur Entwicklung der Stadt im Mittelalter, Kollokium vom 13./14. November in Solothurn*, Zurich, 1990, p. 33-81.

L'écriture hagiographique dans la province de Tarentaise (à partir de la fin du VIIIe siècle)

par

Éric CHEVALLEY

INTRODUCTION.
I. LA VIE DE THÉODORE, ÉVÊQUE DE SION. – A. Auteur. – B. Datation. – C. Structure et contenu. – D. Développement du culte de saint Théodule au Moyen Âge. – E. La critique historique à l'époque moderne et ses conséquences.
II. LE DIOCÈSE D'AOSTE. – A. La Vie de saint Ours. – B. Structure et contenu.
BIBLIOGRAPHIE.

INTRODUCTION

La province ecclésiastique de Tarentaise ne fut organisée comme telle qu'à la fin du VIIIe siècle dans le cadre de la restructuration globale des provinces de l'Empire entreprise par Charlemagne à partir du modèle de la *Notitia Galliarum*. Ainsi, la première mention explicite d'une entité autonome figure dans le testament de l'empereur transmis par Eginhard[1]. La province regroupe alors les évêchés de Tarentaise, de Maurienne jusqu'en 867, de Sion jusqu'en 1513 et d'Aoste jusqu'en 1793. La province rassemblait des évêchés qui lors de leur fondation

---

[1] Au Ve siècle, dans le contexte des rivalités opposant les évêques de Vienne et Arles, un arbitrage du pape Léon Ier place l'évêque de Tarentaise sous l'autorité de celui de Vienne. Au synode de Francfort, en 794, se posa encore la question du statut des évêchés de Tarentaise, Embrun et Aix-en-Provence: on décida alors de s'en remettre à l'autorité du pape dont nous ne connaissons pas la décision. *Helvetia Sacra*, I, 5: *Le diocèse de Sion. L'archidiocèse de Tarentaise*, Bâle, 2001, p. 584-585.

avaient dû appartenir à des zones d'influence différentes, comme Aoste dont le premier titulaire connu se fit représenter au concile de Milan en 451². C'était peut-être aussi le cas de l'évêché d'Octodure, dont l'évêque Théodore participa au concile d'Aquilée présidé par Ambroise de Milan³. Si les traditions hagiographiques se rapportant aux origines des différents évêchés sont assez nombreuses, leur datation est souvent problématique. Ainsi, la fondation de l'évêché de Tarentaise est traditionnellement attribuée à saint Jacques, que sa Vie présente comme un disciple d'Honorat de Lérins, chargé par son maître, devenu évêque d'Arles, de l'évangélisation des Ceutrons. Sa mission aurait eu lieu en 427 ou 428, ce qui n'est pas invraisemblable puisque l'évêché est mentionné par le Pape Léon Ier en 450. En revanche, l'existence même de Jacques reste douteuse car sa Vie semble peu fiable et sa rédaction tardive⁴.

Quant à la production hagiographique ressortissant à cet espace religieux, force est de constater qu'elle est discrète, voire maigre pour la période envisagée dans le cadre de cette parution. La situation est alors différente de celle qui prévalait à l'époque antérieure où le développement de divers cultes, tel celui de saint Maurice et de ses compagnons thébains en Valais, avait donné naissance à plusieurs compositions. De plus, il est admis qu'à l'époque carolingienne les centres d'activité intellectuelle se sont décalés vers le nord de l'Europe, si bien que, malgré certaines exceptions notables, le niveau culturel des provinces du sud-est de la Gaule est alors globalement en baisse. Dans ces conditions, il n'est pas surprenant que l'espace alpin, à l'écart des grands centres du pouvoir, n'ait connu à cette période qu'une modeste production de textes hagiographiques.

Ainsi, les traditions relatives au diocèse de Tarentaise ont été mises en forme à une époque plus tardive (à partir du XIIe). Seuls les évêchés de Sion et d'Aoste font exception. Le premier avec une Vie de saint Théodule attribuée au moine Ruodpert à

---

² Au Xe siècle, Aoste semble à nouveau appartenir à la zone d'influence de Milan.

³ *Theodorus episcopus Octodorensis dixit...* suit la condamnation de Pallade: M. ZELZER éd., *Acta concilii Aquileiensis*, 1, 62 (*Corpus Scriptorum Ecclesiasticorum Latinorum*, 82/3, 1982, p. 362).

⁴ DUCHESNE (1907, p. 244) semble toutefois envisager que la fondation est plus ancienne. La Vie de saint Jacques de Tarentaise (BHL 4112) est éditée dans les *AASS*, Ian. II (16 janvier), 1643, p. 390-392.

la fin du XIe/début du XIIe siècle, et le second avec la Vie de saint Ours, dont on situe la plus ancienne version entre le VIIIe et le Xe siècle.

I. La Vie de Théodore, évêque de Sion

A. Auteur

La *Vita sancti Theodori episcopi Sedunensis* (*BHL* 8088) attribuée par certains de ses témoins manuscrits à un moine dénommé Ruodpert a peu suscité d'enthousiasme chez les historiens et savants qui ont été amenés à l'étudier. C'est ainsi que les Bollandistes omettent tout bonnement son prologue et sa péroraison jugés dénués d'intérêt. Effectivement, l'œuvre est déroutante et semble peu mériter le titre de Vie, car elle ne nous apprend rien sur l'origine ou la mort du personnage principal, l'évêque Théodore que la tradition nomme Théodule. Elle représente toutefois, comme nous le verrons, un développement significatif dans l'histoire du culte rendu au saint vénéré comme figure emblématique de l'évêché de Sion.

De fait, l'édition établie par les Bollandistes, avec l'aide de Pierre-François Chifflet, ne retient que les épisodes centraux de la Vie: le récit de l'intercession de l'évêque de Sion en faveur de Charlemagne, celui du miracle du moût et l'intervention de Théodore dans la découverte des corps des martyrs de la Légion thébaine[5]. Le prologue, quant à lui, a été édité en 1939 par H. Foerster à partir d'un manuscrit provenant de l'abbaye cistercienne de Hauterive dans le canton de Fribourg[6]. Une édition complète a été publiée en 2005 par F. Huot sur la base d'un manuscrit conservé aujourd'hui à Rome (Biblioteca Angelica, 1269, XIIIe siècle), provenant de l'abbaye de Saint-Maurice d'Agaune[7].

---

[5] *AASS*, Aug. III, 1737, p. 278-280.
[6] Foerster (1939).
[7] Le manuscrit de la Biblioteca Angelica n'est pas le plus ancien témoin, mais il contient un texte complet alors que Paris, BnF, lat. 5309 présente un texte amputé dès le XVIIIe siècle du quart du contenu de la Vie: Huot (2005).

L'attribution de l'œuvre à un moine du nom de Ruodpert repose sur le témoignage de l'incipit du prologue tel qu'il figure dans deux manuscrits: *Incipit prologus vite sancti Theodori a quodam Ruodperto peregrino monacho composite* (Fribourg, Bibliothèque cantonale et universitaire, L. 5)[8]. La nature homilétique de l'exorde, adressé à un auditoire ecclésiastique, tissé de citations scripturaires, pourrait suggérer que ce passage soit inspiré d'un sermon tenu par Ruodpert et que seule cette partie de la Vie doive lui être attribuée. Pourtant, il est plus vraisemblable que l'auteur ait rédigé l'ensemble de l'œuvre à partir des traditions qu'il aurait rassemblées sur l'évêque Théodore qui depuis longtemps faisait l'objet d'un culte dans le diocèse de Sion[9]. Le nom Ruodpert suggère peut-être une origine germanique[10].

B. Datation

En l'absence de données concrètes, il est malaisé d'avancer une date précise pour la composition de la Vie de saint Théodule. On rencontre chez les historiens une datation qui s'étend sur un siècle, du milieu du XIe au milieu du XIIe siècle[11]. À partir de l'épisode de l'intercession de l'évêque en faveur de Charlemagne, qui constitue la première partie de la Vie à proprement parler, on a proposé, du fait que le l'empereur n'y est jamais qualifié de saint, de situer la composition avant 1165, date de sa canonisation[12]. Quant au *terminus a quo*, il est indéniable que la demande, formulée avec toute la modestie de rigueur par l'évêque à un souverain débordant de reconnaissance, de la *Vallensium prefectura* en faveur de l'Église de Sion ne peut

---

[8] Le plus ancien témoin de la Vie (Paris, BnF, lat. 5309) contient toutefois la leçon *composito* qui a été considérée comme une lecture fautive, par le copiste, d'un nominatif *compositus*; dans ce cas, seul le prologue devrait être attribué au moine-pèlerin. Huot (2005), p. 20; cependant, il pourrait aussi s'agir d'une lecture fautive de *composite/compositae*.

[9] Dubuis (1981), p. 127-130; cet article offre une synthèse très fouillée des différentes contributions de Dubuis sur ce sujet et reste la référence de base sur le culte de saint Théodule.

[10] Huot (2005), p. 20.

[11] *Ibid.*, p. 18. Dubuis (1981), p. 132.

[12] Werder (1976/1977), p. 329. Huot (2005), p. 18, se montre réservé quant à l'utilisation de cet argument du fait que le culte de Charlemagne n'est pas attesté en Valais avant le XIIIe siècle.

s'expliquer qu'après la donation des droits comtaux sur le Valais de la part du roi Rodolphe III de Bourgogne, datant de 999[13]. Par ailleurs, le rôle que sa Vie attribue à Théodule auprès de Charlemagne a suggéré à de nombreux auteurs l'idée d'associer la figure du saint à celle (historique) de l'évêque Ermanfroid de Sion (1054/1055-1087/1091), qui fut chancelier du royaume de Bourgogne et, à ce titre, proche de l'empereur Henri IV[14]. La possession du glaive à double tranchant, revendiquée expressément par le saint évêque, *qui ecclesiasticus est, si bicipitem gladium in manu portat, in carnali quidem non occidendo, sed terrendo incidit, in spiritali autem quia blandiendo unguentum curationis imponit*, trouverait un sens bien précis dans le contexte de la Querelle des Investitures alors qu'après l'avènement de Grégoire VII, Ermanfroid semble ne plus bénéficier de la faveur pontificale. Ainsi, il serait tentant de situer la composition de la Vie sous l'épiscopat de ce grand personnage (plus précisément dans les années 1070-1080), dont le pouvoir séculier se trouverait en quelque sorte légitimé par l'exemple de son saint prédécesseur. Telle est la position de J. Huber dans son article consacré à la Grande Châsse de Sion[15]. Récemment, l'étude consacrée à Ermanfroid par J. Luther défend aussi cette idée et attribue un rôle déterminant à l'évêque-chancelier aussi bien dans la promotion du culte de Théodule que dans la réalisation de la Grande Châsse de Sion qui devait contenir nombre de reliques du saint évêque[16].

Cette hypothèse s'appuie en particulier sur un passage de la Vie dont M. Werder a donné en 1977 une traduction, qui a été ensuite reprise par Huber, en français, et Luther, en allemand. Après avoir reçu la donation impériale, Théodule revint à Sion, où, nous dit la Vie, ...*tanta, ut prediximus, auctoritate vivendi usus est, ut divine pietatis augmentum illo in tempore in tantum percipere*

---

[13] DUBUIS (1981), p. 132, fait également remarquer que la composition de la Vie ne saurait être proche de l'époque carolingienne, car elle manifeste une totale ignorance de l'identité des évêques de Sion de cette époque: Willicaire et surtout Althée. Cf. *Helvetia Sacra*, I, 5, p. 137-139.

[14] *Helvetia Sacra*, I, 5, p. 149-151; Voir surtout LUTHER (2016), p. 173-234.

[15] Selon HUBER (2005, p. 78-79 et 81), Ermanfroid joua également un rôle moteur dans la révélation *sancti Theoduli* et dans la constitution du trésor de reliques contenues dans la châsse de saint Théodule.

[16] LUTHER (2016), p. 220-223.

meruisset, quo non solum pure conscientie frueretur arbitrio, sed etiam faciendorum signorum non modico dignus haberetur imperio[17]. Or, Werder traduit cette période par: « Er lebte, wie schon gesagt, in so vorbildlicher Haltung, dass er zu jener Zeit so hohe göttliche Gnaden verdiente und er deshalb nicht nur mit reinem Gewissen urteilen konnte, sondern auch für würdig genug erachtet wurde, für das Reich Unterschriften zu machen[18] ». Traduction que reprend Huber en citant la Vie qui, selon lui, dit de Théodule qu'il est en puissance « d'apposer sa signature pour l'Empire[19] ». On le voit, l'historienne a interprété le terme *signum* comme signature (seing) et donné à *imperio* le sens d'Empire. Or, il est plus naturel de donner à *signum* le sens de miracle (très fréquemment attesté) et d'associer en une litote les termes *non modico... imperio*. Aussi peut-on plus vraisemblablement traduire ce passage par: « ...mais aussi qu'il fût digne ‹de bénéficier› d'un pouvoir étendu d'accomplir des miracles »[20]. Il me paraît donc difficile de reconnaître dans ce passage de la Vie une allusion précise au rôle de chancelier de l'Empire tel qu'Ermanfroid l'occupa. Il n'est cependant pas impossible que l'activité diplomatique et politique d'un prélat de son importance ait contribué à imposer aux Valaisans la figure d'un évêque impliqué dans la vie de la cour impériale[21]. Toutefois, on ne saurait légitimement invoquer cet argument pour limiter la datation de la Vie à cette période de l'épiscopat d'Ermanfroid. Quant au *terminus ante quem* proposé habituellement, à savoir 1165, date de

---

[17] HUOT (2005), p. 29.
[18] WERDER (1976/1977), p. 319.
[19] HUBER (2005), p. 79.
[20] Cette interprétation, par ailleurs, convient mieux à une forme de conclusion (fin de l'épisode de Charlemagne) et sert d'introduction à la suite du texte. La Vie, en effet, enchaîne avec une réflexion sur la capacité d'accomplir des miracles et en donne un exemple précis réalisé par Théodule lui-même: celui du moût.
[21] La réserve dont font preuve DUBUIS (1981, p. 133), puis HUOT (2005, p. 18) à ce sujet montre, je pense, qu'ils n'admettent pas la traduction de Werder et l'interprétation que l'on peut en tirer. De même, MORAND, FLÜHLER-KREIS *et al.* (2013, p. 155) interprètent la fin de l'épisode de Charlemagne comme une annonce des miracles qui furent accomplis par Théodore. Il faut cependant noter que WERDER (1976/1977, p. 337-340) ne situe pas la composition de la Vie par Ruodpert sous l'épiscopat d'Ermanfroid, mais au siècle suivant sous celui de Louis de Granges, dans un contexte politique différent dont elle présente les enjeux possibles.

la canonisation de Charlemagne, on peut à la suite de Huot émettre quelques réserves sur sa validité. Surtout la date attribuée par l'éditeur au plus ancien témoin de la Vie (première moitié du XIIe siècle) impliquerait que l'œuvre a été composée au plus tard au début de ce siècle[22]. Il paraît donc raisonnable de situer la composition de la Vie vers la fin du XIe et le commencement du XIIe siècle.

C. Structure et contenu

Le prologue, introduisant les épisodes narratifs de la Vie, est relativement développé et présente une tonalité homilétique très marquée: *Divine pietatis sacramentum cum magna pietate, fratres karissimi, venerari oportet...* L'auteur s'adresse visiblement à une communauté ou, du moins, insère son discours dans une célébration que l'éditeur de la Vie envisage comme la proclamation de la légende de saint Théodule dans l'office choral de l'Église de Sion[23]. Sur la base de citations scripturaires, Ruodpert élabore une histoire du salut à partir de la création et de l'incarnation, suivant un ordre plus ou moins chronologique. Comparant le royaume des cieux à un filet plongé dans la mer, l'auteur développe le thème des chrétiens assimilés aux poissons, dont le premier exemple fut celui de l'apôtre lui-même. Le thème de la nourriture lui permet ensuite d'assembler toutes sortes de citations et de contextes bibliques pour en arriver aux animaux dont le Christ a redressé la nature terrestre et charnelle. Enfin Ruodpert mentionne Théodore qui occupe une place privilégiée parmi les créatures. *De virtute in virtutem eundo, leonem exhibuit, videndo Deum deorum in Syon, aquila fuit.* C'est ainsi qu'il en vient au sujet lui-même: la biographie du héros *juxta historiam quod de eo sentimus*. À ce propos, il avoue en substance ne pas détenir beaucoup d'informations sur le parcours terrestre du saint, mais se dit prêt à combler cette lacune par l'évocation de sa gloire spirituelle: *Pauca nobis omnimodis dicenda*

---

[22] Paris, BnF, lat. 5309. À partir de critères paléographiques Huot (2005, p. 19-20) date ce témoin de la première moitié du XIIe siècle. Il précise, toutefois, qu'il s'agit de son avis personnel, car aussi bien les Bollandistes (*Cat. Paris*, II, p. 74), que Dolbeau (1979, p. 201) datent ce manuscrit du XIIIe siècle.

[23] Huot (2005), p. 18.

sunt, quia et pauciora a nobis intellecta sunt. Si quid autem de corporali per ignorantiam detraximus, de spiritali addere non pigebit, quia in eo detrimentum aut dampnum omnino non erit.

Effectivement, la Vie tout en situant l'existence du saint sous le règne de Charlemagne, en Burgondie, ne dit rien de son origine et de sa jeunesse, mais le présente d'emblée comme un candidat parfait à l'épiscopat. Devenu évêque, sa réputation ne manqua pas de parvenir aux oreilles de l'empereur qui le convoqua à un concile important. À cette occasion, Charlemagne s'accusa lui-même d'un grand crime pour le rachat duquel il demanda à chacun des évêques rassemblés de célébrer des messes. Théodore, malgré la modestie de sa promesse – une seule messe –, obtint par sa ferveur dans la prière qu'au moment de la célébration lui soient révélés le péché du prince et son absolution. De retour auprès de Charlemagne, Théodore informa l'empereur du pardon qu'il avait obtenu. Reconnaissant, celui-ci, à la demande de l'évêque, accorda à l'Église de Sion la *Vallensium prefectura*, que l'évêque souhaitait ne pas voir en mains laïques. Ainsi l'empereur remit à l'évêque le comté du Valais: *eundem comitatum episcopo venerabli Theodoro, suisque successoribus, perpetua stabilitate subnixa contradidit*. À la suite de cet épisode, le saint évêque regagna sa ville, où il put exercer son jugement en toute conscience et réaliser de nombreux miracles.

Ce thème permet au narrateur d'enchaîner avec l'épisode suivant, non sans avoir repris un éloge de Grégoire le Grand qu'il adapte en faveur du bienheureux Théodore[24]. Après une nouvelle adresse à son auditoire, l'auteur rapporte comment, en une année de vendanges maigres, le saint évêque remplit les vases destinés à recevoir le fruit de la vigne d'un excellent vin: c'est le miracle du moût qu'il compare à la multiplication des pains de l'Évangile. Ce récit est suivi par une méditation qui se conclut par l'évocation des deux natures, contemplative et active, de Théodore et sa capacité à révéler ce qui était caché.

Ainsi, se trouve introduit le motif suivant, celui de la découverte des dépouilles des martyrs de la Légion thébaine. L'épisode débute par un bref rappel de la tradition relative au martyre de saint Maurice et de ses compagnons: l'auteur s'attarde quelque peu sur la description du lieu, où, dit-il, les restes

---

[24] HUOT (2005, p. 34) indique comme source la *Règle pastorale* (SC 381-382) et les *Dialogues* (SC 251, 260-265).

des martyrs gisent en proie aux vexations des bêtes sauvages et exposés à l'érosion causée par les eaux du Rhône. L'auteur reprend à ce propos un thème qui lui est cher, celui de l'opposition entre la nature spirituelle des martyrs, qui vivent déjà en Dieu, et la nature charnelle de leurs restes qui reposent dans la terre. C'est Théodore justement qui fut amené à révéler les deux natures des bienheureux martyrs: après avoir contemplé leur gloire dans le ciel, il put découvrir leurs reliques sur terre et leur offrir une demeure digne de leur gloire. L'évocation d'une construction permet à l'auteur d'élaborer une réflexion sur les murs de la Jérusalem céleste, siège des élus au nombre desquels figure le saint évêque Théodore. La Vie se termine par une invocation traditionnelle.

On le voit, la Vie dans son ensemble manifeste un caractère homilétique très marqué: chaque épisode se termine par une réflexion annonçant le suivant, les citations bibliques abondent, permettant de situer l'action du personnage principal dans l'ensemble de la tradition chrétienne et suscitant chez les auditeurs une méditation sur la signification des faits rapportés. Ainsi, il ne semble pas judicieux de chercher à distinguer un auteur pour le prologue et un autre pour les épisodes centraux de la Vie: l'ensemble présente en réalité une très grande unité. Le moine-pèlerin Ruodpert peut donc être considéré comme l'auteur de l'ensemble de la composition [25].

Quant à l'histoire du saint évêque, nous avons vu que le narrateur avouait ne pas avoir beaucoup d'informations sur celle-ci, justifiant ainsi le caractère particulier de la Vie. Jadis, le Père de Gaiffier avait étudié le motif du péché de l'Empereur et de son pardon: son travail montre bien ce que la Vie de Théodule doit à celle de saint Gilles (composée au Xe siècle): le motif est le même, tout comme les modalités de l'aveu et de l'annonce du pardon [26]. Il est donc indéniable que Ruodpert s'est inspiré d'une tradition littéraire qu'il a adaptée en faveur du saint local. L'épisode final, celui qui décrit le rôle de l'évêque en faveur des martyrs d'Agaune, montre que l'inspiration provient également

---

[25] Huot (2005, p. 18) montre que la structure du texte en trois parties, mises en évidence par l'emploi de lettrines au début des différents épisodes, allait fournir à l'Église de Sion les différentes leçons liturgiques des deux fêtes de saint Théodule et servir de source à son Office propre.

[26] de Gaiffier (1955).

de sources hagiographiques, d'origine locale cette fois, en l'occurrence la tradition relative à saint Maurice et ses compagnons. Effectivement, la Passion composée par Eucher de Lyon vers le milieu du Ve siècle précise que les corps des bienheureux martyrs ont été révélés à saint Théodore présenté comme évêque du lieu, c'est-à-dire du Valais: *At vero beatissimorum Acaunensium martyrum corpora post multos passionis annos sancto Theodoro eiusdem loci episcopo revelata traduntur*[27]. Toutefois, le contexte historique évoqué par Ruodpert et sa description des lieux consacrés par le martyre montrent qu'il emprunte de nombreux motifs et citations à la Passion anonyme de saint Maurice[28]. Il est donc très vraisemblable que la tradition sur laquelle il se base avait déjà fusionné les deux textes (Passion d'Eucher et Passion anonyme) afin de constituer un corpus suffisamment important pour fournir des leçons à l'occasion de la commémoration de la saint Maurice à Sion comme à Agaune[29]. Quant au récit du miracle du moût, il est certainement issu d'une tradition locale, qui s'explique par l'importance et les difficultés récurrentes de la culture de la vigne en Valais[30].

Néanmoins, si le moine-pèlerin a pu enrichir son récit d'épisodes empruntés à la tradition hagiographique, il n'a certainement pas totalement inventé ce qu'il rapporte de la vie de l'évêque Théodore. Au contraire, il a dû rassembler les éléments d'une tradition morcelée qui depuis longtemps attribuait au

---

[27] *Passio Acaunensium martyrum*, éd. B. KRUSCH, *MGH, SRM*, III, Hanovre 1884, p. 38.

[28] *Cum rei publice Romane Diocletianus... Qui ibi per angusta Alpium itinera ingressus in loco, cui Aganus nomen est,... planicies campestris habetur...* On trouve des expressions proches dans la Passion anonyme de saint Maurice, CHEVALLEY – RODUIT (2014), p. 82 (l. 1) et p. 83 (l. 3 et 13).

[29] De nombreux témoins de la Passion anonyme contiennent les chapitres d'Eucher consacrés à l'histoire du culte des martyrs et aux miracles opérés par leur intercession. Cf. CHEVALLEY – RODUIT (2014), p. 58-73. C'est en particulier le cas du légendier, Rome, Biblioteca Angelica 1269 provenant de Saint-Maurice d'Agaune, qui contient également la *Vita beati Theodori episcopi Sedunensis*. Il n'est toutefois pas exclu que le récit de la Passion des martyrs d'Agaune ait été si célèbre qu'il finît par constituer une forme de tradition orale.

[30] DUBUIS (1981, p. 137) rappelle qu'à partir du XIVe siècle les bouleversements causés par les intempéries de plus en plus fréquentes expliquent le développement de cette compétence du saint évêque.

saint évêque un rôle central dans les grandes étapes de l'histoire de l'Eglise du Valais.

Effectivement, un culte en l'honneur du saint est attesté à Sion, au moins dès l'époque carolingienne, époque où la crypte de l'église, dédiée, selon la tradition, à saint Théodule, est remaniée de façon à faciliter l'accès à une tombe privilégiée, qui devait contenir les reliques du saint[31]. À la même époque, le rédacteur anonyme de l'Acte de fondation de l'abbaye de Saint-Maurice d'Agaune (fin du VIIIe/début IXe) attribue un rôle important dans la fondation du monastère à l'évêque Théodore: *tunc sanctus Theodorus episcopus Sedunencium ait: Instantia cordis mei est ut proferam sermonem vestris salubribus consiliis quid agendum sit de beatorum martirum thebeorum corporibus...*[32]. L'évêque une fois encore se soucie de la sépulture des saints martyrs. On constate que Théodore est ici censé vivre à l'époque de la fondation de l'abbaye par le roi Sigismond (soit en 515) et s'entretenir avec le prince burgonde et l'évêque Maxime de Genève. Il est alors désigné comme évêque de Sion, à une époque où le souvenir du siège épiscopal d'Octodure s'était éteint[33]. Nous avons ainsi la preuve que dès l'époque carolingienne, au plus tard, celui à qui l'on attribuait l'origine du culte des martyrs thébains était considéré comme évêque de Sion et vénéré dans cette ville. L'auteur de l'Acte de fondation, naturellement lié à l'abbaye d'Agaune, se base sur des sources de natures diverses, parmi lesquelles nous pouvons reconnaître la Vie des Abbés d'Agaune à laquelle il emprunte le personnage de Maxime de Genève ainsi que les noms des évêques cités. Quant à Théodore et son rôle dans le culte des martyrs thébains, il est naturellement inspiré de la Passion des martyrs d'Agaune d'Eucher de Lyon. Nous constatons donc que la figure de Théodore (dès l'origine qualifié de saint), échappant à toute dimension chronologique, se retrouve à deux moments distincts, et cruciaux, de l'histoire de

---

[31] DUBUIS (1981), p. 127. Les fouilles effectuées sous l'église Saint-Théodule ont montré qu'à l'emplacement d'anciens thermes romains utilisé très tôt comme cimetière fut bâtie une église funéraire antérieure à l'époque carolingienne; ce lieu abritait peut-être déjà la sépulture d'un défunt honoré d'un culte.

[32] THEURILLAT (1954); JACCOUD (2013), p. 11.

[33] Selon les signatures apposées aux actes des conciles, le transfert du siège épiscopal de Martigny à Sion eut lieu entre 549 et 585: *Helvetia Sacra*, I, 5, p. 15.

l'abbaye. Il est considéré comme le fondateur, l'instigateur par excellence, du culte des martyrs qui fit la gloire d'Agaune et contribua à l'évangélisation du Valais.

Dans le courant du Xe ou du XIe siècle, l'Église de Sion introduisit des modifications importantes dans les modalités du culte du saint[34]. Les reliques furent alors extraites de la tombe se trouvant dans la crypte et placées dans des reliquaires. Cette nouvelle localisation leur donna une plus grande visibilité, une fois placées sur l'autel, et une certaine mobilité. Il s'agit d'une nouvelle forme de vénération, permettant notamment la participation des reliques aux grandes processions. Il se peut aussi qu'en une période assez agitée, la possibilité de les placer à l'abri dans l'église fortifiée de Valère ait contribué à influencer ce choix[35]. C'est peut-être à cette occasion que fut réalisée la grande châsse de Sion, que l'on peut vraisemblablement identifier avec l'une des deux châsses contenant les reliques de saint Théodule, mentionnées par un inventaire de 1364[36]. En parallèle fut organisée la célébration en l'honneur du saint, comme l'atteste la première mention d'une fête, au 16 août, dans le missel de Granges datant du XIe siècle[37].

Force est donc de constater que le culte du saint connut à cette période un important regain d'intérêt, une nouvelle forme de vénération, l'organisation d'une célébration liturgique. Dans ces circonstances, il n'est pas surprenant que l'on ait cherché à disposer d'une Vie permettant de rassembler ce que l'on savait sur ce personnage qui, depuis longtemps, faisait l'objet d'un culte, mais dont personne n'avait mis par écrit les exploits[38]. Selon Dubuis, il s'agissait essentiellement pour l'Église de Sion de rappeler la vertu de son saint évêque, la pureté et la ferveur de sa foi surpassant le luxe des autres prélats. Il s'agissait aussi de pérenniser le souvenir de l'établissement de l'évêché tel qu'il se présentait alors, à savoir une autorité à la fois spirituelle et

---

[34] DUBUIS (1981), p. 129, n. 27; MORAND – FLÜHLER-KREIS *et al.* (2013), p. 155.

[35] *Ibid.*

[36] HUBER (2005), p. 79-80.

[37] HUOT (1973). Dans le courant du XIIIe siècle une nouvelle célébration, connue sous le nom de *Revelatio Theoduli*, fut introduite au 4 septembre.

[38] *Ibid.*, p. 18: Huot souligne un rapport étroit entre la composition de la Vie et son emploi dans la liturgie: les leçons des deux fêtes de saint Théodule dans l'ordinaire de Sion sont tirées des épisodes distincts de la Vie.

temporelle, dont le souvenir était déjà ancien[39]. C'est aussi la tradition, vivifiée par les sources hagiographiques, qui a fourni à la Vie le rôle de l'évêque dans la quête des corps des martyrs thébains. Ainsi la Vie ne viserait pas tant à légitimer un pouvoir contesté par la réforme grégorienne, mais surtout à montrer que Théodore reste le saint des commencements, le premier bénéficiaire de la donation des droits régaliens, l'instigateur du culte des martyrs thébains[40].

Toutefois, on ne saurait totalement exempter la Vie d'arrière-pensées politiques. De nombreux témoignages attestent, nous l'avons vu, un important renouveau du culte à la fin du XIe siècle, vraisemblablement sous l'épiscopat d'Ermanfroid. Si un lien direct avec la Querelle des Investitures est difficile à démontrer par les textes, reste néanmoins que la Vie insiste expressément sur la légitimité des droits temporels de l'évêque. Elle n'hésite pas à justifier la détention du droit du glaive par l'usage moins sanglant et plus intimidant qu'en ferait un homme d'Église. Cette insistance montre bien que la question n'est pas sans importance au moment de la rédaction de la Vie. De même, le récit de la découverte par Théodule des dépouilles des martyrs d'Agaune peut aussi avoir une implication dans la politique ecclésiastique du temps. En effet, le rôle qu'on lui prête d'«inventeur» et de promoteur du culte lui confère une

---

[39] DUBUIS (1981, p. 129) pense qu'à l'époque carolingienne les évêques de Sion avaient pu bénéficier d'une certaine autorité temporelle dont la tradition aurait gardé le souvenir. Il considère également que la mention de saint Théodule, associée à celle de sainte Marie, comme destinataires de la donation des droits comtaux en faveur de l'Eglise de Sion remonte à une tradition antérieure à la composition de la Vie par Ruodpert. Il s'appuie pour cela sur la donation du comté par le roi Rodolphe III de Bourgogne que l'on connaît par une copie vidimée de 1477: *comitatum vallensem integriter sancte Marie sanctoque Theodolo Sedunensi, cuius tamen studio primum eo loci acquisitus erat, Hugonemque eiusdem loci episcopum presentem...* Si le passage mentionnant Théodule a été considéré avec raison comme une interpolation, Büttener montre qu'il figurait déjà dans le modèle copié en 1477. Il pense plus précisément que l'interpolation serait antérieure à la Vie composée par Ruodpert, car il n'y est pas fait mention de Charlemagne; cf. BÜTTNER (1960). Dubuis, se fondant sur l'ancienneté du culte du saint à Sion, va plus loin et laisse entendre que la mention de Théodule aurait pu déjà se trouver dans l'acte de 999. Voir toutefois COUTAZ (1999) qui pense que l'interpolation mentionnant Théodule a été insérée au moment de la rédaction du vidimus sous l'épiscopat de Walter Supersaxo.

[40] DUBUIS (1981), p. 132-133.

forme d'autorité sur celui-ci, suggérant que sans le saint évêque la victoire des martyrs d'Agaune serait restée totalement ignorée. Ce qui équivaut à placer sous l'autorité, au moins symbolique, de l'Église de Sion un culte dont le noyau se trouvait à l'abbaye de Saint-Maurice d'Agaune. Or, il apparaît qu'au XIe siècle les évêques de Sion ont tenté de mettre la main sur l'abbatiat de Saint-Maurice: Aimon y parvint, après avoir été prévôt, alors qu'Ermanfroid dut, semble-t-il, se contenter d'une simple prébende. Ainsi la figure d'un Théodule évêque de Sion et fondateur du culte des martyrs d'Agaune pouvait servir d'argument de poids aux prétentions des évêques ses successeurs[41].

Qu'un évêque de Sion ait été impliqué dans les affaires de l'Empereur ne devait pas sembler insolite aux Valaisans du XIe siècle: l'activité du chancelier de Bourgogne à la cour pouvait l'expliquer. Peut-être, n'avait-on pas totalement oublié non plus que, dans le passé, des évêques de Sion, abbés également de Saint-Maurice, avaient été proches des princes et de Charlemagne en particulier. C'est le cas justement des prélats qui ont été en quelque sorte évincés par Théodule: Willicaire et Althée[42]. D'ailleurs une tradition attestée par la Chronique de l'abbaye d'Agaune veut que Charlemagne ait séjourné au monastère où, à la suite d'une révélation miraculeuse, il fut invité par l'évêque-abbé, Althée, à célébrer avec lui la messe, ce qu'ils firent pendant quinze jours à la suite desquels l'empereur fit une donation considérable à l'abbaye[43]. Bien que la rédaction de la

---

[41] Dès ses origines, l'abbaye d'Agaune, par sa nature de monastère royal, avait bénéficié de la protection des rois burgondes puis mérovingiens. Cf. HELVÉTIUS (2015). À la suite de la disparition des Rodolphiens, qui avaient porté le titre d'abbés de Saint-Maurice, le pape Léon IX, par un privilège daté du 22 septembre 1050, reprit en quelque sorte cette fonction de protecteur et mit en œuvre des mesures visant à rétablir l'ancien statut de l'établissement. Selon RIPART (2015), il s'agissait en particulier de prémunir la communauté contre les empiètements de l'évêque de Sion, Aimon, qui avait réussi à se faite élire à l'abbatiat de Saint-Maurice. Pour Ripart, c'est l'appartenance d'Aimon à la famille des Humbertiens qui représentait le danger principal. Le cumul des fonctions devait toutefois sembler dangereux à la communauté ce qui explique qu'Ermanfroid n'obtint qu'une prébende.

[42] *Helvetia Sacra*, I, 5, p. 137-139. Sur l'importance des fonctions remplies par Willicaire et Althée voir en dernier lieu HELVÉTIUS (2015), p. 127-130.

[43] JACCOUD (2013), p. 59. La datation de ce passage de la Chronique est délicate: toutefois THEURILLAT (1954, p. 47-53) estime qu'on peut envisager au plus tard le XIIe siècle, car il se retrouve dans une charte de cette

chronique soit difficile à situer, son témoignage montre qu'en Valais Charlemagne était perçu comme un bienfaiteur exceptionnel, notamment en raison des liens qu'il entretenait avec l'évêque de Sion[44]. Cela expliquerait pourquoi la tradition a attribué à l'empereur la donation effectuée par le roi de Bourgogne. Quant aux personnalités des évêques Willicaire et Althée, qui pourtant bénéficiaient d'un grand prestige de leur temps, elles ont été en quelque sorte assimilées par la figure de Théodule dont le culte était solidement établi à Sion. Lui seul devait sembler pouvoir rassembler les principaux événements fondateurs de l'histoire ecclésiatique du Valais.

D. Développement du culte de saint Théodule au Moyen Âge

Dans le courant XIIIe siècle, apparaît une nouvelle fête en l'honneur du saint commémorant au 4 septembre la *Revelatio Theoduli* ou redécouverte des reliques. À cette même époque, un grand nombre de fondations, autels et chapelles, sont dédiées au saint qui, en 1219, est expressément mentionné dans les statuts synodaux de Sion comme patron du diocèse. Doté d'abord de la crosse seule, le saint évêque sera, dès le XVe siècle, représenté muni également du glaive, symbole du pouvoir temporel des évêques de Sion[45]. Le rôle de saint Théodule comme protecteur du diocèse apparaît plus nettement encore lors du conflit avec la Savoie qui se conclut par la victoire valaisanne de la Planta[46]. De façon significative, après la remise du Chablais le 16 mars 1476 par les Bernois, l'ancienne chapelle Saint-Michel qui se trouvait sur la culée du pont de Saint-Maurice est reconstruite sous le vocable de Saint-Théodule, marquant désormais la limite

---

époque. Helvétius (2015, p. 129) se range à cet avis. Werder (1976/1977, p. 401-403) donne une interprétation de cette légende dont elle situe également la composition au XIIe siècle.

[44] Il est difficile de préciser quels rapports unissent les traditions de Sion (Vie de saint Théodule) et d'Agaune (Althée), mais on peut constater que dans les deux cas Charlemagne joue le rôle de bienfaiteur privilégié, à la suite de l'intervention miraculeuse d'un prélat.

[45] Deux études ont été récemment consacrées à la représentation de saint Théodule: Morand, Flühler-Kreis *et al.* (2013) et Elsig (2015).

[46] Truffer (1975). L'armée qui a obtenu cette victoire est nommée par l'évêque Walter Supersaxo *armata militia sancti Theodoli*.

du Valais[47]. Le saint est alors considéré comme le protecteur de l'ensemble du territoire valaisan et comme le garant du pouvoir temporel de l'évêque qui s'étendait désormais sur l'ensemble du diocèse[48].

A la fin du XVe siècle, les vertus du saint évêque furent encore amplifiées par Henri Fischer dans un poème rédigé en allemand à l'intention de l'évêque Josse de Silenen: nous y trouvons en particulier le premier développement littéraire de l'histoire du diable sommé par le saint de le transporter à Rome afin de détourner le pape d'un grave péché et la mention de la récompense reçue du pontife: une cloche miraculeuse, capable de détourner les calamités, qui devint très célèbre même en dehors du Valais[49]. À la fin du Moyen Age, le culte de saint Théodule connut son extension maximale: il était à la fois le protecteur du diocèse, le garant du pouvoir temporel des évêques[50]; il assurait aussi la meilleure protection contre le gel, la grêle et toutes les calamités qui pouvaient affecter les cultures. Sa représentation est désormais fixée avec crosse et glaive, accompagné du diablotin portant la cloche[51].

---

[47] DUBUIS (1981), p. 139, n. 74; MORAND, FLÜHLER-KREIS et al. (2013) p. 164. Pour la diffusion du culte de saint Théodule voir en particulier FOHLEN (2005), p. 39-70. Voir également pour le cas particulier du Voralberg, NACHBAUR (2014).

[48] MORAND, FLÜHLER-KREIS et al. (2013), p. 162-172.

[49] DUBUIS (1981), p. 140-143. La cloche du saint avait la réputation de détenir un si grand pouvoir contre les intempéries qu'on ressentit le besoin de multiplier sa puissance thaumaturgique par l'insertion d'un fragment de la pièce originale dans les nouvelles fontes de cloches. Ainsi à Lucerne en 1397, une particule de la cloche de saint Théodule reçue de l'église de Sion fut mêlée à la fonte d'une nouvelle cloche; cf. DUBUIS (1981), p. 138, n. 62.

[50] Au début du XVIe siècle le cardinal Mathieu Schiner demanda à Charles Quint une confirmation de la Caroline, selon un argumentaire fondé sur la Vie écrite par Ruodpert.

[51] Cette iconographie se retrouve sur les frappes monétaires de l'évêque Mathieu Schiner, dont les thalers, frappés en 1501, présentent une forme d'aboutissement de la vénération du patron du diocèse MORAND, FLÜHLER-KREIS et al. (2013), p. 171-172.

LA PROVINCE DE TARENTAISE 711

E. LA CRITIQUE HISTORIQUE À L'ÉPOQUE MODERNE
ET SES CONSÉQUENCES

Il faudra attendre les travaux de Jean Stumpf, dont la *Chronique* fut publiée en 1547-1548, pour que les idées émises par l'évêché de Sion soient mises en doute. À partir de sources ignorées jusqu'alors, cet érudit rétablit dans le catalogue des évêques de Sion Willicaire, Althée et Abdalon et, de ce fait, ne trouve plus de place pour Théodule à l'époque de Charlemagne. Considérant l'acte de fondation de l'abbaye d'Agaune comme un document authentique, il fait de l'évêque Théodore un contemporain du roi burgonde Sigismond[52]. Dans sa *Description du Valais*, parue en 1574, Josias Simmler reprend cette conclusion et apporte un élément nouveau, oublié depuis longtemps en Valais: la participation d'un évêque d'Octodure nommé *Theodorus* au concile d'Aquilée en 381. Ce personnage lui semble nettement distinct du Théodule contemporain de Sigismond[53].

Si les conclusions des érudits alémaniques furent reçues par les opposants au pouvoir de l'évêque de Sion et contribuèrent à invalider l'autorité de la Caroline comme légitimation des droits épiscopaux[54], elles n'eurent pas d'influence véritable sur le discours officiel de l'Église de Sion. En 1638, le chanoine Jean Stälin dédiait à l'évêque Hildebrand Jost une composition en allemand sur les saints du Valais dans laquelle Théodule occupe une place importante. L'auteur reprend les thèmes principaux de la tradition médiévale auxquels il ajoute quelques précisions comme l'origine familiale de Théodule; il modifie toutefois la légende de la cloche en gommant la faute du pape. En outre Stälin mentionne un Théodore premier évêque de Sion qui vivait sous le pape Damase et les empereurs Gratien et Valens[55]. Finalement les historiens catholiques admirent l'existence de trois évêques distincts: Théodore signataire des actes du concile d'Aquilée, un second Théodore contemporain du roi Sigismond et un troisième Théodore, appelé communément Théodule, à

---

[52] STUMPF (1548), livre XI, fol. 352v.
[53] SIMMLER (1574), comme Stumpf, considère que Charlemagne a cependant pu faire don de quelque pouvoir temporel à l'évêque du Valais en hommage à l'évêque Théodule, mort depuis longtemps mais considéré comme un saint.
[54] DUBUIS (1981), p. 145.
[55] DUBUIS (1981) p. 147-150.

l'époque de Charlemagne[56]. La critique historique finit par battre en brèche cette construction: le contemporain de Charlemagne fut le premier à être relégué au rang de figure légendaire puis ce fut le tour de Théodore II[57]. Depuis lors, seule l'existence de l'évêque d'Octodure attesté à la fin du IVe siècle est admise par les historiens[58].

La légende dont fut auréolée la figure du saint patron du Valais connut au Moyen Age un développement remarquable, hors de toute dimension historique. Dans ce processus, la Vie composée par le moine Ruodpert constitua un jalon fondamental, donnant corps à un culte dont certaines caractéristiques étaient déjà établies. En définitive, si les traditions servant de fondement et de légitimation à l'Église du Valais se sont cristallisées sur la figure du saint évêque Théodore, c'est que son rôle initial dans la découverte des corps des martyrs d'Agaune était resté vivant dans la mémoire collective. La transmission fut assurée par la tradition hagiographique réactivée par la commémoration collective au fil des célébrations. Ainsi, le lien premier entre l'évêché du Valais et le culte des martyrs d'Agaune se trouvait en quelque sorte pérennisé et réactivé en fonction des divers contextes et revendications.

II. Le diocèse d'Aoste

A. La Vie de saint Ours

Parmi les saints du diocèse d'Aoste, la figure d'Ours, prêtre et confesseur, nous est connue par une Vie transmise sous deux rédactions: l'une plus développée (*BHL* 8453) et l'autre plus concise (*BHL* 8453b)[59]. Il ne s'agit pas, en effet, de deux ver-

---

[56] Murer (1648) et della Chiesa (1645). Ces conclusions furent adoptées par l'Église de Sion qui inscrivit à l'*ordo* de 1675 deux nouvelles fêtes en l'honneur de Théodore Ier (26 août) et de Théodore II (27 août).

[57] Besson (1906), p. 7-8, 41 et 117; Theurillat (1954) p. 65 et 70.

[58] Toutefois, la figure du saint évêque, accompagné de son diablotin est loin d'avoir disparu de la tradition populaire valaisanne. Cf. Dubuis (1981), p. 153.

[59] La version brève de la Vie de saint Ours a été éditée par Frutaz (1953 et 1966). La version longue (plus tardive) a été éditée par Jean Bolland dans

sions indépendantes, mais de deux rédactions d'une trame identique. La version b, la plus concise, est la plus ancienne et la version longue une forme d'amplification de la première[60]. Malgré l'importance du culte de saint Ours dans la Vallée d'Aoste[61], la Vie se montre peu généreuse en renseignements précis sur la personnalité du saint. Sa datation est également mal assurée. Selon l'éditeur de la Vie, A. P. Frutaz, l'auteur de celle-ci doit avoir vécu à la fin du VIIIe siècle ou au début du IXe comme l'attestent la qualité de sa langue et sa tournure d'esprit, qu'il compare à celle de Grégoire de Tours. Bien que nous n'ayons aucune information sur son identité (nom, qualité), le rédacteur devait être d'origine valdôtaine, ou du moins avoir composé son texte dans la Vallée, ainsi que l'atteste l'emploi de démonstratifs pour désigner la cité d'Aoste: *Igitur fuit vir Dei confessor in hac Augusta civitate...* (§2) ou la vallée: *Fluvius vero qui iuxta huius loci fines infestare videtur...* (§5) et certainement lié à l'église dont le saint avait été prêtre: *Ita et in huius loci ecclesiam tanta vastitas aquae superabat* (§5)[62].

Le texte de la Vie primitive a connu une diffusion relativement restreinte. Frutaz recense trois témoins de cette version: un manuscrit de Farfa (IXe/Xe s.), un manuscrit du Latran (XIe s.) et un témoin provenant de l'abbaye bénédictine de Saint-Matthias de Trèves (XVIe s.)[63]. Quant à la rédaction longue, qui s'est imposée dans la Vallée, elle est en particulier

---

les *AASS*, Feb. I, 2ª ed., Venise, 1735, p. 97-99. Elle est publiée, accompagnée d'une traduction française par Boson (1929). Il faut noter toutefois que Mgr Frutaz a mené l'étude la plus rigoureuse et la mieux documentée de l'ensemble de la question.

[60] Frutaz (1953, p. 310-311) illustre par deux exemples l'exercice d'amplification littéraire auquel s'est livré l'auteur de la version longue. Celui-ci a cependant ajouté un prologue de son cru situant l'action du saint dans la cité d'Aoste au temps du cruel évêque Ploceanus. Ce prologue présente une description détaillée de la ville et de la Vallée, précisant le nom des deux rivières qui entourent la plaine: *Duria videlicet et Bautegius*. Ces précisions toponymiques attestent vraisemblablement l'origine locale du rédacteur.

[61] Le monastère, puis collégiale, des Saints-Pierre-et-Ours joua un rôle très important dans l'histoire religieuse et culturelle de la Vallée.

[62] Frutaz (1966), p. 162. Dans son étude antérieure (1953, p. 315), Frutaz considérait toutefois l'auteur de la version courte comme étranger à la Vallée, en particulier en raison de son ignorance du nom des rivières dont le saint arrêta la crue.

[63] Frutaz (1953), p. 306.

connue par le légendier datant du XIVᵉ siècle de la collégiale Saints-Pierre-et-Ours d'Aoste[64]. La version longue a vraisemblablement été aussi élaborée dans le centre du culte de saint Ours. Le travail de réécriture a porté essentiellement sur trois aspects: l'ajout d'une introduction, qui situe l'action du saint sous l'épiscopat du perfide et cruel Ploceanus (selon la leçon du manuscrit de la collégiale) en faisant référence au texte de la Vie. L'introduction contient également une description de la vallée qui permet de mieux faire comprendre une intervention miraculeuse du saint lors d'une inondation mettant en péril la ville d'Aoste; l'auteur précise à ce propos les noms des deux cours d'eau qui encerclent la plaine[65]. De même, le rédacteur s'est plu à enrichir la narration soit en amplifiant certaines expressions (ajout de synonymes, d'expressions ampoulées), soit en ajoutant des citations bibliques pour renforcer la parfaite adéquation de l'action du saint avec le message évangélique. Ainsi, à partir du deuxième paragraphe de la Vie primitive, où figure déjà une citation biblique, la version longue poursuit: *Humilitas vero et misericordia semper inventae fuerunt in eo iuxta Salvatoris vocem dicentis: Beati humiles, beati misericordes*[66]. La réécriture vise également à modifier une tournure qui peut sembler erronée ou trop particulière, comme au début du chapitre 7: la version brève introduit un épisode en faisant référence au précédent et dit: *Cumque vir Dei memoratas aviculas annonaret et resideret in atriis dominorum sanctorum martyrum...* La forme verbale *annonaret*, qui rappelle le monde de l'Antiquité tardive, a été remplacée par la tournure: *Cumque aves superius nominatas aleret et resideret ante januam ecclesiae...* On le voit, la réécriture tend à simplifier et normaliser le vocabulaire. De la même façon, la version longue nomme l'église desservie par le saint *ecclesia sancti Petri*, alors que la version courte lui confère l'appellation de *loca sanctorum, limina sanctorum* (§3), *in atriis dominorum sanctorum martyrum* (§7), *concilia dominorum sanctorum martyrum* (§7), *concilia sanctorum* (§8),

---

[64] *Ibid.*, p. 305-323: à la liste de manuscrits décrits dans la publication de 1953, FRUTAZ (1966, p. 162) ajoute un témoin supplémentaire conservé à Novare.

[65] FRUTAZ (1953), p. 312. Dans le récit du miracle transmis par la version longue, le torrent dont la crue menace la ville (anonyme dans la version primitive) porte le nom de Buthier.

[66] BOSON (1929), p. 10-11: les exemples de ce genre sont extrêmement nombreux.

sanctorum ecclesiam (§8). Ce type d'appellation peut se référer à une crypte ou confession où reposent les corps de plusieurs saints, martyrs et confesseurs. Ainsi la version brève atteste que le vénérable Ours desservait une église cémétériale, située comme il se doit en dehors de la cité[67].

B. Structure et contenu

Dans une brève introduction, l'auteur de la Vie annonce son projet: rappeler l'action de Dieu à travers les vertus de son élu. Ainsi, il dit avoir fait un choix parmi de nombreux exemples de miracles du saint dont il présente l'ascèse comme une réalisation du martyre non sanglant. Les deux chapitres suivants décrivent de façon globale les vertus de saint Ours, insistant sur son humilité, sa charité, son assiduité à la prière: lorsqu'il se rend à l'église muni du signe de la croix, les portes du sanctuaire s'ouvrent d'elles-mêmes. La Vie évoque ensuite le travail manuel de l'homme de Dieu, consacré à la culture d'une vigne qu'il avait lui-même plantée. Elle produit un vin capable d'obtenir la guérison de toute maladie. Suivent quelques épisodes plus importants: l'un rapporte comment, par la prière, le saint obtint lors d'une terrible inondation que la rivière regagne son cours normal, sauvant ainsi toute la vallée, le suivant rapporte l'attention du saint à l'égard des oiseaux auxquels il abandonnait une partie de sa moisson. De ce fait, il était toujours entouré de ces créatures célestes, voletant autour de sa tête et se posant dans sa main.

Alors qu'il nourrissait les oiseaux, Ours vit un palefrenier à la recherche d'une monture qu'il avait perdue. Le saint lui demande alors la raison de son passage fréquent et de son inquiétude. Le jeune homme lui révèle son angoisse à l'idée d'avoir

---

[67] Frutaz (1953), p. 312-313. En dehors des murs de la ville, entre la porte prétorienne et l'arc de l'empereur Auguste, se trouvait un important lieu de sépulture de la communauté chrétienne: les restes d'une remarquable église cruciforme y ont été mis au jour (église Saint-Laurent qui servait de nécropole aux évêques de la cité): de ce cimetière provient la très belle épitaphe de l'évêque Gallus, mort le 5 octobre 526, déposée ensuite dans le chœur de la collégiale Saints-Pierre-et-Ours. De même, on a reconnu, sous l'église romane de Saint-Ours, les restes d'un édifice remontant au Ve siècle que Charles Bonnet propose d'identifier avec l'église des martyrs mentionnée à plusieurs reprises dans la Vie de saint Ours: Bonnet, Perinetti (1986).

laissé partir le cheval préféré de son maître. Le saint l'invite à la prière, puis lui fait voir le cheval égaré. Ours encourage alors le jeune homme à fréquenter avec assiduité l'église des saints. Suit un épisode qui relate une nouvelle intervention du saint en faveur d'un serviteur de l'évêque Plotianus (présenté comme évêque d'Aoste). Le jeune homme qui avait commis une faute et redoutait un châtiment de la part de son maître, avait pris la fuite et cherché refuge dans l'église des saints dont Ours était le desservant. Il supplia le saint homme d'intercéder en sa faveur auprès de l'évêque, ce que fit Ours. L'évêque l'assura de son pardon, mais fit saisir le jeune homme : il ordonna ensuite qu'on le frappe presque à mort et, après l'avoir tondu, qu'on lui verse de la poix brûlante sur la tête, se comportant davantage en tyran cruel qu'en chrétien. Le serviteur, rejoignant péniblement le saint, lui révèle ses malheurs. Profondément attristé, Ours le renvoie auprès de l'évêque pour lui annoncer sa mort prochaine et sa réprobation. Il l'encourage également à se préparer à la mort et l'informe qu'ils se retrouveront devant le tribunal de Dieu et que lui-même assisterait à leur audience. La nuit suivante l'évêque mourut, suivi du serviteur. Peu de jours après, le saint, toujours fidèle à la prière, quitta ce monde pour rejoindre le Seigneur et ses élus, dont les saints Sévère et Julien.

On le voit, fort peu d'éléments de ce récit permettent de le situer dans une époque précise. La mention du cruel Plotianus, expressément désigné comme évêque d'Aoste, pourrait fournir quelque indice. En fait, il semble que l'existence de ce prélat ne soit attestée par aucune autre source[68]: on a pensé toutefois retrouver en cette figure négative le souvenir d'un évêque arien et dater l'ensemble de la Vie d'une période où le nord de l'Italie était encore concerné par l'hérésie. Tout cela, de même qu'une tradition voulant que saint Ours ait rejoint le ciel en 529, permettrait de dater la composition du début du VIIe siècle[69]. Selon Frutaz, aucun indice sérieux ne permet de faire de Plotianus un arien, il s'agit tout simplement d'un homme particulière-

---

[68] DUCHESNE (1907, p. 247-248), ne le mentionne même pas. Plotianus figure, en revanche, dans une liste d'évêques retenus par FRUTAZ (1966, p. 14): son épiscopat se situerait entre le VIe et le VIIIe siècle.
[69] *L'insigne collégiale d'Aoste*, p. 24-25. Pour l'auteur, la mention des saints Sévère et Jules (selon le texte transmis par la version longue) qui seraient, l'un, l'évêque Sévère de Ravenne et, pour le second, l'évêque Jules d'Orta (Ve siècle) confirmerait une datation ancienne de la Vie.

ment cruel, tels certains évêques dont Grégoire de Tours dénonce la méchanceté[70].

Malgré le manque de précision sur l'année de la mort du saint, la commémoration de son *dies natalis*, au 1er février, semble bien établie par la tradition liturgique et confirmée par le témoignage de la Vie (§ 10) qui associe précisément le saint confesseur aux prêtres Sévère et Julien (ou Jules): *Talia perseverans confessor Domini migravit ad Dominum... adiunctus est et sacerdotibus Christi Severo et Iuliano, qui ab hodierna die in pace dominica in aeterna requie praecesserunt...* Selon Frutaz, qui propose de remplacer le nom de Julien par celui de Jules, attesté par une leçon du manuscrit de Saint-Matthias de Trèves, Ours aurait été associé à ces deux saints essentiellement en raison de la date de leur mort: en effet, l'évêque Sévère de Ravenne est mort un 1er février et le prêtre Jules d'Orta un 31 janvier[71].

Cependant, la tradition historiographique affirmant que le bienheureux Ours a rejoint sa demeure céleste en 529 semble une conjecture peu fondée[72]. Une autre tradition, très répandue, veut que saint Ours ait été originaire d'Irlande, patrie de bon nombre d'ascètes. Frutaz a de nouveau montré que cette tradition n'était pas antérieure à 1554 et qu'elle est une pure invention de la part du chanoine Jean Louis Vaudan[73]. La copie de la version longue de la Vie du saint confesseur envoyée aux Bollandistes par le père Turinetti avait intégré cette interpolation, lui donnant un forme d'autorité malgré les doutes exprimés par Bolland lui-même[74].

En revanche, la Vie présente plusieurs facettes d'un cadre ecclésiastique et spirituel ancien, vraisemblablement emprunté à

---

[70] FRUTAZ (1966), p. 290. On peut néanmoins envisager que l'image négative de l'évêque transmise par la Vie témoigne d'une forme de réserve face à un pouvoir épiscopal perçu comme autoritaire et mondain.

[71] FRUTAZ (1953), p. 314.

[72] Cette date est à l'origine de la commémoration du 14e centenaire en 1929; cf. BOSON (1929), p. 5.

[73] FRUTAZ (1953, p. 321-323), dresse la liste des biographies du saint qui insistent sur son origine irlandaise. La tradition affirmant l'origine insulaire du saint et le contexte arien de la Vie de saint Ours se trouve aussi dans BERTHET (1951), p. 13-15.

[74] FRUTAZ (1953), p. 322-323: l'éditeur pense que l'on a attribué au saint valdôtain une origine irlandaise parce que le 1er février, date de la commémoration de sa mort, coïncidait avec celle d'une célèbre sainte irlandaise, Brigitte de Kildare.

une tradition autorisée, si la rédaction de la version brève n'est pas antérieure à la fin du VIIIe siècle. Elle révèle en particulier la fonction du saint confesseur, véritable desservant d'une église funéraire édifiée hors les murs de la cité, église qui sera par la suite dédiée à Saint-Pierre-et-Saint-Ours. Cette église fut transformée en collégiale et joua un rôle important dans le développement du culte de son saint patron. Diverses représentations du saint sont inspirées de la Vie, notamment un extraordinaire chapiteau du cloître de la collégiale qui offre un authentique récit en images de ses exploits, accompagné de légendes explicatives[75]. Le saint est fréquemment représenté dans la statuaire de la collégiale, portant une bible avec, parfois, un oiseau perché sur son épaule[76]. Son culte s'est essentiellement diffusé dans les diocèses d'Aoste, Ivrée et Vercelli et en Valais: saint Ours y est invoqué comme protecteur des campagnes, contre les dangers d'inondation, contre la sécheresse et contre les maladies[77].

Bibliographie

BERTHET, A., «Le cloître de la collégiale et la graphie des chapiteaux des prophètes», *Mélange de documents historiques et hagiographiques valdôtains. Miscellanea Augustana*, Aoste, 1951, p. 11-30.

BESSON, M., *Recherches sur les origines des évêchés de Genève, Lausanne et Sion*, Fribourg – Paris, 1906.

BONNET, C. – PERINETTI, R., «Les premiers édifices chrétiens d'Augusta Praetoria (Aoste, Italie)», *Comptes rendus des séances de l'Académie des inscriptions et Belles lettres*, Paris, 1986, p. 489-493.

BOSON, G., *L'insigne collégiale d'Aoste. En souvenir du XIVe centenaire de St. Ours, fondateur de la collégiale*, Ivrée, 1929, p. 9-23.

BÜTTNER, H., «Zur Urkunde des Königs Rudolf III. Von Burgund aus dem Jahre 999 für das Bistum Sitten», *Zeitschrift für schweizerische Kirchengeschichte*, 54 (1960), p. 158-163.

CHEVALLEY, E. – RODUIT, C., *La mémoire hagiographique de l'abbaye de Saint-Maurice d'Agaune*, Lausanne, 2014 (Cahiers lausannois d'histoire médiévale, 53).

---

[75] BERTHET (1951), p. 20.
[76] BOSON (1929), p. 21.
[77] Les visites pastorales montrent qu'au XVe siècle quatre églises du diocèse d'Aoste étaient dédiées à saint Ours: MORAND, FLÜHLER-KREIS *et al.* (2013), p. 35-37.

Coutaz, G., «La donation des droits comtaux à l'évêque de Sion en 999: un texte dévalué de l'histoire du Valais», *Vallesia*, 54 (1999), p. 31-67.

de Gaiffier, B., «La légende de Charlemagne. Le péché de l'empereur et son pardon», dans *Recueil de travaux offerts à M. Clovis Brunel*, Paris, 1955, p. 490-503.

della Chiesa, F. A., *Chronologica historia cardinalium, episcoporum et abbatum Pedemontanae regionis*, Turin, 1645.

Dolbeau, F., «Anciens possesseurs des manuscrits hagiographiques latins conservés à la Bibliothèque nationale de Paris», *Revue d'histoire des textes*, 9 (1979), p. 183-238.

Dubuis, F.-O., «Saint Théodule, patron du diocèse de Sion et fondateur du premier sanctuaire d'Agaune», *Annales Valaisannes*, 2e série, 56 (1981), p. 123-159.

Duchesne, L., *Fastes épiscopaux de l'ancienne Gaule*, I: *Provinces du Sud-Est*, 2e éd., Paris, 1907.

Elsig, P., «L'image de saint Théodule, un exemple de récupération politique», dans S. Abbaléa – F. Elsig, éd., *L'image des saints dans les Alpes occidentales. Actes du colloque international tenu au Musée d'Art et d'Histoire de Genève (17-18 juin 2013)*, Rome, 2015, p. 155-166.

Foerster, H., «Zur *Vita sancti Theodori Sedunensis episcopi*», *Zeitschrift für Schweizerische Kirchengeschichte*, 33 (1939), p. 233-240.

Fohlen, F., «Recherches sur saint Théodule, évêque de Sion en Valais», dans K. Anheuser – C. Werner dir., *La Grande Châsse de Sion*, Paris, 2005, p. 39-70.

Frutaz, A. P., «Redazione inedita della *Vita Beati Ursi presbyteri et confessoris de Augusta Civitate*», *Mélanges historiques et hagiographiques valdôtains*, t. II, Aoste, 1953, p. 305-330.

—, *Le Fonti per la storia della Valle d'Aosta*, Roma, 1966, p. 162-167.

Helvetia Sacra, I, 5: *Le diocèse de Sion*, P. Braun – B. Degler-Spengler – E. Gilomenen-Schenkel, éd., Bâle, 2001.

Helvétius, A.-M., «L'abbaye d'Agaune de la fondation de Sigismond au règne de Charlemagne (515-814)», dans B. Andenmatten – L. Ripart, dir., *L'abbaye de Saint-Maurice d'Agaune 515-2015*, I: *Histoire et archéologie*, Gollion, 2015, p. 111-133.

Huber, J., «La Grande Châsse de Sion et la Querelle des Investitures», dans K. Anheuser – C. Werner, dir., *La Grande Châsse de Sion*, Paris 2005, p. 73-97.

Huot, F., *L'ordinaire du diocèse de Sion. Étude sur sa transmission manuscrite, son cadre historique et sa liturgie*, Fribourg, 1973.

—, «*Vita beati Theodori episcopi Sedunensis*. Légende de saint Théodule. Introduction, édition et notes», dans K. Anheuser – C. Werner, dir., *La Grande Châsse de Sion*, Paris, 2005, p. 17-36.

JACCOUD, S., *Acte de fondation de l'abbaye de St-Maurice d'Agaune*, Mémoire de Maîtrise universitaire, Lausanne, 2013.

LUTHER, J., «Kanzler, Bischof, Legat. Leben und Nachwirken des Bischofs Ermenfried von Sitten», *Blätter aus der Walliser Geschichte*, 48 (2016), p. 173-234.

MORAND, M.-C. – FLÜHLER-KREIS, D. – SYBURRA-BERTELLETTO, R. – PROVIDOLI, S. – ELSIG, P., «La croix et le glaive. Saints et politique en Valais», dans S. BAIOCCO – M. C. MORAND, dir., *Des saints et des hommes. L'image des saints dans les Alpes occidentales à la fin du Moyen Age*, Milan, 2013, p. 154-181.

MURER, H., *Helvetia sancta, H. Schweizer Land, seu paradisus sanctorum Helvetiae florum...*, Luzern, 1648.

NACHBAUR, U., «Der heilige Bischof Theodul. Von der Urkundenfälschung bis zur Käsewerbung», *Montfort. Zeitschrift für Geschichte Vorarlbergs*, 66-1 (2014), p. 5-81.

—, «Der heilige Bischof Theodul als Leitfossil der Walserforschung und Markenzeichen des neuen Walsertums», *Montfort. Zeitschrift für Geschichte Vorarlbergs*, 66-2 (2014), p. 5-125.

RIPART, L., «Le temps des réformes (de l'an mil au début du XIIIe siècle) », dans B. ANDENMATTEN – L. RIPART, dir., *L'abbaye de Saint-Maurice d'Agaune 515-2015*, I: *Histoire et archéologie*, Gollion, 2015, p. 159-161.

SIMMLER, J., *Vallesiae descriptio*, Zürich, 1574.

STUMPF, J., *Gemeiner loblicher Eydgnoschaft Stetten, Landen, und Völckeren chronickwirdiger thaaten beschreybung*, Zürich, 1548.

THEURILLAT, J.-M., «L'Abbaye de Saint-Maurice d'Agaune des origines à la réforme canoniale, 515-830», *Vallesia*, 9 (1954), p. 1-128.

TRUFFER, B., *La bataille de la Planta (500e anniversaire)*, Sion, 1975 (Sedunum nostrum, 12).

WERDER, M., «Das Nachleben Karls des Grossen im Wallis», *Blätter aus der Walliser Geschichte*, 16 (1976/1977), p. 316-476.

L'écriture hagiographique dans le diocèse de Besançon*

par

Anne Wagner

I. Les Vies de disciples de Colomban.
II. Les passions de martyrs.
Bibliographie.

L'hagiographie dans le diocèse de Besançon[1] a connu une floraison précoce avec la Vie des Pères du Jura mais, à l'époque carolingienne, la production hagiographique est très limitée: elle se développe très modestement selon deux axes: la promotion de la vie monastique à travers des disciples directs ou indirects de Colomban et la création de martyrs locaux[2].

I. Les Vies de disciples de Colomban

Sous l'influence des fondations de Colomban, en particulier Luxeuil qui garde un grand prestige[3], l'écriture hagiographique s'efforce donc de consolider, voire de créer, des liens avec l'action de Colomban et de ses disciples.

---

* Au Moyen Âge, Besançon était à la tête d'une province ecclésiastique qui comprenait au sud le diocèse de Belley où, à l'abbaye Saint-Rambert-en-Bugey, était inhumé Rambert, qui fut l'objet de l'écriture d'une *Vita* et dont le culte s'est diffusé depuis Lyon (cf. *supra*, « Le diocèse de Lyon », par M.-C. Isaïa, p. 588-589), à l'est, le diocèse d'Avenche-Lausanne, pour lequel aucune source hagiographique n'a été repérée pour le haut Moyen-Âge et enfin, au-delà de la *Gallia*, le diocèse de Bâle.

[1] Moyse (1973), en part. p. 47-48 pour Ermenfroy et Desle; de Vrégille (1958-59); Zinzius (1927).

[2] Pour le diocèse de Besançon, Usuard, comme Florus et Adon, ne connaît qu'un seul saint, Eustaise, abbé de Luxeuil, cf. Dubois (1965), p. 90.

[3] Wagner (2016).

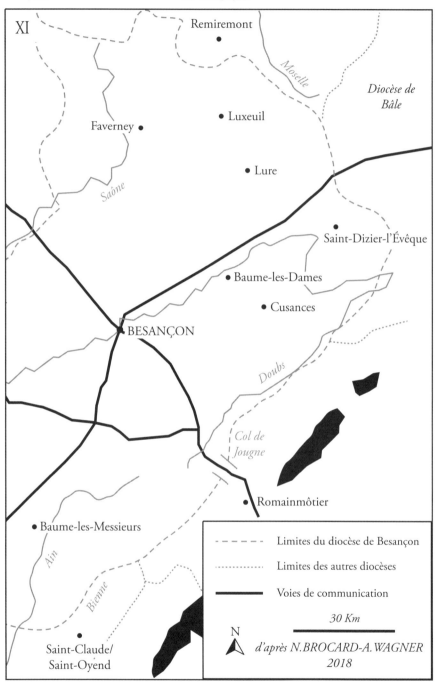

Lieux mentionnés dans le chapitre sur le diocèse de Besançon

La Vie d'Ermenfroy (*Hermenfredus*, BHL 2608), abbé de Cusance vers 670, fut sans doute écrite à Luxeuil à l'époque carolingienne: le nom de l'auteur, Egilbertus, se lit dans la liste relative à Luxeuil du livre de confraternité de Reichenau[4], les noms de deux des quatre dédicataires Leotricus et Mellinus sont mentionnés dans une lettre du moine de Luxeuil Angelomus, écrite vers 840-850[5]. Toutefois, l'auteur prétend avoir connu sept des disciples d'Ermenfroy qui l'ont élevé, ce qui placerait la rédaction au milieu du VIIIe siècle (à moins que l'hagiographe ne reprenne les termes d'une Vie plus ancienne). Ce récit a pour objet de défendre les droits de Luxeuil sur la *cella* de Cusance en soulignant le rôle d'Eustaise, successeur de Colomban à Luxeuil, dans sa fondation: c'est Eustaise qui aurait persuadé un Warasque[6] de rompre un mariage incestueux et de fonder le monastère de Cusance pour sa femme et sa fille, Islia, qui laissa une réputation de sainteté. L'hagiographe relie habilement ce monastère à un aristocrate désigné par Jonas de Bobbio (le biographe de Colomban) comme un disciple de celui-ci, Waldelène[7]: dans la Vie d'Ermenfroy, Waldelène, avec son frère Ermenfroy *nutritus* à la cour de Clothaire II puis chancelier du roi, prend le monastère sous sa protection. Ermenfroy devint ensuite moine à Luxeuil, puis abbé de Cusance qu'il soumit à Luxeuil[8].

---

[4] *MGH, Necrologia Germaniae*, Suppl.: *Libri confraternitatum Sancti Galli, Augiensis, Fabariensis*, éd. P. PIPER, Berlin, 1884, p. 217, col. 208 et 209 et *Libri memoriales et necrologia. Nova series*, 1: *Das Verbrüderungsbuch der Abtei Reichenau*, éd. J. AUTENRIETH, D. GEUENICH et K. SCHMID, Hanovre, 1979, Fac-simile p. 53, col. A et B.

[5] Éd. E. DÜMMLER, *MGH, Epist.*, V, Berlin, 1899, p. 620.

[6] Emprunts à la *Vita Columbani et discipulorum eius* qui montre Eustaise en prédication contre les Warasques: *Vita Columbani*, II, 8 (éd. B. Krusch, *MGH, SRG in usum scholarum*, XXXVII, Hanovre – Leipzig, 1905, p. 243-244): *Progressus ergo Warasquos praedicat, quorum alii idololatriis cultibus diditi, alii Fotini uel Bonosi maculati sunt*.

[7] *Ibid.*, I, 14, p. 174-176.

[8] Y. FOX (2014, p. 101-108) ne mentionne pas, à raison, Ermenfroy, dans la synthèse qu'il effectue des données sur cette famille que Jonas évoque sans toutefois bien la connaître (GAILLARD, 2018); quel que soit le talent de l'hagiographe d'Ermenfroy, il paraît difficile de mesurer la valeur historique de ses propos qui témoignent davantage du prestige de la *Vita Columbani* et de ses héros que de l'histoire de la région. Analyse fine et circonstanciée sur les Warasques et sur la Vie d'Ermenfroy dans DUMÉZIL (2018); voir aussi GEORGY (2013).

Plus tardive, la *Vita Deicoli* (*BHL* 2120-2121), dont les plus anciens manuscrits datent du XIIe siècle[9], s'efforce de placer son héros, Desle, fondateur du monastère de Lure, dans la lignée colombanienne. L'abbé Desles n'est pas attesté auparavant, cependant un abbé *Deicolus* est un des dédicataires de la Vie de saint Germain de Moutier-Grandval (*BHL* 3167), écrite par Bobolenus, dès le VIIe siècle. La Vie de Desle a été commanditée par l'abbé de Lure, Werdolf († 1016) mais rien ne permet d'affirmer qu'elle ait été écrite à Lure ou dans le diocèse de Besançon[10]. L'auteur fait feu de tout bois (utilisation de la Vie de Colomban, des Vies carolingiennes de saint Gall et de celle de saint Goar...) pour inscrire Desle dans la lignée de Colomban; pour l'époque carolingienne, il rattache l'abbaye à la famille des Étichonides, ce qui semble bien correspondre à la réalité[11].

II. LES PASSIONS DE MARTYRS

Comme l'a remarqué Gérard Moyse[12], «l'hagiographie comtoise possède un groupe caractéristique de martyrs, ceux dont la mort est attribuée à des brigands attirés par les objets précieux», et qui, ajouterons-nous, étaient tous des clercs (évêques, prêtres, diacres)[13].

Le récit du martyre de Dizier et Raimfroid (*Desiderius et Reginfridus*, *BHL* 2147) remonte probablement à l'époque carolingienne puisque, en 737, Dizier était l'objet d'un culte, comme l'atteste une charte du comte Eberhard qui donne au monastère

---

[9] Paris, BnF, lat. 16734 et lat. 17005, Dijon, BM 643 et Montpellier, BIU H. 1, t. 4.

[10] La Vie de Desle contient des passages élogieux sur Trèves, ce qui conduit à supposer que son auteur était un moine de Trèves; en la comparant avec les autres œuvres de Thierry, moine de Saint-Euchaire de Trèves, THOMAS (1966/1967) lui a attribué l'écriture de la Vie de Desle qu'il aurait écrite avant d'arriver à Trèves et alors qu'il aurait été moine à Lure; KRÖNERT (2010, p. 140-141) a souligné que cette attribution, qui ne repose que sur des hypothèses, est peu convaincante; la Vie a pu aussi être écrite par un moine de Lure originaire de Trèves.

[11] HUMMER (2006), p. 225-226; GIRARDOT (1946 et 1970).

[12] MOYSE (1973), p. 40-41.

[13] WAGNER (2006); JEANNIN (1988). La transformation de crimes de droit commun en martyres n'est pas l'apanage de la Franche-Comté: BOZOKY (2011).

de Murbach une église dédiée à Dizier[14]. À Saint-Dizier-l'Évêque près de Montbéliard on conserve un sarcophage de la fin du VIIe ou du début du VIIIe siècle[15]. Les reliques furent transférées avant 1041 à Murbach. Ce récit a sans doute inspiré celui de la Passion de Bertaire et Atalein (*Bertharius et Atalenus, BHL* 1272-1273), vénérés à Bleurville, prieuré de Saint-Mansuy de Toul au XIIe siècle, et qui sont censés avoir été martyrisés à Favernay, en 766, sous le règne du roi Pépin. De la même veine, la *Passio* de Maimbœuf (*Maimbodus, BHL* 5176) a sans doute été écrite après l'élévation des reliques du saint dans l'église Saint-Pierre de Montbéliard, au temps de l'archevêque de Besançon, Béranger († 930), qui avait retrouvé son siège en 924 après avoir été aveuglé par son concurrent Aymin, en 895[16]. Aucun élément ne permet de dater ce texte qui, vraisemblablement, a pu être rédigé dans l'entourage de Béranger, mais peut être aussi bien plus tardif[17] et rédigé à une époque où la littérature hagiographique prend son essor à Besançon, en particulier dans l'entourage d'Hugues de Salins[18].

Bibliographie

Bonnassie, P. – Sigal, P. A. – Iogna-Prat, D., «Gallia du Sud, 930-1130», in *Hagiographies*, I (1994), p. 329-331.

Bozoky, E., «La rumeur de sainteté dans l'hagiographie des 'martyrs de faits divers'», in M. Billoré – M. Soria, dir., *La rumeur au Moyen Âge, Du mépris à la manipulation, V[e]-XVe siècle*, Rennes, 2011, p. 191-300.

---

[14] Éd. W. Levison, *Neues Archiv*, 27 (1901), p. 379: *ubi sanctus Desiderius in corpore requiescit*; donation confirmée par Conrad Ier le 12 mars 913 (éd. T. Sickel, *MGH, Diplomata regum et imperatorum Germaniae*, I, Hanovre, 1879, n° 17, p. 16-17).

[15] Jeannin (1994).

[16] Demotz (2008) p. 120, 150 et 204-205; dans l'édition de Chifflet, il est précisé que Béranger fut guéri de sa cécité par Maimboeuf (*AASS*, Ian. II, 1643, p. 544, note q).

[17] C'est l'opinion de G. Moyse (1973, p. 41) qui date ce récit du XIe siècle; l'édition des Bollandistes est issue de la *descriptio* d'anciens manuscrits bisontins par F. Chifflet et aucun manuscrit n'en subsiste.

[18] de Vrégille (1983), p. 196-197; Bonnassie – Sigal – Iogna-Prat (1994), p. 329-331; Wagner (2018).

Demotz, F., *La Bourgogne, dernier des royaumes carolingiens: 855-1056; roi, pouvoirs et élites autour du Léman*, Lausanne, 2008.

de Vrégille, B., «Besançon et ses vieux saints», *Académie des Sciences Belles Lettres et Arts de Besançon*, 173 (1958-1959), p. 123-137.

—, *Hugues de Salins, archevêque de Besançon, 1031-1066*, 3 vol., Lille, 1983

Dubois, J., *Le Martyrologe d'Usuard: texte et commentaire*, Bruxelles, 1965 (Subsidia hagiographica, 40).

Dumézil, B., «La chasse aux Bonosiens en Burgondie, v^e-viie siècle: une affaire d'hérésie?», in I. Rosé – F. Mercier éd., *Aux marges de l'hérésie, Inventions, formes et usages polémiques de l'accusation d'hérésie au Moyen Âge*, Rennes, 2018, p. 187-199.

Fox, Y., *Power and religion in Merovingian Gaul: Columbanian Monasticism and the Frankish Elites*, Cambridge, 2014.

Gaillard, M., «Colomban, un *peregrinus* bien informé», in *Colomban et son influence. Moines et monastères du haut Moyen Âge en Europe*, S. Bully – A. Dubreucq – A. Bully, éd., Rennes, 2018, p. 211-223.

Georgy, P., *Vie de saint Ermenfroy*, Mémoire de Master, Université de Franche-Comté, Besançon, 2013 (dactylographié).

Girardot, J., *La Vie de Saint Desle et les origines de l'abbaye de Lure*, Lure, 1946.

—, *L'abbaye et la ville de Lure. Des origines à 1870*, Vesoul, 1970 (Facsimile, Paris, Le livre d'histoire, 2005).

Hummer, H. J., *Politics and power in early medieval Europe: Alsace and the Frankish Realm, 600-1000*, Cambridge, 2005.

Jeannin, Y., «Des morts célèbres (et célébrés): saints comtois d'avant l'an mil», in *La mort à travers l'archéologie franc-comtoise*, Besançon, 1988, p. 103-106.

—, «Saint-Dizier-l'Évêque (Terr, de Belfort). Église Saint-Dizier», *Archéologie médiévale*, 24 (1994), p. 459-460.

Krönert, K., *L'exaltation de Trèves, Écriture hagiographique et passé historique de la métropole mosellane (viiie-xie siècle)*, Ostfildern, 2010 (Beihefte der Francia, 70).

Moyse, G., «Les origines du monachisme dans le diocèse de Besançon (v^e-xe siècles)», *Bibliothèque de l'École des Chartes*, 131 (1973), p. 21-104.

Thomas, H., «Das Mönch Theoderich von Trier und die *Vita Deicoli*», *Rheinisches Vierteljahresblätter*, 31 (1966/1967), p. 42-63.

Wagner, A., «Meurtres dans les Vosges: pèlerins et martyrs de l'époque carolingienne au xie siècle», *Les cahiers lorrains*, 3/4 (2006), p. 16-21.

—, «Disciples de Colomban en Lorraine et Franche-Comté», in *Le monachisme luxovien à l'époque de saint Eustaise, colloque de Luxeuil 2016*, Les Cahiers Colombaniens, 2016, p. 94-99.

—, «Les évêques de Besançon», in WAGNER, A. – N. BROCARD, éd., *Les royaumes de Bourgogne jusque 1032 à travers la culture et la religion*, Turnhout, 2018 (Culture et société médiévales, 30).

ZINZIUS, H., «Untersuchungen über Heiligenleben der Diözese Besançon», *Zeitschrift fur Kirchengeschichte*, 46 (1927), p. 384-385.

Au-delà de la *Gallia*

L'hagiographie en Germanie (env. 750-950)

suppléments à Klüppel (*Hagiographies*, II, 1996)
et Lotter – Gäbe (*Hagiographies*, IV, 2006)

par

Klaus KRÖNERT

INTRODUCTION.
  I. LE DIOCÈSE DE TRÈVES. – A. Contexte général de la production hagiographique. – B. Saint-Maximin: les trois premières Vies de saint Maximin. – C. La Celle Saint-Goar: les deux Vies de saint Goar et les *Miracula Goaris*. – D. Saint-Euchaire: le dossier de saint Euchaire, le *Sermo in natale S. Celsi* et le *Liber inventionis S. Matthiae*. – E. Textes écrits dans d'autres établissements de Trèves et ses environs: les Vies de Liutrude et Irmina, la *Vita II^a Paulini*, la *Laudatio Paulini*, les Vies de Lubentius et Castor.
  II. LES VIES DE TROIS «ANCIENS» ÉVÊQUES DE COLOGNE. – A. Cologne, métropole de la *Germania Secunda*. – B. La Vie de Séverin. – C. La Vie de Cunibert. – D. La Vie d'Eberigisil.
  III. QUELQUES RÉCITS RÉDIGÉS À LA SUITE DES TRANSLATIONS DE RELIQUES EN GERMANIE. – A. Le phénomène des translations de reliques en Germanie. – B. La *Translatio Marcellini et Petri*, suivie d'une *Passio* en l'honneur des mêmes saints – C. La *Vita et Translatio Severi* – D. La *Translatio Patrocli Susatum an. 959* et *Vita II^a Patrocli*.
  BIBLIOGRAPHIE.
  ANNEXE: La Vie de sainte Odile (par Michèle Gaillard). – Bibliographie.

INTRODUCTION

L'objectif de ce chapitre consiste à apporter des informations supplémentaires et des mises-à-jour à deux chapitres déjà publiés dans *Hagiographies* sur les textes écrits en Germanie aux époques carolingienne, ottonienne et salienne. Quand Theodor Klüppel a présenté en 1996, dans le deuxième volume de la série, la production hagiographique réalisée en Germanie durant les années 750 à 950, il s'est concentré sur les régions situées sur la rive droite du Rhin. En revanche, le chapitre qui est conçu comme suite chronologique de cette partie – celui que Friedrich Lotter et Sabine Gäbe ont écrit en 2006 sur l'espace germanophone sous les Ottoniens et les Saliens (vers 960-1130), publié dans le quatrième volume d'*Hagiographies* – englobe, lui, le diocèse de Trèves[1], et il est complété par l'étude de Guy Philippart et Anne Wagner sur l'hagiographie lorraine (950-1130), qui traite des diocèses de Metz, Toul et Verdun en y intégrant aussi les rares textes déjà écrits sous les Carolingiens[2]. Il existe donc à présent une lacune que ce chapitre souhaite combler: les écrits hagiographiques rédigés dans le diocèse de Trèves dans les années 750 à 950. Par la même occasion, nous compléterons le chapitre de Lotter et Gäbe concernant les diocèses de Trèves et de Cologne et nous présenterons quelques récits hagiographiques rédigés à la suite des translations de reliques en Germanie, qui n'ont jusqu'ici pas encore trouvé l'attention qu'ils méritent. À cela, Michèle Gaillard a ajouté une annexe développant l'étude de la Vie de saint Odile d'Alsace, seulement évoquée par Klüppel[3].

---

[1] Lotter-Gäbe (2006).

[2] PHILIPPART – WAGNER (2006). Les textes carolingiens pour ces trois diocèses se limitent à la *Vita Prima S. Glodesindis* (*BHL* 3562) ainsi qu'au *Liber de episcopis Mettensibus* de Paul Diacre, qui n'est pas à proprement parler une œuvre hagiographique, mais qui contient un récit original relatif à saint Arnoul (*BHL* 694). Pour ces deux textes évoqués par PHILIPPART – WAGNER (2006), voir GOULLET (2006), respectivement p. 283-287 et p. 224-229; on peut y ajouter, pour le diocèse de Toul, la *Vita s. Apri* (*BHL* 617) dont le plus ancien manuscrit date de l'extrême fin du IXe siècle, cf. GOULLET (2001), p. 27-35.

[3] KLÜPPEL (1996), p. 194.

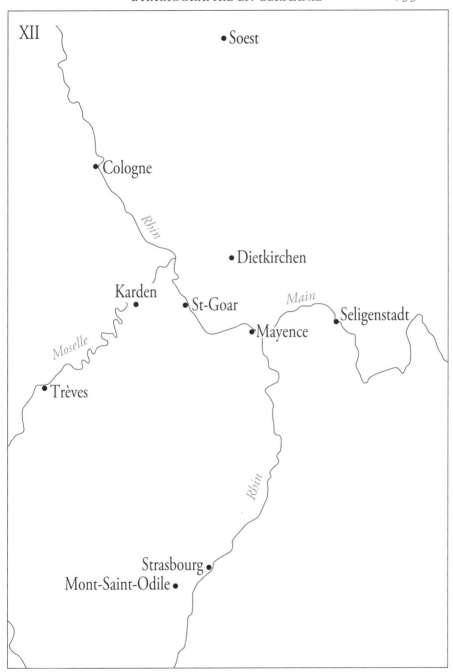

Lieux mentionnés dans le chapitre sur la Germanie

I. Le diocèse de Trèves

A. Contexte général de la production hagiographique

Ancienne cité romaine, Trèves fut aussi l'une des capitales de l'Empire lors des premiers siècles chrétiens. Sous les Carolingiens, ses évêques avaient cependant du mal à maintenir leur position prééminente: c'est seulement vers 800 qu'ils obtinrent le statut de métropolitain contre les prétentions des prélats de Metz, et au cours du IXe siècle, Hincmar de Reims s'avéra aussi un redoutable adversaire. Depuis 925, date à laquelle la Lotharingie fut intégrée dans la Francie orientale, les archevêques de Trèves faisaient partie de l'Église ottonienne et salienne: leurs grands rivaux étaient désormais leurs homologues de Cologne et Mayence[4].

Les principaux établissements religieux de Trèves et de ses environs – ceux qui ont par la suite joué un rôle pour la production hagiographique – étaient, au début de l'époque carolingienne, outre la cathédrale, les abbayes de Saint-Martin et Sainte-Irmina d'Oeren – une communauté de femmes –, situées toutes les deux à l'intérieur des murs, et, à l'extérieur des remparts, Saint-Maximin, dépendant seulement du roi, Saint-Euchaire, toujours proche de l'archevêque, et Saint-Paulin, une communauté de chanoines. À une vingtaine de kilomètres de Trèves se trouvaient des abbayes de Mettlach et d'Echternach. Vers la fin du IXe siècle, l'archevêque Radbod (883-915) mit en place cinq archidiaconés avec pour centre: Saint-Lubentius à Dietkirchen, Sainte-Agathe à Longuyon, Saint-Castor à Karden, Saint-Maurice à Tholey, ainsi que la cathédrale de Trèves elle-même. Plus loin encore, sur les bords du Rhin, se trouvait la Celle Saint-Goar. La seule nouvelle communauté de Trèves fondée au cours des époques ottonienne et salienne, était celle de Saint-Siméon, aménagée dans la *Porta Nigra* de Trèves, qui date de la fin des années 1030[5].

À Trèves, l'activité hagiographique commence véritablement au Xe siècle. Seuls deux centres sont aujourd'hui connus pour

---

[4] Une excellente vue d'ensemble de l'histoire de Trèves au Moyen Âge est présentée par Anton – Haverkamp (1996).
[5] Krönert (2010), p. 29-33.

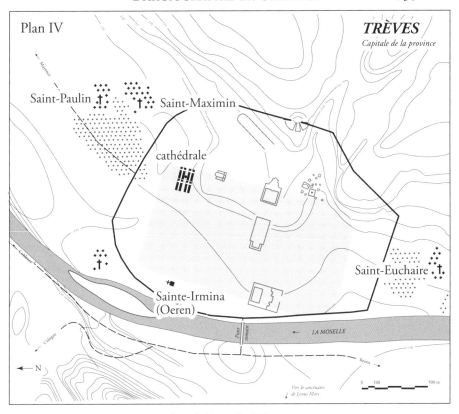

Les églises de Trèves

Plan d'après F. Prévot, M. Gaillard et N. Gauthier (éd.), *Topographie chrétienne des cités de la Gaule des origines au milieu du VIIIe siècle, Quarante ans d'enquête, 1972-2012*, XVI, 2: *Christianisation et espace urbain: atlas, tableaux, index*, Paris, De Boccard, 2014, p. 674-675.

avoir fait écrire des textes en l'honneur des saints dès le milieu du VIIIe siècle: Saint-Maximin et Saint-Goar[6]. Nous présenterons d'abord les œuvres qui y furent rédigées ou commandées, puis nous analyserons ensuite les écrits plus tardifs des autres établissements que la recherche a fait sortir de l'oubli depuis 2006.

---

[6] Krönert (2003).

B. Saint-Maximin

Le texte hagiographique le plus ancien rédigé à Trèves est la *Vita I^a Maximini* (BHL 5822)[7]; il porte sur le cinquième évêque de la cité antique, attesté pour les années 335 à 347. Maximin nous est relativement bien connu grâce à quelques mentions faites par des auteurs contemporains comme Jérôme, Athanase ou Hilaire de Poitiers. En effet, il avait été très engagé dans la lutte contre l'arianisme en accueillant notamment l'évêque d'Alexandrie quand celui-ci fut banni de son siège[8]. Le premier texte hagiographique qui a été consacré à Maximin est issu de la plume de Grégoire de Tours: il s'agit de deux miracles relatés dans le *Liber in gloria confessorum* (BHL 5825)[9]. Tout indique cependant que l'hagiographe anonyme de Trèves qui a rédigé son œuvre, selon toute probabilité entre 751 et 754[10], ignorait cette ancienne documentation: dans la première partie de la Vie, composée sur un plan tripartite, il attribue au saint des origines aquitaines dont l'historicité reste douteuse[11], et il explique que le jeune Maximin fut attiré à Trèves par la réputation de son évêque Agrice. Quant à son épiscopat, il est marqué par deux événements: le synode de Cologne où il destitua l'évêque rhénan arien Euphrates, et un pèlerinage à Rome en compagnie de saint Martin de Tours. Le premier épisode repose sur les souscriptions (peut-être authentiques) des actes du pseudo-concile de Cologne de 346; le pèlerinage – chronologiquement très improbable – a sans aucun doute été inventé. À la fin de sa vie, Maximin se rendit en Aquitaine pour y mourir. La deuxième partie de la Vie porte sur la translation de ses reliques à Trèves – un *furtum sacrum* – et la dernière partie est consacrée aux miracles du saint,

---

[7] La *Vita I^a Maximini* a été éditée par HENSCHEN, *AASS*, Mai. VII, 3^a ed., Anvers, 1866, p. 21-25 et le prologue (BHL 5823) par WINHELLER (1935), p. 10. Les manuscrits les plus anciens de ces textes datent du XIIe siècle: Paris, BnF, lat. 15029, fol. 14-21v et Trèves, StB, 137/50, fol. 192v.

[8] POHLSANDER (1996), p. 170.

[9] GRÉGOIRE DE TOURS, *Liber in gloria confessorum*, c. 91, éd. B. KRUSCH, *MGH*, *SRM*, I-2, Hanovre, 1885, p. 356-357.

[10] La datation de ce texte repose sur des indices: l'auteur appelle Pépin «roi», mais il ne semble pas encore connaître la mort de Boniface. Étant donné que le texte semble avoir été écrit contre les intérêts de l'Église de Cologne, on peut supposer que le martyre de Boniface aurait attiré l'attention de l'auteur; cf. KRÖNERT (2010), p. 48-54.

[11] KRÖNERT (2010), Saint Maximin de Trèves.

essentiellement des guérisons. En ce qui concerne la langue, le texte n'est pas encore sous l'influence carolingienne[12]. Quatre manuscrits connus datant du XIIe au XVe siècle[13] nous prouvent que cette Vie a eu un certain succès malgré l'élaboration d'une nouvelle version au IXe siècle.

En effet, cette première Vie de Maximin a fait l'objet d'une réécriture en 839 (*BHL* 5824)[14]. Son auteur, Loup – sans aucun doute Loup de Ferrières – s'est nommé lui-même et a indiqué également son commanditaire, l'abbé de Saint-Maximin Waldo, ainsi que, dans l'épilogue de son œuvre, l'année de la rédaction[15]. Dans le prologue, il explique que Waldo lui avait demandé de retravailler la Vie de Maximin «dans son style» et de restituer les faits «connus grâce à certains écrits». Tout en gardant le plan tripartite de son modèle, l'hagiographe a surtout élargi la première partie de la *Vita* en citant la Chronique de Jérôme et en apportant des détails et des explications théologiques sur la lutte de Maximin contre l'arianisme. Le principal changement dans la dernière partie, celle qui porte sur les miracles, concerne l'ordre des épisodes: ils sont désormais relatés selon un plan thématique, tandis que le premier hagiographe avait choisi une approche chronologique. Les nouveaux miracles produits après la rédaction de la *Vita I^a*, manquent. Comme Waldo l'avait demandé, Loup a choisi un style très classique, à la fois sur le plan lexical et syntaxique. Les trente-neuf manuscrits de ce texte que Romano a répertoriés témoignent du succès très important de la Vie[16].

L'importance du culte de Maximin à Trèves au Xe siècle se vérifie ensuite par la rédaction d'une collection de miracles, les *Miracula Maximini* (*BHL* 5826), datant de 962, que Lotter a

---

[12] Nous reprenons ici notre analyse dans KRÖNERT (2010), p. 48-54; concernant le style, cf. BERSCHIN (1991), p. 66.

[13] Les manuscrits les plus tardifs sont Tours, BM 157, fol. 50v, et Paris, BnF, lat. 3809A, fol. 249v-251, tous les deux du XVe siècle.

[14] Il existe deux éditions critiques de la *Vita II^a Maximini*: B. KRUSCH, *MGH*, *SRM*, III, Hanovre, 1896, p. 74-82 et ROMANO (1995). Le manuscrit le plus ancien est Metz, BM 523, du XIe siècle.

[15] Nous reprenons ici notre analyse dans KRÖNERT (2010), p. 54-59; cf. également KRÖNERT (2019).

[16] ROMANO (1995), p. 49-54.

présentés dans le volume IV d'*Hagiographies*[17]. Un autre texte en l'honneur du même saint, en revanche, n'a pas retenu son attention, la *Vita III^a* ou *Vita metrica Maximini* (*BHL* 5827)[18]. Composé après 962 – selon une certaine probabilité entre 993 et 1000 – par un moine anonyme, ce texte est le seul du dossier de Maximin qui soit composé en vers, de quarante-trois hexamètres dans l'ensemble[19]. Il a été conçu pour une inscription destinée à commenter une série de peintures murales qui décoraient la salle capitulaire du monastère Saint-Maximin. La fresque a aujourd'hui disparu et le texte ne nous est parvenu que par un seul manuscrit, Gand, Universiteitsbibliotheek 9, fol. 25r-v, datant de la fin du Xe siècle, qui constitue donc le *terminus ante quem* pour la rédaction. Le poète, dont les vers manquent cruellement d'élégance, a utilisé comme sources les deux premières Vies de Maximin (*BHL* 5822, 5824), les deux miracles relatés par Grégoire de Tours (*BHL* 5825), les Miracles de saint Maximin relatés par le moine Sigehard (*BHL* 5826), la *Vita I^a Paulini* (*BHL* 6562-6563) et sans doute aussi la Continuation qu'Adalbert a écrite pour la Chronique de Réginon de Prüm. Réalisé en 966/967, ce dernier texte fixe le *terminus post quem*. Étant donné que l'hagiographe insiste dans la *Vita III^a* sur la tradition impériale de son monastère et que l'archevêque de Trèves, Liudulf, multiplia, à partir de 993, les efforts pour incorporer dans ses droits un autre monastère de Trèves, Sainte-Irmina d'Oeren, il est possible que la Vie métrique de Maximin servît à défendre l'indépendance du monastère, soumis au pouvoir impérial. Dans ce cas, elle fut écrite après 993[20]. Ainsi s'achève la grande époque de l'activité hagiographique à Saint-Maximin[21].

---

[17] LOTTER – GÄBE (2006), p. 284-285; cf. à propos de ce texte aussi KRÖNERT (2005), «Les *Miracula*» et KRÖNERT (2010), p. 66-69 et 390-392.

[18] Édition de référence de la *Vita III^a Maximini*: K. STRECKER, *MGH, Poet. Lat.*, V-1, Leipzig, 1937, p. 147-152.

[19] Nous reprenons ici notre analyse de la *Vita III^a Maximini* dans KRÖNERT (2010), p. 69-77 et 388-390.

[20] Pour compléter l'aperçu sur Maximin, mentionnons ici encore un miracle du saint qui a été individuellement transmis: *BHL* 5826. Une analyse du texte se trouve dans KRÖNERT (2010), p. 392-393.

[21] Pendant la deuxième moitié du XIe siècle, l'abbé de Saint-Maximin, Thierry, fut également abbé des deux monastères de Stavelot et Malmédy. Lors de l'«affaire de Malmédy», il s'opposa fermement à Annon II, arche-

C. La Celle Saint-Goar

Presque au même moment où la première Vie de saint Maximin fut écrite, un autre texte hagiographique a vu le jour dans le diocèse de Trèves: la *Vita I^a* de saint Goar (*BHL* 3565)[22], ermite au début du VIe siècle sur les bords du Rhin, à l'endroit où fut érigée par la suite la Celle-Saint-Goar[23]. L'auteur de ce texte est inconnu et le récit qu'il a fait sur son héros est plus légendaire qu'historique[24]. Dans l'ensemble, la vie de l'ermite est rythmée par les prières et les messes, mais son accueil chaleureux suscitait parfois la méfiance[25]. Le style de la Vie contient un certain nombre de «romanismes», ce qui a conduit Walter Berschin à dater l'œuvre des années 770[26]. L'étude du contexte fournit un argument supplémentaire pour cette datation: selon l'un des passages du texte, Goar aurait fait en sorte que l'identité du père d'un enfant orphelin soit révélée: l'évêque de Trèves, Rustique. Ce miracle peut non seulement être interprété comme critique aux mœurs de l'évêque de Trèves Milon (717-757), mais aussi comme une tentative des frères de la Celle Saint-Goar de prendre leurs distances avec la métropole mosellane: en effet, en 765, Pépin III (751-768) avait donné la Celle, jusque-là uniquement soumis au roi, à l'abbaye de Prüm. Weomad, prélat de Trèves (762-791), commença à contester cette décision à partir de 768. L'«affaire de Saint-Goar» dura jusqu'en 782 quand Charlemagne confirma de façon définitive que la Celle appartenait à Prüm, et il est donc possible que la Vie de l'ermite fût écrite entre 768 et 782[27].

---

vêque de Cologne. Lors de cette querelle, un célèbre texte hagiographique fut rédigé, le *Triumphus sancti Remacli* (*BHL* 7140). Il sera présenté dans la partie consacrée à l'hagiographie de Liège.

[22] La *Vita I^a Goaris* est éditée par I. Pinius, *AASS*, Iul. II, 1721, p. 333-337, et par B. Krusch, *MGH*, *SRM*, IV, Hanovre – Leipzig, 1902, p. 411-423; cf. pour les manuscrits les plus importants Berschin (1991), p. 73, n. 183.

[23] Krönert (2005), *La construction du passé*, p. 90-93.

[24] Il relate ainsi, entre autres, comment le saint a accroché son manteau à un rayon de soleil.

[25] Nous reprenons ici notre analyse dans Krönert (2005), *La construction du passé*, p. 90-92.

[26] Cf. Berschin (1991), p. 74.

[27] Voir Heyen (1961), p. 87-106.

Comme la Vie de saint Maximin, la Vie de saint Goar a été réécrite en 839 (*BHL* 3566)[28]. C'est l'auteur, Wandalbert de Prüm, qui le précise lui-même à la fin du récit. Selon ses propres mots, dans le prologue, le diacre Wandalbert avait agi sur la demande de son abbé, Markward[29]: la nouvelle Vie devrait être plus «polie» car le style «assez vil» de l'ancienne version avait offensé les oreilles des lecteurs et une collection de miracles était nécessaire pour compléter l'œuvre. Sans véritablement toucher au contenu de la Vie, Wandalbert a surtout écrit des récits de miracles très vifs (*BHL* 3567) qui reflètent, entre autres, le commerce sur le Rhin[30] et les tensions qui existaient alors dans la famille impériale[31]. Les douze manuscrits identifiés pour la *Vita II^a Goaris* et les *Miracula* qui lui sont attachés prouvent que cette nouvelle version a connu un certain succès[32]. On ne connaît pas d'autres textes écrits à Saint-Goar ou pour sa communauté pendant le haut Moyen Âge et le Moyen Âge central.

D. Saint-Euchaire

Comme nous avons indiqué plus haut, à Trèves, le véritable essor hagiographique commence seulement au Xe siècle. Le premier texte alors écrit – une œuvre capitale pour la genèse de l'ensemble du futur corpus hagiographique de Trèves – fut la *Vita Eucharii, Valerii et Materni* (*BHL* 2655). Son auteur relate pour la première fois dans un texte continu la légende des origines apostoliques de Trèves selon laquelle Euchaire, son premier évêque, et Valère et Materne, ses deux compagnons et successeurs sur le siège de Trèves, auraient été envoyés par Saint Pierre[33]. Ce texte, présenté par Lotter[34], a fait depuis l'objet de plusieurs recherches qui permettent notamment de préciser sa

---

[28] La *Vita II^a Goaris* a été éditée par O. Holder-Egger, *MGH*, *SS*, XV-1, Hanovre, 1887, p. 362-376 et Stiene (1981), p. 2-89 (liste complète de manuscrits, p. XLI sq.).
[29] Nous reprenons ici notre analyse dans Krönert (2019).
[30] Cf. Lebecq (2011).
[31] Cf. Krönert (2019).
[32] Cf. Stiene (1981) et Krönert (2019).
[33] Cf. Krönert (2010), p. 83-92, où nous montrons que cette légende a déjà existé auparavant et l'hagiographe l'a seulement mise par écrit.
[34] Lotter – Gäbe (2006), p. 291-292.

datation, sa fonction et son importance[35]: rédigée vers 900 – le manuscrit le plus ancien, Paris, BnF, lat. 10864, précisément de cette époque, n'en laisse aucun doute – par un hagiographe anonyme, qui appartenait à la cathédrale de Trèves ou à l'abbaye de Saint-Euchaire, la Vie avait pour l'objectif d'exalter l'évêque fondateur de Trèves et le siège pontifical. La cinquantaine de manuscrits qui nous sont parvenus attestent un succès très important. Plus tard, la Vie d'Euchaire fut instrumentalisée au cours de la querelle de la primatie qui, aux Xe et XIe siècles, opposait Trèves aux métropoles de Cologne et de Mayence. Une analyse détaillée du texte et de ses utilisateurs se trouve dans notre livre *L'exaltation de Trèves*[36].

Amplifiée à deux reprises (*BHL* 2656, 2657, au plus tard sous l'archevêque Egbert, 977-993, et *BHL vacat,* probablement entre 994 et 1008)[37], elle a surtout servi de modèle pour toute une série de panégyriques, dont l'importance ne doit pas être sous-estimée et qu'il convient de présenter ici brièvement: il s'agit d'une *Historia Eucharii* (*BHL vacat*)[38] et d'une homélie en l'honneur d'Euchaire, Valère et Materne (*BHL vacat*), composées toutes les deux sur la commande d'Egbert par Remi, futur abbé de Mettlach[39]. En outre Thierry, moine de Saint-Euchaire, a composé, dans la première moitié du XIe siècle, un *Sermo de festivitate Eucharii* (*BHL* 2659d)[40] et un hagiographe anonyme, qui a travaillé vers le milieu ou dans la deuxième moitié du XIe siècle, est l'auteur de deux sermons en l'honneur d'Euchaire et de Valère (*BHL vacat* pour les deux textes)[41]. Tous ces écrits mettent l'accent sur la proximité du premier prélat de Trèves avec le premier apôtre, ce qui constituait le principal argument pour que l'Église mosellane obtînt

---

[35] Pour les recherches les plus importantes, voir KRÖNERT (2010), p. 80 et 92-94 où nous présentons ces études de façon détaillée.

[36] *Ibid.*, p. 79-101 et 347-356.

[37] *Ibid.*, p. 110-115, 136-138 et 353-356.

[38] *Ibid.*, p. 115-120 et 356-357.

[39] *Ibid.*, p. 120-131 et 357-358.

[40] *Ibid.*, p. 156-154 et 359-361; il s'agit du même Thierry, qui a également écrit le récit sur l'invention (*BHL* 1720) et les miracles de Celse (*BHL* 1721), présentés par LOTTER in LOTTER – GÄBE (2006), p. 289-291; à propos des textes sur Celse et Thierry, voir aussi KRÖNERT (2010), p. 139-156 et 342-345.

[41] *Ibid.*, p. 164-184; 362-365.

en 969 le privilège de la primatie et lui permit de le défendre jusqu'à la fin du XIe siècle[42]. Leur diffusion est cependant restée limitée à Trèves et ses environs.

Le dossier des trois premiers évêques de Trèves n'est pas le seul que les moines de Saint-Euchaire ont enrichi au cours des Xe et XIe siècles: le moine Remi, déjà auteur de deux écrits en l'honneur d'Euchaire, a également écrit un *Sermo in natale Celsi* (*BHL vacat*), probablement peu de temps après la mort d'Egbert († 993)[43]. Avec les deux écrits en l'honneur de Celse qui sont issus de la plume de Thierry de Saint-Euchaire et que F. Lotter a présenté dans le volume IV, le dossier de Celse contient donc au moins trois écrits[44]; ce nombre relativement élevé s'explique par le fait qu'en 980, lors de la nouvelle construction de l'abbatiale à Saint-Euchaire, on découvrit un sarcophage sur lequel on pouvait lire le nom du mort, *Celsus*. Une fois reconnue la sainteté de cet homme jusque-là quasi-inconnu, Egbert et ses successeurs firent des efforts considérables, dont ces trois écrits font partie, pour établir un véritable culte pour ce nouveau saint[45].

Un dernier texte écrit à Saint-Euchaire est communément appelé *Liber inventionis S. Matthiae* (*BHL* 5697)[46]. Il nous est parvenu dans le manuscrit de Trèves, Stadtbibliothek 98[47]; l'auteur, resté anonyme, nous rapporte comment l'empereur Henri III avait demandé, en 1050, à l'archevêque de Trèves Eberhard des reliques de l'apôtre Matthias pour la nouvelle abbaye de Goslar. Eberhard, qui n'était pas au courant que son Église possédait un tel trésor, apprit alors que sainte Hélène avait envoyé l'apôtre à Trèves par l'intermédiaire d'Agrice; sa tombe fut alors découverte dans l'abbaye Saint-Euchaire. Puis, le texte est interrompu, car il manque une page, certainement déjà enlevée au XIIe siècle. Sur la page suivante, le récit reprend au 1er sep-

---

[42] KRÖNERT (2012), p. 185-198.

[43] KRÖNERT (2010), p. 131-136; 340-342.

[44] Un 4ème *Sermo Celsi* (*BHL vacat*), souvent attribué à Thierry de Saint-Euchaire, est probablement plus tardif; cf. KRÖNERT (2010), p. 345-346.

[45] Leur diffusion s'est cependant limitée à Trèves et ses environs.

[46] Nous reprenons ici notre analyse dans KRÖNERT (2005), *La construction du passé*, p. 364-367.

[47] Trèves, Stadtbibliothek 98, fol. 1-12, éd. G. HENSCHEN, *AASS*, Feb. III, 3[a] ed., Anvers, 1858, p. 448-452; édition partielle par G. H. PERTZ, *MGH, SS*, VIII, Hanovre, 1848, p. 227-231.

tembre 1127 quand les reliques de Matthias furent découvertes une nouvelle fois. Comment interpréter ces données codicologiques ? Le clergé de Trèves avait manifestement décidé, après la découverte du saint corps au milieu du Xe siècle et avant son éventuelle translation à Goslar, de ne pas se séparer de lui ; il fut alors décidé de faire oublier la découverte de 1050 en cachant les reliques et en faisant disparaître la page du récit qui en avait fait mention[48]. Le *Liber inventionis S. Matthiae* contient aussi quelques récits de miracles et une brève notice sur un incendie de l'an 1131, ce qui incite à penser qu'il a été écrit très peu de temps après cet événement. Vers la fin du XIIe siècle, il servit de modèle pour Lambert de Liège et son œuvre *De Vita, translatione ac miraculis sancti Matthiae apostoli* en cinq livres (*BHL* 5699-5715)[49].

E. Textes écrits
dans d'autres établissements religieux
de Trèves et ses environs

La vision que nous avons de l'activité hagiographique dans les autres établissements religieux de Trèves sous les Ottoniens et Saliens, n'a pas beaucoup changé depuis la publication de Lotter en 2006. Seules trois Vies – celles de Liutrud, Irmina et Paulin – et un éloge en l'honneur de Paulin, écrits à Trèves ou sur la demande des clercs mosellans, ont été depuis mis en valeur par la recherche. Présentons-les ici, l'un après l'autre.

Le premier, par ordre chronologique, est très atypique pour l'hagiographie de Trèves, qui porte généralement sur les saints locaux de l'époque paléochrétienne. L'archevêque Thierry (965-977) a composé une *Vita metrica sanctae Liutrudis* (*BHL* 4952)[50]. Sainte du Ve/VIe siècle et originaire de la Champagne, Liutrude

---

[48] Nous reprenons ici Kloos (1958), p. 17-28.

[49] Le *Sermo in festivitate s. Mathie apostoli*, copié dans le manuscrit Trèves, Stadtbibliothek 4, fol. 304-311v, qui est systématiquement attribué à Thierry de Saint-Euchaire, est en réalité une copie incomplète d'un sermon, écrit par Autpert du Mont Cassin (*BHL* 5695), cf. Krönert (2005), *La construction du passé*, p. 363-367 et 883-884.

[50] La *Vita metrica Liutrudis* a été éditée par K. Strecker, *MGH, Poetae Lat.*, V, Leipzig, 1937, p. 153-173 ; voir aussi Röckelein (2002), p. 214-224 et Krönert (2010), p. 44.

était vénérée comme l'une des sept sœurs de Pusinne. Selon la Vie, elle avait acquis des reliques de saint Maurice d'Agaune, ce qui constitue peut-être la clef pour comprendre pourquoi l'archevêque de Trèves s'est intéressé à elle: Maurice était l'un des saints favoris d'Otton Ier et Thierry figurait parmi les grands prélats de l'Empire. Quant au texte, il s'agit d'un poème rythmique de 15 syllabes (8p + 7 pp), un mètre plutôt rare pour le Xe siècle, et, selon Karl Strecker, d'une qualité plutôt médiocre[51].

Le texte suivant est également consacré à une sainte alto-médiévale: Irmina, fondatrice et abbesse du monastère de Sainte-Irmina d'Oeren, qui est attestée pour la fin du VIIe et le début du VIIIe siècle et est vénérée le 24 décembre. Il s'agit de la *Vita Irminae* (*BHL* 4471-4472), écrite par Thiofried d'Echternach[52]. Thiofried est devenu abbé d'Echternach en 1081; il est connu pour avoir écrit d'autres textes hagiographiques comme la *Vita II^a Liudwini* (*BHL* 4956)[53], une *Vita Willibrordi* (*BHL* 8940-8941)[54] sous forme d'un *opus geminum*, ainsi que les *Flores epytaphii sanctorum* et s'est fait remarquer par son style très sophistiqué. Bien que le style de la Vie d'Irmina soit beaucoup plus simple que celui de ses autres œuvres, l'identification de l'auteur ne fait pas de doute: il se mentionne lui-même dans le prologue et il semble que ce texte fût une œuvre de jeunesse car l'auteur se désigne comme «disciple». Il faut donc croire que cette vie ait été écrite avant 1081[55].

Les deux derniers textes nous mènent à la collégiale Saint-Paulin: après la découverte de martyrs de Trèves dans leur crypte en 1072, les chanoines de Saint-Paulin ont non seule-

---

[51] Cf. STRECKER, dans l'introduction de l'édition de la Vie de Liutrude, p. 153-155. Le vers employé dans la *Vita Liutrudis* est une imitation du septénaire trochaïque antique, dont les poètes médiévaux ont fait un vers de 15 syllabes.

[52] Pour lire la Vie d'Irmina telle qu'elle a été conçue par son auteur, il faut, semble-t-il, combiner la version du manuscrit Paris, BnF, lat. 9741, avec l'épilogue tel qu'il nous est parvenu dans le *Liber aureus* d'Echternach. HANSEN (1841) reproduit une transcription de la *Vita Irminae* (avec le prologue, mais sans l'épilogue), telle qu'elle se trouve dans le manuscrit de Paris, BnF, lat. 9741, transcription qui a été réalisée par K. DE MONTEYNARD; cf. KRÖNERT (2005), *La construction du passé*, p. 872-873.

[53] LOTTER, in LOTTER – GÄBE (2006), p. 349-351.

[54] *Ibid.*, p. 354-357.

[55] KRÖNERT (2005), *La construction du passé*, p. 610-625 et 872-873.

ment écrit une *Historia martyrum Treverensium* (*BHL* 8284) et une *Passio martyrum Treverensium* (*BHL* 8284c) afin de commémorer cet événement et réécrit la Vie de saint Félix (*BHL* 2892)[56], ils ont également jugé nécessaire de réécrire la Vie de leur saint patron, Paulin, considéré comme sixième évêque de Trèves, attesté en tant que tel pour les années 347-358 et vénéré le 30 août (*BHL* 6565, 6566)[57]. Ce texte fut rédigé entre 1072 et 1101 – date de la rédaction des *Gesta Trevirorum* –, mais avant la *Vita II^a Felicis*, qui a été également écrite avant 1101. L'auteur, appartenant sans doute à la communauté de Saint-Paulin, est resté anonyme; il est fort probable qu'il est identique au deuxième hagiographe de Félix. La *Vita II^a Paulini* exalte bien plus que son modèle principal, la *Vita I^a*, son héros et la cité de Trèves: Paulin est ici consacré évêque par saint Martin lui-même, son rôle dans la lutte contre l'arianisme est davantage mis en valeur en le présentant comme principal acteur du concile de Milan et l'hagiographe n'oublie pas de faire l'éloge des martyrs qui avaient été découverts peu de temps avant dans la crypte de son abbaye[58].

Contrairement à ce que la numérotation de la *BHL* laisse penser, la *Laudatio Paulini* (*BHL* 6567)[59] ne fait pas partie de la *Vita II^a Paulini*. Il s'agit très probablement de l'hymne qui est mentionnée dans l'*Historia martyrum Treverensium* (*BHL* 8284) où il est question d'un *quidam hymnus de santo Paulino* que les chanoines de Saint-Paulin avaient (re-)découvert en 1071/1072 dans la bibliothèque du monastère Sainte-Irmina-Oeren. Le lexique proche du milieu irlandais et le classement alphabétique des strophes font penser que l'éloge date de l'époque carolingienne ou du Xe siècle. L'auteur était peut-être en relation avec l'abbaye d'Echternach où l'influence insulaire était encore forte à cette époque[60].

---

[56] LOTTER, in LOTTER – GÄBE (2006), p. 345-349.

[57] *Editio princeps* et seule édition de ce texte dans KRÖNERT (2005), *La construction du passé*, p. 825-840.

[58] Nous reprenons ici notre analyse dans KRÖNERT (2010), p. 255-262 et 399-401.

[59] *Editio princeps* et seule édition de ce texte: KRÖNERT (2005), *La construction du passé*, p. 841-842, à partir du manuscrit Paris, BnF, lat. 9740, fol. 171v-172v.

[60] Nous reprenons ici notre analyse dans KRÖNERT (2010), p. 401-402.

En ce qui concerne les communautés du diocèse de Trèves situées plus loin de la cité, outre les textes écrits à Mettlach – par Remi – et Echternach – par Thiofried – déjà présentés par Lotter et nous-mêmes, seules deux Vies doivent être mentionnées, celles de Lubentius et de Castor. Il s'agit de deux prêtres, vénérés à Trèves dès le IXe siècle, que leur légende rattache à saint Maximin. Saint patron de l'église de Dietkirchen, Lubentius reçut, au cours du XIIe siècle, sa propre Vie (*BHL* 4968) sans doute écrite par les chanoines du lieu[61]. La *Vita Castoris* (*BHL* 1642) provient de Saint-Castor à Karden; elle date, selon F. Pauly, du XIe/XIIe siècle[62].

II. LES VIES DE TROIS «ANCIENS» ÉVÊQUES DE COLOGNE

A. COLOGNE, MÉTROPOLE DE LA *GERMANIA SECUNDA*

Attestée la première fois tout au début du Ier siècle de notre ère, la ville de Cologne a très vite joué un rôle important dans l'histoire du Bas Empire, si bien qu'elle est devenue plus tard la métropole de Germanie Seconde. Son premier évêque fut Materne, qui participa aux conciles du Latran (313) et d'Arles (314). Un autre évêque du IVe siècle, Euphrates, est connu pour avoir été accusé d'arianisme dans les sources du VIIIe siècle[63]. Après l'épiscopat de Séverin de Cologne, pontife vers la fin du IVe siècle et au début du Ve siècle, aucun autre nom de prélat ne nous est parvenu: cette lacune dans la liste épiscopale pourrait s'expliquer par l'installation des «barbares»,

---

[61] Éd. J.-B. FONSON, *AASS*, Oct. VI, 1794, p. 202-203; voir également Cf. STRUCK (1986), p. 51-55.

[62] Éd. J. BOLLAND, *AASS*, Feb. II, 1658, p. 661-666; cf. également PAULY (1986), p. 9-14. La *Navigatio sancti Brendani*, parfois attribuée à un évêque irlandais nommé Israël, installé à Trèves au milieu du Xe siècle (cf. M. EMBACH, «Einflüsse der irisch-angelsächsischen Schriftkultur des Mittelalters im Raum Trier Echternach, Mit einem Blick auf Bischof Israel», *Kurtrierisches Jahrbuch*, 46 (2006), p. 43-78), fut plus probablement écrite vers 800 ou dans la première moitié du IXe siècle. Cf. à ce sujet aussi la contribution de J.-C. Poulin sur la Bretagne, *supra* p. 199, n. 29.

[63] Voir *supra* notre présentation de la *Vita I[a] Maximini*.

comme c'est le cas pour d'autres sièges de cette région. C'est seulement à partir du VIe siècle que nous sommes à nouveau renseignés sur l'histoire de la ville rhénane, notamment grâce à Venance Fortunat et Grégoire de Tours. L'un des cultes qui a alors pris de plus en plus d'importance, non seulement à cette époque mais aussi durant les siècles à venir, est celui de la Légion Thébaine, dont un grand nombre d'hommes auraient subi le martyre à Cologne sous Dioclétien (284-305). Les textes hagiographiques en l'honneur de ces saints, et en premier lieu de saint Géréon, ont été déjà présentés dans le volume IV d'*Hagiographies*[64]. Aux VIe-VIIe siècles, le siège de Cologne gardait une certaine importance dans le royaume mérovingien, comme le montre notamment la proximité entre les rois et quelques prélats comme Eberigisil et Cunibert. À partir de l'époque carolingienne un autre culte se développa dans la métropole rhénane: celui de sainte Ursule et des onze milles vierges, vénérées comme victimes des Huns. Au Xe siècle, cette légende a pris véritablement consistance grâce à la rédaction de plusieurs textes hagiographiques, dont le *Sermo in natali sanctorum virginum XI milium* (BHL 8426) et la *Passio sanctarum undecim milium virginum* (BHL 8428-84-30)[65]. Ensuite, sous les Ottoniens et les Saliens, les hagiographes de la métropole rhénane se sont de plus en plus consacrés aux prélats de leur temps: Brunon, Héribert, Annon, pour ne mentionner qu'eux, ont ainsi reçu leur biographie sainte. Toutes ces œuvres figurent, dans le volume IV d'*Hagiographies*[66], de même que les nombreux récits de miracles qui étaient alors composés dans les abbayes de Cologne: Deutz, Siegburg ou encore Brauweiler[67]. Ce panorama a cependant fait l'impasse sur trois Vies consacrées à des évêques des premiers siècles de l'histoire de Cologne: celles de Séverin, Cunibert et Eberigisil, textes que nous présenterons ici. Ces écrits prouvent que, dans la métropole rhénane aussi, les clercs

---

[64] Voir notamment la *Passio Gereonis* (BHL 3446), LOTTER, in LOTTER – GÄBE (2006), p. 306-307.

[65] KRÖNERT – MÉRIAUX (2017) p. 38-39 et 45-48.

[66] LOTTER, in LOTTER – GÄBE (2006), p. 304-306 (*sermo in natale virginum*), p. 299-303 (Brunon), p. 359-362 (Héribert); GÄBE (2006), p. 460-464 (Annon).

[67] LOTTER – GÄBE (2006), p. 363-366 (*Miracula Heriberti*), p. 370-373 (*Vita Adelheidis*), p. 467-470 (*Vita Wolfhelmi abb. Brunwilar.*), textes qui sont aussi analysés par KLEINE (2006).

gardaient un intérêt vif pour les prélats «anciens», comme à Trèves[68].

B. La Vie de Séverin

Séverin de Cologne est attesté comme contemporain de Martin de Tours grâce à Grégoire de Tours qui le mentionne dans le premier livre sur les miracles de saint Martin (*BHL* 5621, c. 4)[69]. Ce Séverin quasi-inconnu mais considéré comme troisième évêque de la ville, est vénéré le 23 octobre[70].

Pour expliquer comment sa légende a été écrite, il est nécessaire de parler d'abord d'un homonyme et contemporain, Séverin de Bordeaux, vénéré le 21 octobre: ce Séverin est attesté pour la première fois dans le *In gloria confessorum*, 44 (45) de Grégoire de Tours (*BHL* 327)[71]. Grégoire savait seulement que le saint était venu des «pays orientaux» et qu'il avait été accueilli par Amand, évêque de Bordeaux au Ve siècle. Il est ici important de souligner que Grégoire de Tours n'a jamais confondu les deux Séverin, celui de Cologne et celui de Bordeaux. À peu près à la même époque, Venance Fortunat a consacré une Vie au saint de Bordeaux (*BHL* 7652)[72], avec une différence notable: il précise que Séverin était venu de Trèves[73]. Nous ignorons d'où vient cette information, mais Levison suppose que les clercs de Bordeaux savaient uniquement que leur Séverin était venu d'ailleurs et qu'ils ont essayé de lui trouver une origine prestigieuse[74]. L'origine trévire ne joue cependant aucun rôle dans la

---

[68] Deux autres textes relatifs à saint Patrocle (*BHL* 6521 et 6523) sont sans doute encore écrits à Cologne, cf. *infra* p. 753-755.

[69] Grégoire de Tours, *Virtutes Martini*, I, 4, éd. B. Krusch, *MGH, SRM*, I-2, Hanovre, 1885, p. 590: Grégoire mentionne ici que le vieux Séverin a entendu des voix d'anges à la mort de saint Martin, qui lui ont annoncé cet événement; cf., à propos de Séverin de Cologne, Päffgen (2011), p. 441-534.

[70] Levison (1909), p. 52-53.

[71] Grégoire De Tours, *In Gloria confessorum*, cap. 44, éd. B. Krusch, *MGH, SRM*, I-2, Hanovre, 1885, p. 775; cf. à propos de ce Séverin (et aussi de Séverin de Cologne), Baillet – Henriet – Junique (2009).

[72] Venance Fortunat, *Vita Severini*, éd. W. Levison, *MGH, SRM*, VII, Hanovre – Leipzig, 1920, p. 219-224.

[73] *Ibid.*, cap. 1, p. 219.

[74] Levison (1909), p. 32-51.

Vie, car dès la deuxième leçon (sur neuf) il n'est question que de Bordeaux.

C'est au cours du haut Moyen Âge que les dossiers des deux Séverin commencent à être entremêlés. En effet, à un moment que nous ne pouvons pas déterminer avec certitude, le texte de Fortunat a été lu par des clercs de Cologne, qui n'ont pas hésité à l'utiliser et à l'adapter à leur propre Séverin. Nous avons ainsi plusieurs manuscrits dans lesquels «l'origine trévire» de Séverin de Bordeaux est remplacée par l'origine de Cologne: ceci avait dû paraître crédible, voire probable, aux clercs de Cologne du fait que leur Séverin et le Séverin de Bordeaux étaient contemporains et vénérés presque au même jour. Le plus ancien manuscrit de la Vie de Séverin écrite par Fortunat, qui affirme que le saint est originaire de Cologne, est Paris, BnF, lat. 5308, du XIIe siècle[75]. Il est cependant presque sûr que l'adaptation de la Vie écrite par Fortunat aux besoins de l'Église de Cologne remonte au IXe ou Xe siècle comme le suggère le texte suivant.

Nous possédons, en effet, une *Vita II[a] Severini Coloniensis et Translatio* (BHL 7647-7648)[76] conçue pour l'abbaye Saint-Séverin de Cologne et écrite par un auteur rhénan anonyme qui préserve *grosso modo* la trame narrative du texte de Fortunat. *Vita* (BHL 7647) et *Translatio* (BHL 7648) forment ici, à l'origine, une seule unité, bien que certains copistes plus tardifs se soient contentés de ne reprendre que la Vie[77]. Prédestiné à l'Église de Cologne, Séverin avait lutté sur les bords du Rhin contre les ariens et accompli un grand nombre de miracles, raconte l'hagiographe. Puis, il aborde le séjour bordelais du saint mais, quoique bien accueilli par Amand, il ne serait jamais devenu évêque de Bordeaux. Mort dans cette ville, il aurait dû attendre un certain temps jusqu'à ce que les rhénans se décident à récupérer son corps: après l'invasion des Huns, explique l'hagiographe, une délégation se rendit à Bordeaux et revint à Cologne

---

[75] Paris, BnF, lat. 5308, du XIIe siècle, fol. 196v-197v; voir également LEVISON (1909), p. 46.

[76] *Vita II[a] Severini et Translatio*, éd. SURIUS, *De probatis historiis*, V, Cologne, 1574, p. 920-927 et par J. VAN HECKE, *AASS*, Oct. X, 3[a] ed., Bruxelles, 1861, p. 56-63; une traduction en allemand et un commentaire de ce texte a été réalisé par PÄFFGEN – CARLO PANGERL (2011).

[77] Pour une liste complète de manuscrits, *ibid.*, p. 552-553; les auteurs y signalent toujours si la copie est complète ou partielle.

avec une partie des reliques – chose que les Bordelais n'ont jamais reconnue dans les textes relatifs à leur Séverin[78].

La *Vita II^a Severini Coloniensis et Translatio* (*BHL* 7647-7648), dont le manuscrit le plus ancien date du Xe siècle[79], peut être datée avec une certaine précision: le pape Léon III (795-816) aurait reconnu les reliques lors d'un voyage en Francie, et celles-ci auraient protégé un oratoire du saint lors du raid normand qui eut lieu en 881. Le texte a donc été écrit après 881 et au plus tard au Xe siècle[80]. Une seule question reste sans réponse: est-ce bien l'auteur de la *Vita II^a* qui a modifié les origines de Séverin en déclarant qu'il était de Cologne, ou, plus probablement, avait-il déjà un exemplaire aujourd'hui perdu de la Vie écrite par Fortunat qui lui indiquait les origines rhénanes de son héros[81]? Toujours est-il que les clercs rhénans avaient confectionné, probablement vers la fin du IXe ou au Xe siècle au plus tard, une Vie épiscopale sur le troisième prélat de leur ville et c'est celle-ci qui a connu la plus large diffusion de toutes[82].

C. La Vie de Cunibert

Cunibert appartient à la première génération des évêques francs choisis directement dans l'entourage des princes. Né vers la fin du règne de Childebert II dans une riche famille mosellane, il fut d'abord archidiacre à Trèves avant d'occuper le siège épiscopal de Cologne. Attesté dans beaucoup de documents diplomatiques et narratifs, il est connu pour avoir été le confident de Dagobert, le précepteur de Sigebert III et l'ami d'Arnoul de Metz, de Pépin l'Ancien et de Grimoald. Il a été enterré à Cologne[83].

---

[78] Voir aussi, pour l'analyse du texte,: Baillet – Henriet – Junique (2009), p. 81.

[79] Il s'agit de Bruxelles, KBR, ms. 2764, Xe siècle, fol. 138v-153v; cf. *Cat. Bruxelles*, I, p. 345.

[80] Baillet – Henriet – Junique (2009), p. 81.

[81] Levison (1909), p. 47-49. Levison reprend ici en grande partie le travail de Quentin (1902) dont il fait l'éloge.

[82] Nous avons relevé 18 témoins pour le groupe *BHL* 7652-7652b-7653 et 26 pour la *Vita* et/ou *Translatio BHL* 7647-7648; Baillet – Henriet – Junique (2009), p. 81.

[83] Voir Neuss – Oediger (1964), p. 76.

Les manuscrits de sa Vie sont relativement nombreux et on peut les classer selon deux types, ayant à chaque fois des variantes minimes: les Vies du type 1 (*BHL* 2014-2016) représentent un texte relativement sobre et peu développé[84], les Vies du type 2 (*BHL* 2017) constituent un remaniement littéraire de la version du type 1, un peu plus long et plus orné[85].

Quant au contenu du récit, tous les récits – des types 1 et 2 – suivent le même plan: (1) origine et famille du saint, (2) son éducation à la cour, (3) les mérites de l'adolescent attestés par un prodige lumineux, (4) son accès à l'archidiaconat de Trèves puis à l'épiscopat de Cologne, (5) l'éloge de ses vertus, (6) l'illustration de ses vertus par un miracle (une colombe vient de se poser sur la tête du pontife lors de la messe), (7) de nouvelles louanges, (8) sa mort après quarante ans d'épiscopat et sa sépulture dans l'église Saint-Clément à Cologne.

Hélas, aucune Vie ne nous renseigne sur l'auteur ou sur la date de sa rédaction. Une analyse philologique des principaux manuscrits, menée par M. Coens, suggère que le récit primitif de la Vie a été perdu mais que les textes du type 1 se rapprochent beaucoup de ce type primitif[86]. La datation s'avère ainsi difficile: le manuscrit le plus ancien, Bruxelles, KBR, n° 9636-37, du XIe-XIIe siècle, nous donne un *terminus ante quem*[87]. Celui-ci peut certainement être remonté dans le temps, car Levison a montré que la Vie de Cunibert a servi de modèle pour la Vie d'Eberigisil, qui, elle, a été écrite, semble-t-il, dans la deuxième moitié du XIe siècle[88]. N. Gauthier et H. Hellenkemper proposent ainsi la fin du IXe ou le début du Xe siècle comme moment de rédaction[89].

Quant aux sources, M. Coens a identifié comme modèles certains ou probables pour la *Vita Cuniberti* la lettre 6 des *Ep. Aus-*

---

[84] *BHL* 2014, faisant partie de ce type, a été éditée en appendice à la description du cod. 428-42 de la bibliothèque royale de Bruxelles (*Cat. Bruxelles*, I, p. 244-245).

[85] *BHL* 2017 a été éditée par Surius, *De probatis Sanctorum historiis*, t. VI, 1575, p. 273-276 (= 1581, p. 301-304) et t. XI, 1618, p. 274-275.

[86] Coens (1929), en particulier p. 340.

[87] Bruxelles, KBR, ms. 9636-37, du XIe-XIIe siècle, fol. 223-224; c'est une Vie de type 1, b = *BHL* 2015.

[88] Cf. Levison (1931), p. 61, montre que la *Vita Cuniberti* a servi de modèle pour décrire comment Eberigisil est monté au siège de Cologne.

[89] Gauther – Hellenkemper (2002), p. 33.

trasicae, la Vie de Lambert[90], peut-être la Vie d'Arnoul[91] et très probablement la Vie de Balthilde[92].

D. La Vie d'Eberigisil

L'identité d'Eberigisil a mené à une certaine confusion dans la littérature ancienne en supposant qu'il y avait deux évêques de ce nom sur le siège de Cologne: un premier prélat au début Ve siècle et un deuxième vers la fin du VIe siècle[93]. Aujourd'hui, il ne fait pas de doute qu'il ne faut considérer comme historiquement attesté que le second. Son existence est prouvée par Grégoire de Tours qui parle de lui comme envoyé du roi Childebert II à Poitiers en 590 et qui l'a sûrement connu personnellement[94].

À partir du Xe siècle, différents textes, comme la Passion de Géréon ou la Vie de Brunon de Cologne mentionnent à nouveau Eberigisil, mais souvent seulement en quelques mots: Brunon aurait ainsi fait transférer ses reliques de Tongres à Sainte-Cécile à Cologne[95]. C'est ce qui a sans doute ravivé l'intérêt pour le saint évêque et c'est pour cette raison qu'un hagiographe de Cologne a rédigé, mais pas avant le milieu du XIe siècle et selon Levison sans doute dans la deuxième moitié du XIe siècle, une *Vita Evergisli* (BHL 2365)[96]. Écrite en prose rimée dans un style

---

[90] *Vita Landiberti* (Lambert), éd. B. Krusch, *MGH*, *SRM*, VI, Hanovre – Leipzig, 1913, p. 355-384.

[91] *Vita Arnulfi*, éd. B. Krusch, *MGH*, *SRM*, II, Hanovre, 1888, p. 431-446.

[92] *Vita Balthildis*, *ibid.*, p. 484.

[93] Par exemple, Kleinermanns (1896), p. 33.

[94] Grégoire de Tours, *Libri historiarum X*, X, 15, *MGH*, *SRM*, I-1, Hanovre, 1884, p. 425.

[95] Voir aussi *infra*, p. 753-755.

[96] Éd. *AB*, 6 (1887), p. 93-198; la Translation a été éditée par G. H. Pertz, *MGH*, *SRM*, IV, Hanovre – Leipzig, 1902, p. 279-280, et dans: *AASS*, Oct. X, 1861, p. 660; à propos de la datation, voir Levison (1931), p. 62, où il montre qu'au milieu du XIe siècle, la Vie d'Eberigisil n'existait pas encore. Quant au *terminus ante quem*, il se situe peu de temps après 1167 quand le catalogue des évêques de Cologne fut remplacé par un catalogue annoté qui reprenait des passages de la Vie (le chant des anges annonçant la mort de saint Martin et son martyre à Tongres notamment). Cependant, la tradition manuscrite remonte seulement au XIIIe siècle (Düsseldorf, Landes- und Staatsbibliothek, C. 10a, XIIIe siècle, fol. 294-296v).

assez verbeux, mais avec un contenu très maigre, la Vie rapporte qu'Eberigisil était originaire de Tongres et que Séverin de Cologne l'a ramené avec lui dans la métropole mosellane pour lutter contre l'hérésie d'Euphrates. En tant que disciple, il aurait aussi entendu – comme Séverin – les anges annonçant la mort de saint Martin (397). Après la mort de Séverin, Eberigisil est devenu évêque de Cologne. Quand il retourna dans sa ville natale pour y lutter contre des païens, il fut assassiné par des voleurs et a été enterré à Tongres jusqu'à ce que son corps fut rapatrié par Brunon, au Xe siècle, comme nous l'avons déjà signalé. Les sources de l'hagiographe sont faciles à identifier: il a notamment utilisé la *Vita II^a Severini* avec son récit de translation (*BHL* 7647-7648) pour rapporter que Séverin et Eberigisil ont entendu les anges annonçant la mort de saint Martin ensemble et pour calquer le récit de la translation du corps de son héros à Cologne sur celui du transfert de Séverin dans la même ville. D'autres sources identifiées sont la Passion de Géréon, la Vie de Cunibert[97] et probablement la Passion de sainte Ursule. Le rattachement de la légende d'Eberigisil à celle de Séverin, contemporain de saint Martin, explique pourquoi Eberigisil, en réalité un homme de la fin du VIe siècle, est devenu pour notre hagiographe un homme de la fin du IVe et du début du Ve siècle et pourquoi la recherche moderne a longtemps supposé qu'il y eut deux évêques du même nom à Cologne. Levison a le mérite d'avoir montré comment cette erreur a pu se produire[98].

III. Quelques récits rédigés à la suite de translations de reliques en Germanie

A. Le phénomène des translations de reliques en Germanie

L'intégration des régions germaniques dans l'espace chrétien à l'époque carolingienne nécessitait la mise en place d'une structure ecclésiastique avec, en premier lieu, la construction des

---

[97] Levison (1931), p. 61, qui montre que la Vie de Cunibert a servi de modèle pour relater comment Eberigisil a été élevé sur le siège de Cologne.
[98] Levison (1931).

églises. Celles-ci devaient être dotées de reliques qu'il a fallu apporter d'Italie et de la Francie occidentale. En Saxe, ces translations devinrent si fréquentes au cours du IXe siècle qu'elles suscitèrent une riche production littéraire relatant de façon détaillée les transferts des saints corps. Le prototype de ces récits composés en Francie orientale est la *Translatio Marcellini et Petri* d'Eginhard (*BHL* 5233) qui date de 834 environ et qui rapporte comment le conseiller de Louis le Pieux avait acquis à Rome les reliques de deux martyrs, comment il les fit transporter à Seligenstadt et quelles furent les manifestations divines lors du transfert. En adaptant par la suite ce modèle de façon plus ou moins libre, d'autres hagiographes ont décrit les transferts des reliques de Liboire du Mans à Paderborn en 836 (*BHL* 4911, 4913), de saint Vite de Saint-Denis à Corvey en 836 (*BHL* 8718-8719), d'Alexandre de Rome à Wildeshausen en 851 (*BHL* 283), de sainte Pusinne de Binson à Herford en 860 (*BHL* 6995), de saint Mars d'Auxerre à Corvey en 863 (*BHL* 5544c), et de saint Justin de Paris à Corvey en 891 (*BHL* 4581). Ce phénomène – les «translations de reliques en Saxe» – est désormais bien connu grâce à l'étude de Hedwig Röckelein[99] et la plupart de ces récits ont déjà été présentés par T. Klüppel dans le deuxième volume d'*Hagiographies*[100]. Nous pouvons donc nous contenter d'analyser ici les quelques écrits nécessaires à un panorama complet et dépassant parfois le cadre de la Saxe et de l'époque carolingienne: la *Translatio Marcellini et Petri*, suivie d'une *Passio* relative aux mêmes saints, et la *Vita et Translatio Severi*, datant toutes les deux du IXe siècle ainsi qu'un récit de translation de Patrocle suivi d'une *Passio II^a*, écrits sans doute dans la deuxième moitié du Xe siècle. En effet, à bien des égards, les Ottoniens se sont glissés dans les traditions carolingiennes, dont celle de la politique des reliques.

---

[99] RÖCKELEIN (2002).
[100] Pour la *Translatio Alexandri* (*BHL* 283), voir KLÜPPEL (1996) p. 181-182, pour le *Sermo Marsi* (*BHL* 5544c), *Ibid.*, p. 198, pour les différentes versions de la *Translatio Liborii* (*BHL BHL* 4911 et 4913), *Ibid.*, p. 196, pour la *Translatio Viti* (*BHL* 8718-8719), *Ibid.*, p. 195, pour la *Translatio Pusinnae* (*BHL* 6995), *Ibid.*, p. 195-196 et pour la *Translatio Iustini* (*BHL* 4581), *Ibid.*, p. 195.

B. La *Translatio Marcellini et Petri* (*BHL* 5233), suivie d'une *Passio* en l'honneur des mêmes saints (*BHL* 5232)

Né vers 775, Éginhard fut l'un des grandes figures des règnes de Charlemagne et de Louis le Pieux. Très proche du premier, il devint conseiller du second, jusqu'à ce qu'il se retire, vers 830, dans le monastère de Seligenstadt qu'il avait fondé lui-même et où il est mort en 840. En 830, quelques années après la rédaction de sa *Vita Karoli*, il écrivit, à Seligenstadt, un, voire deux, textes sur Marcellin et Pierre, deux martyrs romains victimes des persécutions sous Dioclétien, dont il avait fait venir les reliques de Rome à Seligenstadt: la *Translatio* (*BHL* 5233)[101] et probablement aussi la *Passio* (*BHL* 5232)[102]. L'attribution du récit de la translation à Éginhard provient des plus anciens manuscrits qui nous donnent son nom dans le titre de l'œuvre[103]. La datation du texte repose sur le dernier miracle daté du 28 août 830, à la suite duquel l'auteur semble avoir terminé la rédaction définitive de l'œuvre[104]. Dans son ensemble, la *Translatio* a un fort caractère historiographique: dans la première partie qui est consacrée au transfert des reliques à proprement parler, l'hagiographe a écrit un récit très détaillé et même captivant, reprenant par exemple en détail comment une délégation envoyée à Rome a pu obtenir les reliques qui, plus tard, dans des conditions peu claires, furent temporairement enlevées par Hilduin, abbé de Saint-Denis[105]. La deuxième partie, qui est dédiée aux miracles qui se sont produits lors et à la suite du transfert, est également élaborée avec beaucoup de minutie: dans le livre IV, Éginhard explique ainsi qu'il s'est fait envoyer des rapports qui relatent les miracles que les reliques de Marcellin et Pierre ont accomplis dans d'autres lieux de vénération:

---

[101] ÉGINHARD, *Translatio Marcellini et Petri*, éd. G. WAITZ, *MGH*, *SS*, XV-1, Hanovre, 1887, p. 239-264.

[102] *Passio Marcellini et Petri*, éd. E. DÜMMLER, *MGH*, *Poet. Lat.*, II, Berlin, 1884, p. 125-135.

[103] Les trois manuscrits les plus anciens de la *Translatio* sont: Paris, BnF, lat. 14143 (IXe siècle), fol. 60r-73v, Vatican, Reg. lat. 711 II (Xe siècle), fol. 96v-103v et Paris, BnF, lat. 5310 (Xe siècle), fol. 40v-48r.

[104] HEINZELMANN (1997), en part. p. 278. Ce travail constitue par ailleurs la principale analyse de l'œuvre; voir également: KRÖNERT (2019).

[105] ÉGINHARD, *Translatio*, éd., WAITZ p. 239-248.

Valenciennes, Gand et Maastricht. Ces rapports étaient ensuite intégrés dans le texte courant de l'œuvre. Ce qui différencie beaucoup le texte d'autres récits de translation, c'est le message à la fois politique et religieux qu'il véhicule de façon clairement affichée: dans le prologue, Éginhard écrit que ceux qui rédigent des biographies de justes et d'hommes vivant selon des préceptes de Dieu, souhaitaient inciter, par de tels exemples, d'autres hommes à corriger leurs mauvaises habitudes et à louer la toute-puissance de Dieu. Non seulement exempts de jalousie, mais aussi débordants d'amour – de *caritas* –, ils doivent être imités par beaucoup d'autres[106]. L'hagiographe fait donc part de son intention d'améliorer, grâce à son œuvre, le comportement de ses contemporains et de participer à un renouvellement moral de la société qui doit s'orienter à la communauté des saints et le corps spirituel du Christ[107]. Étant donné qu'Éginhard fréquentait les très hautes sphères de l'empire, il pouvait effectivement espérer que son œuvre soit lue à la cour et qu'elle exerce par la suite une influence réelle.

Quant à la *Passio Marcellini et Petri*, son attribution à Éginhard, provient d'un seul manuscrit, Vatican, Reg. lat. 711 II, du Xe siècle[108], où l'auteur est mentionné; elle est donc moins sûre que celle de la *Translatio* mais reste probable. Il s'agit d'un poème de 118 strophes composées, chacune, de trois vers de quinze syllabes et, plus précisément, d'une adaptation rythmique de tétramètre trochaïque cataleptique. Très populaire de tous temps, ce mètre nécessitait cependant une excellente maîtrise du latin. Éginhard faisait sans aucun doute partie des quelques personnes capables de composer de tels vers, car il est connu pour avoir eu des qualités de poètes et sa *Vita Karoli* est écrite dans un style très raffiné[109]. Cette attribution n'est d'ailleurs pas exclue par le manuscrit le plus ancien, Paris, BnF, lat. 14143, datant du IXe siècle, ni par l'enjeu du texte: Éginhard a fait des efforts considérables pour obtenir les reliques de Marcellin et Pierre, il les a vénérées avec faveur, comme il l'atteste lui-même dans sa *Translatio Marcellini et Petri*, et, une fois retiré sans le monastère de Seligenstadt et libéré de ses engage-

---

[106] *Ibid.*, p. 239 (prologue).
[107] HEINZELMANN (1997), p. 294-297.
[108] Vatican, Reg. lat. 711 II (Xe siècle), fol. 96v-103v.
[109] BRUNHÖLZL (1991), p. 80.

ments à la cour, il pouvait s'adonner librement à d'autres occupations religieuses et littéraires. Il paraît donc tout à fait possible que la *Passio* ait été composée vers 830 ou peu de temps après à Seligenstadt. Étant donné que l'hagiographe rapporte beaucoup de détails sur les martyres des deux saints, il est presque sûr qu'il s'est appuyé sur une ancienne Passion aujourd'hui perdue et qui, selon F. Brunhölzl, pourrait dater du Ve ou du VIe siècle[110].

C. La Vita et Translatio Severi (*BHL* 7681-7682)

La *Vita et Translatio Severi* (*BHL* 7681, 7682), consacrée à un saint italien qui est censé avoir vécu vers la fin du IVe siècle, ressemble, quant à sa forme, plutôt à un rapport de voyage qui inclut une Vie et un récit de translation qu'à une *Vita* et une *Translatio* telles qu'on les trouve habituellement dans les manuscrits. L'œuvre, écrite vers 860[111], a été éditée dans les *Acta Sanctorum*[112] et les *MGH*[113], et, excepté un seul manuscrit du XIIe siècle qui ne contient que la Vie (*BHL* 7681), les rares témoins répertoriés dans la *BHL*ms datent tous de la fin du Moyen Âge[114].

Dans la phrase introductive de l'œuvre, Liutolf, prêtre à Mayence, s'adresse à un certain Erlarius, diacre dans la même ville, afin de lui relater ce qu'il avait appris sur Sévère dont les reliques étaient vénérées depuis peu de temps dans l'église Saint-Alban de Mayence. À l'occasion d'un pèlerinage à Rome, de passage à Ravenne, il avait décidé, dit-il, de mener une enquête sur ce saint. D'abord déçu, car personne ne pouvait le renseigner, il fut finalement envoyé dans un monastère dans les environs de la ville, Saint-Apollinaire, où un moine lui raconta les hauts faits de la vie du saint[115]. Ce récit, la véritable *Vita*, n'occupe que la moitié du texte de *BHL* 7681, et pour cause: seulement deux épisodes, son élection à l'épiscopat et sa mort, y

---

[110] *Ibid.*
[111] GERLICH (1954), p. 299; à propos de ce texte, voir aussi GEARY (1990), p. 80-81.
[112] Éd. J. BOLLAND, *AASS*, Feb. I, 1658, p. 88-91.
[113] Éd. L. DE HEINEMANN, *MGH, SS*, XV-1, Hanovre, 1887, p. 289-293.
[114] Bruxelles, KBR 20826-20828 (3265), fol. 43v-44v.
[115] *Vita Severi*, cap. 1-3, éd. DE HEINEMANN, p. 290.

sont relatés de façon détaillée; ils correspondent dans leurs grands traits à ce que Agnellus a rapporté sur ce saint dans son *Liber pontificalis ecclesiae Ravennatis*, élaboré dans les années trente et quarante du IXe siècle, mais que Liutolf ne semble pas avoir connu[116]. Sévère y est présenté comme confesseur, et non comme un martyr, comme le souligne l'hagiographe. D'origine modeste et marié à Vincentia avec laquelle il avait une fille, Innocentia, le saint était un ouvrier qui travaillait la laine. Après la mort de l'évêque de Ravenne, il se rendit dans la ville pour savoir qui lui succéderait. C'est alors lui qu'il fut désigné par la volonté divine, sous forme d'une colombe qui se posa sur sa tête. Vers la fin de sa vie, il choisit lui-même sa tombe et s'y allongea pour s'endormir. En effet, lors de son sommeil, son âme s'envola vers le ciel. Pour étoffer cette «biographie» assez maigre, Liutolf y inclut des discours directs ainsi que quelques éloges assez généraux[117]. Puis, il reprend le récit de son propre voyage en ajoutant qu'il s'était enquis du jour de la fête du saint avant de rentrer chez lui[118].

La deuxième partie de l'œuvre, le récit de translation (*BHL* 7682), est le récit très captivant des évènements qui se sont produits en 836: Félix, un prêtre franc, a fait croire aux moines de Saint-Apollinaire qu'il souhaitait intégrer leur communauté. Après avoir gagné leur confiance, il saisit l'occasion pour subtiliser les corps de Sévère, de son épouse et de sa fille. Quand les moines découvrirent le vol, ils se mirent à sa poursuite, mais Félix s'enfuit de nuit. Lors de sa cavale, il croisa par hasard le chemin d'Otgar, archevêque de Mayence, qui était à ce moment-là à Pavie en mission diplomatique pour réconcilier Louis le Pieux avec son fils Lothaire. Très heureux de se voir proposer ces reliques, il les acheta et les transféra dans sa ville épiscopale où elles furent déposées dans l'église Saint-Alban. Mais, peu de temps après, Sévère fut transféré à Erfurt en Thuringe où un miracle d'exorcisme et bien d'autres interventions divines illustrèrent sa vertu[119]. Liutolf termine son récit en

---

[116] Pour AGNELLUS RAVENNATIS, *Liber pontificalis ecclesiae Ravennatis*, cap. 15, 17, éd. D. M. DELIYANNIS, Turnhout, 2006 (*CC CM*, 199).
[117] *Vita Severi*, cap. 4, éd. DE HEINEMANN, p. 290-291.
[118] *Ibid.*, cap. 5-7, p. 291.
[119] *Translatio Severi*, cap. 1-4, éd. DE HEINEMANN, p. 291-293; cf. pour cet épisode également GEARY (1990), p. 80-81, et GERLICH (1954), p. 298-

ajoutant que les reliques d'Innocentia se trouvent désormais dans l'église l'Altenmünster à Mayence et en assurant à Erlarius que c'est tout ce qu'il avait appris lors de ses enquêtes[120].

D. La Translatio Patrocli Susatum (*BHL* 6523) et la Vita ii^a Patrocli (*BHL* 6521)

Patrocle est un saint de la Gaule qui, selon sa *Passio I^a* (*BHL* 6520)[121] – un texte très légendaire qui a été écrit au milieu du vi^e siècle[122] – a subi le martyre à Troyes en Champagne, sa ville natale, au milieu du iiie siècle. En 959, Brunon, frère de l'empereur Otton Ier, archevêque de Cologne et duc de Lotharingie, a fait venir ses reliques à Soest en Westphalie[123]. Cette translation nous est connue grâce à un récit (*BHL* 6523) qui est inclus dans l'un des manuscrits de la *Vita Brunonis* écrite par Ruotger[124], Bruxelles, KBR, 329-341 (3134); originaire de Saint-Pantaléon de Cologne, ce témoin manuscrit date seulement du xive siècle. Une deuxième copie de la *Translatio Patrocli* se trouvait, semble-il, dans le légendaire de Böddeken, du xve siècle, qui nous est connu grâce à une étude de M. Moretus datant de 1908 mais qui a brûlé lors de la Seconde guerre mondiale[125]. L'existence de cette deuxième copie suggère que le récit a aussi circulé indépendamment de la Vie de Brunon. Malgré ces témoins tardifs, il est fort probable que cette *Translatio* a été rédigée seulement peu de temps après l'évènement, au xe siècle

---

302, qui présente une analyse détaillée du contexte politique dans lequel Otgar a ici agi.

[120] *Translatio Severi*, cap. 5, éd. De Heinemann, p. 293.

[121] *Passio I^a Patrocli*, *AASS*, Ian. II, 1643, p. 343-345.

[122] Van Der Straeten (1960) et Jansen (1964), « Der heilige Märtyrer Patroklus ».

[123] Jansen (1964), « Die Reliquienübetragung », discute des dates des translations à Cologne, puis à Soest.

[124] *Vita Brunonis*, éd. G. H. Pertz, *MGH*, *SS*, IV, Hanovre, 1841, p. 252-275 et *Translatio Patrocli*, éd. G. H. Pertz, *ibid.*, p. 280-281; celle-ci est également éditée dans *AASS*, Ian. II, 1643, p. 348-349 et traduite en allemand dans Jansen (1964), « Die Reliquienübetragung », p. 14-16.

[125] Münster, UB, 20, fol. 135v-136v; voir surtout H. Moretus, « De magno legendario Bodecensi », *AB*, 27 (1908), p. 257-358, en particulier p. 287-288; Moretus a identifié ce texte par son numéro de *BHL* 6523, mais curieusement intitulé *Passio*, peut-être parce que l'auteur de la *Translatio* rappelle au début de son œuvre brièvement la passion du saint.

encore, par un clerc qui était d'une façon ou d'une autre impliqué dans ce transfert: seule l'institution qui a accueilli les nouvelles reliques avait véritablement intérêt à garder une trace détaillée des conditions dans lesquelles elles avaient été acquises[126].

L'auteur de la *Translatio Patrocli* rappelle d'abord brièvement le martyre du saint sous Aurélien, puis il explique comment Brunon de Cologne a été envoyé par son frère, Otton Ier, dans la province de Sens pour une mission de paix. Lors de son séjour à Troyes il a obtenu de l'évêque de la ville, Anségise (914-970), l'autorisation de transférer le corps de Patrocle à Cologne. Celui-ci a été identifié grâce à des odeurs douces et incomparables, puis transféré dans la métropole rhénane. C'est là que Brunon décida de l'envoyer à Soest, en Saxe, un lieu riche par son commerce, mais pauvre en connaissance du Christ. En effet, conclut l'hagiographe, Patrocle y a connu, par la suite, une importante vénération[127].

Il est tout-à-fait possible que la *Vita I[a]* de Patrocle (*BHL* 6520) ait été réécrite à l'occasion de la translation des reliques du saint, en 959. Une seule copie de cette *Vita II[a] Patrocli* (*BHL* 6521) a pour l'instant pu être identifiée dans le légendier perdu de Böddeken, du XVe siècle[128]. Selon l'analyse de Moretus, il s'agissait cependant d'une version légèrement modifiée du récit de *BHL* 6521[129]. Cette reprise nous prouve que la *Passio II[a]* est bien plus ancienne que cette seule copie connue et qu'il est tout-à-fait possible qu'elle ait été rédigée en même temps que la *Translatio*, peu de temps après de transfert des re-

---

[126] La version de la Vie de Brunon présente dans le manuscrit Bruxelles, KBR, 329-341 (3134), contient aussi un très bref récit du transfert des reliques d'Eberigisil (*BHL* 2366). Il est trop succinct pour être présenté ici, et il n'y a aucun indice suggérant qu'il ait circulé indépendamment de la Vie de Brunon; signalons donc seulement que l'auteur mentionne comment Brunon a fait venir les reliques de son lointain successeur de Tongres à Cologne. Il est fort probable que cet ajout, édité par Pertz (*MGH*, *SS*, IV, Hanovre, 1841, p. 279-280), date également de la deuxième moitié du Xe siècle. Cf. *supra*, p. 746-747, la Vie d'Eberigisil (*BHL* 2365).

[127] *Vita Patrocli*, éd. G. H. Pertz, p. 280-281.

[128] Münster, UB, 20, fol. 133v-135v.

[129] Cf. Moretus, *De magno legendario Bodecensi*, p. 257-358., et spécialement p. 287: «Haec est retractatio quaedam non iam Passionis *BHL* 6520, sed de supra n. 20, sed Passionis *BHL* 6521»; la *Passio II[a]* est éditée dans *AASS*, Ian. II, 1643, p. 345-347.

liques de Patrocle à Soest en 959. Cette Passion est légèrement plus longue que la *Passio I^a*, mais sur le fond, son auteur n'a rien changé au contenu: l'éloge général du saint, sa double défense face à son persécuteur Aurélien, rapportée en discours direct, sa mise à mort et sa sépulture, tout est repris en préservant même les noms des acteurs secondaires. Le style de cette *Passio II^a* est très clair et plutôt classique ce qui plaide pour une réécriture réalisée par un hagiographe qui était déjà sous l'influence de la «réforme carolingienne». D'où notre hypothèse selon laquelle le clergé de Cologne et/ou de Soest a souhaité avoir un texte relatif à Patrocle qui ait fait, sur le plan stylistique, «peau neuve».

Bibliographie

ANTON, H. H. – HAVERKAMP, A., dir., *2000 Jahre Trier*, II, Trèves, 1996.

BAILLET, C. – HENRIET, P. – JUNIQUE, S., «Le dossier hagiographique de Saint-Seurin», in I. CARTRON – D. BARRAUD – P. HENRIET – A. MICHEL, éd., *Autour de Saint-Seurin: Lieu, Mémoire, Pouvoir. Des premiers temps chrétiens à la fin du Moyen Âge.* Actes du colloque de Bordeaux (12-14 octobre 2006), Bordeaux 2009, p. 79-85 (Mémoires, 21).

BERSCHIN, W., *Biographie und Epochenstil im Lateinischen Mittelalter*, III: *Karolingische Biographie 750-920 n. Chr.*, Stuttgart, 1991.

BRUNHÖLZL, F., *Histoire de la littérature latine*, I-2: *L'époque carolingienne*, Turnhout, 1991.

COENS, M., «Les Vies de S. Cunibert de Cologne et la tradition manuscrite», *AB*, 47 (1929), p. 338-367.

GAUTHER, N. – HELLENKEMPER, H., «Cologne», in EID., dir., *Topographie chrétienne des cités de la Gaule, des origines au milieu du VIIIe siècle*, XII: *Province ecclésiastique de Cologne (Germania secunda)*, p. 25-69.

GEARY, P. J., *Le vol des reliques au Moyen Âge, Furta Sacra*, Paris, 1990.

GERLICH, A., «Die Reichspolitik des Erzbischofs Otgar von Mainz», in *Festschrift Camille Wampach, Rheinische Vierteljahrsblätter*, 19 (1954), p. 286-316.

GOULLET, M., «Les saints du diocèse de Toul (SHG VI)», in M. HEINZELMANN, dir., *L'hagiographie du haut Moyen Âge en Gaule du Nord*, Stuttgart, 2001, p. 11-90 (Beihefte der Francia, 52).

—, «Les saints du diocèse de Metz (SHG X)», In EAD – M. HEINZELMANN, dir., *Miracles, Vies et réécritures dans l'Occident médiéval*, Ostfildern, 2006, p. 149-317 (Beihefte der Francia, 65).

HANSEN, J. A. J., «Kirchengeschichtliche Notizen», *Treviris oder Trierisches Archiv für Vaterlandskunde*, 2 (1841), p. 281-285.
HEINZELMANN, M., «Einhards 'Translatio Marcellini et Petri': Eine hagiographische Reformschrift von 830», in H. SCHEFERS, éd., *Einhard. Studien zu Leben und Werk. Dem Gedenken an Helmut Beumann gewidmet*, Darmstadt 1997, p. 269-299 (Arbeiten der Hessischen Historischen Kommission, Neue Folge, 12).
HEYEN, F.-J., «St. Goar im frühen und hohen Mittelalter», *Kurtrierisches Jahrbuch*, 1 (1961), p. 87-106.
JANSEN, J., «Der heilige Märtyrer Patroklus», in H. SCHWARTZ, éd., *Der heilige Patroklus. Festschrift zur Tausend-Jahrfeier der Reliquienübertragung nach Soest 1964*, Soest, 1964, p. 2-13.
—, «Die Reliquienübetragung von Troyes nach Soest», *Ibid.*, p. 14-17.
KLEINE, U., *Gesta, Fama, Scripta. Rheinische Mirakel des Hochmittelalters zwischen Geschichtsdeutung, Erzählung und sozialer Praxis*, Stuttgart, 2006 (Beitäge zur Hagiographie, 7).
KLEINERMANNS, J., *Die heiligen auf dem bischöflichen bzw. erzbischöflichen Stuhle von Köln*, I: *Erstes Jahrtausend*, Cologne 1896, p. 33.
KLOOS, R. M., *Lambertus de Legia. De Vita, translatione ac miraculis sancti Matthiae apostoli libri quinque*, Trèves, 1958 (Trierer Theologische Studien, 8).
KLÜPPEL, T., «Die Germania (750-950)», in *Hagiographies*, II (1996), p. 161-209.
KRÖNERT, K., «Les *Miracula sancti Maximini* (*BHL* 5826): entre hagiographie et historiographie», *Revue bénédictine*, 115 (2005), p. 112-150.
—, *La construction du passé de la cité de Trèves: VIIIe-XIe siècles. Études d'un corpus hagiographique*, thèse de doctorat soutenue en 2003 à l'université Paris X – Nanterre, Lille, Atelier national de reproduction des thèses, 2005 (dont est issu, avec une thématique resserrée, le livre *L'exaltation de Trèves*).
—, «Production hagiographique et enjeux politiques à Trèves (X^e-XIe siècle)», in E. BOZOKY, éd., *Hagiographie, idéologie et politique au Moyen Âge en Occident, Actes du colloque international du Centre d'Études supérieures de Civilisation médiévale de Poitiers, 11-14 septembre 2008*, Turnhout, 2012, p. 185-198 (Hagiologia, 8).
—, *L'exaltation de Trèves. Écriture hagiographique et passé historique de la métropole mosellane (VIIIe-XIe siècle)*, Ostfildern, 2010 (Beihefte der Francia, 70).
—, «Saint Maximin de Trèves, un Aquitain?», in E. BOZOKY, éd., *Saints aquitains. Missionnaires et pèlerins du haut Moyen Age*, Rennes, 2010, p. 81-102.

—, « La production hagiographique en Germanie à l'époque de Louis le Pieux. Productivité littéraire et crises, mais quel rapport? », in M. GRAVEL – S. KASCHKE, éd., *Regnum semper reformandum*, Ostfildern, Thorbecke, 2019, p. 269-373 (Relectio. Karolingische Perspektiven – Perspectives carolingiennes – Carolingian Perspectives, 2).

KRÖNERT, K. – MÉRIAUX, C., « Saints et barbares en Gaule du Nord pendant le haut Moyen Âge », in E. BOZOKY, éd., *Les saints face aux barbares au haut Moyen Âge. Réalités et légendes* », Rennes, 2017, p. 29-51 (collection « Histoire »).

LEBECQ, S., « Les Frisons de Saint-Goar : présentation, traduction et bref commentaire des chapitres 28 et 29 des 'Miracula sancti Goaris' de Waldalbert de Prüm », in M. GRAVEL – S. ROSSIGNOL, « Ad libros! » *Mélanges d'études médiévales offerts à Denise Angers et Joseph-Claude Poulin*, Montréal, 2011, p. 11-20 (réimp. in ID., *Hommes, mers et terres du Nord au début du Moyen Âge*, 2: *Centres, communications, échanges*, Lille 2011, p. 303-312).

LEVISON, W., « Die Entwicklung der Legende Severins von Köln », *Bonner Jahrbücher*, 118 (1909), p. 34-53 (réimp. in ID., *Aus rheinischer und fränkischer Frühzeit, Ausgewählte Aufsätze*, Düsseldorf, 1948, p. 28-48).

—, « Bischof Eberigisil von Köln », in *Festschrift Albert Brackmann*, Weimar, 1931, p. 40-63 (réimp. *Ibid.*, p. 57-75).

LOTTER, F. – GÄBE, S., « Die hagiographische Literatur im deutschen Sprachraum unter den Ottonen und Saliern (ca. 960-1130) », in *Hagiographies*, IV (2006), p. 273-521.

NEUSS, W., – OEDIGER, F. W., *Das Bistum Köln von den Anfängen bis zum Ende des 12. Jhs.*, Cologne, 1964.

PÄFFGEN, B., « Der heilige Severin im Spiegel der frühen historischen Überlieferung », in J. OEPEN – B. PÄFFGEN – S. SCHRENK – U. TEGTMEIER, *Der heilige Severin von Köln. Verehrung und Legende. Befunde und Forschungen zur Schreinöffung von 1999*, Siegburg, 2011 (Studien zur Kölner Kirchengeschichte, 40).

PÄFFGEN, B. – CARLO PANGERL, D., « Die *Vita et Translatio Sancti Severini* (BHL 7647, 7648) in Kommentar und Übersetzung », in *Ibid.*, p. 543-581.

PAULY, F., « Das Stift St. Kastor in Karden an der Mosel », in *Germania Sacra*, NF 19: *Die Bistümer der Kirchenprovinz Trier, Das Erzbistum Trier III*, Berlin – New York 1986, p. 9-14.

PHILIPPART, G. – WAGNER, A., « Hagiographie lorraine (950-1130). Les diocèses de Metz, Toul et Verdun », in *Hagiographies*, IV (2006), p. 585-744.

POHLSANDER, H. A., «Maximinus und Paulinus», *Trierer Zeitschrift für Geschichte und Kunst des Trierer Landes und seiner Nachbargebiete*, 59 (1996), p. 119-180.

QUENTIN, H., «La plus ancienne Vie de saint Seurin de Bordeaux», in *Mélanges Léonce Couture Études d'histoires méridionales*, Toulouse, 1902, p. 23-63.

RÖCKELEIN, H., *Reliquientranslationen nach Sachsen im 9. Jahrhundert. Über Kommunikation, Mobilität und Öffentlichkeit im Frühmittelalter*, Stuttgart, 2002 (Beihefte der Francia, 48).

ROMANO, A., *L'opera agiografica di Lupo di Ferrières, Testo critico, traduzione e nota della 'Vita Maximini' e, in Appendice, testo e traduzione della 'Vita Wiberti'*, Galatina, Congedo, 1995.

STIENE, H.-E., *Wandalbert de Prüm, Vita sancti Goaris*, Frankfort s .l. M., 1981 (Europäische Hochschulschriften, série I, 399).

STRUCK, W.-H., «Das Stift St. Lubentius in Dietkirchen», in *Germania Sacra*, N.F. 22: *Die Bistümer der Kirchenprovinz Trier, Das Erzbistum Trier*, IV, Berlin – New York 1986, p. 51-55.

VAN DER STRAETEN, J., «La Passion de saint Patrocle de Troyes – ses sources», *AB*, 78 (1960), p. 145-153.

WINHELLER, E., *Die Lebensbeschreibungen der vorkarolingischen Bischöfe von Trier*, Bonn, 1935 (Rheinisches Archiv, 27).

Annexe
La Vie de sainte Odile
(diocèse de Strasbourg)

par

Michèle GAILLARD

De l'écriture hagiographique dans le diocèse de Strasbourg entre 750 et 950 ne nous est parvenue qu'une seule œuvre, la *Vita Odiliae* (*BHL* 6271), connue par de nombreux manuscrits, près de 25, dont les deux plus anciens (Saint-Gall 577 et Bruxelles, KBR 3316) ont été confectionnés au cours du Xe siècle[1].

Selon sa *Vita*, Odile était la fille du duc d'Alsace, Eticho-Adalric (vers 679-700), connu par d'autres sources, en particulier la Vie de saint Germain de Moutier-Grandval, et évoqué par un certain nombre de documents diplomatiques[2]. Elle semble avoir vécu à la fin du VIIe siècle et au début du VIIIe siècle. Un chapitre de la Vie suggère qu'elle a été écrite après le concile d'Aix-la-Chapelle de 816 qui codifia le mode de vie des religieuses par une *Institutio* destinée aux *sanctimoniales canonice degentes*; l'auteur affirme en effet qu'Odile interrogea ses religieuses sur la vie régulière et choisit la vie canoniale parce qu'elle ne voulait pas imposer une règle trop dure à celles qui leur succéderaient. Sainte Odile est connue de l'auteur de la Vie de sainte Ide de Hersfeld (*BHL* 4143), écrite entre 980 et 983, ce qui fournit le premier témoignage du culte de sainte Odile. On peut donc supposer que la Vie a été écrite au IXe siècle quand la vie canoniale devint usuelle dans les grands monastères de Germanie.

---

[1] Saint-Gall 577 daté des IXe-Xe siècles, fol. 71-86,; KBR 3316 daté du IXe siècle, fol. 72-82v (manuscrit en provenance de Stavelot, acquis par la Bibliothèque Royale de Belgique en 1900); éd. B. KRUSCH, *MGH*, *SRM*, VI, Hanovre – Leipzig, 1913, p. 24-50; études historiques d'Odile et de sa famille dans HUMMER (2005) et WEBER (2019).

[2] *Vita Germani auct. Boboleno* (*BHL* 3467), éd. B. KRUSCH, *MGH*, *SRM*, V, Hanovre – Leipzig, 1910, p. 33-40; H. EBLING, *Prosopographie der Amtsträger des Merowingerreiches. Von Chlothar II. (613) bis Karl Martell (741)*, Munich, 1974, n°VIII, p. 33-36 (Beihefte der Francia, 2).

Cette datation fut aussi avancée par Christian Pfister, qui a relevé dans la *Vita Odiliae* quelques épisodes empruntés à la *Vita Sadalbergae*, fondatrice et abbesse de Sainte-Marie-Saint-Jean de Laon, dont la vie fut écrite au VIIe siècle[3]: Salaberge, comme Odile était aveugle et les deux jeunes filles ont été guéries par des religieux venus de Bavière; les deux monastères possédaient une église Sainte-Marie et une église Saint-Jean; Salaberge et Odile étaient filles de ducs d'Alsace. Bien que ce ne fût pas spécifié dans leurs *Vitae*, Gondoin, le père de Salaberge est le premier duc d'Alsace connu et a favorisé la fondation de Moutier-Grandval par Walbert de Luxeuil et Germain. Dans la Vie de Germain, Adalric-Eticho, le père d'Odile, était l'ennemi de la nouvelle abbaye et tua Germain. L'événement n'est pas mentionné dans le Vie de sainte Odile mais Eticho, tout en étant un homme pieux, y apparaît comme un personnage extrêmement violent qui voulut faire tuer sa fille parce qu'elle était aveugle et frappa son fils si violemment qu'il en mourut. Ainsi, le propos de la *Vita Odiliae* ne se conforme pas à celui des Vies d'abbesses du haut Moyen Âge; l'aspect surprenant de cette Vie a déjà été relevé par Christian Pfister qui remarquait que le récit possède «un tour romanesque tout à fait singulier[4]».

Si la structure de la Vie de sainte Odile s'apparente à un conte[5], elle n'en a pas moins été écrite dans le but de promouvoir le culte de la sainte, de mettre en valeur le monastère où celle-ci est inhumée et de résoudre un certain nombre de problèmes qui se posaient à la communauté au moment de sa rédaction. Les données de la *Vita* concernant le monastère et la vie des religieuses participent de la volonté de l'hagiographe d'expliquer la situation de son époque en en attribuant l'origine à la sainte et, ce faisant, de conforter le statut et le pouvoir de la communauté du Mont-Sainte-Odile. L'hagiographe rapporte ainsi au temps d'Odile deux changements majeurs: l'adoption de la règle des chanoinesses et la construction d'un deuxième monastère en contrebas, Niedermunster. Rapporter à l'époque

---

[3] Sur cette datation voir en dernier lieu, M. GAILLARD, «Les saints de l'abbaye Sainte-Marie-Saint-Jean de Laon», in M. GOULLET – M. HEINZELMANN, éd., *Miracles, Vies et réécritures dans l'Occident médiéval*, Ostfildern, 2006, p. 319-340 (Beihefte der Francia, 65).

[4] PFISTER (1891), p. 419.

[5] GAILLARD (2018).

de sainte Odile, le choix de la règle canoniale est particulièrement anachronique[6] mais à l'époque de l'écriture de la *Vita*, il était sans doute plus prestigieux de rapporter ce choix à la sainte fondatrice, plutôt qu'à un texte issu d'un concile carolingien, peut-être ignoré de l'auteur. L'attribution à Odile de la fondation de Niedermunster répond sans doute à d'autres objectifs: affirmer la dépendance de l'établissement du bas vis-à-vis de sainte Odile et combattre du même coup la légende (historiquement fondée) qui rattachait celle-ci à l'époque carolingienne, à Hugues de Tours et à son épouse Abba et lui donnait ainsi autant de prestige qu'à l'abbaye du Mont.

Malgré l'originalité du récit et les analogies avec la *Vita Sadalbergae,* on ne peut totalement exclure la possibilité de l'écriture d'une *Vita antiqua* qui aurait contenu des détails sur la famille d'Odile, d'autant qu'à travers ce récit, les Étichonides paraissent mener une politique similaire à celle d'autres grandes familles aristocratiques qui fondent plusieurs monastères en quelques décennies. La fondation du monastère par Eticho, avant même la naissance d'Odile, participerait donc de ce mouvement de fondations aristocratiques qui visait autant à sacraliser le pouvoir de la famille qu'à protéger ses biens des attaques de familles aristocratiques rivales.

Cependant, la plus ancienne mention du monastère étant une charte de 783, où une certaine Odsindis fait un don au monastère construit en l'honneur de sainte Marie et d'autres saints et ne mentionne pas Odile[7], il est vraisemblable que la légende de sainte Odile s'est progressivement construite depuis l'époque de la renaissance de la famille d'Eticho autour du comte Hugues de Tours dans la première moitié du IXe siècle[8] (qui voit proba-

---

[6] Ce choix n'a pu avoir lieu qu'après la promulgation de l'*Institutio sanctimonialium* en 816; éd. A. WERMINGHOFF, *MGH, Conc.*, II-1, Hanovre – Leipzig, 1906, p. 421-456.

[7] WILSDORFF (1993), p. 207; analyse et extraits de l'acte (connu par une copie du XIIe siècle) dans A. BRÜCKNER, *Regesta Alsatiae aevi merovingici et karolini (496-918)*, Strasbourg, 1949, I, n° 302, p. 189.

[8] Sur la famille d'Hugues de Tours, VOLLMER (1957), p. 163-175. La tradition a gardé le souvenir d'une croix monumentale, offerte par Hugues et son épouse Abba à Niedermunster, cf. WILSDORF (1967) et WILSDORF (2011), en particulier p. 306-307, 318-320 et 323-327; sur la volonté d'Hugues de Tours de se rattacher à la famille d'Odile, voir HUMMER (2005), p. 218.

blement aussi l'adoption de la règle canoniale et la construction de Niedermunster) jusqu'à l'écriture de la Vie. L'auteur a alors éprouvé le besoin d'amarrer la fondation à l'histoire, de développer les mérites d'Odile pour l'insérer dans la communauté des saints et de forger un récit susceptible de plaire à son auditoire, tout en mettant en valeur l'originalité de la vie de son héroïne, ce qui explique le succès du culte pendant tout le Moyen Âge et au-delà. Ce succès se reflète dans le grand nombre de manuscrits conservé, ainsi que l'essor de son culte à partir du XIe siècle au moins, suivi par l'écriture, au XIIIe siècle seulement, de la Vie de sa nièce Attala (*BHL* 739m, 740-741), abbesse du monastère Saint-Étienne de Strasbourg, qui aurait été fondé par le frère d'Odile, le duc Adalbert. On comprend aussi pourquoi, sous réserve d'inventaire, aucune autre Vie de sainte mérovingienne ne ressemble à celle d'Odile: seule la Vie d'Adilia d'Orp connue par des manuscrits de la fin du Moyen Âge, relate des faits similaires mais c'est un plagiat de la Vie d'Odile[9].

Bibliographie

Cardot, F., «Le pouvoir aristocratique et le sacré au haut Moyen Âge. Sainte Odile et les Étichonides dans la *Vita Odiliae*», *Le Moyen Âge*, 89, 1983, p. 173-193.

Gaillard, M., «Conte et hagiographie: étude sur la Vie de sainte Odile d'Alsace», *Revue belge de philologie et d'histoire*, 95 (2018), p. 403-416.

Hummer, H., *Politics and power in early medieval Europe: Alsace and the Frankish Realm, 600-1000*, Cambridge, 2005, en particulier p. 46-47 et 218-224 (Cambridge studies in medieval life and thought. Fourth series, 65).

Pfister, C., «Le duché mérovingien d'Alsace et la légende de sainte Odile», *Annales de l'Est*, 4 (1890), p. 433-455; 5 (1891), p. 392-484; 6 (1892), p. 27-119 (en particulier, 5, p. 402-405).

—, «La vie de sainte Odile», *AB*, 13 (1894), p. 5-33.

Vollmer, F., «Die Etichonen. Ein Beitrag zur Frage der Kontinuität früher Adelsfamilien», in G. Tellenbach, *Studien und Vorarbeiten*

---

[9] Adilia ou Odilia (*BHL* 6277-6278); D. Papebroch, «De s. Adilia virgine, sanctimoniali Orpii in Brabantia», dans *AASS*, Iun. V, 1709, p. 587-588; Pfister (1894), p. 7, n° 25 et p. 8, n 43.

zur Geschichte des großfränkischen und frühdeutschen Adels, Fribourg, 1957, p. 137-184 (Forschungen zur oberrheinischen Landesgeschichte, 4).

WEBER, K., Die Formierung des Elsass im Regnum Francorum: Adel, Kirche und Königtum am Oberrhein in merowingischer und frühkarolingischer Zeit, Ostfildern, 2011, p. 100-111 (Archäologie und Geschichte, 19).

WILSDORF, C., «Les Étichonides aux temps carolingiens et ottoniens», dans Bulletin philologique et historique, 1967, p. 1-33

—, «Les très anciennes forteresses du Mont-Saint-Odile et de Frankenburg dans les textes du haut Moyen Âge», in Mélanges J.-J. Hatt, Cahiers alsaciens d'archéologie, d'art et d'histoire, 36 (1993), p. 207-221.

—, «Comment la sainte Croix parvint à Niedermunster (Alsace). Une légende carolingienne écrite au XVe siècle. Édition critique et commentaire d'un texte retrouvé», in ID., L'Alsace des Mérovingiens à Léon IX, Strasbourg, 2011, p. 288-346 (Recherches et documents, 82).

Les auteurs

Maddalena BETTI, née à Florence (Italie) en 1979, a obtenu son diplôme d'histoire à l'Université de Florence en 2003 avec une thèse intitulée «S. Adalberto, vescovo di Praga e la *Renovatio Imperii* di Ottone III». En 2008 elle a soutenu sa thèse de doctorat en Histoire du Christianisme et des Églises au Moyen Âge à l'Université de Padova et de Paris I, Panthéon-Sorbonne (titre de la thèse: La formazione della sancta Ecclesia Marabensis, 858-882. Fonti e linguaggi di un progetto papale). Depuis 2008, elle a conduit des recherches sur les relations diplomatique entre la papauté et les nouvelles formations politiques en Europe centrale et sud-orientale (IXe siècle), l'histoire ecclésiastique de l'Europe centrale, les stratégies identitaires des élites (Rome et Ravenna, VIII-Xe siècles), l'histoire de la parenté au Haut Moyen Âge, l'histoire de la papauté (VIIIe-Xe siècles). Depuis 2008 elle collabore à la rédaction centrale du Bulletin bibliographique «MEL – Medio Evo Latino», publié par la SISMEL, Florence.

Dernières publications: *The Making of Christian Moravia (858-882). Papal Power and Political Reality*, praef. T. X. Noble, Leiden – Boston, 2014 (East Central and Eastern Europe in the Middle Ages, 450-1450, 24); – *I centri urbani nella regione medio-danubiana (VII-IX secolo): la rappresentazione della «Conversio Bagoariorum et Carantanorum»*, in *Le identità urbane in Italia settentrionale (secoli IX-XI). Padova, 17-19 ottobre 2013*, Turnhout, p. 403-428; – «Incestuous Marriages in the Late Carolingian Ravenna. The causa Deusdedit (878-881)», *Early Medieval Europe*, 23 (2015), p. 457-477; – «Le ragioni di una caduta. Il collasso della Grande Moravia tra fonti scritte e archeologiche», *Reti medievali*, 17, p. [1]-[16]; – «Affari di frontiera. Politica e commercio in Europa centrale tra VII e fine IX secolo», in *The Age of Affirmation: Venice, the Adriatic and the Hinterland between the 9th and 10th Centuries*, Turnhout, p. 59-78; – «Rome and the heritage of ancient Illyricum in the 9th century», in *Imperial Spheres and the Adriatic: Byzantium, the Carolingians and the Treaty of Aachen (812)*, cur. M. ANCIC, J. SHEPARD, T. VEDRIS, Abingdon – New York, p. 243-252; – «*Iacobellus de Misa*», in *C.A.L.M.A. – Compendium Auctorum Latinorum Medii Aevii (500-1500)*, cur. M. LAPIDGE, p. 314-330.

Anne-Marie BULTOT-VERLEYSEN, née à Bruxelles en 1960. Études d'histoire et de philosophie aux Facultés universitaires Saint-Louis (Bruxelles) et à l'Université catholique de Louvain (Louvain-la-Neuve). Assistante au Département d'Histoire puis collaboratrice scientifique au Centre d'études sur le Moyen Âge et la Renaissance de l'UCLouvain.

Recherches sur l'hagiographie médiolatine de la France méridionale.

Principales publications: *Odon de Cluny. Vita sancti Geraldi Auriliacensis.* Édition critique, traduction française, introduction et commentaires, Bruxelles, 2009 (Subidia hagiographica, 89); «Hagiographie d'Aquitaine

(750-1130)», dans *Hagiographies*, t. VI, dir. M. GOULLET, Turnhout, 2014, p. 521-704.

Hélène CAILLAUD, née à Limoges (France) en 1985, est spécialiste d'hagiographie latine médiévale du haut Moyen Âge et du Moyen Âge central, elle effectue l'ensemble de son cursus universitaire en Histoire à l'Université de Limoges avant de poursuivre en doctorat en cotutelle avec l'Université de Tübingen en Allemagne, sous la direction de Philippe Depreux et de Stephen Patzold. Soutenue en 2016, sa thèse de doctorat intitulée *Violences hagiographiques* porte sur l'étude des discours et des représentations de la violence dans les sources hagiographiques de la province ecclésiastique de Sens (V^e-XIIe siècle). Par la suite, elle a notamment participé au projet de recherche CBMA dirigé par Eliana Magnani, en tant qu'ingénieure de recherche et pris une part active dans le PCR sur la cathédrale Sainte-Croix d'Orléans dirigé par Pierre Martin, tout en menant divers travaux de recherche sur les sources hagiographiques orléanaises notamment concernant saint Aignan et saint Euverte.

Bibliographie sélective: «La postérité des œuvres de Grégoire de Tours dans les sources hagiographiques de la province ecclésiastique de Sens (VIe-XIIe siècle)», *Revue des études tardo-antiques*, 6 (2016-2017), p. 207-236; – «Saint Israël et saint Théobald. Réexamen d'un dossier hagiographique», dans É. SPARHUBERT – A. MASSONI, dir., *Israël du Dorat. Être chanoine en l'an mil*, actes du colloque *Saint Israël*, Limoges, 2019, p. 215-232; – «L'abbaye de Micy et le pouvoir épiscopal au prisme de l'hagiographie orléanaise. Construction et déconstruction du discours hagiographique (IXe-XIe siècle)», dans A. MASSONI – N. DEFLOU-LECA, dir., *Évêques et communautés religieuses dans le royaume de France et ses marges (816-1563)*, à paraître.

Marianna CERNO, née à Udine (Italie) en 1978. Études d'histoire et littérature chrétienne à l'Université de Udine, PhD 2008 en philologie et littérature latine médiévale à la SISMEL, Florence. Depuis 2008, elle mène des recherches sur la littérature hagiographique latine (occasionnellement sur la grecque), les manuscrits médiévaux (description, catalogage, bases de données), la tradition manuscrite des collections homilétiques et des Pères de l'Église. Récemment, ses recherches ont porté sur les sermons de l'Antiquité tardive et du haut Moyen Âge (études des textes de Chromace d'Aquilée (env. 388-408) et d'Ambroise Autpert); elle participe au projet TraPat sur la tradition et la traduction des Pères latins et grecques en Occident. Depuis 2008, elle est membre de la rédaction centrale du Bulletin bibliographique «MEL – Medio Evo Latino», publié par SISMEL, Florence.

Intérêts de recherche: littérature hagiographique latine et grecque; sermons latins et collections homilétique médiévales; histoire et littérature du Patriarcat d'Aquilée; tradition littéraire et manuscrite des œuvres des Pères latins et grecques en Occident.

Principales publications récentes: *Cromazio di Aquileia in mezzo ai Padri. Il destino medievale dei sermoni*, Roma, 2019 (Fonti per la Storia della Chiesa in Friuli. Serie medievale, 22); – *Cromazio di Aquileia. I sermoni. Nuova edizione con traduzione a fronte*, Roma, 2019 (Fonti per la Storia della Chiesa in Friuli. Serie medievale, 23); – «When the 'Other' Has Another God: Christians towards Saracens in Italian Hagiography before the First Crusade», in J. LA-

GOUANÈRE (éd.), *La naissance d'autrui de l'Antiquité à la Renaissance*, Paris, 2019 (Rencontres, 415. Colloques, congrès et conférences sur la Renaissance européenne, 104), p. 333-357 ; « La più antica agiografia latina della Slovenia (IX-XV secolo). Con una nota sulla letteratura religiosa vernacolare », in M. GOULLET, dir., *Hagiographies. Histoire internationale de la littérature hagiographique latine et vernaculaire en Occident des origines à 1550*, VII, Turnhout, 2017, p. 505-564 ; – « Holding the Aquileian Patriarchate's Title: The Key Role of Local Early-Ninth-Century Hagiography », in M. ANČIĆ – J. SHEPARD – T. VEDRIŠ, ed., *Imperial spheres and the Adriatic. Byzantium, the Carolingians and the Treaty of Aachen (812)*, London – New York, 2018, p. 140-151 ; – « Un'agiografia 'dimenticata' del vescovo Domnione, martire di Salona », *Mélanges de l'École française de Rome – Moyen Âge*, 127, 2 (2015), p. 365-406.

Paul CHAFFENET, né à L'Isle-Adam (France) en 1988 : docteur en histoire médiévale de l'Université de Lille et de l'Université Libre de Bruxelles, ingénieur d'études à l'IRHT (section de Paléographie latine). Dans la continuité de sa thèse, traitant des rapports entre les aristocraties et les communautés religieuses dans le diocèse de Noyon, ses recherches actuelles portent principalement sur les abbayes et chapitres du Noyonnais et du Vermandois ainsi que sur la diplomatique privée. À l'IRHT, il collabore au projet européen « HOME » (sous la direction de Dominique Stutzmann) consacré au traitement et à la valorisation numériques des cartulaires.

Bibliographie : « De la conversion monastique au châtiment divin : l'exemple du comte Albert II de Vermandois (début du XIe siècle) », dans C. MÉRIAUX (dir.), *Les représentations de l'autorité épiscopale au XIe siècle : Gérard de Cambrai et les* Gesta episcoporum Cameracensium, *Revue du Nord*, 97 (2015), n° 410, p. 357-384 ; – « Un acte inédit de Guy, archevêque de Reims, en faveur de l'abbaye Saint-Vincent de Laon [vers 1048] », *Revue belge de philologie et d'histoire*, 93 (2015), p. 619-645 ; – « Imitation et innovation dans les politiques religieuses des comtes de Vermandois (XIe siècle) », *Trajectoires* (2017), https://journals.openedition.org/trajectoires/2179. – « Aristocratie et communautés religieuses aux marges septentrionales du royaume de France (fin IXe-début XIIe siècles). Le cas du diocèse de Noyon », thèse dirigée par Michèle Gaillard (Université de Lille) et Alain Dierkens (Université Libre de Bruxelles), dactylographiée, https://tel.archives-ouvertes.fr/tel-01779139.

Éric CHEVALLEY, né en 1962, à Lausanne (Suisse), est Maître d'enseignement et de recherche à l'Université de Lausanne et membre de l'Institut d'Archéologie et des Sciences de l'Antiquité. Il a fait ses études dans cette ville jusqu'à la licence universitaire, obtenue en octobre 1988. Son mémoire de licence portait sur la Passion anonyme de saint Maurice d'Agaune. Grâce à une bourse du FNRS, il put ensuite compléter sa formation à l'École Pratique des Hautes Études à Paris auprès de François Dolbeau et de Jean-Pierre Callu. Devenu membre de l'Institut suisse de Rome, Éric Chevalley a poursuivi ses recherches à la Bibliothèque Vaticane, dans le cadre d'une thèse consacrée à la Passion de saint Symphorien d'Autun. Il partage maintenant son temps entre l'enseignement du latin et de l'histoire au Gymnase Auguste Piccard de Lausanne et celui du latin à la Faculté des Lettres. Ses domaines d'enseignement et de recherche sont essentiellement axés sur la littérature tardo-antique et les textes hagiographiques.

Bibliographie sélective: «Passion anonyme de saint Maurice», «Vie des abbés d'Agaune»: *La mémoire hagiographique de l'abbaye de Saint-Maurice d'Agaune*, Lausanne, 2014 (Cahiers lausannois d'histoire médiévale, 53); – en collaboration avec C. RODUIT, «La naissance du culte des saints d'Agaune et les premiers textes hagiographiques», *L'abbaye de Saint-Maurice d'Agaune, 515-2015*, I: *Histoire et archéologie*, B. ANDENMATTEN – L. RIPART, dir., Gollion, 2015, p. 33-57.

Michèle GAILLARD, née à Noisy-le-Sec (France) en 1954 est professeur émérite d'histoire du Moyen Âge à l'université de Lille. Ses recherches sur les monastères du haut Moyen Âge, en particulier en Lorraine, et sur la topographie des villes de l'Antiquité tardive et du haut Moyen Âge, l'ont amenée à s'intéresser de près à l'hagiographie et aussi aux données archéologiques, comme en témoignent ses plus récentes publications.

Bibliographie sélective: «Remarques sur les plus anciennes versions manuscrites de la *Passio* et de l'*Inventio* des saints Fuscien, Victoric et Gentien dans les manuscrits Paris, BnF, lat. 12598 et Wien ÖnB 371», in *Parva pro magnis munera, Mélanges offerts à F. Dolbeau par ses élèves et auditeurs*, M. GOULLET *et al.*, éd., 2009, p. 397-409; – «Erhard, évêque de Ratisbonne, un saint aquitain en Bavière?», dans *Saints d'Aquitaine, missionnaires et pèlerins du haut Moyen Âge*, E. BOZOKY, dir., Rennes, 2010, p. 159-171; – «Les *Vitae* des saintes Salaberge et Anstrude de Laon, deux sources exceptionnelles pour l'étude de la construction hagiographique et du contexte socio-politique», *Revue du Nord*, 93 (2011), n°s 293-294, p. 655-670 (= *Mélanges Stéphane Lebecq*); – «Les deux *vitae* anciennes de saint Éleuthère, évêque de Tournai: tradition manuscrite et contextes d'écriture», dans M. CAVALIERI – E. DE WAELE, éd., *Industria apium. L'archéologie: une démarche singulière, des pratiques multiples. Hommages à Raymond Brulet*, Louvain-la-Neuve, 2013, p. 345-369; – «Un 'cycle' hagiographique du haut Moyen Âge en Gaule septentrionale: les Passions des martyrs de Riciovar», *Hagiographica*, 21 (2014), p. 1-28; – «La *Passio* de saint Quentin» et «La *Passio* des saints Crépin et Crépinien», dans *Le Légendier de Turin, Torino, Biblioteca Nazionale e Universitaria D.V.3*, M. GOULLET, éd., Florence, 2014, p. 211-228 et 311-332; – En collaboration avec C. SAPIN, «Autour de la tombe de saint Quentin: histoire et archéologie d'un culte (milieu IVe-début VIIIe s.)», in *L'empreinte chrétienne en Gaule (fin IVe-début VIIIe s.)*, M. GAILLARD, éd., Turnhout, 2014, p. 273-290; – «Conte et hagiographie: étude sur la Vie de sainte Odile d'Alsace», dans *Revue belge de philologie et d'histoire*, 95 (2018), p. 403-416 (= *Mélanges Alain Dierkens*).

Marie-Céline ISAÏA, née à Paris (France) en 1977, ancienne élève de l'École normale Supérieure de la rue d'Ulm, est docteur en histoire de l'Université Paris X – Nanterre pour une thèse publiée à Paris en 2010 sous le titre *Remi de Reims. Mémoire d'un saint, histoire d'une Église (v^e-xie s.)*. Élue maître de conférences en histoire par l'Université Jean-Moulin Lyon3/Université de Lyon en 2006, elle est habilitée à diriger des recherches depuis 2018. Membre junior de l'Institut Universitaire de France (2019-2024), elle consacre ses travaux au sein du CIHAM – UMR 5648 aux hagiographes du haut Moyen Âge et à leurs écoles. Les premiers résultats de ce projet sont à paraître sous le titre «L'enfance dans l'hagiographie latine», *L'infanzia nell'alto medioevo. Sessantottesima Settiamana di Studio,* Spoleto, 2021. Avec Florence Bret, elle vient de publier la traduction de trois *Vies* latines dans *Vie de Geneviève,* Paris, 2020 (Sources chrétiennes, 610). Une liste complète de ses travaux est en ligne https://facdeslettres.univ-lyon3.fr/isaia-marie-celine.

Klaus KRÖNERT, né à Hanovre (Allemagne) en 1970, est maître de conférences à l'université de Lille. Après avoir passé le 'Staatsexamen' allemand en Histoire et en Latin à l'université de Göttingen en 1997, il a soutenu, en 2003, une thèse de doctorat, à l'université Paris X – Nanterre, sur la production hagiographique à Trèves, qui a été dirigée par les professeurs Michel Sot (Paris X – Nanterre) et François Dolbeau (É.P.H.É, 4e section). Ses travaux, réalisés avec une double approche historique et philologique, portent sur l'hagiographie et l'historiographie du haut Moyen Âge. Ils prolongent, en partie, les recherches de sa thèse sur Trèves, et couvrent également d'autres régions de la Germanie et de la Francie. Ses périodes de prédilection sont celles des Carolingiens et des Ottoniens. Récemment, il s'est aussi ouvert à de nouveaux sujets comme la communication orale au haut Moyen Âge.

Bibliographie sélective: – *L'exaltation de Trèves, Ecriture hagiographique et passé historique de la métropole mosellane (VIIIe-XIe siècle),* avec en annexe, l'équivalent de *SHG* XIV, Ostfildern 2010 (Beihefte der Francia, 70); – *Rerum gestarum scriptor. Histoire et historiographie au Moyen Age,* Mélanges Michel Sot, M. COUMERT, M.-C. ISAÏA, K. KRÖNERT, S. SHIMAHARA, éd., Paris, 2012 (Collection Cultures et civilisations médiévales, 58); – «La Passion de saint Denys écrite par Hilduin (*BHL* 2175). Le travail d'un historiographe ou l'œuvre d'un faussaire?», *Bibliothèque de l'Ecole des chartes,* 172 (2014), p. 61-99; – «Une compilation historiographique attribuée à Méthode (Trèves, début du XIIe siècle)», *Revue des études augustiniennes,* 62 (2016), p. 335-368; – avec D. KEMPF, «La Vie de saint Memmie de Châlons et les légendes apostoliques des diocèses de Gaule au début du IXe siècle», *Revue de l'histoire de l'Église de France,* 103 (2017), p. 5-25; – «Le dossier hagiographique de saint Godehard, évêque de Hildesheim au XIe siècle», *Analecta Bollandiana,* 135 (2017), p. 359-401; – «Communiquer avec l'autre: les langues de l'Europe centrale et septentrionale», in B. DUMÉZIL – S. JOYE – C. MÉRIAUX, dir., *Confrontation, échanges et connaissance de l'autre au nord et à l'est de l'Europe de la fin du VIIe siècle au milieu du XIe siècle,* Rennes, 2017, p. 151-170 (collection «Didact histoire»); – «Between Identity, History, and Rivalry: Hagiographic Legends in Trier, Cologne and Liège», in *Medieval Liège at the Crossroads of Europe. Monastic Society and Culture, 1000-1300,* S. VANDERPUTTEN – T. SNIJDERS – J. DIEHL, éd., Turnhout, 2017, p. 49-68 (Medieval Church Studies, 37); – «La production hagiographique en Germanie à l'époque de Louis le Pieux. Productivité littéraire et crises, mais quel rapport?», in *Politische Kultur und Textproduktion unter Ludwig dem Fromme. Culture politique et production littéraire sous Louis le Pieux,* M. GRAVEL – S. KASCHKE, éd., Ostfildern, 2019, p. 269-373 (Relectio. Karolingische Perspektiven – Perspectives carolingiennes – Carolingian Perspectives, 2); – «Hagiography and Inter-Urban Rivalry: The Life of Saint Eucharius (*BHL* 2655), first bishop of Trier, and its use in 'political' quarrels during the 10th century», S. KAHN-HERRICK, éd., *Hagiography and the History of Latin Christendom, 500-1500*, Leiden – Boston, 2020, p. 297-313.

Charles MÉRIAUX, né à Troyes (France) en 1973, est professeur d'histoire du Moyen Âge à l'Université de Lille. Ses recherches portent sur le culte des saints, les récits hagiographiques et l'encadrement religieux dans l'Occident du haut Moyen Âge – et plus spécialement dans la province ecclésiastique de Reims – auxquels il a consacré près de 70 articles.

Bibliographie sélective: Gallia irradiata. *Saints et sanctuaires dans le nord de la Gaule du haut Moyen Âge*, Stuttgart, (Beiträge zur Hagiographie, 4), 2006; avec S. GIOANNI, dir., *Réforme(s) et hagiographie dans l'Occident latin, VIe-XIIIe siècle, Médiévales*, 62 (2012); (dir.), *Les représentations de l'autorité épiscopale au XIe siècle, Revue du Nord*, 97 (2015), n° 410.

Fernand PELOUX, né à Valence (France), 1987. Études à Grenoble et Toulouse, agrégé et docteur en histoire avec une thèse soutenue en 2016 sous la direction d'Hélène Débax et Monique Goullet, intitulée *Les saints évêques du Languedoc. Construction et déconstruction d'une mémoire hagiographique au Moyen Âge* (en cours de publication). Il a enseigné l'histoire du Moyen Âge dans les universités de Toulouse, Montpellier et Lille. Après un post-doctorat à l'université de Namur, et comme membre de l'École des Hautes Études hispaniques et Ibériques (EHEHI – Casa de Velázquez). Il est actuellement chargé de recherches au CNRS (FRAMESPA – UMR 5136, Toulouse). Il porte une attention particulière à la fabrique et aux usages des manuscrits hagiographiques ainsi qu'à l'ancrage territorial des cultes et de l'écriture hagiographique, notamment dans le cadre de programmes de recherches archéologiques.

Bibliographie sélective: Direction de *Le légendier de Moissac et la culture hagiographique méridionale autour de l'an mil*, Turnhout, 2018; – «Le récit retrouvé du vol des reliques de saint Eudald, martyr d'Ax-les-Thermes, par les moines de Ripoll en 978. Édition et commentaire d'un texte fragmentaire», *Miscellania liturgica catalana*, 27 (2019), p. 239-271; – «Les agglomérations secondaires et leur topographie religieuse dans le Gévaudan du haut Moyen Âge. Hagiographie, transformations territoriales et construction chrétienne de l'espace», *Siècles* [En ligne], 48 (2020).

Joseph-Claude POULIN, né à Québec en 1943. Licence d'histoire à l'Université Laval (Québec, 1965); diplôme d'études supérieures à l'Université de Poitiers (CÉSCM, 1967); doctorat de troisième cycle en histoire médiévale à l'Université d'Aix-en-Provence, sous la direction de Georges Duby (1969). Professeur d'histoire à l'Université Laval de 1969 à 2000; professeur associé à l'Université de Montréal depuis 2000.

Publications principales: *L'idéal de sainteté dans l'Aquitaine carolingienne* (1975); – avec M. HEINZELMANN, dir., *Les Vies anciennes de sainte Geneviève de Paris* (1986); – *L'hagiographie bretonne du haut Moyen Âge* (2009); – «La circulation des œuvres hagiographiques d'Alcuin», Hagiographica, 22 (2015) et 23 (2016).

Lucile TRÂN DUC, née en 1977 à Caen (France), est professeur agrégée en lycée et docteur en Histoire médiévale.

Bibliographie sélective: *Le culte des saints en Normandie (IXe-XIIe siècle). Enjeux de pouvoir dans les établissements bénédictins du diocèse de Rouen*, thèse soutenue en 2015 à l'Université de Caen; – «Le *Miraculum quo B. Mariae subvenit Guillemo Crispino de Miles Crespin*: entre hagiographie et généalogie», *Annales des Normandie*, 67-1 (2017), p. 43-56; – «Fontenelle et Saint-Pierre de Gand: rivalités et échanges (IXe-XIIe siècles)», dans S. Excoffon, D.-O. Hurel, A. Peters-Custot, dir., *Interactions, emprunts, confrontations chez les religieux (Antiquité tardive-fin du XIXe siècle)*, Saint-Étienne, 2015, p. 153-162; – «Enjeux de pouvoir dans le Livre Noir de l'abbaye Saint-Ouen de Rouen (Rouen, Bibl. mun. ms Y 41)», dans E. Bozoky, dir., *Hagiographie, idéologie et pouvoir au Moyen Age. L'écriture de la sainteté, instrument politique*, Turnhout, 2012 (Hagiologia, 8), p. 199-210.

Anne Wagner, née à Metz (France) en 1958, est maître de conferences à l'Université de Besançon depuis 1994. Après une thèse de 3e cycle sur l'abbaye de Gorze au XIe siècle, elle a travaillé sur le monachisme en Lorraine et sur les relations entre réforme monastique et hagiographie, en particulier à Verdun, ainsi que sur le culte des reliques des saints Maurice et Gotthard notamment.

Bibliographie sélective: *Autour de saint Maurice. Actes du colloque «Politique, société et construction identitaire: Autour de saint Maurice»*, N. Brocard, Fr. Vannotti, A. Wagner, éd., Besançon – Saint-Maurice, 2011; – *L'abbaye de Gorze au XIe siècle*, Turnhout, 1997; – *Les saints et l'histoire: Sources hagiographiques du haut Moyen Âge*, A. Wagner, éd., Bréal, 2004; – *Les Royaumes de Bourgogne jusqu'en 1032 à travers la culture et la religion*, A. Wagner, N. Brocard, éd., Turnhout, 2018; – «Richard de Saint-Vanne (1004-1046) et l'impact de sa réforme à Verdun», in *L'écrit et le livre peint en Lorraine, de Saint-Mihiel à Verdun (IXe-XVe siècles). Actes du colloque de Saint-Mihiel (25-26 octobre 2010)*, A.-O. Poilpré, éd., Turnhout, 2014, p. 105-120.

Table des cartes et des plans

Carte I	Distribution des cartes du tome VIII	13
Carte II	Churches and monasteries of medieval Bohemia and Moravia	17
Carte III	Provinces et diocèses de la Gallia à l'époque carolingienne	142
Carte IV	Lieux mentionnés dans le chapitre «Alcuin hagiographe»	146
Carte V	Lieux mentionnés dans les chapitres sur la province de Tours	187
Carte VI	Lieux mentionnés dans les chapitres sur la province de Rouen	260
Carte VII	Lieux mentionnés dans les chapitres sur la province de Reims	312
Carte VIII	Lieux mentionnés dans les chapitres sur la province de Sens	452
Carte IX	Lieux mentionnés dans les chapitres sur la province de Lyon	592
Carte X	Lieux mentionnés dans les chapitres sur les provinces de Vienne et de Tarentaise	612
Carte XI	Lieux mentionnés dans le chapitre sur le diocèse de Besançon	722
Carte XII	Lieux mentionnés dans le chapitre sur la Germanie	733
Plan I	Les églises de Soissons	317
Plan II	Les églises de Reims	318
Plan III	Les églises de Paris	519
Plan IV	Les églises de Trèves	735

Table des matières
du huitième volume

Table générale des matières 5

Sigles et abréviations 11

Marianna CERNO and Maddalena BETTI, Latin Hagiography and the Cult of Saints in Czech Territories in the Middle Ages (tenth-fifteenth Centuries) 15

I. INTRODUCTION. – A. Geo-historical Framework and Terminology. – B. Political and Ecclesiastical History of Moravia and Bohemia in the Middle Ages. – 1. At First Great Moravia. – 2. Bohemia: Christianization and the Formation of the Přemyslid Duchy. – 3. The Foundation of the Bishopric of Prague. – 4. The Eleventh Century: Towards the Kingdom (and the Foundation of the Diocese of Olomouc). – 5. King Vladislav II and Jindřich Zdík, Bishop of Olomouc. The Hereditary Kingdom. – 6. The Last Přemyslids. – 7. Luxemburg's Dinasty. – 8. Jan Hus and the Hussite Wars.

II. LATIN HAGIOGRAPHY OF BOHEMIA AND MORAVIA. – A. Features and Protagonists of Bohemian and Moravian Latin Hagiography. – 1. Preliminary Note on Czech Modern Historiography. – 2. Latin Hagiography for the Czech Saints. – 3. Hussitica. – 4. Imported Sainthood (Vitus martyr. – Mauritius Agaunensis seu Thebaeus martyr. – Emmerammus episcopus martyr. – Godehardus Hildesheimensis episcopus. – Victorinus martyr. – *Legenda aurea*. – Clemens I papa. – Hieronymus Stridonius/Eusebius Hieronymus). – 5. Cyrillo-Methodiana. – 6. The Parodies of the Manuscript PRAHA, *Národní Knihovna*, III.E.27. – 7. The *Passio Iudeorum Pragensium*. – B. Alphabetical Inventory of the Czech Saints' Hagiographies. – 1. Adalbertus (Vojtechus) Pragensis episcopus. – 2. Agnes de Bohemia O.S.Cl. – 3. Arnestus seu Ernestus Pragensis episcopus. – 4. Benedictus, Iohannes et socii (Quinque fratres) in Polonia martyres. – 5. Guntherus eremita. – 6. Hieronymus de Praga magister. – 7. Hieronymus Stridonius (Eusebius Hieronymus). – 8. Hroznata Ord. Praem. martyr. – 9. Iohannes Hus. – 10. Iohannes de Ienzenstein Pragensis episcopus. – 11. Iohannes Milicius de Chremsir. – 12. Iohannes Nepomucenus Pragae presbyter. – 13. Passio Iudeorum Pragensium. – 14. Ivanus eremita. – 15. Ludmilla Bohemiae ducissa. – 16. Milada Pragensis abbatissa OSB. – 17. Procopius Pragensis abbas. – 18. *Sigismundus rex Burgundionum m.* – 19. Wenceslaus Bohemiae dux et martyr. – 20. Zdislava OP.

III. SELECTED SUPPLEMENTARY BIBLIOGRAPHY. – A. Political and Ecclesiastical History of Moravia and Bohemia in the Middle Ages. – B. Latin Hagiography of Moravia and Bohemia. – 1. General Studies. – 2. Adalbertus

(Vojtechus) Pragensis episcopus. – 3. Agnes de Bohemia O.S.Cl. – 4. Arnestus seu Ernestus Pragensis episcopus. – 5. Benedictus, Iohannes et socii (Quinque fratres) in Polonia martyres. – 6. Guntherus eremita. – 7. Hieronymus de Praga magister. – 8. Hieronymus Stridonius (Eusebius Hieronymus). – 9. Hroznata Ord. Praem. martyr. – 10. Iohannes Hus. – 11. *Iohannes Nepomucenus Pragae presbyter.* – 12. Passio Iudaeorum Pragensium. – 13. Ivanus eremita. – 14. Karolus Magnus rex. – 15. Procopius Pragensis abbas. – 16. Sigismundus rex Burgundionum m. – 17. Wenceslaus Bohemiae dux et martyr. – C. Webography of the published sources.

BIBLIOGRAPHY.

Michèle Gaillard et Monique Goullet, Avant-propos 143

Joseph-Claude POULIN, Alcuin hagiographe 145

INTRODUCTION.
I. HAGIOGRAPHIE EN PROSE. – A. Saint Willibrord († 739). – B. Saint Vaast († 540). – C. Saint Riquier († milieu VIIe s.). – E. Saint Martin († 397).
II. HAGIOGRAPHIE MÉTRIQUE.
III. MESSES ET OFFICES PROPRES. – A. Saint Willibrord. – B. Saint Vaast. – C. Saint Riquier. – D. Saint Martin. – E. Autres saints.
CONCLUSION.
ANNEXE: Poèmes d'Alcuin pour des saints.
BIBLIOGRAPHIE.

L'ÉCRITURE HAGIOGRAPHIQUE
DANS LA PROVINCE DE TOURS (ENV. 750-950)

Joseph-Claude POULIN, L'hagiographie bretonne avant l'an mil 189

I. PRÉSENTATION GÉNÉRALE. – A. Cadre géographique. – B. Cadre chronologique. – C. Typologie de la sainteté. – D. Sources et transmission. – E. Modalités de mise en écriture. – F. Conclusion. – G. Bibliographie.
II. RÉPERTOIRE DE L'HAGIOGRAPHIE BRETONNE ANTÉRIEURE À L'AN MIL. – A. Tableau de la production hagiographique. – B. Bibliographie générale complémentaire. – C. Dossiers individuels. – 1. Conwoion de Redon († 868). – 2. Ethbinus/Idunetus. – 3. Judocus de Saint-Josse-sur-Mer. – 4. Lenoverius/Leonorius. – 5. Machutes d'Alet. – 6. Maglorius de Dol. – 7. Melanius de Rennes († *c.* 530). – 8. Meroveus; – 9. Paulus Aurelianus de Saint-Pol de Léon – 10. Samson de Dol († *c.* 565?). – 11. Turiavus de Dol. – 12. Wenailus. – 13. Winnocus. – 14. Winwaloeus de Landévennec.

Lucile TRÂN DUC, avec la collaboration de Charles MÉRIAUX, L'écriture hagiographique dans les diocèses du mans et d'Angers 243

 I. LE DIOCÈSE DU MANS. – A. Les *Actus pontificum Cenomannis* et les *Gesta Aldrici*. – B. Les saints compagnons d'Avit. – C. Les saints fondateurs de monastères (par C. Mériaux).
 II. LE DIOCÈSE D'ANGERS
 BIBLIOGRAPHIE.

L'ÉCRITURE HAGIOGRAPHIQUE DANS LA PROVINCE DE ROUEN (ENV. 750-950)

Lucile TRÂN DUC, L'écriture hagiographique dans le diocèse de Rouen (env. 750-950) 261

 INTRODUCTION.
 I. L'ÉCRITURE HAGIOGRAPHIQUE À L'ABBAYE DE FONTENELLE. – A. Les *Gesta abbatum Fontanellensium*. – B. Le dossier de saint Wandrille. – C. Le dossier des saints Ansbert et Lambert. – D. Le dossier de saint Vulfran. – E. Le dossier des saints Condède et Erembert.
 II. L'ÉCRITURE HAGIOGRAPHIQUE À L'ABBAYE DE JUMIÈGES. – A. Le dossier des saints Aychard et Hugues. – B. Le dossier de sainte Austreberte.
 III. DANS L'ORBITE DE LA CATHÉDRALE DE ROUEN: le dossier de saint Ouen.
 CONCLUSION.
 BIBLIOGRAPHIE. – A. SOURCES. – B. ÉTUDES.

Joseph-Claude POULIN, L'hagiographie de Basse-Normandie (env. 750-950) 287

 INTRODUCTION.
 I. EBRULFUS D'OUCHE. – Bibliographie spéciale.
 II. LEUTFREDUS D'ÉVREUX. – Bibliographie spéciale.
 III. MARCULFUS DE NANTEUIL. – Bibliographie spéciale.
 IV. MICHAEL ARCHANGELUS – Bibliographie spéciale.
 V. OPPORTUNA DE SÉES – Bibliographie spéciale.
 VI. TAURINUS D'ÉVREUX – Bibliographie spéciale.
 CONCLUSION.
 BIBLIOGRAPHIE GÉNÉRALE SUR L'HAGIOGRAPHIE DE BASSE-NORMANDIE – 1. Catalogues, répertoires, instruments de travail – 2. Études d'ensemble pour l'hagiographie bas-normande, 750-950

L'ÉCRITURE HAGIOGRAPHIQUE
DANS LA PROVINCE DE REIMS (ENV. 750-950)

Marie-Céline ISAÏA, L'écriture hagiographique dans les
diocèses de Reims, Soissons et Laon (env. 750-950) 315

INTRODUCTION.
I. SOISSONS. – A. Les Vies de saint Voüé. – B. L'écriture hagiographique à Saint-Médard. – 1. Translation et Miracles de saint Grégoire le Grand et saint Sébastien. – 2. Vie de l'évêque saint Médard. – 3. Odilon de Saint-Médard hagiographe.
II. LES PASSIONS S'INSCRIVANT DANS LE CYCLE DE RICIOVARE. – A. La Passion de sainte Macre. – B. La Passion des saints Rufin et Valère. – C. La Passion des saints Crépin et Crépinien.
III. REIMS. – A. Les Vies des saints évêques de Reims. – 1. La Passion de saint Nicaise. – 2. La Vie de saint Remi de Reims. – 3. La Vie de saint Rigobert et le dossier des translations rémoises. – 4. La Vie de saint Maternien évêque de Reims. – B. Autour des monastères bénédictins du diocèse de Reims. – 1. Les Vies de saint Thierry et saint Thiou. – 2. L'œuvre d'Almann de Hautvillers. – 3. Les Vies des abbesses Bova et Doda. – C. Flodoard hagiographe.
BIBLIOGRAPHIE.

Paul CHAFFENET et Michèle GAILLARD, L'écriture hagiographique dans le diocèse de Noyon (env. 750-950) 367

I. LES RÉÉCRITURES CAROLINGIENNES. – A. La Vie de saint Éloi. – B. Les Passions de saint Quentin (en vers et en prose).
II. DES TEXTES ORIGINAUX – A. Autour du culte de saint Quentin. – B. Les miracles de saint Fursy. – C. Le dossier hagiographique de sainte Hunégonde d'Homblières.
III. LA POURSUITE DE L'ACTIVITÉ HAGIOGRAPHIQUE AU MOYEN ÂGE CENTRAL.
BIBLIOGRAPHIE.

Klaus KRÖNERT, avec la collaboration de Michèle
GAILLARD, L'écriture hagiographique dans le diocèse de
Châlons (env. 750-950) 379

I. MEMMIE, PREMIER ÉVÊQUE DE CHÂLONS: sa *Vita I^a* (BHL 5907).
II. LES LÉGENDES DE L'ÉVÊQUE ALPIN, DE PUSINNE ET DE SES SŒURS.
BIBLIOGRAPHIE.

Charles MÉRIAUX, L'écriture hagiographique dans les
diocèses de Senlis et de Beauvais (env. 750-950) 389

I. LE DIOCÈSE DE SENLIS.

II. LE DIOCÈSE DE BEAUVAIS. – A. Saint Lucien. – B. Saint Just. – C. Les saints d'Orër et de Fly: Germer, Angadrême et Évroult. – D. Le légendier de Saint-Quentin de Beauvais.
BIBLIOGRAPHIE.

Fernand PELOUX, L'écriture hagiographique dans le diocèse d'Amiens (ca. VIIIe-XIIe s.) 409

I. L'HAGIOGRAPHIE ÉPISCOPALE AUX ÉPOQUES CAROLINGIENNE ET FÉODALE. – A. Les Passions de saint Firmin. – B. L'invention des reliques de Firmin. – C. La Vie de l'évêque et confesseur Firmin. – D. La Vie de l'évêque Sauve, découvreur des reliques de saint Firmin. – E. Les Miracles de saint Firmin. – F. Vie et miracles de l'évêque Honoré.
II. L'HAGIOGRAPHIE MONASTIQUE ET CANONIALE AU MOYEN ÂGE CENTRAL. – A. Corbie: les translations des reliques de Gentien et Précord. – B. Saint-Josse sur Mer et le dossier hagiographique de Josse. – C. Montdidier: le récit de la translation des reliques des saints Lugle et Luglien. – D. Saint-Germain sur Bresle: la Vie de Germain l'Écossais. – E. Saint-Valery-sur-Somme: Vie et translation de Walaricus. – F. Le monastère cistercien du Paraclet. Les Vies de la vierge Ulphe et de l'ermite Domice.
CONCLUSION.
BIBLIOGRAPHIE.

L'ÉCRITURE HAGIOGRAPHIQUE
DANS LA PROVINCE DE SENS (ENV. 750-950)

Michèle GAILLARD, L'écriture hagiographique dans les diocèses de Sens, Troyes et Nevers (env. 750-950) 453

I. DIOCÈSE DE SENS. – A. Les Vies d'évêques. – B. Les Vies de saints du «cycle d'Aurélien. – C. La Vie de Sidronius – D. Les Passions des saints Savinien et Potentien.
II. DIOCÈSE DE TROYES. – A. Sabine et Sabinien. – B. Le lien avec Sens: Potentien et les deux Sabiniens. – C. Écritures et réécritures attribuables sans certitude à l'époque carolingienne. – D. Le sermon de Prudence sur sainte Maure.
III. DIOCÈSE DE NEVERS.
BIBLIOGRAPHIE.

Anne-Marie BULTOT-VERLEYSEN, L'écriture hagiographique dans le diocèse d'Auxerre (env. 750-950) 473

I. LA VIE ET LES MIRACLES DE GERMAIN, PAR HEIRIC.
II. UNE ŒUVRE COMPOSITE: LES GESTES DES ÉVÊQUES D'AUXERRE.
III. LA TRANSLATION DE SAINT BAUDILLE ET LA VIE DE SAINT MARIEN.
BIBLIOGRAPHIE.

Hélène CAILLAUD, avec la collaboration de Klaus
KRÖNERT et Michèle GAILLARD, L'écriture hagiographique dans le diocèse d'Orléans (env. 750-950) 493

I. DES SAINTS ÉVÊQUES: AIGNAN; EUVERTE ET EUCHER. – A. Les Vies d'Aignan et d'Euverte. – B. La Vie d'Eucher, une production orléanaise? II. DES SAINTS CONFESSEURS. – A. Saint Avit. – B. Saint Mesmin. – C. Saint Liphard. – D. L'œuvre d'Adrévald de Fleury.
CONCLUSION
BIBLIOGRAPHIE.

Klaus KRÖNERT, L'activité hagiographique à Paris à l'époque carolingienne (env. 750-950) 515

INTRODUCTION: Paris à l'époque carolingienne.
I. SAINT-GERMAIN-DES-PRÉS. – A. Contexte historique. – B. Le martyrologe d'Usuard. – C. Des textes rédigés par des auteurs anonymes. – 1. *Translatio et Miracula sancti Germani episcopi Parisiaci anno 756* (BHL 3472-3473).– 2. Réécriture et continuation des récits de miracles de la *Translatio et Miracula sancti Germani sp. Parisiaci anno 756* (BHL 3474-3476). – 3. *Rhythmi* (BHL 3470, 3471, 3477) – 4. *Translatio sancti Germani espiscopi anno 845* (BHL 3479). – 5. *Vita et Miracula Turiani* (BHL 8342, 8343). – C. Les textes attribués à Aimoin. – 1. *Translationes an. 845, 857-863 et Miracula, auctore Aimoino* (BHL 3480). – 2. *Inventio et translatio beati Vincentii levitae et martyris* (BHL 8644-8645). – 3. *Carmen de translatione sancti Vincentii* (BHL 8646). – 4. *Translatio sanctorum Cordubensium martyrum Georgii atque Aurelii* (BHL 3409). – 5. *Translatio Savini martyris* (BHL 7450). – D. La *Vita Droctovei* rédigée par Gislemar (BHL 2336).
II. SAINTE-GENEVIÈVE. – A. *Vita I^a Genovefae* (recension *A*), modèle des hagiographes carolingiens de sainte Geneviève (BHL 3335). – B. Les réécritures de la *Vita Genovefae*. – 1. *Vita Genovefae*, recension *C* (BHL 3336). – 2. *Vita Genovefae*, recension *B* (BHL 3334). – 3. *Vita Genovefae*, recension *D* (BHL vacat). – 4. *Vita Genovefae*, recension *E* (BHL 3338). – C. *Miracula Genovefae* (BHL 3341, 3342).
III. TEXTES PARISIENS DONT LE LIEU EXACT DE LA RÉDACTION N'A PAS PU ÊTRE IDENTIFIÉ. – A. Textes carolingiens. – 1. *Marcellus*: *Vita II^a* (BHL 5249). – 2. *Justinus: Passio* (BHL 4579), *Passio rhythmica* (BHL 4580) et *Translatio Corbeiam anno 891* (BHL 4581). – 3. *Vita sancti Meredici et translatio a. 884* (BHL 5875-5876). – 4. *Chlodoaldus ou Chlodovaldus: Vitae I^a – II^a* (BHL 1732-1733). – B. Textes dont la datation est incertaine. – 1. *Translatio sancti Maglorii* (BHL 5147). – 2. *Aurea abb. Parisiis, Sermo de Vita* (BHL 814-817). – 3. *Passio* en l'honneur d'*Agoardus, Aglibertus et soc. mm. Christolii in agro Parisiensi* (BHL 168).
BIBLIOGRAPHIE.

L'ÉCRITURE HAGIOGRAPHIQUE DANS LA PROVINCE DE LYON (ENV. 750-950)

Marie-Céline ISAÏA, L'écriture hagiographique dans le diocèse de Lyon (env. 750-950) 593

INTRODUCTION.
I. DE RARES TEXTES DE DATATION INCERTAINE CONCERNANT DES SAINTS D'ÉPOQUE MÉROVINGIENNE.
II. LES MARTYROLOGES (ANONYME, FLORUS, ADON).

Michèle GAILLARD, avec la collaboration d'Alain RAUWEL, L'écriture hagiographique dans les diocèses suffragants de Lyon (env. 750-950) 599

INTRODUCTION.
I. LE DIOCÈSE DE LANGRES (avec A. RAUWEL). – A. La Vie de Valentin de Griselles. – B. La Passion de Gengoul. – C. L'activité hagiographique autour de Moutiers-Saint-Jean. – D. Une activité hagiographique autour de Saint-Bénigne de Dijon?
II LE DIOCÈSE D'AUTUN. – A. *Translatio* et *Miracula* de sainte Reine. – B. Incertitudes d'attribution et de datation.
III. LE DIOCÈSE DE CHALON-SUR-SAÔNE. – A. L'activité hagiographique autour de l'évêque Girbaldus. – B. Gratus: une Vie tardive? – C. La Passion de saint Valérien (Tournus).

BIBLIOGRAPHIE (ensemble de la province de Lyon)

L'ÉCRITURE HAGIOGRAPHIQUE DANS LES PROVINCES DE VIENNE, TARENTAISE ET BESANÇON (ENV. 750-950)

Anne-Marie BULTOT-VERLEYSEN, L'écriture hagiographique dans le diocèse de Vienne (env. 750-950) 613

I. L'ŒUVRE D'ADON. – A. Adon compilateur: le Martyrologe. – B. Adon auteur: Les Vies de Theudère, Sévère (?) et Didier. – C. Adon éditeur: le manuscrit de Saint-Gall.
II. VIES ET MIRACLES D'ÉVÊQUES: AVIT ET BARNARD.
III. VIES D'ABBÉS: LÉONIEN, CLAIR ET MAXIME.
CONCLUSION.
BIBLIOGRAPHIE.

Fernand PELOUX, L'écriture hagiographique dans les diocèses suffragants de la métropole viennoise (c. VIIIe-XIe s.) 639

    I. DIE: Marcel.
    II. GRENOBLE. – A. Aper. – B. Ferréol.
    III. MAURIENNE. – A. Marin. – B. Tigre.
    IV. VALENCE. – A. Apollinaire. – B. Galla.
    V. VIVIERS. – A. La transmission des textes. – B. Andéol. – C. Aule. – D. Hostian. – E. Montan. – F. Venance.
    CONCLUSION.
    BIBLIOGRAPHIE.

Éric CHEVALLEY, La Passion des saints Victor et Ours (Genève) 681

    I. ÉCRITURE, TRADITION MANUSCRITE ET ÉDITION DE LA PASSION.
    II. STRUCTURE ET CONTENU DE LA PASSION.
    III. VALEUR HISTORIQUE.
    BIBLIOGRAPHIE.

Éric CHEVALLEY, L'écriture hagiographique dans la province de Tarentaise (à partir de la fin du VIIIe siècle) 695

    INTRODUCTION.
    I. LA VIE DE THÉODORE, ÉVÊQUE DE SION. – A. Auteur. – B. Datation. – C. Structure et contenu. – D. Développement du culte de saint Théodule au Moyen Âge. – E. La critique historique à l'époque moderne et ses conséquences.
    II. LE DIOCÈSE D'AOSTE. – A. La Vie de saint Ours. – B. Structure et contenu.
    BIBLIOGRAPHIE.

Anne WAGNER, L'écriture hagiographique dans le diocèse de Besançon 721

    I. LES VIES DE DISCIPLES DE COLOMBAN.
    II. LES PASSIONS DE MARTYRS.
    BIBLIOGRAPHIE.

AU-DELÀ DE LA GALLIA

Klaus KRÖNERT, L'hagiographie en Germanie (env. 750-950): suppléments à Klüppel (*Hagiographies*, II, 1996) et Lotter – Gäbe (*Hagiographies*, IV, 2006) 731

    INTRODUCTION.

I. Le diocèse de Trèves. – A. Contexte général de la production hagiographique. – B. Saint-Maximin: les trois premières Vies de saint Maximin. – C. La Celle Saint-Goar: les deux Vies de saint Goar et les *Miracula Goaris*. – D. Saint-Euchaire: le dossier de saint Euchaire, le *Sermo in natale S. Celsi* et le *Liber inventionis S. Matthiae*. – E. Textes écrits dans d'autres établissements de Trèves et ses environs: les Vies de Liutrude et Irmina, la *Vita II^a Paulini*, la *Laudatio Paulini*, les Vies de Lubentius et Castor.

II. Les Vies de trois «anciens» évêques de Cologne. – A. Cologne, métropole de la *Germania Secunda*. – B. La Vie de Séverin. – C. La Vie de Cunibert. – D. La Vie d'Eberigisil.

III. Quelques récits rédigés à la suite des translations de reliques en Germanie. – A. Le phénomène des translations de reliques en Germanie. – B. La *Translatio Marcellini et Petri*, suivie d'une Passio en l'honneur des mêmes saints – C. La *Vita et Translatio Severi* – D. La *Translatio Patrocli Susatum an. 959 et Vita II^a Patrocli*.

Bibliographie.

Annexe: La Vie de sainte Odile (par Michèle Gaillard). – Bibliographie.

Les auteurs 771

Table des cartes et des plans 779

Printed in Belgium – Impimé en Belgique
D/2020/0095/235
978-2-503-58912-1 HB – relié